INDIVIDUAL RIGHTS AND THE AMERICAN CONSTITUTION
Fourth Edition

INDIVIDUAL RIGHTS AND THE AMERICAN CONSTITUTION

FOURTH EDITION

DOUGLAS W. KMIEC
U.S. Ambassador (ret.)
Caruso Family Chair in Constitutional Law & Human Rights
Pepperdine University

STEPHEN B. PRESSER
Raoul Berger Professor of Legal History
Northwestern University School of Law

JOHN C. EASTMAN
Henry Salvatori Professor of Law & Community Service and Former Dean
Chapman University Dale E. Fowler School of Law

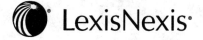

ISBN: 978–1–6304–3611–7
Looseleaf ISBN: 978-1-6304-3613-1
ebook ISBN: 978-1-6304-3612-4

Library of Congress Cataloging-in-Publication Data

Kmiec, Douglas W., author.
Individual rights and the American constitution / Douglas W. Kmiec, Professor of Constitutional Law and Caruso Family Chair in Constitutional Law, Pepperdine University School of Law, Ambassador of the United States (Ret.); Stephen B. Presser, Raoul Berger Professor of Legal History, Northwestern University School of Law; John C. Eastman, Henry Salvatori Professor of Law & Community Service and former Dean, Chapman University Dale E. Fowler School of Law. -- Fourth Edition.
pages cm
Includes index.
ISBN 978-1-63043-611-7 (hard cover)
1. Constitutional law--United States. 2. Civil rights--United States. I. Presser, Stephen B., 1946- author. II. Eastman, John C., 1960- author. III. Title.
KF4550.K554 2014
342.7308'5--dc23

2014018346

This publication is designed to provide authoritative information in regard to the subject matter covered. It is sold with the understanding that the publisher is not engaged in rendering legal, accounting, or other professional services. If legal advice or other expert assistance is required, the services of a competent professional should be sought.

NOTE TO USERS

To ensure that you are using the latest materials available in this area, please be sure to periodically check the LexisNexis Law School web site for downloadable updates and supplements at www.lexisnexis.com/lawschool.

Editorial Offices
121 Chanlon Rd., New Providence, NJ 07974 (908) 464-6800
201 Mission St., San Francisco, CA 94105-1831 (415) 908-3200
www.lexisnexis.com

MATTHEW◆BENDER

DEDICATION

For our students.

TABLE OF CONTENTS

Table of Contents

Table of Contents

Table of Contents

Table of Contents

Table of Contents

Table of Contents

Table of Contents

PREFACE TO THE FOURTH EDITION

This entirely revised fourth edition arrives on your doorstep at a time when United States has, depending on your party affiliation, either a constitutional scholar or a dangerous revolutionary as president. The House of Representatives is controlled by the President's antagonists; the Senate narrowly held by his apologists. The two Houses of Congress have permitted increasing budget deficits and occasionally allowed fiscal deadlines to go unmet, thereby allowing the closure of the government. The politics of the day is rancorous and divisive and often in need of honesty and civility.

Honest assessment of case development is what we have prided ourselves in the past, and teachers and students will find that quality of getting to the point still very much present from the previous three editions. Since its inception, this work has faithfully kept to the purpose of presenting the full statement of the "law" of the Constitution in the context of its philosophical and historical origins, without either narrowed originalist glint or undisclosed progressive bias.

Because we teach — among the three of us — legal history, human rights, appellate advocacy/Supreme Court litigation as well as constitutional law, the note materials are enriched with many sub-disciplines. The book is designed for the individual rights semester of a two semester required constitutional law survey and makes an ideal book as well as the core casebook around which advanced courses in legal history, economic liberties, or jurisprudence might be organized. In whatever setting, teachers will enjoy the depth and collaboration of the accompanying teacher's manual, for which we have received many compliments.

What's new in the Fourth edition — primarily, the inclusion of cases of importance decided since 2009, sensibly edited (and they have to be since 80+ page opinions are now commonplace on the bench). Unless you have, like one of our co-authors, been on an island in the Mediterranean during that time, you know the important areas touched by the Roberts Court, are still being mediated by Justice Kennedy, who remains firmly ensconced as the Court's principal center swing vote.

In truth, those of us writing or assembling this volume love our work because we appreciate the institutional role of the judiciary, the only branch of government that writes opinions to explain its actions, opinions that can be tested for their factual claims, legal authority, historical accuracy and logic, even if we are occasionally (perhaps of late frequently) disappointed when the arguments fall short. Say all you want about health care as a right or as the proximate cause of Armageddon, there is something well-ordered and meritorious about a branch of government that has to explain its reasoning.

The new cases have contributed substantially to the developments with respect to the Second Amendment, some still as yet to be fully applied reaffirmation of the Takings Clause, and of course, developments in both the Establishment Clause and free exercise aspects of the First Amendment guaranteeing freedom of, not from, religion. There have been some landmark developments concerning justiciability and the claims of same-sex individuals seeking to redefine marriage. The Court also has new members. Since our last edition Justices Sotomayor and Kagan were confirmed, inheriting the seats previously held by Justices Stevens and Souter on the ideological left side of the bench. But for rare occasions, they have not disappointed jurisprudential expectations, so the ideological balance of the Court has remained generally the same as it was before their arrival. That could change dramatically in the near future, with one octagenerian already on the Court and two more who will hit that milestone before the next presidential election. With one of them from the left, one from the right, and one from the center, the next round of confirmation battles may well test our institutions in ways we have not seen for decades.

Nevertheless, the Court under the administratively efficient and ever cordial John Roberts continues to give the appearance of being the best run branch of the federal government, which may explain why the Justices decline to be televised. No reason to poke one's judicial head up while so many are grousing about (err, browsing for) — health insurance. There is something quaint and reassuring to be employed by the branch of government where "droning on" has its customary meaning. In truth, the Court reflects a remarkable collegiality notwithstanding the ideological origins of all of its appointments and the expected differences addressing some of society's genuine legal puzzlers.

It may not be fashionable in academe, but we admire the lot of the Justices, even though as a diverse set of authors we, too, are seldom in complete agreement, which we think you'll find, if you are open-minded, the very strength of the book, the enjoyment of the subject matter, and frankly its importance to the common good. Topics like religious freedom, affirmative action, and sexual orientation do not lend themselves to glib answer. In a democracy, the judicial, nonpolitical branch acquits itself with the subtlety, candor and persuasiveness of its reasoning, as long as it remembers its role of interpreting rather than making the law, of exercising judgment rather than will. We continue to hope that the historical foundations of this text inspire both current judges and future ones to keep that role evermost in mind, no matter whose president signed their commission, and that makes new editions a labor of love.

This edition reflects the blessing it has been for the co-authors to spend our lives in teaching. We have especially benefited from those who have become special friends and colleagues in adopting one of the earlier editions, and it is in that friendship and with gratitude for your suggested improvements, many of which are included and all of which were considered, that we present our Fourth Edition of Individual Rights and the American Constitution.

DWK
SBP
JCE

The Declaration of Independence

In Congress, July 4, 1776

(The Unanimous Declaration of the Thirteen United States of America)

WHEN in the Course of human events, it becomes necessary for one people to dissolve the political bands which have connected them with another, and to assume among the powers of the earth, the separate and equal station to which the Laws of Nature and of Nature's God entitle them, a decent respect to the opinions of mankind requires that they should declare the causes which impel them to the separation.

We hold these truths to be self-evident, that all men are created equal, that they are endowed by their Creator with certain unalienable Rights, that among these are Life, Liberty and the pursuit of Happiness. That to secure these rights, Governments are instituted among Men, deriving their just powers from the consent of the governed, That whenever any Form of Government becomes destructive of these ends, it is the Right of the People to alter or to abolish it, and to institute new Government, laying its foundation on such principles and organizing its powers in such form, as to them shall seem most likely to effect their Safety and Happiness. Prudence, indeed, will dictate that Governments long established should not be changed for light and transient causes; and accordingly all experience hath shown, that mankind are more disposed to suffer, while evils are sufferable, than to right themselves by abolishing the forms to which they are accustomed. But when a long train of abuses and usurpations, pursuing invariably the same Object evinces a design to reduce them under absolute Despotism, it is their right, it is their duty, to throw off such Government, and to provide new Guards for their future security. — Such has been the patient sufferance of these Colonies; and such is now the necessity which constrains them to alter their former Systems of Government. The history of the present King of Great Britain is a history of repeated injuries and usurpations, all having in direct object the establishment of an absolute Tyranny over these States. To prove this, let Facts be submitted to a candid world.

He has refused his Assent to Laws, the most wholesome and necessary for the public good.

He has forbidden his Governors to pass Laws of Immediate and pressing importance, unless suspended in their operation till his Assent should be obtained; and when so suspended, he has utterly neglected to attend to them.

He has refused to pass other Laws for the accommodation of large districts of people, unless those people would relinquish the right of Representation in the Legislature, a right inestimable to them and formidable to tyrants only.

He has called together legislative bodies at places unusual, uncomfortable, and distant from the depository of their Public Records, for the sole purpose of fatiguing them into compliance with his measures.

He has dissolved Representative Houses repeatedly, for opposing with manly firmness his invasions on the rights of the people.

He has refused for a long time, after such dissolutions, to cause others to be elected; whereby the Legislative Powers, incapable of Annihilation, have returned to the People at large for their exercise; the State remaining in the mean time exposed to all the dangers of invasion from without, and convulsions within.

He has endeavoured to prevent the population of these States; for that purpose obstructing the Laws for Naturalization of Foreigners; refusing to pass others to encourage their migration hither, and raising the conditions of new Appropriations of Lands.

The Declaration of Independence

He has obstructed the Administration of Justice, by refusing his Assent to Laws for establishing Judiciary Powers.

He has made Judges dependent on his Will alone, for the tenure of their offices, and the amount and payment of their salaries.

He has erected a multitude of New Offices, and sent hither swarms of Officers to harrass our People, and eat out their substance.

He has kept among us, in times of peace, Standing Armies, without the Consent of our legislatures.

He has affected to render the Military independent of and superior to the Civil Power.

He has combined with others to subject us to a jurisdiction foreign to our constitution, and unacknowledged by our laws; giving his Assent to their acts of pretended Legislation:

For quartering large bodies of armed troops among us:

For protecting them, by a mock Trial, from Punishment for any Murders which they should commit on the Inhabitants of these States:

For cutting off our Trade with all parts of the world:

For imposing taxes on us without our Consent:

For depriving us in many cases, of the benefits of Trial by Jury:

For transporting us beyond Seas to be tried for pretended offences:

For abolishing the free System of English Laws in a neighbouring Province, establishing therein an Arbitrary government, and enlarging its Boundaries so as to render it at once an example and fit instrument for introducing the same absolute rule into these Colonies:

For taking away our Charters, abolishing our most valuable Laws, and altering fundamentally the Forms of our Governments:

For suspending our own Legislatures, and declaring themselves invested with Power to legislate for us in all cases whatsoever.

He has abdicated Government here, by declaring us out of his Protection and waging War against us.

He has plundered our seas, ravaged our Coasts, burnt our towns, and destroyed the lives of our people.

He is at this time transporting large Armies of foreign mercenaries to compleat the works of death, desolation and tyranny, already begun with circumstances of Cruelty & perfidy scarcely paralleled in the most barbarous ages, and totally unworthy the Head of a civilized nation.

He has constrained our fellow Citizens taken Captive on the high Seas to bear Arms against their Country, to become the executioners of their friends and Brethren, or to fall themselves by their Hands.

He has excited domestic insurrections amongst us, and has endeavoured to bring on the inhabitants of our frontiers, the merciless Indian Savages, whose known rule of war-fare, is an undistinguished destruction of all ages, sexes and conditions.

In every stage of these Oppressions We have Petitioned for Redress in the most humble terms: Our repeated Petitions have been answered only by repeated injury. A Prince, whose character is thus marked by every act which may define a Tyrant, is unfit to be the ruler of a free people.

Nor have We been wanting in attentions to our Brittish brethren. We have warned them from time to time of attempts by their legislature to extend an unwarrantable jurisdiction over us. We have reminded them of the circumstances of our emigration and settlement here. We have appealed to their native justice and magnanimity, and we have conjured them by the ties of our common kindred to disavow these usurpations, which, would inevitably interrupt our connections and correspondence. They too have been deaf to the voice of justice and of consanguinity. We must, therefore, acquiesce in the necessity, which denounces our Separation, and hold them, as we hold the rest of mankind, Enemies in War, in Peace Friends.

WE, THEREFORE, the REPRESENTATIVES of the UNITED STATES OF AMERICA, in General Congress, Assembled, appealing to the Supreme Judge of the world for the rectitude of our intentions, do, in the Name, and by Authority of the good People of these Colonies, solemnly publish and declare, That these United Colonies are, and of Right ought to be FREE AND INDEPENDENT STATES; that they are Absolved from all Allegiance to the British Crown, and that all political connection between them and the State of Great Britain, is and ought to be totally dissolved; and that as Free and Independent States, they have full Power to levy War, conclude Peace, contract Alliances, establish Commerce, and to do all other Acts and Things which Independent States may of right do. And for the support of this Declaration, with a firm reliance on the protection of Divine Providence, we mutually pledge to each other our Lives, our Fortunes and our sacred Honor.

JOHN HANCOCK

New Hampshire
JOSIAH BARTLETT
WM. WHIPPLE
MATTHEW THORNTON

Connecticut
ROGER SHERMAN
SAM'EL HUNTINGTON
WM. WILLIAMS
OLIVER WOLCOTT

Massachusetts Bay
SAML. ADAMS
JOHN ADAMS
ROBT. TREAT PAINE
ELBRIDGE GERRY

New York
WM. FLOYD
PHIL. LIVINGSTON
FRANS. LEWIS
LEWIS MORRIS

Rhode Island
STEP. HOPKINS
WILLIAM ELLERY

Virginia
GEORGE WYTHE
RICHARD HENRY LEE
TH. JEFFERSON
BENJA. HARRISON
THS. NELSON, JR.
FRANCIS LIGHTFOOT LEE
CARTER BRAXTON

New Jersey
RICHD. STOCKTON
JNO. WITHERSPOON
FRAS. HOPKINSON
JOHN HART
ABRA. CLARK

North Carolina
WM. HOOPER
JOSEPH HEWES
JOHN PENN

The Declaration of Independence

Pennsylvania
ROBT. MORRIS
BENJAMIN RUSH
BENJA. FRANKLIN
JOHN MORTON
GEO. CLYMER
JAS. SMITH
GEO. TAYLOR
JAMES WILSON
GEO. ROSS

South Carolina
EDWARD RUTLEDGE
THOS. HEYWARD, JUNR.
THOMAS LYNCH, JUNR.
ARTHUR MIDDLETON

Delaware
CAESAR RODNEY
GEO. READ
THO. M'KEAN

Georgia
BUTTON GWINNETT
LYMAN HALL
GEO. WALTON

Maryland
SAMUEL CHASE
WM. PACA
THOS. STONE
CHARLES CARROLL of Carrollton

The Constitution of the United States

We the People of the United States, in Order to form a more perfect Union, establish Justice, insure domestic Tranquility, provide for the common defence, promote the general Welfare, and secure the Blessings of Liberty to ourselves and our Posterity, do ordain and establish this Constitution for the United States of America.

Article I.

Section 1. All legislative Powers herein granted shall be vested in a Congress of the United States, which shall consist of a Senate and House of Representatives.

Section 2. The House of Representatives shall be composed of Members chosen every second Year by the People of the several States, and the Electors in each State shall have the Qualifications requisite for Electors of the most numerous Branch of the State Legislature.

No person shall be a Representative who shall not have attained to the Age of twenty five Years, and been seven Years a Citizen of the United States, and who shall not, when elected, be an Inhabitant of that State in which he shall be chosen.

[Representatives and direct Taxes shall be apportioned among the several States which may be included within this Union, according to their respective Numbers, which shall be determined by adding to the whole Number of free Persons, including those bound to Service for a Term of Years, and excluding Indians not taxed, three fifths of all other Persons.] The actual Enumeration shall be made within three Years after the first Meeting of the Congress of the United States, and within every subsequent Term of ten Years, in such Manner as they shall by Law direct. The Number of Representatives shall not exceed one for every thirty Thousand, but each State shall have at Least one Representative; and until such enumeration shall be made, the State of New Hampshire shall be entitled to chuse three, Massachusetts eight, Rhode-Island and Providence Plantations one, Connecticut five, New-York six, New Jersey four, Pennsylvania eight, Delaware one, Maryland six, Virginia ten, North Carolina five, South Carolina five, and Georgia three.

When vacancies happen in the Representation from any State, the Executive Authority thereof shall issue Writs of Election to fill such Vacancies.

The House of Representatives shall chuse their Speaker and other Officers; and shall have the sole Power of Impeachment.

Section 3. The Senate of the United States shall be composed of two Senators from each State, chosen by the Legislature thereof, for six Years; and each Senator shall have one Vote.

Immediately after they shall be assembled in Consequence of the first Election, they shall be divided as equally as may be into three Classes. The Seats of the Senators of the first Class shall be vacated at the Expiration of the second Year, of the second Class at the Expiration of the fourth Year, and of the third Class at the Expiration of the sixth Year, so that one third may be chosen every second Year; and if Vacancies happen by Resignation, or otherwise, during the Recess of the Legislature of any State, the Executive thereof may make temporary Appointments until the next Meeting of the Legislature, which shall then fill such Vacancies.

No Person shall be a Senator who shall not have attained to the Age of thirty Years, and been nine Years a Citizen of the United States, and who shall not, when elected, be an Inhabitant of that State for which he shall be chosen.

The Vice President of the United States shall be President of the Senate, but shall have no Vote, unless they be equally divided.

The Senate shall chuse their other Officers, and also a President pro tempore, in the Absence of the Vice President, or when he shall exercise the Office of President of the United States.

The Constitution of the United States

The Senate shall have the sole Power to try all Impeachments. When sitting for that Purpose, they shall be on Oath or Affirmation. When the President of the United States is tried, the Chief Justice shall preside: and no Person shall be convicted without the Concurrence of two thirds of the Members present.

Judgment in Cases of Impeachment shall not extend further than to removal from Office, and disqualification to hold and enjoy any Office of honor, Trust or Profit under the United States: but the Party convicted shall nevertheless be liable and subject to Indictment, Trial, Judgment and Punishment, according to Law.

Section 4. The Times, Places and Manner of holding Elections for Senators and Representatives, shall be prescribed in each State by the Legislature thereof; but the Congress may at any time by Law make or alter such Regulations, except as to the Places of chusing Senators.

The Congress shall assemble at least once in every Year, and such Meeting shall be on the first Monday in December, unless they shall be Law appoint a different Day.

Section 5. Each House shall be the Judge of the Elections, Returns and Qualifications of its own Members, and a Majority of each shall constitute a Quorum to do Business; but a smaller Number may adjourn from day to day, and may be authorized to compel the Attendance of absent Members, in such Manner, and under such Penalties as each House may provide.

Each House may determine the Rules of its Proceedings, punish its Members for disorderly Behaviour, and, with the Concurrence of two thirds, expel a Member.

Each House shall keep a Journal of its Proceedings, and from time to time publish the same, excepting such Parts as may in their Judgment require Secrecy; and the Yeas and Nays of the Members of either House on any question shall, at the Desire of one fifth of those Present, be entered on the Journal.

Neither House, during the Session of Congress, shall, without the consent of the other, adjourn for more than three days, nor to any other Place than that in which the two Houses shall be sitting.

Section 6. The Senators and Representatives shall receive a Compensation for their Services, to be ascertained by Law, and paid out of the Treasury of the United States. They shall in all Cases, except Treason, Felony and Breach of the Peace, be privileged from Arrest during their Attendance at the Session of their respective Houses, and in going to and returning from the same; and for any Speech or Debate in either House, they shall not be questioned in any other Place.

No Senator or Representative shall, during the Time for which he was elected, be appointed to any civil Office under the Authority of the United States, which shall have been created, or the Emoluments whereof shall have been encreased during such time; and no Person holding any Office under the United States, shall be a Member of either House during his Continuance in Office.

Section 7. All Bills for raising Revenue shall originate in the House of Representatives; but the Senate may propose or concur with Amendments as on other Bills.

Every Bill which shall have passed the House of Representatives and the Senate, shall, before it become a Law, be presented to the President of the United States; If he approve he shall sign it, but if not he shall return it, with his Objections to that House in which it shall have originated, who shall enter the Objections at large on their Journal, and proceed to reconsider it. If after such Reconsideration two thirds of that House shall agree to pass the Bill, it shall be sent, together with the Objections, to the other House, by which it shall likewise be reconsidered, and if approved by two thirds of that House, it shall become a Law. But in all such Cases the Votes of both Houses shall be determined by yeas and Nays, and the Names of the Persons voting for and against the Bill shall be entered on the Journal of each House respectively. If any Bill shall not be returned by the President within ten days (Sundays excepted) after it shall have been presented to him, the Same shall be a Law, in like Manner as if he had signed it, unless the Congress by their Adjournment prevent its Return in which Case it shall not be a Law.

Every Order, Resolution, or Vote to which the Concurrence of the Senate and House of Representatives may be necessary (except on a question of Adjournment) shall be presented to the President of the United States; and before the Same shall take Effect, shall be approved by him, or being disapproved by him, shall be repassed by two thirds of the Senate and House of Representatives, according to the Rules and Limitations prescribed in the Case of a Bill.

Section 8. The Congress shall have Power To lay and collect Taxes, Duties, Imposts and Excises, to pay the Debts and provide for the common Defence and general Welfare of the United States; but all Duties, Imposts and Excises shall be uniform throughout the United States;

To borrow Money on the credit of the United States;

To regulate Commerce with foreign Nations, and among the several States, and with the Indian Tribes;

To establish an uniform Rule of Naturalization, and uniform Laws on the subject of Bankruptcies throughout the United States;

To coin Money, regulate the Value thereof, and of foreign Coin, and fix the Standard of Weights and Measures;

To provide for the Punishment of counterfeiting the Securities and current Coin of the United States;

To establish Post Offices and post Roads;

To promote the Progress of Science and useful Arts, by securing for limited Times to Authors and Inventors the exclusive Right to their respective Writings and Discoveries;

To constitute Tribunals inferior to the supreme Court;

To define and punish Piracies and Felonies committed on the high Seas, and Offences against the Law of Nations;

To declare War, grant Letters of Marque and Reprisal, and make Rules concerning Captures on Land and Water;

To raise and support Armies, but no Appropriation of Money to that Use shall be for a longer Term than two Years;

To provide and maintain a Navy;

To make Rules for the Government and Regulation of the land and naval Forces;

To provide for calling forth the Militia to execute the Laws of the Union, suppress Insurrections and repel Invasions;

To provide for organizing, arming, and disciplining, the Militia, and for governing such Part of them as may be employed in the Service of the United States, reserving to the States respectively, the Appointment of the Officers, and the Authority of training the Militia according to the discipline prescribed by Congress;

To exercise exclusive Legislation in all Cases whatsoever, over such District (not exceeding ten Miles square) as may, by Cession of particular States, and the Acceptance of Congress, become the Seat of the Government of the United States, and to exercise like Authority over all Places purchased by the Consent of the Legislature of the State in which the Same shall be, for the Erection of Forts, Magazines, Arsenals, dock-Yards, and other needful Buildings; -And

To make all Laws which shall be necessary and proper for carrying into Execution the foregoing Powers, and all other Powers vested by this Constitution in the Government of the United States, or in any Department or Officer thereof.

Section 9. The Migration or Importation of such Persons as any of the States now existing shall think proper to admit, shall not be prohibited by the Congress prior to the Year one thousand eight hundred and eight, but a Tax or duty may be imposed on such Importation, not exceeding ten dollars for each Person.

The Privilege of the Writ of Habeas Corpus shall not be suspended, unless when in Cases of Rebellion or Invasion the public Safety may require it.

No Bill of Attainder or ex post facto Law shall be passed.

No Capitation, or other direct, Tax shall be laid, unless in Proportion to the Census or Enumeration herein before directed to be taken.

No Tax or Duty shall be laid on Articles exported from any State.

No Preference shall be given by any Regulation of Commerce or Revenue to the Ports of one State over those of another: nor shall Vessels bound to, or from, one State, be obliged to enter, clear, or pay Duties in another.

No Money shall be drawn from the Treasury, but in Consequence of Appropriations made by Law; and a regular Statement and Account of the Receipts and Expenditures of all public Money shall be published from time to time.

No Title of Nobility shall be granted by the United States: And no Person holding any Office of Profit or Trust under them, shall, without the Consent of the Congress, accept of any present, Emolument, Office, or Title, of any kind whatever, from any King, Prince, or foreign State.

Section 10. No State shall enter into any Treaty, Alliance, or Confederation; grant Letters of Marque and Reprisal; coin Money; emit Bills of Credit; make any Thing but gold and silver Coin a Tender in Payment of Debts; pass any Bill of Attainder, ex post facto Law, or Law impairing the Obligation of Contracts, or grant any Title of Nobility.

No State shall, without the Consent of the Congress, lay any Imposts or Duties on Imports or Exports, except what may be absolutely necessary for executing it's inspection Laws: and the net Produce of all Duties and Imposts, laid by any State on Imports or Exports, shall be for the Use of the Treasury of the United States; and all such Laws shall be subject to the Revision and Controul of the Congress.

No State shall, without the Consent of Congress, lay any Duty of Tonnage, keep Troops, or Ships of War in time of Peace, enter into any Agreement or Compact with another State, or with a foreign Power, or engage in War, unless actually invaded, or in such imminent Danger as will not admit of delay.

Article II

Section 1. The executive Power shall be vested in a President of the United States of America. He shall hold his Office during the Term of four Years, and, together with the Vice President, chosen for the same Term, be elected as follows

Each State shall appoint, in such Manner as the Legislature thereof may direct, a Number of Electors, equal to the whole Number of Senators and Representatives to which the State may be entitled in the Congress: but no Senator or Representative, or Person holding an Office of Trust or Profit under the United States, shall be appointed an Elector.

The Electors shall meet in their respective States, and vote by Ballot for two Persons, of whom one at least shall not be an Inhabitant of the same State with themselves. And they shall make a List of all the Persons voted for, and of the Number of Votes for each; which List they shall sign and certify, and transmit sealed to the Seat of the Government of the United States, directed to the President of the Senate. The President of the Senate shall, in the Presence of the Senate and House of Representatives, open all the Certificates, and the Votes shall then be counted. The Person having the greatest Number of Votes shall be the President, if such Number be a Majority of the whole Number of Electors appointed; and if there be more than one who have such Majority, and have an equal Number of Votes, then the House of Representatives shall immediately chuse by

Ballot one of them for President; and if no Person have a Majority, then from the five highest on the List the said House shall in like Manner chuse the President. But in chusing the President, the Votes shall be taken by States, the Representation from each State having one Vote; A quorum for this Purpose shall consist of a Member or Members from two thirds of the States, and a Majority of all the States shall be necessary to a Choice. In every Case, after the Choice of the President, the Person having the greatest Number of Votes of the Electors shall be the Vice President. But if there should remain two or more who have equal Votes, the Senate shall chuse from them by Ballot the Vice President.

The Congress may determine the Time of chusing the Electors, and the Day on which they shall give their Votes; which Day shall be the same throughout the United States.

No Person except a natural born Citizen, or a Citizen of the United States, at the time of the Adoption of this Constitution, shall be eligible to the Office of President; neither shall any Person be eligible to that Office who shall not have attained to the Age of thirty five Years, and been fourteen Years a Resident within the United States.

In Case of the Removal of the President from Office, or of his Death, Resignation, or Inability to discharge the Powers and Duties of the said Office, the Same shall devolve on the Vice president, and the Congress may by Law provide for the Case of Removal, Death, Resignation or Inability, both of the President and Vice President, declaring what Officer shall then act as President, and such Officer shall act accordingly, until the Disability be removed, or a President shall be elected.

The President shall, at stated Times, receive for his Services, a Compensation, which shall neither be encreased nor diminished during the Period for which he shall have been elected, and he shall not receive within that Period any other Emolument from the United States, or any of them.

Before he enter on the Execution of his Office, he shall take the following Oath or Affirmation: -"I do solemnly swear (or affirm) that I will faithfully execute the Office of President of the United States, and will to the best of my Ability, preserve, protect and defend the Constitution of the United States."

Section 2. The president shall be Commander in Chief of the Army and Navy of the United States, and of the Militia of the several States, when called into the actual service of the United States; he may require the Opinion, in writing, of the principal Officer in each of the executive Departments, upon any Subject relating to the Duties of their respective Offices, and he shall have Power to grant Reprieves and Pardons for Offences against the United States, except in Cases of Impeachment.

He shall have Power, by and with the Advice and Consent of the Senate, to make Treaties, provided two thirds of the Senators present concur; and he shall nominate, and by and with the Advice and Consent of the Senate, shall appoint Ambassadors, other public Ministers and Consuls, Judges of the supreme Court, and all other Officers of the United States, whose Appointments are not herein otherwise provided for, and which shall be established by Law but the Congress may by Law vest the Appointment of such inferior Officers, as they think proper, in the President alone, in the Courts of Law, or in the Heads of Departments.

The President shall have Power to fill up all Vacancies that may happen during the Recess of the Senate, by granting Commissions which shall expire at the End of their next Session.

Section 3. He shall from time to time give to the Congress Information of the State of the Union, and recommend to their Consideration such Measures as he shall judge necessary and expedient; he may, on extraordinary Occasions, convene both Houses, or either of them, and in Case of Disagreement between them, with Respect to the Time of Adjournment, he may adjourn them to such Time as he shall think proper; he shall receive Ambassadors and other public Ministers; he shall take Care that the Laws be faithfully executed, and shall Commission all the Officers of the United States.

Section 4. The President, Vice President and all civil Officers of the United States, shall be removed from Office on Impeachment for, and Conviction of, Treason, Bribery, or other high Crimes and Misdemeanors.

Article III

Section 1. The judicial Power of the United States, shall be vested in one supreme Court, and in such inferior Courts as the Congress may from time to time ordain and establish. The Judges, both of the supreme and inferior Courts, shall hold their Offices during good Behaviour, and shall, at stated Times, receive for their Services, a Compensation, which shall not be diminished during their Continuance in Office.

Section 2. The judicial Power shall extend to all Cases, in Law and Equity, arising under this Constitution, the Laws of the United States, and Treaties made, or which shall be made, under their Authority; -to all Cases affecting Ambassadors, other public Ministers and Consuls; -to all Cases of admiralty and maritime Jurisdiction; -to Controversies to which the United States shall be a Party; -to Controversies between two or more States; -between a State and Citizens of another State; -between Citizens of different States,-between Citizens of the same State claiming Lands under Grants of different States, and between a State, or the Citizens thereof, and foreign States, Citizens or Subjects.

In all cases affecting Ambassadors, other public Ministers and Consuls, and those in which a State shall be Party, the supreme Court shall have original Jurisdiction. In all the other Cases before mentioned, the supreme Court shall have appellate Jurisdiction, both as to Law and Fact, with such Exceptions, and under such Regulations as the Congress shall make.

The Trial of all Crimes, except in Cases of Impeachment, shall be by Jury; and such Trial shall be held in the State where the said Crimes shall have been committed; but when not committed within any State, the Trial shall be at such Place or Places as the Congress may by Law have directed.

Section 3. Treason against the United States, shall consist only in levying War against them, or in adhering to their Enemies, giving them Aid and Comfort. No Person shall be convicted of Treason unless on the Testimony of two Witnesses to the same overt Act, or on Confession in open Court.

The Congress shall have Power to declare the Punishment of Treason, but no Attainder of Treason shall work Corruption of Blood, or Forfeiture except during the Life of the Person attainted.

Article IV

Section 1. Full Faith and Credit shall be given in each State to the public Acts, Records, and judicial Proceedings of every other State. And the Congress may by general Laws prescribe the Manner in which such Acts, Records and Proceedings shall be proved, and the Effect thereof.

Section 2. The Citizens of each State shall be entitled to all Privileges and Immunities of Citizens in the several States.

A Person charged in any State with Treason, Felony, or other Crime, who shall flee from Justice, and be found in another State, shall on Demand of the executive Authority of the State from which he fled, be delivered up, to be removed to the State having Jurisdiction of the Crime.

No Person held to Service or Labour in one State, under the Laws thereof, escaping into another, shall, in Consequence of any Law or Regulation therein, be discharged from such Service or Labour, but shall be delivered up on Claim of the Party to whom such Service or Labour may be due.

Section 3. New States may be admitted by the Congress into this Union; but no new State shall be formed or erected within the Jurisdiction of any other State; nor any State be formed by the Junction of two or more States, or Parts of States, without the Consent of the Legislatures of the States concerned as well as of the Congress.

The Congress shall have Power to dispose of and make all needful Rules and Regulations respecting the Territory or other Property belonging to the United States; and nothing in this

Constitution shall be so construed as to Prejudice any Claims of the United States, or of any particular State.

Section 4. The United States shall guarantee to every State in this Union a Republican Form of Government, and shall protect each of them against Invasion; and on Application of the Legislature, or of the Executive (when the Legislature cannot be convened) against domestic Violence.

Article V

The Congress, whenever two thirds of both Houses shall deem it necessary, shall propose Amendments to this Constitution, or, on the Application of the Legislatures of two thirds of the several States, shall call a Convention for proposing Amendments, which, in either Case, shall be valid to all Intents and Purposes, as Part of this Constitution, when ratified by the Legislatures of three fourths of the several States, or by Conventions in three fourths thereof, as the one or the other Mode of Ratification may be proposed by the Congress; provided that no Amendment which may be made prior to the Year One thousand eight hundred and eight shall in any Manner affect the first and fourth Clauses in the Ninth Section of the first Article; and that no State, without its Consent, shall be deprived of it's equal Suffrage in the Senate.

Article VI

All Debts contracted and Engagements entered into, before the adoption of this Constitution, shall be as valid against the United States under this Constitution, as under the Confederation.

This Constitution, and the Laws of the United States which shall be made in Pursuance thereof; and all Treaties made, or which shall be made, under the Authority of the United States, shall be the supreme Law of the Land; and the Judges in every State shall be bound thereby, any Thing in the Constitution or Laws of any State to the Contrary notwithstanding.

The Senators and Representatives before mentioned, and the Members of the several State Legislatures, and all executive and judicial Officers, both of the United States and of the several States, shall be bound by Oath or Affirmation, to support this Constitution; but no religious Test shall ever be required as a Qualification to any Office or public Trust under the United States.

Article VII

The Ratification of the Conventions of nine States, shall be sufficient for the Establishment of this Constitution between the States so ratifying the Same.

The Word, "the," being interlined between the seventh and eighth Lines of the first Page, The Word "Thirty" being partly written on an Erazure in the fifteenth Line of the first Page, The Words "is tried" being interlined between the thirty second and thirty third Lines of the first Page and the Word "the" being interlined between the forty third and forty fourth Lines of the second Page.

Attest WILLIAM JACKSON Secretary done in Convention by the Unanimous Consent of the States present the Seventeenth Day of September in the Year of our Lord one thousand seven hundred and Eighty seven and of the Independence of the United States of America the Twelfth In witness whereof We have hereunto subscribed our Names,

Go: WASHINGTON

Amendment I

Congress shall make no law respecting an establishment of religion, or prohibiting the free exercise thereof; or abridging the freedom of speech, or of the press; or the right of the people peaceably to assemble, and to petition the government for a redress of grievances.

The Constitution of the United States

Amendment II

A well regulated militia, being necessary to the security of a free state, the right of the people to keep and bear arms, shall not be infringed.

Amendment III

No soldier shall, in time of peace be quartered in any house, without the consent of the owner, nor in time of war, but in a manner to be prescribed by law.

Amendment IV

The right of the people to be secure in their persons, houses, papers, and effects, against unreasonable searches and seizures, shall not be violated, and no warrants shall issue, but upon probable cause, supported by oath or affirmation, and particularly describing the place to be searched, and the persons or things to be seized.

Amendment V

No person shall be held to answer for a capital, or otherwise infamous crime, unless on a presentment or indictment of a grand jury, except in cases arising in the land or naval forces, or in the militia, when in actual service in time of war or public danger; nor shall any person be subject for the same offense to be twice put in jeopardy of life or limb; nor shall be compelled in any criminal case to be a witness against himself, nor be deprived of life, liberty, or property, without due process of law; nor shall private property be taken for public use, without just compensation.

Amendment VI

In all criminal prosecutions, the accused shall enjoy the right to a speedy and public trial, by an impartial jury of the state and district wherein the crime shall have been committed, which district shall have been previously ascertained by law, and to be informed of the nature and cause of the accusation; to be confronted with the witnesses against him; to have compulsory process for obtaining witnesses in his favor, and to have the assistance of counsel for his defense.

Amendment VII

In suits at common law, where the value in controversy shall exceed twenty dollars, the right of trial by jury shall be preserved, and no fact tried by a jury, shall be otherwise reexamined in any court of the United States, than according to the rules of the common law.

Amendment VIII

Excessive bail shall not be required, nor excessive fines imposed, nor cruel and unusual punishments inflicted.

Amendment IX

The enumeration in the Constitution, of certain rights, shall not be construed to deny or disparage others retained by the people.

Amendment X

The powers not delegated to the United States by the Constitution, nor prohibited by it to the states, are reserved to the states respectively, or to the people.

The Constitution of the United States

Amendment XI

(1798)

The judicial power of the United States shall not be construed to extend to any suit in law or equity, commenced or prosecuted against one of the United States by citizens of another state, or by citizens or subjects of any foreign state.

Amendment XII

(1804)

The electors shall meet in their respective states and vote by ballot for President and Vice-President, one of whom, at least, shall not be an inhabitant of the same state with themselves; they shall name in their ballots the person voted for as President, and in distinct ballots the person voted for as Vice-President, and they shall make distinct lists of all persons voted for as President, and of all persons voted for as Vice-President, and of the number of votes for each, which lists they shall sign and certify, and transmit sealed to the seat of the government of the United States, directed to the President of the Senate; — The President of the Senate shall, in the presence of the Senate and House of Representatives, open all the certificates and the votes shall then be counted; — the person having the greatest number of votes for President, shall be the President, if such number be a majority of the whole number of electors appointed; and if no person have such majority, then from the persons having the highest numbers not exceeding three on the list of those voted for as President, the House of Representatives shall choose immediately, by ballot, the President. But in choosing the President, the votes shall be taken by states, the representation from each state having one vote; a quorum for this purpose shall consist of a member or members from two-thirds of the states, and a majority of all the states shall be necessary to a choice. And if the House of Representatives shall not choose a President whenever the right of choice shall devolve upon them, before the fourth day of March next following, then the Vice-President shall act as President, as in the case of the death or other constitutional disability of the President. The person having the greatest number of votes as Vice-President, shall be the Vice-President, if such number be a majority of the whole number of electors appointed, and if no person have a majority, then from the two highest numbers on the list, the Senate shall choose the Vice-President; a quorum for the purpose shall consist of two-thirds of the whole number of Senators, and a majority of the whole number shall be necessary to a choice. But no person constitutionally ineligible to the office of President shall be eligible to that of Vice-President of the United States.

Amendment XIII

(1865)

Section 1. Neither slavery nor involuntary servitude, except as a punishment for crime whereof the party shall have been duly convicted, shall exist within the United States, or any place subject to their jurisdiction.

Section 2. Congress shall have power to enforce this article by appropriate legislation.

Amendment XIV

(1868)

Section 1. All persons born or naturalized in the United States, and subject to the jurisdiction thereof, are citizens of the United States and of the state wherein they reside. No state shall make or enforce any law which shall abridge the privileges or immunities of citizens of the United States; nor shall any state deprive any person of life, liberty, or property, without due process of law; nor deny to any person within its jurisdiction the equal protection of the laws.

Section 2. Representatives shall be apportioned among the several states according to their

The Constitution of the United States

respective numbers, counting the whole number of persons in each state, excluding Indians not taxed. But when the right to vote at any election for the choice of electors for President and Vice President of the United States, Representatives in Congress, the executive and judicial officers of a state, or the members of the legislature thereof, is denied to any of the male inhabitants of such state, being twenty-one years of age, and citizens of the United States, or in any way abridged, except for participation in rebellion, or other crime, the basis of representation therein shall be reduced in the proportion which the number of such male citizens shall bear to the whole number of male citizens twenty-one years of age in such state.

Section 3. No person shall be a Senator or Representative in Congress, or elector of President and Vice President, or hold any office, civil or military, under the United States, or under any state, who, having previously taken an oath, as a member of Congress, or as an officer of the United States, or as a member of any state legislature, or as an executive or judicial officer of any state, to support the Constitution of the United States, shall have engaged in insurrection or rebellion against the same, or given aid or comfort to the enemies thereof. But Congress may by a vote of two-thirds of each House, remove such disability.

Section 4. The validity of the public debt of the United States, authorized by law, including debts incurred for payment of pensions and bounties for services in suppressing insurrection or rebellion, shall not be questioned. But neither the United States nor any state shall assume or pay any debt or obligation incurred in aid of insurrection or rebellion against the United States, or any claim for the loss or emancipation of any slave; but all such debts, obligations and claims shall be held illegal and void.

Section 5. The Congress shall have power to enforce, by appropriate legislation, the provisions of this article.

Amendment XV

(1870)

Section 1. The right of citizens of the United States to vote shall not be denied or abridged by the United States or by any state on account of race, color, or previous condition of servitude.

Section 2. The Congress shall have power to enforce this article by appropriate legislation.

Amendment XVI

(1913)

The Congress shall have power to lay and collect taxes on incomes, from whatever source derived, without apportionment among the several states, and without regard to any census of enumeration.

Amendment XVII

(1913)

The Senate of the United States shall be composed of two Senators from each state, elected by the people thereof, for six years; and each Senator shall have one vote. The electors in each state shall have the qualifications requisite for electors of the most numerous branch of the state legislatures.

When vacancies happen in the representation of any state in the Senate, the executive authority of such state shall issue writs of election to fill such vacancies: Provided, that the legislature of any state may empower the executive thereof to make temporary appointments until the people fill the vacancies by election as the legislature may direct.

This amendment shall not be so construed as to affect the election or term of any Senator chosen before it becomes valid as part of the Constitution.

Amendment XVIII

The Constitution of the United States

(1919)

Section 1. After one year from the ratification of this article the manufacture, sale, or transportation of intoxicating liquors within, the importation thereof into, or the exportation thereof from the United States and all territory subject to the jurisdiction thereof for beverage purposes is hereby prohibited.

Section 2. The Congress and the several states shall have concurrent power to enforce this article by appropriate legislation.

Section 3. This article shall be inoperative unless it shall have been ratified as an amendment to the Constitution by the legislatures of the several states, as provided in the Constitution, within seven years from the date of the submission hereof to the states by the Congress.

Amendment XIX

(1920)

The right of citizens of the United States to vote shall not be denied or abridged by the United States or by any state on account of sex.

Congress shall have power to enforce this article by appropriate legislation.

Amendment XX

(1933)

Section 1. The terms of the President and Vice President shall end at noon on the 20th day of January, and the terms of Senators and Representatives at noon on the 3d day of January, of the years in which such terms would have ended if this article had not been ratified; and the terms of their successors shall then begin.

Section 2. The Congress shall assemble at least once in every year, and such meeting shall begin at noon on the 3d day of January, unless they shall by law appoint a different day.

Section 3. If, at the time fixed for the beginning of the term of the President, the President elect shall have died, the Vice President elect shall become President. If a President shall not have been chosen before the time fixed for the beginning of his term, or if the President elect shall have failed to qualify, then the Vice President elect shall act as President until a President shall have qualified; and the Congress may by law provide for the case wherein neither a President elect nor a Vice President elect shall have qualified, declaring who shall then act as President, or the manner in which one who is to act shall be selected, and such person shall act accordingly until a President or Vice President shall have qualified.

Section 4. The Congress may by law provide for the case of the death of any of the persons from whom the House of Representatives may choose a President whenever the right of choice shall have devolved upon them, and for the case of the death of any of the persons from whom the Senate may choose a Vice President whenever the right of choice shall have devolved upon them.

Section 5. Sections 1 and 2 shall take effect on the 15th day of October following the ratification of this article.

Section 6. This article shall be inoperative unless it shall have been ratified as an amendment to the Constitution by the legislatures of three-fourths of the several states within seven years from the date of its submission.

Amendment XXI

(1933)

Section 1. The eighteenth article of amendment to the Constitution of the United States is hereby repealed.

xxix

The Constitution of the United States

Section 2. The transportation or importation into any state, territory, or possession of the United States for delivery or use therein of intoxicating liquors, in violation of the laws thereof, is hereby prohibited.

Section 3. This article shall be inoperative unless it shall have been ratified as an amendment to the Constitution by conventions in the several states, as provided in the Constitution, within seven years from the date of the submission hereof to the states by the Congress.

Amendment XXII

(1951)

Section 1. No person shall be elected to the office of the President more than twice, and no person who has held the office of President, or acted as President, for more than two years of a term to which some other person was elected President shall be elected to the office of the President more than once. But this article shall not apply to any person holding the office of President when this article was proposed by the Congress, and shall not prevent any person who may be holding the office of President, or acting as President, during the term within which this article becomes operative from holding the office of President or acting as President during the remainder of such term.

Section 2. This article shall be inoperative unless it shall have been ratified as an amendment to the Constitution by the legislatures of three-fourths of the several states within seven years from the date of its submission to the states by the Congress.

Amendment XXIII

(1961)

Section 1. The District constituting the seat of government of the United States shall appoint in such manner as the Congress may direct:

A number of electors of President and Vice President equal to the whole number of Senators and Representatives in Congress to which the District would be entitled if it were a state, but in no event more than the least populous state; they shall be in addition to those appointed by the states, but they shall be considered, for the purposes of the election of President and Vice President, to be electors appointed by a state; and they shall meet in the District and perform such duties as provided by the twelfth article of amendment.

Section 2. The Congress shall have power to enforce this article by appropriate legislation.

Amendment XXIV

(1964)

Section 1. The right of citizens of the United States to vote in any primary or other election for President or Vice President, for electors for President or Vice President, or for Senator or Representative in Congress, shall not be denied or abridged by the United States or any state by reason of failure to pay any poll tax or other tax.

Section 2. The Congress shall have power to enforce this article by appropriate legislation.

Amendment XXV

(1967)

Section 1. In case of the removal of the President from office or of his death or resignation, the Vice President shall become President.

Section 2. Whenever there is a vacancy in the office of the Vice President, the President shall nominate a Vice President who shall take office upon confirmation by a majority vote of bot Houses of Congress.

Section 3. Whenever the President transmits to the President pro tempore of the Senate and the Speaker of the House of Representatives his written declaration that he is unable to discharge the powers and duties of his office, and until he transmits to them a written declaration to the contrary, such powers and duties shall be discharged by the Vice President as Acting President.

Section 4. Whenever the Vice President and a majority of either the principal officers of the executive departments or of such other body as Congress may by law provide, transmit to the President pro tempore of the Senate and the Speaker of the House of Representatives their written declaration that the President is unable to discharge the powers and duties of his office, the Vice President shall immediately assume the powers and duties of the office as Acting President.

Thereafter, when the President transmits to the President pro tempore of the Senate and the Speaker of the House of Representatives his written declaration that no inability exists, he shall resume the powers and duties of his office unless the Vice President and a majority of either the principal officers of the executive department or of such other body as Congress may by law provide, transmit within four days to the President pro tempore of the Senate and the Speaker of the House of Representatives their written declaration that the President is unable to discharge the powers and duties of his office.

Thereupon Congress shall decide the issue, assembling within forty-eight hours for that purpose if not in session. If the Congress, within twenty-one days after receipt of the latter written declaration, or, if Congress is not in session, within twenty-one days after Congress is required to assemble, determines by two-thirds vote of both Houses that the President is unable to discharge the powers and duties of his office, the Vice President shall continue to discharge the same as Acting President; otherwise, the President shall resume the powers and duties of his office.

Amendment XXVI

(1971)

Section 1. The right of citizens of the United States, who are 18 years of age or older, to vote, shall not be denied or abridged by the United States or any state on account of age.

Section 2. The Congress shall have the power to enforce this article by appropriate legislation.

Amendment XXVII

(1992)

No law varying the compensation for the services of the Senators and Representatives shall take effect until an election of Representatives shall have intervened.

Supreme Court Justices

Samuel Anthony Alito, Jr.

Associate Justice, born in Trenton, New Jersey, April 1, 1950. He married Martha-Ann Bomgardner in 1985, and they have two children, Philip and Laura. He received an A.B. from Princeton University in 1972 and a J.D. from Yale Law School in 1975. He served as a law clerk for Leonard I. Garth of the United States Court of Appeals for the Third Circuit from 1976–1977. He was Assistant U.S. Attorney, District of New Jersey, 1977–1981, Assistant to the Solicitor General, U.S. Department of Justice, 1981–1985, Deputy Assistant Attorney General, Office of Legal Counsel, U.S. Department of Justice, 1985–1987, and U.S. Attorney, District of New Jersey, 1987–1990. He was appointed to the United States Court of Appeals for the Third Circuit in 1990. President George W. Bush nominated him as an Associate Justice of the Supreme Court, and he took his seat on January 31, 2006. Since joining the Court, Justice Alito has been a Distinguished Visiting Professor at Pepperdine University, teaching courses on executive power and methods of interpretation.

Stephen Breyer

Born August 15, 1938, in San Francisco, California. Married, three children. Education. Stanford University, A.B., 1959, Great Distinction; Oxford University, B.A., 1961; Harvard Law School, LL.B., magna cum laude, 1964. Clerk to the Honorable Arthur J. Goldberg, Associate Justice of the United States, 1964–65. Harvard University, Assistant Professor, 1967–70; Professor of Law, 1970–80; Professor, Kennedy School of Government, 1977–80; Lecturer, 1980–present. Visiting Professor, College of Law, Sydney, Australia, 1975; University of Rome, 1993. Nominated by President Jimmy Carter to the United States Court of Appeals for the First Circuit, took oath of office December 10, 1980. Nominated by President Bill Clinton as Associate Justice of the United States; took oath of office August 3, 1994.

Ruth Bader Ginsburg

Born March 15, 1933, in Brooklyn, New York. Married, two children. Education. Cornell University, B.A., 1954, with high honors in Government and distinction in all subjects; attended Harvard Law School (1956–58), Harvard Law Review; Columbia Law School, LL.B. (J.D.) 1959. Clerk to the Honorable Edmund L. Palmieri, United States District Court, Southern District of New York, 1959–61; Columbia Law School Project on International Procedure: Research Associate, 1961–62, Associate Director, 1962–63; Rutgers University School of Law, Professor, 1963–72; Columbia Law School, Professor, 1972–80; General counsel and founder of women's rights project, ACLU, 1973–80. Nominated by President Jimmy Carter to United States Court of Appeals for the District of Columbia Circuit, took oath of office June 30, 1980. Nominated by President Bill Clinton as Associate Justice of the United States, took oath of office August 10, 1993.

Elena Kagan

Born in New York, New York, on April 28, 1960. She received an A.B. from Princeton in 1981, an M. Phil. from Oxford in 1983, and a J.D. from Harvard Law School in 1986. She clerked for Judge AbnerMikva of the U.S. Court of Appeals for the D.C. Circuit from 1986-1987 and for Justice Thurgood Marshall of the U.S. Supreme Court during the 1987 Term. After briefly practicing law at a Washington, D.C. law firm, she became a law professor, first at the University of Chicago Law School and later at Harvard Law School. She also served for four years in the Clinton Administration, as Associate Counsel to the President and then as Deputy Assistant to the President for Domestic Policy. Between 2003 and 2009, she served as the Dean of Harvard Law School. In 2009, President Obama nominated her as the Solicitor General of the United States. After serving in that role for a year, the President nominated her as an Associate Justice of the Supreme Court on

Supreme Court Justices

May 10, 2010. She took her seat on August 7, 2010.

Anthony M. Kennedy

Born July 23, 1936 in Sacramento, California. Married, three children. Education. Stanford University, B.A., 1958; Harvard Law School, LL.B., 1961. Private Practice in Sacrament, 1961–75. Professor of constitutional law, McGeorge School of Law, University of the Pacific, 1965–88. Nominated by President Gerald Ford to United States Court of Appeals for the Ninth Circuit, took oath of office May 30, 1975. Nominated by President Ronald Reagan as Associate Justice of the United States, took oath of office February 18, 1988.

John G. Roberts, Jr.

Chief Justice of the United States, born January 27, 1955, in Buffalo, New York. He married Jane Marie Sullivan in 1996; they have two children — Josephine and John. He received an A.B. from Harvard College in 1976 and a J.D. from Harvard Law School in 1979. He served as a law clerk for Henry J. Friendly of the United States Court of Appeals for the Second Circuit from 1979–1980 and as a law clerk for then-Associate Justice William H. Rehnquist of the Supreme Court of the United States during the 1980 Term. He was Special Assistant to the Attorney General, U.S. Department of Justice from 1981–1982, Associate Counsel to President Ronald Reagan, White House Counsel's Office from 1982–1986, and Principal Deputy Solicitor General, U.S. Department of Justice from 1989–1993. From 1986–1989 and 1993–2003, he practiced law in Washington, D.C. He was appointed to the United States Court of Appeals for the District of Columbia Circuit in 2003. President George W. Bush nominated him as Chief Justice of the United States, and he took his seat on September 29, 2005.

Antonin Scalia

Born March 11, 1936 in Trenton, N.J. Married, with nine children. Education. Georgetown University, A.B., 1957; Harvard, LL.B., 1960; note editor. General counsel, Office of Telecommunications Policy, Executive Office of the President, 1971–72. Chairman, Administrative Conference of the United States, 1972–74. Assistant Attorney General, Office of Legal Counsel, U.S. Department of Justice, 1974–77. Law Teaching. Professor of Law, University of Virginia, 1967–74 (on leave 1971–74); scholar in residence, American Enterprise Institute, 1977; visiting professor of law, Georgetown University, 1977; professor of law, University of Chicago, 1977–82; visiting professor of law, Stanford University, 1980–81; Straus Distinguished Visiting Professor, Pepperdine University, Summer 1990. Nominated by President Ronald Reagan to the United States Court of Appeals for the District of Columbia Circuit, took the oath of office August 17, 1982. Nominated by President Reagan as Associate Justice of the United States, took the oath of office September 26, 1986.

Sonia Sotomayor

Born June 25, 1954, in Bronx, New York. She earned a B.A. in 1976 from Princeton University, graduating summa cum laude and receiving the university's highest academic honor. In 1979, she earned a J.D. from Yale Law School where she served as an editor of the Yale Law Journal. She served as Assistant District Attorney in the New York County District Attorney's Office from 1979–1984. She then litigated international commercial matters in New York City at Pavia & Harcourt, where she served as an associate and then partner from 1984–1992. In 1991, President George H.W. Bush nominated her to the U.S. District Court, Southern District of New York, and she served in that role from 1992–1998. She served as a judge on the United States Court of Appeals for the Second Circuit from 1998–2009. President Barack Obama nominated her as an Associate Justice of the Supreme Court on May 26, 2009, notably making the case for empathy as a prime consideration for appointment. See Douglas W Kmiec, The Case for Empathy, America magazine (May 11, 2009). She assumed by bench August 8, 2009.

Supreme Court Justices

Clarence Thomas

Born June 28, 1948 in the Pinpoint community, near Savannah, Georgia. Married, one child. Education. Conception Seminary, 1967–68; Holy Cross College, A.B., cum laude; Yale Law School, J.D., 1974. Assistant Attorney General of Missouri, 1974–77; Attorney, Monsanto Company, 1977–79. Government Service. Legislative assistant to Senator John C. Danforth of Missouri, 1979–81; Assistant Secretary for Civil Rights, U.S. Department of Education, 1981–82; Chairman U.S. Equal Employment Opportunity Commission, 1982–90. Nominated by President George Bush to the United States Court of Appeals for the District of Columbia Circuit, took oath of office, March 12, 1990. Nominated by President George Bush as Associate Justice of the United States, took oath of office October 23, 1991.

Chapter 1

THE DECLARATION AND ITS CONSTITUTION

A. THE CONSTITUTION — MEANS OR END?

Is the Constitution a means to advance particular fundamental ends or principles, or is it a freestanding means to any end, democratically chosen? This is the question taken up in this Chapter. The beginning of an answer is to be found in the English common law tradition. Common law lawyers followed a distinct pattern of legal thinking: the law of God, the law of nature, and the law of the land. Chapter Two addresses all three aspects of the American common law tradition, but concentrates in Part I on the law of nature, or our ability as thinking human beings to reason to good result. Part II of this Chapter turns toward the law of God, at least insofar as it manifests itself in matters of religion. The Declaration of Independence squarely rests the American constitutional order upon both sources, or in its words, "the Laws of Nature and of Nature's God." But from the beginning (see especially, the book of *Genesis*), it has been the nature of human beings to become a law unto themselves through the third source, "the law of the land," or as we know it, positive law. At times, the positive law seemingly has denied not only the relevance of God, but also the very nature of human beings (*e.g.*, slavery). In Part I, we see this turn toward self-centeredness, in the perennial struggle over whether natural law is sufficiently knowable or definite to guide human action, and in particular, constitutional litigation. In Part II, a similar pattern emerges in the struggle to interpret the First Amendment Religion Clauses ("Congress shall make no law respecting an establishment of religion, or prohibiting the free exercise thereof"). At our nation's founding and for a considerable period thereafter, these Clauses preserved, free of an established national church or sect-based favoritism, the individual freedom to choose how best to know and worship God. More recently, however, the Clauses have been transformed into a claim of neutrality between religion and no religion at all. Some say this "neutrality" manifests a hostility to public acknowledgment of the significance of private religious faith.

B. THE COMMON LAW AND THE NATURAL LAW

The common law thought pattern — law of God, law of nature, and law of the land — suffered a major disruption when Henry VIII, in order to secure a divorce contrary to the teaching of the Roman Catholic Church, declared the King of England to be the supreme head of the Church on earth. Thomas More, the King's Lord Chancellor at the time, disagreed, and ultimately for his disagreement, would pay with his life. But as British barrister Richard O'Sullivan reflects below, even as Thomas More died, the idea that the King or Parliament could legislate without limit, or in disregard of some conception of God or our reasoned discovery of human nature, has refused to die.

Richard O'Sullivan, *The Natural Law and Common Law* in 3 NATURAL LAW INSTITUTE PROCEEDINGS 9, 31–37 (Edward F. Barrett ed., 1950)

In 1468 the Lord Chancellor [Thomas More] told the assembled peers that Justice "was ground, well, and root of all prosperity, peace and public rule of every realm, whereupon all the law of the world had been ground and set, which resteth in three; that is to say, the law of God, the law of nature, and the positive law."

* * *

The Year Books bear witness to the same order or hierarchy of laws. There is in Plowden a report of the well-known case of *Hales vs. Petit* in which the Common Bench declared that suicide (in this case the suicide of one of the King's judges) is an offense against God, against Nature and against the King.

1.) Against God, in that it is a breach of His commandment, "Thou shalt not kill" and to kill oneself, by which act he kills in presumption his own soul, is a greater offense than killing another.

2.) Against Nature; because it is contrary to the rule of self-preservation which is the principle of nature, for every living thing does by instinct of nature defend itself against destruction and then to destroy oneself is contrary to nature and a thing most horrible.

3.) Against the King in that hereby he has lost a subject . . . he being the head has lost one of his mystical members.

At the crisis of English history . . . [a] statute dictated by Thomas Cromwell had declared the King to be the Supreme Head on earth of the Ecclesia Anglicana. It gave the King authority to reform and redress all errors and heresies in the land. A second Statute made it treason for anyone maliciously to wish, will or desire by words or in writing to deprive the King of his dignity, title or name of his royal state.

In the first of the four counts of the Indictment [against Thomas More, the Lord Chancellor,] it was alleged that the prisoner, being asked in the Tower, by the Secretary of State whether he "accepted and reputed the King as the Supreme Head of the Church in England," remained silent and declined to make answer. . . .

To this count in the Indictment, the prisoner took exception: "Touching, I say, this challenge and accusation, I answer that for this my taciturnity and silence neither you nor your law nor any law in the world is able justly and rightly to punish me unless you may beside it lay to my charge either some word or some fact in deed."

The objection was overruled, and the pretended trial proceeded to its close on all four counts in the Indictment. After a verdict of guilty on each count had been returned, Thomas More claimed the right to speak his mind: "seeing that I see ye are determined to condemn me (God knoweth how) I will now in discharge of my conscience speak my mind plainly and freely touching my Indictment and your Statute withal."

He proceeded to argue that the Act under which he had been charged and condemned was contrary to the law of God, the law of reason, and the law of the land.

"And forasmuch as this Indictment is grounded upon an Act of Parliament directly repugnant to the laws of God and His Holy Church . . . it is therefore in law among Christian men insufficient to charge any Christian man."

The Statute was against the law of reason: "For this realm being but one member and a small part of the Church, might not make a particular law, disagreeable with the general law of the Church, no more than the City of London being but one poor member in respect of the whole realm, might make a law against an Act of Parliament to bind the whole realm."

The Statute was against the law of the land. It was "contrary to the law and Statutes of this our land, yet unrepealed, as they might evidently perceive in Magna Carta . . . . ["]

In the reign of Henry VIII, says Professor Holdsworth, Vinerian Professor of English Law at the University of Oxford, "It was realized that the Acts of Parliament, whether public or private, were legislative in character and the judges were obligated to admit that these acts however morally unjust must be obeyed. . . . The legislation which had deposed the Pope and made the Church an integral part of the State, had made it clear that the morality of the provisions of a law, or the reasons which induced the legislature to pass it, could not be regarded by the courts."

It was obviously difficult to assign any limits to the power of the Acts of a body which had effected changes so sweeping as those effected by the Reformation Parliament. Lord Burleigh is reported by James I to have said that he knew not what an Act of Parliament could not do in England. When an Act of Parliament had acquired this authority, says Professor Holdsworth, the last remnants of the idea that there might be fundamental laws, which could not be changed by any person or body of persons in the State necessarily disappears.

After the Reformation, the Parliament of England was no longer bound by the laws of nature or the law of God.

* * *

Now, though the theory (or the supposition) of the Omnipotence of Parliament was implicit in the Reformation Statutes, the process of translating this new theory into a practical rule of jurisprudence was not easy or simple. This new theory threatened the whole existence of the Common Law which had its foundation in the natural law . . . .

NOTES AND QUESTIONS

1.   Why did the legislation formalizing England's break with the Roman Catholic church also provides, as Professor Holdsworth reports, that henceforth "the morality of the provisions of the law . . . could not be regarded by the courts"? Isn't it the idea of the natural law that truth is knowable and universal regardless of religious denomination? Why would the formation of the Anglican Church threaten the "whole existence of the Common Law"? What is the relationship between natural law and common law?

2.   Professor Holdsworth was the Vinerian Professor of English Law at Oxford. This position was first occupied by Sir William Blackstone (1723–1780), whose famous *Commentaries on the Laws of England* was widely regarded by the leading American colonists as the best treatise on the English common law, which became the foundation of American law. The following passage from the *Commentaries* was thus most familiar to the American founders. Note, in particular, how Blackstone coins the terminology "pursuit of happiness," which later finds its way into the Declaration of Independence. Note as well how Blackstone indicates that the natural law, man's reasoned deduction of that impressed by God within the design of human nature, became interwoven with the common law (natural law "is branched in our systems").

1 WILLIAM BLACKSTONE, COMMENTARIES ON THE LAWS OF ENGLAND *38–41 (James Dewitt Andrews ed., Callaghan Co. 4th ed. 1899)

[W]hen the Supreme Being formed the universe, and created matter out of nothing, he impressed certain principles upon that matter, from which it can never depart, and without which it would cease to be . . . .

* * *

This then is the general significance of law, a rule of action dictated by some superior being; and in those creatures that have neither the power to think, nor to will, such laws must be invariably obeyed, so long as the creature itself subsists, for its existence depends on that obedience. But laws, in their more confined sense, and in which it is our present business to consider them, denote the rules, not of action in general, but of *human* action or conduct: that is, the precepts by which man . . . endowed with both reason and free will, is commanded to make use of those faculties in the general regulation of his behaviour.

Man, considered as a creature, must necessarily be subject to the laws of his creator, for he is entirely a dependent being. . . . [A] state of dependence will inevitably oblige the inferior to take the will of him, on whom he depends, as the rule of his conduct . . . in all those points wherein his dependence consists. . . . [C]onsequently, [since] man depends absolutely upon his maker for every thing, it is necessary that he should in all points conform to his maker's will.

This will of his maker is called the law of nature. [Emphasis added.] For as God, when he created matter, and endued it with a principle of mobility, established certain rules for the perpetual direction of that motion; so, when he created man, and endued him with free will to conduct himself in all parts of life, he laid down certain immutable laws of human nature, whereby that free will is in some degree regulated and restrained, and gave him also the faculty of *reason* to discover the purport of those laws . . . .

* * *

. . . [T]he Creator is a being, not only of infinite *power*, and *wisdom*, but also of infinite *goodness*, [therefore,] he has been pleased so to contrive the constitution and frame of humanity, that we should want no other prompter to inquire after and pursue the rule of right, but only our own self love, that universal principle of action. For he has so intimately connected, so inseparably interwoven the laws of eternal justice with the happiness of each individual, that [happiness] cannot be attained but by observing the former; and, if the former be punctually obeyed, it cannot but induce [happiness]. In consequence of which mutual connection of justice and human felicity, [God] has not perplexed the law of nature with a multitude of abstracted rules and precepts . . . but has graciously reduced the rule of obedience to this one paternal precept, *"that man shall pursue his own true and substantial happiness."* [Emphasis added.] This is the foundation of what we call ethics, or natural law. For the several articles into which it is branched in our systems, amount to no more than demonstrating, that this or that action tends to man's real happiness, and therefore very justly concluding that the performance of it is a part of the law of nature; or, on the other hand, that this or that action is destructive of man's real happiness, and therefore that the law of nature forbids it.

NOTES AND QUESTIONS

1.   How might Blackstone prove especially useful in the American colonies' dispute with England over representation and related matters, such as trade and taxation? Blackstone described natural law as "binding over all the globe in all countries, and at all times; no human laws are of any validity, if contrary to this; and such of them as are valid derive all of their force, and all of their authority, mediately or immediately, from this origin." *Id.* at *41. For American colonies looking for persuasive authority to dispute adverse English Parliamentary measures such as the Stamp Act, Blackstone was invaluable. When Blackstone declares the absolute rights of individuals as "the right of personal security, the right of personal liberty, and the right of private property," *id.* at *129, he virtually prescribes the trilogy of unalienable rights in the Declaration of Independence.

2.   Blackstone easily saw the natural law as explicated through the application of the common law as binding in theory on all. Thus, returning to the question at issue in this Chapter — whether or not the Constitution must be construed to advance particular fundamental ends — it would thus far appear that Blackstone would be inclined to say that it must. Legislative power no more than the arbitrary prerogatives asserted by the Stuart Kings can contradict the natural law. As Blackstone writes, "acts of Parliament that are impossible to be performed are of no validity; and if there arise out of them . . . any absurd consequences, . . . contradictory to common reason [informed by the natural law, of course — Eds.], they are, with regard to those collateral consequences, void." *Id.* at *91. In other words, *all* of government — even that derived from consent in the legislature — is

subject to (or if you will, must advance) particular fundamental (natural law) ends.

3.   But there's a problem, *who* was to tell a given government entity that it has acted beyond its authority or in derogation of fundamental principle? As suggested in Chapter 1, this question emerged in England when the Stuart monarchs in the 17th century declared themselves to be superior to the common law and Acts of Parliament. In the words of Lord Chancellor Ellesmere in *Calvin's Case*, "the monarch is the law; the King is the law speaking." 77 Eng. Rep. 377 (K.B. 1608). As we learned, Parliament contested this brazen assertion and would ultimately prevail in the so-called Glorious Revolution of 1688 in which James II fled the country to be replaced by William and Mary, who, in the 1689 English Bill of Rights, acquiesced to legislative supremacy. But what if the legislative body disregards fundamental right? Here, Blackstone posits that "if the parliament will positively enact [an unreasonable thing, there is] no power in the ordinary forms of the constitution, that is vested with authority to control it." 1 Blackstone, *supra*, at *91. Uncomfortably, from the standpoint of principled argumentation, Blackstone appears to stand for the asymmetrical proposition that the King or executive must be under the enacted law, and yes, the legislature is bound by the common (natural) law in the enactment of law, but there is no entity known to man able to correct the legislature when it, itself, exceeds these boundaries. Blackstone explicitly rejects judicial review, arguing "the judges are [not] at liberty to reject it; for that were to set the judicial power above that of the legislature, which would be subversive of all government." *Id.*

4.   A recurring question in this book will ask you to evaluate whether there is an inability to constrain legislative action contrary to fundamental natural law in the United States. Acclaimed Law School Deans Roscoe Pound of Harvard and Clarence Manion of Notre Dame argue that Blackstone's view did not carry over to America. Pound wrote:

> [T]here are three points of origin of what has been called the American doctrine of [judicial review:] . . . [Coke's] idea of the law of the land[,] . . . . Coke's doctrine that statutes contrary to common right and reason . . . were void[,] . . . [and] the practice . . . of appeals to the Privy Council in which statutes enacted by colonial legislatures were held void . . . . That statutes could be scrutinized to look into the basis of their authority and if in conflict with fundamental law must be disregarded was as much a matter of course to the American lawyer of the era of the Revolution as the doctrine of the absolute binding force of an act of Parliament is to the English lawyer of today. American lawyers were taught to believe in a fundamental law which, after the [American] Revolution, they found declared in written constitutions.

Roscoe Pound, *The Development of Constitutional Guarantees of Liberty*, 20 Notre Dame L. Rev. 347, 367 (1945). Dean Pound's proposition that America rejected legislative supremacy, and thus, deliberately linked its written Constitution to the fundamental natural law has been repeated by many. The most concise summation of natural law proximate to the founding was the Declaration of Independence. The late Dean Clarence Manion of the University of Notre Dame put it this way:

The fact is that the Declaration is the best possible condensation of [Anglo-American] natural law-common law doctrines as they were developed . . . for hundreds of years prior to the American Revolution. By pushing and pursuing the principle of parliamentary absolutism it was England and not America who abandoned the ancient traditions of English liberty. In 1776 the British Government was insisting that "the law of the land" and "the immemorial rights of English subjects" were exclusively and precisely what the British Parliament from time to time declared them to be. This claim . . . was at variance with all the great traditions of the natural law and common law . . . from Bracton to Blackstone. By abandoning their ingrained concepts of the natural law, the colonists undoubtedly could have made a comfortable settlement of their . . . difficulties with England, but they chose the alternatives so well and so logically declared in the Declaration of Independence.

Clarence E. Manion, *The Natural Law Philosophy of the Founding Fathers*, 1 NATURAL LAW INSTITUTE PROCEEDINGS 3, 16 (Alfred L. Scanlan ed., 1949). But as we will see later in this Chapter, today's Supreme Court is ambivalent over the scope of judicial review, and in particular, whether it is to be guided by natural law. Of course, even if Pound, Manion or others convince you to accept judicial review based upon higher or natural law principle, who then is to check the *judiciary* when it goes astray? In this regard, many modern legal historians and commentators perceive the greatest danger to democratic governance and natural law principle to lie with the judiciary. What do you think?

C. THE DECLARATION OF INDEPENDENCE — A SUMMARY OF AMERICAN FUNDAMENTAL PRINCIPLE

THE DECLARATION OF INDEPENDENCE
para. 2 (U.S. 1776) (Preamble)

We hold these truths to be self-evident, that all men are created equal, that they are endowed by their Creator with certain unalienable Rights, that among these are Life, Liberty, and the pursuit of Happiness. That to secure these rights, Governments are instituted among Men, deriving their just powers from the consent of the governed — That whenever any Form of Government becomes destructive of these ends, it is the Right of the People to alter or to abolish it, and to institute new Government, laying its foundation on such principles and organizing its powers in such form, as to them shall seem most likely to effect their Safety and Happiness.

NOTES AND QUESTIONS

1. These relatively few words are viewed by notable political theorists to summarize, as the late political philosopher Russell Kirk revealed in a book by the same name, *The Roots of the American Order*. Chapter One and this Chapter have introduced you to these sources. The Declaration recites that we as a Nation hold at least some *truths to be self-evident*: that is, every proposition isn't equally valid.

Some opinions are right; others, wrong. In the phraseology, "the Laws of Nature and of Nature's God," we are further instructed that the measure of the validity of any opinion is to be found in one of two sources — either reasoned reflection upon the intrinsic design of human nature, "the laws of nature," or the "law of Nature's God," that is, the revealed word of God. These are the very same sources of authority relied upon by Thomas More to evaluate the actions of Henry VIII.

Nevertheless, you will shortly learn, if you do not already know from previous study, that referencing God, revelation, or religion generally in terms of constitutional study has been made controversial, in part, as a result of highly contested Supreme Court opinions since about 1940, and especially since 1960. These case developments are explored in Part II.B. of this Chapter. Nevertheless, in 1776 — and indeed throughout much of the history of America — the existence of God (as a "Creator") is an accepted postulate of the American order. Of course, much of God's revealed word, be it located in the Old or New Testaments or informed by other religious instruction, is basic guidance into how to "pursue happiness" — that is, live a good and happy life. The framers recognized as much. In his first inaugural address, for example, George Washington observed that "the propitious smiles of Heaven can never be expected on a nation that disregards the eternal rules of order and right, which Heaven itself has ordained." GEORGE WASHINGTON, FIRST INNAUGURAL ADDRESS (Apr. 30, 1789), *reprinted in* GEORGE WASHINGTON: A COLLECTION 460, 462 (W.B. Allen ed., 1988).

Human knowledge being imperfect, we differ in how we come to know God. But arguably, these denominational differences merely reveal the founders' justification for narrowing the role of government by prudently enumerating federal power, and securing religious freedom in the Bill of Rights. More on First Amendment religious freedoms later, but it is enough to observe here that the drafters of the Declaration, and the framers of the Constitution, believed that government authority must necessarily be limited to leave room for individuals to pursue moral instruction within their freely chosen religious community. They anticipated, maybe better than they knew, that where God is banished, the state — as a substitute source of ultimate authority — expands rapidly. This is the totalitarian history of the former Soviet Union, where the exact opposite of the Declaration of Independence was asserted — "man makes religion," claimed Karl Marx arrogantly, "religion does not make man."

The Declaration affirms one further creation-based proposition of some importance: "all men are created equal." This does not mean that all men and women have the very same talents or leanings, but it does mean that no one of us has any better claim to govern than any other. There is no divine kingship in America. We are all equal before God, and therefore, only those persons can lead who are chosen with our consent. Those we consent to be governed by, are bound, as we all are, to observe the "unalienable rights of life, liberty, and the pursuit of happiness." These human rights pre-date all governments, including our own, and entitlement to them stems simply from the intrinsic worth of each created human being.

2. Do these principles embedded within the Declaration have continuing validity, or have they been superseded by events? To give a full answer, one would need not only a responsible approach to constitutional interpretation, but also entire courses in epistemology, theology, philosophy, and jurisprudence. A less elaborate, but arguably workable response, is simply to observe that the United States Code includes the Declaration of Independence as one of the Organic Laws upon which all statutory law rests. *See* 1 U.S.C., at xli (1994). In other words, the Declaration has not been repealed. As Lincoln said to Stephen A. Douglas in debate, "[i]f th[e D]eclaration is not the truth, let us get the statute book, in which we find it, and tear it out!" Abraham Lincoln, Speech in reply to Senator Douglas (July 10, 1858), *in* THE POLITICAL DEBATES BETWEEN ABRAHAM LINCOLN AND STEPHEN A. DOUGLAS 20, 35 (Cleveland, O.S. Hubbel & Co. 1895).

 3. But doesn't modern science undermine our founders' belief in a Creator as the ultimate source of unalienable rights? Judging by the consistently high reports of faith belief in the United States (well over 90%), the answer would seem to be no. Scientific developments in evolutionary and genetic theory have not undermined belief in transcendent values or the view that some truth can be known. Perhaps this is so because advances in scientific research and theory neither prove, nor must they depend upon proving, the denial of God. *See* PHILIP E. JOHNSON, REASON IN THE BALANCE (1995); PATRICK GLYNN, GOD — THE EVIDENCE (1997). President Calvin Coolidge once reflected that

> no progress can be made beyond [the propositions of the Declaration]. If anyone wishes to deny their truth or their soundness, the only direction in which he can proceed historically is not forward, but backward toward the time when there was no equality, no rights of the individual, no rule of the people. Those who wish to proceed in this direction cannot claim to progress, they are reactionary.

CALVIN COOLIDGE, FOUNDATIONS OF THE REPUBLIC: SPEECHES & ADDRESSES 451–52 (1928).

 4. For a contemporary account of the significance of the natural law by a respected elder statesman of constitutional law, see CHARLES E. RICE, FIFTY QUESTIONS ON THE NATURAL LAW (1993). Modern commentary on a broad range of natural law issues can also be found in the American Journal of Jurisprudence.

1. The Declaration and the Formation of the Constitution

 The principal author of the Declaration, Thomas Jefferson, appears to have anticipated a continuing interpretative role for the Declaration. In correspondence, Jefferson first acknowledged that the Declaration was not intended "to invent new ideas," but to re-state well-grounded common or natural law ideas. To the notion that following the successful American Revolution, the Declaration should be set aside "to spare the feeling of our English friends," Jefferson retorted, "it is not to wound them that we wish to keep it in mind; but to cherish the principles of the instrument in the bosoms of our own citizens. . . . I pray God that these principles may be eternal." Letter from Thomas Jefferson to James Madison (Sept. 4, 1823), *in* 15 THE WRITINGS OF THOMAS JEFFERSON 460, 463–64 (Andrew A. Lipscomb & Albert Ellery Bergh eds., 1904). Madison shared this view. In a letter to Jefferson, for example, Madison recommended the Declaration as the first of the "best guides" to the "distinctive principles" of government. Letter from James Madison to Thomas Jefferson (Feb. 8, 1825), *in* 9 THE WRITINGS OF JAMES MADISON 218, 221 (Gaillard Hunt ed., 1910). Similarly, Abraham Lincoln would call the equality principle of the Declaration "the great fundamental principle upon which our free institutions rest." Letter from Abraham Lincoln to James N. Brown (Oct. 18, 1858), *in* 3 THE COLLECTED WORKS OF ABRAHAM LINCOLN 327, 327 (Roy P. Basler ed., 1953). The Reverend Martin Luther King, Jr. called the Declaration the "promissory note to which every American was to fall heir." Martin Luther King, Jr., *I Have a Dream* (Aug. 28, 1963), *in* A TESTAMENT OF HOPE: THE ESSENTIAL WRITINGS OF MARTIN LUTHER KING, JR. 217 (James M. Washington ed., 1986).

The importance of the Declaration is largely assumed in THE FEDERALIST, a collection of 85 letters written to the general public from October 1787 to August 1788 in an effort to win ratification for the proposed Constitution in New York. Most of these letters, printed under the pseudonym Publius, first appeared in newsprint. They were written chiefly by Alexander Hamilton, who was aided by James Madison, and to a lesser extent, by a distinguished New York lawyer, John Jay. Noted political historian Clinton Rossiter places THE FEDERALIST

> third only to the Declaration of Independence and the Constitution itself among all the sacred writings of American political history. It has a quality of legitimacy, of authority and authenticity, that gives it the high status of a public document, one to which, as Thomas Jefferson put it, "appeal is habitually made by all, and rarely declined or denied by any" as to the "genuine meaning" of the Constitution.

Clinton Rossiter, *Introduction* to THE FEDERALIST PAPERS, at vii (Clinton Rossiter ed., 1961). The fundamental principles of the Declaration logically preceded THE FEDERALIST argument because, as the distinguished authors of the papers repeatedly illustrate, the constitutional means there explained depend upon agreement upon governmental ends, such as the "security of liberty," *id.* at Nos. 1, 70 (Hamilton), No. 51 (Madison); guarding the rights of individuals with an independent judiciary, *id.* at No. 78 (Hamilton); and protecting civil and religious rights, *id.* at No. 51 (Madison). The language of the Declaration is directly referenced in THE FEDERALIST NO. 43, where Madison addresses the difficult issue of how a Constitution proposed to be ratified by less than the unanimity required by Article 13 of the Articles of Confederation could be binding and what the relation of any dissenting states would be to the others. Madison's answer to both questions depends, in significant part, on his direct reference to fundamental principles of natural law or the "transcendent law of nature and of nature's God" (the precise language of the Declaration), which delimits the object of all political institutions.

THE FEDERALIST NO. 43 (James Madison)
(Clinton Rossiter ed., 1961)

> 9. "The ratification of the conventions of nine States shall be sufficient for the establishment of this Constitution between the States, ratifying the same."

This article speaks for itself. The express authority of the people alone could give due validity to the Constitution. To have required the unanimous ratification of the thirteen States would have subjected the essential interests of the whole to the caprice or corruption of a single member. It would have marked a want of foresight in the convention, which our own experience would have rendered inexcusable.

Two questions of a very delicate nature present themselves on this occasion: 1. On what principle the Confederation, which stands in the solemn form of a compact among the States, can be superseded without the unanimous consent of the parties to it? 2. What relation is to subsist between the nine or more States ratifying the Constitution, and the remaining few who do not become parties to it?

The first question is answered at once by recurring to the absolute necessity of the case; to the great principle of self-preservation; to the transcendent law of nature and of nature's God, which declares that the safety and happiness of society are the objects at which all political institutions aim and to which all such institutions must be sacrificed. *Perhaps*, also, an answer may be found without searching beyond the principles of the compact itself. It has been heretofore noted among the defects of the Confederation that in many of the States it had received no higher sanction than a mere legislative ratification. The principle of reciprocity seems to require that its obligation on the other States should be reduced to the same standard. A compact between independent sovereigns, founded on ordinary acts of legislative authority, can pretend to no higher validity than a league or treaty between the parties. It is an established doctrine on the subject of treaties that all the articles are mutually conditions of each other; that a breach of any one article is a breach of the whole treaty; and that a breach, committed by either of the parties, absolves the others, and authorizes them, if they please, to pronounce the compact violated and void. Should it unhappily be necessary to appeal to these delicate truths for a justification for dispensing with the consent of particular States to a dissolution of the federal pact, will not the complaining parties find it a difficult task to answer the *multiplied* and *important* infractions with which they may be confronted? The time has been when it was incumbent on us all to veil the ideas which this paragraph exhibits. The scene is now changed, and with it the part which the same motives dictate.

The second question is not less delicate; and the flattering prospect of its being merely hypothetical forbids an over-curious discussion of it. It is one of those cases which must be left to provide for itself. In general, it may be observed that although no political relation can subsist between the assenting and dissenting States, yet the moral relations will remain uncanceled. The claims of justice, both on one side and on the other, will be in force, and must be fulfilled; the rights of humanity must in all cases be duly and mutually respected; whilst considerations of a common interest, and, above all, the remembrance of the endearing scenes which are past, and the anticipation of a speedy triumph over the obstacles to reunion, will, it is hoped, not urge in vain *moderation* on one side, and *prudence* on the other.

NOTES AND QUESTIONS

1. The Anti-Federalists who opposed the ratification of the Constitution similarly relied upon the principles of the Declaration. Throughout Anti-Federalist materials there is a reference to how the primary object of any new government must be "to secure . . . natural rights." *Essay by the Impartial Examiner to the Free People of Virginia* (Feb. 20, 1788), *reprinted in* 5 THE COMPLETE ANTI-

FEDERALIST 173, 176 (Herbert J. Storing ed., 1981). Indeed, it was with that object in mind that Anti-Federalist opposition was written; the essential complaint being that the proposed union would not guarantee the unalienable natural rights of individuals. Like both the Declaration and THE FEDERALIST (No. 22), Anti-Federalist leaders assumed that the only legitimate government was one premised upon consent of the governed. In arguing that the proposed constitution did not sufficiently sustain this principle, the Anti-Federalist "Brutus" appears to make direct reference to the language of the Declaration, writing:

> [T]he people of America . . . hold this truth as self evident, that all men are by nature free. No one man, therefore, or any class of men, have a right, by the law of nature, . . . to assume or exercise authority over their fellows. The origin of society then is to be sought . . . in the united consent of those who associate.

Essay of Brutus to the Citizens of New York (Nov. 1, 1787) *reprinted in* 2 THE COMPLETE ANTI-FEDERALIST, *supra*, at 372–73.

2.   The significance of the Declaration continues to the present. Dr. Harry Jaffa, whose scholarly career has been substantially devoted to exploring the profound implications of the Declaration for the Constitution, writes:

> *Acts of Congress* admitting new states into the Union are of the highest constitutional standing. Since the Civil War every enabling act has laid down the identical relationship of Constitution and Declaration. For example:

> That the Constitution when formed shall be republican, and not repugnant to the Constitution of the United States and the principles of the Declaration of Independence. [Nebraska, 1864]

> The Constitution of the State of Alaska shall always be republican in form and shall not be repugnant to the Constitution of the United States and the principles of the Declaration of Independence. [1959]

> The Constitution of the State of Hawaii shall always be republican in form and shall not be repugnant to the Constitution of the United States and the principles of the Declaration of Independence. [1959]

Harry V. Jaffa, *Slaying the Dragon of Bad Originalism: Jaffa Answers Cooper,* 1995 PUB. INTEREST L. REV. 209, 218 n.20 (emphasis added).

After surveying the founders' reliance upon the Declaration in some depth, Dan Himmelfarb concludes:

> [T]he Declaration of Independence is more than a propaganda instrument or legal brief . . . in fact it is fundamental to a proper understanding of the Constitution. . . . Indeed, it would hardly be an exaggeration to say that the most fundamental pronouncements made in connection with the framing and ratification of the Constitution are restatements of the principles articulated in the second sentence of the Declaration of Independence.

. . . [T]hose whose constitutional theories rest on the premise that the essential feature of American government is popular rule must confront [this evidence] that it is the security of rights that is the essential feature of American government; that democracy is merely a means toward that end, one of several forms of government to which a people might consent; that the American regime, in short, is liberal primarily, democratic only secondarily.

Dan Himmelfarb, *The Constitutional Relevance of the Second Sentence of the Declaration of Independence*, 100 YALE L.J. 169, 170–71, 186–87 (1990) (footnotes omitted).

2.   The Written Constitution — A Substitute for the Declaration?

The Declaration is a concise summation of natural law principle and, as reflected above, it had continuing significance throughout the founding period. But, notwithstanding the admonitions of Jefferson and Madison, should the Declaration and the vast body of common and natural law tradition it represents have governing significance today? Another way of asking this question is: Did the participants at the federal constitutional convention envision that they were displacing the fundamental principles of the Declaration with a written Constitution?

The short answer is no, or at least, not entirely. The delegates coming into the constitutional convention of 1787 understood a constitution not as a written document, but as the embodiment of long-established laws, traditions, and first principles consistent with natural law. As one writer put it, the "Magna Charta, doth not give the privileges therein mentioned, nor doth our Charters, but must be considered as only declaratory of our rights, and in affirmance of them." Silas Downer, *A Discourse at the Dedication of the Tree of Liberty* (1798), *in* 1 AMERICAN POLITICAL WRITING DURING THE FOUNDING ERA, 1760–1805, at 97, 100 (Charles S. Hyneman & Donald S. Lutz eds., 1983). Judicial cases prior to the constitutional convention similarly make reference to principles of fundamental law without regard to whether the source of the fundamental law was written or not. For example, in the New York case of *Rutgers v. Waddington* (N.Y. City Mayor's Ct. 1784), *reprinted in* 1 THE LAW PRACTICE OF ALEXANDER HAMILTON 392 (Julius Goebel, Jr., ed., 1964), Alexander Hamilton defended a British citizen against a trespass complaint for occupation of property during the Revolutionary War. Hamilton argued not only that the natural law, or "law of nations," justified the defendant's actions in time of war, but also that the New York courts were bound to give effect to such "universal" principles in adjudication. *Id.* at 399–400. The court agreed. New York could enact its trespass statute, but it could not be employed in a manner inconsistent with the unwritten, but nevertheless fundamental, law of nations obligatory upon all. *Id.* at 411. In response to the landowner's argument that "the *customary and voluntary law of nations*" did not bind New York, the court answered, "[b]y our excellent constitution, the common law is declared to be part of the law of the land; and the [law of nations] is a branch of the common law." *Id.* at 402.

Mid-way through the convention in Philadelphia, however, the idea began to take hold that the constitutional document being drafted might itself be fundamental law. As Suzanna Sherry has pointed out in a particularly illuminating article, Alexander Hamilton in a "rambling speech" on June 18 suggested to the convention delegates that the written Constitution could itself be a self-executing source of law — "[a]ll laws of the particular States contrary to the Constitution or laws of the United States [shall] be utterly void." 1 JAMES MADISON, DEBATES IN THE FEDERAL CONVENTION OF 1787, at 119 (Gaillard Hunt & James Brown Scott eds., Promethius Books 1987) (1920). However, Hamilton then obscured the point of self-enforcement by suggesting that the national legislature would be given a negative over state laws. *See* Suzanna Sherry, *The Founders' Unwritten Constitution*, 54 U. CHI. L. REV. 1127, 1147 (1987). In mid-July, Luther Martin introduced what was later to become the Constitution's Supremacy Clause (Article VI, Clause 2), but his proposal made only legislative acts, not the Constitution itself, the supreme law of the land. In late August, however, John Rutledge added the Constitution to this assertion of supremacy, and William Samuel Johnson successfully moved to amend the concept of federal jurisdiction to include cases "arising under the Constitution." *See* Sherry, *supra*, at 1148–50.

Thus, the concept of the Constitution as a written, freestanding, enforceable document of positive law came to life. It got a further boost when the convention discussed how the new Constitution would be ratified. The convention's handiwork well-exceeded "amendments" to the existing Articles of Confederation, even though that is how the draft was disingenuously labeled for reasons of strategy, and there was a practical realization among the delegates that the new Constitution might well go down to defeat if submitted to state legislatures, whose power would be diminished by the new charter. *See id.* at 1150–51. As a cover plan for this practical difficulty, George Mason and later James Madison posited that the product of the convention should not be submitted to state legislatures that were mere creatures of their own state constitutions, but to "the clear [and] undisputed authority of the people." 2 MADISON, *supra*, at 305. Madison elaborated:

> He considered the difference between a system founded on the Legislatures only, and one founded on the people, to be the true difference between a *league* or *treaty*, and a *Constitution*. The former in point of *moral obligation* might be as inviolable as the latter. . . . [However, a] law violating a treaty ratified by a pre-existing law, might be respected by the Judges as a law, though an unwise or perfidious one. A law violating a constitution established by the people themselves, would be considered by the Judges as null [and] void.

Id. at 308–9.

Madison's convention speech supporting popular ratification is an obvious foundation for judicial review, but did it mean that the judges should interpret the ratified Constitution as a self-contained positive enactment or as a document to be construed in light of the Declaration and the natural law principles it summarized? Much modern commentary at various points on the political spectrum suggests only the former. In fairly substantial disregard of the historical record just canvassed, former Judge Robert Bork wrote in his book *The Tempting of America*:

[I]f the Founders intended judges to apply natural law, they certainly kept quiet about it. Many historians are not even sure the Founders as a group contemplated any form of judicial review, even review confined to enforcement of the text, much less review according to an unmentioned natural law. No one at the time suggested any such power in the courts, and early courts made no claim that such a power had been delegated to them.

ROBERT H. BORK, THE TEMPTING OF AMERICA 209 (1990). Likewise, Jefferson Powell has written that the framers linked " 'the Constitution' with a single normative document instead of a historical tradition, . . . thus . . . creat[ing] the possibility of treating constitutional interpretation as an exercise in the traditional legal activity of construing a written instrument." H. Jefferson Powell, *The Original Understanding of Original Intent*, 98 HARV. L. REV. 885, 902 (1985) (footnote omitted). Both Bork and Powell may seriously understate the accomplishments of the framers: yes, they did establish the written Constitution as a source of authority in itself, but in doing so, there is considerable evidence that they had no intention of displacing the fundamental natural law principles in the Declaration or the common law tradition that preceded its ratification. *See* Eugene V. Rostow, *The Perils of Positivism: A Response to Professor Quigley*, 2 DUKE J. COMP. & INT'L L. 229 (1992) (arguing that positivism is jurisprudentially flawed because it divorces legal rules from their historical and political context). That those who drafted the Constitution thought interpretative reference would continue to be made to the natural law — in giving substance to such clauses as the Privileges and Immunities Clause and the Republican Guarantee Clause of Article IV, for example — can be gleaned from a variety of sources: the convention debates generally, the specific debate in the convention and during ratification over the necessity of an express bill of rights, Madison's comments introducing his draft of the Bill of Rights in the first Congress, the earliest decisions of the Supreme Court, and actions taken by the first Congresses. *See* John C. Eastman, *The Declaration of Independence as Viewed from the States, in* SCOTT D. GERBER, ED., THE DECLARATION OF INDEPENDENCE: ORIGINS AND IMPACT 96 (CQ Press 2002). Each of these sources are briefly examined in the materials that follow.

a.   Natural Law at the Constitutional Convention

In the convention, several critical discussions reveal the continuing significance of natural law to constitutional interpretation. In Chapter Three, we take up directly the issue of judicial review. Much of what we know about the founders' view of that subject comes from the convention's discussion, and rejection on four separate occasions, of a proposed Council of Revision. As contemplated and promoted by Madison, the Council would consist of members of both the executive and judicial branches, and a primary function would be to review federal legislation before it took effect. The Council would have been empowered to veto or preclude new laws from taking effect, subject to legislative override for laws re-passed by the national legislature. As noted, the Council was rejected and the convention instead gave a qualified veto to the President alone. The rejection of the Council did not mean a rejection of judicial review, though it did signal that the delegates did not see such review including a revisionary power in judges *before* laws took effect. For present purposes, the Council is relevant because the multiple debates surrounding it suggest that judges were expected to make reference to principles of natural justice in assaying constitutionality.

DEBATES IN THE CONSTITUTIONAL CONVENTION
Saturday, July 21, 1787, *available in*
2 JAMES MADISON, DEBATES IN THE FEDERAL CONVENTION OF 1787 at 294–99
(Gaillard Hunt & James Brown Scott eds.,
Prometheus Books 1987) (1920)
(emphasis added)

* * *

MR. WILSON moved as an amendment to Resol[utio]n. 10. that the supreme Nat[iona]l. Judiciary should be associated with the Executive in the Revisionary power. This proposition had been before made and failed: but he was so confirmed by reflection in the opinion of its utility, that he thought it incumbent on him to make another effort: The Judiciary ought to have an opportunity of remonstrating ag[ain]st. projected encroachments on the people as well as on themselves. It had been said that the Judges, as expositors of the Laws would have an opportunity of defending their constitutional rights. There was weight in this observation; *but this power of the Judges did not go far enough. Laws may be unjust, may be unwise, may be dangerous, may be destructive; and yet may not be so unconstitutional as to justify the Judges in refusing to give them effect.* Let them have a share in the Revisionary power, and they will have an opportunity of taking notice of these characters of a law, and of counteracting, by the weight of their opinions the improper views of the Legislature. —

MR. MADISON [seconded] the motion.

MR. GHORUM did not see the advantage of employing the Judges in this way. As Judges they are not to be presumed to possess any peculiar knowledge of the mere policy of public measures . . . .

MR. ELSEWORTH [*sic*] approved heartily of the motion. The aid of the Judges will give more wisdom [and] firmness to the Executive. They will possess a systematic and accurate knowledge of the Laws, which the Executive can not be expected always to possess. *The law of Nations also will frequently come into question. Of this the Judges alone will have competent information.*

MR. MADISON considered the object of the motion as of great importance to the meditated Constitution. . . . It would moreover be useful to the Community at large as an additional *check ag[ain]st. a pursuit of those unwise [and] unjust measures* which constituted so great a portion of our calamities.

MR. GERRY did not expect to see this point which had undergone full discussion, again revived. . . . *It was making Statesmen of the Judges; and setting them up as the guardians of the Rights of the People.* He relied for his part on the Representatives of the people as the guardians of their Rights [and] interests. It was making the Expositors of the Laws, the Legislators which ought never to be done. . . .

MR. STRONG thought with Mr. Gerry that the *power of making ought to be kept distinct from that of expounding,* the laws. No maxim was better established. The

Judges in exercising the function of expositors might be influenced by the part they had taken, in framing the laws.

Mr. L. Martin considered the association of the Judges with the Executive as a dangerous innovation; as well as one which could not produce the particular advantage expected from it. A knowledge of Mankind, and of Legislative affairs cannot be presumed to belong in a higher degree to the Judges than to the Legislature. *And as to the Constitutionality of laws, that point will come before the Judges in their proper official character. In this character they have a negative on the laws* . . . .

Col. Mason observed that the defence of the Executive was not the sole object of the Revisionary power. He expected even greater advantages from it. Notwithstanding the precautions taken in the Constitution of the Legislature, it would still so much resemble that of the individual States, that it must be expected frequently *to pass unjust and pernicious laws.* This restraining power was therefore essentially necessary. It would have the effect not only of hindering the final passage of such laws; but would discourage demagogues from attempting to get them passed. It had been said [by Mr. L. Martin] that if the judges were joined in this check on the laws, they would have a double negative, since in their expository capacity of Judges they would have one negative. He would reply that in this capacity they could impede in one case only, the operation of laws. *They could declare an unconstitutional law void. But with regard to every law however unjust oppressive or pernicious, which did not come plainly under this description, they would be under the necessity as Judges to give it a free course.*

NOTES AND QUESTIONS

1.   In the July 21 debate, James Wilson makes plain that the concept of unconstitutionality is not limited to constitutional text. In particular, Wilson relates unconstitutionality to injustice, ill-wisdom, and dangerousness. Ellesworth and Madison second this broader conception of unconstitutionality by making reference to "the law of nations," which as in the *Rutgers* case, *supra*, was merely the natural law differently expressed, and by repeating how a constitutional inquiry is one aimed at avoiding "calamity." Similarly, Mason can logically be read as supporting Wilson, but expressing the worry that not every law may be so plainly "unjust oppressive or pernicious" as to allow judges in the normal exercise of their constitutional review function alone to address such defect. No one in the debates challenges this understanding of constitutional evaluation, and thus the fact that the delegates were simultaneously developing the idea that the constitutional text was a separate source of authoritative, declared, positive law did not mean that they saw this development as repealing the inherent or undeclared natural law. It is true that Mr. Gerry argues against the Council, fearing that it would make "Statesmen of the Judges," but in context, this opposition is directed more at the difficulties of al lying judges to the executive and inviting such alliance to perform a lawmaking, rather than interpretative, function — namely, the evaluation of laws before they went into effect and unrelated to actual cases or disputes.

2.   Late in the convention, long after the written, declared nature of the new constitutional framework had fully taken shape in the Supremacy Clause, the

delegates turned their attention to whether the document should prohibit bills of attainder and ex post facto laws. (A bill of attainder is legislation that singles out individuals for criminal punishment. Ex post facto laws make criminal actions that were lawful when performed.) Professor Sherry reports that bills of attainder were commonplace in the states, so an explicit prohibition was readily thought necessary to alter this practice. *See* Sherry, *supra*, at 1157. However, the delegates did not immediately see the necessity of writing down a prohibition against ex post facto laws. As Wilson relates in the debate, such laws contravene the first principles of legislation, and to include a prohibition of them would make the delegates appear "ignorant." James McHenry, who along with Eldridge Gerry initiated the proposal, recorded the opposition to it this way:

> Gouverneur Morris Wilson Dr. Johnson etc thought the [ex post facto prohibition] an unnecessary guard as the principles of justice law et[c] were a perpetual bar to such. To say that the legislature shall not pass an ex post facto law is the same as to declare they shall not do a thing contrary to common sense — that they shall not cause that to be crime which is no crime.

2 The Records of the Federal Convention of 1787, at 378–79 (Max Farrand ed., rev. ed. 1966).

b. Was There a Need for a Declaration or Bill of Rights in the Constitution?

The continuing significance of the natural law to constitutional interpretation is also revealed in the debate which occurred over whether to include within the Constitution an explicit bill or declaration of rights. The word "declaration" is deliberate; the founding generation understood rights to exist prior to government, inherent in human nature, discovered through reason, and thus declared, *not enacted*. Virtually all of the new American states wrote declarations of rights, most patterned directly upon the Declaration of Independence. *See* Eastman, *The Declaration of Independence as Viewed from the States, supra,* at 97–102. For example, Pennsylvania wrote in its Declaration of Rights:

> That all men are born equally free and independent, and have certain natural, inherent and inalienable rights, amongst which are, the enjoying and defending life and liberty, acquiring, possessing and protecting property, and pursuing and obtaining happiness and safety.

Pennsylvania Declaration of Rights (1776), *reprinted in* Daniel A. Farber & Suzanna Sherry, A History of the American Constitution 220 (1990).

Near the end of the convention, delegate Charles Pinckney raised the possibility of including a declaration or bill of rights in the Constitution itself, but the drafting committees did not include any of Pinckney's suggestions, which would have included specific mention of the liberty of the press and the prohibition of religious tests. The issue was raised briefly again in the convention's final week. Again, however, the convention unanimously rejected adding a list of rights.

2 THE RECORDS OF THE FEDERAL CONVENTION OF 1787
at 587–88 (Max Farrand ed., rev. ed. 1966)

MR. WILLIAMSON, observed to the House that no provision was yet made for juries in Civil cases and suggested the necessity of it.

MR. GORHAM. It is not possible to discriminate equity cases from those in which juries are proper. The Representatives of the people may be safely trusted in this matter.

MR. GERRY urged the necessity of Juries to guard ag[ain]st. corrupt Judges. He proposed that the Committee last appointed should be directed to provide a clause for securing the trial by Juries.

COL. MASON perceived the difficulty mentioned by Mr. Gorham. The jury cases cannot be specified. A general principle laid down on this and some other points would be sufficient. He wished the plan had been prefaced with a Bill of Rights, [and] would second a Motion if made for the purpose — it would give great quiet to the people; and with the aid of the State declarations, a bill might be prepared in a few hours.

MR. GERRY concurred in the idea [and] moved for a Committee to prepare a Bill of Rights. Col Mason [seconded] the motion.

MR. SHERMAN was for securing the rights of the people where requisite. The State Declarations of Rights are not repealed by this Constitution; and being in force are sufficient — There are many cases where juries are proper which cannot be discriminated. The Legislature may be safely trusted.

COL. MASON. The Laws of the U.S. are to be paramount to State Bills of Rights. On the question for a Com[mitte]e to prepare a Bill of Rights.

N.H. no. Mas. abst. Ct. no. N.J. no. Pa. no. Del. no. Md. no. Va. no. N.C. no. S.C no. Geo. no. [Ayes — 0; noes — 10; absent — 1]

NOTES AND QUESTIONS

1. George Mason of Virginia, who had a variety of objections to the final document and refused to sign it, saying he would "sooner chop off his right hand than put it to the Constitution as it now stands," *id.* at 479, wrote on blank pages of his copy of the September 12, 1787 draft:

> There is no Declaration of Rights, and the laws of the general government being paramount to the laws and constitution of the several States, the Declaration of Rights in the separate States are no security. Nor are the people secured even in the enjoyment of the benefit of the common law (which stands here upon no other foundation than its having been adopted by the respective acts forming the constitutions of the several States).

George Mason, *Objections to the Constitution of Government formed by the Convention* (1787), *reprinted in* 2 THE COMPLETE ANTI-FEDERALIST, *supra*, at 11.

2.   Was Mason right? Take a look at James Iredell's response to Mason below. He argued that express declarations of right were necessary in England because they were responses to usurpations by the Crown in a context where there was no written constitution. In America, there is a written constitution of enumerated power, and thus, a declaration of rights is about as necessary has having a judge enjoin the sheriff to not behead a man who is to be hanged. Iredell later served as an Associate Justice of the Supreme Court, and his response to Mason in this respect seems at first consistent with his later opinion in *Calder v. Bull, infra,* where he admonished Justice Chase that in Supreme Court adjudication, the written Constitution had replaced what he claimed were ill-defined concepts of natural justice. Significantly, however, Iredell also responded to Mason's further complaint that the new Constitution does not secure to the people the benefit of common law by positing that the new Constitution only displaces the common law where there is an enumeration of federal authority. Since we know from Blackstone that the common law is derived from natural law, Iredell thus seems at once to be denying and affirming natural law's continuing constitutional importance. As we shall see, this confusion gets compounded by Justice Iredell's successors on the modern Court.

James Iredell, *Reply to Mr. Mason's Objections* (1788) *reprinted in* 2 Life and Correspondence of James Iredell 186–88 (Griffith J. McRee ed., 1857)

Answers to Mr. Mason's Objections to the New Constitution recommended by the late Convention at Philadelphia. By Marcus (James Iredell).

I. OBJECTION

"There is no declaration of rights, and the laws of the general government being paramount to the laws and constitutions of the several States, the declarations of rights in the separate States are no security. Nor are the people secured even in the enjoyment of the benefit of the common law, which stands here upon no other foundation than its having been adopted by the respective acts forming the Constitutions of the several States."

ANSWER

1. As to the want of a declaration of rights. The introduction of these in England, from which the idea was originally taken, was in consequence of usurpations of the Crown, contrary, as was conceived, to the principles of their government. But there no original constitution is to be found, and the only meaning of a declaration of rights in that country is, that in certain particulars specified, the Crown had no authority to act. Could this have been necessary had there been a constitution in being by which it could have been clearly discerned whether the Crown had such authority or not? Had the people, by a solemn instrument, delegated particular powers to the Crown at the formation of their government, surely the Crown, which in that case could claim under that instrument only, could not have contended for

more power than was conveyed by it. So it is in regard to the New Constitution here: the future government which may be formed under that authority certainly cannot act beyond the warrant of that authority. As well might they attempt to impose a King upon America, as go one step in any other respect beyond the terms of their institution. The question then only is, whether more power will be vested in the future government than is necessary for the general purposes of the union. This may occasion a ground of dispute — but after expressly defining the powers that are to be exercised, to say that they shall exercise no other powers (either by a general or particular enumeration) would seem to me both nugatory and ridiculous. As well might a Judge when he condemns a man to be hanged, give strong injunctions to the Sheriff that he should not be beheaded.

2. As to the common law, it is difficult to know what is meant by that part of the objection. So far as the people are now entitled to the benefit of the common law, they certainly will have a right to enjoy it under the new Constitution until altered by the general legislature, which even in this point has some cardinal limits assigned to it. What are most acts of Assembly but a deviation in some degree from the principles of the common law? The people are expressly secured (contrary to Mr. Mason's wishes) against *ex post facto* laws; so that the tenure of any property at any time held under the principles of the common law, cannot be altered by any future act of the general legislature. The principles of the common law, as they now apply, must surely always hereafter apply, except in those particulars in which express authority is given by this Constitution; in no other particulars can the Congress have authority to change it, and I believe it cannot be shown that any one power of this kind given is unnecessarily given, or that the power would answer its proper purpose if the legislature was restricted from any innovations on the principles of the common law, which would not in all cases suit the vast variety of incidents that might arise out of it.

c. Natural Law and the Ratification Debate

The debate on the necessity or not of an express declaration of rights thus spilled over to the ratification debates. Again, as mentioned earlier with respect to the Declaration of Independence, Federalists and Anti-Federalists were in agreement over the origin of human rights — these came from God and human nature. The question was how to best protect or secure such rights — with or without written declaration. The Anti-Federalists wanted it in writing.

Essay of Brutus to the Citizens of New York
(Nov. 1, 1787)

If we may collect the sentiments of the people of America, from their own most solemn declarations, they hold this truth as self evident, that all men are by nature free. No one man, therefore, or any class of men, have a right, by the law of nature, or of God, to assume or exercise authority over their fellows. The origin of society then is to be sought, not in any natural right which one man has to exercise authority over another, but in the united consent of those who associate. The mutual wants of men, at first dictated the propriety of forming societies; and when they were established, protection and defence pointed out the necessity of instituting government. In a state of nature every individual pursues his own interest; in this pursuit it frequently happened, that the possessions or enjoyments of one were sacrificed to the views and designs of another; thus the weak were a prey to the strong, the simple and unwary were subject to impositions from those who were more crafty and designing. In this state of things, every individual was insecure; common interest therefore directed, that government should be established, in which the force of the whole community should be collected, and under such directions, as to protect and defend every one who composed it. The common good, therefore, is the end of civil government, and common consent, the foundation on which it is established. To effect this end, it was necessary that a certain portion of natural liberty should be surrendered, in order, that what remained should be preserved: how great a proportion of natural freedom is necessary to be yielded by individuals, when they submit to government, I shall not now enquire. So much, however, must be given up, as will be sufficient to enable those, to whom the administration of the government is committed, to establish laws for the promoting the happiness of the community, and to carry those laws into effect. But it is not necessary, for this purpose, that individuals should relinquish all their natural rights. Some are of such a nature that they cannot be surrendered. Of this kind are the rights of conscience, the right of enjoying and defending life, etc. Others are not necessary to be resigned, in order to attain the end for which government is instituted, these therefore ought not to be given up. To surrender them, would counteract the very end of government, to wit, the common good. From these observations it appears, that in forming a government on its true principles, the foundation should be laid in the manner I before stated, by expressly reserving to the people such of their essential natural rights, as are not necessary to be parted with. The same reasons which at first induced mankind to associate and institute government, will operate to influence them to observe this precaution. If they had been disposed to conform themselves to the rule of immutable righteousness, government would not have been requisite. It was because one part exercised fraud, oppression, and violence on the other, that men came together, and agreed that certain rules should be formed, to regulate the conduct of all, and the power of the whole community lodged in the hands of rulers to enforce an obedience to them. But rulers have the same propensities as other men; they are as likely to use the power with which they are vested for private purposes, and to the injury and oppression of those over whom they are placed, as individuals in a state of nature are to injure and oppress one another. It is therefore as proper that bounds should be set to their authority, as that government should have at first been instituted to restrain private injuries.

This principle, which seems so evidently founded in the reason and nature of things, is confirmed by universal experience. Those who have governed, have been found in all ages ever active to enlarge their powers and abridge the public liberty. This has induced the people in all countries, where any sense of freedom remained, to fix barriers against the encroachments of their rulers. The country from which we have derived our origin, is an eminent example of this. Their magna charta and bill of rights have long been the boast, as well as the security, of that nation. I need say no more, I presume, to an American, than, that this principle is a fundamental one, in all the constitutions of our own states; there is not one of them but what is either founded on a declaration or bill of rights, or has certain express reservation of rights interwoven in the body of them. From this it appears, that at a time when the pulse of liberty beat high and when an appeal was made to the people to form constitutions for the government of themselves, it was their universal sense, that such declarations should make a part of their frames of government. It is therefore the more astonishing, that this grand security, to the rights of the people, is not to be found in this constitution.

The Federalists responded that putting it in writing would be "dangerous" because no enumeration could capture all of the natural rights of man, and those not mentioned would then be argued to be conceded to the government.

The Federalist No. 84 (Alexander Hamilton) (Clinton Rossiter ed., 1961)

In the course of the foregoing review of the Constitution, I have taken notice of, and endeavoured to answer most of the objections which have appeared against it. . . .

The most considerable of these remaining objections is that the plan of the convention contains no bill of rights. . . .

It has been several times truly remarked that bills of rights are, in their origin, stipulations between kings and their subjects, abridgements of prerogative in favor of privilege, reservations of rights not surrendered to the prince. Such was MAGNA CHARTA [1215], obtained by the barons, sword in hand, from King John. Such were the subsequent confirmations of that charter by subsequent princes. Such was the *Petition of Right* [1628] assented to by Charles the First in the beginning of his reign. Such, also, was the Declaration of Right presented by the Lords and Commons to the Prince of Orange in 1688, and afterwards thrown into the form of an act of Parliament called the Bill of Rights [1689]. It is evident, therefore, that, according to their primitive signification, they have no application to constitutions, professedly founded upon the power of the people and executed by their immediate representatives and servants. Here, in strictness, the people surrender nothing; and as they retain everything they have no need of particular reservations, "WE, THE PEOPLE of the United States, to secure the blessings of liberty to ourselves and our posterity, do *ordain* and *establish* this Constitution for the United States of America." Here is a better recognition of popular rights than volumes of those aphorisms which make the principal figure in several of our State bills of rights and which would sound much better in a treatise of ethics than in a constitution of government.

But a minute detail of particular rights is certainly far less applicable to a Constitution like that under consideration, which is merely intended to regulate the general political interests of the nation, than to a constitution which has the regulation of every species of personal and private concerns. If, therefore, the loud clamours against the plan of the convention, on this score, are well founded, no epithets of reprobation will be too strong for the constitution of this State. But the truth is that both of them contain all which, in relation to their objects, is reasonably to be desired.

I go further and affirm that bills of rights, in the sense and to the extent in which they are contended for, are not only unnecessary in the proposed Constitution but would even be dangerous. They would contain various exceptions to powers which are not granted; and, on this very account, would afford a colourable pretext to claim more than were granted. For why declare that things shall not be done which there is no power to do? Why, for instance, should it be said that the liberty of the press shall not be restrained, when no power is given by which restrictions may be imposed? I will not contend that such a provision would confer a regulating power; but it is evident that it would furnish, to men disposed to usurp, a plausible pretence for claiming that power. They might urge with a semblance of reason that the Constitution ought not to be charged with the absurdity of providing against the abuse of an authority which was not given, and that the provision against restraining the liberty of the press afforded a clear implication that a power to prescribe proper regulations concerning it was intended to be vested in the national government. This may serve as a specimen of the numerous handles which would be given to the doctrine of constructive powers, by the indulgence of an injudicious zeal for bills of rights.

There remains but one other view of this matter to conclude the point. The truth is, after all the declamations we have heard, that the Constitution is itself, in every rational sense, and to every useful purpose, A BILL OF RIGHTS. The several bills of rights in Great Britain form its Constitution, and conversely the constitution of each State is its bill of rights. And the proposed Constitution, if adopted, will be the bill of rights of the union. Is it one object of a bill of rights to declare and specify the political privileges of the citizens in the structure and administration of the government? This is done in the most ample and precise manner in the plan of the convention; comprehending various precautions for the public security which are not to be found in any of the State constitutions. Is another object of a bill of rights to define certain immunities and modes of proceeding, which are relative to personal and private concerns? This we have seen has also been attended to in a variety of cases in the same plan. Adverting therefore to the substantial meaning of a bill of rights, it is absurd to allege that it is not to be found in the work of the convention. It may be said that it does not go far enough though it will not be easy to make this appear; but it can with no propriety be contended that there is no such thing. It certainly must be immaterial what mode is observed as to the order of declaring the rights of the citizens if they are to be found in any part of the instrument which establishes the government. And hence it must be apparent that much of what has been said on this subject rests merely on verbal and nominal distinctions, entirely foreign from the substance of the thing.

3. The Bill of Rights Introduced: Unenumerated Natural Law Rights Preserved

Politically, the competing arguments of whether or not to enumerate rights were eclipsed when Rhode Island and North Carolina refused to ratify the new Constitution, and Virginia and New York threatened and then submitted calls for a new convention. To blunt this possibility, which would have likely meant chaos, Madison promised that if ratification was achieved, he would bring amendments before the House so that a declaration of rights could be added by amendment to the new Constitution. In doing so, Madison did not give up his fear that putting rights down on paper might disparage unenumerated rights. To meet this lingering concern, when Madison rose to get the attention of the House of Representatives on June 8, 1789, to introduce his draft of a bill of rights, he first reiterated the purposes of the new Constitution as those found in the language of the Declaration; second, he listed the specific rights which had been pressed by the ratifying states; finally, and most importantly, he reaffirmed that the origin of these rights are not the written Constitution itself. Instead, he indicated that "[t]he exceptions here or elsewhere in the Constitution, made in favor of particular rights, shall not be so construed as to diminish the just importance of other rights retained by the people." 1 ANNALS OF CONG. 435 (Joseph Gales ed., 1789). What follows is an excerpt of that speech.

1 Annals of Cong. 431–40
(Joseph Gales ed., 1789)

MR. MADISON —

. . . There have been objections of various kinds made against the Constitution. . . . I believe that the great mass of the people who opposed it, disliked it because it did not contain effectual provisions against the encroachments on particular rights, and those safeguards which they have been long accustomed to have interposed between them and the magistrate who exercises the sovereign power; nor ought we to consider them safe, while a great number of our fellow-citizens think these securities necessary.

It is a fortunate thing that the objection to the Government has been made on the ground I stated; because it will be practicable, on that ground, to obviate the objection, so far as to satisfy the public mind that their liberties will be perpetual, and this without endangering any part of the Constitution, which is considered as essential to the existence of the Government by those who promoted its adoption.

The amendments which have occurred to me, proper to be recommended by Congress to the State Legislatures, are these:

First. That there be prefixed to the Constitution a declaration that all power is originally vested in, and consequently derived from, the people.

That Government is instituted and ought to be exercised for the benefit of the people; which consists in the enjoyment of life and liberty, with the right of acquiring and using property, and generally of pursuing and obtaining happiness and safety.

That the people have an indubitable, unalienable, and indefeasible right to reform or change their Government, whenever it be found adverse or inadequate to the purposes of its institution.

Fourthly. That in article 1st, section 9, between clauses 3 and 4, be inserted these clauses, to wit: The civil rights of none shall be abridged on account of religious belief or worship, nor shall the full and equal rights of conscience be in any manner, or on any pretext, infringed.

The people shall not be deprived or abridged of their right to speak, to write, or to publish their sentiments; and the freedom of the press, as one of the great bulwarks of liberty, shall be inviolable.

The right of the people to keep and bear arms shall not be infringed; a well armed and well regulated militia being the best security of a free country: but no person religiously scrupulous of bearing arms shall be compelled to render military service in person.

No soldier shall in time of peace be quartered in any house without the consent of the owner; nor at any time, but in a manner warranted by law.

No person shall be subject, except in cases of impeachment, to more than one punishment or one trial for the same offence; nor shall be compelled to be a witness against himself; nor be deprived of life, liberty, or property, without due process of law; nor be obliged to relinquish his property, where it may be necessary for public use, without a just compensation.

Excessive bail shall not be required, nor excessive fines imposed, nor cruel and unusual punishments inflicted.

The rights of the people to be secured in their persons, their houses, their papers, and their other property, from all unreasonable searches and seizures, shall not be violated by warrants issued without probable cause, supported by oath or affirmation, or not particularly describing the places to be searched, or the persons or things to be seized.

In all criminal prosecutions, the accused shall enjoy the right to a speedy and public trial, to be informed of the cause and nature of the accusation, to be confronted with his accusers, and the witnesses against him; to have a compulsory process for obtaining witnesses in his favor; and to have the assistance of counsel for his defence.

The exceptions here or elsewhere in the Constitution, made in favor of particular rights, shall not be so construed as to diminish the just importance of other rights retained by the people, or as to enlarge the powers delegated by the Constitution; but either as actual limitations of such powers, or as inserted merely for greater caution.

The first of these amendments relates to what may be called a bill of rights. I will own that I never considered this provision so essential to the Federal Constitution as to make it improper to ratify it, until such an amendment was added; at the same time, I always conceived, that in a certain form, and to a certain extent, such a provision was neither improper nor altogether useless. I am aware that a great number of the most respectable friends to the Government, and champions for republican liberty, have thought such a provision not only unnecessary, but even improper; nay, I believe some have gone so far as to think it even dangerous. Some policy has been made use of, perhaps, by gentlemen on both sides of the question: I acknowledge the ingenuity of those arguments which were drawn against the Constitution, by a comparison with the policy of Great Britain, in establishing a declaration of rights; but there is too great a difference in the case to warrant the comparison: therefore, the arguments drawn from that source were in a great measure inapplicable. In the declaration of rights which that country has established, the truth is, they have gone no farther than to raise a barrier against the power of the Crown; the power of the Legislature is left altogether indefinite. Although I know whenever the great rights, the trial by jury, freedom of the press, or liberty of conscience, come in question in that body, the invasion of them is resisted by able advocates, yet their Magna Charta does not contain any one provision for the security of those rights, respecting which the people of America are most alarmed. The freedom of the press and rights of conscience, those choicest privileges of the people, are unguarded in the British Constitution.

But although the case may be widely different, and it may not be thought necessary to provide limits for the legislative power in that country, yet a different opinion prevails in the United States. The people of many States have thought it necessary to raise barriers against power in all forms and departments of Government, and I am inclined to believe, if once bills of rights are established in all the States as well as the Federal Constitution, we shall find, that, although some of them are rather unimportant, yet, upon the whole, they will have a salutary tendency. It may be said, in some instances, they do no more than state the perfect equality of mankind. This, to be sure, is an absolute truth, yet it is not absolutely necessary to be inserted at the head of a Constitution.

In some instances they assert those rights which are exercised by the people in forming and establishing a plan of Government. In other instances, they specify those rights which are retained when particular powers are given up to be exercised by the Legislature. In other instances, they specify positive rights, which may seem to result from the nature of the compact. Trial by jury cannot be considered as a natural right, but a right resulting from a social compact, which regulates the action of the community, but is as essential to secure the liberty of the people as any one of the pre-existent rights of nature. In other instances, they lay down dogmatic maxims with respect to the construction of the Government; declaring that the Legislative, Executive, and Judicial branches, shall be kept separate and distinct. Perhaps the best way of securing this in practice is, to provide such checks as will prevent the encroachment of the one upon the other.

But, whatever may be the form which the several States have adopted in making declarations in favor of particular rights, the great object in view is to limit and qualify the powers of Government, by excepting out of the grant of power those cases in which the Government ought not to act, or to act only in a particular mode. They point these exceptions sometimes against the abuse of the Executive power, sometimes against the Legislative, and, in some cases, against the community itself; or, in other words, against the majority in favor of the minority.

It has been said, by way of objection to a bill of rights, by many respectable gentlemen out of doors, and I find opposition on the same principles likely to be made by gentlemen on this floor, that they are unnecessary articles of a Republican Government, upon the presumption that the people have those rights in their own hands, and that is the proper place for them to rest. It would be a sufficient answer to say, that this objection lies against such provisions under the State Governments, as well as under the General Government; and there are, I believe, but few gentlemen who are inclined to push their theory so far as to say that a declaration of rights in those cases is either ineffectual or improper. It has been said, that in the Federal Government they are unnecessary, because the powers are enumerated, and it follows, that all that are not granted by the Constitution are retained; that the Constitution is a bill of powers, the great residuum being the rights of the people; and, therefore, a bill of rights cannot be so necessary as if the residuum was thrown into the hands of the Government. I admit that these arguments are not entirely without foundation; but they are not conclusive to the extent which has been supposed. It is true, the powers of the General Government are circumscribed, they are directed to particular objects; but even if Government keeps within those limits, it has certain discretionary powers with respect to the means, which may admit of abuse to a certain extent, in the same manner as the powers of the State Governments under their constitutions may to an indefinite extent; because in the Constitution of the United States, there is a clause granting to Congress the power to make all laws which shall be necessary and proper for carrying into execution all the powers vested in the Government of the United States, or in any department or officer thereof; this enables them to fulfil every purpose for which the Government was established. Now, may not laws be considered necessary and proper by Congress, (for it is for them to judge of the necessity and propriety to accomplish those special purposes which they may have in contemplation), which laws in themselves are neither necessary nor proper; as well as improper laws could be enacted by the State Legislatures, for fulfilling the more extended objects of those Governments? I will state an instance, which I think in point, and proves that this might be the case. The General Government has a right to pass all laws which shall be necessary to collect its revenue; the means for enforcing the collection are within the direction of the Legislature: may not general warrants be considered necessary for this purpose, as well as for some purposes which it was supposed at the framing of their constitutions the State Governments had in view? If there was reason for restraining the State Governments from exercising this power, there is likely reason for restraining the Federal Government.

It may be said, indeed it has been said, that a bill of rights is not necessary, because the establishment of this Government has not repealed those declarations of rights which are added to the several State constitutions; that those rights of the people which had been established by the most solemn act, could not be annihilated by a subsequent act of that people, who meant and declared at the head of the instrument, that they ordained and established a new system, for the express purpose of securing to themselves and posterity the liberties they had gained by an arduous conflict.

I admit the force of this observation, but I do not look upon it to be conclusive. In the first place, it is too uncertain ground to leave this provision upon, if a provision is at all necessary to secure rights so important as many of those I have mentioned are conceived to be, by the public in general, as well as those in particular who opposed the adoption of this Constitution. Besides, some States have no bills of rights, there are others provided with very defective ones, and there are others whose bills of rights are not only defective, but absolutely improper; instead of securing some in the full extent which republican principles would require, they limit them too much to agree with the common ideas of liberty.

It has been objected also against a bill of rights, that, by enumerating particular exceptions to the grant of power, it would disparage those rights which were not placed in that enumeration; and it might follow by implication, that those rights which were not singled out, were intended to be assigned into the hands of the General Government, and were consequently insecure. This is one of the most plausible arguments I have ever heard urged against the admission of a bill of rights into this system; but, I conceive, that it may be guarded against. I have attempted it, as gentlemen may see by turning to the last clause of the fourth resolution.

It has been said that it is unnecessary to load the Constitution with this provision, because it was not found effectual in the constitution of the particular States. It is true, there are a few particular States in which some of the most valuable articles have not, at one time or other, been violated; but it does not follow but they have, to a certain degree, a salutary effect against the abuse of power. If they are incorporated into the Constitution, independent tribunals of justice will consider themselves in a peculiar manner the guardians of those rights; they will be an impenetrable bulwark against every assumption of power in the Legislative or Executive; they will be naturally led to resist every encroachment upon rights expressly stipulated for in the Constitution by the declaration of rights. Besides this security, there is a great probability that such a declaration in the federal system would be enforced; because the State Legislatures will jealously and closely watch the operations of this Government, and be able to resist with more effect every assumption of power, than any other power on earth can do; and the greatest opponents to a Federal Government admit the State Legislatures to be sure guardians of the people's liberty. I conclude, from this view of the subject, that it will be proper in itself, and highly politic, for the tranquillity of the public mind, and the stability of the Government, that we should offer something, in the form I have proposed, to be incorporated in the system of Government, as a declaration of the rights of the people.

4. Natural Law in the Early Supreme Court

Madison's fourth resolution became the Ninth Amendment, which provides, "[t]he enumeration in the Constitution, of certain rights, shall not be construed to deny or disparage others retained by the people." By this provision, do the vast body of unenumerated common or natural law rights become judicially enforceable against the Congress? This is, of course, just another formulation of the underlying question of this Chapter — whether the Constitution must be construed in accordance with fundamental principle. As will be discussed in Chapter Three, judicial review is an American innovation confirmed in the celebrated case of *Marbury v. Madison*, 5 U.S. (1 Cranch) 137 (1803). At least in part, *Marbury* reflects the American rejection of Blackstonian legislative supremacy, which itself had circumscribed the earlier claims of executive or monarchial prerogative. But by what standards are judges to undertake this review? Do they, in particular, include the standards of natural law as summarized in the Declaration, or are they limited to the text of the Constitution, assuming (and it is a big assumption) that the text always has a uniform and plain meaning? Madison includes natural law, pointing out that "independent tribunals of justice will consider themselves in a peculiar manner the guardians of those [unenumerated but retained] rights; they will be an unpenetrable bulwark against every assumption of power in the Legislative or Executive. . . ."

But not every one agrees that the Ninth Amendment and unenumerated natural rights were to be enforced by the federal judiciary, as Madison plainly seems to prescribe. Judge Bork asserts that:

> Madison, who wrote the amendments, and who wrote with absolute clarity elsewhere, had he meant to put a freehand power concerning rights in the hands of judges, could easily have drafted an amendment that said something like "The courts shall determine what rights, in addition to those enumerated here, are retained by the people," or "The courts shall create new rights as required. . . ."

ROBERT H. BORK, THE TEMPTING OF AMERICA 183 (1990). With respect, Judge Bork may misperceive the judicial role envisioned by Madison. Judges were not to create "new rights" under the Ninth Amendment, but they were to be a guardian of pre-existing common law or natural rights. The need for a Ninth Amendment that would be enforceable by federal judges against the federal government in all of its parts also makes sense of Madison's analogy to the equivalent importance of state bills of rights that were enforceable against the states by state judges. As Madison writes, "there are but few gentlemen who are inclined to push their theory so far as to say that a declaration of rights in those [state] cases is either ineffectual or improper."

Whatever the scope of judicial enforcement envisioned by the founders, it is undeniable that natural law was important to early constitutional interpretation. In no decision in the first three decades of its existence, did the early Supreme Court uphold a legislative act contrary to natural law principles. Coincident with the founders' understanding of the Constitution as drawn from multiple sources, written text as well as universal principles of justice, early opinions often relied upon both. Often, the written Constitution would be referenced to answer questions of the allocation of government power, while natural law principles would be employed to weigh claims of individual right. What's more, natural law inquiry was made in a wide variety of disputes, implicating a number of constitutional provisions. For example, in *Corfield v. Coryell*, 6 F. Cas. 546 (C.C.E.D. Pa. 1823) (No. 3,230), Justice Washington, sitting as a circuit justice, employed natural law reasoning to partially identify the fundamental rights of individuals encompassed by the Privileges and Immunities Clause of Article IV, Section 2, which was intended — at least with respect to certain fundamental rights and occupations — to moderate if not disallow distinctions a state might draw between its own citizens and those of another state. The listing devised by Justice Washington:

> The inquiry is, what are the privileges and immunities of citizens in the several states? We feel no hesitation in confining these expressions to those privileges and immunities which are, in their nature, fundamental; which belong, of right, to the citizens of all free governments; and which have, at all times, been enjoyed by the citizens of the several states which compose this Union, from the time of their becoming free, independent, and sovereign. What these fundamental principles are, it would perhaps be more tedious than difficult to enumerate. They may, however, be all

comprehended under the following general heads: Protection by the government; the enjoyment of life and liberty, with the right to acquire and possess property of every kind, and to pursue and obtain happiness and safety; subject nevertheless to such restraints as the government may justly prescribe for the general good of the whole. The right of a citizen of one state to pass through, or to reside in any other state, for purposes of trade, agriculture, professional pursuits, or otherwise; to claim the benefit of the writ of habeas corpus; to institute and maintain actions of any kind in the courts of the state; to take, hold and dispose of property, either real or personal; and an exemption from higher taxes or impositions than are paid by the other citizens of the state; may be mentioned as some of the particular privileges and immunities of citizens, which are clearly embraced by the general description of privileges deemed to be fundamental: to which may be added, the elective franchise, as regulated and established by the laws or constitution of the state in which it is to be exercised. These, and many others which might be mentioned, are, strictly speaking, privileges and immunities, and the enjoyment of them by the citizens of each state, in every other state, was manifestly calculated (to use the expressions of the preamble of the corresponding provision in the old articles of confederation) "the better to secure and perpetuate mutual friendship and intercourse among the people of the different states of the Union."

The *Corfield* listing of privileges and immunities is a classic elaboration of the more general principles of the Declaration of Independence. Indeed, we will see that after the Civil War, Congress returns to the *Corfield* list in passing the Fourteenth Amendment, in order to better secure natural rights for freed slaves and all American citizens against encroachments from the state governments. Environmentally-conscious students will also recognize how natural law reasoning is employed to address the so-called "tragedy of the commons," that is, the exhaustion or over-use of commonly held resources.

In *Ware v. Hylton*, future Chief Justice John Marshall represented Daniel Hylton and other citizens of Virginia who claim that certain debts owed a British creditor were discharged by a Virginia Act of October 20, 1777, which allowed such debts to be paid to the state instead. The British subjects counter that the Treaty settling the Revolutionary War in September 1783 provided that "creditors on either side, shall meet with no lawful impediment to the recovery of the full value in sterling money, of all bona fide debts heretofore contracted." Marshall lost his case attempting to make an argument contrary to the natural law. Marshall claimed there was no debt for the Treaty to revive because it had been discharged. Justices Chase, Patterson, and Wilson observed at some length how the extinguishment of debts would transgress the natural law which is "obligatory" on Virginia and "all the Courts of the United States."

In *Fletcher v. Peck*, 10 U.S. (6 Cranch) 87 (1810), Chief Justice Marshall confronted an enormous land swindle. In 1795, members of the Georgia legislature conveyed the better part of what is today Alabama and Mississippi to four corporations (the Yazoo Land companies) for about 1.5 cents per acre. All but one member of the Georgia legislature owned stock in these companies at the time. The public was outraged, and in 1796, a new legislature passed legislation purporting to repeal the earlier grant. There was a problem, however, in that some of the original, though tainted grantees, had conveyed parcels to innocent purchasers. These purchasers argued that the subsequent Georgia legislature could not constitutionally divest their title. Calling into question both individual property rights and federalism (state legislative authority versus that of the federal judiciary), Chief Justice Marshall relies upon both natural law and constitutional text to reach his decision upholding the vested rights of the innocent purchasers. He writes:

> It is, then, the unanimous opinion of the court, that, in this case, the estate having passed into the hands of a purchaser for a valuable consideration, without notice, the state of Georgia was restrained, *either by general principles which are common to our free institutions, or by the particular provisions of the constitution of the United States*, from passing a law whereby the estate of the plaintiff in the premises so purchased could be constitutionally and legally impaired and rendered null and void.

Id. at 139 (emphasis added). We examine *Fletcher* more closely in Chapter Six.

In *Calder v. Bull* — the next case in our brief, early Supreme Court natural law sampler — the facts are less significant for our purpose than the debate between Chase and Iredell over the ascertainability of the natural law. Connecticut passed a law allowing Bull to re-open a probate or decedent estate administration judgment after the time for appeal had expired. Calder protested this untimely second bite at the apple unsuccessfully in the Connecticut courts, and came to the Supreme Court arguing that the state legislature passed an unconstitutional, retrospective enactment. Calder lost again, but Justices Chase and Iredell differed significantly as to whether the text of the Constitution alone, or the text in conjunction with natural law, determines the outcome.

CALDER v. BULL
3 U.S. (3 Dall.) 386 (1798)

CHASE, JUSTICE. . . .

The counsel for the plaintiffs in error, contend, that the . . . law of the legislature of Connecticut, granting a *new hearing*, in the above case, is *an ex post facto law*, prohibited by the Constitution of the United States; that any law of the Federal government, or of any of the State governments, contrary to the Constitution of the United States, is *void*; and that this court possess the power to declare *such* law void. . . .

Whether the legislature of any of the States can revise and correct by law, a decision of any of its Courts of Justice, although not prohibited by the Constitution of the State, is a question of very great importance, and not necessary now to be determined; *because the resolution or law in question does not go so far*. I cannot subscribe to the *omnipotence* of a *state legislature*, or that it is *absolute and without controul*; although its authority should not be *expressly* restrained by the Constitution, or *fundamental law*, of the State. The people of the United States erected their Constitutions, or forms of government, to establish justice, to promote the general welfare, to secure the blessings of liberty; and to protect their *persons* and *property* from violence. The purposes for which men enter into society will determine the *nature* and *terms* of the *social* compact; and as *they* are the foundation of the *legislative* power, *they* will decide what are the *proper* objects of it: The *nature* and *ends* of *legislative* power will limit the *exercise* of it. This *fundamental* principle flows from the very nature of our free *Republican* governments, that no man should be compelled to do what the laws do *not* require, *nor to refrain from acts which the laws permit*. There are acts which the *Federal*, or *State*, Legislature cannot do, *without exceeding their authority*. There are certain *vital* principles in our *free Republican governments*, which will determine and over-rule an *apparent and flagrant* abuse of *legislative* power; as to authorize *manifest injustice by positive law*; or to take away that security for *personal liberty*, or *private property*, for the protection whereof the government was established. An act of the legislature (for I cannot call it a *law*), contrary to the *great first principles* of the *social compact*, cannot be considered a *rightful exercise* of *legislative* authority. The obligation of a law in governments established on *express compact, and on republican principles*, must be determined by the *nature* of the *power*, on which it is founded. A few instances will suffice to explain what I mean. A law that punished a citizen for an *innocent* action, or, in other words, for an act, which, when done, was in violation of no *existing* law; a law that destroys, or impairs, the *lawful private* contracts of citizens; a law that makes a man *a judge in his own cause*; or a law that takes *property* from A, and gives it to B: It is against all reason and justice, for a people to intrust a Legislature with such powers; and, therefore, it cannot be presumed that they have done it. The *genius*, the *nature*, and the *spirit*, of our State Governments, amount to a prohibition of *such acts of legislation*; and the *general principles of law and reason* forbid them. The legislature may enjoin, permit, forbid, and punish; they may declare *new* crimes; and establish rules of conduct for *all* its citizens in *future* cases; they may *command* what is right, and *prohibit* what is wrong; but they cannot change *innocence* into *guilt*, or punish *innocence* as a *crime*; or violate the right of an *antecedent lawful private contract*; or the *right of private property*. To maintain that our Federal, or State, Legislature possesses *such powers*, if they had not been *expressly* restrained; would, in my opinion, be a *political heresy*, altogether inadmissible in our *free republican governments*.

I will state *what laws* I consider *ex post facto laws*, within the *words* and the *intent* of the prohibition. 1st. Every law that makes an action done before the passing of the law, and which was *innocent* when done, criminal; and punishes such action. 2d. Every law that *aggravates* a *crime*, or makes it *greater* than it was, when committed. 3d. Every law that *changes the punishment*, and inflicts a *greater punishment*, than the law annexed to the crime, when committed. 4th. Every law that alters the *legal* rules of *evidence*, and receives less, or different, testimony, than the law required at the time of the commission of the offense, *in order to convict the offender*. All these, and similar laws, are manifestly *unjust and oppressive*. In my opinion, the true distinction is between *ex post facto laws*, and *retrospective laws*. Every *ex post facto law* must necessarily be *retrospective*; but every *retrospective law* is not an *ex post facto law*: the former, only, are prohibited. Every law that takes away, or impairs, *rights vested*, agreeably to existing laws, is retrospective, and is generally unjust, and may be oppressive; and it is a good general rule, that a law should have no *retrospect*: but there are cases in which laws may justly, and for the benefit of the community, and also of individuals, relate to a time antecedent to their commencement; as statutes of oblivion, or of *pardon*. They are certainly *retrospective*, and literally both *concerning, and after, the facts committed*. But I do not consider any law *ex post facto*, within the prohibition, that mollifies the rigor of the *criminal* law; but only those that *create*, or *aggravate*, the *crime*; or increase the punishment, or change the rules of evidence, *for the purpose of conviction*. Every law that is to have an operation before the making thereof, as to commence at an antecedent time; or to save time from the statute of limitations; or to excuse acts which were unlawful, and before committed, and the like; is *retrospective*. But such laws may be proper or necessary, as the case may be. There is a great and apparent difference between making an UNLAWFUL act LAWFUL; and the making an *innocent* action *criminal*, and punishing it as a CRIME. . . .

. . . The restraint against making any *ex post facto laws* was not considered, by the framers of the constitution, as extending to prohibit the depriving a citizen even of a *vested right to property*; or the provision, "that *private* property should not be taken for PUBLIC use, without just compensation," was unnecessary.

It seems to me that the *right of property*, in its origin, could only arise from *compact express*, or *implied*, and I think it the better opinion, that the *right*, as well as the *mode*, or *manner*, of acquiring property, and of alienating or transferring, inheriting, or transmitting it, is conferred by society; is regulated by *civil* institution, and is always subject to the rules prescribed *by positive law*. When I say that a *right* is vested in a citizen, I mean, that he has the *power* to do *certain actions*; or to possess *certain things, according to the law of the land*.

I am of opinion, that the decree of the Supreme Court of Errors of Connecticut be affirmed, with costs.

IREDELL, JUSTICE. . . .

. . . It is true, that some speculative jurists have held, that a legislative act against natural justice must, in itself, be void; but I cannot think that, under such a government, any Court of Justice would possess a power to declare it so. . . .

[I]t has been the policy of all the American states, which have, individually, framed their state constitutions since the revolution, and of the people of the United States, when they framed the Federal Constitution, to define with precision the objects of the legislative power, and to restrain its exercise within marked and settled boundaries. If any act of Congress, or of the Legislature of a state, violates those constitutional provisions, it is unquestionably void; though, I admit, that as the authority to declare it void is of a delicate and awful nature, the court will never resort to that authority, but in a clear and urgent case. If, on the other hand, the Legislature of the Union, or the Legislature of any member of the Union, shall pass a law, within the general scope of their constitutional power, the Court cannot pronounce it to be void, merely because it is, in their judgment, contrary to the principles of natural justice. The ideas of natural justice are regulated by no fixed standard: the ablest and the purest men have differed upon the subject; and all that the Court could properly say, in such an event, would be, that the Legislature (possessed of an equal right of opinion) had passed an act which, in the opinion of the judges, was inconsistent with the abstract principles of natural justice. . . .

Still, however, in the present instance, the act or resolution of the Legislature of Connecticut, cannot be regarded as an *ex post facto* law; for the true construction of the prohibition extends to criminal, not to civil, cases. . . .

The policy, the reason and humanity, of the prohibition, do not . . . extend to civil cases, to cases that merely affect the private property of citizens. Some of the most necessary and important acts of legislation are, on the contrary, founded upon the principle, that private rights must yield to public exigencies. . . . Without the possession of this power the operations of Government would often be obstructed, and society itself would be endangered. It is not sufficient to urge, that the power may be abused, for, such is the nature of all power, — such is the tendency of every human institution. . . . We must be content to limit power where we can, and where we cannot, consistently with its use, we must be content to repose a salutary confidence. It is our consolation that there never existed a Government, in ancient or modern times, more free from danger in this respect, than the Governments of America.

Judgment Affirmed.

NOTE AND QUESTION

In 1993, California enacted a new criminal statute of limitations that allowed prosecution for sex-related child abuse where the prior limitations period had expired. Marion Stogner was prosecuted under the new statute for abuse he allegedly committed between 1955 and 1973, for which the three-year statute of limitations that was applicable at the time of the alleged abuse had long since expired. In *Stogner v. California*, 539 U.S. 607 (2003), the Court held that California's revived statute of limitations violated the Ex Post Facto Clause. Both Justice Breyer for the five-member majority, and Justice Kennedy for the four Justices in dissent relied on *Calder v. Bull* and its English common law precedents and natural rights principles to argue their respective positions. Should judges rely on such common law precedent and natural law principle standing alone, or is their recourse to them limited to gleaning the meaning of express constitutional provisions?

5. The Declaration, Natural Law, and the Modern Court

Throughout the later readings in this book, we will see that the modern Supreme Court arguably uses a form of natural-law jurisprudence whenever it extends constitutional protection to a right that seems to be important or fundamental but is not articulated in the text of the Constitution, except in the vaguest, most general terms, *e.g.*, the Ninth Amendment ("certain rights . . . retained by the people") or the word "liberty" in the Due Process Clauses of the Fifth and Fourteenth Amendments.

Focusing on that word "liberty" — which is the source most often seized upon by the Supreme Court when it declares certain rights which are not otherwise mentioned in the Constitution to be "constitutional" rights (for example, the well-known and yet still controversial right to personal privacy in matters of procreation) — the difficulty has been to identify those "liberties" which are important or fundamental enough to justify the conclusion that they are indeed protected by that word "liberty" in the Fifth and Fourteenth Amendments. Certainly not every "liberty" receives full constitutional protection. To give every "liberty" full constitutional protection would mean that we would have to jettison drug-abuse laws, seat-belt requirements, and a host of other interferences with one's "liberty." That might sit well with a strongly doctrinaire libertarian, but the Supreme Court has not seen fit to adopt such an absolutist view. It does, however, identify some personal rights as being worthy of protection, but not others. Example — the right to privacy in the abortion decision is strongly protected. The right to engage in private, adult, consensual homosexual activity is also now similarly protected. The right to ingest marijuana or other narcotic substances is not so protected. How do we identify which rights receive strong protection, and which do not? The modern Supreme Court purports to use a history and tradition type of test. What are the rights that have been regarded as being fundamentally important in the history and traditions of the Anglo-American people? What are the rights that have been implicit in the Anglo-American concept of ordered liberty?

To the extent that the Supreme Court adheres to that "history and tradition" approach in its efforts to identify so-called fundamental rights, the richly historical ideals written into the Declaration of Independence and the richly traditional principles of Anglo-American common-law jurisprudence, both of which are grounded in natural-law jurisprudence, would seem to be relevant aids. To the extent that the Supreme Court departs from that history-and-tradition approach, its decisions as to which rights are to be strongly protected as "fundamental" become controversial and subject to the criticism that rights so found are mere predilections in the political or moral opinions of the individual Justices.

The enterprise of departing from the Constitution in an effort to identify what it is that the Constitution protects is difficult and fraught with danger, if not illogic. And yet, as we shall see, the modern Supreme Court engages in exactly that enterprise.

The dangers (and perhaps the illogic) are so apparent that some of the Justices have called the whole natural-law-based enterprise into question, and have come to identify themselves as "textualists" or "original intentists" in their approach to identifying "fundamental" rights. The logic of the approach used by textualist and original-intent Justices is that if outside-the-Constitution rights are to be placed in the Constitution, the deed should be done in the only way the original framers, authors, and ratifiers of the Constitution provided: The amendatory process in Article Five of the Constitution itself.

Those Justices (often in the majority on the modern Court) who embrace the enterprise despite its difficulty sometimes manage to avoid crossing the thin line between, on the one hand, an objectively verifiable history-and-tradition approach grounded in the Declaration and the natural law and, on the other hand, the imposition of personal political or moral predilections. Interestingly, however, when the Justices are engaging in that objectively verifiable history-and-tradition approach grounded in the natural law, they are usually very much averse to admitting that that is what they are doing. Those Justices who manage to avoid crossing the line likely view themselves as engaging in an original-intent or purpose approach to the Constitution.

To the extent that the Justices occasionally free-lancingly depart from the grounding in text, history, and tradition, and wander into the politics of the day, they often seek to justify their extra-constitutional action by appeals to the supposition that we have, or at least ought to have, a "living," "evolving" Constitution, with scant thought for any responsibility to defer to the amendatory process set forth in Article Five of the Constitution.

Chapter 2

A GOVERNMENT RESPECTFUL OF INDIVIDUAL CONSCIENCE

A. THE SPECIAL SIGNIFICANCE OF PREFERRED RELIGIOUS FREEDOM

In Chapter 1, we explored whether the interpretation of the Constitution was to be accomplished in accordance with fundamental ends or principles. We saw how the founders looked to the English common law to define these principles, and how the common law, itself, was often a reflection of the natural law — that is, reasoned deductions about actions that either are, or are not, in accord with human nature. In writing the Declaration of Independence, Jefferson traced the unalienable rights of man to "the Laws of Nature and of Nature's God," and thus, the founding generation anchored fundamental principle in both reason and God's revealed word. This Chapter, therefore, takes up Jefferson's second source, and with it, the issue of religion. In Section B, labeled "The Public Affirmation of God and the Importance of Religion," we first explore how the framers understood that the nation's civic morality and well-being depended upon a corporate or sovereign affirmation of God's existence, while leaving individuals free to worship and to come to understand God in their own uncoerced fashion. In Section C, entitled "Public Neutrality Toward God and Religion," we examine Supreme Court opinion as it relates to the interpretation of the Establishment Clause of the First Amendment ("Congress shall make no law respecting an establishment of religion"). Finally, in Section D, we study the complementary Free Exercise Clause that prevents Congress from "prohibiting the free exercise thereof" — that is, religious belief and some, but not all, religious practices. We will see that by judicial interpretation both the Establishment and Free Exercise Clauses have been extended to limit the states, as well as Congress, and that the interpretation of the two Clauses in judicial opinion has been both difficult and controversial. Noticeably, modern interpretations of the no establishment limitation have become, contrary to the framers' inclinations, increasingly exclusionary, and perhaps even hostile to religion. Similarly, many perceive the protections under the Free Exercise Clause also to be less protective of religion, either because its application has been diluted to include beliefs that are sincerely held, but not necessarily religious in any formal sense, or because, under recent Court precedent, religious practice is more susceptible to prohibition under generally applicable laws.

B. THE PUBLIC AFFIRMATION OF GOD AND THE IMPORTANCE OF RELIGION

1. Pre-Founding; Colonial America

Colonial America was Christian, largely Protestant Christian. Religious dissension nevertheless arose within Christian denominations. To alleviate this, a measure of religious freedom was conferred by Toleration Acts. The Acts were decidedly intolerant of blasphemy, however, which was punishable, at least according to the letter of the law, "with death and confiscation or forfeiture. . . ." Maryland Toleration Act (1649), *reprinted in* 5 THE FOUNDERS' CONSTITUTION 49 (Philip B. Kurland & Ralph Lerner eds., 1987) (reproduced below). Historians report that the blasphemy provisions were not enforced strictly.

Maryland Toleration Act of 1649

Forasmuch as in a well governed and [Christian] Common Wealth matters concerning Religion and the honor of God ought in the first place to bee taken, into serous considerat[ion] and endeavoured to bee settled. Bee it therefore . . . enacted . . . that whatsoever [per]son or [per]sons within this Province . . . shall from henceforth blaspheme God, . . . or shall deny our Saviour Jesus Christ to bee the sonne of God, or shall deny the holy Trinity the father sonne and holy Ghost, or the Godhead of any of the said Three [per]sons of the trinity or the Unity of the Godhead . . . [shall be] punished with death and confiscat[ion] or forfeiture of all his or her lands. . . . And whereas the inforceing of the conscience in matters of Religion hath frequently fallen out to be of dangerous Consequence in those commonwealthes where it hath been practised, And for the more quiett and peaceable governe[ment] of this Province, and the better to [pre]serve mutuall Love and amity amongst the Inhabitants thereof. Bee it Therefore . . . enacted (except as in this [pre]sent Act is before Declared and sett forth) that noe person or [per]sons whatsoever within this Province, . . . professing to beleive in Jesus Christ, shall from henceforth bee any waies troubled, Molested or discountenanced for or in respect of his or her religion nor in the free exercise thereof within this Province . . . nor any way compelled to the beleife or exercise of any other Religion against his or her consent, soe as they be not unfaithful to the Lord Proprietary, or molest or conspire against the civill Govern[ment] established . . . in this Province under him or his heires.

2. At the Founding

The early state constitutions, framed contemporaneously with the Declaration of Independence, further reflected both belief in God as a sovereign or governmental premise and individual freedom of conscience in matters of denominational choice. These state documents are fully within the natural law tradition, listing rights that pre-exist government as a matter of human nature. Thus, in the Pennsylvania Constitution of 1776, a government is instituted for securing that which already exists; namely "to enable the individuals who compose it to enjoy their natural rights, and other blessings which the Author of existence has bestowed upon man. . . ." Pa. Const. of 1776 para. 1, *reprinted in* 5 FEDERAL

AND STATE CONSTITUTIONS, COLONIAL CHARTERS, AND OTHER ORGANIC LAWS 3081, 3082 (Francis W. Thorpe ed., 1909) (reproduced below). Religious freedom consisted not of the denial of God or revelation, but of abolishing specific denominational religious tests or qualifications beyond a general agreement in the Divine.

Constitution of Pennsylvania
(1776)

WHEREAS all government ought to be instituted and supported for the security and protection of the community as such, and to enable the individuals who compose it to enjoy their natural rights, and the other blessings which the Author of existence has bestowed upon man; and whenever these great ends of government are not obtained, the people have a right, by common consent to change it, and take such measures as to them may appear necessary to promote their safety and happiness. . . . We, the representatives of the freemen of Pennsylvania, in general convention met, for the express purpose of framing such a government, confessing the goodness of the great Governor of the universe (who alone knows to what degree of earthly happiness mankind may attain, by perfecting the arts of government) in permitting the people of this State, by common consent, and without violence, deliberately to form for themselves such just rules as they shall think best, for governing their future society. . . .

SECT. 10. A quorum of the house of representatives shall consist of two-thirds of the whole number of members elected; and having met and chosen their speaker, shall each of them before they proceed to business take and subscribe, as well the oath or affirmation of fidelity and allegiance hereinafter directed, as the following oath or affirmation, viz:

I _____ do swear (or affirm) that as a member of this assembly, I will not propose or assent to any bill, vote, or resolution, which shall appear to me injurious to the people; nor do or consent to any act or thing whatever, that shall have a tendency to lessen or abridge their rights and privileges, as declared in the constitution of this state; but will in all things conduct myself as a faithful honest representative and guardian of the people, according to the best of my judgment and abilities.

And each member, before he takes his seat, shall make and subscribe the following declaration, viz:

I do believe in one God, the creator and governor of the universe, the rewarder of the good and the punisher of the wicked. And I do acknowledge the Scriptures of the Old and New Testament to be given by Divine inspiration.

NOTES AND QUESTIONS

1. Three states (New Hampshire, New York, and Virginia) ratified the Constitution on condition that it be amended to include guarantees of religious freedom. Similarly, Rhode Island and North Carolina would accept the already ratified Constitution only upon acceptance of the proposed guarantee of religious freedom in the Bill of Rights that was then being debated. With the exception of the New

Hampshire resolution, which sweepingly called upon Congress to "make no laws touching religion," 1 THE DEBATES IN THE SEVERAL STATE CONVENTIONS ON THE ADOPTION OF THE FEDERAL CONSTITUTION 325, 326 (photo. reprint 1996) (Jonathan Elliot ed., 2d ed. 1891), the others all focused on precluding the federal government from establishing a national church and preventing any federal interference with individual religious exercise. New York's language was typical: "That the people have an equal, natural, and unalienable right freely and peaceably to exercise their religion, according to the dictates of conscience; and that no religious sect or society ought to be favored or established by law in preference to others." *Id.* at 327, 328.

2. Madison brought these ratification concerns to the House of Representatives. On June 8, 1789, Madison submitted a first draft of what would later become the First Amendment Religion Clauses. He wrote: "The civil rights of none shall be abridged on account of religious belief or worship, nor shall any national religion be established, nor shall the full and equal rights of conscience be in any manner, or on any pretext, infringed." 1 ANNALS OF CONG. 434 (Joseph Gales ed., 1789) (reproduced *supra*). After a somewhat meandering debate in the full House, this language, and the other provisions of Madison's suggested bill of rights, went to a drafting committee. What emerged in most cases was language similar, but more concise, than Madison's original. Thus, the committee condensed Madison's religion clauses to: "[N]o religion shall be established by law, nor shall the equal rights of conscience be infringed." *Id.* at 729 (reproduced below). There is nothing in the committee report to suggest that the language change was intended to be substantive. The revised language became the subject of debate in the House on August 15, 1789. As seen in the discussion below, the concern of the House was whether the language failed to convey that its focus was precluding the imposition of a national church, and not to be "hurtful to the cause of religion" or "to patronise those who profess no religion at all." Madison clearly proclaims such not to be his intent, but his efforts to make that more explicit by using the adjective "national," are thwarted by the lingering Federalist/Anti-Federalist debate over the exact nature (and scope of authority) of the newly-created central government.

1 ANNALS OF CONG. 729–31 (Joseph Gales ed., 1789)
August 15, 1789

The fourth proposition being under consideration, as follows:

Article 1. Section 9. Between paragraphs two and three insert "no religion shall be established by law, nor shall the equal rights of conscience be infringed."

Mr. SYLVESTER had some doubts of the propriety of the mode of expression used in this paragraph. He apprehended that it was liable to a construction different from what had been made by the committee. He feared it might be thought to have a tendency to abolish religion altogether.

Mr. VINING suggested the propriety of transposing the two members of the sentence.

Mr. GERRY said it would read better if it was, that no religious doctrine shall be established by law.

Mr. SHERMAN thought the amendment altogether unnecessary, inasmuch as

Congress had no authority whatever delegated to them by the Constitution to make religious establishments; he would, therefore, move to have it struck out.

Mr. CARROLL. — As the rights of conscience are, in their nature, of peculiar delicacy, and will little bear the gentlest touch of governmental hand; and as many sects have concurred in opinion that they are not well secured under the present Constitution, he said he was much in favor of adopting the words. He thought it would tend more towards conciliating the minds of the people to the Government than almost any other amendment he had heard proposed. He would not contend with gentlemen about the phraseology, his object was to secure the substance in such a manner as to satisfy the wishes of the honest part of the community.

Mr. MADISON said, he apprehended the meaning of the words to be, that Congress should not establish a religion, and enforce the legal observation of it by law, nor compel men to worship God in any manner contrary to their conscience. Whether the words are necessary or not, he did not mean to say, but they had been required by some of the State Conventions, who seemed to entertain an opinion that under the clause of the Constitution, which gave power to Congress to make all laws necessary and proper to carry into execution the Constitution, and the laws made under it, enabled them to make laws of such a nature as might infringe the rights of conscience, and establish a national religion; to prevent these effects he presumed the amendment was intended, and he thought it as well expressed as the nature of the language would admit.

Mr. HUNTINGTON said that he feared, with the gentleman first up on this subject, that the words might be taken in such latitude as to be extremely hurtful to the cause of religion. He understood the amendment to mean what had been expressed by the gentleman from Virginia; but others might find it convenient to put another construction upon it. The ministers of their congregations to the Eastward were maintained by the contributions of those who belonged to their society; the expense of building meeting-houses was contributed in the same manner. These things were regulated by by-laws. If an action was brought before a Federal Court on any of these cases, the person who had neglected to perform his engagements could not be compelled to do it; for a support of ministers or building of places of worship might be construed into a religious establishment.

By the charter of Rhode Island, no religion could be established by law; he could give a history of the effects of such a regulation; indeed the people were now enjoying the blessed fruits of it. He hoped, therefore, the amendment would be made in such a way as to secure the rights of conscience, and a free exercise of the rights of religion, but not to patronise those who professed no religion at all.

Mr. MADISON thought, if the word "national" was inserted before religion, it would satisfy the minds of honorable gentlemen. He believed that the people feared one sect might obtain a pre-eminence, or two combine together, and establish a religion to which they would compel others to conform. He thought if the word "national" was introduced, it would point the amendment directly to the object it was intended to prevent.

Mr. LIVERMORE was not satisfied with that amendment; but he did not wish them to dwell long on the subject. He thought it would be better if it were altered, and made to read in this manner, that Congress shall make no laws touching religion, or infringing the rights of conscience.

Mr. GERRY did not like the term national, proposed by the gentleman from Virginia, and he hoped it would not be adopted by the House. It brought to his mind some observations that had taken place in the conventions at the time they were considering the present Constitution. It had been insisted upon by those who were called anti-federalists, that this form of Government consolidated the Union; the honorable gentleman's motion shows that he considers it in the same light. Those who were called anti-federalists at that time, complained that they had injustice done them by the title, because they were in favor of a Federal Government, and the others were in favor of a national one; the federalists were for ratifying the Constitution as it stood, and the others not until amendments were made. Their names then ought not to have been distinguished by federalists and anti-federalists, but rats and anti-rats.

Mr. MADISON withdrew his motion, but observed that the words "no national religion shall be established by law," did not imply that the Government was a national one; the question was then taken on Mr. Livermore's motion, and passed in the affirmative, thirty-one for, and twenty against it.

NOTE

While the Anti-Federalists (or opponents of the new Constitution) feared the unstated, and probably unintended, implications of the word "national" in Madison's proposal to make clear that the Religion Clauses were aimed at precluding a national church, the Anti-Federalists clearly recognized the importance of religion generally to the maintenance of civic virtue. They understood that for most people, a good or virtuous life, one directed toward individual happiness and responsible participation in community, was unlikely to result solely from reasoned reflection on the natural law. In part, this reflected the criticism of Justice Iredell and modern positivists like John Hart Ely and Robert Bork, discussed in Chapter 1, that the natural law is too indefinite to be applied. While positivists, liberal or conservative, look to the state to supply answers where reason is unclear, the framers — Federalist and Anti-Federalist — had another source — God's revealed word. Reliance upon religious source was especially important to Anti-Federalists, however, as — given the separation of church and state — the greater the role of religion in the life of the individual citizen, the lesser the role of the new federal government. Religion thus supplied reinforcement for a structurally limited government of enumerated power as well as nourishment for the individual and civic virtue necessary to sustain democratic government. Herbert Storing summarizes the Anti-Federalist position this way:

> [M]any Anti-Federalists were concerned with the maintenance of religious conviction as a support of republican government. . . . The Anti-Federalists feared that the Americans would follow the example of the Europeans as described by Mercy Warren: "Bent on gratification, at the expense of every moral tie, they have broken down the barriers of religion, and the spirit of infidelity is nourished at the fount; thence the poisonous streams run through every grade that constitutes the mass of nations."

Warren insisted that skepticism is not, as some hold, necessarily fostered by republican liberty. Indeed, the history of republics is the history of strict regard to religion.

. . . They saw no inconsistency between liberty of conscience and the public support of the religious, and generally Protestant, community as the basis of public and private morality.

HERBERT J. STORING, WHAT THE ANTI-FEDERALISTS WERE FOR 22–23 (1981) (endnotes omitted).

The First Amendment was adopted, and as already mentioned, consists of two clauses — "Congress shall make no law respecting an Establishment of Religion" (the Establishment Clause); "nor prohibiting the free exercise thereof" (the Free Exercise Clause). Later, we will consider the modern Supreme Court's "non-coercion" view of the Establishment Clause, one of several competing contemporary interpretations. This view is arguably the interpretation most consistent with the founders' posture of general religious support and individual denominational freedom. It is also an interpretation that is consistent with Madison's articulations of religious freedom, even as his efforts, along with Jefferson's in Virginia, would later be misidentified in Supreme Court opinion as being wholly separatist or exclusionary of religion. This insight was perceived early by Anti-Federalist Richard Henry Lee, who wrote in 1784 that "[the Virginia] declaration of Rights, it seems to me, rather contends against forcing modes of faith and forms of worship, than against compelling contribution for the support of religion in general." Letter from Richard Henry Lee to James Madison (Nov. 26, 1784), *in* 2 THE LETTERS OF RICHARD HENRY LEE 304 (photo. reprint 1970) (James Curtis Ballagh ed., 1914).

This pattern of denominational tolerance and general support for religion was thus well set at the founding. It became further evident in the original Northwest Ordinance that both pre-dated the Constitution, and was re-enacted several times thereafter, recognizing "[r]eligion, morality, and knowledge, [as] necessary to good government and the happiness of mankind." Northwest Territory Ordinance of 1787, art. III, 1 Stat. 51 n.a, 52 (1789). There was also the funding for legislative chaplains ("There shall be allowed to each chaplain of Congress . . . five hundred dollars per annum during the session of Congress." Act of September 22, 1789, ch. 17, § 4, 1 Stat. 70, 71 (1789). The significance of religion to the well-being of the new republic was also not lost upon George Washington; it is prominent within his farewell guidance to the nation.

George Washington, *Farewell Address*
(Sept. 19, 1796), *reprinted in*
GEORGE WASHINGTON: A COLLECTION 512 (W.B. Allen ed., 1988)

Of all the dispositions and habits which lead to political prosperity, Religion and morality are indispensable supports. In vain would that man claim the tribute of Patriotism, who should labor to subvert these great Pillars of human happiness, these firmest props of the duties of Men and citizens. The mere Politician, equally with the pious man ought to respect and to cherish them. A volume could not trace all their connections with private and public felicity. Let it simply be asked where is the security for property, for reputation, for life, if the sense of religious obligation *desert* the oaths, which are the instruments of investigation in Courts of Justice? And let us with caution indulge the supposition, that morality can be maintained without religion. Whatever may be conceded to the influence of refined education on minds of peculiar structure, reason and experience both forbid us to expect, that National morality can prevail in exclusion of religious principle.

. . . Can it be, that Providence has not connected the permanent felicity of a Nation with its virtue? The experiment, at least, is recommended by every sentiment which ennobles human Nature. Alas! is it rendered impossible by its vices?

Though in reviewing the incidents of my Administration, I am unconscious of intentional error, I am nevertheless too sensible of my defects not to think it probable that I may have committed many errors. Whatever they may be I fervently beseech the Almighty to avert or mitigate the evils to which they may tend. I shall also carry with me the hope that my Country will never cease to view them with indulgence; and that after forty-five years of my life dedicated to its Service, with an upright zeal, the faults of incompetent abilities will be consigned to oblivion, as myself must soon be to the Mansions of rest.

Relying on its kindness in this as in other things, and actuated by that fervent love towards it, which is so natural to a Man, who views it in the native soil of himself and his progenitors for several Generations; I anticipate with pleasing expectation that retreat, in which I promise myself to realize, without alloy, the sweet enjoyment of partaking, in the midst of my fellow Citizens, the benign influence of good laws under a free Government, the ever favorite object of my heart, and the happy reward, as I trust, of our mutual cares, labors and dangers.

Washington was not alone in his recognition of the significance of religion to the well-being of the American republic. In the following excerpt, Alexis de Tocqueville, a French political theorist who came to America in 1831 to study the penal system, and as a result wrote a brilliant, two-part account of the American experiment with democracy entitled *De la dèmocratie en Ameriquè* [*Democracy in America*], grasps the essential fact that separation of church and state was not intended to lessen the civil significance of religion, but to enhance it. A descendant of St. Joan of Arc, Tocqueville was one of the first to clearly perceive that French socialist thought of the 1840s, like modern demands of the social and economic welfare state, inevitably lead to heightened dependence upon the state and a loss of economic and political freedom.

Tocqueville's observations give us a special insight into the attitude of the American population at large to whom the political framers, Madison, Jefferson and the like, were responding in public action. In this, Tocqueville might be considered the equivalent of the framer's polling data, although with considerably more erudition than pollsters supply modernly. As to the special place of religion in America, Tocqueville concludes:

1. the success of a democratic political system depends upon a proper moral formation of its people;

2. there are multiple religious sects in America, but all acknowledge a Creator God;

3. the importance of religion to American political society is not that a particular religion is divinely true [although this is certainly important to the individual], but that it supplies "habits of restraint" or general morality; religion regulates where law cannot effectively; democracy needs this moral or religious infrastructure in ways that more statist or despotic governments do not;

4. to deny faith is to deny man's inherent nature to hope;

5. religion is strengthened by its separation from the state because it is then immune from the state's failings and partisans; religion draws directly on the universal nature of the human person;

6. since religion is beyond the reach of the state, it can bind Americans together when their leaders fail or when the people fail each other;

7. in America, unbelievers hide their disbelief recognizing the utility of religion, and believers openly rely upon their faith; religious difference does not occasion hostility, but thoughtful concern.

ALEXIS DE TOCQUEVILLE, DEMOCRACY IN AMERICA
(translation by Henry Reeve, 1835)

I have previously remarked that the manners of the people may be considered as one of the general causes to which the maintenance of a democratic republic in the United States is attributable. I here used the word manners with the meaning which the ancients attached to the word mores, for I apply it not only to manners in their proper sense of what constitutes the character of social intercourse, but I extend it to the various notions and opinions current among men, and to the mass of those ideas which constitute their character of mind. I comprise, therefore, under this term the whole moral and intellectual condition of a people. My intention is not to draw a picture of American manners, but simply to point out such features of them as are favorable to the maintenance of political institutions.

*   *   *

[Religion's] indirect influence appears to me to be still more considerable, and it never instructs the Americans more fully in the art of being free than when it says nothing of freedom.

The sects which exist in the United States are innumerable. They all differ in respect to the worship which is due from man to his Creator, but they all agree in respect to the duties which are due from man to man. Each sect adores the Deity in its own peculiar manner, but all the sects preach the same moral law in the name of God. If it be of the highest importance to man, as an individual, that his religion should be true, the case of society is not the same. Society has no future life to hope for or to fear; and provided the citizens profess a religion, the peculiar tenets of that religion are of very little importance to its interests.

*   *   *

In the United States religion exercises but little influence upon the laws and upon the details of public opinion, but it directs the manners of the community, and by regulating domestic life it regulates the State.

I do not question that the great austerity of manners which is observable in the United States, arises, in the first instance, from religious faith. Religion is often unable to restrain man from the numberless temptations of fortune; nor can it check that passion for gain which every incident of his life contributes to arouse, but its influence over the mind of woman is supreme, and women are the protectors of morals. There is certainly no country in the world where the tie of marriage is so much respected as in America, or where conjugal happiness is more highly or worthily appreciated. In Europe almost all the disturbances of society arise from the irregularities of domestic life. To despise the natural bonds and legitimate pleasures of home, is to contract a taste for excesses, a restlessness of heart, and the evil of fluctuating desires. Agitated by the tumultuous passions which frequently disturb his dwelling, the European is galled by the obedience which the legislative powers of the State exact. But when the American retires from the turmoil of public life to the bosom of his family, he finds in it the image of order and of peace. There his pleasures are simple and natural, his joys are innocent and calm; and as he finds that an orderly life is the surest path to happiness, he accustoms himself without difficulty to moderate his opinions as well as his tastes. Whilst the European endeavors to forget his domestic troubles by agitating society, the American derives from his own home that love of order which he afterwards carries with him into public affairs.

In the United States the influence of religion is not confined to the manners, but it extends to the intelligence of the people. Amongst the Anglo-Americans, there are some who profess the doctrines of Christianity from a sincere belief in them, and others who do the same because they are afraid to be suspected of unbelief. Christianity, therefore, reigns without any obstacle, by universal consent; the consequence is, as I have before observed, that every principle of the moral world is fixed and determinate, although the political world is abandoned to the debates and the experiments of men. Thus the human mind is never left to wander across a boundless field; and, whatever may be its pretensions, it is checked from time to time by barriers which it cannot surmount. Before it can perpetrate innovation, certain primal and immutable principles are laid down, and the boldest conceptions of human device are subjected to certain forms which retard and stop their completion.

The imagination of the Americans, even in its greatest flights, is circumspect and undecided; its impulses are checked, and its works unfinished. These habits of restraint recur in political society, and are singularly favorable both to the tranquillity of the people and to the durability of the institutions it has established. Nature and circumstances concurred to make the inhabitants of the United States bold men, as is sufficiently attested by the enterprising spirit with which they seek for fortune. If the mind of the Americans were free from all trammels, they would very shortly become the most daring innovators and the most implacable disputants in the world. But the revolutionists of America are obliged to profess an ostensible respect for Christian morality and equity, which does not easily permit them to violate the laws that oppose their designs; nor would they find it easy to surmount the scruples of their partisans, even if they were able to get over their own. Hitherto no one in the United States has dared to advance the maxim, that everything is permissible with a view to the interests of society; an impious adage which seems to have been invented in an age of freedom to shelter all the tyrants of future ages. Thus whilst the law permits the Americans to do what they please, religion prevents them from conceiving, and forbids them to commit, what is rash or unjust.

Religion in America takes no direct part in the government of society, but it must nevertheless be regarded as the foremost of the political institutions of that country; for if it does not impart a taste for freedom, it facilitates the use of free institutions. Indeed, it is in this same point of view that the inhabitants of the United States themselves look upon religious belief. I do not know whether all the Americans have a sincere faith in their religion, for who can search the human heart? but I am certain that they hold it to be indispensable to the maintenance of republican institutions. This opinion is not peculiar to a class of citizens or to a party, but it belongs to the whole nation, and to every rank of society.

In the United States, if a political character attacks a sect, this may not prevent even the partisans of that very sect from supporting him; but if he attacks all the sects together, everyone abandons him, and he remains alone.

Whilst I was in America, a witness, who happened to be called at the assizes of the county of Chester (State of New York), declared that he did not believe in the existence of God, or in the immortality of the soul. The judge refused to admit his evidence, on the ground that the witness had destroyed beforehand all the confidence of the Court in what he was about to say. The newspapers related the fact without any further comment.

The Americans combine the notions of Christianity and of liberty so intimately in their minds, that it is impossible to make them conceive the one without the other; and with them this conviction does not spring from that barren traditionary faith which seems to vegetate in the soul rather than to live.

I have known of societies formed by the Americans to send out ministers of the Gospel into the new Western States to found schools and churches there, lest religion should be suffered to die away in those remote settlements, and the rising States be less fitted to enjoy free institutions than the people from which they emanated. I met with wealthy New Englanders who abandoned the country in which they were born in order to lay the foundations of Christianity and of freedom on the banks of the Missouri, or in the prairies of Illinois. Thus religious zeal is perpetually stimulated in the United States by the duties of patriotism. These men do not act from an exclusive consideration of the promises of a future life; eternity is only one motive of their devotion to the cause; and if you converse with these missionaries of Christian civilization, you will be surprised to find how much value they set upon the goods of this world, and that you meet with a politician where you expected to find a priest. They will tell you that "all the American republics are collectively involved with each other; if the republics of the West were to fall into anarchy, or to be mastered by a despot, the republican institutions which now flourish upon the shores of the Atlantic Ocean would be in great peril. It is, therefore, our interest that the new States should be religious, in order to maintain our liberties."

Such are the opinions of the Americans, and if any hold that the religious spirit which I admire is the very thing most amiss in America, and that the only element wanting to the freedom and happiness of the human race is to believe in some blind cosmogony, or to assert with Cabanis the secretion of thought by the brain, I can only reply that those who hold this language have never been in America, and that they have never seen a religious or a free nation. When they return from their expedition, we shall hear what they have to say.

*   *   *

Despotism may govern without faith, but liberty cannot. Religion is much more necessary in the republic which they set forth in glowing colors than in the monarchy which they attack; and it is more needed in democratic republics than in any others. How is it possible that society should escape destruction if the moral tie be not strengthened in proportion as the political tie is relaxed? and what can be done with a people which is its own master, if it be not submissive to the Divinity?

*   *   *

The philosophers of the eighteenth century explained the gradual decay of religious faith in a very simple manner. Religious zeal, said they, must necessarily fail, the more generally liberty is established and knowledge diffused. Unfortunately, facts are by no means in accordance with their theory. There are certain populations in Europe whose unbelief is only equalled by their ignorance and their debasement, whilst in America one of the freest and most enlightened nations in the world fulfils all the outward duties of religious fervor.

Upon my arrival in the United States, the religious aspect of the country was the first thing that struck my attention; and the longer I stayed there the more did I perceive the great political consequences resulting from this state of things, to which I was unaccustomed. In France I had almost always seen the spirit of religion and the spirit of freedom pursuing courses diametrically opposed to each other; but in America I found that they were intimately united, and that they reigned in common over the same country. My desire to discover the causes of this phenomenon increased from day to day. In order to satisfy it I questioned the members of all the different sects; and . . . I found that they differed upon matters of detail alone; and that they mainly attributed the peaceful dominion of religion in their country to the separation of Church and State. I do not hesitate to affirm that during my stay in America I did not meet with a single individual, of the clergy or of the laity, who was not of the same opinion upon this point.

. . . [I then] inquire[d] how it happened that the real authority of religion was increased by a state of things which diminished its apparent force: these causes did not long escape my researches.

The short space of threescore years can never content the imagination of man; nor can the imperfect joys of this world satisfy his heart. Man alone, of all created beings, displays a natural contempt of existence, and yet a boundless desire to exist; he scorns life, but he dreads annihilation. These different feelings incessantly urge his soul to the contemplation of a future state, and religion directs his musings thither. Religion, then, is simply another form of hope; and it is no less natural to the human heart than hope itself.]Men cannot abandon their religious faith without a kind of aberration of intellect, and a sort of violent distortion of their true natures; but they are invincibly brought back to more pious sentiments; for unbelief is an accident, and faith is the only permanent state of mankind. If we only consider religious institutions in a purely human point of view, they may be said to derive an inexhaustible element of strength from man himself, since they belong to one of the constituent principles of human nature.

I am aware that at certain times religion may strengthen this influence, which originates in itself, by the artificial power of the laws, and by the support of those temporal institutions which direct society. Religions, intimately united to the governments of the earth, have been known to exercise a sovereign authority derived from the twofold source of terror and of faith; but when a religion contracts an alliance of this nature, I do not hesitate to affirm that it commits the same error as a man who should sacrifice his future to his present welfare; and in obtaining a power to which it has no claim, it risks that authority which is rightfully its own. When a religion founds its empire upon the desire of immortality which lives in every human heart, it may aspire to universal dominion; but when it connects itself with a government, it must necessarily adopt maxims which are only applicable to certain nations. Thus, in forming an alliance with a political power, religion augments its authority over a few, and forfeits the hope of reigning over all.

As long as a religion rests upon those sentiments which are the consolation of all affliction, it may attract the affections of mankind. But if it be mixed up with the bitter passions of the world, it may be constrained to defend allies whom its interests, and not the principle of love, have given to it; or to repel as antagonists men who are still attached to its own spirit, however opposed they may be to the powers to which it is allied. The Church cannot share the temporal power of the State without being the object of a portion of that animosity which the latter excites.

The political powers which seem to be most firmly established have frequently no better guarantee for their duration than the opinions of a generation, the interests of the time, or the life of an individual. A law may modify the social condition which seems to be most fixed and determinate; and with the social condition everything else must change. The powers of society are more or less fugitive, like the years which we spend upon the earth; they succeed each other with rapidity, like the fleeting cares of life; and no government has ever yet been founded upon an invariable disposition of the human heart, or upon an imperishable interest.

As long as a religion is sustained by those feelings, propensities, and passions which are found to occur under the same forms, at all the different periods of history, it may defy the efforts of time; or at least it can only be destroyed by another religion. But when religion clings to the interests of the world, it becomes almost as fragile a thing as the powers of earth. It is the only one of them all which can hope for immortality; but if it be connected with their ephemeral authority, it shares their fortunes, and may fall with those transient passions which supported them for a day. The alliance which religion contracts with political powers must needs be onerous to itself; since it does not require their assistance to live, and by giving them its assistance to live, and by giving them its assistance it may be exposed to decay.

The danger which I have just pointed out always exists, but it is not always equally visible. In some ages governments seem to be imperishable; in others, the existence of society appears to be more precarious than the life of man. Some constitutions plunge the citizens into a lethargic somnolence, and others rouse them to feverish excitement. When governments appear to be so strong, and laws so stable, men do not perceive the dangers which may accrue from a union of Church and State. When governments display so much weakness, and laws so much inconstancy, the danger is self-evident, but it is no longer possible to avoid it; to be effectual, measures must be taken to discover its approach.

In proportion as a nation assumes a democratic condition of society, and as communities display democratic propensities, it becomes more and more dangerous to connect religion with political institutions; for the time is coming when authority will be bandied from hand to hand, when political theories will succeed each other, and when men, laws, and constitutions will disappear, or be modified from day to day, and this, not for a season only, but unceasingly. Agitation and mutability are inherent in the nature of democratic republics, just as stagnation and inertness are the law of absolute monarchies.

If the Americans, who change the head of the Government once in four years, who elect new legislators every two years, and renew the provincial officers every twelvemonth; if the Americans, who have abandoned the political world to the attempts of innovators, had not placed religion beyond their reach, where could it abide in the ebb and flow of human opinions? where would that respect which belongs to it be paid, amidst the struggles of faction? and what would become of its immortality, in the midst of perpetual decay?

*   *   *

But if the unbeliever does not admit religion to be true, he still considers it useful. Regarding religious institutions in a human point of view, he acknowledges their influence upon manners and legislation. He admits that they may serve to make men live in peace with one another, and to prepare them gently for the hour of death. He regrets the faith which he has lost; and as he is deprived of a treasure which he has learned to estimate at its full value, he scruples to take it from those who still possess it.

On the other hand, those who continue to believe are not afraid openly to avow their faith. They look upon those who do not share their persuasion as more worthy of pity than of opposition; and they are aware that to acquire the esteem of the unbelieving, they are not obliged to follow their example. They are hostile to no one in the world; and as they do not consider the society in which they live as an arena in which religion is bound to face its thousand deadly foes, they love their contemporaries, whilst they condemn their weaknesses and lament their errors.

As those who do not believe, conceal their incredulity; and as those who believe, display their faith, public opinion pronounces itself in favor of religion: love, support, and honor are bestowed upon it, and it is only by searching the human soul that we can detect the wounds which it has received. The mass of mankind, who are never without the feeling of religion, do not perceive anything at variance with the established faith. The instinctive desire of a future life brings the crowd about the altar, and opens the hearts of men to the precepts and consolations of religion.

But this picture is not applicable to us: for there are men amongst us who have ceased to believe in Christianity, without adopting any other religion; others who are in the perplexities of doubt, and who already affect not to believe; and others, again, who are afraid to avow that Christian faith which they still cherish in secret.

Amidst these lukewarm partisans and ardent antagonists a small number of believers exist, who are ready to brave all obstacles and to scorn all dangers in defence of their faith. They have done violence to human weakness, in order to rise superior to public opinion. Excited by the effort they have made, they scarcely knew where to stop; and as they know that the first use which the French made of independence was to attack religion, they look upon their contemporaries with dread, and they recoil in alarm from the liberty which their fellow-citizens are seeking to obtain. As unbelief appears to them to be a novelty, they comprise all that is new in one indiscriminate animosity. They are at war with their age and country, and they look upon every opinion which is put forth there as the necessary enemy of the faith.

Such is not the natural state of men with regard to religion at the present day; and some extraordinary or incidental cause must be at work in France to prevent the human mind from following its original propensities and to drive it beyond the limits at which it ought naturally to stop. I am intimately convinced that this extraordinary and incidental cause is the close connection of politics and religion. The unbelievers of Europe attack the Christians as their political opponents, rather than as their religious adversaries; they hate the Christian religion as the opinion of a party, much more than as an error of belief; and they reject the clergy less because they are the representatives of the Divinity than because they are the allies of authority.

In Europe, Christianity has been intimately united to the powers of the earth. Those powers are now in decay, and it is, as it were, buried under their ruins. The living body of religion has been bound down to the dead corpse of superannuated polity: cut but the bonds which restrain it, and that which is alive will rise once more.

3. Early Establishment Clause Interpretation — America as a "Religious People" Assumed

For the better part of a century, the Supreme Court confronted no Establishment Clause challenges. The few cases that did arise found no violation in providing public support to a religious body to carry out a secular function (*Bradfield v. Roberts*, 175 U.S. 291 (1899)) or to recognize the religious character of the people as a whole (*Zorach v. Clauson*, 343 U.S. 306 (1952)). *Bradfield* and *Zorach* more or less constitute the judicial book-ends for this period, in which an original understanding supportive of the importance of religion was accepted. *Bradfield* involved a grant to a religious society to run a public hospital. The Court found it unnecessary to inquire into the religious nature of the grantee so long as the hospital function was being performed. Indeed, there was some suggestion that even to inquire into the religious nature of the grantee would be an interference with free exercise. So long as the grantee met its grant obligations there could be no constitutional objection. Likewise, *Zorach* over a half-century later well into the middle of the 20th century found no difficulty with an early release program that allowed public school teachers to assist in the early exit from class of those students who wanted instruction in their faith tradition. It is true that the Court had earlier objected to the provision of religious instruction in the public school house itself with public school personnel but that early ruling was rather quickly tempered by the decision in *Zorach*.

Justice Douglas, writing for the majority stressed that there was little involvement of the school with the religious organizations, and the slight amount of interaction was within a "common sense" understanding of the Establishment Clause, stressing that a separation of church and state in any and all respects would make the state and the church "aliens to each other, hostile, suspicious, and even unfriendly." Such that rendering police and fire services to a church would be a violation of the First Amendment. Douglas goes on to state that "[w]e are a religious people whose institutions presuppose a Supreme Being." Believing that when "the state encourages religious instruction or cooperates with religious authorities by adjusting the schedule of public events to sectarian needs, it follows the best of our traditions." Going further by stating that to do otherwise would be to both favor those without religion over those that follow a faith tradition by showing "callous indifference" to religious groups.

In the second half of the 20th century however, more questions would begin to emerge. In *Everson v. Board of Education*, the Court upheld the provision of school buses to religious schools but it did so with a rationale that contains within it the seed — not of neutrality and accommodation — but of affirmative secularity and exclusion — which presumably meant that there was an obligation on the part of the government to be neutral not just among religions but between religion and no religion. As a moral principle of nondiscrimination that might be argued as an attractive ideal, but it's not necessarily consistent with a First Amendment Establishment Clause which was carefully framed to so as not to manifest exclusion of or hostility toward religion. As is modernly said, the framing of the First Amendment was aimed at protecting freedom of religion not freedom from it.

4. Incorporation of the Religion Clauses Against the States

As will be discussed later, from 1950 through roughly the late 1980s, the Court had particular difficulty straddling the line of accommodation on the one hand with exclusion on the other — especially in the context of public grammar and secondary schools where students were said to be particularly susceptible or impressionable — that impressionability becoming a substitute for the coercion that worried the framers when religion was advanced in the form of far harsher blasphemy similar statutory punishments. But education and the protection of culture represented by blasphemy enactments were the province of the state so very few cases at first troubled Supreme Court.

Alas, this difficulty ended up at the Supreme Court when the religion clauses were said to be "incorporated against the states." As a textual matter, the Bill of Rights are limitations upon Congress. *Barron v. Mayor of Baltimore*, 32 U.S. (7

Pet.) 243, 247–48 (1833). Following the Fourteenth Amendment which placed limitations upon the several states after the Civil War, however, it became the habit of the Court to read initially some and then most of the Bill of Rights as applying to both the federal and state governments. In essence the Court would make a judicial determination of which of the rights listed were essential to the concept of "ordered liberty" or some similarly capacious formulation.

The Supreme Court specifically held that the Free Exercise Clause did not apply to the states in *Permoli v. First Municipality*, 44 U.S. (3 How.) 589, 610 (1845). Some have argued that the drafters of the Fourteenth Amendment intended to extend all of the provisions of the Bill of Rights to the states. *See Adamson v. California*, 332 U.S. 46, 71–75 (1947) (Black, J., dissenting). Justice Black relied principally upon some persuasive testimony by the sponsors of the Fourteenth Amendment to that effect in the 39th Congress. *See* Hugo Black, *The Bill of Rights*, 35 N.Y.U. L. REV. 865 (1960). Black's view and those like it never gained a majority of the Court, however, and it was also disputed in the law reviews. *See, e.g.*, Stanley Morrison, *Does the Fourteenth Amendment Incorporate the Bill of Rights? The Judicial Interpretation*, 2 STAN. L. REV. 140 (1949); Charles Fairman, *Does the Fourteenth Amendment Incorporate the Bill of Rights? The Original Understanding*, 2 STAN. L. REV. 5 (1949).

In the Congress, a few years after the Fourteenth Amendment on December 14, 1875, Representative James G. Blaine introduced the so-called "Blaine Amendment," which was largely an anti-immigrant, anti-Catholic measure to preclude public aid from going to Catholic schools, but it also provided in its first clause that "[n]o State shall make any law respecting an establishment of religion or prohibiting the free exercise thereof." 4 CONG. REC. 205 (1875). In so providing, it is evident that members of the 44th Congress, which debated the Blaine Amendment, including the holdover members from the 39th Congress that had drafted the Fourteenth Amendment, did not believe that the Fourteenth Amendment had already applied the Bill of Rights, including the Religion Clauses, to the states. *See generally*, Alfred W. Meyer, *The Blaine Amendment and the Bill of Rights* , 64 HARV. L. REV. 939 (1951); F. William O'Brien, *The Blaine Amendment 1875–1876*, 41 U. DET. L.J. 137 (1963). So the Blaine Amendment presumably would have done the job, along with specifically prohibiting the public funding of sectarian schools. But the Blaine Amendment never went to the states for ratification, as it failed to get the requisite two-thirds majority in the Senate.

Today, the issue of extending the Religion Clauses to the states is practically moot in light of the Court's practice of selectively incorporating most of the Bill of Rights into the word "liberty" in the Fourteenth Amendment's Due Process Clause with the pseudo-natural law theory that liberty must necessarily include the fundamental freedoms in our concept of civilization. *Palko v. Connecticut*, 302 U.S. 319, 323–25 (1937). By this means, the Court in *Cantwell v. Connecticut*, 310 U.S. 296, 303 (1940), applied the Free Exercise Clause to the states and in *Illinois ex rel. McCollum v. Board of Education*, 333 U.S. 203, 210–11 (1948), applied the Establishment Clause. In neither case did the Supreme Court offer much reasoning to support incorporation of the Establishment Clause to the states.

When the Bill of Rights come to apply against the states do they have the same meaning? Justice Thomas, and former Justice John Paul Stevens, two members of the Court who were normally not in agreement on most matters, discerned that the no Establishment Clause was intended to preclude the Congress from interfering with state established churches. In other words, the no Establishment Clause could be seen as a principle of law protecting the states, not protecting individuals, except insofar as it was honoring the decision of individuals within a particular state to favor one religion over another in that state. This is not the modern interpretation of the Establishment Clause, however. Nevertheless, there are still intriguing questions to be asked whether there are circumstances in which the Religion Clauses or perhaps other portions of the Bill of Rights should apply differently to the federal and state governments. The possibility of this is discussed in a concurring opinion from Justice Thomas in the case of *Zelman v. Simmons-Harris*, a decision upholding public funding for private religious schools when it is the result of individual decisions in the expenditure of "vouchers" rather than direct funding by the state. We will examine the voucher idea more closely, but here we read Justice Thomas' explanation of how some amendments when applied to the states could plausibly mean something different than when applied against the federal government.

ZELMAN v. SIMMONS-HARRIS
536 U.S. 639 (2002)

JUSTICE THOMAS, concurring.

*   *   *

[I]n the context of the Establishment Clause, it may well be that state action should be evaluated on different terms than similar action by the Federal Government. "States, while bound to observe strict neutrality, should be freer to experiment with involvement [in religion] — on a neutral basis — than the Federal Government." *Walz v. Tax Comm'n of City of New York* (1970) (Harlan, J., concurring). Thus, while the Federal Government may "make no law respecting an establishment of religion," the States may pass laws that include or touch on religious matters so long as these laws do not impede free exercise rights or any other individual religious liberty interest. By considering the particular religious liberty right alleged to be invaded by a State, federal courts can strike a proper balance between the demands of the Fourteenth Amendment on the one hand and the federalism prerogatives of States on the other.[1]

---

[1] [3] Several Justices have suggested that rights incorporated through the Fourteenth Amendment apply in a different manner to the States than they do to the Federal Government. For instance, Justice Jackson stated, "the inappropriateness of a single standard for restricting State and Nation is indicated by the disparity between their functions and duties in relation to those freedoms." *Beauharnais v. Illinois*, 343 U.S. 250, 294 (1952) (dissenting opinion). Justice Harlan noted: "The Constitution differentiates between those areas of human conduct subject to the regulation of the States and those subject to the powers of the Federal Government. The substantive powers of the two governments, in many instances, are distinct. And in every case where we are called upon to balance the interest in free expression against other interests, it seems to me important that we should keep in the forefront the

* * *

II

The wisdom of allowing States greater latitude in dealing with matters of religion and education can be easily appreciated in this context. Respondents advocate using the Fourteenth Amendment to handcuff the State's ability to experiment with education. But without education one can hardly exercise the civic, political, and personal freedoms conferred by the Fourteenth Amendment. Faced with a severe educational crisis, the State of Ohio enacted wide-ranging educational reform that allows voluntary participation of private and religious schools in educating poor urban children otherwise condemned to failing public schools. The program does not force any individual to submit to religious indoctrination or education. It simply gives parents a greater choice as to where and in what manner to educate their children.[2] This is a choice that those with greater means have routinely exercised.

Justice Thomas' opinion was not joined by any other member of the Court, but he has continued to press the point, in *Elk Grove Unified School District v. Newdow*, 542 U.S. 1 (2004) (the Pledge of Allegiance case), and *Van Orden v. Perry*, 545 U.S. 677 (2005) (the Ten Commandments case). Does he raise a challenge to existing Establishment Clause orthodoxy that the Court will one day have to address? The sparring over the issue seems already to have begun. *Compare McCreary County, Kentucky v. ACLU of Kentucky*, 545 U.S. 844 (2005) (Scalia, J., dissenting), *with Van Orden v. Perry*, 545 U.S. 677 (2005) (Stevens, J., dissenting) (challenging Justice Scalia's views in *McCreary County* as requiring him to repudiate the incorporation of the Establishment Clause, but also noting that Justice Thomas has offered "some persuasive evidence" that incorporation of the Establishment Clause "ran contrary to the core of the Clause's original understanding" and that the Free Exercise Clause is a more appropriate source to protect individuals from any coercion of belief or practice).

C.   PUBLIC NEUTRALITY TOWARD GOD AND RELIGION

There is ample historical evidence that the word "establishment," as used by the framers of the First Amendment in 1791 meant what it had in Europe — government's "exclusive patronage" of one church. *See generally* LEO PFEFFER, CHURCH, STATE AND FREEDOM 63–70 (1953). The framers were most disturbed by laws that prescribed worship of one favored denomination, provided special subsidies therefore, or imposed disabilities on members of other religious sects, in particular for public office. As discussed in Part A, however, the framers nevertheless

---

question of whether those other interests are state or federal." *Roth v. United States* (1957) (dissenting opinion). See also *Gitlow v. New York* (1925) (Holmes, J., dissenting).

[2] [5] This Court has held that parents have the fundamental liberty to choose how and in what manner to educate their children. "The fundamental theory of liberty upon which all governments in this Union repose excludes any general power of the State to standardize its children by forcing them to accept instruction from public teachers only. The child is not the mere creature of the State; those who nurture him and direct his destiny have the right, coupled with the high duty, to recognize and prepare him for additional obligations." *Pierce v. Society of Sisters* (1925). But see *Troxel v. Granville* (2000) (THOMAS, J., concurring in judgment).

understood and encouraged the importance of religious belief generally. This was consistent with the natural law tradition of the Declaration. As Justice Joseph Story wrote: "[t]he real object of the [First] amendment was, not to countenance, much less to advance Mohametanism, or Judaism, or infidelity, by prostrating Christianity; but to exclude all rivalry among Christian sects, and to prevent any national ecclesiastical establishment, which should give to an hierarchy the exclusive patronage of the national government." 3 JOSEPH STORY, COMMENTARIES ON THE CONSTITUTION OF THE UNITED STATES § 1871 (photo. reprint 1991) (Boston, Hilliard, Gray & Co. 1833). From 1791 to 1947, this understanding went unchallenged. In 1947, however, in *Everson v. Board of Education*, 330 U.S. 1 (1947), the Supreme Court took a radical turn. In the guise of neutrality, *Everson* articulated the exclusionary view that government may not aid religion generally — a truly extraordinary proposition for a nation founded upon the "Laws of Nature and of Nature's God." Subsequent to *Everson*, the Establishment Clause case law has taken numerous other twists and turns. There is no single, agreed upon Establishment Clause test on the Court. Instead, the Justices ask whether a law: (1) has a secular legislative purpose; (2) its principal or primary effect is either inducing or inhibiting religion; and (3) fosters an excessive government entanglement with religion. This three part test is sometimes described by the shorthand of the *Lemon* test from a case of that name, though the three inquiries are broader than that case, itself. What might those inquiries be? By way of overview, the Establishment Clause has been interpreted in the following ways:

1. (The no coercion view; sometimes referred to as "non-preferentialism"). By the framers, as prohibiting the establishment of a national church, the coercion under law of a particular religious belief or practice, or the showing of any favoritism to a particular religious sect.

2. (The exclusionary view, no coercion as well as a duty to exclude religion — *i.e.*, to promote secularism). *Everson* is the 20th century root of the exclusionary view and later *Lemon v. Kurtzman*, 403 U.S. 602 (1971).

3. (The no endorsement view). This ideas was put forth by the former Justice O'Connor and today makes sporadic appearance in Establishment cases. It asks whether a reasonably informed observer would perceive government action as an endorsement of religion generally.

4. (The equal protectionview). This view which is also an outgrowth of a basic "free speech" principle that it is not up to the government to favor one private speaker over another — *e.g.*, the essence of the modern protection of free speech is to keep the government from being a censor.

5. (The "Just Say No" view). This view basically finds even the slightest support — symbolic, monetary or otherwise — for religion to be contrary to the Constitution.

Let's take a closer look at the judicial argumentation for each of these positions:

1. Modern Judicial Application of the No Establishment Principle

a. The Exclusionary View

EVERSON v. BOARD OF EDUCATION
330 U.S. 1 (1947)

MR. JUSTICE BLACK delivered the opinion of the Court.

A New Jersey statute authorizes its local school districts to make rules and contracts for the transportation of children to and from schools. The appellee, a township board of education, acting pursuant to this statute, authorized reimbursement to parents of money expended by them for the bus transportation of their children on regular busses operated by the public transportation system. Part of this money was for the payment of transportation of some children in the community to Catholic parochial schools. These church schools give their students, in addition to secular education, regular religious instruction conforming to the religious tenets and modes of worship of the Catholic Faith. The superintendent of these schools is a Catholic priest.

The appellant, in his capacity as a district taxpayer, filed suit in a state court challenging the right of the Board to reimburse parents of parochial school students. He contended that the statute and the resolution passed pursuant to it violated both the State and the Federal Constitutions. That court held that the legislature was without power to authorize such payment under the state constitution. The New Jersey Court of Errors and Appeals reversed, holding that neither the statute nor the resolution passed pursuant to it was in conflict with the State constitution or the provisions of the Federal Constitution in issue. The case is here on appeal. . . .

A large proportion of the early settlers of this country came here from Europe to escape the bondage of laws which compelled them to support and attend government-favored churches. . . .

The movement toward this end reached its dramatic climax in Virginia in 1785–86 when the Virginia legislative body was about to renew Virginia's tax levy for the support of the established church. Thomas Jefferson and James Madison led the fight against this tax. Madison wrote his great Memorial and Remonstrance against the law. In it, he eloquently argued that a true religion did not need the support of law; that no person, either believer or non-believer, should be taxed to support a religious institution of any kind; that the best interest of a society required that the minds of men always be wholly free; and that cruel persecutions were the inevitable result of government-established religions. Madison's Remonstrance received strong support throughout Virginia, and the Assembly postponed consideration of the proposed tax measure until its next session. When the proposal came up for consideration at that session, it not only died in committee, but the Assembly enacted the famous "Virginia Bill for Religious Liberty" originally written by Thomas Jefferson.

The meaning and scope of the First Amendment, preventing establishment of religion or prohibiting the free exercise thereof, in the light of its history and the evils it was designed forever to suppress, have been several times elaborated by the decisions of this Court prior to the application of the First Amendment to the states by the Fourteenth. . . .

The "establishment of religion" clause of the First Amendment means at least this: Neither a state nor the Federal Government can set up a church. Neither can pass laws which aid one religion, aid all religions, or prefer one religion over another. Neither can force nor influence a person to go to or to remain away from church against his will or force him to profess a belief or disbelief in any religion. No person can be punished for entertaining or professing religious beliefs or disbeliefs, for church attendance or non-attendance. No tax in any amount, large or small, can be levied to support any religious activities or institutions, whatever they may be called, or whatever form they may adopt to teach or practice religion. Neither a state nor the Federal Government can, openly or secretly, participate in the affairs of any religious organizations or groups and *vice versa*. In the words of Jefferson, the clause against establishment of religion by law was intended to erect "a wall of separation between church and State."

We must consider the New Jersey statute in accordance with the foregoing limitations imposed by the First Amendment. But we must not strike that state statute down if it is within the State's constitutional power even though it approaches the verge of that power. . . .

Measured by these standards, we cannot say that the First Amendment prohibits New Jersey from spending tax-raised funds to pay the bus fares of parochial school pupils as a part of a general program under which it pays the fares of pupils attending public and other schools. . . . Of course, cutting off church schools from these services, so separate and so indisputably marked off from the religious function, would make it far more difficult for the schools to operate. But such is obviously not the purpose of the First Amendment. That Amendment requires the state to be a neutral in its relations with groups of religious believers and non-believers; it does not require the state to be their adversary. State power is no more to be used so as to handicap religions than it is to favor them.

This Court has said that parents may, in the discharge of their duty under state compulsory education laws, send their children to a religious rather than a public school if the school meets the secular educational requirements which the state has power to impose. See *Pierce v. Society of Sisters* [(1925)]. It appears that these parochial schools meet New Jersey's requirements. The State contributes no money to the schools. It does not support them. Its legislation, as applied, does no more than provide a general program to help parents get their children, regardless of their religion, safely and expeditiously to and from accredited schools.

The First Amendment has erected a wall between church and state. That wall must be kept high and impregnable. We could not approve the slightest breach. New Jersey has not breached it here.

Affirmed.

MR. JUSTICE JACKSON, dissenting. [Omitted.]

MR. JUSTICE RUTLEDGE, with whom MR. JUSTICE FRANKFURTER, MR. JUSTICE JACKSON and MR. JUSTICE BURTON agree, dissenting. [Omitted]

NOTES AND QUESTIONS

1. Do you see why *Everson*'s rationale, but not its result, is exclusionary? At first blush, the opinion in *Everson* may not seem all that exclusionary. In terms of result, the Court upholds governmentally-provided bus service to religious schools. What's more the Court's opinion is phrased in terms of "neutrality," not exclusion. The exclusionary impact of *Everson* will be felt later, however, most notably as the Court struggles with other forms of aid to religious elementary schools. In any event, neutrality between religion and no religion is far different than say, Washington's decidedly non-neutral postulate that "religion and morality" were necessary supports for the political well-being of the republic. *See* John H. Garvey, *Is There a Principle of Religious Liberty?*, 94 MICH. L. REV. 1379 (1996) (discussing theories of religious liberty and arguing that they need not be neutral because nonneutral theories simply explain why society supports the right to do certain things and not others).

2. Revisionist History: The *Everson* opinion is historically questionable. Justice Black makes reference to Jefferson's Statute of Religious Freedom (reprinted below under the noncoercion view), but fails to recognize, as did the Anti-Federalist Richard Henry Lee earlier, that its aim was completing the work of Virginia's disestablishment of the Anglican Church, not mandating that government disavow all support for religion. Not surprisingly, therefore, contemporaneous with the Statute of Religious Freedom, Virginia was continuing in law to support religion generally. For example, fines were imposed for violating the Sabbath, *see* Act of December 26, 1792, ch 141, 1 VA. REV. CODE 554, 555 (1819), and public officials took oaths that ended with the language, "So help me God," or with such other language that was in accord with "the religion in which such person professeth to believe." *See* Act of January 7, 1818, ch. 28, 1 VA. REV. CODE 72, 73 (1819). The Anglican Church in Virginia had received special lands, called glebe lands, as an established church. Such lands were taken away by the Act of January 12, 1802, ch. 32b, 1 VA. REV. CODE 79 (1819). In *Terrett v. Taylor*, 13 U.S. (9 Cranch) 43 (1815), Justice Story held the act unconstitutional at least as applied to lands received by the church prior to the creation of the state of Virginia. In so doing, Story opined on the difference between disestablishment and the continuing importance of even-handed government support for religious corporations:

> It is conceded on all sides that, at the revolution, the Episcopal church no longer retained its character as an exclusive religious establishment. And there can be no doubt that it was competent to the people and to the legislature to deprive it of its superiority over other religious sects, and to withhold from it any support by public taxation. But, although it may be true that "religion can be directed only by reason and conviction, not by force or violence," and that "all men are equally entitled to the free exercise of religion according to the dictates of conscience," as the bill of rights of

Virginia declares, yet it is difficult to perceive how it follows as a consequence that the legislature may not enact laws more effectually to enable all sects to accomplish the great objects of religion by giving them corporate rights for the management of their property, and the regulation of their temporal as well as spiritual concerns. Consistent with the constitution of Virginia the legislature could not create or continue a religious establishment which should have exclusive rights and prerogatives, or compel the citizens to worship under a stipulated form or discipline, or to pay taxes to those whose creed they could not conscientiously believe. But the free exercise of religion cannot be justly deemed to be restrained by aiding with equal attention the votaries of every sect to perform their own religious duties, or by establishing funds for the support of ministers, for public charities, for the endowment of churches, or for the sepulture of the dead. And that these purposes could be better secured and cherished by corporate powers, cannot be doubted by any person who has attended to the difficulties which surround all voluntary associations. While, therefore, the legislature might exempt the citizens from a compulsive attendance and payment of taxes in support of any particular sect, it is not perceived that either public or constitutional principles required the abolition of all religious corporations.

13 U.S. (9 Cranch) at 48–49.

3. The "Wall of Separation" Metaphor: *Everson*'s perspective is far different from *Terrett v. Taylor*'s. It is a judicial attitude less congenial to public reliance upon the work of religion than at any previous time in our nation's history. For example, it is in *Everson* where Jefferson's absolutist phraseology, "a wall of separation between church and state," first appears in Supreme Court Establishment Clause jurisprudence (it first appeared in free exercise case law in *Reynolds v. United States*, 98 U.S. 145, 164 (1878), considered in Part C). As forbidding as the metaphor sounds, even this "wall" was misconstructed in *Everson*. Justice Black does not explain that Jefferson employed the phrase in a letter to the Danbury, Connecticut Baptist Association, not to diminish public support for religion generally, but to decry the establishment of the Congregationalist Church in Connecticut. *See* Thomas Jefferson, Reply to a Committee of the Danbury Baptist Association (Jan. 1, 1802), *in* 16 THE WRITINGS OF THOMAS JEFFERSON 281–82 (Andrew A. Lipscomb & Albert Ellery Bergh eds., 1905).

Despite its historical imperfection, *Everson* has troubled the Court's Establishment Clause jurisprudence ever since, and perhaps the American culture at large. As Washington and Tocqueville implicitly warned, the exclusion of religious influence may be seen in dramatically increased levels of violence, divorce, illegitimacy, and other manifestations of cultural dysfunction. At first, the extreme nature of *Everson*'s exclusionary theory was masked by its expedient, if not inclusionary result, allowing public funds to be used for the bus transportation of all students, including those attending religious schools. Shortly thereafter, however, *Everson* would spawn an ever more mechanically exclusionary formula in *Lemon v. Kurtzman*, 403 U.S. 602 (1971). Under the "*Lemon* test," a law does not violate the Establishment Clause only if it (1) has a secular purpose; (2) neither advances nor inhibits religion as its primary effect; and (3) does not "excessively entangle" the government with religion. *Id.* at 612–13. This multi-prong *Lemon* formula satisfied few of the Justices, and yielded highly inconsistent results over what assistance, if any, the government may render to religious schools, especially at the elementary level.

Outside of the grammar school in other substantive contexts, the ahistorical re-direction of *Everson* has been mitigated somewhat by various Establishment Clause theories that either re-direct the clause to its original purpose of no legal coercion of denominational faith and the equal treatment of religious sects, or less predictably and more subjectively, attempt to measure whether government activity can be perceived as too much "endorsement" of faith.

b. The Noncoercion View

Jefferson justifiably regarded the Virginia Statute of Religious Liberty to be one of his three most memorable contributions, the others being the Declaration of Independence and the founding of the University of Virginia. Jefferson was aided in this pursuit by Madison, as the *Everson* dissenters suggest. But the dissenters overlook that Jefferson and Madison together saw the struggle for religious freedom, not as a limitation of the significance or importance of religion, but as an affirmation of religion's importance to "the natural rights of mankind." That religion has this high place is signaled at the very beginning of Virginia's statute which calls first upon Almighty God. Nothing in this statute is at odds with sovereign acknowledgment of the existence of a Creator God in the Declaration. Indeed, given the common authorship of the two documents, it would be extraordinary for there to be a conflict. The Statute of Religious Liberty is primarily directed at ending the vestiges of Anglicanism (which had been the established church in Virginia) and other similar forms of compelled denominationalism. As you read the Statute, note especially the following testimonials to the importance of faith, freely embraced:

1. God endowed all human persons with free will, aided by a free mind;

2. It is contrary to God's will to coerce religious belief, whether that coercion comes at the hands of the state or the church;

3. Coercion includes not only forced belief, but the compelled financial support of a particular religious opinion or pastor over those religious ministers a person "feels most persuasive to righteousness" [notice the implicit assumption that some pastor or religious body would be freely supported by all moral men — Eds.];

4. Civil rights, including the right to hold public office, do not depend upon holding a particular religious opinion;

5. Religious belief and practice ought to remain free up to the point such "principles break out into overt acts against peace and good order." Thus, note: even religious liberty, as exalted as it is, is not absolute or without limit.

We take up what general laws maintaining "peace and good order" may be applied to religious beliefs and practices in Part C of this Chapter dealing with the interpretation of the Free Exercise Clause.

Virginia Statute of Religious Liberty
(Jan. 16, 1786), *reprinted in* THE VIRGINIA STATUTE FOR RELIGIOUS FREEDOM at xvii (Merrill D Peterson & Robert C. Vaughan eds., 1988)

. . . An Act for establishing Religious Freedom.

I. WHEREAS Almighty God hath created the mind free; that all attempts to influence it by temporal punishments or burthens, or by civil incapacitations, tend only to beget habits of hypocrisy and meanness, and are a departure from the plan of the Holy author of our religion, who being Lord both of body and mind, yet chose not to propagate it by coercions either, as was in his Almighty power to do; that the impious presumption of legislators and rulers, civil as well as ecclesiastical, who being themselves but fallible and uninspired men, have assumed dominion over the faith of others, setting up their own opinions and modes of thinking as the only true and infallible, and as such endeavouring to impose them on others, hath established and maintained false religions over the greatest part of the world, and through all time; that to compel a man to furnish contributions of money for the propagation of opinions which he disbelieves, is sinful and tyrannical; that even the forcing him to support this or that teacher of his own religious persuasion, is depriving him of the comfortable liberty of giving his contributions to the particular pastor, whose morals he would make his pattern, and whose powers he feels most persuasive to righteousness, and is withdrawing from the ministry those temporary rewards, which proceeding from an approbation of their personal conduct, are an additional incitement to earnest and unremitting labours for the instruction of mankind; that our civil rights have no dependence on our religious opinions, any more than our opinions in physics or geometry; that therefore the proscribing any citizen as unworthy the public confidence by laying upon him an incapacity of being called to offices of trust and emolument, unless he profess or renounce this or that religious opinion, is depriving him injuriously of those privileges and advantages to which in common with his fellow-citizens he has a natural right; that it tends only to corrupt the principles of that religion it is meant to encourage, by bribing with a monopoly of worldly honours and emoluments, those who will externally profess and conform to it; that though indeed these are criminal who do not withstand such temptation, yet neither are those innocent who lay the bait in their way; that to suffer the civil magistrate to intrude his powers into the field of opinion, and to restrain the profession or propagation of principles on supposition of their ill tendency, is a dangerous fallacy, which at once destroys all religious liberty, because he being of course judge of that tendency will make his opinions the rule of judgment, and approve or condemn the sentiments of others only as they shall square with or differ from his own; that it is time enough for the rightful purposes of civil government, for its officers to interfere when principles break out into overt acts against peace and good order; and finally, that truth is great and will prevail if left to herself, that she is the proper and sufficient antagonist to error, and has nothing to fear from the conflict, unless by human interposition disarmed of her natural weapons, free argument and debate, errors ceasing to be dangerous when it is permitted freely to contradict them:

II. *Be it enacted by the General Assembly,* that no man shall be compelled to frequent or support any religious worship, place, or ministry whatsoever, nor shall be enforced, restrained, molested, or burthened in his body or goods, nor shall otherwise suffer on account of his religious opinions or belief; but that all men shall be free to profess, and by argument to maintain, their opinion in matters of religion, and that the same shall in no way diminish, enlarge, or affect their civil capacities.

III. And though we well know that this assembly elected by the people for the ordinary purposes of legislation only, have no power to restrain the acts of succeeding assemblies, constituted with powers equal to our own, and that therefore to declare this act to be irrevocable would be of no effect in law; yet we are free to declare, and do declare, that the rights hereby asserted are to the natural rights of mankind, and that if any act shall be hereafter passed to repeal the present, or to narrow its operation, such act will be an infringement of natural right.

NOTE

In *Lee v. Weisman*, the issue before the Court was whether a graduation prayer violated the Establishment Clause. In the context of considering this issue, a fairly evenly-divided Court debates whether coercion is a necessary element of an Establishment Clause case. Five members of the Court (Justice Kennedy writing for the majority and the four dissenting justices) believe coercion is necessary. Unlike the dissenters, though, Justice Kennedy extends the concept to include psychological coercion — an analogue, perhaps, of Justice O'Connor's no endorsement speculation considered later in this Chapter.

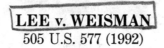

LEE v. WEISMAN
505 U.S. 577 (1992)

JUSTICE KENNEDY delivered the opinion of the Court.

School principals in the public school system of the city of Providence, Rhode Island, are permitted to invite members of the clergy to offer invocation and benediction prayers as part of the formal graduation ceremonies for middle schools and for high schools. The question before us is whether including clerical members who offer prayers as part of the official school graduation ceremony is consistent with the Religion Clauses of the First Amendment, provisions the Fourteenth Amendment makes applicable with full force to the States and their school districts.

[Robert E. Lee, the principal of Nathan Bishop Middle School, invited Rabbi Leslie Gutterman to deliver prayers at the school's graduation ceremony in June 1989. Gutterman accepted, and offered both the invocation and benediction. Daniel Weisman, whose 14 year-old daughter graduated in the ceremony, challenged the practice on behalf of himself and his daughter as an unconstitutional establishment of religion.]

I
A

It has been the custom of Providence school officials to provide invited clergy with a pamphlet entitled "Guidelines for Civic Occasions," prepared by the National

Conference of Christians and Jews. . . .

Rabbi Gutterman's prayers were as follows:

"INVOCATION

"God of the Free, Hope of the Brave:

"For the legacy of America where diversity is celebrated and the rights of minorities are protected, we thank You. May these young men and women grow up to enrich it.

"For the liberty of America, we thank You. May these new graduates grow up to guard it.

"For the political process of America in which all its citizens may participate, for its court system where all may seek justice we thank You. May those we honor this morning always turn to it in trust.

"For the destiny of America we thank You. May the graduates of Nathan Bishop Middle School so live that they might help to share it.

"May our aspirations for our country and for these young people, who are our hope for the future, be richly fulfilled.

AMEN"

"BENEDICTION = utterance or bestowing of a blessing

"O God, we are grateful to You for having endowed us with the capacity for learning which we have celebrated on this joyous commencement.

"Happy families give thanks for seeing their children achieve an important milestone. Send Your blessings upon the teachers and administrators who helped prepare them.

"The graduates now need strength and guidance for the future, help them to understand that we are not complete with academic knowledge alone. We must each strive to fulfill what You require of us all: To do justly, to love mercy, to walk humbly.

"We give thanks to You, Lord, for keeping us alive, sustaining us and allowing us to reach this special, happy occasion.

AMEN"

*   *   *

B

* * *

. . . The District Court held that petitioners' practice of including invocations and benedictions in public school graduations violated the Establishment Clause of the First Amendment, and it enjoined petitioners from continuing the practice. The court applied the three-part Establishment Clause test set forth in *Lemon v. Kurtzman* (1971). Under that test as described in our past cases, to satisfy the Establishment Clause a governmental practice must (1) reflect a clearly secular purpose; (2) have a primary effect that neither advances nor inhibits religion; and (3) avoid excessive government entanglement with religion. The District Court held that petitioners' actions violated the second part of the test, and so did not address either the first or the third. The court decided, based on its reading of our precedents, that the effects test of *Lemon* is violated whenever government action "creates an identification of the state with a religion, or with religion in general," or when "the effect of the governmental action is to endorse one religion over another, or to endorse religion in general." The court determined that the practice of including invocations and benedictions, even so-called nonsectarian ones, in public school graduations creates an identification of governmental power with religious practice, endorses religion, and violates the Establishment Clause. In so holding the court expressed the determination not to follow *Stein v. Plainwell Community Schools* (6th Cir. 1987), in which the Court of Appeals for the Sixth Circuit, relying on our decision in *Marsh v. Chambers* (1983), held that benedictions and invocations at public school graduations are not always unconstitutional. In *Marsh* we upheld the constitutionality of the Nebraska State Legislature's practice of opening each of its sessions with a prayer offered by a chaplain paid out of public funds. The District Court in this case disagreed with the Sixth Circuit's reasoning because it believed that *Marsh* was a narrow decision, "limited to the unique situation of legislative prayer," and did not have any relevance to school prayer cases.

On appeal, the United States Court of Appeals for the First Circuit affirmed. . . . We granted certiorari, and now affirm.

II

These dominant facts mark and control the confines of our decision: State officials direct the performance of a formal religious exercise at promotional and graduation ceremonies for secondary schools. Even for those students who object to the religious exercise, their attendance and participation in the state-sponsored religious activity are in a fair and real sense obligatory, though the school district does not require attendance as a condition for receipt of the diploma.

The principle that government may accommodate the free exercise of religion does not supersede the fundamental limitations imposed by the Establishment Clause. It is beyond dispute that, at a minimum, the Constitution guarantees that government may not coerce anyone to support or participate in religion or its exercise, or otherwise act in a way which "establishes a [state] religion or religious faith, or tends to do so." The State's involvement in the school prayers challenged today violates these central principles.

That involvement is as troubling as it is undenied. A school official, the principal, decided that an invocation and a benediction should be given; this is a choice attributable to the State, and from a constitutional perspective it is as if a state statute decreed that the prayers must occur. The principal chose the religious participant, here a rabbi, and that choice is also attributable to the State. The reason for the choice of a rabbi is not disclosed by the record, but the potential for divisiveness over the choice of a particular member of the clergy to conduct the ceremony is apparent.

Divisiveness, of course, can attend any state decision respecting religions, and neither its existence nor its potential necessarily invalidates the State's attempts to accommodate religion in all cases. The potential for divisiveness is of particular relevance here though, because it centers around an overt religious exercise in a secondary school environment where, as we discuss below, subtle coercive pressures exist and where the student had no real alternative which would have allowed her to avoid the fact or appearance of participation.

We are asked to recognize the existence of a practice of nonsectarian prayer, prayer within the embrace of what is known as the Judeo-Christian tradition, prayer which is more acceptable than one which, for example, makes explicit references to the God of Israel, or to Jesus Christ, or to a patron saint. There may be some support, as an empirical observation, to the statement of the Court of Appeals for the Sixth Circuit, picked up by Judge Campbell's dissent in the Court of Appeals in this case, that there has emerged in this country a civic religion, one which is tolerated when sectarian exercises are not. If common ground can be defined which permits once conflicting faiths to express the shared conviction that there is an ethic and a morality which transcend human invention, the sense of community and purpose sought by all decent societies might be advanced. But though the First Amendment does not allow the government to stifle prayers which aspire to these ends, neither does it permit the government to undertake that task for itself.

. . . The undeniable fact is that the school district's supervision and control of a high school graduation ceremony places public pressure, as well as peer pressure, on attending students to stand as a group or, at least, maintain respectful silence during the Invocation and Benediction. This pressure, though subtle and indirect, can be as real as any overt compulsion. Of course, in our culture standing or remaining silent can signify adherence to a view or simple respect for the views of others. And no doubt some persons who have no desire to join a prayer have little objection to standing as a sign of respect for those who do. But for the dissenter of high school age, who has a reasonable perception that she is being forced by the State to pray in a manner her conscience will not allow, the injury is no less real. There can be no doubt that for many, if not most, of the students at the graduation, the act of standing or remaining silent was an expression of participation in the rabbi's prayer. That was the very point of the religious exercise. It is of little comfort to a dissenter, then, to be told that for her the act of standing or remaining in silence signifies mere respect, rather than participation. What matters is that, given our social conventions, a reasonable dissenter in this milieu could believe that the group exercise signified her own participation or approval of it.]

Finding no violation under these circumstances would place objectors in the dilemma of participating, with all that implies, or protesting. We do not address whether that choice is acceptable if the affected citizens are mature adults, but we think the State may not, consistent with the Establishment Clause, place primary and secondary school children in this position. Research in psychology supports the common assumption that adolescents are often susceptible to pressure from their peers towards conformity, and that the influence is strongest in matters of social convention. To recognize that the choice imposed by the State constitutes an unacceptable constraint only acknowledges that the government may no more use social pressure to enforce orthodoxy than it may use more direct means.

The injury caused by the government's action, and the reason why Daniel and Deborah Weisman object to it, is that the State, in a school setting, in effect required participation in a religious exercise. It is, we concede, a brief exercise during which the individual can concentrate on joining its message, meditate on her own religion, or let her mind wander. But the embarrassment and the intrusion of the religious exercise cannot be refuted by arguing that these prayers, and similar ones to be said in the future, are of a *de minimis* character. To do so would be an affront to the rabbi who offered them and to all those for whom the prayers were an essential and profound recognition of divine authority. . . .

There was a stipulation in the District Court that attendance at graduation and promotional ceremonies is voluntary. Petitioners and the United States, as *amicus*, made this a center point of the case, arguing that the option of not attending the graduation excuses any inducement or coercion in the ceremony itself. The argument lacks all persuasion. Law reaches past formalism. And to say a teenage student has a real choice not to attend her high school graduation is formalistic in the extreme. True, Deborah could elect not to attend commencement without renouncing her diploma; but we shall not allow the case to turn on this point. Everyone knows that in our society and in our culture high school graduation is one of life's most significant occasions. A school rule which excuses attendance is beside the point. . . .

Our society would be less than true to its heritage if it lacked abiding concern for the values of its young people, and we acknowledge the profound belief of adherents to many faiths that there must be a place in the student's life for precepts of a morality higher even than the law we today enforce. We express no hostility to those aspirations, nor would our oath permit us to do so. A relentless and all-pervasive attempt to exclude religion from every aspect of public life could itself become inconsistent with the Constitution. We recognize that, at graduation time and throughout the course of the educational process, there will be instances when religious values, religious practices, and religious persons will have some interaction with the public schools and their students. But these matters, often questions of accommodation of religion, are not before us. The sole question presented is whether a religious exercise may be conducted at a graduation ceremony in circumstances where, as we have found, young graduates who object are induced to conform. No holding by this Court suggests that a school can persuade or compel a student to participate in a religious exercise. That is being done here, and it is forbidden by the Establishment Clause of the First Amendment.

Kennedy
Blackmun
Stevens
O'Connor

+

concurring
opinion:

Souter

For the reasons we have stated, the judgment of the Court of Appeals is Affirmed.

JUSTICE BLACKMUN, with whom JUSTICE STEVENS and JUSTICE O'CONNOR join, concurring. [Omitted.]

JUSTICE SOUTER, with whom JUSTICE STEVENS and JUSTICE O'CONNOR join, concurring.

I join the whole of the Court's opinion, and fully agree that prayers at public school graduation ceremonies indirectly coerce religious observance. I write separately nonetheless on two issues of Establishment Clause analysis that underlie my independent resolution of this case: whether the Clause applies to governmental practices that do not favor one religion or denomination over others, and whether state coercion of religious conformity, over and above state endorsement of religious exercise or belief, is a necessary element of an Establishment Clause violation.

I

Forty-five years ago, this Court announced a basic principle of constitutional law from which it has not strayed: the Establishment Clause forbids not only state practices that "aid one religion . . . or prefer one religion over another," but also those that "aid all religions." *Everson v. Board of Education of Ewing* (1947). Today we reaffirm that principle, holding that the Establishment Clause forbids state-sponsored prayers in public school settings no matter how nondenominational the prayers may be. . . .

B

Some have challenged this precedent by reading the Establishment Clause to permit "nonpreferential" state promotion of religion. The challengers argue that, as originally understood by the Framers, "[t]he Establishment Clause did not require government neutrality between religion and irreligion nor did it prohibit the Federal Government from providing nondiscriminatory aid to religion." *Wallace [v. Jaffree* (1985)] (REHNQUIST, J., dissenting); see also R. CORD, SEPARATION OF CHURCH AND STATE: HISTORICAL FACT AND CURRENT FICTION (1988). While a case has been made for this position, it is not [] convincing. . . .

. . . [H]istory neither contradicts nor warrants reconsideration of the settled principle that the Establishment Clause forbids support for religion in general no less than support for one religion or some.[3]

---

[3] [3] In his dissent in *Wallace v. Jaffree* (1985), THE CHIEF JUSTICE rested his nonpreferentialist interpretation partly on the post-ratification actions of the early National Government. Aside from the willingness of some (but not all) early Presidents to issue ceremonial religious proclamations, which were at worst trivial breaches of the Establishment Clause, he cited such seemingly preferential aid as a treaty provision, signed by Jefferson, authorizing federal subsidization of a Roman Catholic priest and church for the Kaskaskia Indians. But this proves too much, for if the Establishment Clause permits a special appropriation of tax money for the religious activities of a particular sect, it forbids virtually

C

While these considerations are, for me, sufficient to reject the nonpreferentialist position, one further concern animates my judgment. In many contexts, including this one, nonpreferentialism requires some distinction between "sectarian" religious practices and those that would be, by some measure, ecumenical enough to pass Establishment Clause muster. Simply by requiring the enquiry, nonpreferentialists invite the courts to engage in comparative theology. I can hardly imagine a subject less amenable to the competence of the federal judiciary, or more deliberately to be avoided where possible.

II
A

Our precedents may not always have drawn perfectly straight lines. They simply cannot, however, support the position that a showing of coercion is necessary to a successful Establishment Clause claim.

III

While the Establishment Clause's concept of neutrality is not self-revealing, our recent cases have invested it with specific content: the state may not favor or endorse either religion generally over nonreligion or one religion over others. . . .

JUSTICE SCALIA, with whom THE CHIEF JUSTICE, JUSTICE WHITE, and JUSTICE THOMAS join, dissenting.

Three Terms ago, I joined an opinion recognizing that the Establishment Clause must be construed in light of the "[g]overnment policies of accommodation, acknowledgment, and support for religion [that] are an accepted part of our political and cultural heritage." That opinion affirmed that "the meaning of the Clause is to be determined by reference to historical practices and understandings. . . ."

These views of course prevent me from joining today's opinion, which is conspicuously bereft of any reference to history. In holding that the Establishment Clause prohibits invocations and benedictions at public school graduation ceremonies, the Court — with nary a mention that it is doing so — lays waste a tradition that is as old as public school graduation ceremonies themselves, and that is a component of an even more longstanding American tradition of nonsectarian prayer to God at public celebrations generally. As its instrument of destruction, the bulldozer of its social engineering, the Court invents a boundless, and boundlessly manipulable, test of psychological coercion. . . .

---

nothing. Although evidence of historical practice can indeed furnish valuable aid in the interpretation of contemporary language, acts like the one in question prove only that public officials, no matter when they serve, can turn a blind eye to constitutional principle.

I

From our Nation's origin, prayer has been a prominent part of governmental ceremonies and proclamations. The Declaration of Independence, the document marking our birth as a separate people, "appeal[ed] to the Supreme Judge of the world for the rectitude of our intentions" and avowed "a firm reliance on t he protection of divine Providence." In his first inaugural address, after swearing his oath of office on a Bible, George Washington deliberately made a prayer a part of his first official act as President:

> "it would be peculiarly improper to omit in this first official act my fervent supplications to that Almighty Being who rules over the universe, who presides in the councils of nations, and whose providential aids can supply every human defect, that His benediction may consecrate to the liberties and happiness of the people of the United States a Government instituted by themselves for these essential purposes." INAUGURAL ADDRESSES OF THE PRESIDENTS OF THE UNITED STATES 2 (1989).

Such supplications have been a characteristic feature of inaugural addresses ever since. . . .

The other two branches of the Federal Government also have a long-established practice of prayer at public events. As we detailed in *Marsh* [*v. Chambers* (1983)], Congressional sessions have opened with a chaplain's prayer ever since the First Congress. And this Court's own sessions have opened with the invocation "God save the United States and this Honorable Court" since the days of Chief Justice Marshall. 1 C. WARREN, THE SUPREME COURT IN UNITED STATES HISTORY 469 (1922).

II

The Court presumably would separate graduation invocations and benedictions from other instances of public "preservation and transmission of religious beliefs" on the ground that they involve "psychological coercion." I find it a sufficient embarrassment that our Establishment Clause jurisprudence regarding holiday displays, see *Allegheny County v. Greater Pittsburgh ACLU* (1989), has come to "requir[e] scrutiny more commonly associated with interior decorators than with the judiciary." *American Jewish Congress v. Chicago* (7th Cir. 1987) (Easterbrook, J., dissenting). But interior decorating is a rock-hard science compared to psychology practiced by amateurs. A few citations of "research in psychology" that have no particular bearing upon the precise issue here, cannot disguise the fact that the Court has gone beyond the realm where judges know what they are doing. The Court's argument that state officials have "coerced" students to take part in the invocation and benediction at graduation ceremonies is, not to put too fine a point on it, incoherent.

The Court identifies two "dominant facts" that it says dictate its ruling that invocations and benedictions at public-school graduation ceremonies violate the Establishment Clause. Neither of them is in any relevant sense true.

A

The Court declares that students' "attendance and participation in the [invocation and benediction] are in a fair and real sense obligatory." But what exactly is this "fair and real sense"? According to the Court, students at graduation who want "to avoid the fact or appearance of participation," in the invocation and benediction are *psychologically* obligated by "public pressure, as well as peer pressure, . . . to stand as a group or, at least, maintain respectful silence" during those prayers. This assertion — *the very linchpin of the Court's opinion* — is almost as intriguing for what it does not say as for what it says. It does not say, for example, that students are psychologically coerced to bow their heads, place their hands in a Dürer-like prayer position, pay attention to the prayers, utter "Amen," or in fact pray. (Perhaps further intensive psychological research remains to be done on these matters.) It claims only that students are psychologically coerced "to stand . . . *or*, at least, maintain respectful silence." Both halves of this disjunctive (*both* of which must amount to the fact or appearance of participation in prayer if the Court's analysis is to survive on its own terms) merit particular attention.

To begin with the latter: The Court's notion that a student who simply *sits* in "respectful silence" during the invocation and benediction (when all others are standing) has somehow joined — or would somehow be perceived as having joined — in the prayers is nothing short of ludicrous. We indeed live in a vulgar age. But surely "our social conventions," have not coarsened to the point that anyone who does not stand on his chair and shout obscenities can reasonably be deemed to have assented to everything said in his presence. Since the Court does not dispute that students exposed to prayer at graduation ceremonies retain (despite "subtle coercive pressures") the free will to sit, there is absolutely no basis for the Court's decision. It is fanciful enough to say that "a reasonable dissenter," standing head erect in a class of bowed heads, "could believe that the group exercise signified her own participation or approval of it." It is beyond the absurd to say that she could entertain such a belief while pointedly declining to rise.

But let us assume the very worst, that the nonparticipating graduate is "subtly coerced" . . . to stand! Even that half of the disjunctive does not remotely establish a "participation" (or an "appearance of participation") in a religious exercise. The Court acknowledges that "in our culture standing . . . can signify adherence to a view or simple respect for the views of others." (Much more often the latter than the former, I think, except perhaps in the proverbial town meeting, where one votes by standing.) But if it is a permissible inference that one who is standing is doing so simply out of respect for the prayers of others that are in progress, then how can it possibly be said that a "reasonable dissenter . . . could believe that the group exercise signified her own participation or approval"? Quite obviously, it cannot. I may add, moreover, that maintaining respect for the religious observances of others is a fundamental civic virtue that government (including the public schools) can and should cultivate — so that even if it were the case that the displaying of such respect might be mistaken for taking part in the prayer, I would deny that the dissenter's interest in avoiding *even the false appearance of participation* constitutionally trumps the government's interest in fostering respect for religion generally.

The opinion manifests that the Court itself has not given careful consideration to its test of psychological coercion. For if it had, how could it observe, with no hint of concern or disapproval, that students stood for the Pledge of Allegiance, which immediately preceded Rabbi Gutterman's invocation? . . . Moreover, since the Pledge of Allegiance has been revised . . . to include the phrase "under God," recital of the Pledge would appear to raise the same Establishment Clause issue as the invocation and benediction. If students were psychologically coerced to remain standing during the invocation, they must also have been psychologically coerced, moments before, to stand for (and thereby, in the Court's view, take part in or appear to take part in) the Pledge. Must the Pledge therefore be barred from the public schools (both from graduation ceremonies and from the classroom)? . . .

B

The other "dominant fac[t]" identified by the Court is that "state officials direct the performance of a formal religious exercise" at school graduation ceremonies. "Direct[ing] the performance of a formal religious exercise" has a sound of liturgy to it, summoning up images of the principal directing acolytes where to carry the cross, or showing the rabbi where to unroll the Torah. A Court professing to be engaged in a "delicate and fact-sensitive" line-drawing, would better describe what it means as "prescribing the content of an invocation and benediction." But even that would be false. All the record shows is that principals of the Providence public schools, acting within their delegated authority, have invited clergy to deliver invocations and benedictions at graduations; and that Principal Lee invited Rabbi Gutterman, provided him a two-page pamphlet, prepared by the National Conference of Christians and Jews, giving general advice on inclusive prayer for civic occasions, and advised him that his prayers at graduation should be nonsectarian. How these facts can fairly be transformed into the charges that Principal Lee "directed and controlled the content of [Rabbi Gutterman's] prayer," that school officials "monitor prayer," and attempted to "compose official prayers," and that the "government involvement with religious activity in this case is pervasive," is difficult to fathom. The Court identifies nothing in the record remotely suggesting that school officials have ever drafted, edited, screened, or censored graduation prayers, or that Rabbi Gutterman was a mouthpiece of the school officials.

These distortions of the record are, of course, not harmless error: without them the Court's solemn assertion that the school officials could reasonably be perceived to be "enforc[ing] a religious orthodoxy," would ring as hollow as it ought.

III

The deeper flaw in the Court's opinion does not lie in its wrong answer to the question whether there was state-induced "peer-pressure" coercion; it lies, rather, in the Court's making violation of the Establishment Clause hinge on such a precious question. The coercion that was a hallmark of historical establishments of religion was coercion of religious orthodoxy and of financial support *by force of law and threat of penalty*. Typically, attendance at the state church was required; only clergy of the official church could lawfully perform sacraments; and dissenters, if tolerated, faced an array of civil disabilities. L. LEVY, THE ESTABLISHMENT CLAUSE 4 (1986). Thus, for example, in the colony of Virginia, where the Church of England had been established, ministers were required by law to conform to the doctrine and rites of the Church of England; and all persons were required to attend church and observe the Sabbath, were tithed for the public support of Anglican ministers, and were taxed for the costs of building and repairing churches.

The Establishment Clause was adopted to prohibit such an establishment of religion at the federal level (and to protect state establishments of religion from federal interference). I will further acknowledge for the sake of argument that, as some scholars have argued, by 1790 the term "establishment" had acquired a n additional meaning — "financial support of religion generally, by public taxation" — that reflected the development of "general or multiple" establishments, not limited to a single church. But that would still be an establishment coerced *by force of law*. And I will further concede that our constitutional tradition, from the Declaration of Independence and the first inaugural address of Washington, quoted earlier, down to the present day, has, with a few aberrations, see *Holy Trinity Church v. United States* (1892), ruled out of order government-sponsored endorsement of religion — even when no legal coercion is present, and indeed even when no ersatz, "peer-pressure" psycho-coercion is present — where the endorsement is sectarian, in the sense of specifying details upon which men and women who believe in a benevolent, omnipotent Creator and Ruler of the world are known to differ (for example, the divinity of Christ). But there is simply no support for the proposition that the officially sponsored nondenominational invocation and benediction read by Rabbi ✶ Gutterman — with no one legally coerced to recite them — violated the Constitution of the United States. To the contrary, they are so characteristically American they could have come from the pen of George Washington or Abraham Lincoln himself.

Thus, while I have no quarrel with the Court's general proposition that the Establishment Clause "guarantees that government may not coerce anyone to support or participate in religion or its exercise," I see no warrant for expanding the concept of coercion beyond acts backed by threat of penalty — a brand of coercion that, happily, is readily discernible to those of us who have made a career of reading the disciples of Blackstone rather than of Freud. The Framers were indeed opposed to coercion of religious worship by the National Government; but, as their own sponsorship of nonsectarian prayer in public events demonstrates, they understood that "[s]peech is not coercive; the listener may do as he likes." *American Jewish Congress v. Chicago* (Easterbrook, J., dissenting).

The Court relies on our "school prayer" cases, *Engel v. Vitale* (1962), and *Abington School District v. Schempp* (1963). But whatever the merit of those cases, they do not support, much less compel, the Court's psycho-journey. In the first place, *Engel* and *Schempp* do not constitute an exception to the rule, distilled from historical practice, that public ceremonies may include prayer; rather, they simply do not fall within the scope of the rule (for the obvious reason that school instruction is not a public ceremony). Second, we have made clear our understanding that school prayer occurs within a framework in which legal coercion to attend school (*i.e.*, coercion under threat of penalty) provides the ultimate backdrop. In *Schempp*, for example, we emphasized that the prayers were "prescribed as part of the curricular activities of students who are *required by law* to attend school." (emphasis added). *Engel*'s suggestion that the school prayer program at issue there

— which permitted students "to remain silent or be excused from the room," — involved "indirect coercive pressure," should be understood against this backdrop of legal coercion. . . .

IV

Our Religion Clause jurisprudence has become bedeviled (so to speak) by reliance on formulaic abstractions that are not derived from, but positively conflict with, our long-accepted constitutional traditions. Foremost among these has been the so-called *Lemon* test, see *Lemon v. Kurtzman* (1971), which has received well-earned criticism from many members of this Court. The Court today demonstrates the irrelevance of *Lemon* by essentially ignoring it, and the interment of that case may be the one happy by product of the Court's otherwise lamentable decision. Unfortunately, however, the Court has replaced *Lemon* with its psycho-coercion test, which suffers the double disability of having no roots whatever in our people's historic practice, and being as infinitely expandable as the reasons for psychotherapy itself.

Another happy aspect of the case is that it is only a jurisprudential disaster and not a practical one. Given the odd basis for the Court's decision, invocations and benedictions will be able to be given at public school graduations next June, as they have for the past century and a half, so long as school authorities make clear that anyone who abstains from screaming in protest does not necessarily participate in the prayers. All that is seemingly needed is an announcement, or perhaps a written insertion at the beginning of the graduation Program, to the effect that, while all are asked to rise for the invocation and benediction, none is compelled to join in them, nor will be assumed, by rising, to have done so. That obvious fact recited, the graduates and their parents may proceed to thank God, as Americans have always done, for the blessings He has generously bestowed on them and on their country.

The reader has been told much in this case about the personal interest of Mr. Weisman and his daughter, and very little about the personal interests on the other side. They are not inconsequential. Church and state would not be such a difficult subject if religion were, as the Court apparently thinks it to be, some purely personal avocation that can be indulged entirely in secret, like pornography, in the privacy of one's room. For most believers it is *not* that, and has never been. Religious men and women of almost all denominations have felt it necessary to acknowledge and beseech the blessing of God as a people, and not just as individuals, because they believe in the "protection of divine Providence," as the Declaration of Independence put it, not just for individuals but for societies; because they believe God to be, as Washington's first Thanksgiving Proclamation put it, the "Great Lord and Ruler of Nations." One can believe in the effectiveness of such public worship, or one can deprecate and deride it. But the longstanding American tradition of prayer at official ceremonies displays with unmistakable clarity that the Establishment Clause does not forbid the government to accommodate it.

The narrow context of the present case involves a community's celebration of one of the milestones in its young citizens' lives, and it is a bold step for this Court to seek to banish from that occasion, and from thousands of similar celebrations throughout this land, the expression of gratitude to God that a majority of the community wishes to make. The issue before us today is not the abstract philosophical question whether the alternative of frustrating this desire of a religious majority is to be preferred over the alternative of imposing "psychological coercion," or a feeling of exclusion, upon nonbelievers. Rather, the question is whether a mandatory choice in favor of the former has been imposed by the United States Constitution. As the age-old practices of our people show, the answer to that question is not at all in doubt.

I must add one final observation: The founders of our Republic knew the fearsome potential of sectarian religious belief to generate civil dissension and civil strife. And they also knew that nothing, absolutely nothing, is so inclined to foster among religious believers of various faiths a toleration — no, an affection — for one another than voluntarily joining in prayer together, to the God whom they all worship and seek. Needless to say, no one should be compelled to do that, but it is a shame to deprive our public culture of the opportunity, and indeed the encouragement, for people to do it voluntarily. The Baptist or Catholic who heard and joined in the simple and inspiring prayers of Rabbi Gutterman on this official and patriotic occasion was inoculated from religious bigotry and prejudice in a manner that can not be replicated. To deprive our society of that important unifying mechanism, in order to spare the nonbeliever what seems to me the minimal inconvenience of standing or even sitting in respectful nonparticipation, is as senseless in policy as it is unsupported in law.

For the foregoing reasons, I dissent.

c. The No Endorsement Speculation

Religious displays in public places are difficult cases only because the Court has made them so. The cases, often dealing with a Christmas nativity scene or Menorah, crystalize the garbled posture of a nation entering the 21st century that historically recognizes the importance of religion, but now putatively must remain neutral toward it because of Supreme Court opinion. In *Lynch v. Donnelly*, 465 U.S. 668 (1984), the Court confronted a display erected by the City of Pawtucket, Rhode Island that featured a Santa Claus house, reindeer, candy-striped poles, carolers, clowns, elephants, a teddy bear, lots of lights, and a creche or nativity scene. *Id.* at 671. The lower courts found an Establishment Clause violation because of the overtly religious nature of the creche, but the Supreme Court, per Chief Justice Burger, reversed. The Chief Justice's analysis, while nominally applying the three-part *Lemon* test (secular purpose, effect that neither advances nor inhibits religion, no entanglement of church and state), largely relied upon the mostly secular, and even commercial, context of the bulk of the display and a conception of Christmas as an historical, rather than a religious tradition. *Id.* at 681–86. *Lynch's* concern with the make-up of the display probably accounts for Justice Scalia's observation in *Lee* that the outcome of these cases seems to depend more on "interior decorating," than on constitutional analysis. The *Lynch* case is significant, however, because it occasioned some speculation on the part of Justice O'Connor, concurring separately, that many establishment cases can be resolved by examining whether there has been a government endorsement that "sends a message to nonadherents that they are outsiders, not full members of the political community, and an accompanying message to adherents that they are insiders, [or] favored members of the political community." *Id.* at 688 (O'Connor, J., concurring). This is the no endorsement speculation, and since *Lynch*, Justice O'Connor has been proselytizing in its favor. She has won a few converts, but never a clear majority of the Court.

Applying this speculation in *Lynch*, Justice O'Connor found no endorsement, but only a celebration of a public holiday that like the printing of "In God We Trust" on coins serves only to "solemniz[e] public occasions, express[] confidence in the future, and encourag[e] the recognition of what is worthy of appreciation in society." *Id.* at 693 (O'Connor, J., concurring).

In a subsequent case, *Allegheny County v. Greater Pittsburgh ACLU*, 492 U.S. 573 (1989), Justice Blackmun wrote for a highly-divided Court that borrowed from Justice O'Connor's no endorsement speculation. *Allegheny County* involved two displays — another nativity scene, this time set on the main staircase of a county courthouse and one block away, a Jewish Menorah, evergreen tree, and sign saluting liberty in front of the main city-county office building. The local government erected both displays, although the creche had been donated by a Catholic organization, and there was a sign to that effect. The Court allowed the menorah, but not the creche.

Writing partly for a majority, occasionally for a plurality, and sometimes alone, Justice Blackmun found the creche to violate the three-part *Lemon* test, *id.* at 598–602, but found that test satisfied in relation to the menorah, because he asserted the latter display was not exclusively a religious one, in light of the object's history, the sign and evergreen tree, *id.* at 613–21. Justice Blackmun also made reference to Justice O'Connor's no endorsement speculation in *Lynch*, noting that "[i]n recent years, we have paid particularly close attention to whether the challenged governmental practice either has the purpose or effect of 'endorsing' religion." *Id.* at 592. Maybe so, but the entire Court was not prepared to make the no endorsement speculation the "controlling endorsement inquiry," as Justice Blackmun called it. *Id.* at 597. Justice O'Connor agreed with Blackmun's result, though she emphasized that the reason the menorah display was acceptable related to her belief that there was no "message of endorsement of Judaism or of religion in general." *Id.* at 634 (O'Connor, J., concurring).

Justice O'Connor had to defend her no endorsement speculation from a strong challenge from Justice Kennedy, who wrote in dissent in *Allegheny County* for himself, Chief Justice Rehnquist, and Justices White and Scalia. Drawing upon the no coercion view he articulated in *Lee v. Weisman*, Justice Kennedy wrote: "The creche and the menorah are purely passive symbols of religious holidays. Passersby who disagree with the message conveyed by these displays are free to ignore them, or even to turn their backs, just as they are free to do so when they disagree with any other form of government speech." *Id.* at 664 (Kennedy, J., dissenting).

Justice Kennedy saw little future for the no endorsement speculation, as he found it "flawed in its fundamentals and unworkable in practice. The uncritical adoption of this standard is every bit as troubling as the bizarre result it produces in the cases before us." *Id.* at 669 (Kennedy, J., dissenting). Nevertheless, as the decision in *Capitol Square Review and Advisory Board v. Pinette*, 515 U.S. 753 (1995), illustrates, Justice O'Connor continues to promote this conception of the

Establishment Clause. Unlike *Lynch* and *Allegheny County, Capitol Square* involved a private display on public property, and a plurality written by Justice Scalia indicated that if the public property is a public forum where the private expression of views by word or symbol are allowed, there is no meaningful Establishment Clause problem. In this sense, the public forum is merely an extension of the no coercion view — citizens can speak freely and others may agree, disagree, or ignore as they wish. The mere fact that the government facilitates general expression cannot be said to be an establishment of religion. The matter becomes complicated, however, if the no endorsement speculation is indulged. Refining her prior speculations, Justice O'Connor argued that the Establishment Clause "imposes affirmative obligations that may require a State, in some situations, to take steps to avoid being perceived as supporting or endorsing a private religious message." *Id.* at 777 (O'Connor, J., concuring). In other words, according to Justice O'Connor, the government must actively distance itself even from private religious expression if some "hypothetical observer" who is "aware of the history and context of the community" might perceive the private speech or display as a government endorsement of religion. *Id.* at 780 (O'Connor, J., concurring). Justice Scalia rejects the refined concept of "transferred endorsement." *Id.* at 764. In this, Justice Scalia's opinion reminds us that active discrimination against private religious expression is a good distance from Tocqueville's observation of religion as "the first of [America's] political institutions," fostering the proper use of liberty. Justices Stevens and Ginsburg separately dissented. Justice Stevens argued that:

> the Establishment Clause should be construed to create a strong presumption against the installation of unattended religious symbols on public property. Although the State of Ohio has allowed Capitol Square, the area around the seat of its government, to be used as a public forum, and although it has occasionally allowed private groups to erect other sectarian displays there, neither fact provides a sufficient basis for rebutting that presumption. On the contrary, the sequence of sectarian displays disclosed by the record in this case illustrates the importance of rebuilding the "wall of separation between church and State" that Jefferson envisioned.

Justice Ginsburg inquired whether the establishment clause could be satisfied by a disclaimer sign. Because the Ku Klux Klan's sign was "unsturdy" and it didn't identify the Klan as the sponsor and failed to state unequivocally that Ohio didn't endorse the message of the display, the sign was insufficient to satisfy her constitutional concerns.

> If the aim of the Establishment Clause is genuinely to uncouple government from church, see *Everson v. Board of Ed. of Ewing*, a State may not permit, and a court may not order, a display of this character. *Cf.* Sullivan, *Religion and Liberal Democracy*, 59 U. CHI. L. REV. 195, 197–214 (1992) (negative bar against establishment of religion implies affirmative establishment of secular public order). JUSTICE SOUTER, in the final paragraphs of his opinion, suggests two arrangements that might have distanced the State from "the principal symbol of Christianity around the

world": a sufficiently large and clear disclaimer;[4] or an area reserved for unattended displays carrying no endorsement from the State, a space plainly and permanently so marked. Neither arrangement is even arguably present in this case. The District Court's order did not mandate a disclaimer. ("Plaintiffs are entitled to an injunction requiring the defendants to issue a permit to erect a cross on Capitol Square"). And the disclaimer the Klan appended to the foot of the cross was unsturdy: it did not identify the Klan as sponsor; it failed to state unequivocally that Ohio did not endorse the display's message; and it was not shown to be legible from a distance. The relief ordered by the District Court thus violated the Establishment Clause.

Whether a court order allowing display of a cross, but demanding a sturdier disclaimer, could withstand Establishment Clause analysis is a question more difficult than the one this case poses. I would reserve that question for another day and case. . . .

NOTE AND QUESTION

In *Salazar v. Buono*, 559 U.S. 700 (2010), a plurality led by Justice Kennedy reversed a Court of Appeals judgment that a federal statute transferring ownership of a replacement Latin cross (the original of which had originally been placed by private citizens on federal land in a remote section of the Mojave Desert to honor American soldiers who fell during World War I) and the land on which it stands to a private party is unconstitutional. There had been prior litigation before enactment of the federal statute which had resulted in a federal district court ruling enjoining the continued presence of the cross on federal land because, in the opinion of the court, it created the public perception that the federal government was endorsing the Christian religion. Congress then enacted the statute in question, and a federal district court then enjoined the statute's land transfer on the basis of its suspicion that Congress had "an illicit government purpose" in enacting the statute. The Court of Appeals affirmed, and the United States Supreme Court, in a plurality ruling, reversed and remanded the case with the instruction that the district court should undertake an analysis of the effect that public knowledge of the transfer of the land to private ownership would have on any perceived governmental endorsement of religion. Five justices concurred in the judgment of reversal, but two of the five, Justices Scalia and Thomas, would have ruled that the plaintiff lacked standing to sue, thus rendering the plurality status of the Court's rationale.

---

[1] *Cf. American Civil Liberties Union v. Wilkinson* (6th Cir. 1990) (approving disclaimer ordered by District Court, which had to be " 'prominently displayed immediately in front of' " the religious symbol and " 'readable from an automobile passing on the street directly in front of the structure' "; the approved sign read: " 'This display was not constructed with public funds and does not constitute an endorsement by the Commonwealth [of Kentucky] of any religion or religious doctrine.' ") (quoting District Court); *McCreary v. Stone* (2d Cir. 1984) (disclaimers must meet requirements of size, visibility, and message; disclaimer at issue was too small), Parish, *Private Religious Displays in Public Fora*, 61 U. CHI. L. REV. 253, 285–286 (1994) (disclaimer must not only identify the sponsor, it must say "in no uncertain language" that the government's permit "in no way connotes [government] endorsement of the display's message"; the "disclaimer's adequacy should be measured by its visibility to the average person viewing the religious display").

The federal government's position in the *Salazar* case was that it was merely trying to comply with the then outstanding injunctive order when it enacted the ownership-transfer statute. In 1985, in *Wallace v. Jaffre*, the Court had ruled that a similar argument made by the State of Alabama regarding its enactment of a moment-of-silence law for its public schools was ineffective against an Establishment Clause challenge. Curiously, none of the opinions in *Salazar* referenced the *Wallace* case. Should the district court on remand of the *Salazar* ruling reference *Wallace*? If it were to do so, what ruling?

d. The Equal Protection Idea

The equal protection idea is implicit in Justice Scalia's plurality opinion in *Capitol Square*. In several decisions cited by him in Part III of the *Capitol Square* opinion, *e.g.*, *Lamb's Chapel* and *Widmar v. Vincent*, the Court addressed the issue of whether a government school or public university was compelled by the Establishment Clause to exclude religious groups from making use of facilities within educational contexts that were open forums, either in a limited or general sense. These cases were largely resolved on the free speech basis that governmental entities may not draw viewpoint- or content-based distinctions. But along the way, the Court made plain that the Establishment Clause did not excuse such abridgement of speech or denial of equal access to public facilities.

The next case, *Rosenberger v. Rector*, 515 U.S. 819 (1995), is like *Lamb's Chapel* and *Widmar* insofar as it involves equal, religiously neutral access to the equivalent of a public forum — this time, not a physical place, but a common fund available for use by student organizations of the University of Virginia. The Court concludes that the Establishment Clause does not mandate that the University scan publications for religious content and exclude those publications from funding any more than the prior cases established that religious groups could not use university or school meeting rooms for sectarian activities, whether or not accompanied by devotional exercises.

Four dissenting Justices, Souter, Stevens, Ginsburg, and Breyer, reject the equal protection idea, or as they call it, "evenhandedness," as sufficient to meet the requirements of the Establishment Clause. The fact that the student organization publishing the religious magazine acquired its public funds on an evenhanded basis does not, for the dissent, alleviate the fact that the funds were used for a religious purpose. Writes the dissent, "we never held that evenhandedness might be sufficient to render direct aid to religion constitutional." *Id.* at 880 (Souter, J., dissenting).

The dissent's claim, however, is ahistorical, as Justice Thomas' concurring opinion demonstrates. Recognizing the importance the framers assigned to general support for religion, Thomas combs the history yet again to demonstrate that "the Framers saw the Establishment Clause simply as a prohibition on governmental preferences for some religious faiths over others." *Id.* at 855 (Thomas, J., concurring). Moreover, as Thomas points out, even if one rejects the nonpreferential view (which, as students should remember, largely coincides with the no coercion position), there is nothing to warrant the outright hostility that is represented by "the dissent's extreme view that the government must discriminate against religious adherents by excluding them from more generally available financial subsidies." *Id.* at 857 (Thomas, J., concurring).

ROSENBERGER v. RECTOR
515 U.S. 819 (1995)

MR. JUSTICE KENNEDY delivered the opinion of the Court.

The University of Virginia, an instrumentality of the Commonwealth for which it is named and thus bound by the First and Fourteenth Amendments, authorizes the payment of outside contractors for the printing costs of a variety of student publications. It withheld any authorization for payments on behalf of petitioners for the sole reason that their student paper "primarily promotes or manifests a particular belie[f] in or about a deity or an ultimate reality." That the paper did promote or manifest views within the defined exclusion seems plain enough. The challenge is to the University's regulation and its denial of authorization, the case raising issues under the Speech and Establishment Clauses of the First Amendment.

I

The public corporation we refer to as the "University" is denominated by state law as "the Rector and Visitors of the University of Virginia," and it is responsible for governing the school. Founded by Thomas Jefferson in 1819, and ranked by him, together with the authorship of the Declaration of Independence and of the Virginia Act for Religious Freedom, Va. Code Ann. § 57-1, as one of his proudest achievements, the University is among the Nation's oldest and most respected seats of higher learning. It has more than 11,000 undergraduate students, and 6,000 graduate and professional students. An understanding of the case requires a somewhat detailed description of the program the University created to support extracurricular student activities on its campus.

Before a student group is eligible to submit bills from its outside contractors for payment by the fund described below, it must become a "Contracted Independent Organization" (CIO). CIO status is available to any group the majority of whose members are students, whose managing officers are fulltime students, and that complies with certain procedural requirements. . . .

All CIOs may exist and operate at the University, but some are also entitled to apply for funds from the Student Activities Fund (SAF). . . .

Some, but not all, CIOs may submit disbursement requests to the SAF. The Guidelines recognize 11 categories of student groups that may seek payment to third-party contractors because they "are related to the educational purpose of the University of Virginia." The Guidelines also specify, however, that the costs of certain activities of CIOs that are otherwise eligible for funding will not be reimbursed by the SAF. The student activities which are excluded from SAF support are religious activities, philanthropic contributions and activities, political activities, activities that would jeopardize the University's tax exempt status, those which involve payment of honoraria or similar fees, or social entertainment or related expenses. The prohibition on "political activities" is defined so that it is limited to electioneering and lobbying. The Guidelines provide that "[t]hese restrictions on funding political activities are not intended to preclude funding of any otherwise eligible student organization which . . . espouses particular positions or ideological viewpoints, including those that may be unpopular or are not generally accepted." A "religious activity," by contrast, is defined as any activity that "primarily promotes or manifests a particular belie[f] in or about a deity or an ultimate reality."

The Guidelines prescribe these criteria for determining the amounts of third-party disbursements that will be allowed on behalf of each eligible student organization: the size of the group, its financial self-sufficiency, and the University-wide benefit of its activities. If an organization seeks SAF support, it must submit its bills to the Student Council, which pays the organization's creditors upon determining that the expenses are appropriate. No direct payments are made to the student groups. During the 1990–1991 academic year, 343 student groups qualified as CIOs. One hundred thirty-five of them applied for support from the SAF, and 118 received funding. Fifteen of the groups were funded as "student news, information, opinion, entertainment, or academic communications media groups."

Petitioners' organization, Wide Awake Productions (WAP), qualified as a CIO. Formed by petitioner Ronald Rosenberger and other undergraduates in 1990, WAP was established "[t]o publish a magazine of philosophical and religious expression," "[t]o facilitate discussion which fosters an atmosphere of sensitivity to and tolerance of Christian viewpoints," and "[t]o provide a unifying focus for Christians of multicultural backgrounds." . . .

A few months after being given CIO status, WAP requested the SAF to pay its printer $5,862 for the costs of printing its newspaper. The Appropriations Committee of the Student Council denied WAP's request on the ground that Wide Awake was a "religious activity" within the meaning of the Guidelines, *i.e.*, that the newspaper "promote[d] or manifest[ed] a particular belie[f] in or about a deity or an ultimate reality." It made its determination after examining the first issue. WAP appealed the denial to the full Student Council, contending that WAP met all the applicable Guidelines and that denial of SAF support on the basis of the magazine's religious perspective violated the Constitution. The appeal was denied without further comment, and WAP appealed to the next level, the Student Activities Committee. In a letter signed by the Dean of Students, the committee sustained the denial of funding.

Having no further recourse within the University structure, WAP, Wide Awake, and three of its editors and members filed suit in the United States District Court for the Western District of Virginia, challenging the SAF's action. . . . They alleged that refusal to authorize payment of the printing costs of the publication, [was] solely on the basis of its religious editorial viewpoint. . . .

. . . [T]he District Court ruled for the University, holding that denial of SAF support was not an impermissible content or viewpoint discrimination against petitioners' speech, and that the University's Establishment Clause concern over its "religious activities" was a sufficient justification for denying payment to third-party contractors. . . .

The United States Court of Appeals for the Fourth Circuit, in disagreement with the District Court, held that the Guidelines did discriminate on the basis of content. It ruled that, while the State need not underwrite speech, there was a presumptive violation of the Speech Clause when viewpoint discrimination was invoked to deny third-party payment otherwise available to CIOs. The Court of Appeals affirmed the judgment of the District Court nonetheless, concluding that the discrimination by the University was justified by the "compelling interest in maintaining strict separation of church and state." ✳

II

It is axiomatic that the government may not regulate speech based on its substantive content or the message it conveys. . . .

The SAF is a forum more in a metaphysical than in a spatial or geographic sense, but the same principles are applicable. . . .

The University's denial of WAP's request for third-party payments in the present case is based upon viewpoint discrimination not unlike the discrimination the school district relied upon in *Lamb's Chapel* [*v. Center Moriches Union Free School Dist.* (1993)] and that we found invalid. . . .

The University tries to escape the consequences of our holding in *Lamb's Chapel* by urging that this case involves the provision of funds rather than access to facilities. . . .

It does not follow, . . . that viewpoint-based restrictions are proper when the University does not itself speak or subsidize transmittal of a message it favors but instead expends funds to encourage a diversity of views from private speakers. . . .

Based on the principles we have discussed, we hold that the regulation invoked to deny SAF support, both in its terms and in its application to these petitioners, is a denial of their right of free speech guaranteed by the First Amendment. It remains to be considered whether the violation following from the University's action is excused by the necessity of complying with the Constitution's prohibition against state establishment of religion. We turn to that question.

III

A central lesson of our decisions is that a significant factor in upholding governmental programs in the face of Establishment Clause attack is their neutrality towards religion. We have decided a series of cases addressing the receipt of government benefits where religion or religious views are implicated in some degree. The first case in our modern Establishment Clause jurisprudence was *Everson v. Board of Ed. of Ewing* (1947). . . .

The neutrality of the program distinguishes the student fees from a tax levied for the direct support of a church or group of churches. A tax of that sort, of course, would run contrary to Establishment Clause concerns dating from the earliest days of the Republic. The apprehensions of our predecessors involved the levying of taxes upon the public for the sole and exclusive purpose of establishing and supporting specific sects. The exaction here, by contrast, is a student activity fee designed to reflect the reality that student life in its many dimensions includes the necessity of wide-ranging speech and inquiry and that student expression is an integral part of the University's educational mission. . . .

Government neutrality is apparent in the State's overall scheme in a further meaningful respect. The program respects the critical difference "between *government* speech endorsing religion, which the Establishment Clause forbids, and *private* speech endorsing religion, which the Free Speech and Free Exercise Clauses protect." In this case, "the government has not willfully fostered or encouraged" any mistaken impression that the student newspapers speak for the University. *Capitol Square Review and Advisory Bd. v. Pinette.* The University has taken pains to disassociate itself from the private speech involved in this case. . . .

The Court of Appeals (and the dissent) are correct to extract from our decisions the principle that we have recognized special Establishment Clause dangers where the government makes direct money payments to sectarian institutions. The error is not in identifying the principle but in believing that it controls this case. Even assuming that WAP is no different from a church and that its speech is the same as the religious exercises conducted in *Widmar* [*v. Vincent* (1981)] (two points much in doubt), the Court of Appeals decided a case that was, in essence, not before it, and the dissent would have us do the same. We do not confront a case where, even under a neutral program that includes nonsectarian recipients, the government is making direct money payments to an institution or group that is engaged in religious activity. Neither the Court of Appeals nor the dissent, we believe, takes sufficient cognizance of the undisputed fact that no public funds flow directly to WAP's coffers.

It does not violate the Establishment Clause for a public university to grant access to its facilities on a religion-neutral basis to a wide spectrum of student groups, including groups which use meeting rooms for sectarian activities, accompanied by some devotional exercises. . . . Given our holdings in [*Widmar, Lamb's Chapel,* and *Board of Education v. Mergens* (1990)], it follows that a public university may maintain its own computer facility and give student groups access to that facility, including the use of the printers, on a religion-neutral, say first-come-first-served, basis. If a religious student organization obtained access on that religion-neutral basis and used a computer to compose or a printer or copy machine to print speech with a religious content or viewpoint, the State's action in providing the group with access would no more violate the Establishment Clause than would giving those groups access to an assembly hall. There is no difference in logic or principle, and no difference of constitutional significance, between a school using its funds to operate a facility to which students have access, and a school paying a third-party contractor to operate the facility on its behalf. The latter occurs here. . . .

Were the dissent's view to become law, it would require the University, in order to avoid a constitutional violation, to scrutinize the content of student speech, lest the expression in question — speech otherwise protected by the Constitution — contain too great a religious content. The dissent, in fact, anticipates such censorship as "crucial" in distinguishing between "works characterized by the evangelism of Wide Awake and writing that merely happens to express views that a given religion might approve." That eventuality raises the specter of governmental censorship, to ensure that all student writings and publications meet some baseline standard of secular orthodoxy. . . .

To obey the Establishment Clause, it was not necessary for the University to deny eligibility to student publications because of their viewpoint. The neutrality commanded of the State by the separate Clauses of the First Amendment was compromised by the University's course of action. The viewpoint discrimination inherent in the University's regulation required public officials to scan and interpret student publications to discern their underlying philosophic assumptions respecting religious theory and belief. That course of action was a denial of the right of free speech and would risk fostering a pervasive bias or hostility to religion, which could undermine the very neutrality the Establishment Clause requires. There is no Establishment Clause violation in the University's honoring its duties under the Free Speech Clause.

The judgment of the Court of Appeals must be, and is, reversed.

It is so ordered.

JUSTICE O'CONNOR, concurring.

"We have time and again held that the government generally may not treat people differently based on the God or gods they worship, or don't worship." . . . Neutrality, in both form and effect, is one hallmark of the Establishment Clause.

As JUSTICE SOUTER demonstrates, however, there exists another axiom in the history and precedent of the Establishment Clause. "Public funds may not be used to endorse the religious message." Our cases have permitted some government funding of secular functions performed by sectarian organizations. *Bradfield v. Roberts* (1899) (funding of health care for indigent patients). These decisions, however, provide no precedent for the use of public funds to finance religious activities.

This case lies at the intersection of the principle of government neutrality and the prohibition on state funding of religious activities. It is clear that the University has established a generally applicable program to encourage the free exchange of ideas by its students, an expressive marketplace that includes some 15 student publications with predictably divergent viewpoints. It is equally clear that petitioners' viewpoint is religious and that publication of Wide Awake is a religious activity, under both the University's regulation and a fair reading of our precedents. Not to finance Wide Awake, according to petitioners, violates the principle of neutrality by sending a message of hostility toward religion. To finance Wide Awake, argues the University, violates the prohibition on direct state funding of religious activities.

When two bedrock principles so conflict, understandably neither can provide the definitive answer. Reliance on categorical platitudes is unavailing. Resolution instead depends on the hard task of judging — sifting through the details and determining whether the challenged program offends the Establishment Clause. . . .

In *Witters v. Washington Dept. of Services for Blind* (1986), for example, we unanimously held that the State may, through a generally applicable financial aid program, pay a blind student's tuition at a sectarian theological institution. The Court so held, however, only after emphasizing that "vocational assistance provided under the Washington program is paid directly to the student, who transmits it to the educational institution of his or her choice."

The Court's decision today therefore neither trumpets the supremacy of the neutrality principle nor signals the demise of the funding prohibition in Establishment Clause jurisprudence. As I observed last Term, "[e]xperience proves that the Establishment Clause, like the Free Speech Clause, cannot easily be reduced to a single test." *Kiryas Joel* [*Village Sch. Dist. v. Grumet* (1994)] (O'CONNOR, J., concurring in part and concurring in judgment). When bedrock principles collide, they test the limits of categorical obstinacy and expose the flaws and dangers of a Grand Unified Theory that may turn out to be neither grand nor unified. The Court today does only what courts must do in many Establishment Clause cases — focus on specific features of a particular government action to ensure that it does not violate the Constitution. By withholding from Wide Awake assistance that the University provides generally to all other student publications, the University has discriminated on the basis of the magazine's religious viewpoint in violation of the Free Speech Clause. And particular features of the University's program — such as the explicit disclaimer, the disbursement of funds directly to third-party vendors, the vigorous nature of the forum at issue, and the possibility for objecting students to opt out — convince me that providing such assistance in this case would not carry the danger of impermissible use of public funds to endorse Wide Awake's religious message.

Subject to these comments, I join the opinion of the Court.

JUSTICE THOMAS, concurring.

I agree with the Court's opinion and join it in full, but I write separately to express my disagreement with the historical analysis put forward by the dissent. Although the dissent starts down the right path in consulting the original meaning of the Establishment Clause, its misleading application of history yields a principle that is inconsistent with our Nation's long tradition of allowing religious adherents to participate on equal terms in neutral government programs.

Even assuming that the Virginia debate on the so-called "Assessment Controversy" was indicative of the principles embodied in the Establishment Clause, this incident hardly compels the dissent's conclusion that government must actively discriminate against religion. The dissent's historical discussion glosses over the fundamental characteristic of the Virginia assessment bill that sparked the controversy: The assessment was to be imposed for the support of clergy in the performance of their function of teaching religion. Thus, the "Bill Establishing a Provision for Teachers of the Christian Religion" provided for the collection of a specific tax, the proceeds of which were to be appropriated "by the Vestries, Elders, or Directors of each religious society . . . to a provision for a Minister or Teacher of the Gospel of their denomination, or the providing places of divine worship, and to none other use whatsoever." See *Everson v. Board of Ed. of Ewing* (1947) (appendix to dissent of Rutledge, J.).

James Madison's Memorial and Remonstrance Against Religious Assessments (hereinafter Madison's Remonstrance) must be understood in this context. Contrary to the dissent's suggestion, Madison's objection to the assessment bill did not rest on the premise that religious entities may never participate on equal terms in neutral government programs. Nor did Madison embrace the argument that forms the linchpin of the dissent: that monetary subsidies are constitutionally different from other neutral benefits programs. Instead, Madison's comments are more consistent with the neutrality principle that the dissent inexplicably discards. According to Madison, the Virginia assessment was flawed because it "violate[d] that equality which ought to be the basis of every law." The assessment violated the "equality" principle not because it allowed religious groups to participate in a generally available government program, but because the bill singled out religious entities for special benefits. See [*Everson, supra*] (arguing that the assessment violated the equality principle "by subjecting some to peculiar burdens" and "by granting to others peculiar exemptions").

Legal commentators have disagreed about the historical lesson to take from the Assessment Controversy. For some, the experience in Virginia is consistent with the view that the Framers saw the Establishment Clause simply as a prohibition on governmental preferences for some religious faiths over others. Other commentators have rejected this view, concluding that the Establishment Clause forbids not only government preferences for some religious sects over others, but also government preferences for religion over irreligion.

I find much to commend the former view. Madison's focus on the preferential nature of the assessment was not restricted to the fourth paragraph of the Remonstrance discussed above. The funding provided by the Virginia assessment was to be extended only to Christian sects, and the Remonstrance seized on this defect:

> "Who does not see that the same authority which can establish Christianity,
> in exclusion of all other Religions, may establish with the same ease any
> particular sect of Christians, in exclusion of all other Sects."

Madison's Remonstrance, reprinted in *Everson*. In addition to the third and fourth paragraphs of the Remonstrance, "Madison's seventh, ninth, eleventh, and twelfth arguments all speak, in some way, to the same intolerance, bigotry, unenlightenment, and persecution that had generally resulted from previous exclusive religious establishments." The conclusion that Madison saw the principle of nonestablishment as barring governmental preferences for *particular* religious faiths seems especially clear in light of statements he made in the more-relevant context of the House debates on the First Amendment. See *Wallace v. Jaffree* (1985) (REHNQUIST, J., dissenting) (Madison's views "as reflected by actions on the floor of the House in 1789, [indicate] that he saw the [First] Amendment as designed to prohibit the establishment of a national religion, and perhaps to prevent discrimination among sects," but not "as requiring neutrality on the part of government between religion and irreligion"). . . .

But resolution of this debate is not necessary to decide this case. Under any understanding of the Assessment Controversy, the history cited by the dissent cannot support the conclusion that the Establishment Clause "categorically condemn[s] state programs directly aiding religious activity" when that aid is part of a neutral program available to a wide array of beneficiaries. Even if Madison believed that the principle of nonestablishment of religion precluded government financial support for religion *per se* (in the sense of government benefits specifically targeting religion), there is no indication that at the time of the framing he took the dissent's extreme view that the government must discriminate against religious adherents by excluding them from more generally available financial subsidies.

In fact, Madison's own early legislative proposals cut against the dissent's suggestion. In 1776, when Virginia's Revolutionary Convention was drafting its Declaration of Rights, Madison prepared an amendment that would have disestablished the Anglican Church. This amendment (which went too far for the Convention and was not adopted) is not nearly as sweeping as the dissent's version of disestablishment; Madison merely wanted the Convention to declare that "no man or class of men ought, on account of religion[,] to be invested with *peculiar* emoluments or privileges. . . ." Madison's Amendments to the Declaration of Rights (May 29–June 12, 1776), *in* 1 Papers of James Madison 174 (W. Hutchinson & W. Rachal eds., 1962) (emphasis added). Likewise, Madison's Remonstrance stressed that "just government" is "best supported by protecting every citizen in the enjoyment of his Religion with the same equal hand which protects his person and his property; by neither invading the equal rights of any Sect, nor suffering any Sect to invade those of another." Madison's Remonstrance ¶ 8, reprinted in *Everson, supra; cf. Terrett v. Taylor* (1815) (holding that the Virginia constitution did not prevent the government from "aiding the votaries of every sect to . . . perform their own religious duties," or from "establishing funds for the support of ministers, for public charities, for the endowment of churches, or for the sepulture of the dead").

Stripped of its flawed historical premise, the dissent's argument is reduced to the claim that our Establishment Clause jurisprudence permits neutrality in the context of access to government *facilities* but requires discrimination in access to government *funds*. The dissent purports to locate the prohibition against "direct public funding" at the "heart" of the Establishment Clause, but this conclusion fails to confront historical examples of funding that date back to the time of the founding. To take but one famous example, both Houses of the First Congress elected chaplains, and that Congress enacted legislation providing for an annual salary of $500 to be paid out of the Treasury. Madison himself was a member of the committee that recommended the chaplain system in the House. See H.R. Jour., at 11–12; 1 Annals of Cong. 891 (1789); [R.] Cord, [Separation of Church and State: Historical Fact and Current Fiction] 25 [(1982)]. This same system of "direct public funding" of congressional chaplains has "continued without interruption ever since that early session of Congress." *Marsh v. Chambers* (1983).[5]

---

[5] [3] A number of other, less familiar examples of what amount to direct funding appear in early Acts

The historical evidence of government support for religious entities through property tax exemptions is also overwhelming. . . . In my view, the dissent's acceptance of this tradition puts to rest the notion that the Establishment Clause bars monetary aid to religious groups even when the aid is equally available to other groups. A tax exemption in many cases is economically and functionally indistinguishable from a direct monetary subsidy. . . .

Though our Establishment Clause jurisprudence is in hopeless disarray, this case provides an opportunity to reaffirm one basic principle that has enjoyed an uncharacteristic degree of consensus: The Clause does not compel the exclusion of religious groups from government benefits programs that are generally available to a broad class of participants. . . .

Our Nation's tradition of allowing religious adherents to participate in even-handed government programs is hardly limited to the class of "essential public benefits" identified by the dissent. . . .

. . . The dissent identifies no evidence that the Framers intended to disable religious entities from participating on neutral terms in evenhanded government programs. The evidence that does exist points in the opposite direction and provides ample support for today's decision.

JUSTICE SOUTER, with whom JUSTICE STEVENS, JUSTICE GINSBURG and JUSTICE BREYER join, dissenting.

I

A

The Court, . . . has never before upheld direct state funding of the sort of proselytizing published in Wide Awake and, in fact, has categorically condemned state programs directly aiding religious activity, *School Dist. v. Ball* [(1985)] (striking programs providing secular instruction to nonpublic school students on nonpublic school premises because they are "indistinguishable from the provision of a direct cash subsidy to the religious school that is most clearly prohibited under the Establishment Clause"). . . .

Even when the Court has upheld aid to an institution performing both secular and sectarian functions, it has always made a searching enquiry to ensure that the institution kept the secular activities separate from its sectarian ones, with any

of Congress. See, *e.g.*, Act of Feb. 20, 1833, ch. 42, 4 Stat. 618–619 (authorizing the State of Ohio to sell "all or any part of the lands heretofore reserved and appropriated by Congress for the support of religion within the Ohio Company's . . . purchases . . . and to invest the money arising from the sale thereof, in some productive fund; the proceeds of which shall be for ever annually applied . . . for the support of religion within the several townships for which said lands were originally reserved and set apart, and for no other use or purpose whatsoever"); Act of Mar. 2, 1833, ch. 86, §§ 1, 3, 6 Stat. 538 (granting to Georgetown College — a Jesuit institution — "lots in the city of Washington, to the amount, in value, of twenty-five thousand dollars," and directing the College to sell the lots and invest the proceeds, thereafter using the dividends to establish and endow such professorships as it saw fit); see also *Wallace v. Jaffree* (1985) (REHNQUIST, J., dissenting) ("As the United States moved from the 18th into the 19th century, Congress appropriated time and again public moneys in support of sectarian Indian education carried on by religious organizations").

direct aid flowing only to the former and never the latter. *Bowen v. Kendrick* (1988) (upholding grant program for services related to premarital adolescent sexual relations on ground that funds cannot be "used by the grantees in such a way as to advance religion"); *Roemer v. Board of Pub. Works of Md.* (1976) (plurality opinion) (upholding general aid program restricting uses of funds to secular activities only); *Hunt v. McNair* (1973) (upholding general revenue bond program excluding from participation facilities used for religious purposes); *Tilton v. Richardson* (1971) (plurality opinion) (upholding general aid program for construction of academic facilities as "[t]here is no evidence that religion seeps into the use of any of these facilities"); see *Board of Ed. of Central School Dist. No. 1 v. Allen* (1968) (upholding textbook loan program limited to secular books requested by individual students for secular educational purposes).

B

. . . At the heart of the Establishment Clause stands the prohibition against direct public funding, but that prohibition does not answer the questions that occur at the margins of the Clause's application. Is any government activity that provides any incidental benefit to religion likewise unconstitutional? Would it be wrong to put out fires in burning churches, wrong to pay the bus fares of students on the way to parochial schools, wrong to allow a grantee of special education funds to spend them at a religious college? These are the questions that call for drawing lines, and it is in drawing them that evenhandedness becomes important. However the Court may in the past have phrased its line-drawing test, the question whether such benefits are provided on an evenhanded basis has been relevant, for the question addresses one aspect of the issue whether a law is truly neutral with respect to religion. . . .

Three cases permitting indirect aid to religion, *Mueller v. Allen* (1983), *Witters v. Washington Dept. of Services for Blind* (1986), and *Zobrest v. Catalina Foothills School Dist.* (1993), are among the latest of those to illustrate this relevance of evenhandedness when advancement is not so obvious as to be patently unconstitutional. Each case involved a program in which benefits given to individuals on a religion-neutral basis ultimately were used by the individuals, in one way or another, to support religious institutions. In each, the fact that aid was distributed generally and on a neutral basis was a necessary condition for upholding the program at issue. But the significance of evenhandedness stopped there. We did not, in any of these cases, hold that satisfying the condition was sufficient, or dispositive. Even more importantly, we never held that evenhandedness might be sufficient to render direct aid to religion constitutional. Quite the contrary. Critical to our decisions in these cases was the fact that the aid was indirect; it reached religious institutions "only as a result of the genuinely independent and private choices of aid recipients." In noting and relying on this particular feature of each of the programs at issue, we in fact reaffirmed the core prohibition on direct funding of religious activities. Thus, our holdings in these cases were little more than extensions of the unremarkable proposition that "a State may issue a paycheck to one of its employees, who may then donate all or part of that paycheck to a religious institution, all without constitutional barrier. . . ." Such "attenuated financial benefit[s], ultimately controlled by the private choices of individual[s]," we have found, are simply not within the contemplation of the Establishment Clause's broad prohibition.

Evenhandedness as one element of a permissibly attenuated benefit is, of course, a far cry from evenhandedness as a sufficient condition of constitutionality for direct financial support of religious proselytization, and our cases have unsurprisingly repudiated any such attempt to cut the Establishment Clause down to a mere prohibition against unequal direct aid.

D

Nothing in the Court's opinion would lead me to end this enquiry into the application of the Establishment Clause any differently from the way I began it. The Court is ordering an instrumentality of the State to support religious evangelism with direct funding. This is a flat violation of the Establishment Clause.

II

Given the dispositive effect of the Establishment Clause's bar to funding the magazine, there should be no need to decide whether in the absence of this bar the University would violate the Free Speech Clause by limiting funding as it has done. *Widmar*, 454 U.S. at 271 (university's compliance with its Establishment Clause obligations can be a compelling interest justifying speech restriction).

NOTES AND QUESTIONS

1. Michael McConnell, a prominent constitutional scholar in matters of religious freedom, has made the following argument in the context of religious equality:

> 1. Tolerance has become a one-way street; a government tolerant of secular views has been intolerant of religious expression;

> 2. In matters of government funding, the federal government often excludes or discriminates against religious entities, even as the First Amendment (the Establishment Clause) has been interpreted not to require that discrimination, and the Free Speech Clause often prohibits it; and

> 3. Even if the federal government did not engage in religious discrimination in funding programs, the First Amendment has, troublingly, not yet been interpreted to preclude state anti-religious discrimination in funding.

And he elaborated:

> Religious and traditionalist parents are finding that their viewpoints and concerns are ruled out of order, while at the same time the schools can be used to promote ideas and values that are sometimes offensive and hostile to their own.

> Tolerance and diversity, it often seems, are one-way streets. There is scrupulous concern lest any child (and increasingly any adult) be exposed to unwanted religious influence, but little or no concern for the religious or

traditionalist child (or adult) who objects to the far-more-prevalent proselytizing that is carried on under the banner of progressive causes.

In the marketplace of ideas, secular viewpoints and ideologies are in
competition with religious viewpoints and ideologies. . . . It is no more
neutral to favor the secular over the religious than it is to favor the religious
over the secular.

*See Examining the Status of Religious Liberty in the States and Whether There is
a Need for Further Protection: Hearings on S.J. Res. 45 Before the Senate
Judiciary Comm.*, 104th Cong. 79 (testimony of Michael W. McConnell). Do you
agree with Professor McConnell? For a concurring view, see Michael S. Paulsen,
*Religion, Equality and the Constitution: An Equal Protection Approach to
Establishment Clause Adjudication*, 61 NOTRE DAME L. REV. 311 (1986) (discussing
the Supreme Court's historical and conceptual errors that resulted in an errant
Establishment Clause doctrine and arguing that the religion clauses advance
fundamentally similar interests and are best understood in terms of nondiscrimination and equality). The less favorable, but not totally unsympathetic, view of
Professor Douglas Laycock of the University of Virginia posits that religious
expression is well protected under free speech case law — discrimination against
private religious speech, he says, is unconstitutional viewpoint discrimination.
Professor Laycock nevertheless agrees with Professor McConnell that religious
and secular organizations should be treated equally in funding decisions, but he
does not think this extends to cases where the government itself supplies the good.
See Hearings on S.J. 45 Before the Senate Judiciary Committee, 104 Cong. 68
(1995) (Statement of Professor Laycock). Do you agree with Professor Laycock? Or
is government obliged, once it decides to fund education at all, to make education
funds it collects from all citizens available for the school of their choice, religious or
nonreligious? We take up the issue of school funding next.

2. In *Good News Club v. Milford Central School*, 533 U.S. 98 (2001), the Court
applies the equality principle to the after hours use of a public elementary school
finding that it was improper to exclude a voluntary bible club, where children ages
6 to 12 wanted to hold after-school meetings at which children would sing songs,
hear Bible stories, and memorize scriptural passages. The Court, following *Rosenberger*, found that excluding the Club violates the Club's free speech rights and that
no Establishment Clause concern justifies that violation.

3. Should it matter whether other non-religious groups have actually been
using the classrooms after school? Justices Breyer and Souter both seem to think
so. Justice Souter suggests that the Court cannot determine whether there would
be an Establishment Clause violation unless it knows when, and to what extent,
other groups use the facilities. In a footnote to his opinion, Justice Thomas remarks
that "[w]hen a limited public forum is available for use by groups presenting any
viewpoint, . . . we would not find an Establishment Clause violation simply because
only groups presenting a religious viewpoint have opted to take advantage of the
forum at a particular time." Keep this point in mind as you read later about school
vouchers. One of the issues raised in *Zelman v. Simmons-Harris, infra,* was
whether the Establishment Clause was violated by a voucher program designed to
include both public and private religious schools was used primarily by private

religious schools because the public schools refused to participate.

4. What about the impressionability of young students? Justice O'Connor is the principal author of the no-endorsement view and she fully joined the majority in *Good News*, in part, because the nature of the forum avoids endorsement, and implicitly because the parents have given permission for student participation. Does that mean that the relevant objective observer is the parent, not the youngster? Justice Souter in dissent points out that "[t]he cohort addressed by *Good News* is not university students with relative maturity, or even high school pupils, but elementary school children as young as six." He insists that this difference between college students and grade school pupils warrants "a difference in constitutional results." The proper focus, says Justice Souter, are the elementary school students who see peers attending religious meetings. Do you agree?

5. The dissent is also bothered by the fact that Milford's limited forum was less robust than the sites for wide-ranging intellectual exchange in related cases that the Court relies upon like *Lamb's Chapel* or *Rosenberger*. But why again should actual use matter within the framework of the established forum, where all views are welcome. Doesn't the failure of other groups to present their ideas then amount to a "heckler's veto" as the majority fears?

6. How important is the following observation made by the majority in a footnote: "In any event, we conclude that the Club's activities do not constitute mere religious worship, divorced from any teaching of moral values." Does this mean that worship activities could not constitutionally occur in public school classrooms after hours? In California and other states, public educational facilities are used for religious liturgies on weekends. Isn't the Court on dangerous ground if it tries to distinguish religious viewpoint from religious activity or worship?

7. Whether it is constitutionally permissible to recite the pledge of allegiance with the phrase "one nation under God" in a public school came before the Court in *Elk Grove Unified School District v. Newdow*, 542 U.S. 1 (2004). The challenge was brought by Michael Newdow, a non-married father who had some custodial rights, but not final decision making authority over his daughter's education. After the Ninth Circuit ruled in Newdow's favor and triggered a firestorm of criticism, including a 99-0 rebuke from the Senate reaffirming the pledge, the Supreme Court found Newdow not to have standing to object to his daughter being invited to recite the pledge of allegiance at the beginning of a public school day. California law did not preclude Mr. Newdow from exposing his daughter to his atheistic beliefs, but, said Justice Stevens, speaking for five members of the Court, he had no standing to veto the desire of either the girl's mother who had been given broader custodial authority under state law or the school to make such religious reference. The majority did not reach the issue of whether the religious reference in the pledge would be constitutional, but the case prompted three Justices to discuss why, under three different theories, they believed the Establishment Clause would not be violated.

The Chief Justice, joined by Justice O'Connor, thought Newdow had sufficient standing, not premised upon his daughter's rights, but upon his relationship with his daughter. On the merits, these Justices thought the pledge of allegiance to be merely an historical summary of the founder's belief and reliance upon God. This historical foundation has been repeated frequently by American leaders. It was fitting to see the pledge, said these Justices, as a patriotic exercise, not a prayer.

Justice O'Connor indicated that she joined the Chief Justice's opinion in full, but she also took the occasion to re-emphasize her "no endorsement" view based on a reasonable observer — who, Justice O'Connor suggested, Mr. Newdow was not, even as she described his challenge as "well intentioned." A reasonable observer thinks objectively, not subjectively, taking full account of the role of religion in our national culture. To take a hypersensitive view toward religion given the pluralistic nature of the republic, she opined, would be an "absurdity." Justice O'Connor specifically mentioned a number of factors that a reasonable observer would take into account: the history and ubiquity of the reference; the absence of worship or prayer; the absence of reference to a particular religion; and the minimal nature of the reference. All of these factors favored leaving the pledge unaltered.

Applying these considerations, Justice O'Connor gave explicit approval to ceremonial deism, which "most clearly encompasses such things as the national motto ('In God We Trust'), religious references in traditional patriotic songs such as the Star-Spangled Banner, and the words with which the Marshal [of the Supreme] Court opens each of its sessions ('God save the United States and this honorable Court'). These references are not minor trespasses upon the Establishment Clause to which [Justice O'Connor] turn[s] a blind eye. Instead, their history, character, and context prevent [these references] from being constitutional violations at all."

Finally, Justice Thomas took the occasion to suggest again that the Court needs to re-think its Establishment Clause jurisprudence more comprehensively. In this regard, Justice Thomas' dissenting view in *Newdow* elaborates upon analytical points he made in his *Zelman* concurrence discussed earlier in this Chapter. Justice Thomas first notes that under the Court's previous decision in *Lee v. Weisman* (1989), he would be required to find the pledge to be an unacceptable form of coercion. Finding *Lee* to be "wrongly decided," Thomas argues that as originally understood, the Establishment Clause was a federalism guarantee only and not an individual right. Specifically, that the Congress would not establish a national religion or interfere with state establishments concerning religion (of which there were six at the time of the founding). After judicial incorporation, Justice Thomas admits it is hard to know what to make of the Establishment Clause, since it then prohibits (state establishments) exactly what he believes the Clause sought to protect. Nevertheless, if one assumes that the Establishment Clause does prohibit state establishments, it is necessary then to know what would constitute such an establishment. Justice Thomas supposes that the Clause means no coercion of religious belief or practice "by force of law and threat of penalty" (obviously mere psychological or peer pressure coercion posited in *Lee* would not be enough), no imbuing religion with governmental authority (*e.g.*, by delegating political or governmental power to a religious body) or no religious favoritism among particular religious beliefs. Since the pledge implicates none of these, Justice Thomas answered that the pledge should be seen as fully constitutional.

Justice Thomas elaborated on his originalist understanding of the Establishment Clause in *Cutter v. Wilkinson*, 544 U.S. 707 (2005), where Ohio unsuccessfully tried to employ his view that the Establishment Clause is a federalism guarantee to suggest that the federal government had overstepped its authority in imposing the Religious Land Use and Institutionalized Persons Act (RLUIPA) against the states. RLUIPA requires greater accommodation of the religious practices of institution-alized persons (prisoners) and in land use decision-making than would be constitu-tionally required under the Free Exercise Clause. Ohio tried to argue that, even though it could no longer establish a church since the no establishment injunction had been judicially incorporated against the states as well as the federal govern-ment, Congress could not generally legislate on state choices regarding religious policy. Justice Thomas responded that this "overread" the original understanding. Congress was forbidden from legislating with respect to state establishments, but could legislate on state religious topics if it had alternative sources of power to do so. Agreeing with the rest of the Court in *Cutter*, that RLUIPA is "a law respecting religion, but not one respecting an establishment of religion," the issue for Justice Thomas became whether Congress had alternative enumerated spending or commerce authority to act. He doubted that they did, but the balance of the Court thought the enumerated power issue not squarely before it to decide.

8.   Postscript. The Milford School District apparently did not cheerfully comply with the spirit of the Court's ruling in *Good News*. The AP reported that public school officials were contemplating "pushing starting times back for all clubs until 5 p.m. or 6 p.m., a few hours after students are dismissed." Rick Stevens, *Despite Supreme Court Ruling, Christian Youth Group Still May Not Meet at Public School* (June 18, 2001). In response to a decision by the California Court of Appeal holding that it would not violate the Establishment Clause for a religiously-oriented student group, the Fellowship of Christian Athletes, to have equal access to school facilities, the Saddleback Unified School District in Mission Viejo, California, similarly banned all student clubs from campus. See *Van Schoick v. Saddleback Valley Unified School Dist.*, 87 Cal. App. 4th 522 (2001); Charles Adamson, *School Clubs Lose Status*, THE ORANGE COUNTY REGISTER (June 14, 2001). Why do you think that some school board officials would rather ban all student clubs than provide access to a religious club? Is it simply animosity toward religious clubs, or concern about the school board's loss of discretion to determine which clubs should be permitted on school grounds? The Fellowship of Christian Athletes relied upon the Federal Equal Access Act, 20 U.S.C. § 4071, in *Van Schoick*. The Act has also been relied upon by student groups seeking to promote gay and lesbian issues. *See, e.g., Colin ex rel. Colin v. Orange Unified Sch. Dist.*, 83 F. Supp. 2d 1135 (C.D. Cal. 2000). The Orange school board's effort to ban all non-curricular clubs from its El Modina High School rather than grant access to the Gay-Straight Alliance club was rebuffed by the court. Should it have been? One of your casebook authors, in an essay following the *Good News Club* decision, argued that the case represented a "larger battle . . . of philosophic ideas, between the natural rights principles of the Declaration of Independence and the moral relativism of the late Twentieth century," suggesting that in that context "the 'equal access' rationale upon which the Court relied may well represent a defeat, rather than a victory, for the moral views fostered by our nation's Founders" because "[t]he non-preferential, neutrality principle that is the hallmark of the Court's modern-day Establishment Clause doctrine makes it impossible . . . to make [moral] distinctions." John C. Eastman, *Bad News for Good News Clubs?*, LOS ANGELES DAILY JOURNAL (July 2, 2001). Do you agree?

2. The Special Context of the Private, Religious School

Nowhere have disputes over the meaning of the Establishment Clause been more pointed than with regard to the issue of whether private religious schools should have equal access to public education funds. As the materials in this section indicate, it is out of these controversies that the three-part Establishment Clause test inquiring into secular purpose, effect, and entanglement emerges in *Lemon v. Kurtzman*, 403 U.S. 602 (1971). As implemented, *Lemon* precluded most, but somewhat inexplicably on its own terms, not all public funding from being equitably apportioned with private religious schools, even as, time and again, the Court would compliment these schools for their contribution to the educational process. While private religious schools are still excluded from a good deal of direct public funding, a considerable portion of the constitutional fussiness in this area has subsided with the recognition, first in *Zobrest v. Catalina Foothills School District* and most recently in *Zelman v. Simmons-Harris*, that nothing in the Constitution precludes states from allowing parents to freely choose to spend their pro rata share of public education tax dollars on a private religious school.

a. Direct Funding of Religious Schools

Earlier mention was made of the failed Blaine Amendment that had been proposed in 1876 in part to apply the Religion Clauses to the states. The same proposed amendment provided that "no money raised by taxation in any State for the support of public schools or derived from any public fund therefor, nor any public lands devoted thereto, shall ever be under the control of any religious sect, nor shall any money so raised or lands so devoted be divided between religious sects or denominations." 4 CONG. REC. 205 (1875). This denial of public funding for religiously provided education was a considerable break from precedent.

At the time of the founding until the mid-19th century, elementary schools in America were largely religious schools. As one writer explains: "[t]his plan of elementary education was frankly religious in its aims, and pious books constituted the basic materials of instruction. The religious orientation persisted for at least two centuries, in New England and in other sections. . . ." NELSON R. BURR, A CRITICAL BIBLIOGRAPHY OF RELIGION IN AMERICA 654 (James Ward Smith & Leland Jamison eds., 1961). Many teachers were also ministers, and even in the common or public school, the Bible was the principal textbook. It was the Protestant Bible, however, and problems arose with the substantial emigration of Catholics and persons of other faiths to the United States beginning in the 1840s. The problem was temporarily mitigated, however, by the establishment of private sectarian schools that often were recipients of public funds. The federal government had long given aid to religious schools. 2 ANSON PHELPS STOKES, CHURCH AND STATE 57–58 (1950). For example, land grants were made on the condition that each township set aside two sections for purposes of religion and education. 32 J. CONTINENTAL CONG. 312 (1787). An 1801 New York law directed that public educational funds be given to the Episcopal, Reformed Dutch, Methodist Episcopal, Scotch Presbyterian, Lutheran, Baptist, and Moravian Churches. Thus, there was little evidence before the mid-19th century of a constitutional objection to the direct public funding of religious schools. After that, such objections as arose came not from the Constitution, but from the fact that by 1870 the number of private Protestant schools was rapidly being eclipsed by Catholic schools. It is evident that Representative Blaine did not think the no establishment language of the First Amendment or the parallel language in his proposal banned public assistance for sectarian schools. If it had, the specialized language of Blaine's proposed amendment banning school funding would have been surplusage. As one commentator put it,

> It is of great significance that not a single voice was raised to suggest that the no establishment and/or the " free exercise" clause in the first section of the [Blaine] resolution ruled out the aforesaid use of public funds. It was assumed by all that they did not — an assumption stated explicitly by many Senators, implicitly by others.

F. William O'Brien, *The Blaine Amendment 1875–1876*, 41 U. Det. L.J. 137, 203–04 (1963). Professor O'Brien also notes that detractors of the Blaine proposal asserted that it did nothing to stop *federal* appropriations for religious schools, confirming again the original understanding that the First Amendment did not preclude such direct funding.*Id.* at 204.

That the original understanding did not prohibit, and indeed in practice, was supportive of the funding of religious schools should not be surprising with regard to a Constitution framed in the natural law tradition. Accordingly:

> The natural law principle assumes that there exist some external axioms. Whether they be the beliefs advocated by the Catholic, Jewish, or Lutheran [faith, by way of example,] is not relevant; instead, what is important is that the persons who drafted the Constitution viewed religion as one of the conduits for determining right conduct.

Henry T. Miller, Comment, *Constitutional Fiction: An Analysis of the Supreme Court's Interpretation of the Religion Clauses*, 47 La. L. Rev. 169, 174 (1986).

The distance from that tradition to modern Supreme Court jurisprudence can be measured in *Lemon v. Kurtzman*, 403 U.S. 602 (1971), which supplies the three-part *Lemon* test asking if the spending program has a secular legislative purpose, whether that program has the primary or principal effect of advancing or inhibiting religion and whether or not the program results in excessive entanglement between religion and the government. To answer, especially the middle question with regard to the effect of the program either inhibiting or advancing religion, the Court will normally employ one of the versions of the Establishment Clause already discussed — *i.e.*, exclusionary, equal protection; no endorsement; no coercion. Thus, as it is used presently, the *Lemon* standard is really little more than a vehicle or organizing chart to apply the elements of other Establishment Clause theory.

NOTES AND QUESTIONS

1. *Lemon's* purpose prong provides that, in order to be valid, government action must have "*a* secular . . . purpose" (emphasis added), language that has generally been interpreted as permitting government action unless there was *no* secular purpose or if the proffered secular purpose was merely a sham. However, in *McCreary County v. ACLU of Kentucky*, 545 U.S. 844 (2005), a closely divided Court

held that the display of the Ten Commandments in a county courthouse was an unconstitutional establishment of religion because the display was originally motivated by a religious purpose and that government's secular purpose must "predominate." This led Justice Scalia to argue in dissent that the Court had imposed a "heightened requirement" under the purpose prong. As invalidated by the Court, the display was denominated as a "Foundations of American Law and Government Display" and the government expressly stated its purpose as depicting "documents that played a significant role in the foundation of our system of law and government." Will the Court's new purpose requirement lead to a more searching inquiry into legislative motives under *Lemon*? Should it? Justice Breyer joined the majority opinion in *McCreary County*, but provided the critical fifth vote upholding a Texas Ten Commandments display in *Van Orden v. Perry*, 545 U.S. 677 (2005). In Texas, "the tablets have been used as part of a display that communicates not simply a religious message, but a secular message as well," Justice Breyer wrote in his opinion concurring in the judgment, noting that "[t]he circumstances surrounding the display's placement on the capitol grounds and its physical setting [among other, non-religious monuments] suggest that the State itself intended the latter, nonreligious aspects of the tablets' message to predominate." Does Justice Breyer's opinion in *Van Orden* shed any additional light on the new inquiry into predominance of purpose?

2.   What if the government changes its position out of concern that its initial purpose or motivation was too pro-religious and thereby renders a display unconstitutional? Should the history of alteration matter? In *McCreary County v. ACLU of Kentucky, supra*, Justice Souter, writing for the Court and joined by Justices Stevens, O'Connor, Ginsburg, and Breyer, held that the display of the Ten Commandments in a county courthouse was an unconstitutional establishment of religion because the display was originally motivated by a religious purpose. After the suit was filed, the county legislative body adopted a resolution calling for a more extensive display of significant documents in American history, including a central passage from the Declaration of Independence announcing the "self-evident truth" that all people are "endowed by their Creator"; the preamble to the Kentucky Constitution ("We, the people of the Commonwealth of Kentucky, grateful to Almighty God. . . ."); the national motto ("In God We Trust"); and the Mayflower Compact. When the district court held the expanded display unconstitutional, the County expanded the display yet again, this time to include, alongside the Ten Commandments, "framed copies of the Magna Carta, the Declaration of Independence, the Bill of Rights, the lyrics of the Star Spangled Banner, the Mayflower Compact, the National Motto, the Preamble to the Kentucky Constitution, and a picture of Lady Justice," in a collection titled "The Foundations of American Law and Government Display." The district court enjoined that display, too, holding that it still had a religious purpose in light of the "history of [the] litigation." A panel of the Sixth Circuit affirmed over the dissent of Judge Ryan, who denied that the prior displays should have any bearing on the constitutionality of the third one. The Supreme Court affirmed 5-4, rejecting, in light of the litigation history, the County's claim that the purpose of the third exhibit was "to educate the citizens of the county regarding some of the documents that played a significant role in the foundation of our system of law and government." The Court recognized, though, that one consequence of its inquiry into the purpose of "past actions was that the same

government action may be constitutional if taken in the first instance and unconstitutional if it has a sectarian heritage," suggesting that Kentucky's third display may have been constitutional had it been erected first. Having been found initially to have exhibited an "unconstitutional" religious purpose, are there any alterations Kentucky can now make to render constitutional a display that would have been constitutional at the outset?

b. School Vouchers or the Equivalent — The Permissible Evenhanded Funding of Students or Parents

In the years following *Lemon*, the courts continued to grapple with drawing the line between permissible and impermissible attempts to provide state aid for educational purposes to parents who choose to send their children to religious schools. In *Zobrest v. Catalina Foothills Sch. Dist.*, 509 U.S. 1 (1993), the Supreme Court held that the Establishment Clause did not prevent the public provision of a sign language interpreter to a deaf child attending a religious high school. With some hedging, it held that so long as educational funds are made available directly to parents or students as part of a government program "that neutrally provide[s] benefits to a broad class of citizens defined without reference to religion" then no Establishment Clause issue arises. *Zobrest*, 509 U.S. at 8. Thus, presumably, a state, if it so chose, could tax all of its citizens (usually through a combination of property and income taxes) to create a general education fund and then return those funds to parents for public or private (including private religious) schooling either in the form of a tax credit or cash payment (voucher).

The hedging in *Zobrest* was removed in *Agostini v. Felton*, 521 U.S. 203 (1997), in which the Supreme Court reopened its previous rulings in *Aguilar v. Felton*, 473 U.S. 402 (1985), and *Grand Rapids Sch. Dist. v. Ball*, 473 U.S. 373 (1985), largely overruling both and holding that "a federally funded program providing supplemental, remedial instruction to disadvantaged children on a neutral basis is not invalid under the Establishment Clause when such instruction is given on the premises of sectarian schools by government employees." *Agostini*, 521 U.S. at 234–35. Since *Agostini* lends further strength to the equal protection idea, it is significant that the Court's opinion was written by Justice O'Connor, who explicitly rejected Justice Souter's dissenting analysis that the neutral, generally available educational assistance in reading, English and mathematics created an impermissible "symbolic union" between church and state. *Id.* at 224. Justice O'Connor, of course, has been a consistent advocate of the no endorsement view in other cases. In his dissent, Justice Souter strenuously argued that earlier cases, such as *Zobrest* and *Witters*, involved only individuals receiving isolated services, while the program in *Agostini* assumed the core teaching responsibility of the religious schools. *Id.* at 248–52 (Souter, J., dissenting). The majority refused to engage in what it called the dissent's speculations, and stated that it was also unwilling "to conclude that the constitutionality of an aid program depends on the number of sectarian school students who happen to receive the otherwise neutral aid." *Id.* at 229.

Finally, in *Mitchell v. Helms*, 530 U.S. 793 (2000), the Court in a fractured, 4-2-3 opinion, upheld Louisiana's provision of library books, computers, and video equipment to private religious schools on the same terms as they were provided to public schools. Justice Thomas, writing for the plurality, held that the aid did not run afoul of *Lemon*'s effects prong because the aid was provided to the religious schools "only as a result of the genuinely independent and private choices of individua[l parents]," and because the aid was "allocated on the basis of neutral, secular criteria that neither favor[ed] nor disfavor[ed] religion, and [was] made available to both religious and secular beneficiaries on a nondiscriminatory basis." Justice O'Connor, joined by Justice Breyer, concurred only in the judgment, contending that the plurality opinion treated the neutrality of the aid program as dispositive, when in her view (as well as that of Justice Souter, joined by Justices Stevens and Ginsburg, in dissent) it was a necessary but not a sufficient condition for surviving an Establishment Clause challenge. Justice O'Connor was also troubled by what she described as the plurality's rejection of "the distinction between direct and indirect aid," and its holding "that the actual diversion of secular aid by a religious school to the advancement of its religious mission is permissible." *Agostini* and *Mitchell* were both decided with cases addressing the constitutionality of school voucher programs on the immediate horizon. Can you predict from them the outcome and reasoning of the following case?

ZELMAN v. SIMMONS-HARRIS
536 U.S. 639 (2002)

CHIEF JUSTICE REHNQUIST delivered the opinion of the Court.

The State of Ohio has established a pilot program designed to provide educational choices to families with children who reside in the Cleveland City School District. The question presented is whether this program offends the Establishment Clause of the United States Constitution. We hold that it does not.

The program provides two basic kinds of assistance to parents of children in a covered district. First, the program provides tuition aid for students in kindergarten through third grade, expanding each year through eighth grade, to attend a participating public or private school of their parent's choosing. Second, the program provides tutorial aid for students who choose to remain enrolled in public school.

The tuition aid portion of the program is designed to provide educational choices to parents who reside in a covered district. Any private school, whether religious or nonreligious, may participate in the program and accept program students so long as the school is located within the boundaries of a covered district and meets statewide educational standards. Participating private schools must agree not to discriminate on the basis of race, religion, or ethnic background, or to "advocate or foster unlawful behavior or teach hatred of any person or group on the basis of race, ethnicity, national origin, or religion." Any public school located in a school district adjacent to the covered district may also participate in the program. Adjacent public schools are eligible to receive a $2,250 tuition grant for each program student accepted in addition to the full amount of per-pupil state funding attributable to each additional student.[11]

---

[11] [1] Although the parties dispute the precise amount of state funding received by suburban school

Tuition aid is distributed to parents according to financial need. Families with incomes below 200% of the poverty line are given priority and are eligible to receive 90% of private school tuition up to $2,250. . . . If parents choose a private school, checks are made payable to the parents who then endorse the checks over to the chosen school.

The program has been in operation within the Cleveland City School District since the 1996–1997 school year. In the 1999–2000 school year, 56 private schools participated in the program, 46 (or 82%) of which had a religious affiliation. None of the public schools in districts adjacent to Cleveland have elected to participate. More than 3,700 students participated in the scholarship program, most of whom (96%) enrolled in religiously affiliated schools. . . .

The Establishment Clause of the First Amendment, applied to the States through the Fourteenth Amendment, prevents a State from enacting laws that have the "purpose" or "effect" of advancing or inhibiting religion. *Agostini v. Felton* ("[W]e continue to ask whether the government acted with the purpose of advancing or inhibiting religion [and] whether the aid has the 'effect' of advancing or inhibiting religion" (citations omitted)). There is no dispute that the program challenged here was enacted for the valid secular purpose of providing educational assistance to poor children in a demonstrably failing public school system. Thus, the question presented is whether the Ohio program nonetheless has the forbidden "effect" of advancing or inhibiting religion.

To answer that question, our decisions have drawn a consistent distinction between government programs that provide aid directly to religious schools, . . . and programs of true private choice, in which government aid reaches religious schools only as a result of the genuine and independent choices of private individuals, *Mueller v. Allen* . . . . While our jurisprudence with respect to the constitutionality of direct aid programs has "changed significantly" over the past two decades, our jurisprudence with respect to true private choice programs has remained consistent and unbroken. Three times we have confronted Establishment Clause challenges to neutral government programs that provide aid directly to a broad class of individuals, who, in turn, direct the aid to religious schools or institutions of their own choosing. Three times we have rejected such challenges.

In *Mueller*, we rejected an Establishment Clause challenge to a Minnesota program authorizing tax deductions for various educational expenses, including private school tuition costs, even though the great majority of the program's beneficiaries (96%) were parents of children in religious schools. We began by focusing on the class of beneficiaries, finding that because the class included "*all* parents," including parents with "children [who] attend nonsectarian private schools or sectarian private schools," the program was "not readily subject to challenge under the Establishment Clause." Then, viewing the program as a whole, we emphasized the principle of private choice, noting that public funds were made available to religious schools "only as a result of numerous, private choices of individual parents of school-aged children." This, we said, ensured that " 'no

---

districts adjacent to the Cleveland City School District, there is no dispute that any suburban district agreeing to participate in the program would receive a $2,250 tuition grant *plus* the ordinary allotment of per-pupil state funding for each program student enrolled in a suburban public school.

imprimatur of state approval' can be deemed to have been conferred on any particular religion, or on religion generally." We thus found it irrelevant to the constitutional inquiry that the vast majority of beneficiaries were parents of children in religious schools, saying:

> "We would be loath to adopt a rule grounding the constitutionality of a facially neutral law on annual reports reciting the extent to which various classes of private citizens claimed benefits under the law."

That the program was one of true private choice, with no evidence that the State deliberately skewed incentives toward religious schools, was sufficient for the program to survive scrutiny under the Establishment Clause.

In *Witters*, we used identical reasoning to reject an Establishment Clause challenge to a vocational scholarship program that provided tuition aid to a student studying at a religious institution to become a pastor. Looking at the program as a whole, we observed that "[a]ny aid . . . that ultimately flows to religious institutions does so only as a result of the genuinely independent and private choices of aid recipients." Five Members of the Court, in separate opinions, emphasized the general rule from *Mueller* that the amount of government aid channeled to religious institutions by individual aid recipients was not relevant to the constitutional inquiry. Our holding thus rested not on whether few or many recipients chose to expend government aid at a religious school but, rather, on whether recipients generally were empowered to direct the aid to schools or institutions of their own choosing.

Finally, in *Zobrest*, we applied *Mueller* and *Witters* to reject an Establishment Clause challenge to a federal program that permitted sign-language interpreters to assist deaf children enrolled in religious schools. Reviewing our earlier decisions, we stated that "government programs that neutrally provide benefits to a broad class of citizens defined without reference to religion are not readily subject to an Establishment Clause challenge."

Mueller, Witters, and *Zobrest* thus make clear that where a government aid program is neutral with respect to religion, and provides assistance directly to a broad class of citizens who, in turn, direct government aid to religious schools wholly as a result of their own genuine and independent private choice, the program is not readily subject to challenge under the Establishment Clause. A program that shares these features permits government aid to reach religious institutions only by way of the deliberate choices of numerous individual recipients. The incidental advancement of a religious mission, or the perceived endorsement of a religious message, is reasonably attributable to the individual recipient, not to the government, whose role ends with the disbursement of benefits. . . . It is precisely for these reasons that we have never found a program of true private choice to offend the Establishment Clause.

We believe that the program challenged here is a program of true private choice, consistent with *Mueller, Witters*, and *Zobrest*, and thus constitutional. As was true in those cases, the Ohio program is neutral in all respects toward religion. It is part of a general and multifaceted undertaking by the State of Ohio to provide educational opportunities to the children of a failed school district. It confers educational assistance directly to a broad class of individuals defined without reference to religion, *i.e.*, any parent of a school-age child who resides in the Cleveland City School District. The program permits the participation of *all* schools within the district, religious or nonreligious. Adjacent public schools also may participate and have a financial incentive to do so. Program benefits are available to participating families on neutral terms, with no reference to religion. The only preference stated anywhere in the program is a preference for low-income families, who receive greater assistance and are given priority for admission at participating schools.

Respondents suggest that even without a financial incentive for parents to choose a religious school, the program creates a "public perception that the State is endorsing religious practices and beliefs." But we have repeatedly recognized that no reasonable observer would think a neutral program of private choice, where state aid reaches religious schools solely as a result of the numerous independent decisions of private individuals, carries with it the *imprimatur* of government endorsement. . . . Any objective observer familiar with the full history and context of the Ohio program would reasonably view it as one aspect of a broader undertaking to assist poor children in failed schools, not as an endorsement of religious schooling in general. . . .

That 46 of the 56 private schools now participating in the program are religious schools does not condemn it as a violation of the Establishment Clause. The Establishment Clause question is whether Ohio is coercing parents into sending their children to religious schools, and that question must be answered by evaluating *all* options Ohio provides Cleveland schoolchildren, only one of which is to obtain a program scholarship and then choose a religious school.

Respondents and JUSTICE SOUTER claim that even if we do not focus on the number of participating schools that are religious schools, we should attach constitutional significance to the fact that 96% of scholarship recipients have enrolled in religious schools. They claim that this alone proves parents lack genuine choice, even if no parent has ever said so. We need not consider this argument in detail, since it was flatly rejected in *Mueller*, where we found it irrelevant that 96% of parents taking deductions for tuition expenses paid tuition at religious schools.

The 96% figure upon which respondents and JUSTICE SOUTER rely discounts entirely (1) the more than 1,900 Cleveland children enrolled in alternative community schools, (2) the more than 13,000 children enrolled in alternative magnet schools, and (3) the more than 1,400 children enrolled in traditional public schools with tutorial assistance. Including some or all of these children in the denominator of children enrolled in nontraditional schools during the 1999–2000 school year drops the percentage enrolled in religious schools from 96% to under 20%.[12]

---

[12] [6] JUSTICE SOUTER and JUSTICE STEVENS claim that community schools and magnet schools are separate and distinct from program schools, simply because the program itself does not include community and magnet school options. But none of the dissenting opinions explain how there is any perceptible difference between scholarship schools, community schools, or magnet schools from the perspective of Cleveland parents looking to choose the best educational option for their school-age children. Parents who choose a program school in fact receive from the State precisely what parents who choose a community or magnet school receive — the opportunity to send their children largely at state

In sum, the Ohio program is entirely neutral with respect to religion. It provides benefits directly to a wide spectrum of individuals, defined only by financial need and residence in a particular school district. It permits such individuals to exercise genuine choice among options public and private, secular and religious. The program is therefore a program of true private choice. In keeping with an unbroken line of decisions rejecting challenges to similar programs, we hold that the program does not offend the Establishment Clause.

The judgment of the Court of Appeals is reversed.

It is so ordered.

JUSTICE O'CONNOR, concurring.

While I join the Court's opinion, I write separately for two reasons. First, although the Court takes an important step, I do not believe that today's decision, when considered in light of other longstanding government programs that impact religious organizations and our prior Establishment Clause jurisprudence, marks a dramatic break from the past. Second, given the emphasis the Court places on verifying that parents of voucher students in religious schools have exercised "true private choice," I think it is worth elaborating on the Court's conclusion that this inquiry should consider all reasonable educational alternatives to religious schools that are available to parents. To do otherwise is to ignore how the educational system in Cleveland actually functions.

I

These cases are different from prior indirect aid cases in part because a significant portion of the funds appropriated for the voucher program reach religious schools without restrictions on the use of these funds. The share of public resources that reach religious schools is not, however, as significant as respondents suggest. . . . These statistics do not take into account all of the reasonable educational choices that may be available to students in Cleveland public schools. When one considers the option to attend community schools, the percentage of students enrolled in religious schools falls to 62.1 percent. If magnet schools are included in the mix, this percentage falls to 16.5 percent. . . .

Although $8.2 million is no small sum, it pales in comparison to the amount of funds that federal, state, and local governments already provide religious institutions. Religious organizations may qualify for exemptions from the federal corporate income tax, the corporate income tax in many States, and property taxes in all 50 States.

These tax exemptions, which have "much the same effect as [cash grants] . . . of the amount of tax [avoided]," are just part of the picture. Federal dollars also reach religiously affiliated organizations through public health programs such as Medicare, and Medicaid, through educational programs such as the Pell Grant program, and the G.I. Bill of Rights, and through child care programs such as the Child Care and Development Block Grant Program (CCDBG).

---

expense to schools they prefer to their local public school. . . .

A significant portion of the funds appropriated for these programs reach religiously affiliated institutions, typically without restrictions on its subsequent use. . . . Against this background, the support that the Cleveland voucher program provides religious institutions is neither substantial nor atypical of existing government programs. While this observation is not intended to justify the Cleveland voucher program under the Establishment Clause, it places in broader perspective alarmist claims about implications of the Cleveland program and the Court's decision in these cases. . . .

II

Nor does today's decision signal a major departure from this Court's prior Establishment Clause jurisprudence. A central tool in our analysis of cases in this area has been the *Lemon* test. As originally formulated, a statute passed this test only if it had "a secular legislative purpose," if its "principal or primary effect" was one that "neither advance[d] nor inhibit[ed] religion," and if it did "not foster an excessive government entanglement with religion." *Lemon v. Kurtzman* (1971). In *Agostini v. Felton* (1997), we folded the entanglement inquiry into the primary effect inquiry. This made sense because both inquiries rely on the same evidence, and the degree of entanglement has implications for whether a statute advances or inhibits religion. . . .

The Court's opinion in these cases focuses on a narrow question related to the *Lemon* test: how to apply the primary effects prong in indirect aid cases? Specifically, it clarifies the basic inquiry when trying to determine whether a program that distributes aid to beneficiaries, rather than directly to service providers, has the primary effect of advancing or inhibiting religion, *Lemon v. Kurtzman*, or, as I have put it, of "endors[ing] or disapprov[ing] . . . religion," *Lynch v. Donnelly* (concurring opinion); see also *Wallace v. Jaffree* (1985) (O'CONNOR, J., concurring in judgment). Courts are instructed to consider two factors: first, whether the program administers aid in a neutral fashion, without differentiation based on the religious status of beneficiaries or providers of services; second, and more importantly, whether beneficiaries of indirect aid have a genuine choice among religious and nonreligious organizations when determining the organization to which they will direct that aid. If the answer to either query is "no," the program should be struck down under the Establishment Clause.

JUSTICE SOUTER portrays this inquiry as a departure from *Everson*. A fair reading of the holding in that case suggests quite the opposite. Justice Black's opinion for the Court held that the "[First] Amendment requires the state to be a neutral in its relations with groups of religious believers and non-believers; it does not require the state to be their adversary." *Everson, supra.* How else could the Court have upheld a state program to provide students transportation to public and religious schools alike? What the Court clarifies in these cases is that the Establishment Clause also requires that state aid flowing to religious organizations through the hands of beneficiaries must do so only at the direction of those beneficiaries. Such a refinement of the *Lemon* test surely does not betray *Everson*.

III

Based on the reasoning in the Court's opinion, which is consistent with the realities of the Cleveland educational system, I am persuaded that the Cleveland voucher program affords parents of eligible children genuine nonreligious options and is consistent with the Establishment Clause.

JUSTICE THOMAS, concurring. [*See supra*, part II.A.4]

JUSTICE STEVENS, dissenting. [Omitted]

[The "Just Say No" View — Eds.]

JUSTICE SOUTER, with whom JUSTICE STEVENS, JUSTICE GINSBERG, and JUSTICE BREYER, join, dissenting.

How can a Court consistently leave *Everson* on the books and approve the Ohio vouchers? The answer is that it cannot. It is only by ignoring *Everson* that the majority can claim to rest on traditional law in its invocation of neutral aid provisions and private choice to sanction the Ohio law. It is, moreover, only by ignoring the meaning of neutrality and private choice themselves that the majority can even pretend to rest today's decision on those criteria.

I

The majority's statements of Establishment Clause doctrine cannot be appreciated without some historical perspective on the Court's announced limitations on government aid to religious education, and its repeated repudiation of limits previously set. . . .

Viewed with the necessary generality, the cases can be categorized in three groups. In the period from 1947 to 1968, the basic principle of no aid to religion through school benefits was unquestioned. Thereafter for some 15 years, the Court termed its efforts as attempts to draw a line against aid that would be divertible to support the religious, as distinct from the secular, activity of an institutional beneficiary. Then, starting in 1983, concern with divertibility was gradually lost in favor of approving aid in amounts unlikely to afford substantial benefits to religious schools, when offered evenhandedly without regard to a recipient's religious character, and when channeled to a religious institution only by the genuinely free choice of some private individual. Now, the three stages are succeeded by a fourth, in which the substantial character of government aid is held to have no constitutional significance, and the espoused criteria of neutrality in offering aid, and private choice in directing it, are shown to be nothing but examples of verbal formalism.

A

Everson v. Board of Ed. of Ewing inaugurated the modern development of Establishment Clause doctrine at the behest of a taxpayer challenging state provision of "tax-raised funds to pay the bus fares of parochial school pupils" on regular city buses as part of a general scheme to reimburse the public-transportation costs of children attending both public and private nonprofit schools. Although the Court split, no Justice disagreed with the basic doctrinal principle already quoted, that "[n]o tax in any amount . . . can be levied to support any religious activities or institutions, . . . whatever form they may adopt to teach . . . religion." Nor did any Member of the Court deny the tension between the New Jersey program and the aims of the Establishment Clause. The majority upheld the state law on the strength of rights of religious-school students under the Free Exercise Clause, which was thought to entitle them to free public transportation when offered as a "general government servic[e]" to all schoolchildren. Despite the indirect benefit to religious education, the transportation was simply treated like "ordinary police and fire protection, connections for sewage disposal, public highways and sidewalks," and, most significantly, "state-paid policemen, detailed to protect children going to and from church schools from the very real hazards of traffic." The dissenters, however, found the benefit to religion too pronounced to survive the general principle of no establishment, no aid, and they described it as running counter to every objective served by the establishment ban. . . .

The difficulty of drawing a line that preserved the basic principle of no aid was no less obvious some 20 years later in *Board of Ed. of Central School Dist. No. 1 v. Allen* (1968), which upheld a New York law authorizing local school boards to lend textbooks in secular subjects to children attending religious schools, a result not self-evident from *Everson*'s "general government services" rationale. The Court relied instead on the theory that the in-kind aid could only be used for secular educational purposes, and found it relevant that "no funds or books are furnished [directly] to parochial schools, and the financial benefit is to parents and children, not to schools."[13] Justice Black, who wrote *Everson*, led the dissenters.

B

Allen recognized the reality that "religious schools pursue two goals, religious instruction and secular education," if state aid could be restricted to serve the second, it might be permissible under the Establishment Clause. But in the retrenchment that followed, the Court saw that the two educational functions were so intertwined in religious primary and secondary schools that aid to secular education could not readily be segregated, and the intrusive monitoring required to enforce the line itself raised Establishment Clause concerns about the entanglement of church and state. See *Lemon v. Kurtzman* (1971) (striking down program supplementing salaries for teachers of secular subjects in private schools). To avoid the entanglement, the Court's focus in the post-*Allen* cases was on the principle of divertibility, on discerning when ostensibly secular government aid to religious schools was susceptible to religious uses. The greater the risk of diversion to

---

[13] [4] The Court noted that "the record contains no evidence that any of the private schools . . . previously provided textbooks for their students," and "there is some evidence that at least some of the schools did not." *Allen*, 392 U.S. at 244, n.6. This was a significant distinction: if the parochial schools provided secular textbooks to their students, then the State's provision of the same in their stead might have freed up church resources for allocation to other uses, including, potentially, religious indoctrination.

religion (and the monitoring necessary to avoid it), the less legitimate the aid scheme was under the no-aid principle. On the one hand, the Court tried to be practical, and when the aid recipients were not so "pervasively sectarian" that their secular and religious functions were inextricably intertwined, the Court generally upheld aid earmarked for secular use.

C

Like all criteria requiring judicial assessment of risk, divertibility is an invitation to argument, but the object of the arguments provoked has always been a realistic assessment of facts aimed at respecting the principle of no aid. In *Mueller v. Allen*, however, that object began to fade, for *Mueller* started down the road from realism to formalism.

School Dist. of Grand Rapids v. Ball (1985), overruled in part by *Agostini v. Felton* (1997), clarified that the notions of evenhandedness, neutrality, and private choice in *Mueller* did not apply to cases involving direct aid to religious schools, which were still subject to the divertibility test. But in *Agostini*, where the substance of the aid was identical to that in *Ball*, public employees teaching remedial secular classes in private schools, the Court rejected the 30-year-old presumption of divertibility, and instead found it sufficient that the aid "supplement[ed]" but did not "supplant" existing educational services. The Court, contrary to *Ball*, viewed the aid as aid "directly to the eligible students . . . no matter where they choose to attend school."

In the 12 years between *Ball* and *Agostini*, the Court decided two other cases emphasizing the form of neutrality and private choice over the substance of aid to religious uses, but always in circumstances where any aid to religion was isolated and insubstantial. *Zobrest v. Catalina Foothills School Dist.* (1993) involved one student's choice to spend funds from a general public program at a religious school (to pay for a sign-language interpreter). As in *Witters*, the Court reasoned that "[d]isabled children, not sectarian schools, [were] the primary beneficiaries . . . ; to the extent sectarian schools benefit at all . . . , they are only incidental beneficiaries."

To be sure, the aid in *Agostini* was systemic and arguably substantial, but, as I have said, the majority there chose to view it as a bare "supplement." And this was how the controlling opinion described the systemic aid in our most recent case, *Mitchell v. Helms* (2000), as aid going merely to a "portion" of the religious schools' budgets. (O'Connor, J., concurring in judgment). The plurality in that case did not feel so uncomfortable about jettisoning substance entirely in favor of form, finding it sufficient that the aid was neutral and that there was virtual private choice, since any aid "first passes through the hands (literally or figuratively) of numerous private citizens who are free to direct the aid elsewhere." But that was only the plurality view.

Hence it seems fair to say that it was not until today that substantiality of aid has clearly been rejected as irrelevant by a majority of this Court, just as it has not been until today that a majority, not a plurality, has held purely formal criteria to suffice for scrutinizing aid that ends up in the coffers of religious schools. Today's cases are notable for their stark illustration of the inadequacy of the majority's chosen formal analysis.

II

Although it has taken half a century since *Everson* to reach the majority's twin standards of neutrality and free choice, the facts show that, in the majority's hands, even these criteria cannot convincingly legitimize the Ohio scheme.

A

Consider first the criterion of neutrality. As recently as two Terms ago, a majority of the Court recognized that neutrality conceived of as evenhandedness toward aid recipients had never been treated as alone sufficient to satisfy the Establishment Clause, *Mitchell* (O'CONNOR, J., concurring in judgment); (SOUTER, J., dissenting). But at least in its limited significance, formal neutrality seemed to serve some purpose. Today, however, the majority employs the neutrality criterion in a way that renders it impossible to understand.

In order to apply the neutrality test, it makes sense to focus on a category of aid that may be directed to religious as well as secular schools, and ask whether the scheme favors a religious direction. Here, one would ask whether the voucher provisions, allowing for as much as $2,250 toward private school tuition (or a grant to a public school in an adjacent district), were written in a way that skewed the scheme toward benefiting religious schools.

This, however, is not what the majority asks. The majority looks not to the provisions for tuition vouchers, but to every provision for educational opportunity: "The program permits the participation of *all* schools within the district [as well as public schools in adjacent districts], religious or nonreligious." The majority then finds confirmation that "participation of *all* schools" satisfies neutrality by noting that the better part of total state educational expenditure goes to public schools, thus showing there is no favor of religion.

The illogic is patent. If regular, public schools (which can get no voucher payments) "participate" in a voucher scheme with schools that can, and public expenditure is still predominantly on public schools, then the majority's reasoning would find neutrality in a scheme of vouchers available for private tuition in districts with no secular private schools at all. "Neutrality" as the majority employs the term is, literally, verbal and nothing more. This, indeed, is the only way the majority can gloss over the very nonneutral feature of the total scheme covering *"all* schools": public tutors may receive from the State no more than $324 per child to support extra tutoring (that is, the State's 90% of a total amount of $360), whereas the tuition voucher schools (which turn out to be mostly religious) can receive up to $2,250.[14]

----

[14] [7] The majority's argument that public school students within the program "direct almost twice as much state funding to their chosen school as do program students who receive a scholarship and attend a private school," was decisively rejected in *Committee for Public Ed. & Religious Liberty v. Nyquist* (1973):

B

The majority addresses the issue of choice the same way it addresses neutrality, by asking whether recipients or potential recipients of voucher aid have a choice of public schools among secular alternatives to religious schools. Again, however, the majority asks the wrong question and misapplies the criterion. The majority has confused choice in spending scholarships with choice from the entire menu of possible educational placements, most of them open to anyone willing to attend a public school. I say "confused" because the majority's new use of the choice criterion, which it frames negatively as "whether Ohio is coercing parents into sending their children to religious schools," ignores the reason for having a private choice enquiry in the first place. Cases since *Mueller* have found private choice relevant under a rule that aid to religious schools can be permissible so long as it first passes through the hands of students or parents. The majority's view that all educational choices are comparable for purposes of choice thus ignores the whole point of the choice test: it is a criterion for deciding whether indirect aid to a religious school is legitimate because it passes through private hands that can spend or use the aid in a secular school. The question is whether the private hand is genuinely free to send the money in either a secular direction or a religious one. The majority now has transformed this question about private choice in channeling aid into a question about selecting from examples of state spending (on education) including direct spending on magnet and community public schools that goes through no private hands and could never reach a religious school under any circumstance. When the choice test is transformed from where to spend the money to where to go to school, it is cut loose from its very purpose.

Defining choice as choice in spending the money or channeling the aid is, moreover, necessary if the choice criterion is to function as a limiting principle at all. If "choice" is present whenever there is any educational alternative to the religious school to which vouchers can be endorsed, then there will always be a choice and the voucher can always be constitutional, even in a system in which there is not a single private secular school as an alternative to the religious school. And because it is unlikely that any participating private religious school will enroll more pupils than the generally available public system, it will be easy to generate numbers suggesting that aid to religion is not the significant intent or effect of the voucher scheme.

Confining the relevant choices to spending choices, on the other hand, is not vulnerable to comparable criticism. Although leaving the selection of alternatives for choice wide open, as the majority would, virtually guarantees the availability of a "choice" that will satisfy the criterion, limiting the choices to spending choices will not guarantee a negative result in every case. There may, after all, be cases in which

---

"We do not agree with the suggestion . . . that tuition grants are an analogous endeavor to provide comparable benefits to all parents of schoolchildren whether enrolled in public or nonpublic schools. . . . The grants to parents of private school children are given in addition to the right that they have to send their children to public schools 'totally at state expense.' And in any event, the argument proves too much, for it would also provide a basis for approving through tuition grants the *complete subsidization* of all religious schools on the ground that such action is necessary if the State is fully to equalize the position of parents who elect such schools — a result wholly at variance with the Establishment Clause."

a voucher recipient will have a real choice, with enough secular private school desks in relation to the number of religious ones, and a voucher amount high enough to meet secular private school tuition levels. But, even to the extent that choice-to-spend does tend to limit the number of religious funding options that pass muster, the choice criterion has to be understood this way in order, as I have said, for it to function as a limiting principle. Otherwise there is surely no point in requiring the choice to be a true or real or genuine one.

III

I do not dissent merely because the majority has misapplied its own law, for even if I assumed *arguendo* that the majority's formal criteria were satisfied on the facts, today's conclusion would be profoundly at odds with the Constitution. Proof of this is clear on two levels. The first is circumstantial, in the now discarded symptom of violation, the substantial dimension of the aid. The second is direct, in the defiance of every objective supposed to be served by the bar against establishment.

A

The scale of the aid to religious schools approved today is unprecedented, both in the number of dollars and in the proportion of systemic school expenditure supported. Each measure has received attention in previous cases.

On the other hand, the Court has found the gross amount unhelpful for Establishment Clause analysis when the aid afforded a benefit solely to one individual, however substantial as to him, but only an incidental benefit to the religious school at which the individual chose to spend the State's money. When neither the design nor the implementation of an aid scheme channels a series of individual students' subsidies toward religious recipients, the relevant beneficiaries for establishment purposes, the Establishment Clause is unlikely to be implicated. The majority's reliance on the observations of five Members of the Court in *Witters* as to the irrelevance of substantiality of aid in that case, is therefore beside the point in the matter before us, which involves considerable sums of public funds systematically distributed through thousands of students attending religious elementary and middle schools in the city of Cleveland.

The Cleveland voucher program has cost Ohio taxpayers $33 million since its implementation in 1996 ($28 million in voucher payments, $5 million in administrative costs), and its cost was expected to exceed $8 million in the 2001-2002 school year.

The gross amounts of public money contributed are symptomatic of the scope of what the taxpayers' money buys for a broad class of religious-school students. In paying for practically the full amount of tuition for thousands of qualifying students, the scholarships purchase everything that tuition purchases, be it instruction in math or indoctrination in faith.

B

It is virtually superfluous to point out that every objective underlying the prohibition of religious establishment is betrayed by this scheme, but something has to be said about the enormity of the violation. I anticipated these objectives earlier, in discussing *Everson*, which cataloged them, the first being respect for freedom of conscience. Jefferson described it as the idea that no one "shall be compelled to . . . support any religious worship, place, or ministry whatsoever," even a "teacher of his own religious persuasion," and Madison thought it violated by any " 'authority which can force a citizen to contribute three pence . . . of his property for the support of any . . . establishment.' "

As for the second objective, to save religion from its own corruption, Madison wrote of the " 'experience . . . that ecclesiastical establishments, instead of maintaining the purity and efficacy of Religion, have had a contrary operation.' " In Madison's time, the manifestations were "pride and indolence in the Clergy; ignorance and servility in the laity[,] in both, superstition, bigotry and persecution," in the 21st century, the risk is one of "corrosive secularism" to religious schools, and the specific threat is to the primacy of the schools' mission to educate the children of the faithful according to the unaltered precepts of their faith. Even "[t]he favored religion may be compromised as political figures reshape the religion's beliefs for their own purposes; it may be reformed as government largesse brings government regulation."

The risk is already being realized. In Ohio, for example, a condition of receiving government money under the program is that participating religious schools may not "discriminate on the basis of . . . religion," which means the school may not give admission preferences to children who are members of the patron faith; children of a parish are generally consigned to the same admission lotteries as non-believers. This indeed was the exact object of a 1999 amendment repealing the portion of a predecessor statute that had allowed an admission preference for "[c]hildren . . . whose parents are affiliated with any organization that provides financial support to the school, at the discretion of the school." Nor is the State's religious antidiscrimination restriction limited to student admission policies: by its terms, a participating religious school may well be forbidden to choose a member of its own clergy to serve as teacher or principal over a layperson of a different religion claiming equal qualification for the job.[15] Indeed, a separate condition that "[t]he school . . . not . . . teach hatred of any person or group on the basis of . . . religion," could be understood (or subsequently broadened) to prohibit religions from teaching traditionally legitimate articles of faith as to the error, sinfulness, or ignorance of

---

[15] [23] And the courts will, of course, be drawn into disputes about whether a religious school's employment practices violated the Ohio statute. In part precisely to avoid this sort of involvement, some Courts of Appeals have held that religious groups enjoy a First Amendment exemption for clergy from state and federal laws prohibiting discrimination on the basis of race or ethnic origin. *See, e.g., Rayburn v. General Conference of Seventh-Day Adventists* (4th Cir. 1985) ("The application of Title VII to employment decisions of this nature would result in an intolerably close relationship between church and state both on a substantive and procedural level"); *EEOC v. Catholic Univ. of America* (D.C. Cir. 1996) . . . .

others,[16] if they want government money for their schools.

When government aid goes up, so does reliance on it; the only thing likely to go down is independence. . . . A day will come when religious schools will learn what political leverage can do, just as Ohio's politicians are now getting a lesson in the leverage exercised by religion.

Increased voucher spending is not, however, the sole portent of growing regulation of religious practice in the school, for state mandates to moderate religious teaching may well be the most obvious response to the third concern behind the ban on establishment, its inextricable link with social conflict. . . .

JUSTICE BREYER has addressed this issue in his own dissenting opinion, which I join, and here it is enough to say that the intensity of the expectable friction can be gauged by realizing that the scramble for money will energize not only contending sectarians, but taxpayers who take their liberty of conscience seriously.

If the divisiveness permitted by today's majority is to be avoided in the short term, it will be avoided only by action of the political branches at the state and national levels. Legislatures not driven to desperation by the problems of public education may be able to see the threat in vouchers negotiable in sectarian schools. Perhaps even cities with problems like Cleveland's will perceive the danger, now that they know a federal court will not save them from it.

My own course as a judge on the Court cannot, however, simply be to hope that the political branches will save us from the consequences of the majority's decision. *Everson*'s statement is still the touchstone of sound law, even though the reality is that in the matter of educational aid the Establishment Clause has largely been read away. True, the majority has not approved vouchers for religious schools alone, or aid earmarked for religious instruction. But no scheme so clumsy will ever get before us, and in the cases that we may see, like these, the Establishment Clause is largely silenced. I do not have the option to leave it silent, and I hope that a future Court will reconsider today's dramatic departure from basic Establishment Clause principle.

JUSTICE BREYER, with whom JUSTICE STEVENS and JUSTICE SOUTER join, dissenting.

I join JUSTICE SOUTER's opinion, and I agree substantially with JUSTICE STEVENS. I write separately, however, to emphasize the risk that publicly financed voucher programs pose in terms of religiously based social conflict. I do so because I believe that the Establishment Clause concern for protecting the Nation's social fabric from

---

16 [24] *See, e.g.,* Christian New Testament (2 Corinthians 6:14) (King James Version) ("Be ye not unequally yoked together with unbelievers: for what fellowship hath righteousness with unrighteousness? and what communion hath light with darkness?"); The Book of Mormon (2 Nephi 9:24) ("And if they will not repent and believe in his name, and be baptized in his name, and endure to the end, they must be damned; for the Lord God, the Holy One of Israel, has spoken it"); Pentateuch (Deut. 29:18) (The New Jewish Publication Society Translation) (for one who converts to another faith, "the LORD will never forgive him; rather will the LORD's anger and passion rage against that man, till every sanction recorded in this book comes down upon him, and the LORD blots out his name from under heaven"); The Koran 334 (The Cow Ch. 2:1) (N. Dawood transl. 4th rev. ed. 1974) ("As for the unbelievers, whether you forewarn them or not, they will not have faith. Allah has set a seal upon their hearts and ears; their sight is dimmed and a grievous punishment awaits them").

religious conflict poses an overriding obstacle to the implementation of this well-intentioned school voucher program.

I

When it decided these 20th century Establishment Clause cases, the Court did not deny that an earlier American society might have found a less clear-cut church/state separation compatible with social tranquility. Indeed, historians point out that during the early years of the Republic, American schools — including the first public schools — were Protestant in character. Their students recited Protestant prayers, read the King James version of the Bible, and learned Protestant religious ideals. Those practices may have wrongly discriminated against members of minority religions, but given the small number of such individuals, the teaching of Protestant religions in schools did not threaten serious social conflict.

The 20th century Court was fully aware, however, that immigration and growth had changed American society dramatically since its early years. By 1850, 1.6 million Catholics lived in America, and by 1900 that number rose to 12 million. There were similar percentage increases in the Jewish population. Not surprisingly, with this increase in numbers, members of non-Protestant religions, particularly Catholics, began to resist the Protestant domination of the public schools. Scholars report that by the mid-19th century religious conflict over matters such as Bible reading "grew intense," as Catholics resisted and Protestants fought back to preserve their domination. "Dreading Catholic domination," native Protestants "terrorized Catholics." In some States "Catholic students suffered beatings or expulsions for refusing to read from the Protestant Bible, and crowds . . . rioted over whether Catholic children could be released from the classroom during Bible reading."

The 20th century Court was also aware that political efforts to right the wrong of discrimination against religious minorities in primary education had failed; in fact they had exacerbated religious conflict. Catholics sought equal government support for the education of their children in the form of aid for private Catholic schools. But the "Protestant position" on this matter, scholars report, "was that public schools must be 'nonsectarian' (which was usually understood to allow Bible reading and other Protestant observances) and public money must not support 'sectarian' schools (which in practical terms meant Catholic)." . . .

These historical circumstances suggest that the Court, applying the Establishment Clause through the Fourteenth Amendment to 20th century American society, faced an interpretive dilemma that was in part practical. The Court appreciated the religious diversity of contemporary American society. It realized that the status quo favored some religions at the expense of others. And it understood the Establishment Clause to prohibit (among other things) any such favoritism. Yet *how* did the Clause achieve that objective? Did it simply require the government to give each religion an equal chance to introduce religion into the primary schools — a kind of "equal opportunity" approach to the interpretation of the Establishment Clause? Or, did that Clause avoid government favoritism of some religions by insisting upon "separation" — that the government achieve equal treatment by removing itself from the business of providing religious education for children? This interpretive choice arose in respect both to religious activities in public schools and government aid to private education.

In both areas the Court concluded that the Establishment Clause required "separation," in part because an "equal opportunity" approach was not workable. With respect to religious activities in the public schools, how could the Clause require public primary and secondary school teachers, when reading prayers or the Bible, *only* to treat all religions alike? In many places there were too many religions, too diverse a set of religious practices, too many whose spiritual beliefs denied the virtue of formal religious training. This diversity made it difficult, if not impossible, to devise meaningful forms of "equal treatment" by providing an "equal opportunity" for all to introduce their own religious practices into the public schools.

With respect to government aid to private education, did not history show that efforts to obtain equivalent funding for the private education of children whose parents did not hold popular religious beliefs only exacerbated religious strife? . . .

The upshot is the development of constitutional doctrine that reads the Establishment Clause as avoiding religious strife, *not* by providing every religion with an *equal opportunity* (say, to secure state funding or to pray in the public schools), but by drawing fairly clear lines of *separation* between church and state — at least where the heartland of religious belief, such as primary religious education, is at issue.

II

The principle underlying these cases — avoiding religiously based social conflict — remains of great concern. As religiously diverse as America had become when the Court decided its major 20th century Establishment Clause cases, we are exponentially more diverse today. America boasts more than 55 different religious groups and subgroups with a significant number of members.

III

I concede that the Establishment Clause currently permits States to channel various forms of assistance to religious schools, for example, transportation costs for students, computers, and secular texts. States now certify the nonsectarian educational content of religious school education. . . .

School voucher programs differ, however, in both *kind* and *degree* from aid programs upheld in the past. They differ in kind because they direct financing to a core function of the church: the teaching of religious truths to young children.

Vouchers also differ in *degree*. The aid programs recently upheld by the Court involved limited amounts of aid to religion. But the majority's analysis here appears to permit a considerable shift of taxpayer dollars from public secular schools to private religious schools. That fact, combined with the use to which these dollars will be put, exacerbates the conflict problem. State aid that takes the form of peripheral secular items, with prohibitions against diversion of funds to religious teaching, holds significantly less potential for social division. In this respect as well, the secular aid upheld in *Mitchell* differs dramatically from the present case. Although it was conceivable that minor amounts of money could have, contrary to the statute, found their way to the religious activities of the recipients, that case is at worst the camel's nose, while the litigation before us is the camel itself.

IV

I do not believe that the "parental choice" aspect of the voucher program sufficiently offsets the concerns I have mentioned. Parental choice cannot help the taxpayer who does not want to finance the religious education of children. It will not always help the parent who may see little real choice between inadequate nonsectarian public education and adequate education at a school whose religious teachings are contrary to his own. It will not satisfy religious minorities unable to participate because they are too few in number to support the creation of their own private schools. It will not satisfy groups whose religious beliefs preclude them from participating in a government-sponsored program, and who may well feel ignored as government funds primarily support the education of children in the doctrines of the dominant religions. And it does little to ameliorate the entanglement problems or the related problems of social division. Consequently, the fact that the parent may choose which school can cash the government's voucher check does not alleviate the Establishment Clause concerns associated with voucher programs.

V

The Court, in effect, turns the clock back. It adopts, under the name of "neutrality," an interpretation of the Establishment Clause that this Court rejected more than half a century ago. In its view, the parental choice that offers each religious group a kind of equal opportunity to secure government funding overcomes the Establishment Clause concern for social concord. An earlier Court found that "equal opportunity" principle insufficient; it read the Clause as insisting upon greater separation of church and state, at least in respect to primary education. In a society composed of many different religious creeds, I fear that this present departure from the Court's earlier understanding risks creating a form of religiously based conflict potentially harmful to the Nation's social fabric. Because I believe the Establishment Clause was written in part to avoid this kind of conflict, and for reasons set forth by JUSTICE SOUTER and JUSTICE STEVENS, I respectfully dissent.

NOTES AND QUESTIONS

1. *Zelman* has the potential for changing the landscape of American education by its approval of parent-directed vouchers or scholarships. It remains to be seen whether other methods of providing assistance raise different constitutional questions. The Supreme Court indirectly took up this question in *Hibbs v. Winn*, 542 U.S. 88 (2004). *Hibbs* was a federal challenge to an Arizona tax credit for donations to school tuition organizations (STO). State law permitted tax credits up to $625 for joint filers who contributed to an STO. STOs must disburse as scholarship grants at least 90 percent of contributions received, may allow donors to direct scholarships to individual students, may not allow donors to name their own dependents, must designate at least two schools whose students will receive funds, and must not designate schools that "discriminate on the basis of race, color, handicap, familial status or national origin." STOs may designate schools that provide religious instruction or that give admissions preference on the basis of religion or religious affiliation. In essence, the STO gives a taxpayer a choice: to direct tax payments up to the approved amount either to an STO or to the general state treasury.

In a 5-4 opinion by Justice Ginsburg, the Supreme Court refused to block a suit claiming such support violated the Establishment Clause. The suit was sought to be enjoined as contrary to the federal Tax Injunction Act (TIA) which precludes federal court challenges to state tax assessments. The majority reasoned that the TIA applies only in cases where "state taxpayers seek federal-court orders enabling them to avoid paying state taxes." The Court observed further that "the Senate Report commented that the Act had two closely related, state-revenue-protective objectives: (1) to eliminate disparities between taxpayers who could seek injunctive relief in federal court — usually out-of-state corporations asserting diversity jurisdiction — and taxpayers with recourse only to state courts, which generally required taxpayers to pay first and litigate later; and (2) to stop taxpayers, with the aid of a federal injunction, from withholding large sums, thereby disrupting state government finances." These considerations were not implicated in the present matter, said Justice Ginsburg, since the purpose of the suit is a third-party challenge on constitutional grounds which would enlarge, not diminish, state revenues.

The four dissenters lead by Justice Kennedy thought the Court to be disregarding the plain text of the federal statute, and further argued that "the Court shows great skepticism for the state courts' ability to vindicate constitutional wrongs." Thus, this *as applied* challenge to the Arizona credit was permitted to proceed, even as the Arizona Supreme Court had already upheld the *facial* validity of the program. *Kotterman v. Killian*, 972 P.2d 606 (Ariz. 1999) (en banc) (finding that the tuition tax credit did not prefer one religion over another, or religion over non-religion. Rather, the state high court found it to aid a broad spectrum of citizens by allowing for a wide range of private choices and any perceived state connection to private religious schools was indirect and attenuated).

2.   It is now clear that the Establishment Clause does not *require* discrimination in the allocation of public funds for education. *If* a State decides to extend these funds to parents and parents may freely choose among public, private, and religious schools (in the words of Justice O'Connor, exercise "true private choice"), there is neither an impermissible establishment nor endorsement. But what if a state decides not to allow parents to pursue religious educational options? Can it be argued that states not only need not be exclusionary, but also must be inclusionary? Certainly, many would argue that states are entirely free to structure their own educational programs, and given that, are under no obligation to expand educational options beyond the public ones. After all, it is well established that no one can obligate the government to subsidize exercise of constitutional liberty, including religious liberty. However, is it a different question if the reason the government excludes religious participants is animus or bias?

3.   Unfortunately, religious discrimination or animus toward 19th century immigrant populations, most notably Catholics and Jews, is the modern day source of many state exclusions of religious schools from the education fund contributed to by all taxpayers. Approximately thirty-seven state constitutions contain provisions commonly known as Blaine Amendments. While the language varies, a reasonably typical formulation forbids "draw[ing money] from the treasury for the benefit of religious societies, or religious or theological seminaries." The term "seminaries" is generally understood to include all religiously affiliated schools. New York's provision reads: "Neither the state nor any subdivision thereof, shall use its property or credit or any public money, or authorize or permit either to be used, *directly or indirectly*, in aid or maintenance, other than for examination or inspection, of any school or institution of learning wholly or in part under the control or direction of any religious denomination, or in which any denominational tenet or doctrine is taught, but the legislature may provide for the transportation of children to and from any school or institution of learning." (Art. 11, Sec. 3, N.Y. Const.; emphasis supplied).

If interpreted literally, provisions like New York's would seemingly prohibit the indirect funding of religious schools, exactly what is permitted under *Zelman*. The notion that the Blaine Amendments may be more restrictive than the Establishment Clause finds support in *Witters v. Washington Department of Services for the Blind*, 771 P.2d 1119 (Wash.), *cert. denied*, 493 U.S. 850 (1989). While the U.S. Supreme Court found no federal Establishment Clause violation for the use of state vocational assistance, as a matter of individual private choice, for religious training, on remand the Washington Supreme Court denied the assistance on state constitutional grounds. The state court rested its holding on the language of the state's Blaine Amendment, which contained language not unlike that of New York noted above. The court concluded that "apply[ing] federal establishment clause analysis . . . would be inappropriate" and also rebuffed Witters' contention that the denial of funding violated the federal Equal Protection Clause. It is not clear that the state court fully grasped the equal protection challenge, but even assuming that it did, the court found a "compelling" interest in maintaining the separation of church and state set forth in the state constitution. Witters petitioned for certiorari, but the United States Supreme Court denied his petition. Would that petition be differently treated in light of *Zelman*? Might such facial religious discrimination now be acknowledged as an equal protection or free exercise violation or considered the censorship of religious thought contrary to First Amendment free speech principles?

4.   In a narrowly written, but 7-2, opinion, the Supreme Court rejected the notion that a state was obligated to fund the training of clergy under an otherwise generally available public scholarship program. *Locke v. Davey*, 540 U.S. 712 (2004). Washington had created a scholarship program — the Promise Scholarship — to help academically talented but underprivileged students attend college. Washington excepted devotional theology from qualifying courses of study because its state constitution provides in Article I, section 11 that "No public money or property shall be appropriated for or applied to any religious worship, exercise or instruction, or the support of any religious establishment." To the state this meant that public assistance for tuition to train clergy, even if passed through a private hand through

the exercise of private choice, would be a violation of the state constitution.

When Joshua Davey sought to double major in business and devotional theology, he was denied assistance and initially persuaded the Ninth Circuit that this denial was discriminatory and a violation of the *federal* Free Exercise Clause. In an opinion by Chief Justice Rehnquist, the Court reversed. Relying upon the historical exclusion of the public funding for the training of religious clerics and the "play in the joints" between the Establishment and Free Exercise Clauses, Washington was permitted to discriminate in this instance. The Court found that Washington's interest in complying with the terms of its own constitution was substantial and that the burden Davey alleged was minimal since he could study theology more generally (that is, as an academic subject apart from preparation for the ministry) without losing his scholarship. Thus, the Court felt this was not a case akin the imposition of a criminal or civil penalty because of religion or the denial of participation in public assembly because of religious belief, both of which have been held to violate free exercise. Moreover, Davey did not have to choose between his religious belief and the scholarship, since he could receive the state money for use at a wide array of public or religious colleges. Davey simply had to forego "devotional training" with public money. Seeming to write to cabin the holding as much as possible, the Chief Justice opined that "[s]ince the founding of our country, there have been popular uprisings against procuring taxpayer funds to support church leaders, which is one of the hallmarks of an 'established' religion." In this respect, "training someone to lead a congregation is an essentially religious endeavor. Indeed, majoring in devotional theology is akin to a religious calling as well as an academic pursuit."

Justices Scalia and Thomas dissented, criticizing the Court for backing away from earlier precedent where the Court said, that "[a] law burdening religious practice that is not neutral . . . must undergo the most rigorous of scrutiny" and that "the minimum requirement of neutrality is that a law not discriminate on its face." Further, the dissenters argued that "[w]hen the State makes a public benefit generally available, that benefit becomes part of the baseline against which burdens on religion are measured; and when the State withholds that benefit from some individuals solely on the basis of religion, it violates the Free Exercise Clause no less than if it had imposed a special tax." The dissent also questioned the legitimacy of the state's purported interest in the case, asking: "What is the nature of the State's asserted interest here? It can not be protecting the pocketbooks of its citizens; given the tiny fraction of Promise Scholars who would pursue theology degrees. . . . It cannot be preventing mistaken appearance of endorsement [since everyone who qualifies receives the scholarship without regard to course of study]." Rather, Justice Scalia saw the state's interest as "a pure philosophical one: the State's opinion that it would violate taxpayers' freedom of conscience *not* to discriminate against candidates for the ministry."

5.   In *Davey*, the Court expressly reserved the question of whether the outcome would be different if the State of Washington had relied on its Blaine Amendment to preclude the scholarship aid. Wrote the Chief Justice in footnote: "Neither Davey nor *amici* have established a credible connection between the Blaine Amendment and Article I, § 11, the relevant constitutional provision," used to deny Joshua Davey assistance for his devotional theology study. "Accordingly," said the Court, "the

Blaine Amendment's history [of bigotry] is simply not before us." If the Court does take up a Blaine-inspired case in the future, it may be argued that Blaine Amendment discrimination has dissipated. Passage of time, standing alone, is insufficient to purge the taint of an originally invidious purpose. In *Hunter v. Underwood*, 471 U.S. 222 (1985), the Supreme Court unanimously struck down a provision of the Alabama Constitution that disenfranchised any person convicted of an offense involving moral turpitude. It was not seriously disputed that the provision had been enacted to "establish white supremacy in [Alabama]." The Supreme Court brushed aside Alabama's argument that the provision's original intent was too historically remote to be dispositive because the provision conceivably could serve legitimate, nondiscriminatory state interests:

> Without deciding whether [the provision] would be valid if enacted today without any impermissible motivation, we simply observe that its original enactment was motivated by a desire to discriminate against blacks on account of race and the section continues to this day to have that effect. As such, it violates equal protection. . . .

Hunter thus teaches that the impermissible anti-Catholic motivations that created the Blaine Amendments should not be excused simply because many decades have elapsed since the provisions were enacted.

3. School Prayer

USC law professor Erwin Chemerinsky writes: "[f]ew Supreme Court decisions have been as controversial as those which declared unconstitutional prayers and Bible readings in public schools." ERWIN CHEMERINSKY, CONSTITUTIONAL LAW — PRINCIPLES AND POLICIES 997 (1997). In *Engel v. Vitale*, 370 U.S. 421 (1962), the Court found a non-denominational prayer composed by the New York Board of Regents ("Almighty God, we acknowledge our dependence upon Thee, and we beg Thy blessings upon us, our parents, our teachers and our Country") to violate the Establishment Clause. What would George Washington have thought? In some ways, *Engel* was predictable because it extended the exclusionary foundation laid in *Everson*. Once again, Justice Black argued that the " Establishment Clause, unlike the Free Exercise Clause, does not depend upon any showing of direct governmental compulsion." *Engel*, 370 U.S. at 430. Justice Stewart in dissent maintained the contrary originalist view, with numerous references to prayers by courts, congressmen and presidents, and his argument that the establishment limitation is aimed at faith coerced by law, not the expression of faith generally, whether that expression is by a public or private person.

The year following *Engel*, Black's view would once again prevail in *School District v. Schempp*, 374 U.S. 203 (1963), invalidating a Pennsylvania law that provided that "At least ten verses from the Holy Bible shall be read, without comment, at the opening of each public school on each school day. Any child shall be excused from such Bible reading, or attending such Bible reading, upon the written request of his parent or guardian." *Id.* at 205. Writing for the majority, Justice Clark defined neutrality as a "purpose and a primary effect that neither advances nor inhibits religion." *Id.* at 222. This recital should be familiar. It was to become the second, and most excluding, prong of the Court's establishment standard in *Lemon*. Again Justice Stewart dissented, calling the exclusionary view "doctrinaire" and indicating that it fails to understand the countless ways in which religion and the government interact. *Id.* at 309 (Stewart, J., dissenting). Stewart concluded, "[i]n the absence of coercion upon those who do not wish to participate, . . . such provisions cannot . . . be held to represent the type of support of religion barred by the Establishment Clause." *Id.* at 316 (Stewart, J., dissenting).

Fundamentally, the allowance or disallowance of school prayer raises issues of religious tolerance in a pluralistic society. While popularly it may be thought that any recital of prayer is intolerant of different prayer traditions, Erwin Griswold, a dean of the Harvard Law School and later Solicitor General, had a different perspective:

> When the prayer is recited, if [a] child or his parents feel that he cannot participate, he may stand or sit, in respectful attention . . . . It is said that this is bad, because it sets him apart from other children. It is even said that there is an element of compulsion in this. . . . But is this the way it should be looked at? The child of a nonconforming or minority group is, to be sure, different in his beliefs. That is what it means to be a member of a minority. . . . And is it not desirable that, at the same time, he experiences and learns the fact that his difference is tolerated and accepted? . . . But he, too, has the opportunity to be tolerant. He allows the majority of the group to follow their own tradition, perhaps coming to understand and to respect what they feel is significant to them.

Erwin Griswold, *Absolute Is in the Dark — A Discussion of the Approach of the Supreme Court to Constitutional Questions*, 8 Utah L. Rev. 167, 177 (1963).

In *Wallace v. Jaffree*, 472 U.S. 38 (1985), below, the Court fully disapproves of even the hint of religion in striking down an Alabama law allowing schools to set aside one minute "for meditation or voluntary prayer." *Id.* at 40. Justice Stevens asserts that "the individual freedom of conscience protected by the First Amendment embraces the right to select any religious faith or none at all." *Id.* at 53. Justice Stevens admits that this was not the original meaning of the Constitution, but it is the interpretation that has emerged from the "crucible of litigation." *Id.* at 52. Justice Rehnquist supplies a substantial historical criticism of the Stevens' exclusionary view in his dissent. *Id.* at 91–114 (Rehnquist, J., dissenting).

WALLACE v. JAFFREE
472 U.S. 38 (1985)

Justice Stevens delivered the opinion of the Court.

At an early stage of this litigation, the constitutionality of three Alabama statutes was questioned: (1) § 16-1-20, enacted in 1978, which authorized a 1-minute period of silence in all public schools "for meditation"; (2) § 16-1-20.1, enacted in 1981, which authorized a period of silence "for meditation or voluntary prayer"; and (3) § 16-1-20.2, enacted in 1982, which authorized teachers to lead "willing students" in a prescribed prayer to "Almighty God . . . the Creator and Supreme Judge of the world."

At the preliminary-injunction stage of this case, the District Court distinguished § 16-1-20 from the other two statutes. It then held that there was "nothing wrong" with § 16-1-20. . . .

The Court of Appeals agreed with the District Court's initial interpretation of the purpose of both § 16-1-20.1 and § 16-1-20.2, and held them both unconstitutional. We have already affirmed the Court of Appeals' holding with respect to § 16-1-20.2. Moreover, appellees have not questioned the holding that § 16-1-20 is valid. Thus, the narrow question for decision is whether § 16-1-20.1, which authorizes a period of silence for "meditation or voluntary prayer," is a law respecting the establishment of religion within the meaning of the First Amendment.

I

. . . With respect to § 16-1-20.1 [meditation or voluntary prayer] and § 16-1-20.2, [which permitted teachers to lead willing students in the prescribed prayer to "Almighty God . . . the Creator and Supreme Judge of the World,"] the Court of Appeals stated that "both statutes advance and encourage religious activities."

II

Our unanimous affirmance of the Court of Appeals' judgment concerning § 16-1-20.2 makes it unnecessary to comment at length on the District Court's remarkable conclusion that the Federal Constitution imposes no obstacle to Alabama's establishment of a state religion. Before analyzing the precise issue that is presented to us, it is nevertheless appropriate to recall how firmly embedded in our constitutional jurisprudence is the proposition that the several States have no greater power to restrain the individual freedoms protected by the First Amendment than does the Congress of the United States.

As is plain from its text, the First Amendment was adopted to curtail the power of Congress to interfere with the individual's freedom to believe, to worship, and to express himself in accordance with the dictates of his own conscience. Until the Fourteenth Amendment was added to the Constitution, the First Amendment's restraints on the exercise of federal power simply did not apply to the States. But when the Constitution was amended to prohibit any State from depriving any person of liberty without due process of law, that Amendment imposed the same substantive limitations on the States' power to legislate that the First Amendment had always imposed on the Congress' power. This Court has confirmed and endorsed this elementary proposition of law time and time again.

. . . At one time it was thought that [the Establishment Clause] merely proscribed the preference of one Christian sect over another, but would not require equal respect for the conscience of the infidel, the atheist, or the adherent of a non-Christian faith such as Islam or Judaism. But when the underlying principle has been examined in the crucible of litigation, the Court has unambiguously concluded that the individual freedom of conscience protected by the First Amendment embraces the right to select any religious faith or none at all. This conclusion derives support not only from the interest in respecting the individual's freedom of conscience, but also from the conviction that religious beliefs worthy of respect are the product of free and voluntary choice by the faithful[17]

. . . .

IV

The legislative intent to return prayer to the public schools is, of course, quite different from merely protecting every student's right to engage in voluntary prayer during an appropriate moment of silence during the schoolday. The 1978 statute already protected that right, containing nothing that prevented any student from engaging in voluntary prayer during a silent minute of meditation. Appellants have not identified any secular purpose that was not fully served by § 16-1-20 before the enactment of § 16-1-20.1. Thus, only two conclusions are consistent with the text of § 16-1-20.1: (1) the statute was enacted to convey a message of state endorsement and promotion of prayer; or (2) the statute was enacted for no purpose. No one suggests that the statute was nothing but a meaningless or irrational act.

. . . The legislature enacted § 16-1-20.1, despite the existence of § 16-1-20 for the sole purpose of expressing the State's endorsement of prayer activities for one minute at the beginning of each schoolday. The addition of "or voluntary prayer" indicates that the State intended to characterize prayer as a favored practice. Such an endorsement is not consistent with the established principle that the government must pursue a course of complete neutrality toward religion.

The judgment of the Court of Appeals is affirmed.

It is so ordered.

JUSTICE POWELL, concurring. [Omitted.]

JUSTICE O'CONNOR, concurring in the judgment. [Omitted.]

CHIEF JUSTICE BURGER, dissenting.

Some who trouble to read the opinions in these cases will find it ironic — perhaps even bizarre — that on the very day we heard arguments in the cases, the Court's session opened with an invocation for Divine protection. . . .

. . . . [A]ll of the opinions fail to mention that the sponsor also testified that one of his purposes in drafting and sponsoring the moment-of-silence bill was to clear up a widespread misunderstanding that a schoolchild is legally *prohibited* from engaging in silent, individual prayer once he steps inside a public school building. . . .

---

[17] [*] [Justice Stevens overlooks a possibility. As salutary, and wise, as individual choice in matters of conscience may be, might it not be possible to see the framers as *both* allowing individuals the right to select any religious faith or none at all *and* simultaneously endorsing, as a matter of governing philosophy in the Declaration and myriad other legislative actions, the importance of religion for civic virtue? — Eds.]

The several preceding opinions conclude that the principal difference between § 16-1-20.1 and its predecessor statute proves that the sole purpose behind the inclusion of the phrase "or voluntary prayer" in § 16-1-20.1 was to endorse and promote prayer. This reasoning is simply a subtle way of focusing exclusively on the religious component of the statute rather than examining the statute as a whole. Such logic — if it can be called that — would lead the Court to hold, for example, that a state may enact a statute that provides reimbursement for bus transportation to the parents of all schoolchildren, but may not *add* parents of parochial school students to an existing program providing reimbursement for parents of public school students. Congress amended the statutory Pledge of Allegiance 31 years ago to add the words "under God." Do the several opinions in support of the judgment today render the Pledge unconstitutional? That would be the consequence of their method of focusing on the difference between § 16-1-20.1 and its predecessor statute rather than examining § 16-1-20.1 as a whole. Any such holding would of course make a mockery of our decisionmaking in Establishment Clause cases. . . .

(d) The notion that the Alabama statute is a step toward creating an established church borders on, if it does not trespass into, the ridiculous. The statute does not remotely threaten religious liberty; it affirmatively furthers the values of religious freedom and tolerance that the Establishment Clause was designed to protect. Without pressuring those who do not wish to pray, the statute simply creates an opportunity to think, to plan, or to pray if one wishes — as Congress does by providing chaplains and chapels. It accommodates the purely private, voluntary religious choices of the individual pupils who wish to pray while at the same time creating a time for nonreligious reflection for those who do not choose to pray. . . .

The mountains have labored and brought forth a mouse.[18]

Justice White, dissenting.

. . . As I read the filed opinions, a majority of the Court would approve statutes that provided for a moment of silence but did not mention prayer. But if a student asked whether he could pray during that moment, it is difficult to believe that the teacher could not answer in the affirmative. If that is the case, I would not invalidate a statute that at the outset provided the legislative answer to the question "May I pray?" This is so even if the Alabama statute is infirm, which I do not believe it is, because of its peculiar legislative history.

I appreciate Justice Rehnquist's explication of the history of the Religion Clauses of the First Amendment. Against that history, it would be quite under-standable if we undertook to reassess our cases dealing with these Clauses, particularly those dealing with the Establishment Clause. Of course, I have been out of step with many of the Court's decisions dealing with this subject matter, and it is thus not surprising that I would support a basic reconsideration of our precedents.

---

[18] [6] Horace, Epistles, bk. III (Ars Poetica), line 139.

JUSTICE REHNQUIST, dissenting.

Thirty-eight years ago this Court, in *Everson v. Board of Education* (1947), summarized its exegesis of Establishment Clause doctrine thus:

> "In the words of Jefferson, the clause against establishment of religion by law was intended to erect 'a wall of separation between church and State.' *Reynolds v. United States* [(1879)]."

This language from *Reynolds*, a case involving the Free Exercise Clause of the First Amendment rather than the Establishment Clause, quoted from Thomas Jefferson's letter to the Danbury Baptist Association the phrase "I contemplate with sovereign reverence that act of the whole American people which declared that their legislature should 'make no law respecting an establishment of religion, or prohibiting the free exercise thereof,' thus building a wall of separation between church and State." 8 WRITINGS OF THOMAS JEFFERSON 113 (H. Washington ed., 1861).

It is impossible to build sound constitutional doctrine upon a mistaken understanding of constitutional history, but unfortunately the Establishment Clause has been expressly freighted with Jefferson's misleading metaphor for nearly 40 years. Thomas Jefferson was of course in France at the time the constitutional Amendments known as the Bill of Rights were passed by Congress and ratified by the States. His letter to the Danbury Baptist Association was a short note of courtesy, written 14 years after the Amendments were passed by Congress. He would seem to any detached observer as a less than ideal source of contemporary history as to the meaning of the Religion Clauses of the First Amendment.

Jefferson's fellow Virginian, James Madison, with whom he was joined in the battle for the enactment of the Virginia Statute of Religious Liberty of 1786, did play as large a part as anyone in the drafting of the Bill of Rights. He had two advantages over Jefferson in this regard: he was present in the United States, and he was a leading Member of the First Congress. But when we turn to the record of the proceedings in the First Congress leading up to the adoption of the Establishment Clause of the Constitution, including Madison's significant contributions thereto, we see a far different picture of its purpose than the highly simplified "wall of separation between church and State."

During the debates in the Thirteen Colonies over ratification of the Constitution, one of the arguments frequently used by opponents of ratification was that without a Bill of Rights guaranteeing individual liberty the new general Government carried with it a potential for tyranny. The typical response to this argument on the part of those who favored ratification was that the general Government established by the Constitution had only delegated powers, and that these delegated powers were so limited that the Government would have no occasion to violate individual liberties. This response satisfied some, but not others, and of the 11 Colonies which ratified the Constitution by early 1789, 5 proposed one or another amendments guaranteeing individual liberty. Three — New Hampshire, New York, and Virginia — included in one form or another a declaration of religious freedom. Rhode Island and North Carolina flatly refused to ratify the Constitution in the absence of amendments in the nature of a Bill of Rights. Virginia and North Carolina proposed identical guarantees of religious freedom:

"[A]ll men have an equal, natural and unalienable right to the free exercise of religion, according to the dictates of conscience, and . . . no particular religious sect or society ought to be favored or established, by law, in preference to others."

On June 8, 1789, James Madison rose in the House of Representatives and "reminded the House that this was the day that he had heretofore named for bringing forward amendments to the Constitution." 1 ANNALS OF CONG. 424 (Joseph Gales ed., 1789). Madison's subsequent remarks in urging the House to adopt his drafts of the proposed amendments were less those of a dedicated advocate of the wisdom of such measures than those of a prudent statesman seeking the enactment of measures sought by a number of his fellow citizens which could surely do no harm and might do a great deal of good. . . .

The language Madison proposed for what ultimately became the Religion Clauses of the First Amendment was this:

"The civil rights of none shall be abridged on account of religious belief or worship, nor shall any national religion be established, nor shall the full and equal rights of conscience be in any manner, or on any pretext, infringed."

[Justice Rehnquist then reviewed the debate in Congress and various amendments to Madison's initial proposal, reprinted above at Part I.B.3, which ultimately produced the language of the Religion Clauses of the First Amendment:]

"Congress shall make no law respecting an establishment of religion, or prohibiting the free exercise thereof."

The House and the Senate both accepted this language on successive days, and the Amendment was proposed in this form.

On the basis of the record of these proceedings in the House of Representatives, James Madison was undoubtedly the most important architect among the Members of the House of the Amendments which became the Bill of Rights. . . . His original language "nor shall any national religion be established" obviously does not conform to the "wall of separation" between church and State idea which latter-day commentators have ascribed to him. His explanation on the floor of the meaning of his language — "that Congress should not establish a religion, and enforce the legal observation of it by law" is of the same ilk. When he replied to Huntington in the debate over the proposal which came from the Select Committee of the House, he urged that the language "no religion shall be established by law" should be amended by inserting the word "national" in front of the word "religion."

It seems indisputable from these glimpses of Madison's thinking, as reflected by actions on the floor of the House in 1789, that he saw the Amendment as designed to prohibit the establishment of a national religion, and perhaps to prevent discrimination among sects. He did not see it as requiring neutrality on the part of government between religion and irreligion. Thus the Court's opinion in *Everson* — while correct in bracketing Madison and Jefferson together in their exertions in their home State leading to the enactment of the Virginia Statute of Religious Liberty — is totally incorrect in suggesting that Madison carried these views onto the floor of the United States House of Representatives when he proposed the language which would ultimately become the Bill of Rights.

The repetition of this error in the Court's opinion in *Illinois ex rel. McCollum v. Board of Education* (1948), and, *inter alia, Engel v. Vitale* (1962), does not make it any sounder historically. Finally, in *Abington School District v. Schempp* (1963), the Court made the truly remarkable statement that "the views of Madison and Jefferson, preceded by Roger Williams, came to be incorporated not only in the Federal Constitution but likewise in those of most of our States" (footnote omitted). On the basis of what evidence we have, this statement is demonstrably incorrect as a matter of history. And its repetition in varying forms in succeeding opinions of the Court can give it no more authority than it possesses as a matter of fact; *stare decisis* may bind courts as to matters of law, but it cannot bind them as to matters of history.

None of the other Members of Congress who spoke during the August 15th debate expressed the slightest indication that they thought the language before them from the Select Committee, or the evil to be aimed at, would require that the Government be absolutely neutral as between religion and irreligion. The evil to be aimed at, so far as those who spoke were concerned, appears to have been the establishment of a national church, and perhaps the preference of one religious sect over another; but it was definitely not concerned about whether the Government might aid all religions evenhandedly. If one were to follow the advice of JUSTICE BRENNAN, concurring in *Abington School District v. Schempp*, and construe the Amendment in the light of what particular "practices . . . challenged threaten those consequences which the Framers deeply feared; whether, in short, they tend to promote that type of interdependence between religion and state which the First Amendment was designed to prevent," one would have to say that the First Amendment Establishment Clause should be read no more broadly than to prevent the establishment of a national religion or the governmental preference of one religious sect over another.

The actions of the First Congress, which reenacted the Northwest Ordinance for the governance of the Northwest Territory in 1789, confirm the view that Congress did not mean that the Government should be neutral between religion and irreligion. The House of Representatives took up the Northwest Ordinance on the same day as Madison introduced his proposed amendments which became the Bill of Rights; while at that time the Federal Government was of course not bound by draft amendments to the Constitution which had not yet been proposed by Congress, to say nothing of ratified by the States, it seems highly unlikely that the House of Representatives would simultaneously consider proposed amendments to the Constitution and enact an important piece of territorial legislation which conflicted with the intent of those proposals. The Northwest Ordinance, 1 Stat. 50 (1789), reenacted the Northwest Ordinance of 1787 and provided that "[r]eligion, morality, and knowledge, being necessary to good government and the happiness of mankind, schools and the means of education shall forever be encouraged." Land grants for schools in the Northwest Territory were not limited to public schools. It was not until 1845 that Congress limited land grants in the new States and Territories to nonsectarian schools.

As the United States moved from the 18th into the 19th century, Congress appropriated time and again public moneys in support of sectarian Indian education carried on by religious organizations. Typical of these was Jefferson's treaty with the Kaskaskia Indians, which provided annual cash support for the Tribe's Roman Catholic priest and church. It was not until 1897, when aid to sectarian education for Indians had reached $500,000 annually, that Congress decided thereafter to cease appropriating money for education in sectarian schools. This history shows the fallacy of the notion found in *Everson* that "no tax in any amount" may be levied for religious activities in any form.

Joseph Story, a Member of this Court from 1811 to 1845, and during much of that time a professor at the Harvard Law School, published by far the most comprehensive treatise on the United States Constitution that had then appeared. Volume 2 of Story's COMMENTARIES ON THE CONSTITUTION OF THE UNITED STATES 630–632 (5th ed. 1891) discussed the meaning of the Establishment Clause of the First Amendment this way:

> "Probably at the time of the adoption of the Constitution, and of the amendment to it now under consideration [First Amendment], the general if not the universal sentiment in America was, that Christianity ought to receive encouragement from the State so far as was not incompatible with the private rights of conscience and the freedom of religious worship. An attempt to level all religions, and to make it a matter of state policy to hold all in utter indifference, would have created universal disapprobation, if not universal indignation."

Thomas Cooley's eminence as a legal authority rivaled that of Story. Cooley stated in his treatise entitled CONSTITUTIONAL LIMITATIONS that aid to a particular religious sect was prohibited by the United States Constitution, but he went on to say:

> "But while thus careful to establish, protect, and defend religious freedom and equality, the American constitutions contain no provisions which prohibit the authorities from such solemn recognition of a superintending Providence in public transactions and exercises as the general religious sentiment of mankind inspires, and as seems meet and proper in finite and dependent beings. Whatever may be the shades of religious belief, all must acknowledge the fitness of recognizing in important human affairs the superintending care and control of the Great Governor of the Universe, and of acknowledging with thanksgiving his boundless favors, or bowing in contrition when visited with the penalties of his broken laws. No principle of constitutional law is violated when thanksgiving or fast days are appointed; when chaplains are designated for the army and navy; when legislative sessions are opened with prayer or the reading of the Scriptures; or when religious teaching is encouraged by a general exemption of the houses of religious worship from taxation for the support of State government. Undoubtedly the spirit of the Constitution will require, in all these cases, that care be taken to avoid discrimination in favor of or against any one religious denomination or sect; but the power to do any of these things does not become unconstitutional simply because of its susceptibility to abuse. . . ."

Cooley added that

> "[t]his public recognition of religious worship, however, is not based entirely, perhaps not even mainly, upon a sense of what is due to the Supreme Being himself as the author of all good and of all law; but the same reasons of state policy which induce the government to aid institutions of charity and seminaries of instruction will incline it also to foster religious worship and religious institutions, as conservators of the public morals and valuable, if not indispensable, assistants to the preservation of the public order."

It would seem from this evidence that the Establishment Clause of the First Amendment had acquired a well-accepted meaning: it forbade establishment of a national religion, and forbade preference among religious sects or denominations. Indeed, the first American dictionary defined the word "establishment" as "the act of establishing, founding, ratifying or ordaining," such as in "[t]he episcopal form of religion, so called, in England." The Establishment Clause did not require government neutrality between religion and irreligion nor did it prohibit the Federal Government from providing nondiscriminatory aid to religion. There is simply no historical foundation for the proposition that the Framers intended to build the "wall of separation" that was constitutionalized in *Everson.*

Notwithstanding the absence of a historical basis for this theory of rigid separation, the wall idea might well have served as a useful albeit misguided analytical concept, had it led this Court to unified and principled results in Establishment Clause cases. The opposite, unfortunately, has been true; in the 38 years since *Everson* our Establishment Clause cases have been neither principled nor unified. Our recent opinions, many of them hopelessly divided pluralities, have with embarrassing candor conceded that the "wall of separation" is merely a "blurred, indistinct, and variable barrier," which "is not wholly accurate" and can only be "dimly perceived."

Whether due to its lack of historical support or its practical unworkability, the *Everson* "wall" has proved all but useless as a guide to sound constitutional adjudication. It illustrates only too well the wisdom of Benjamin Cardozo's observation that "[m]etaphors in law are to be narrowly watched, for starting as devices to liberate thought, they end often by enslaving it."

But the greatest injury of the "wall" notion is its mischievous diversion of judges from the actual intentions of the drafters of the Bill of Rights. The "crucible of litigation," is well adapted to adjudicating factual disputes on the basis of testimony presented in court, but no amount of repetition of historical errors in judicial opinions can make the errors true. The "wall of separation between church and State" is a metaphor based on bad history, a metaphor which has proved useless as a guide to judging. It should be frankly and explicitly abandoned.

The Court has more recently attempted to add some mortar to *Everson*'s wall through the three-part test of *Lemon v. Kurtzman,* which served at first to offer a more useful test for purposes of the Establishment Clause than did the "wall" metaphor. Generally stated, the *Lemon* test proscribes state action that has a sectarian purpose or effect, or causes an impermissible governmental entanglement with religion.

Lemon cited *Board of Education v. Allen* (1968), as the source of the "purpose" and "effect" prongs of the three-part test. The *Allen* opinion explains, however, how it inherited the purpose and effect elements from *Schempp* and *Everson*, both of which contain the historical errors described above. Thus the purpose and effect prongs have the same historical deficiencies as the wall concept itself: they are in no way based on either the language or intent of the drafters.

The secular purpose prong has proven mercurial in application because it has never been fully defined, and we have never fully stated how the test is to operate. If the purpose prong is intended to void those aids to sectarian institutions accompanied by a stated legislative purpose to aid religion, the prong will condemn nothing so long as the legislature utters a secular purpose and says nothing about aiding religion. Thus the constitutionality of a statute may depend upon what the legislators put into the legislative history and, more importantly, what they leave out. The purpose prong means little if it only requires the legislature to express any secular purpose and omit all sectarian references, because legislators might do just that. Faced with a valid legislative secular purpose, we could not properly ignore that purpose without a factual basis for doing so.

However, if the purpose prong is aimed to void all statutes enacted with the intent to aid sectarian institutions, whether stated or not, then most statutes providing any aid, such as textbooks or bus rides for sectarian school children, will fail because one of the purposes behind every statute, whether stated or not, is to aid the target of its largesse. In other words, if the purpose prong requires an absence of *any* intent to aid sectarian institutions, whether or not expressed, few state laws in this area could pass the test, and we would be required to void some state aids to religion which we have already upheld.

The entanglement prong of the *Lemon* test came from *Walz v. Tax Comm'n* (1970). *Walz* involved a constitutional challenge to New York's time-honored practice of providing state property tax exemptions to church property used in worship. The *Walz* opinion refused to "undermine the ultimate constitutional objective [of the Establishment Clause] as illuminated by history," and upheld the tax exemption. The Court examined the historical relationship between the State and church when church property was in issue, and determined that the challenged tax exemption did not so entangle New York with the church as to cause an intrusion or interference with religion. Interferences with religion should arguably be dealt with under the Free Exercise Clause, but the entanglement inquiry in *Walz* was consistent with that case's broad survey of the relationship between state taxation and religious property.

We have not always followed *Walz*'s reflective inquiry into entanglement, however. One of the difficulties with the entanglement prong is that, when divorced from the logic of *Walz*, it creates an "insoluable paradox" in school aid cases: we have required aid to parochial schools to be closely watched lest it be put to sectarian use, yet this close supervision itself will create an entanglement. For example, in *Wolman* [*v. Walter* (1977)], the Court in part struck the State's nondiscriminatory provision of buses for parochial school field trips, because the state supervision of sectarian officials in charge of field trips would be too onerous. This type of self-defeating result is certainly not required to ensure that States do not establish religions.

The entanglement test as applied in cases like *Wolman* also ignores the myriad state administrative regulations properly placed upon sectarian institutions such as curriculum, attendance, and certification requirements for sectarian schools, or fire and safety regulations for churches. Avoiding entanglement between church and State may be an important consideration in a case like *Walz*, but if the entanglement prong were applied to all state and church relations in the automatic manner in which it has been applied to school aid cases, the State could hardly require anything of church-related institutions as a condition for receipt of financial assistance.

These difficulties arise because the *Lemon* test has no more grounding in the history of the First Amendment than does the wall theory upon which it rests. The three-part test represents a determined effort to craft a workable rule from a historically faulty doctrine; but the rule can only be as sound as the doctrine it attempts to service. The three-part test has simply not provided adequate standards for deciding Establishment Clause cases, as this Court has slowly come to realize. Even worse, the *Lemon* test has caused this Court to fracture into unworkable plurality opinions, depending upon how each of the three factors applies to a certain state action. The results from our school services cases show the difficulty we have encountered in making the *Lemon* test yield principled results.

For example, a State may lend to parochial school children geography textbooks[19] that contain maps of the United States, but the State may not lend maps of the United States for use in geography class.[20] A State may lend textbooks on American colonial history, but it may not lend a film on George Washington, or a film projector to show it in history class. A State may lend classroom workbooks, but may not lend workbooks in which the parochial school children write, thus rendering them nonreusable.[21] A State may pay for bus transportation to religious schools[22] but may not pay for bus transportation from the parochial school to the public zoo or natural history museum for a field trip.[23] A State may pay for diagnostic services conducted in the parochial school but therapeutic services must be given in a different building; speech and hearing "services" conducted by the State inside the sectarian school are forbidden, *Meek v. Pittenger* (1975), but the State may conduct speech and hearing diagnostic testing inside the sectarian school. *Wolman.* Exceptional parochial school students may receive counseling, but it must take place outside of the parochial school,[24] such as in a trailer parked down the street. A State may give cash to a parochial school to pay for the administration

---

[19] [7] *Board of Education v. Allen* (1968).

[20] [8] *Meek [v. Pittenger* (1975)]. A science book is permissible, a science kit is not.

[21] [9] *See Meek, supra.*

[22] [10] *Everson v. Board of Education* (1947).

[23] [11] *Wolman, supra*

[24] [12] *Wolman, supra; Meek, supra.*

of state-written tests and state-ordered reporting services,[25] but it may not provide funds for teacher-prepared tests on secular subjects.[26] Religious instruction may not be given in public school,[27] but the public school may release students during the day for religion classes elsewhere, and may enforce attendance at those classes with its truancy laws.[28]

These results violate the historically sound principle "that the Establishment Clause does not forbid governments . . . to [provide] general welfare under which benefits are distributed to private individuals, even though many of those individuals may elect to use those benefits in ways that 'aid' religious instruction or worship." It is not surprising in the light of this record that our most recent opinions have expressed doubt on the usefulness of the *Lemon* test.

Although the test initially provided helpful assistance, we soon began describing the test as only a "guideline". . . . We have noted that the *Lemon* test is "not easily applied," and . . . under the *Lemon* test we have "sacrifice[d] clarity and predictability for flexibility." In *Lynch* [*v. Donnelly* (1984),] we reiterated that the *Lemon* test has never been binding on the Court, and we cited two cases where we had declined to apply it.

If a constitutional theory has no basis in the history of the amendment it seeks to interpret, is difficult to apply and yields unprincipled results, I see little use in it. The "crucible of litigation," has produced only consistent unpredictability, and today's effort is just a continuation of "the sisyphean task of trying to patch together the 'blurred, indistinct and variable barrier' described in *Lemon v. Kurtzman*." We have done much straining since 1947, but still we admit that we can only "dimly perceive" the *Everson* wall. Our perception has been clouded not by the Constitution but by the mists of an unnecessary metaphor.

The true meaning of the Establishment Clause can only be seen in its history. As drafters of our Bill of Rights, the Framers inscribed the principles that control today. Any deviation from their intentions frustrates the permanence of that Charter and will only lead to the type of unprincipled decisionmaking that has plagued our Establishment Clause cases since *Everson*.

The Framers intended the Establishment Clause to prohibit the designation of any church as a "national" one. The Clause was also designed to stop the Federal Government from asserting a preference for one religious denomination or sect over others. Given the "incorporation" of the Establishment Clause as against the States via the Fourteenth Amendment in *Everson*, States are prohibited as well from establishing a religion or discriminating between sects. As its history abundantly shows, however, nothing in the Establishment Clause requires government to be strictly neutral between religion and irreligion, nor does that Clause prohibit Congress or the States from pursuing legitimate secular ends through nondiscriminatory sectarian means.

---

[25] [13] [*Comm. For Pub. Educ. and Religious Liberty v.*] *Regan* [(1980)].

[26] [14] *Levitt* [*v. Committee For Pub. Educ. and Religious Liberty* (1973)].

[27] [15] *Illinois ex rel. McCollum v. Board of Education* (1948).

[28] [16] *Zorach v. Clauson* (1952).

The Court strikes down the Alabama statute because the State wished to "characterize prayer as a favored practice." It would come as much of a shock to those who drafted the Bill of Rights as it will to a large number of thoughtful Americans today to learn that the Constitution, as construed by the majority, prohibits the Alabama Legislature from "endorsing" prayer. George Washington himself, at the request of the very Congress which passed the Bill of Rights, proclaimed a day of "public thanksgiving and prayer, to be observed by acknowledging with grateful hearts the many and signal favors of Almighty God." History must judge whether it was the Father of his Country in 1789, or a majority of the Court today, which has strayed from the meaning of the Establishment Clause.

The State surely has a secular interest in regulating the manner in which public schools are conducted. Nothing in the Establishment Clause of the First Amendment, properly understood, prohibits any such generalized "endorsement" of prayer. I would therefore reverse the judgment of the Court of Appeals.

NOTES AND QUESTIONS

1.   Is the Rehnquist view in *Wallace* non-preferentialist? Non-preferentialism is the view that the Establishment Clause prohibits discrimination among religious sects, but that nothing requires government to be strictly neutral between religion and irreligion. Non-preferentialism received its most recent exposition in Justice Thomas' concurrence in *Rosenberger v. Rector*, considered earlier as part of the equal protection idea. However, as seen above, this ground was first broken by then-Justice Rehnquist in *Wallace v. Jaffree*. Both Justice Rehnquist and later Justice Thomas argue that Madison and the Framers intended the Establishment Clause to prohibit a national religion as well as discrimination among denominations. They rely especially upon Madison's *Memorial and Remonstrance Against Religious Assessments*, in which Madison criticized a Virginia plan to assess a tax in order to "support . . . clergy in the performance of their function of teaching religion." *Rosenberger*, 515 U.S. at 853 (Thomas, J., concurring).

2.   In response to litigation challenging the constitutionality of the practice at the public high school in Santa Fe, Texas, allowing the "student council chaplain" to deliver a prayer over the public address system before each varsity football game, the Santa Fe Independent School District adopted a series of policies by which it was left entirely to the students to decide, first, if there should be a "message, statement, or invocation" prior to football games and, if so, who should deliver it. In *Santa Fe Independent Sch. Dist. v. Doe*, 530 U.S. 290 (2000), Justice Stevens, writing for the Court, invalidated the policy. Rejecting the school's contention that the pre-game invocation was private speech rather than government prayer because of the election mechanism, Justice Stevens found that the facially neutral majority-rule policy afforded no access to the pre-game invocation slot for minority views, and that the school had not sufficiently distanced itself from the student-led prayer. How well does Justice Stevens reconcile the competing constitutional considerations — preventing government or public schools from coercing religious belief while ensuring that the free speech interests of students, which might voluntarily include prayer, not be censored? In dissent, Chief Justice Rehnquist, joined by Justices Scalia and Thomas, found the tone of Justice Stevens' majority opinion

"disturbing" because "it bristles with hostility to all things religious in public life." *Id.* at 318. "Neither the holding nor the tone of the opinion is faithful to the meaning of the Establishment Clause," the Chief Justice continued, "when it is recalled that George Washington himself, at the request of the very Congress which passed the Bill of Rights, proclaimed a day of 'public thanksgiving and prayer, to be observed by acknowledging with grateful hearts the many and signal favors of Almighty God.'" *Id.* (quoting Presidential Proclamation, 1 MESSAGES AND PAPERS OF THE PRESIDENTS, 1789–1897, p. 64 (J. Richardson ed. 1897)).

3. Does the case give adequate guidance to school officials? Before this case, several lower courts had suggested to school principals seeking to navigate the equally important duties of avoiding religious preference and religious censorship that they could successfully do so by letting the students decide by vote. *See, e.g., Jones v. Clear Creek Independent School District*, 977 F.2d 963 (5th Cir. 1992). Is this still possible? According to the *Santa Fe* majority, granting the student body the power to elect a speaker that may choose to pray, "regardless of the students' ultimate use of it, is not acceptable." The reason elections are off-limits is ascribed by the Court to a supposed free speech duty of the government to remain viewpoint neutral. The government, indeed, has this duty, but doesn't it turn matters on its head to say that the government has a duty to insure that private individuals remain viewpoint neutral? The majority does state that it is not its intent to invalidate all student elections. Rather, it says, it is forbidden where a religious message is attributable to the school, not just the student. Because that happened in *Santa Fe* only because of the school's pre-policy behavior, the Court may be less inclined to censor private religious speech in a context where school officials were more circumspect.

4. Is resolving the scope of school prayer important? In a dissent to a lower court decision pre-dating *Santa Fe*, Judge Edith Jones of the Fifth Circuit explains why she thinks it is.

IV. *Why This Case Matters*

. . . The panel's decision [in *Ingebretsen v. Jackson Public School District*, 88 F. 3d 274 (5th Cir. 1996),] is the latest in a long line of cases whose inevitable consequence has been to remake society in a secular image. Two examples suffice: courts have held that the mere existence of a Good Friday holiday "establishes" the Christian religion, and the venerable inscription on a courthouse "The World Needs God" likewise constitution-ally offends . . . someone. Only by recognizing the absurdity of holding otherwise have courts allowed us still to pledge that we are "one nation under God, indivisible" and to maintain "In God We Trust" on the currency. When our cultural heritage and tradition, indeed the three-millennial history of the Western world threatens to be erased by three decades of federal court pronouncements, something is amiss. As Prof. Stephen Carter arrestingly concluded, our elite cultural institutions, including federal courts, have imposed on us an historically unprecedented "culture of disbelief."[29]

The elites' tin ear for religious belief and practice has been particularly evident in cases regarding the public schools. Federal courts often seem unable to draw fundamental distinctions between school-sponsored religious "establishment" and benign teaching about religion or, in this case, students' constitutionally protected free exercise of speech and religion. School officials, averse to the emotional and financial costs of litigation, have systematically excised religious references from school curricula and activities in response to the caselaw. This widespread Establishment Clause misconstruction occurs notwithstanding that Supreme Court justices have repeatedly acknowledged the importance of teaching about religion in public schools and that no Supreme Court authority limits students' nondisruptive religious self-expression. Not to belabor the point, I note that Congress passed and the Supreme Court upheld the Equal Access Act, a law guaranteeing students' rights to meet in religious clubs on school property, in order to overturn lower federal court decisions to the contrary. Only last summer, President Clinton spoke of the problem of hostility to religion in public schools and instructed the Departments of Justice and Education to formulate guidelines for the protection of public schools students' religious speech and conduct.[30] Every time a federal court writes an unduly broad Establishment Clause decision concerning public schools, we encourage further misunderstandings, to the detriment of students' constitutional rights and the goal of teaching about religion in public schools.

The courts' broad decisions in this area are not only in my view, uncompelled by precedent, they are also extraordinarily shortsighted. Decisions fostering rigidly secular public education strip school officials of moral tools that lie at the heart of the educational process. As the Reverend Martin Luther King explained:

> "The function of education, therefore, is to teach one to think intensively and to think critically. But education which stops with efficiency may prove the greatest menace to society. The most dangerous criminal may be the man gifted with reason but with no morals.

> "We must remember that intelligence is not enough. Intelligence plus character — that is the goal of true education."

THE WORDS OF MARTIN LUTHER KING, JR. 41 (Coretta Scott King ed., 1993).

---

[29] [15] STEPHEN L. CARTER, THE CULTURE OF DISBELIEF: HOW AMERICAN LAW AND POLITICS TRIVIALIZE RELIGIOUS DEVOTION (1993).

[30] [19] See President's Directive to the Education Dept., and News Release of U.S. Dept. of Education, Aug. 17, 1995. The Directive states that the President "share[s] the concern and frustration that many Americans feel about situations where the protections accorded by the First Amendment are not recognized or understood." President Clinton instructed the Departments of Justice and Education "to provide school officials with guidance [concerning] the extent to which religious expression and activities are permitted in public schools."

Ingebretsen, 88 F.3d at 286–87 (Jones, J., dissenting).

5. Of course, what Judge Jones described as an "absurdity" has come to pass. In *Newdow v. U.S. Congress*, 292 F.3d 597 (9th Cir. 2002), the Ninth Circuit held that the recitation of the Pledge of Allegiance in public schools was an unconstitutional establishment of religion because of the phrase, "under God," in the Pledge. The decision set off a national firestorm — bills were even introduced in Congress prohibiting the Department of Justice from using any of its appropriations to enforce the decision — but the Ninth Circuit held its ground, denying the government's petition for rehearing. (The Supreme Court reversed for lack of standing, see discussion, *supra.*) Is the Ninth Circuit's decision "absurd," or is it the natural outgrowth of the Supreme Court's Establishment Clause precedent since *Everson*?

D.   THE FREE EXERCISE CLAUSE — GOVERNMENT MAY NOT PROHIBIT RELIGIOUS EXPRESSION

The First Amendment Religion Clauses have a common goal — advancing religious liberty — even as they accomplish that goal in two different ways. As discussed in Part B, all agree the Establishment Clause at least precludes government from setting up a national or state church or granting special favors to some, but not all, religions. By contrast, the Free Exercise Clause is aimed at advancing religious freedom by preventing the government from prohibiting the holding of religious beliefs or engaging in religious practices.

Today, it is extraordinary for laws to be enacted specifically to disable religious belief or practice. Rather, free exercise disputes arise commonly when a law that is religiously neutral and generally applicable on its face is argued to prevent or burden what someone's religious faith requires, or alternatively, requires someone to undertake an act that faith would preclude. In essence, then, free exercise arguments contemplate religious exemptions from otherwise general laws. As you might guess, this poses a problem for the fair administration of law since manifold faith traditions seemingly necessitate an equal number of exceptions. Relatedly, there is the difficulty of knowing what a given religion requires, and how it is that a court is to inquire into that without getting enmeshed in theological doctrine or commenting upon the sometimes unusual beliefs of someone else's faith. Finally, there is the simple problem of maintaining public order, and evaluating where a religious practice can fairly be said to threaten that order.

1. Distinguishing Between Religious Belief and Religious Practice

Reynolds v. United States, 98 U.S. 145 (1878), addresses the issue of whether a general federal law criminalizing polygamy can be applied to a Mormon whose religion included that practice. Traditionally, matters of marriage and family are state law issues; however, *Reynolds* involved Utah, at the time a federal territory, and hence, Congress was the regulatory body. The federal prohibition of polygamy is justified, according to the Court, because of the importance of monogamous, heterosexual marriage, a practice, says the Court, "[u]pon [which] society may be said to be built," and perhaps even, upon which democratic traditions depend. *Id.* at 165. This important societal interest prevails over the countervailing religious practice by a rather strict, and ultimately unsustainable, distinction between religious belief and practice. This distinction begins to crumble in 1963 with the Court's decision in *Sherbert v. Verner*, 374 U.S. 398 (1963), considered below in Part 4. The difference between belief (fully protected) and conduct (protected if not threatening of public order) is not entirely abandoned, however, as the discussion in the case of *Wisconsin v. Yoder*, 406 U.S. 205 (1972), immediately following *Reynolds*, reveals. The very word, "exercise," in the Free Exercise Clause sustains Chief Justice Burger's conclusion in *Yoder* that "belief and action cannot be neatly confined in logic-tight compartments." *Id.* at 220.

REYNOLDS v. UNITED STATES
98 U.S. 145 (1878)

This is an indictment found in the District Court for the third judicial district of the Territory of Utah, charging George Reynolds with bigamy, in violation of sect. 5352 of the Revised Statutes, which, omitting its exceptions, is as follows:

"Every person having a husband or wife living, who marries another, whether married or single, in a Territory, or other place over which the United States have exclusive jurisdiction, is guilty of bigamy, and shall be punished by a fine of not more than $500, and by imprisonment for a term of not more than five years."

*   *   *

Mr. Chief Justice Waite delivered the opinion of the court.

*   *   *

5. Should the accused have been acquitted if he married the second time, because he believed it to be his religious duty?

*   *   *

5. As to the defence of religious belief or duty.

On the trial, the plaintiff in error, the accused, proved that at the time of his alleged second marriage he was, and for many years before had been, a member of the Church of Jesus Christ of Latter-Day Saints, commonly called the Mormon Church, and a believer in its doctrines; that it was an accepted doctrine of that church "that it was the duty of male members of said church, circumstances permitting, to practise polygamy; . . . that this duty was enjoined by different books which the members of said church believed to be of divine origin, and among others the Holy Bible, and also that the members of the church believed that the practice of polygamy was directly enjoined upon the male members thereof by the Almighty God, in a revelation to Joseph Smith, the founder and prophet of said church; that the failing or refusing to practise polygamy by such male members of said church, when circumstances would admit, would be punished, and that the penalty for such failure and refusal would be damnation in the life to come." He also proved "that he had received permission from the recognized authorities in said church to enter into polygamous marriage; . . . that Daniel H. Wells, one having authority in said church to perform the marriage ceremony, married the said defendant on or about the time the crime is alleged to have been committed, to some woman by the name of Schofield, and that such marriage ceremony was performed under and pursuant to the doctrines of said church."

* * *

Congress cannot pass a law for the government of the Territories which shall prohibit the free exercise of religion. The first amendment to the Constitution expressly forbids such legislation. Religious freedom is guaranteed everywhere throughout the United States, so far as congressional interference is concerned. The question to be determined is, whether the law now under consideration comes within this prohibition.

The word "religion" is not defined in the Constitution. We must go elsewhere, therefore, to ascertain its meaning, and nowhere more appropriately, we think, than to the history of the times in the midst of which the provision was adopted. The precise point of the inquiry is, what is the religious freedom which has been guaranteed.

Before the adoption of the Constitution, attempts were made in some of the colonies and States to legislate not only in respect to the establishment of religion, but in respect to its doctrines and precepts as well. The people were taxed, against their will, for the support of religion, and sometimes for the support of particular sects to whose tenets they could not and did not subscribe. Punishments were prescribed for a failure to attend upon public worship, and sometimes for entertaining heretical opinions. The controversy upon this general subject was animated in many of the States, but seemed at last to culminate in Virginia. In 1784, the House of Delegates of that State having under consideration "a bill establishing provision for teachers of the Christian religion," postponed it until the next session, and directed that the bill should be published and distributed, and that the people be requested "to signify their opinion respecting the adoption of such a bill at the next session of assembly."

This brought out a determined opposition. Amongst others, Mr. Madison prepared a "Memorial and Remonstrance," which was widely circulated and signed, and in which he demonstrated "that religion, or the duty we owe the Creator," was not within the cognizance of civil government. . . .

. . . Mr. Jefferson was not a member [of the Constitutional Convention], he being then absent as minister to France. As soon as he saw the draft of the Constitution proposed for adoption, he, in a letter to a friend, expressed his disappointment at the absence of an express declaration insuring the freedom of religion, but was willing to accept it as it was, trusting that the good sense and honest intentions of the people would bring about the necessary alterations. . . . Accordingly, at the first session of the first Congress the amendment now under consideration was proposed with others by Mr. Madison. It met the views of the advocates of religious freedom, and was adopted. Mr. Jefferson afterwards, in reply to an address to him by a committee of the Danbury Baptist Association, took occasion to say: "Believing with you that religion is a matter which lies solely between man and his God; that he owes account to none other for his faith or his worship; that the legislative powers of the government reach actions only, and not opinions, — I contemplate with sovereign reverence that act of the whole American people which declared that their legislature should 'make no law respecting an establishment of religion or prohibiting the free exercise thereof'. . . ." Coming as this does from an acknowledged leader of the advocates of the measure, it may be accepted almost as an authoritative declaration of the scope and effect of the amendment thus secured. Congress was deprived of all legislative power over mere opinion, but was left free to reach actions which were in violation of social duties or subversive of good order.

Polygamy has always been odious among the northern and western nations of Europe, and, until the establishment of the Mormon Church, was almost exclusively a feature of the life of Asiatic and of African people. At common law, the second marriage was always void (2 Kent, Com. 79), and from the earliest history of England polygamy has been treated as an offence against society. . . .

By the statute of 1 James I. (c. 11), the offence, if committed in England or Wales, was made punishable in the civil courts, and the penalty was death. As this statute was limited in its operation to England and Wales, it was at a very early period re-enacted, generally with some modifications, in all the colonies. In connection with the case we are now considering, it is a significant fact that on the 8th of December, 1788, after the passage of the act establishing religious freedom, and after the convention of Virginia had recommended as an amendment to the Constitution of the United States the declaration in a bill of rights that "all men have an equal, natural, and unalienable right to the free exercise of religion, according to the dictates of conscience," the legislature of that State substantially enacted the statute of James I., death penalty included, because, as recited in the preamble, "it hath been doubted whether bigamy or poligamy be punishable by the laws of this Commonwealth." 12 Hening's Stat. 691. From that day to this we think it may safely be said there never has been a time in any State of the Union when polygamy has not been an offence against society, cognizable by the civil courts and punishable with more or less severity. In the face of all this evidence, it is impossible to believe that the constitutional guaranty of religious freedom was intended to prohibit legislation in respect to this most important feature of social life. Marriage, while from its very nature a sacred obligation, is nevertheless, in most civilized nations, a civil contract, and usually regulated by law. Upon it society may be said to be built, and out of its fruits spring social relations and social obligations and duties, with which government is necessarily required to deal. In fact, according as monogamous or polygamous marriages are allowed, do we find the principles on which the government of the people, to a greater or less extent, rests. Professor Lieber says, polygamy leads to the patriarchal principle, and which, when applied to large communities, fetters the people in stationary despotism, while t hat principle cannot long exist in connection with monogamy. . . .

In our opinion, the statute immediately under consideration is within the legislative power of Congress. It is constitutional and valid as prescribing a rule of action for all those residing in the Territories, and in places over which the United States have exclusive control. This being so, the only question which remains is, whether those who make polygamy a part of their religion are excepted from the operation of the statute. If they are, then those who do not make polygamy a part of their religious belief may be found guilty and punished, while those who do, must be acquitted and go free. This would be introducing a new element into criminal law. Laws are made for the government of actions, and while they cannot interfere with mere religious belief and opinions, they may with practices. Suppose one believed that human sacrifices were a necessary part of religious worship, would it be seriously contended that the civil government under which he lived could not interfere to prevent a sacrifice? Or if a wife religiously believed it was her duty to burn herself upon the funeral pile of her dead husband, would it be beyond the power of the civil government to prevent her carrying her belief into practice?

So here, as a law of the organization of society under the exclusive dominion of the United States, it is provided that plural marriages shall not be allowed. Can a man excuse his practices to the contrary because of his religious belief? To permit this would be to make the professed doctrines of religious belief superior to the law of the land, and in effect to permit every citizen to become a law unto himself. Government could exist only in name under such circumstances.

Upon a careful consideration of the whole case, we are satisfied that no error was committed by the court below.

Judgment affirmed, [except that by later action of the Court, imprisonment was not at hard labor].

Mr. Justice Field, [concurring]. [Omitted.]

NOTES AND QUESTIONS

1.   Does *Reynolds* stand for the proposition that society has a special interest in heterosexual marriage? If so, how would you articulate that interest? What would such special interest mean for homosexual relationships, which, unlike the Mormon interest in polygamy, is usually presented without religious basis? We take up the consideration of homosexuality in Chapter 8 dealing with equality.

2.   As you read the next case, *Wisconsin v. Yoder*, 406 U.S. 205 (1972), note not only the already mentioned partial abandonment of the belief/conduct distinction, but also the manner in which the religious claim is weighed against the state interest. The state in *Yoder* was insisting upon compulsory education through the age of 16, and its justification was one largely premised upon ensuring individual competence. The Amish, who as a matter of faith, live as separately from the world as possible, asked for exemption from this state requirement after the 8th grade. In upholding the Amish claim for constitutional exemption, the Court weighs: the centrality of the religious belief (a "life aloof from the world and its values is central to their faith," *id.* at 210); the partial compliance with the state interest, and hence, the reasonableness of the religious claim ("Amish accept compulsory elementary education generally," *id.* at 212); the ability of the state's interest to be accomplished in less religiously-intrusive ways ("the evidence adduced . . . that an additional one or two years of formal high school for Amish children in place of their long-established program of informal vocational education would do little to serve [state] interests. . . ." *id.* at 222); and the fact that more than one constitutional interest was at stake ("when the interests of parenthood are combined with a free exercise

claim of the nature revealed by this record, more than merely a 'reasonable relation to some purpose within the competency of the State' is required," *id.* at 233). The last factor, conjoining free exercise with other constitutional interests like parental rights, takes an even greater significance in *Employment Division v. Smith*, 494 U.S. 872 (1990), considered later in this Chapter.

WISCONSIN v. YODER
406 U.S. 205 (1972)

MR. CHIEF JUSTICE BURGER delivered the opinion of the Court.

On petition of the State of Wisconsin, we granted the writ of certiorari in this case to review a decision of the Wisconsin Supreme Court holding that respondents' convictions for violating the State's compulsory school-attendance law were invalid under the Free Exercise Clause of the First Amendment to the United States Constitution made applicable to the States by the Fourteenth Amendment. For the reasons hereafter stated we affirm the judgment of the Supreme Court of Wisconsin.

Respondents Jonas Yoder and Wallace Miller are members of the Old Order Amish religion. . . . They and their families are residents of Green County, Wisconsin. Wisconsin's compulsory school-attendance law required them to cause their children to attend public or private school until reaching age 16 but the respondents declined to send their children, ages 14 and 15, to public school after they completed the eighth grade. The children were not enrolled in any private school, or within any recognized exception to the compulsory-attendance law, and they are conceded to be subject to the Wisconsin statute.

On complaint of the school district administrator for the public schools, respondents were charged, tried, and convicted of violating the compulsory-attendance law in Green County Court and were fined the sum of $5 each.[31]

Respondents defended on the ground that the application of the compulsory-attendance law violated their rights under the First and Fourteenth Amendments. The trial testimony showed that respondents believed, in accordance with the tenets of Old Order Amish communities generally, that their children's attendance at high school, public or private, was contrary to the Amish religion and way of life. They believed that by sending their children to high school, they would not only expose themselves to the danger of the censure of the church community, but, as found by the county court, also endanger their own salvation and that of their children. The

---

[31] [3] Prior to trial, the attorney for respondents wrote the State Superintendent of Public Instruction in an effort to explore the possibilities for a compromise settlement. Among other possibilities, he suggested that perhaps the State Superintendent could administratively determine that the Amish could satisfy the compulsory-attendance law by establishing their own vocational training plan similar to one that has been established in Pennsylvania. Under the Pennsylvania plan, Amish children of high school age are required to attend an Amish vocational school for three hours a week, during which time they are taught such subjects as English, mathematics, health, and social studies by an Amish teacher. For the balance of the week, the children perform farm and household duties under parental supervision, and keep a journal of their daily activities. The major portion of the curriculum is home projects in agriculture and homemaking.

State stipulated that respondents' religious beliefs were sincere.

. . . As a result of their common heritage, Old Order Amish communities today are characterized by a fundamental belief that salvation requires life in a church community separate and apart from the world and worldly influence. This concept of life aloof from the world and its values is central to their faith.

A related feature of Old Order Amish communities is their devotion to a life in harmony with nature and the soil, as exemplified by the simple life of the early Christian era that continued in America during much of our early national life. Amish beliefs require members of the community to make their living by farming or closely related activities. Broadly speaking, the Old Order Amish religion pervades and determines the entire mode of life of its adherents. Their conduct is regulated in great detail by the *Ordnung*, or rules, of the church community. Adult baptism, which occurs in late adolescence, is the time at which Amish young people voluntarily undertake heavy obligations, not unlike the Bar Mitzvah of the Jews, to abide by the rules of the church community.

Amish objection to formal education beyond the eighth grade is firmly grounded in these central religious concepts. They object to the high school, and higher education generally, because the values they teach are in marked variance with Amish values and the Amish way of life; they view secondary school education as an impermissible exposure of their children to a "worldly" influence in conflict with their beliefs. . . .

The Amish do not object to elementary education through the first eight grades as a general proposition because they agree that their children must have basic skills in the "three R's" in order to read the Bible, to be good farmers and citizens, and to be able to deal with non-Amish people when necessary in the course of daily affairs. They view such a basic education as acceptable because it does not significantly expose their children to worldly values or interfere with their development in the Amish community during the crucial adolescent period. While Amish accept compulsory elementary education generally, wherever possible they have established their own elementary schools in many respects like the small local schools of the past. In the Amish belief higher learning tends to develop values they reject as influences that alienate man from God.

. . . The testimony of Dr. Donald A. Erickson, an expert witness on education, also showed that the Amish succeed in preparing their high school age children to be productive members of the Amish community. He described their system of learning through doing the skills directly relevant to their adult roles in the Amish community as "ideal" and perhaps superior to ordinary high school education. The evidence also showed that the Amish have an excellent record as law-abiding and generally self-sufficient members of society.

Although the trial court in its careful findings determined that the Wisconsin compulsory school-attendance law "does interfere with the freedom of the Defendants to act in accordance with their sincere religious belief" it also concluded that the requirement of high school attendance until age 16 was a "reasonable and constitutional" exercise of governmental power, and therefore denied the motion to dismiss the charges. The Wisconsin Circuit Court affirmed the convictions. The

Wisconsin Supreme Court, however, sustained respondents' claim under the Free Exercise Clause of the First Amendment and reversed the convictions. . . .

I

. . . As [*Pierce v. Society of Sisters* (1925)] suggests, the values of parental direction of the religious upbringing and education of their children in their early and formative years have a high place in our society. Thus, a State's interest in universal education, however highly we rank it, is not totally free from a balancing process when it impinges on fundamental rights and interests, such as those specifically protected by the Free Exercise Clause of the First Amendment, and the traditional interest of parents with respect to the religious upbringing of their children so long as they, in the words of *Pierce*, "prepare [them] for additional obligations."

It follows that in order for Wisconsin to compel school attendance beyond the eighth grade against a claim that such attendance interferes with the practice of a legitimate religious belief, it must appear either that the State does not deny the free exercise of religious belief by its requirement, or that there is a state interest of sufficient magnitude to override the interest claiming protection under the Free Exercise Clause. . . .

II

. . . In evaluating those claims we must be careful to determine whether the Amish religious faith and their mode of life are, as they claim, inseparable and interdependent. A way of life, however virtuous and admirable, may not be interposed as a barrier to reasonable state regulation of education if it is based on purely secular considerations; to have the protection of the Religion Clauses, the claims must be rooted in religious belief. Although a determination of what is a "religious" belief or practice entitled to constitutional protection may present a most delicate question, the very concept of ordered liberty precludes allowing every person to make his own standards on matters of conduct in which society as a whole has important interests. Thus, if the Amish asserted their claims because of their subjective evaluation and rejection of the contemporary secular values accepted by the majority, much as Thoreau rejected the social values of his time and isolated himself at Walden Pond, their claims would not rest on a religious basis. Thoreau's choice was philosophical and personal rather than religious, and such belief does not rise to the demands of the Religion Clauses.

. . . That the Old Order Amish daily life and religious practice stem from their faith is shown by the fact that it is in response to their literal interpretation of the Biblical injunction from the Epistle of Paul to the Romans, "be not conformed to this world. . . ." This command is fundamental to the Amish faith. Moreover, for the Old Order Amish, religion is not simply a matter of theocratic belief. As the expert witnesses explained, the Old Order Amish religion pervades and determines virtually their entire way of life, regulating it with the detail of the Talmudic diet through the strictly enforced rules of the church community.

. . . As the record so strongly shows, the values and programs of the modern secondary school are in sharp conflict with the fundamental mode of life mandated by the Amish religion; modern laws requiring compulsory secondary education have accordingly engendered great concern and conflict. . . .

The impact of the compulsory-attendance law on respondents' practice of the Amish religion is not only severe, but inescapable, for the Wisconsin law affirmatively compels them, under threat of criminal sanction, to perform acts undeniably at odds with fundamental tenets of their religious beliefs. Nor is the impact of the compulsory-attendance law confined to grave interference with important Amish religious tenets from a subjective point of view. It carries with it precisely the kind of objective danger to the free exercise of religion that the First Amendment was designed to prevent. As the record shows, compulsory school attendance to age 16 for Amish children carries with it a very real threat of undermining the Amish community and religious practice as they exist today; they must either abandon belief and be assimilated into society at large, or be forced to migrate to some other and more tolerant region.

III

Wisconsin concedes that under the Religion Clauses religious beliefs are absolutely free from the State's control, but it argues that "actions," even though religiously grounded, are outside the protection of the First Amendment. But our decisions have rejected the idea that religiously grounded conduct is always outside the protection of the Free Exercise Clause. It is true that activities of individuals, even when religiously based, are often subject to regulation by the States in the exercise of their undoubted power to promote the health, safety, and general welfare, or the Federal Government in the exercise of its delegated powers. But to agree that religiously grounded conduct must often be subject to the broad police power of the State is not to deny that there are areas of conduct protected by the Free Exercise Clause of the First Amendment and thus beyond the power of the State to control, even under regulations of general applicability. This case, therefore, does not become easier because respondents were convicted for their "actions" in refusing to send their children to the public high school; in this context belief and action cannot be neatly confined in logic-tight compartments.

Nor can this case be disposed of on the grounds that Wisconsin's requirement for school attendance to age 16 applies uniformly to all citizens of the State and does not, on its face, discriminate against religions or a particular religion, or that it is motivated by legitimate secular concerns. A regulation neutral on its face may, in its application, nonetheless offend the constitutional requirement for governmental neutrality if it unduly burdens the free exercise of religion. . . .

We turn, then, to the State's broader contention that its interest in its system of compulsory education is so compelling that even the established religious practices of the Amish must give way. . . .

The State advances two primary arguments in support of its system of compulsory education. It notes, as Thomas Jefferson pointed out early in our history, that some degree of education is necessary to prepare citizens to participate effectively and intelligently in our open political system if we are to preserve freedom and independence. Further, education prepares individuals to be self-reliant and self-sufficient participants in society. We accept these propositions.

However, the evidence adduced by the Amish in this case is persuasively to the effect that an additional one or two years of formal high school for Amish children in place of their long-established program of informal vocational education would do little to serve those interests. . . .

The State attacks respondents' position as one fostering "ignorance" from which the child must be protected by the State. No one can question the State's duty to protect children from ignorance but this argument does not square with the facts disclosed in the record. Whatever their idiosyncrasies as seen by the majority, this record strongly shows that the Amish community has been a highly successful social unit within our society, even if apart from the conventional "mainstream." Its members are productive and very law-abiding members of society; they reject public welfare in any of its usual modern forms. The Congress itself recognized their self-sufficiency by authorizing exemption of such groups as the Amish from the obligation to pay social security taxes.[32]

It is neither fair nor correct to suggests that the Amish are opposed to education beyond the eighth grade level. What this record shows is that they are opposed to conventional formal education of the type provided by a certified high school because it comes at the child's crucial adolescent period of religious development. Dr. Donald Erickson, for example, testified that their system of learning-by-doing was an "ideal system" of education in terms of preparing Amish children for life as adults in the Amish community, and that "I would be inclined to say they do a better job in this than most of the rest of us do." . . .

The State, however, supports its interest in providing an additional one or two years of compulsory high school education to Amish children because of the possibility that some such children will choose to leave the Amish community, and that if this occurs they will be ill-equipped for life. . . .

There is nothing in this record to suggest that the Amish qualities of reliability, self-reliance, and dedication to work would fail to find ready markets in today's society. Absent some contrary evidence supporting the State's position, we are unwilling to assume that persons possessing such valuable vocational skills and habits are doomed to become burdens on society should they determine to leave the Amish faith, nor is there any basis in the record to warrant a finding that an additional one or two years of formal school education beyond the eighth grade would serve to eliminate any such problem that might exist.

---

[32] [11] Title 26 U.S.C. § 1402(h) authorizes the Secretary of Health, Education, and Welfare to exempt members of "a recognized religious sect" existing at all times since December 31, 1950, from the obligation to pay social security taxes if they are, by reason of the tenets of their sect, opposed to receipt of such benefits and agree to waive them, provided the Secretary finds that the sect makes reasonable provision for its dependent members. The history of the exemption shows it was enacted with the situation of the Old Order Amish specifically in view. H.R. Rep. No. 213, 89th Cong., 1st Sess., 101–102 (1965). The record in this case establishes without contradiction that the Green County Amish had never been known to commit crimes, that none had been known to receive public assistance, and that none were unemployed.

. . . Indeed, the Amish communities singularly parallel and reflect many of the virtues of Jefferson's ideal of the "sturdy yeoman" who would form the basis of what he considered as the ideal of a democratic society.[33]

. . .

IV

Finally, the State, on authority of *Prince v. Massachusetts*, argues that a decision exempting Amish children from the State's requirement fails to recognize the substantive right of the Amish child to a secondary education, and fails to give due regard to the power of the State as *parens patriae* to extend the benefit of secondary education to children regardless of the wishes of their parents. Taken at its broadest sweep, the Court's language in *Prince* might be read to give support to the State's position. However, the Court was not confronted in *Prince* with a situation comparable to that of the Amish as revealed in this record; this is shown by the Court's severe characterization of the evils that it thought the legislature could legitimately associate with child labor, even when performed in the company of an adult. The Court later took great care to confine *Prince* to a narrow scope in *Sherbert v. Verner*, when it stated:

> "On the other hand, the Court has rejected challenges under the Free Exercise Clause to governmental regulation of certain overt acts prompted by religious beliefs or principles, for 'even when the action is in accord with one's religious convictions, [it] is not totally free from legislative restrictions.' *Braunfeld v. Brown* (1961). The conduct or actions so regulated have invariably posed some substantial threat to public safety, peace or order. *See, e.g., Reynolds v. United States* [(1878)]; *Jacobson v. Massachusetts* [(1905)]; *Prince v. Massachusetts* [(1944)]. . . ."

This case, of course, is not one in which any harm to the physical or mental health of the child or to the public safety, peace, order, or welfare has been demonstrated or may be properly inferred. The record is to the contrary, and any reliance on that theory would find no support in the evidence.

. . . The dissent argues that a child who expresses a desire to attend public high school in conflict with the wishes of his parents should not be prevented from doing so. There is no reason for the Court to consider that point since it is not an issue in the case. The children are not parties to this litigation. . . .

Our holding in no way determines the proper resolution of possible competing interests of parents, children, and the State in an appropriate state court proceeding in which the power of the State is asserted on the theory that Amish parents are preventing their minor children from attending high school despite their expressed desires to the contrary. Recognition of the claim of the State in such a proceeding

---

[33] [14] While Jefferson recognized that education was essential to the welfare and liberty of the people, he was reluctant to directly force instruction of children "in opposition to the will of the parent." Instead he proposed that state citizenship be conditioned on the ability to "read readily in some tongue, native or acquired." Letter from Thomas Jefferson to Joseph Cabell, Sept. 9, 1817, in 17 WRITINGS OF THOMAS JEFFERSON 417, 423–424 (Mem. ed. 1904). . . .

would, of course, call into question traditional concepts of parental control over the religious upbringing and education of their minor children recognized in this Court's past decisions. It is clear that such an intrusion by a State into family decisions in the area of religious training would give rise to grave questions of religious freedom comparable to those raised here and those presented in *Pierce v. Society of Sisters* (1925). On this record we neither reach nor decide those issues.

. . . [P]erhaps the most significant statements of the Court in this area are found in *Pierce v. Society of Sisters*, in which the Court observed:

> "Under the doctrine of *Meyer v. Nebraska* [(1923)], we think it entirely plain that the Act of 1922 unreasonably interferes with the liberty of parents and guardians to direct the upbringing and education of children under their control. As often heretofore pointed out, rights guaranteed by the Constitution may not be abridged by legislation which has no reasonable relation to some purpose within the competency of the State. The fundamental theory of liberty upon which all governments in this Union repose excludes any general power of the State to standardize its children by forcing them to accept instruction from public teachers only. The child is not the mere creature of the State; those who nurture him and direct his destiny have the right, coupled with the high duty, to recognize and prepare him for additional obligations."

The duty to prepare the child for "additional obligations," referred to by the Court, must be read to include the inculcation of moral standards, religious beliefs, and elements of good citizenship. *Pierce*, of course, recognized that where nothing more than the general interest of the parent in the nurture and education of his children is involved, it is beyond dispute that the State acts "reasonably" and constitutionally in requiring education to age 16 in some public or private school meeting the standards prescribed by the State.

However read, the Court's holding in *Pierce* stands as a charter of the rights of parents to direct the religious upbringing of their children. And, when the interests of parenthood are combined with a free exercise claim of the nature revealed by this record, more than merely a "reasonable relation to some purpose within the competency of the State" is required to sustain the validity of the State's requirement under the First Amendment. . . .

V

For the reasons stated we hold, with the Supreme Court of Wisconsin, that the First and Fourteenth Amendments prevent the State from compelling respondents to cause their children to attend formal high school to age 16.

Affirmed.

MR. JUSTICE POWELL and MR. JUSTICE REHNQUIST took no part in the consideration or decision of this case.

MR. JUSTICE STEWART, with whom MR. JUSTICE BRENNAN joins, concurring. [Omitted.]

MR. JUSTICE WHITE, with whom MR. JUSTICE BRENNAN and MR. JUSTICE STEWART join, concurring.

Decision in cases such as this and the administration of an exemption for Old Order Amish from the State's compulsory school-attendance laws will inevitably involve the kind of close and perhaps repeated scrutiny of religious practices, as is exemplified in today's opinion, which the Court has heretofore been anxious to avoid. But such entanglement does not create a forbidden establishment of religion where it is essential to implement free exercise values threatened by an otherwise neutral program instituted to foster some permissible, nonreligious state objective. I join the Court because the sincerity of the Amish religious policy here is uncontested, because the potentially adverse impact of the state requirement is great, and because the State's valid interest in education has already been largely satisfied by the eight years the children have already spent in school.

MR. JUSTICE DOUGLAS, dissenting in part.

I

. . . It is, of course, beyond question that the parents have standing as defendants in a criminal prosecution to assert the religious interests of their children as a defense. Although the lower courts and a majority of this Court assume an identity of interest between parent and child, it is clear that they have treated the religious interest of the child as a factor in the analysis.

II

The views of the two children in question were not canvassed by the Wisconsin courts. The matter should be explicitly reserved so that new hearings can be held on remand of the case.

III

The Court rightly rejects the notion that actions, even though religiously grounded, are always outside the protection of the Free Exercise Clause of the First Amendment. In so ruling, the Court departs from the teaching of *Reynolds v. United States* (1879) where it was said concerning the reach of the Free Exercise Clause of the First Amendment, "Congress was deprived of all legislative power over mere opinion, but was left free to reach actions which were in violation of social duties or subversive of good order." In that case it was conceded that polygamy was a part of the religion of the Mormons. Yet the Court said, "It matters not that his belief [in polygamy] was a part of his professed religion: it was still belief and belief only."

Action, which the Court deemed to be antisocial, could be punished even though it was grounded on deeply held and sincere religious convictions. What we do today, at least in this respect, opens the way to give organized religion a broader base than it has ever enjoyed; and it even promises that in time *Reynolds* will be overruled.

In another way, however, the Court retreats when in reference to Henry Thoreau it says his "choice was philosophical and personal rather than religious, and such belief does not rise to the demands of the Religion Clauses." That is contrary to what we held in *United States v. Seeger* (1964), where we were concerned with the meaning of the words "religious training and belief" in the Selective Service Act, which were the basis of many conscientious objector claims. We said:

> "Within that phrase would come all sincere religious beliefs which are based upon a power or being, or upon a faith, to which all else is subordinate or upon which all else is ultimately dependent. The test might be stated in these words: A sincere and meaningful belief which occupies in the life of its possessor a place parallel to that filled by the God of those admittedly qualifying for the exemption comes within the statutory definition. This construction avoids imputing to Congress an intent to classify different religious beliefs, exempting some and excluding others, and is in accord with the well-established congressional policy of equal treatment for those whose opposition to service is grounded in their religious tenets."

I adhere to these exalted views of "religion" and see no acceptable alternative to them now that we have become a Nation of many religions and sects, representing all of the diversities of the human race. *United States v. Seeger* (concurring opinion).

NOTES AND QUESTIONS

1. Why do the Mormons lose in *Reynolds*, but the Amish win in *Yoder*? Is it a principled distinction or one that turns on religious preference or the favorable perception of one sect over another? Is public order threatened in one instance, but not the other? All religious belief is protected, but protection is extended only to conduct that does not threaten public order. In his article *The Origins and Historical Understanding of Free Exercise of Religion*, Professor Michael McConnell summarizes the historical understanding of the public order exception as a limitation on the free exercise of religion in the United States:

> [S]tate constitutions provide the most direct evidence of the original understanding [of the Free Exercise Clause], for it is reasonable to infer that those who drafted and adopted the first amendment assumed the term "free exercise of religion" meant what it had meant in their states. . . .

> The most common feature of the state provisions was the government's right to protect public peace and safety. . . . [A] believer has no license to invade the private rights of others or to disturb public peace and order, no matter how conscientious the belief or how trivial the private right on the other side.

Michael McConnell, *The Origins and Historical Understanding of Free Exercise of Religion*, 103 HARV. L. REV. 1409, 1456–58, 1464 (1990).

As we saw, the Supreme Court endorsed this historical understanding of the public order exception in *Reynolds v. United States*, 98 U.S. 145 (1878), which held that the Free Exercise Clause did not exempt Reynolds, a Mormon, from a territorial statute making polygamy a criminal offense. The opinion explains the practical basis of the public order exception:

> Laws are made for the government of actions, and while they cannot interfere with mere religious belief and opinions, they may with practices. . . .
>
> . . . Can a man excuse his practices to the contrary [of the law] because of his religious belief? To permit this would be to make the professed doctrines of religious belief superior to the law of the land, and in effect to permit every citizen to become a law unto himself.

Id. at 166–67.

2. In *Cantwell v. Connecticut*, 310 U.S. 296 (1940), the court overturned the convictions of three Jehovah's Witnesses for violations of a state law prohibiting the solicitation of money for religious organizations without prior licensing by a state official. The Court discussed the extent of public order exception:

> The state is . . . free to regulate the time and manner of solicitation generally, in the interest of public safety, peace, comfort or convenience. But to condition the solicitation of aid for the perpetuation of religious views or systems upon a license, the grant of which rests in the exercise of a determination by state authority as to what is a religious cause, is to lay a forbidden burden upon the exercise of liberty protected by the Constitution.

Id. at 306–07. Because Connecticut's regulation went beyond that which was necessary to protect the public order, the Court found that it was an unnecessary, and therefore unconstitutional, burden on the defendants' free exercise of their faith.

The Court expanded on *Cantwell* in *Watchtower Bible and Tract Society of New York, Inc. v. Village of Stratton*, 536 U.S. 150 (2002), holding in an 8-1 decision that a city ordinance requiring individuals engaged in religious proselytizing, anonymous political speech, and handbill distribution, among other things, to first register with the mayor and obtain a permit facially violated the First Amendment because the ordinance intruded upon the freedom of speech and the free exercise of religion much more broadly than necessary to serve the government's interest in protecting citizen privacy and preventing fraud.

3. By contrast, in *Prince v. Massachusetts*, 321 U.S. 158 (1943), the Court upheld the conviction of Mrs. Prince, a Jehovah's Witness, under state child labor laws for permitting her nine year old ward, Betty Simmons, to sell religious materials on a public street. Mrs. Prince argued that she and Betty were fulfilling their religious obligation by selling the magazines, and that, therefore, their conduct was constitutionally protected by a combination of the Free Exercise

Clause and Mrs. Prince's parental rights. The Court, however, found that neither the Free Exercise Clause nor Mrs. Prince's parental rights limited the state's ability to control Mrs. Prince and Betty's conduct in this matter. "[T]he state has a wide range of power for limiting parental freedom and authority in things affecting the child's welfare; and . . . this includes, to some extent, matters of conscience and religious conviction." *Id.* at 167. The Court's conclusion that the state's interest in Betty's welfare outweighed Mrs. Prince and Betty's interest in the free exercise of their faith is another example of the public order exception to the Free Exercise Clause.

4. Can you discern at what point an individual's interest in the free exercise of conduct motivated by religious faith overcomes the government's interest in preserving the public order? Some commentators believe there is an absence of a substantive principal of limitation for the public order exception. Notre Dame's Gerard V. Bradley writes:

> Defenders of the conduct exemption do not deny that it is a bit fuzzy. . . .

> Even so appealing a formulation as Madison's (which McConnell endorses), "that free exercise should be protected in every case where it does not trespass on private rights or the public peace," is inconclusive. Do the people enjoy a collective right to a decent society? . . .

> . . . Americans in the founding and antebellum eras [believed that] they enjoyed a nearly perfect freedom of conscience. And they brought blasphemy prosecutions, and compelled ministerial support, as well as sabbath observance. Quite likely, McConnell means "public order" to exclude all perfectionistic state action, in favor of liberal neutrality. Be that as it may, we need to know if that corresponds to the original understanding. Already, the answer appears to be no.

Gerard V. Bradley, *Beguiled: Free Exercise Exemptions and the Siren Song of Liberalism*, 20 HOFSTRA L. REV. 245, 259–60 (1991).

5. The extent of the public order exception is at the core of modern free exercise disagreement. In *Employment Division v. Smith*, 494 U.S. 872 (1990), which we will encounter in Part 5, the Court refused to find drug use in a religious ceremony to merit a free exercise exemption from a generally applicable criminal prohibition. Both Justices O'Connor and Blackmun, however, would have provided that exemption, but they differed over the application of the public order exception. In her concurring opinion, Justice O'Connor found that Oregon's criminal prohibition placed a "severe burden on the ability of respondents to freely exercise their religion." *Id.* at 903. However, she concluded that the state's interest in public safety and order was sufficiently compelling to justify the burden placed on claimants:

> [U]niform application of Oregon's criminal prohibition is "essential to accomplish" its overriding interest in preventing the physical harm caused by the use of a Schedule I controlled substance. Oregon's criminal prohibition represents that State's judgment that the possession and use of controlled substances, even by only one person, is inherently harmful and dangerous. Because the health effects caused by the use of controlled substances exist regardless of the motivation of the user, the use of such

substances, even for religious purposes, violates the very purpose of the laws that prohibit them. Moreover, in view of the societal interest in preventing trafficking in controlled substances, uniform application of the criminal prohibition at issue is essential to the effectiveness of Oregon's stated interest in preventing any possession of peyote.

Id. at 905 (O'Connor, J., concurring) (citations omitted).

In his dissenting opinion, Justice Blackmun also applied the "compelling interest" test. However, Justice Blackmun differed with Justice O'Connor regarding the nature of the state interest involved. Justice Blackmun defined it as the "State's narrow interest in refusing to make an exception for the religious, ceremonial use of peyote." *Id.* at 910 (Blackmun, J., dissenting). Because the state had provided only a "symbolic" and "speculative" interest in "enforcing its drug laws against religious users of peyote," and "no evidence that the religious use of peyote [had] ever harmed anyone," Justice Blackmun found the state's interest "not sufficiently compelling to outweigh respondent's right to the free exercise of their religion." *Id.* at 910–12, 921.

6. The difference between accommodation and establishment: In Justice White's concurring opinion, he notes: "entanglement does not create a forbidden establishment of religion where it is essential to implement free exercise values threatened by an otherwise neutral program instituted to foster some permissible, nonreligious state objective." *Yoder,* 406 U.S. at 240–41 (White, J., concurring). Justice White's comment suggests that some state efforts could be too accommodating of free exercise values and lead a state to violate the Establishment Clause. Thus, in *Estate of Thornton v. Calder,* 472 U.S. 703 (1984), the Court invalidated a Connecticut statute that gave employees a choice to be absent from work on the sabbath of their choice. Similarly, in *Board of Education v. Grummett,* 512 U.S. 687 (1994), New York's effort to allow Hasidic Jews, who live in a concentrated area, to form their own public school district was seen as favoritism not mandated by free exercise requirements. Notice that in both *Thornton* and *Grummett,* the state was not seeking to exempt religious practice from neutral state laws, but to enact state laws facilitating religious practice. As we have seen, this facilitation would be inoffensive to our Constitutional framers absent a clear showing of sect-based favoritism, but it does not coincide with the exclusionary posture of establishment case law in the latter third of the 20th century. By contrast, the Court upheld the religious exemption from the otherwise generally applicable employment discrimination provisions of Title VII of the Civil Rights Act of 1964, 42 U.S.C. § 2000e-1(a) (1994), in *Corporation of the Presiding Bishop of the Church of Jesus Christ of Latter Day Saints v. Amos,* 483 U.S. 327 (1984).

2. Judicial Inquiry into the Sincerity, But Not the Validity, of Religious Belief

Religious belief is often very personal and beyond the standards of proof associated with law or science. By nature, that which is spiritual is not material. Not everyone, of course, holding themselves out as spiritual leaders are completely honest, and *United States v. Ballard* deals with allegations of fraud against certain claimed faith-healers. The appellate court in *Ballard* thought the "truth of religious doctrines" could be submitted to the jury. *See Ballard v. United States*, 138 F.2d 540, 545 (9th Cir. 1943). Here, the Supreme Court reverses, indicating that in evaluating free exercise claims or defenses, an honest, sincere belief is all temporal judges can measure.

UNITED STATES v. BALLARD
322 U.S. 78 (1944)

MR. JUSTICE DOUGLAS delivered the opinion of the Court.

Respondents were indicted and convicted for using, and conspiring to use, the mails to defraud. The indictment was in twelve counts. It charged a scheme to defraud by organizing and promoting the I Am movement through the use of the mails. . . . The false representations charged were eighteen in number. It is sufficient at this point to say that they covered respondents' alleged religious doctrines or beliefs. They were all set forth in the first count. The following are representative:

> . . . that Guy W. Ballard, during his lifetime, and Edna W. Ballard and Donald Ballard had, by reason of supernatural attainments, the power to heal persons of ailments and diseases and to make well persons afflicted with any diseases, injuries, or ailments, and did falsely represent to persons intended to be defrauded that the three designated persons had the ability and power to cure persons of those diseases normally classified as curable and also of diseases which are ordinarily classified by the medical profession as being incurable diseases; and did further represent that the three designated persons had in fact cured either by the activity of one, either, or all of said persons, hundreds of persons afflicted with diseases and ailments. . . .

Each of the representations enumerated in the indictment was followed by the charge that respondents "well knew" it was false. . . .

. . . [T]he [District C]ourt advised the jury . . . in the following language:

> "[T]he defendants in this case made certain representations of belief in a divinity and in a supernatural power. . . ."

The District Court . . . [also charged to the jury]:

> "The question of the defendants' good faith is the cardinal question in this case. You are not to be concerned with the religious belief of the defendants, or any of them. The jury will be called upon to pass on the question of whether or not the defendants honestly and in good faith believed the representations which are set forth in the indictment, and honestly and in good faith believed that the benefits which they represented would flow from their belief to those who embraced and followed their teachings, or whether these representations were mere pretenses without honest belief on the part of the defendants or any of them, and, were the representations made for the purpose of procuring money, and were the mails used for this purpose. . . ."

. . . [T]he Circuit Court of Appeals held that the question of the truth of the representations concerning respondent's religious doctrines or beliefs should have been submitted to the jury. . . . [W]e do not agree that the truth or verity of respondents' religious doctrines or beliefs should have been submitted to the jury. Whatever this particular indictment might require, the First Amendment precludes such a course, as the United States seems to concede. "The law knows no heresy, and is committed to the support of no dogma, the establishment of no sect." . . . Men may believe what they cannot prove. They may not be put to the proof of their religious doctrines or beliefs. . . . The miracles of the New Testament, the Divinity of Christ, life after death, the power of prayer are deep in the religious convictions of many. If one could be sent to jail because a jury in a hostile environment found those teachings false, little indeed would be left of religious freedom. . . . The religious views espoused by respondents might seem incredible, if not preposterous, to most people. But if those doctrines are subject to trial before a jury charged with finding their truth or falsity, then the same can be done with the religious beliefs of any sect. . . . So we conclude that the District Court ruled properly when it withheld from the jury all questions concerning the truth or falsity of the religious beliefs or doctrines of respondents.

MR. CHIEF JUSTICE STONE, [and JUSTICES ROBERTS and FRANKFURTER wrote a separate opinion reversing the appellate court and re-instating the trial court conviction].

. . . With the assent of the prosecution and the defense the trial judge withdrew from the consideration of the jury the question whether the alleged religious experiences had in fact occurred, but submitted to the jury the single issue whether petitioners honestly believed that they had occurred, with the instruction that if the jury did not so find, then it should return a verdict of guilty. . . .

On the issue submitted to the jury in this case it properly rendered a verdict of guilty. . . .

MR. JUSTICE JACKSON, dissenting.

The Ballard family claimed miraculous communication with the spirit world and supernatural power to heal the sick. They were brought to trial for mail fraud on an indictment which charged that their representations were false and that they "well knew" they were false. The trial judge, obviously troubled, ruled that the court could not try whether the statements were untrue, but could inquire whether the defendants knew them to be untrue; and, if so, they could be convicted.

I find it difficult to reconcile this conclusion with our traditional religious freedoms.

In the first place, as a matter of either practice or philosophy I do not see how we can separate an issue as to what is believed from considerations as to what is believable. The most convincing proof that one believes his statements is to show that they have been true in his experience. Likewise, that one knowingly falsified is best proved by showing that what he said happened never did happen. How can the Government prove these persons knew something to be false which it cannot prove to be false? If we try religious sincerity severed from religious verity, we isolate the dispute from the very considerations which in common experience provide its most reliable answer.

Prosecutions of this character easily could degenerate into religious persecution. I do not doubt that religious leaders may be convicted of fraud for making false representations on matters other than faith or experience, as for example if one represents that funds are being used to construct a church when in fact they are being used for personal purposes. But that is not this case, which reaches into wholly dangerous ground. When does less than full belief in a professed credo become actionable fraud if one is soliciting gifts or legacies? Such inquiries may discomfort orthodox as well as unconventional religious teachers, for even the most regular of them are sometimes accused of taking their orthodoxy with a grain of salt.

I would dismiss the indictment and have done with this business of judicially examining other people's faiths.

NOTE

Does a free exercise claim depend on others holding similar beliefs? Following *Ballard*, the Court made it clear that sincerity also does not depend upon a religious belief being held or share by others. *Thomas v. Review Bd. of the Ind. Employment Sec. Div.*, 450 U.S. 707, 715–16 (1981). This focus on the individual is consistent with the view of the framers. Madison's *Memorial and Remonstrance* plainly states that it is "the duty of every man to render to the Creator such homage, and such only, as he believes to be acceptable to him." JAMES MADISON, MEMORIAL AND REMON-STRANCE AGAINST RELIGIOUS ASSESSMENTS ¶ 1 (1785), *reprinted in Everson v. Board of Education*, 330 U.S. 1, 64 (1947) (appendix to dissenting opinion of Justice Rutledge). The government can disprove sincerity, however, by showing that the claimant has an ulterior motive, such as greed or immorality, *see, e.g, United States v. Daly*, 756 F.2d 1076, 1081 (5th Cir. 1985) (personal church as tax dodge); or personal drug use, *United States v. Kuch*, 288 F. Supp. 439, 443–45 (D.D.C. 1968).

3. More than Theism, But How Much More?

The Court has not been entirely clear on what counts as religion for purposes of the Free Exercise Clause. For example, in *Torcaso v. Watkins*, 367 U.S. 488, 495 & n.11 (1961), the Court suggested that Ethical Culture and Secular Humanism were religions, while in *Wisconsin v. Yoder*, it will be recalled that Thoreau's philosophy was said not to count as religious belief. In the next case, the Court takes a particularly liberal view of this definitional question for purposes of construction of a federal statute allowing conscientious objection to military service. While the Court proclaims that religion excludes "essentially political, sociological, or philosophical views," it nevertheless includes "belief that is sincere and meaningful [and that] occupies a place in the life of its possessor parallel to that filled by the orthodox belief in God." *United States v. Seeger*, 380 U.S. 163, 165–66 (1964).

UNITED STATES v. SEEGER
380 U.S. 163 (1964)

MR. JUSTICE CLARK delivered the opinion of the Court.

These cases involve claims of conscientious objectors under § 6(j) of the Universal Military Training and Service Act, 50 U.S.C. App. § 456(j) (1958 ed.), which exempts from combatant training and service in the armed forces of the United States those persons who by reason of their religious training and belief are conscientiously opposed to participation in war in any form. The cases were consolidated for argument and we consider them together although each involves different facts and circumstances. The parties raise the basic question of the constitutionality of the section which defines the term "religious training and belief," as used in the Act, as "an individual's belief in a relation to a Supreme Being involving duties superior to those arising from any human relation, but [not including] essentially political, sociological, or philosophical views or a merely personal moral code." The constitutional attack is launched under the First Amendment's Establishment and Free Exercise Clauses and is twofold: (1) The section does not exempt nonreligious conscientious objectors; and (2) it discriminates between different forms of religious expression in violation of the Due Process Clause of the Fifth Amendment. Jakobson (No. 51) and Peter (No. 29) also claim that their beliefs come within the meaning of the section. Jakobson claims that he meets the standards of § 6(j) because his opposition to war is based on belief in a Supreme Reality and is therefore an obligation superior to one resulting from man's relationship to his fellow man. Peter contends that his opposition to war derives from his acceptance of the existence of a universal power beyond that of man and that this acceptance in fact constitutes belief in a Supreme Being, qualifying him for exemption. We granted certiorari in each of the cases because of their importance in the administration of the Act.

We have concluded that Congress, in using the expression "Supreme Being" rather than the designation "God," was merely clarifying the meaning of religious training and belief so as to embrace all religions and to exclude essentially political, sociological, or philosophical views. We believe that under this construction, the test of belief "in a relation to a Supreme Being" is whether a given belief that is sincere and meaningful occupies a place in the life of its possessor parallel to that filled by the orthodox belief in God of one who clearly qualifies for the exemption. Where such beliefs have parallel positions in the lives of their respective holders we cannot say that one is "in a relation to a Supreme Being" and the other is not. We have concluded that the beliefs of the objectors in these cases meet these criteria. . . .

Governmental recognition of the moral dilemma posed for persons of certain religious faiths by the call to arms came early in the history of this country. Various methods of ameliorating their difficulty were adopted by the Colonies, and were later perpetuated in state statutes and constitutions. Thus by the time of the Civil War there existed a state pattern of exempting conscientious objectors on religious grounds. . . . With the Federal Conscription Act of 1863, . . . the Federal Government occupied the field entirely, and in the 1864 Draft Act, 13 Stat. 9, it extended exemptions to those conscientious objectors who were members of religious denominations opposed to the bearing of arms and who were prohibited from doing so by the articles of faith of their denominations. . . .

The need for conscription did not again arise until World War I. The Draft Act of 1917, 40 Stat. 76, 78, afforded exemptions to conscientious objectors who were affiliated with a "well-recognized religious sect or organization [then] organized and existing and whose existing creed or principles [forbade] its members to participate in war in any form. . . ." The Act required that all persons be inducted into the armed services, but allowed the conscientious objectors to perform noncombatant service in capacities designated by the President of the United States. . . .

In adopting the 1940 Selective Training and Service Act Congress broadened the exemption afforded in the 1917 Act by making it unnecessary to belong to a pacifist religious sect if the claimant's own opposition to war was based on "religious training and belief." 54 Stat. 889. Those found to be within the exemption were not inducted into the armed services but were assigned to noncombatant service under the supervision of the Selective Service System. . . .

Between 1940 and 1948 two courts of appeals held that the phrase "religious training and belief" did not include philosophical, social or political policy. Then in 1948 the Congress amended the language of the statute and declared that "religious training and belief" was to be defined as "an individual's belief in a relation to a Supreme Being involving duties superior to those arising from any human relation, but [not including] essentially political, sociological, or philosophical views or a merely personal moral code." The only significant mention of this change in the provision appears in the report of the Senate Armed Services Committee recommending adoption. It said simply this: "This section reenacts substantially the same provisions as were found in subsection 5(g) of the 1940 act. Exemption extends to anyone who, because of religious training and belief in his relation to a Supreme Being, is conscientiously opposed to combatant military service or to both combatant and non-combatant military service."

2.

Few would quarrel, we think, with the proposition that in no field of human endeavor has the tool of language proved so inadequate in the communication of ideas as it has in dealing with the fundamental questions of man's predicament in life, in death or in final judgment and retribution. This fact makes the task of discerning the intent of Congress in using the phrase "Supreme Being" a complex one. Nor is it made the easier by the richness and variety of spiritual life in our country. Over 250 sects inhabit our land. Some believe in a purely personal God, some in a supernatural deity; others think of religion as a way of life envisioning as its ultimate goal the day when all men can live together in perfect understanding and peace. There are those who think of God as the depth of our being; others, such as the Buddhists, strive for a state of lasting rest through self-denial and inner purification; in Hindu philosophy, the Supreme Being is the transcendental reality which is truth, knowledge and bliss. Even those religious groups which have traditionally opposed war in every form have splintered into various denominations: from 1940 to 1947 there were four denominations using the name "Friends"; the "Church of the Brethren" was the official name of the oldest and largest church body of four denominations composed of those commonly called Brethren; and the "Mennonite Church" was the largest of 17 denominations, including the Amish and Hutterites, grouped as "Mennonite bodies" in the 1936 report on the Census of Religious Bodies. This vast panoply of beliefs reveals the magnitude of the problem which faced the Congress when it set about providing an exemption from armed service. It also emphasizes the care that Congress realized was necessary in the fashioning of an exemption which would be in keeping with its long-established policy of not picking and choosing among religious beliefs.

In spite of the elusive nature of the inquiry, we are not without certain guidelines. In amending the 1940 Act, Congress adopted almost intact the language of Chief Justice Hughes in *United States v. Macintosh* [(1931)]:

> "The essence of religion is belief in a relation to *God* involving duties superior to those arising from any human relation." 283 U.S. at 633–34 (emphasis supplied.)

By comparing the statutory definition with those words, however, it becomes readily apparent that the Congress deliberately broadened them by substituting the phrase "Supreme Being" for the appellation "God." And in so doing it is also significant that Congress did not elaborate on the form or nature of this higher authority which it chose to designate as "Supreme Being." By so refraining it must have had in mind the admonitions of the Chief Justice when he said in the same opinion that even the word "God" had myriad meanings for men of faith:

> "[P]utting aside dogmas with their particular conceptions of deity, freedom of conscience itself implies respect for an innate conviction of paramount duty. The battle for religious liberty has been fought and won with respect to religious beliefs and practices, which are not in conflict with good order, upon the very ground of the supremacy of conscience within its proper field."

Section 6(j), then, is no more than a clarification of the 1940 provision . . . .

4.

Moreover, we believe this construction embraces the ever-broadening understanding of the modern religious community. The eminent Protestant theologian, Dr. Paul Tillich, whose views the Government concedes would come within the statute, identifies God not as a projection "out there" or beyond the skies but as the ground of our very being.

Dr. David Saville Muzzey, a leader in the Ethical Culture Movement, states in his book, ETHICS AS A RELIGION (1951), that "[e]verybody except the avowed atheists (and they are comparatively few) believes in some kind of God," and that "The proper question to ask, therefore, is not the futile one, Do you believe in God? but rather, What *kind* of God do you believe in?"

5.

We recognize the difficulties that have always faced the trier of fact in these cases. We hope that the test that we lay down proves less onerous. The examiner is furnished a standard that permits consideration of criteria with which he has had considerable experience. While the applicant's words may differ, the test is simple of application. It is essentially an objective one, namely, does the claimed belief occupy the same place in the life of the objector as an orthodox belief in God holds in the life of one clearly qualified for exemption?

. . . The validity of what he believes cannot be questioned. Some theologians, and indeed some examiners, might be tempted to question the existence of the registrant's "Supreme Being" or the truth of his concepts. But these are inquiries foreclosed to Government. . . .

But we hasten to emphasize that while the "truth" of a belief is not open to question, there remains the significant question whether it is "truly held." This is the threshold question of sincerity which must be resolved in every case. . . .

APPLICATION OF § 6(j) TO THE INSTANT CASES

As we noted earlier, the statutory definition excepts those registrants whose beliefs are based on a "merely personal moral code." The records in these cases, however, show that at no time did any one of the applicants suggest that his objection was based on a "merely personal moral code." Indeed at the outset each of them claimed in his application that his objection was based on a religious belief. We have construed the statutory definition broadly and it follows that any exception to it must be interpreted narrowly. The use by Congress of the words "merely personal" seems to us to restrict the exception to a moral code which is not only personal but which is the sole basis for the registrant's belief and is in no way related to a Supreme Being. . . .

MR. JUSTICE DOUGLAS, concurring.

When the present Act was adopted in 1948 we were a nation of Buddhists, Confucianists, and Taoists, as well as Christians. Hawaii, then a Territory, was indeed filled with Buddhists, Buddhism being "probably the major faith, if Protestantism and Roman Catholicism are deemed different faiths." . . .

In the continental United States Buddhism is found "in real strength" in Utah, Arizona, Washington, Oregon, and California. "Most of the Buddhists in the United States are Japanese or Japanese-Americans; however, there are 'English' departments in San Francisco, Los Angeles, and Tacoma." . . .

When the Congress spoke in the vague general terms of a Supreme Being I cannot, therefore, assume that it was so parochial as to use the words in the narrow sense urged on us. I would attribute tolerance and sophistication to the Congress, commensurate with the religious complexion of our communities. In sum, I agree with the Court that any person opposed to war on the basis of a sincere belief, which in his life fills the same place as a belief in God fills in the life of an orthodox religionist, is entitled to exemption under the statute. None comes to us an avowedly irreligious person or as an atheist. . . .

NOTES AND QUESTIONS

Is the *Seeger* opinion too expansive, and therefore, dilutive of the significance of religion? Does a liberalized definition of religion abet the exclusionary Establishment Clause view? Just as religion is removed and deemphasized in terms of public importance under the Court's exclusionary view, formal religion may lose its significance when it becomes indistinguishable from other orientations or motivations for human action. As a Department of Justice Report summarized: "It does not strain credulity to see that [the *Seeger*] approach might ultimately enshrine materialism, narcissism, or even nudism as the ethical or moral motivation for personal action, and hence, 'religion' — a step that seems wholly inconsistent with the intent of the religion clauses." OFFICE OF LEGAL POLICY, U.S. DEP'T. OF JUSTICE, RELIGIOUS LIBERTY UNDER THE FREE EXERCISE CLAUSE 26 (1986). Similarly, a respected American jurisprudence teacher, the late Edward J. Murphy, once wrote:

> In a sense this is a very "religious" society. There are all sorts of gods. . . . [T]he question for all of us is not *whether* we will be guided by an ultimate authority, but *who* or *what* that authority will be. Is it to be God? Or is it to be ourselves? Or the State? Or a political party? Or a race? Or an economic class? Or the Stars? Or Satan? Or what? Clearly, each of us will choose, and the choice will be consequential.

Edward J. Murphy, *Conflicting Ultimates: Jurisprudence as Religious Controversy*, 35 AM. J. JURIS. 129, 129–30 (1990). As a cultural matter, Professor Murphy is undoubtedly correct that who or what we aim our lives toward matters greatly. This again was Washington and Tocqueville's observation about the inumerable connections between religion and morality. It is important, therefore, not to have the Free Exercise Clause patronizing false gods. But which gods are false? In a religiously pluralistic nation, especially one guaranteeing religious freedom, are any and all conceptions of religion entitled to constitutional protection?

4. Prohibitions or Burdens?

Two cases decided in the same year, *Braunfeld v. Brown*, 366 U.S. 398 (1963), and *Sherbert v. Verner*, 374 U.S. 398 (1963), may seem in direct conflict, because they are. Both deal with more or less generally applicable laws or regulations — *Braunfeld* with a Sunday closing law that adversely affected orthodox Jews who for religious reasons closed on Saturday, and thus lost an entire weekend's worth of business, and *Sherbert* with a general state law precluding employment compensation for those who refuse to work "without good cause," including by application, a Seventh Day Adventist who, in accord with her faith, would not work on Saturday. Both laws "burdened" the exercise of religious practice, but *Braunfeld* held that it merely made the exercise of faith "more expensive," 366 U.S. at 605, while *Sherbert* reasoned that the Free Exercise Clause precludes forcing a person to "choose between" her religion and government benefits. 374 U.S. at 404. The majority claims *Sherbert* is "wholly dissimilar" from *Braunfeld*, in that the state had a compelling interest in a uniform day of rest in the latter, but not in avoiding fraudulent employment claims in the former. *Id.* at 408. Maybe, but Justice Stewart, concurring only in the result of *Sherbert*, highlights that Mr. Braunfeld's loss of his business far outweighed Mrs. Sherbert's denial of compensation payments. *Id.* at 417–18 (Stewart, J., concurring). The *Sherbert* opinion is included below because it will have continuing relevance as an exception to the rule established in the subsequent case, *Employment Division v. Smith*, 494 U.S. 872 (1990) (discussed in Part 5).

Sherbert will be distinguished differently, as a particularized denial of compensation based upon religion — that is, Mrs. Sherbert lost her benefits only after a government administrator concluded that declining work for religious reasons wasn't a "good cause." *Id.* at 884. That distinction at least makes sense; however, there is a lingering problem. Both *Braunfeld* and *Sherbert* assume that government action which indirectly *burdens* a religious practice falls within a constitutional limitation on *prohibiting* religious practice. When the framers wanted to use a word suggesting burden, they knew how to do it, say, in the Free Speech Clause precluding its "abridgment." Thus, it is possible to argue that the words "or prohibiting the free exercise" mean actually forbidding a religious belief or preventing a religious practice — as in *Wisconsin v. Yoder*, above — not merely making it more expensive [*Braunfeld*] or difficult [*Sherbert*]. Nominally, the Court has not been this textualist; after all, Mrs. Sherbert won with only a burden. However, *Employment Division v. Smith* suggests a retrenchment by the Court from protecting religious exercise from religiously neutral, generally applicable statutes. Might this retrenchment not have occurred, had the Court applied the Free Exercise Clause only to prohibitions, thus lessening the occasion for conflict between religious value and government edict?

SHERBERT v. VERNER
374 U.S. 398 (1963)

MR. JUSTICE BRENNAN delivered the opinion of the Court.

Appellant, a member of the Seventh-Day Adventist Church, was discharged by her South Carolina employer because she would not work on Saturday, the Sabbath Day of her faith. When she was unable to obtain other employment because from conscientious scruples she would not take Saturday work, she filed a claim for unemployment compensation benefits under the South Carolina Unemployment Compensation Act. That law provides that, to be eligible for benefits, a claimant must be "able to work and . . . available for work"; and, further, that a claimant is ineligible for benefits "[i]f . . . he has failed, without good cause . . . to accept available suitable work when offered him by the employment office or the employer. . . ." The appellee Employment Security Commission, in administrative proceedings under the statute, found that appellant's restriction upon her availability for Saturday work brought her within the provision disqualifying for benefits insured workers who fail, without good cause, to accept "suitable work when offered . . . by the employment office or the employer. . . ." The Commission's finding was sustained by the Court of Common Pleas for Spartanburg County. That court's judgment was in turn affirmed by the South Carolina Supreme Court, which rejected appellant's contention that, as applied to her, the disqualifying provisions of the South Carolina statute abridged her right to the free exercise of her religion secured under the Free Exercise Clause of the First Amendment through the Fourteenth Amendment. The State Supreme Court held specifically that appellant's ineligibility infringed no constitutional liberties because such a construction of the statute "places no restriction upon the appellant's freedom of religion nor does it in any way prevent her in the exercise of her right and freedom to observe her religious beliefs in accordance with the dictates of her conscience." We noted probable jurisdiction of appellant's appeal. We reverse the judgment of the South Carolina Supreme Court and remand for further proceedings not inconsistent with this opinion.

I

The door of the Free Exercise Clause stands tightly closed against any governmental regulation of religious *beliefs* as such, *Cantwell v. Connecticut* [(1940)]. Government may neither compel affirmation of a repugnant belief, *Torcaso v. Watkins* [(1961)]; nor penalize or discriminate against individuals or groups because they hold religious views abhorrent to the authorities, *Fowler v. Rhode Island* [(1953)]; nor employ the taxing power to inhibit the dissemination of particular religious views, *Murdock v. Pennsylvania* [(1943)]; *Follett v. McCormick* [(1944)]; *cf. Grosjean v. American Press Co.* [(1936)]. On the other hand, the Court has rejected challenges under the Free Exercise Clause to governmental regulation of certain overt acts prompted by religious beliefs or principles, for "even when the action is in accord with one's religious convictions, [it] is not totally free from legislative restrictions." *Braunfeld v. Brown* [(1961)]. The conduct or actions so regulated have invariably posed some substantial threat to public safety, peace or order. *See, e.g., Reynolds v. United States* [(1878)]; *Jacobson v. Massachusetts* [(1905)]; *Prince v. Massachusetts* [(1944)]; *Cleveland v. United States* [(1946)].

Plainly enough, appellant's conscientious objection to Saturday work constitutes no conduct prompted by religious principles of a kind within the reach of state legislation. If, therefore, the decision of the South Carolina Supreme Court is to withstand appellant's constitutional challenge, it must be either because her disqualification as a beneficiary represents no infringement by the State of her constitutional rights of free exercise, or because any incidental burden on the free exercise of appellant's religion may be justified by a "compelling state interest in the regulation of a subject within the State's constitutional power to regulate. . . ." *NAACP v. Button* [(1963)].

II

We turn first to the question whether the disqualification for benefits imposes any burden on the free exercise of appellant's religion. We think it is clear that it does. In a sense the consequences of such a disqualification to religious principles and practices may be only an indirect result of welfare legislation within the State's general competence to enact; it is true that no criminal sanctions directly compel appellant to work a six-day week. But this is only the beginning, not the end, of our inquiry. For "[i]f the purpose or effect of a law is to impede the observance of one or all religions or is to discriminate invidiously between religions, that law is constitutionally invalid even though the burden may be characterized as being only indirect." *Braunfeld.* Here not only is it apparent that appellant's declared ineligibility for benefits derives solely from the practice of her religion, but the pressure upon her to forego that practice is unmistakable. The ruling forces her to choose between following the precepts of her religion and forfeiting benefits, on the one hand, and abandoning one of the precepts of her religion in order to accept work, on the other hand. Governmental imposition of such a choice puts the same kind of burden upon the free exercise of religion as would a fine imposed against appellant for her Saturday worship.

Nor may the South Carolina court's construction of the statute be saved from constitutional infirmity on the ground that unemployment compensation benefits are not appellant's "right" but merely a "privilege." It is too late in the day to doubt that the liberties of religion and expression may be infringed by the denial of or placing of conditions upon a benefit or privilege. . . .

Significantly South Carolina expressly saves the Sunday worshipper from having to make the kind of choice which we here hold infringes the Sabbatarian's religious liberty. When in times of "national emergency" the textile plants are authorized by the State Commissioner of Labor to operate on Sunday, "no employee shall be required to work on Sunday . . . who is conscientiously opposed to Sunday work; and if any employee should refuse to work on Sunday on account of conscientious . . . objections he or she shall not jeopardize his or her seniority by such refusal or be discriminated against in any other manner." S.C. Code, § 64-4. No question of the disqualification of a Sunday worshipper for benefits is likely to arise, since we cannot suppose that an employer will discharge him in violation of this statute. The unconstitutionality of the disqualification of the Sabbatarian is thus compounded by the religious discrimination which South Carolina's general statutory scheme necessarily effects.

III

We must next consider whether some compelling state interest enforced in the eligibility provisions of the South Carolina statute justifies the substantial infringement of appellant's First Amendment right. . . . The appellees suggest no more than a possibility that the filing of fraudulent claims by unscrupulous claimants feigning religious objections to Saturday work might not only dilute the unemployment compensation fund but also hinder the scheduling by employers of necessary Saturday work. But that possibility is not apposite here because no such objection appears to have been made before the South Carolina Supreme Court, and we are unwilling to assess the importance of an asserted state interest without the views of the state court. Nor, if the contention had been made below, would the record appear to sustain it; there is no proof whatever to warrant such fears of malingering or deceit as those which the respondents now advance. Even if consideration of such evidence is not foreclosed by the prohibition against judicial inquiry into the truth or falsity of religious beliefs, *United States v. Ballard* [(1944)] — a question as to which we intimate no view since it is not before us — it is highly doubtful whether such evidence would be sufficient to warrant a substantial infringement of religious liberties. For even if the possibility of spurious claims did threaten to dilute the fund and disrupt the scheduling of work, it would plainly be incumbent upon the appellees to demonstrate that no alternative forms of regulation would combat such abuses without infringing First Amendment rights.

In these respects, then, the state interest asserted in the present case is wholly dissimilar to the interests which were found to justify the less direct burden upon religious practices in *Braunfeld v. Brown, supra.* The Court recognized that the Sunday closing law which that decision sustained undoubtedly served "to make the practice of [the Orthodox Jewish merchants'] . . . religious beliefs more expensive." But the statute was nevertheless saved by a countervailing factor which finds no equivalent in the instant case — a strong state interest in providing one uniform day of rest for all workers. That secular objective could be achieved, the Court found, only by declaring Sunday to be that day of rest. Requiring exemptions for Sabbatarians, while theoretically possible, appeared to present an administrative problem of such magnitude, or to afford the exempted class so great a competitive advantage, that such a requirement would have rendered the entire statutory scheme unworkable. . . .

IV

In holding as we do, plainly we are not fostering the "establishment" of the Seventh-Day Adventist religion in South Carolina, for the extension of unemployment benefits to Sabbatarians in common with Sunday worshippers reflects nothing more than the governmental obligation of neutrality in the face of religious differences, and does not represent that involvement of religious with secular institutions which it is the object of the Establishment Clause to forestall.

. . . Our holding today is only that South Carolina may not constitutionally apply the eligibility provisions so as to constrain a worker to abandon his religious convictions respecting the day of rest. This holding but reaffirms a principle that we announced a decade and a half ago, namely that no State may "exclude individual Catholics, Lutherans, Mohammedans, Baptists, Jews, Methodists, Non-believers, Presbyterians, or the members of any other faith, *because of their faith, or lack of it,* from receiving the benefits of public welfare legislation." *Everson v. Board of Education* (1947).

In view of the result we have reached under the First and Fourteenth Amendments' guarantee of free exercise of religion, we have no occasion to consider appellant's claim that the denial of benefits also deprived her of the equal protection of the laws in violation of the Fourteenth Amendment.

The judgment of the South Carolina Supreme Court is reversed and the case is remanded for further proceedings not inconsistent with this opinion.

It is so ordered.

MR. JUSTICE DOUGLAS, concurring.

This case is resolvable not in terms of what an individual can demand of government, but solely in terms of what government may not do to an individual in violation of his religious scruples. The fact that government cannot exact from me a surrender of one iota of my religious scruples does not, of course, mean that I can demand of government a sum of money, the better to exercise them. For the Free Exercise Clause is written in terms of what the government cannot do to the individual, not in terms of what the individual can exact from the government.

MR. JUSTICE STEWART, concurring in the result.

Although fully agreeing with the result which the Court reaches in this case, I cannot join the Court's opinion. This case presents a double-barreled dilemma, which in all candor I think the Court's opinion has not succeeded in papering over. The dilemma ought to be resolved.

I

I am convinced that no liberty is more essential to the continued vitality of the free society which our Constitution guarantees than is the religious liberty protected by the Free Exercise Clause explicit in the First Amendment and imbedded in the Fourteenth. And I regret that on occasion, and specifically in *Braunfeld v. Brown, supra*, the Court has shown what has seemed to me a distressing insensitivity to the appropriate demands of this constitutional guarantee. By contrast I think that the Court's approach to the Establishment Clause has on occasion . . . and specifically in *Engel [v. Vitale*, (1962)], [*Sch. Dist. v.*] *Schempp* [(1963)] and *Murray [v. Curlett* (companion case to *Schempp*)], been not only insensitive, but positively wooden, and that the Court has accorded to the Establishment Clause a meaning which neither the words, the history, nor the intention of the authors of that specific constitutional provision even remotely suggests.

But my views as to the correctness of the Court's decisions in these cases are beside the point here. The point is that the decisions are on the books. And the result is that there are many situations where legitimate claims under the Free Exercise Clause will run into head-on collision with the Court's insensitive and sterile construction of the Establishment Clause. The controversy now before us is clearly such a case.

Because the appellant refuses to accept available jobs which would require her to work on Saturdays, South Carolina has declined to pay unemployment compensation benefits to her. Her refusal to work on Saturdays is based on the tenets of her religious faith. The Court says that South Carolina cannot under these circumstances declare her to be not "available for work" within the meaning of its statute because to do so would violate her constitutional right to the free exercise of her religion.

Yet what this Court has said about the Establishment Clause must inevitably lead to a diametrically opposite result. If the appellant's refusal to work on

Saturdays were based on indolence, or on a compulsive desire to watch the Saturday television programs, no one would say that South Carolina could not hold that she was not "available for work" within the meaning of its statute. That being so, the Establishment Clause as construed by this Court not only *permits* but affirmatively *requires* South Carolina equally to deny the appellant's claim for unemployment compensation when her refusal to work on Saturdays is based upon her religious creed. For, as said in *Everson v. Board of Education* [(1947)], the Establishment Clause bespeaks "a government . . . stripped of all power . . . to support, or otherwise to assist any or all religions . . . ," and no State "can pass laws which aid one religion . . . ." . . .

To require South Carolina to so administer its laws as to pay public money to the appellant under the circumstances of this case is thus clearly to require the State to violate the Establishment Clause as construed by this Court. This poses no problem for me, because I think the Court's mechanistic concept of the Establishment Clause is historically unsound and constitutionally wrong. I think the process of constitutional decision in the area of the relationships between government and religion demands considerably more than the invocation of broad-brushed rhetoric of the kind I have quoted. And I think that the guarantee of religious liberty embodied in the Free Exercise Clause affirmatively requires government to create an atmosphere of hospitality and accommodation to individual belief or disbelief. In short, I think our Constitution commands the positive protection by government of religious freedom — not only for a minority, however small — not only for the majority, however large — but for each of us.

South Carolina would deny unemployment benefits to a mother unavailable for work on Saturdays because she was unable to get a babysitter. Thus, we do not have before us a situation where a State provides unemployment compensation generally, and singles out for disqualification only those persons who are unavailable for work on religious grounds. This is not, in short, a scheme which operates so as to discriminate against religion as such. But the Court nevertheless holds that the State must prefer a religious over a secular ground for being unavailable for work — that state financial support of the appellant's religion is constitutionally required to carry out "the governmental obligation of neutrality in the face of religious differences . . . ."

II

My second difference with the Court's opinion is that I cannot agree that today's decision can stand consistently with *Braunfeld v. Brown.* The Court says that there was a "less direct burden upon religious practices" in that case than in this. With all respect, I think the Court is mistaken, simply as a matter of fact. The *Braunfeld* case involved a state *criminal* statute. The undisputed effect of that statute, as pointed out by MR. JUSTICE BRENNAN in his dissenting opinion in that case, was that " 'Plaintiff, Abraham Braunfeld, will be unable to continue in his business if he may not stay open on Sunday and he will thereby lose his capital investment.' In other words, the issue in this case — and we do not understand either appellees or the Court to contend otherwise — is whether a State may put an individual to a choice between his business and his religion."

The impact upon the appellant's religious freedom in the present case is considerably less onerous. We deal here not with a criminal statute, but with the particularized administration of South Carolina's Unemployment Compensation Act. Even upon the unlikely assumption that the appellant could not find suitable non-Saturday employment, the appellant at the worst would be denied a maximum of 22 weeks of compensation payments. I agree with the Court that the possibility of that denial is enough to infringe upon the appellant's constitutional right to the free exercise of her religion. But it is clear to me that in order to reach this conclusion the court must explicitly reject the reasoning of *Braunfeld v. Brown*. I think the *Braunfeld* case was wrongly decided and should be overruled, and accordingly I concur in the result reached by the Court in the case before us.

Mr. Justice Harlan, whom Mr. Justice White joins, dissenting.

Today's decision is disturbing both in its rejection of existing precedent and in its implications for the future. . . .

. . . Since virtually all of the mills in the Spartanburg area were operating on a six-day week, the appellant was "unavailable for work," and thus ineligible for benefits, when personal considerations prevented her from accepting employment on a full-time basis in the industry and locality in which she had worked. The fact that these personal considerations sprang from her religious convictions was wholly without relevance to the state court's application of the law. Thus in no proper sense can it be said that the State discriminated against the appellant on the basis of her religious beliefs or that she was denied benefits *because* she was a Seventh-Day Adventist. She was denied benefits just as any other claimant would be denied benefits who was not "available for work" for personal reasons.

With this background, this Court's decision comes into clearer focus. What the Court is holding is that if the State chooses to condition unemployment compensation on the applicant's availability for work, it is constitutionally compelled to *carve out an exception* — and to provide benefits — for those whose unavailability is due to their religious convictions. Such a holding has particular significance in two respects.

First, despite the Court's protestations to the contrary, the decision necessarily overrules *Braunfeld v. Brown*, which held that it did not offend the "Free Exercise" Clause of the Constitution for a State to forbid a Sabbatarian to do business on Sunday. . . .

Second, the implications of the present decision are far more troublesome than its apparently narrow dimensions would indicate at first glance. The meaning of today's holding, as already noted, is that the State must furnish unemployment benefits to one who is unavailable for work if the unavailability stems from the exercise of religious convictions. The State, in other words, must *single out* for financial assistance those whose behavior is religiously motivated, even though it denies such assistance to others whose identical behavior (in this case, inability to work on Saturdays) is not religiously motivated.

It has been suggested that such singling out of religious conduct for special treatment may violate the constitutional limitations on state action. My own view, however, is that at least under the circumstances of this case it would be a permissible accommodation of religion for the State, if it *chose* to do so, to create an exception to its eligibility requirements for persons like the appellant. The constitutional obligation of "neutrality," see *School District of Abington Township v. Schempp* [(1963)], is not so narrow a channel that the slightest deviation from an absolutely straight course leads to condemnation. . . .

For very much the same reasons, however, I cannot subscribe to the conclusion that the State is constitutionally *compelled* to carve out an exception to its general rule of eligibility in the present case. Those situations in which the Constitution may require special treatment on account of religion are, in my view, few and far between, and this view is amply supported by the course of constitutional litigation in this area. Such compulsion in the present case is particularly inappropriate in light of the indirect, remote, and insubstantial effect of the decision below on the exercise of appellant's religion and in light of the direct financial assistance to religion that today's decision requires.

For these reasons I respectfully dissent from the opinion and judgment of the Court.

5. No Religious Exemption from Neutral, Generally Applicable Laws

EMPLOYMENT DIVISION v. SMITH
494 U.S. 872 (1990)

JUSTICE SCALIA delivered the opinion of the Court.

This case requires us to decide whether the Free Exercise Clause of the First Amendment permits the State of Oregon to include religiously inspired peyote use within the reach of its general criminal prohibition on use of that drug, and thus permits the State to deny unemployment benefits to persons dismissed from their jobs because of such religiously inspired use.

I

Oregon law prohibits the knowing or intentional possession of a "controlled substance" unless the substance has been prescribed by a medical practitioner. . . .

Respondents Alfred Smith and Galen Black (hereinafter respondents) were fired from their jobs with a private drug rehabilitation organization because they ingested peyote [a controlled substance] for sacramental purposes at a ceremony of the Native American Church, of which both are members. When respondents applied to petitioner Employment Division (hereinafter petitioner) for unemployment compensation, they were determined to be ineligible for benefits because they had been discharged for work-related "misconduct." . . .

. . . [T]he Oregon Supreme Court held that respondents' religiously inspired use of peyote fell within the prohibition of the Oregon statute, which "makes no exception for the sacramental use" of the drug. It then considered whether that prohibition was valid under the Free Exercise Clause, and concluded that it was not. The court therefore reaffirmed its previous ruling that the State could not deny unemployment benefits to respondents for having engaged in that practice.

We . . . granted certiorari.

II

A

. . . [T]he "exercise of religion" often involves not only belief and profession but the performance of (or abstention from) physical acts: assembling with others for a worship service, participating in sacramental use of bread and wine, proselytizing, abstaining from certain foods or certain modes of transportation. It would be true, we think (though no case of ours has involved the point), that a State would be "prohibiting the free exercise [of religion]" if it sought to ban such acts or abstentions only when they are engaged in for religious reasons, or only because of the religious belief that they display. It would doubtless be unconstitutional, for example, to ban the casting of "statues that are to be used for worship purposes," or to prohibit bowing down before a golden calf.

Respondents in the present case, however, seek to carry the meaning of "prohibiting the free exercise [of religion]" one large step further. They contend that their religious motivation for using peyote places them beyond the reach of a criminal law that is not specifically directed at their religious practice, and that is concededly constitutional as applied to those who use the drug for other reasons. . . .

. . . We have never held that an individual's religious beliefs excuse him from compliance with an otherwise valid law prohibiting conduct that the State is free to regulate. On the contrary, the record of more than a century of our free exercise jurisprudence contradicts that proposition. . . . We first had occasion to assert that principle in *Reynolds v. United States* (1879), where we rejected the claim that criminal laws against polygamy could not be constitutionally applied to those whose religion commanded the practice. "Laws," we said, "are made for the government of actions, and while they cannot interfere with mere religious belief and opinions, they may with practices. . . . Can a man excuse his practices to the contrary because of his religious belief? To permit this would be to make the professed doctrines of religious belief superior to the law of the land, and in effect to permit every citizen to become a law unto himself."

Subsequent decisions have consistently held that the right of free exercise does not relieve an individual of the obligation to comply with a "valid and neutral law of general applicability on the ground that the law proscribes (or prescribes) conduct that his religion prescribes (or proscribes)." In *Prince v. Massachusetts* (1944), we held that a mother could be prosecuted under the child labor laws for using her children to dispense literature in the streets, her religious motivation notwithstanding. We found no constitutional infirmity in "excluding [these children] from doing there what no other children may do." In *Braunfeld v. Brown* (1961) (plurality opinion), we upheld Sunday-closing laws against the claim that they burdened the religious practices of persons whose religions compelled them to refrain from work on other days. . . .

The only decisions in which we have held that the First Amendment bars application of a neutral, generally applicable law to religiously motivated action have involved not the Free Exercise Clause alone, but the Free Exercise Clause in conjunction with other constitutional protections, such as freedom of speech and of the press, see *Cantwell v. Connecticut* [(1940)] (invalidating a licensing system for religious and charitable solicitations under which the administrator had discretion to deny a license to any cause he deemed nonreligious); *Murdock v. Pennsylvania* (1943) (invalidating a flat tax on solicitation as applied to the dissemination of religious ideas); *Follett v. McCormick* (1944) (same), or the right of parents, acknowledged in *Pierce v. Society of Sisters* (1925), to direct the education of their children, see *Wisconsin v. Yoder* (1972) (invalidating compulsory school-attendance laws as applied to Amish parents who refused on religious grounds to send their children to school). Some of our cases prohibiting compelled expression, decided exclusively upon free speech grounds, have also involved freedom of religion, *cf. Wooley v. Maynard* (1977) (invalidating compelled display of a license plate slogan that offended individual religious beliefs); *West Virginia Bd. of Education v. Barnette* (1943) (invalidating compulsory flag salute statute challenged by religious objectors). . . .

The present case does not present such a hybrid situation, but a free exercise claim unconnected with any communicative activity or parental right. Respondents urge us to hold, quite simply, that when otherwise prohibitable conduct is accompanied by religious convictions, not only the convictions but the conduct itself must be free from governmental regulation. We have never held that, and decline to do so now. There being no contention that Oregon's drug law represents an attempt to regulate religious beliefs, the communication of religious beliefs, or the raising of one's children in those beliefs, the rule to which we have adhered ever since *Reynolds* plainly controls. . . .

B

Respondents argue that even though exemption from generally applicable criminal laws need not automatically be extended to religiously motivated actors, at least the claim for a religious exemption must be evaluated under the balancing test set forth in *Sherbert v. Verner* (1963). Under the *Sherbert* test, governmental actions that substantially burden a religious practice must be justified by a compelling governmental interest. Applying that test we have, on three occasions, invalidated state unemployment compensation rules that conditioned the availability of benefits upon an applicant's willingness to work under conditions forbidden by his religion. We have never invalidated any governmental action on the basis of the *Sherbert* test except the denial of unemployment compensation. Although we have sometimes purported to apply the *Sherbert* test in contexts other than that, we have always found the test satisfied. In recent years we have abstained from applying the *Sherbert* test (outside the unemployment compensation field) at all. In *Bowen v. Roy* (1986), we declined to apply *Sherbert* analysis to a federal statutory scheme that required benefit applicants and recipients to provide their Social Security numbers. The plaintiffs in that case asserted that it would violate their religious beliefs to obtain and provide a Social Security number for their daughter. We held the statute's application to the plaintiffs valid regardless of whether it was necessary to effectuate a compelling interest. In *Lyng v. Northwest Indian Cemetery Protective Assn.* (1988), we declined to apply *Sherbert* analysis to the Government's logging and road construction activities on lands used for religious purposes by several Native American Tribes, even though it was undisputed that the activities "could have devastating effects on traditional Indian religious practices." In *Goldman v. Weinberger* (1986), we rejected application of the *Sherbert* test to military dress regulations that forbade the wearing of yarmulkes. In *O'Lone v. Estate of Shabazz* (1987), we sustained, without mentioning the *Sherbert* test, a prison's refusal to excuse inmates from work requirements to attend worship services.

Even if we were inclined to breathe into *Sherbert* some life beyond the unemployment compensation field, we would not apply it to require exemptions from a generally applicable criminal law. The *Sherbert* test, it must be recalled, was developed in a context that lent itself to individualized governmental assessment of the reasons for the relevant conduct. As a plurality of the Court noted in *Roy*, a distinctive feature of unemployment compensation programs is that their eligibility criteria invite consideration of the particular circumstances behind an applicant's unemployment: "The statutory conditions [in *Sherbert* and *Thomas v. Review Bd. of Indiana Employment Division* (1981)] provided that a person was not eligible for unemployment compensation benefits if, 'without good cause,' he had quit work or refused available work. The 'good cause' standard created a mechanism for individualized exemptions." As the plurality pointed out in *Roy*, our decisions in the unemployment cases stand for the proposition that where the State has in place a system of individual exemptions, it may not refuse to extend that system to cases of "religious hardship" without compelling reason.

Whether or not the decisions are that limited, they at least have nothing to do with an across-the-board criminal prohibition on a particular form of con duct. . . . We conclude today that the sounder approach, and the approach in accord with the vast majority of our precedents, is to hold the [*Sherbert*] test inapplicable to such challenges. The government's ability to enforce generally applicable prohibitions of socially harmful conduct, like its ability to carry out other aspects of public policy, "cannot depend on measuring the effects of a governmental action on a religious objector's spiritual development." To make an individual's obligation to obey such a law contingent upon the law's coincidence with his religious beliefs, except where the State's interest is "compelling" — permitting him, by virtue of his beliefs, "to become a law unto himself," *Reynolds v. United States* — contradicts both constitutional tradition and common sense.

The "compelling government interest" requirement seems benign, because it is familiar from other fields. But using it as the standard that must be met before the government may accord different treatment on the basis of race, or before the government may regulate the content of speech, is not remotely comparable to using it for the purpose asserted here. What it produces in those other fields — equality of treatment and an unrestricted flow of contending speech — are constitutional norms; what it would produce here — a private right to ignore generally applicable laws — is a constitutional anomaly.

Nor is it possible to limit the impact of respondents' proposal by requiring a "compelling state interest" only when the conduct prohibited is "central" to the individual's religion. It is no more appropriate for judges to determine the "centrality" of religious beliefs before applying a "compelling interest" test in the free exercise field, than it would be for them to determine the "importance" of ideas before applying the "compelling interest" test in the free speech field. What principle of law or logic can be brought to bear to contradict a believer's assertion that a particular act is "central" to his personal faith? Judging the centrality of different religious practices is akin to the unacceptable "business of evaluating the relative merits of differing religious claims." . . .

If the "compelling interest" test is to be applied at all, then, it must be applied across the board, to all actions thought to be religiously commanded. Moreover, if "compelling interest" really means what it says (and watering it down here would subvert its rigor in the other fields where it is applied), many laws will not meet the test. Any society adopting such a system would be courting anarchy, but that danger increases in direct proportion to the society's diversity of religious beliefs, and its determination to coerce or suppress none of them. Precisely because "we are a cosmopolitan nation made up of people of almost every conceivable religious preference," and precisely because we value and protect that religious divergence, we cannot afford the luxury of deeming *presumptively invalid*, as applied to the religious objector, every regulation of conduct that does not protect an interest of the highest order. The rule respondents favor would open the prospect of constitutionally required religious exemptions from civic obligations of almost every conceivable kind — ranging from compulsory military service, to the payment of taxes, to health and safety regulation such as manslaughter and child neglect laws, compulsory vaccination laws, drug laws, and traffic laws, to social welfare legislation such as minimum wage laws, child labor laws, animal cruelty laws, see, *e.g., Church of the Lukumi Babalu Aye Inc. v. City of Hialeah* (S.D. Fla. 1989), environmental protection laws, and laws providing for equality of opportunity for the races. The First Amendment's protection of religious liberty does not require this.[35]

Values that are protected against government interference through enshrinement in the Bill of Rights are not thereby banished from the political process. Just as a society that believes in the negative protection accorded to the press by the First Amendment is likely to enact laws that affirmatively foster the dissemination of the printed word, so also a society that believes in the negative protection

---

[35] [5] JUSTICE O'CONNOR contends that the "parade of horribles" in the text only "demonstrates . . . that courts have been quite capable of . . . strik[ing] sensible balances between religious liberty and competing state interests." But the cases we cite have struck "sensible balances" only because they have all applied the general laws, despite the claims for religious exemption. In any event, JUSTICE O'CONNOR mistakes the purpose of our parade: it is not to suggest that courts would necessarily permit harmful exemptions from these laws (though they might), but to suggest that courts would constantly be in the business of determining whether the "severe impact" of various laws on religious practice (to use JUSTICE BLACKMUN's terminology), or the "constitutiona[l] significan[ce]" of the "burden on the specific plaintiffs" (to use JUSTICE O'CONNOR's terminology) suffices to permit us to confer an exemption. It is a parade of horribles because it is horrible to contemplate that federal judges will regularly balance against the importance of general laws the significance of religious practice.

accorded to religious belief can be expected to be solicitous of that value in its legislation as well. It is therefore not surprising that a number of States have made an exception to their drug laws for sacramental peyote use. But to say that a nondiscriminatory religious-practice exemption is permitted, or even that it is desirable, is not to say that it is constitutionally required, and that the appropriate occasions for its creation can be discerned by the courts. It may fairly be said that leaving accommodation to the political process will place at a relative disadvantage those religious practices that are not widely engaged in; but that unavoidable consequence of democratic government must be preferred to a system in which each conscience is a law unto itself or in which judges weigh the social importance of all laws against the centrality of all religious beliefs.

Because respondents' ingestion of peyote was prohibited under Oregon law, and because that prohibition is constitutional, Oregon may, consistent with the Free Exercise Clause, deny respondents unemployment compensation when their dismissal results from use of the drug. The decision of the Oregon Supreme Court is accordingly reversed.

It is so ordered.

JUSTICE O'CONNOR, with whom JUSTICE BRENNAN, JUSTICE MARSHALL, and JUSTICE BLACKMUN join as to Parts I and II, concurring in the judgment. [Although JUSTICE BRENNAN, JUSTICE MARSHALL, and JUSTICE BLACKMUN join Parts I and II of this opinion, they do not concur in the judgment.]

Although I agree with the result the Court reaches in this case, I cannot join its opinion. In my view, today's holding dramatically departs from well-settled First Amendment jurisprudence, appears unnecessary to resolve the question presented, and is incompatible with our Nation's fundamental commitment to individual religious liberty.

I

Respondents contend that, because the Oregon Supreme Court declined to decide whether the Oregon Constitution prohibits criminal prosecution for the religious use of peyote, any ruling on the federal constitutional question would be premature. Respondents are of course correct that the Oregon Supreme Court may eventually decide that the Oregon Constitution requires the State to provide an exemption from its general criminal prohibition for the religious use of peyote. Such a decision would then reopen the question whether a State may nevertheless deny unemployment compensation benefits to claimants who are discharged for engaging in such conduct. As the case comes to us today, however, the Oregon Supreme Court has plainly ruled that Oregon's prohibition against possession of controlled substances does not contain an exemption for the religious use of peyote. . . . [T]his finding [is] a "necessary predicate to a correct evaluation of respondents' federal claim," [and thus] the question presented and addressed is properly before the Court.

II

The Court today extracts from our long history of free exercise precedents the single categorical rule that "if prohibiting the exercise of religion . . . is . . . merely the incidental effect of a generally applicable and otherwise valid provision, the First Amendment has not been offended." Indeed, the Court holds that where the law is a generally applicable criminal prohibition, our usual free exercise jurisprudence does not even apply. To reach this sweeping result, however, the Court must not only give a strained reading of the First Amendment but must also disregard our consistent application of free exercise doctrine to cases involving generally applicable regulations that burden religious conduct.

A

The Court today . . . interprets the Clause to permit the government to prohibit, without justification, conduct mandated by an individual's religious beliefs, so long as that prohibition is generally applicable. But a law that prohibits certain conduct — conduct that happens to be an act of worship for someone — manifestly does prohibit that person's free exercise of his religion. A person who is barred from engaging in religiously motivated conduct is barred from freely exercising his religion. . . .

The Court responds that generally applicable laws are "one large step" removed from laws aimed at specific religious practices. The First Amendment, however, does not distinguish between laws that are generally applicable and laws that target particular religious practices. Indeed, few States would be so naive as to enact a law directly prohibiting or burdening a religious practice as such. Our free exercise cases have all concerned generally applicable laws that had the effect of significantly burdening a religious practice. . . .

To say that a person's right to free exercise has been burdened, of course, does not mean that he has an absolute right to engage in the conduct. Under our established First Amendment jurisprudence, we have recognized that the freedom to act, unlike the freedom to believe, cannot be absolute. Instead, we have respected both the First Amendment's express textual mandate and the governmental interest in regulation of conduct by requiring the government to justify any substantial burden on religiously motivated conduct by a compelling state interest and by means narrowly tailored to achieve that interest. . . .

. . . [I]n [*Wisconsin v.*] *Yoder* [(1972),] we expressly rejected the interpretation the Court now adopts:

> "[O]ur decisions have rejected the idea that religiously grounded conduct is always outside the protection of the Free Exercise Clause. It is true that activities of individuals, even when religiously based, are often subject to regulation by the States in the exercise of their undoubted power to promote the health, safety, and general welfare, or the Federal Government in the exercise of its delegated powers. But to agree that religiously grounded conduct must often be subject to the broad police power of the State is not to deny that there are areas of conduct protected by the Free

Exercise Clause of the First Amendment and thus beyond the power of the State to control, *even under regulations of general applicability.* . . .

". . . A regulation neutral on its face may, in its application, nonetheless offend the constitutional requirement for government neutrality if it unduly burdens the free exercise of religion." (emphasis added).

The Court endeavors to escape from our decision[] in . . . *Yoder* by labeling [it a] "hybrid" decision[], but there is no denying that [it and others] expressly relied on the Free Exercise Clause. . . .

B

In my view, however, the essence of a free exercise claim is relief from a burden imposed by government on religious practices or beliefs, whether the burden is imposed directly through laws that prohibit or compel specific religious practices, or indirectly through laws that, in effect, make abandonment of one's own religion or conformity to the religious beliefs of others the price of an equal place in the civil community. . . .

Legislatures, of course, have always been "left free to reach actions which were in violation of social duties or subversive of good order." . . .

The Court today gives no convincing reason to depart from settled First Amendment jurisprudence. There is nothing talismanic about neutral laws of general applicability or general criminal prohibitions, for laws neutral toward religion can coerce a person to violate his religious conscience or intrude upon his religious duties just as effectively as laws aimed at religion. Although the Court suggests that the compelling interest test, as applied to generally applicable laws, would result in a "constitutional anomaly," the First Amendment unequivocally makes freedom of religion, like freedom from race discrimination and freedom of speech, a "constitutional nor[m]," not an "anomaly." . . .

Finally, the Court today suggests that the disfavoring of minority religions is an "unavoidable consequence" under our system of government and that accommodation of such religions must be left to the political process. In my view, however, the First Amendment was enacted precisely to protect the rights of those whose religious practices are not shared by the majority and may be viewed with hostility. The history of our free exercise doctrine amply demonstrates the harsh impact majoritarian rule has had on unpopular or emerging religious groups such as the Jehovah's Witnesses and the Amish. . . .

III

The Court's holding today not only misreads settled First Amendment precedent; it appears to be unnecessary to this case. I would reach the same result applying our established free exercise jurisprudence.

A

There is . . . no dispute that Oregon has a significant interest in enforcing laws that control the possession and use of controlled substances by its citizens. . . .

B

. . . Although the question is close, I would conclude that uniform application of Oregon's criminal prohibition is "essential to accomplish" its overriding interest in preventing the physical harm caused by the use of a Schedule I controlled substance. Oregon's criminal prohibition represents that State's judgment that the possession and use of controlled substances, even by only one person, is inherently harmful and dangerous. . . .

I would therefore adhere to our established free exercise jurisprudence and hold that the State in this case has a compelling interest in regulating peyote use by its citizens and that accommodating respondents' religiously motivated conduct "will unduly interfere with fulfillment of the governmental interest." Accordingly, I concur in the judgment of the Court.

JUSTICE BLACKMUN, with whom JUSTICE BRENNAN and JUSTICE MARSHALL join, dissenting.

This Court over the years painstakingly has developed a consistent and exacting standard to test the constitutionality of a state statute that burdens the free exercise of religion. Such a statute may stand only if the law in general, and the State's refusal to allow a religious exemption in particular, are justified by a compelling interest that cannot be served by less restrictive means.

I

In weighing the clear interest of respondents Smith and Black (hereinafter respondents) in the free exercise of their religion against Oregon's asserted interest in enforcing its drug laws, it is important to articulate in precise terms the state interest involved. It is not the State's broad interest in fighting the critical "war on drugs" that must be weighed against respondents' claim, but the State's narrow interest in refusing to make an exception for the religious, ceremonial use of peyote. . . .

The State's interest in enforcing its prohibition, in order to be sufficiently compelling to outweigh a free exercise claim, cannot be merely abstract or symbolic. The State cannot plausibly assert that unbending application of a criminal prohibition is essential to fulfill any compelling interest, if it does not, in fact, attempt to enforce that prohibition. In this case, the State actually has not evinced any concrete interest in enforcing its drug laws against religious users of peyote. Oregon has never sought to prosecute respondents, and does not claim that it has made significant enforcement efforts against other religious users of peyote. The State's asserted interest thus amounts only to the symbolic preservation of an unenforced prohibition. . . .

Similarly, this Court's prior decisions have not allowed a government to rely on mere speculation about potential harms, but have demanded evidentiary support for a refusal to allow a religious exception. . . .

The fact that peyote is classified as a Schedule I controlled substance does not, by itself, show that any and all uses of peyote, in any circumstance, are inherently harmful and dangerous. The Federal Government, which created the classifications of unlawful drugs from which Oregon's drug laws are derived, apparently does not find peyote so dangerous as to preclude an exemption for religious use. . . .

The carefully circumscribed ritual context in which respondents used peyote is far removed from the irresponsible and unrestricted recreational use of unlawful drugs. . . .

Moreover, just as in *Yoder*, the values and interests of those seeking a religious exemption in this case are congruent, to a great degree, with those the State seeks to promote through its drug laws. Not only does the church's doctrine forbid nonreligious use of peyote; it also generally advocates self-reliance, familial responsibility, and abstinence from alcohol. . . .

The State also seeks to support its refusal to make an exception for religious use of peyote by invoking its interest in abolishing drug trafficking. There is, however, practically no illegal traffic in peyote. . . .

Finally, the State argues that granting an exception for religious peyote use would erode its interest in the uniform, fair, and certain enforcement of its drug laws. The State fears that, if it grants an exemption for religious peyote use, a flood of other claims to religious exemptions will follow. It would then be placed in a dilemma, it says, between allowing a patchwork of exemptions that would hinder its law enforcement efforts, and risking a violation of the Establishment Clause by arbitrarily limiting its religious exemptions. This argument, however, could be made in almost any free exercise case. . . .

The State's apprehension of a flood of other religious claims is purely speculative. Almost half the States, and the Federal Government, have maintained an exemption for religious peyote use for many years, and apparently have not found themselves overwhelmed by claims to other religious exemptions. . . .

II

Finally, although I agree with JUSTICE O'CONNOR that courts should refrain from delving into questions whether, as a matter of religious doctrine, a particular practice is "central" to the religion, I do not think this means that the courts must turn a blind eye to the severe impact of a State's restrictions on the adherents of a minority religion.

Respondents believe, and their sincerity has *never* been at issue, that the peyote plant embodies their deity, and eating it is an act of worship and communion. Without peyote, they could not enact the essential ritual of their religion.

III

For these reasons, I conclude that Oregon's interest in enforcing its drug laws against religious use of peyote is not sufficiently compelling to outweigh respondents' right to the free exercise of their religion. Since the State could not constitutionally enforce its criminal prohibition against respondents, the interests underlying the State's drug laws cannot justify its denial of unemployment benefits.

. . .

I dissent.

NOTE

Do you find *Smith* consistent with the importance of religious faith to the framers? The *Smith* decision stirred considerable controversy, both in and outside Congress. Congress directly reacted with the passage of the Religious Freedom Restoration Act (RFRA) of 1993, Pub. L. No. 103-141, 107 Stat. 1488 (codified at 42 U.S.C. §§ 2000bb to bb-4 (1994)). However, in *City of Boerne v. Flores*, 521 U.S. 507 (1997), the Court found RFRA to be unconstitutional. *Boerne* involved the application of a garden-variety zoning ordinance to a local church that had been placed within an historic zone. The City of Boerne, Texas, had refused to grant the church a demolition or alteration permit in order to expand because of its negative impact on the historic structure, which sat on a hill as a focal point within the community. Archbishop Flores sued on behalf of the church under RFRA.

Writing for seven members of the Court, Justice Kennedy observed that "Congress enacted RFRA in direct response to the Court's decision in [*Smith*]," and the *Smith* Court's declination to apply the balancing test from *Sherbert v. Verner*. *Id.* at 2160. Justice Kennedy continued:

> The application of the *Sherbert* test, the *Smith* decision explained, would have produced an anomaly in the law, a constitutional right to ignore neutral laws of general applicability. The anomaly would have been accentuated, the Court reasoned, by the difficulty of determining whether a particular practice was central to an individual's religion.

Id. at 2161. Justice Kennedy explained that the Court did not view *Smith* as a substantial break from precedent, since, pre-*Smith*, "[t]he only instances where a neutral, generally applicable law had failed to pass constitutional muster were cases in which other constitutional protections were at stake." *Id.*

This did not satisfy Congress, however, and in passing RFRA Congress announced:

> (1) [T]he framers of the Constitution, recognizing free exercise of religion as an unalienable right, secured its protection in the First Amendment to the Constitution;

> (2) laws "neutral" toward religion may burden religious exercise as surely as laws intended to interfere with religious exercise;

(3) governments should not substantially burden religious exercise without compelling justification;

(4) in *Employment Division v. Smith*, 494 U.S. 872 (1990), the Supreme Court virtually eliminated the requirement that the government justify burdens on religious exercise imposed by laws neutral toward religion; and

(5) the compelling interest test as set forth in prior Federal court rulings is a workable test for striking sensible balances between religious liberty and competing prior governmental interests.

42 U.S.C. § 2000bb(a). Congress further declared the purposes of RFRA as being:

(1) to restore the compelling interest test as set forth in *Sherbert v. Verner*, 374 U.S. 398 (1963) and *Wisconsin v. Yoder*, 406 U.S. 205 (1972) and to guarantee its application in all cases where free exercise of religion is substantially burdened; and

(2) to provide a claim or defense to persons whose religious exercise is substantially burdened by government.

Id. § 2000bb(b).

Rather blatantly, RFRA attempted to reverse *Smith* by prohibiting government from "substantially burden[ing] a person's exercise of religion even if the burden results from a rule of general applicability," unless the government could show that the burden "(1) [wa]s in furtherance of a compelling governmental interest; and (2) [wa]s the least restrictive means of furthering that compelling governmental interest." *Id.* § 2000bb-1. RFRA's scope encompassed any "branch, department, agency, instrumentality, and official (or other person acting under color of law) of the United States," as well as any "State, or . . . subdivision of a State." § 2000bb-2(1). RFRA further applied "to all Federal and State law, and the implementation of that law, whether statutory or otherwise, and whether adopted before or after [RFRA's enactment]." *Id.* § 2000bb-3(a). Accordingly, RFRA's broad coverage reached local and municipal ordinances.

The proponents of RFRA argued that RFRA was not a reversal of *Smith*, but a proper exercise of Congress' power under section 5 of the Fourteenth Amendment. This power is discussed more fully in Chapter Four, but briefly it provides that Congress has the power "to enforce" the provisions of section 1 of the amendment, including the provision that no state can deprive anyone of "liberty . . . without due process of law." U.S. Const. amend. XIV, § 1. The Court agreed that Congress can enact legislation under § 5 enforcing the constitutional right to the free exercise of religion, because the Free Exercise Clause has been "incorporated" against the states through the Fourteenth Amendment's Due Process Clause. *Boerne*, 521 U.S. at 519 (citing *Cantwell v. Connecticut*, 310 U.S. 296, 303 (1940)). However, the Court concluded that RFRA went too far because it was not remedial, but substantive. In the Court's words:

Legislation which alters the meaning of the Free Exercise Clause cannot be said to be enforcing the Clause. Congress does not enforce a constitutional right by changing what the right is. It has been given the power "to enforce," not the power to determine what constitutes a constitutional violation. Were it not so, what Congress would be enforcing would no longer be, in any meaningful sense, the "provisions of [the Fourteenth Amendment]."

Id. at 519.

In particular, RFRA was not a proper exercise of remedial or preventive power, because it lacked "congruence between the means used and the ends to be achieved." *Id.* at 530. There was no showing in the legislative record that generally applicable laws had been passed out of religious bigotry. Concluded the Court:

> The stringent test RFRA demands of state laws reflects a lack of proportionality or congruence between the means adopted and the legitimate end to be achieved. If an objector can show a substantial burden on his free exercise, the State must demonstrate a compelling governmental interest and show that the law is the least restrictive means of furthering its interest. . . . If " 'compelling interest' really means what it says . . . many laws will not meet the test. . . . [The test] would open the prospect of constitutionally required religious exemptions from civic obligations of almost every conceivable kind." Laws valid under *Smith* would fall under RFRA without regard to whether they had the object of stifling or punishing free exercise. We make these observations not to reargue the position of the majority in *Smith* but to illustrate the substantive alteration of its holding attempted by RFRA. Even assuming RFRA would be interpreted in effect to mandate some lesser test, say one equivalent to intermediate scrutiny, the statute nevertheless would require searching judicial scrutiny of state law with the attendant likelihood of invalidation. This is a considerable congressional intrusion into the States' traditional prerogatives and general authority to regulate for the health and welfare of their citizens.

Id. at 533–34 (quoting *Smith*, 494 U.S. at 888).

The Court in *Boerne* did not reargue the merits of *Smith* as a whole, but assumed its continuing validity. Nevertheless, Justice Scalia defended *Smith* in a separate opinion while Justices O'Connor, Breyer, and Souter indicated a desire to have the principle in *Smith* reargued, even as Justice O'Connor fully shared the Court's discussion of the proper scope of Congress' § 5 authority in *Boerne*. Here is part of the colloquy between Justices Scalia and O'Connor:

CITY OF BOERNE v. FLORES
521 U.S. 507 (1997)

[The majority opinion dealing with Congress' § 5 power to define religious freedom is discussed more fully in Chapter Five.]

Justice Scalia, with whom Justice Stevens joins, concurring in part.

I write to respond briefly to the claim of Justice O'Connor's dissent (hereinafter "the dissent") that historical materials support a result contrary to the one reached in *Employment Div, Dept. of Human Resources of Ore. v. Smith*. . . . The material that the dissent claims is at odds with *Smith* either has little to say about the issue or is in fact more consistent with *Smith* than with the dissent's interpretation of the Free Exercise Clause. . . .

. . . The Free Exercise Clause, the dissent claims, "is best understood as an affirmative guarantee of the right to participate in religious practices and conduct without impermissible governmental interference, even when such conduct conflicts with a neutral, generally applicable law"; thus, even neutral laws of general application may be invalid if they burden religiously motivated conduct. However, the early "free exercise" enactments cited by the dissent protect only against action that is taken "for" or "in respect of" religion. . . . It is eminently arguable that application of neutral, generally applicable laws of the sort the dissent refers to — such as zoning laws — would not constitute action taken "for," "in respect of," or "on account of" one's religion, or "discriminatory" action.

Assuming, however, that the affirmative protection of religion accorded by the early "free exercise" enactments sweeps as broadly as the dissent's theory would require, those enactments do not support the dissent's view, since they contain "provisos" that significantly qualify the affirmative protection they grant. According to the dissent, the "provisos" support its view because they would have been "superfluous" if "the Court was correct in *Smith* that generally applicable laws are enforceable regardless of religious conscience." I disagree. In fact, the most plausible reading of the "free exercise" enactments (if their affirmative provisions are read broadly, as the dissent's view requires) is a virtual restatement of *Smith*: Religious exercise shall be permitted so long as it does not violate general laws governing conduct. The "provisos" in the enactments negate a license to act in a manner "unfaithfull to the Lord Proprietary" (Maryland Act Concerning Religion of 1649), or "behav[e]" in other than a "peaceabl[e] and quie[t]" manner (Rhode Island Charter of 1663), or "disturb the public peace" (New Hampshire Constitution), or interfere with the "peace [and] safety of th[e] State" (New York, Maryland, and Georgia Constitutions), or "demea[n]" oneself in other than a "peaceable and orderly manner" (Northwest Ordinance of 1787). At the time these provisos were enacted, keeping "peace" and "order" seems to have meant, precisely, obeying the laws. . . . This limitation upon the scope of religious exercise would have been in accord with the background political philosophy of the age (associated most prominently with John Locke), which regarded freedom as the right "to do only what was not lawfully prohibited," Ellis West, *The Case Against a Right to Religion-Based Exemptions*, 4 NOTRE DAME J. L. ETHICS & PUB. POL'Y 591, 624 (1990). . . .

The dissent's final source of claimed historical support consists of statements of certain of the Framers in the context of debates about proposed legislative enactments or debates over general principles (not in connection with the drafting of State or Federal Constitutions). Those statements are subject to the same objection as was the evidence about legislative accommodation: There is no reason to think they were meant to describe what was constitutionally required (and judicially enforceable), as opposed to what was thought to be legislatively or even morally desirable. . . .

It seems to me that the most telling point made by the dissent is to be found, not in what it says, but in what it fails to say. Had the understanding in the period surrounding the ratification of the Bill of Rights been that the various forms of accommodation discussed by the dissent were constitutionally required (either by State Constitutions or by the Federal Constitution), it would be surprising not to find a single state or federal case refusing to enforce a generally applicable statute because of its failure to make accommodation. Yet the dissent cites none — and to my knowledge, and to the knowledge of the academic defenders of the dissent's position, none exists. The closest one can come in the period prior to 1850 is the decision of a New York City municipal court in 1813, holding that the New York Constitution of 1777 required acknowledgment of a priest-penitent privilege, to protect a Catholic priest from being compelled to testify as to the contents of a confession. *People v. Philips*, Court of General Sessions, City of New York (June 14, 1813), *excerpted in Privileged Communications to Clergymen*, 1 CATH. LAW. 199 (1955). Even this lone case is weak authority, not only because it comes from a minor court, but also because it did not involve a statute, and the same result might possibly have been achieved (without invoking constitutional entitlement) by the court's simply modifying the common-law rules of evidence to recognize such a privilege. On the other side of the ledger, moreover, there are two cases, from the Supreme Court of Pennsylvania, flatly rejecting the dissent's view. In *Philips v. Gratz* (Pa. 1831), the court held that a litigant was not entitled to a continuance of trial on the ground that appearing on his Sabbath would violate his religious principles. And in *Stansbury v. Marks* (Pa. 1793), decided just two years after the ratification of the Bill of Rights, the court imposed a fine on a witness who "refused to be sworn, because it was his Sabbath."

   . . . The issue presented by *Smith* is, quite simply, whether the people, through their elected representatives, or rather this Court, shall control the outcome of concrete cases [like this one]. For example, shall it be the determination of this Court, or rather of the people, whether church construction will be exempt from zoning laws? The historical evidence put forward by the dissent does nothing to undermine the conclusion we reached in *Smith*: It shall be the people.

JUSTICE O'CONNOR, with whom JUSTICE BREYER joins except as to a portion of Part I, dissenting.

   I dissent from the Court's disposition of this case. I agree with the Court that the issue before us is whether the Religious Freedom Restoration Act (RFRA) is a proper exercise of Congress' power to enforce § 5 of the Fourteenth Amendment. But as a yardstick for measuring the constitutionality of RFRA, the Court uses its holding in *Employment Div., Dept. of Human Resources of Ore. v. Smith*, the decision that prompted Congress to enact RFRA as a means of more rigorously enforcing the Free Exercise Clause. I remain of the view that *Smith* was wrongly decided, and I would use this case to reexamine the Court's holding there. Therefore, I would direct the parties to brief the question whether *Smith* represents the correct understanding of the Free Exercise Clause and set the case for reargument. If the Court were to correct the misinterpretation of the Free Exercise Clause set forth in *Smith*, it would simultaneously put our First Amendment jurisprudence back on course and allay the legitimate concerns of a majority in Congress who believed that *Smith* improperly restricted religious liberty. We would then be in a position to review RFRA in light of a proper interpretation of the Free Exercise Clause.

I

I agree with much of the reasoning set forth in Part III-A of the Court's opinion. Indeed, if I agreed with the Court's standard in *Smith*, I would join the opinion. As the Court's careful and thorough historical analysis shows, Congress lacks the "power to decree the substance of the Fourteenth Amendment's restrictions on the States." Rather, its power under § 5 of the Fourteenth Amendment extends only to enforcing the Amendment's provisions. In short, Congress lacks the ability independently to define or expand the scope of constitutional rights by statute. Accordingly, whether Congress has exceeded its § 5 powers turns on whether there is a "congruence and proportionality between the injury to be prevented or remedied and the means adopted to that end." This recognition does not, of course, in any way diminish Congress' obligation to draw its own conclusions regarding the Constitution's meaning. Congress, no less than this Court, is called upon to consider the requirements of the Constitution and to act in accordance with its dictates. But when it enacts legislation in furtherance of its delegated powers, Congress must make its judgments consistent with this Court's exposition of the Constitution and with the limits placed on its legislative authority by provisions such as the Fourteenth Amendment.

. . . [Nevertheless] I continue to believe that *Smith* adopted an improper standard for deciding free exercise claims. . . . Before *Smith*, our free exercise cases were generally in keeping with this idea: where a law substantially burdened religiously motivated conduct — regardless whether it was specifically targeted at religion or applied generally — we required government to justify that law with a compelling state interest and to use means narrowly tailored to achieve that interest.

The Court's rejection of this principle in *Smith* is supported neither by precedent nor . . . by history. . . .

II

B

The principle of religious "free exercise" and the notion that religious liberty deserved legal protection were by no means new concepts in 1791, when the Bill of Rights was ratified. To the contrary, these principles were first articulated in this country in the colonies of Maryland, Rhode Island, Pennsylvania, Delaware, and Carolina, in the mid-1600's. These colonies, though established as sanctuaries for particular groups of religious dissenters, extended freedom of religion to groups — although often limited to Christian groups — beyond their own. Thus, they encountered early on the conflicts that may arise in a society made up of a plurality of faiths.

The term "free exercise" appeared in an American legal document as early as

1648, when Lord Baltimore extracted from the new Protestant governor of Maryland and his councilors a promise not to disturb Christians, particularly Roman Catholics, in the "free exercise" of their religion. Soon after, in 1649, the Maryland Assembly enacted the first free exercise clause by passing the Act Concerning Religion: "[N]oe person . . . professing to beleive in Jesus Christ, shall from henceforth bee any waies troubled, Molested or discountenanced for or in respect of his or her religion nor in the free exercise thereof . . . nor any way [be] compelled to the beleife or exercise of any other Religion against his or her consent, soe as they be not unfaithfull to the Lord Proprietary, or molest or conspire against the civill Government." Act Concerning Religion of 1649. . . .

These documents suggest that, early in our country's history, several colonies acknowledged that freedom to pursue one's chosen religious beliefs was an essential liberty. Moreover, these colonies appeared to recognize that government should interfere in religious matters only when necessary to protect the civil peace or to prevent "licentiousness." In other words, when religious beliefs conflicted with civil law, religion prevailed unless important state interests militated otherwise. Such notions parallel the ideas expressed in our pre-*Smith* cases — that government may not hinder believers from freely exercising their religion, unless necessary to further a significant state interest.

E

. . . By its very nature, Madison wrote, the right to free exercise is "unalienable," both because a person's opinion "cannot follow the dictates of other[s]," and because it entails "a duty toward the Creator." Madison continued:

> "This duty [owed the Creator] is precedent both in order of time and degree of obligation, to the claims of Civil Society. . . . [E]very man who becomes a member of any Civil Society, [must] do it with a saving of his allegiance to the Universal Sovereign. We maintain therefore that in matters of Religion, no man's right is abridged by the institution of Civil Society, and that Religion is wholly exempt from its cognizance."

To Madison, then, duties to God were superior to duties to civil authorities — the ultimate loyalty was owed to God above all. Madison did not say that duties to the Creator are precedent only to those laws specifically directed at religion, nor did he strive simply to prevent deliberate acts of persecution or discrimination. The idea that civil obligations are subordinate to religious duty is consonant with the notion that government must accommodate, where possible, those religious practices that conflict with civil law.

These are but a few examples of various perspectives regarding the proper relationship between church and government that existed during the time the First Amendment was drafted and ratified. Obviously, since these thinkers approached the issue of religious freedom somewhat differently, it is not possible to distill their thoughts into one tidy formula. Nevertheless, a few general principles may be discerned. Foremost, these early leaders accorded religious exercise a special constitutional status. The right to free exercise was a substantive guarantee of individual liberty, no less important than the right to free speech or the right to just compensation for the taking of property. . . .

Second, all agreed that government interference in religious practice was not to be lightly countenanced. Finally, all shared the conviction that" 'true religion and good morals are the only solid foundation of public liberty and happiness.' " To give meaning to these ideas — particularly in a society characterized by religious pluralism and pervasive regulation — there will be times when the Constitution requires government to accommodate the needs of those citizens whose religious practices conflict with generally applicable law.

III

The Religion Clauses of the Constitution represent a profound commitment to religious liberty. Our Nation's Founders conceived of a Republic receptive to voluntary religious expression, not of a secular society in which religious expression is tolerated only when it does not conflict with a generally applicable law. As the historical sources discussed above show, the Free Exercise Clause is properly understood as an affirmative guarantee of the right to participate in religious activities without impermissible governmental interference, even where a believer's conduct is in tension with a law of general application. Certainly, it is in no way anomalous to accord heightened protection to a right identified in the text of the First Amendment. For example, it has long been the Court's position that freedom of speech — a right enumerated only a few words after the right to free exercise — has special constitutional status. Given the centrality of freedom of speech and religion to the American concept of personal liberty, it is altogether reasonable to conclude that both should be treated with the highest degree of respect.

Although it may provide a bright line, the rule the Court declared in *Smith* does not faithfully serve the purpose of the Constitution. Accordingly, I believe that it is essential for the Court to reconsider its holding in *Smith* — and to do so in this very case. I would therefore direct the parties to brief this issue and set the case for reargument.

NOTES AND QUESTIONS

1. Should *Smith* be overruled or would that be a misunderstanding of originalism insofar as an individual's free exercise of religious practice was always subject to "public order" limitations? *Compare* Douglas W. Kmiec, *The Original Understanding of the Free Exercise Clause and Religious Diversity*, 59 UMKC L. REV. 591 (1991) (arguing that *Smith* is correct as to laws that burden, but do not prohibit religious exercise, but that as to true prohibitions a compelling governmental purpose of the public order variety must be demonstrated), *with* Edward McGlynn Gaffney, Jr., *The Religion Clause: A Double Guarantee of Religious Liberty*, 1993 B.Y.U. L. REV. 189 (1993) (discussing the adverse impact of Supreme Court jurisprudence, including primarily *Employment Division v. Smith*, on religious freedom and concluding that remedial legislation is needed "to restore the first of civil liberties to the position of honor it deserves in our republic"). The perspective of John Roberts and Samuel Alito, Jr., may yet cast doubt on the long-term viability of *Smith*. Most notably, Justice Alito in his previous appellate work on the Third

Circuit appeared to give the holding in *Smith* a narrow application.

2. Some state legislatures, in light of *Boerne*, adopted RFRA-like statutes under state law. Rhode Island, Illinois, Texas, South Carolina, Arizona, Connecticut, Florida, Alabama, Idaho, New Mexico, and Oklahoma all have state enactments requiring a "compelling state interest" to burden religious belief. Other states are discussing the topic, though not without considerable confusion and disagreement. In California, for example, a state RFRA passed the House, but it did not exempt "an act or refusal to act that is substantially motivated by religious belief, whether or not the religious exercise is compulsory or central to a larger system of religious belief" from the state's other anti-discrimination laws, such as those precluding decision making on the basis of marital status. This has led a director of the Christian Legal Society's Center for Laws and Religious Freedom to characterize the measure as "an unmitigated disaster." Press Release, *California Assembly passes religious freedom act*, The Freedom Forum on Line (Jan. 23, 1998) (quoting Steve McFarland). The prohibition of marital status discrimination had been earlier applied by the California Supreme Court to deny a widow the right to refuse on religious grounds to rent part of her property to an unmarried heterosexual couple. *Smith v. FEHC*, 913 P.2d 909 (Cal. 1996).

3. The next case reveals that RFRA has continuing viability as against the federal government, and perhaps, indicate Chief Justice Roberts' inclinations on the *Smith* decision.

GONZALES v. O CENTRO ESPIRITA BENEFICENTE UNIAO DO VEGETAL
546 U.S. 418 (2006)

CHIEF JUSTICE ROBERTS delivered the unanimous opinion of the Court.

I

In *Employment Div., Dept. of Human Resources of Ore. v. Smith* (1990), this Court held that the Free Exercise Clause of the First Amendment does not prohibit governments from burdening religious practices through generally applicable laws. In *Smith*, we rejected a challenge to an Oregon statute that denied unemployment benefits to drug users, including Native Americans engaged in the sacramental use of peyote. In so doing, we rejected the interpretation of the Free Exercise Clause announced in *Sherbert v. Verner* (1963), and held that the Constitution does not require judges to engage in a case-by-case assessment of the religious burdens imposed by facially constitutional laws.

Congress responded by enacting the Religious Freedom Restoration Act of 1993 (RFRA), which adopts a statutory rule comparable to the constitutional rule rejected in *Smith*. Under RFRA, the Federal Government may not, as a statutory matter, substantially burden a person's exercise of religion, "even if the burden results from a rule of general applicability." The only exception recognized by the statute requires the Government to satisfy the compelling interest test — to "demonstrat[e] that application of the burden to the person — (1) is in furtherance of a compelling government interest; and (2) is the least restrictive means of furthering that compelling governmental interest." A person whose religious practices are burdened in violation of RFRA "may assert that violation as a claim or defense in a judicial proceeding and obtain appropriate relief."[36]

The Controlled Substances Act regulates the importation, manufacture, distribution, and use of psychotropic substances. The Act classifies substances into five schedules based on their potential for abuse, the extent to which they have an accepted medical use, and their safety. Substances listed in Schedule I of the Act are subject to the most comprehensive restrictions, including an outright ban on all importation and use, except pursuant to strictly regulated research projects.

O Centro Espírita Beneficente Uniã do Vegetal (UDV) is a Christian Spiritist sect based in Brazil, with an American branch of approximately 130 individuals. Central to the UDV's faith is receiving communion through *hoasca* (pronounced "wass-ca"), a sacramental tea made from two plants unique to the Amazon region. One of the plants, *psychotria viridis*, contains dimethyltryptamine (DMT), a hallucinogen whose effects are enhanced by alkaloids from the other plant, *banisteriopsis caapi*. DMT, as well as "any material, compound, mixture, or preparation, which contains any quantity of [DMT]," is listed in Schedule I of the Controlled Substances Act.

In 1999, United States Customs inspectors intercepted a shipment to the American UDV containing three drums of *hoasca*. A subsequent investigation revealed that the UDV had received 14 prior shipments of *hoasca*. The inspectors seized the intercepted shipment and threatened the UDV with prosecution.

The UDV filed suit against the Attorney General and other federal law enforcement officials, seeking declaratory and injunctive relief. The complaint alleged, *inter alia*, that applying the Controlled Substances Act to the UDV's sacramental use of *hoasca* violates RFRA. Prior to trial, the UDV moved for a preliminary injunction, so that it could continue to practice its faith pending trial on the merits. . . .

The [lower] courts entered a preliminary injunction prohibiting the Government from enforcing the Controlled Substances Act with respect to the UDV's importation and use of *hoasca*. . . .

II

Although its briefs contain some discussion of the potential for harm and diversion from the UDV's use of *hoasca*, the Government does not challenge the District Court's factual findings or its conclusion that the evidence submitted on these issues was evenly balanced. Instead, the Government maintains that such evidentiary equipoise is an insufficient basis for issuing a preliminary injunction against enforcement of the Controlled Substances Act . . .

The Government argues that, although it would bear the burden of demonstrat-

---

[36] [2] As originally enacted, RFRA applied to States as well as the Federal Government. In *City of Boerne v. Flores* (1997), we held the application to States to be beyond Congress' legislative authority under § 5 of the 14th Amendment.

ing a compelling interest as part of its affirmative defense at trial on the merits, the UDV should have borne the burden of disproving the asserted compelling interests at the hearing on the preliminary injunction. This argument is foreclosed by our recent decision in *Ashcroft v. American Civil Liberties Union* (2004). In *Ashcroft*, we affirmed the grant of a preliminary injunction in a case where the Government had failed to show a likelihood of success under the compelling interest test. We reasoned that "[a]s the Government bears the burden of proof on the ultimate question of [the challenged Act's] constitutionality, respondents [the movants] must be deemed likely to prevail unless the Government has shown that respondents' proposed less restrictive alternatives are less effective than [enforcing the Act]." That logic extends to this case; here the Government failed on the first prong of the compelling interest test, and did not reach the least restrictive means prong, but that can make no difference. The point remains that the burdens at the preliminary injunction stage track the burdens at trial . . .

III

The Government's second line of argument rests on the Controlled Substances Act itself. The Government contends that the Act's description of Schedule I substances as having "a high potential for abuse," "no currently accepted medical use in treatment in the United States," and "a lack of accepted safety for use . . . under medical supervision," by itself precludes any consideration of individualized exceptions such as that sought by the UDV. . . . Under the Government's view, there is no need to assess the particulars of the UDV's use or weigh the impact of an exemption for that specific use, because the Controlled Substances Act serves a compelling purpose and simply admits of no exceptions.

A

RFRA, and the strict scrutiny test it adopted, contemplate an inquiry more focused than the Government's categorical approach. RFRA requires the Government to demonstrate that the compelling interest test is satisfied through application of the challenged law "to the person" — the particular claimant whose sincere exercise of religion is being substantially burdened. RFRA expressly adopted the compelling interest test "as set forth in *Sherbert v. Verner* (1963) and *Wisconsin v. Yoder* (1972)." In each of those cases, this Court looked beyond broadly formulated interests justifying the general applicability of government mandates and scrutinized the asserted harm of granting specific exemptions to particular religious claimants. In *Yoder*, for example, we permitted an exemption for Amish children from a compulsory school attendance law. We recognized that the State had a "paramount" interest in education, but held that "despite its admitted validity in the generality of cases, we must searchingly examine the interests that the State seeks to promote . . . and the impediment to those objectives that would flow from recognizing *the claimed Amish exemption*." The Court explained that the State needed "to show with more particularity how its admittedly strong interest . . . would be adversely affected by granting an exemption *to the Amish*."

In *Sherbert*, the Court upheld a particular claim to a religious exemption from a state law denying unemployment benefits to those who would not work on

Saturdays, but explained that it was not announcing a constitutional right to unemployment benefits for "*all* persons whose religious convictions are the cause of their unemployment." The Court distinguished the case "in which an employee's religious convictions serve to make him a nonproductive member of society." . . .

B

Under the more focused inquiry required by RFRA and the compelling interest test, the Government's mere invocation of the general characteristics of Schedule I substances, as set forth in the Controlled Substances Act, cannot carry the day. It is true, of course, that Schedule I substances such as DMT are exceptionally dangerous. Nevertheless, there is no indication that Congress, in classifying DMT, considered the harms posed by the particular use at issue here — the circumscribed, sacramental use of *hoasca* by the UDV. . . .

This conclusion is reinforced by the Controlled Substances Act itself. The Act contains a provision authorizing the Attorney General to "waive the requirement for registration of certain manufacturers, distributors, or dispensers if he finds it consistent with the public health and safety." The fact that the Act itself contemplates that exempting certain people from its requirements would be "consistent with the public health and safety" indicates that congressional findings with respect to Schedule I substances should not carry the determinative weight, for RFRA purposes, that the Government would ascribe to them.

And in fact an exception has been made to the Schedule I ban for religious use. For the past 35 years, there has been a regulatory exemption for use of peyote — a Schedule I substance — by the Native American Church. . . .

C

The Government points to some pre-*Smith* cases relying on a need for uniformity in rejecting claims for religious exemptions under the Free Exercise Clause, but those cases strike us as quite different from the present one. Those cases did not embrace the notion that a general interest in uniformity justified a substantial burden on religious exercise; they instead scrutinized the asserted need and explained why the denied exemptions could not be accommodated. . . . The whole point of a "uniform day of rest for all workers" would have been defeated by exceptions. See *Sherbert* (discussing *Braunfeld*). These cases show that the Government can demonstrate a compelling interest in uniform application of a particular program by offering evidence that granting the requested religious accommodations would seriously compromise its ability to administer the program.

Here the Government's argument for uniformity is different; it rests not so much on the particular statutory program at issue as on slippery-slope concerns that could be invoked in response to any RFRA claim for an exception to a generally applicable law. The Government's argument echoes the classic rejoinder of bureaucrats throughout history: If I make an exception for you, I'll have to make one for everybody, so no exceptions. But RFRA operates by mandating consideration, under the compelling interest test, of exceptions to "rule[s] of general applicability." Congress determined that the legislated test "is a workable test for striking sensible balances between religious liberty and competing prior governmental interests." This determination finds support in our cases; in *Sherbert*, for example, we rejected a slippery-slope argument similar to the one offered in this case, dismissing as "no more than a possibility" the State's speculation "that the filing of fraudulent claims by unscrupulous claimants feigning religious objections to Saturday work" would drain the unemployment benefits fund.

We reaffirmed just last Term the feasibility of case-by-case consideration of religious exemptions to generally applicable rules. In *Cutter v. Wilkinson* (2005), we held that the Religious Land Use and Institutionalized Persons Act of 2000, which allows federal and state prisoners to seek religious accommodations pursuant to the same standard as set forth in RFRA, does not violate the Establishment Clause . . .

IV

Before the District Court, the Government also asserted an interest in compliance with the 1971 United Nations Convention on Psychotropic Substances. The Convention, signed by the United States and implemented by the Controlled Substances Act, calls on signatories to prohibit the use of hallucinogens, including DMT. The Government argues that it has a compelling interest in meeting its international obligations by complying with the Convention. . . .

The fact that *hoasca* is covered by the Convention, however, does not automatically mean that the Government has demonstrated a compelling interest in applying the Controlled Substances Act, which implements the Convention, to the UDV's sacramental use of the tea. At the present stage, it suffices to observe that the Government did not even *submit* evidence addressing the international consequences of granting an exemption for the UDV. The Government simply submitted two affidavits by State Department officials attesting to the general importance of honoring international obligations and of maintaining the leadership position of the United States in the international war on drugs. We do not doubt the validity of these interests, any more than we doubt the general interest in promoting public health and safety by enforcing the Controlled Substances Act, but under RFRA invocation of such general interests, standing alone, is not enough.

The Government repeatedly invokes Congress' findings and purposes underlying the Controlled Substances Act, but Congress had a reason for enacting RFRA, too. Congress recognized that "laws 'neutral' toward religion may burden religious exercise as surely as laws intended to interfere with religious exercise," and legislated "the compelling interest test" as the means for the courts to "strik[e] sensible balances between religious liberty and competing prior governmental interests."

We have no cause to pretend that the task assigned by Congress to the courts under RFRA is an easy one. Indeed, the very sort of difficulties highlighted by the Government here were cited by this Court in deciding that the approach later mandated by Congress under RFRA was not required as a matter of constitutional law under the Free Exercise Clause. See *Smith*. But Congress has determined that courts should strike sensible balances, pursuant to a compelling interest test that requires the Government to address the particular practice at issue. Applying that test, we conclude that the courts below did not err in determining that the Government failed to demonstrate, at the preliminary injunction stage, a compelling interest in barring the UDV's sacramental use of *hoasca*.

The judgment of the United States Court of Appeals for the Tenth Circuit is affirmed, and the case is remanded for further proceedings consistent with this opinion.

It is so ordered.

JUSTICE ALITO took no part in the consideration or decision of this case.

6.   The "Ministerial Exception"

HOSANNA-TABOR v. EEOC
132 S. Ct. 694, 181 L. Ed. 2d 650 (2012)

CHIEF JUSTICE ROBERTS delivered the opinion of the Court. [Some footnotes have been omitted.]

Certain employment discrimination laws authorize employees who have been wrongfully terminated to sue their employers for reinstatement and damages. The question presented is whether the Establishment and Free Exercise Clauses of the First Amendment bar such an action when the employer is a religious group and the employee is one of the group's ministers.

I

A

Petitioner Hosanna-Tabor Evangelical Lutheran Church and School is a member congregation of the Lutheran Church-Missouri Synod . . . . Hosanna-Tabor operated a small school in Redford, Michigan, offering a "Christ-centered education" to students in kindergarten through eighth grade. . . .

The Synod classifies teachers into two categories: "called" and "lay." "Called" teachers are regarded as having been called to their vocation by God through a congregation. To be eligible to receive a call from a congregation, a teacher must satisfy certain academic requirements. One way of doing so is by completing a "colloquy" program at a Lutheran college or university. The program requires candidates to take eight courses of theological study, obtain the endorsement of their local Synod district, and pass an oral examination by a faculty committee. A teacher who meets these requirements may be called by a congregation. Once called, a teacher receives the formal title "Minister of Religion, Commissioned." . . . A commissioned minister serves for an open-ended term; at Hosanna-Tabor, a call could be rescinded only for cause and by a supermajority vote of the congregation.

"Lay" or "contract" teachers, by contrast, are not required to be trained by the Synod or even to be Lutheran. At Hosanna-Tabor, they were appointed by the school board, without a vote of the congregation, to one-year renewable terms.

Although teachers at the school generally performed the same duties regardless of whether they were lay or called, lay teachers were hired only when called teachers were unavailable.

Respondent Cheryl Perich was first employed by Hosanna-Tabor as a lay teacher in 1999. After Perich completed her colloquy later that school year, Hosanna-Tabor asked her to become a called teacher. Perich accepted the call and received a "diploma of vocation" designating her a commissioned minister. . . .

Perich taught kindergarten during her first four years at Hosanna-Tabor and fourth grade during the 2003–2004 school year. She taught math, language arts, social studies, science, gym, art, and music. She also taught a religion class four days a week, led the students in prayer and devotional exercises each day, and attended a weekly school-wide chapel service. Perich led the chapel service herself about twice a year. Perich became ill in June 2004 with what was eventually diagnosed as narcolepsy. Symptoms included sudden and deep sleeps from which she could not be roused. Because of her illness, Perich began the 2004–2005 school year on disability leave. On January 27, 2005, however, Perich notified the school principal, Stacey Hoeft, that she would be able to report to work the following month. Hoeft responded that the school had already contracted with a lay teacher to fill Perich's position for the remainder of the school year. Hoeft also expressed concern that Perich was not yet ready to return to the classroom.

On January 30, Hosanna-Tabor held a meeting of its congregation at which school administrators stated that Perich was unlikely to be physically capable of returning to work that school year or the next. The congregation voted to offer Perich a "peaceful release" from her call, whereby the congregation would pay a portion of her health insurance premiums in exchange for her resignation as a called teacher. . . . Perich refused to resign and produced a note from her doctor stating that she would be able to return to work on February 22. The school board urged Perich to reconsider, informing her that the school no longer had a position for her, but Perich stood by her decision not to resign. On the morning of February 22 — the first day she was medically cleared to return to work — Perich presented herself at the school. Hoeft asked her to leave but she would not do so until she obtained written documentation that she had reported to work. Later that afternoon, Hoeft called Perich at home and told her that she would likely be fired. Perich responded that she had spoken with an attorney and intended to assert her legal rights. Following a school board meeting that evening, board chairman Scott Salo sent Perich a letter stating that Hosanna-Tabor was reviewing the process for rescinding her call in light of her "regrettable" actions. . . . Salo subsequently followed up with a letter advising Perich that the congregation would consider whether to rescind her call at its next meeting. As grounds for termination, the letter cited Perich's "insubordination and disruptive behavior" on February 22, as well as the damage she had done to her "working relationship" with the school by "threatening to take legal action." . . . The congregation voted to rescind Perich's call on April 10, and Hosanna-Tabor sent her a letter of termination the next day.

B

Perich filed a charge with the Equal Employment Opportunity Commission, alleging that her employment had been terminated in violation of the Americans with Disabilities Act . . . . The ADA prohibits an employer from discriminating against a qualified individual on the basis of disability. . . . It also prohibits an employer from retaliating "against any individual because such individual has opposed any act or practice made unlawful by [the ADA] or because such individual made a charge, testified, assisted, or participated in any manner in an investigation, proceeding, or hearing under [the ADA]." . . .[37]

The EEOC brought suit against Hosanna-Tabor, alleging that Perich had been fired in retaliation for threatening to file an ADA lawsuit. Perich intervened in the litigation, claiming unlawful retaliation under both the ADA and the Michigan Persons with Disabilities Civil Rights Act. The EEOC and Perich sought Perich's reinstatement to her former position (or frontpay in lieu thereof), along with backpay, compensatory and punitive damages, attorney's fees, and other injunctive relief.Hosanna-Tabor moved for summary judgment. Invoking what is known as the "ministerial exception," the Church argued that the suit was barred by the First Amendment because the claims at issue concerned the employment relationship between a religious institution and one of its ministers. According to the Church, Perich was a minister, and she had been fired for a religious reason — namely, that her threat to sue the Church violated the Synod's belief that Christians should resolve their disputes internally.

The District Court agreed that the suit was barred by the ministerial exception [a case-law principle that precludes application of employment discrimination legislation to claims concerning the employment relationship between a religious institution and its ministers — Eds.] and granted summary judgment in Hosanna-Tabor's favor. . . .

The Court of Appeals for the Sixth Circuit vacated and remanded, directing the District Court to proceed to the merits of Perich's retaliation claims. . . . The court concluded . . . that Perich did not qualify as a "minister" under the exception, noting in particular that her duties as a called teacher were identical to her duties as a lay teacher. . . . We granted certiorari. . . .

II

*   *   *

---

[37] [1] The ADA itself provides religious entities with two defenses to claims of discrimination that arise under subchapter I of the Act. The first provides that "[t]his subchapter shall not prohibit a religious corporation, association, educational institution, or society from giving preference in employment to individuals of a particular religion to perform work connected with the carrying on by such [entity] of its activities." . . . The second provides that "[u]nder this subchapter, a religious organization may require that all applicants and employees conform to the religious tenets of such organization." . . . The ADA's prohibition against retaliation, § 12203(a), appears in a different subchapter — subchapter IV. The EEOC and Perich contend, and Hosanna-Tabor does not dispute, that these defenses therefore do not apply to retaliation claims.

C

Until today, we have not had occasion to consider whether this freedom of a religious organization to select its ministers is implicated by a suit alleging discrimination in employment. The Courts of Appeals, in contrast, have had extensive experience with this issue. Since the passage of Title VII of the Civil Rights Act of 1964 . . . and other employment discrimination laws, the Courts of Appeals have uniformly recognized the existence of a "ministerial exception," grounded in the First Amendment, that precludes application of such legislation to claims concerning the employment relationship between a religious institution and its ministers. [Citations omitted.]

We agree that there is such a ministerial exception. The members of a religious group put their faith in the hands of their ministers. Requiring a church to accept or retain an unwanted minister, or punishing a church for failing to do so, intrudes upon more than a mere employment decision. Such action interferes with the internal governance of the church, depriving the church of control over the selection of those who will personify its beliefs. By imposing an unwanted minister, the state infringes the Free Exercise Clause, which protects a religious group's right to shape its own faith and mission through its appointments.

According the state the power to determine which individuals will minister to the faithful also violates the Establishment Clause, which prohibits government involvement in such ecclesiastical decisions. The EEOC and Perich acknowledge that employment discrimination laws would be unconstitutional as applied to religious groups in certain circumstances. They grant, for example, that it would violate the First Amendment for courts to apply such laws to compel the ordination of women by the Catholic Church or by an Orthodox Jewish seminary. . . . According to the EEOC and Perich, religious organizations could successfully defend against employment discrimination claims in those circumstances by invoking the constitutional right to freedom of association — a right "implicit" in the First Amendment. . . . The EEOC and Perich thus see no need — and no basis — for a special rule for ministers grounded in the Religion Clauses themselves.

We find this position untenable. The right to freedom of association is a right enjoyed by religious and secular groups alike. It follows under the EEOC's and Perich's view that the First Amendment analysis should be the same, whether the association in question is the Lutheran Church, a labor union, or a social club. . . . That result is hard to square with the text of the First Amendment itself, which gives special solicitude to the rights of religious organizations. We cannot accept the remarkable view that the Religion Clauses have nothing to say about a religious organization's freedom to select its own ministers.

The EEOC and Perich also contend that our decision in *Employment Div., Dept. of Human Resources of Ore. v. Smith* . . . (1990), precludes recognition of a ministerial exception. In *Smith*, two members of the Native American Church were denied state unemployment benefits after it was determined that they had been fired from their jobs for ingesting peyote, a crime under Oregon law. We held that this did not violate the Free Exercise Clause, even though the peyote had been ingested for sacramental purposes, because the "right of free exercise does not relieve an individual of the obligation to comply with a valid and neutral law of general applicability on the ground that the law proscribes (or prescribes) conduct that his religion prescribes (or proscribes)." . . .

It is true that the ADA's prohibition on retaliation, like Oregon's prohibition on peyote use, is a valid and neutral law of general applicability. But a church's selection of its ministers is unlike an individual's ingestion of peyote. Smith involved government regulation of only outward physical acts. The present case, in contrast, concerns government interference with an internal church decision that affects the faith and mission of the church itself. . . . The contention that *Smith* forecloses recognition of a ministerial exception rooted in the Religion Clauses has no merit.

III

Having concluded that there is a ministerial exception grounded in the Religion Clauses of the First Amendment, we consider whether the exception applies in this case. We hold that it does.

Every Court of Appeals to have considered the question has concluded that the ministerial exception is not limited to the head of a religious congregation, and we agree. We are reluctant, however, to adopt a rigid formula for deciding when an employee qualifies as a minister. It is enough for us to conclude, in this our first case involving the ministerial exception, that the exception covers Perich, given all the circumstances of her employment.

To begin with, Hosanna-Tabor held Perich out as a minister, with a role distinct from that of most of its members. When Hosanna-Tabor extended her a call, it issued her a "diploma of vocation" according her the title "Minister of Religion, Commissioned." . . . She was tasked with performing that office "according to the Word of God and the confessional standards of the Evangelical Lutheran Church as drawn from the Sacred Scriptures." . . . The congregation prayed that God "bless [her] ministrations to the glory of His holy name, [and] the building of His church." . . . In a supplement to the diploma, the congregation undertook to periodically review Perich's "skills of ministry" and "ministerial responsibilities," and to provide for her "continuing education as a professional person in the ministry of the Gospel." . . .

Perich's title as a minister reflected a significant degree of religious training followed by a formal process of commissioning. To be eligible to become a commissioned minister, Perich had to complete eight college-level courses in subjects including biblical interpretation, church doctrine, and the ministry of the Lutheran teacher. She also had to obtain the endorsement of her local Synod district by submitting a petition that contained her academic transcripts, letters of recommendation, personal statement, and written answers to various ministry-related questions. Finally, she had to pass an oral examination by a faculty committee at a Lutheran college. It took Perich six years to fulfill these require-ments. And when she eventually did, she was commissioned as a minister only upon election by the congregation, which recognized God's call to her to teach. At that point, her call could be rescinded only upon a supermajority vote of the congrega-tion — a protection designed to allow her to "preach the Word of God boldly." . . .

Perich held herself out as a minister of the Church by accepting the formal call to religious service, according to its terms. She did so in other ways as well. For example, she claimed a special housing allowance on her taxes that was available only to employees earning their compensation "in the exercise of the ministry." . . . In a form she submitted to the Synod following her termination, Perich again indicated that she regarded herself as a minister at Hosanna-Tabor, stating: "I feel that God is leading me to serve in the teaching ministry . . . . I am anxious to be in the teaching ministry again soon." . . . Perich's job duties reflected a role in conveying the Church's message and carrying out its mission. Hosanna-Tabor expressly charged her with "lead[ing] others toward Christian maturity" and "teach[ing] faithfully the Word of God, the Sacred Scriptures, in its truth and purity and as set forth in all the symbolical books of the Evangelical Lutheran Church." . . . In fulfilling these responsibilities, Perich taught her students religion four days a week, and led them in prayer three times a day. Once a week, she took her students to a school-wide chapel service, and — about twice a year — she took her turn leading it, choosing the liturgy, selecting the hymns, and delivering a short message based on verses from the Bible. During her last year of teaching, Perich also led her fourth graders in a brief devotional exercise each morning. As a source of religious instruction, Perich performed an important role in transmitting the Lutheran faith to the next generation.

In light of these considerations — the formal title given Perich by the Church, the substance reflected in that title, her own use of that title, and the important religious functions she performed for the Church — we conclude that Perich was a minister covered by the ministerial exception.

*   *   *

Because Perich was a minister within the meaning of the exception, the First Amendment requires dismissal of this employment discrimination suit against her religious employer. The EEOC and Perich originally sought an order reinstating Perich to her former position as a called teacher. By requiring the Church to accept a minister it did not want, such an order would have plainly violated the Church's freedom under the Religion Clauses to select its own ministers.

Perich no longer seeks reinstatement, having abandoned that relief before this Court. . . . But that is immaterial. Perich continues to seek frontpay in lieu of reinstatement, backpay, compensatory and punitive damages, and attorney's fees. An award of such relief would operate as a penalty on the Church for terminating an unwanted minister, and would be no less prohibited by the First Amendment than an order overturning the termination. Such relief would depend on a determination that Hosanna-Tabor was wrong to have relieved Perich of her position, and it is precisely such a ruling that is barred by the ministerial exception.[38]

The EEOC and Perich suggest that Hosanna-Tabor's asserted religious reason for firing Perich — that she violated the Synod's commitment to internal dispute resolution — was pretextual. That suggestion misses the point of the ministerial exception. The purpose of the exception is not to safeguard a church's decision to

---

[38] [3] Perich does not dispute that if the ministerial exception bars her retaliation claim under the ADA, it also bars her retaliation claim under Michigan law.

fire a minister only when it is made for a religious reason. The exception instead ensures that the authority to select and control who will minister to the faithful — a matter "strictly ecclesiastical," *Kedroff*, 344 U.S., at 119 — is the church's alone.[39]

IV

The EEOC and Perich foresee a parade of horribles that will follow our recognition of a ministerial exception to employment discrimination suits. According to the EEOC and Perich, such an exception could protect religious organizations from liability for retaliating against employees for reporting criminal misconduct or for testifying before a grand jury or in a criminal trial. What is more, the EEOC contends, the logic of the exception would confer on religious employers "unfettered discretion" to violate employment laws by, for example, hiring children or aliens not authorized to work in the United States. . . . Hosanna-Tabor responds that the ministerial exception would not in any way bar criminal prosecutions for interfering with law enforcement investigations or other proceedings. Nor, according to the Church, would the exception bar government enforcement of general laws restricting eligibility for employment, because the exception applies only to suits by or on behalf of ministers themselves. Hosanna-Tabor also notes that the ministerial exception has been around in the lower courts for 40 years . . . and has not given rise to the dire consequences predicted by the EEOC and Perich.

The case before us is an employment discrimination suit brought on behalf of a minister, challenging her church's decision to fire her. Today we hold only that the ministerial exception bars such a suit. We express no view on whether the exception bars other types of suits, including actions by employees alleging breach of contract or tortious conduct by their religious employers. There will be time enough to address the applicability of the exception to other circumstances if and when they arise.

* * *

The interest of society in the enforcement of employment discrimination statutes is undoubtedly important. But so too is the interest of religious groups in choosing who will preach their beliefs, teach their faith, and carry out their mission. When a minister who has been fired sues her church alleging that her termination was discriminatory, the First Amendment has struck the balance for us. The church must be free to choose those who will guide it on its way.

The judgment of the Court of Appeals for the Sixth Circuit is reversed.

JUSTICE THOMAS, concurring.

I join the Court's opinion. I write separately to note that, in my view, the Religion Clauses require civil courts to apply the ministerial exception and to defer to a religious organization's good-faith understanding of who qualifies as its minister. As

---

[39] [4] A conflict has arisen in the Courts of Appeals over whether the ministerial exception is a jurisdictional bar or a defense on the merits. [Citations omitted.] We conclude that the exception operates as an affirmative defense to an otherwise cognizable claim, not a jurisdictional bar. . . .

the Court explains, the Religion Clauses guarantee religious organizations autonomy in matters of internal governance, including the selection of those who will minister the faith. A religious organization's right to choose its ministers would be hollow, however, if secular courts could second-guess the organization's sincere determination that a given employee is a"minister" under the organization's theological tenets. Our country's religious landscape includes organizations with different leadership structures and doctrines that influence their conceptions of ministerial status. The question whether an employee is a minister is itself religious in nature, and the answer will vary widely. Judicial attempts to fashion a civil definition of "minister" through a bright-line test or multi-factor analysis risk disadvantaging those religious groups whose beliefs, practices, and membership are outside of the "mainstream" or unpalatable to some. Moreover, uncertainty about whether its ministerial designation will be rejected, and a corresponding fear of liability, may cause a religious group to conform its beliefs and practices regarding "ministers" to the prevailing secular understanding. . . . These are certainly dangers that the First Amendment was designed to guard against. The Court thoroughly sets forth the facts that lead to its conclusion that Cheryl Perich was one of Hosanna-Tabor's ministers, and I agree that these facts amply demonstrate Perich's ministerial role. But the evidence demonstrates that Hosanna-Tabor sincerely considered Perich a minister. That would be sufficient for me to conclude that Perich's suit is properly barred by the ministerial exception.

JUSTICE ALITO, with whom JUSTICE KAGAN joins, concurring. [Some footnotes have been omitted.]

I join the Court's opinion, but I write separately to clarify my understanding of the significance of formal ordination and designation as a "minister" in determining whether an "employee" of a religious group falls within the so-called "ministerial" exception. The term "minister" is commonly used by many Protestant denominations to refer to members of their clergy, but the term is rarely if ever used in this way by Catholics, Jews, Muslims, Hindus, or Buddhists. In addition, the concept of ordination as understood by most Christian churches and by Judaism has no clear counterpart in some Christian denominations and some other religions. Because virtually every religion in the world is represented in the population of the United States, it would be a mistake if the term "minister" or the concept of ordination were viewed as central to the important issue of religious autonomy that is presented in cases like this one. Instead, courts should focus on the function performed by persons who work for religious bodies.

The First Amendment protects the freedom of religious groups to engage in certain key religious activities, including the conducting of worship services and other religious ceremonies and rituals, as well as the critical process of communicating the faith. Accordingly, religious groups must be free to choose the personnel who are essential to the performance of these functions. The "ministerial" exception should be tailored to this purpose. It should apply to any "employee" who leads a religious organization, conducts worship services or important religious ceremonies or rituals, or serves as a messenger or teacher of its faith. If a religious group believes that the ability of such an employee to perform these key functions has been compromised, then the constitutional guarantee of religious freedom protects the group's right to remove the employee from his or her position.

I

Throughout our Nation's history, religious bodies have been the preeminent example of private associations that have "act[ed] as critical buffers between the individual and the power of the State." *Roberts v. United States Jaycees* . . . (1984). In a case like the one now before us — where the goal of the civil law in question, the elimination of discrimination against persons with disabilities, is so worthy — it is easy to forget that the autonomy of religious groups, both here in the United States and abroad, has often served as a shield against oppressive civil laws. To safeguard this crucial autonomy, we have long recognized that the Religion Clauses protect a private sphere within which religious bodies are free to govern themselves in accordance with their own beliefs. The Constitution guarantees religious bodies "independence from secular control or manipulation — in short, power to decide for themselves, free from state interference, matters of church government as well as those of faith and doctrine." *Kedroff v. Saint Nicholas Cathedral of Russian Orthodox Church in North America* . . . (1952).

Religious autonomy means that religious authorities must be free to determine who is qualified to serve in positions of substantial religious importance. Different religions will have different views on exactly what qualifies as an important religious position, but it is nonetheless possible to identify a general category of "employees" whose functions are essential to the independence of practically all religious groups. These include those who serve in positions of leadership, those who perform important functions in worship services and in the performance of religious ceremonies and rituals, and those who are entrusted with teaching and conveying the tenets of the faith to the next generation.

Applying the protection of the First Amendment to roles of religious leadership, worship, ritual, and expression focuses on the objective functions that are important for the autonomy of any religious group, regardless of its beliefs. As we have recognized in a similar context, "[f]orcing a group to accept certain members may impair [its ability] to express those views, and only those views, that it intends to express." *Boy Scouts of America v. Dale* . . . (2000). That principle applies with special force with respect to religious groups, whose very existence is dedicated to the collective expression and propagation of shared religious ideals. . . . As the Court notes, the First Amendment "gives special solicitude to the rights of religious organizations," . . . but our expressive-association cases are nevertheless useful in pointing out what those essential rights are. Religious groups are the archetype of associations formed for expressive purposes, and their fundamental rights surely include the freedom to choose who is qualified to serve as a voice for their faith.

When it comes to the expression and inculcation of religious doctrine, there can be no doubt that the messenger matters. Religious teachings cover the gamut from moral conduct to metaphysical truth, and both the content and credibility of a religion's message depend vitally on the character and conduct of its teachers. A religion cannot depend on someone to be an effective advocate for its religious vision if that person's conduct fails to live up to the religious precepts that he or she espouses. For this reason, a religious body's right to self-governance must include the ability to select, and to be selective about, those who will serve as the very "embodiment of its message" and "its voice to the faithful." . . . A religious body's control over such "employees" is an essential component of its freedom to speak in its own voice, both to its own members and to the outside world.

The connection between church governance and the free dissemination of religious doctrine has deep roots in our legal tradition: "The right to organize voluntary religious associations to assist in the expression and dissemination of any religious doctrine, and to create tribunals for the decision of controverted questions of faith within the association, and for the ecclesiastical government of all the individual members, congregations, and officers within the general association, is unquestioned. All who unite themselves to such a body do so with an implied consent to this government, and are bound to submit to it. But it would be a vain consent and would lead to the total subversion of such religious bodies, if any one aggrieved by one of their decisions could appeal to the secular courts and have them reversed." [Citation omitted.] The "ministerial" exception gives concrete protection to the free "expression and dissemination of any religious doctrine." The Constitution leaves it to the collective conscience of each religious group to determine for itself who is qualified to serve as a teacher or messenger of its faith.

II

A

The Court's opinion today holds that the "ministerial" exception applies to Cheryl Perich (hereinafter respondent), who is regarded by the Lutheran Church — Missouri Synod as a commissioned minister. But while a ministerial title is undoubtedly relevant in applying the First Amendment rule at issue, such a title is neither necessary nor sufficient. As previously noted, most faiths do not employ the term "minister," and some eschew the concept of formal ordination.[40] And at the opposite end of the spectrum, some faiths consider the ministry to consist of all or a very large percentage of their members.[41] Perhaps this explains why, although every circuit to consider the issue has recognized the "ministerial" exception, no circuit has made ordination status or formal title determinative of the exception's applicability.

* * *

---

[40] [3] In Islam, for example, "every Muslim can perform the religious rites, so there is no class or profession of ordained clergy. Yet there are religious leaders who are recognized for their learning and their ability to lead communities of Muslims in prayer, study, and living according to the teaching of the Qur'an and Muslim law." 10 ENCYCLOPEDIA OF RELIGION 6858 (2d ed. 2005).

[41] [4] For instance, Jehovah's Witnesses consider all baptized disciples to be ministers. *See* THE WATCHTOWER, *Who Are God's Ministers Today?* Nov. 15, 2000, p. 16 ("According to the Bible, all Jehovah's worshippers — heavenly and earthly — are ministers").

B

The ministerial exception applies to respondent because, as the Court notes, she played a substantial role in "conveying the Church's message and carrying out its mission." . . . She taught religion to her students four days a week and took them to chapel on the fifth day. She led them in daily devotional exercises, and led them in prayer three times a day. She also alternated with the other teachers in planning and leading worship services at the school chapel, choosing liturgies, hymns, and readings, and composing and delivering a message based on Scripture.

It makes no difference that respondent also taught secular subjects. While a purely secular teacher would not qualify for the "ministerial" exception, the constitutional protection of religious teachers is not somehow diminished when they take on secular functions in addition to their religious ones. What matters is that respondent played an important role as an instrument of her church's religious message and as a leader of its worship activities. Because of these important religious functions, Hosanna-Tabor had the right to decide for itself whether respondent was religiously qualified to remain in her office. Hosanna-Tabor discharged respondent because she threatened to file suit against the church in a civil court. This threat contravened the Lutheran doctrine that disputes among Christians should be resolved internally without resort to the civil court system and all the legal wrangling it entails.[42] In Hosanna-Tabor's view, respondent's disregard for this doctrine compromised her religious function, disqualifying her from serving effectively as a voice for the church's faith. Respondent does not dispute that the Lutheran Church subscribes to a doctrine of internal dispute resolution, but she argues that this was a mere pretext for her firing, which was really done for nonreligious reasons.

For civil courts to engage in the pretext inquiry that respondent and the Solicitor General urge us to sanction would dangerously undermine the religious autonomy that lower court case law has now protected for nearly four decades. In order to probe the real reason for respondent's firing, a civil court — and perhaps a jury — would be required to make a judgment about church doctrine. The credibility of Hosanna-Tabor's asserted reason for terminating respondent's employment could not be assessed without taking into account both the importance that the Lutheran Church attaches to the doctrine of internal dispute resolution and the degree to which that tenet compromised respondent's religious function. If it could be shown that this belief is an obscure and minor part of Lutheran doctrine, it would be much more plausible for respondent to argue that this doctrine was not the real reason for her firing. If, on the other hand, the doctrine is a central and universally known tenet of Lutheranism, then the church's asserted reason for her discharge would seem much more likely to be nonpretextual. But whatever the truth of the matter might be, the mere adjudication of such questions would pose grave problems for religious autonomy: It would require calling witnesses to testify about the impor-

---

[42] [5] *See* THE LUTHERAN CHURCH — MISSOURI SYNOD, COMMISSION ON THEOLOGY AND CHURCH RELATIONS, 1 CORINTHIANS 6:1–11: AN EXEGETICAL STUDY, p. 10 (Apr. 1991) (stating that instead of suing each other, Christians should seek "an amicable settlement of differences by means of a decision by fellow Christians"). See also 1 *Corinthians* 6:1–7 ("If any of you has a dispute with another, dare he take it before the ungodly for judgment instead of before the saints?").

tance and priority of the religious doctrine in question, with a civil factfinder sitting in ultimate judgment of what the accused church really believes, and how important that belief is to the church's overall mission.

At oral argument, both respondent and the United States acknowledged that a pretext inquiry would sometimes be prohibited by principles of religious autonomy, and both conceded that a Roman Catholic priest who is dismissed for getting married could not sue the church and claim that his dismissal was actually based on a ground forbidden by the federal antidiscrimination laws. . . . But there is no principled basis for proscribing a pretext inquiry in such a case while permitting it in a case like the one now before us. The Roman Catholic Church's insistence on clerical celibacy may be much better known than the Lutheran Church's doctrine of internal dispute resolution, but popular familiarity with a religious doctrine cannot be the determinative factor.

What matters in the present case is that Hosanna-Tabor believes that the religious function that respondent performed made it essential that she abide by the doctrine of internal dispute resolution; and the civil courts are in no position to second-guess that assessment. This conclusion rests not on respondent's ordination status or her formal title, but rather on her functional status as the type of employee that a church must be free to appoint or dismiss in order to exercise the religious liberty that the First Amendment guarantees.

NOTES AND QUESTIONS

1. As a result of the decision in *Hosanna-Tabor* the all-male Catholic priesthood is now apparently immune from state or federal antidiscrimination challenge. Until the year 1978, The Church of Jesus Christ of Latter-day Saints (Mormon) had a policy against ordaining black men to the priesthood. If the Mormon Church or any other religious denomination had such a policy today, would that policy now be immune from state or federal antidiscrimination challenge?

2. There were two concurring opinions in *Hosanna-Tabor*. What are the differences between the two concurrences of Justice Thomas and Justice Alito? One of the differences may be that Justice Thomas seemed to adopt the "sincerity" test that the Court used in *United States v. Seeger* as part of the judicial inquiry into whether "a religious organization's understanding of who qualifies as its minister is in "good-faith" and to use that test in arriving at his conclusion that "the evidence demonstrates that Hosanna-Tabor *sincerely* considered Perich a minister [emphasis added]." Justice Alito, on the other hand, seemed to object strenuously to the sort of "pretext" inquiry that a "sincerity" test would entail in ministerial-exception cases when he wrote, "For civil courts to engage in the pretext inquiry that respondent and the Solicitor General urge us to sanction would dangerously undermine the religious autonomy that lower court case law has now protected for nearly four decades." What approach did Chief Justice Roberts for the majority take on this issue?

Chapter 3

A FAIR GOVERNMENT

I.

THE SUBSTANTIVE PROTECTION
OF VESTED RIGHTS

Law is perceived as substantively unfair when it disappoints well-settled and reasonable expectations — that is, when it undermines vested rights. In his influential *Second Treatise on Civil Government*, John Locke reflects that no person would yield liberty to a civil society, if government thereafter could apply laws retrospectively to conduct that conformed to the law at the time it was undertaken. The Constitution reflects this precept in favor of a rule of law (general enactments, prospectively applied) through a number of provisions: In Article I, Sections 9 and 10, the Constitution prohibits ex post facto laws, laws punishing individuals for conduct that was legal at the time they committed it, as well as bills of attainder, laws where the legislature singles out an individual or discrete group for punishment; the Fifth Amendment protects against the taking of property without just compensation; and the Contract Clause in Article I, Section 10, Clause 1 states that "no state shall . . . pass any . . . Law impairing the Obligation of Contracts." Matters of ex post facto legislation and bills of attainder are normally taken up with the study of criminal law. Here, we turn first to the protection of contract and then property.

A. THE PROTECTION OF CONTRACT AGAINST STATE IMPAIRMENT

1. The Precipitating Hardship

Harvard historian Benjamin Wright concludes after exhaustive study that "[d]uring the nineteenth century no constitutional clause was so frequently the basis of decisions by the Supreme Court of the United States as that forbidding the states to pass laws impairing the obligation of contracts." BENJAMIN WRIGHT, THE CONTRACT CLAUSE OF THE CONSTITUTION at xiii (1938). The immediate need for the Clause originated out of the economic depression following the Revolutionary War. These sour economic times were especially difficult for small farmers, who in great numbers were losing their lands to foreclosure. A number of states sought to rectify the plight of the farmers by enacting debtor relief or "stay" laws that deferred foreclosure. Some states allowed debts to be paid with paper currency of little or no value that effectively canceled underlying debt. Farmers in

Massachusetts petitioned the legislature for such economic relief, but to no avail. In September 1786, farmer and former army captain Daniel Shays organized a small force to capture an arsenal to provide farmers with military protection from their creditors. "Shays' Rebellion," as it was called, lasted for three weeks. Pointing to this insurrection, creditors and property owners advanced the need to rework the Articles of Confederation to prevent states from pursuing policies that undermined commerce and vested economic rights. Congress responded by passing a resolution calling for the constitutional convention.

Wright reports that the delegates to the constitutional convention were indeed greatly distressed by the "evils" of debtor relief laws and the like, as Madison called them. WRIGHT, *supra*, at 3–6. However, it should not be assumed that our founders were unsympathetic to their less well-off countrymen. The constitutional delegates recognized that farmers faced difficult economic times, but prudently supposed that these could not be overcome with counterfeit accounting. Such would merely jeopardize the commercial reputation of the young republic and curtail lines of credit. The sounder course, the delegates reasoned, would be to address the underlying cause: the unstructured state sovereignty of the Articles of Confederation which yielded an inadequate supply of money of fixed value. Fairly early in the convention, the drafters directly addressed this problem by forbidding the states from issuing bills of credit or coining money. It was the national government that would do that and regulate its value.

Having addressed the issue of the supply and value of money, the framers did not at first perceive any additional need to secure the vested rights of contract. However, six weeks into the convention on July 13, 1787, the Congress under the Articles sitting in New York passed the Northwest Ordinance regulating territories that eventually became several midwestern states. Among other provisions, that Ordinance provided that "in the just preservation of rights and property, it is understood and declared, that no law ought ever to be made or have force in the said territory, that shall, in any manner whatever, interfere with or affect private contracts . . . previously formed." Northwest Territory Ordinance of 1787, art. II, 1 Stat. 51, 52 (1789). Richard Henry Lee sent a copy of the Ordinance to George Washington urging that such a clause was necessary to secure vested rights against "licentious" settlers who might use legislative power to divest them. Shortly thereafter, a similar provision was brought before the convention.

2.   Debate in Convention

2 THE RECORDS OF THE FEDERAL CONVENTION 434, 439–40 (Max Farrand ed., 1911)

Tuesday, August 28, 1787

MR. KING moved to add . . . a prohibition on the States to interfere in private contracts.

MR. GOVR. MORRIS. This would be going too far. There are a thousand laws relating to bringing actions — limitations of actions [and] which affect contracts —

The Judicial power of the [United States] will be a protection in cases within their jurisdiction; and within the State itself a majority must rule, whatever may be the mischief done among themselves.

MR. SHERMAN. Why then prohibit bills of credit?

MR. WILSON was in favor of Mr. King's motion.

MR. MADISON admitted that inconveniences might arise from such a prohibition but thought on the whole it would be overbalanced by the utility of it. He conceived however that a negative on the State laws could alone secure the effect. Evasions might and would be devised by the ingenuity of the Legislatures —

COL. MASON. This is carrying the restraint too far. Cases will happen that can not be foreseen, where some kind of interference will be proper, [and] essential — He mentioned the case of limiting the period for bringing actions on open account — that of bonds after a certain (lapse of time,) — asking whether it was proper to tie the hands of the States from making provisions in such cases?

MR. WILSON. The answer to these objections is that *retrospective* interferences only are to be prohibited.

MR. MADISON. Is not that already done by the prohibition of ex post facto laws, which will oblige the Judges to declare such interferences null [and] void?

MR. RUTLIDGE moved instead of Mr. King's Motion to insert — "nor pass bills of attainder nor retrospective laws" . . . .

*   *   *

Wednesday, August 29, 1787

*   *   *

MR. DICKENSON mentioned to the House that on examining Blackstone's Commentaries, he found that the terms "ex post facto" related to criminal cases only; that they would not consequently restrain the States from retrospective laws in civil cases, and that some further provision for this purpose would be requisite.

*   *   *

Friday, September 14, 1787

*   *   *

MR. GERRY entered into observations inculcating the importance of public faith, and the propriety of the restraint put on the States from impairing the obligation of contracts — Alledging that Congress ought to be laid under the like prohibitions.

3.   Post-Convention Justification

The Federalist No. 7 (Alexander Hamilton)

*   *   *

Laws in violation of private contracts as they amount to aggressions on the rights of those States, whose citizens are injured by them, may be considered as another probable source of hostility. We are not authorized to expect, that a more liberal or more equitable spirit would preside over the legislations of the individual States hereafter, if unrestrained by any additional checks, than we have heretofore seen, in too many instances, disgracing their several codes. We have observed the disposition to retaliation excited in Connecticut, in consequence of the enormities perpetrated by the legislature of Rhode Island; and we may reasonably infer, that in similar cases, under other circumstances, a war not of *parchment* but of the sword would chastise such atrocious breaches of moral obligation and social justice.

The Federalist No. 44 (James Madison)

A *fifth* class of provisions in favor of the federal authority, consists of the following restrictions on the authority of the several States:

1. "No State shall enter into any treaty, alliance, or confederation, grant letters of marque and reprisal, coin money, emit bills of credit, make any thing but gold and silver a legal tender in payment of debts; pass any bill of attainder, ex post facto law, or law impairing the obligation of contracts, or grant any title of nobility."

*   *   *

Bills of attainder, ex post facto laws, and laws impairing the obligation of contracts, are contrary to the first principles of the social compact, and to every principle of sound legislation. The two former are expressly prohibited by the declarations prefixed to some of the State Constitutions, and all of them are prohibited by the spirit and scope of these fundamental charters. Our own experience has taught us nevertheless, that additional fences against these dangers ought not to be omitted. Very properly therefore have the Convention added this constitutional bulwark in favor of personal security and private rights; and I am much deceived if they have not in so doing as faithfully consulted the genuine sentiments, as the undoubted interests of their constituents. The sober people of America are weary of the fluctuating policy which has directed the public councils. They have seen with regret and with indignation, that sudden changes and legislative interferences in cases affecting personal rights, become jobs in the hands of enterprising and influential speculators; and snares to the more industrious and less informed part of the community. They have seen, too, that legislative interference, is but the first link of a long chain of repetitions; every subsequent interference being naturally produced by the effects of the preceding. They very rightly infer, therefore, that some thorough reform is wanting which will banish speculations on public measures, inspire a general prudence and industry, and give a regular course to the business of society.

NOTE

The objectives of the founders in adding the Contract Clause are ably summarized by Joseph Story. Appointed as an Associate Justice of the Supreme Court by Madison in 1811, Story was named to the Court at the age of 32 and served until his death in 1845. A serious student of the law, his *Commentaries* are accepted by many as a classic exposition of original meaning. GERARD DUNNE, JUSTICE JOSEPH STORY AND THE RISE OF THE SUPREME COURT (1970). As Story reflects in the excerpt below and in a number that will be referred to throughout this Chapter, contract was a mixed natural law/positive law concept. Society through the positive law gives application, says Story, to contractual obligations that arise by promise — conferring moral right under natural or universal law. Law, then, does not create the obligation, it merely supplies a means of enforcement so long as the agreement, itself, does not transgress the public policy.

3 JOSEPH STORY, COMMENTARIES ON THE CONSTITUTION (1833)

§ 1372 [Will] or actions, which I, by my contract, confer on another. And that right and power will be found to be measured, neither by moral law alone, nor by universal law alone, nor by the laws of society alone; but by a combination of the three; an operation, in which the moral law is explained, and applied by the law of nature, and both modified and adapted to the exigencies of society by positive law.

* * *

§ 1379. In the next place, what may properly be deemed impairing the obligation of contracts in the sense of the constitution? It is perfectly clear, that any law, which enlarges, abridges, or in any manner changes the intention of the parties, resulting from the stipulations in the contract, necessarily impairs it. The manner or degree, in which this change is effected, can in no respect influence the conclusion; for whether the law affect the validity, the construction, the duration, the discharge, or the evidence of the contract, it impairs its obligation, though it may not do so to the same extent in all the supposed cases. Any deviation from its terms by postponing, or accelerating the period of performance, which it prescribes; imposing conditions not expressed in the contract; or dispensing with the performance of those, which are a part of the contract; however minute or apparently immaterial in their effect upon it, impair its obligation. *A fortiori*, a law, which makes the contract wholly invalid, or extinguishes, or releases it, is a law impairing it. Nor is this all. Although there is a distinction between the obligation of a contract, and a remedy upon it; yet if there are certain remedies existing at the time, when it is made, all of which are afterwards wholly extinguished by new laws, so that there remain no means of enforcing its obligation, and no redress; such an abolition of all remedies, operating *in presenti*, is also an impairing of the obligation of such contract.

* * *

§ 1392. Before quitting this subject it may be proper to remark, that as the prohibition, respecting *ex post facto* laws, applies only to criminal cases; and the other is confined to impairing the obligation of contracts; there are many laws of a retrospective character, which may yet be constitutionally passed by the state legislatures, however unjust, oppressive, or impolitic they may be. Retrospective laws are, indeed, generally unjust; and, as has been forcibly said, neither accord with sound legislation, nor with the fundamental principles of the social compact. Still they are, with the exceptions above stated, left open to the states, according to their own constitutions of government; and become obligatory, if not prohibited by the latter. Thus, for instance, where the legislature of Connecticut, in 1795, passed a resolve, setting aside a decree of a court of probate disapproving of a will, and granted a new hearing; it was held, that the resolve, not being against any constitutional principle in that state, was valid; and that the will, which was approved upon the new hearing, was conclusive, as to the rights obtained under it [*See Calder v. Bull*, 3 U.S. (3 Dall.) 386 (1798), discussed *supra* in Chapter 1 — Eds.]. There is nothing in the constitution of the United States, which forbids a state legislature from exercising judicial functions; nor from divesting rights, vested by law in an individual; provided its effect be not to impair the obligation of a contract. If such a law be void, it is upon principles derived from the general nature of free governments, and the necessary limitations created thereby, or from the state restrictions upon the legislative authority, and not from the prohibitions of the constitution of the United States.

a. Prohibiting Retrospective Debtor Relief

In *Sturges v. Crowninshield*, 17 U.S. (4 Wheat.) 122 (1819), the Court considered at length the respective powers of state and federal governments over bankruptcy and what constitutes an impairment of the obligation of contract that the Constitution forbids. Ruling on the constitutionality of a New York State bankruptcy law, the Supreme Court maintained that state bankruptcy laws were permitted since congressional legislation was at that point lacking. The Court also concluded that the power of Congress to enact "uniform laws on the subject of bankruptcies" was supreme. The New York law was nevertheless declared invalid because it applied retroactively to contracts made prior to its enactment.

Following *Sturges*, the issue arose whether a bankruptcy act that *preceded* a contract was valid. In *Ogden v. Saunders*, 25 U.S. (12 Wheat.) 213 (1827), the Court held that such an act did not offend the Contract Clause. For the only time in his thirty-four years as Chief Justice, John Marshall was in dissent. In separate opinions, the majority in *Ogden* reasoned that a statute, including a bankruptcy statute, in effect at the time a contract is formed becomes "the law of the contract" and is in fact a "part of the contract." Justice Johnson wrote that the Contract Clause was intended solely as "a general provision against arbitrary and tyrannical legislation over existing rights, whether of person or property." *Id.* at 286. The majority's argument seems reasonable enough in context and generally in terms of notice to contracting parties. However, if carried to an extreme, the majority position incorporating the law of the place into all subsequent contracts can be problematic. As will be seen below in the discussion of the reserved police power, the majority's principle is too unrefined. Theoretically, it would allow a state to have general laws in place prohibiting all private contracting regardless of police power interest or public harm.

For this and other reasons, Marshall strongly disagreed with the majority. The interpretation of the majority, he wrote, "convert[ed] an inhibition to pass laws impairing the obligation of contracts, into an inhibition to pass retrospective laws."

Id. at 355–56 (Marshall, C.J., dissenting). Marshall argued that the Contract Clause was intended as a far more substantial limitation on state authority, one that would preclude all legislation impairing contractual obligations, whether prospective or retrospective. Marshall's dissenting position avoids the risk of unlimited police power seemingly invited by the majority with the opposite extreme. In other words, it is, itself, an unrefined limitation upon state legislative power to address economic subject matter.

The constitutional convention provides little, if any, support for the extreme positions put forward by either the majority or Marshall. Douglas W. Kmiec & John O. McGinnis, *The Contract Clause: A Return to the Original Understanding*, 14 HASTINGS CONST. L.Q. 525, 538 (1987). Similarly, the natural law tradition of the founding fathers only partially supports Marshall, even as, in his *Ogden* dissent, Marshall expressly relies upon natural law to bolster his case for broader economic freedom. Wrote Marshall, "individuals do not derive from government their right to contract, but bring that right with them into society." *Ogden*, 25 U.S. (12 Wheat.) at 346 (Marshall, C.J., dissenting). Professor Wright at Harvard speculated that "[h]ad this case come to the Court a few years earlier [Marshall] might have had his way and made the obligation of contract as inclusive as the later interpretation of liberty of contract under the due process clause." BENJAMIN WRIGHT, THE CONTRACT CLAUSE OF THE CONSTITUTION 52 (1938). If Professor Wright is correct, it would have been interesting to learn whether Marshall's conception of economic freedom premised upon natural law would have had a more discernible or principled foundation than the later suspect judicial activism of substantive economic due process of the industrial age, whereby judges second-guessed state legislatures at will.

In theory, natural law might have been more capable of balancing individual economic freedom with needful economic regulation than personal judicial bias. For example, the natural law might have been looked to for limits upon legislative acts that contradict fundamental aspects of human nature — say, those that promote public monopoly or totally foreclose entry to legitimate occupation. However, this high moral principle could not be relied upon to determine the advisability of the day-to-day economic decisions modernly considered by legislatures, such as whether or not to raise the minimum wage. The founders did not understand the natural law to be a detailed codebook, but a set of principles derived from human reason that could then be freely applied in often innumerable, and from the standpoint of philosophical principle, indifferent ways.

Apart from the text or foundational principles of the Contract Clause, Professor Richard Epstein makes an economic case that the inability to limit prospective legislative impediments to contract invites the misuse of power for covert wealth redistribution and other forms of "rent-seeking" behavior. Richard A. Epstein, *Toward a Revitalization of the Contract Clause*, 51 U. CHI. L. REV. 703, 723–30 (1984). Epstein's argument in favor of having the Contract Clause apply to both retrospective and prospective impairment might be seen as partially derived from James Madison's concern that factions would capture local legislatures to disadvantage particular commercial actors. In THE FEDERALIST No. 10 (James Madison), Madison speculates that oppression is less likely in a large body like that governing the entire republic because no one faction, or special interest, will easily come to dominate. However, in correspondence with Jefferson, he opined that the Contract Clause is necessary to prevent oppression by states or smaller republics.

This observation remains valid, but the problem of oppression that Madison feared, or rent-seeking in Professor Epstein's words, is greater with legislation interfering with pre-existing, rather than future, contracts. This is so, since with new laws applied to existing contracts, a faction capturing the legislature can clearly impose losses on the identifiable group who has earlier invested. Sensible political action is more likely in the prospective context, because any losses associated with the public policy are less concentrated or identified, and thus, the chance of passing self-serving, faction-dominated laws is also less.

An argument was made in *Sturges* that the language of the Contract Clause should be applied only to the specific type of state legislative enactments of concern to the framers. Chief Justice Marshall soundly rejected this narrowing of general principle, writing: "[t]his question will scarcely admit of discussion. If this was the only remaining mischief against which the constitution intended to provide, it would undoubtedly have been, like paper money and tender laws, expressly forbidden. At any rate, terms more directly applicable to the subject, more appropriately expressing the intention of the convention, would have been used." *Sturges*, 17 U.S. (4 Wheat.) at 205.

Similarly, Justice Story writes in his COMMENTARIES, *supra*, at § 1389:

> It is probable, that the other great evils, already alluded to, constituted the main inducement to insert [the Contract Clause], where the temptations were more strong, and the interest more immediate and striking, to induce a violation of contracts. But though the motive may thus have been to reach other more pressing mischiefs, the prohibition itself is made general. It is applicable to all contracts, and not confined to the forms then most known, and most divided. Although a rare or particular case may not of itself be of sufficient magnitude to induce the establishment of a constitutional rule; yet it must be governed by that rule, when established, unless some plain and strong reason for excluding it can be given. It is not sufficient to show, that it may not have been foreseen, or intentionally provided for. To exclude it, it is necessary to go farther, and show, that if the case had been suggested, the language of the convention would have been varied so, as to exclude and except it. Where a case falls within the words of a rule or prohibition, it must be held within its operation, unless there is something obviously absurd, or mischievous, or repugnant to the general spirit of the instrument, arising from such a construction.

b. Extension to Public Contracts

Fletcher v. Peck, 10 U.S. (6 Cranch) 87 (1810), is a case that we mentioned briefly in Chapter 1, Section [C][4], to illustrate natural law reasoning in the early Supreme Court. We return to the case now to learn whether the Contract Clause applies to property conveyances. The Court decides that it does, and in so doing also expands the Clause to contracts with the government. Looking first at the aspects of the case that extends the Clause to the conveyance of property, perhaps Marshall felt no hesitancy in giving the Clause this sweep because doing so coincided with natural law principle, or as Marshall puts it, "by general principles which are common to our free institutions." *Id.* at 139.

In *Fletcher*, Chief Justice John Marshall determined that the Ex Post Facto Clause was applicable only in the criminal context so that was of no help in terms of the protection of a vested interest. Instead, Marshall reasons that a property conveyance was simply a form of executed contract. Marshall continued: "[s]ince, then, in fact, a grant is a contract executed, the obligation of which still continues, and since the constitution uses the general term contract, without distinguishing between those which are executory and those which are executed, it must be construed to comprehend the latter as well as the former. A law annulling conveyances between individuals, and declaring that the grantors should stand seized of their former estates, notwithstanding those grants, would be as repugnant to the constitution as a law discharging the vendors of property from the obligation of executing their contracts by conveyances. It would be strange if a contract to convey was secured by the constitution, while an absolute conveyance remained unprotected." The reader can see the excellence of John Marshall's reasoning and why over a span of over 30 years as Chief Justice, he was in the majority all but once."

However, extending the Contract Clause to contracts with public entities is more problematic. That application can pose difficulty since the government will be conflicted wherever its police power role would void a contract, but doing so would result in the government losing its own contractual advantage. This is what happened in *Fletcher* as the government as an entity was cheated out of fair market value by legislators who schemed to sell government land to themselves at well below market price and then sold it at market level to bona fide purchasers without knowledge of the fraud. In *Fletcher*, the government was seemingly precluded by the extension of the Contract Clause from exercising its police power to set aside the entire transaction. Nevertheless, Marshall reasoned: "if, under a fair construction of the constitution, grants are comprehended under the term contracts, is a grant from the state excluded from the operation of the provision? Is the Clause to be considered as inhibiting the state from impairing the obligation of contracts between two individuals, but as excluding from that inhibition contracts made with itself?"

Because Marshall's reasoning is so pellucid, we will stop interrupting it to allow you to savor the quality of his legal reasoning to its conclusion before you raise the objection that Marshall ended up favoring private right over public regulatory authority too greatly. Nevertheless, exploding any difference between the application of the Clause to contracts between private parties and contracts with public entities, Marshall continues:

> The words themselves contain no such distinction. They are general, and are applicable to contracts of every description. If contracts made with the state are to be exempted from their operation, the exception must arise from the character of the contracting party, not from the words which are employed. . . .

> In this form the power of the legislature over the lives and fortunes of individuals is expressly restrained. What motive, then, for implying, in

words which import a general prohibition to impair the obligation of contracts, an exception in favour of the right to impair the obligation of those contracts into which the state may enter?

The state legislatures can pass no *ex post facto* law. An *ex post facto* law is one which renders an act punishable in a manner in which it was not punishable when it was committed. Such a law may inflict penalties on the person, or may inflict pecuniary penalties which swell the public treasury. The legislature is then prohibited from passing a law by which a man's estate, or any part of it, shall be seized for a crime which was not declared, by some previous law, to render him liable to that punishment. Why, then, should violence be done to the natural meaning of words for the purpose of leaving to the legislature the power of seizing, for public use, the estate of an individual in the form of a law annulling the title by which he holds that estate? The court can perceive no sufficient grounds for making this distinction. This rescinding act would have the effect of an *ex post facto* law. It forfeits the estate of Fletcher for a crime not committed by himself, but by those from whom he purchased. This cannot be effected in the form of an *ex post facto* law, or bill of attainder; why, then, is it allowable in the form of a law annulling the original grant?

The argument in favour of presuming an intention to except a case, not excepted by the words of the constitution, is susceptible of some illustration from a principle originally ingrafted in that instrument, though no longer a part of it. The constitution, as passed, gave the courts of the United States jurisdiction in suits brought against individual states. A state, then, which violated its own contract was suable in the courts of the United States for that violation. Would it have been a defence in such a suit to say that the state had passed a law absolving itself from the contract? It is scarcely to be conceived that such a defence could be set up. And yet, if a state is neither restrained by the general principles of our political institutions, nor by the words of the constitution, from impairing the obligation of its own contracts, such a defence would be a valid one. This feature is no longer found in the constitution; but it aids in the construction of those clauses with which it was originally associated.

It is, then, the unanimous opinion of the court, that, in this case, the estate having passed into the hands of a purchaser for a valuable consideration, without notice, the state of Georgia was restrained, either by general principles which are common to our free institutions, or by the particular provisions of the constitution of the United States, from passing a law whereby the estate of the plaintiff in the premises so purchased could be constitutionally and legally impaired and rendered null and void.

10 U.S. 87, at 137–39.

John Marshall's reasoning in *Fletcher* leaves no room for the police power which is reserved to the states to allow it to regulate use of property in pursuit of the general welfare of the community. Because it failed to reconcile this retained power, later cases would opine that the Contract Clause cannot be used as an estoppel to prevent exercise of police power or as alternatively phrased the local government can contract away its police power. In a brief concurrence in *Fletcher*, Justice Johnson raised a related concern in cautioning that Marshall's reasoning went too far. Said Johnson: "To give it the general effect of a restriction of the state powers in favour of private rights, is certainly going very far beyond the obvious and necessary import of the words, and would operate to restrict the states in the exercise of that right which every community must exercise, of possessing itself of the property of the individual, when necessary for public uses; a right which a magnanimous and just government will never exercise without amply indemnifying the individual, and which perhaps amounts to nothing more than a power to oblige him to sell and convey, when the public necessities require it." 10 U.S. 87, at 145. Indeed, it might be argued that Marshall conflated the Contract Clause with the limitation on government from taking property for public use without the payment of just compensation. Failure to apply the most apt limitation upon state power to construe another can be said to be a lapse that undermines the rest of the reasoning put forth by Marshall.

NOTES AND QUESTIONS

1.   Note that the lawsuit in *Fletcher* was not brought directly against the state of Georgia in federal court, a proceeding precluded after the passage of the Eleventh Amendment in 1791.

2.   The lawsuit, as it was, existed between grantor, John Peck, and grantee, Robert Fletcher. Since both stood to gain by upholding title (Fletcher would have title and Peck consideration), where was the case or controversy? In a portion of his concurring opinion not reprinted, Justice Johnson indicates that he was reluctant "to proceed . . . at all" since the proceeding appeared to be "a mere feigned case." *Fletcher*, 10 U.S. (6 Cranch) at 147 (Johnson, J., concurring). Johnson said he concurred since he had confidence that "the respectable gentlemen who have been engaged for the parties . . . would never consent to impose a mere feigned case upon this court." *Id.* at 147–48.

3.   In his concurrence, Justice Johnson declines to rely upon the Contract Clause, preferring instead to rely upon "the reason and nature of things." This natural law ground was preferable to Johnson because he anticipated that bringing a public contract within the phraseology of the Contract Clause would cause "much difficulty." "[W]here to draw the line, or how to define or limit the words, 'obligation of contracts,' will be found a subject of extreme difficulty." As you read the balance of cases dealing with the Contract Clause, ask yourself whether or not Johnson has been proven correct. If Johnson was right, does that account for, or justify, the modern reluctance to judicially enforce the Clause?

4.   Marshall confirmed and enlarged his extension of the Contract Clause to public contracts in *Dartmouth College v. Woodward*, 17 U.S. (4 Wheat) 518 (1819). *Dartmouth* involved a charter granted originally in 1769 by Governor Wentworth of New Hampshire on behalf of George III. In 1815, a dispute arose between the existing board of trustees and the school's president. The legislature sided with the president and, to bolster his position, altered the charter of the school by, among other things, increasing the number of trustees and providing for a Board of Overseers that could veto acts by the trustees. The New Hampshire court of

appeals approved the modification, reasoning that the charter of the college was a civil institution, not a private contract, in the nature of a public trust. Marshall disagreed and applied the Contract Clause to disallow the changes in the charter, even as he admitted that a public charter was not likely in the minds of the framers in the drafting of the Contract Clause. Marshall writes:

> It is not enough to say, that this particular case was not in the mind of the convention, when the article was framed, nor of the American people, when it was adopted. It is necessary to go further, and to say that, had this particular case been suggested, the language would have been so varied, as to exclude it, or it would have been made a special exception. The case being within the words of the rule, must be within its operation likewise, unless there be something in the literal construction, so obviously absurd or mischievous, or repugnant to the general spirit of the instrument, as to justify those who expound the constitution in making it an exception.
>
> On what safe and intelligible ground, can this exception stand? There is no expression in the constitution, no sentiment delivered by its contemporaneous expounders, which would justify us in making it. In the absence of all authority of this kind, is there, in the nature and reason of the case itself, that which would sustain a construction of the constitution, not warranted by its words? Are contracts of this description of a character to excite so little interest, that we must exclude them from the provisions of the constitution, as being unworthy of the attention of those who framed the instrument? Or does public policy so imperiously demand their remaining exposed to legislative alteration, as to compel us, or rather permit us, to say, that these words, which were introduced to give stability to contracts, and which in their plain import comprehend this contract, must yet be so construed as to exclude it?

17 U.S. (4 Wheat.) at 644–45.

Separate and apart from what it tells us about the Contract Clause, this method of reasoning is interesting for what it reveals to us about constitutional interpretation. Justice Antonin Scalia insists that the only legitimate basis for construing the Constitution is its original understanding, and yet, here is the great Chief Justice John Marshall much closer to the understanding of the founders taking a very progressive/purposive approach to the interpretation of the Constitution's text. Of course, Marshall did use textual approaches closer to that recommended by the good Justice Scalia in other cases, so it's not that Justice Scalia can be declared or written off as entirely wrong; rather, to the extent that Justice Scalia ignores competing interpretive approaches at the founding or now can be accepted as a helpful reminder that it is often best to forgo ideological and partisan consistency in order to understand how competing means of interpretation are not precluded by anything in the text or original understanding of our institutions.

5. The impact of *Dartmouth College* was muted somewhat by the later opinion in *Charles River Bridge v. Warren Bridge*, 36 U.S. (11 Pet.) 420 (1837), which held that the grant of a charter to one private company to operate a toll bridge did not prevent the state from authorizing the construction of a competing free bridge. In an opinion by Chief Justice Roger Taney, Marshall's successor, the Court held that

"ambiguity in the terms of the contract, must operate against the adventurers, and in favour of the public." *Id.* at 544.

6.   Modernly, the protection of public contracts under the Clause has continued, invertedly, to the effect that government now needs greater justification for such interference than it does with regard to private contracts. In *United States Trust Co. v. New Jersey*, 431 U.S. 1 (1977), the Court found New York and New Jersey's attempt to welsh on a bond covenant to violate the Contract Clause. Writing for the Court, Justice Blackmun opined that a state impairment of its own contract must be shown to be "reasonable and necessary to serve an important public purpose." *Id.* at 25. While this is the same standard modernly applied to private contracts, Justice Blackmun held that the state would be given less deference when it was self-interested. In dissent, Justice Brennan argued that the Court stood the Clause "completely on its head," *id.* at 53 (Brennan, J., dissenting), but arguably, Justice Brennan's complaint should have been directed not at his brother Blackmun, but toward the legacy of Chief Justice Marshall and the extension of the Clause to public contracts.

c.   The Reserved Police Power

While states are precluded from impairing the obligation of contract, public or private, the Court has held that a state may not contract away its police power, or its ability to deal with fundamental issues of health and safety. In *Stone v. Mississippi*, 101 U.S. 814 (1879), the State passed an act in 1867 authorizing a lottery. In December 1869, the state constitution was amended providing that "the legislature shall never authorize any lottery; . . . nor shall any lottery heretofore authorized be permitted to be drawn, or tickets therein to be sold." When the 1869 provision rendered the earlier grant a nullity, it was argued to be an impairment of contract. Indeed, it was said that the court was well justified by the police power desire to suppress the evil of gambling. Said the Court: "All agree that the legislature cannot bargain away the police power of a State. 'Irrevocable grants of property and franchises may be made if they do not impair the supreme authority to make laws for the right government of the State; but no legislature can curtail the power of its successors to make such laws as they may deem proper in matters of police.' Many attempts have been made in this court and elsewhere to define the police power, but never with entire success. It is always easier to determine whether a particular case comes within the general scope of the power, than to give an abstract definition of the power itself which will be in all respects accurate. No one denies, however, that it extends to all matters affecting the public health or the public morals. . . . Neither can it be denied that lotteries are proper subjects for the exercise of this power."

Stone did recognize that it was possible for the government to bargain away its taxation authority — at least in part. In other words, a state government that grants a corporation tax-exempt status can be held to the bargain. The Court reasoned that while taxation is in general necessary for the support of government, it is not part of the government itself. Taxation is an incident to the exercise of the legitimate functions of government, said the Court, "but nothing more." *Stone*, 101 U.S. at 820.

The Modern Non-Enforcement of the Contract Clause.

When your authors began teaching this course, none of us contemplated a mortgage lending crisis of a magnitude similar to the Great Depression of the 1930s. All of us heard stories of this desperately hard time within our own families. Because the type of loan commonly available at the turn of the 20th century was a non-amortized interest-only product, banking institutions that were largely unregulated at the federal level often chose to call these notes when deposit money was lost in the stock market. When the market really hit the skids and portfolio positions had to be paid or risk institutional insolvency, thousands committed suicide, others turned to the bread lines, odd jobs, even petty crime. Then as now a great many found themselves without work — up to 10 million in the years after the crash of October 29.

Ambassador Kmiec's grandfather who came to the United States having been educated as a historian had been outspoken and of great courage in his frequent and open criticism of the Nazi treatment of the Jews. Unlike others of his generation who lacked the temerity to challenge Hitler and his irrational hatreds, grandfather never lost his voice even years later as the world mourned the millions lost.

Lest you forget that the law of the contract clause is the purpose of this note, and while you are encouraged to learn and retell the narrative of your own family's economic challenges, permit us to humanize the law of the Constitution that it is real flesh and blood people ("we the people") who are the intended beneficiaries of the human rights arguably preserved by the document. We are willing to venture that some of your kin who were first to arrive in the US opened a small business within a few months or years of arrival. Our ancestors were an industrious lot. Like so many businesses of that era, these ventures were heavily leveraged. When times were good, the large amount owed seemed a minor detail. When times turned bad, the amounts owed became multiples of that asked previously. Often, the loan was called in a downturn. Coming to America allowed escape from Nazi terror not challenging economic circumstances. The family that stayed behind would ultimately confront the Nazi terror directly.

In Menachem Katz's *Path of Hope* (yad Vashem 2008), the story of Piotr Kmiec would be told "Kmiec and his wife and their two daughters were among those few local people willing to assist Jews endangering their own lives." One of those assisted by Piotr was Menachem Katz, now an architect in Israel. Katz writes that "it was the early evening of 4 April (1944) and it was an especially cold night. Suddenly, the sounds of rapid footsteps made by several pairs of iron shod boots were heard from above, followed by a bang on the apartment floor as if a sack of wheat had been thrown from above. The sounds of steps renewed, and stopped again. Murderers! Murderers! Murderers! They killed him! The scream was heard and repeated several times, till it gradually dwindled. [Piotr Kmiec had been shot twice point blank by Nazi soldiers in front of his wife and daughters; martyred]. There are those that say that human rights cannot exist without the performance of duty; there is no duty to lay down one's life for another but there is a duty to educate a culture that makes that act of selfless nobility more rather than less likely.] The Kmiec name is said because of those valiant actions to be "righteous among all the nations."

How does this relate to the contract clause? It relates to the inquiry of whether or not the American Constitution is responsive to the needs and truth of the human person. Ambassador's father did not author a published book like that of Menachem Katz recounting the courage and bravery of a Kmiec left in the old country, but he did pen poetry and several chapters of an autobiography. One of the most poignant scenes recounted by Ambassador Kmiec's father was the day of foreclosure when the Sheriff removed the family of eight from their Chicago home. Walter Kmiec wrote: "the day was dark and cold like so many Chicago days in the run-up to the bleak winter which to this child always seem to arrive before its scheduled arrival. It was raining. Raining so hard that mother was pleading with the Sheriff to just wait an hour so all the furnishings would not be lost. But the brusque Sheriff's men no doubt having seen it all before either wouldn't — or couldn't — wait and they literally pried mother's hands from the pillow embroidery that she had done so lovingly in the quiet of the evenings. As all was tossed into the street and all was lost, the ambassador's father recalls finding it difficult to differentiate the rush of water pouring from the sky and that which fell unceasingly mother's eyes."

To relieve the anguish of moments like this, a good number of states in the 1930s passed laws that left mortgages as intact loans by provided an extended period to repay provided some current value was otherwise delivered to the business. Such modification of contract was the subject of the next case.

HOME BUILDING & LOAN ASS'N v. BLAISDELL
290 U.S. 398 (1933)

Mr. Chief Justice Hughes delivered the opinion of the Court.

Appellant contests the validity of . . . the Minnesota Mortgage Moratorium Law, as being repugnant to the contract clause (Article 1, Section 10) . . . of the Federal Constitution. . . .

The Act provides that, during the emergency declared to exist, relief may be had through authorized judicial proceedings with respect to foreclosures of mortgages, and execution sales, of real estate; that sales may be postponed and periods of redemption may be extended. The Act does not apply to mortgages subsequently made nor to those made previously which shall be extended for a period ending more than a year after the passage of the Act. . . . The act is to remain in effect "only during the continuance of the emergency and in no event beyond May 1, 1935." No extension of the period for redemption and no postponement of sale is to be allowed which would have the effect of extending the period of redemption beyond that date. Part 2, Section 8.

The Act declares that the various provisions for relief are severable; that each is to stand on its own footing with respect to validity. Part 1, Section 9. We are here concerned with the provisions of Part 1, Section 4, authorizing the District Court of the county to extend the period of redemption from foreclosure sales "for such additional time as the court may deem just and equitable," subject to the above-described limitation. The extension is to be made upon application to the court, on notice, for an order determining the reasonable value of the income on the property involved in the sale, or, if it has no income, then the reasonable rental value of the property, and directing the mortgagor "to pay all or a reasonable part of such income or rental value, in or toward the payment of taxes, insurance, interest, mortgage . . . indebtedness at such times and in such manner" as shall be determined by the court. The section also provides that the time for redemption from foreclosure sales theretofore made, which otherwise would expire less than thirty days after the approval of the Act, shall be extended to a date thirty days after its approval, and application may be made to the court within that time for a further extension as provided in the section. By another provision of the Act, no action, prior to May 1, 1935, may be maintained for a deficiency judgment until the period of redemption as allowed by existing law or as extended under the provisions of the Act has expired. . . .

Invoking the relevant provision of the statute, appellees applied to the District Court of Hennepin County for an order extending the period of redemption from a foreclosure sale. Their petition stated that they owned a lot in Minneapolis which they had mortgaged to appellant; that the mortgage contained a valid power of sale by advertisement, and that by reason of their default the mortgage had been foreclosed and sold to appellant on May 2, 1932, for $3,700.98; that appellant was the holder of the sheriff's certificate of sale; that, because of the economic depression, appellees had been unable to obtain a new loan or to redeem, and that, unless the period of redemption were extended, the property would be irretrievably lost; and that the reasonable value of the property greatly exceeded the amount due on the mortgage, including all liens, costs, and expenses.

*   *   *

Justice Olsen of the state court, in a concurring opinion, stated:

"The present nation wide and world wide business and financial crisis has the same results as if it were caused by flood, earthquake, or disturbance in nature. It has deprived millions of persons in this nation of their employment and means of earning a living for themselves and their families; it has destroyed the value of and the income from all property on which thousands of people depended for a living; it actually has resulted in the loss of their homes by a number of our people, and threatens to result in the loss of their homes by many other people, in this state; it has resulted in such widespread want and suffering among our people that private, state, and municipal agencies are unable to adequately relieve the want and suffering, and Congress has found it necessary to step in and attempt to remedy the situation by federal aid. Millions of the people's money were and are yet tied up in closed banks and in business enterprises."

*   *   *

. . . The statute does not impair the integrity of the mortgage indebtedness. The obligation for interest remains. The statute does not affect the validity of the sale or the right of a mortgagee-purchaser to title in fee, or his right to obtain a deficiency judgment, if the mortgagor fails to redeem within the prescribed period. Aside from the extension of time, the other conditions of redemption are unaltered. While the mortgagor remains in possession he must pay the rental value as that value has been determined, upon notice and hearing, by the court. The rental value so paid is devoted to the carrying of the property by the application of the required payments to taxes, insurance, and interest on the mortgage indebtedness. While the mortgagee-purchaser is debarred from actual possession, he has, so far as rental value is concerned, the equivalent of possession during the extended period.

In determining whether the provision for this temporary and conditional relief exceeds the power of the State by reason of the clause in the Federal Constitution prohibiting impairment of the obligations of contracts, we must consider the relation of emergency to constitutional power, the historical setting of the contract clause, the development of the jurisprudence of this Court in the construction of that clause, and the principles of construction which we may consider to be established.

While emergency does not create power, emergency may furnish the occasion for the exercise of power. "Although an emergency may not call into life a power which has never lived, nevertheless emergency may afford a reason for the exertion of a living power already enjoyed." . . . When the provisions of the Constitution, in grant or restriction, are specific, so particularized as not to admit of construction, no question is presented. Thus, emergency would not permit a State to have more than two Senators in the Congress, or permit the election of President by a general popular vote without regard to the number of electors to which the States are respectively entitled, or permit the States to "coin money" or to "make anything but gold and silver coin a tender in payment of debts." But, where constitutional grants and limitations of power are set forth in general clauses, which afford a broad outline, the process of construction is essential to fill in the details. That is true of the contract clause. . . .

. . . The occasion and general purpose of the contract clause are summed up in the terse statement of Chief Justice Marshall in *Ogden v. Saunders* [(1827)]:

"The power of changing the relative situation of debtor and creditor, of interfering with contracts, a power which comes home to every man, touches the interest of all, and controls the conduct of every individual in those things which he supposes to be proper for his own exclusive management, had been used to such an excess by the state legislatures, as to break in upon the ordinary intercourse of society, and destroy all confidence between man and man. This mischief had become so great, so alarming, as not only to impair commercial intercourse, and threaten the existence of credit, but to sap the morals of the people, and destroy the sanctity of private faith. To guard against the continuance of the evil was an object of deep interest with all the truly wise, as well as the virtuous, of this great community, and was one of the important benefits expected from a reform of the government."

But full recognition of the occasion and general purpose of the clause does not suffice to fix its precise scope. Nor does an examination of the details of prior legislation in the States yield criteria which can be considered controlling. To ascertain the scope of the constitutional prohibition, we examine the course of judicial decisions in its application. These put it beyond question that the prohibition is not an absolute one and is not to be read with literal exactness like a mathematical formula. . . .

The inescapable problems of construction have been: What is a contract?[1] What are the obligations of contracts? What constitutes impairment of these obligations? What residuum of power is there still in the States in relation to the operation of contracts, to protect the vital interests of the community? Questions of this character, "of no small nicety and intricacy, have vexed the legislative halls, as well as the judicial tribunals, with an uncounted variety and frequency of litigation and speculation." STORY ON THE CONSTITUTION, § 13[69].

The obligation of a contract is the "law which binds the parties to perform their agreement." *Sturges v. Crowninshield* [(1819)]. This Court has said that "the laws which subsist at the time and place of the making of a contract, and where it is to be performed, enter into and form a part of it, as if they were expressly referred to or incorporated in its terms. This principle embraces alike those which affect its validity, construction, discharge, and enforcement. . . . Nothing can be more material to the obligation than the means of enforcement. . . ." [However,] the general statement above quoted was limited by the further observation that "It is competent for the States to change the form of the remedy, or to modify it otherwise, as they may see fit, provided no substantial right secured by the contract is thereby impaired. No attempt has been made to fix definitely the line between alterations of the remedy, which are to be deemed legitimate, and those which, under the form of modifying the remedy, impair substantial rights. Every case must be determined upon its own circumstances." . . .

The obligations of a contract are impaired by a law which renders them invalid, or releases or extinguishes them and impairment, as above noted, has been predicated of laws which without destroying contracts derogate from substantial contractual rights. . . .

*   *   *

Not only is the constitutional provision qualified by the measure of control which the State retains over remedial processes, but the State also continues to possess authority to safeguard the vital interests of its people. It does not matter that legislation appropriate to that end "has the result of modifying or abrogating contracts already in effect." *Stephenson v. Binford* [(1932)]. Not only are existing laws read into contracts in order to fix obligations as between the parties, but the reservation of essential attributes of sovereign power is also read into contracts as a postulate of the legal order. The policy of protecting contracts against impairment presupposes the maintenance of a government by virtue of which contractual relations are worth while, — a government which retains adequate authority to secure the peace and good order of society. This principle of harmonizing the constitutional prohibition with the necessary residuum of state power has had progressive recognition in the decisions of this Court.

*   *   *

---

[1] [8] Contracts, within the meaning of the clause, have been held to embrace those that are executed, that is, grants, as well as those that are executory. They embrace the charters of private corporations. But not the marriage contract, so as to limit the general right to legislate on the subject of divorce. Nor are judgments, though rendered upon contracts, deemed to be within the provision. Nor does a general law, giving the consent of a State to be sued, constitute a contract.

. . . [S]peaking through Mr. Justice Brewer, . . . in *Long Island Water Supply Co. v. Brooklyn* [(1897)], [this Court stated]:

> "But into all contracts, whether made between States and individuals, or between individuals only, there enter conditions which arise, not out of the literal terms of the contract itself, they are superinduced by the pre-existing and higher authority of the laws of nature, of nations, or of the community to which the parties belong. They are always presumed, and must be presumed, to be known and recognized by all, are binding upon all, and need never, therefore, be carried into express stipulation, for this could add nothing to their force. Every contract is made in subordination to them, and must yield to their control, as conditions inherent and paramount, wherever a necessity for their execution shall occur."

The Legislature cannot "bargain away the public health or the public morals." Thus, the constitutional provision against the impairment of contracts was held not to be violated by an amendment of the state constitution which put an end to a lottery theretofore authorized by the Legislature. *Stone v. Mississippi* [(1879)]. The lottery was a valid enterprise when established under express state authority, but the legislature in the public interest could put a stop to it. A similar rule has been applied to the control by the state of the sale of intoxicating liquors. *Beer Company v. Massachusetts* [(1877)]; *Mugler v. Kansas* [(1887)]. The states retain adequate power to protect the public health against the maintenance of nuisances despite insistence upon existing contracts. *Fertilizing Compan. v. Hyde Park* [(1878)]. . . .

* * *

The argument is pressed that in the cases we have cited the obligation of contracts was affected only incidentally. This argument proceeds upon a misconception. The question is not whether the legislative action affects contracts incidentally, or directly or indirectly, but whether the legislation is addressed to a legitimate end and the measures taken are reasonable and appropriate to that end. Another argument, which comes more closely to the point, is that the state power may be addressed directly to the prevention of the enforcement of contracts only when these are of a sort which the legislature in its discretion may denounce as being in themselves hostile to public morals, or public health, safety, or welfare, or where the prohibition is merely of injurious practices; that interference with the enforcement of other and valid contracts according to appropriate legal procedure, although the interference is temporary and for a public purpose, is not permissible. This is but to contend that in the latter case the end is not legitimate in the view that it cannot be reconciled with a fair interpretation of the constitutional provision.

Undoubtedly, whatever is reserved of state power must be consistent with the fair intent of the constitutional limitation of that power. The reserved power cannot be construed so as to destroy the limitation, nor is the limitation to be construed to destroy the reserved power in its essential aspects. They must be construed in harmony with each other. This principle precludes a construction which would permit the state to adopt as its policy the repudiation of debts or the destruction of contracts or the denial of means to enforce them. But it does not follow that conditions may not arise in which a temporary restraint of enforcement may be consistent with the spirit and purpose of the constitutional provision and thus be found to be within the range of the reserved power of the state to protect the vital interests of the community. It cannot be maintained that the constitutional prohibition should be so construed as to prevent limited and temporary interpositions with respect to the enforcement of contracts if made necessary by a great public calamity such as fire, flood, or earthquake. The reservation of state power appropriate to such extraordinary conditions may be deemed to be as much a part of all contracts, as is the reservation of state power to protect the public interest in the other situations to which we have referred. And, if state power exists to give temporary relief from the enforcement of contracts in the presence of disasters due to physical causes such as fire, flood, or earthquake, that power cannot be said to be non-existent when the urgent public need demanding such relief is produced by other and economic causes.

Whatever doubt there may have been that the protective power of the state, its police power, may be exercised — without violating the true intent of the provision of the Federal Constitution — in directly preventing the immediate and literal enforcement of contractual obligations, by a temporary and conditional restraint, where vital public interests would otherwise suffer, was removed by our decisions relating to the enforcement of provisions of leases during a period of scarcity of housing. . . .

* * *

Applying the criteria established by our decisions, we conclude:

1. An emergency existed in Minnesota which furnished a proper occasion for the exercise of the reserved power of the state to protect the vital interests of the community. . . .

2. The legislation was addressed to a legitimate end; that is, the legislation was not for the mere advantage of particular individuals but for the protection of a basic interest of society.

3. In view of the nature of the contracts in question — mortgages of unquestionable validity — the relief afforded and justified by the emergency, in order not to contravene the constitutional provision, could only be of a character appropriate to that emergency, and could be granted only upon reasonable conditions.

4. The conditions upon which the period of redemption is extended do not appear to be unreasonable. The initial extension of the time of redemption for thirty days from the approval of the Act was obviously to give a reasonable opportunity for the authorized application to the court. As already noted, the integrity of the mortgage indebtedness is not impaired; interest continues to run; the validity of the sale and the right of a mortgagee-purchaser to title or to obtain a deficiency judgment, if the mortgagor fails to redeem within the extended period, are maintained; and the conditions of redemption, if redemption there be, stand as they were under the prior law. The mortgagor during the extended period is not ousted from possession, but he must pay the rental value of the premises as ascertained in judicial proceedings and this amount is applied to the carrying of the property and to interest upon the indebtedness. . . .

5. The legislation is temporary in operation. It is limited to the exigency which

called it forth. While the postponement of the period of redemption from the foreclosure sale is to May 1, 1935, that period may be reduced by the order of the court under the statute, in case of a change in circumstances, and the operation of the statute itself could not validly outlast the emergency or be so extended as virtually to destroy the contracts.

We are of the opinion that the Minnesota statute as here applied does not violate the contract clause of the Federal Constitution. Whether the legislation is wise or unwise as a matter of policy is a question with which we are not concerned.

Judgment affirmed.

Mr. Justice Sutherland, dissenting.

Few questions of greater moment than that just decided have been submitted for judicial inquiry during this generation. He simply closes his eyes to the necessary implications of the decision who fails to see in it the potentiality of future gradual but ever-advancing encroachments upon the sanctity of private and public contracts. . . .

It is quite true that an emergency may supply the occasion for the exercise of power, dependent upon the nature of the power and the intent of the Constitution with respect thereto. The emergency of war furnishes an occasion for the exercise of certain of the war powers. This the Constitution contemplates, since they cannot be exercised upon any other occasion. The existence of another kind of emergency authorizes the United States to protect each of the states of the Union against domestic violence. Const. Article 4, Section 4. But we are here dealing, not with a power granted by the Federal Constitution, but with the state police power, which exists in its own right. Hence the question is, not whether an emergency furnishes the occasion for the exercise of that state power, but whether an emergency furnishes an occasion for the relaxation of the restrictions upon the power imposed by the contract impairment clause; and the difficulty is that the contract impairment clause forbids state action under any circumstances, if it have the effect of impairing the obligation of contracts. That clause restricts every state power in the particular specified, no matter what may be the occasion. It does not contemplate that an emergency shall furnish an occasion for softening the restriction or making it any the less a restriction upon state action in that contingency than it is under strictly normal conditions.

I am authorized to say that Mr. Justice Van Devanter, Mr. Justice McReynolds, and Mr. Justice Butler concur in this opinion.

NOTES AND QUESTIONS

1.   While the original mortgage contract is not fully protected in *Blaisdell*, note that, notwithstanding the profound economic emergency that the Great Depression of the 1930s represented, the Court did not merely assume that the contract could be set aside under a broad, undifferentiated claim of reserved police power. Rather, the Court carefully circumscribed its opinion in its own five-point summary to fit the emergency circumstance. Likewise, the cases the *Blaisdell* Court relied upon are

similarly limited in language. For example, in *Block v. Hirsh*, 256 U.S. 135 (1921), the Court upheld a law that suspended the removal of tenants after the expiration of leases in light of a well-documented housing shortage. The *Blaisdell* Court correctly noted that the relief afforded was temporary and conditional. It was sustained because of the emergency due to scarcity of housing, and because the statute made provision for reasonable compensation to the landlord during the period he was prevented from regaining possession.

Even this temporary explanation did not satisfy four members of the Court. Justice Sutherland wrote in dissent:

> The rent cases — *Block v. Hirsh* [(1921)]; *Marcus Brown Holding Co. v. Feldman* [(1921)]; *Edgar A. Levy Leasing Co. v. Siegel* [(1922)] — which are here relied upon, dealt with an exigent situation due to a period of scarcity of housing caused by the war. I do not stop to consider the distinctions between them and the present case or to do more than point out that the question of contract impairment received little, if any, more than casual consideration. The writer of the opinions in the first two cases [Justice Oliver Wendell Holmes], speaking for this Court in a later case, *PennsylvaniaCoal Co. v. Mahon* [(1922)], characterized all of them as having gone "to the verge of the law." It, therefore, seems pertinent to say that decisions which confessedly escape the limbo of unconstitutionality by the exceedingly narrow margin suggested by this characterization should be applied toward the solution of a doubtful question arising in a different field with a very high degree of caution. Reasonably considered, they do not foreclose the question here involved, and it should be determined upon its merits without regard to those cases.

Blaisdell, 290 U.S. at 478–79 (Sutherland, J., dissenting).

2. One of the limiting features the Court highlights is the difference between modification of remedy and impairment of obligation of contract. This distinction was made quite early by Justice Joseph Story who wrote:

> [E]very change and modification of the remedy does not involve such a consequence. No one will doubt, that the legislature may vary the nature and extent of remedies, so always, that some substantive remedy be in fact left. Nor can it be doubted, that the legislature may prescribe the times and modes, in which remedies may be pursued; and bar suits not brought within such periods, and not pursued in such modes. Statutes of limitations are of this nature; and have never been supposed to destroy the obligation of contracts, but to prescribe the times, within which that obligation shall be enforced by a suit; and in default to deem it either satisfied, or abandoned. The obligation to perform a contract is coequal with the undertaking to perform it. It originates with the contract itself, and operates anterior to the time of performance. The remedy acts upon the broken contract, and enforces a pre-existing obligation.

JOSEPH STORY, COMMENTARIES ON THE CONSTITUTION OF THE UNITED STATES § 1379 (1833).

3. Beyond emergency and the difference between obligation and remedy, Chief Justice Hughes further suggests another important way for distinguishing between unconstitutional impairments and valid modifications pursuant to the police power. Hughes emphasizes that the legislation "was not for the mere advantage of particular individuals." *Blaisdell*, 290 U.S. at 4445. Recall that Madison was greatly concerned with factions using legislative power to secure self-interested advantages for themselves. THE FEDERALIST NOS. 10 & 44 (James Madison). While such factions will always attempt to dress their self-interest in public terms, where the effect of a law is to do little other than to redistribute the benefit of a contractual right from one private party to another, Chief Justice Hughes — like Madison — properly instructs that such law should be invalidated.

4.   Obviously, all of the qualifications that attend *Blaisdell* help define what the scope of the reserved police power is with respect to the Contract Clause. In dissent, Justice Sutherland sought to add another qualification in the difference between a total prohibition of a contractual activity and a selective interference. For Sutherland, the essential attributes of reserved sovereign power that are read into contracts includes the former, but not the latter. He gives an example:

> [L]et us revert to the example already given with respect to an agreement for the manufacture and sale of intoxicating liquor. And let us suppose that the state, instead of passing legislation prohibiting the manufacture and sale of the commodity, in which event the doctrine of implied conditions would be pertinent, continues to recognize the general lawfulness of the business, but, because of what it conceives to be a justifying emergency, provides that the time for the performance of existing contracts for future manufacture and sale shall be extended for a specified period of time. It is perfectly admissible, in view of the state power to prohibit the business, to read into the contract an implied proviso to the effect that the business of manufacturing and selling intoxicating liquors shall not, prior to the date when performance is due, become unlawful; but in the case last put, to read into the contract a pertinent provisional exception in the event of inter- meddling state action would be more than unreasonable, it would be absurd, since we must assume that the contract was made on the footing that, so long as the obligation remained lawful, the impairment clause would effectively preclude a law altering or nullifying it however exigent the occasion might be.

Blaisdell, 290 U.S. at 477–78 (Sutherland, J., dissenting).

5.   The empathy demonstrated in *Blaisdell* in essence qualified the absolutist nature of the Contract Clause text and subjected it to judicial balancing in context. This did not signify that the Contract Clause did not still prevail in some cases. For example, in *W.B. Worthen Co. v. Thomas*, 292 U.S. 426 (1934), the Court dealt with an Arkansas law that exempted the proceeds of a life insurance policy from collection by the beneficiary's judgment creditors. Stressing the retroactive effect of the state law, the Court held that it was invalid under the Contract Clause, since it was not precisely and reasonably designed to meet a grave temporary emergency in the interest of the general welfare. In *W.B. Worthen Co. v. Kavanaugh*, 295 U.S. 56 (1935), the Court was confronted with another Arkansas law that diluted the rights and remedies of mortgage bondholders. The Court held the law invalid under the Contract Clause. "Even when the public welfare is invoked as an excuse," Mr.

Justice Cardozo wrote for the Court, the security of a mortgage cannot be cut down "without moderation or reason or in a spirit of oppression." *Id.* at 60. And finally, in *Treigle v. Acme Homestead Assn.*, 297 U.S. 189 (1936), the Court held invalid under the Contract Clause a Louisiana law that modified the existing withdrawal rights of the members of a building and loan association. "Such an interference with the right of contract," said the Court, "cannot be justified by saying that in the public interest the operations of building associations may be controlled and regulated, or that in the same interest their charters may be amended." *Id.* at 196.

In the 1960s, the Court addressed a Texas statute that limited statutory rights to reclaim title to land that had been forfeited because of certain delinquent interest payments. *City of El Paso v. Simmons*, 379 U.S. 497 (1965). In the early 20th century, desirous to have its territory settled, Texas made unusually generous credit sales of public lands into private hands. These sales required little upfront capital and often only interest payment. Further, if interest went unpaid, the purchaser could redeem at any time until third party interests intervened. With oil discoveries, these lands became more valuable, and Texas limited the right of redemption to five years. Texas sought to justify the limitation as a mere change in remedy, not obligation. Breaking from earlier case law, the Court held that it was unnecessary to make that distinction since even if the state was impairing its obligation, such impairment was not "substantial." In the majority's judgment, the right of reinstatement was not an essential element of the bargain Texas made, and hence, in light of the changed land values and need to eliminate title uncertainty, the reinstatement right could be limited. *Id.* at 513–16.

In *Allied Structural Steel Company v. Spannaus*, 438 U.S. 234 (1978), Minnesota rather radically adjusted the terms of a private pension contract in response to the announcement that the company was leaving the state. The Court found that the proposed changes violated the Contract Clause distinguishing *Blaisdell* by virtue of lack of emergency and widespread economic dislocation. In this regard, the original understanding of the Contract Clause preventing the unfair redistribution of wealth and isolated incidents as opposed to addressing a society-wide problem prevailed. The court emphasized that the statutory modification was both severe and unexpected.

A similar result obtained in *United States Trust Co. v. New Jersey* [(1977)]. In that case the Court again recognized that although the absolute language of the Clause must leave room for "the 'essential attributes of sovereign power,' . . . necessarily reserved by the States to safeguard the welfare of their citizens," *id.* at 21, that power has limits when its exercise effects substantial modifications of private contracts. . . .

In a footnote [n.13], the Court in *Allied* noted in addition to the list of qualifications to the Contract Clause, namely, whether the contract was made in "an enterprise already regulated." 438 U.S. at 292 n.13 (quoting *Veix v. Sixth Ward Building & Loan Ass'n*, 310 U.S. 32, 38 (1940)). In several cases subsequent to *Allied*, this factor proved to be important or dispositive. For example, in *Energy Reserves Group v. Kansas Power and Light Co.*, 459 U.S. 400 (1982), the Court upheld a Kansas statute that precluded certain gas price increases by suppliers of natural gas. The statute's provision contradicted existing contractual provisions between the Energy Reserves Group, a natural gas provider, and the Kansas Power and Light Company, a public utility, that authorized periodic price increases. Justice Blackmun, writing for the Court, wrote that "[s]ignificant here is the fact that the parties are operating in a heavily regulated industry." *Energy Reserves Group*, 459 U.S. at 413. Moreover, said the Court, "the contracts expressly recognize the existence of extensive regulation by providing that any contractual terms are subject to relevant present and future state and federal law. This latter provision could be interpreted to incorporate all future state regulation, and thus dispose of the Contract Clause claim." *Id.* at 416.

Another decision, *Exxon Corp v. Eagerton*, 462 U.S. 176 (1983), was resolved in a similar way. In *Exxon*, the Court upheld an Alabama statute that increased an oil severance tax and precluded passing on the increase to purchasers. Provisions of existing contracts would have allowed the increased taxes to be passed on, but the Court analogized the position of the oil producer to that of a highly-regulated common carrier limited by rate regulation. *Id.* at 193–94. The Court somewhat gratuitously added that the denial of the pass through was a generally applicable law not targeted at a particular contract obligation, *id.* at 191–92, but this feature of the state law does not explain the case. While Marshall was surely correct that the police power allows the states to eliminate some types of contract opportunities altogether (*see, e.g., Stone v. Mississippi, supra*, and the elimination of the state lottery), such police power exercises, concerned as they are with the health, safety and welfare, are qualitatively different than the redistribution of a tax increase. Nevertheless, since Justice Thurgood Marshall saw no difference between the cases, *Exxon* muddies the water of modern Contract Clause interpretation.

6.   In *General Motors Corp. v. Romein*, 503 U.S. 181 (1992), the Court rejected a Contract Clause challenge to a 1987 Michigan law that effectively repealed the "coordination of benefits" that employers were permitted to do under a prior 1981 Michigan law. Under the 1981 law, employers were coordinating, or reducing, the benefits of disabled or injured workers who had multiple compensation sources. The Court held there was no contractual agreement with regard to the coordination of benefits, and therefore, there was nothing impaired by the 1987 law. *Id.* at 186–87. To the employers' argument that the 1981 law had been impliedly incorporated into private contracts, the Court stated "we have not held that all state regulations are implied terms of every contract entered into while they are effective, especially when the regulations themselves cannot be fairly interpreted to require such incorporation." *Id.* at 189. Justice O'Connor went on to say that state laws are implied into private contract regardless of the assent of the parties only when that law affects "the validity, construction, and enforcement of contracts." *Id.* The 1987 repeal in *General Motors* did not affect the legal validity of the underlying employment contracts.

7.   As noted throughout, by its express terms, the Contract Clause applies only to the states, and not to the federal government. However, some early case law employs the Due Process Clause to limit federal interferences with contract. *Lynch v. United States*, 292 U.S. 571 (1934) (invalidating federal cancellation of life insurance policies). However, other more recent cases indicate that the Due Process Clause standards are less searching than those applied under the Contract Clause. *Pension Benefit Guaranty Corp. v. R.A. Gray & Co.*, 467 U.S. 717, 733 (1984)

(upholding retroactive "withdrawal liability" imposed by federal law upon private companies leaving a multi-employer pension plan). *See also Usery v. Turner Elkhorn Mining Co.*, 428 U.S. 1, 14–20 (1976) (validating a federal statute that required the operators of coal mines to compensate employees who had contracted pneumoconiosis even though the employees had terminated their work in the coal-mining industry before the Act was passed. This federal statute imposed this new duty on operators based on past acts and applied even though the coal mine operators might not have known of the danger that their employees would contract pneumoconiosis at the time of a particular employee's service).

United States v. Winstar, 518 U.S. 839 (1996), applied a type of Contract Clause analysis to a breach of contract by the federal government itself. The case arose out of the savings and loan crisis of the late 1980s. Because the Federal Savings and Loan Insurance Corporation (FSLIC) was insufficiently funded to liquidate all of the failing thrifts, the Federal Home Loan Bank Board induced healthy thrifts and outside investors to purchase the failing thrifts by permitting the acquiring entities to treat the amount that the purchase price of the thrifts exceeded their fair market value as "supervisory goodwill." The purchasers were further permitted to treat the goodwill and other capital credits as "capital reserves," in satisfaction of their capital reserve requirements established by federal regulations. Subsequently, Congress passed the Financial Institutions Reform, Recovery, and Enforcement Act of 1989 (FIRREA). FIRREA prevented thrifts from treating goodwill and capital credits as capital reserves. Three thrifts created by way of supervisory mergers, two of which later failed because of the government change of regulation, and one which survived only with a great infusion of private capital, brought suit against the United States seeking damages for breach of contract.

In a plurality opinion for the Court, Justice Souter rejected several variants of the reserved power doctrine — that is, to allow recovery for the breach would impede valid regulatory authority — with the proposition that the government is free to regulate, but it must bear the cost of any regulatory changes that result in a breach of its existing contracts. *Id.* at 871–91. Interestingly, Justice Souter, who has been hostile to natural law reasoning in other opinions, relied in his opinion upon several distinctly natural law sources — for example, Chief Justice John Marshall's opinion in *Fletcher v. Peck*. Justice Souter wrote:

> In England, of course, Parliament was historically supreme in the sense that no "higher law" limited the scope of legislative action or provided mechanisms for placing legally enforceable limits upon it in specific instances; the power of American legislative bodies, by contrast, is subject to the overriding dictates of the Constitution and the obligations that it authorizes. Hence, although we have recognized that "a general law . . . may be repealed, amended or disregarded by the legislature which enacted it," and "is not binding upon any subsequent legislature," on this side of the Atlantic, the principle has always lived in some tension with the constitutionally created potential for a legislature, under certain circumstances, to place effective limits on its successors, or to authorize executive action resulting in such a limitation.

The development of this latter, American doctrine in federal litigation began in cases applying limits on state sovereignty imposed by the National Constitution. Thus Chief Justice Marshall's exposition in *Fletcher v. Peck*, where the Court held that the Contract Clause, U.S. Const., Art. I, § 10, cl. 1, barred the State of Georgia's effort to rescind land grants made by a prior state legislature.

Id. at 871–73.

With regard to the reserved power doctrine, Justice Souter concluded that it was not implicated because the government did not contract away its sovereign authority, it merely (to the tune of $140 billion dollars or so) agreed to indemnify the private thrifts for losses sustained by later regulatory change which limited use of supervisory goodwill as an asset. In Justice Souter's words:

> The [argument] rests on the reserved powers doctrine, developed in the course of litigating claims that States had violated the Contract Clause. It holds that a state government may not contract away "an essential attribute of its sovereignty," *United States Trust*, 431 U.S. at 23, with the classic example of its limitation on the scope of the Contract Clause being found in *Stone v. Mississippi*, 101 U.S. 814 (1880). There a corporation bargained for and received a state legislative charter to conduct lotteries, only to have them outlawed by statute a year later. This Court rejected the argument that the charter immunized the corporation from the operation of the statute, holding that "the legislature cannot bargain away the police power of a State." *Id.* at 817. The Government says that "[t]he logic of the doctrine . . . applies equally to contracts alleged to have been made by the federal government." This may be so but is also beside the point, for the reason that the Government's ability to set capital requirements is not limited by the Bank Board's and FSLIC's promises to make good any losses arising from subsequent regulatory changes. The answer to the Government's contention that the State cannot barter away certain elements of its sovereign power is that a contract to adjust the risk of subsequent legislative change does not strip the Government of its legislative sovereignty.

Id. at 888–89.

8. The Contract Clause is not the only substantive constitutional protection of vested rights. The Fifth Amendment also precludes the taking of private property for public use without the payment of just compensation. Since contract is a species of property, cases brought under the Contract Clause frequently implicate the so-called "Takings Clause" as well. For example, in his *El Paso* dissent, *supra*, Justice Black observed:

> In spite of all the Court's discussion of clouds on land titles and need for "efficient utilization" of land, the real issue in this case is not whether Texas has constitutional power to pass legislation to correct these problems, by limiting reinstatements to five years following forfeiture. I think that there was and is a constitutional way for Texas to do this. But I think the Fifth Amendment forbids Texas to do so without compensating the holders of

contractual rights for the interests it wants to destroy. Contractual rights, this Court has held, are property, and the Fifth Amendment requires that property shall not be taken for public use without just compensation. [Citations omitted.] This constitutional requirement is made applicable to the States by the Fourteenth Amendment. The need to clear titles and stabilize the market in land would certainly be a valid public purpose to sustain exercise of the State's power of eminent domain, and while the Contract Clause protects the value of the property right in contracts, it does not stand in the way of a State's taking those property rights as it would any other property, provided it is willing to pay for what it has taken.

. . .

The Court seems to say that because it was "necessary" to raise money and clear titles, Texas was not obligated to pay for rights which it took. I suppose that if Texas were building a highway and a man's house stood in the way, it would be "necessary" to tear it down. Until today I had thought there could be no doubt that he would be entitled to just compensation. Yet the Fifth and Fourteenth Amendments protect his rights no more nor less than they do those of people to whom Texas was contractually obligated. Texas' "necessity" as seen by this Court is the mother of a regrettable judicial invention which I think has no place in our constitutional law. Our Constitution provides that property needed for public use, whether for schools or highways or any other public purpose, shall be paid for out of tax-raised funds fairly contributed by all the taxpayers, not just by a few purchasers of land who trusted the State not wisely but too well. It is not the happiest of days for me when one of our wealthiest States is permitted to enforce a law that breaks faith with those who contracted with it.

379 U.S. at 533–35 (Black, J., dissenting). We now take a closer look at why the framers assigned high importance to the protection of property, and the Court's application of the Takings Clause.

B. THE PROTECTION OF PROPERTY

1. Historical and Philosophical Justification

The founders understood the importance of property both from their grounding in natural law (see the excerpt from Locke, *infra*) and practical experience, reflected below in William Bradford's reflection on the relationship between private property and industriousness in the Plymouth colony. In Madison's words, "[g]overnment is instituted to protect property of every sort. . . . This being the end of government, that alone is a *just* government, which *impartially* secures to every man, whatever is his *own*." JAMES MADISON, *Property, in* 14 THE PAPERS OF JAMES MADISON 266 (William T. Hutchinson ed., 1977) (emphasis in the original). The protection of vested rights, especially private property and contract, advanced liberty and invited greater participation in the political life of the community, upon which the new republic would depend.

William Bradford, Of Plymouth Plantation
120–21 (Samuel Eliot Morison ed., 1952)

. . . So they began to think how they might raise as much corn as they could, and obtain a better crop than they had done, that they might not still thus languish in misery. At length, after much debate of things, the Governor . . . gave way that they should set corn every man for his own particular, and in that regard trust to themselves; in all other things to go on in the general way as before. And so assigned to every family a parcel of land . . . . This had very good success, for it made all hands very industrious . . . .

The experience that was had in this common course and condition . . . may well evince the vanity of that conceit of Plato's . . . that the taking away of property and bringing in community into a commonwealth would make them happy and flourishing; as if they were wiser than God.

NOTES AND QUESTIONS

1. Governor Bradford chastises ancient philosophers for suggesting that commonly-held property, rather than private, individually-vested allocations would allow a people to flourish. The hard experience of the Plymouth Plantation conclusively demonstrated to Bradford the contrary and that these ancients were wrong to presume themselves "wiser than God." But didn't God bestow the entire earth as a gift in common? Or is the commandment "not to steal," as illustrated in Judeo-Christian Scriptures, sufficient to indicate God's support for the division of the common into separately owned shares? Much of the Judeo-Christian tradition familiar to the framers supported private property as a means to secure the lives of men and women from both poverty and violence. Nevertheless, recognizing property's common, Divine origin, the private allocations were owned subject to an accompanying stewardship obligation. Stewardship entailed both using property in its highest and best use (making it fruitful) as well as reserving and sharing any surplus with those less well off. The latter obligation was reinforced by additional religious teaching that promoted the virtue of temperance, including having only a moderate attachment to earthly goods.

2. In the next excerpt, philosopher John Locke explains how man comes to have a justifiable vested right to particular property, apart from the positive laws of any government. In this, Locke states the natural law justification for property that the framers brought with them into the constitutional convention.

John Locke, Second Treatise of Government
§§ 25–51 (1690)

§ 25. Whether we consider natural *reason*, which tells us, that men, being once born, have a right to their preservation, and consequently to meat and drink, and such other things as nature affords for their subsistence: or *revelation*, which gives us an account of those grants God made of the world to *Adam*, and to *Noah*, and his sons, it is very clear, that God, as King *David* says, *Psal.* cxv. 16. *has given the earth to the children of men*; given it to mankind in common. But this being supposed, it seems to some a very great difficulty, how any one should ever come to have a *property* in any thing: I will not content myself to answer, that if it be difficult to make out *property*, upon a supposition that God gave the world to *Adam*, and his posterity in common, it is impossible that any man, but one universal monarch, should have any *property* upon a supposition, that God gave the world to *Adam*, and his heirs in succession, exclusive of all the rest of his posterity. But I shall endeavour to shew, how men might come to have a *property* in several parts of that which God gave to mankind in common, and that without any express compact of all the commoners.

§ 26. God, who hath given the world to men in common, hath also given them reason to make use of it to the best advantage of life, and convenience. The earth, and all that is therein, is given to men for the support and comfort of their being. And tho' all the fruits it naturally produces, and beasts it feeds, belong to mankind in common, as they are produced by the spontaneous hand of nature; and no body has originally a private dominion, exclusive of the rest of mankind, in any of them, as they are thus in their natural state: yet being given for the use of men, there must of necessity be *a means to appropriate* them some way or other, before they can be of any use, or at all beneficial to any particular man. The fruit, or venison, which nourishes the wild *Indian*, who knows no inclosure, and is still a tenant in common, must be his, and so his, *i.e.* a part of him, that another can no longer have any right to it, before it can do him any good for the support of his life.

§ 27. Though the earth, and all inferior creatures be common to all men, yet every man has a *property* in his own *person*: this no body has any right to but himself. The *labour* of his body, and the *work* of his hands, we may say, are properly his. Whatsoever then he removes out of the state that nature hath provided, and left it in, he hath mixed his *labour* with, and joined to it something that is his own, and thereby makes it his *property*. It being by him removed from the common state nature hath placed it in, it hath by this *labour* something annexed to it, that excludes the common right of other men: for this *labour* being the unquestionable property of the labourer, no man but he can have a right to what that is once joined to, at least where there is enough, and as good, left in common for others.

§ 28. He that is nourished by the acorns he picked up under an oak, or the apples he gathered from the trees in the wood, has certainly appropriated them to himself. No body can deny but the nourishment is his. I ask then, when did they begin to be his? when he digested? or when he eat? or when he boiled? or when he brought them home? or when he picked them up? and it is plain, if the first gathering made them not his, nothing else could. That *labour* put a distinction between them and common: that added something to them more than nature, the common mother of all, had done; and so they became his private right. And will any one say, he had no right to those acorns or apples he thus appropriated, because he had not the consent of all mankind to make them his? Was it a robbery thus to assume to himself what belonged to all in common? If such a consent as that was necessary, man had starved, notwithstanding the plenty God had given him. We see in *commons*, which remain so by compact, that it is the taking any part of what is common, and removing it out of the state nature leaves it in, which *begins the property*; without which the common is of no use. And the taking of this or that part, does not depend on the express consent of all the commoners. Thus the grass my horse has bit; the turfs my servant has cut; and the ore I have digged in any place, where I have a right to them in common with others, become my *property*, without the assignation or consent of any body. The *labour* that was mine, removing them out of that common state they were in, hath *fixed* my *property* in them.

§ 29. By making an explicit consent of every commoner, necessary to any one's appropriating to himself any part of what is given in common, children or servants could not cut the meat which their father or master had provided for them in common, without assigning to every one his peculiar part. Though the water running in the fountain be every one's, yet who can doubt, but that in the pitcher is his only who drew it out? His *labour* hath taken it out of the hands of nature, where it was common, and belonged equally to all her children, and *hath* thereby *appropriated* it to himself.

§ 30. Thus this law of reason makes the deer that *Indian's* who hath killed it; it is allowed to be his goods, who hath bestowed his labour upon it, though before it was the common right of every one. And amongst those who are counted the civilized part of mankind, who have made and multiplied positive laws to determine *property*, this original law of nature, for the *beginning of property*, in what was before common, still takes place. . . .

§ 31. It will perhaps be objected to this, that if gathering the acorns, or other fruits of the earth, *&c.* makes a right to them, then any one may *ingross* as much as he will. To which I answer, Not so. The same law of nature, that does by this means give us property, does also *bound* that *property* too. *God has given us all things richly*, 1 *Tim.* vi. 12. is the voice of reason confirmed by inspiration. But how far has he given it us? *To enjoy.* As much as any one can make use of to any advantage of life before it spoils, so much he may by his labour fix a property in: whatever is beyond this, is more than his share, and belongs to others. Nothing was made by God for man to spoil or destroy. And thus, considering the plenty of natural provisions there was a long time in the world, and the few spenders; and to how small a part of that provision the industry of one man could extend itself, and ingross it to the prejudice of others; especially keeping within the *bounds*, set by reason, of what might serve for his *use*; there could be then little room for quarrels or contentions about property so established.

§ 32. But the *chief matter of property* being now not the fruits of the earth, and the beasts that subsist on it, but *the earth itself*; as that which takes in and carries with it all the rest; I think it is plain, that *property* in that too is acquired as the former. *As much land* as a man tills, plants, improves, cultivates, and can use the product of, so much is his *property*. He by his labour does, as it were, inclose it from the common. Nor will it invalidate his right, to say every body else has an equal title to it; and therefore he cannot appropriate, he cannot inclose, without the consent of all his fellow-commoners, all mankind. God, when he gave the world in common to all mankind, commanded man also to labour, and the penury of his condition required it of him. God and his reason commanded him to subdue the earth, *i.e.* improve it for the benefit of life, and therein lay out something upon it that was his own, his labour. He that in obedience to this command of God, subdued, tilled and sowed any part of it, thereby annexed to it something that was his *property*, which another had no title to, nor could without injury take from him.

§ 33. Nor was this *appropriation* of any parcel of *land*, by improving it, any prejudice to any other man, since there was still enough, and as good left; and more than the yet unprovided could use. So that, in effect, there was never the less left for others because of his inclosure for himself: for he that leaves as much as another can make use of, does as good as take nothing at all. No body could think himself injured by the drinking of another man, though he took a good draught, who had a whole river of the same water left him to quench his thirst: and the case of land and water, where there is enough of both, is perfectly the same.

*   *   *

§ 36. . . . [T]hat the same *rule of property, (viz.)* that every man should have as much as he could make use of, would hold still in the world, without straitening any body; since there is land enough in the world to suffice double the inhabitants, had not the *invention of money*, and the tacit agreement of men to put a value on it, introduced (by consent) larger possessions, and a right to them; which, how it has done, I shall by and by shew more at large.

*   *   *

§ 47. And thus *came in the use of money*, some lasting thing that men might keep without spoiling, and that by mutual consent men would take in exchange for the truly useful, but perishable supports of life.

§ 48. And as different degrees of industry were apt to give men possessions in different proportions, so this *invention of money* gave them the opportunity to continue and enlarge them . . . : Where there is not some thing, both lasting and scarce, and so valuable to be hoarded up, there men will not be apt to enlarge their *possessions of land*, were it never so rich, never so free for them to take: for I ask, what would a man value ten thousand, or an hundred thousand acres of excellent *land*, ready cultivated, and well stocked too with cattle, in the middle of the inland parts of *America*, where he had no hopes of commerce with other parts of the world, to draw *money* to him by the sale of the product? It would not be worth the inclosing, and we should see him give up again to the wild common of nature, whatever was more than would supply the conveniencies of life to be had there for him and his family.

§ 49. Thus in the beginning all the world was *America*, and more so than that is now; for no such thing as *money* was any where known. Find out something that hath the *use and value of money* amongst his neighbours, you shall see the same man will begin presently to enlarge his possessions.

§ 50. But since gold and silver, being little useful to the life of man in proportion to food, raiment, and carriage, has its *value* only from the consent of men, whereof *labour* yet *makes*, in great part, *the measure*, it is plain, that men have agreed to disproportionate and unequal *possession of the earth*, they having, by a tacit and voluntary consent, found out a way how a man may fairly possess more land than he himself can use the product of, by receiving in exchange for the overplus gold and silver, which may be hoarded up without injury to any one; these metals not spoiling or decaying in the hands of the possessor. . . .

§ 51. And thus, I think, it is very easy to conceive, without any difficulty, *how labour could at first begin a title of property* in the common things of nature, and how the spending it upon our uses bounded it. So that there could then be no reason of quarrelling about title, nor any doubt about the largeness of possession it gave. Right and conveniency went together; for as a man had a right to all he could employ his labour upon, so he had no temptation to labour for more than he could make use of. This left no room for controversy about the title, nor for incroachment on the right of others; what portion a man carved to himself, was easily seen; and it was useless, as well as dishonest, to carve himself too much, or take more than he needed.

*   *   *

Chap. IX. Of the Ends of Political Society and Government

§ 123. If man in the state of nature be so free, as has been said; if he be absolute lord of his own person and possessions, equal to the greatest, and subject to no body, why will he part with his freedom? why will he give up this empire, and subject himself to the dominion and controul of any other power? To which it is obvious to answer, that though in the state of nature he hath such a right, yet the enjoyment of it is very uncertain, and constantly exposed to the invasion of others: for all being kings as much as he, every man his equal, and the greater part no strict observers of equity and justice, the enjoyment of the property he has in this state is very unsafe, very unsecure. This makes him willing to quit a condition, which, however free, is full of fears and continual dangers: and it is not without reason, that he seeks out, and is willing to join in society with others, who are already united, or have a mind to unite, for the mutual *preservation* of their lives, liberties and estates, which I call by the general name, *property*.

§ 124. The great and *chief end*, therefore, of men's uniting into common-wealths, and putting themselves under government, *is the preservation of their property*. To which in the state of nature there are many things wanting.

First, There wants an *establshed*, settled, known *law*, received and allowed by common consent to be the standard of right and wrong, and the common measure to decide all controversies between them: for though the law of nature be plain and intelligible to all rational creatures; yet men being biassed by their interest, as well as ignorant for want of study of it, are not apt to allow of it as a law binding to them in the application of it to their particular cases.

§ 125. *Secondly*, In the state of nature there wants *a known and indifferent judge*, with authority to determine all differences according to the established law: for every one in that state being both judge and executioner of the law of nature, men being partial to themselves, passion and revenge is very apt to carry them too far, and with too much heat, in their own cases; as well as negligence, and unconcernedness, to make them too remiss in other men's.

§ 126. *Thirdly*, In the state of nature there often wants *power* to back and support the sentence when right, and to *give* it due *execution*. They who by any injustice offended, will seldom fail, where they are able, by force to make good their injustice; such resistance many times makes the punishment dangerous, and frequently destructive, to those who attempt it.

NOTES AND QUESTIONS

1. Locke premises individual ownership on the claim that "every man has a *property* in his own *person*: this nobody has any right to but himself." LOCKE, *supra*, at § 27. This proposition is often viewed as self-evident, yet, is it contrary to St. Paul's admonition that no person owns himself or herself? 1 *Corinthians* 6:19? In scripture, it is made plain that man is God's creature, not an independent contractor. *e.g.*, *Psalm* 100:3, 139:13–16. Did Locke fail to reaffirm this religious point, thereby steering private property in America onto an overly individualistic or self-centered course? Was this less of a problem at the time of the founding since both the nature of earth and individual life as gift, rather than entitlement, was then manifest in the duties individuals were impliedly expected to fulfill toward their community? In fact, Locke himself rejected the idea that inherent in the human person is right divorced from obligation, although the framers were likely unaware of any such proclamation from Locke's pen. In a manuscript that remarkably remained unpublished until 1954, Locke writes:

> [S]ince it is necessary to conclude . . . that there exists some creator of all these things, . . . it follows from this that he has not made this world at random and to no end before it. . . . [And] [c]an man believe that all of these things have been given to him by a most wise creator, ready for use, so that he can do nothing . . . ? From this is perfectly clear that God wills him to do something. . . . It seems that the function of man is what he is naturally equipped to do[:] . . . to form and preserve a union of his life with other men, not only by the needs and necessities of life, but [he perceives also that] he is driven by a certain natural propensity to enter society and is fitted to preserve it by the gift of speech and the commerce of language.

JOHN LOCKE, QUESTIONS CONCERNING THE LAW OF NATURE 167, 169 (Robert Horwitz et al. trans., Cornell Univ. Press 1990) (1954).

2. Under Locke's natural law theory, prior to the invention of money, there is a natural limit on acquisition which helps to reinforce the virtue of moderation and to leave sufficient property ownership opportunities for others. The limit, of course, is how much property an individual person can "enjoy" without waste or spoilage. Money, however, allows men and women to enlarge their possessions beyond that which they can enjoy presently. Does Locke suggest any limit on the inequality of possessions resulting from the invention of money? Note Locke's argument that "putting a value on gold and silver, and tacitly agreeing in the use of money" arose without benefit of law "out of the bounds of society." LOCKE, SECOND TREATISE OF GOVERNMENT, *supra*, at § 50. Modernly, does this remain true given the role played by such institutions as the Federal Reserve, which controls the domestic money supply, and the International Monetary Fund, influencing the same internationally?

3. Finally, with regard to Locke, note that he squarely identifies the purpose of government as the preservation of property. LOCKE, *supra*, at § 124. While human reason would know the "right and wrong" in property dealings in the state of nature, controversies are better settled in society where the contesting claimants are not also the judge. Nevertheless, even when the function of protecting vested rights or property is given over to society, the impartial judge is to decide matters

in accordance with "the law of nature [that is] plain and intelligible to all rational creatures." *Id.* at §§ 124–25.

4.   The Constitution mentions the word property four times. Article IV, Section 2, grants Congress plenary authority to regulate and dispose of property belonging to the United States. Of greater interest to us in this Chapter, though, is how the Fifth and Fourteenth Amendments expressly protect privately held property from some government interference. In Part II of this Chapter, our focus will be upon the Due Process Clauses of the Fifth and Fourteenth Amendments, which prohibit both the federal government and the states from depriving any person of property without constitutionally adequate procedures.

Our immediate attention, however, is the Fifth Amendment Takings Clause, which precludes the taking of private property for public use without the payment of just compensation. This provision is relatively unproblematic when government physically assumes or desires possession of private property. Compensation in such case must be paid for the title taken or the physical occupancy. This is studied in courses on property, under the law of eminent domain, or condemnation. The most important issue in physical takings is an understanding of the qualifier, "public use." While some states by constitution, and many states by statute, require actual ownership by the public (say, a road or government building) or an actual right of use by the public (as in land condemned for a common carrier like a rail line), the Supreme Court has virtually read the public use limitation out of the Federal Constitution. *Hawaii Housing Authority v. Midkiff*, 467 U.S. 229 (1984) (sustaining a Hawaiian law that allowed tenants to use public condemnation to force owners of large estates to sell them the property the tenants occupied). In *Midkiff*, the Court described its review of what constitutes a public use as "extremely narrow." *Id.* at 240 (quoting *Berman v. Parker*, 348 U.S. 26, 32 (1954)). Further, the Court wrote that "[t]he mere fact that property taken outright by eminent domain is transferred in the first instance to private beneficiaries does not condemn that taking as having only a private purpose. The Court long ago rejected any literal requirement that condemned property be put into use for the general public." *Id.* at 243–44.

There are strong reasons to believe that *Midkiff* is a substantial departure from the natural law tradition as explicated by Locke and followed in early Supreme Court cases. In *Vanhorne's Lessee v. Dorrance*, 2 U.S. (2 Dall.) 304 (1795), for example, Justice Paterson wrote that that the Legislature had no "authority to make an act, divesting one citizen of his freehold and vesting it in another, even with compensation." And in *Calder v. Bull*, 3 U.S. (3 Dall.) 386 (1798), the Court noted that a "law that takes property from A and gives it to B" would be "against all reason and justice." Professor Richard Epstein makes this point elegantly and comprehensively in his book, Takings — Private Property and the Power of Eminent Domain 161 (1985). Professor Epstein carefully explains how the public use limitation was intended as a strict limitation upon the power of government, even when accompanied by compensation. In addition, writing in the law and economics tradition, he argues that the public use limitation ought to be informed by the economic concept of public good — that is, those goods which are nonexclusive and in which one person's consumption does not significantly reduce or preclude enjoyment by another. National defense needs are the stock example, but public highways and parks generally fit this description as well.

Recently, the lower courts have begun to put some teeth back in the "public use" limitation on the eminent domain power. In *99 Cents Only Stores v. Lancaster Redevelopment Agency*, 237 F. Supp. 2d 1123 (C.D. Cal. 2001), for example, the court held that condemnation could not be used to transfer a lease from one privately-owned store to another because such was for private gain and not a public use. In *County of Wayne County v. Hathcock*, 471 Mich. 415 (2004), the Michigan Supreme Court overturned the landmark case, *Poletown Neighborhood Council v. City of Detroit*, 410 Mich. 616 (1981), that allowed Detroit to condemn a low-income neighborhood known as Poletown and sell the land at a discount to General Motors Corporation in 1981. And in *Southwestern Illinois Development Authority v. National City Environmental, LLC*, 768 N.E.2d 1 (Ill. 2002), the Illinois Supreme Court rejected an Illinois redevelopment agency's condemnation of private property to make way for a parking lot for a privately-owned speedway as not a permissible public use. These lower court and state court developments prompted the Supreme Court to re-examine its thinking in *Berman* and *Midkiff* in the following case:

KELO v. CITY OF NEW LONDON, CONNECTICUT
545 U.S. 469 (2005)

JUSTICE STEVENS delivered the opinion of the Court.

In 2000, the city of New London approved a development plan that, in the words of the Supreme Court of Connecticut, was "projected to create in excess of 1,000 jobs, to increase tax and other revenues, and to revitalize an economically distressed city, including its downtown and waterfront areas." In assembling the land needed for this project, the city's development agent has purchased property from willing sellers and proposes to use the power of eminent domain to acquire the remainder of the property from unwilling owners in exchange for just compensation. The question presented is whether the city's proposed disposition of this property qualifies as a "public use" within the meaning of the Takings Clause of the Fifth Amendment to the Constitution.[4]

I

* * *

[Poor economic] conditions prompted state and local officials to target New London, and particularly its Fort Trumbull area, for economic revitalization. To this end, respondent New London Development Corporation (NLDC), a private non-profit entity established some years earlier to assist the City in planning economic development, was reactivated. In January 1998, the State authorized a $5.35 million bond issue to support the NLDC's planning activities and a $10 million bond issue toward the creation of a Fort Trumbull State Park. In February, the pharmaceutical company Pfizer Inc. announced that it would build a $300 million research facility on

---

[4] [1] "[N]or shall private property be taken for public use, without just compensation." U.S. Const., Amdt. 5. That Clause is made applicable to the States by the Fourteenth Amendment. [*Chicago, B. & Q.R. Co. v. Chicago* (1897)].

a site immediately adjacent to Fort Trumbull; local planners hoped that Pfizer would draw new business to the area, thereby serving as a catalyst to the area's rejuvenation.

*   *   *

The NLDC intended the development plan to capitalize on the arrival of the Pfizer facility and the new commerce it was expected to attract. In addition to creating jobs, generating tax revenue, and helping to "build momentum for the revitalization of downtown New London," the plan was also designed to make the City more attractive and to create leisure and recreational opportunities on the waterfront and in the park.

II

Petitioner Susette Kelo has lived in the Fort Trumbull area since 1997. She has made extensive improvements to her house, which she prizes for its water view. Petitioner Wilhelmina Dery was born in her Fort Trumbull house in 1918 and has lived there her entire life. Her husband Charles (also a petitioner) has lived in the house since they married some 60 years ago. In all, the nine petitioners own 15 properties in Fort Trumbull — 4 in parcel 3 of the development plan and 11 in parcel 4A. Ten of the parcels are occupied by the owner or a family member; the other five are held as investment properties. There is no allegation that any of these properties is blighted or otherwise in poor condition; rather, they were condemned only because they happen to be located in the development area.

The disposition of this case . . . turns on the question whether the City's development plan serves a "public purpose." Without exception, our cases have defined that concept broadly, reflecting our longstanding policy of deference to legislative judgments in this field.

In *Berman v. Parker* (1954), this Court upheld a redevelopment plan targeting a blighted area of Washington, D.C., in which most of the housing for the area's 5,000 inhabitants was beyond repair. Under the plan, the area would be condemned and part of it utilized for the construction of streets, schools, and other public facilities. The remainder of the land would be leased or sold to private parties for the purpose of redevelopment, including the construction of low-cost housing.

The owner of a department store located in the area challenged the condemnation, pointing out that his store was not itself blighted and arguing that the creation of a "better balanced, more attractive community" was not a valid public use. Writing for a unanimous Court, Justice Douglas refused to evaluate this claim in isolation, deferring instead to the legislative and agency judgment that the area "must be planned as a whole" for the plan to be successful.

*   *   *

In *Hawaii Housing Authority v. Midkiff* (1984), the Court considered a Hawaii statute whereby fee title was taken from lessors and transferred to lessees (for just compensation) in order to reduce the concentration of land ownership. We unanimously upheld the statute and rejected the Ninth Circuit's view that it was "a naked attempt on the part of the state of Hawaii to take the property of A and transfer it to B solely for B's private use and benefit." Reaffirming *Berman*'s deferential approach to legislative judgments in this field, we concluded that the State's purpose of eliminating the "social and economic evils of a land oligopoly" qualified as a valid public use. Our opinion also rejected the contention that the mere fact that the State immediately transferred the properties to private individuals upon condemnation somehow diminished the public character of the taking. "[I]t is only the taking's purpose, and not its mechanics," we explained, that matters in determining public use.

* * *

IV

* * *

[P]etitioners urge us to adopt a new bright-line rule that economic development does not qualify as a public use. Putting aside the unpersuasive suggestion that the City's plan will provide only purely economic benefits, neither precedent nor logic supports petitioners' proposal. Promoting economic development is a traditional and long accepted function of government. There is, moreover, no principled way of distinguishing economic development from the other public purposes that we have recognized. . . . In *Berman*, we endorsed the purpose of transforming a blighted area into a "well-balanced" community through redevelopment, and in *Midkiff*, we upheld the interest in breaking up a land oligopoly that "created artificial deterrents to the normal functioning of the State's residential land market." It would be incongruous to hold that the City's interest in the economic benefits to be derived from the development of the Fort Trumbull area has less of a public character than any of those other interests. Clearly, there is no basis for exempting economic development from our traditionally broad understanding of public purpose.

Petitioners contend that using eminent domain for economic development impermissibly blurs the boundary between public and private takings. Again, our cases foreclose this objection. Quite simply, the government's pursuit of a public purpose will often benefit individual private parties. For example, in *Midkiff*, the forced transfer of property conferred a direct and significant benefit on those lessees who were previously unable to purchase their homes. . . . The owner of the department store in *Berman* objected to "taking from one businessman for the benefit of another businessman," referring to the fact that under the redevelopment plan land would be leased or sold to private developers for redevelopment. . . .

It is further argued that without a bright-line rule nothing would stop a city from transferring citizen A's property to citizen B for the sole reason that citizen B will put the property to a more productive use and thus pay more taxes. Such a one-to-one transfer of property, executed outside the confines of an integrated development plan, is not presented in this case. While such an unusual exercise of government power would certainly raise a suspicion that a private purpose was afoot, the hypothetical cases posited by petitioners can be confronted if and when they arise. They do not warrant the crafting of an artificial restriction on the concept of public use.

Alternatively, petitioners maintain that for takings of this kind we should require a "reasonable certainty" that the expected public benefits will actually accrue. Such a rule, however, would represent an even greater departure from our precedent. "When the legislature's purpose is legitimate and its means are not irrational, our cases make clear that empirical debates over the wisdom of takings — no less than debates over the wisdom of other kinds of socioeconomic legislation(are not to be carried out in the federal courts." . . . The disadvantages of a heightened form of review are especially pronounced in this type of case. Orderly implementation of a comprehensive redevelopment plan obviously requires that the legal rights of all interested parties be established before new construction can be commenced. A constitutional rule that required postponement of the judicial approval of every condemnation until the likelihood of success of the plan had been assured would unquestionably impose a significant impediment to the successful consummation of many such plans.

*   *   *

In affirming the City's authority to take petitioners' properties, we do not minimize the hardship that condemnations may entail, notwithstanding the payment of just compensation.[5] We emphasize that nothing in our opinion precludes any State from placing further restrictions on its exercise of the takings power. Indeed, many States already impose "public use" requirements that are stricter than the federal baseline. Some of these requirements have been established as a matter of state constitutional law, while others are expressed in state eminent domain statutes that carefully limit the grounds upon which takings may be exercised. . . .[6]

The judgment of the Supreme Court of Connecticut is affirmed.

It is so ordered.

JUSTICE KENNEDY, concurring.

I join the opinion for the Court and add these further observations.

*   *   *

A court applying rational-basis review under the Public Use Clause should strike down a taking that, by a clear showing, is intended to favor a particular private party, with only incidental or pretextual public benefits, just as a court applying rational-basis review under the Equal Protection Clause must strike down a government classification that is clearly intended to injure a particular class of

---

[5] [21] The *amici* raise questions about the fairness of the measure of just compensation. While important, these questions are not before us in this litigation.

[6] [23] Under California law, for instance, a city may only take land for economic development purposes in blighted areas. Cal. Health & Safety Code Ann. §§ 33030–33037 (1997). *e.g.*, *Redevelopment Agency of Chula Vista v. Rados Bros.*, 95 Cal. App. 4th 309, 115 Cal. Rptr. 2d 234 (2002).

private parties, with only incidental or pretextual public justifications. *Cleburne v. Cleburne Living Center, Inc.*. . . .

A court confronted with a plausible accusation of impermissible favoritism to private parties should treat the objection as a serious one and review the record to see if it has merit, though with the presumption that the government's actions were reasonable and intended to serve a public purpose. Here, the trial court conducted a careful and extensive inquiry into "whether, in fact, the development plan is of primary benefit to . . . the developer [*i.e.*, Corcoran Jennison], and private businesses which may eventually locate in the plan area [*e.g.*, Pfizer], and in that regard, only of incidental benefit to the city." . . .

* * *

My agreement with the Court that a presumption of invalidity is not warranted for economic development takings in general, or for the particular takings at issue in this case, does not foreclose the possibility that a more stringent standard of review than that announced in *Berman* and *Midkiff* might be appropriate for a more narrowly drawn category of takings. There may be private transfers in which the risk of undetected impermissible favoritism of private parties is so acute that a presumption (rebuttable or otherwise) of invalidity is warranted under the Public Use Clause. *Eastern Enterprises v. Apfel* (1998) (KENNEDY, J., concurring in judgment and dissenting in part) (heightened scrutiny for retroactive legislation under the Due Process Clause). This demanding level of scrutiny, however, is not required simply because the purpose of the taking is economic development.

* * *

For the foregoing reasons, I join in the Court's opinion.

JUSTICE O'CONNOR, with whom THE CHIEF JUSTICE, JUSTICE SCALIA, and JUSTICE THOMAS join, dissenting.

Over two centuries ago, just after the Bill of Rights was ratified, Justice Chase wrote:

> "An ACT of the Legislature (for I cannot call it a law) contrary to the great first principles of the social compact, cannot be considered a rightful exercise of legislative authority. . . . A few instances will suffice to explain what I mean. . . . [A] law that takes property from A. and gives it to B: It is against all reason and justice, for a people to entrust a Legislature with SUCH powers; and, therefore, it cannot be presumed that they have done it." *Calder v. Bull*, (1798) (emphasis deleted).

Today the Court abandons this long-held, basic limitation on government power. Under the banner of economic development, all private property is now vulnerable to being taken and transferred to another private owner, so long as it might be upgraded — *i.e.*, given to an owner who will use it in a way that the legislature deems more beneficial to the public — in the process. To reason, as the Court does, that the incidental public benefits resulting from the subsequent ordinary use of private property render economic development takings "for public use" is to wash out any distinction between private and public use of property — and thereby effectively to delete the words "for public use" from the Takings Clause of the Fifth Amendment. Accordingly I respectfully dissent.

I

To save their homes, petitioners sued New London and the NLDC. . . . Theirs is an objection in principle: They claim that the NLDC's proposed use for their confiscated property is not a "public" one for purposes of the Fifth Amendment. While the government may take their homes to build a road or a railroad or to eliminate a property use that harms the public, say petitioners, it cannot take their property for the private use of other owners simply because the new owners may make more productive use of the property.

II

*   *   *

While the Takings Clause presupposes that government can take private property without the owner's consent, the just compensation requirement spreads the cost of condemnations and thus "prevents the public from loading upon one individual more than his just share of the burdens of government." The public use requirement, in turn, imposes a more basic limitation, circumscribing the very scope of the eminent domain power: Government may compel an individual to forfeit her property for the *public's* use, but not for the benefit of another private person. This requirement promotes fairness as well as security.

Where is the line between "public" and "private" property use? We give considerable deference to legislatures' determinations about what governmental activities will advantage the public. But were the political branches the sole arbiters of the public-private distinction, the Public Use Clause would amount to little more than hortatory fluff. . . .

Our cases have generally identified three categories of takings that comply with the public use requirement, though it is in the nature of things that the boundaries between these categories are not always firm. Two are relatively straightforward and uncontroversial. First, the sovereign may transfer private property to public ownership — such as for a road, a hospital, or a military base. Second, the sovereign may transfer private property to private parties, often common carriers, who make the property available for the public's use — such as with a railroad, a public utility, or a stadium. But "public ownership" and "use-by-the-public" are sometimes too constricting and impractical ways to define the scope of the Public Use Clause. Thus we have allowed that, in certain circumstances and to meet certain exigencies, takings that serve a public purpose also satisfy the Constitution even if the property is destined for subsequent private use. *e.g.*, *Berman v. Parker* (1954); *Hawaii Housing Authority v. Midkiff* (1984).

This case returns us for the first time in over 20 years to the hard question of when a purportedly "public purpose" taking meets the public use requirement. It presents an issue of first impression: Are economic development takings constitutional? I would hold that they are not.

*   *   *

The Court's holdings in *Berman* and *Midkiff* were true to the principle underlying the Public Use Clause. In both those cases, the extraordinary, precondemnation use of the targeted property inflicted affirmative harm on society — in *Berman* through blight resulting from extreme poverty and in *Midkiff* through oligopoly resulting from extreme wealth. And in both cases, the relevant legislative body had found that eliminating the existing property use was necessary to remedy the harm. Thus a public purpose was realized when the harmful use was eliminated. Because each taking *directly* achieved a public benefit, it did not matter that the property was turned over to private use. Here, in contrast, New London does not claim that Susette Kelo's and Wilhelmina Dery's well-maintained homes are the source of any social harm. Indeed, it could not so claim without adopting the absurd argument that any single-family home that might be razed to make way for an apartment building, or any church that might be replaced with a retail store, or any small business that might be more lucrative if it were instead part of a national franchise, is inherently harmful to society and thus within the government's power to condemn.

In moving away from our decisions sanctioning the condemnation of harmful property use, the Court today significantly expands the meaning of public use. It holds that the sovereign may take private property currently put to ordinary private use, and give it over for new, ordinary private use, so long as the new use is predicted to generate some secondary benefit for the public — such as increased tax revenue, more jobs, maybe even aesthetic pleasure. But nearly any lawful use of real private property can be said to generate some incidental benefit to the public. Thus, if predicted (or even guaranteed) positive side-effects are enough to render transfer from one private party to another constitutional, then the words "for public use" do not realistically exclude *any* takings, and thus do not exert any constraint on the eminent domain power.

. . . There is a sense in which this troubling result follows from errant language in *Berman* and *Midkiff*. In discussing whether takings within a blighted neighborhood were for a public use, *Berman* began by observing: "We deal, in other words, with what traditionally has been known as the police power." From there it declared that "[o]nce the object is within the authority of Congress, the right to realize it through the exercise of eminent domain is clear." Following up, we said in *Midkiff* that "[t]he 'public use' requirement is coterminous with the scope of a sovereign's police powers." This language was unnecessary to the specific holdings of those decisions. *Berman* and *Midkiff* simply did not put such language to the constitutional test, because the takings in those cases were within the police power but also for "public use" for the reasons I have described. The case before us now demonstrates why, when deciding if a taking's purpose is constitutional, the police power and "public use" cannot always be equated. The Court protests that it does not sanction the bare transfer from A to B for B's benefit. It suggests two limitations on what can be taken after today's decision. First, it maintains a role for courts in ferreting out takings whose sole purpose is to bestow a benefit on the private transferee — without detailing how courts are to conduct that complicated inquiry. For his part, JUSTICE KENNEDY suggests that courts may divine illicit purpose by a careful review of the record and the process by which a legislature arrived at the decision to take — without specifying what courts should look for in a case with different facts, how they will know if they have found it, and what to do if they do not. Whatever the details of JUSTICE KENNEDY's as-yet-undisclosed test, it is difficult to envision anyone but the "stupid staff[er]" failing it. The trouble with economic development takings is that private benefit and incidental public benefit are, by definition, merged and mutually reinforcing. In this case, for example, any boon for Pfizer or the plan's developer is difficult to disaggregate from the promised public gains in taxes and jobs.

Even if there were a practical way to isolate the motives behind a given taking, the gesture toward a purpose test is theoretically flawed. If it is true that incidental public benefits from new private use are enough to ensure the "public purpose" in a taking, why should it matter, as far as the Fifth Amendment is concerned, what inspired the taking in the first place? How much the government does or does not desire to benefit a favored private party has no bearing on whether an economic development taking will or will not generate secondary benefit for the public. And whatever the reason for a given condemnation, the effect is the same from the constitutional perspective — private property is forcibly relinquished to new private ownership.

A second proposed limitation is implicit in the Court's opinion. The logic of today's decision is that eminent domain may only be used to upgrade — not downgrade — property. At best this makes the Public Use Clause redundant with the Due Process Clause, which already prohibits irrational government action. *Lingle* [*v. Chevron* (2005)]. The Court rightfully admits, however, that the judiciary cannot get bogged down in predictive judgments about whether the public will actually be better off after a property transfer. In any event, this constraint has no realistic import. For who among us can say she already makes the most productive or attractive possible use of her property? The specter of condemnation hangs over all property. Nothing is to prevent the State from replacing any Motel 6 with a Ritz-Carlton, any home with a shopping mall, or any farm with a factory.

. . . If legislative prognostications about the secondary public benefits of a new use can legitimate a taking, there is nothing in the Court's rule or in JUSTICE KENNEDY's gloss on that rule to prohibit property transfers generated with less care, that are less comprehensive, that happen to result from less elaborate process, whose only projected advantage is the incidence of higher taxes, or that hope to transform an already prosperous city into an even more prosperous one.

Finally, in a coda, the Court suggests that property owners should turn to the States, who may or may not choose to impose appropriate limits on economic development takings. This is an abdication of our responsibility. States play many important functions in our system of dual sovereignty, but compensating for our refusal to enforce properly the Federal Constitution (and a provision meant to curtail state action, no less) is not among them.

*   *   *

JUSTICE THOMAS, dissenting.

The most natural reading of the Clause is that it allows the government to take property only if the government owns, or the public has a legal right to use, the property, as opposed to taking it for any public purpose or necessity whatsoever. At the time of the founding, dictionaries primarily defined the noun "use" as "[t]he act of employing any thing to any purpose." When the government takes property and gives it to a private individual, and the public has no right to use the property, it strains language to say that the public is "employing" the property, regardless of the incidental benefits that might accrue to the public from the private use. The term "public use," then, means that either the government or its citizens as a whole must actually "employ" the taken property.

* * *

. . . Blackstone rejected the idea that private property could be taken solely for purposes of any public benefit. "So great . . . is the regard of the law for private property," he explained, "that it will not authorize the least violation of it; no, not even for the general good of the whole community." He continued: "If a new road . . . were to be made through the grounds of a private person, it might perhaps be extensively beneficial to the public; but the law permits no man, or set of men, to do this without the consent of the owner of the land." Only "by giving [the landowner] full indemnification" could the government take property, and even then "[t]he public [was] now considered as an individual, treating with an individual for an exchange." When the public took property, in other words, it took it as an individual buying property from another typically would: for one's own use. The Public Use Clause, in short, embodied the Framers' understanding that property is a natural, fundamental right, prohibiting the government from "tak[ing] *property* from A. and giv[ing] it to B."

* * *

III

Our current Public Use Clause jurisprudence, as the Court notes, has rejected this natural reading of the Clause. The Court adopted its modern reading blindly, with little discussion of the Clause's history and original meaning, in two distinct lines of cases: first, in cases adopting the "public purpose" interpretation of the Clause, and second, in cases deferring to legislatures' judgments regarding what constitutes a valid public purpose. Those questionable cases converged in the boundlessly broad and deferential conception of "public use" adopted by this Court in *Berman v. Parker* (1954), and *Hawaii Housing Authority v. Midkiff* (1984), cases that take center stage in the Court's opinion. The weakness of those two lines of cases, and consequently *Berman* and *Midkiff*, fatally undermines the doctrinal foundations of the Court's decision. Today's questionable application of these cases is further proof that the "public purpose" standard is not susceptible of principled application. This Court's reliance by rote on this standard is ill advised and should be reconsidered.

[I]t is backwards to adopt a searching standard of constitutional review for nontraditional property interests, such as welfare benefits, *e.g.*, *Goldberg, supra,* while deferring to the legislature's determination as to what constitutes a public use when it exercises the power of eminent domain, and thereby invades individuals' traditional rights in real property. The Court has elsewhere recognized "the overriding respect for the sanctity of the home that has been embedded in our traditions since the origins of the Republic," when the issue is only whether the government may search a home. Yet today the Court tells us that we are not to "second-guess the City's considered judgments," when the issue is, instead, whether the government may take the infinitely more intrusive step of tearing down petitioners' homes. Something has gone seriously awry with this Court's interpretation of the Constitution. Though citizens are safe from the government in their homes, the homes themselves are not. Once one accepts, as the Court at least nominally does, that the Public Use Clause is a limit on the eminent domain power of the Federal Government and the States, there is no justification for the almost complete deference it grants to legislatures as to what satisfies it.

C

Berman and *Midkiff* erred by equating the eminent domain power with the police power of States. Traditional uses of that regulatory power, such as the power to abate a nuisance, required no compensation whatsoever, *Mugler v. Kansas* (1887), in sharp contrast to the takings power, which has always required compensation. The question whether the State can take property using the power of eminent domain is therefore distinct from the question whether it can regulate property pursuant to the police power. To construe the Public Use Clause to overlap with the States' police power conflates these two categories.

The "public purpose" test applied by *Berman* and *Midkiff* also cannot be applied in principled manner. "When we depart from the natural import of the term 'public use,' and substitute for the simple idea of a public possession and occupation, that of public utility, public interest, common benefit, general advantage or convenience . . . we are afloat without any certain principle to guide us." . . . The Court is wrong to criticize the "actual use" test as "difficult to administer." It is far easier to analyze whether the government owns or the public has a legal right to use the taken property than to ask whether the taking has a "purely private purpose" — unless the Court means to eliminate public use scrutiny of takings entirely. Obliterating a provision of the Constitution, of course, guarantees that it will not be misapplied.

For all these reasons, I would revisit our Public Use Clause cases and consider returning to the original meaning of the Public Use Clause: that the government may take property only if it actually uses or gives the public a legal right to use the property.

NOTES AND QUESTIONS

1. So what judicial limits, if any, does the majority place on the power of eminent domain? Very few. Justice Stevens conceded that the City would no doubt be forbidden from taking petitioners' land for the purpose of conferring a private benefit on a particular private party. *Midkiff* ("A purely private taking could not withstand the scrutiny of the public use requirement; it would serve no legitimate purpose of government and would thus be void"). In addition, the City would not be allowed to take property under the mere pretext of a public purpose, when its actual purpose was to bestow a private benefit. The Court was not inclined to see such private benefit if the taking was the result of a "carefully considered development plan. . . ." With plan in hand, Justice Stevens concluded that, notwithstanding the text of the Fifth Amendment, all that was necessary was a sufficient "public purpose," giving broad deference to legislative judgments in this field. Other limits, if any, would have to be supplied by the legislature.

2.   The opinion triggered a national uproar and the introduction of legislation in Congress. The Protection of Homes, Small Businesses, and Private Property Act of 2005 would declare Congress' view that the power of eminent domain should be exercised only "for public use," as guaranteed by the Fifth Amendment, and that this power to seize homes, small businesses, and other private property should be reserved only for true public uses. Specifically, the power of eminent domain should not be used simply to further private economic development. The Act would apply this standard to two areas of government action which are clearly within Congress' authority to regulate: (1) all exercises of eminent domain power by the federal government, and (2) all exercises of eminent domain power by state and local government through the use of federal funds.

3.   In dissent, Justice O'Connor finds three tenable bases for a finding of public use: where government retains ownership (*e.g.*, parks, roads); where ownership is transferred to a private entity, but public use is ensured (*e.g.*, common carriers, like railways and utilities); and a very narrow and exceptional third category, where an idiosyncratic exigency must be met. Obviously, the third category can be the most problematic, but it is here, where Justice O'Connor locates government's ability to remove blighted tenements as in *Berman* or to address highly unusual land concentrations or oligopolies, as in *Midkiff*. Unlike the majority, the dissent understands that *no precedent* ever categorically approved of economic development takings as an unexamined or unexceptional public use. To accept this deferential posture is not only unconstitutional, writes Justice O'Connor, but absurd (her word). Indulging this overly permissive conception of public use would mean "that any single-family home . . . might be razed to make way for an apartment building, or any church might be replaced with a retail store." The alarm in Justice O'Connor's normally quite moderate judicial voice may explain some of the public anxiety in response to the opinion.

4.   Justice Thomas in dissent shares the alarm of Justice O'Connor, but thinks the roots of eminent domain abuse is anchored in a failure to follow the original understanding. In particular, Justice Thomas assails the notion that deference is appropriate by reminding the Court that the public use limitation is in the Bill of Rights. It would be unthinkable, argues Thomas, that the Court would defer on the question of whether a search is reasonable; why is deference to legislative judgment appropriate here? In a clever bit of writing, Thomas posits that "[t]he Court has elsewhere recognized 'the overriding respect for the sanctity of the home that has been embedded in our traditions since the origins of the Republic,' when the issue is only whether the government may search a home. Yet today the Court tells us that we are not to 'second-guess the City's considered judgments,' when the issue is,

instead, whether the government may take the infinitely more intrusive step of tearing down petitioners' homes. Something has gone seriously awry with this Court's interpretation of the Constitution. Though citizens are safe from the government in their homes, the homes themselves are not." Ineluctably, Thomas is led by his search for original meaning to revisit, and not just distinguish as extraordinary, *Berman v. Parker* (1954) and *Hawaii Housing Authority v. Midkiff* (1984). Yes, it is true that blight and oligopoly are far more "harmful" than New London's desire to have upscale development in place of modest homes, but Thomas doubts that this distinction will permit long-term adherence to the public use limitation. "When we depart from the natural import of the term 'public use,' and substitute for the simple idea of a public possession and occupation, that of public utility, public interest, common benefit, general advantage or convenience . . . we are afloat without any certain principle to guide us."

2. Regulatory Takings and the Supreme Court

The application of the Takings Clause becomes even more difficult when it is sought to be applied to government regulation. As a structural matter, you will recall that the Takings Clause initially applied only to the federal government. *Barron v. Mayor of Baltimore*, 32 U.S. (7 Pet.) 243 (1833). Subsequently, either the Takings Clause directly or its substantive meaning was incorporated into the Fourteenth Amendment Due Process Clause and applied to the states. *Chicago, Burlington & Quincy R.R. Co. v. City of Chicago*, 166 U.S. 226 (1897). As Chief Justice Rehnquist writes in *Dolan v. City of Tigard*, 512 U.S. 374, 384 n.5 (1994), considered below, "there is no doubt that later cases have held that the Fourteenth Amendment does make the Takings Clause . . . applicable to the States." For related commentary on these developments, see Jan. G. Laitos, *The Public Use Paradox and the Takings Clause*, 13 J. ENERGY NAT. RESOURCES & ENVTL. L. 9 (1993) (analyzing the police power takings test and concluding that to require "just compensation" only when a taking is *not* for public use is to ignore the language of the Fifth Amendment and that doing so removes an effective check on the police power).

As a matter of definition, the Constitution is silent about what constitutes property. Sir William Blackstone in the 18th Century, however, described property as being both an absolute, pre-societal natural right and a relative right dependent upon positive law. 1 WILLIAM BLACKSTONE, COMMENTARIES *138 ("The third absolute right, inherent in every Englishman, is that of property[; but its] free use, enjoyment, and disposal [is subject to] the laws of the land."). Douglas W. Kmiec, *The Coherence of the Natural Law of Property*, 26 VAL. U. L. REV. 367 (1991). That property has elements of both characteristics goes a good distance toward explaining the constitutional difficulty. A member of the constitutional convention, James Wilson, sought to reconcile the seeming contradiction, writing: "[o]ur law recognizes no such thing as absolute power or absolute rights, but does recognize the distinction between the abstract right to acquire property as one of the civil rights of persons and the right of property as applied to things." 2 THE WORKS OF JAMES WILSON 309 n.1 (James DeWitt Andrews ed., 1896). Knowing where the natural right to acquire and own ends, and where the relative right of specific ownership activities begins is the modern story of the conflict between private property and its limitation by governmental police or regulatory power.

Courses in property regularly introduce the concept of regulatory taking and we refresh your memory with a few of those cases and then some modern developments. *Pennsylvania Coal Company v. Mahon*, 260 U.S. 393 (1922) is an opinion by Justice Oliver Wendell Holmes dealing with the regulation of subsidence from the extraction of coal. The statute involved sought to protect a property owner even though the coal company had reserved a distinct mining right under the owner's property. Suggesting that "taking" calculus is governed by diminution in value, all mischaracterized what had been taken as a complete, distinct property right and pronounced that while regulation could go to a point, it could not go "too far." Of course, the remaining puzzler is how far is too far? Justice Brandeis in dissent thought the value-based inquiry mistaken, reasoning that local government has no obligation to compensate for the termination of a nuisance. He had a point and it illustrates effectively the equivalent of the reservation of the police power in the context of Contract Clause analysis. Justice Holmes wrote: "The general rule at least is, that while property may be regulated to a certain extent, if regulation goes too far it will be recognized as a taking. . . . We are in danger of forgetting that a strong public desire to improve the public condition is not enough to warrant achieving the desire by a shorter cut than the constitutional way of paying for the change. . . ."

Pennsylvania Coal is sometimes characterized as the first time the Takings or Just Compensation Clause was extended as a limit upon police power regulation. *See* William M. Treanor, *The Original Understanding of the Takings Clause and the Political Process*, 95 COLUM. L. REV. 782 (1995). In fact, Justice Holmes' reasoning reflects the high importance assigned to the protection of property by the framers. *See* Douglas W. Kmiec, *The Coherence of the Natural Law of Property*, 26 VAL. U. L. REV. 367 (1991). As a common law right that is part natural law (all entering society have a right by human nature to acquire, possess, and use property) and part positive law (the those particular features of ownership and use are elaborated and specified by state common and statutory law), the right of property has never been assumed to include the right to harm others with that property. The question is how to define what constitutes a "harm." Both Holmes for the majority and Brandeis for the dissent largely premise that definition upon the common law concept of nuisance. Defined at the state level incrementally through the adjudication of particular cases, nuisance seemingly allows each local community to keep the rights of property and the limitations on those rights in reasonable balance. Moreover, from the standpoint of federalism, that balance can be differently defined in different locations, and of course, differently over time as the perception of harm changes. Holmes and Brandeis fundamentally disagree over whether preventing subsidence should be viewed as a nuisance. Unfortunately, neither makes particular reference to Pennsylvania nuisance law to decide the issue, relying instead upon prior federal treatments of the issue. That was likely a misstep in light of both the interests in federalism and the protection of property, though in context probably a small one given the similarity between Holmes' conclusions and the common law at the time.

In *Penn Central Transp. Co. v. City of New York*, 438 U.S. 104 (1978), the landowner — following refusal of New York City's Landmarks Preservation

Commission to approve plans for construction of a 50-story office building over Grand Central Terminal, which had been designated a "landmark" — filed suit charging that the application of the Landmarks Preservation Law constituted a "taking" of the property without just compensation and arbitrarily deprived owners of their property without due process. Justice Brennan, writing for a 5-4 Court, held against the terminal owner, and established the modern taking test to be premised upon the balancing of several factors. Brennan wrote:

> The question of what constitutes a "taking" for purposes of the Fifth Amendment has proved to be a problem of considerable difficulty. While this Court has recognized that the "Fifth Amendment's guarantee . . . [is] designed to bar Government from forcing some people alone to bear public burdens which, in all fairness and justice, should be borne by the public as a whole," this Court, quite simply, has been unable to develop any "set formula" for determining when "justice and fairness" require that economic injuries caused by public action be compensated by the government, rather than remain disproportionately concentrated on a few persons. Indeed, we have frequently observed that whether a particular restriction will be rendered invalid by the government's failure to pay for any losses proximately caused by it depends largely "upon the particular circumstances [in that] case."

> In engaging in these essentially ad hoc, factual inquiries, the Court's decisions have identified several factors that have particular significance. The economic impact of the regulation on the claimant and, particularly, the extent to which the regulation has interfered with distinct investment-backed expectations are, of course, relevant considerations. So, too, is the character of the governmental action. A "taking" may more readily be found when the interference with property can be characterized as a physical invasion by government, than when interference arises from some public program adjusting the benefits and burdens of economic life to promote the common good. . . .

Noting the claim by the terminal owner that the discrete "air rights" property interest had been completely taken or deprived of value, Justice Brennan continued,

> "Taking" jurisprudence does not divide a single parcel into discrete segments and attempt to determine whether rights in a particular segment have been entirely abrogated. In deciding whether a particular governmental action has effected a taking, this Court focuses rather both on the character of the action and on the nature and extent of the interference with rights in the parcel as a whole — here, the city tax block designated as the "landmark site."

> . . . Appellants concede that the decisions sustaining other land-use regulations, which, like the New York City law, are reasonably related to the promotion of the general welfare, uniformly reject the proposition that diminution in property value, standing alone, can establish a "taking," see *Euclid v. Ambler Realty Co.* (1926) (75% diminution in value caused by zoning law); *Hadacheck v. Sebastian* (1915) (87% diminution in value). . . .

Next, appellants observe that New York City's law differs from zoning laws and historic-district ordinances in that the Landmarks Law does not impose identical or similar restrictions on all structures located in particular physical communities. It follows, they argue, that New York City's law is inherently incapable of producing the fair and equitable distribution of benefits and burdens of governmental action which is characteristic of zoning laws and historic-district legislation and which they maintain is a constitutional requirement if "just compensation" is not to be afforded. It is, of course, true that the Landmarks Law has a more severe impact on some landowners than on others, but that in itself does not mean that the law effects a "taking." Legislation designed to promote the general welfare commonly burdens some more than others. The owners of the brickyard in *Hadacheck*, of the cedar trees in *Miller v. Schoene* [(1928)], and of the gravel and sand mine in *Goldblatt v. Hempstead* [(1962)], were uniquely burdened by the legislation sustained in those cases.[7]

Unlike the governmental acts in [other cases], the New York City law does not interfere in any way with the present uses of the Terminal. Its designation as a landmark not only permits but contemplates that appellants may continue to use the property precisely as it has been used for the past 65 years: as a railroad terminal containing office space and concessions. So the law does not interfere with what must be regarded as Penn Central's primary expectation concerning the use of the parcel. More importantly, on this record, we must regard the New York City law as permitting Penn Central not only to profit from the Terminal but also to obtain a "reasonable return" on its investment.

Second, to the extent appellants have been denied the right to build above the Terminal, it is not literally accurate to say that they have been denied all use of even those pre-existing air rights. Their ability to use these rights has not been abrogated; they are made transferable to at least eight parcels in the vicinity of the Terminal, one or two of which have been found suitable for the construction of new office buildings. Although appellants and others have argued that New York City's transferable development-

---

[7] [30] Appellants attempt to distinguish these cases on the ground that, in each, government was prohibiting a "noxious" use of land, and that, in the present case, in contrast, appellants' proposed construction above the Terminal would be beneficial. We observe that the uses in issue in Hadacheck, Miller, and Goldblatt were perfectly lawful in themselves. They involved no

"blameworthiness, . . . moral wrongdoing or conscious act of dangerous risk-taking which induce[d society] to shift the cost to a pa[rt]icular individual."

Sax, *Takings and the Police Power*, 74 YALE L.J. 36, 50 (1964). These cases are better understood as resting not on any supposed "noxious" quality of the prohibited uses, but rather on the ground that the restrictions were reasonably related to the implementation of a policy — not unlike historic preservation — expected to produce a widespread public benefit and applicable to all similarly situated property.

Nor, correlatively, can it be asserted that the destruction or fundamental alteration of a historic landmark is not harmful. The suggestion that the beneficial quality of appellants' proposed construction is established by the fact that the construction would have been consistent with applicable zoning laws ignores the development in sensibilities and ideals reflected in landmark legislation like New York City's. *Cf. West Bros. Brick Co. v. Alexandria*, 169 Va. 271, 282–283, 192 S.E. 881, 885–886, *appeal dismissed for want of a substantial federal question*, 302 U.S. 658 (1937).

rights program is far from ideal, the New York courts here supportably found that, at least in the case of the Terminal, the rights afforded are valuable. While these rights may well not have constituted "just compensation" if a "taking" had occurred, the rights nevertheless undoubtedly mitigate whatever financial burdens the law has imposed on appellants and, for that reason, are to be taken into account in considering the impact of regulation.

Justice Rehnquist wrote in dissent for himself and Chief Justice Burger and Justice Stevens arguing that "the cost associated with the city of New York's desire to preserve a limited number of 'landmarks' within its borders must be borne by all of its taxpayers" and not "imposed entirely on the owners of the individual properties." This was because the landmark law was "not a prevention of a misuse or illegal use but the prevention of a legal and essential use, an attribute of its ownership."

> [The owners] are not prohibiting a nuisance. The record is clear that the proposed addition to the Grand Central Terminal would be in full compliance with zoning, height limitations, and other health and safety requirements. Instead, appellees are seeking to preserve what they believe to be an outstanding example of beaux arts architecture. Penn Central is prevented from further developing its property basically because *too good* a job was done in designing and building it. The city of New York, because of its unadorned admiration for the design, has decided that the owners of the building must preserve it unchanged for the benefit of sightseeing New Yorkers and tourists.

> Unlike land-use regulations, appellees' actions do not merely *prohibit* Penn Central from using its property in a narrow set of noxious ways. Instead, appellees have placed an *affirmative* duty on Penn Central to maintain the Terminal in its present state and in "good repair." . . .

> Even where the government prohibits a noninjurious use, the Court has ruled that a taking does not take place if the prohibition applies over a broad cross section of land and thereby "secure[s] an average reciprocity of advantage." *Pennsylvania Coal Co. v. Mahon.* It is for this reason that zoning does not constitute a "taking." While zoning at times reduces *individual* property values, the burden is shared relatively evenly and it is reasonable to conclude that on the whole an individual who is harmed by one aspect of the zoning will be benefited by another.

> Here, however, a multimillion dollar loss has been imposed on [one owner]; it is uniquely felt and is not offset by any benefits flowing from the preservation of some 400 other "landmarks" in New York City . . . The Fifth Amendment:

>> "prevents the public from loading upon one individual more than his just share of the burdens of government, and says that when he surrenders to the public something more and different from that which is exacted from other members of the public, a full and just equivalent shall be returned to him."

The Zeitgeist was at work in Justice Brennan's majority opinion in *Penn Central*. Without comment, Brennan adopts Justice Brandeis' dissenting opinion in *Pennsylvania Coal* with respect to the calculation of loss. Unlike the holding in *Pennsylvania Coal*, losses associated with regulatory takings are to be calculated in reference to the whole property, not merely the regulated portion. As Justice Rehnquist reflected in footnote 13 of his dissent, this disregard of prior precedent poses "difficult conceptual and legal problems" regarding the definition of the property interest for purposes of regulatory taking assessment which the majority chooses to ignore or state inconsistently. As we will see, the Court will return to this difficulty in *Lucas v. South Carolina Coastal Council* considered later in this Chapter.

The entire difficulty of calculating loss is, as mentioned in earlier notes, traceable to the unfortunate reliance by Justice Holmes upon this factor as a measure of a regulatory taking. The more apt inquiry is whether property is being regulated for a genuine police power purpose — that is, the prevention of something equivalent to a common law nuisance. On this issue, Justice Brennan revises both the majority and dissenting opinions of *Pennsylvania Coal*; both Holmes and Brandeis linked the police power with the avoidance of nuisance-like harms. As Justice Rehnquist relates, this is not the purpose of the New York landmark preservation ordinance. He writes: "Appellees are not prohibiting a nuisance. . . . Instead, appellees have placed an *affirmative* duty on Penn Central to maintain the Terminal in its present state and in 'good repair.' " 438 U.S. at 146 (Rehnquist, J., dissenting).

Does this mean the police power is confined to the prevention of harm? A case can be made for this. Douglas W. Kmiec, *Inserting the Last Remaining Pieces into the Takings Puzzle*, 38 WM. & MARY L. REV. 995 (1997). Justice Rehnquist is somewhat more deferential to broader exercises of the police power, writing that in addition to the prevention of harm, the police power can be used to impose a broadly applicable regulation that secures an "average reciprocity of advantage" and de minimis losses in value. 438 U.S. at 147 (Rehnquist, J., dissenting). By virtue of this statement, Justice Rehnquist would allow garden-variety zoning ordinances that are generally applied and do not involve substantial, individualized losses. By contrast, it is not immediately clear whether any regulation falls outside the undifferentiated conception of the police power nursed along by Justice Brennan. Justice Brennan writes in footnote 30 that there is no difference in his mind between the prohibition of noxious uses and regulation designed to produce a widespread public benefit. Note that the only authority Justice Brennan cites for this assertion is a law review article. In footnote 7 of the dissent, Justice Rehnquist answers that Justice Brennan's novel construction makes the police power " 'an authority for invasion of private right under the pretext of public good, which had no warrant in the laws or practices of our ancestors.' " *Id.* at 144 n.7 (Rehnquist, J., dissenting) (quoting *United States v. Lynah*, 188 U.S. 445, 470 (1903)).

The Court had an opportunity to anchor the police power clearly on the prevention of harm in *Lingle v. Chevron USA Inc.*, 544 U.S. 528 (2005). It unanimously declined. In an opinion by Justice O'Connor, the Court was presented with an Hawaiian commercial rent limitation which, by expert testimony, did not prevent any of the harms driving lessee gas stations out of business or high retail gas prices) the state legislature sought to mitigate. Because of this, the Ninth

Circuit invalidated the law as a regulatory taking, citing *Agins v. City of Tiburon*, 447 U.S. 255, 260 (1980), where the Court had created a shorthand takings law summary; that is — takings occur either where regulation "does not substantially advance legitimate state interests or denies an owner economically viable use of his land." The Court reversed the Ninth Circuit, concluding that the "substantially advance" portion of the shorthand formulation was not a proper takings inquiry. Unless regulation invites physical occupation by uninvited third parties, or (as in the *Lucas* case below) deprives a landowner of *all* economic value, the *ad hoc* factors of *Penn Central* should govern the regulatory takings inquiry. And, said the Court, "the *Penn Central* inquiry turns, in large part, albeit not exclusively, upon the magnitude of a regulation's economic impact and the degree to which it interferes with legitimate property interests." In the notes following the *Lucas* case, you will also see that the Court continues to allow for greater regulatory takings scrutiny in so-called "exaction cases," where a governmental permission is conditioned upon the landowner involuntarily giving up a property interest. There the Court finds it appropriate to inquire whether the exaction substantially advances the *same* interest as regulation that could have been relied upon to deny permission altogether. This is judicial inquiry into the nexus between regulatory means and ends, *not* inquiry into whether the end is an appropriate police power/harm prevention purpose. Justice Kennedy wrote a brief concurrence in *Lingle* noting that regulation might separately violate substantive due process if it is wholly arbitrary or irrational, but this had not been argued by the parties.

So, then, is there any substantive limit on regulatory takings? Yes, but it is highly qualified and that substantive limit thus far only appears in unique circumstances. Those circumstances include: a stipulation or finding that the regulation results to the total deprivation of economic value; physical occupation; and the conditioning of a permit on the sacrifice of a property interest. In *Lucas v. South Carolina Coastal Council*, 505 U.S. 1003 (1992), a 5 to 4 majority written by Justice Scalia found that a total deprivation of value could be justified only by an antecedent inquiry that demonstrated that the regulation was in essence performing the same function as a finding of nuisance. There are some problems hidden in the analysis including how to calculate whether there has been a total deprivation.

Justice Scalia noted:

> Regrettably, the rhetorical force of our "deprivation of all economically feasible use" rule is greater than its precision, since the rule does not make clear the "property interest" against which the loss of value is to be measured. When, for example, a regulation requires a developer to leave 90% of a rural tract in its natural state, it is unclear whether we would analyze the situation as one in which the owner has been deprived of all economically beneficial use of the burdened portion of the tract, or as one in which the owner has suffered a mere diminution in value of the tract as a whole. (For an extreme — and, we think, unsupportable — view of the relevant calculus, *Penn Central Transportation Co. v. New York City* (N.Y. 1977), *aff'd* (1978), where the state court examined the diminution in a particular parcel's value produced by a municipal ordinance in light of total value of the takings claimant's other holdings in the vicinity.) Unsurprisingly, this uncertainty regarding the composition of the denominator in our

"deprivation" fraction has produced inconsistent pronouncements by the Court. Compare *Pennsylvania Coal Co. v. Mahon* (1922) (law restricting subsurface extraction of coal held to effect a taking), with *Keystone Bituminous Coal Assn. v. DeBenedictis* (1987) (nearly identical law held not to effect a taking). The answer to this difficult question may lie in how the owner's reasonable expectations have been shaped by the State's law of property — *i.e.*, whether and to what degree the State's law has accorded legal recognition and protection to the particular interest in land with respect to which the takings claimant alleges a diminution in (or elimination of) value. In any event, we avoid this difficulty in the present case, since the "interest in land" that Lucas has pleaded (a fee simple interest) is an estate with a rich tradition of protection at common law, and since the South Carolina Court of Common Pleas found that the Beachfront Management Act left each of Lucas's beachfront lots without economic value.

Relying upon the finding that there was reason to believe all economic value had in fact been subtracted by the regulation, the court examined whether there was any regulatory justification that could be given for such severity:

Where the State seeks to sustain regulation that deprives land of all economically beneficial use, we think it may resist compensation only if the logically antecedent inquiry into the nature of the owner's estate shows that the proscribed use interests were not part of his title to begin with. This accords, we think, with our "takings" jurisprudence, which has traditionally been guided by the understandings of our citizens regarding the content of, and the State's power over, the "bundle of rights" that they acquire when they obtain title to property. It seems to us that the property owner necessarily expects the uses of his property to be restricted, from time to time, by various measures newly enacted by the State in legitimate exercise of its police powers; "[a]s long recognized, some values are enjoyed under an implied limitation and must yield to the police power." *Pennsylvania Coal Co. v. Mahon.* And in the case of personal property, by reason of the State's traditionally high degree of control over commercial dealings, he ought to be aware of the possibility that new regulation might even render his property economically worthless (at least if the property's only economically productive use is sale or manufacture for sale). In the case of land, however, we think the notion pressed by the Council that title is somehow held subject to the "implied limitation" that the State may subsequently eliminate all economically valuable use is inconsistent with the historical compact recorded in the Takings Clause that has become part of our constitutional culture.

Where "permanent physical occupation" of land is concerned, we have refused to allow the government to decree it anew (without compensation), no matter how weighty the asserted "public interests" involved. . . . Any limitation so severe cannot be newly legislated or decreed (without compensation), but must inhere in the title itself, in the restrictions that background principles of the State's law of property and nuisance already place upon land ownership. A law or decree with such an effect must, in other words, do no more than duplicate the result that could have been achieved in the courts — by adjacent landowners (or other uniquely affected persons) under the State's law of private nuisance, or by the State under its complementary power to abate nuisances that affect the public generally, or otherwise.

On this analysis, the owner of a lake-bed, for example, would not be entitled to compensation when he is denied the requisite permit to engage in a landfilling operation that would have the effect of flooding others' land. Nor the corporate owner of a nuclear generating plant, when it is directed to remove all improvements from its land upon discovery that the plant sits astride an earthquake fault. Such regulatory action may well have the effect of eliminating the land's only economically productive use, but it does not proscribe a productive use that was previously permissible under relevant property and nuisance principles. The use of these properties for what are now expressly prohibited purposes was *always* unlawful, and (subject to other constitutional limitations) it was open to the State at any point to make the implication of those background principles of nuisance and property law explicit. In light of our traditional resort to "existing rules or understandings that stem from an independent source such as state law" to define the range of interests that qualify for protection as "property" under the Fifth and Fourteenth Amendments, this recognition that the Takings Clause does not require compensation when an owner is barred from putting land to a use that is proscribed by those "existing rules or understandings" is surely unexceptional. When, however, a regulation that declares "off-limits" all economically productive or beneficial uses of land goes beyond what the relevant background principles would dictate, compensation must be paid to sustain it.[9]

The "total taking" inquiry we require today will ordinarily entail (as the application of state nuisance law ordinarily entails) analysis of, among other things, the degree of harm to public lands and resources, or adjacent private property, posed by the claimant's proposed activities, see, *e.g.*, §§ 826, 827, the social value of the claimant's activities and their suitability to the locality in question, see, *e.g.*, *id.*, §§ 828(a) and (b), 831, and the relative ease with which the alleged harm can be avoided through measures taken by the claimant and the government (or adjacent private landowners) alike, see, *e.g.*, *id.*, §§ 827(e), 828(c), 830. The fact that a particular use has long been engaged in by similarly situated owners ordinarily imports a lack of any common-law prohibition (though changed circumstances or new knowledge may make what was previously permissible no longer so, see, *id.*, § 827, Comment *g*). So also does the fact that other landowners, similarly situated, are permitted to continue the use denied to the claimant.

---

9 [17] Of course, the State may elect to rescind its regulation and thereby avoid having to pay compensation for a permanent deprivation. See *First English Evangelical Lutheran Church* [*of Glendale v. County of Los Angeles* (1987)]. But "where the [regulation has] already worked a taking of all use of property, no subsequent action by the government can relieve it of the duty to provide compensation for the period during which the taking was effective." *Ibid.*

It seems unlikely that common-law principles would have prevented the erection of any habitable or productive improvements on petitioner's land; they rarely support prohibition of the "essential use" of land. The question, however, is one of state law to be dealt with on remand. We emphasize that to win its case, South Carolina must do more than proffer the legislature's declaration that the uses Lucas desire are inconsistent with the public interest, or the conclusory assertion that they violate a common-law maxim such as *sic utere tuo ut alienum non laedas*. As we have said, a "State, by *ipse dixit*, may not transform private property into public property without compensation . . . ." Instead, as it would be required to do if it sought to restrain Lucas in a common-law action for public nuisance, South Carolina must identify background principles of nuisance and property law that prohibit the uses he now intend in the circumstances in which the property is presently found. Only on this showing can the State fairly claim that, in proscribing all such beneficial uses, the Beachfront Management Act is taking nothing.

NOTES AND QUESTIONS

1. The linchpin of *Lucas* is its establishment of a relationship between the application of the Takings Clause and the meaning of property under state law. This "solved" the takings puzzle by effectively letting the Court check legislative and regulatory abuse under the text of the Fifth Amendment without seeming to usurp legislative function. The reasons why the *Lucas* antecedent inquiry solves the takings puzzle is a long story, but its essence is this: reliance upon an objective, third party source or definition for property and corresponding police power limits thereon (primarily state judges in common law proceedings) precludes the Justices from substituting their own will a la *Lochner*, and avoids the abdication of judicial enforcement of the Takings Clause that is entailed when the Court deferentially allows the legislature to redefine private property as it sees fit, even post-investment. *See* Douglas W. Kmiec, *At Last, The Supreme Court Solves the Takings Puzzle*, 19 Harv. J. L. & Pub. Pol'y 147, 151–54 (1995); Douglas W. Kmiec, *Inserting the Last Remaining Pieces into the Takings Puzzle*, 38 Wm. & Mary L. Rev. 995, 1009–10 (1997).

2. As the Court noted in *Lucas*, even minor physical occupations are takings for which just compensation must be paid. *See Loretto v. Teleprompter Manhattan CATV Corp.*, 458 U.S. 419 (1982) (invalidating a New York ordinance which authorized the coercive installation of cable television. Such regulations are invalid without regard to assessment of public purpose or economic impact). But what of physical occupations made pursuant to a regulatory policy, exacted as a condition on a governmental permit? Are they to be treated as regulatory takings or as physical takings? In *Nollan v. California Coastal Commission*, 483 U.S. 825 (1987), the Court considered whether the California Coastal Commission could require an ocean-front property owner to convey a public-access easement as a condition on obtaining a building permit. The Commission contended that because it had a legitimate governmental interest in protecting the public's view of the ocean, which it could further by denying Nollan's building permit altogether, the easement was a permissible permit condition. Justice Scalia, writing for a 5-4 majority of the

Court, held that the exaction was a compensable taking. "[U]nless the permit condition serves the same governmental purpose as the development ban," he noted, "the building restriction is not a valid regulation of land use but 'an out-and-out plan of extortion.' "

3. Even when a permit condition has a nexus to a legitimate governmental interest, the exaction must bear a "roughly proportionality" to the impact to the public posed by the permitted use. *Dolan v. City of Tigard*, 512 U.S. 374 (1994), involved whether the City of Tigard, Oregon, could require Dolan to convey a 15-foot strip of land — about 10% of his property — as a condition on granting Dolan a permit to expand his plumbing and electric supply store. The City wanted the land for flood control purposes (to help mitigate the additional run-off that would be caused by Dolan's additional paving on his property) and also for a bike path (to help mitigate the increased traffic that would result from the expanded business use of the property). The Court held that both conditions had a sufficient nexus to the proposed expansion, but that they were invalid because not "roughly proportional" to the impact posed by the development. An open space requirement would have sufficed to address the City's flood control concerns, noted the Court, "[b]ut the city demanded more — it not only wanted petitioner not to build in the floodplain, but it also wanted petitioner's property along Fanno Creek for its greenway system. The city has never said why a public greenway, as opposed to a private one, was required in the interest of flood control." As for the bike path, the Court held that the City had "not met its burden of demonstrating that the additional number of vehicle and bicycle trips generated by the development" was reasonably related to the requirement that Dolan dedicate a bike path easement. For more on the issues addressed in *Nollan* and *Dolan*, see Douglas W. Kmiec, *The Original Understanding of the Taking Clause Is Neither Weak Nor Obtuse*, 88 COLUM. L. REV. 1630, 1650–52 (1988).

4. Takings claims are not ripe in federal court until a state fails in a final decision to provide adequate compensation for the taking. *Williamson County Regional Planning Comm'n v. Hamilton Bank*, 473 U.S. 172 (1985). In *San Remo Hotel v. City and County of San Francisco*, 545 U.S, 32 (2005), San Francisco required the owners of a residential hotel to contribute $567,000 to an affordable housing fund in order to obtain a permit to change the use of the hotel to a tourist facility. Since the hotel owners had not caused the housing shortage in any significant degree, they argued a taking of property equivalent to a *Nollan* or *Dolan* exactions case. Procedural reasons kept the Supreme Court from addressing the merits of that pleading. Specifically, when the hotel filed suit in federal court, the district court found it unripe under *Williamson County*, as the hotelier had not pursued just compensation in state court. Returning to state court, the hotelier expressly reserved its federal taking claim, and was denied compensation by the California courts. Rather than seeking review by writ of *certiorari* of the state court judgment in the Supreme Court, the hoteliers went to federal district court first in order to present their federal taking claim before a federal forum. A unanimous Court, per Justice Stevens, found the claim to be precluded by the state court judgment, since the state court had proclaimed state takings law to be coextensive with federal law. Said Justice Stevens, it is an erroneous assumption that there is a "right to vindicate[] federal claims in a federal forum." It did not matter that it was the Court's ripeness rule that had initially sent the hotel back to state court involuntarily. Four Justices, led by Chief Justice Rehnquist, said that they were open to reconsidering *Williamson County* since it is "not obvious" that it is either a constitutional or prudential principle to require claimants to utilize all state compensation procedures before they can bring a federal takings claim.

KOONTZ v. ST. JOHNS RIVER WATER MANAGEMENT DISTRICT
133 S. Ct. 2586, 186 L. Ed. 2d 697 (2013)

* * *

Justice Alito delivered the opinion of the Court.

Our decisions in *Nollan v. California Coastal Comm'n*, (1987), and *Dolan v. City of Tigard*, (1994), provide important protection against the misuse of the power of land-use regulation. In those cases, we held that a unit of government may not condition the approval of a land-use permit on the owner's relinquishment of a portion of his property unless there is a "nexus" and "rough proportionality" between the government's demand and the effects of the proposed land use. In this case, the St. Johns River Water Management District (District) believes that it circumvented *Nollan* and *Dolan* because of the way in which it structured its handling of a permit application submitted by Koontz (petitioner). The District did not approve his application on the condition that he surrender an interest in his land. Instead, the District, after suggesting that he could obtain approval by signing over such an interest, denied his application because he refused to yield. The Florida Supreme Court blessed this maneuver and thus effectively interred those important decisions. Because we conclude that *Nollan* and *Dolan* cannot be evaded in this way, the Florida Supreme Court's decision must be reversed.

I

A

In 1972, petitioner purchased an undeveloped 14.9-acre tract of land on the south side of Florida State Road 50, a divided four-lane highway east of Orlando. The property is located less than 1,000 feet from that road's intersection with Florida State Road 408, a tolled expressway that is one of Orlando's major thoroughfares.

A drainage ditch runs along the property's western edge, and high-voltage power lines bisect it into northern and southern sections. The combined effect of the ditch, a 100–foot wide area kept clear for the power lines, the highways, and other construction on nearby parcels is to isolate the northern section of petitioner's property from any other undeveloped land. Although largely classified as wetlands by the State, the northern section drains well; the most significant standing water forms in ruts in an unpaved road used to access the power lines. The natural topography of the property's southern section is somewhat more diverse, with a small creek, forested uplands, and wetlands that sometimes have water as much as a foot deep. A wildlife survey found evidence of animals that often frequent developed areas: raccoons, rabbits, several species of bird, and a turtle. The record also indicates that the land may be a suitable habitat for opossums.

The same year that petitioner purchased his property, Florida enacted the Water Resources Act, which divided the State into five water management districts and authorized each district to regulate "construction that connects to, draws water from, drains water into, or is placed in or across the waters in the state." 1972 Fla. Laws ch. 72–299, pt. IV, § 1(5), pp. 1115, 1116 (codified as amended at Fla. Stat. § 373.403(5) (2010)). Under the Act, a landowner wishing to undertake such construction must obtain from the relevant district a Management and Storage of Surface Water (MSSW) permit, which may impose "such reasonable conditions" on the permit as are "necessary to assure" that construction will "not be harmful to the water resources of the district." 1972 Fla. Laws § 4(1), at 1118 (codified as amended at Fla. Stat. § 373.413(1)).

In 1984, in an effort to protect the State's rapidly diminishing wetlands, the Florida Legislature passed the Warren S. Henderson Wetlands Protection Act, which made it illegal for anyone to "dredge or fill in, on, or over surface waters" without a Wetlands Resource Management (WRM) permit. 1984 Fla. Laws ch. 84–79, pt. VIII, § 403.905(1), pp. 204–205. Under the Henderson Act, permit applicants are required to provide "reasonable assurance" that proposed construction on wetlands is "not contrary to the public interest," as defined by an enumerated list of criteria. See Fla. Stat. § 373.414(1). Consistent with the Henderson Act, the St. Johns River Water Management District, the district with jurisdiction over petitioner's land, requires that permit applicants wishing to build on wetlands offset the resulting environmental damage by creating, enhancing, or preserving wetlands elsewhere.

Petitioner decided to develop the 3.7-acre northern section of his property, and in 1994 he applied to the District for MSSW and WRM permits. Under his proposal, petitioner would have raised the elevation of the northernmost section of his land to make it suitable for a building, graded the land from the southern edge of the building site down to the elevation of the high-voltage electrical lines, and installed a dry-bed pond for retaining and gradually releasing stormwater runoff from the building and its parking lot. To mitigate the environmental effects of his proposal, petitioner offered to foreclose any possible future development of the approximately 11-acre southern section of his land by deeding to the District a conservation easement on that portion of his property.

The District considered the 11-acre conservation easement to be inadequate, and it informed petitioner that it would approve construction only if he agreed to one of two concessions. First, the District proposed that petitioner reduce the size of his development to 1 acre and deed to the District a conservation easement on the remaining 13.9 acres. To reduce the development area, the District suggested that petitioner could eliminate the dry-bed pond from his proposal and instead install a more costly subsurface stormwater management system beneath the building site. The District also suggested that petitioner install retaining walls rather than gradually sloping the land from the building site down to the elevation of the rest of his property to the south.

In the alternative, the District told petitioner that he could proceed with the development as proposed, building on 3.7 acres and deeding a conservation easement to the government on the remainder of the property, if he also agreed to hire contractors to make improvements to District-owned land several miles away. Specifically, petitioner could pay to replace culverts on one parcel or fill in ditches on another. Either of those projects would have enhanced approximately 50 acres of District-owned wetlands. When the District asks permit applicants to fund offsite mitigation work, its policy is never to require any particular offsite project, and it did not do so here. Instead, the District said that it "would also favorably consider" alternatives to its suggested offsite mitigation projects if petitioner proposed something "equivalent." App. 75.

Believing the District's demands for mitigation to be excessive in light of the environmental effects that his building proposal would have caused, petitioner filed suit in state court. Among other claims, he argued that he was entitled to relief under Fla. Stat. § 373.617(2), which allows owners to recover "monetary damages" if a state agency's action is "an unreasonable exercise of the state's police power constituting a taking without just compensation."

B

The Florida Circuit Court granted the District's motion to dismiss on the ground that petitioner had not adequately exhausted his state-administrative remedies, but the Florida District Court of Appeal for the Fifth Circuit reversed. On remand, the State Circuit Court held a 2-day bench trial. After considering testimony from several experts who examined petitioner's property, the trial court found that the property's northern section had already been "seriously degraded" by extensive construction on the surrounding parcels. App. to Pet. for Cert. D-3. In light of this finding and petitioner's offer to dedicate nearly three-quarters of his land to the District, the trial court concluded that any further mitigation in the form of payment for offsite improvements to District property lacked both a nexus and rough proportionality to the environmental impact of the proposed construction. It accordingly held the District's actions unlawful under our decisions in *Nollan* and *Dolan*.

The Florida District Court affirmed, 5 So.3d 8 (2009), but the State Supreme Court reversed, (2011). A majority of that court distinguished *Nollan* and *Dolan* on two grounds. First, the majority thought it significant that in this case, unlike *Nollan* or *Dolan*, the District did not approve petitioner's application on the condition that he accede to the District's demands; instead, the District denied his application because he refused to make concessions. Second, the majority drew a distinction between a demand for an interest in real property (what happened in *Nollan* and *Dolan*) and a demand for money. The majority acknowledged a division of authority over whether a demand for money can give rise to a claim under *Nollan* and *Dolan*, and sided with those courts that have said it cannot. Compare, *e.g.*, *McClung v. Sumner*, (C.A.9 2008), with *Ehrlich v. Culver City*, (1996); *Flower Mound v. Stafford Estates Ltd. Partnership*, (Tex. 2004). Two justices concurred in the result, arguing that petitioner had failed to exhaust his administrative remedies as required by state law before bringing an inverse condemnation suit that challenges the propriety of an agency action. *See Key Haven Associated Enterprises, Inc. v. Board of Trustees of Internal Improvement Trust Fund,* (Fla. 1982).

Recognizing that the majority opinion rested on a question of federal constitutional law on which the lower courts are divided, we granted the petition and now reverse.

II

A

* * *

[Our] cases reflect an overarching principle, known as the unconstitutional conditions doctrine, that vindicates the Constitution's enumerated rights by preventing the government from coercing people into giving them up.

Nollan and *Dolan* "involve a special application" of this doctrine that protects the Fifth Amendment right to just compensation for property the government takes when owners apply for land-use permits. *Lingle v. Chevron U.S.A. Inc.,* (2005); *Dolan,* (invoking "the well-settled doctrine of 'unconstitutional conditions' "). Our decisions in those cases reflect two realities of the permitting process. The first is that land-use permit applicants are especially vulnerable to the type of coercion that the unconstitutional conditions doctrine prohibits because the government often has broad discretion to deny a permit that is worth far more than property it would like to take. By conditioning a building permit on the owner's deeding over a public right-of-way, for example, the government can pressure an owner into voluntarily giving up property for which the Fifth Amendment would otherwise require just compensation. So long as the building permit is more valuable than any just compensation the owner could hope to receive for the right-of-way, the owner is likely to accede to the government's demand, no matter how unreasonable. Extortionate demands of this sort frustrate the Fifth Amendment right to just compensation, and the unconstitutional conditions doctrine prohibits them.

A second reality of the permitting process is that many proposed land uses threaten to impose costs on the public that dedications of property can offset. Where a building proposal would substantially increase traffic congestion, for example, officials might condition permit approval on the owner's agreement to deed over the land needed to widen a public road. Respondent argues that a similar rationale justifies the exaction at issue here: petitioner's proposed construction project, it submits, would destroy wetlands on his property, and in order to compensate for this loss, respondent demands that he enhance wetlands elsewhere. Insisting that landowners internalize the negative externalities of their conduct is a hallmark of responsible land-use policy, and we have long sustained such regulations against constitutional attack. *See Village of Euclid v. Ambler Realty Co.,* (1926).

Nollan and *Dolan* accommodate both realities by allowing the government to condition approval of a permit on the dedication of property to the public so long as there is a "nexus" and "rough proportionality" between the property that the government demands and the social costs of the applicant's proposal. Our precedents thus enable permitting authorities to insist that applicants bear the full costs of their proposals while still forbidding the government from engaging in "out-and-out . . . extortion" that would thwart the Fifth Amendment right to just compensation. *Ibid.* (internal quotation marks omitted). Under *Nollan* and *Dolan* the government may choose whether and how a permit applicant is required to mitigate the impacts of a proposed development, but it may not leverage its legitimate interest in mitigation to pursue governmental ends that lack an essential nexus and rough proportionality to those impacts.

B

The principles that undergird our decisions in *Nollan* and *Dolan* do not change depending on whether the government *approves* a permit on the condition that the applicant turn over property or *denies* a permit because the applicant refuses to do so. We have often concluded that denials of governmental benefits were impermissible under the unconstitutional conditions doctrine.

* * *

A contrary rule would be especially untenable in this case because it would enable the government to evade the limitations of *Nollan* and *Dolan* simply by phrasing its demands for property as conditions precedent to permit approval. Under the Florida Supreme Court's approach, a government order stating that a permit is "approved if" the owner turns over property would be subject to *Nollan* and *Dolan*, but an identical order that uses the words "denied until" would not. Our unconstitutional conditions cases have long refused to attach significance to the distinction between conditions precedent and conditions subsequent.

* * *

The Florida Supreme Court puzzled over how the government's demand for property can violate the Takings Clause even though " 'no property of any kind was ever taken.' " [But] extortionate demands for property in the land-use permitting context run afoul of the Takings Clause not because they take property but because they impermissibly burden the right not to have property taken without just compensation. As in other unconstitutional conditions cases in which someone refuses to cede a constitutional right in the face of coercive pressure, the impermissible denial of a governmental benefit is a constitutionally cognizable injury.

Nor does it make a difference, as respondent suggests, that the government might have been able to deny petitioner's application outright without giving him the option of securing a permit by agreeing to spend money to improve public lands. *See Penn Central Transp. Co. v. New York City,* (1978). . . . Yet we have repeatedly rejected the argument that if the government need not confer a benefit at all, it can withhold the benefit because someone refuses to give up constitutional rights. *E.g., United States v. American Library Assn., Inc.,* (2003) ("[T]he government may not deny a benefit to a person on a basis that infringes his constitutionally protected . . . freedom of speech *even if he has no entitlement to that benefit*" Even if respondent would have been entirely within its rights in denying the permit for some other reason, that greater authority does not imply a lesser power to condition permit approval on petitioner's forfeiture of his constitutional rights.

That is not to say, however, that there is *no* relevant difference between a consummated taking and the denial of a permit based on an unconstitutionally extortionate demand. Where the permit is denied and the condition is never imposed, nothing has been taken. While the unconstitutional conditions doctrine recognizes that this *burdens* a constitutional right, the Fifth Amendment mandates a particular *remedy* — just compensation — only for takings. In cases where there is an excessive demand but no taking, whether money damages are available is not a question of federal constitutional law but of the cause of action — whether state or federal — on which the landowner relies. Because petitioner brought his claim pursuant to a state law cause of action, the Court has no occasion to discuss what remedies might be available for a *Nollan/Dolan* unconstitutional conditions violation either here or in other cases.

C

At oral argument, respondent conceded that the denial of a permit could give rise to a valid claim under *Nollan* and *Dolan*, Tr. of Oral Arg. 33–34, but it urged that we should not review the particular denial at issue here because petitioner sued in the wrong court, for the wrong remedy, and at the wrong time. Most of respondent's objections to the posture of this case raise questions of Florida procedure that are not ours to decide. *See Mullaney v. Wilbur*, (1975); *Murdock v. Memphis*, 20 Wall. (1875). But to the extent that respondent suggests that the posture of this case creates some federal obstacle to adjudicating petitioner's unconstitutional conditions claim, we remand for the Florida courts to consider that argument in the first instance.

*   *   *

For similar reasons, we decline to reach respondent's argument that its demands for property were too indefinite to give rise to liability under *Nollan* and *Dolan*. The Florida Supreme Court did not reach the question whether respondent issued a demand of sufficient concreteness to trigger the special protections of *Nollan* and *Dolan*. It relied instead on the Florida District Court of Appeals' characterization of respondent's behavior as a demand for *Nollan/Dolan* purposes. Whether that characterization is correct is beyond the scope of the questions the Court agreed to take up for review. If preserved, the issue remains open on remand for the Florida Supreme Court to address. This Court therefore has no occasion to consider how concrete and specific a demand must be to give rise to liability under *Nollan* and *Dolan*.

Finally, respondent argues that we need not decide whether its demand for offsite improvements satisfied *Nollan* and *Dolan* because it gave petitioner another avenue for obtaining permit approval. Specifically, respondent said that it would have approved a revised permit application that reduced the footprint of petitioner's proposed construction site from 3.7 acres to 1 acre and placed a conservation easement on the remaining 13.9 acres of petitioner's land. Respondent argues that regardless of whether its demands for offsite mitigation satisfied *Nollan* and *Dolan*, we must separately consider each of petitioner's options, one of which did not require any of the offsite work the trial court found objectionable.

Respondent's argument is flawed because the option to which it points — developing only 1 acre of the site and granting a conservation easement on the rest — involves the same issue as the option to build on 3.7 acres and perform offsite mitigation. We agree with respondent that, so long as a permitting authority offers the landowner at least one alternative that would satisfy *Nollan* and *Dolan*, the landowner has not been subjected to an unconstitutional condition. But respondent's suggestion that we should treat its offer to let petitioner build on 1 acre as an alternative to offsite mitigation misapprehends the governmental benefit that petitioner was denied. Petitioner sought to develop 3.7 acres, but respondent in effect told petitioner that it would not allow him to build on 2.7 of those acres unless he agreed to spend money improving public lands. Petitioner claims that he was wrongfully denied a permit to build on those 2.7 acres. For that reason, respondent's offer to approve a less ambitious building project does not obviate the need to determine whether the demand for offsite mitigation satisfied *Nollan* and *Dolan*.

III

We turn to the Florida Supreme Court's alternative holding that petitioner's claim fails because respondent asked him to spend money rather than give up an easement on his land. A predicate for any unconstitutional conditions claim is that the government could not have constitutionally ordered the person asserting the claim to do what it attempted to pressure that person into doing. For that reason, we began our analysis in both *Nollan* and *Dolan* by observing that if the government had directly seized the easements it sought to obtain through the permitting process, it would have committed a *per se* taking. The Florida Supreme Court held that petitioner's claim fails at this first step because the subject of the exaction at issue here was money rather than a more tangible interest in real property. Respondent and the dissent take the same position, citing the concurring and dissenting opinions in *Eastern Enterprises v. Apfel*, (1998), for the proposition that an obligation to spend money can never provide the basis for a takings claim.

We note as an initial matter that if we accepted this argument it would be very easy for land-use permitting officials to evade the limitations of *Nollan* and *Dolan*. Because the government need only provide a permit applicant with one alternative that satisfies the nexus and rough proportionality standards, a permitting authority wishing to exact an easement could simply give the owner a choice of either surrendering an easement or making a payment equal to the easement's value. Such so-called "in lieu of" fees are utterly commonplace and they are functionally equivalent to other types of land use exactions. For that reason and those that follow, we reject respondent's argument and hold that so-called "monetary exactions" must satisfy the nexus and rough proportionality requirements of *Nollan* and *Dolan*.

A

In *Eastern Enterprises*, the United States retroactively imposed on a former mining company an obligation to pay for the medical benefits of retired miners and their families. A four-Justice plurality concluded that the statute's imposition of retroactive financial liability was so arbitrary that it violated the Takings Clause. Although Justice KENNEDY concurred in the result on due process grounds, he joined four other Justices in dissent in arguing that the Takings Clause does not apply to government-imposed financial obligations that "d[o] not operate upon or alter an identified property interest." Relying on the concurrence and dissent in *Eastern Enterprises*, respondent argues that a requirement that petitioner spend money improving public lands could not give rise to a taking.

Respondent's argument rests on a mistaken premise. Unlike the financial obligation in *Eastern Enterprises*, the demand for money at issue here did "operate upon . . . an identified property interest" by directing the owner of a particular piece of property to make a monetary payment. (opinion of KENNEDY, J.). In this case, unlike *Eastern Enterprises*, the monetary obligation burdened petitioner's ownership of a specific parcel of land. In that sense, this case bears resemblance to our cases holding that the government must pay just compensation when it takes a lien — a right to receive money that is secured by a particular piece of property. The fulcrum this case turns on is the direct link between the government's demand and a specific parcel of real property. Because of that direct link, this case implicates the central concern of *Nollan* and *Dolan*: the risk that the government may use its substantial power and discretion in land-use permitting to pursue governmental ends that lack an essential nexus and rough proportionality to the effects of the proposed new use of the specific property at issue, thereby diminishing without justification the value of the property.

In this case, moreover, petitioner does not ask us to hold that the government can commit a *regulatory* taking by directing someone to spend money. As a result, we need not apply *Penn Central*'s "essentially ad hoc, factual inquir[y]" at all, much less extend that "already difficult and uncertain rule" to the "vast category of cases" in which someone believes that a regulation is too costly. *Eastern Enterprises*, (opinion of KENNEDY, J.). Instead, petitioner's claim rests on the more limited proposition that when the government commands the relinquishment of funds linked to a specific, identifiable property interest such as a bank account or parcel of real property, a *"per se* [takings] approach" is the proper mode of analysis under the Court's precedent.

Finally, it bears emphasis that petitioner's claim does not implicate "normative considerations about the wisdom of government decisions." *Eastern Enterprises*, (opinion of KENNEDY, J). We are not here concerned with whether it would be "arbitrary or unfair" for respondent to order a landowner to make improvements to public lands that are nearby. (BREYER, J., dissenting). Whatever the wisdom of such a policy, it would transfer an interest in property from the landowner to the government. For that reason, any such demand would amount to a *per se* taking similar to the taking of an easement or a lien.

B

Respondent and the dissent argue that if monetary exactions are made subject to scrutiny under *Nollan* and *Dolan*, then there will be no principled way of distinguishing impermissible land-use exactions from property taxes. We think they exaggerate both the extent to which that problem is unique to the land-use permitting context and the practical difficulty of distinguishing between the power to tax and the power to take by eminent domain.

It is beyond dispute that "[t]axes and user fees . . . are not 'takings,' " and our cases have been clear on that point ever since. *United States v. Sperry Corp.*, (1989). This case therefore does not affect the ability of governments to impose property taxes, user fees, and similar laws and regulations that may impose financial burdens on property owners.

At the same time, we have repeatedly found takings where the government, by confiscating financial obligations, achieved a result that could have been obtained by imposing a tax. Most recently, in *Brown*, we were unanimous in concluding that a State Supreme Court's seizure of the interest on client funds held in escrow was a taking despite the unquestionable constitutional propriety of a tax that would have raised exactly the same revenue. Our holding in *Brown* followed from *Phillips v. Washington Legal Foundation*, (1998), and *Webb's Fabulous Pharmacies, Inc. v. Beckwith*, (1980), two earlier cases in which we treated confiscations of money as takings despite their functional similarity to a tax. Perhaps most closely analogous to the present case, we have repeatedly held that the government takes property when it seizes liens, and in so ruling we have never considered whether the government could have achieved an economically equivalent result through taxation.

Two facts emerge from those cases. The first is that the need to distinguish taxes from takings is not a creature of our holding today that monetary exactions are subject to scrutiny under *Nollan* and *Dolan*. Rather, the problem is inherent in this Court's long-settled view that property the government could constitutionally demand through its taxing power can also be taken by eminent domain.

Second, our cases show that teasing out the difference between taxes and takings is more difficult in theory than in practice. *Brown* is illustrative. Similar to respondent in this case, the respondents in *Brown* argued that extending the protections of the Takings Clause to a bank account would open a Pandora's Box of constitutional challenges to taxes. But also like respondent here, the *Brown* respondents never claimed that they were exercising their power to levy taxes when they took the petitioners' property. Any such argument would have been implausible under state law; in Washington, taxes are levied by the legislature, not the courts. (SCALIA, J dissenting).

The same dynamic is at work in this case because Florida law greatly circumscribes respondent's power to tax. If respondent had argued that its demand for money was a tax, it would have effectively conceded that its denial of petitioner's permit was improper under Florida law. Far from making that concession, respondent has maintained throughout this litigation that it considered petitioner's money to be a substitute for his deeding to the public a conservation easement on a larger parcel of undeveloped land.[10]

This case does not require us to say more. We need not decide at precisely what point a land-use permitting charge denominated by the government as a "tax" becomes "so arbitrary . . . that it was not the exertion of taxation but a confiscation of property." For present purposes, it suffices to say that despite having long recognized that "the power of taxation should not be confused with the power of eminent domain," we have had little trouble distinguishing between the two.

C

Finally, we disagree with the dissent's forecast that our decision will work a revolution in land use law by depriving local governments of the ability to charge reasonable permitting fees. Numerous courts — including courts in many of our Nation's most populous States — have confronted constitutional challenges to monetary exactions over the last two decades and applied the standard from *Nollan* and *Dolan* or something like it.

*   *   *

The dissent criticizes the notion that the Federal Constitution places any meaningful limits on "whether one town is overcharging for sewage, or another is setting the price to sell liquor too high." But only two pages later, it identifies three constraints on land use permitting fees that it says the Federal Constitution imposes and suggests that the additional protections of *Nollan* and *Dolan* are not needed. In any event, the dissent's argument that land use permit applicants need no further protection when the government demands money is really an argument for overruling *Nollan* and *Dolan*. After all, the Due Process Clause protected the Nollans from an unfair allocation of public burdens, and they too could have argued that the government's demand for property amounted to a taking under the *Penn Central* framework. See *Nollan.* We have repeatedly rejected the dissent's contention that other constitutional doctrines leave no room for the nexus and rough proportionality requirements of *Nollan* and *Dolan*. Mindful of the special vulnerability of land use permit applicants to extortionate demands for money, we do so again today.

*   *   *

We hold that the government's demand for property from a land-use permit applicant must satisfy the requirements of *Nollan* and *Dolan* even when the government denies the permit and even when its demand is for money. The Court expresses no view on the merits of petitioner's claim that respondent's actions here failed to comply with the principles set forth in this opinion and those two cases. The

---

[10] [1] Citing cases in which state courts have treated similar governmental demands for money differently, the dissent predicts that courts will "struggle to draw a coherent boundary" between taxes and excessive demands for money that violate *Nollan* and *Dolan*. But the cases the dissent cites illustrate how the frequent need to decide whether a particular demand for money qualifies as a tax under state law, and the resulting state statutes and judicial precedents on point, greatly reduce the practical difficulty of resolving the same issue in federal constitutional cases like this one.

Florida Supreme Court's judgment is reversed, and this case is remanded for further proceedings not inconsistent with this opinion.

It is so ordered.

JUSTICE KAGAN, with whom JUSTICE GINSBURG, JUSTICE BREYER, and JUSTICE SOTO-MAYOR join, dissenting.

*   *   *

I think the Court gets the first question it addresses right. The *Nollan — Dolan* standard applies not only when the government approves a development permit conditioned on the owner's conveyance of a property interest (*i.e.,* imposes a condition subsequent), but also when the government denies a permit until the owner meets the condition (*i.e.,* imposes a condition precedent). That means an owner may challenge the denial of a permit on the ground that the government's condition lacks the "nexus" and "rough proportionality" to the development's social costs that *Nollan* and *Dolan* require. Still, the condition-subsequent and condition-precedent situations differ in an important way. When the government grants a permit subject to the relinquishment of real property, and that condition does not satisfy *Nollan* and *Dolan*, then the government has taken the property and must pay just compensation under the Fifth Amendment. But when the government denies a permit because an owner has refused to accede to that same demand, nothing has actually been taken. The owner is entitled to have the improper condition removed; and he may be entitled to a monetary remedy created by state law for imposing such a condition; but he cannot be entitled to constitutional compensation for a taking of property. So far, we all agree.

Our core disagreement concerns the second question the Court addresses. The majority extends *Nollan* and *Dolan* to cases in which the government conditions a permit not on the transfer of real property, but instead on the payment or expenditure of money. That runs roughshod over *Eastern Enterprises v. Apfel,* (1998), which held that the government may impose ordinary financial obligations without triggering the Takings Clause's protections. The boundaries of the majority's new rule are uncertain. But it threatens to subject a vast array of land-use regulations, applied daily in States and localities throughout the country, to heightened constitutional scrutiny. I would not embark on so unwise an adventure, and would affirm the Florida Supreme Court's decision.

I also would affirm for two independent reasons establishing that Koontz cannot get the money damages he seeks. First, respondent St. Johns River Water Management District (District) never demanded *anything* (including money) in exchange for a permit; the *Nollan — Dolan* standard therefore does not come into play (even assuming that test applies to demands for money). Second, no taking occurred in this case because Koontz never acceded to a demand (even had there been one), and so no property changed hands; as just noted, Koontz therefore cannot claim just compensation under the Fifth Amendment. The majority does not take issue with my first conclusion, and affirmatively agrees with my second. But the majority thinks Koontz might still be entitled to money damages, and remands to the Florida Supreme Court on that question. I do not see how, and expect that court will so rule.

I

*   *   *

In sum, *Nollan* and *Dolan* restrain governments from using the permitting process to do what the Takings Clause would otherwise prevent — *i.e.*, take a specific property interest without just compensation. Those cases have no application when governments impose a general financial obligation as part of the permitting process, because under *Apfel* such an action does not otherwise trigger the Takings Clause's protections. By extending *Nollan* and *Dolan*'s heightened scrutiny to a simple payment demand, the majority threatens the heartland of local land-use regulation and service delivery, at a bare minimum depriving state and local governments of "necessary predictability." *Apfel*. That decision is unwarranted — and deeply unwise. I would keep *Nollan* and *Dolan* in their intended sphere and affirm the Florida Supreme Court.

NOTES AND QUESTIONS

1. The unconstitutional conditions doctrine is mostly associated with freedom of speech cases. Government can specify ideological conditions that need to be observed in the spending of government resources, but it cannot leverage those resources to impose an ideology to be observed by the government grantee generally — that is outside the funding received from the government. Is Justice Alito right to apply that doctrine here in the highly sensitive regulation of environmental development? Is it not reasonable to assume that all landowners in the use of their property are expected to observe an environmental ethic that is consistent with the fragility of the human environment? In other words, are there really competing ideologies here or is there simply a fundamental application of what common sense requires as a good citizen? In this regard, takings cases are less about the government imposing a point of view than they are about ensuring that our commitment to wetlands and the like is shared in rough proportion to the external effects upon environmental resources that everyone pretty much agrees should be preserved.

2. How could anyone think the phrasing of the condition as either precedent or subsequent would matter?

3. And what exactly is the property interest being taken in this case? Justice Alito says the right to compensation is triggered not because property is taken giving rise to a claim of compensation for that property but because there has been an unconstitutional burden imposed on the right to not have property taken without just compensation. Does this transform the takings clause into a general right of damages for what the Court will now consider a governmental burden? Isn't this a revival of *Lochner v. New York*, with all of its accompanying perils involving judges in the day to day administration of these environmental resources. *Lochner v. New York*, 198 U.S. 45 (1905).

4.   In *Stop the Beach Renourishment, Inc. v. Florida Department of Environmental Protection*, 560 U.S. 702 (2010), the Court divided sharply and evenly on the issue of whether the decision of a state's court of last resort can amount to a taking of private property. After several hurricanes had eroded a 6.9-mile stretch of beachfront, the City of Destin and County of Walton, Florida, sought to restore the beachfront in such a way that 75 feet of dry sand would be added seaward of the mean high-water line. The Stop the Beach Renourishment group, a nonprofit corporation formed by people who own beachfront property bordering the project area challenged the restoration project as an unconstitutional taking of their common-law riparian rights to receive accretions to their property and to have the contact of their property with the water remain intact. Justice Stevens, who owned land in the affected area recused himself, thus setting up the potential for an even split on the Court. The remaining eight members of the Court had no difficulty with the substantive issue in the case. No taking had occurred. The government was filling in land below high-water mark — land that had been taken from it by avulsion. The court below — *i.e.*, the Florida Supreme Court — had essentially held the same. The Stop the Beach Renourishment group, however, had sought a rehearing in the Florida Supreme Court on the ground that the Florida Supreme Court's decision itself effected a taking. Hence the contentious issue that beset the Court was whether the decision of a state's highest court can constitute a taking. Four Justices, Scalia, Thomas, Alito, and the Chief Justice held that, although no taking had occurred in this case, such a judicial decision could, in proper circumstances, constitute a taking. Two justices, Kennedy and Sotomayor, saw the plurality's ruling that the Takings Clause applies to judicial action as being a "bold and risky step" and cautioned that the taking-by-judicial-action issue should be less boldly and less riskily handled under the Due Process Clause rather than the Takings Clause. Justices Breyer and Ginsburg opined that the taking-by-judicial-action issue "unnecessarily addresses questions of constitutional law that are better left for another day."

5.   A fair government is assured not only by the protection of vested contract and property rights, but also by the observance of fair procedures. This idea is embodied in the Due Process Clauses of the Fifth and Fourteenth Amendments, a topic to which we now turn. Our initial inquiry is into a concept called "state action," reflecting the fact that the obligation of fair process is one that applies to governmental entities, not individuals. The natural law obligations of individuals to do justice are not capable of enforcement under law since, as the great natural law thinker Thomas Aquinas observed, the law is not to enact every virtue or prohibit every vice. It is instead to legislate against the "more grievous vices . . . chiefly those that are to the hurt of others, without the prohibition of which human society could not be maintained: thus human law prohibits murder, theft, and suchlike." II THOMAS AQUINAS, SUMMA THEOLOGICA, Q. 96, art. 2 (Fathers of the English Dominican Province trans., Benzinger Brothers 1947). Consider as you read the due process materials whether the Constitution has been interpreted to prohibit more or less of the grievous vices.

II.

PROCEDURAL DUE PROCESS

A. WHAT CONSTITUTES STATE ACTION?

We will be looking at the topic "What Constitutes State Action?" from two slightly different vantage points. In the introductory material on *The Civil Rights Cases* (1883), we will be focusing on the extent of Congress's powers to go beyond regulating state action in using § 5 of the Fourteenth Amendment. There is, however, another, subtler feature of the concept of "state action." There is a line of cases, typified by *Shelley v. Kraemer* (1948), in which the Court has explored the extent to which otherwise private activity can become subject to the self-executing provisions of the Fourteenth Amendment, depending roughly on the closeness of the connectedness between the private activity and the operations of a state government. The first case, *The Civil Rights Cases*, it might be thought, discusses "state action" as a *shield* against the legitimacy of congressional civil rights legislation — a *limitation* on congressional power. The second case, *Shelley*, discusses "state action" as a *sword*, extending the affirmative, direct, "self-implementing" protections of the Fourteenth Amendment to many forms of private activity that adversely affect persons on the basis of race.

In the *Civil Rights Cases*, 109 U.S. 3 (1883), *United States v. Stanley et al.*, semi-officially and generally known as *The Civil Rights Cases*, access to public accommodations [private property, such as a theater, restaurant, hotel held out for general use by the public] was being denied on the basis of race. The Court ruled that the public accommodations portions of that Civil Rights Act of 1875 are unconstitutional, as being beyond Congress' powers under either § 2 of the Thirteenth Amendment or § 5 of the Fourteenth Amendment. Those sections authorize Congress to "enforce," by appropriate legislation, the provisions of the Thirteenth and Fourteenth Amendments. The Thirteenth Amendment prohibits slavery and involuntary servitude. The Fourteenth Amendment, in relevant parts, prohibits states from making or enforcing any law that abridges the privileges or immunities of citizens of the United States, from depriving any person of life, liberty, or property without due process of law, and from denying to any person within its jurisdiction the equal protection of the laws.

The Court ruled that Congress, in enforcing the provisions of the Fourteenth Amendment, is limited to remedial or corrective legislation redressing "state action," *i.e.*, actions done by state governments. Congress' powers under § 5 of the Fourteenth Amendment do not extend to actions done by private individuals or private corporations.

The Thirteenth Amendment, the Court acknowledged, is a somewhat different story. It is not confined to outlawing state action; it applies directly to private actions, but it is confined to outlawing slavery and involuntary servitude, and Congress' power to enforce that Amendment is limited to outlawing what the Court referred to as the "badges and incidents" of slavery or involuntary servitude, construed narrowly.

Justice Bradley, writing for the majority, summarized the essence of the Court's Fourteenth Amendment ruling:

> The truth is, [Justice Bradley wrote] that the implication of a power to legislate in this manner [*i.e.*, the implication of recognizing in Congress a power to outlaw private acts of racial discrimination unaided by state action] is based upon the assumption that if the states are forbidden to legislate or act in a particular way on a particular subject, and the power is conferred upon Congress to enforce the prohibition [the reference here is to the fact that the 14th Amendment operates as a prohibition on the states and an empowerment of Congress — eds.], this gives Congress power to legislate generally upon that subject, and not merely power to provide modes of redress against such state legislation or action.

One might be inclined to stop right here and answer: "Yes! Exactly! That is exactly the meaning of § 5 of the 14th Amendment." Justice Bradley, however, continued: "Th[at] assumption is certainly unsound. It is repugnant to the Tenth Amendment of the Constitution."

The Court was saying that Congress, acting under the powers given it in § 5 of the Fourteenth Amendment, is limited to outlawing racially discriminatory acts by the state governments. Purely private acts of racial discrimination are beyond Congress' § 5 powers of redress, and outlawing private acts of racial discrimination, as of 1883, must be left to the tender mercies of state laws. Congress, of course, has since done exactly what the Civil Rights Act of 1875 did in its Civil Rights Act of 1964, invoking its powers not only under § 5 of the Fourteenth Amendment, but also under the Commerce Clause in Article 1 § 8.

The first Justice Harlan dissented, and he answered what he felt to be the majority's somewhat crabbed approach to the extent of Congress's § 5 powers:

> I cannot resist the conclusion [wrote Harlan] that the substance and spirit of the recent amendments of the Constitution [*i.e.*, the post Civil War Amendments] have been sacrificed by a subtle and ingenious criticism. It is not the words of the law but the internal sense of it that makes the law: the letter of the law is the body; the sense and reason of the law is the soul.

Perhaps a tactful way of suggesting that the majority had gutted the Fourteenth Amendment of its soul.

Under its powers under § 2 of the Thirteenth Amendment, Justice Bradley acknowledged, Congress can reach private activity: "The amendment is not a mere prohibition of State laws establishing or upholding slavery, but an absolute declaration that slavery or involuntary servitude shall not exist in any part of the United States." He also acknowledged, perhaps surprisingly, that the Thirteenth Amendment has an affirmative character to it: "It has a reflex character also, establishing and decreeing universal civil and political freedom throughout the United States." Moreover, he went on to assume that Congress, under § 2 of the Thirteenth Amendment, has the power to outlaw the "badges and incidents" of slavery. Writing for the majority, he even mentioned some of those badges and incidents, quoting from an 1866 Civil Rights Act: "the same right to make and enforce contracts, to sue, be parties, give evidence, and to inherit, purchase, lease, sell and convey property, as is enjoyed by white citizens." Those rights, the majority reasoned, are the ones that undo the badges and incidents of slavery — but the right to be free from racial discrimination in access to places of public accommodation, according to the Court in 1883, is not a right that undoes the badges and incidents of slavery. The Court's interesting explanation:

> It may be that by the Black Code (as it was called), in the times when slavery prevailed, the proprietors of inns and public conveyances were forbidden to receive persons of the African race, because it might assist slaves to escape from the control of their masters. This was merely a means of preventing such escapes, and was no part of the servitude itself.

There is one interesting suggestion from the majority opinion that seems to convey the idea that by 1883 the Court saw no further need for what today is referred to as "affirmative action":

> When a man has emerged from slavery, and by the aid of beneficent legislation has shaken off the inseparable concomitants of that state, there must be some stage in the progress of his elevation when he takes the rank of a mere citizen, and ceases to be the special favorite of the laws, and when his rights as a citizen, or a man, are to be protected in the ordinary modes by which other men's rights are protected.

What happened in the wake of that sentiment was the "separate-but-equal" doctrine, segregation, and another century of oppression.

Justice Harlan's dissent was more representative of the current approach in today's jurisprudence. What follows is perhaps the essence of Harlan's position:

> I hold [wrote Harlan] that since slavery, as the court has repeatedly declared, . . . was the moving or principal cause of the adoption of [the Thirteenth] amendment, and since that institution rested wholly upon the inferiority, as a race, of those held in bondage, their freedom necessarily involved immunity from, and protection against, all discrimination against them, because of their race, in respect of such civil rights as belong to freemen of other races. Congress, therefore, under its express power to enforce that amendment, by appropriate legislation, may enact laws to protect that people against the deprivation, *because of their race*, of any civil rights granted to other freemen in the same State; and such legislation may be of a direct and primary character, operating upon States, their officers and agents, and, also, upon, at least, such individuals and corporations as exercise public functions and wield power and authority under the State.

Harlan was not quite arguing that Congress can reach purely private acts of racial discrimination, although his use of the phrase "at least" suggests that he would be comfortable arguing for that proposition as well. His main contention was that Congress can outlaw racial discrimination by places of public accommodation because places of public accommodation "exercise public functions and wield power and authority under the State." He argued that public conveyances use public highways, innkeepers exercise "a quasi public employment," and places of public amusement are licensed by state law.

As you may have guessed, Justice Harlan's dissenting opinion on this point was, in our own time, to become the view of a majority of the members of the court, as indicated in the case that follows.

SHELLEY v. KRAEMER
334 U.S. 1 (1948)

Mr. Chief Justice Vinson delivered the opinion of the Court.

These cases present for our consideration questions relating to the validity of court enforcement of private agreements, generally described as restrictive covenants, which have as their purpose the exclusion of persons of designated race or color from the ownership or occupancy of real property. . . .

The first of these cases comes to this Court on certiorari to the Supreme Court of Missouri. On February 16, 1911, thirty out of a total of thirty-nine owners of property fronting both sides of Labadie Avenue between Taylor Avenue and Cora Avenue in the city of St. Louis, signed an agreement, which was subsequently recorded, providing in part:

> ". . . the said property is hereby restricted to the use and occupancy for
> the term of Fifty (50) years from this date, so that it shall be a condition all
> the time and whether recited and referred to as [*sic*] not in subsequent
> conveyances and shall attach to the land as a condition precedent to the sale
> of the same, that hereafter no part of said property or any portion thereof
> shall be, for said term of Fifty-years, occupied by any person not of the
> Caucasian race, it being intended hereby to restrict the use of said property
> for said period of time against the occupancy as owners or tenants of any
> portion of said property for resident or other purpose by people of the
> Negro or Mongolian Race."

*   *   *

The Supreme Court of Missouri . . . held the agreement effective and concluded that enforcement of its provisions violated no rights guaranteed to petitioners by the Federal Constitution. . . .

The second of the cases under consideration comes to this Court from the Supreme Court of Michigan. The circumstances presented do not differ materially from the Missouri case. . . .

*   *   *

Petitioners have placed primary reliance on their contentions, first raised in the state courts, that judicial enforcement of the restrictive agreements in these cases has violated rights guaranteed to petitioners by the Fourteenth Amendment of the Federal Constitution and Acts of Congress passed pursuant to that Amendment. Specifically, petitioners urge that they have been denied the equal protection of the laws. . . .

I.

Whether the equal protection clause of the Fourteenth Amendment inhibits judicial enforcement by state courts of restrictive covenants based on race or color is a question which this Court has not heretofore been called upon to consider. . . .

*   *   *

It should be observed that these covenants do not seek to proscribe any particular use of the affected properties. Use of the properties for residential occupancy, as such, is not forbidden. The restrictions of these agreements, rather, are directed toward a designated class of persons and seek to determine who may and who may not own or make use of the properties for residential purposes. . . .

It cannot be doubted that among the civil rights intended to be protected from discriminatory state action by the Fourteenth Amendment are the rights to acquire, enjoy, own and dispose of property. Equality in the enjoyment of property rights was regarded by the framers of that Amendment as an essential pre-condition to the realization of other basic civil rights and liberties which the Amendment was intended to guarantee. Thus, § 1978 of the Revised Statutes, derived from § 1 of the Civil Rights Act of 1866 which was enacted by Congress while the Fourteenth Amendment was also under consideration, provides:

> "All citizens of the United States shall have the same right, in every State
> and Territory, as is enjoyed by white citizens thereof to inherit, purchase,
> lease, sell, hold, and convey real and personal property." . . .

It is likewise clear that restrictions on the right of occupancy of the sort sought to be created by the private agreements in these cases could not be squared with the requirements of the Fourteenth Amendment if imposed by state statute or local ordinance. . . . In the case of *Buchanan v. Warley* [(1917)], a unanimous Court declared unconstitutional the provisions of a city ordinance which denied to colored persons the right to occupy houses in blocks in which the greater number of houses were occupied by white persons, and imposed similar restrictions on white persons with respect to blocks in which the greater number of houses were occupied by colored persons. During the course of the opinion in that case, this Court stated: "The Fourteenth Amendment and these statutes enacted in furtherance of its purpose operate to qualify and entitle a colored man to acquire property without state legislation discriminating against him solely because of color."

In *Harmon v. Tyler* (1927), a unanimous court, on the authority of *Buchanan v. Warley, supra,* declared invalid an ordinance which forbade any Negro to establish a home on any property in a white community or any white person to establish a home in a Negro community, "except on the written consent of a majority of the persons of the opposite race inhabiting such community or portion of the City to be affected."

*   *   *

But the present cases, unlike those just discussed, do not involve action by state legislatures or city councils. Here the particular patterns of discrimination and the areas in which the restrictions are to operate, are determined, in the first instance, by the terms of agreements among private individuals. Participation of the State consists in the enforcement of the restrictions so defined. The crucial issue with which we are here confronted is whether this distinction removes these cases from the operation of the prohibitory provisions of the Fourteenth Amendment.

Since the decision of this Court in the *Civil Rights Cases* (1883), the principle has become firmly embedded in our constitutional law that the action inhibited by the first section of the Fourteenth Amendment is only such action as may fairly be said to be that of the States. That Amendment erects no shield against merely private conduct, however discriminatory or wrongful.

We conclude, therefore, that the restrictive agreements standing alone cannot be regarded as violative of any rights guaranteed to petitioners by the Fourteenth Amendment. So long as the purposes of those agreements are effectuated by voluntary adherence to their terms, it would appear clear that there has been no action by the State and the provisions of the Amendment have not been violated.

But here there was more. These are cases in which the purposes of the agreements were secured only by judicial enforcement by state courts of the restrictive terms of the agreements. The respondents urge that judicial enforcement of private agreements does not amount to state action; or, in any event, the participation of the State is so attenuated in character as not to amount to state action within the meaning of the Fourteenth Amendment. Finally, it is suggested, even if the States in these cases may be deemed to have acted in the constitutional sense, their action did not deprive petitioners of rights guaranteed by the Fourteenth Amendment. We move to a consideration of these matters.

II.

That the action of state courts and judicial officers in their official capacities is to be regarded as action of the State within the meaning of the Fourteenth Amendment, is a proposition which has long been established by decisions of this Court. That principle was given expression in the earliest cases involving the construction of the terms of the Fourteenth Amendment. Thus, in *Virginia v. Rives* (1880), this Court stated: "It is doubtless true that a State may act through different agencies, — either by its legislative, its executive, or its judicial authorities; and the prohibitions of the amendment extend to all action of the State denying equal protection of the laws, whether it be action by one of these agencies or by another." In *Ex parte Virginia* (1880), the Court observed: "A State acts by its legislative, its executive, or its judicial authorities. It can act in no other way." In the *Civil Rights Cases* (1883), this Court pointed out that the Amendment makes void "State action of every kind" which is inconsistent with the guaranties therein contained, and extends to manifestations of "State authority in the shape of laws, customs, or judicial or executive proceedings." . . .

Similar expressions, giving specific recognition to the fact that judicial action is to be regarded as action of the State for the purposes of the Fourteenth Amendment, are to be found in numerous cases which have been more recently decided. In *Twining v. New Jersey* (1908), the Court said: "The judicial act of the highest court of the State, in authoritatively construing and enforcing its laws, is the act of the State." In *Brinkerhoff-Faris Trust & Savings Co. v. Hill* (1930), the Court, through Mr. Justice Brandeis, stated: "The federal guaranty of due process extends to state action through its judicial as well as through its legislative, executive or administrative branch of government." . . .

One of the earliest applications of the prohibitions contained in the Fourteenth Amendment to action of state judicial officials occurred in cases in which Negroes had been excluded from jury service in criminal prosecutions by reason of their race or color. These cases demonstrate, also, the early recognition by this Court that state action in violation of the Amendment's provisions is equally repugnant to the constitutional commands whether directed by state statute or taken by a judicial official in the absence of statute. Thus, in *Strauder v. West Virginia* (1880), this Court declared invalid a state statute restricting jury service to white persons as amounting to a denial of the equal protection of the laws to the colored defendant in that case. In the same volume of the reports, the Court in *Ex parte Virginia, supra*, held that a similar discrimination imposed by the action of a state judge denied rights protected by the Amendment, despite the fact that the language of the state statute relating to jury service contained no such restrictions.

The action of state courts in imposing penalties or depriving parties of other substantive rights without providing adequate notice and opportunity to defend, has, of course, long been regarded as a denial of the due process of law guaranteed by the Fourteenth Amendment.

* * *

But the examples of state judicial action which have been held by this Court to violate the Amendment's commands are not restricted to situations in which the judicial proceedings were found in some manner to be procedurally unfair. It has been recognized that the action of state courts in enforcing a substantive common-law rule formulated by those courts, may result in the denial of rights guaranteed by the Fourteenth Amendment, even though the judicial proceedings in such cases may have been in complete accord with the most rigorous conceptions of procedural due process. Thus, in *American Federation of Labor v. Swing* (1941), enforcement by state courts of the common-law policy of the State, which resulted in the restraining of peaceful picketing, was held to be state action of the sort prohibited by the Amendment's guaranties of freedom of discussion. In *Cantwell v. Connecticut* (1940), a conviction in a state court of the common-law crime of breach of the peace was, under the circumstances of the case, found to be a violation of the Amendment's commands relating to freedom of religion. In *Bridges v. California* (1941), enforcement of the state's common-law rule relating to contempts by publication was held to be state action inconsistent with the prohibitions of the Fourteenth Amendment.

The short of the matter is that from the time of the adoption of the Fourteenth Amendment until the present, it has been the consistent ruling of this Court that the action of the States to which the Amendment has reference includes action of state courts and state judicial officials. . . .

III.

*   *   *

We have no doubt that there has been state action in these cases in the full and complete sense of the phrase. The undisputed facts disclose that petitioners were willing purchasers of properties upon which they desired to establish homes. The owners of the properties were willing sellers; and contracts of sale were accordingly consummated. It is clear that but for the active intervention of the state courts, supported by the full panoply of state power, petitioners would have been free to occupy the properties in question without restraint.

These are not cases, as has been suggested, in which the States have merely abstained from action, leaving private individuals free to impose such discriminations as they see fit. Rather, these are cases in which the States have made available to such individuals the full coercive power of government to deny to petitioners, on the grounds of race or color, the enjoyment of property rights in premises which petitioners are willing and financially able to acquire and which the grantors are willing to sell. The difference between judicial enforcement and non-enforcement of the restrictive covenants is the difference to petitioners between being denied rights of property available to other members of the community and being accorded full enjoyment of those rights on an equal footing.

*   *   *

We hold that in granting judicial enforcement of the restrictive agreements in these cases, the States have denied petitioners the equal protection of the laws and that, therefore, the action of the state courts cannot stand. We have noted that freedom from discrimination by the States in the enjoyment of property rights was among the basic objectives sought to be effectuated by the framers of the Fourteenth Amendment. That such discrimination has occurred in these cases is clear. Because of the race or color of these petitioners they have been denied rights of ownership or occupancy enjoyed as a matter of course by other citizens of different race or color. The Fourteenth Amendment declares "that all persons, whether colored or white, shall stand equal before the laws of the States, and, in regard to the colored race, for whose protection the amendment was primarily designed, that no discrimination shall be made against them by law because of their color.". . . Nor may the discriminations imposed by the state courts in these cases be justified as proper exertions of state police power.

Respondents urge, however, that since the state courts stand ready to enforce restrictive covenants excluding white persons from the ownership or occupancy of property covered by such agreements, enforcement of covenants excluding colored persons may not be deemed a denial of equal protection of the laws to the colored persons who are thereby affected. This contention does not bear scrutiny. The parties have directed our attention to no case in which a court, state or federal, has been called upon to enforce a covenant excluding members of the white majority from ownership or occupancy of real property on grounds of race or color. But there are more fundamental considerations. The rights created by the first section of the Fourteenth Amendment are, by its terms, guaranteed to the individual. The rights established are personal rights. It is, therefore, no answer to these petitioners to say that the courts may also be induced to deny white persons rights of ownership and occupancy on grounds of race or color. Equal protection of the laws is not achieved through indiscriminate imposition of inequalities.

Nor do we find merit in the suggestion that property owners who are parties to these agreements are denied equal protection of the laws if denied access to the courts to enforce the terms of restrictive covenants and to assert property rights which the state courts have held to be created by such agreements. The Constitution confers upon no individual the right to demand action by the State which results in the denial of equal protection of the laws to other individuals. And it would appear beyond question that the power of the State to create and enforce property interests must be exercised within the boundaries defined by the Fourteenth Amendment.

* * *

The historical context in which the Fourteenth Amendment became a part of the Constitution should not be forgotten. Whatever else the framers sought to achieve, it is clear that the matter of primary concern was the establishment of equality in the enjoyment of basic civil and political rights and the preservation of those rights from discriminatory action on the part of the States based on considerations of race or color. Seventy-five years ago this Court announced that the provisions of the Amendment are to be construed with this fundamental purpose in mind. Upon full consideration, we have concluded that in these cases the States have acted to deny petitioners the equal protection of the laws guaranteed by the Fourteenth Amendment. . . .

* * *

Mr. Justice Reed, Mr. Justice Jackson, and Mr. Justice Rutledge took no part in the consideration or decision of these cases.

NOTES AND QUESTIONS

1. Do you understand why enforcement by the state courts of racially-restrictive covenants is "state action" within the meaning of the Fourteenth Amendment? Is this what you suppose the framers of the Fourteenth Amendment had in mind? There is no denying that when the courts are used to enforce racially-restrictive covenants, they have been used as instruments for employing "the full coercive power of government to deny to petitioners, on the grounds of race or color, the enjoyment of property rights in premises which petitioners are willing and financially able to acquire and which the grantors are willing to sell." 334 U.S. at 19. There is also no denying that at the time the Fourteenth Amendment was passed, "the matter of primary concern was the establishment of equality in the enjoyment of basic civil and political rights and the preservation of those rights from discriminatory action on the part of the States based on considerations of race or color." *Id.* at 23. Does it necessarily follow, however, that the Fourteenth Amendment prohibits the use of the courts by individuals who seek racially to discriminate? Would it have been clearer if the Amendment had stated "No *person*

. . . shall deny to any person . . . the equal protection of the laws"? Is there force in the claim that so long as whites may be discriminated against as well by racially-restrictive covenants, there is no equal protection problem?

2.   The court concludes that there is no violation of the Fourteenth Amendment when parties agree to racially restrictive covenants, but only when they seek to use the courts to enforce such agreements. But if such agreements are not unconstitutional when made, why do they violate the Constitution when they are enforced? Indeed, if they cannot be enforced in the courts, can they really be regarded as binding contracts? Could the meaning of the Fourteenth Amendment be that individuals are free to discriminate and can use the courts to effect that discrimination, though legislators may not pass discriminatory legislation? This was the conclusion apparently reached in a famous critique of *Shelley v. Kraemer*, Herbert Wechsler, *Toward Neutral Principles of Constitutional Law*, 73 HARV. L. REV. 1 (1959). Professor Wechsler asked, "[a]ssuming that the Constitution speaks to state discrimination on the ground of race but not to such discrimination by an individual . . . , why is the enforcement of the private covenant a state discrimination rather than a legal recognition of the freedom of the individual?" *Id.* at 29. Can you answer Wechsler's question?

3.   One analyst of the opinion, apparently conceding Wechsler's point, stated that "[t]he facts surrounding the covenant cases, however, suggest that in enforcing the racial covenants the states did more than provide neutral enforcement of private contracts, but had, in fact, adopted policies of racial residential segregation in the supposed interests of protecting property values, suppressing crime, and promoting racial purity." Francis A. Allen, Shelley v. Kramer, *in* THE OXFORD COMPANION TO THE SUPREME COURT OF THE UNITED STATES 781 (Kermit L. Hall et al. eds., 1992). Should this make a difference in your view of the case? Allen further notes that "[u]nfortunately these matters were not fully canvassed in the Court's opinion, nor were adequate indicia suggested to determine the point at which enforcement of private agreements becomes transmuted into state action to advance public policies." *Id.* You may have noticed that these matters were not "canvassed" at all in the Court's opinion that you have read, but do you agree with Allen's observation that "adequate indicia" of the public/private distinction were not provided? Allen still concludes that the opinion was "an important event in modern constitutional history." *Id.* at 782. Why do you suppose that was, and do you agree?

4.   *Shelley* is not the only case to find state action on the basis of entanglement. All of these cases are premised on the fact that the government is somehow authorizing, encouraging, or facilitating private conduct that, if performed directly by government, would violate the Constitution. Other judicial activities beyond the peremptory and covenant contexts already studied include use of judicial process in the context of pre-judgment attachment. *Lugar v. Edmonson Oil Co.*, 457 U.S. 922 (1982) (due process required to be observed where state law creates attachment privilege and sheriff enforces it on behalf of private party). It is less clear whether government licensing is sufficient entanglement. In an early case, *Burton v. Wilmington Parking Authority*, 365 U.S. 715 (1961), the Court found a "symbiotic relationship" between a private discriminating restaurant in a public building. The government was partially dependent upon the revenue of the restaurant. However, in *Moose Lodge Number 107 v. Irvis*, 407 U.S. 163 (1972), the Court found the mere

grant of liquor license to a discriminating private club did not make the club a state actor. Similarly, licensed television stations can refuse to accept advertisements on the basis of content without violating the First Amendment. *Columbia Broad. Sys. v. Democratic Nat'l Comm.*, 412 U.S. 94 (1972). And private utilities operating with a state charter can terminate service for nonpayment without the provision of notice and hearing. *Jackson v. Metropolitan Edison Co.*, 419 U.S. 345 (1974).

State law, however, cannot encourage private discriminatory behavior. In *Reitman v. Mulkey*, 387 U.S. 369 (1967), the Court invalidated a California initiative that authorized total private discretion in the sale or lease of real property. This, reasoned the Court, would too greatly implicate the courts in private racial discrimination. However, another California initiative prohibiting school busing unless needed to remedy a Fourteenth Amendment violation was upheld because it did not impede remedies required by the Constitution. *Crawford v. Board of Education*, 458 U.S. 527 (1982).

5. In *Edmonson v. Leesville Concrete Co., Inc.*, 500 U.S. 614 (1991), Justice Kennedy, for a 6-3 Court, held that private attorneys in civil litigation between private parties could not use their peremptory challenges to strike prospective jurors based on race. The Court had previously held race-based peremptory challenges by a government prosecutor to violate the Equal Protection rights of jurors, *see Batson v. Kentucky*, 476 U.S. 79 (1986), but Justice Kennedy rightly pointed out that whether "an act violates the Constitution when committed by a government official . . . does not answer the question whether the same act offends constitutional guarantees if committed by a private litigant or his attorney." Is there a difference between the use of peremptory challenges by the government prosecutor — clearly a state actor — and a private attorney representing private clients? Here is the test the Court applied to determine whether action by a private actor should be deemed state action for purposes of the Fourteenth Amendment:

> Our precedents establish that, in determining whether a particular action or course of conduct is governmental in character, it is relevant to examine the following: the extent to which the actor relies on governmental assistance and benefits; whether the actor is performing a traditional governmental function; and whether the injury caused is aggravated in a unique way by the incidents of governmental authority. . . .

Justice Kennedy thought the involvement of the court in the jury selection process, and of the legislature in authorizing peremptory challenges in the first place, to be enough to bring the private attorney's actions under the state action umbrella, and that the race-based peremptories violated the equal protection rights of jurors.

Justice O'Connor, joined by Chief Justice Rehnquist and Justice Scalia, dissented:

> Not everything that happens in a courtroom is state action. A trial, particularly a civil trial is by design largely a stage on which private parties may act; it is a forum through which they can resolve their disputes in a peaceful and ordered manner. The government erects the platform; it does not thereby become responsible for all that occurs upon it. As much as we would like to eliminate completely from the courtroom the specter of racial

discrimination, the Constitution does not sweep that broadly. Because I believe that a peremptory strike by a private litigant is fundamentally a matter of private choice and not state action, I dissent.

Justice Scalia also noted in a separate dissenting opinion that the Court's new rule "will not necessarily be a net help rather than hindrance to minority litigants in obtaining racially diverse juries. In criminal cases, *Batson v. Kentucky* (1986), already prevents the *prosecution* from using race-based strikes. The effect of today's decision (which logically must apply to criminal prosecutions) will be to prevent the *defendant* from doing so — so that the minority defendant can no longer seek to prevent an all-white jury, or to seat as many jurors of his own race as possible."

6. In *Johnson v. California*, 545 U.S. 162 (2005), the Court elaborated upon *Batson*, finding that California case law which required an initial showing of a "strong likelihood that a peremptory was based upon a group rather than an individual basis," was inconsistent with the simple inference articulated as sufficient to raise the objection in *Batson*. Johnson, a black man, had been convicted of murdering a 19-month-old white child. The prosecutor used three peremptories to strike the three blacks in the jury pool. Reviewing the record, but not asking the prosecutor for an explanation, the trial judge was satisfied that there were race-neutral reasons for the strikes. The California Supreme Court agreed, but an 8-1 opinion by Justice Stevens reversed. The Court summarized the *Batson* procedure as: "First, the defendant must make out a prima facie case 'by showing that the totality of the relevant facts gives rise to an inference of discriminatory purpose.' citing *Washington v. Davis* (1976). Second, once the defendant has made out a prima facie case, the 'burden shifts to the State to explain adequately the racial exclusion.' Third, '[i]f a race-neutral explanation is tendered, the trial court must then decide . . . whether the opponent of the strike has proved purposeful racial discrimination.' " The California "strong likelihood" or "more likely than not" initial step was too rigorous. The Court said that it "assumed in *Batson* that the trial judge would have the benefit of all relevant circumstances, including the prosecutor's explanation, before deciding whether it was more likely than not that the challenge was improperly motivated. We did not intend the first step to be so onerous that a defendant would have to persuade the judge — on the basis of all the facts, some of which are impossible for the defendant to know with certainty — that the challenge was more likely than not the product of purposeful discrimination. Instead, a defendant satisfies the requirements of *Batson*'s first step by producing evidence sufficient to permit the trial judge to draw an inference that discrimination has occurred." The ultimate burden of persuasion with regard to the challenged strike is on the defendant. In a short dissent, Justice Thomas would have given California and the states more latitude to decide how best to decide if a strike was improperly made. Said Justice Thomas: "According to *Batson*, the Equal Protection Clause requires that prosecutors select juries based on factors other than race — not that litigants bear particular burdens of proof or persuasion."

7. Why is the use of race-based peremptory challenges "state action" as that term is understood in the Fourteenth Amendment? Would Justice Harlan have agreed? How, if at all, does this affect the holding in the *Civil Rights Cases*? Are race-based peremptories closer to state action than the conduct rejected as state action in the *Civil Rights Cases*? Undeniably there is some government action involved here, as the majority points out. Is it as *de minimus* as Justice O'Connor suggests in her dissent?

8.   What do you make of the institution of peremptory challenges itself? Is it something that should be encouraged? Do you understand the argument that peremptory challenges contribute to the perceived "fairness" of a trial? Are there different implications with regard to barring race-based peremptories in criminal trials as opposed to civil trials? In which are they the more odious? Clarence Thomas, currently the only black Justice on the Supreme Court, and a one-time champion of natural law, has spoken out strongly against the holdings rejecting race-based peremptories, *especially* in criminal trials. Why do you suppose that is?

9.   The majority was striving, through its rejection of race-based peremptories, to build a color-blind society, or at least to lessen the amount of state-sanctioned racial discrimination. This is obviously a worthy goal. Is it furthered by the majority's decision? Justice O'Connor has been a strong foe of racial classifications drawn by governmental bodies (even those which favor racial minorities). Why might even she oppose barring race-based peremptories? In the case, Justice Scalia opined that the costs of banning race-based peremptories far outweigh the benefits. Was he correct?

10.   In *Felkner v. Jackson*, 131 S. Ct. 1305, 179 L. Ed. 2d 374 (2011), the Court, in a *per curiam* opinion in a case in which a California trial judge had accepted a prosecutor's proffered race-neutral explanations for striking several black jurors, and the state's appellate courts, as well as the lower federal court on habeas corpus, had upheld the trial judge, reversed the Ninth Circuit's flimsily explained reversal of the lower federal court. The Court reasoned that a trial court's determination on the issue of proffered race-neutral explanations is entitled to great deference and must be sustained unless it is clearly erroneous.

11.   By now, you realize that the Constitution's protection of equal protection — like other provisions of the Fourteenth Amendment — textually only limits the government. However, over time, as the *Edmonson* case reflects, the Court has developed a number of doctrines treating private individuals as if they were state actors. If a private entity has been given a public function or it has become too entangled with government activity, it may be treated as a state actor. *Edmonson* is built on both of these foundations. The public function doctrine is premised on the belief that the government ought not to avoid the strictures of the Constitution merely by contracting its duty to the private sector. The public function exception originated with *Marsh v. Alabama*, 326 U.S. 501 (1946), where a private company town performing virtually all municipal duties was precluded from excluding religious leafletters exercising their First Amendment rights. In addition, the Court invalidated several attempts to allow private political bodies to discriminate on the basis of race. *Smith v. Allwright*, 321 U.S. 649 (1944) (the Democratic party of Texas, a private entity, could not conduct discriminatory primary elections). *See also Terry v. Adams*, 345 U.S. 461 (1953) (holding that the rule stated in *Allwright* could not be avoided by conducting a pre-primary through a private group called the Jaybirds).

To be a public function, it must be the type of activity that is *exclusively* run by the government. Thus, in *Rendell-Baker v. Kohn*, 457 U.S. 830 (1982), the Court refused to find a private school to be a state actor, in part, because schooling has never been an exclusive government function; indeed, just the opposite, public schools were the Johnny-come-latelys. The *Kohn* case also involved the question of whether the receipt of government funding makes a private entity into a state actor. *Kohn* held that it did not, however, the case is in tension with *Norwood v. Harrison*, 413 U.S. 455 (1973), finding it unconstitutional for a state to provide textbooks to a discriminatory private school. Effectively, *Norwood* meant the school, a private entity, had to stop discriminating if it wanted the state textbooks, and in this sense, the equal protection requirement was extended to the private sector. Of course, the restriction on the private school is derivative of the prohibition of the state. In *Kohn* there was no state activity to directly restrict, since the issue was whether a private school could fire a teacher on speech grounds.

12. In *Brentwood Academy v. Tennessee*, 531 U.S. 288 (2001), the Court addressed the issue of whether a statewide association incorporated to regulate interscholastic athletic competition among public and private secondary schools may be regarded as engaging in state action when it enforces a rule against a member school. 5-4, the Court, per Justice Souter, held that since the association in question here includes most public schools located within the state, acts through their representatives, draws it officers from them, is largely funded by their dues and income received in their stead, and has historically been seen to regulate in lieu of the State Board of Education's exercise of its own authority, the association's regulatory activity may and should be treated as state action. Justice Souter summarized these factors as "pervasive entwinement of state school officials in the structure of the association." Justice Souter described the Court's obligation as directed at not only to " 'preserv[e] an area of individual freedom by limiting the reach of federal law' and avoi[d] the imposition of responsibility on a State for conduct it could not control," but also to assure that constitutional standards are invoked "when it can be said that the State is *responsible* for the specific conduct of which the plaintiff complains."

The Court opined that what is fairly attributable to the state is a matter of normative judgment, and the criteria lack rigid simplicity. And by now, you certainly appreciate the fluidity of the Court's state action inquiries. According to the Justices, they have treated a nominally private entity as a state actor when it is controlled by an "agency of the State," when it has been delegated a public function by the state, *cf., Edmonson v Leesville Concrete Co.* (1991), when it is "entwined with governmental policies" or when government is "entwined in [its] management or control." Nevertheless, the *Brentwood* case stands in some tension with a previous decision in which the Court held that the National Collegiate Athletic Association (NCAA) was not a state actor. *National Collegiate Athletic Assoc. v. Tarkanian* (1988).

Tarkanian arose when an undoubted state actor, the University of Nevada, suspended its basketball coach, Tarkanian, in order to comply with rules and recommendations of the NCAA. The coach charged the NCAA with state action, arguing that the state university had delegated its own functions to the NCAA, clothing the latter with the authority to make and apply the university's rules, the result being joint action making the NCAA a state actor, but the Court disagreed. Nevertheless, the majority in *Brentwood* saw a difference: the NCAA's policies were shaped not by the University of Nevada alone, but by several hundred member organizations, most of them having no connection with Nevada, and exhibiting no color of Nevada law. It was difficult to see the NCAA as anything other than a collective membership, and not as surrogate for the one state. There was, however, this dictum in *Tarkanian*: "The situation would, of course, be different if the [Association's] membership consisted entirely of institutions located within the same State, many of them public institutions created by the same sovereign."

Justice Thomas, writing with the Chief Justice, and Justices Scalia and Kennedy in dissent noted that the Court had never found state action based upon mere "entwinement." Until *Brentwood*, they said, a private organization's acts constituted state action only when the organization performed a public function; was created, coerced, or encouraged by the government; or acted in a symbiotic relationship with the government. To the dissent, the majority's holding that the private association's enforcement of its recruiting rule was state action not only extends state-action doctrine beyond its permissible limits but also encroaches upon the realm of individual freedom that the doctrine was meant to protect.

The dissent also laments that the majority never defines "entwinement," and that the scope of its holding is unclear. While the dissenters thought the development of this new theory was fact-specific analysis having little bearing beyond that case, they also worried that if the entwinement test develops in future years, it could affect many organizations that foster activities, enforce rules, and sponsor extra-curricular competition among high schools — not just in athletics, but in such diverse areas as agriculture, mathematics, music, marching bands, forensics, and cheerleading. Indeed, this entwinement test may extend to other organizations that are composed of, or controlled by, public officials or public entities, such as firefighters, policemen, teachers, cities, or counties.

13. With *Shelley* and *Edmonson*, we get expansive readings of state action that are similar in spirit to Justice Harlan's opinion in the *Civil Rights Cases*. Are there any limits to what is now construed as state action? Consider the heart-wrenching case which follows.

DESHANEY v. WINNEBAGO COUNTY DEPARTMENT OF SOCIAL SERVICES
489 U.S. 189 (1989)

CHIEF JUSTICE REHNQUIST delivered the opinion of the Court.

Petitioner is a boy who was beaten and permanently injured by his father, with whom he lived. Respondents are social workers and other local officials who received complaints that petitioner was being abused by his father and had reason to believe that this was the case, but nonetheless did not act to remove petitioner from his father's custody. Petitioner sued respondents claiming that their failure to act deprived him of his liberty in violation of the Due Process Clause of the Fourteenth Amendment to the United States Constitution. We hold that it did not.

I

The facts of this case are undeniably tragic. Petitioner Joshua DeShaney was born in 1979. In 1980, a Wyoming court granted his parents a divorce and awarded custody of Joshua to his father, Randy DeShaney. The father shortly thereafter moved to Neenah, a city located in Winnebago County, Wisconsin, taking the infant Joshua with him. There he entered into a second marriage, which also ended in divorce.

The Winnebago County authorities first learned that Joshua DeShaney might be a victim of child abuse in January 1982, when his father's second wife complained to the police, at the time of their divorce, that he had previously "hit the boy causing marks and [was] a prime case for child abuse." The Winnebago County Department of Social Services (DSS) interviewed the father, but he denied the accusations, and DSS did not pursue them further. In January 1983, Joshua was admitted to a local hospital with multiple bruises and abrasions. The examining physician suspected child abuse and notified DSS, which immediately obtained an order from a Wisconsin juvenile court placing Joshua in the temporary custody of the hospital. Three days later, the county convened an ad hoc "Child Protection Team" — consisting of a pediatrician, a psychologist, a police detective, the county's lawyer, several DSS caseworkers, and various hospital personnel — to consider Joshua's situation. At this meeting, the Team decided that there was insufficient evidence of child abuse to retain Joshua in the custody of the court. The Team did, however, decide to recommend several measures to protect Joshua, including enrolling him in a preschool program, providing his father with certain counselling services, and encouraging his father's girlfriend to move out of the home. Randy DeShaney entered into a voluntary agreement with DSS in which he promised to cooperate with them in accomplishing these goals.

Based on the recommendation of the Child Protection Team, the juvenile court dismissed the child protection case and returned Joshua to the custody of his father. A month later, emergency room personnel called the DSS caseworker handling Joshua's case to report that he had once again been treated for suspicious injuries. The caseworker concluded that there was no basis for action. For the next six months, the caseworker made monthly visits to the DeShaney home, during which she observed a number of suspicious injuries on Joshua's head; she also noticed that he had not been enrolled in school, and that the girlfriend had not moved out. The caseworker dutifully recorded these incidents in her files, along with her continuing suspicions that someone in the DeShaney household was physically abusing Joshua, but she did nothing more. In November 1983, the emergency room notified DSS that Joshua had been treated once again for injuries that they believed to be caused by child abuse. On the caseworker's next two visits to the DeShaney home, she was told that Joshua was too ill to see her. Still DSS took no action.

In March 1984, Randy DeShaney beat 4-year-old Joshua so severely that he fell into a life-threatening coma. Emergency brain surgery revealed a series of hemorrhages caused by traumatic injuries to the head inflicted over a long period of time. Joshua did not die, but he suffered brain damage so severe that he is expected to spend the rest of his life confined to an institution for the profoundly retarded. Randy DeShaney was subsequently tried and convicted of child abuse.

Joshua and his mother brought this action under 42 U.S.C. § 1983 in the United States District Court for the Eastern District of Wisconsin against respondents Winnebago County, DSS, and various individual employees of DSS. The complaint alleged that respondents had deprived Joshua of his liberty without due process of law, in violation of his rights under the Fourteenth Amendment, by failing to intervene to protect him against a risk of violence at his father's hands of which they knew or should have known. The District Court granted summary judgment for respondents.

The Court of Appeals for the Seventh Circuit affirmed. . . .

*   *   *

II

The Due Process Clause of the Fourteenth Amendment provides that "[n]o State shall . . . deprive any person of life, liberty, or property, without due process of law." Petitioners contend that the State deprived Joshua of his liberty interest in "free[dom] from . . . unjustified intrusions on personal security," by failing to provide him with adequate protection against his father's violence. The claim is one invoking the substantive rather than the procedural component of the Due Process Clause; petitioners do not claim that the State denied Joshua protection without according him appropriate procedural safeguards, but that it was categorically obligated to protect him in these circumstances.

But nothing in the language of the Due Process Clause itself requires the State to protect the life, liberty, and property of its citizens against invasion by private actors. The Clause is phrased as a limitation on the State's power to act, not as a guarantee of certain minimal levels of safety and security. It forbids the State itself to deprive individuals of life, liberty, or property without "due process of law," but its language cannot fairly be extended to impose an affirmative obligation on the State to ensure that those interests do not come to harm through other means. Nor does history support such an expansive reading of the constitutional text. Like its counterpart in the Fifth Amendment, the Due Process Clause of the Fourteenth Amendment was intended to prevent government "from abusing [its] power, or employing it as an instrument of oppression." Its purpose was to protect the people from the State, not to ensure that the State protected them from each other. The Framers were content to leave the extent of governmental obligation in the latter area to the democratic political processes.

Consistent with these principles, our cases have recognized that the Due Process Clauses generally confer no affirmative right to governmental aid, even where such aid may be necessary to secure life, liberty, or property interests of which the government itself may not deprive the individual. *e.g., Harris v. McRae* (1980) (no obligation to fund abortions or other medical services) . . . ; *Lindsey v. Normet* (1972) (no obligation to provide adequate housing). . . . As we said in *Harris v. McRae*: "Although the liberty protected by the Due Process Clause affords protection against unwarranted *government* interference . . . , it does not confer an entitlement to such [governmental aid] as may be necessary to realize all the advantages of that freedom." (emphasis added). If the Due Process Clause does not require the State to provide its citizens with particular protective services, it follows that the State cannot be held liable under the Clause for injuries that could have been averted had it chosen to provide them. As a general matter, then, we conclude that a State's failure to protect an individual against private violence simply does not constitute a violation of the Due Process Clause.

Petitioners contend, however, that even if the Due Process Clause imposes no affirmative obligation on the State to provide the general public with adequate protective services, such a duty may arise out of certain "special relationships" created or assumed by the State with respect to particular individuals. Petitioners argue that such a "special relationship" existed here because the State knew that Joshua faced a special danger of abuse at his father's hands, and specifically proclaimed, by word and by deed, its intention to protect him against that danger. Having actually undertaken to protect Joshua from this danger — which petitioners concede the State played no part in creating — the State acquired an affirmative "duty," enforceable through the Due Process Clause, to do so in a reasonably competent fashion. Its failure to discharge that duty, so the argument goes, was an abuse of governmental power that so "shocks the conscience," *Rochin v. California* (1952), as to constitute a substantive due process violation.

We reject this argument. It is true that in certain limited circumstances the Constitution imposes upon the State affirmative duties of care and protection with respect to particular individuals. In *Estelle v. Gamble* (1976), we recognized that the Eighth Amendment's prohibition against cruel and unusual punishment, made applicable to the States through the Fourteenth Amendment's Due Process Clause, *Robinson v. California* (1962), requires the State to provide adequate medical care to incarcerated prisoners. We reasoned that because the prisoner is unable " 'by reason of the deprivation of his liberty [to] care for himself,' " it is only " 'just' " that the State be required to care for him.

In *Youngberg v. Romeo* (1982), we extended this analysis beyond the Eighth Amendment setting, holding that the substantive component of the Fourteenth Amendment's Due Process Clause requires the State to provide involuntarily committed mental patients with such services as are necessary to ensure their "reasonable safety" from themselves and others. As we explained: "If it is cruel and unusual punishment to hold convicted criminals in unsafe conditions, it must be unconstitutional [under the Due Process Clause] to confine the involuntarily committed — who may not be punished at all — in unsafe conditions."

But these cases afford petitioners no help. Taken together, they stand only for the proposition that when the State takes a person into its custody and holds him there against his will, the Constitution imposes upon it a corresponding duty to assume some responsibility for his safety and general well-being. The rationale for this principle is simple enough: when the State by the affirmative exercise of its power so restrains an individual's liberty that it renders him unable to care for himself, and at the same time fails to provide for his basic human needs — *e.g.*, food, clothing, shelter, medical care, and reasonable safety — it transgresses the substantive limits on state action set by the Eighth Amendment and the Due Process Clause. The affirmative duty to protect arises not from the State's knowledge of the individual's predicament or from its expressions of intent to help him, but from the limitation which it has imposed on his freedom to act on his own behalf. In the substantive due process analysis, it is the State's affirmative act of restraining the individual's freedom to act on his own behalf — through incarceration, institutionalization, or other similar restraint of personal liberty — which is the "deprivation of liberty" triggering the protections of the Due Process Clause, not its failure to act to protect his liberty interests against harms inflicted by other means.

The *Estelle-Youngberg* analysis simply has no applicability in the present case. . . .

It may well be that, by voluntarily undertaking to protect Joshua against a danger it concededly played no part in creating, the State acquired a duty under state tort law to provide him with adequate protection against that danger. See RESTATEMENT (SECOND) OF TORTS § 323 (1965) (one who undertakes to render services to another may in some circumstances be held liable for doing so in a negligent fashion). . . . But the claim here is based on the Due Process Clause of the Fourteenth Amendment, which, as we have said many times, does not transform every tort committed by a state actor into a constitutional violation. . . .

*   *   *

The people of Wisconsin may well prefer a system of liability which would place upon the State and its officials the responsibility for failure to act in situations such as the present one. They may create such a system, if they do not have it already, by changing the tort law of the State in accordance with the regular lawmaking process. But they should not have it thrust upon them by this Court's expansion of the Due Process Clause of the Fourteenth Amendment.

Affirmed.

JUSTICE BRENNAN, with whom JUSTICE MARSHALL and JUSTICE BLACKMUN join, dissenting.

"The most that can be said of the state functionaries in this case," the Court today concludes, "is that they stood by and did nothing when suspicious circumstances dictated a more active role for them." Because I believe that this description of respondents' conduct tells only part of the story and that, accordingly, the Constitution itself "dictated a more active role" for respondents in the circumstances presented here, I cannot agree that respondents had no constitutional duty to help Joshua DeShaney.

It may well be, as the Court decides, that the Due Process Clause as construed by our prior cases creates no general right to basic governmental services. That however, is not the question presented here. . . . No one . . . has asked the Court to proclaim that, as a general matter, the Constitution safeguards positive as well as negative liberties.

*   *   *

The Court's baseline is the absence of positive rights in the Constitution and a concomitant suspicion of any claim that seems to depend on such rights. From this perspective, the DeShaneys' claim is first and foremost about inaction (the failure, here, of respondents to take steps to protect Joshua), and only tangentially about action (the establishment of a state program specifically designed to help children like Joshua). And from this perspective, holding these Wisconsin officials liable — where the only difference between this case and one involving a general claim to protective services is Wisconsin's establishment and operation of a program to protect children — would seem to punish an effort that we should seek to promote.

I would begin from the opposite direction. I would focus first on the action that Wisconsin *has* taken with respect to Joshua and children like him, rather than on the actions that the State failed to take. Such a method is not new to this Court. Both *Estelle v. Gamble* (1976), and *Youngberg v. Romeo* (1982), began by emphasizing that the States [had confined J.W. Gamble to prison and Nicholas Romeo to a psychiatric hospital]. This initial action rendered these people helpless to help themselves or to seek help from persons unconnected to the government. Cases from the lower courts also recognize that a State's actions can be decisive in assessing the constitutional significance of subsequent inaction. For these purposes, moreover, actual physical restraint is not the only state action that has been considered relevant. *See, e.g., White v. Rochford* (7th Cir. 1979) (police officers violated due process when, after arresting the guardian of three young children, they abandoned the children on a busy stretch of highway at night).

Because of the Court's initial fixation on the general principle that the Constitution does not establish positive rights, it is unable to appreciate our recognition in *Estelle* and *Youngberg* that this principle does not hold true in all circumstances. Thus, in the Court's view, *Youngberg* can be explained (and dismissed) in the following way: "In the substantive due process analysis, it is the State's affirmative act of restraining the individual's freedom to act on his own behalf — through incarceration, institutionalization, or other similar restraint of personal liberty — which is the 'deprivation of liberty' triggering the protections of the Due Process Clause, not its failure to act to protect his liberty interests against harms inflicted by other means." This restatement of *Youngberg*'s holding should come as a surprise when one recalls our explicit observation in that case that Romeo did not challenge his commitment to the hospital, but instead "argue[d] that he ha[d] a constitutionally protected liberty interest in safety, freedom of movement, and training within the institution; and that petitioners infringed these rights *by failing to provide* constitutionally required conditions of confinement." (emphasis added). I do not mean to suggest that "the State's affirmative act of restraining the individual's freedom to act on his own behalf," was irrelevant in *Youngberg*; rather, I emphasize that this conduct would have led to no injury, and consequently no cause of action under § 1983, unless the State then had failed to take steps to protect Romeo from himself and from others. In addition, the Court's exclusive attention to state-imposed restraints of "the individual's freedom to act on his own behalf," suggests that it was the State that rendered Romeo unable to care for himself, whereas in fact — with an I.Q. of between 8 and 10, and the mental capacity of an 18-month-old child — he had been quite incapable of taking care of himself long before the State stepped into his life. Thus, the fact of hospitalization was critical in *Youngberg* not because it rendered Romeo helpless to help himself, but because it separated him from other sources of aid that, we held, the State was obligated to replace. Unlike the Court, therefore, I am unable to see in *Youngberg* a neat and decisive divide between action and inaction.

Moreover, to the Court, the only fact that seems to count as an "affirmative act of restraining the individual's freedom to act on his own behalf" is direct physical control. I would not, however, give *Youngberg* and *Estelle* such a stingy scope. I would recognize, as the Court apparently cannot, that "the State's knowledge of [an] individual's predicament [and] its expressions of intent to help him" can amount to a "limitation . . . on his freedom to act on his own behalf" or to obtain help from others. Thus, I would read *Youngberg* and *Estelle* to stand for the much more generous proposition that, if a State cuts off private sources of aid and then refuses aid itself, it cannot wash its hands of the harm that results from its inaction.

Youngberg and *Estelle* are not alone in sounding this theme. In striking down a filing fee as applied to divorce cases brought by indigents, see *Boddie v. Connecticut* (1971), and in deciding that a local government could not entirely foreclose the opportunity to speak in a public forum, see *e.g.*, *Schneider v. State* (1939); *Hague v. Committee for Industrial Organization* (1939); *United States v. Grace* (1983), we have acknowledged that a State's actions — such as the monopolization of a particular path of relief — may impose upon the State certain positive duties. Similarly, *Shelley v. Kraemer* (1948), and *Burton v. Wilmington Parking Authority* (1961) [racial discrimination by private lessee of restaurant space in state-owned parking garage constituted "state action" because the state's ownership of the building carried with it a responsibility to prevent such discrimination], suggest that a State may be found complicit in an injury even if it did not create the situation that caused the harm.

Arising as they do from constitutional contexts different from the one involved here, cases like *Boddie* and *Burton* are instructive rather than decisive in the case before us. But they set a tone equally well established in precedent as, and contradictory to, the one the Court sets by situating the DeShaneys' complaint within the class of cases epitomized by the Court's decision in *Harris v. McRae* (1980). The cases that I have cited tell us that *Goldberg v. Kelly* (1970) (recognizing entitlement to welfare under state law), can stand side by side with *Dandridge v. Williams* (1970) (implicitly rejecting idea that welfare is a fundamental right), and that *Goss v. Lopez* (1975) (entitlement to public education under state law), is perfectly consistent with *San Antonio Independent School Dist. v. Rodriguez* (1973) (no fundamental right to education). To put the point more directly, these cases signal that a State's prior actions may be decisive in analyzing the constitutional significance of its inaction. I thus would locate the DeShaneys' claims within the framework of cases like *Youngberg* and *Estelle*, and more generally, *Boddie* and *Schneider*, by considering the actions that Wisconsin took with respect to Joshua.

Wisconsin has established a child-welfare system specifically designed to help children like Joshua. Wisconsin law places upon the local departments of social services such as respondent (DSS or Department) a duty to investigate reported instances of child abuse. While other governmental bodies and private persons are largely responsible for the reporting of possible cases of child abuse, Wisconsin law channels all such reports to the local departments of social services for evaluation and, if necessary, further action. Even when it is the sheriff's office or police department that receives a report of suspected child abuse, that report is referred to local social services departments for action; the only exception to this occurs when the reporter fears for the child's *immediate* safety. In this way, Wisconsin law invites — indeed, directs — citizens and other governmental entities to depend on local departments of social services such as respondent to protect children from abuse.

* * *

In these circumstances, a private citizen, or even a person working in a government agency other than DSS, would doubtless feel that her job was done as soon as she had reported her suspicions of child abuse to DSS. Through its child-welfare program, in other words, the State of Wisconsin has relieved ordinary citizens and governmental bodies other than the Department of any sense of obligation to do anything more than report their suspicions of child abuse to DSS. If DSS ignores or dismisses these suspicions, no one will step in to fill the gap. Wisconsin's child-protection program thus effectively confined Joshua DeShaney within the walls of Randy DeShaney's violent home until such time as DSS took action to remove him. Conceivably, then, children like Joshua are made worse off by the existence of this program when the persons and entities charged with carrying it out fail to do their jobs.

It simply belies reality, therefore, to contend that the State "stood by and did nothing" with respect to Joshua. Through its child-protection program, the State actively intervened in Joshua's life and, by virtue of this intervention, acquired ever more certain knowledge that Joshua was in grave danger. These circumstances, in my view, plant this case solidly within the tradition of cases like *Youngberg* and *Estelle*.

It will be meager comfort to Joshua and his mother to know that, if the State had "selectively den[ied] its protective services" to them because they were "disfavored minorities," their § 1983 suit might have stood on sturdier ground. Because of the posture of this case, we do not know why respondents did not take steps to protect Joshua; the Court, however, tells us that their reason is irrelevant so long as their inaction was not the product of invidious discrimination. Presumably, then, if respondents decided not to help Joshua because his name began with a "J," or because he was born in the spring, or because they did not care enough about him even to formulate an intent to discriminate against him based on an arbitrary reason, respondents would not be liable to the DeShaneys because they were not the ones who dealt the blows that destroyed Joshua's life.

* * *

As the Court today reminds us, "the Due Process Clause of the Fourteenth Amendment was intended to prevent government 'from abusing [its] power, or employing it as an instrument of oppression.'" My disagreement with the Court arises from its failure to see that inaction can be every bit as abusive of power as action, that oppression can result when a State undertakes a vital duty and then ignores it. Today's opinion construes the Due Process Clause to permit a State to displace private sources of protection and then, at the critical moment, to shrug its shoulders and turn away from the harm that it has promised to try to prevent.

Because I cannot agree that our Constitution is indifferent to such indifference, I respectfully dissent.

JUSTICE BLACKMUN, dissenting [omitted].

NOTES AND QUESTIONS

1.   Our concern is still what constitutes "state action" of a sort the Fourteenth Amendment is designed to guard against. "Poor Joshua!" said the dissenters in this case, believing that the state of Wisconsin child welfare authorities had horribly failed him. And so, even Justice Rehnquist in his recitation of the excruciating facts of the case, makes clear. Why then, if the state social worker was clearly at fault for failing to do her job, was the relief sought in the case denied? "The complaint alleged that respondents had deprived Joshua of his liberty without due process of law, in violation of his rights under the Fourteenth Amendment, by failing to intervene to protect him against a risk of violence at his father's hands of which they knew or should have known." 489 U.S. at 193. The statute under which relief was sought provides a remedy for a state's depriving one of one's civil rights under color of law, and was passed pursuant to the authority of the Fourteenth Amendment. Why, if the state officials, in effect, could have prevented the harm that took place, are they not liable? Why, in short, was this not "state action"?

2.   Note that the majority explains that we are dealing with the "substantive" component of "due process." There is no doubt, really, that state action, or perhaps state "inaction" is involved, but the question the Court is addressing is whether a failure to prevent someone else from doing harm is a deprivation of the "life, liberty, or property" interest protected by the Due Process Clause. What would be your answer? For a view highly critical of the Chief Justice in this case and others, see Alan R. Madry, *State Action and the Obligation of the States to Prevent Private Harm: The Rehnquist Transformation and the Betrayal of Fundamental Commitments,* 65 So. CAL. L. REV. 781 (1992) ("If there is at least one right [the right to private property] that the states must protect against invasion by private agents, then one cannot claim that the Fourteenth Amendment as a general matter imposes no responsibility on the states to provide such protection. The burden would then shift to the proponents of state discretion to show how and why rights or interests other than property are not protected by the Amendment"). Would Joshua's claim have been more successful had he asserted that Wisconsin failed to afford him the equal *protection* of the law?

3.   The majority is willing to concede that "[i]t is true that in certain limited circumstances the Constitution imposes upon the state affirmative duties of care and protection with respect to particular individuals." 489 U.S. at 198. Why isn't "poor Joshua" one of those individuals?

4.   You may have been struck by the fact that the dissent cites *Shelley v. Kramer* in support of its position. Do you see the connection? How might Justice Harlan have voted in this case? The majority makes much of the historical reasons for the passage of the Fourteenth Amendment. Are they relevant here?

5. The critics of the *DeShaney* decision (and there are many) have sought to portray the majority as insufficiently sensitive to the plight of children such as Joshua. Are such children left, however, with no legal remedy after the majority's opinion? What policies are served by leaving Joshua's family only to the state tort system for redress? Why would anyone want to regard the father's conduct as implicating federally-protected rights? Does the dissenters' focus on cases involving the welfare system and indigents give you any clues? In the dissenters' view, should the Fourteenth Amendment be used only as a means of improving the lot of African Americans, as the Amendment's framers had most prominent in their minds, or does it express a different vision of American society? In order to understand just what vision of American society is inherent in the Fourteenth Amendment, it is useful to spend some time trying to outline with more precision the meaning of the protected sphere of "life, liberty, and property." This is the subject of the next case.

B.   WHAT CONSTITUTES "LIFE, LIBERTY, OR PROPERTY"?

BOARD OF REGENTS v. ROTH
408 U.S. 564 (1972)

MR. JUSTICE STEWART delivered the opinion of the Court.

In 1968 the respondent, David Roth, was hired for his first teaching job as assistant professor of political science at Wisconsin State University-Oshkosh. He was hired for a fixed term of one academic year. . . . The respondent completed that term. But he was informed that he would not be rehired for the next academic year.

The respondent had no tenure rights to continued employment. Under Wisconsin statutory law a state university teacher can acquire tenure as a "permanent" employee only after four years of year-to-year employment. Having acquired tenure, a teacher is entitled to continued employment "during efficiency and good behavior." A relatively new teacher without tenure, however, is under Wisconsin law entitled to nothing beyond his one-year appointment. There are no statutory or administrative standards defining eligibility for re-employment. State law thus clearly leaves the decision whether to rehire a nontenured teacher for another year to the unfettered discretion of university officials.

The procedural protection afforded a Wisconsin State University teacher before he is separated from the University corresponds to his job security. As a matter of statutory law, a tenured teacher cannot be "discharged except for cause upon written charges" and pursuant to certain procedures. A nontenured teacher, similarly, is protected to some extent *during* his one-year term. Rules promulgated by the Board of Regents provide that a nontenured teacher "dismissed" before the end of the year may have some opportunity for review of the "dismissal." But the Rules provide no real protection for a nontenured teacher who simply is not re-employed for the next year. He must be informed by February 1 "concerning retention or nonretention for the ensuing year." But "no reason for non-retention need be given. No review or appeal is provided in such case."

In conformance with these Rules, the President of Wisconsin State University-Oshkosh informed the respondent before February 1, 1969, that he would not be rehired for the 1969–1970 academic year. He gave the respondent no reason for the decision and no opportunity to challenge it at any sort of hearing.

The respondent then brought this action in Federal District Court alleging that the decision not to rehire him for the next year infringed his Fourteenth Amendment rights. He attacked the decision both in substance and procedure. First, he alleged that the true reason for the decision was to punish him for certain statements critical of the University administration, and that it therefore violated his right to freedom of speech. Second, he alleged that the failure of University officials to give him notice of any reason for nonretention and an opportunity for a hearing violated his right to procedural due process of law.

The District Court granted summary judgment for the respondent on the procedural issue, ordering the University officials to provide him with reasons and a hearing. The Court of Appeals, with one judge dissenting, affirmed this partial summary judgment. We granted certiorari. The only question presented to us at this stage in the case is whether the respondent had a constitutional right to a statement of reasons and a hearing on the University's decision not to rehire him for another year. We hold that he did not.

I

The requirements of procedural due process apply only to the deprivation of interests encompassed by the Fourteenth Amendment's protection of liberty and property. When protected interests are implicated, the right to some kind of prior hearing is paramount. But the range of interests protected by procedural due process is not infinite.

The District Court decided that procedural due process guarantees apply in this case by assessing and balancing the weights of the particular interests involved. It concluded that the respondent's interest in re-employment at Wisconsin State University-Oshkosh outweighed the University's interest in denying him re-employment summarily. Undeniably, the respondent's re-employment prospects were of major concern to him — concern that we surely cannot say was insignificant. And a weighing process has long been a part of any determination of the *form* of hearing required in particular situations by procedural due process. But, to determine whether due process requirements apply in the first place, we must look not to the "weight" but to the nature of the interest at stake. We must look to see if the interest is within the Fourteenth Amendment's protection of liberty and property.

"Liberty" and "property" are broad and majestic terms. They are among the "[g]reat [constitutional] concepts . . . purposely left to gather meaning from experience. . . . [T]hey relate to the whole domain of social and economic fact, and the statesmen who founded this Nation knew too well that only a stagnant society remains unchanged." For that reason, the Court has fully and finally rejected the wooden distinction between "rights" and "privileges" that once seemed to govern the applicability of procedural due process rights. The Court has also made clear that the property interests protected by procedural due process extend well beyond actual ownership of real estate, chattels, or money. By the same token, the Court has required due process protection for deprivations of liberty beyond the sort of formal constraints imposed by the criminal process.

Yet, while the Court has eschewed rigid or formalistic limitations on the protection of procedural due process, it has at the same time observed certain boundaries. . . .

II

"While this Court has not attempted to define with exactness the liberty . . . guaranteed [by the Fourteenth Amendment], the term has received much consideration and some of the included things have been definitely stated. Without doubt, it denotes not merely freedom from bodily restraint but also the right of the individual to contract, to engage in any of the common occupations of life, to acquire useful knowledge, to marry, establish a home and bring up children, to worship God according to the dictates of his own conscience, and generally to enjoy those privileges long recognized . . . as essential to the orderly pursuit of happiness by free men." *Meyer v. Nebraska* (1923). In a Constitution for a free people, there can be no doubt that the meaning of "liberty" must be broad indeed.

There might be cases in which a State refused to reemploy a person under such circumstances that interests in liberty would be implicated. But this is not such a case.

The State, in declining to rehire the respondent, did not make any charge against him that might seriously damage his standing and associations in his community. It did not base the nonrenewal of his contract on a charge, for example, that he had been guilty of dishonesty, or immorality. Had it done so, this would be a different case. For "[w]here a person's good name, reputation, honor, or integrity is at stake because of what the government is doing to him, notice and an opportunity to be heard are essential." In such a case, due process would accord an opportunity to refute the charge before University officials. In the present case, however, there is no suggestion whatever that the respondent's "good name, reputation, honor, or integrity" is at stake.

Similarly, there is no suggestion that the State, in declining to re-employ the respondent, imposed on him a stigma or other disability that foreclosed his freedom to take advantage of other employment opportunities. The State, for example, did not invoke any regulations to bar the respondent from all other public employment in state universities. . . .

To be sure, the respondent has alleged that the nonrenewal of his contract was based on his exercise of his right to freedom of speech. But this allegation is not now before us. The District Court stayed proceedings on this issue, and the respondent has yet to prove that the decision not to rehire him was, in fact, based on his free speech activities.

Hence, on the record before us, all that clearly appears is that the respondent was not rehired for one year at one university. It stretches the concept too far to suggest that a person is deprived of "liberty" when he simply is not rehired in one job but remains as free as before to seek another.

III

The Fourteenth Amendment's procedural protection of property is a safeguard of the security of interests that a person has already acquired in specific benefits. These interests — property interests — may take many forms.

Thus, the Court has held that a person receiving welfare benefits under statutory and administrative standards defining eligibility for them has an interest in continued receipt of those benefits that is safeguarded by procedural due process. *Goldberg v. Kelly* (1970). Similarly, in the area of public employment, the Court has held that a public college professor dismissed from an office held under tenure provisions, and college professors and staff members dismissed during the terms of their contracts, have interests in continued employment that are safeguarded by due process. Only last year, the Court held that this principle "proscribing summary dismissal from public employment without hearing or inquiry required by due process" also applied to a teacher recently hired without tenure or a formal contract, but nonetheless with a clearly implied promise of continued employment.

Certain attributes of "property" interests protected by procedural due process emerge from these decisions. To have a property interest in a benefit, a person clearly must have more than an abstract need or desire for it. He must have more than a unilateral expectation of it. He must, instead, have a legitimate claim of entitlement to it. It is a purpose of the ancient institution of property to protect those claims upon which people rely in their daily lives, reliance that must not be arbitrarily undermined. It is a purpose of the constitutional right to a hearing to provide an opportunity for a person to vindicate those claims.

Property interests, of course, are not created by the Constitution. Rather, they are created and their dimensions are defined by existing rules or understandings that stem from an independent source such as state law — rules or understandings that secure certain benefits and that support claims of entitlement to those benefits. Thus, the welfare recipients in *Goldberg v. Kelly, supra,* had a claim of entitlement to welfare payments that was grounded in the statute defining eligibility for them. The recipients had not yet shown that they were, in fact, within the statutory terms of eligibility. But we held that they had a right to a hearing at which they might attempt to do so.

Just as the welfare recipients' "property" interest in welfare payments was created and defined by statutory terms, so the respondent's "property" interest in employment at Wisconsin State University-Oshkosh was created and defined by the terms of his appointment. Those terms secured his interest in employment up to June 30, 1969. But the important fact in this case is that they specifically provided that the respondent's employment was to terminate on June 30. They did not provide for contract renewal absent "sufficient cause." Indeed, they made no provision for renewal whatsoever.

Thus, the terms of the respondent's appointment secured absolutely no interest in re-employment for the next year. They supported absolutely no possible claim of entitlement to re-employment. Nor, significantly, was there any state statute or University rule or policy that secured his interest in re-employment or that created any legitimate claim to it. In these circumstances, the respondent surely had an abstract concern in being rehired, but he did not have a *property* interest sufficient to require the University authorities to give him a hearing when they declined to renew his contract of employment.

IV

Our analysis of the respondent's constitutional rights in this case in no way indicates a view that an opportunity for a hearing or a statement of reasons for nonretention would, or would not, be appropriate or wise in public colleges and universities. For it is a written Constitution that we apply. Our role is confined to interpretation of that Constitution.

*   *   *

MR. JUSTICE DOUGLAS, dissenting.

. . . Though Roth was rated by the faculty as an excellent teacher, he had publicly criticized the administration for suspending an entire group of 94 black students without determining individual guilt. He also criticized the university's regime as being authoritarian and autocratic. He used his classroom to discuss what was being done about the black episode; and one day, instead of meeting his class, he went to the meeting of the Board of Regents.

In this case . . . an action was started in Federal District Court under 42 U.S.C. § 1983[10] claiming in part that the decision of the school authorities not to rehire was in retaliation for his expression of opinion. . . .

Professor Will Herberg, of Drew University, in writing of "academic freedom" recently said:

> "[I]t is sometimes conceived as a basic constitutional right guaranteed and protected under the First Amendment.
>
> "But, of course, this is not the case. Whereas a man's right to speak out on this or that may be guaranteed and protected, he can have no imaginable human or constitutional right to remain a member of a university faculty. Clearly, the right to academic freedom is an acquired one, yet an acquired right of such value to society that in the minds of many it has verged upon the constitutional."

There may not be a constitutional right to continued employment if private schools and colleges are involved. But Prof. Herberg's view is not correct when

---

[10] [18] Section 1983 reads as follows:

"Every person who, under color of any statute, ordinance, regulation, custom, or usage, of any State or Territory, subjects, or causes to be subjected, any citizen of the United States or other person within the jurisdiction thereof to the deprivation of any rights, privileges, or immunities secured by the Constitution and laws, shall be liable to the party injured in an action at law, suit in equity, or other proper proceeding for redress."

public schools move against faculty members. For the First Amendment, applicable to the States by reason of the Fourteenth Amendment, protects the individual against state action when it comes to freedom of speech and of press and the related freedoms guaranteed by the First Amendment; and the Fourteenth protects "liberty" and "property". . . .

No more direct assault on academic freedom can be imagined than for the school authorities to be allowed to discharge a teacher because of his or her philosophical, political, or ideological beliefs. The same may well be true of private schools, if through the device of financing or other umbilical cords they become instrumentalities of the State. . . .

* * *

When a violation of First Amendment rights is alleged, the reasons for dismissal or for nonrenewal of an employment contract must be examined to see if the reasons given are only a cloak for activity or attitudes protected by the Constitution. A statutory analogy is present under the National Labor Relations Act. While discharges of employees for "cause" are permissible, discharges because of an employee's union activities are banned. So the search is to ascertain whether the stated ground was the real one or only a pretext.

In the case of teachers whose contracts are not renewed, tenure is not the critical issue. . . . [C]onditioning renewal of a teacher's contract upon surrender of First Amendment rights is beyond the power of a State.

There is sometimes a conflict between a claim for First Amendment protection and the need for orderly administration of the school system. . . . That is one reason why summary judgments in this class of cases are seldom appropriate. Another reason is that careful factfinding is often necessary to know whether the given reason for nonrenewal of a teacher's contract is the real reason or a feigned one.

It is said that since teaching in a public school is a privilege, the State can grant it or withhold it on conditions. We have, however, rejected that thesis in numerous cases. . . .

. . . [W]hen a State proposes to deny a privilege to one who it alleges has engaged in unprotected speech, Due Process requires that the State bear the burden of proving that the speech was not protected. "[T]he 'protection of the individual against arbitrary action' . . . [is] the very essence of due process," but where the State is allowed to act secretly behind closed doors and without any notice to those who are affected by its actions, there is no check against the possibility of such "arbitrary action."

Moreover, where "important interests" of the citizen are implicated they are not to be denied or taken away without due process. [One such case] involved a driver's license. But also included are disqualification for unemployment compensation, discharge from public employment, denial of tax exemption, and withdrawal of welfare benefits (*Goldberg v. Kelly* (1970)). We should now add that nonrenewal of a teacher's contract, whether or not he has tenure, is an entitlement of the same importance and dignity.

Nonrenewal of a teacher's contract is tantamount in effect to a dismissal and the consequences may be enormous. Nonrenewal can be a blemish that turns into a permanent scar and effectively limits any chance the teacher has of being rehired as a teacher, at least in his State.

If this nonrenewal implicated the First Amendment, then Roth was deprived of constitutional rights because his employment was conditioned on a surrender of First Amendment rights; and, apart from the First Amendment, he was denied due process when he received no notice and hearing of the adverse action contemplated against him. Without a statement of the reasons for the discharge and an opportunity to rebut those reasons — both of which were refused by petitioners — there is no means short of a lawsuit to safeguard the right not to be discharged for the exercise of First Amendment guarantees.

*   *   *

MR. JUSTICE MARSHALL, dissenting.

*   *   *

While I agree with Part I of the Court's opinion, setting forth the proper framework for consideration of the issue presented, and also with those portions of Parts II and III of the Court's opinion that assert that a public employee is entitled to procedural due process whenever a State stigmatizes him by denying employment, or injures his future employment prospects severely, or whenever the State deprives him of a property interest, I would go further than the Court does in defining the terms "liberty" and "property."

The prior decisions of this Court . . . establish a principle that is as obvious as it is compelling — i.e., federal and state governments and governmental agencies are restrained by the Constitution from acting arbitrarily with respect to employment opportunities that they either offer or control. Hence, it is now firmly established that whether or not a private employer is free to act capriciously or unreasonably with respect to employment practices, at least absent statutory or contractual controls, a government employer is different. The government may only act fairly and reasonably.

This Court has long maintained that "the right to work for a living in the common occupations of the community is of the very essence of the personal freedom and opportunity that it was the purpose of the [Fourteenth] Amendment to secure." It has also established that the fact that an employee has no contract guaranteeing work for a specific future period does not mean that as the result of action by the government he may be "discharged at any time for any reason or for no reason."

In my view, every citizen who applies for a government job is entitled to it unless the government can establish some reason for denying the employment. This is the "property" right that I believe is protected by the Fourteenth Amendment and that cannot be denied "without due process of law." And it is also liberty — liberty to work — which is the "very essence of the personal freedom and opportunity" secured by the Fourteenth Amendment.

This Court has often had occasion to note that the denial of public employment is a serious blow to any citizen. Thus, when an application for public employment is denied or the contract of a government employee is not renewed, the government must say why, for it is only when the reasons underlying government action are known that citizens feel secure and protected against arbitrary government action.

Employment is one of the greatest, if not the greatest, benefits that governments offer in modern-day life. When something as valuable as the opportunity to work is at stake, the government may not reward some citizens and not others without demonstrating that its actions are fair and equitable. And it is procedural due process that is our fundamental guarantee of fairness, our protection against arbitrary, capricious, and unreasonable government action.

MR. JUSTICE DOUGLAS has written that:

> "It is not without significance that most of the provisions of the Bill of Rights are procedural. It is procedure that spells much of the difference between rule by law and rule by whim or caprice. Steadfast adherence to strict procedural safeguards is our main assurance that there will be equal justice under law."

And Mr. Justice Frankfurter has said that "[t]he history of American freedom is, in no small measure, the history of procedure." With respect to occupations controlled by the government, one lower court has said that "[t]he public has the right to expect its officers . . . to make adjudications on the basis of merit." The first step toward insuring that these expectations are realized is to require adherence to the standards of due process; absolute and uncontrolled discretion invites abuse.

We have often noted that procedural due process means many different things in the numerous contexts in which it applies. Prior decisions have held that an applicant for admission to practice as an attorney before the United States Board of Tax Appeals may not be rejected without a statement of reasons and a chance for a hearing on disputed issues of fact; that a tenured teacher could not be summarily dismissed without notice of the reasons and a hearing; that an applicant for admission to a state bar could not be denied the opportunity to practice law without notice of the reasons for the rejection of his application and a hearing; and even that a substitute teacher who had been employed only two months could not be dismissed merely because she refused to take a loyalty oath without an inquiry into the specific facts of her case and a hearing on those in dispute. I would follow these cases and hold that respondent was denied due process when his contract was not renewed and he was not informed of the reasons and given an opportunity to respond.

NOTES AND QUESTIONS

1.   The subject of this case, as indicated, is what sort of "rights" are protected by the terms "liberty and property" under the Fourteenth Amendment. Note that even the majority (which denies the relief sought) is careful to suggest that there is no easy answer to this question, and that it is not a matter of "rigid or formalistic" categorization — the sort of thinking which might say, for example, that "rights" are protected but "privileges" are not. Is "rigid or formalistic" thinking inconsistent

with the interpretation of the Constitution? Has this always been the case?

2. Quoting from a famous case on the point, the majority observes that the Fourteenth Amendment term, "liberty,"

> denotes not merely freedom from bodily restraint but also the right of the individual to contract, to engage in any of the common occupations of life, to acquire useful knowledge, to marry, establish a home and bring up children, to worship God according to the dictates of his own conscience, and generally to enjoy those privileges long recognized . . . as essential to the orderly pursuit of happiness by free men.

408 U.S. at 572 (quoting *Meyer v. Nebraska*, 262 U.S. 390, 399 (1923)). This is very much a definition informed by the natural law rights of individuals. Modernly, why isn't job security in a nontenured academic position such a protected "right," or is it? Is it the object in controversy — the teacher's job — or the manner in which he lost it that is important?

3. The majority finally appears to zero in on the concept of protected "property" interests under the Fourteenth Amendment, and then describes those interests as follows:

> Property interests, of course, are not created by the Constitution. Rather, they are created and their dimensions are defined by existing rules or understandings that stem from an independent source such as state law — rules or understandings that secure certain benefits and that support claims of entitlement to those benefits.

408 U.S. at 577. Note, then, that this means that one cannot fully understand the law of the federal Constitution, at least insofar as one studies the Fourteenth Amendment, without having an appreciation of state law as well. Note further, that the meaning of this passage is that what is protected under the Fourteenth Amendment may vary from state to state. Is this appropriate? Is the dissent in agreement with the majority on this point? Are you? What is it that leads to dissents in the case? Is it the point about what constitutes protected "property" interests, is it about the supposed "First Amendment" implications (not addressed by the majority), or is it, as seems to be implicit in Justice Marshall's dissent, the notion that "public employment" of any kind cannot be terminated without due process?

4. In *DeShaney*, the Court suggested in a footnote that the Fourteenth Amendment might support a cause of action against state government for failure to protect *if* the state had itself created a *Roth*-type property interest. That proposition was tested in *Town of Castle Rock v. Gonzales*, 545 U.S. 748 (2005), another case that, like *DeShaney* itself, began with very tragic facts.

Simon and Jessica Gonzales were in the middle of divorce proceedings, and the divorce court issued a restraining order barring Simon from "disturbing the peace" of his estranged wife and their children except during specified parenting time every other weekend and during a pre-arranged mid-week dinner visit. In violation of the restraining order, Mr. Gonzales took the three daughters while they played outside. No advance arrangements had been made for him to see the daughters that evening. When Mrs. Gonzales noticed the children were missing, she suspected her husband had taken them. At about 7:30 p.m., she called the Castle Rock Police Department, which dispatched two officers. When the officers arrived, she showed them a copy of the restraining order which contained pre-printed language seemingly requiring its enforcement. The officers stated that there was nothing they could do about the restraining order and suggested that Mrs. Gonzales call the Police Department again if the three children did not return home by 10:00 p.m. At approximately 8:30 p.m., Mrs. Gonzales talked to her husband on his cellular telephone. He told her "he had the three children [at an] amusement park in Denver. She called the police again and asked them to 'have someone check for' her husband or his vehicle at the amusement park and 'put out an [all points bulletin]' for her husband, but the officer with whom she spoke 'refused to do so,' again telling her to 'wait until 10:00 p.m. and see if'" her husband returned the girls. At approximately 10:10 p.m., Mrs. Gonzales called the police and said her children were still missing, but she was now told to wait until midnight. She called at midnight and told the dispatcher her children were still missing. She went to her husband's apartment and, finding nobody there, called the police at 12:10 a.m.; she was told to wait for an officer to arrive. When none came, she went to the police station at 12:50 a.m. and submitted an incident report. The officer who took the report "made no reasonable effort to enforce the [restraining order] or locate the three children. Instead, he went to dinner." At approximately 3:20 a.m., the husband arrived at the police station and opened fire with a semiautomatic handgun he had purchased earlier that evening. Police shot back, killing him. Inside the cab of his pickup truck, they found the bodies of all three daughters, whom he had already murdered.

Mrs. Gonzales sued police and the town itself, contending that she was deprived of *procedural* due process when police failed to enforce the restraining order, in which she claimed she had a property interest because of statutory language providing that police "*shall* arrest" or seek a warrant for an arrest if they have probable cause to believe that the order had been violated. Justice Scalia, writing for seven members of the Court, held that Colorado's use of the word "shall" did not create a property interest, particularly when read in the context of the discretion traditionally afforded to police. Explained Justice Scalia:

> Respondent's alleged interest stems only from a State's *statutory* scheme — from a restraining order that was authorized by and tracked precisely the statute on which the Court of Appeals relied. She does not assert that she has any common-law or contractual entitlement to enforcement. If she was given a statutory entitlement, we would expect to see some indication of that in the statute itself. Although Colorado's statute spoke of "protected person[s]" such as respondent, it did so in connection with matters other than a right to enforcement. It said that a "protected person shall be provided with a copy of [a restraining] order" when it is issued; that a law enforcement agency "shall make all reasonable efforts to contact the protected party upon the arrest of the restrained person"; and that the agency "shall give [to the protected person] a copy" of the report it submits to the court that issued the order. Perhaps most importantly, the statute spoke directly to the protected person's power to "initiate contempt proceedings against the restrained person if the order [was] issued in a civil

action or request the prosecuting attorney to initiate contempt proceedings if the order [was] issued in a criminal action." The protected person's express power to "initiate" civil contempt proceedings contrasts tellingly with the mere ability to "request" initiation of criminal contempt proceedings — and even more dramatically with the complete silence about any power to "request" (much less demand) that an arrest be made.

Justice Souter, concurring, went even further, stating that one never has a property interest in mere procedure. Justice Stevens, joined by Justice Ginsburg, dissented, contending that the State of Colorado, like a number of other states in the decade and a half since *DeShaney* was decided, had deliberately intended to deprive police of their traditional discretion and mandate enforcement of domestic abuse restraining orders, and that police should therefore be constitutionally liable (rather than just liable under state tort law) for failure to perform that statutory duty.

The dissent explained:

> . . . Neither the tragic facts of the case, nor the importance of according proper deference to law enforcement professionals, should divert our attention from that issue. That issue is whether the restraining order entered by the Colorado trial court on June 4, 1999, created a "property" interest that is protected from arbitrary deprivation by the Due Process Clause of the Fourteenth Amendment.

> It is perfectly clear, on the one hand, that neither the Federal Constitution itself, nor any federal statute, granted respondent or her children any individual entitlement to police protection. See *DeShaney v. Winnebago County Dept. of Social Servs.* (1989). Nor, I assume, does any Colorado statute create any such entitlement for the ordinary citizen. On the other hand, it is equally clear that federal law imposes no impediment to the creation of such an entitlement by Colorado law. Respondent certainly could have entered into a contract with a private security firm, obligating the firm to provide protection to respondent's family; respondent's interest in such a contract would unquestionably constitute "property" within the meaning of the Due Process Clause. If a Colorado statute enacted for her benefit, or a valid order entered by a Colorado judge, created the functional equivalent of such a private contract by granting respondent an entitlement to mandatory individual protection by the local police force, that state-created right would also qualify as "property" entitled to constitutional protection.

> *   *   *

> Given that Colorado law has quite clearly eliminated the police's discretion to deny enforcement, respondent is correct that she had much more than a "unilateral expectation" that the restraining order would be enforced; rather, she had a "legitimate claim of entitlement" to enforcement, *citing Roth.* Recognizing respondent's property interest in the enforcement of her restraining order is fully consistent with our precedent. This Court has "made clear that the property interests protected by

procedural due process extend well beyond actual ownership of real estate, chattels, or money." The "types of interests protected as 'property' are varied and, as often as not, intangible, 'relating to the whole domain of social and economic fact.' " *Logan v. Zimmerman Brush Co.*, 455 U.S. 422, 430 (1982); see also *Perry v. Sindermann*, 408 U.S. 593, 601 (1972) (" '[P]roperty' interests subject to procedural due process protection are not limited by a few rigid, technical forms. Rather, 'property' denotes a broad range of interests that are secured by 'existing rules or understandings' "). Thus, our cases have found "property" interests in a number of state-conferred benefits and services, including welfare benefits, *Goldberg v. Kelly* (1970); disability benefits, *Mathews v. Eldridge* (1976); public education, *Goss v. Lopez*, 419 U.S. 565 (1975); utility services, *Memphis Light, Gas & Water Div. v. Craft*, 436 U.S. 1 (1978); government employment, *Cleveland Bd. of Ed. v. Loudermill*, 470 U.S. 532 (1985); as well as in other entitlements that defy easy categorization, see, *e.g.*, *Bell v. Burson*, 402 U.S. 535 (1971) (due process requires fair procedures before a driver's license may be revoked pending the adjudication of an accident claim); *Logan*, 455 U.S., at 431 (due process prohibits the arbitrary denial of a person's interest in adjudicating a claim before a state commission).

Police enforcement of a restraining order is a government service that is no less concrete and no less valuable than other government services, such as education. The relative novelty of recognizing this type of property interest is explained by the relative novelty of the domestic violence statutes creating a mandatory arrest duty; before this innovation, the unfettered discretion that characterized police enforcement defeated any citizen's "legitimate claim of entitlement" to this service. Novel or not, respondent's claim finds strong support in the principles that underlie our due process jurisprudence. In this case, Colorado law *guaranteed* the provision of a certain service, in certain defined circumstances, to a certain class of beneficiaries, and respondent reasonably relied on that guarantee. As we observed in *Roth*, "[i]t is a purpose of the ancient institution of property to protect those claims upon which people rely in their daily lives, reliance that must not be arbitrarily undermined." . . .

Because respondent had a property interest in the enforcement of the restraining order, state officials could not deprive her of that interest without observing fair procedures. Her description of the police behavior in this case and the department's callous policy of failing to respond properly to reports of restraining order violations clearly alleges a due process violation. At the very least, due process requires that the relevant state decisionmaker *listen* to the claimant and then *apply the relevant criteria* in reaching his decision. The failure to observe these minimal procedural safeguards creates an unacceptable risk of arbitrary and "erroneous deprivation[s]," *Mathews*. . . .

Who is right here? If, as asserted in the Declaration of Independence, the very purpose of government is to secure to individuals the unalienable rights of life and liberty, shouldn't government be liable for failing to provide that security? Or would creating a property right to police enforcement for some matters shift police resources away from other, perhaps more urgent claims?

5. Thus far, we have seen that due process protection requires both a finding of state action and a protectible life, liberty or property interest. It should be kept in mind that due process arises only when the subject is the application of an already enacted law to a particular person or group. Long ago, the Court made it clear that due process cannot be raised against general legislative activity. *Bi-Metallic Investment Co. v. State Board of Equalization*, 239 U.S. 441 (1915) (increasing the valuation of all property in Denver by 40 percent without notice or hearing; the remedy, said the Court, is to throw the bums out). We turn next to the issue of just what constitutes "due process" if one is entitled to it. The dissenters in *Roth* suggest that some notification of charges for dismissal, at the very least, ought to be required. What else constitutes "due process," and does it vary depending on the type of interest protected? This is the subject of the next section.

C. WHAT PROCESS IS DUE?

GOLDBERG v. KELLY
397 U.S. 254 (1970)

MR. JUSTICE BRENNAN delivered the opinion of the Court.

* * *

I

The constitutional issue to be decided . . . is . . . whether the Due Process Clause requires that [a welfare] recipient be afforded an evidentiary hearing *before* the termination of benefits. The District Court held that only a pre-termination evidentiary hearing would satisfy the constitutional command, and rejected the argument of the state and city officials that the combination of the post-termination "fair hearing" with the informal pre-termination review disposed of all due process claims. The court said: "While post-termination review is relevant, there is one overpowering fact which controls here. By hypothesis, a welfare recipient is destitute, without funds or assets. . . . Suffice it to say that to cut off a welfare recipient in the face of . . . 'brutal need' without a prior hearing of some sort is unconscionable, unless overwhelming considerations justify it." The court rejected the argument that the need to protect the public's tax revenues supplied the requisite "overwhelming consideration." "Against the justified desire to protect public funds must be weighed the individual's overpowering need in this unique situation not to be wrongfully deprived of assistance. . . . While the problem of additional expense must be kept in mind, it does not justify denying a hearing meeting the ordinary standards of due process. . . ."

Appellant does not contend that procedural due process is not applicable to the termination of welfare benefits. Such benefits are a matter of statutory entitlement for persons qualified to receive them. Their termination involves state action that adjudicates important rights. The constitutional challenge cannot be answered by an argument that public assistance benefits are "a 'privilege' and not a 'right.'"

Relevant constitutional restraints apply as much to the withdrawal of public assistance benefits as to disqualification for unemployment compensation, or to denial of a tax exemption, or to discharge from public employment. The extent to which procedural due process must be afforded the recipient is influenced by the extent to which he may be "condemned to suffer grievous loss," and depends upon whether the recipient's interest in avoiding that loss outweighs the governmental interest in summary adjudication. Accordingly, . . . "consideration of what procedures due process may require under any given set of circumstances must begin with a determination of the precise nature of the government function involved as well as of the private interest that has been affected by governmental action."

It is true, of course, that some governmental benefits may be administratively terminated without affording the recipient a pre-termination evidentiary hearing. But we agree with the District Court that when welfare is discontinued, only a pre-termination evidentiary hearing provides the recipient with procedural due process. For qualified recipients, welfare provides the means to obtain essential food, clothing, housing, and medical care. Thus the crucial factor in this context — a factor not present in the case of the blacklisted government contractor, the discharged government employee, the taxpayer denied a tax exemption, or virtually anyone else whose governmental entitlements are ended — is that termination of aid pending resolution of a controversy over eligibility may deprive an eligible recipient of the very means by which to live while he waits. Since he lacks independent resources, his situation becomes immediately desperate. His need to concentrate upon finding the means for daily subsistence, in turn, adversely affects his ability to seek redress from the welfare bureaucracy.

*   *   *

Appellant does not challenge the force of these considerations but argues that they are outweighed by countervailing governmental interests in conserving fiscal and administrative resources. These interests, the argument goes, justify the delay of any evidentiary hearing until after discontinuance of the grants. Summary adjudication protects the public fisc by stopping payments promptly upon discovery of reason to believe that a recipient is no longer eligible. Since most terminations are accepted without challenge, summary adjudication also conserves both the fisc and administrative time and energy by reducing the number of evidentiary hearings actually held.

We agree with the District Court, however, that these governmental interests are not overriding in the welfare context. The requirement of a prior hearing doubtless involves some greater expense, and the benefits paid to ineligible recipients pending decision at the hearing probably cannot be recouped, since these recipients are likely to be judgment-proof. But the State is not without weapons to minimize these increased costs. . . . Thus, the interest of the eligible recipient in uninterrupted receipt of public assistance, coupled with the State's interest that his payments not be erroneously terminated, clearly outweighs the State's competing concern to prevent any increase in its fiscal and administrative burdens. . . .

II

We also agree with the District Court, however, that the pre-termination hearing need not take the form of a judicial or quasi-judicial trial. We bear in mind that the statutory "fair hearing" will provide the recipient with a full administrative review. Accordingly, the pre-termination hearing has one function only: to produce an initial determination of the validity of the welfare department's grounds for discontinuance of payments in order to protect a recipient against an erroneous termination of his benefits. Thus, a complete record and a comprehensive opinion, which would serve primarily to facilitate judicial review and to guide future decisions, need not be provided at the pre-termination stage. . . . We wish to add that we, no less than the dissenters, recognize the importance of not imposing upon the States or the Federal Government in this developing field of law any procedural requirements beyond those demanded by rudimentary due process.

"The fundamental requisite of due process of law is the opportunity to be heard." . . . The hearing must be "at a meaningful time and in a meaningful manner." . . . In the present context these principles require that a recipient have timely and adequate notice detailing the reasons for a proposed termination, and an effective opportunity to defend by confronting any adverse witnesses and by presenting his own arguments and evidence orally. . . .

*   *   *

The city's procedures presently do not permit recipients to appear personally with or without counsel before the official who finally determines continued eligibility. Thus a recipient is not permitted to present evidence to that official orally, or to confront or cross-examine adverse witnesses. These omissions are fatal to the constitutional adequacy of the procedures.

The opportunity to be heard must be tailored to the capacities and circumstances of those who are to be heard. It is not enough that a welfare recipient may present his position to the decision maker in writing or secondhand through his caseworker. Written submissions are an unrealistic option for most recipients, who lack the educational attainment necessary to write effectively and who cannot obtain professional assistance. Moreover, written submissions do not afford the flexibility of oral presentations; they do not permit the recipient to mold his argument to the issues the decision maker appears to regard as important. Particularly where credibility and veracity are at issue, as they must be in many termination proceedings, written submissions are a wholly unsatisfactory basis for decision. . . . Therefore a recipient must be allowed to state his position orally. Informal procedures will suffice; in this context due process does not require a particular order of proof or mode of offering evidence.

In almost every setting where important decisions turn on questions of fact, due process requires an opportunity to confront and cross-examine adverse witnesses. . . .

"The right to be heard would be, in many cases, of little avail if it did not comprehend the right to be heard by counsel." We do not say that counsel must be provided at the pre-termination hearing, but only that the recipient must be allowed to retain an attorney if he so desires. . . .

Finally, the decisionmaker's conclusion as to a recipient's eligibility must rest solely on the legal rules and evidence adduced at the hearing. To demonstrate compliance with this elementary requirement, the decision maker should state the reasons for his determination and indicate the evidence he relied on, though his statement need not amount to a full opinion or even formal findings of fact and conclusions of law. And, of course, an impartial decision maker is essential. We agree with the District Court that prior involvement in some aspects of a case will not necessarily bar a welfare official from acting as a decision maker. He should not, however, have participated in making the determination under review.

*   *   *

MR. JUSTICE BLACK, dissenting.

In the last half century the United States, along with many, perhaps most, other nations of the world, has moved far toward becoming a welfare state, that is, a nation that for one reason or another taxes its most affluent people to help support, feed, clothe, and shelter its less fortunate citizens. The result is that today more than nine million men, women, and children in the United States receive some kind of state or federally financed public assistance in the form of allowances or gratuities, generally paid them periodically, usually by the week, month, or quarter. Since these gratuities are paid on the basis of need, the list of recipients is not static, and some people go off the lists and others are added from time to time. These ever-changing lists put a constant administrative burden on government and it certainly could not have reasonably anticipated that this burden would include the additional procedural expense imposed by the Court today.

The dilemma of the ever-increasing poor in the midst of constantly growing affluence presses upon us and must inevitably be met within the framework of our democratic constitutional government, if our system is to survive as such. It was largely to escape just such pressing economic problems and attendant government repression that people from Europe, Asia, and other areas settled this country and formed our Nation. Many of those settlers had personally suffered from persecutions of various kinds and wanted to get away from governments that had unrestrained powers to make life miserable for their citizens. It was for this reason, or so I believe, that on reaching these new lands the early settlers undertook to curb their governments by confining their powers within written boundaries, which eventually became written constitutions. They wrote their basic charters as nearly as men's collective wisdom could do so as to proclaim to their people and their officials an emphatic command that: "Thus far and no farther shall you go; and where we neither delegate powers to you, nor prohibit your exercise of them, we the people are left free."

Representatives of the people of the Thirteen Original Colonies spent long, hot months in the summer of 1787 in Philadelphia, Pennsylvania, creating a government of limited powers. They divided it into three departments — Legislative, Judicial, and Executive. The Judicial Department was to have no part whatever in making any laws. In fact proposals looking to vesting some power in the Judiciary to take part in the legislative process and veto laws were offered, considered, and rejected by the Constitutional Convention. In my judgment there is not one word, phrase, or sentence from the beginning to the end of the Constitution from which it can be inferred that judges were granted any such legislative power. True, *Marbury v. Madison* (1803), held, and properly, I think, that courts must be the final interpreters of the Constitution, and I recognize that the holding can provide an opportunity to slide imperceptibly into constitutional amendment and law making. But when federal judges use this judicial power for legislative purposes, I think they wander out of their field of vested powers and transgress into the area constitutionally assigned to the Congress and the people. That is precisely what I believe the Court is doing in this case. Hence my dissent.

The more than a million names on the relief rolls in New York, and the more than nine million names on the rolls of all the 50 States were not put there at random. The names are there because state welfare officials believed that those people were eligible for assistance. Probably in the officials' haste to make out the lists many names were put there erroneously in order to alleviate immediate suffering, and undoubtedly some people are drawing relief who are not entitled under the law to do so. Doubtless some draw relief checks from time to time who know they are not eligible, either because they are not actually in need or for some other reason. Many of those who thus draw undeserved gratuities are without sufficient property to enable the government to collect back from them any money they wrongfully receive. But the Court today holds that it would violate the Due Process Clause of the Fourteenth Amendment to stop paying those people weekly or monthly allowances unless the government first affords them a full "evidentiary hearing" even though welfare officials are persuaded that the recipients are not rightfully entitled to receive a penny under the law. In other words, although some recipients might be on the lists for payment wholly because of deliberate fraud on their part, the Court holds that the government is helpless and must continue, until after an evidentiary hearing, to pay money that it does not owe, never has owed, and never could owe. I do not believe there is any provision in our Constitution that should thus paralyze the government's efforts to protect itself against making payments to people who are not entitled to them.

Particularly do I not think that the Fourteenth Amendment should be given such an unnecessarily broad construction. That Amendment came into being primarily to protect Negroes from discrimination, and while some of its language can and does protect others, all know that the chief purpose behind it was to protect ex-slaves. The Court, however, relies upon the Fourteenth Amendment and in effect says that failure of the government to pay a promised charitable instalment to an individual deprives that individual *of his own property*, in violation of the Due Process Clause of the Fourteenth Amendment. It somewhat strains credulity to say that the government's promise of charity to an individual is property belonging to that individual when the government denies that the individual is honestly entitled to receive such a payment.

I would have little, if any, objection to the majority's decision in this case if it were written as the report of the House Committee on Education and Labor, but as an opinion ostensibly resting on the language of the Constitution I find it woefully deficient. Once the verbiage is pared away it is obvious that this Court today adopts the views of the District Court "that to cut off a welfare recipient in the face of . . . 'brutal need' without a prior hearing of some sort is unconscionable," and therefore, says the Court, unconstitutional. The majority reaches this result by a process of weighing "the recipient's interest in avoiding" the termination of welfare benefits against "the governmental interest in summary adjudication." Today's balancing act requires a "pre-termination evidentiary hearing," yet there is nothing that indicates what tomorrow's balance will be. . . . [I]t is obvious that today's result does not depend on the language of the Constitution itself or the principles of other decisions, but solely on the collective judgment of the majority as to what would be a fair and humane procedure in this case.

This decision is thus only another variant of the view often expressed by some members of this Court that the Due Process Clause forbids any conduct that a majority of the Court believes "unfair," "indecent," or "shocking to their consciences." Neither these words nor any like them appear anywhere in the Due Process Clause. If they did, they would leave the majority of Justices free to hold any conduct unconstitutional that they should conclude on their own to be unfair or shocking to them. Had the drafters of the Due Process Clause meant to leave judges such ambulatory power to declare laws unconstitutional, the chief value of a written constitution, as the Founders saw it, would have been lost. In fact, if that view of due process is correct, the Due Process Clause could easily swallow up all other parts of the Constitution. And truly the Constitution would always be "what the judges say it is" at a given moment, not what the Founders wrote into the document. A written constitution, designed to guarantee protection against governmental abuses, including those of judges, must have written standards that mean something definite and have an explicit content. I regret very much to be compelled to say that the Court today makes a drastic and dangerous departure from a Constitution written to control and limit the government and the judges and moves toward a constitution designed to be no more and no less than what the judges of a particular social and economic philosophy declare on the one hand to be fair or on the other hand to be shocking and unconscionable.

The procedure required today as a matter of constitutional law finds no precedent in our legal system. Reduced to its simplest terms, the problem in this case is similar to that frequently encountered when two parties have an ongoing legal relationship that requires one party to make periodic payments to the other. Often the situation arises where the party "owing" the money stops paying it and justifies his conduct by arguing that the recipient is not legally entitled to payment. The recipient can, of course, disagree and go to court to compel payment. But I know of no situation in our legal system in which the person alleged to owe money to another is required by law to continue making payments to a judgment-proof claimant without the benefit of any security or bond to insure that these payments can be recovered if he wins his legal argument. Yet today's decision in no way obligates the welfare recipient to pay back any benefits wrongfully received during the pre-termination evidentiary hearings or post any bond, and in all "fairness" it could not do so. These recipients are by definition too poor to post a bond or to repay the benefits that, as the majority assumes, must be spent as received to insure survival.

The Court apparently feels that this decision will benefit the poor and needy. In my judgment the eventual result will be just the opposite. While today's decision requires only an administrative, evidentiary hearing, the inevitable logic of the approach taken will lead to constitutionally imposed, time-consuming delays of a full adversary process of administrative and judicial review. In the next case the welfare recipients are bound to argue that cutting off benefits before judicial review of the agency's decision is also a denial of due process. Since, by hypothesis, termination of aid at that point may still "deprive an *eligible* recipient of the very means by which to live while he waits," I would be surprised if the weighing process did not compel the conclusion that termination without full judicial review would be unconscionable. After all, at each step, as the majority seems to feel, the issue is only one of weighing the government's pocketbook against the actual survival of the recipient, and surely that balance must always tip in favor of the individual. Similarly today's decision requires only the opportunity to have the benefit of counsel at the administrative hearing, but it is difficult to believe that the same reasoning process would not require the appointment of counsel, for otherwise the right to counsel is a meaningless one since these people are too poor to hire their own advocates. Thus the end result of today's decision may well be that the government, once it decides to give welfare benefits, cannot reverse that decision until the recipient has had the benefits of full administrative and judicial review, including, of course, the opportunity to present his case to this Court. Since this process will usually entail a delay of several years, the inevitable result of such a constitutionally imposed burden will be that the government will not put a claimant on the rolls initially until it has made an exhaustive investigation to determine his eligibility. While this Court will perhaps have insured that no needy person will be taken off the rolls without a full "due process" proceeding, it will also have insured that many will never get on the rolls, or at least that they will remain destitute during the lengthy proceedings followed to determine initial eligibility.

. . . The operation of a welfare state is a new experiment for our Nation. For this reason, among others, I feel that new experiments in carrying out a welfare program should not be frozen into our constitutional structure. They should be left, as are other legislative determinations, to the Congress and the legislatures that the people elect to make our laws.

NOTES AND QUESTIONS

1. *Goldberg v. Kelly* is one of the most frequently-cited of the "procedural due process" cases. Note, first of all, that the Justice Black disagrees even with the majority's assumption that the receipt of welfare is a protected property interest under the Fourteenth Amendment, claiming that it "strains credulity" to treat the government's promise of charitable payments as "property" even though the government has determined that the claimant is ineligible. What view of "property" is the majority putting forward, and is it consistent with Locke's? *See* Richard A. Epstein, *No New Property*, 56 BROOK. L. REV. 747 (1990) (discussing the efforts of Justice Brennan to create and defend the concept of "new property" and arguing that the term is meaningless because property rights are the result of the activity of individuals, not governmental dictates). More important, perhaps, why should the requirements of procedural due process include a hearing prior to termination of benefits? Of what relevance are Justice Brennan's assertions that "[f]rom its

founding the Nation's basic commitment has been to foster the dignity and well-being of all persons within its borders. We have come to recognize that forces not within the control of the poor contribute to their poverty"? 397 U.S. at 264–65. Are those two sentences correct, by the way? Is the nation's basic commitment to "dignity and well-being of all persons within its borders"? The pledge of allegiance speaks of "one nation under God, indivisible, with liberty and justice for all." Is this the same thing? Would all agree on the proposition that "forces not within the control of the poor contribute to their poverty"? Is it a helpful statement with regard to decisions to be made concerning procedural due process? Is Justice Brennan advocating that there should be a different constitutional law for the poor and the rich? Would you? The French satirist, Anatole France, praised the majesty of his country's law, which forbids, with equal force, the rich or the poor from sleeping under bridges.

Is Justice Brennan reflecting similar insight? Should the law?

2.   Note that Justice Brennan also justifies the welfare system on the grounds that it tends to "promote the general Welfare, and secure the Blessings of Liberty to ourselves and our Posterity." 397 U.S. at 265. How exactly does providing aid to the poorest in society do this? Is this persuasive? Is this constitutional law? Suppose there were more effective means of improving the economic conditions of the poor than state-supplied welfare payments. Would that have any bearing on procedural due process?

3.   Why does Justice Black dissent? Surely he cannot object to the notion that the Due Process Clause requires that particular procedures be followed. What is one to make of his quite emphatic suggestions that:

> The Judicial Department was to have no part whatever in making any laws. In fact proposals looking to vesting some power in the Judiciary to take part in the legislative process and veto laws were offered, considered, and rejected by the Constitutional Convention. In my judgment there is not one word, phrase, or sentence from the beginning to the end of the Constitution from which it can be inferred that judges were granted any such legislative power.

397 U.S. at 273–74 (Black, J., dissenting). What does that have to do with "procedural due process" as applied in the case at hand? Could it be that "procedural due process" also has substantive aspects? How does Justice Brennan know, for example, that the kind of hearing required before welfare benefits can be suspended is not the same as the kind to be seen in courtrooms or formal proceedings of administrative agencies? The late Justice Brennan was regarded by liberals and conservatives alike as the foremost champion of the view that the meaning of the Constitution changed with the times. Do you see that view in evidence here? What do you suppose the essential elements of Justice Black's jurisprudence were? With whose perspective are you the most comfortable?

4.   Note, in particular, Justice Black's charge that the "balancing act" in which the majority engages — balancing the needs of the state government to conserve the funds available for welfare, and to pay them only to deserving recipients, with the needs of the individual recipients — is an improper means of deciding

constitutional law questions. Why is that, and do you agree? Justice Black's criticism of the majority minces no words. Is his tone justified?

MATHEWS v. ELDRIDGE
424 U.S. 319 (1976)

Mr. Justice Powell delivered the opinion of the Court.

The issue in this case is whether the Due Process Clause of the Fifth Amendment requires that prior to the termination of Social Security disability benefit payments the recipient be afforded an opportunity for an evidentiary hearing.

I

Cash benefits are provided to workers during periods in which they are completely disabled under the disability insurance benefits program created by the 1956 amendments to Title II of the Social Security Act. 42 U.S.C. § 423. Respondent Eldridge was first awarded benefits in June 1968 [but they were terminated in July 1972 after extensive review of Eldridge's medical records by the Social Security Administration]. . . . [Eldridge was advised] of his right to seek reconsideration by the state agency of this initial determination within six months.

Instead of requesting reconsideration Eldridge commenced this action challenging the constitutional validity of the administrative procedures established by the Secretary of Health, Education, and Welfare for assessing whether there exists a continuing disability. He sought an immediate reinstatement of benefits pending a hearing on the issue of his disability.[11] . . . In support of his contention that due process requires a pretermination hearing, Eldridge relied exclusively upon this Court's decision in *Goldberg v. Kelly* (1970), which established a right to an "evidentiary hearing" prior to termination of welfare benefits. The Secretary contended that *Goldberg* was not controlling since eligibility for disability benefits, unlike eligibility for welfare benefits, is not based on financial need and since issues of credibility and veracity do not play a significant role in the disability entitlement decision, which turns primarily on medical evidence.

. . . Reasoning that disability determinations may involve subjective judgments based on conflicting medical and nonmedical evidence, the District Court held that prior to termination of benefits Eldridge had to be afforded an evidentiary hearing of the type required for welfare beneficiaries under Title IV of the Social Security Act. . . . We reverse.

* * *

---

[11] [3] The District Court ordered reinstatement of Eldridge's benefits pending its final disposition on the merits.

III

A

*   *   *

. . . " '[D]ue process,' unlike some legal rules, is not a technical conception with a fixed content unrelated to time, place and circumstances." "[D]ue process is flexible and calls for such procedural protections as the particular situation demands." Accordingly, resolution of the issue whether the administrative procedures provided here are constitutionally sufficient requires analysis of the governmental and private interests that are affected. . . .

*   *   *

B

*   *   *

The principal reasons for benefits terminations are that the worker is no longer disabled or has returned to work. As Eldridge's benefits were terminated because he was determined to be no longer disabled, we consider only the sufficiency of the procedures involved in such cases.

The continuing-eligibility investigation is made by a state agency acting through a "team" consisting of a physician and a nonmedical person trained in disability evaluation. The agency periodically communicates with the disabled worker, usually by mail — in which case he is sent a detailed questionnaire — or by telephone, and requests information concerning his present condition, including current medical restrictions and sources of treatment, and any additional information that he considers relevant to his continued entitlement to benefits.

Information regarding the recipient's current condition is also obtained from his sources of medical treatment. If there is a conflict between the information provided by the beneficiary and that obtained from medical sources such as his physician, or between two sources of treatment, the agency may arrange for an examination by an independent consulting physician. Whenever the agency's tentative assessment of the beneficiary's condition differs from his own assessment, the beneficiary is informed that benefits may be terminated, provided a summary of the evidence upon which the proposed determination to terminate is based, and afforded an opportunity to review the medical reports and other evidence in his case file. He also may respond in writing and submit additional evidence.

The state agency then makes its final determination, which is reviewed by an examiner in the SSA Bureau of Disability Insurance. If, as is usually the case, the SSA accepts the agency determination it notifies the recipient in writing, informing him of the reasons for the decision, and of his right to seek *de novo* reconsideration by the state agency. Upon acceptance by the SSA, benefits are terminated effective two months after the month in which medical recovery is found to have occurred.

If the recipient seeks reconsideration by the state agency and the determination is adverse, the SSA reviews the reconsideration determination and notifies the recipient of the decision. He then has a right to an evidentiary hearing before an SSA administrative law judge. The hearing is nonadversary, and the SSA is not represented by counsel. As at all prior and subsequent stages of the administrative process, however, the claimant may be represented by counsel or other spokesmen. If this hearing results in an adverse decision, the claimant is entitled to request discretionary review by the SSA Appeals Council, and finally may obtain judicial review.

Should it be determined at any point after termination of benefits, that the claimant's disability extended beyond the date of cessation initially established, the worker is entitled to retroactive payments. If, on the other hand, a beneficiary receives any payments to which he is later determined not to be entitled, the statute authorizes the Secretary to attempt to recoup these funds in specified circumstances.

C

Despite the elaborate character of the administrative procedures provided by the Secretary, the courts below held them to be constitutionally inadequate, concluding that due process requires an evidentiary hearing prior to termination. In light of the private and governmental interests at stake here and the nature of the existing procedures, we think this was error.

Since a recipient whose benefits are terminated is awarded full retroactive relief if he ultimately prevails, his sole interest is in the uninterrupted receipt of this source of income pending final administrative decision on his claim. . . .

Only in *Goldberg* has the Court held that due process requires an evidentiary hearing prior to a temporary deprivation. It was emphasized there that welfare assistance is given to persons on the very margin of subsistence. . . . Eligibility for disability benefits, in contrast, is not based upon financial need. Indeed, it is wholly unrelated to the worker's income or support from many other sources. . . .

* * *

In view of the torpidity of this administrative review process, and the typically modest resources of the family unit of the physically disabled worker, the hardship imposed upon the erroneously terminated disability recipient may be significant. Still, the disabled worker's need is likely to be less than that of a welfare recipient. In addition to the possibility of access to private resources, other forms of government assistance will become available where the termination of disability benefits places a worker or his family below the subsistence level. In view of these potential sources of temporary income, there is less reason here than in *Goldberg* to depart from the ordinary principle, established by our decisions, that something less than an evidentiary hearing is sufficient prior to adverse administrative action.

D

An additional factor to be considered here is the fairness and reliability of the existing pretermination procedures, and the probable value, if any, of additional procedural safeguards. Central to the evaluation of any administrative process is the nature of the relevant inquiry. In order to remain eligible for benefits the disabled worker must demonstrate by means of "medically acceptable clinical and laboratory diagnostic techniques," that he is unable "to engage in any substantial gainful activity by reason of any *medically determinable* physical or mental impairment. . . ." In short, a medical assessment of the worker's physical or mental condition is required. This is a more sharply focused and easily documented decision than the typical determination of welfare entitlement. In the latter case, a wide variety of information may be deemed relevant, and issues of witness credibility and veracity often are critical to the decisionmaking process. *Goldberg* noted that in such circumstances "written submissions are a wholly unsatisfactory basis for decision."

By contrast, the decision whether to discontinue disability benefits will turn, in most cases, upon "routine, standard, and unbiased medical reports by physician specialists," concerning a subject whom they have personally examined. In [an earlier case we] recognized the "reliability and probative worth of written medical reports," emphasizing that while there may be "professional disagreement with the medical conclusions" the "specter of questionable credibility and veracity is not present." To be sure, credibility and veracity may be a factor in the ultimate disability assessment in some cases. But procedural due process rules are shaped by the risk of error inherent in the truthfinding process as applied to the generality of cases, not the rare exceptions. The potential value of an evidentiary hearing, or even oral presentation to the decisionmaker, is substantially less in this context than in *Goldberg*.

E

In striking the appropriate due process balance the final factor to be assessed is the public interest. This includes the administrative burden and other societal costs that would be associated with requiring, as a matter of constitutional right, an evidentiary hearing upon demand in all cases prior to the termination of disability benefits. The most visible burden would be the incremental cost resulting from the increased number of hearings and the expense of providing benefits to ineligible recipients pending decision. No one can predict the extent of the increase, but the fact that full benefits would continue until after such hearings would assure the exhaustion in most cases of this attractive option. Nor would the theoretical right of the Secretary to recover undeserved benefits result, as a practical matter, in any substantial offset to the added outlay of public funds. The parties submit widely varying estimates of the probable additional financial cost. We only need say that experience with the constitutionalizing of government procedures suggests that the ultimate additional cost in terms of money and administrative burden would not be insubstantial.

Financial cost alone is not a controlling weight in determining whether due process requires a particular procedural safeguard prior to some administrative decision. But the Government's interest, and hence that of the public, in conserving scarce fiscal and administrative resources is a factor that must be weighed. At some point the benefit of an additional safeguard to the individual affected by the administrative action and to society in terms of increased assurance that the action is just, may be outweighed by the cost. . . .

But more is implicated in cases of this type than ad hoc weighing of fiscal and administrative burdens against the interests of a particular category of claimants. The ultimate balance involves a determination as to when, under our constitutional system, judicial-type procedures must be imposed upon administrative action to assure fairness. We reiterate the wise admonishment of Mr. Justice Frankfurter that differences in the origin and function of administrative agencies "preclude wholesale transplantation of the rules of procedure, trial, and review which have evolved from the history and experience of courts." The judicial model of an evidentiary hearing is neither a required, nor even the most effective, method of decisionmaking in all circumstances. The essence of due process is the requirement that "a person in jeopardy of serious loss [be given] notice of the case against him and opportunity to meet it." All that is necessary is that the procedures be tailored, in light of the decision to be made, to "the capacities and circumstances of those who are to be heard," to insure that they are given a meaningful opportunity to present their case. In assessing what process is due in this case, substantial weight must be given to the good-faith judgments of the individuals charged by Congress with the administration of social welfare programs that the procedures they have provided assure fair consideration of the entitlement claims of individuals. This is especially so where, as here, the prescribed procedures not only provide the claimant with an effective process for asserting his claim prior to any administrative action, but also assure a right to an evidentiary hearing, as well as to subsequent judicial review, before the denial of his claim becomes final.

We conclude that an evidentiary hearing is not required prior to the termination of disability benefits and that the present administrative procedures fully comport with due process.

The judgment of the Court of Appeals is

Reversed.

Mr. Justice Brennan, with whom Mr. Justice Marshall concurs, dissenting.

. . . [T]he Court's consideration that a discontinuance of disability benefits may cause the recipient to suffer only a limited deprivation is no argument. It is speculative. Moreover, the very legislative determination to provide disability benefits, without any prerequisite determination of need in fact, presumes a need by the recipient which is not this Court's function to denigrate. Indeed, in the present case, it is indicated that because disability benefits were terminated there was a foreclosure upon the Eldridge home and the family's furniture was repossessed, forcing Eldridge, his wife, and their children to sleep in one bed. Finally, it is also no argument that a worker, who has been placed in the untenable position of having been denied disability benefits, may still seek other forms of public assistance.

NOTES AND QUESTIONS

1.   You will have noticed that the argument in favor of a pretermination hearing which succeeded in *Goldberg v. Kelly* fails in *Mathews v. Eldridge*. Why is that? Did

Justice Powell adopt Justice Black's dissenting position in *Goldberg* or did he accept Justice Brennan's balancing test and just balance things differently? How can the procedural due process requirements differ in the two cases? Why weren't the dissenters convinced?

2.   While *Goldberg* and *Mathews* differ over when due process must be provided, the basic elements of due process have long been regarded as notice, meaningful hearing, and impartial decisionmaker. *Mullane v. Central Hanover Bank & Trust Co.*, 339 U.S. 306, 313 (1950). There are many hidden issues, however. Some relate to the timing of the proceeding. Others explore whether the hearing must be akin to a trial or more informal. Still others apply to whether the claimant can be represented by a lawyer, and even, whether, as in criminal trials and appeals, an attorney must be appointed for an indigent person. Finally, issues of standards of proof also have a bearing on the issue of due process. At one time it was thought that government had a relatively free hand in defining the elements of due process in the same way that it might define other entitlements. In *Arnett v. Kennedy*, 416 U.S. 134 (1974), a plurality of the Court argued that the grant of a substantive right is inextricably linked with the procedures to be applied. The Court later rejected this view, however. Now, the minimum procedures required are said to be a constitutional question to be answered by the judiciary, not a statutory question for the legislature. *Cleveland Bd. of Educ. v. Loudermill*, 470 U.S. 532 (1985). You may have noticed that *Mathews* supplies a balancing test for determining what process is due. The factors listed as being balanced are:

> First, the private interest that will be affected by the official action; second, the risk of an erroneous deprivation of such interest through the procedures used, and the probable value, if any, of additional or substitute procedural safeguards; and finally, the Government's interest, including the function involved and the fiscal and administrative burdens that the additional or substitute procedural requirements would entail.

470 U.S. at 535. Are you convinced that the *Mathews* balancing formulation provides a genuine standard? Justice Rehnquist has remarked that under *Mathews* "[t]he balance is simply an ad hoc weighing which depends to a great extent upon how the Court subjectively views the underlying interests at stake." *Cleveland Bd. of Educ. v. Loudermill*, 470 U.S. 532, 562 (1985) (Rehnquist, J., dissenting).

3.   You may be getting the sense that the rules regarding procedural due process are amorphous indeed. So far you have seen two cases where plaintiffs sought to recover government benefits, but the language of procedural due process is ambiguous enough so that other victims of "undue process" might logically seek the aid of the courts. This has been especially true with regard to process that has resulted in large punitive damage awards. In *Browning-Ferris Industries of Vermont v. Kelco Disposal, Inc.*, 492 U.S. 257 (1989), the Court both rejected a challenge to punitive damages under the Eighth Amendment's Excessive Fines Clause and declined to address any due process implications. However, Justice Brennan in a separate concurrence said the Court was leaving "the door open for a holding that the Due Process Clause constrains the imposition of punitive damages." That was especially true, said Brennan, if those damages could be said to be "grossly excessive" or "so severe and oppressive as to be wholly dispropor-

tioned to the offense and obviously unreasonable."

4. It should be stressed that the *Mathews v. Eldridge* test applies to *procedural* due process problems. The test for alleged violations of the *substantive* element in the Due Process Clauses is usually the strict scrutiny test. There is one area of the law, however, in which a different approach is taken with respect to both procedural and substantive due process problems — punitive damages. In a series of modern cases, the Court laid out the appropriate tests and exhibited the divisions of opinion among the Justices on the issue. First, in 1991, in *Pacific Mutual Life Insurance Co. v. Haslip*, 499 U.S. 1 (1991), the Court ruled that neither the concept of punitive damages nor the procedures used by the State of Alabama (Alabama allowed punitive damages to be assessed against employers of tortfeasors under the *respondeat superior* doctrine) violated the Die Process Clause of the 14th Amendment. In dissent, Justice O'Connor applied the *Matthews v. Eldridge* test. The majority, led by Justice Blackmun, however, did not. Without identifying by name the test that it was using, the majority reasoned that punitive damages, considered in the abstract, do not violate due process, in part at least because of their historic pedigree:

> In view of this consistent history, we cannot say that the common-law method for assessing punitive damages is so inherently unfair as to deny due process and be *per se* unconstitutional. If a thing has been practiced for two hundred years by common consent, it will need a strong case for the Fourteenth Amendment to affect it.

In terms of *procedural* due process, *i.e.*, the fairness of the award of punitive damages under the procedures used by the State of Alabama, the majority focused on the availability, under Alabama law, of judicial and appellate review of the award of punitive damages, and concluded that due process was not violated.

Justice Scalia's approach in concurrence eschewed the majority's focus on inherent fairness. Scalia reasoned that the punitive-damages practice used from time immemorial (1) has a strong historic pedigree, and (2) does not violate any specific provision of the Bill of Rights. Thus punitive damages (or at least the historic procedures for the awarding of punitive damages) cannot possibly be a violation of Due Process of Law. He wrote:

> Since it has been the traditional practice of American courts to leave punitive damages . . . to the discretion of the jury, and since in my view a process that accords with such a tradition and does not violate the Bill of Rights necessarily constitutes "due process"; I would approve the procedure challenged here without further inquiry into its "fairness" or "reasonableness."

In recent years the Court has been active in what might be called a judicial effort at tort reform in the context of punitive damages — reining in the tendency of juries to render "jackpot"-sized punitive-damages awards. In the 1991 *Pacific Mutual* case, the Court expressed its "concern about punitive damages that 'run wild' " while at the same time sustaining the award of punitive damages that bore a 4 to 1 ratio to compensatories in that case. Two years later, in *TXO Production Corp v. Alliance Resources Corp.*, 509 U.S. 443 (1993), the Court once again expressed its concern, while sustaining a $10 million award. In *TXO*, the Court contented itself with ruling that Due Process required an adequate jury instruction and a post-verdict review (*e.g.*, *remittitur*) procedure. The implication seemed to be that as long as those *procedural* Due Process requirements were met, the *substantive* size of the punitive damages award didn't really matter.

In *BMW of North America, Inc. v. Gore*, 517 U.S. 559 (1996), the Court ruled that the size of the award can be so great that it will violate the *substantive* element in the Due Process Clause. In determining whether an award of punitive damages is so high as to be unconstitutional, the Court looks to three factors: (1) the degree of reprehensibility of the defendant's conduct, (2) the disparity between the harm or potential harm suffered by the plaintiff and the punitive damage award (in essence, the disparity between the amount of compensatory damages and the amount of punitive damages awarded), and (3) the difference between the punitive damages awarded by the jury and the any civil penalties authorized or imposed in comparable cases. The *BMW* Court also looked at what might be considered a fourth factor, namely the existence or nonexistence of less drastic alternatives to the punitive damages remedy. One of the issues in *BMW* was whether the Due Process Clause allowed a state court to consider evidence of tortious activity committed in other states in assessing a punitive damages amount, and the Court ruled in the negative on that issue.

In *Cooper Industries Inc. v. Leatherman Tool Group, Inc.*, 532 U.S. 424 (2001), the Court returned to the *procedural* due process concept and tightened its analysis a bit. It ruled that due process required that an appellate court's handling of a punitive damages award had to be by a *de novo* review, rather than by the abuse-of-discretion standard. Then, in 2003, in *State Farm v. Campbell*, 538 U.S. 408 (2003), the Court reiterated and applied the approach that it took in *BMW* and took the occasion to suggest that any disparity between punitive damages and compensatory damages that gets above the single-digit level, (*i.e.*, above 9 to 1) is going to be suspect. The Court cautioned, however, that it was not drawing a bright line.

The Court's latest skirmish in the punitive damages arena occurred in the context of the war on tobacco, and it resulted in an unusual alignment of the justices. In *Philip Morris v. Williams*, 549 U.S. 346 (2007), Justices Breyer, Kennedy, Souter, Alito, and Chief Justice Roberts comprised the majority of 5, and Justices Stevens, Thomas, Ginsburg, and Scalia dissented. Led by Justice Breyer, the Court held that *procedural* due process is violated when a jury bases the amount its award of punitive damages on harm to anyone other than the plaintiff or plaintiffs before the court. The holding, however, was not actually that simple — because the Court recognized that juries can consider harm to others when assessing the reprehensibility of the defendant's conduct. *i.e.*, a jury can take harm to nonparties into account when assessing reprehensibility, but not when assessing the amount of punitive damages. That seems to mean something like this: A jury can look at harm to others and reach the conclusion that the defendant's conduct was, say, doubly or triply "reprehensible" because it caused harm to so many persons, but the jury cannot assess a higher punitive-damages amount because of that higher degree of reprehensibility. The Court — perhaps sensing what bothered the dissenters (and perhaps other readers of its opinion) — posed the question to itself:

How can we know whether a jury, in taking account of harm caused others under the rubric of reprehensibility, also seeks to *punish* the defendant for having caused injury to others? Our answer is that state courts cannot authorize procedures that create an unreasonable and unnecessary risk of any such confusion occurring.

Presumably, the Court had in mind proper jury instructions and proper rules for what counsel may or may not say in argumentation and summation. The Court's rationale was perhaps a bit clearer than its holding. A jury cannot base an award of punitive damages upon its desire to punish the defendant for harming persons who are not before the court because:

> [A] defendant threatened with punishment for injuring a nonparty victim has no opportunity to defend against the charge, by showing, for example in a case such as this, that the other victim was not entitled to damages because he or she knew that smoking was dangerous [and therefore presumably assumed the risk] or did not rely upon the defendant's statements to the contrary.

> . . . [T]o permit punishment for injuring a nonparty victim would add a near standardless dimension to the punitive damages equation. . . . [and skip about 5 lines to where the Court said] . . . [T]he fundamental due process concerns to which our punitive damages cases refer — risks of arbitrariness, uncertainty and lack of notice — will be magnified.

On the *substantive* due process issue, the Court balked on the question of the amount of punitive damages awarded in this case — $79.5 million as compared to less than $1 million in compensatories. At the very end of the majority opinion, the Court opined that there may be a need for a new trial, and if so, it would handle the question of whether an 80 to 1 ratio or punitives to compensatories was or was not constitutionally excessive.

Chapter 4

A GOVERNMENT COMMITMENT TO FREEDOM

A. FIRST AMENDMENT SPEECH

This Chapter returns us to the very First Amendment to the Constitution. That Amendment protects the right to freedom of religion and freedom of expression from government interference. In an earlier chapter we examined the Religion Clauses (Establishment and Free Exercise); in this Chapter, we examine freedom of speech or more broadly expression. Within the ambit of this Amendment are the rights to freedom of speech, press, assembly and to petition the government for a redress of grievances, and the implied right of association. While partially grounded in history, the meaning of these freedoms is principally the product of the Supreme Court. While the rights are often specified as being "fundamental," and thereby meriting a form of heightened, even strict, scrutiny, we will see very quickly that there are various answers given to the question: how strict? By its terms, the expression-related aspect of the Amendment applied only to Congress, but by judicial incorporation, the First Amendment protects against like interference by state governments via the Due Process Clause of the Fourteenth Amendment.

While our presentation will soon reveal how the jurisprudence in this area consists of separate frames of analysis or "tests" applied to the individual ways in which governments seek to limit expressive activities, students should not lose the underlying reason for this constitutional protection. First Amendment scholar Dean Rodney Smolla nicely captures that underlying purpose by referencing the comment of Justice Oliver Wendell Holmes in dissent in *Abrams v. United States* (1919), where Holmes relates that "persecution for the expression of opinions seems . . . perfectly logical if you have no doubt of your premises or your power." Under such circumstances, it is natural to "express your wishes in law and sweep away all opposition." Censorship, Dean Smolla speculates, thus begins as the seemingly confident view of the social good of a responsible citizen. The problem is that how ever responsible a given perspective may seem, it is not necessarily built on truth. Of course, it might be. For example, keeping a book about bomb making off the Internet could be premised upon the simple truth that no one has a right to endanger the life of another. Yet very little can be assumed. Upon examination, the suppression of the book might have more to do with covering-up a governmental misdeed in which case the issue would take on a very different complexion.

Speech is a necessary support of democracy, or as Justice Louis Brandeis put it concurring in *Whitney v. California* (1927), "freedom to think as you will and to speak as you think are means indispensable to the discovery and spread of political truth." In this regard, it is rightly said that the First Amendment protection of expression serves as an indispensable check against government abuse. More than a few governmental abuses of power have come to light only because a dissenting voice has been free to object and has had access to a free press.

Finally, in terms of underlying philosophy, it is common to see the constitutional protection of expression linked with honoring the individual dignity and creativity of each person. Indeed, First Amendment freedom of expression is vital for giving due respect to the benefits and inventiveness that arises when an individual sets off in previously untried directions and is able to contribute to a "marketplace of ideas."

Thus far, we have been speaking of the protection afforded "expressive activity," but this is a category regularly broken down in the Court's cases. The most basic component of freedom of expression is the right of freedom of speech. The right to freedom of speech allows individuals to express themselves without interference or constraint by the government. The Supreme Court requires the government to provide substantial justification for the interference with the right of free speech where the government attempts to regulate the *content* of the speech. A less stringent test is applied for content-neutral legislation, particularly that which controls the "time, place, or manner" of the expression. The government is also given greater latitude over content — but not viewpoint — where it creates a public forum limited to a certain subject matter. Thus, a bookstore located in the Supreme Court may be devoted exclusively to books on the Court, but it may not exclude this volume or others because the Court may dislike, say, our candid inquiry into whether original understanding really supports a non-militia-related gun right under the Second Amendment. The Supreme Court has also recognized that the government may prohibit some speech that may cause an imminent breach of the peace or cause violence. Relatedly, and more deferentially, the government may limit the speech of a government employee to avoid workplace disruption.

The right to free speech includes the various mediums of expression that communicate a message. While freedom of the press is sometimes thought to be a greater expressive freedom, in fact, it is not. Indeed, it is still good law, though questionable physics, that because of the limits of the electromagnetic spectrum, government has greater latitude to regulate the licensees it permits to use that spectrum. The First Amendment by and large does not give members of the media any special rights or privileges not afforded to citizens in general, even as an individual legislature may give members of the press some specialized statutory protections for their sources under so-called "shield laws."

The right to assemble allows people to gather for peaceful and lawful purposes. Implicit within this right are the rights to association and belief. The right to associate prohibits the government from requiring a group to register or disclose its members or from denying government benefits on the basis of an individual's current or past membership in a particular group. There are exceptions to this rule where the Court finds that governmental interests in disclosure or registration outweigh interference with First Amendment rights. The government may also, generally, not compel individuals to express themselves, hold certain beliefs, or belong to particular associations or groups.

The right to petition the government for a redress of grievances guarantees people the right to ask the government to provide relief for a wrong through the courts (litigation) or other governmental action. It works with the right of assembly by allowing people to join together and seek change from the government.

In addition to the substantive scope of the protection of the First Amendment, there are certain procedural safeguards that maintain the constitutional adequacy of this protection. One of the most important is independent judicial review, by appellate courts when reviewing a verdict and by trial courts on motions for judgment notwithstanding the verdict or for summary judgment. Under Court precedent, appellate courts may not just turn over vague phrases such as "actual malice," "incitement," or "sexually explicit expression" to fact-finders, and then defer to the fact-finders' conclusions about what constitutes libel, incitement, or obscenity. Instead, courts must conduct an independent review of the record both to be sure that the speech in question actually is unprotected and to confine the parameters of any unprotected category within acceptably narrow limits in an effort to ensure that protected expression will not be inhibited. It is via this independent review that errors are avoided and the line between protected and unprotected speech can be better discerned.

1. The Presumption Against Prior Restraint

As a matter of original understanding, the First Amendment "has meant, principally although not exclusively, immunity from previous restraints or censorship." *Near v. Minnesota ex rel. Olson* (1931). "Any system of prior restraints of expression comes to this Court bearing a heavy presumption against its constitutional validity." *Bantam Books v. Sullivan* (1963). Government thus carries a heavy burden of showing justification for the imposition of such a restraint. Under the English licensing system, which expired in 1695, all printing presses and printers were licensed and nothing could be published without prior approval of the state or church authorities. The great struggle for liberty of the press was for the right to publish without a license that which for a long time could be published only with a license.

The Court unfortunately has never undertaken to explore the kinds of restrictions to which the term "prior restraint" can apply or to do more than assert that only in "exceptional circumstances" would prior restraint be permissible. Nevertheless, the doctrine has been relied upon to invalidate poorly drafted statutes and ordinances requiring licenses to hold meetings and parades and to distribute literature if unfettered discretion is conferred upon the licensor. As a general matter, prior licensing is constitutional if the discretion of the issuing official is limited to questions of times, places, and manners. Not surprisingly, the Court has had to wrestle with the concept of prior restraint in the context of national security when the Government attempted to enjoin press publication of classified documents.

In *New York Times Co. v. United States* (1971), the Court rejected the effort to enjoin publication even as applied to documents stolen from the Pentagon (the so-called "Pentagon Papers") that somehow came into the possession of the *New York Times* and the *Washington Post*. That said, six Justices concurred over the principle that in some circumstances prior restraint of publication would be constitutional. Unfortunately, there was little agreement on those circumstances and a short *per curiam* merely recited that "any system of prior restraints of expression comes to this Court bearing a heavy presumption against its constitutional validity. . . . [T]he Government ha[s] not met that burden." Here is a sample of some of the individual opinions:

MR. JUSTICE BLACK, with whom MR. JUSTICE DOUGLAS joins, concurring.

. . . I believe that every moment's continuance of the injunctions against these newspapers amounts to a flagrant, indefensible, and continuing violation of the First Amendment. . . . In my view it is unfortunate that some of my Brethren are apparently willing to hold that the publication of news may sometimes be enjoined. Such a holding would make a shambles of the First Amendment.

Our Government was launched in 1789 with the adoption of the Constitution. The Bill of Rights, including the First Amendment, followed in 1791. Now, for the first time in the 182 years since the founding of the Republic, the federal courts are asked to hold that the First Amendment does not mean what it says, but rather means that the Government can halt the publication of current news of vital importance to the people of this country.

In seeking injunctions against these newspapers and in its presentation to the Court, the Executive Branch seems to have forgotten the essential purpose and history of the First Amendment. When the Constitution was adopted, many people strongly opposed it because the document contained no Bill of Rights to safeguard certain basic freedoms. They especially feared that the new powers granted to a central government might be interpreted to permit the government to curtail freedom of religion, press, assembly, and speech. In response to an overwhelming public clamor, James Madison offered a series of amendments to satisfy citizens that these great liberties would remain safe and beyond the power of government to abridge. Madison proposed what later became the First Amendment in three parts, . . . one of which proclaimed "The people shall not be deprived or abridged of their right to speak, to write, or to publish their sentiments; *and the freedom of the press, as one of the great bulwarks of liberty, shall be inviolable."* (Emphasis added.) The amendments were offered to *curtail* and *restrict* the general powers granted to the Executive, Legislative, and Judicial Branches two years before in the original Constitution. . . .

The Government's case here is based on premises entirely different from those that guided the Framers of the First Amendment. The Solicitor General has carefully and emphatically stated:

"Now, MR. JUSTICE [BLACK], your construction of . . . [the First Amendment] is well known, and I certainly respect it. You say that no law means no law, and that should be obvious. I can only say, Mr. Justice, that to me it is equally obvious that 'no law' does not mean 'no law', and I would seek to persuade the Court that that is true. . . . [T]here are other parts of the Constitution that grant powers and responsibilities to the Executive, and . . . the First Amendment was not intended to make it impossible for the Executive to function or to protect the security of the United States."

. . . The word "security" is a broad, vague generality whose contours should not be invoked to abrogate the fundamental law embodied in the First Amendment. The guarding of military and diplomatic secrets at the expense of informed representative government provides no real security for our Republic. The Framers of the First Amendment, fully aware of both the need to defend a new nation and the abuses of the English and Colonial governments, sought to give this new society strength and security by providing that freedom of speech, press, religion, and assembly should not be abridged. . . .

MR. JUSTICE DOUGLAS, with whom MR. JUSTICE BLACK joins, concurring.

. . . So any power that the Government possesses must come from its "inherent power."

The power to wage war is "the power to wage war successfully." But the war power stems from a declaration of war. The Constitution by Art. I, § 8, gives Congress, not the President, power "[t]o declare War." Nowhere are presidential wars authorized. We need not decide therefore what leveling effect the war power of Congress might have.

These disclosures may have a serious impact. But that is no basis for sanctioning a previous restraint on the press. . . .

The Government says that it has inherent powers to go into court and obtain an injunction to protect the national interest, which in this case is alleged to be national security. . . .

The dominant purpose of the First Amendment was [to prohibit the widespread practice of governmental suppression of embarrassing information.] It is common knowledge that the First Amendment was adopted against the widespread use of the common law of seditious libel to punish the dissemination of material that is embarrassing to the powers-that-be. The present cases will, I think, go down in history as the most dramatic illustration of that principle. A debate of large proportions goes on in the Nation over our posture in Vietnam. That debate antedated the disclosure of the contents of the present documents. The latter are highly relevant to the debate in progress.

Secrecy in government is fundamentally anti-democratic, perpetuating bureaucratic errors. Open debate and discussion of public issues are vital to our national health. On public questions there should be "uninhibited, robust, and wide-open" debate. . . .

MR. JUSTICE BRENNAN, concurring.

I write separately in these cases only to emphasize what should be apparent: that our judgments in the present cases may not be taken to indicate the propriety, in the future, of issuing temporary stays and restraining orders to block the publication of material sought to be suppressed by the Government . . .

Mr. Justice White, with whom Mr. Justice Stewart joins, concurring.

I concur in today's judgments, but only because of the concededly extraordinary protection against prior restraints enjoyed by the press under our constitutional system. . . .

At least in the absence of legislation by Congress, based on its own investigations and findings, I am quite unable to agree that the inherent powers of the Executive and the courts reach so far as to authorize remedies having such sweeping potential for inhibiting publications by the press. Much of the difficulty inheres in the "grave and irreparable danger" standard suggested by the United States. If the United States were to have judgment under such a standard in these cases, our decision would be of little guidance to other courts in other cases, for the material at issue here would not be available from the Court's opinion or from public records, nor would it be published by the press. Indeed, even today where we hold that the United States has not met its burden, the material remains sealed in court records and it is properly not discussed in today's opinions. Moreover, because the material poses substantial dangers to national interests and because of the hazards of criminal sanctions, a responsible press may choose never to publish the more sensitive materials. To sustain the Government in these cases would start the courts down a long and hazardous road that I am not willing to travel, at least without congressional guidance and direction.

Mr. Justice Marshall, concurring.

. . . The problem here is whether in these particular cases the Executive Branch has authority to invoke the equity jurisdiction of the courts to protect what it believes to be the national interest. The Government argues that in addition to the inherent power of any government to protect itself, the President's power to conduct foreign affairs and his position as Commander in Chief give him authority to impose censorship on the press to protect his ability to deal effectively with foreign nations and to conduct the military affairs of the country. . . .

It would, however, be utterly inconsistent with the concept of separation of powers for this Court to use its power of contempt to prevent behavior that Congress has specifically declined to prohibit. . . .

Mr. Chief Justice Burger, dissenting.

. . . It is not disputed that the Times has had unauthorized possession of the documents for three to four months, during which it has had its expert analysts studying them, presumably digesting them and preparing the material for publication. During all of this time, the Times, presumably in its capacity as trustee of the public's "right to know," has held up publication for purposes it considered proper and thus public knowledge was delayed. No doubt this was for a good reason; the analysis of 7,000 pages of complex material drawn from a vastly greater volume of material would inevitably take time and the writing of good news stories takes time. But why should the United States Government, from whom this information was illegally acquired by someone, along with all the counsel, trial judges, and appellate judges be placed under needless pressure? After these months of deferral, the alleged "right to know" has somehow and suddenly become a right that must be vindicated instanter.

Would it have been unreasonable, since the newspaper could anticipate the Government's objections to release of secret material, to give the Government an opportunity to review the entire collection and determine whether agreement could be reached on publication? Stolen or not, if security was not in fact jeopardized, much of the material could no doubt have been declassified, since it spans a period ending in 1968. With such an approach — one that great newspapers have in the past practiced and stated editorially to be the duty of an honorable press — the newspapers and Government might well have narrowed the area of disagreement as to what was and was not publishable, leaving the remainder to be resolved in orderly litigation, if necessary. To me it is hardly believable that a newspaper long regarded as a great institution in American life would fail to perform one of the basic and simple duties of every citizen with respect to the discovery or possession of stolen property or secret government documents. That duty, I had thought — perhaps naively — was to report forthwith, to responsible public officers. This duty rests on taxi drivers, Justices, and the New York Times. The course followed by the Times, whether so calculated or not, removed any possibility of orderly litigation of the issues. . . .

Mr. Justice Harlan, with whom The Chief Justice and Mr. Justice Blackmun join, dissenting.

These cases forcefully call to mind the wise admonition of Mr. Justice Holmes, dissenting in *Northern Securities Co. v. United States* (1904):

"Great cases like hard cases make bad law. For great cases are called great, not by reason of their real importance in shaping the law of the future, but because of some accident of immediate overwhelming interest which appeals to the feelings and distorts the judgment. These immediate interests exercise a kind of hydraulic pressure which makes what previously was clear seem doubtful, and before which even well settled principles of law will bend."

With all respect, I consider that the Court has been almost irresponsibly feverish in dealing with these cases.

Both the Court of Appeals for the Second Circuit and the Court of Appeals for the District of Columbia Circuit rendered judgment on June 23. The New York Times' petition for certiorari, its motion for accelerated consideration thereof, and its application for interim relief were filed in this Court on June 24 at about 11 a.m. The application of the United States for interim relief in the *Post* case was also filed here on June 24 at about 7:15 p.m. This Court's order setting a hearing before us on June 26 at 11 a.m., a course which I joined only to avoid the possibility of even more peremptory action by the Court, was issued less than 24 hours before. The record in the *Post* case was filed with the Clerk shortly before 1 p.m. on June 25; the record in the *Times* case did not arrive until 7 or 8 o'clock that same night. The briefs of the parties were received less than two hours before argument on June 26.

This frenzied train of events took place in the name of the presumption against prior restraints created by the First Amendment. Due regard for the extraordinarily important and difficult questions involved in these litigations should have led the Court to shun such a precipitate timetable. In order to decide the merits of these cases properly, some or all of the following questions should have been faced:

1. Whether the Attorney General is authorized to bring these suits in the name of the United States. This question involves as well the construction and validity of a singularly opaque statute — the Espionage Act, 18 U.S.C. § 793(e).

2. Whether the First Amendment permits the federal courts to enjoin publication of stories which would present a serious threat to national security.

3. Whether the threat to publish highly secret documents is of itself a sufficient implication of national security to justify an injunction on the theory that regardless of the contents of the documents harm enough results simply from the demonstration of such a breach of secrecy.

4. Whether the unauthorized disclosure of any of these particular documents would seriously impair the national security.

5. What weight should be given to the opinion of high officers in the Executive Branch of the Government with respect to questions 3 and 4.

6. Whether the newspapers are entitled to retain and use the documents notwithstanding the seemingly uncontested facts that the documents, or the originals of which they are duplicates, were purloined from the Government's possession and that the newspapers received them with knowledge that they had been feloniously acquired.

7. Whether the threatened harm to the national security or the Government's possessory interest in the documents justifies the issuance of an injunction against publication in light of —

     a. The strong First Amendment policy against prior restraints on publication;

     b. The doctrine against enjoining conduct in violation of criminal statutes; and

     c. The extent to which the materials at issue have apparently already been otherwise disseminated.

These are difficult questions of fact, of law, and of judgment; the potential consequences of erroneous decision are enormous. The time which has been available to us, to the lower courts, and to the parties has been wholly inadequate for giving these cases the kind of consideration they deserve. . . .

*   *   *

Accordingly, I would vacate the judgment of the Court of Appeals for the District of Columbia Circuit on this ground and remand the case for further proceedings in the District Court. Before the commencement of such further proceedings, due opportunity should be afforded the Government for procuring from the Secretary of State or the Secretary of Defense or both an expression of their views on the issue of national security. The ensuing review by the District Court should be in accordance with the views expressed in this opinion. And for the reasons stated above I would affirm the judgment of the Court of Appeals for the Second Circuit.

Pending further hearings in each case conducted under the appropriate ground rules, I would continue the restraints on publication. I cannot believe that the doctrine prohibiting prior restraints reaches to the point of preventing courts from maintaining the *status quo* long enough to act responsibly in matters of such national importance as those involved here.

Mr. Justice Blackmun, dissenting.

. . . I strongly urge, and sincerely hope, that these two newspapers will be fully aware of their ultimate responsibilities to the United States of America. Judge Wilkey, dissenting in the District of Columbia case, after a review of only the affidavits before his court (the basic papers had not then been made available by either party), concluded that there were a number of examples of documents that, if in the possession of the Post, and if published, "could clearly result in great harm to the nation," and he defined "harm" to mean "the death of soldiers, the destruction of alliances, the greatly increased difficulty of negotiation with our enemies, the inability of our diplomats to negotiate. . . ." I, for one, have now been able to give at least some cursory study not only to the affidavits, but to the material itself. I regret to say that from this examination I fear that Judge Wilkey's statements have possible foundation. I therefore share his concern. I hope that damage has not already been done. If, however, damage has been done, and if, with the Court's action today, these newspapers proceed to publish the critical documents and there results therefrom "the death of soldiers, the destruction of alliances, the greatly increased difficulty of negotiation with our enemies, the inability of our diplomats to negotiate," to which list I might add the factors of prolongation of the war and of further delay in the freeing of United States prisoners, then the Nation's people will know where the responsibility for these sad consequences rests.

NOTES AND QUESTIONS

1. Do you understand why the government was not permitted to suppress the information contained within the Pentagon Papers? Why should citizens be able to publish material critical of the government? Suppose that even true information critical of the government, if published, will fundamentally impair the ability of the government to preserve order and carry out its duties to the people — should that information be allowed to be published? In England, until the late eighteenth century, even truthful criticism of the government was not permitted, pursuant to the doctrine of seditious libel. Under traditional English common law seditious libel doctrine, one could be criminally punished for the publication of any information, true or false, which tended to turn the sentiments of the people against the government. Did that doctrine make any sense? In colonial America the doctrine of seditious libel early came under fire, most notably in the trial of John Peter Zenger, a New York printer, who was prosecuted for seditious libel in the 1730s for comments critical of the New York Governor (then a Crown appointee). There was no doubt that Zenger had published the critical articles in question, nor was there any doubt that under the English common law of seditious libel Zenger was guilty of the crime whether what he published was true or not. "The greater the truth, the greater the libel," was the English common law maxim. Did it make any sense? What sort of a view of government did the English common law of seditious libel reveal?

Zenger's lawyer, a hoary barrister from Philadelphia, one Andrew Hamilton, argued to the jury that whatever the law was in England, in America citizens needed more freedom to criticize their governors, who were not, after all, members of the royal family, but just their representatives in the colonies. Hamilton was not permitted to prove the truth of Zenger's allegations, since the common law rule was that truth was no defense to a charge of seditious libel. In a famous and elegant move, Hamilton then argued to the jury that they should take the fact that he was not permitted to prove truth as a strong argument for the truth of what Zenger published. Remarkably, Hamilton was not censured by the court. What Hamilton argued — that truth ought to be a defense — was clearly not then the law, but he did manage to get the jury to acquit Zenger, even though, under the law as it then was, he should have been convicted. Can you understand what is meant by the term "Philadelphia lawyer"? From that time to this the Zenger trial has been taken to stand for the proposition that freedom of the press is one of the most important features of American law.

2. Just what was meant by "freedom of the press," as that term was used in the First Amendment, is far from clear, however. By 1798 several American theorists, most notably Jefferson and Madison, had begun to argue that the First Amendment forbade any American law of seditious libel. Nevertheless, in 1798 in the famous Alien and Sedition Laws, the United States Congress, controlled by the partisans of John Adams and Alexander Hamilton, fearing subversive activities on the part of a press hostile to the administration and friendly to France, with whom we were engaged in an undeclared naval war, passed a federal statute making it a crime to publish criticism of the government which tended to excite the people of the United States against the government. Alien and Sedition Laws, ch. 74, § 2, 1 Stat. 596, 596–97 (1798) (expired 1801). The 1798 statute departed from the English common

law, and made truth a defense to the crime, but approximately 15 editors and publishers critical of the Adams administration were convicted under the statute and served several months in jail and had fines of up to two thousand dollars levied against them. Jefferson argued that the federal seditious libel law was unconstitutional (under the First Amendment), and succeeded in winning the Presidency in 1800 in part because of his campaign against the act. Once in office, he swiftly pardoned all who had been convicted under the act, although there is evidence that he began state prosecutions for seditious libel against some of *his* critics. Jefferson's and Madison's views — that the First Amendment forbade seditious libel prosecutions — were very much in the minority in the late eighteenth century. What then, did the First Amendment's preservation of "freedom of the press" mean? Most likely it simply meant freedom from what the English called "prior restraint." As Blackstone, the great exponent of the English common law, made clear, for a long time in England there had been a requirement that anyone seeking to publish anything first receive permission from the government. 4 WILLIAM BLACKSTONE, COMMENTARIES *152. This was the so-called law of prior restraint. Under that law, no one could publish anything without the Crown's permission. The late eighteenth-century freedom of the press, achieved at roughly the same time in America and England, was simply freedom from licensing, from prior restraint. In both England and America at that time, the ideal notion was that one should be free to publish anything one wanted, but that one's publications might nevertheless — after publication — subject one to liability for criminal or civil libel. Criminal libel resulted when one published pieces critical of the government, civil libel when one criticized one's fellow subject or citizen. Criminal libel could result in fine and/or imprisonment, civil libel could result in the payment of damages to the person wronged. Another common development — in both England and America in the 1790s — was to establish truth as a defense to seditious libel, and as a matter that was for the determination of the jury. Seditious libel, as late as 1800, however, was alive (if not completely well) in both places.

The Pentagon Papers case reveals how far American society had come on the issue of freedom of the press by the middle of the twentieth century. Should there have been a prior restraint on the publication of the Pentagon Papers?

3. Do you understand from the Pentagon Papers case whether prior restraint is ever permissible? Would it be permissible to publish information regarding our troop movements during time of war? Why was it permissible to publish information critical of the war effort in Vietnam while that war still raged? How does 9-11 and the modern challenge of terrorism figure into this.

For a re-consideration of the Pentagon Papers case in light of the subsequently disclosed "secret brief" filed by Solicitor General Erwin Griswold in the matter, see Douglas W. Kmiec, *The Supreme Court in Times of Hot and Cold War*, 28 J. SUP. CT. HISTORY 270, 290–92 (2003). Professor Kmiec observes:

> While it would later be learned that the negotiating volumes had not, in fact, been leaked to the news organizations, there was ample other classified information of potentially great value to our enemies that had. For example, the stolen materials sought to be enjoined contained: the names of CIA and National Security Agency operatives still active in

Southeast Asia; military plans for dealing with armed aggression in Laos; a discussion of our intelligence methods not then known to the Soviet Union; a Joint Chiefs memorandum recommending "a nuclear response" in the event of a Chinese attack on Thailand; and a fulsome discussion of the extent to which the National Security Agency had been able to break the codes of other nations. With respect to the last item, the Solicitor General pointed out the obvious: disclosure of our code-breaking abilities would permit an enemy nation " 'to minimize our chance of successful interception' with adverse consequences for current U.S. military operations."

Why wasn't this enough to warrant injunctive relief? Largely for reasons that had developed separately in the First Amendment cases during cold war periods — specifically, the need to show that advocacy (or publication) would result in *immediate* or *imminent* harm. Not fully realizing how this nuance of speech jurisprudence might trump inherent executive power over foreign affairs, Griswold lost his case at oral argument when he conceded:

> the materials specified in my closed brief . . . materially affect the security of the United States. It will affect lives. It will affect the process of termination of the war. It will affect the process of recovering prisoners of war. However, I cannot say that the termination of the war, or recovering prisoners of war, is something which has an "immediate" effect on the security of the United States. Nevertheless, I say that it has such an effect on the security of the United States that it ought to be the basis of an injunction in this case.

Why did Griswold not see this as a fatal concession? Perhaps it was because the need for immediacy or imminent lawless action to punish speech or publication is a later judicial graft on the First Amendment. Proximate to the founding, Joseph Story writes: "the language of [the First Amendment] imports no more, than that every man shall have a right to speak, write, and print his opinions upon any subject whatsoever, without any prior restraint. . . ." But Story also observes that the speech right exists *only if* the speaker "does not injure any other person in his rights, person, property, or reputation; and so always that he does not thereby disturb the public peace, or attempt to subvert the government. That this amendment was intended to secure to every citizen an absolute right to speak, or write, or print, whatever he might please, without any responsibility, public or private, therefor, is a supposition too wild to be indulged by any rational man." In Griswold's day, the accepted reading of this passage condemned prior restraints, but it did not necessarily make them all unconstitutional. Griswold might well have understood the Story passage as confirming a right to speak without restraint only if there is no disturbance of public peace or no subversion of the government. After *New York Times*, by contrast, speech or publication can be punished only after the fact, and only when harm is immediately upon us. This is now standard doctrine, but is it completely faithful to the original understanding and sustainable in the national security context? Erwin Griswold, I believe, was suggesting otherwise in a time of cold war. . . .

Does the terrorist threat now undermine the standard academic commentary that reflexively immunizes all speech activity short of imminent harm from illegal action? What would Solicitor General Griswold tell us? My supposition is that it was startling to Solicitor General Griswold that a lack of immediate or imminent damage to national security would preclude the injunctive relief he sought in *New York Times*. Griswold argued that an imminence standard was overly narrow and that it would be better phrased as "great and irreparable harm to the security of the United States." Griswold did not know the diabolical nature of the present al-Qaida threat, of course, but with extraordinary prescience, he further stated, "In the whole diplomatic area the things don't happen at 8:15 tomorrow morning. It may be weeks or months." Indeed, al-Qaida would bring it to New York at 8:48 a.m. one unexceptional September morning, and an anxious nation is still uncertain what dangers lie ahead.

4. Note the arguments of the dissenters. Why do they object to the speed with which this issue found its way to the court and resulted in a decision? Do they also disagree with the substantive law as the majority lays it down? What, if anything, is left of the doctrine of prior restraint? What, precisely, is the public's right to know with regard to the war effort in Vietnam?

You will have noticed the government's argument that the publication of the Pentagon Papers would endanger the lives of United States soldiers in Vietnam, jeopardize the release of prisoners of war, and put in peril the peace process then underway. Why wasn't this persuasive to the court?

5. A noted First Amendment scholar, Thomas Emerson, wrote:

A system of prior restraint is in many ways more inhibiting than a system of subsequent punishment: It is likely to bring under government scrutiny a far wider range of expression; it shuts off communication before it takes place; suppression by a stroke of the pen is more likely to be applied than suppression through a criminal process; the procedures do not require attention to the safeguards of the criminal process; the system allows less opportunity for public appraisal and criticism; the dynamics of the system drive toward excesses, as the history of all censorship shows.

THOMAS EMERSON, THE SYSTEM OF FREEDOM OF EXPRESSION 506 (1970).

6. One reason prior restraints are viewed with distaste is that they are frequently incapable of being challenged even if unconstitutional. In other words, a person violating an unconstitutional prior restraint, especially if issued by a court, may be punished, and precluded from raising the "collateral" issue of unconstitutionality as a defense to contempt of court charges. Thus, in *Walker v. City of Birmingham*, 388 U.S. 307 (1967), Dr. Martin Luther King, Jr. and several other civil rights protestors were not permitted to challenge the punishment meted out for violating a court order that arguably violated the Constitution by preventing them from undertaking a demonstration on a city street without a permit. Why? Because, reasoned the Court, "petitioners were not free to ignore all procedures of the law and carry their battle to the streets. . . . [R]espect for judicial process is a small price to pay for the civilizing hand of law, which alone can give abiding meaning to constitutional freedom." *Id.* at 321.

7.   Technically, a prior restraint is any administrative requirement (*e.g.*, license or permit) or judicial order directed at suppressing speech before it is undertaken. However, the Court has allowed such restraints in the context of abortion protests. *Schenck v. Pro-Choice Network*, 519 U.S. 357 (1997) (upholding an injunction against sidewalk counseling where a request is made to cease and desist), and *Madsen v. Women's Health Center*, 512 U.S. 753 (1994) (upholding a 36-foot buffer zone around an abortion clinic). In both cases, the Court asserted that the judicial orders suppressing the demonstrations or counseling was not aimed at that expression, but at prior unlawful conduct that had impeded the free access of patients and staff to the abortion facility.

8.   The guarantee of a fair trial may also implicate the prior restraint issue. Courts have fairly frequently directed attorneys and other trial participants not to talk with the media. While the Supreme Court has not passed on the constitutionality of this, the logic of such action is bolstered not only by the defendant's rights, but also by the control courts have over attorneys as "officer[s] of the court." By contrast, the Supreme Court has all but eliminated the enforceability of orders regarding pretrial publicity directed at the media, itself. In *Nebraska Press Association v. Stuart*, 427 U.S. 539 (1976), the Court held there is a strong presumption against such orders, absent a showing that the publicity will jeopardize the fairness of the trial, that alternative measures, such as changing location, postponement, or juror screening are unavailing, and that such order would in fact be observed and workable.

2.   Content-Neutral Regulatory Authority in and Outside a "Public Forum"

First Amendment analysis often requires an evaluation of both the place where speech is occurring (a public forum where expression is anticipated by tradition; a nonpublic forum where speech may be prohibited; or a "limited" public forum where the government holds out an area not traditionally subject to expression but now finds it acceptable so long as the limitation is one of subject matter, and not viewpoint, and the limitation makes sense in terms of the nature of the government property). "Limited" public forum restrictions can include, *e.g.*, limiting speech in a courthouse to speech related to judicial proceedings; instruction in the classroom limited to that which relates the subject matter being examined; and many other numerous examples that one could think of. In both public forums and nonpublic forums, the government is able to have reasonable regulation that is content neutral regulating the time place and manner of expression. Expression has a relationship to the place itself.

Nonpublic forums are not intended by the government for public gatherings or expression at all. Examples would be a military base, most public streets and grounds adjacent to school buildings, interoffice mail systems, and public utility poles, just to mention a few. As with public forums and limited public forums, reasonable time place and manner restrictions that are content neutral can also apply, but significantly, in a nonpublic forum, speech can be blocked altogether. Nonpublic forums which the government has not opened for purposes of public gatherings or expression include most prisons and prison grounds, the advertising space on municipal buses, military bases, home mailboxes, public utility poles and even various sidewalk areas like that in front of United States Supreme Court or post office. Speech in limited public forums is invited so long as that expression is matched with the purpose of the government property, *e.g.*, a bookstore run by the National Park Service at the Gettysburg Memorial limited to selling books on the Civil War or on Gettysburg in particular would be an inoffensive limitation in the context of a limited public forum. Aside from observing the subject matter limitation, the only regulation permitted in a public forum or limited public forum is that which meets a compelling governmental interest. Usually, the limitation must be reasonable in relation to "the nature of speech" and advance its objective by a regulatory means no greater than necessary leaving alternative channels of communication open.

In *International Society for Krishna Consciousness, Inc. v. Lee*, 505 U.S. 672 (1992), the Court found that an airport terminal was not a public forum. For the Krishnas, giving away materials and soliciting money is an expressive and religious activity protected by the First Amendment Speech and Religion Clauses. Moreover, the value of allowing expressive activity had to be weighed against the discomfort one feels when approached for money versus the relatively uncomplicated handing off of literature. The place where the solicitation was pursued — an airport — was not intended as a place for public speech gathering but for the expeditious movement of people from check-in to departing aircraft and then back again, which sensibly rendered the airport a nonpublic forum, although modern airport design with shopping centers, restaurants, and much more commercial activity may be changing this over time. In a pair of 5 to 4 votes, with Justice O'Connor playing the switch hitter, the Court held that social solicitation for funds was could be prohibited but distribution of literature in the terminals must be allowed. Thus, the airport was effectively being held to be a public forum in some respects and a limited or nonpublic forum in others.

INTERNATIONAL SOCIETY FOR KRISHNA CONSCIOUSNESS, INC. v. LEE
505 U.S. 672 (1992)

CHIEF JUSTICE REHNQUIST delivered the opinion of the Court.

In this case we consider whether an airport terminal operated by a public authority is a public forum and whether a regulation prohibiting solicitation in the interior of an airport terminal violates the First Amendment.

The relevant facts in this case are not in dispute. Petitioner International Society for Krishna Consciousness, Inc. (ISKCON), is a not-for-profit religious corporation whose members perform a ritual known as *sankirtan*. The ritual consists of " 'going into public places, disseminating religious literature and soliciting funds to support the religion.' " The primary purpose of this ritual is raising funds for the movement.

Respondent Walter Lee, now deceased, was the police superintendent of the Port Authority of New York and New Jersey and was charged with enforcing the regulation at issue. The Port Authority owns and operates three major airports in the greater New York City area. . . .

The airports are funded by user fees and operated to make a regulated profit. Most space at the three airports is leased to commercial airlines, which bear primary responsibility for the leasehold. The Port Authority retains control over unleased portions . . . (we refer to these areas collectively as the "terminals"). The terminals are generally accessible to the general public and contain various commercial establishments such as restaurants, snack stands, bars, newsstands, and stores of various types. Virtually all who visit the terminals do so for purposes related to air travel. . . .

The Port Authority has adopted a regulation forbidding within the terminals the repetitive solicitation of money or distribution of literature. . . .

The regulation governs only the terminals; the Port Authority permits solicitation and distribution on the sidewalks outside the terminal buildings. The regulation effectively prohibits ISKCON from performing *sankirtan* in the terminals. As a result, ISKCON brought suit seeking declaratory and injunctive relief under 42 U.S.C. § 1983, alleging that the regulation worked to deprive its members of rights guaranteed under the First Amendment. The District Court analyzed the claim under the "traditional public forum" doctrine. It concluded that the terminals were akin to public streets, the quintessential traditional public fora. This conclusion in turn meant that the Port Authority's terminal regulation could be sustained only if it was narrowly tailored to support a compelling state interest. In the absence of any argument that the blanket prohibition constituted such narrow tailoring, the District Court granted ISKCON summary judgment.

The Court of Appeals affirmed in part and reversed in part. Relying on our recent decision in *United States v. Kokinda* (1990), a divided panel concluded that the terminals are not public fora. As a result, the restrictions were required only to satisfy a standard of reasonableness. The Court of Appeals then concluded that, presented with the issue, this Court would find that the ban on solicitation was reasonable, but the ban on distribution was not. ISKCON and one of its members, also a petitioner here, sought certiorari respecting the Court of Appeals' decision that the terminals are not public fora and upholding the solicitation ban. Respondent cross-petitioned respecting the court's holding striking down the distribution ban. We granted both petitions, to resolve whether airport terminals are public fora, a question on which the Circuits have split. . . .

It is uncontested that the solicitation at issue in this case is a form of speech protected under the First Amendment. But it is also well settled that the government need not permit all forms of speech on property that it owns and controls. Where the government is acting as a proprietor, managing its internal operations, rather than acting as lawmaker with the power to regulate or license, its action will not be subjected to the heightened review to which its actions as a lawmaker may be subject. Thus, we have upheld a ban on political advertisements in city-operated transit vehicles, even though the city permitted other types of advertising on those vehicles. Similarly, we have permitted a school district to limit access to an internal mail system used to communicate with teachers employed by the district.

These cases reflect, either implicitly or explicitly, a "forum based" approach for assessing restrictions that the government seeks to place on the use of its property. Under this approach, regulation of speech on government property that has traditionally been available for public expression is subject to the highest scrutiny. Such regulations survive only if they are narrowly drawn to achieve a compelling state interest. The second category of public property is the designated public forum, whether of a limited or unlimited character — property that the State has opened for expressive activity by part or all of the public. Regulation of such property is subject to the same limitations as that governing a traditional public forum. Finally, there is all remaining public property. Limitations on expressive activity conducted on this last category of property must survive only a much more limited review. The challenged regulation need only be reasonable, as long as the regulation is not an effort to suppress the speaker's activity due to disagreement with the speaker's view.

The parties do not disagree that this is the proper framework. Rather, they disagree whether the airport terminals are public fora or nonpublic fora. They also disagree whether the regulation survives the "reasonableness" review governing nonpublic fora, should that prove the appropriate category. Like the Court of Appeals, we conclude that the terminals are nonpublic fora and that the regulation reasonably limits solicitation.

The suggestion that the government has a high burden in justifying speech restrictions relating to traditional public fora made its first appearance in *Hague v. Committee for Industrial Organization* (1939). Justice Roberts, concluding that individuals have a right to use "streets and parks for communication of views," reasoned that such a right flowed from the fact that "streets and parks . . . have immemorially been held in trust for the use of the public and, time out of mind, have been used for purposes of assembly, communicating thoughts between citizens, and discussing public questions." We confirmed this observation in *Frisby v. Schultz* (1988), where we held that a residential street was a public forum.

Our recent cases provide additional guidance on the characteristics of a public forum. In *Cornelius* [*v. NAACP Legal Defense & Ed. Fund, Inc.* (1985),] we noted that a traditional public forum is property that has as "a principal purpose . . . the free exchange of ideas." Moreover, consistent with the notion that the government — like other property owners — "has power to preserve the property under its control for the use to which it is lawfully dedicated," the government does not create a public forum by inaction. Nor is a public forum created "whenever members of the public are permitted freely to visit a place owned or operated by the Government." The decision to create a public forum must instead be made "by intentionally opening a nontraditional forum for public discourse." Finally, we have recognized that the location of property also has bearing because separation from acknowledged public areas may serve to indicate that the separated property is a special enclave, subject to greater restriction.

These precedents foreclose the conclusion that airport terminals are public fora. Reflecting the general growth of the air travel industry, airport terminals have only recently achieved their contemporary size and character. But given the lateness with which the modern air terminal has made its appearance, it hardly qualifies for the description of having "immemorially . . . time out of mind" been held in the public trust and used for purposes of expressive activity. Moreover, even within the rather short history of air transport, it is only "[i]n recent years [that] it has become a common practice for various religious and nonprofit organizations to use commercial airports as a forum for the distribution of literature, the solicitation of funds, the proselytizing of new members, and other similar activities." Thus, the tradition of airport activity does not demonstrate that airports have historically been made available for speech activity. Nor can we say that these particular terminals, or airport terminals generally, have been intentionally opened by their operators to such activity; the frequent and continuing litigation evidencing the operators' objections belies any such claim. In short, there can be no argument that society's time-tested judgment, expressed through acquiescence in a continuing practice, has resolved the issue in petitioners' favor.

Petitioners attempt to circumvent the history and practice governing airport activity by pointing our attention to the variety of speech activity that they claim historically occurred at various "transportation nodes" such as rail stations, bus stations, wharves, and Ellis Island. Even if we were inclined to accept petitioners' historical account describing speech activity at these locations, an account respondent contests, we think that such evidence is of little import for two reasons. First, much of the evidence is irrelevant to *public* fora analysis, because sites such as bus and rail terminals traditionally have had *private* ownership. The development of privately owned parks that ban speech activity would not change the public fora status of publicly held parks. But the reverse is also true. The practices of privately held transportation centers do not bear on the government's regulatory authority over a publicly owned airport.

Second, the relevant unit for our inquiry is an airport, not "transportation nodes" generally. When new methods of transportation develop, new methods for accommodating that transportation are also likely to be needed. And with each new step, it therefore will be a new inquiry whether the transportation necessities are compatible with various kinds of expressive activity. To make a category of "transportation nodes," therefore, would unjustifiably elide what may prove to be critical differences of which we should rightfully take account. The "security magnet," for example, is an airport commonplace that lacks a counterpart in bus terminals and train stations. And public access to air terminals is also not infrequently restricted — just last year the Federal Aviation Administration required airports for a 4-month period to limit access to areas normally publicly accessible. To blithely equate airports with other transportation centers, therefore, would be a mistake.

The differences among such facilities are unsurprising since, as the Court of Appeals noted, airports are commercial establishments funded by users fees and designed to make a regulated profit, and where nearly all who visit do so for some travel related purpose. As commercial enterprises, airports must provide services attractive to the marketplace. In light of this, it cannot fairly be said that an airport terminal has as a principal purpose promoting "the free exchange of ideas." To the contrary, the record demonstrates that Port Authority management considers the purpose of the terminals to be the facilitation of passenger air travel, not the promotion of expression. Even if we look beyond the intent of the Port Authority to the manner in which the terminals have been operated, the terminals have never been dedicated (except under the threat of court order) to expression in the form sought to be exercised here: *i.e.*, the solicitation of contributions and the distribution of literature.

The terminals here are far from atypical. Airport builders and managers focus their efforts on providing terminals that will contribute to efficient air travel. The Federal Government is in accord; the Secretary of Transportation has been directed to publish a plan for airport development necessary "to anticipate and meet the needs *of civil aeronautics*, to meet requirements in support of the national defense . . . and to meet identified needs of the Postal Service." (emphasis added). Although many airports have expanded their function beyond merely contributing to efficient air travel, few have included among their purposes the designation of a forum for solicitation and distribution activities. Thus, we think that neither by tradition nor purpose can the terminals be described as satisfying the standards we have previously set out for identifying a public forum.

The restrictions here challenged, therefore, need only satisfy a requirement of reasonableness. . . . The restriction " 'need only be *reasonable*; it need not be the most reasonable or the only reasonable limitation.' " We have no doubt that under this standard the prohibition on solicitation passes muster.

We have on many prior occasions noted the disruptive effect that solicitation may have on business. "Solicitation requires action by those who would respond: The individual solicited must decide whether or not to contribute (which itself might involve reading the solicitor's literature or hearing his pitch), and then, having decided to do so, reach for a wallet, search it for money, write a check, or produce a credit card." Passengers who wish to avoid the solicitor may have to alter their paths, slowing both themselves and those around them. The result is that the normal flow of traffic is impeded. This is especially so in an airport, where "[a]ir travelers, who are often weighted down by cumbersome baggage . . . may be hurrying to catch a plane or to arrange ground transportation." Delays may be particularly costly in this setting, as a flight missed by only a few minutes can result in hours worth of subsequent inconvenience.

In addition, face-to-face solicitation presents risks of duress that are an appropriate target of regulation. The skillful, and unprincipled, solicitor can target the most vulnerable, including those accompanying children or those suffering physical impairment and who cannot easily avoid the solicitation. The unsavory solicitor can also commit fraud through concealment of his affiliation or through deliberate efforts to shortchange those who agree to purchase. Compounding this problem is the fact that, in an airport, the targets of such activity frequently are on tight schedules. This in turn makes such visitors unlikely to stop and formally complain to airport authorities. As a result, the airport faces considerable difficulty in achieving its legitimate interest in monitoring solicitation activity to assure that travelers are not interfered with unduly.

The Port Authority has concluded that its interest in monitoring the activities can best be accomplished by limiting solicitation and distribution to the sidewalk areas outside the terminals. This sidewalk area is frequented by an overwhelming percentage of airport users. Thus the resulting access of those who would solicit the general public is quite complete. In turn we think it would be odd to conclude that the Port Authority's terminal regulation is unreasonable despite the Port Authority having otherwise assured access to an area universally traveled.

The inconveniences to passengers and the burdens on Port Authority officials flowing from solicitation activity may seem small, but viewed against the fact that "pedestrian congestion is one of the greatest problems facing the three terminals," the Port Authority could reasonably worry that even such incremental effects would prove quite disruptive. Moreover, "[t]he justification for the Rule should not be measured by the disorder that would result from granting an exemption solely to ISKCON." For if ISKCON is given access, so too must other groups. "Obviously, there would be a much larger threat to the State's interest in crowd control if all other religious, nonreligious, and noncommercial organizations could likewise move freely." As a result, we conclude that the solicitation ban is reasonable.

* * *

JUSTICE SOUTER, with whom JUSTICE BLACKMUN and JUSTICE STEVENS join, . . . dissenting. . . .

* * *

II

From the Court's conclusion . . . sustaining the total ban on solicitation of money for immediate payment, I respectfully dissent. "We have held the solicitation of money by charities to be fully protected as the dissemination of ideas. It is axiomatic that, although fraudulent misrepresentation of facts can be regulated, the dissemination of ideas cannot be regulated to prevent it from being unfair or unreasonable."

Even if I assume, *arguendo*, that the ban on the petitioners' activity at issue here is both content neutral and merely a restriction on the manner of communication, the regulation must be struck down for its failure to satisfy the requirements of narrow tailoring to further a significant state interest, and availability of "ample alternative channels for communication."

. . . [R]espondent comes closest to justifying the restriction as one furthering the government's interest in preventing coercion and fraud. The claim to be preventing coercion is weak to start with. While a solicitor can be insistent, a pedestrian on the street or airport concourse can simply walk away or walk on. In any event, we have held in a far more coercive context than this one, that of a black boycott of white stores in Claiborne County, Mississippi, that "[s]peech does not lose its protected character . . . simply because it may embarrass others or coerce them into action." Since there is here no evidence of any type of coercive conduct, over and above the merely importunate character of the open and public solicitation, that might justify a ban, the regulation cannot be sustained to avoid coercion.

As for fraud, our cases do not provide government with plenary authority to ban solicitation just because it could be fraudulent. "Broad prophylactic rules in the area of free expression are suspect," and more than a laudable intent to prevent fraud is required to sustain the present ban. The evidence of fraudulent conduct here is virtually nonexistent. It consists of one affidavit describing eight complaints, none of them substantiated, "involving some form of fraud, deception, or larceny" over an entire 11-year period between 1975 and 1986, during which the regulation at issue here was, by agreement, not enforced. Petitioners claim, and respondent does not dispute, that by the Port Authority's own calculation, there has not been a single claim of fraud or misrepresentation since 1981. As against these facts, respondent's brief is ominous in adding that "[t]he Port Authority is also aware that members of [International Society for Krishna Consciousness] have engaged in misconduct elsewhere." This is precisely the type of vague and unsubstantiated allegation that could never support a restriction on speech. Finally, the fact that other governmental bodies have also enacted restrictions on solicitation in other places, is not evidence of fraudulent conduct.

Even assuming a governmental interest adequate to justify some regulation, the present ban would fall when subjected to the requirement of narrow tailoring. "Precision of regulation must be the touchstone. . . ." Thus, . . . we [have] said:

"The Village's legitimate interest in preventing fraud can be better served by measures less intrusive than a direct prohibition on solicitation. Fraudulent misrepresentations can be prohibited and the penal laws used to punish such conduct directly. Efforts to promote disclosure of the finances of charitable organizations also may assist in preventing fraud by informing the public of the ways in which their contributions will be employed. Such measures may help make contribution decisions more informed, while leaving to individual choice the decision whether to contribute. . . ."

Similarly, in [another case] we required the State to cure its perceived fraud problem by more narrowly tailored means than compelling disclosure by professional fundraisers of the amount of collected funds that were actually turned over to charity during the previous year:

"In contrast to the prophylactic, imprecise, and unduly burdensome rule the State has adopted to reduce its alleged donor misperception, more benign and narrowly tailored options are available. For example, as a general rule, the State may itself publish the detailed financial disclosure forms it requires professional fund-raisers to file. This procedure would communicate the desired information to the public without burdening a speaker with unwanted speech during the course of a solicitation. Alternatively, the State may vigorously enforce its antifraud laws to prohibit professional fund-raisers from obtaining money on false pretenses or by making false statements."

Finally, I do not think the Port Authority's solicitation ban leaves open the "ample" channels of communication required of a valid content-neutral time, place, and manner restriction. A distribution of preaddressed envelopes is unlikely to be much of an alternative. The practical reality of the regulation, which this Court can never ignore, is that it shuts off a uniquely powerful avenue of communication for organizations like the International Society for Krishna Consciousness, and may, in effect, completely prohibit unpopular and poorly funded groups from receiving funds in response to protected solicitation.

Accordingly, I would . . . strike down the ban on solicitation.

NOTES AND QUESTIONS

1. Why did the parties in the case who sought to raise funds in airports to support their religious faith believe that they were entitled so to do because of the First Amendment? What has the First Amendment got to do with airports? Do you find the reasoning of the majority — that the airport can bar solicitations by the Krishna group if it has a "reasonable basis" for doing so — persuasive? Why don't the dissenters?

2. Does this case present an issue in freedom of speech, in freedom of religion, or a hybrid of both? What does it mean to suggest that time, place, and manner restrictions of the exercise of freedom of speech (in an airport) are permissible, so long as they are "content neutral"? Will such restrictions really ever be "content neutral"?

3. As an abstract matter, government can control, and decide the use of, its property. However, long ago, the Court decided that some public property must remain open for public assembly. Thus, in *Hague v. CIO*, 307 U.S. 496 (1939), the Court invalidated an ordinance which sought to limit the availability of public streets and sidewalks without a permit. Modernly, the extent of the government's control over public property often depends on whether the property is a public forum, a designated or limited public forum, or a non-public forum. The distinctions were articulated in *Perry Education Association v. Perry Local Educators' Association*, 460 U.S. 37 (1983), where the Court upheld limiting access to an inter-school mail system. There, the Court defined a public forum as a place, where by long tradition, assembly and debate have been permitted, such as streets, sidewalks, and parks. In a public forum, any government regulation must be content-neutral. This means neutral as to subject matter and viewpoint. Any content-based regulation would need to have a compelling governmental justification. In only one modern case, has a content restriction of this type survived strict scrutiny. In *Burson v. Freeman*, 504 U.S. 191 (1992), the Court upheld a prohibition of the distribution of campaign literature within 100 feet of the entrance of a polling place. Also allowed in a public forum are time, place, and manner restrictions. These, too, must be content-neutral, though they must merely serve a significant governmental interest and leave open ample channels of communication. Thus, in *Grayned v. Rockford*, 408 U.S. 104 (1972), the Court sustained a noise control ordinance in a school zone. However, a government regulating a public forum need not employ the least restrictive means. The question is whether the regulation is not substantially broader than necessary to achieve the government's interest. The issue is not whether the Court could envision a less restrictive alternative. *Ward v. Rock Against Racism*, 491 U.S. 781 (1989) (upholding the requirement that those using a public park use the public sound system and engineers).

A designated public forum is an area voluntarily opened by the government as a place for expressive activity. The government need not retain it indefinitely in that status, though as long as it does so, it will be treated by the same rules that govern a public forum. Thus, in *Lamb's Chapel v. Center Moriches Union Free School Dist.*, 508 U.S. 384 (1993), school facilities that were made generally available after hours could not exclude certain viewpoints. "[A]bove all else, the First Amendment means that government has no power to restrict expression because of its message, its ideas, its subject matter or its content." *Police Department of Chicago v. Mosley*, 408 U.S. 92, 95–96 (1972). Thus, content restrictions are presumptively invalid and can be justified only by meeting the strict scrutiny with a compelling governmental interest. When it is said that a government regulation must be content-neutral, it means both neutrality as to viewpoint and subject matter. Viewpoint restrictions regulate on the ideology of the message. For example, in *Boos v. Berry*, 485 U.S. 312 (1988), the Court invalidated a District of Columbia ordinance that prohibited signs critical of a foreign government within 500 feet of an embassy. By comparison, in *Carey v. Brown*, 447 U.S. 455 (1980), the Court invalidated a ban on all picketing in residential areas other than that related to the subject of labor or employment. Unlike viewpoint and subject matter restrictions that result in strict scrutiny, a regulation that affects speech but is not aimed at content or viewpoint is subject to an intermediate level of scrutiny or review.

The government may also designate a public forum limited to particular purposes. In a sense, it can limit the subject matter, or content, of the forum, but even here it cannot discriminate on the basis of viewpoint, a point we address in the next section.

By contrast to either public fora (traditional or designated) or limited public fora, a non-public forum can be closed to speech activity, pursuant to any reasonable regulation that is viewpoint neutral. Thus, in *Members of the City Council of the City of Los Angeles v. Taxpayers for Vincent*, 466 U.S. 789 (1984), the Court upheld the prohibition of the posting of signs on public property. Within a non-public forum, the government may also draw distinctions on the basis of subject-matter or speaker identity, but not viewpoint. In *Cornelius v. NAACP Legal Defense and Education Fund, Inc.*, 473 U.S. 788 (1985), the Court allowed the federal government to exclude from its charitable fund raising campaign, legal defense and political organizations. Of course, as the principal case reveals, not every regulation in a non-public forum will be held reasonable.

4. What then determines the status of a forum? This somewhat divides the Court in *Krishna*, with some members of the Court holding onto tradition as the primary, if not dispositive, criterion, and others seeking to evaluate more contextually whether speech activities would be compatible with the general functioning of the enterprise.

5. Even though the Court in *Krishna* found the airport to be a non-public forum, that did not mean that all regulation of this public space would be deemed "reasonable." In a portion of the opinion not reprinted, the Court held a similar ban on mere distribution of literature as invalid under the First Amendment. Justice O'Connor had supported the characterization of the airport as non-public and the ban on solicitation, but she switched sides when the issue was prohibiting the distribution of literature. "Leafletting does not entail the same kinds of problems presented by face-to-face solicitation," wrote Justice O'Connor, who was supported in this view by Justices Kennedy, Souter, Blackmun, and Stevens, the last three of which, were in dissent on the earlier solicitation ban. Chief Justice Rehnquist who wrote the majority opinion for the solicitation aspects of the regulation dissented along with Justices White, Scalia, and Thomas, fearing that the split result would be overly burdensome on the Port Authority.

6. The next section considers time, place, and manner restrictions on speech that are permitted even in public fora, as long as they do not discriminate on the basis of either content or viewpoint.

3. Ascertaining Content and Viewpoint Discrimination by the Government

HILL v. COLORADO
530 U.S. 703 (2000)

Justice Stevens delivered the opinion of the Court.

At issue is the constitutionality of a 1993 Colorado statute that regulates speech-related conduct within 100 feet of the entrance to any health care facility. The specific section of the statute that is challenged, . . . makes it unlawful within the regulated areas for any person to "knowingly approach" within eight feet of another person, without that person's consent, "for the purpose of passing a leaflet or handbill to, displaying a sign to, or engaging in oral protest, education, or counseling with such other person. . . ."[1] . . . [The Statute] makes it more difficult to give unwanted advice, particularly in the form of a handbill or leaflet, to persons entering or leaving medical facilities.

The question is whether the First Amendment rights of the speaker are abridged

---

[1] § 18-9-122 reads [in part] as follows:

"(1) The general assembly recognizes that access to health care facilities for the purpose of obtaining medical counseling and treatment is imperative for the citizens of this state; that the exercise of a person's right to protest or counsel against certain medical procedures must be balanced against another person's right to obtain medical counseling and treatment in an unobstructed manner; and that preventing the willful obstruction of a person's access to medical counseling and treatment at a health care facility is a matter of statewide concern. The general assembly therefore declares that it is appropriate to enact legislation that prohibits a person from knowingly obstructing another person's entry to or exit from a health care facility.

"(2) A person commits a class 3 misdemeanor if such person knowingly obstructs, detains, hinders, impedes, or blocks another person's entry to or exit from a health care facility.

"(3) No person shall knowingly approach another person within eight feet of such person, unless such other person consents, for the purpose of passing a leaflet or handbill to, displaying a sign to, or engaging in oral protest, education, or counseling with such other person in the public way or sidewalk area within a radius of one hundred feet from any entrance door to a health care facility. Any person who violates this subsection (3) commits a class 3 misdemeanor.

*   *   *

"(6) In addition to, and not in lieu of, the penalties set forth in this section, a person who violates the provisions of this section shall be subject to civil liability, as provided in section 13-21-106.7, C.R.S."

by the protection the statute provides for the unwilling listener.

I

Five months after the statute was enacted, petitioners filed a complaint in the District Court for Jefferson County, Colorado, praying for a declaration that [it] was facially invalid and seeking an injunction against its enforcement. They stated that prior to the enactment of the statute, they had engaged in "sidewalk counseling" on the public ways and sidewalks within 100 feet of the entrances to facilities where human abortion is practiced or where medical personnel refer women to other facilities for abortions. "Sidewalk counseling" consists of efforts "to educate, counsel, persuade, or inform passersby about abortion and abortion alternatives by means of verbal or written speech, including conversation and/or display of signs and/or distribution of literature." They further alleged that such activities frequently entail being within eight feet of other persons and that their fear of prosecution under the new statute caused them "to be chilled in the exercise of fundamental constitutional rights."

. . . . [Petitioners contended the law] was content based for two reasons: The content of the speech must be examined to determine whether it "constitutes oral protest, counseling and education"; and that it is "viewpoint-based" because the statute "makes it likely that prosecution will occur based on displeasure with the position taken by the speaker."

. . . There was no evidence that the "sidewalk counseling" conducted by petitioners in this case was ever abusive or confrontational.

*   *   *

In 1996, the Supreme Court of Colorado denied review, and petitioners sought a writ of certiorari from our Court. While their petition was pending, we decided *Schenck v. Pro-Choice Network of Western N.Y.* (1997). Because we held in that case that an injunctive provision creating a speech-free "floating buffer zone" with a 15-foot radius violates the First Amendment, we granted certiorari, vacated the judgment of the Colorado Court of Appeals, and remanded the case to that court for further consideration in light of *Schenck.*

On remand the Court of Appeals reinstated its judgment upholding the statute. It noted that in *Schenck* we had "expressly declined to hold that a valid governmental interest in ensuring ingress and egress to a medical clinic may never be sufficient to justify a zone of separation between individuals entering and leaving the premises and protesters" and that our opinion in *Ward* [*v. Rock Against Racism* (1989)] provided the standard for assessing the validity of a content-neutral, generally applicable statute. Under that standard, even though a 15-foot floating buffer might preclude protesters from expressing their views from a normal conversational distance, a lesser distance of eight feet was sufficient to protect such speech on a public sidewalk.

The Colorado Supreme Court granted certiorari and affirmed the judgment of the Court of Appeals. . . . It noted that both the trial court and the Court of Appeals had concluded that the statute was content neutral, that petitioners no longer contended otherwise, and that they agreed that the question for decision was whether the statute was a valid time, place, and manner restriction under the test announced in *Ward*.

The court identified two important distinctions between this case and *Schenck*. First, *Schenck* involved a judicial decree and therefore, as explained in *Madsen*, posed "greater risks of censorship and discriminatory application than do general ordinances." Second, unlike the floating buffer zone in *Schenck*, which would require a protester either to stop talking or to get off the sidewalk whenever a patient came within 15 feet, the "knowingly approaches" requirement in the Colorado statute allows a protester to stand still while a person moving towards or away from a health care facility walks past her. Applying the test in *Ward*, the court concluded that the statute was narrowly drawn to further a significant government interest. It rejected petitioners' contention that it was not narrow enough because it applied to all health care facilities in the State. In the court's view, the comprehensive coverage of the statute was a factor that supported its content neutrality. Moreover, the fact that the statute was enacted, in part, because the General Assembly "was concerned with the safety of individuals seeking wide-ranging health care services, not merely abortion counseling and procedures," added to the substantiality of the government interest that it served. Finally, it concluded that ample alternative channels remain open. . . . We now affirm.

II

Before confronting the question whether the Colorado statute reflects an acceptable balance between the constitutionally protected rights of law-abiding speakers and the interests of unwilling listeners, it is appropriate to examine the competing interests at stake. A brief review of both sides of the dispute reveals that each has legitimate and important concerns.

The First Amendment interests of petitioners are clear and undisputed. . . . There is no disagreement on this point, even though the legislative history makes it clear that its enactment was primarily motivated by activities in the vicinity of abortion clinics. Second, they correctly state that their leafletting, sign displays, and oral communications are protected by the First Amendment. The fact that the messages conveyed by those communications may be offensive to their recipients does not deprive them of constitutional protection. Third, the public sidewalks, streets, and ways affected by the statute are "quintessential" public forums for free speech. Finally, although there is debate about the magnitude of the statutory impediment to their ability to communicate effectively with persons in the regulated zones, that ability, particularly the ability to distribute leaflets, is unquestionably lessened by this statute.

On the other hand, petitioners do not challenge the legitimacy of the state interests that the statute is intended to serve. It is a traditional exercise of the States' "police powers to protect the health and safety of their citizens." That interest may justify a special focus on unimpeded access to health care facilities and the avoidance of potential trauma to patients associated with confrontational protests. See *Madsen v. Women's Health Center, Inc.* . . .

The right to free speech, of course, includes the right to attempt to persuade others to change their views, and may not be curtailed simply because the speaker's message may be offensive to his audience. But the protection afforded to offensive messages does not always embrace offensive speech that is so intrusive that the unwilling audience cannot avoid it. *Frisby v. Schultz* (1988).

* * *

The unwilling listener's interest in avoiding unwanted communication has been repeatedly identified in our cases. It is an aspect of the broader "right to be let alone" that one of our wisest Justices characterized as "the most comprehensive of rights and the right most valued by civilized men." The right to avoid unwelcome speech has special force in the privacy of the home, *Rowan v. United States Post Office Dept.* (1970), and its immediate surroundings, *Frisby v. Schultz*, but can also be protected in confrontational settings.

We have since recognized that the "right to persuade" discussed in that case is protected by the First Amendment, *Thornhill v. Alabama* (1940), as well as by federal statutes. Yet we have continued to maintain that "no one has a right to press even 'good' ideas on an unwilling recipient." None of our decisions has minimized the enduring importance of "the right to be free" from persistent "importunity, following and dogging" after an offer to communicate has been declined.

* * *

III

All four of the state court opinions upholding the validity of this statute concluded that it is a content-neutral time, place, and manner regulation. Moreover, they all found support for their analysis in *Ward v. Rock Against Racism* (1989). It is therefore appropriate to comment on the "content neutrality" of the statute. As we explained in *Ward*:

> "The principal inquiry in determining content neutrality, in speech cases generally and in time, place, or manner cases in particular, is whether the government has adopted a regulation of speech because of disagreement with the message it conveys."

The Colorado statute passes that test for three independent reasons. First, it is not a "regulation of speech." Rather, it is a regulation of the places where some speech may occur. Second, it was not adopted "because of disagreement with the message it conveys." This conclusion is supported not just by the Colorado courts' interpretation of legislative history, but more importantly by the State Supreme Court's unequivocal holding that the statute's "restrictions apply equally to all demonstrators, regardless of viewpoint, and the statutory language makes no reference to the content of the speech." Third, the State's interests in protecting access and privacy, and providing the police with clear guidelines, are unrelated to the content of the demonstrators' speech. As we have repeatedly explained, government regulation of expressive activity is "content neutral" if it is justified without reference to the content of regulated speech. . . .

. . . Petitioners contend that an individual near a health care facility who knowingly approaches a pedestrian to say "good morning" or to randomly recite lines from a novel would not be subject to the statute's restrictions. Because the content of the oral statements made by an approaching speaker must sometimes be examined to determine whether the knowing approach is covered by the statute, petitioners argue that the law is "content-based."

* * *

It is common in the law to examine the content of a communication to determine the speaker's purpose. Whether a particular statement constitutes a threat, blackmail, an agreement to fix prices, a copyright violation, a public offering of securities, or an offer to sell goods often depends on the precise content of the statement. We have never held, or suggested, that it is improper to look at the content of an oral or written statement in order to determine whether a rule of law applies to a course of conduct. With respect to the conduct that is the focus of the Colorado statute, it is unlikely that there would often be any need to know exactly what words were spoken in order to determine whether "sidewalk counselors" are engaging in "oral protest, education, or counseling" rather than pure social or random conversation.

Theoretically, of course, cases may arise in which it is necessary to review the content of the statements made by a person approaching within eight feet of an unwilling listener to determine whether the approach is covered by the statute. But that review need be no more extensive than a determination of whether a general prohibition of "picketing" or "demonstrating" applies to innocuous speech. The regulation of such expressive activities, by definition, does not cover social, random, or other everyday communications. . . . Nevertheless, we have never suggested that the kind of cursory examination that might be required to exclude casual conversation from the coverage of a regulation of picketing would be problematic.

In *Carey v. Brown* we examined a general prohibition of peaceful picketing that contained an exemption for picketing of a place of employment involved in a labor dispute. We concluded that this statute violated the Equal Protection Clause of the Fourteenth Amendment, because it discriminated between lawful and unlawful conduct based on the content of the picketers' messages. That discrimination was impermissible because it accorded preferential treatment to expression concerning one particular subject matter — labor disputes — while prohibiting discussion of all other issues. Although our opinion stressed that "it is the content of the speech that determines whether it is within or without the statute's blunt prohibition," we appended a footnote to that sentence explaining that it was the fact that the statute placed a prohibition on discussion of particular topics, while others were allowed, that was constitutionally repugnant. Regulation of the subject matter of messages, though not as obnoxious as viewpoint-based regulation, is also an objectionable form of content-based regulation.

The Colorado statute's regulation of the location of protests, education, and counseling is easily distinguishable from *Carey*. It places no restrictions on — and clearly does not prohibit — either a particular viewpoint or any subject matter that may be discussed by a speaker. Rather, it simply establishes a minor place restriction on an extremely broad category of communications with unwilling listeners. Instead of drawing distinctions based on the subject that the approaching speaker may wish to address, the statute applies equally to used car salesmen, animal rights activists, fundraisers, environmentalists, and missionaries. Each can attempt to educate unwilling listeners on any subject, but without consent may not approach within eight feet to do so.

*   *   *

IV

We also agree with the state courts' conclusion that [the law] is a valid time, place, and manner regulation under the test applied in *Ward* because it is "narrowly tailored." We already have noted that the statute serves governmental interests that are significant and legitimate and that the restrictions are content neutral. We are likewise persuaded that the statute is "narrowly tailored" to serve those interests and that it leaves open ample alternative channels for communication. As we have emphasized on more than one occasion, when a content-neutral regulation does not entirely foreclose any means of communication, it may satisfy the tailoring requirement even though it is not the least restrictive or least intrusive means of serving the statutory goal.

The three types of communication regulated are the display of signs, leafletting, and oral speech. The 8-foot separation between the speaker and the audience should not have any adverse impact on the readers' ability to read signs displayed by demonstrators. In fact, the separation might actually aid the pedestrians' ability to see the signs by preventing others from surrounding them and impeding their view. Furthermore, the statute places no limitations on the number, size, text, or images of the placards. And, as with all of the restrictions, the 8-foot zone does not affect demonstrators with signs who remain in place.

. . . Unlike the 15-foot zone in *Schenck*, this 8-foot zone allows the speaker to communicate at a "normal conversational distance." Additionally, the statute allows the speaker to remain in one place, and other individuals can pass within eight feet of the protester without causing the protester to violate the statute. Finally, here there is a "knowing" requirement that protects speakers "who thought they were keeping pace with the targeted individual" at the proscribed distance from inadvertently violating the statute.

*   *   *

The burden on the ability to distribute handbills is more serious because it seems possible that an 8-foot interval could hinder the ability of a leafletter to deliver handbills to some unwilling recipients. The statute does not, however, prevent a leafletter from simply standing near the path of oncoming pedestrians and proffering his or her material, which the pedestrians can easily accept. And, as in all leafletting situations, pedestrians continue to be free to decline the tender. In *Heffron v. International Soc. for Krishna Consciousness, Inc* (1981), we upheld a state fair regulation that required a religious organization desiring to distribute literature to conduct that activity only at an assigned location — in that case booths. As in this case, the regulation primarily burdened the distributors' ability to communicate with unwilling readers. We concluded our opinion by emphasizing that the First Amendment protects the right of every citizen to "reach the minds of willing listeners and to do so there must be opportunity to win their attention." The Colorado statute adequately protects those rights.

Finally, in determining whether a statute is narrowly tailored, we have noted that "[w]e must, of course, take account of the place to which the regulations apply in determining whether these restrictions burden more speech than necessary." States and municipalities plainly have a substantial interest in controlling the activity around certain public and private places. For example, we have recognized the special governmental interests surrounding schools, courthouses, polling places, and private homes. Additionally, we previously have noted the unique concerns that surround health care facilities.

* * *

The statute takes a prophylactic approach; it forbids all unwelcome demonstrators to come closer than eight feet. We recognize that by doing so, it will sometimes inhibit a demonstrator whose approach in fact would have proved harmless. But the statute's prophylactic aspect is justified by the great difficulty of protecting, say, a pregnant woman from physical harassment with legal rules that focus exclusively on the individual impact of each instance of behavior, demanding in each case an accurate characterization (as harassing or not harassing) of each individual movement within the 8-foot boundary. Such individualized characterization of each individual movement is often difficult to make accurately. A bright-line prophylactic rule may be the best way to provide protection, and, at the same time, by offering clear guidance and avoiding subjectivity, to protect speech itself.

* * *

V

[Petitioners also contend that the law] is invalid because it is "overbroad." There are two parts to petitioners' "overbreadth" argument. On the one hand, they argue that the statute is too broad because it protects too many people in too many places, rather than just the patients at the facilities where confrontational speech had occurred. Similarly, it burdens all speakers, rather than just persons with a history of bad conduct. On the other hand, petitioners also contend that the statute is overbroad because it "bans virtually the universe of protected expression, including displays of signs, distribution of literature, and mere verbal statements."

The first part of the argument does not identify a constitutional defect. . . . In this case, it is not disputed that the regulation affects protected speech activity, the question is thus whether it is a "reasonable restrictio[n] on the time, place, or manner of protected speech."

. . . . The second part of the argument is based on a misreading of the statute and an incorrect understanding of the overbreadth doctrine. As we have already noted, [the law] simply does not "ban" any messages, and likewise it does not "ban" any signs, literature, or oral statements. It merely regulates the places where communications may occur. As we explained in *Broadrick v. Oklahoma* (1973), the overbreadth doctrine enables litigants "to challenge a statute, not because their own rights of free expression are violated, but because of a judicial prediction or assumption that the statute's very existence may cause others not before the court to refrain from constitutionally protected speech or expression." Moreover, "particularly where conduct and not merely speech is involved, we believe that the overbreadth of a statute must not only be real, but substantial as well, judged in relation to the statute's plainly legitimate sweep." Petitioners have not persuaded us that the impact of the statute on the conduct of other speakers will differ from its impact on their own sidewalk counseling. Like petitioners' own activities, the conduct of other protesters and counselors at all health care facilities are encompassed within the statute's "legitimate sweep." Therefore, the statute is not overly broad.

VI

Petitioners also claim that [the law] is unconstitutionally vague. They find a lack of clarity in three parts of the section: the meaning of "protest, education, or counseling"; the "consent" requirement; and the determination of whether one is "approaching" within eight feet of another.

A statute can be impermissibly vague for either of two independent reasons. First, if it fails to provide people of ordinary intelligence a reasonable opportunity to understand what conduct it prohibits. Second, if it authorizes or even encourages arbitrary and discriminatory enforcement. *Chicago v. Morales* (1999).

In this case, the first concern is ameliorated by the fact that [the law] contains a scienter requirement. The statute only applies to a person who "knowingly" approaches within eight feet of another, without that person's consent, for the purpose of engaging in oral protest, education, or counseling. The likelihood that anyone would not understand any of those common words seems quite remote.

* * *

For the same reason, we are similarly unpersuaded by the suggestion that [the law] fails to give adequate guidance to law enforcement authorities. Indeed, it seems to us that one of the section's virtues is the specificity of the definitions of the zones described in the statute. "As always, enforcement requires the exercise of some degree of police judgment," and the degree of judgment involved here is acceptable.

VII

Finally, petitioners argue that [the law's] consent requirement is invalid because it imposes an unconstitutional "prior restraint" on speech. We rejected this argument previously in *Schenck*, and *Madsen*. Moreover, the restrictions in this case raise an even lesser prior restraint concern than those at issue in *Schenck* and *Madsen* where particular speakers were at times completely banned within certain zones. Under this statute, absolutely no channel of communication is foreclosed. No speaker is silenced. And no message is prohibited. Petitioners are simply wrong when they assert that "[t]he statute compels speakers to obtain consent to speak and it authorizes private citizens to deny petitioners' requests to engage in expressive activities." To the contrary, this statute does not provide for a "heckler's veto" but rather allows every speaker to engage freely in any expressive activity communicating all messages and viewpoints subject only to the narrow place requirement imbedded within the "approach" restriction.

Furthermore, our concerns about "prior restraints" relate to restrictions imposed by official censorship. The regulations in this case, however, only apply if the pedestrian does not consent to the approach. Private citizens have always retained the power to decide for themselves what they wish to read, and within limits, what oral messages they want to consider. This statute simply empowers private citizens entering a health care facility with the ability to prevent a speaker, who is within eight feet and advancing, from communicating a message they do not wish to hear. Further, the statute does not authorize the pedestrian to affect any other activity at any other location or relating to any other person. These restrictions thus do not constitute an unlawful prior restraint.

* * *

The judgment of the Colorado Supreme Court is affirmed.

It is so ordered.

JUSTICE SOUTER, with whom JUSTICE O'CONNOR, JUSTICE GINSBURG, and JUSTICE BREYER join, concurring.

I join the opinion of the Court and add this further word. The key to determining whether [the law], makes a content-based distinction between varieties of speech lies in understanding that content-based discriminations are subject to strict scrutiny because they place the weight of government behind the disparagement or suppression of some messages, whether or not with the effect of approving or promoting others. . . .

Concern about employing the power of the State to suppress discussion of a subject or a point of view is not, however, raised in the same way when a law addresses not the content of speech but the circumstances of its delivery. The right to express unpopular views does not necessarily immunize a speaker from liability for resorting to otherwise impermissible behavior meant to shock members of the speaker's audience, *United States v. O'Brien* (1968) (burning draft card), or to guarantee their attention, *Kovacs v. Cooper* (1949) (sound trucks); *Frisby v. Schultz* (1988) (residential picketing); *Heffron v. International Soc. for Krishna Consciousness, Inc.* (1981) (soliciting). Unless regulation limited to the details of a speaker's delivery results in removing a subject or viewpoint from effective discourse (or otherwise fails to advance a significant public interest in a way narrowly fitted to that objective), a reasonable restriction intended to affect only the time, place, or manner of speaking is perfectly valid. *See Ward v. Rock Against Racism*, (1989).

* * *

JUSTICE SCALIA, with whom JUSTICE THOMAS joins, dissenting.

The Court today concludes that a regulation requiring speakers on the public thoroughfares bordering medical facilities to speak from a distance of eight feet is "not a 'regulation of speech,'" but "a regulation of the places where some speech may occur," and that a regulation directed to only certain categories of speech (protest, education, and counseling) is not "content-based." For these reasons, it says, the regulation is immune from the exacting scrutiny we apply to content-based suppression of speech in the public forum. The Court then determines that the regulation survives the less rigorous scrutiny afforded content-neutral time, place, and manner restrictions because it is narrowly tailored to serve a government interest — protection of citizens' "right to be let alone" — that has explicitly been disclaimed by the State, probably for the reason that, as a basis for suppressing peaceful private expression, it is patently incompatible with the guarantees of the First Amendment.

. . . If one accepts the Court's description of the interest served by this regulation, it is clear that the regulation is both based on content and justified by reference to content. Constitutionally proscribable "secondary effects" of speech are directly addressed in subsection (2) of the statute, which makes it unlawful to obstruct, hinder, impede, or block access to a health care facility — a prohibition broad enough to include all physical threats and all physically threatening approaches. The purpose of subsection (3), however (according to the Court), is to protect "[t]he unwilling listener's interest in avoiding unwanted communication." On this analysis, Colorado has restricted certain categories of speech — protest, counseling, and education — out of an apparent belief that only speech with this content is sufficiently likely to be annoying or upsetting as to require consent before it may be engaged in at close range. It is reasonable enough to conclude that even the most gentle and peaceful close approach by a so-called "sidewalk counselor" — who wishes to "educate" the woman entering an abortion clinic about the nature of the procedure, to "counsel" against it and in favor of other alternatives, and perhaps even (though less likely if the approach is to be successful) to "protest" her taking of a human life — will often, indeed usually, have what might be termed the "secondary effect" of annoying or deeply upsetting the woman who is planning the abortion. But that is not an effect which occurs "without reference to the content" of the speech. This singling out of presumptively "unwelcome" communications fits precisely the description of prohibited regulation set forth in *Boos v. Barry* (1988): It "targets the direct impact of a particular category of speech, not a secondary feature that happens to be associated with that type of speech."

In sum, it blinks reality to regard this statute, in its application to oral communications, as anything other than a content-based restriction upon speech in the public forum. As such, it must survive that stringent mode of constitutional analysis our cases refer to as "strict scrutiny," which requires that the restriction be narrowly tailored to serve a compelling state interest. . . . Since the Court does not even attempt to support the regulation under this standard, I shall discuss it only briefly. Suffice it to say that if protecting people from unwelcome communications (the governmental interest the Court posits) is a compelling state interest, the First Amendment is a dead letter. And if forbidding peaceful, nonthreatening, but uninvited speech from a distance closer than eight feet is a "narrowly tailored" means of preventing the obstruction of entrance to medical facilities (the governmental interest the State asserts) narrow tailoring must refer not to the standards of Versace, but to those of Omar the tentmaker. . . .

I dissent.

JUSTICE KENNEDY, dissenting.

The Court's holding contradicts more than a half century of well-established First Amendment principles. For the first time, the Court approves a law which bars a private citizen from passing a message, in a peaceful manner and on a profound moral issue, to a fellow citizen on a public sidewalk. If from this time forward the Court repeats its grave errors of analysis, we shall have no longer the proud tradition of free and open discourse in a public forum. In my view, JUSTICE SCALIA's First Amendment analysis is correct and mandates outright reversal. In addition to undermining established First Amendment principles, the Court's decision conflicts with the essence of the joint opinion in *Planned Parenthood of Southeastern Pa. v. Casey* (1992).

I

*   *   *

The statute is content based for an additional reason: It restricts speech on particular topics. Of course, the enactment restricts "oral protest, education, or counseling" on any subject; but a statute of broad application is not content neutral if its terms control the substance of a speaker's message. If oral protest, education, or counseling on every subject within an 8-foot zone present a danger to the public, the statute should apply to every building entrance in the State. It does not. It applies only to a special class of locations: entrances to buildings with health care facilities. We would close our eyes to reality were we to deny that "oral protest, education, or counseling" outside the entrances to medical facilities concern a narrow range of topics — indeed, one topic in particular. By confining the law's application to the specific locations where the prohibited discourse occurs, the State has made a content-based determination. The Court ought to so acknowledge. Clever content-based restrictions are no less offensive than censoring on the basis of content. *See, e.g., United States v. Eichman* (1990). If, just a few decades ago, a State with a history of enforcing racial discrimination had enacted a statute like this one, regulating "oral protest, education, or counseling" within 100 feet of the entrance to any lunch counter, our predecessors would not have hesitated to hold it was content based or viewpoint based. It should be a profound disappointment to defenders of the First Amendment that the Court today refuses to apply the same structural analysis when the speech involved is less palatable to it.

*   *   *

After the Court errs in finding the statute content neutral, it compounds the mistake by finding the law viewpoint neutral. Viewpoint-based rules are invidious speech restrictions, yet the Court approves this one. The purpose and design of the statute — as everyone ought to know and as its own defenders urge in attempted justification — are to restrict speakers on one side of the debate: those who protest abortions. The statute applies only to medical facilities, a convenient yet obvious mask for the legislature's true purpose and for the prohibition's true effect. One need read no further than the statute's preamble to remove any doubt about the question. The Colorado Legislature sought to restrict "a person's right to protest or counsel against certain medical procedures." The word "against" reveals the legislature's desire to restrict discourse on one side of the issue regarding "certain medical procedures." The testimony to the Colorado Legislature consisted, almost in its entirety, of debates and controversies with respect to abortion, a point the majority acknowledges. The legislature's purpose to restrict unpopular speech should be beyond dispute.

* * *

II

The Colorado statute offends settled First Amendment principles in another fundamental respect. It violates the constitutional prohibitions against vague or overly broad criminal statutes regulating speech. The enactment's fatal ambiguities are multiple and interact to create further imprecisions. The result is a law more vague and overly broad than any criminal statute the Court has sustained as a permissible regulation of speech. The statute's imprecisions are so evident that this, too, ought to have ended the case without further discussion.

* * *

The 8-foot no-approach zone is so unworkable it will chill speech. Assume persons are about to enter a building from different points and a protestor is walking back and forth with a sign or attempting to hand out leaflets. If she stops to create the 8-foot zone for one pedestrian, she cannot reach other persons with her message; yet if she moves to maintain the 8-foot zone while trying to talk to one patron she may move knowingly closer to a patron attempting to enter the facility from a different direction. In addition, the statute requires a citizen to give affirmative consent before the exhibitor of a sign or the bearer of a leaflet can approach. . . . The only sure way to avoid violating the law is to refrain from picketing, leafleting, or oral advocacy altogether. Scienter cannot save so vague a statute as this.

A statute is vague when the conduct it forbids is not ascertainable. *See Chicago v. Morales* (1999).

* * *

III

Even aside from the erroneous, most disturbing assumptions that the statute is content neutral, viewpoint neutral, and neither vague nor overbroad, the Court falls into further serious error when it turns to the time, place, and manner rules set forth in *Ward*. . . .

NOTES AND QUESTIONS

1. The majority sees this case as an unexceptional extension of *Madsen* and *Schenck*, while the dissent perceives it as a troubling disregard of longstanding free speech precedent. Which is it? Are you bothered by the fact that the activity suppressed here was stipulated to be entirely peaceful (educational counseling), and not aimed at prior unlawful conduct as was the limited injunctive relief in prior cases?

2.   Was the Colorado statute content-based? The dissent argues that it is because before it can be applied, the content (counseling, education, protest) must be determined. But aren't these categories simply broad descriptions of the prohibited conduct? Or is the real problem the fact that the statute is limited to protest *against* certain medical procedures? Is the generality of that phrasing merely a disguise designed to preserve a prior restraint of not only a disfavored content (abortion counseling), but also a disfavored viewpoint (counseling *against* obtaining the procedure)? Certainly, the dissent is right that if in the midst of the civil rights movement of the 1950s and 1960s, Alabama passed a statute outlawing protests in front of lunch counters, everyone would have known its purpose was not to regulate café accessibility, but to maintain racial segregation. Can these examples be distinguished?

3.   Do you understand the limits of the majority's proposition that the government can protect people from unwelcome communication? Later in this Chapter we will see the Court find that even the "unwelcome-ness" of flag-burning must be tolerated in a free republic. Why is the abortion protest different? Isn't the wounded military veteran or the mother of soldier killed in action to be as deeply troubled by flag destruction as a woman contemplating terminating a pregnancy by counseling? The dissent writes that: "[t]oday's decision is an unprecedented departure from this Court's teachings respecting unpopular speech in public fora." Do you agree?

4.   In *Rosenberger v. Rector*, 515 U.S. 819 (1995), which you read in Chapter 2, the Court invalidated the University of Virginia's restriction that student activity fees could not be used by a student group to publish a newsletter that "primarily promotes or manifests a particular belie[f] in or about a deity or an ultimate reality," though student newsletters expressing other viewpoints were readily permitted:

> It is axiomatic that the government may not regulate speech based on its substantive content or the message it conveys. *Police Dept. of Chicago v. Mosley* (1972). Other principles follow from this precept. In the realm of private speech or expression, government regulation may not favor one speaker over another. *Members of City Council of Los Angeles v. Taxpayers for Vincent* (1984). Discrimination against speech because of its message is presumed to be unconstitutional. *Turner Broadcasting System, Inc. v. FCC* (1994). These rules informed our determination that the government offends the First Amendment when it imposes financial burdens on certain speakers based on the content of their expression. *Simon & Schuster, Inc. v. Members of N.Y. State Crime Victims Bd.* (1991). When the government targets not subject matter, but particular views taken by speakers on a subject, the violation of the First Amendment is all the more blatant. *R.A.V. v. St. Paul* (1992). Viewpoint discrimination is thus an egregious form of content discrimination. The government must abstain from regulating speech when the specific motivating ideology or the opinion

or perspective of the speaker is the rationale for the restriction. *Perry Ed. Assn. v. Perry Local Educators' Assn.* (1983).

Rosenberger, 515 U.S. at 828–29. The Court treated the University's student activities fee fund as a "limited public forum," which, as noted above, differs from a traditional public forum in that the government may impose restrictions on subject matter in order to further the purpose of the limited forum it has created. The University's restrictions were unconstitutional, though, because they were not just content-based restrictions, but viewpoint-based restrictions, which are unconstitutional even in the more confined limited public forum:

> The necessities of confining a forum to the limited and legitimate purposes for which it was created may justify the State in reserving it for certain groups or for the discussion of certain topics. *e.g.*, *Cornelius v. NAACP Legal Defense & Ed. Fund, Inc.* (1985). Once it has opened a limited forum, however, the State must respect the lawful boundaries it has itself set. The State may not exclude speech where its distinction is not "reasonable in light of the purpose served by the forum," nor may it discriminate against speech on the basis of its viewpoint. . . . Thus, in determining whether the State is acting to preserve the limits of the forum it has created so that the exclusion of a class of speech is legitimate, we have observed a distinction between, on the one hand, content discrimination, which may be permissible if it preserves the purposes of that limited forum, and, on the other hand, viewpoint discrimination, which is presumed impermissible when directed against speech otherwise within the forum's limitations.
>
> . . . By the very terms of the [student activity fund] prohibition, the University does not exclude religion as a subject matter but selects for disfavored treatment those student journalistic efforts with religious editorial viewpoints. Religion may be a vast area of inquiry, but it also provides, as it did here, a specific premise, a perspective, a standpoint from which a variety of subjects may be discussed and considered. The prohibited perspective, not the general subject matter, resulted in the refusal to make third-party payments, for the subjects discussed were otherwise within the approved category of publications.

Does *Rosenberger*'s holding of unconstitutional viewpoint discrimination in a limited public forum context bolster Justice Scalia's dissenting position that the Court has crafted a First Amendment exception for speech *against* abortion in *Hill v. Colorado*? After all, *Hill* involved the more protected, traditional public forum of public sidewalks, where even content restrictions are subject to strict scrutiny and are presumptively invalid unless narrowly tailored to further a compelling governmental interest. When it is said that a government regulation must be content-neutral, it means both neutrality as to viewpoint and subject matter. Viewpoint restrictions regulate on the ideology of the message. For example, in *Boos v. Berry*, 485 U.S. 312 (1988), the Court invalidated a District of Columbia ordinance that prohibited signs critical of a foreign government within 500 feet of an embassy. By comparison, in *Carey v. Brown*, 447 U.S. 455 (1980), the Court invalidated a ban on all picketing in residential areas other than that related to the subject of labor or employment. Unlike viewpoint and subject matter restrictions that result in strict scrutiny, a regulation that affects speech but is not aimed at content or viewpoint is subject to an intermediate level of scrutiny or review.

5. As we will discuss later in this Chapter, government may favor some content over others when it is either speaking itself or subsidizing private speakers to transmit its information. *See Rust v. Sullivan*, 500 U.S. 173 (1991) (upholding a limitation on abortion counseling with federal money). Why then, couldn't the University of Virginia refuse to fund religious speech in *Rosenberger*? Is it because the University was not seeking to speak itself, or articulate a particular point of view, but to facilitate a diversity of views? Does that distinction support or undermine the Court's holding in *Hill*?

6. Does the funding of partisan political speech through the use of mandatory student fees amount to unconstitutional viewpoint discrimination? In *Board of Regents of the University of Wisconsin v. Southworth*, 529 U.S. 217 (2000), the Court upheld the University of Wisconsin's mandatory student fee program against a challenge that it compelled students to support speech with which they disagreed. The parties had stipulated in the lower courts that the primary means of allocating the fees to student groups were viewpoint neutral, so the Court did not consider the students' contention that the program lacked viewpoint neutrality by funding partisan political speech. Nevertheless, the Court remanded for consideration whether one aspect of the program — a mechanism for funding some viewpoints pursuant to student referendum — did amount to unconstitutional viewpoint discrimination.

7. *Southworth* signifies that the university is a special forum unlike a bar association or labor union. Other special contexts or distinctions are drawn in the First Amendment area among different types of media, most notably between print and over-the-air broadcasting. In *Red Lion Broadcasting Co. v. FCC*, 395 U.S. 367 (1969), the Court upheld the so-called fairness doctrine requiring commercial over-the-air broadcast stations to present an even-handed discussion of public issues. This content-limitation is clearly inappropriate outside this context, but the Court asserted that broadcasting was different because of the inherent scarcity of broadcast frequencies. By contrast, the Court invalidated in *Miami Herald v. Tornillo*, 418 U.S. 241 (1974), a right of reply statute that required newspapers to print a reply from a political candidate whose character or official record had been attacked in its pages. This requirement would chill editors and writers, reasoned the Court. Why isn't the same true in broadcasting? And, for that matter, are broadcast opportunities really more scarce than those in the print media? In 1987, the FCC repealed the fairness doctrine because of the vast explosion of cable and satellite television operations. If the print and broadcast media are equivalent, doesn't the First Amendment preclude content limitation in either context? Cable television, by the way, is treated somewhat more generously — in theory — than broadcast television. In *Turner Broadcasting System Inc. v. Federal Communication Commission*, 512 U.S. 622 (1994), Justice Kennedy for the Court stated: "[t]he rationale for applying a less rigorous standard of First Amendment scrutiny to broadcast regulation does not apply in the context of cable regulation. . . . The broadcast cases are inapposite in the present context because cable television does not suffer from the inherent limitations that characterize the broadcast medium." *Id.* at

638–39. However, the more rigorous protection was not sufficient to immunize the cable industry from Congress's requirement that cable operators set aside one-third of their channel capacity for use by over-the-air-broadcasters. *Turner Broadcasting System, Inc. v. Federal Communications Commission*, 520 U.S. 180 (1997). The cable industry argued that this was effectively a content regulation, since commercial broadcasts were subject to greater government scrutiny and licensing. The Court disagreed finding the "must-carry" law to be justified by an important government purpose — preserving the broadcast industry and promoting fair competition — by a means that was no broader than necessary (the usual intermediate standard of review). Regulation of the Internet has been held by the Court to merit First Amendment protection equivalent to the print media. *Reno v. ACLU*, 521 U.S. 844 (1997). Said Justice Stevens for the Court: "unlike the conditions that prevailed when Congress first authorized regulation of the broadcast spectrum, the Internet can hardly be considered a 'scarce' expressive commodity. It provides relatively unlimited, low-cost capacity for communication of all kinds. . . . We agree . . . that our cases provide no basis for qualifying the level of First Amendment scrutiny that should be applied to this medium." *Id.* at 897 For a thoughtful appraisal of old law applied to new technology, see Marie A. Failinger, *New Wine, New Bottles: Private Property Metaphors and Public Forum Speech*, 71 St. John's L. Rev. 217 (1997) (suggesting that the "public forum" metaphor in free speech analysis is not suited for new communication methods like the Internet).

4. Qualified Speech Protection

a. Libel and the "Actual Malice" Standard

NEW YORK TIMES CO. v. SULLIVAN
376 U.S. 254 (1964)

Mr. Justice Brennan delivered the opinion of the Court.

*   *   *

Respondent L. B. Sullivan is one of the three elected Commissioners of the City of Montgomery, Alabama. He testified that he was "Commissioner of Public Affairs and the duties are supervision of the Police Department, Fire Department, Department of Cemetery and Department of Scales." He brought this civil libel action against the four individual petitioners, who are Negroes and Alabama clergymen, and against petitioner the New York Times Company. . . . A jury in the Circuit Court of Montgomery County awarded him damages of $500,000, the full amount claimed, against all the petitioners, and the Supreme Court of Alabama affirmed.

Respondent's complaint alleged that he had been libeled by statements in a full-page advertisement that was carried in the New York Times on March 29, 1960. Entitled "Heed Their Rising Voices," the advertisement began by stating that "As the whole world knows by now, thousands of Southern Negro students are engaged in widespread non-violent demonstrations in positive affirmation of the right to live in human dignity as guaranteed by the U.S. Constitution and the Bill of Rights." It went on to charge that "in their efforts to uphold these guarantees, they are being met by an unprecedented wave of terror by those who would deny and negate that document which the whole world looks upon as setting the pattern for modern freedom . . . ." Succeeding paragraphs purported to illustrate the "wave of terror" by describing certain alleged events. The text concluded with an appeal for funds for three purposes: support of the student movement, "the struggle for the right-to-vote," and the legal defense of Dr. Martin Luther King, Jr., leader of the movement, against a perjury indictment then pending in Montgomery.

* * *

Of the 10 paragraphs of text in the advertisement, the third and a portion of the sixth were the basis of respondent's claim of libel. They read as follows:

Third paragraph:

> "In Montgomery, Alabama, after students sang 'My Country, 'Tis of Thee' on the State Capitol steps, their leaders were expelled from school, and truckloads of police armed with shotguns and tear-gas ringed the Alabama State College Campus. When the entire student body protested to state authorities by refusing to re-register, their dining hall was padlocked in an attempt to starve them into submission."

Sixth paragraph:

> "Again and again the Southern violators have answered Dr. King's peaceful protests with intimidation and violence. They have bombed his home almost killing his wife and child. They have assaulted his person. They have arrested him seven times — for 'speeding,' 'loitering' and similar 'offenses.' And now they have charged him with 'perjury' — a *felony* under which they could imprison him for *ten years*. . . ."

Although neither of these statements mentions respondent by name, he contended that the word "police" in the third paragraph referred to him as the Montgomery Commissioner who supervised the Police Department, so that he was being accused of "ringing" the campus with police. He further claimed that the paragraph would be read as imputing to the police, and hence to him, the padlocking of the dining hall in order to starve the students into submission. As to the sixth paragraph, he contended that since arrests are ordinarily made by the police, the statement "They have arrested [Dr. King] seven times" would be read as referring to him; he further contended that the "They" who did the arresting would be equated with the "They" who committed the other described acts and with the "Southern violators." Thus, he argued, the paragraph would be read as accusing the Montgomery police, and hence him, of answering Dr. King's protests with "intimidation and violence," bombing his home, assaulting his person, and charging him with perjury. Respondent and six other Montgomery residents testified that they read some or all of the statements as referring to him in his capacity as Commissioner.

It is uncontroverted that some of the statements contained in the two paragraphs were not accurate descriptions of events which occurred in Montgomery. Although Negro students staged a demonstration on the State Capitol steps, they sang the

National Anthem and not "My Country, 'Tis of Thee." Although nine students were expelled by the State Board of Education, this was not for leading the demonstration at the Capitol, but for demanding service at a lunch counter in the Montgomery County Courthouse on another day. Not the entire student body, but most of it, had protested the expulsion, not by refusing to register, but by boycotting classes on a single day; virtually all the students did register for the ensuing semester. The campus dining hall was not padlocked on any occasion, and the only students who may have been barred from eating there were the few who had neither signed a preregistration application nor requested temporary meal tickets. Although the police were deployed near the campus in large numbers on three occasions, they did not at any time "ring" the campus, and they were not called to the campus in connection with the demonstration on the State Capitol steps, as the third paragraph implied. Dr. King had not been arrested seven times, but only four; and although he claimed to have been assaulted some years earlier in connection with his arrest for loitering outside a courtroom, one of the officers who made the arrest denied that there was such an assault.

On the premise that the charges in the sixth paragraph could be read as referring to him, respondent was allowed to prove that he had not participated in the events described. Although Dr. King's home had in fact been bombed twice when his wife and child were there, both of these occasions antedated respondent's tenure as Commissioner, and the police were not only not implicated in the bombings, but had made every effort to apprehend those who were. Three of Dr. King's four arrests took place before respondent became Commissioner. Although Dr. King had in fact been indicted (he was subsequently acquitted) on two counts of perjury, each of which carried a possible five-year sentence, respondent had nothing to do with procuring the indictment.

Respondent made no effort to prove that he suffered actual pecuniary loss as a result of the alleged libel. One of his witnesses, a former employer, testified that if he had believed the statements, he doubted whether he "would want to be associated with anybody who would be a party to such things that are stated in that ad," and that he would not re-employ respondent if he believed "that he allowed the Police Department to do the things that the paper say he did." But neither this witness nor any of the others testified that he had actually believed the statements in their supposed reference to respondent.

The cost of the advertisement was approximately $4800, and it was published by the Times upon an order from a New York advertising agency. . . . The agency submitted the advertisement with a letter from A. Philip Randolph . . . certifying that the persons whose names appeared on the advertisement had given their permission. Mr. Randolph was known to the Times' Advertising Acceptability Department as a responsible person, and in accepting the letter as sufficient proof of authorization it followed its established practice. . . . The manager of the Advertising Acceptability Department testified that he had approved the advertisement for publication because he knew nothing to cause him to believe that anything in it was false, and because it bore the endorsement of "a number of people who are well known and whose reputation" he "had no reason to question." Neither he nor anyone else at the Times made an effort to confirm the accuracy of the advertisement. . . .

Alabama law denies a public officer recovery of punitive damages in a libel action brought on account of a publication concerning his official conduct unless he first makes a written demand for a public retraction and the defendant fails or refuses to comply. Respondent served such a demand upon each of the petitioners. . . . The Times did not publish a retraction in response to the demand, but wrote respondent a letter stating, among other things, that "we . . . are somewhat puzzled as to how you think the statements in any way reflect on you," and "you might, if you desire, let us know in what respect you claim that the statements in the advertisement reflect on you." Respondent filed this suit a few days later without answering the letter. The Times did, however, subsequently publish a retraction of the advertisement upon the demand of Governor John Patterson of Alabama, who asserted that the publication charged him with "grave misconduct and . . . improper actions and omissions as Governor of Alabama and Ex-Officio Chairman of the State Board of Education of Alabama." When asked to explain why there had been a retraction for the Governor but not for respondent, the Secretary of the Times testified: "We did that because we didn't want anything that was published by The Times to be a reflection on the State of Alabama and the Governor was, as far as we could see, the embodiment of the State of Alabama and the proper representative of the State and, furthermore, we had by that time learned more of the actual facts which the ad purported to recite and, finally, the ad did refer to the action of the State authorities and the Board of Education presumably of which the Governor is the ex-officio chairman. . . ." On the other hand, he testified that he did not think that "any of the language in there referred to Mr. Sullivan."

The trial judge submitted the case to the jury under instructions that the statements in the advertisement were "libelous per se" and were not privileged, so that petitioners might be held liable if the jury found that they had published the advertisement and that the statements were made "of and concerning" respondent. The jury was instructed that, because the statements were libelous *per se*, "the law . . . implies legal injury from the bare fact of publication itself," "falsity and malice are presumed," "general damages need not be alleged or proved but are presumed," and "punitive damages may be awarded by the jury even though the amount of actual damages is neither found nor shown." An award of punitive damages — as distinguished from "general" damages, which are compensatory in nature — apparently requires proof of actual malice under Alabama law, and the judge charged that "mere negligence or carelessness is not evidence of actual malice or malice in fact, and does not justify an award of exemplary or punitive damages." He refused to charge, however, that the jury must be "convinced" of malice, in the sense of "actual intent" to harm or "gross negligence and recklessness," to make such an award, and he also refused to require that a verdict for respondent differentiate between compensatory and punitive damages. The judge rejected petitioners' contention that his rulings abridged the freedoms of speech and of the press that are guaranteed by the First and Fourteenth Amendments.

In affirming the judgment, the Supreme Court of Alabama sustained the trial judge's rulings and instructions in all respects. . . .

* * *

Because of the importance of the constitutional issues involved, we granted the separate petitions for certiorari of the individual petitioners and of the Times. We reverse the judgment. We hold that the rule of law applied by the Alabama courts is constitutionally deficient for failure to provide the safeguards for freedom of speech and of the press that are required by the First and Fourteenth Amendments in a libel action brought by a public official against critics of his official conduct. We further hold that under the proper safeguards the evidence presented in this case is constitutionally insufficient to support the judgment for respondent.

I.

We may dispose at the outset of two grounds asserted to insulate the judgment of the Alabama courts from constitutional scrutiny. The first is the proposition relied on by the State Supreme Court — that "The Fourteenth Amendment is directed against State action and not private action." That proposition has no application to this case. Although this is a civil lawsuit between private parties, the Alabama courts have applied a state rule of law which petitioners claim to impose invalid restrictions on their constitutional freedoms of speech and press. It matters not that that law has been applied in a civil action and that it is common law only, though supplemented by statute. The test is not the form in which state power has been applied but, whatever the form, whether such power has in fact been exercised.

The second contention is that the constitutional guarantees of freedom of speech and of the press are inapplicable here, at least so far as the Times is concerned, because the allegedly libelous statements were published as part of a paid, "commercial" advertisement. . . .

The publication here was not a [purely] "commercial" advertisement. . . . It communicated information, expressed opinion, recited grievances, protested claimed abuses, and sought financial support on behalf of a movement whose existence and objectives are matters of the highest public interest and concern. That the Times was paid for publishing the advertisement is as immaterial in this connection as is the fact that newspapers and books are sold. Any other conclusion would discourage newspapers from carrying "editorial advertisements" of this type, and so might shut off an important outlet for the promulgation of information and ideas by persons who do not themselves have access to publishing facilities — who wish to exercise their freedom of speech even though they are not members of the press. The effect would be to shackle the First Amendment in its attempt to secure "the widest possible dissemination of information from diverse and antagonistic sources." To avoid placing such a handicap upon the freedoms of expression, we hold that if the allegedly libelous statements would otherwise be constitutionally protected from the present judgment, they do not forfeit that protection because they were published in the form of a paid advertisement.

II.

Under Alabama law as applied in this case, a publication is "libelous per se" if the words "tend to injure a person . . . in his reputation" or to "bring [him] into public contempt"; the trial court stated that the standard was met if the words are such as to "injure him in his public office, or impute misconduct to him in his office, or want of official integrity, or want of fidelity to a public trust . . . ." The jury must find that the words were published "of and concerning" the plaintiff, but where the plaintiff is a public official his place in the governmental hierarchy is sufficient evidence to support a finding that his reputation has been affected by statements that reflect upon the agency of which he is in charge. Once "libel per se" has been established, the defendant has no defense as to stated facts unless he can persuade the jury that they were true in all their particulars. . . . Unless he can discharge the burden of proving truth, general damages are presumed, and may be awarded without proof of pecuniary injury. A showing of actual malice is apparently a prerequisite to recovery of punitive damages, and the defendant may in any event forestall a punitive award by a retraction meeting the statutory requirements. Good motives and belief in truth do not negate an inference of malice, but are relevant only in mitigation of punitive damages if the jury chooses to accord them weight.

The question before us is whether this rule of liability, as applied to an action brought by a public official against critics of his official conduct, abridges the freedom of speech and of the press that is guaranteed by the First and Fourteenth Amendments.

Respondent relies heavily, as did the Alabama courts, on statements of this Court to the effect that the Constitution does not protect libelous publications. Those statements do not foreclose our inquiry here. . . .

*   *   *

. . . [W]e consider this case against the background of a profound national commitment to the principle that debate on public issues should be uninhibited, robust, and wide-open, and that it may well include vehement, caustic, and sometimes unpleasantly sharp attacks on government and public officials. The present advertisement, as an expression of grievance and protest on one of the major public issues of our time, would seem clearly to qualify for the constitutional protection. The question is whether it forfeits that protection by the falsity of some of its factual statements and by its alleged defamation of respondent.

Authoritative interpretations of the First Amendment guarantees have consistently refused to recognize an exception for any test of truth — whether administered by judges, juries, or administrative officials — and especially one that puts the burden of proving truth on the speaker. The constitutional protection does not turn upon "the truth, popularity, or social utility of the ideas and beliefs which are offered." *N.A.A.C.P. v. Button*, 371 U.S. 415, 445. As Madison said, "Some degree of abuse is inseparable from the proper use of every thing; and in no instance is this more true than in that of the press." 4 ELLIOT'S DEBATES ON THE FEDERAL CONSTITUTION 571 (1876). . . . That erroneous statement is inevitable in free debate, and that it must be protected if the freedoms of expression are to have the "breathing space" that they "need . . . to survive," *N.A.A.C.P. v. Button*, was also recognized by the Court of Appeals for the District of Columbia Circuit in *Sweeney v. Patterson* (D.C. Cir. 1942). Judge Edgerton spoke for a unanimous court which affirmed the dismissal of a Congressman's libel suit based upon a newspaper article charging him with anti-Semitism in opposing a judicial appointment. He said:

"Cases which impose liability for erroneous reports of the political conduct of officials reflect the obsolete doctrine that the governed must not criticize their governors. . . . The interest of the public here outweighs the interest of appellant or any other individual. The protection of the public requires not merely discussion, but information. Political conduct and views which some respectable people approve, and others condemn, are constantly imputed to Congressmen. Errors of fact, particularly in regard to a man's mental states and processes, are inevitable. . . . Whatever is added to the field of libel is taken from the field of free debate."

Injury to official reputation affords no more warrant for repressing speech that would otherwise be free than does factual error. Where judicial officers are involved, this Court has held that concern for the dignity and reputation of the courts does not justify the punishment as criminal contempt of criticism of the judge or his decision. This is true even though the utterance contains "half-truths" and "misinformation." Such repression can be justified, if at all, only by a clear and present danger of the obstruction of justice. If judges are to be treated as "men of fortitude, able to thrive in a hardy climate," surely the same must be true of other government officials, such as elected city commissioners. Criticism of their official conduct does not lose its constitutional protection merely because it is effective criticism and hence diminishes their official reputations.

If neither factual error nor defamatory content suffices to remove the constitutional shield from criticism of official conduct, the combination of the two elements is no less inadequate. This is the lesson to be drawn from the great controversy over the Sedition Act of 1798, 1 Stat. 596, which first crystallized a national awareness of the central meaning of the First Amendment. That statute made it a crime, punishable by a $5,000 fine and five years in prison, "if any person shall write, print, utter or publish . . . any false, scandalous and malicious writing or writings against the government of the United States, or either house of the Congress . . . , or the President . . . , with intent to defame . . . or to bring them, or either of them, into contempt or disrepute; or to excite against them, or either or any of them, the hatred of the good people of the United States." The Act allowed the defendant the defense of truth, and provided that the jury were to be judges both of the law and the facts. Despite these qualifications, the Act was vigorously condemned as unconstitutional in an attack joined in by Jefferson and Madison. In the famous Virginia Resolutions of 1798, the General Assembly of Virginia resolved that it

"doth particularly protest against the palpable and alarming infractions of the Constitution, in the two late cases of the 'Alien and Sedition Acts,' passed at the last session of Congress. . . . [The Sedition Act] exercises . . . a power not delegated by the Constitution, but, on the contrary, expressly and positively forbidden by one of the amendments thereto — a power which, more than any other, ought to produce universal alarm, because it is levelled against the right of freely examining public characters and measures, and of free communication among the people thereon, which has ever been justly deemed the only effectual guardian of every other right."

Madison prepared the Report in support of the protest. His premise was that the

Constitution created a form of government under which "The people, not the government, possess the absolute sovereignty." The structure of the government dispersed power in reflection of the people's distrust of concentrated power, and of power itself at all levels. This form of government was "altogether different" from the British form, under which the Crown was sovereign and the people were subjects. "Is it not natural and necessary, under such different circumstances," he asked, "that a different degree of freedom in the use of the press should be contemplated?" Earlier, in a debate in the House of Representatives, Madison had said: "If we advert to the nature of Republican Government, we shall find that the censorial power is in the people over the Government, and not in the Government over the people." Of the exercise of that power by the press, his Report said: "In every state, probably, in the Union, the press has exerted a freedom in canvassing the merits and measures of public men, of every description, which has not been confined to the strict limits of the common law. On this footing the freedom of the press has stood; on this foundation it yet stands. . . ." The right of free public discussion of the stewardship of public officials was thus, in Madison's view, a fundamental principle of the American form of government.

Although the Sedition Act was never tested in this Court, the attack upon its validity has carried the day in the court of history. Fines levied in its prosecution were repaid by Act of Congress on the ground that it was unconstitutional. Calhoun, reporting to the Senate on February 4, 1836, assumed that its invalidity was a matter "which no one now doubts." . . . Jefferson, as President, pardoned those who had been convicted and sentenced under the Act and remitted their fines, stating: "I discharged every person under punishment or prosecution under the sedition law, because I considered, and now consider, that law to be a nullity, as absolute and as palpable as if Congress had ordered us to fall down and worship a golden image." . . . The invalidity of the Act has also been assumed by Justices of this Court. . . . These views reflect a broad consensus that the Act, because of the restraint it imposed upon criticism of government and public officials, was inconsistent with the First Amendment.

There is no force in respondent's argument that the constitutional limitations implicit in the history of the Sedition Act apply only to Congress and not to the States. It is true that the First Amendment was originally addressed only to action by the Federal Government, and that Jefferson, for one, while denying the power of Congress "to controul the freedom of the press," recognized such a power in the States. But this distinction was eliminated with the adoption of the Fourteenth Amendment and the application to the States of the First Amendment's restrictions.

What a State may not constitutionally bring about by means of a criminal statute is likewise beyond the reach of its civil law of libel. The fear of damage awards under a rule such as that invoked by the Alabama courts here may be markedly more inhibiting than the fear of prosecution under a criminal statute. . . .

The state rule of law is not saved by its allowance of the defense of truth. . . . A rule compelling the critic of official conduct to guarantee the truth of all his factual assertions — and to do so on pain of libel judgments virtually unlimited in amount — leads to a comparable "self-censorship." Allowance of the defense of truth, with the burden of proving it on the defendant, does not mean that only false speech will be deterred. Even courts accepting this defense as an adequate safeguard have recognized the difficulties of adducing legal proofs that the alleged libel was true in all its factual particulars. Under such a rule, would-be critics of official conduct may be deterred from voicing their criticism, even though it is believed to be true and even though it is in fact true, because of doubt whether it can be proved in court or fear of the expense of having to do so. . . . The rule thus dampens the vigor and limits the variety of public debate. It is inconsistent with the First and Fourteenth Amendments.

The constitutional guarantees require, we think, a federal rule that prohibits a public official from recovering damages for a defamatory falsehood relating to his official conduct unless he proves that the statement was made with "actual malice" — that is, with knowledge that it was false or with reckless disregard of whether it was false or not. An oft-cited statement of a like rule, which has been adopted by a number of state courts, is found in the Kansas case of *Coleman v. MacLennan* (Kan. 1908). The State Attorney General, a candidate for re-election and a member of the commission charged with the management and control of the state school fund, sued a newspaper publisher for alleged libel in an article purporting to state facts relating to his official conduct in connection with a school-fund transaction. The defendant pleaded privilege and the trial judge, over the plaintiff's objection, instructed the jury that

> "where an article is published and circulated among voters for the sole purpose of giving what the defendant believes to be truthful information concerning a candidate for public office and for the purpose of enabling such voters to cast their ballot more intelligently, and the whole thing is done in good faith and without malice, the article is privileged, although the principal matters contained in the article may be untrue in fact and derogatory to the character of the plaintiff; and in such a case the burden is on the plaintiff to show actual malice in the publication of the article."

In answer to a special question, the jury found that the plaintiff had not proved actual malice, and a general verdict was returned for the defendant. On appeal the Supreme Court of Kansas, in an opinion by Justice Burch, reasoned as follows:

> "It is of the utmost consequence that the people should discuss the character and qualifications of candidates for their suffrages. The importance to the state and to society of such discussions is so vast, and the advantages derived are so great, that they more than counterbalance the inconvenience of private persons whose conduct may be involved, and occasional injury to the reputations of individuals must yield to the public welfare, although at times such injury may be great. The public benefit from publicity is so great, and the chance of injury to private character so small, that such discussion must be privileged."

*   *   *

Such a privilege for criticism of official conduct is appropriately analogous to the protection accorded a public official when *he* is sued for libel by a private citizen. In *Barr v. Matteo* (1959), this Court held the utterance of a federal official to be absolutely privileged if made "within the outer perimeter" of his duties. The States accord the same immunity to statements of their highest officers, although some differentiate their lesser officials and qualify the privilege they enjoy. But all hold that all officials are protected unless actual malice can be proved. The reason for the official privilege is said to be that the threat of damage suits would otherwise "inhibit the fearless, vigorous, and effective administration of policies of government" and "dampen the ardor of all but the most resolute, or the most irresponsible, in the unflinching discharge of their duties." Analogous considerations support the privilege for the citizen-critic of government. It is as much his duty to criticize as it is the official's duty to administer. . . . It would give public servants an unjustified preference over the public they serve, if critics of official conduct did not have a fair equivalent of the immunity granted to the officials themselves.

We conclude that such a privilege is required by the First and Fourteenth Amendments.

III.

We hold today that the Constitution delimits a State's power to award damages for libel in actions brought by public officials against critics of their official conduct. Since this is such an action, the rule requiring proof of actual malice is applicable. While Alabama law apparently requires proof of actual malice for an award of punitive damages, where general damages are concerned malice is "presumed." Such a presumption is inconsistent with the federal rule. "The power to create presumptions is not a means of escape from constitutional restrictions"; "the showing of malice required for the forfeiture of the privilege is not presumed but is a matter for proof by the plaintiff. . . ." Since the trial judge did not instruct the jury to differentiate between general and punitive damages, it may be that the verdict was wholly an award of one or the other. But it is impossible to know, in view of the general verdict returned. Because of this uncertainty, the judgment must be reversed and the case remanded.

Since respondent may seek a new trial, we deem that considerations of effective judicial administration require us to review the evidence in the present record to determine whether it could constitutionally support a judgment for respondent. This Court's duty is not limited to the elaboration of constitutional principles; we must also in proper cases review the evidence to make certain that those principles have been constitutionally applied. . . .

Applying these standards, we consider that the proof presented to show actual malice lacks the convincing clarity which the constitutional standard demands, and hence that it would not constitutionally sustain the judgment for respondent under the proper rule of law. . . .

As to the Times, we . . . conclude that the facts do not support a finding of actual malice. The statement by the Times' Secretary that, apart from the padlocking allegation, he thought the advertisement was "substantially correct," affords no constitutional warrant for the Alabama Supreme Court's conclusion that it was a "cavalier ignoring of the falsity of the advertisement [from which] the jury could not have but been impressed with the bad faith of The Times, and its maliciousness inferable therefrom." The statement does not indicate malice at the time of the publication; even if the advertisement was not "substantially correct" — although respondent's own proofs tend to show that it was — that opinion was at least a reasonable one, and there was no evidence to impeach the witness' good faith in holding it. The Times' failure to retract upon respondent's demand, although it later retracted upon the demand of Governor Patterson, is likewise not adequate evidence of malice for constitutional purposes. Whether or not a failure to retract may ever constitute such evidence, there are two reasons why it does not here. *First*, the letter written by the Times reflected a reasonable doubt on its part as to whether the advertisement could reasonably be taken to refer to respondent at all. *Second*, it was not a final refusal, since it asked for an explanation on this point — a request that respondent chose to ignore. Nor does the retraction upon the demand of the Governor supply the necessary proof. It may be doubted that a failure to retract which is not itself evidence of malice can retroactively become such by virtue of a retraction subsequently made to another party. But in any event that did not happen here, since the explanation given by the Times' Secretary for the distinction drawn between respondent and the Governor was a reasonable one, the good faith of which was not impeached.

Finally, there is evidence that the Times published the advertisement without checking its accuracy against the news stories in the Times' own files. The mere presence of the stories in the files does not, of course, establish that the Times "knew" the advertisement was false, since the state of mind required for actual malice would have to be brought home to the persons in the Times' organization having responsibility for the publication of the advertisement. With respect to the failure of those persons to make the check, the record shows that they relied upon their knowledge of the good reputation of many of those whose names were listed as sponsors of the advertisement, and upon the letter from A. Philip Randolph, known to them as a responsible individual, certifying that the use of the names was authorized. There was testimony that the persons handling the advertisement saw nothing in it that would render it unacceptable under the Times' policy of rejecting advertisements containing "attacks of a personal character"; their failure to reject it on this ground was not unreasonable. We think the evidence against the Times supports at most a finding of negligence in failing to discover the misstatements, and is constitutionally insufficient to show the recklessness that is required for a finding of actual malice.

We also think the evidence was constitutionally defective in another respect: it was incapable of supporting the jury's finding that the allegedly libelous statements were made "of and concerning" respondent. Respondent relies on the words of the advertisement and the testimony of six witnesses to establish a connection between it and himself. . . . There was no reference to respondent in the advertisement, either by name or official position. . . . [The Supreme Court of Alabama], in holding that the trial court "did not err in overruling the demurrer [of the Times] in the aspect that the libelous matter was not of and concerning the [plaintiff,]" based its ruling on the proposition that:

> "We think it common knowledge that the average person knows that municipal agents, such as police and firemen, and others, are under the control and direction of the city governing body, and more particularly under the direction and control of a single commissioner. In measuring the

performance or deficiencies of such groups, praise or criticism is usually attached to the official in complete control of the body."

This proposition has disquieting implications for criticism of governmental conduct. For good reason, "no court of last resort in this country has ever held, or even suggested, that prosecutions for libel on government have any place in the American system of jurisprudence." . . . The present proposition would sidestep this obstacle by transmuting criticism of government, however impersonal it may seem on its face, into personal criticism, and hence potential libel, of the officials of whom the government is composed. There is no legal alchemy by which a State may thus create the cause of action that would otherwise be denied for a publication which, as respondent himself said of the advertisement, "reflects not only on me but on the other Commissioners and the community." Raising as it does the possibility that a good-faith critic of government will be penalized for his criticism, the proposition relied on by the Alabama courts strikes at the very center of the constitutionally protected area of free expression. We hold that such a proposition may not constitutionally be utilized to establish that an otherwise impersonal attack on governmental operations was a libel of an official responsible for those operations. Since it was relied on exclusively here, and there was no other evidence to connect the statements with respondent, the evidence was constitutionally insufficient to support a finding that the statements referred to respondent.

*   *   *

MR. JUSTICE BLACK, with whom MR. JUSTICE DOUGLAS joins, concurring.

. . . I base my vote to reverse on the belief that the First and Fourteenth Amendments not merely "delimit" a State's power to award damages to "public officials against critics of their official conduct" but completely prohibit a State from exercising such a power. The Court goes on to hold that a State can subject such critics to damages if "actual malice" can be proved against them. "Malice," even as defined by the Court, is an elusive, abstract concept, hard to prove and hard to disprove. The requirement that malice be proved provides at best an evanescent protection for the right critically to discuss public affairs and certainly does not measure up to the sturdy safeguard embodied in the First Amendment. Unlike the Court, therefore, I vote to reverse exclusively on the ground that the Times and the individual defendants had an absolute, unconditional constitutional right to publish in the Times advertisement their criticisms of the Montgomery agencies and officials. . . .

*   *   *

MR. JUSTICE GOLDBERG, with whom MR. JUSTICE DOUGLAS joins, concurring in the result.

The Court today announces a constitutional standard which prohibits "a public official from recovering damages for a defamatory falsehood relating to his official conduct unless he proves that the statement was made with 'actual malice' — that is, with knowledge that it was false or with reckless disregard of whether it was false or not." The Court thus rules that the Constitution gives citizens and newspapers a "conditional privilege" immunizing nonmalicious misstatements of fact regarding the official conduct of a government officer. The impressive array of history and precedent marshaled by the Court, however, confirms my belief that the Constitution affords greater protection than that provided by the Court's standard to citizen and press in exercising the right of public criticism.

In my view, the First and Fourteenth Amendments to the Constitution afford to the citizen and to the press an absolute, unconditional privilege to criticize official conduct despite the harm which may flow from excesses and abuses. . . . Such criticism cannot, in my opinion, be muzzled or deterred by the courts at the instance of public officials under the label of libel.

NOTES AND QUESTIONS

1. *New York Times v. Sullivan* is surely one of the most important First Amendment decisions ever rendered by the Supreme Court. It is both a product of the times, and deeply anchored in a particular view of American history. You have had a very small bit of historical introduction to the time of the framing of the First Amendment. Putting to the side the highly problematical nature of applying the First Amendment against the states in the first place (the problem of "incorporation," which we have dealt with elsewhere), do you think the framers of the First Amendment would have believed that they were declaring a qualified immunity for newspapers engaging in the criticism of public figures? Do you agree with the Court's reading of the relevant history? Recall that at the time of the First Amendment's passage it was believed by all but a few (though among that few were counted Jefferson and Madison) that the English doctrine of seditious libel was not obliterated by the First Amendment, which, with regard to the press, was only supposed to have prohibited prior restraint. How does the majority deal with this?

We have here, of course, a private libel case, but if what the New York Times published would have been seditious libel in the late eighteenth century (would it have?), isn't it pretty clear that it also would have been a violation of private libel law? Private libel law, simply stated, allows private persons who have been damaged in reputation by a publication to recover from the publisher for such damage. Truth is a defense for the publisher, but note that truth is unavailable as a defense in *New York Times v. Sullivan*, because of the inaccuracy of the items published. Where does the Court come up with its notion that there is no liability for civil libel in the case of a public official such as Sullivan, even if the publication falsely criticizes him, so long as the publication was not done with actual malice? If you were making up the rules of libel, would this be your solution? How do you account for the fact that the Court's decision, at least in terms of the result, is unanimous?

2. Before *New York Times v. Sullivan*, it was generally believed that libel (of a kind that the New York Times had clearly been guilty of) was unprotected speech, just as obscenity, or child pornography, or, for most of our history, commercial advertising was. If libel were not to be thought to be something that came under the protection of the First Amendment, of course, the Times or any other newspaper would have been subject to litigation whenever a public official was falsely criticized. Would this have been such a bad thing?

3. By its facts, *New York Times v. Sullivan* is limited to the case of governmental officials, but should it be so limited? Within a few years, the logic of *New York Times v. Sullivan* was extended to grant the press freedom from libel suits (save when malice could be shown) in the case not just of public officials, but also of "public figures" generally, including all sorts of celebrities — TV and motion picture stars, sports figures, and even ordinary citizens whom catastrophic or serendipitous events had placed in the public eye. *See Curtis Publ'g Co. v. Butts*, 388 U.S. 130, 162–65 (1967) (Warren, C.J., concurring in result). Was this a felicitous development?

4. Do you believe that decisions such as *New York Times v. Sullivan* have led to a situation in which the press, with impunity, can destroy the reputations or even the privacy of too many American citizens? On the other hand, do you suppose potential press irresponsibility really entered into the calculation of the Court which decided the case? What other features of the case, and of the time in which it was decided explain the outcome? Does it have anything to do with the contemporary challenge to racial segregation in the South?

5. Summarizing then, understand that there is an enormous difference between a libel action brought by a public figure or official and an action initiated by a private party. Under *New York Times*, a case brought by a public official or figure must prove with clear and convincing evidence that the statement was false and that the defendant knew it was false or at least acted with reckless disregard of the truth — that is, with actual malice. By contrast, a private citizen bringing a defamation action must prove merely negligence on the part of the defendant and that the statement was false. One qualification: if a private citizen is suing for punitive damages, in addition to compensatory damages, and the matter involved is an issue of public concern, then those punitive damages cannot be awarded without proof of actual malice. *Gertz v. Welch*, 418 U.S. 323, 349 (1974).

Many other issues complicate this area. On the question of falsity, for example, the question arises whether labeling a statement "opinion" is enough to insulate from libel liability. In *Milkovich v. Lorain Journal Co.*, 497 U.S. 1 (1990), the Court held that the label was not dispositive. Nevertheless, in order for opinion to be the basis of a defamation action, it must contain within it a false statement of fact.

However, even the partial fabrication of quotations may not be sufficient to demonstrate falsity. In *Masson v. New Yorker*, 501 U.S. 496 (1991), the Court indicated that quotation marks do not signify that the material therein is a verbatim transcription of the words. Rather, quotation marks signify substantial accuracy. There is also some difficulty in ascertaining whether a person is or is not a public figure. Generally, such persons enjoy particularly good access to channels of communication and have involved themselves significantly in matters of public debate. In addition, if the subject is not a matter of public concern, then punitive damages may be awarded without a showing of actual malice. *Dunn & Bradstreet v. Greenmoss Builders*, 472 U.S. 749 (1985) (false credit report indicating inaccurately that a company had filed bankruptcy; the Court found the matter to be one of private concern since it was distributed narrowly and of interest only to a narrow business audience).

6. The Supreme Court dealt with another media issue: the presence of media as "ride alongs" in the serving of an arrest warrant. In *Wilson v. Layne*, 526 U.S. 603 (1999), the Court held that it violates the privacy protected by the Fourth Amendment for the police to bring members of the media or other third parties into arrestees' homes during the execution of the warrant. "[T]he presence of reporters inside the home was not related to the objectives of the authorized intrusion." This was true since the reporters were not in any way assisting in the warrant's execution. The argument that the media would facilitate efforts to combat crime or the accurate reporting of law enforcement activities was not enough to overcome the residential privacy protected by the Fourth Amendment.

b. Commercial Speech

CENTRAL HUDSON GAS & ELECTRIC CORP. v. PUBLIC SERVICE COMMISSION OF NEW YORK
447 U.S. 557 (1980)

Mr. Justice Powell delivered the opinion of the Court.

This case presents the question whether a regulation of the Public Service Commission of the State of New York violates the First and Fourteenth Amendments because it completely bans promotional advertising by an electrical utility.

I

In December 1973, the Commission . . . ordered electric utilities in New York State to cease all advertising that "promot[es] the use of electricity." The order was based on the Commission's finding that "the interconnected utility system in New York State does not have sufficient fuel stocks or sources of supply to continue furnishing all customer demands for the 1973–1974 winter."

Three years later, when the fuel shortage had eased, the Commission requested comments from the public on its proposal to continue the ban on promotional advertising. Central Hudson Gas & Electric Corp. . . . . opposed the ban on First Amendment grounds. After reviewing the public comments, the Commission extended the prohibition. . . .

*   *   *

Appellant challenged the order in state court, arguing that the Commission had restrained commercial speech in violation of the First and Fourteenth Amendments. The Commission's order was upheld by the trial court and at the intermediate appellate level. The New York Court of Appeals affirmed. It found little value to advertising in "the noncompetitive market in which electric corporations operate." Since consumers "have no choice regarding the source of their electric power," the court denied that "promotional advertising of electricity might contribute to society's interest in 'informed and reliable' economic decisionmaking." The court also observed that by encouraging consumption, promotional advertising would only exacerbate the current energy situation. The court concluded that the governmental interest in the prohibition outweighed the limited constitutional value of the commercial speech at issue. We . . . now reverse.

II

The Commission's order restricts only commercial speech, that is, expression related solely to the economic interests of the speaker and its audience. The First Amendment, as applied to the States through the Fourteenth Amendment, protects commercial speech from unwarranted governmental regulation. Commercial expression not only serves the economic interest of the speaker, but also assists consumers and furthers the societal interest in the fullest possible dissemination of information. In applying the First Amendment to this area, we have rejected the "highly paternalistic" view that government has complete power to suppress or regulate commercial speech. "[P]eople will perceive their own best interests if only they are well enough informed, and . . . the best means to that end is to open the channels of communication, rather than to close them. . . ." Even when advertising communicates only an incomplete version of the relevant facts, the First Amendment presumes that some accurate information is better than no information at all.

Nevertheless, our decisions have recognized "the 'commonsense' distinction between speech proposing a commercial transaction, which occurs in an area traditionally subject to government regulation, and other varieties of speech." The Constitution therefore accords a lesser protection to commercial speech than to other constitutionally guaranteed expression. The protection available for particular commercial expression turns on the nature both of the expression and of the governmental interests served by its regulation.

The First Amendment's concern for commercial speech is based on the informational function of advertising. Consequently, there can be no constitutional objection to the suppression of commercial messages that do not accurately inform the public about lawful activity. The government may ban forms of communication more likely to deceive the public than to inform it, or commercial speech related to illegal activity.

If the communication is neither misleading nor related to unlawful activity, the government's power is more circumscribed. The State must assert a substantial interest to be achieved by restrictions on commercial speech. Moreover, the regulatory technique must be in proportion to that interest. The limitation on expression must be designed carefully to achieve the State's goal. Compliance with this requirement may be measured by two criteria. First, the restriction must directly advance the state interest involved; the regulation may not be sustained if it provides only ineffective or remote support for the government's purpose. Second, if the governmental interest could be served as well by a more limited restriction on commercial speech, the excessive restrictions cannot survive.

Under the first criterion, the Court has declined to uphold regulations that only indirectly advance the state interest involved. In [two cases], the Court concluded that an advertising ban could not be imposed to protect the ethical or performance standards of a profession. The Court noted in [one case] that "[t]he advertising ban does not directly affect professional standards one way or the other." In [the other,] the Court overturned an advertising prohibition that was designed to protect the "quality" of a lawyer's work. "Restraints on advertising . . . are an ineffective way of deterring shoddy work."

The second criterion recognizes that the First Amendment mandates that speech restrictions be "narrowly drawn." The regulatory technique may extend only as far as the interest it serves. The State cannot regulate speech that poses no danger to the asserted state interest, nor can it completely suppress information when narrower restrictions on expression would serve its interest as well. . . .

In commercial speech cases, then, a four-part analysis has developed. At the outset, we must determine whether the expression is protected by the First Amendment. For commercial speech to come within that provision, it at least must concern lawful activity and not be misleading. Next, we ask whether the asserted governmental interest is substantial. If both inquiries yield positive answers, we must determine whether the regulation directly advances the governmental interest asserted, and whether it is not more extensive than is necessary to serve that interest.

III

We now apply this four-step analysis for commercial speech to the Commission's arguments in support of its ban on promotional advertising.

A

The Commission does not claim that the expression at issue either is inaccurate or relates to unlawful activity. . . .

*   *   *

Even in monopoly markets, the suppression of advertising reduces the information available for consumer decisions and thereby defeats the purpose of the First Amendment. . . .

B

The Commission offers two state interests as justifications for the ban on promotional advertising. The first concerns energy conservation. Any increase in demand for electricity — during peak or off-peak periods — means greater consumption of energy. The Commission argues, and the New York court agreed, that the State's interest in conserving energy is sufficient to support suppression of advertising designed to increase consumption of electricity. In view of our country's dependence on energy resources beyond our control, no one can doubt the importance of energy conservation. Plainly, therefore, the state interest asserted is substantial.

The Commission also argues that promotional advertising will aggravate inequities caused by the failure to base the utilities' rates on marginal cost. The utilities argued to the Commission that if they could promote the use of electricity in periods of low demand, they would improve their utilization of generating capacity. The Commission responded that promotion of off-peak consumption also would increase consumption during peak periods. . . .

C

Next, we focus on the relationship between the State's interests and the advertising ban. Under this criterion, the Commission's laudable concern over the equity and efficiency of appellant's rates does not provide a constitutionally adequate reason for restricting protected speech. The link between the advertising prohibition and appellant's rate structure is, at most, tenuous. The impact of promotional advertising on the equity of appellant's rates is highly speculative. Advertising to increase off-peak usage would have to increase peak usage, while other factors that directly affect the fairness and efficiency of appellant's rates remained constant. Such conditional and remote eventualities simply cannot justify silencing appellant's promotional advertising.

In contrast, the State's interest in energy conservation is directly advanced by the Commission order at issue here. There is an immediate connection between advertising and demand for electricity. Central Hudson would not contest the advertising ban unless it believed that promotion would increase its sales. Thus, we find a direct link between the state interest in conservation and the Commission's order.

D

We come finally to the critical inquiry in this case: whether the Commission's complete suppression of speech ordinarily protected by the First Amendment is no more extensive than necessary to further the State's interest in energy conservation. The Commission's order reaches all promotional advertising, regardless of the impact of the touted service on overall energy use. But the energy conservation rationale, as important as it is, cannot justify suppressing information about electric devices or services that would cause no net increase in total energy use. In addition, no showing has been made that a more limited restriction on the content of promotional advertising would not serve adequately the State's interests.

Appellant insists that but for the ban, it would advertise products and services that use energy efficiently. These include the "heat pump," which both parties acknowledge to be a major improvement in electric heating, and the use of electric heat as a "backup" to solar and other heat sources. Although the Commission has questioned the efficiency of electric heating before this Court, neither the Commission's Policy Statement nor its order denying rehearing made findings on this issue. In the absence of authoritative findings to the contrary, we must credit as within the realm of possibility the claim that electric heat can be an efficient alternative in some circumstances.

The Commission's order prevents appellant from promoting electric services that would reduce energy use by diverting demand from less efficient sources, or that would consume roughly the same amount of energy as do alternative sources. In neither situation would the utility's advertising endanger conservation or mislead the public. To the extent that the Commission's order suppresses speech that in no way impairs the State's interest in energy conservation, the Commission's order violates the First and Fourteenth Amendments and must be invalidated.

The Commission also has not demonstrated that its interest in conservation cannot be protected adequately by more limited regulation of appellant's commercial expression. To further its policy of conservation, the Commission could attempt to restrict the format and content of Central Hudson's advertising. It might, for example, require that the advertisements include information about the relative efficiency and expense of the offered service, both under current conditions and for the foreseeable future. In the absence of a showing that more limited speech regulation would be ineffective, we cannot approve the complete suppression of Central Hudson's advertising.

Mr. Justice Brennan, concurring in the judgment [omitted].

Mr. Justice Blackmun, with whom Mr. Justice Brennan joins, concurring in the judgment.

I agree with the Court that the Public Service Commission's ban on promotional advertising of electricity by public utilities is inconsistent with the First and Fourteenth Amendments. I concur only in the Court's judgment, however, because I believe the test now evolved and applied by the Court is not consistent with our prior cases and does not provide adequate protection for truthful, nonmisleading, noncoercive commercial speech.

The Court asserts, that "a four-part analysis has developed" from our decisions concerning commercial speech. Under this four-part test a restraint on commercial "communication [that] is neither misleading nor related to unlawful activity" is subject to an intermediate level of scrutiny, and suppression is permitted whenever it "directly advances" a "substantial" governmental interest and is "not more extensive than is necessary to serve that interest." I agree with the Court that this level of intermediate scrutiny is appropriate for a restraint on commercial speech designed to protect consumers from misleading or coercive speech, or a regulation related to the time, place, or manner of commercial speech. I do not agree, however, that the Court's four-part test is the proper one to be applied when a State seeks to suppress information about a product in order to manipulate a private economic decision that the State cannot or has not regulated or outlawed directly.

*   *   *

If the First Amendment guarantee means anything, it means that, absent clear and present danger, government has no power to restrict expression because of the effect its message is likely to have on the public. Our cases indicate that this guarantee applies even to commercial speech. In *Virginia Pharmacy Board v. Virginia Consumer Council* (1976), we held that Virginia could not pursue its goal of encouraging the public to patronize the "professional pharmacist" (one who provided individual attention and a stable pharmacist-customer relationship) by "keeping the public in ignorance of the entirely lawful terms that competing pharmacists are offering." We noted that our decision left the State free to pursue its goal of maintaining high standards among its pharmacists by "requir[ing] whatever professional standards it wishes of its pharmacists."

We went on in *Virginia Pharmacy Board* to discuss the types of regulation of commercial speech that, due to the "commonsense differences" between this form of speech and other forms, are or may be constitutionally permissible. We indicated that government may impose reasonable "time, place, and manner" restrictions, and that it can deal with false, deceptive, and misleading commercial speech. . . .

Concluding with a restatement of the type of restraint that is not permitted, we said: "What is at issue is whether a State may completely suppress the dissemination of concededly truthful information about entirely lawful activity, fearful of that information's effect upon its disseminators and its recipients. . . . [W]e conclude that the answer to this [question] is in the negative."

*   *   *

Carey v. Population Services International (1977), also applied to content-based restraints on commercial speech the same standard of review we have applied to other varieties of speech. There the Court held that a ban on advertising of contraceptives could not be justified by the State's interest in avoiding" 'legitimation' of illicit sexual behavior" because the advertisements could not be characterized as " 'directed to inciting or producing imminent lawless action and . . . likely to incite or produce such action.' "

Our prior references to the " 'commonsense differences' " between commercial speech and other speech " 'suggest that a different degree of protection is necessary to insure that the flow of truthful and legitimate commercial information is unimpaired.' " We have not suggested that the "commonsense differences" between commercial speech and other speech justify relaxed scrutiny of restraints that suppress truthful, nondeceptive, noncoercive commercial speech. The differences articulated by the Court justify a more permissive approach to regulation of the manner of commercial speech for the purpose of protecting consumers from deception or coercion, and these differences explain why doctrines designed to prevent "chilling" of protected speech are inapplicable to commercial speech. No differences between commercial speech and other protected speech justify suppression of commercial speech in order to influence public conduct through manipulation of the availability of information. . . .

It appears that the Court would permit the State to ban all direct advertising of air conditioning, assuming that a more limited restriction on such advertising would not effectively deter the public from cooling its homes. In my view, our cases do not support this type of suppression. If a governmental unit believes that use or overuse of air conditioning is a serious problem, it must attack that problem directly, by prohibiting air conditioning or regulating thermostat levels. Just as the Commonwealth of Virginia may promote professionalism of pharmacists directly, so too New York may *not* promote energy conservation "by keeping the public in ignorance."

MR. JUSTICE STEVENS, with whom MR. JUSTICE BRENNAN joins, concurring in the judgment.

Because "commercial speech" is afforded less constitutional protection than other forms of speech, it is important that the commercial speech concept not be defined too broadly lest speech deserving of greater constitutional protection be inadvertently suppressed. . . .

In my judgment one of the two definitions the Court uses in addressing that issue is too broad and the other may be somewhat too narrow. The Court first describes commercial speech as "expression related solely to the economic interests of the speaker and its audience." Although it is not entirely clear whether this definition uses the subject matter of the speech or the motivation of the speaker as the limiting factor, it seems clear to me that it encompasses speech that is entitled to the maximum protection afforded by the First Amendment. Neither a labor leader's exhortation to strike, nor an economist's dissertation on the money supply, should receive any lesser protection because the subject matter concerns only the economic interests of the audience. Nor should the economic motivation of a speaker qualify his constitutional protection; even Shakespeare may have been motivated by the prospect of pecuniary reward. Thus, the Court's first definition of commercial speech is unquestionably too broad.

The Court's second definition refers to " 'speech proposing a commercial transaction.' " A saleman's solicitation, a broker's offer, and a manufacturer's publication of a price list or the terms of his standard warranty would unquestionably fit within this concept. Presumably, the definition is intended to encompass advertising that advises possible buyers of the availability of specific products at specific prices and describes the advantages of purchasing such items. Perhaps it also extends to other communications that do little more than make the name of a product or a service more familiar to the general public. Whatever the precise contours of the concept, and perhaps it is too early to enunciate an exact formulation, I am persuaded that it should not include the entire range of communication that is embraced within the term "promotional advertising."

This case involves a governmental regulation that completely bans promotional advertising by an electric utility. This ban encompasses a great deal more than mere proposals to engage in certain kinds of commercial transactions. It prohibits all advocacy of the immediate or future use of electricity. It curtails expression by an informed and interested group of persons of their point of view on questions relating to the production and consumption of electrical energy — questions frequently discussed and debated by our political leaders. For example, an electric company's advocacy of the use of electric heat for environmental reasons, as opposed to wood-burning stoves, would seem to fall squarely within New York's promotional advertising ban and also within the bounds of maximum First Amendment protection. . . .

The justification for the regulation is nothing more than the expressed fear that the audience may find the utility's message persuasive. Without the aid of any coercion, deception, or misinformation, truthful communication may persuade some citizens to consume more electricity than they otherwise would. I assume that such a consequence would be undesirable and that government may therefore prohibit and punish the unnecessary or excessive use of electricity. But if the perceived harm associated with greater electrical usage is not sufficiently serious to justify direct regulation, surely it does not constitute the kind of clear and present danger that can justify the suppression of speech.

* * *

In sum, I concur in the result because I do not consider this to be a "commercial speech" case. Accordingly, I see no need to decide whether the Court's four-part analysis adequately protects commercial speech — as properly defined — in the face of a blanket ban of the sort involved in this case.

MR. JUSTICE REHNQUIST, dissenting.

The Court today invalidates an order issued by the New York Public Service Commission designed to promote a policy that has been declared to be of critical national concern. The order was issued by the Commission in 1973 in response to the Mideastern oil embargo crisis. It prohibits electric corporations "from *promoting* the use of electricity through the use of advertising, subsidy payments . . . , or employee incentives." (emphasis added). Although the immediate crisis created by the oil embargo has subsided, the ban on promotional advertising remains in effect. The regulation was re-examined by the New York Public Service Commission in 1977. Its constitutionality was subsequently upheld by the New York Court of Appeals, which concluded that the paramount national interest in energy conservation justified its retention.

The Court's asserted justification for invalidating the New York law is the public interest discerned by the Court to underlie the First Amendment in the free flow of commercial information. Prior to this Court's recent decision in *Virginia Pharmacy Board v. Virginia Citizens Consumer Council* (1976), however, commercial speech was afforded no protection under the First Amendment whatsoever. Given what seems to me full recognition of the holding of *Virginia Pharmacy Board* that commercial speech is entitled to some degree of First Amendment protection, I think the Court is nonetheless incorrect in invalidating the carefully considered state ban on promotional advertising in light of pressing national and state energy needs.

* * *

II

This Court has previously recognized that although commercial speech may be entitled to First Amendment protection, that protection is not as extensive as that accorded to the advocacy of ideas. Thus, we stated in *Ohralik v. Ohio State Bar Assn.* (1978):

"Expression concerning purely commercial transactions has come within the ambit of the Amendment's protection only recently. In rejecting the notion that such speech 'is wholly outside the protection of the First Amendment,' we were careful not to hold 'that it is wholly undifferentiable from other forms' of speech. We have not discarded the 'common-sense' distinction between speech proposing a commercial transaction, which occurs in an area traditionally subject to government regulation, and other varieties of speech. To require a parity of constitutional protection for commercial and noncommercial speech alike could invite dilution, simply by a leveling process, of the force of the Amendment's guarantee with respect to the latter kind of speech. Rather than subject the First Amendment to such a devitalization, we instead have afforded commercial speech a limited measure of protection, commensurate with its subordinate position in the scale of First Amendment values, while allowing modes of regulation that might be impermissible in the realm of noncommercial expression."

*   *   *

I remain of the view that the Court unlocked a Pandora's Box when it "elevated" commercial speech to the level of traditional political speech by according it First Amendment protection in *Virginia Pharmacy Board*. The line between "commercial speech," and the kind of speech that those who drafted the First Amendment had in mind, may not be a technically or intellectually easy one to draw, but it surely produced far fewer problems than has the development of judicial doctrine in this area since *Virginia Pharmacy Board*. For in the world of political advocacy and *its* marketplace of ideas, there is no such thing as a "fraudulent" idea: there may be useless proposals, totally unworkable schemes, as well as very sound proposals that will receive the imprimatur of the "marketplace of ideas" through our majoritarian system of election and representative government. The free flow of information is important in this context not because it will lead to the discovery of any objective "truth," but because it is essential to our system of self-government.

The notion that more speech is the remedy to expose falsehood and fallacies is wholly out of place in the commercial bazaar, where if applied logically the remedy of one who was defrauded would be merely a statement, available upon request, reciting the Latin maxim *"caveat emptor."* But since "fraudulent speech" in this area is to be remediable under *Virginia Pharmacy Board, supra*, the remedy of one defrauded is a lawsuit or an agency proceeding based on common-law notions of fraud that are separated by a world of difference from the realm of politics and government. What time, legal decisions, and common sense have so widely severed, I declined to join in *Virginia Pharmacy Board*, and regret now to see the Court reaping the seeds that it there sowed. For in a democracy, the economic is subordinate to the political, a lesson that our ancestors learned long ago, and that our descendants will undoubtedly have to relearn many years hence.

III

*   *   *

It is in my view inappropriate for the Court to invalidate the State's ban on commercial advertising here, based on its speculation that in some cases the advertising may result in a net savings in electrical energy use, and in the cases in which it is clear a net energy savings would result from utility advertising, the Public Service Commission would apply its ban so as to proscribe such advertising.

Even assuming that the Court's speculation is correct, I do not think it follows that facial invalidation of the ban is the appropriate course. As stated in *Parker v. Levy* (1974), "even if there are marginal applications in which a statute would infringe on First Amendment values, facial invalidation is inappropriate if the 'remainder of the statute . . . covers a whole range of easily identifiable and constitutionally proscribable . . . conduct. . . .' " This is clearly the case here.

NOTES AND QUESTIONS

1. Note that we do not here have the same kind of unanimity we found in cases like *New York Times v. Sullivan*, or even the nearly-unanimous attitude in cases like *New York Times v. United States*. Still, can you discern a doctrinal movement, at least in the opinion of the majority, that is close in spirit to those other cases?

2. Before the 1970s, as you may have been able to discern, commercial speech was simply unprotected under the First Amendment. Are all types of commercial speech equally subject to First Amendment protection once the decision is made to remove commercial speech from the unprotected category? If only some kinds of commercial speech are to be protected, which are deserving, and why? Is it the interests of the speaker that are accorded protection, or those of the audience? Which is the traditionally First Amendment-protected interest?

Only in one case has the Court attempted a definition of commercial speech. In *Bolger v. Young Drug Products Corp.*, 463 U.S. 60 (1983), the Court opined that commercial speech must have three elements: that of advertisement; referring to specific product; where the speaker is economically motivated. If a tobacco company decided to undertake advertisements discussing the reliability of various scientific studies of the tobacco-cancer risk, would such advertisements be commercial speech?

3. You will have noted that the doctrine of protecting commercial speech results in, for example, forbidding the states from banning the advertisement of prescription drug prices, or from banning advertising by lawyers. Are these conclusions unequivocal goods for society? Who should be balancing the harm and benefits of such regulatory moves? The court or the legislature? What does the dissent in this case suggest on this question? Does the fact that the majority has formulated an involved four-part test for determining when commercial speech is to be protected make you more or less sanguine about having courts rather than legislatures make the ultimate determinations here?

4. The Court has not consistently applied the elements of the *Central Hudson* test. In *Board of Trustees of the State of New York v. Fox*, 492 U.S. 469 (1989), the Court suggested that the fourth element did not require the least restrictive regulatory means. Rather, the government must merely choose a means that is narrowly tailored to achieve the desired objective. In contrast, in *Rubin v. Coors Brewing Co.*, 514 U.S. 476 (1995), dealing with a federal regulation that prevented labels with a listing of alcohol content, the Court said the regulation must advance the government's interest in a "direct and material" way, that the harms addressed by the regulation be real, and the restriction will alleviate them in a material fashion. *Id.* at 1592. The Court invalidated the regulation since it could conceive of more effective alternatives to the labeling restriction. Similarly, in *44 Liquormart Inc. v. Rhode Island*, 517 U.S. 484 (1996), a Court plurality found a prohibition on liquor prices not to be the best alternative for promoting temperance. *Fox* seems to have been overruled in everything but name.

5. In *Greater New Orleans Broadcasting Ass'n, Inc. v. United States*, 527 U.S. 173 (1999), the Court continues its close examination of the third and fourth elements of *Central Hudson* — namely, whether regulation directly advances a substantial governmental interest and whether the restriction is no more extensive than necessary. The Court found that a prohibition of private casino gambling advertising in states where such gaming is lawful is unconstitutional. While admitting that casino gambling has enormous social costs, the Court was unwilling to accept limits on speech as the way to address them, especially where the government has been ambivalent, exempting advertising about state-run casinos and lotteries, certain occasional commercial gambling, and tribal casino gambling even when the broadcaster is located in a strict anti-gambling locale. Distinguishing on the basis of the identity of a casino's owner, reasoned the Court, is no way to directly advance the government's interests in avoiding the manifold harms gambling produces, including corruption and organized crime, bribery, narcotics trafficking, diversion of the least affluent families' scarce resources, and the serious abetting of pathological or compulsive gambling by close to three million Americans. Justice Thomas, concurring in the judgment, would find any suppression of speech about a lawful subject — commercial or noncommercial — to be incapable of justification, even under *Central Hudson*. Does the logic of the Court's opinion suggest that the only way the gambling epidemic in the United States can be addressed is by banning or limiting gaming directly?

6. The Court confronted commercial speech again in *Lorillard Tobacco Co. v. Reilly*, 533 U.S. 525 (2001), invalidating a Massachusetts law limiting various tobacco advertising on preemption and free speech grounds, but sustaining sale regulations. The Attorney General of Massachusetts (Attorney General) promulgated comprehensive regulations governing the advertising and sale of cigarettes, smokeless tobacco, and cigars, all of which were challenged by tobacco manufacturers and retailers. The cigarette advertising restrictions were preempted by the Federal Cigarette Labeling and Advertising Act of 1969 (FCLAA), said the Court, which prescribes mandatory health warnings for cigarette packaging and advertising, and precludes similar state regulations. Massachusetts had argued that the FCLAA only pre-empted regulations of the content of cigarette advertising and that its exclusion of cigarette billboards from school zones and the like was a form of zoning, a traditional area of state power, and thus, the presumption against preemption should apply. The Court rejected that view. In addition, while Massachusetts' outdoor and point-of-sale advertising regulations relating to smokeless tobacco and cigars were not preempted, those were found to violate the First Amendment.

No one contested the importance of the state's interest in preventing the use of tobacco by minors, and the Court found that interest directly advanced by the regulations in issue. The problem was the fourth — or "reasonable fit" — step of *Central Hudson*. Because the record indicated that the regulations prohibit advertising in a substantial portion of Massachusetts' major metropolitan areas, and that "outdoor" advertising included not only advertising located outside an establishment, but also advertising inside a store if visible from outside, the regulations were insufficiently tailored. Said Justice O'Connor for the Court: "The State's interest in preventing underage tobacco use is substantial, and even compelling, but it is no less true that the sale and use of tobacco products by adults is a legal activity. We must consider that tobacco retailers and manufacturers have an interest in conveying truthful information about their products to adults, and adults have a corresponding interest in receiving truthful information about tobacco products." In other words, since adults would have a harder time finding tobacco products, the compelling interest of lessening underage tobacco addiction is outweighed. This is a curiously myopic, if not self-centered, calculus in light of the unhealthy, life-threatening qualities of the (nevertheless still lawful) product, but here are the Court's own words, "[a] careful calculation of the costs of a speech regulation does not mean that a State must demonstrate that there is no incursion on legitimate speech interests, but a speech regulation cannot unduly impinge on the speaker's ability to propose a commercial transaction and the adult listener's opportunity to obtain information about products. After reviewing the outdoor advertising regulations, we find the calculation in this case insufficient for purposes of the First Amendment."

The Court also invalidated on free speech grounds a restriction requiring point of sale advertising to be placed above five feet. Some kids are taller or would look up, reasoned the Justices, so the Court thought neither the third (directly advance) or fourth (reasonable fit) aspects of *Central Hudson* were met. By contrast, Massachusetts' sales provisions regulating the placement of the products within the store were sustained. While such conduct may have a communicative component, Massachusetts sought only to regulate the placement of tobacco products for reasons unrelated to the communication of ideas. Under the *O'Brien* expressive conduct standard, the Court concluded that the state had demonstrated a substantial interest in preventing access to tobacco products by minors and had adopted an appropriately narrow means of advancing that interest. "Unattended displays of tobacco products present an opportunity for access without the proper age verification required by law. Thus, the State prohibits self-service and other displays that would allow an individual to obtain tobacco products without direct contact with a salesperson. It was clear that the regulations leave open ample channels of communication. The regulations do not significantly impede adult access to tobacco products."

Concurring, Justice Thomas noted that he continues to believe that when the government seeks to restrict truthful speech in order to suppress the ideas it conveys, strict scrutiny is appropriate, whether or not the speech in question may be characterized as "commercial." He would subject all of the advertising restrictions to strict scrutiny and would hold that they violate the First Amendment. Justices Kennedy and Scalia in a separate concurrence implied agreement. Assuming the Thomas view were the Court's position, is it as clear to you (as apparently it is to Justice Thomas) that strict scrutiny could not be fulfilled given the "compelling" interest in preventing underage addiction to tobacco? Justice Stevens wrote one of the several dissenting opinions from the preemption ruling, but the dissenters (perhaps subject to further fact-finding) largely accepted the

First Amendment analysis because the regulations "unduly restrict[ed] the ability of cigarette manufacturers to convey lawful information to adult consumers."

7.   In *Sorrell v. IMS Health, Inc.*, 131 S. Ct. 2653, 180 L. Ed. 2d 544 (2011), the Court struck down a Vermont statute that had restricted the sale, disclosure, and use of pharmacy records that reveal the prescribing practices of individual doctors. In 2007, Vermont's legislature enacted a "Prescription Confidentiality Law" aimed apparently at protecting physicians and presumably their patients from the marketing practices of pharmaceutical manufacturers and companies in the business of selling prescription medicines, especially those selling brand-name prescription medicines. A portion of the law authorized funds for programs to promote the use of generic as opposed to brand-name pharmaceuticals. Apparently an industry of sorts had developed around the information that pharmacies obtained from the filling of prescriptions. Prior to the enactment of the law, pharmacies were engaging in the practice of selling the information obtained from filling prescriptions to so-called "data miners" who then produced reports on the prescribing habits of physicians and other "prescribers". The data miners would then lease the reports to brand-name pharmaceutical manufacturers. The manufacturers would use the reports to enhance their marketing strategies for convincing physicians and other prescribers to specify their brand-name pharmaceuticals when prescribing for patients. The manufacturers' marketing representatives executed those specially developed marketing strategies by engaging in a practice known in the industry as "detailing" and involving the representatives visiting physicians' offices with free samples and a marketing pitch "detailed" nicely to the individual physician's prescribing habits and practices. Vermont's law is referred to in the opinion as "Act 80" and its central provision is § 4631(d), which read as follows:

> A health insurer, a self-insured employer, an electronic transmission intermediary, a pharmacy, or other similar entity shall not sell, license, or exchange for value regulated records containing prescriber-identifiable information, nor permit the use of regulated records containing prescriber-identifiable information for marketing or promoting a prescription drug, unless the prescriber consents. . . . Pharmaceutical manufacturers and pharmaceutical marketers shall not use prescriber-identifiable information for marketing or promoting a prescription drug unless the prescriber consents.

The Court saw § 4631(d) as imposing more than an incidental burden on protected expression:

> Both on its face and in its practical operation, Vermont's law imposes a burden based on the content of speech and the identity of the speaker. [Citing, *inter alia*, *New York Times v. Sullivan*] . . . While the burdened speech results from an economic motive, so too does a great deal of vital expression. . . . Vermont's law does not simply have an effect on speech, but is directed at certain content and is aimed at particular speakers. The Constitution "does not enact Mr. Herbert Spencer's Social Statics." *Lochner v. New York* . . . (1905) (Holmes, J., dissenting). It does enact the First Amendment.

Having found a content and speaker-based burden in the statute, the Court, while acknowledging that so-called "commercial speech" was involved, nonetheless applied a heightened-scrutiny analysis in striking down the Vermont law:

> To sustain the targeted, content-based burden § 4631(d) imposes on protected expression, the State must show at least that the statute directly advances a substantial governmental interest and that the measure is drawn to achieve that interest. . . . There must be a "fit between the legislature's ends and the means chosen to accomplish those ends." . . . As in other contexts, these standards ensure not only that the State's interests are proportional to the resulting burdens placed on speech but also that the law does not seek to suppress a disfavored message.

8.   In *Golan v. Holder*, 132 S. Ct. 873, 181 L. Ed. 2d 835 (2012), the Court sustained the constitutionality of an act of Congress under the Copyright Clause and the First Amendment's Freedom of Expression. The Copyright Clause in Article I, § 8 empowers Congress "To promote the Progress of Science and useful Arts, by securing for limited Times to Authors . . . the exclusive Right to their . . . Writings."

Prior to 1994, the United States, under the Berne Convention Implementation Act of 1988, had taken a "minimalist approach" in its implementation of the principal accord governing international copyright relations, known as the Berne Convention for the Protection of Literary and Artistic Works. When the United States joined the Berne Convention, it chose not to give copyright protection to foreign works that were then in the public domain under the then-existing United States law. As a result, many works which, under a substantive provision of the Berne Convention known as Article 18, should have received copyright protection in the United States, did not do so, but remained in the public domain. At the time there was no effective international enforcement mechanism. In 1994, however, during its participation in the Uruguay round of multilateral trade negotiations, the United States joined in the Agreement on Trade-Related Aspects of Intellectual Property Rights, an agreement that provided an effective enforcement mechanism before the World Trade Organization for the implementation of Article 18 of the Berne Convention.

With the adoption of the Agreement on Trade-Related Aspects of Intellectual Property Rights, Congress saw the need to abandon its "minimalist approach" and bring the United States into compliance with Article 18 of the Berne Convention, and so it enacted the Uruguay Round Agreements Act, § 514 of which extended copyright protection, with a few ameliorative limitations, to works protected in their countries of origin that had been in the public domain in the United States under the now-abandoned "minimalist approach."

Several orchestra conductors, musicians, publishers, and others who had been enjoying free access to the now-protected works challenged the constitutionality of § 514 as being in excess of Congress's power under the Copyright Clause and as being a violation of their First Amendment rights to Freedom of Expression. The challenge under the Copyright Clause was based on the fact that since Congress was protecting previously unprotected works, it could not be said to be promoting the progress of science. The Court, noting that the first Copyright Act of 1790 necessarily protected previously unprotected works, dismissed the argument on historical grounds, and used a rational-basis form of analysis:

> § 514 falls comfortably within Congress' authority under the Copyright Clause. Congress rationally could have concluded that adherence to [the] Berne [Convention] "promotes the diffusion of knowledge." . . . A well-functioning international copyright system would likely encourage the dissemination of existing and future works. . . . We have no warrant to reject the rational judgment Congress made.

The more serious challenge was the First Amendment argument. The challengers asserted that since the works in question had been in the public domain, a new burden placed on the use of those works must pass muster under a heightened-scrutiny analysis. Led by Justice Ginsburg, however, the majority, noting that "some restriction on expression is the inherent and intended effect of every grant of copyright" and that the Copyright Clause and the First Amendment "were adopted close in time," reasoned that

> the Framers regarded copyright protection not simply as a limit on the manner in which expressive works may be used. They also saw copyright as an "engine of free expression . . .".

Moreover, the majority also noted that two doctrines inherent in copyright protection and indeed codified in the Copyright Act itself, "the 'idea/expression dichotomy' and the 'fair use' defense," operate as "built-in First Amendment accommodations."

> The idea/expression dichotomy is codified at 17 U.S.C. § 102(b): "In no case does copyright protec[t] . . . any idea, procedure, process, system, method of operation, concept, principle, or discovery . . . described, explained, illustrated, or embodied in [the copyrighted] work." [T]he author's expression alone gains copyright protection.
>
> The . . . fair use defense is codified at 17 U.S.C. § 107: "[T]he fair use of a copyrighted work, including such use by reproduction in copies . . . for purposes such as criticism, comment, news reporting, teaching (including multiple copies for classroom use), scholarship, or research, is not an infringement of copyright." This limitation on exclusivity "allows the public to use not only facts and ideas contained in a copyrighted work, but also [the author's] expression itself in certain circumstances." [Citing *Eldred* v. *Ashcroft* (2003).]

The majority reasoned that "[g]iven the 'speech-protective purposes and safeguards' embraced by copyright law, we concluded in *Eldred* that there was no call for the heightened review petitioners sought in that case. We reach the same conclusion here."

5. Do Actions Speak as Loud as Words? Expressive Conduct and the First Amendment

a. Draft Card Burning

UNITED STATES v. O'BRIEN
391 U.S. 367 (1968)

MR. CHIEF JUSTICE WARREN delivered the opinion of the Court.

On the morning of March 31, 1966, David Paul O'Brien and three companions burned their Selective Service registration certificates on the steps of the South Boston Courthouse. A sizable crowd, including several agents of the Federal Bureau of Investigation, witnessed the event. Immediately after the burning, members of the crowd began attacking O'Brien and his companions. An FBI agent ushered O'Brien to safety inside the courthouse. After he was advised of his right to counsel and to silence, O'Brien stated to FBI agents that he had burned his registration certificate because of his beliefs, knowing that he was violating federal law. He produced the charred remains of the certificate, which, with his consent, were photographed.

For this act, O'Brien was indicted, tried, convicted, and sentenced in the United States District Court for the District of Massachusetts. He did not contest the fact that he had burned the certificate. He stated in argument to the jury that he burned the certificate publicly to influence others to adopt his antiwar beliefs, as he put it, "so that other people would reevaluate their positions with Selective Service, with the armed forces, and reevaluate their place in the culture of today, to hopefully [sic] consider my position."

The indictment upon which he was tried charged that he "willfully and knowingly did mutilate, destroy, and change by burning . . . [his] Registration Certificate . . . in violation of Title 50, App., United States Code, Section 462(b)." Section 462(b) is part of the Universal Military Training and Service Act of 1948. Section 462(b)(3), one of six numbered subdivisions of § 462(b), was amended by Congress in 1965, so that at the time O'Brien burned his certificate an offense was committed by any person,

> "who forges, alters, *knowingly destroys, knowingly mutilates*, or in any manner changes any such certificate. . . ." (Italics supplied.)

In the District Court, O'Brien argued that the 1965 Amendment prohibiting the knowing destruction or mutilation of certificates was unconstitutional because it was enacted to abridge free speech, and because it served no legitimate legislative purpose. The District Court rejected these arguments, holding that the statute on its face did not abridge First Amendment rights, that the court was not competent to inquire into the motives of Congress in enacting the 1965 Amendment, and that the Amendment was a reasonable exercise of the power of Congress to raise armies.

On appeal, the Court of Appeals for the First Circuit held the 1965 Amendment unconstitutional as a law abridging freedom of speech. . . . The court ruled, however, that O'Brien's conviction should be affirmed under the statutory provision, 50 U.S.C. App. § 462(b)(6), which in its view made violation of the nonpossession regulation a crime, because it regarded such violation to be a lesser included offense of the crime defined by the 1965 Amendment.

* * *

I.

When a male reaches the age of 18, he is required by the Universal Military Training and Service Act to register with a local draft board. He is assigned a Selective Service number, and within five days he is issued a registration certificate. . . . Subsequently, and based on a questionnaire completed by the registrant, he is assigned a classification denoting his eligibility for induction, and "[a]s soon as practicable" thereafter he is issued a Notice of Classification. . . .

Both the registration and classification certificates are small white cards, approximately 2 by 3 inches. The registration certificate specifies the name of the registrant, the date of registration, and the number and address of the local board with which he is registered. Also inscribed upon it are the date and place of the registrant's birth, his residence at registration, his physical description, his signature, and his Selective Service number. The Selective Service number itself indicates his State of registration, his local board, his year of birth, and his chronological position in the local board's classification record.

The classification certificate shows the registrant's name, Selective Service number, signature, and eligibility classification. It specifies whether he was so classified by his local board, an appeal board, or the President. It contains the address of his local board and the date the certificate was mailed.

Both the registration and classification certificates bear notices that the registrant must notify his local board in writing of every change in address, physical condition, and occupational, marital, family, dependency, and military status, and of any other fact which might change his classification. Both also contain a notice that the registrant's Selective Service number should appear on all communications to his local board.

Congress demonstrated its concern that certificates issued by the Selective Service System might be abused well before the 1965 Amendment here challenged. The 1948 Act, 62 Stat. 604, itself prohibited many different abuses involving "any registration certificate, . . . or any other certificate issued pursuant to or prescribed by the provisions of this title, or rules or regulations promulgated hereunder. . . ." Under §§ 12(b)(1)–(5) of the 1948 Act, it was unlawful (1) to transfer a certificate to aid a person in making false identification; (2) to possess a certificate not duly issued with the intent of using it for false identification; (3) to forge, alter, "or in any manner" change a certificate or any notation validly inscribed thereon; (4) to photograph or make an imitation of a certificate for the purpose of false identification; and (5) to possess a counterfeited or altered certificate. In addition, as previously mentioned, regulations of the Selective Service System required registrants to keep both their registration and classification certificates in their personal possession at all times. . . .

By the 1965 Amendment, Congress added to § 12(b)(3) of the 1948 Act the provision here at issue, subjecting to criminal liability not only one who "forges, alters, or in any manner changes" but also one who "knowingly destroys, [or] knowingly mutilates" a certificate. We note at the outset that the 1965 Amendment plainly does not abridge free speech on its face, and we do not understand O'Brien to argue otherwise. Amended § 12(b)(3) on its face deals with conduct having no connection with speech. It prohibits the knowing destruction of certificates issued by the Selective Service System, and there is nothing necessarily expressive about such conduct. The Amendment does not distinguish between public and private destruction, and it does not punish only destruction engaged in for the purpose of expressing views. A law prohibiting destruction of Selective Service certificates no more abridges free speech on its face than a motor vehicle law prohibiting the destruction of drivers' licenses, or a tax law prohibiting the destruction of books and records.

O'Brien nonetheless argues that the 1965 Amendment is unconstitutional in its application to him, and is unconstitutional as enacted because what he calls the "purpose" of Congress was "to suppress freedom of speech." We consider these arguments separately.

II.

O'Brien first argues that the 1965 Amendment is unconstitutional as applied to him because his act of burning his registration certificate was protected "symbolic speech" within the First Amendment. His argument is that the freedom of expression which the First Amendment guarantees includes all modes of "communication of ideas by conduct," and that his conduct is within this definition because he did it in "demonstration against the war and against the draft."

We cannot accept the view that an apparently limitless variety of conduct can be labeled "speech" whenever the person engaging in the conduct intends thereby to express an idea. However, even on the assumption that the alleged communicative element in O'Brien's conduct is sufficient to bring into play the First Amendment, it does not necessarily follow that the destruction of a registration certificate is constitutionally protected activity. This Court has held that when "speech" and "nonspeech" elements are combined in the same course of conduct, a sufficiently important governmental interest in regulating the nonspeech element can justify incidental limitations on First Amendment freedoms. To characterize the quality of the governmental interest which must appear, the Court has employed a variety of descriptive terms: compelling; substantial; subordinating; paramount; cogent; strong. Whatever imprecision inheres in these terms, we think it clear that a government regulation is sufficiently justified if it is within the constitutional power of the Government; if it furthers an important or substantial governmental interest; if the governmental interest is unrelated to the suppression of free expression; and if the incidental restriction on alleged First Amendment freedoms is no greater than is essential to the furtherance of that interest. We find that the 1965 Amendment to § 12(b)(3) of the Universal Military Training and Service Act meets all of these requirements, and consequently that O'Brien can be constitutionally convicted for violating it.

The constitutional power of Congress to raise and support armies and to make all laws necessary and proper to that end is broad and sweeping. . . .

* * *

2. The information supplied on the certificates facilitates communication between registrants and local boards, simplifying the system and benefiting all concerned. To begin with, each certificate bears the address of the registrant's local board, an item unlikely to be committed to memory. Further, each card bears the registrant's Selective Service number, and a registrant who has his number readily available so that he can communicate it to his local board when he supplies or requests information can make simpler the board's task in locating his file. Finally, a registrant's inquiry, particularly through a local board other than his own, concerning his eligibility status is frequently answerable simply on the basis of his classification certificate. . . .

3. Both certificates carry continual reminders that the registrant must notify his local board of any change of address, and other specified changes in his status. The smooth functioning of the system requires that local boards be continually aware of the status and whereabouts of registrants, and the destruction of certificates deprives the system of a potentially useful notice device.

4. The regulatory scheme involving Selective Service certificates includes clearly valid prohibitions against the alteration, forgery, or similar deceptive misuse of certificates. The destruction or mutilation of certificates obviously increases the difficulty of detecting and tracing abuses such as these. Further, a mutilated certificate might itself be used for deceptive purposes.

The many functions performed by Selective Service certificates establish beyond doubt that Congress has a legitimate and substantial interest in preventing their wanton and unrestrained destruction and assuring their continuing availability by punishing people who knowingly and wilfully destroy or mutilate them. . . .

* * *

We think it apparent that the continuing availability to each registrant of his Selective Service certificates substantially furthers the smooth and proper functioning of the system that Congress has established to raise armies. We think it also apparent that the Nation has a vital interest in having a system for raising armies that functions with maximum efficiency and is capable of easily and quickly responding to continually changing circumstances. For these reasons, the Government has a substantial interest in assuring the continuing availability of issued Selective Service certificates.

It is equally clear that the 1965 Amendment specifically protects this substantial governmental interest. We perceive no alternative means that would more precisely and narrowly assure the continuing availability of issued Selective Service certificates than a law which prohibits their wilful mutilation or destruction. The 1965 Amendment prohibits such conduct and does nothing more. In other words, both the governmental interest and the operation of the 1965 Amendment are limited to the noncommunicative aspect of O'Brien's conduct. . . .

The case at bar is therefore unlike one where the alleged governmental interest in regulating conduct arises in some measure because the communication allegedly integral to the conduct is itself thought to be harmful. In *Stromberg v. California* (1931), for example, this Court struck down a statutory phrase which punished people who expressed their "opposition to organized government" by displaying "any flag, badge, banner, or device." Since the statute there was aimed at suppressing communication it could not be sustained as a regulation of noncommunicative conduct.

In conclusion, we find that because of the Government's substantial interest in assuring the continuing availability of issued Selective Service certificates, because amended § 462(b) is an appropriately narrow means of protecting this interest and condemns only the independent noncommunicative impact of conduct within its reach, and because the noncommunicative impact of O'Brien's act of burning his registration certificate frustrated the Government's interest, a sufficient governmental interest has been shown to justify O'Brien's conviction.

III.

O'Brien finally argues that the 1965 Amendment is unconstitutional as enacted because what he calls the "purpose" of Congress was "to suppress freedom of speech." We reject this argument because under settled principles the purpose of Congress, as O'Brien uses that term, is not a basis for declaring this legislation unconstitutional.

It is a familiar principle of constitutional law that this Court will not strike down an otherwise constitutional statute on the basis of an alleged illicit legislative motive. As the Court long ago stated:

> "The decisions of this court from the beginning lend no support whatever to the assumption that the judiciary may restrain the exercise of lawful power on the assumption that a wrongful purpose or motive has caused the power to be exerted." . . .

Inquiries into congressional motives or purposes are a hazardous matter. When the issue is simply the interpretation of legislation, the Court will look to statements by legislators for guidance as to the purpose of the legislature, because the benefit to sound decision-making in this circumstance is thought sufficient to risk the possibility of misreading Congress' purpose. It is entirely a different matter when we are asked to void a statute that is, under well-settled criteria, constitutional on its face, on the basis of what fewer than a handful of Congressmen said about it. What motivates one legislator to make a speech about a statute is not necessarily what motivates scores of others to enact it, and the stakes are sufficiently high for us to eschew guesswork. We decline to void essentially on the ground that it is unwise legislation which Congress had the undoubted power to enact and which could be reenacted in its exact form if the same or another legislator made a "wiser" speech about it.

* * *

We think it not amiss, in passing, to comment upon O'Brien's legislative-purpose argument. There was little floor debate on this legislation in either House. [In the Senate debate only one Senator, Thurmond, spoke.] In the House debate only two Congressmen addressed themselves to the Amendment — Congressmen Rivers and Bray. The bill was passed after their statements without any further debate by a vote of 393 to 1. It is principally on the basis of the statements by these three Congressmen that O'Brien makes his congressional — "purpose" argument. We note that if we were to examine legislative purpose in the instant case, we would be obliged to consider not only these statements but also the more authoritative reports of the Senate and House Armed Services Committees. . . . While both reports make clear a concern with the "defiant" destruction of so-called "draft cards" and with "open" encouragement to others to destroy their cards, both reports also indicate that this concern stemmed from an apprehension that unrestrained destruction of cards would disrupt the smooth functioning of the Selective Service System.

*   *   *

Mr. Justice Marshall took no part in the consideration or decision of these cases.

Mr. Justice Harlan, concurring.

The crux of the Court's opinion, which I join, is of course its general statement, that:

> "a government regulation is sufficiently justified if it is within the constitutional power of the Government; if it furthers an important or substantial governmental interest; if the governmental interest is unrelated to the suppression of free expression; and if the incidental restriction on alleged First Amendment freedoms is no greater than is essential to the furtherance of that interest."

[handwritten: 4 prongs of O'Brien Test]

I wish to make explicit my understanding that this passage does not foreclose consideration of First Amendment claims in those rare instances when an "incidental" restriction upon expression, imposed by a regulation which furthers an "important or substantial" governmental interest and satisfies the Court's other criteria, in practice has the effect of entirely preventing a "speaker" from reaching a significant audience with whom he could not otherwise lawfully communicate. This is not such a case, since O'Brien manifestly could have conveyed his message in many ways other than by burning his draft card.

Mr. Justice Douglas, dissenting.

The Court states that the constitutional power of Congress to raise and support armies is "broad and sweeping" and that Congress' power "to classify and conscript manpower for military service is 'beyond question.'" This is undoubtedly true in times when, by declaration of Congress, the Nation is in a state of war. The underlying and basic problem in this case, however, is whether conscription is permissible in the absence of a declaration of war. That question has not been briefed nor was it presented in oral argument; but it is, I submit, a question upon which the litigants and the country are entitled to a ruling. I have discussed in *Holmes v. United States* the nature of the legal issue and it will be seen from my dissenting opinion in that case that this Court has never ruled on the question. . . .

The rule that this Court will not consider issues not raised by the parties is not inflexible and yields in "exceptional cases" to the need correctly to decide the case before the court.

In such a case it is not unusual to ask for reargument even on a constitutional question not raised by the parties [citing four cases]. . . .

These precedents demonstrate the appropriateness of restoring the instant case to the calendar for reargument on the question of the constitutionality of a peacetime draft.

NOTES AND QUESTIONS

1.   Why wasn't Mr. O'Brien successful in his claim that burning his draft card was speech protected by the First Amendment? Was there any doubt that he intended to communicate a political message by his actions? When the government forbids him to communicate this message by his chosen method why isn't the First Amendment infringed? Why did Justice Douglas dissent?

2.   To what extent can the government abridge Mr. O'Brien's First Amendment rights? Suppose the congressional purpose in passing the legislation in question was to suppress dissent? We will next examine the Supreme Court's 1989 decision that announced that flag burning was speech protected by the First Amendment. Would you have anticipated this result after reading *O'Brien*? Using only what you have learned from the *O'Brien* case, would a statute which punished those who burned the flag intentionally seeking to outrage onlookers, but not those who burned aged and soiled flags ceremoniously to dispose of them, pass constitutional muster?

3.   It is possible to find some communicative content in virtually every activity. That said, the Court does not treat all conduct as expressive. Only that conduct which is intended to convey a message and which has a substantial likelihood of having that message understood falls within the expressive category. A good example of communicative conduct is *Tinker v. Des Moines Independent Community School District*, 393 U.S. 503 (1969), where the Court held that wearing a black armband to school as an anti-war protest was protected speech.

4.   However, as O'Brien indicates, the mere fact that conduct is communicative does not mean that it is beyond all regulation. O'Brien allows regulation of communicative conduct if the purpose of the regulation is other than suppression of speech and if the impact of the regulation is no greater than necessary to achieve the government's purpose. Many constitutional scholars conclude that the standard is basically one of intermediate scrutiny.

5.   In *Holder v. Humanitarian Law Project*, 130 S. Ct. 2705, 177 L. Ed. 2d 355 (2010), the Court sustained the constitutionality of a federal statute that prohibits the giving of "material support or resources" to "foreign terrorist organizations," so designated by the Secretary of State. The Chief Justice, writing for the Court, saw the Act's prohibitions as being directed at communicative *conduct*. Roberts then

applied the test that had been used in *United States v. O'Brien* (1968) — which he referred to as "more rigorous scrutiny." Roberts's "more rigorous scrutiny" then took account of "[t]he experience and analysis of the U.S. government agencies charged with combating terrorism" and he expressed deference to "Congress's finding that all contributions to foreign terrorist organizations further their terrorism." Seemingly recognizing that deference-to-the-legislature is not one of the hallmarks of "more rigorous" scrutiny, Roberts went on to stress "the lack of competence on the part of the courts" in "collecting evidence and drawing factual inferences" where "concerns of national security and foreign relations" are at stake.

On the freedom-of-association issue, Roberts saw the associational rights of the Humanitarian Law Project as being less directly undercut by the statute's prohibitions. The statute may, in a sense, burden communicative conduct (although not unconstitutionally so), but it does not prohibit the Humanitarian Law Project from *associating* with the foreign terrorist groups. And insofar as the associating that the Humanitarian Law Project wished to do with the foreign terrorist groups might be seen as something like "communicative association," the case law on "communicative conduct" that Roberts had just applied governed.

b. Flag Burning

TEXAS v. JOHNSON
491 U.S. 397 (1989)

Justice Brennan delivered the opinion of the Court.

*   *   *

I

While the Republican National Convention was taking place in Dallas in 1984, respondent Johnson participated in a political demonstration dubbed the "Republican War Chest Tour." . . .

The demonstration ended in front of Dallas City Hall, where Johnson unfurled the American flag, doused it with kerosene, and set it on fire. While the flag burned, the protestors chanted: "America, the red, white, and blue, we spit on you." After the demonstrators dispersed, a witness to the flag burning collected the flag's remains and buried them in his backyard. No one was physically injured or threatened with injury, though several witnesses testified that they had been seriously offended by the flag burning.

Of the approximately 100 demonstrators, Johnson alone was charged with a crime. The only criminal offense with which he was charged was the desecration of a venerated object in violation of Tex. Penal Code Ann. § 42.09(a)(3) (1989).[2] After a trial, he was convicted, sentenced to one year in prison, and fined $2,000. . . .

---

[2] [1] Texas Penal Code Ann. § 42.09 (1989) provides in full:

"§ 42.09. Desecration of Venerated Object.

* * *

II

Johnson was convicted of flag desecration for burning the flag rather than for uttering insulting words. This fact somewhat complicates our consideration of his conviction under the First Amendment. We must first determine whether Johnson's burning of the flag constituted expressive conduct, permitting him to invoke the First Amendment in challenging his conviction. If his conduct was expressive, we next decide whether the State's regulation is related to the suppression of free expression. *See, e.g., United States v. O'Brien* (1968). If the State's regulation is not related to expression, then the less stringent standard we announced in *United States v. O'Brien* for regulations of noncommunicative conduct controls. If it is, then we are outside of *O'Brien*'s test, and we must ask whether this interest justifies Johnson's conviction under a more demanding standard. A third possibility is that the State's asserted interest is simply not implicated on these facts, and in that event the interest drops out of the picture.

The First Amendment literally forbids the abridgment only of "speech," but we have long recognized that its protection does not end at the spoken or written word. While we have rejected "the view that an apparently limitless variety of conduct can be labeled 'speech' whenever the person engaging in the conduct intends thereby to express an idea," we have acknowledged that conduct may be "sufficiently imbued with elements of communication to fall within the scope of the First and Fourteenth Amendments."

In deciding whether particular conduct possesses sufficient communicative elements to bring the First Amendment into play, we have asked whether "[a]n intent to convey a particularized message was present, and [whether] the likelihood was great that the message would be understood by those who viewed it." Hence, we have recognized the expressive nature of students' wearing of black armbands to protest American military involvement in Vietnam; of a sit-in by blacks in a "whites only" area to protest segregation; of the wearing of American military uniforms in a dramatic presentation criticizing American involvement in Vietnam; and of picketing about a wide variety of causes.

Especially pertinent to this case are our decisions recognizing the communicative nature of conduct relating to flags. Attaching a peace sign to the flag; refusing to salute the flag; and displaying a red flag, we have held, all may find shelter under the First Amendment. That we have had little difficulty identifying an expressive element in conduct relating to flags should not be surprising. . . . Pregnant with

---

"(a) A person commits an offense if he intentionally or knowingly desecrates:

"(1) a public monument;

"(2) a place of worship or burial; or

"(3) a state or national flag.

"(b) For purposes of this section, 'desecrate' means deface, damage, or otherwise physically mistreat in a way that the actor knows will seriously offend one or more persons likely to observe or discover his action."

expressive content, the flag as readily signifies this Nation as does the combination of letters found in "America."

We have not automatically concluded, however, that any action taken with respect to our flag is expressive. Instead, in characterizing such action for First Amendment purposes, we have considered the context in which it occurred. In *Spence* [*v. Washington* (1974)], for example, we emphasized that Spence's taping of a peace sign to his flag was "roughly simultaneous with and concededly triggered by the Cambodian incursion and the Kent State tragedy." The State of Washington had conceded, in fact, that Spence's conduct was a form of communication, and we stated that "the State's concession is inevitable on this record."

The State of Texas conceded for purposes of its oral argument in this case that Johnson's conduct was expressive conduct, and this concession seems to us as prudent as was Washington's in *Spence*. Johnson burned an American flag as part — indeed, as the culmination — of a political demonstration that coincided with the convening of the Republican Party and its renomination of Ronald Reagan for President. The expressive, overtly political nature of this conduct was both intentional and overwhelmingly apparent. At his trial, Johnson explained his reasons for burning the flag as follows: "The American Flag was burned as Ronald Reagan was being renominated as President. And a more powerful statement of symbolic speech, whether you agree with it or not, couldn't have been made at that time. It's quite a just position [juxtaposition]. We had new patriotism and no patriotism." In these circumstances, Johnson's burning of the flag was conduct "sufficiently imbued with elements of communication," to implicate the First Amendment.

III

The government generally has a freer hand in restricting expressive conduct than it has in restricting the written or spoken word. It may not, however, proscribe particular conduct *because* it has expressive elements. "[W]hat might be termed the more generalized guarantee of freedom of expression makes the communicative nature of conduct an inadequate *basis* for singling out that conduct for proscription. A law *directed* at the communicative nature of conduct must, like a law directed at speech itself, be justified by the substantial showing of need that the First Amendment requires." It is, in short, not simply the verbal or nonverbal nature of the expression, but the governmental interest at stake, that helps to determine whether a restriction on that expression is valid.

Thus, although we have recognized that where " 'speech' and 'nonspeech' elements are combined in the same course of conduct, a sufficiently important governmental interest in regulating the nonspeech element can justify incidental limitations on First Amendment freedoms," *O'Brien*, we have limited the applicability of *O'Brien*'s relatively lenient standard to those cases in which "the governmental interest is unrelated to the suppression of free expression." In stating, moreover, that *O'Brien*'s test "in the last analysis is little, if any, different from the standard applied to time, place, or manner restrictions," we have highlighted the requirement that the governmental interest in question be unconnected to expression in order to come under *O'Brien*'s less demanding rule.

In order to decide whether *O'Brien*'s test applies here, therefore, we must decide whether Texas has asserted an interest in support of Johnson's conviction that is unrelated to the suppression of expression. . . . The State offers two separate interests to justify this conviction: preventing breaches of the peace and preserving the flag as a symbol of nationhood and national unity. We hold that the first interest is not implicated on this record and that the second is related to the suppression of expression.

A

Texas claims that its interest in preventing breaches of the peace justifies Johnson's conviction for flag desecration. However, no disturbance of the peace actually occurred or threatened to occur because of Johnson's burning of the flag. Although the State stresses the disruptive behavior of the protestors during their march toward City Hall, it admits that "no actual breach of the peace occurred at the time of the flagburning or in response to the flagburning." . . .

The State's position, therefore, amounts to a claim that an audience that takes serious offense at particular expression is necessarily likely to disturb the peace and that the expression may be prohibited on this basis. Our precedents do not countenance such a presumption. On the contrary, they recognize that a principal "function of free speech under our system of government is to invite dispute. It may indeed best serve its high purpose when it induces a condition of unrest, creates dissatisfaction with conditions as they are, or even stirs people to anger." It would be odd indeed to conclude *both* that "if it is the speaker's opinion that gives offense, that consequence is a reason for according it constitutional protection," *and* that the government may ban the expression of certain disagreeable ideas on the unsupported presumption that their very disagreeableness will provoke violence.

Thus, we have not permitted the government to assume that every expression of a provocative idea will incite a riot, but have instead required careful consideration of the actual circumstances surrounding such expression, asking whether the expression "is directed to inciting or producing imminent lawless action and is likely to incite or produce such action." *Brandenburg v. Ohio* (1969) (reviewing circumstances surrounding rally and speeches by Ku Klux Klan). To accept Texas' arguments that it need only demonstrate "the potential for a breach of the peace," and that every flag burning necessarily possesses that potential, would be to eviscerate our holding in *Brandenburg*. This we decline to do.

Nor does Johnson's expressive conduct fall within that small class of "fighting words" that are "likely to provoke the average person to retaliation, and thereby cause a breach of the peace." *Chaplinsky v. New Hampshire* (1942). No reasonable onlooker would have regarded Johnson's generalized expression of dissatisfaction with the policies of the Federal Government as a direct personal insult or an invitation to exchange fisticuffs.

We thus conclude that the State's interest in maintaining order is not implicated on these facts. The State need not worry that our holding will disable it from preserving the peace. We do not suggest that the First Amendment forbids a State to prevent "imminent lawless action." *Brandenburg*. And, in fact, Texas already has a statute specifically prohibiting breaches of the peace, which tends to confirm that Texas need not punish this flag desecration in order to keep the peace.

B

Answers #2

The State also asserts an interest in preserving the flag as a symbol of nationhood and national unity. In *Spence*, we acknowledged that the government's interest in preserving the flag's special symbolic value "is directly related to expression in the context of activity" such as affixing a peace symbol to a flag. We are equally persuaded that this interest is related to expression in the case of Johnson's burning of the flag. The State, apparently, is concerned that such conduct will lead people to believe either that the flag does not stand for nationhood and national unity, but instead reflects other, less positive concepts, or that the concepts reflected in the flag do not in fact exist, that is, that we do not enjoy unity as a Nation. These concerns blossom only when a person's treatment of the flag communicates some message, and thus are related "to the suppression of free expression" within the meaning of *O'Brien*. We are thus outside of *O'Brien*'s test altogether.

IV

It remains to consider whether the State's interest in preserving the flag as a symbol of nationhood and national unity justifies Johnson's conviction.

As in *Spence*, "[w]e are confronted with a case of prosecution for the expression of an idea through activity," and "[a]ccordingly, we must examine with particular care the interests advanced by [petitioner] to support its prosecution." Johnson was not, we add, prosecuted for the expression of just any idea; he was prosecuted for his expression of dissatisfaction with the policies of this country, expression situated at the core of our First Amendment values.

Moreover, Johnson was prosecuted because he knew that his politically charged expression would cause "serious offense." If he had burned the flag as a means of disposing of it because it was dirty or torn, he would not have been convicted of flag desecration under this Texas law: federal law designates burning as the preferred means of disposing of a flag "when it is in such condition that it is no longer a fitting emblem for display," and Texas has no quarrel with this means of disposal. The Texas law is thus not aimed at protecting the physical integrity of the flag in all circumstances, but is designed instead to protect it only against impairments that would cause serious offense to others. Texas concedes as much: "Section 42.09(b) reaches only those severe acts of physical abuse of the flag carried out in a way likely to be offensive. . . ."

Whether Johnson's treatment of the flag violated Texas law thus depended on the likely communicative impact of his expressive conduct. Our decision in *Boos v. Barry* [(1988)] tells us that this restriction on Johnson's expression is content based. In *Boos*, we considered the constitutionality of a law prohibiting "the display of any sign within 500 feet of a foreign embassy if that sign tends to bring that foreign government into 'public odium' or 'public disrepute.'" Rejecting the argument that the law was content neutral because it was justified by "our international law obligation to shield diplomats from speech that offends their dignity," we held that "[t]he emotive impact of speech on its audience is not a 'secondary effect'" unrelated to the content of the expression itself.

According to the principles announced in *Boos*, Johnson's political expression was restricted because of the content of the message he conveyed. We must therefore subject the State's asserted interest in preserving the special symbolic character of the flag to "the most exacting scrutiny."

Texas argues that its interest in preserving the flag as a symbol of nationhood and national unity survives this close analysis. Quoting extensively from the writings of this Court chronicling the flag's historic and symbolic role in our society, the State emphasizes the "'special place'" reserved for the flag in our Nation. The State's argument is not that it has an interest simply in maintaining the flag as a symbol of *something*, no matter what it symbolizes; indeed, if that were the State's position, it would be difficult to see how that interest is endangered by highly symbolic conduct such as Johnson's. Rather, the State's claim is that it has an interest in preserving the flag as a symbol of *nationhood* and *national unity*, a symbol with a determinate range of meanings. According to Texas, if one physically treats the flag in a way that would tend to cast doubt on either the idea that nationhood and national unity are the flag's referents or that national unity actually exists, the message conveyed thereby is a harmful one and therefore may be prohibited.

If there is a bedrock principle underlying the First Amendment, it is that the government may not prohibit the expression of an idea simply because society finds the idea itself offensive or disagreeable.

We have not recognized an exception to this principle even where our flag has been involved. In *Street v. New York* (1969), we held that a State may not criminally punish a person for uttering words critical of the flag. Rejecting the argument that the conviction could be sustained on the ground that Street had "failed to show the respect for our national symbol which may properly be demanded of every citizen," we concluded that "the constitutionally guaranteed 'freedom to be intellectually . . . diverse or even contrary,' and the 'right to differ as to things that touch the heart of the existing order,' encompass the freedom to express publicly one's opinions about our flag, including those opinions which are defiant or contemptuous." Nor may the government, we have held, compel conduct that would evince respect for the flag. "To sustain the compulsory flag salute we are required to say that a Bill of Rights which guards the individual's right to speak his own mind, left it open to public authorities to compel him to utter what is not in his mind."

In holding . . . that the Constitution did not leave this course open to the government, Justice Jackson described one of our society's defining principles in words deserving of their frequent repetition: "If there is any fixed star in our constitutional constellation, it is that no official, high or petty, can prescribe what shall be orthodox in politics, nationalism, religion, or other matters of opinion or force citizens to confess by word or act their faith therein." In *Spence*, we held that the same interest asserted by Texas here was insufficient to support a criminal conviction under a flag-misuse statute for the taping of a peace sign to an American flag. "Given the protected character of [Spence's] expression and in light of the fact that no interest the State may have in preserving the physical integrity of a privately owned flag was significantly impaired on these facts," we held, "the conviction must be invalidated."

In short, nothing in our precedents suggests that a State may foster its own view of the flag by prohibiting expressive conduct relating to it. To bring its argument outside our precedents, Texas attempts to convince us that even if its interest in preserving the flag's symbolic role does not allow it to prohibit words or some expressive conduct critical of the flag, it does permit it to forbid the outright destruction of the flag. The State's argument cannot depend here on the distinction between written or spoken words and nonverbal conduct. That distinction, we have shown, is of no moment where the nonverbal conduct is expressive, as it is here, and where the regulation of that conduct is related to expression, as it is here. . . .

* * *

We never before have held that the Government may ensure that a symbol be used to express only one view of that symbol or its referents. Indeed, in *Schacht v. United States*, we invalidated a federal statute permitting an actor portraying a member of one of our Armed Forces to " 'wear the uniform of that armed force if the portrayal does not tend to discredit that armed force.' " This proviso, we held, "which leaves Americans free to praise the war in Vietnam but can send persons like Schacht to prison for opposing it, cannot survive in a country which has the First Amendment."

We perceive no basis on which to hold that the principle underlying our decision in *Schacht* does not apply to this case. To conclude that the government may permit designated symbols to be used to communicate only a limited set of messages would be to enter territory having no discernible or defensible boundaries. Could the government, on this theory, prohibit the burning of state flags? Of copies of the Presidential seal? Of the Constitution? In evaluating these choices under the First Amendment, how would we decide which symbols were sufficiently special to warrant this unique status? To do so, we would be forced to consult our own political preferences, and impose them on the citizenry, in the very way that the First Amendment forbids us to do.

There is, moreover, no indication — either in the text of the Constitution or in our cases interpreting it — that a separate juridical category exists for the American flag alone. Indeed, we would not be surprised to learn that the persons who framed our Constitution and wrote the Amendment that we now construe were not known for their reverence for the Union Jack. The First Amendment does not guarantee that other concepts virtually sacred to our Nation as a whole — such as the principle that discrimination on the basis of race is odious and destructive — will go unquestioned in the market-place of ideas. See *Brandenburg v. Ohio* (1969). We decline, therefore, to create for the flag an exception to the joust of principles protected by the First Amendment. . . .

* * *

We are tempted to say, in fact, that the flag's deservedly cherished place in our community will be strengthened, not weakened, by our holding today. Our decision is a reaffirmation of the principles of freedom and inclusiveness that the flag best reflects, and of the conviction that our toleration of criticism such as Johnson's is a sign and source of our strength. Indeed, one of the proudest images of our flag, the one immortalized in our own national anthem, is of the bombardment it survived at Fort McHenry. It is the Nation's resilience, not its rigidity, that Texas sees reflected in the flag — and it is that resilience that we reassert today.

The way to preserve the flag's special role is not to punish those who feel differently about these matters. It is to persuade them that they are wrong. "To courageous, self-reliant men, with confidence in the power of free and fearless reasoning applied through the processes of popular government, no danger flowing from speech can be deemed clear and present, unless the incidence of the evil apprehended is so imminent that it may befall before there is opportunity for full discussion. If there be time to expose through discussion the falsehood and fallacies, to avert the evil by the processes of education, the remedy to be applied is more speech, not enforced silence." And, precisely because it is our flag that is involved, one's response to the flag burner may exploit the uniquely persuasive power of the flag itself. We can imagine no more appropriate response to burning a flag than waving one's own, no better way to counter a flag burner's message than by saluting the flag that burns, no surer means of preserving the dignity even of the flag that burned than by — as one witness here did — according its remains a respectful burial. We do not consecrate the flag by punishing its desecration, for in doing so we dilute the freedom that this cherished emblem represents.

*   *   *

JUSTICE KENNEDY, concurring. [Omitted.]

CHIEF JUSTICE REHNQUIST, with whom JUSTICE WHITE and JUSTICE O'CONNOR join, dissenting.

In holding this Texas statute unconstitutional, the Court ignores Justice Holmes' familiar aphorism that "a page of history is worth a volume of logic." For more than 200 years, the American flag has occupied a unique position as the symbol of our Nation, a uniqueness that justifies a governmental prohibition against flag burning in the way respondent Johnson did here.

. . . But the Court insists that the Texas statute prohibiting the public burning of the American flag infringes on respondent Johnson's freedom of expression. Such freedom, of course, is not absolute. In *Chaplinsky v. New Hampshire* (1942), a unanimous Court said:

> "Allowing the broadest scope to the language and purpose of the Fourteenth Amendment, it is well understood that the right of free speech is not absolute at all times and under all circumstances. There are certain well-defined and narrowly limited classes of speech, the prevention and punishment of which have never been thought to raise any Constitutional problem. These include the lewd and obscene, the profane, the libelous, and the insulting or 'fighting' words — those which by their very utterance inflict injury or tend to incite an immediate breach of the peace. It has been

well observed that such utterances are no essential part of any exposition of ideas, and are of such slight social value as a step to truth that any benefit that may be derived from them is clearly outweighed by the social interest in order and morality."

The Court upheld Chaplinsky's conviction under a state statute that made it unlawful to "address any offensive, derisive or annoying word to any person who is lawfully in any street or other public place." Chaplinsky had told a local marshal, "You are a God damned racketeer" and a "damned Fascist and the whole government of Rochester are Fascists or agents of Fascists."

Here it may equally well be said that the public burning of the American flag by Johnson was no essential part of any exposition of ideas, and at the same time it had a tendency to incite a breach of the peace. Johnson was free to make any verbal denunciation of the flag that he wished; indeed, he was free to burn the flag in private. He could publicly burn other symbols of the Government or effigies of political leaders. He did lead a march through the streets of Dallas, and conducted a rally in front of the Dallas City Hall. He engaged in a "die-in" to protest nuclear weapons. He shouted out various slogans during the march, including: "Reagan, Mondale which will it be? Either one means World War III"; "Ronald Reagan, killer of the hour, Perfect example of U.S. power"; and "red, white and blue, we spit on you, you stand for plunder, you will go under." For none of these acts was he arrested or prosecuted; it was only when he proceeded to burn publicly an American flag stolen from its rightful owner that he violated the Texas statute.

The Court could not, and did not, say that Chaplinsky's utterances were not expressive phrases — they clearly and succinctly conveyed an extremely low opinion of the addressee. The same may be said of Johnson's public burning of the flag in this case; it obviously did convey Johnson's bitter dislike of his country. But his act, like Chaplinsky's provocative words, conveyed nothing that could not have been conveyed and was not conveyed just as forcefully in a dozen different ways. As with "fighting words," so with flag burning, for purposes of the First Amendment: It is "no essential part of any exposition of ideas, and [is] of such slight social value as a step to truth that any benefit that may be derived from [it] is clearly outweighed" by the public interest in avoiding a probable breach of the peace. The highest courts of several States have upheld state statutes prohibiting the public burning of the flag on the grounds that it is so inherently inflammatory that it may cause a breach of public order.

The result of the Texas statute is obviously to deny one in Johnson's frame of mind one of many means of "symbolic speech." Far from being a case of "one picture being worth a thousand words," flag burning is the equivalent of an inarticulate grunt or roar that, it seems fair to say, is most likely to be indulged in not to express any particular idea, but to antagonize others. Only five years ago we said in *City Council of Los Angeles v. Taxpayers for Vincent* (1984), that "the First Amendment does not guarantee the right to employ every conceivable method of communication at all times and in all places." The Texas statute deprived Johnson of only one rather inarticulate symbolic form of protest — a form of protest that was profoundly offensive to many — and left him with a full panoply of other symbols and every conceivable form of verbal expression to express his deep disapproval of national policy. Thus, in no way can it be said that Texas is punishing him because his hearers — or any other group of people — were profoundly opposed to the message that he sought to convey. Such opposition is no proper basis for restricting speech or expression under the First Amendment. It was Johnson's use of this particular symbol, and not the idea that he sought to convey by it or by his many other expressions, for which he was punished.

Our prior cases dealing with flag desecration statutes have left open the question that the Court resolves today. In *Street v. New York* (1969), the defendant burned a flag in the street, shouting "We don't need no damned flag" and "[i]f they let that happen to Meredith we don't need an American flag." The Court ruled that since the defendant might have been convicted solely on the basis of his words, the conviction could not stand, but it expressly reserved the question whether a defendant could constitutionally be convicted for burning the flag.

Chief Justice Warren, in dissent, stated: "I believe that the States and Federal Government do have the power to protect the flag from acts of desecration and disgrace. . . . [I]t is difficult for me to imagine that, had the Court faced this issue, it would have concluded otherwise." Justices Black and Fortas also expressed their personal view that a prohibition on flag burning did not violate the Constitution. ([Said Justice Black in dissent,] "It passes my belief that anything in the Federal Constitution bars a State from making the deliberate burning of the American Flag an offense"); ([Said Justice Fortas in his dissent,] "[T]he States and the Federal Government have the power to protect the flag from acts of desecration committed in public. . . . [T]he flag is a special kind of personality. Its use is traditionally and universally subject to special rules and regulation. . . . A person may 'own' a flag, but ownership is subject to special burdens and responsibilities. A flag may be property, in a sense; but it is property burdened with peculiar obligations and restrictions. Certainly . . . these special conditions are not *per se* arbitrary or beyond governmental power under our Constitution").

In *Spence v. Washington* (1974), the Court reversed the conviction of a college student who displayed the flag with a peace symbol affixed to it by means of removable black tape from the window of his apartment. Unlike the instant case, there was no risk of a breach of the peace, no one other than the arresting officers saw the flag, and the defendant owned the flag in question. The Court concluded that the student's conduct was protected under the First Amendment, because "no interest the State may have in preserving the physical integrity of a privately owned flag was significantly impaired on these facts." The Court was careful to note, however, that the defendant "was not charged under the desecration statute, nor did he permanently disfigure the flag or destroy it."

In another related case, *Smith v. Goguen* (1974), the appellee, who wore a small flag on the seat of his trousers, was convicted under a Massachusetts flag-misuse statute that subjected to criminal liability anyone who "publicly . . . treats contemptuously the flag of the United States." The Court affirmed the lower court's reversal of appellee's conviction, because the phrase "treats contemptuously" was unconstitutionally broad and vague. The Court was again careful to point out that "[c]ertainly nothing prevents a legislature from defining with substantial specificity what constitutes forbidden treatment of United States flags." ([Justice White said, in his concurring opinion,] "The flag is a national property, and the Nation may regulate those who would make, imitate, sell, possess, or use it. I would not question those statutes which proscribe mutilation, defacement, or burning of the flag or which otherwise protect its physical integrity, without regard to whether such conduct might provoke violence. . . . There would seem to be little question about the power of Congress to forbid the mutilation of the Lincoln Memorial. . . . The flag is itself a monument, subject to similar protection"); ([Justice Blackmun, dissenting, said,] "Goguen's punishment was constitutionally permissible for harming the physical integrity of the flag by wearing it affixed to the seat of his pants").

But the Court today will have none of this. The uniquely deep awe and respect for our flag felt by virtually all of us are bundled off under the rubric of "designated symbols," that the First Amendment prohibits the government from "establishing." But the government has not "established" this feeling; 200 years of history have done that. . . .

The Court concludes its opinion with a regrettably patronizing civics lecture, presumably addressed to the Members of both Houses of Congress, the members of the 48 state legislatures that enacted prohibitions against flag burning, and the troops fighting under that flag in Vietnam who objected to its being burned: "The way to preserve the flag's special role is not to punish those who feel differently about these matters. It is to persuade them that they are wrong." The Court's role as the final expositor of the Constitution is well established, but its role as a Platonic guardian admonishing those responsible to public opinion as if they were truant schoolchildren has no similar place in our system of government. The cry of "no taxation without representation" animated those who revolted against the English Crown to found our Nation — the idea that those who submitted to government should have some say as to what kind of laws would be passed. Surely one of the high purposes of a democratic society is to legislate against conduct that is regarded as evil and profoundly offensive to the majority of people — whether it be murder, embezzlement, pollution, or flag burning.

Our Constitution wisely places limits on powers of legislative majorities to act, but the declaration of such limits by this Court "is, at all times, a question of much delicacy, which ought seldom, if ever, to be decided in the affirmative, in a doubtful case." *Fletcher v. Peck* (1810) (Marshall, C.J.). Uncritical extension of constitutional protection to the burning of the flag risks the frustration of the very purpose for which organized governments are instituted. The Court decides that the American flag is just another symbol, about which not only must opinions pro and con be tolerated, but for which the most minimal public respect may not be enjoined. The government may conscript men into the Armed Forces where they must fight and perhaps die for the flag, but the government may not prohibit the public burning of the banner under which they fight. I would uphold the Texas statute as applied in this case.

JUSTICE STEVENS, dissenting.

As the Court analyzes this case, it presents the question whether the State of Texas, or indeed the Federal Government, has the power to prohibit the public desecration of the American flag. The question is unique. In my judgment rules that apply to a host of other symbols, such as state flags, armbands, or various privately promoted emblems of political or commercial identity, are not necessarily controlling. Even if flag burning could be considered just another species of symbolic speech under the logical application of the rules that the Court has developed in its interpretation of the First Amendment in other contexts, this case has an intangible dimension that makes those rules inapplicable.

[A country's flag is a symbol of more than "nationhood and national unity." It also signifies the ideas that characterize the society that has chosen that emblem as well as the special history that has animated the growth and power of those ideas.] The fleurs-de-lis and the tricolor both symbolized "nationhood and national unity," but they had vastly different meanings. The message conveyed by some flags — the swastika, for example — may survive long after it has outlived its usefulness as a symbol of regimented unity in a particular nation.

So it is with the American flag. It is more than a proud symbol of the courage, the determination, and the gifts of nature that transformed 13 fledgling Colonies into a world power. It is a symbol of freedom, of equal opportunity, of religious tolerance, and of good will for other peoples who share our aspirations. The symbol carries its message to dissidents both at home and abroad who may have no interest at all in our national unity or survival.

The value of the flag as a symbol cannot be measured. Even so, I have no doubt that the interest in preserving that value for the future is both significant and legitimate. Conceivably that value will be enhanced by the Court's conclusion that our national commitment to free expression is so strong that even the United States as ultimate guarantor of that freedom is without power to prohibit the desecration of its unique symbol. But I am unpersuaded. The creation of a federal right to post bulletin boards and graffiti on the Washington Monument might enlarge the market for free expression, but at a cost I would not pay. Similarly, in my considered judgment, sanctioning the public desecration of the flag will tarnish its value — both for those who cherish the ideas for which it waves and for those who desire to don the robes of martyrdom by burning it.] That tarnish is not justified by the trivial burden on free expression occasioned by requiring that an available, alternative mode of expression — including uttering words critical of the flag — be employed.

*   *   *

The Court is . . . quite wrong in blandly asserting that respondent "was prosecuted for his expression of dissatisfaction with the policies of this country, expression situated at the core of our First Amendment values." [Respondent was prosecuted because of the method he chose to express his dissatisfaction with those policies.] Had he chosen to spray-paint — or perhaps convey with a motion picture projector — [his message of dissatisfaction on the facade of the Lincoln Memorial, there would be no question about the power of the Government to prohibit his means of expression.] The prohibition would be supported by the legitimate interest in preserving the quality of an important national asset. Though the asset at stake in this case is intangible, given its unique value, the same interest supports a prohibition on the desecration of the American flag.

NOTES AND QUESTIONS

1. The result in *Texas v. Johnson*, that for the first time the Supreme Court rejected as unconstitutional flag protection or flag "desecration" statutes, was met with a political firestorm. The first President Bush called for a Constitutional Amendment to protect the flag, as did several veterans' groups. Congress held hearings on the Amendment, but instead decided to pass the Flag Protection Act of 1989, Pub. L. No. 101-131, 103 Stat. 777, which, in carefully crafted language avoiding the term "desecration," sought to be a measure which would not be content discrimination of speech, but would prohibit the knowing "mutilat[ion], deface-[ment], physical[] defile[ment], burn[ing of], or trampl[ing] upon" any American flag. *Id.* Several law professors and legal scholars had assured Congress that such a statute could pass constitutional muster. Others, including former Judge Robert Bork and one of the authors of your casebook, told Congress that any such statute would be declared unconstitutional by the Supreme Court. See *Statutory and Constitutional Responses to the Supreme Court Decision in* Texas v. Johnson: *Hearings Before the Subcomm. on Civil and Constitutional Rights of the House Comm. on the Judiciary,* 101st Cong. (1989); *Hearings on Measures to Protect the Physical Integrity of the American Flag: Hearings Before the Senate Comm. on the Judiciary,* 101st Cong. (1989). Roughly one year after *Johnson,* in *United States v. Eichman,* 496 U.S. 310 (1990), the Supreme Court, by the same 5 to 4 votes in *Johnson,* held that the new federal statute was as invalid as was the Texas measure rejected in *Johnson.* A proposed Amendment to the Constitution, the Flag Protection Amendment, was then introduced into both Houses of Congress. The Amendment would have given both Congress and the state legislatures "the power to prohibit the physical desecration of the Flag of the United States." See H.R.J. Res. 350, 101st Cong. (1990); S.J. Res. 332, 101st Cong. (1990). After that proposed Amendment failed to win the required two-thirds majority in either House of Congress, proponents went to the state legislatures, and over the course of the next five years secured resolutions from forty-nine of the state legislatures asking Congress to pass the Flag Protection Amendment. Then, following the election of Republican majorities to both Houses of Congress in 1994, the proponents of the Amendment returned to Congress. The new Amendment had been slightly revised to focus only on federal power, and its text then was, "Congress shall have power to prohibit the physical desecration of the flag of the United States." S.J. Res. 31, 104th Cong. (1995). The Amendment easily garnered the required two-thirds majority in the House of Representatives, but failed by three votes in the Senate. See Helen Dewar, *Senate Falls Short on Flag Amendment,* Wash. Post, Dec. 13, 1995, at A1. Proponents of the Amendment, which has the support of approximately 80% of the American people (and approximately 1% of the press and the legal academy), argue that the Amendment would simply correct an erroneous Supreme Court decision that wrongly regarded an inarticulate act as protected speech. They also stress, as did the dissenting Justices in *Johnson,* that the Amendment would reaffirm a traditional American commitment to the exercise of rights tempered by responsibilities, and the traditional American high regard in which the flag is held as a symbol of the sacrifice of members of the American armed forces. However, only one national newspaper, the Wall Street Journal, endorsed the Amendment, and that was more on the theory that something ought to be done to indicate to the Supreme Court that the people — and not it — still rule than it was in support of

the principles behind the Amendment itself. See *Sending Judges a Message*, WALL ST. J., Nov. 18, 1996, at A12.

2. Some of the Court's greatest champions of First Amendment liberty, including Earl Warren and Hugo Black, saw no constitutional problem with flag desecration statutes. One of your co-authors agrees and has suggested a government speech or property-based theory (the government of the United States owns the design of the flag) as a basis for protecting the standard without constitutional amendment. See Douglas W. Kmiec, *In the Aftermath of* Johnson *and* Eichman: *The Constitution Need Not Be Mutilated to Preserve the Government's Speech and Property Interests in the Flag*, 1990 B.Y.U. L. REV. 577.

3. Returning to the strictly legal issues for a moment, you will have observed that the majority distinguishes *Johnson* from *O'Brien* on the basis that the criminal provision at issue in the latter was not targeted at the suppression of speech, while that in the former was. Note that the dissenters do not agree with the assumption that flag desecration statutes regulate "speech," but rather, in Justice Rehnquist's memorable words, seek to regulate an act that is more like "an inarticulate grunt ." Still, if the majority was correct, instead of applying the lesser *O'Brien* standard, which upheld a criminal provision not aimed at speech, but which incidentally affected speech, if there was a "valid and important" state interest at stake, a different standard would have to be applied. That different standard was the "compelling interest" standard. The "compelling interest" standard recognizes that First Amendment rights are not absolute, but are so important that any measure seeking to restrict their exercise has to be justified by a "compelling" government interest. You may have sensed by now that a frequent tactic to defeat a piece of legislation is to raise the "compelling interest" standard to defeat it, since almost no legislation can ever survive this "strict scrutiny test." Even so, why isn't the interest of the state or federal government in reinforcing the nation's symbolic commitment (which the flag represents) to the sacrifice of its men and women in arms, a "compelling interest"? Why isn't the state or federal government's interest in promoting the idea that with liberty comes responsibility a "compelling interest"? Or, most simply, why isn't the state's interest in preventing breaches of the peace, the ostensible justification for the Texas legislation at issue, a "compelling interest"?

4. In one of the most interesting and curious side arguments related to this issue, a student note in the Yale Law Journal, written by an individual who would soon become the New Republic's principal writer on Constitutional issues and a law professor, argued that if the Flag Protection Amendment passed it should be declared unconstitutional by the Supreme Court, since it was a violation of natural law. This would have been the nation's first case, the author argued, of an unconstitutional amendment. *See* Jeffrey Rosen, Note, *Was the Flag Burning Amendment Unconstitutional?*, 100 YALE L.J. 1073 (1991). Does that concept make any sense? Does the natural law invoked against the Flag Amendment seem like the natural law we have seen at work in any other cases?

c. Obscenity and Pornography

BARNES v. GLEN THEATRE, INC.
501 U.S. 560 (1991)

CHIEF JUSTICE REHNQUIST announced the judgment of the Court, and delivered an opinion, in which JUSTICE O'CONNOR and JUSTICE KENNEDY join.

Respondents are two establishments in South Bend, Indiana, that wish to provide totally nude dancing as entertainment, and individual dancers who are employed at these establishments. They claim that the First Amendment's guarantee of freedom of expression prevents the State of Indiana from enforcing its public indecency law to prevent this form of dancing. We reject their claim.

. . . The Kitty Kat Lounge, Inc. (Kitty Kat), is located in the city of South Bend. It sells alcoholic beverages and presents "go-go dancing." Its proprietor desires to present "totally nude dancing," but an applicable Indiana statute regulating public nudity requires that the dancers wear "pasties" and "G-strings" when they dance. The dancers are not paid an hourly wage, but work on commission. They receive a 100 percent commission on the first $60 in drink sales during their performances. Darlene Miller, one of the respondents in the action, had worked at the Kitty Kat for about two years at the time this action was brought. Miller wishes to dance nude because she believes she would make more money doing so.

Respondent Glen Theatre, Inc., is an Indiana corporation with a place of business in South Bend. Its primary business is supplying so-called adult entertainment through written and printed materials, movie showings, and live entertainment at an enclosed "bookstore." The live entertainment at the "bookstore" consists of nude and seminude performances and showings of the female body through glass panels. Customers sit in a booth and insert coins into a timing mechanism that permits them to observe the live nude and seminude dancers for a period of time. One of Glen Theatre's dancers, Gayle Ann Marie Sutro, has danced, modeled, and acted professionally for more than 15 years, and in addition to her performances at the Glen Theatre, can be seen in a pornographic movie at a nearby theater.

Respondents sued in the United States District Court for the Northern District of Indiana to enjoin the enforcement of the Indiana public indecency statute, asserting that its prohibition against complete nudity in public places violated the First Amendment. . . . [T]he District Court concluded that "the type of dancing these plaintiffs wish to perform is not expressive activity protected by the Constitution of the United States," and rendered judgment in favor of the defendants. The case was . . . appealed to the Seventh Circuit, and a panel of that court reversed the District Court, holding that the nude dancing involved here was expressive conduct protected by the First Amendment. The Court of Appeals then heard the case en banc, and the court rendered a series of comprehensive and thoughtful opinions. The majority concluded that non-obscene nude dancing performed for entertainment is expression protected by the First Amendment, and that the public indecency statute was an improper infringement of that expressive activity because its purpose was to prevent the message of eroticism and sexuality conveyed by the dancers. . . .

Several of our cases contain language suggesting that nude dancing of the kind involved here is expressive conduct protected by the First Amendment. . . . This, of course, does not end our inquiry. We must determine the level of protection to be afforded to the expressive conduct at issue, and must determine whether the Indiana statute is an impermissible infringement of that protected activity.

Indiana, of course, has not banned nude dancing as such, but has proscribed public nudity across the board. The Supreme Court of Indiana has construed the Indiana statute to preclude nudity in what are essentially places of public accommodation such as the Glen Theatre and the Kitty Kat Lounge. In such places, respondents point out, minors are excluded and there are no nonconsenting viewers. Respondents contend that while the State may license establishments such as the ones involved here, and limit the geographical area in which they do business, it may not in any way limit the performance of the dances within them without violating the First Amendment. The petitioners contend, on the other hand, that Indiana's restriction on nude dancing is a valid "time, place, or manner" restriction. . . .

The "time, place, or manner" test was developed for evaluating restrictions on expression taking place on public property which had been dedicated as a "public forum," although we have on at least one occasion applied it to conduct occurring on private property. . . . [T]his test has been interpreted to embody much the same standards as those set forth in *United States v. O'Brien* (1968), and we turn, therefore, to the rule enunciated in *O'Brien*.

O'Brien . . . claimed that his conviction was contrary to the First Amendment because his act was "symbolic speech" — expressive conduct. The Court rejected his contention that symbolic speech is entitled to full First Amendment protection. . . .

Applying the four-part *O'Brien* test . . . we find that Indiana's public indecency statute is justified despite its incidental limitations on some expressive activity. [1] The public indecency statute is clearly within the constitutional power of the State and [2] furthers substantial governmental interests. It is impossible to discern, other than from the text of the statute, exactly what governmental interest the Indiana legislators had in mind when they enacted this statute, for Indiana does not record legislative history, and the State's highest court has not shed additional light on the statute's purpose. Nonetheless, the statute's purpose of protecting societal order and morality is clear from its text and history. Public indecency statutes of this sort are of ancient origin and presently exist in at least 47 States. Public indecency, including nudity, was a criminal offense at common law, and this Court recognized the common-law roots of the offense of "gross and open indecency" in *Winters v. New York* (1948). Public nudity was considered an act *malum in se. Le Roy v. Sidley* (K.B. 1664). Public indecency statutes such as the one before us reflect moral disapproval of people appearing in the nude among strangers in public places.

This public indecency statute follows a long line of earlier Indiana statutes banning all public nudity. The history of Indiana's public indecency statute shows that it predates bar-room nude dancing and was enacted as a general prohibition.

At least as early as 1831, Indiana had a statute punishing "open and notorious lewdness, or . . . any grossly scandalous and public indecency." A gap during which no statute was in effect was filled by the Indiana Supreme Court in *Ardery v. State* (1877), which held that the court could sustain a conviction for exhibition of "privates" in the presence of others. The court traced the offense to the Bible story of Adam and Eve. In 1881, a statute was enacted that would remain essentially unchanged for nearly a century:

> "Whoever, being over fourteen years of age, makes an indecent exposure of his person in a public place, or in any place where there are other persons to be offended or annoyed thereby, . . . is guilty of public indecency. . . ."

The language quoted above remained unchanged until it was simultaneously repealed and replaced with the present statute in 1976.

This and other public indecency statutes were designed to protect morals and public order. The traditional police power of the States is defined as the authority to provide for the public health, safety, and morals, and we have upheld such a basis for legislation. In *Paris Adult Theatre I v. Slaton* (1973), we said:

> "In deciding *Roth* [*v. United States* (1957)], this Court implicitly accepted that a legislature could legitimately act on such a conclusion to protect 'the social interest in order and morality.'"

And in *Bowers v. Hardwick* (1986), we said:

> "The law, however, is constantly based on notions of morality, and if all laws representing essentially moral choices are to be invalidated under the Due Process Clause, the courts will be very busy indeed."

Thus, the public indecency statute furthers a substantial government interest in protecting order and morality.

This interest is unrelated to the suppression of free expression. Some may view restricting nudity on moral grounds as necessarily related to expression. We disagree. It can be argued, of course, that almost limitless types of conduct — including appearing in the nude in public — are "expressive," and in one sense of the word this is true. People who go about in the nude in public may be expressing something about themselves by so doing. But the court rejected this expansive notion of "expressive conduct" in *O'Brien*, saying: "We cannot accept the view that an apparently limitless variety of conduct can be labeled 'speech' whenever the person engaging in the conduct intends thereby to express an idea."

*   *   *

Respondents contend that even though prohibiting nudity in public generally may not be related to suppressing expression, prohibiting the performance of nude dancing is related to expression because the State seeks to prevent its erotic message. Therefore, they reason that the application of the Indiana statute to the nude dancing in this case violates the First Amendment, because it fails the third part of the *O'Brien test*, viz: the governmental interest must be unrelated to the suppression of free expression.

But we do not think that when Indiana applies its statute to the nude dancing in these nightclubs it is proscribing nudity because of the erotic message conveyed by the dancers. Presumably numerous other erotic performances are presented at these establishments and similar clubs without any interference from the State, so long as the performers wear a scant amount of clothing. Likewise, the requirement that the dancers don pasties and G-strings does not deprive the dance of whatever erotic message it conveys; it simply makes the message slightly less graphic. The perceived evil that Indiana seeks to address is not erotic dancing, but public nudity. The appearance of people of all shapes, sizes and ages in the nude at a beach, for example, would convey little if any erotic message, yet the State still seeks to prevent it. Public nudity is the evil the State seeks to prevent, whether or not it is combined with expressive activity.

This conclusion is buttressed by a reference to the facts of *O'Brien*. An Act of Congress provided that anyone who knowingly destroyed a Selective Service registration certificate committed an offense. O'Brien burned his certificate on the steps of the South Boston Courthouse to influence others to adopt his antiwar beliefs. This Court upheld his conviction, reasoning that the continued availability of issued certificates served a legitimate and substantial purpose in the administration of the Selective Service system. O'Brien's deliberate destruction of his certificate frustrated this purpose and "[f]or this noncommunicative impact of his conduct, and for nothing else, he was convicted." . . .

The fourth part of the *O'Brien* test requires that the incidental restriction on First Amendment freedom be no greater than is essential to the furtherance of the governmental interest. As indicated in the discussion above, the governmental interest served by the text of the prohibition is societal disapproval of nudity in public places and among strangers. The statutory prohibition is not a means to some greater end, but an end in itself. It is without cavil that the public indecency statute is "narrowly tailored"; Indiana's requirement that the dancers wear at least pasties and G-strings is modest, and the bare minimum necessary to achieve the State's purpose.

* * *

JUSTICE SCALIA, concurring in the judgment.

. . . In my view, . . . the challenged regulation must be upheld, not because it survives some lower level of First Amendment scrutiny, but because, as a general law regulating conduct and not specifically directed at expression, it is not subject to First Amendment scrutiny at all.

I

Indiana's public indecency statute provides:

"(a) A person who knowingly or intentionally, in a public place:

"(1) engages in sexual intercourse;

"(2) engages in deviate sexual conduct;

"(3) appears in a state of nudity; or

"(4) fondles the genitals of himself or another person; commits public indecency, a Class A misdemeanor.

"(b) 'Nudity' means the showing of the human male or female genitals, pubic area, or buttocks with less than a fully opaque covering, the showing of the female breast with less than a fully opaque covering of any part of the nipple, or the showing of covered male genitals in a discernibly turgid state."

On its face, this law is not directed at expression in particular. As Judge Easterbrook put it in his dissent below: "Indiana does not regulate dancing. It regulates public nudity. . . . Almost the entire domain of Indiana's statute is unrelated to expression, unless we view nude beaches and topless hot dog vendors as speech." The intent to convey a "message of eroticism" (or any other message) is not a necessary element of the statutory offense of public indecency; nor does one commit that statutory offense by conveying the most explicit "message of eroticism," so long as he does not commit any of the four specified acts in the process.

Indiana's statute is in the line of a long tradition of laws against public nudity, which have never been thought to run afoul of traditional understanding of "the freedom of speech." Public indecency — including public nudity — has long been an offense at common law. Indiana's first public nudity statute (1831), predated by many years the appearance of nude barroom dancing. It was general in scope, directed at all public nudity, and not just at public nude expression; and all succeeding statutes, down to the present one, have been the same. Were it the case that Indiana *in practice* targeted only expressive nudity, while turning a blind eye to nude beaches and unclothed purveyors of hot dogs and machine tools, it might be said that what posed as a regulation of conduct in general was in reality a regulation of only communicative conduct. Respondents have adduced no evidence of that. Indiana officials have brought many public indecency prosecutions for activities having no communicative element.

The dissent confidently asserts that the purpose of restricting nudity in public places in general is to protect nonconsenting parties from offense; and argues that since only consenting, admission-paying patrons see respondents dance, that purpose cannot apply and the only remaining purpose must relate to the communicative elements of the performance. Perhaps the dissenters believe that "offense to others" *ought* to be the only reason for restricting nudity in public places generally, but there is no basis for thinking that our society has ever shared that Thoreauvian "you-may-do-what-you-like-so-long-as-it-does-not-injure-someone-else" beau ideal — much less for thinking that it was written into the Constitution. The purpose of Indiana's nudity law would be violated, I think, if 60,000 fully consenting adults crowded into the Hoosier Dome to display their genitals to one another, even if there were not an offended innocent in the crowd. Our society prohibits, and all human societies have prohibited, certain activities not because they harm others but because they are considered, in the traditional phrase, "*contra bonos mores*," *i.e.*, immoral. In American society, such prohibitions have included, for example, sadomasochism, cockfighting, bestiality, suicide, drug use, prostitution, and sodomy. While there may be great diversity of view on whether various of these prohibitions should exist (though I have found few ready to abandon, in principle, all of them), there is no doubt that, absent specific constitutional protection for the conduct involved, the Constitution does not prohibit them simply because they regulate "morality." See *Bowers v. Hardwick* (1986) (upholding prohibition of private homosexual sodomy enacted solely on "the presumed belief of a majority of the electorate in [the jurisdiction] that homosexual sodomy is immoral and unacceptable"). The purpose of the Indiana statute, as both its text and the manner of its enforcement demonstrate, is to enforce the traditional moral belief that people should not expose their private parts indiscriminately, regardless of whether those who see them are disedified. Since that is so, the dissent has no basis for positing that, where only thoroughly edified adults are present, the purpose must be repression of communication.

II

Since the Indiana regulation is a general law not specifically targeted at expressive conduct, its application to such conduct does not in my view implicate the First Amendment.

*   *   *

All our holdings . . . support the conclusion that "the only First Amendment analysis applicable to laws that do not directly or indirectly impede speech is the threshold inquiry of whether the purpose of the law is to suppress communication. If not, that is the end of the matter so far as First Amendment guarantees are concerned; if so, the court then proceeds to determine whether there is substantial justification for the proscription." Such a regime ensures that the government does not act to suppress communication, without requiring that all conduct-restricting regulation . . . survive an enhanced level of scrutiny.

We have explicitly adopted such a regime in another First Amendment context: that of free exercise. In *Employment Div., Dept. of Human Resources of Ore. v. Smith* (1990), we held that general laws not specifically targeted at religious practices did not require heightened First Amendment scrutiny even though they diminished some people's ability to practice their religion. "The government's ability to enforce generally applicable prohibitions of socially harmful conduct, like its ability to carry out other aspects of public policy, 'cannot depend on measuring the effects of a governmental action on a religious objector's spiritual development.'" See also *Minersville School District v. Gobitis* (1940) (Frankfurter, J.) ("Conscientious scruples have not, in the course of the long struggle for religious toleration, relieved the individual from obedience to a general law not aimed at the promotion or restriction of religious beliefs"). There is even greater reason to apply this approach to the regulation of expressive conduct. Relatively few can plausibly assert that their illegal conduct is being engaged in for religious reasons; but almost anyone can violate almost any law as a means of expression. In the one case, as in the other, if the law is not directed against the protected value (religion or expression) the law must be obeyed.

III

While I do not think the plurality's conclusions differ greatly from my own, I cannot entirely endorse its reasoning. The plurality purports to apply to this general law, insofar as it regulates this allegedly expressive conduct, an intermediate level of First Amendment scrutiny: The government interest in the regulation must be " 'important or substantial.' " As I have indicated, I do not believe such a heightened standard exists. I think we should avoid wherever possible, moreover, a method of analysis that requires judicial assessment of the "importance" of government interests — and especially of government interests in various aspects of morality.

Neither of the cases that the plurality cites to support the "importance" of the State's interest here is in point. *Paris Adult Theatre I v. Slaton* and *Bowers v. Hardwick* did uphold laws prohibiting private conduct based on concerns of decency and morality; but neither opinion held that those concerns were particularly "important" or "substantial," or amounted to anything more than a *rational basis* for regulation. *Slaton* involved an exhibition which, since it was obscene and at least to some extent public, was unprotected by the First Amendment; the State's prohibition could therefore be invalidated only if it had no rational basis. We found that the State's "right . . . to maintain a decent society" provided a "legitimate" basis for regulation — even as to obscene material viewed by consenting adults. In *Bowers*, we held that since homosexual behavior is not a fundamental right, a Georgia law prohibiting private homosexual intercourse needed only a rational basis in order to comply with the Due Process Clause. Moral opposition to homosexuality, we said, provided that rational basis. I would uphold the Indiana statute on precisely the same ground: Moral opposition to nudity supplies a rational basis for its prohibition, and since the First Amendment has no application to this case no more than that is needed.

*   *   *

Indiana may constitutionally enforce its prohibition of public nudity even against those who choose to use public nudity as a means of communication. The State is regulating conduct, not expression, and those who choose to employ conduct as a means of expression must make sure that the conduct they select is not generally forbidden. For these reasons, I agree that the judgment should be reversed.

JUSTICE SOUTER, concurring in the judgment.

*   *   *

I . . . agree with the plurality that the appropriate analysis to determine the actual protection required by the First Amendment is the four-part enquiry described in *United States v. O'Brien*. . . . I nonetheless write separately to rest my concurrence in the judgment, not on the possible sufficiency of society's moral views to justify the limitations at issue, but on the State's substantial interest in combating the secondary effects of adult entertainment establishments of the sort typified by respondents' establishments.

*   *   *

Quote from class

[In *Renton v. Playtime Theatres, Inc.* (1986), we upheld a city's zoning ordinance designed to prevent the occurrence of harmful secondary effects, including the crime associated with adult entertainment, by protecting approximately 95% of the city's area from the placement of motion picture theaters emphasizing " 'matter depicting, describing or relating to "specified sexual activities" or "specified anatomical areas" . . . for observation by patrons therein.' " Of particular importance to the present enquiry, we held that the city of Renton was not compelled to justify its restrictions by studies specifically relating to the problems that would be caused by adult theaters in that city. Rather, "Renton was entitled to rely on the experiences of Seattle and other cities," which demonstrated the harmful secondary effects correlated with the presence "of even one [adult] theater in a given neighborhood."

The type of entertainment respondents seek to provide is plainly of the same character as that at issue in *Renton*. . . . It therefore is no leap to say that live nude dancing of the sort at issue here is likely to produce the same pernicious secondary effects as the adult films displaying "specified anatomical areas" at issue in *Renton*. Other reported cases from the Circuit in which this litigation arose confirm the conclusion. In light of *Renton*'s recognition that legislation seeking to combat the secondary effects of adult entertainment need not await localized proof of those effects, the State of Indiana could reasonably conclude that forbidding nude entertainment of the type offered at the Kitty Kat Lounge and the Glen Theatre's "bookstore" furthers its interest in preventing prostitution, sexual assault, and associated crimes. Given our recognition that "society's interest in protecting this type of expression is of a wholly different, and lesser, magnitude than the interest in untrammeled political debate," I do not believe that a State is required affirmatively to undertake to litigate this issue repeatedly in every case. . . .

*   *   *

JUSTICE WHITE, with whom JUSTICE MARSHALL, JUSTICE BLACKMUN, and JUSTICE STEVENS join, dissenting.

*   *   *

We are told by the attorney general of Indiana that, in *State v. Baysinger* (1979), the Indiana Supreme Court held that the statute at issue here cannot and does not prohibit nudity as a part of some larger form of expression meriting protection when the communication of ideas is involved. Petitioners also state that the evils sought to be avoided by applying the statute in this case would not obtain in the case of theatrical productions, such as "Salome" or "Hair." Neither is there any evidence that the State has attempted to apply the statute to nudity in performances such as plays, ballets, or operas. "No arrests have ever been made for nudity as part of a play or ballet."

Thus, the Indiana statute is not a *general* prohibition of the type we have upheld in prior cases. As a result, the plurality and JUSTICE SCALIA's simple references to the State's general interest in promoting societal order and morality is not sufficient justification for a statute which concededly reaches a significant amount of protected expressive activity. Instead, in applying the *O'Brien* test, we are obligated to carefully examine the reasons the State has chosen to regulate this expressive conduct in a less than general statute. In other words, when the State enacts a law which draws a line between expressive conduct which is regulated and nonexpressive conduct of the same type which is not regulated, *O'Brien* places the burden on the State to justify the distinctions it has made. Closer inquiry as to the purpose of the statute is surely appropriate.

Legislators do not just randomly select certain conduct for proscription; they have reasons for doing so and those reasons illuminate the purpose of the law that is passed. Indeed, a law may have multiple purposes. The purpose of forbidding people from appearing nude in parks, beaches, hot dog stands, and like public places is to protect others from offense. But that could not possibly be the purpose of preventing nude dancing in theaters and barrooms since the viewers are exclusively consenting adults who pay money to see these dances. The purpose of the proscription in these contexts is to protect the viewers from what the State believes is the harmful message that nude dancing communicates. This is why *Clark v. Community for Creative Non-Violence* (1984), is of no help to the State: "In *Clark* . . . the damage to the parks was the same whether the sleepers were camping out for fun, were in fact homeless, or wished by sleeping in the park to make a symbolic statement on behalf of the homeless." (Posner, J., concurring). That cannot be said in this case: The perceived damage to the public interest caused by appearing nude on the streets or in the parks, as I have said, is not what the State seeks to avoid in preventing nude dancing in theaters and taverns. There the perceived harm is the communicative aspect of the erotic dance. As the State now tells us, and as JUSTICE SOUTER agrees, the State's goal in applying what it describes as its "content neutral" statute to the nude dancing in this case is "deterrence of prostitution, sexual assaults, criminal activity, degradation of women, and other activities which break down family structure." The attainment of these goals, however, depends on preventing an expressive activity.

* * *

That the performances in the Kitty Kat Lounge may not be high art, to say the least, and may not appeal to the Court, is hardly an excuse for distorting and ignoring settled doctrine. The Court's assessment of the artistic merits of nude dancing performances should not be the determining factor in deciding this case. In the words of Justice Harlan: "[I]t is largely because governmental officials cannot make principled decisions in this area that the Constitution leaves matters of taste and style so largely to the individual." "[W]hile the entertainment afforded by a nude ballet at Lincoln Center to those who can pay the price may differ vastly in content (as viewed by judges) or in quality (as viewed by critics), it may not differ in substance from the dance viewed by the person who . . . wants some 'entertainment' with his beer or shot of rye."

The plurality and JUSTICE SOUTER do not go beyond saying that the state interests asserted here are important and substantial. But even if there were compelling interests, the Indiana statute is not narrowly drawn. If the State is genuinely concerned with prostitution and associated evils, as JUSTICE SOUTER seems to think, . . . it can adopt restrictions that do not interfere with the expressiveness of nonobscene nude dancing performances. For instance, the State could perhaps require that, while performing, nude performers remain at all times a certain minimum distance from spectators, that nude entertainment be limited to certain hours, or even that establishments providing such entertainment be dispersed throughout the city. Likewise, the State clearly has the authority to criminalize prostitution and obscene behavior. Banning an entire category of expressive activity, however, generally does not satisfy the narrow tailoring requirement of strict First Amendment scrutiny. Furthermore, if nude dancing in barrooms, as compared with other establishments, is the most worrisome problem, the State could invoke its Twenty-first Amendment powers and impose appropriate regulation.

* * *

Justice Scalia's views are similar to those of the plurality and suffer from the same defects. The Justice asserts that a general law barring specified conduct does not implicate the First Amendment unless the purpose of the law is to suppress the expressive quality of the forbidden conduct, and that, absent such purpose, First Amendment protections are not triggered simply because the incidental effect of the law is to proscribe conduct that is unquestionably expressive. The application of the Justice's proposition to this case is simple to state: The statute at issue is a general law banning nude appearances in public places, including barrooms and theaters. There is no showing that the purpose of this general law was to regulate expressive conduct; hence, the First Amendment is irrelevant and nude dancing in theaters and barrooms may be forbidden, irrespective of the expressiveness of the dancing.

As I have pointed out, however, the premise for the Justice's position — that the statute is a *general* law of the type our cases contemplate — is nonexistent in this case. Reference to Justice Scalia's own hypothetical makes this clear. We agree with Justice Scalia that the Indiana statute would not permit 60,000 consenting Hoosiers to expose themselves to each other in the Hoosier Dome. No one can doubt, however, that those same 60,000 Hoosiers would be perfectly free to drive to their respective homes all across Indiana and, once there, to parade around, cavort, and revel in the nude for hours in front of relatives and friends. It is difficult to see why the State's interest in morality is any less in that situation, especially if, as Justice Scalia seems to suggest, nudity is inherently evil, but clearly the statute does not reach such activity. As we pointed out earlier, the State's failure to enact a truly general proscription requires closer scrutiny of the reasons for the distinctions the State has drawn.

As explained previously, the purpose of applying the law to the nude dancing performances in respondents' establishments is to prevent their customers from being exposed to the distinctive communicative aspects of nude dancing. That being the case, Justice Scalia's observation is fully applicable here: "Where the government prohibits conduct *precisely because of its communicative attributes*, we hold the regulation unconstitutional."

The *O'Brien* decision does not help Justice Scalia. Indeed, his position, like the Court's, would eviscerate the *O'Brien* test. *Employment Div., Dept. of Human Resources of Ore. v. Smith* (1990), is likewise not on point. The Indiana law, as applied to nude dancing, targets the expressive activity itself; in Indiana nudity in a dancing performance is a crime because of the message such dancing communicates. In *Smith*, the use of drugs was not criminal because the use was part of or occurred within the course of an otherwise protected religious ceremony, but because a general law made it so and was supported by the same interests in the religious context as in others.

Accordingly, I would affirm the judgment of the Court of Appeals, and dissent from this Court's judgment.

NOTES AND QUESTIONS

1.   We learned in the *O'Brien* case that if there is a valid governmental purpose in legislation which regulates communicative acts in the interests of some other non-speech related goal, that legislation will not infringe the First Amendment if it is narrowly tailored to accomplish its goal and minimally restricts the speech protected by the First Amendment. Is nude dancing speech protected by the First Amendment? Is the legislation in question narrowly tailored? Prior to this case, as you will soon see, Justice Scalia joined with the majority in *Texas v. Johnson* (1989) to hold that flag-burning was speech protected by the First Amendment. Why doesn't he hold that nude dancing is similarly-protected speech? Is he discriminating on the basis of content?

2.   Chief Justice Rehnquist apparently believed that the *O'Brien* test dictated that the statute be upheld. Why didn't Justice White agree? *O'Brien*, you will remember, indicated that under certain circumstances legislation which had the effect of curtailing speech could be upheld, particularly if the legislation was not actually targeted at the suppression of free expression. Why does Justice White believe that an act which generally prohibits public nudity "cannot be said [to be] unrelated to expressive conduct"? Is *Barnes* a case in which First Amendment doctrine is neutrally applied, or does it result from particular prejudices on the part of the majority?

3.   In *Pap's A.M. v. City of Erie*, 719 A.2d 273 (Pa. 1998), *rev'd.*, 529 U.S. 277 (2000), the Pennsylvania Supreme Court struck down a public indecency ordinance as constitutionally overbroad. Although the Pennsylvania court agreed that Justice Souter's opinion in *Barnes* stood for the "narrowest grounds," that opinion, argued the state court, did not command the majority of the Court. Therefore, the Pennsylvania court found that *Barnes* offered no precedential effect aside from the agreement that nude dancing is entitled to some First Amendment protection. The court then independently determined that the public indecency ordinance acted to suppress constitutionally protected freedom of expression as there were other more narrowly tailored means to curb adverse secondary effects while not infringing on what the state judges to be freedom of expression protected by the First Amendment.

In reversing, the Supreme Court reaffirmed *Barnes*, but again without a clear majority favoring a single rationale. A majority did accept, however, that Erie's ordinance was a content-neutral regulation that satisfies the four-part test of *United States v. O'Brien*, (1968). Explained Justice O'Connor:

The ordinance here, like the statute in *Barnes*, is on its face a general prohibition on public nudity. By its terms, the ordinance regulates conduct alone. It does not target nudity that contains an erotic message; rather, it bans all public nudity, regardless of whether that nudity is accompanied by expressive activity. And like the statute in *Barnes*, the Erie ordinance replaces and updates provisions of an "Indecency and Immorality" ordinance that has been on the books since 1866, predating the prevalence of nude dancing establishments such as Kandyland.

*   *   *

. . . The ordinance prohibiting public nudity is aimed at combating crime and other negative secondary effects caused by the presence of adult entertainment establishments like Kandyland and not at suppressing the erotic message conveyed by this type of nude dancing. Put another way, the ordinance does not attempt to regulate the primary effects of the expression, *i.e.*, . . . of watching nude erotic dancing, but rather the secondary effects, such as the impacts on public health, safety, and welfare, which we have previously recognized are "caused by the presence of even one such" establishment.

In meeting the *O'Brien* standard, Justice O'Connor indicated that the city need not "conduct new studies or produce evidence independent of that already generated by other cities" to demonstrate the problem of secondary effects, "so long as whatever evidence the city relies upon is reasonably believed to be relevant to the problem that the city addresses." Because the nude dancing at Kandyland is of the same character as the adult entertainment at issue in *Renton, Young v. American Mini Theatres, Inc.* (1976) (see Note 4 below), it was reasonable for Erie to conclude that such nude dancing was likely to produce the same secondary effects. And Erie could reasonably rely on the evidentiary foundation set forth in *Renton* and *American Mini Theatres* to the effect that secondary effects are caused by the presence of even one adult entertainment establishment in a given neighborhood.

The Pennsylvania Supreme Court did correctly perceive Justice Souter to be ambivalent in *Barnes*, but his ambivalence made no difference to the outcome. In *Pap's*, Justice Souter attempted to disavow his opinion in *Barnes* at least to the extent of requiring greater empirical evidence of secondary effect. The Court disagreed saying bluntly: the evidentiary standard described in *Renton* controls here, and Erie meets that standard.

Justice Scalia repeated his view from *Barnes* (but now shared by Justice Thomas) that when conduct other than speech itself is regulated, the First Amendment is violated only "[w]here the government prohibits conduct precisely because of its communicative attributes." Here, said Justice Scalia, even if one hypothesizes that the city's object was to suppress only nude dancing, that would not establish an intent to suppress what (if anything) nude dancing communicates. Under the Scalia and Thomas view, the city would not be obligated to identify some "secondary effects" associated with nude dancing that the city could properly seek to eliminate since the traditional power of government to foster good morals has not been repealed by the First Amendment. *Bonos mores*, and the acceptability of the traditional judgment (if Erie wishes to endorse it) that nude public dancing itself is immoral, have not been repealed by the First Amendment.

Justices Stevens and Ginsburg dissented. They would have confined the secondary effects rationale to the regulation of the location of adult establishments. Moreover, claim the dissenters, "Nude dancing fits well within a broad, cultural tradition recognized as expressive in nature and entitled to First Amendment protection. The nudity of the dancer is both a component of the protected expression and the specific target of the ordinance. It is pure sophistry to reason from the premise that the regulation of the nudity component of nude dancing is unrelated to the message conveyed by nude dancers. . . ."

4.   Apart from a community's ability to preclude public nudity, as *Barnes* allows, laws may also prohibit obscenity. Obscenity has been declared by the Court to be a category of speech that is unprotected by the First Amendment. *Roth v. United States*, 354 U.S. 476 (1957). As a general matter, obscenity laws reflect the obvious desire of a community to set minimum standards of civil behavior. In addition, there is some evidence that exposure to obscene or violent pornographic material increases a willingness to undertake such dysfunctional conduct. *See generally*, Report of the Attorney General's Commission on Pornography (1986). As Professor Catherine MacKinnon has argued, "[r]ecent experimental research on pornography shows that . . . exposure to [it] increases normal men's immediately subsequent willingness to aggress against women under laboratory conditions. . . . It also significantly increases attitudinal measures known to correlate with rape." Catherine R. MacKinnon, *Pornography, Civil Rights, and Speech*, 20 Harv. C.R.-C.L. L. Rev. 1, 52, 54 (1985). Professor Fred Schauer argues that pornographic material is less speech (a mental exercise), than a rather blatant physical stimulus. Frederick Schauer, *Speech and "Speech" — Obscenity and "Obscenity": An Exercise in the Interpretation of Constitutional Language*, 67 Geo. L.J. 899, 922 (1979).

In *Miller v. California*, 413 U.S. 15 (1973), the Court defined obscenity as material that (1) the average person would find "taken as a whole, appeals to the prurient interest"; (2) describes or depicts, "in a patently offensive way, sexual conduct specifically defined by state law"; and (3) "as a whole, lacks serious literary, artistic, political or scientific value." *Id.* at 24. The first two issues of fact are determined in relation to local community standards, allowing the religious and moral standards of different communities to be reflected in a healthy federalist sense. The third issue is determined by a national standard — that is, how a given work would be evaluated as a literary document, etc. across the entire country. *Pope v. Illinois*, 481 U.S. 497 (1987). Something that is "prurient" is said to be that which reflects a shameful or morbid, rather than a normal, interest in sex. Patently offensive representations can be differently defined from state to state, but the Court in *Miller* suggested by way of example normal or perverted sexual acts whether real or simulated and masturbation, excretory functions and lewd exhibition of the genitals.

This description of obscenity may well not include a variety of other sexually explicit materials. For this reason, some commentators argue that a broader class of pornography simply be recognized as demeaning and discriminatory toward women. Professor MacKinnon proposes an ordinance, for example, that would outlaw portraying women as "sexual objects." A federal court of appeals rejected this approach, *American Booksellers Assn., Inc. v. Hudnut*, 771 F.2d 323 (7th Cir. 1985) (describing the MacKinnon ordinance in more detail), but one can certainly appreciate how pornography generally diminishes the human person in the natural law sense and thus would historically be well outside the First Amendment as envisioned by the founders. For a different view see Nadine Strossen, *Hate Speech and Pornography: Do We Have to Choose Between Freedom of Speech and Equality?*, 46 CASE W. RES. L. REV. 449 (1996) (outlining the traditional approach to hate speech and pornography and arguing that the censorship of these forms of speech would not foster equality for targeted groups, but could actually undermine it).

The Court does allow non-obscene pornographic material to be addressed in another way. In particular, local governments may use land use controls such as zoning to regulate the location of adult theaters and bookstores. *Young v. American Mini-Theaters, Inc.*, 427 U.S. 50 (1976) (keeping these uses away from residential areas). The Court posits that such regulation is not directed at content, but the secondary effects of such uses in terms of crime and urban blight. *City of Renton v. Playtime Theaters, Inc.*, 475 U.S. 41 (1986) (upholding the exclusion of pornographic uses from roughly 95 percent of the land area of the city); *City of Los Angeles v. Alameda Books, Inc.*, 535 U.S. 425 (2002) (upholding ordinance banning multiple adult uses in a single building).

Efforts to zone out pornographic speech from the internet have been less successful, and presently the information superhighway is littered with what many would find to be denigrating depictions and descriptions of both men and women. *Reno v. American Civil Liberties Union*, 521 U.S. 844 (1997) (invalidating provisions of the federal Communications Decency Act that punished knowingly making an indecent communication to a person under the age of 18). The Court had previously upheld laws that criminalized the sale of pornographic materials, like *Playboy*, to children, *Ginsberg v. New York*, 390 U.S. 629 (1968), and in *FCC v. Pacifica Foundation*, 438 U.S. 736 (1978), sustained a ban on indecent speech over the airwaves except late at night when children would normally be expected to be asleep. The Court reasoned that the internet was less invasive than broadcasting, and theoretically, more controllable by parents and others. The Court also found that the use of the terms "patently offensive" or "indecent" was too vague. Fundamentally, however, there was no practicable way for the supplier of information to the internet to know in many circumstances if the recepient of that information was a minor. Thus, the law was also held to be overbroad, suppressing speech that adults are entitled to receive, whether it is harmful to them or not.

FCC v. Pacifica Foundation had decided that the FCC's order banning George Carlin's "Filthy Words" monologue passed First Amendment scrutiny, but it had specifically left open and undecided the question of whether "an occasional expletive . . . would justify any sanction," 438 U.S. at 750. In the years after the Court's *Pacifica* decision, the FCC's regulatory focus was uniformly on the full context of allegedly indecent broadcasts, and in a 2001 policy statement, the FCC even included, as one of the factors significant to the determination of what was patently offensive, "whether the material *dwells on* or *repeats at length*" (emphasis added) the offending description or depiction. Then there occurred two instances of isolated utterance of obscene words on the Fox network and an incident of isolated nudity on ABC. At that point (after the incidents), the FCC changed its policy and declared for the first time that fleeting expletives could be a statutory violation. It then applied its new principle to the Fox and ABC incidents. The case reached the Supreme Court in *FCC v. Fox*, 132 S. Ct. 2307, 183 L. Ed. 2d 234 (2012). In a majority opinion written by Justice Kennedy, the Court avoided ruling directly on the First Amendment implications of the FCC's new policy and instead held that because the FCC had failed to give Fox or ABC fair notice prior to the broadcasts in question that fleeting expletives and momentary nudity could be found actionably indecent, the FCC's standards as applied to these broadcasts were unconstitutionally vague under the Due Process Clause.

Congress attempted to address the Court's concerns with the Child Online Protection Act. Unlike the Communications Decency Act invalidated in *Reno*, COPA applies only to material displayed on the World Wide Web, covers only communications made for commercial purposes, and restricts only "material that is harmful to minors," defined by drawing on the three-part obscenity test in *Miller*. The Third Circuit held that COPA's use of the *Miller* "contemporary community standard" test was unconstitutionally overbroad in the context of the internet, but the Supreme Court disagreed, holding in a split decision in *Ashcroft v. American Civil Liberties Union*, 535 U.S. 564 (2002), that COPA's reliance on contemporary community standards — which by definition vary from community to community — did not itself render the statute substantially overbroad. The Court remanded for further consideration by the lower courts, which again enjoined the statute on the supposition that COPA was not the least restrictive means to protect minors from this material. In *Ashcroft v. American Civil Liberties Union (II)*, 542 U.S. 656 (2004), the Court, 5-4, affirmed. Admitting that the constitutional question was a close one, the majority opinion per Justice Kennedy held that it was not an abuse of discretion for the lower court to preliminarily enjoin the statute. In the context of a content-based restriction, the government must prove that proposed alternatives are not as effective as the challenged statute. The Court believed that filtering devices available to parents were likely better alternatives, since they would block all pornography, not just the estimated sixty percent or so originating from the United States. Nominally, the case will now go to trial on whether filtering is in fact as effective as believed. A strongly worded dissent written by Justice Breyer, and joined by the Chief Justice and Justice O'Connor, and supported by Justice Scalia who separately dissented, pointed out that filtering had worse problems — over- and under-blocking sites, cost, and in terms of the overall government interest of protecting minors, was far less effective, since children could access the Internet from multiple, unfiltered locations. Pointing out that COPA regulates the obscene or near obscene and that COPA does not censor the material but only requires it to be placed behind age verification screens, the dissent found the statute to achieve the compelling congressional goal with a modest burden on protected speech. "After eight years of legislative effort, two statutes, and three Supreme Court cases, the Court sent the case back to the District Court for further proceedings. What proceedings? . . . What remains to be litigated?"

Finally, the Court has allowed the prohibition, sale, or distribution of child pornography even if it does not meet the *Miller* test for obscenity. *New York v.*

Ferber, 458 U.S. 747 (1982). The Court had little difficulty recognizing that the use of children "as subjects of pornographic materials is harmful to the physiological, emotional, and mental health of the child." *Id.* at 757–58. It is, said the Court, while nigh equivalent to child abuse. But the Court drew the line at "virtual" child pornography — pornography that uses computer-generated images of children or youthful-looking adults rather than actual children. Justice Kennedy, writing for five members of the Court in *Ashcroft v. Free Speech Coalition*, claimed that, as written, the "virtual porn" provisions of the Child Pornography Prevention Act of 1996 prohibited a substantial amount of lawful speech (including, according to Justice Kennedy, Shakespeare's Romeo and Juliet, and the recent Academy Award-winning films Traffic and American Beauty) and were thus unconstitutionally overbroad. Justice Thomas concurred in the judgment, leaving open the possibility that advances in technology might well require government to ban virtual child pornography in order to enforce laws against actual child pornography effectively. Justice O'Connor, dissenting in part, would have upheld the ban on computer-generated child pornography but not the ban on youthful-looking adult pornography. Chief Justice Rehnquist, joined by Justice Scalia, also dissented, contending that the statute was constitutional with a reasonable narrowing construction.

5.   In *United States v. Playboy Entertainment Group, Inc.*, 529 U.S. 803 (2000), Justice Kennedy writing for the Court invalidated § 505 of the Telecommunications Act of 1996, which required cable television operators who provide channels "primarily dedicated to sexually-oriented programming" either to "fully scramble or otherwise fully block" those channels or to limit their transmission to hours when children are unlikely to be viewing, set by administrative regulation as the time between 10 p.m. and 6 a.m. The purpose of § 505 was to shield children from hearing or seeing images resulting from signal bleed. All parties to the case assumed Playboy's programming not to be obscene. However, since § 505 is a content-based speech restriction, it could stand only if it satisfied strict scrutiny. *Sable Communications of Cal., Inc. v. FCC* (1989). If a statute regulates speech based on its content, it must be narrowly tailored to promote a compelling Government interest. If a less restrictive alternative would serve the Government's purpose, the legislature must use that alternative.

Justice Kennedy found that less restrictive alternative in § 504, which requires cable operators to block undesired channels at individual households upon request. It was the government's obligation to prove that this was ineffective, and it failed to meet that burden to the majority's satisfaction. The Government failed to establish a pervasive, nationwide problem justifying its nationwide daytime speech ban, concluded the majority.

Justice Breyer wrote in dissent for himself and the Chief Justice and Justices O'Connor and Scalia. He started out by noting that the Court has recognized that material the First Amendment guarantees adults the right to see may not be suitable for children. And it has consequently held that legislatures maintain a limited power to protect children by restricting access to, but not banning, adult material. *Compare Ginsberg v. New York* (1968) (upholding ban on sale of pornographic magazines to minors), *with Butler v. Michigan* (1957) (invalidating ban on all books unfit for minors). Moreover, the case concerned only the regulation of commercial actors who broadcast "virtually 100% sexually explicit" material. The channels do not broadcast more than trivial amounts of more serious material such as birth control information, artistic images, or the visual equivalents of classical or serious literature. This case therefore does not present the kind of narrow tailoring concerns seen in other cases. *See, e.g., Reno* [and the consideration of an Indecency limitation applied to the Internet] ("The breadth of the [statute's] coverage is wholly unprecedented. . . . [It] covers] large amounts of non-pornographic material with serious educational or other value").

The dissent thought the majority "flat-out wrong" on the facts. 29 million children are potentially exposed to audio and video bleed from adult programming. Unlike the majority, the dissent thought that § 504's opt-out was not a similarly effective alternative. The opt-out mechanism is less effective because it fails to inhibit the transmission of adult cable channels to children whose parents may be unaware of what they are watching, whose parents cannot easily supervise television viewing habits, whose parents do not know of their § 504 "opt-out" rights, or whose parents are simply unavailable at critical times. In this respect, § 505 serves the same interests as the laws that deny children access to adult cabarets or X-rated movies. These laws, and § 505, all act in the absence of direct parental supervision. Wrote Justice Breyer:

> This legislative objective is perfectly legitimate. Where over 28 million school age children have both parents or their only parent in the work force, where at least 5 million children are left alone at home without supervision each week, and where children may spend afternoons and evenings watching television outside of the home with friends, § 505 offers independent protection for a large number of families. I could not disagree more when the majority implies that the Government's independent interest in offering such protection — preventing, say, an 8-year-old child from watching virulent pornography without parental consent — might not be "compelling." No previous case in which the protection of children was at issue has suggested any such thing. They make clear that Government has a compelling interest in helping parents by preventing minors from accessing sexually explicit materials in the absence of parental supervision. *See Ginsberg, supra.*

Justice Thomas concurred in the judgment, but reminded the government that it might well pursue blocking this material as obscene in the future. Though perhaps not all of the programming at issue in the case is obscene as this Court defined the term in *Miller v. California* (1973), one could fairly conclude that, under the standards applicable in many communities, some of the programming meets the *Miller* test, he said.

As part of the dissent, Justice Scalia took a different tack. He agreed with Justice Breyer and the principal dissent, but would have sustained § 505 simply as a regulation of the business of obscenity. Even if not all of the material is obscene under *Miller*, Justice Scalia pointed out that the Court had previously recognized that commercial entities which engage in "the sordid business of pandering" by "deliberately emphasi[zing] the sexually provocative aspects of [their nonobscene products], in order to catch the salaciously disposed," engage in constitutionally unprotected behavior. *Ginzburg v. United States* (1966). "We are more permissive of government regulation in these circumstances because it is clear from the context in which exchanges between such businesses and their customers occur that neither the merchant nor the buyer is interested in the work's literary, artistic, political, or scientific value. . . . The deliberate representation of petitioner's publications as erotically arousing . . . stimulate[s] the reader to accept them as prurient; he looks for titillation, not for saving intellectual content." Section 505 was just this sort of business.

Playboy's advertisements reveal its status as commercial pornographer, said Justice Scalia, calling on viewers to "Enjoy the sexiest, hottest adult movies in the privacy of your own home." "Thus, while I agree with JUSTICE BREYER's child-protection analysis, it leaves me with the same feeling of true-but-inadequate as the conclusion that Al Capone did not accurately report his income. It is not only children who can be protected from occasional uninvited exposure to what appellee calls 'adult-oriented programming'; we can all be."

Justice Scalia concluded that since the Government is entirely free to block these transmissions, it may certainly take the less drastic step of dictating how, and during what times, they may occur. Justice Stevens, in a separate concurrence, disagreed, reasoning that what Justice Scalia was proposing was a regulation of commercial speech based on *Ginzburg*, which pre-dated the Court opinions extending greater protection to commercial speech.

6. Regardless of whether one sides with Justice Kennedy or Breyer in the disposition of the *Playboy* case, Justice Kennedy's majority opinion contained the following interesting observation for students of free speech doctrine:

> When a student first encounters our free speech jurisprudence, he or she might think it is influenced by the philosophy that one idea is as good as any other, and that in art and literature objective standards of style, taste, decorum, beauty, and esthetics are deemed by the Constitution to be inappropriate, indeed unattainable. Quite the opposite is true. The Constitution no more enforces a relativistic philosophy or moral nihilism than it does any other point of view. The Constitution exists precisely so that opinions and judgments, including esthetic and moral judgments about art and literature, can be formed, tested, and expressed. What the Constitution says is that these judgments are for the individual to make, not for the Government to decree, even with the mandate or approval of a majority. Technology expands the capacity to choose; and it denies the potential of this revolution if we assume the Government is best positioned to make these choices for us.

Does this sentiment suggest that there are objective standards, perhaps even standards anchored in the natural law, by which artistic expression can be measured? Do you believe that one can fairly call pornographic material demeaning to the human body and spirit? If you do, should there be a role for the government where young children are likely to be unsupervised and exposed to material that may be psychologically harmful or denigrating, especially in its portrayal of women? Or is freedom so important that no government role can be trusted to stay benign and free from the inclination toward censorship? Is freedom a good in itself, or is what we value the freedom to do good?

7. In *United States v. Stevens*, 559 U.S. 460 (2010), the Court struck down, as unconstitutional on its face, a federal statute that had criminalized the commercial creation, sale, or possession of certain depictions of animal cruelty, *i.e.*, depictions "in which a living animal is intentionally maimed, mutilated, tortured, wounded, or killed," if that conduct violates federal or state law where "the creation, sale, or possession takes place." The statute also contained an exceptions clause, indicating that the prohibitions did not apply to depictions that have "serious religious, political, scientific, educational, journalistic, historical, or artistic value." Despite the intentionality requirement and the exceptions clause, an 8-member majority (Alito alone dissenting) struck the statute down as being unconstitutional *on its face*, taking the occasion to disavow an extensive reading of the Court's 1982 decision in *New York v. Ferber*. Chief Justice Roberts, writing for the Court, announced, "Our decisions in *Ferber* and other cases cannot be taken as establishing a freewheeling authority to declare new categories of speech outside the scope of the First Amendment."

Facial challenges, of course, bear a heavier burden than *as-applied* challenges, and the Court acknowledged as much: "To succeed in a typical facial attack, [the Court said] Stevens would have to establish 'that no set of circumstances exists under which [the statute] would be valid,' . . . or that the statute lacks any 'plainly legitimate sweep'." Since the Court struck the statute down as being invalid on its face, we must believe that Stevens, the challenger, succeeded in discharging that heavy burden of proof. It was important in the Court's reasoning that the two parts of the facial-invalidity test that it used are joined by the disjunctive "or". Stevens likely could not have proven that there was *no* set of circumstances that exists under which it would be valid. Indeed, the statute might well have been considered valid *as applied* to Stevens's own business of selling so-called animal "crush videos," let alone a host of other depictions of animal-cruelty horrors. What Stevens was apparently able to show (and what the Court eventually ruled on) was the *other* alternative in the facial-invalidity test — that the statute *lacked any plainly legitimate sweep*. The statute was overbroad. The statute's wording went overboard in that it conceivably applied to depictions of such things as the sport hunting and killing of animals and the slaughter of animals for food (depictions not exempted in the statute's exceptions clause).

8. In *Brown v. Entertainment Merchants Association*, 131 S. Ct. 2729, 180 L. Ed. 2d 708 (2011), the Court struck down, as facially unconstitutional, a state law that prohibits the direct sale or rental of certain video games to minors because the law abridges the freedom of speech. The California law in question, Cal. Civ. Code Ann. §§ 1746–1746.5, prohibits the sale or rental of "violent video games" to minors, and requires their packaging to be labeled "18." The Act covers games "in which the range of options available to a player includes killing, maiming, dismembering, or sexually assaulting an image of a human being, if those acts are depicted" in a manner that "[a] reasonable person, considering the game as a whole, would find appeals to a deviant or morbid interest of minors," that is "patently offensive to prevailing standards in the community as to what is suitable for minors," and that "causes the game, as a whole, to lack serious literary, artistic, political, or scientific value for minors."

The Court first had to deal with its *Ginsburg* precedent. In *Ginsberg v. New York* (1968), the Court had approved, as constitutional, a prohibition on the sale to minors of *sexual* material that would be obscene from the perspective of a child. In that *Ginsburg* case, the Court had held that a state legislature could "adjus[t] the definition of obscenity 'to social realities by permitting the appeal of this type of material to be assessed in terms of the sexual interests . . . 'of . . . minors'." . . . And because "obscenity is not protected expression," the New York statute could be sustained so long as the legislature's judgment that the proscribed materials were harmful to children "was not irrational." But, the Court noted in *Brown*, "speech about violence is not obscene." In *Brown*, the Court saw the California law as creating "a wholly new category of content-based regulation that is permissible only for speech directed at children." And that, in an area of protected speech. In the Court's words,

> No doubt a State possesses legitimate power to protect children from harm, . . . but that does not include a free-floating power to restrict the ideas to which children may be exposed. "Speech that is neither obscene as to youths nor subject to some other legitimate proscription cannot be suppressed solely to protect the young from ideas or images that a legislative body thinks unsuitable for them" [quoting from *Erznoznik v. City of Jacksonville* . . . (1975)].

Having found that the California law imposed a restriction on the content of protected speech, the Court ruled that "it is invalid unless California can demonstrate that it passes strict scrutiny — that is, unless it is justified by a compelling government interest and is narrowly drawn to serve that interest." Applying that test, the Court reasoned that

> California has (wisely) declined to restrict Saturday morning cartoons, the sale of games rated for young children, or the distribution of pictures of guns. The consequence is that its regulation is wildly underinclusive when judged against its asserted justification, which in our view is alone enough to defeat it. Underinclusiveness raises serious doubts about whether the government is in fact pursuing the interest it invokes, rather than disfavoring a particular speaker or viewpoint. . . . Here, California has singled out the purveyors of video games for disfavored treatment — at least when compared to booksellers, cartoonists, and movie producers — and has given no persuasive reason why. . . .

> [And moreover,] the Act's purported aid to parental authority is vastly overinclusive. Not all of the children who are forbidden to purchase violent video games on their own have parents who *care* whether they purchase violent video games. . . .

> . . . Legislation such as this, which is neither fish nor fowl, cannot survive strict scrutiny.

d.   Expressions of Hate

In addition to obscenity, there are a number of categories of speech that are described as unprotected — the advocacy of illegal activity and fighting words. In recent years, there has been an effort to extend these unprotected categories to include expressions of hatred more generally. By and large, this effort has not met with success. With respect to illegal activity and fighting words, these categories of unprotected speech reflect the view of the Court that these forms of speech add very little, if anything, to a correct understanding of human nature or political discussion. *See generally*, Robert Bork, *Neutral Principles and Some First Amendment Problems*, 47 IND. L.J. 1, 31 (1971).

Much of the law of **illegal advocacy** is traceable to war time or times of social unrest. During World War I, Congress passed the Espionage Act of 1917, which made it a crime to promote the success of the enemies of the United States. The Sedition Act of 1918 prohibited individuals from saying or writing anything that was intended to cause contempt for the government of the United States. The Court upheld both acts. For example, in *Schenck v. United States*, 249 U.S. 17 (1919), the Court sustained the convictions of those who had circulated a leaflet against the draft. Writing for the Court, Justice Holmes articulated the view that the place and the times have much to do with the successful prosecution. Said Holmes:

> [T]he character of every act depends upon the circumstance in which it is done. The most stringent protection of free speech would not protect a man in falsely shouting fire in a theatre, and causing a panic. . . . The question in every case is whether the words used are used in such circumstances and are of such a nature as to create a clear and present danger that they will bring about the substantive evils that Congress has a right to prevent.

Id. at 52.

The clear and present danger test for illegal advocacy has not always been consistently applied. In the 1950s during the so-called "red scare," when there were efforts to identify and remove any communist influence in government, the Court sustained the Smith Act in *Dennis v. United States*, 341 U.S. 494 (1951). The Smith Act made it a crime to knowingly or willfully advocate the necessity or desirability "of overthrowing or destroying any government in the United States by force or violence, or by the assassination of any officer of any such government." Act of June 28, 1940, 54 Stat. 670, 671. Writing for a Court plurality, Chief Justice Vinson said that the clear and present danger test was to be understood in light of a formula articulated by a well-regarded lower court judge, Learned Hand, namely, that "[i]n each case [courts] must ask whether the gravity of the 'evil,' discounted by its improbability, justifies such invasion of free speech as is necessary to avoid the danger." 341 U.S. at 570. Obviously under that formulation, the supposed danger need not be "clear and present" if it is great enough. Somewhat later in this period, the clear and present danger test was again refined to draw a distinction between "advocacy of abstract doctrine and advocacy directed at promoting unlawful action." *Yates v. United States*, 354 U.S. 298, 318 (1957) (overturning convictions under the Smith Act, and distinguishing *Dennis*). In order for advocacy to be punished, said the Court, there must be an urging to "*do* something, now or in the future, rather than merely to *believe* in something." *Id.* at 324–25 (emphasis in the original).

The view in *Yates* ultimately crystallized in *Brandenburg v. Ohio*, 395 U.S. 444 (1966), where the Court was of the view that only where advocacy is directed and intended toward "inciting or producing imminent lawless action and is likely to incite or produce such action," may it be punished. *Id.* at 447. *Brandenburg* remains the key test in the illegal advocacy area, though it does not make clear whether risk is to be measured in relation to the gravity of the harm. *Brandenburg* was applied in *Hess v. Indiana*, 414 U.S. 105 (1973), where the Court overturned the conviction of an anti-war protestor for declaring "We'll take the f — g street later." Under *Brandenburg*, the Court found no evidence that there was a likelihood of imminent disruption of the peace. Similarly, in *NAACP v. Claiborne Hardware Co.*, 458 U.S. 886 (1982), the Court reversed a judgment against an NAACP official (Charles Evers) who had threatened violence against anyone not observing a boycott against white businesses. This was mere advocacy of violence, not proof of the likelihood of imminent illegal conduct and intent to cause such conduct.

Fighting words is defined under the few Court decisions to consider it as speech that is directed at another that is likely to provoke a violent response. The notion originated with *Chaplinsky v. New Hampshire*, 315 U.S. 568, 569 (1942) (upholding the conviction of a speaker for speech that does not seem to meet the Court's own definition — *e.g.*, "You are a God damned racketeer" and a "damned Facist and the whole government of Rochester are Fascists or agents of Fascists."). They would have to be awfully thin-skinned Fascists for that feeble statement to provoke a fight. Nevertheless, whether *Chaplinsky*'s facts fit its test or not, the test is reasonably plain — speech directed at another, calculated to cause a violent response, and whose "very utterance inflict[s] injury or tend[s] to incite an immediate breach of the peace." *Id.* at 571–72. The importance that the fighting words being directed at a specific person was made plain in *Cohen v. California*, 403 U.S. 15 (1971), where a disturbing the peace conviction was overturned for the wearing of a jacket with the words "F — k the Draft" on its back. Obviously, the uncivil language was not directed at anyone in particular.

The *Chaplinsky* "fighting words" doctrine has been examined closely in recent years to see if it can sustain codes against hate speech. In *R.A.V. v. City of St. Paul*, 505 U.S. 377 (1992), distinguished below in *Wisconsin v. Mitchell*, the Court invalidated a criminal prohibition for placing, among other things, a burning cross or Nazi swastika, where the person doing so could reasonably know it would arouse "anger, alarm or resentment in others on the basis of race, color, creed, religion or gender." *Id.* at 380. The Court held that to describe a category of speech as unprotected means that it is subject to regulation because of its constitutionally proscribable content, but not that it is "entirely invisible to the First Amendment so that [it] may be made the vehicl[e] for content discrimination unrelated to [its] distinctly proscribable content. Thus, the government may proscribe libel; but it may not make the further content discrimination of proscribing only libel critical of the government." *Id.* at 383–84.

The *R.A.V.* case makes it difficult, if not impossible, for public colleges and universities to promulgate campus codes against hate speech. It also raises questions about "hostile work environment" claims. *See* Eugene Volokh, *What Speech Does "Hostile Work Environment" Harassment Law Restrict?*, 85 Geo. L.J. 627 (1997) (arguing that "hostile work environment" harassment law is overly suppressive of speech because it draws no distinction among differing forms of speech and defines itself with vague terms that have been interpreted broadly); Jules B. Gerard, *The First Amendment in a Hostile Environment: A Primer on Free Speech and Sexual Harassment*, 68 NOTRE DAME L. REV. 1003 (1993) (suggesting that federal regulations under Title VII's sexual discrimination prohibitions are overly broad and are misapplied to situations where constitutionally protected speech is the sole basis for establishing a sexually hostile environment). Generally, campus codes and anti-harrassment rules may only prohibit certain categories of speech, and thus, under *R.A.V.*, present an impermissible content line. When the categories are broadened to include more generalized expressions of hate, a challenge can be brought on vagueness or overbreadth grounds.

In *Virginia v. Black*, 538 U.S. 343 (2003), the Court held, per Justice O'Connor, that a state may, consistent with the First Amendment, ban cross burning carried out with the intent to intimidate. A plurality of the Court found the aspect of the statute that characterized the burning, itself, as evidence of intimidation to be unconstitutional. Virginia's cross-burning statute made it a felony offense for any person or persons, with the intent of intimidating any person or group of persons, to burn a cross on the property of another, a highway, or another public place.

The majority noted that "[c]ross burning in the United States is inextricably intertwined with the history of the Ku Klux Klan." The Klan was responsible for " 'a veritable reign of terror' throughout the South." It frequently employed tactics ranging from whipping to murder and it burned a cross to threaten such violence. Categorically, cross burning, said the Court, is a "symbol of hate." First Amendment protections, reasoned the Justices, are not absolute, and the states are permitted to prohibit "fighting words," "true threats," and speech directed at inciting imminent lawless action. "The First Amendment permits Virginia to outlaw cross burnings done with the intent to intimidate because burning a cross is a particularly virulent form of intimidation," Justice O'Connor wrote, in distinguishing the Court's previous decision in *R.A.V. v. St. Paul* (1992), which banned cross burning done with knowledge that such action would arouse alarm in others on the basis of race, color, creed, religion, or gender. Unlike the St. Paul ordinance that specified particular content for disfavor, the Virginia statute "does not single out for opprobrium only that speech directed toward 'one of the specified disfavored topics.' " Virginia can prohibit all forms of intimidation or a subset thereof. "[J]ust as a State may regulate only that obscenity which is the most obscene due to its prurient content, so too may a State choose to prohibit only those forms of intimidation that are most likely to inspire fear of bodily harm," the majority concluded. However, Virginia cannot presume intimidation from the burning, itself. It must be separately proven beyond a reasonable doubt. To allow the presumption, said the plurality, would "strip away the very reason why a State may ban cross burning with the intent to intimidate," Justice O'Connor stated. The provision makes no attempt to distinguish among the different motivations for cross burnings. By permitting the state to arrest, prosecute, and convict a person based solely on the fact of cross burning itself, the provision would create an unacceptable risk of the suppression of ideas, given the possibility that a state would prosecute and convict somebody engaging only in lawful political speech at the core of what the First Amendment is designed to protect, Justice O'Connor wrote. Justice Stevens filed a brief concurring opinion. Justice Scalia, joined in part by Justice Thomas, believed that there was no justification for the plurality's apparent decision to invalidate the statute's prima facie evidence provision on its face, but agreed that the Court should vacate and remand the Virginia Supreme Court's judgment so that the state court could have an opportunity authoritatively to construe its own law.

Three Justices, Souter, Kennedy, and Ginsburg, would have invalidated the law in its entirety. The dissenters agreed hypothetically with the majority that the Virginia statute makes a content-based distinction within the category of punishable intimidating or threatening expression, "the very type of distinction . . . considered [appropriate in *dicta*] in *R.A.V.*," but disagreed that this statute could be saved. The dissent thought the so-called virulence exception ill-fitting, since "the statute fits poorly with the illustrative examples given in *R.A.V.*, none of which involves communication generally associated with a particular message, and [thus] the majority's discussion of a special virulence exception here moves that exception toward a more flexible conception than the version" contemplated in the earlier case.

For example, wrote Justice Souter, *R.A.V.* had explained the special virulence exception to the rule barring content-based subclasses of categorically proscribable expression this way: prohibition by subcategory is nonetheless constitutional if it is made "entirely" on the "basis" of "the very reason" that "the entire class of speech at issue is proscribable" at all. This is okay since where the subcategory is confined to the most obviously proscribable instances, "no significant danger of idea or viewpoint discrimination exists."

Comparing examples from *R.A.V.*, Justice Souter noted that one permissible distinction is for a prohibition of particularly virulent obscenity, such as the difference between obscene depictions of actual people and simulations. Such a prohibition does not suggest a desire to suppress any particular message. Here, however, "the cross may have been selected because of its special power to threaten, but it may also have been singled out because of disapproval of its message of white supremacy, either because a legislature thought white supremacy was a pernicious doctrine or because it found that dramatic, public espousal of it was a civic embarrassment."

Justice Thomas, in a partial dissent, would not have applied the First Amendment at all to what he considered pure intimidation, rather than expressive conduct. He also thought that it was permissible to construe the presumption as merely permitting the jury to draw an inference of intent to intimidate from the cross burning itself.

WISCONSIN v. MITCHELL
508 U.S. 476 (1993)

CHIEF JUSTICE REHNQUIST delivered the opinion of the Court.

Respondent Todd Mitchell's sentence for aggravated battery was enhanced because he intentionally selected his victim on account of the victim's race. The question presented in this case is whether this penalty enhancement is prohibited by the First and Fourteenth Amendments. We hold that it is not.

On the evening of October 7, 1989, a group of young black men and boys, including Mitchell, gathered at an apartment complex in Kenosha, Wisconsin. Several members of the group discussed a scene from the motion picture "Mississippi Burning," in which a white man beat a young black boy who was praying. The group moved outside and Mitchell asked them: " 'Do you all feel hyped up to move on some white people?' " Shortly thereafter, a young white boy approached the group on the opposite side of the street where they were standing. As the boy walked by, Mitchell said: " 'You all want to fuck somebody up? There goes a white boy; go get him.' " Mitchell counted to three and pointed in the boy's direction. The group ran toward the boy, beat him severely, and stole his tennis shoes. The boy was rendered unconscious and remained in a coma for four days.

After a jury trial in the Circuit Court for Kenosha County, Mitchell was convicted of aggravated battery. That offense ordinarily carries a maximum sentence of two years' imprisonment. But because the jury found that Mitchell had intentionally selected his victim because of the boy's race, the maximum sentence for Mitchell's offense was increased to seven years. . . . That provision [of Wisconsin's criminal statutes] enhances the maximum penalty for an offense whenever the defendant "[i]ntentionally selects the person against whom the crime . . . is committed . . . because of the race, religion, color, disability, sexual orientation, national origin or ancestry of that person. . . ." The Circuit Court sentenced Mitchell to four years' imprisonment for the aggravated battery.

Mitchell . . . appealed his conviction and sentence, challenging the constitutionality of Wisconsin's penalty-enhancement provision on First Amendment grounds. The Wisconsin Court of Appeals rejected Mitchell's challenge, but the Wisconsin Supreme Court reversed. The Supreme Court held that the statute "violates the First Amendment directly by punishing what the legislature has deemed to be offensive thought." It rejected the State's contention "that the statute punishes only the 'conduct' of intentional selection of a victim." According to the court, "[t]he statute punishes the 'because of' aspect of the defendant's selection, the *reason* the defendant selected the victim, the *motive* behind the selection." And under *R.A.V. v. St. Paul* (1992), "the Wisconsin legislature cannot criminalize bigoted thought with which it disagrees."

The Supreme Court also held that the penalty-enhancement statute was unconstitutionally overbroad. It reasoned that, in order to prove that a defendant intentionally selected his victim because of the victim's protected status, the State would often have to introduce evidence of the defendant's prior speech, such as racial epithets he may have uttered before the commission of the offense. This evidentiary use of protected speech, the court thought, would have a "chilling effect" on those who feared the possibility of prosecution for offenses subject to penalty enhancement. Finally, the court distinguished antidiscrimination laws, which have long been held constitutional, on the ground that the Wisconsin statute punishes the "subjective mental process" of selecting a victim because of his protected status, whereas antidiscrimination laws prohibit "objective acts of discrimination."

* * *

Mitchell argues that we are bound by the Wisconsin Supreme Court's conclusion that the statute punishes bigoted thought and not conduct. There is no doubt that we are bound by a state court's construction of a state statute. . . . But here the Wisconsin Supreme Court did not, strictly speaking, [construe the Wisconsin statute in the sense of defining the meaning of a particular statutory word or phrase. Rather, it merely characterized the "practical effect" of the statute for First Amendment purposes.] This assessment does not bind us. Once any ambiguities as to the meaning of the statute are resolved, we may form our own judgment as to its operative effect.

The State argues that the statute does not punish bigoted thought, as the Supreme Court of Wisconsin said, but instead punishes only conduct. While this argument is literally correct, it does not dispose of Mitchell's First Amendment challenge. To be sure, our cases reject the "view that an apparently limitless variety of conduct can be labeled 'speech' whenever the person engaging in the conduct intends thereby to express an idea." *United States v. O'Brien.* Thus, a physical assault is not by any stretch of the imagination expressive conduct protected by the First Amendment.

But the fact remains that under the Wisconsin statute the same criminal conduct may be more heavily punished if the victim is selected because of his race or other protected status than if no such motive obtained. Thus, although the statute punishes criminal conduct, it enhances the maximum penalty for conduct motivated by a discriminatory point of view more severely than the same conduct engaged in for some other reason or for no reason at all. Because the only reason for the enhancement is the defendant's discriminatory motive for selecting his victim, Mitchell argues (and the Wisconsin Supreme Court held) that the statute violates the First Amendment by punishing offenders' bigoted beliefs.

Traditionally, sentencing judges have considered a wide variety of factors in addition to evidence bearing on guilt in determining what sentence to impose on a convicted defendant. The defendant's motive for committing the offense is one important factor. . . . Thus, in many States the commission of a murder, or other capital offense, for pecuniary gain is a separate aggravating circumstance under the capital sentencing statute.

[But it is equally true that a defendant's abstract beliefs, however obnoxious to most people, may not be taken into consideration by a sentencing judge.] *Dawson v. Delaware* (1992). In *Dawson,* the State introduced evidence at a capital sentencing hearing that the defendant was a member of a white supremacist prison gang. Because "the evidence proved nothing more than [the defendant's] abstract beliefs," we held that its admission violated the defendant's First Amendment rights. In so holding, however, we emphasized that ["the Constitution does not erect a *per se* barrier to the admission of evidence concerning one's beliefs and associations at sentencing simply because those beliefs and associations are protected by the First Amendment."] Thus, in *Barclay v. Florida* (1983) (plurality opinion), we allowed the sentencing judge to take into account the defendant's racial animus towards his victim. The evidence in that case showed that the defendant's membership in the Black Liberation Army and desire to provoke a "race war" were related to the murder of a white man for which he was convicted. Because "the elements of racial hatred in [the] murder" were relevant to several aggravating factors, we held that the trial judge permissibly took this evidence into account in sentencing the defendant to death.

Mitchell suggests that *Dawson* and *Barclay* are inapposite because they did not involve application of a penalty-enhancement provision. But in *Barclay* we held that it was permissible for the sentencing court to consider the defendant's racial animus in determining whether he should be sentenced to death, surely the most severe "enhancement" of all. And the fact that the Wisconsin Legislature has decided, as a general matter, that bias-motivated offenses warrant greater maximum penalties across the board does not alter the result here. For the primary responsibility for fixing criminal penalties lies with the legislature.

Mitchell argues that the Wisconsin penalty-enhancement statute is invalid because it punishes the defendant's discriminatory motive, or reason, for acting. But motive plays the same role under the Wisconsin statute as it does under federal and state antidiscrimination laws, which we have previously upheld against constitutional challenge. Title VII of the Civil Rights Act of 1964, for example, makes it unlawful for an employer to discriminate against an employee "*because of* such individual's race, color, religion, sex, or national origin." (emphasis added). . . . [W]e [have previously] rejected the argument that Title VII infringed employers' First Amendment rights. And more recently, in *R.A.V. v. St. Paul* we cited Title VII . . . as an example of a permissible content-neutral regulation of conduct.

Nothing in our decision last Term in *R.A.V.* compels a different result here. That case involved a First Amendment challenge to a municipal ordinance prohibiting the use of " 'fighting words' that insult, or provoke violence, 'on the basis of race, color, creed, religion or gender.' " Because the ordinance only proscribed a class of "fighting words" deemed particularly offensive by the city — *i.e.*, those "that contain . . . messages of 'bias-motivated' hatred" — we held that it violated the rule against content-based discrimination. But whereas the ordinance struck down in *R.A.V.* was explicitly directed at expression (*i.e.*, "speech" or "messages"), the statute in this case is aimed at conduct unprotected by the First Amendment.

Moreover, the Wisconsin statute singles out for enhancement bias-inspired conduct because this conduct is thought to inflict greater individual and societal harm. For example, according to the State and its *amici*, bias-motivated crimes are more likely to provoke retaliatory crimes, inflict distinct emotional harms on their victims, and incite community unrest. The State's desire to redress these perceived harms provides an adequate explanation for its penalty-enhancement provision over and above mere disagreement with offenders' beliefs or biases. As Blackstone said long ago, "it is but reasonable that among crimes of different natures those should be most severely punished, which are the most destructive of the public safety and happiness." 4 W. BLACKSTONE, COMMENTARIES *16.

Finally, there remains to be considered Mitchell's argument that the Wisconsin statute is unconstitutionally overbroad because of its "chilling effect" on free speech. Mitchell argues (and the Wisconsin Supreme Court agreed) that the statute is "overbroad" because evidence of the defendant's prior speech or associations may be used to prove that the defendant intentionally selected his victim on account of the victim's protected status. Consequently, the argument goes, the statute impermissibly chills free expression with respect to such matters by those concerned about the possibility of enhanced sentences if they should in the future commit a criminal offense covered by the statute. We find no merit in this contention.

The sort of chill envisioned here is far more attenuated and unlikely than that contemplated in traditional "over-breadth" cases. We must conjure up a vision of a Wisconsin citizen suppressing his unpopular bigoted opinions for fear that if he later commits an offense covered by the statute, these opinions will be offered at trial to establish that he selected his victim on account of the victim's protected status, thus qualifying him for penalty enhancement. To stay within the realm of rationality, we must surely put to one side minor misdemeanor offenses covered by the statute, such as negligent operation of a motor vehicle; for it is difficult, if not impossible, to conceive of a situation where such offenses would be racially motivated. We are left, then, with the prospect of a citizen suppressing his bigoted beliefs for fear that evidence of such beliefs will be introduced against him at trial if he commits a more serious offense against person or property. This is simply too speculative a hypothesis to support Mitchell's overbreadth claim.

The First Amendment, moreover, does not prohibit the evidentiary use of speech to establish the elements of a crime or to prove motive or intent. Evidence of a defendant's previous declarations or statements is commonly admitted in criminal trials subject to evidentiary rules dealing with relevancy, reliability, and the like. Nearly half a century ago, in *Haupt v. United States* (1947), we rejected a contention similar to that advanced by Mitchell here. Haupt was tried for the offense of treason, which, as defined by the Constitution (Art. III, § 3), may depend very much on proof of motive. To prove that the acts in question were committed out of "adherence to the enemy" rather than "parental solicitude," the Government introduced evidence of conversations that had taken place long prior to the indictment, some of which consisted of statements showing Haupt's sympathy with Germany and Hitler and hostility towards the United States. We rejected Haupt's argument that this evidence was improperly admitted. While "[s]uch testimony is to be scrutinized with care to be certain the statements are not expressions of mere lawful and permissible difference of opinion with our own government or quite proper appreciation of the land of birth," we held that "these statements . . . clearly were admissible on the question of intent and adherence to the enemy."

For the foregoing reasons, we hold that Mitchell's First Amendment rights were not violated by the application of the Wisconsin penalty-enhancement provision in sentencing him. The judgment of the Supreme Court of Wisconsin is therefore reversed, and the case is remanded for further proceedings not inconsistent with this opinion.

NOTES AND QUESTIONS

1. We know that there is no proposition more central to the Court's First Amendment thinking than that the government may not favor certain types of speech over others based on the content of the message they advance. For example, the government clearly would not be permitted to outlaw one particular view about racial issues confronting American society. This attitude on the part of the courts

not only led to the *R.A.V.* decision discussed in Chief Justice Rehnquist's opinion, but also has led to the declaring unconstitutional so-called "campus speech codes," which penalize racially derogatory or sexually suggestive remarks. This is done pursuant to classic First Amendment theory, especially that put forward by Brandeis and Holmes, that the best remedy for speech you dislike is more speech, *see Whitney v. California*, 274 U.S. 357, 377 (1927) (Brandeis, J., concurring); or the equally classic notion that freedom of speech, in order to be effective, must include freedom for the ideas you hate as well as those you love. Why then, is Wisconsin permitted to punish crimes more severely when they are motivated by beliefs the expression of which would be protected under the First Amendment? Why is this not content discrimination of a kind that is unconstitutional?

2.   Why were there no dissenters in the case? Could the reason have something to do with the particular species of hate crime of which the defendant was guilty? *New York Times v. Sullivan* may have been influenced by contemporary civil rights struggles, particularly of Blacks in the South. Is something similar (or different) at work in *Wisconsin v. Mitchell*?

3.   In *Wisconsin v. Mitchell*, the Court considered and rejected the claim that the statute was unconstitutionally overbroad. Vagueness and overbreadth challenges are frequently brought together, though they need not be. A law is vague if it cannot be understood by a person of ordinary intelligence. The idea is to ensure that laws give adequate notice of what is expected and also to avoid selective prosecution. This is a special concern for the Court in the area of free speech. Thus, the Court invalidated a law that made it a crime to treat a flag "contemptuously," since the law failed to convey what type of behavior that terminology covered. *Smith v. Goguen*, 415 U.S. 566, 569 (1974). By comparison, overbreadth deals with a law that regulates *substantially* more speech than is allowed. An overbreadth challenge may be brought even by a person to whom the statute may be constitutionally applied. This is characterized by the Court as an exception to the usual standing principle that one may only raise one's own claims and not those of third parties. In *Schad v. Borough of Mt. Ephraim*, 452 U.S. 61 (1981), the Court invalidated a city ordinance that prohibited all live entertainment. The challenge was brought by an adult bookstore that had live nude dancers. In the *Barnes* case below, the Court finds nude dancing to be outside the protection of the First Amendment; nevertheless, in *Schad* the bookstore was allowed to raise the interests of a wide range of others who would be affected by the overbroad law, such as those seeking to run live sporting or theater events. A finding that a statute is vague or overbroad will render it void in all applications, and thus, a finding of either vagueness or overbreadth is viewed by the Court as "strong medicine." *Broadrick v. Oklahoma*, 413 U.S. 601, 613 (1973) (upholding an Oklahoma law that prohibited political activities by government employees). To avoid taking this medicine, the Court requires *substantial* overbreadth and will often try to construe a statute narrowly.

4.   In *Los Angeles Police Department v. United Reporting Publishing Company*, 528 U.S. 32 (1999), the Court per Chief Justice Rehnquist refused to apply the overbreadth doctrine in a facial challenge to California Government Code § 6254(f)(3), which places two conditions on public access to arrestees' addresses — that the person requesting an address declare that the request is being made for one of five prescribed purposes, and that the requestor also declare that the address

will not be used directly or indirectly to sell a product or service. United Reporting Publishing Corporation is a private publishing service that provides the names and addresses of recently arrested individuals to its customers, who include attorneys, insurance companies, drug and alcohol counselors, and driving schools. The Ninth Circuit had concluded that the statute restricted commercial speech, and while the government interest in privacy was substantial, the numerous exceptions to § 6254(f)(3) for journalistic, scholarly, political, governmental, and investigative purposes rendered the statute unconstitutional under the First Amendment.

The Court refused to apply the overbreadth doctrine because the traditional rule is that "a person to whom a statute may constitutionally be applied may not challenge that statute on the ground that it may conceivably be applied unconstitutionally to others in situations not before the Court." This traditional rule, said the Court, should only be set aside under the overbreadth doctrine "as a last resort." That was not true in *LAPD*, because the government was not prohibiting a speaker from conveying information that the speaker already possesses. *See Rubin v. Coors Brewing Co.* (1995). The California statute in question merely requires that if respondent wished to obtain the addresses of arrestees it must qualify under the statute to do so. Respondent did not attempt to qualify and was therefore denied access to the addresses. For purposes of assessing the propriety of a facial invalidation, the Court thus saw the case as little more than a governmental denial of access to information in its possession. California could decide not to give out arrestee information at all without violating the First Amendment. Concurring, Justice Ginsburg pointed out that California could not release address information only to those whose political views were in line with the party in power. But absent an illegitimate criterion such as viewpoint, California is free to support some speech without supporting other speech.

SNYDER v. PHELPS
131 S. Ct. 1207, 179 L. Ed. 2d 172 (2011)

ROBERTS, C. J., delivered the opinion of the Court, in which SCALIA, KENNEDY, THOMAS, GINSBURG, BREYER, SOTOMAYOR, and KAGAN, JJ., joined. BREYER, J., filed a concurring opinion. ALITO, J., filed a dissenting opinion. [Some footnotes have been omitted.]

CHIEF JUSTICE ROBERTS delivered the opinion of the Court.

A jury held members of the Westboro Baptist Church liable for millions of dollars in damages for picketing near a soldier's funeral service. The picket signs reflected the church's view that the United States is overly tolerant of sin and that God kills American soldiers as punishment. The question presented is whether the First Amendment shields the church members from tort liability for their speech in this case.

I

A

Fred Phelps founded the Westboro Baptist Church in Topeka, Kansas, in 1955. The church's congregation believes that God hates and punishes the United States for its tolerance of homosexuality, particularly in America's military. The church frequently communicates its views by picketing, often at military funerals. In the more than 20 years that the members of Westboro Baptist have publicized their message, they have picketed nearly 600 funerals. . . .

Marine Lance Corporal Matthew Snyder was killed in Iraq in the line of duty. Lance Corporal Snyder's father selected the Catholic church in the Snyders' hometown of Westminster, Maryland, as the site for his son's funeral. Local newspapers provided notice of the time and location of the service.

Phelps became aware of Matthew Snyder's funeral and decided to travel to Maryland with six other Westboro Baptist parishioners (two of his daughters and four of his grandchildren) to picket. On the day of the memorial service, the Westboro congregation members picketed on public land adjacent to public streets near the Maryland State House, the United States Naval Academy, and Matthew Snyder's funeral. The Westboro picketers carried signs that were largely the same at all three locations. They stated, for instance: "God Hates the USA/Thank God for 9/11," "America is Doomed," "Don't Pray for the USA," "Thank God for IEDs [Improvised Explosive Devices, *i.e.*, exploding booby traps (reputed to be the deadliest weapon in the enemy's arsenal in the Afghanistan theatre)]," "Thank God for Dead Soldiers," "Pope in Hell," "Priests Rape Boys," "God Hates Fags," "You're Going to Hell," and "God Hates You."

The church had notified the authorities in advance of its intent to picket at the time of the funeral, and the picketers complied with police instructions in staging their demonstration. The picketing took place within a 10-by-25-foot plot of public land adjacent to a public street, behind a temporary fence. . . . That plot was approximately 1,000 feet from the church where the funeral was held. Several buildings separated the picket site from the church. . . . The Westboro picketers displayed their signs for about 30 minutes before the funeral began and sang hymns and recited Bible verses. None of the picketers entered church property or went to the cemetery. They did not yell or use profanity, and there was no violence associated with the picketing. . . .

The funeral procession passed within 200 to 300 feet of the picket site. Although Snyder testified that he could see the tops of the picket signs as he drove to the funeral, he did not see what was written on the signs until later that night, while watching a news broadcast covering the event.[3] . . .

---

[3] [1] A few weeks after the funeral, one of the picketers posted a message on Westboro's Web site discussing the picketing and containing religiously oriented denunciations of the Snyders, interspersed among lengthy Bible quotations. Snyder discovered the posting, referred to by the parties as the "epic," during an Internet search for his son's name. The epic is not properly before us and does not factor in our analysis. Although the epic was submitted to the jury and discussed in the courts below, Snyder never

B

* * *

In the Court of Appeals, Westboro's primary argument was that the church was entitled to judgment as a matter of law because the First Amendment fully protected Westboro's speech. The Court of Appeals agreed. . . .

II

To succeed on a claim for intentional infliction of emotional distress in Maryland, a plaintiff must demonstrate that the defendant intentionally or recklessly engaged in extreme and outrageous conduct that caused the plaintiff to suffer severe emotional distress. . . . The Free Speech Clause of the First Amendment — "Congress shall make no law . . . abridging the freedom of speech" — can serve as a defense in state tort suits, including suits for intentional infliction of emotional distress. . . .[4]

Whether the First Amendment prohibits holding Westboro liable for its speech in this case turns largely on whether that speech is of public or private concern, as determined by all the circumstances of the case. Speech on matters of public concern . . . is at the heart of the First Amendment's protection. The First Amendment reflects a profound national commitment to the principle that debate on public issues should be uninhibited, robust, and wide-open. That is because speech concerning public affairs is more than self-expression; it is the essence of self-government. Accordingly, speech on public issues occupies the highest rung of the hierarchy of First Amendment values, and is entitled to special protection. [Citations and internal quotation marks omitted.]

* * *

. . . Speech deals with matters of public concern when it can be fairly considered as relating to any matter of political, social, or other concern to the community, or when it is a subject of legitimate news interest; that is, a subject of general interest and of value and concern to the public. The arguably inappropriate or controversial character of a statement is irrelevant to the question whether it deals with a matter of public concern. [Citations and internal quotation marks omitted.]

* * *

Deciding whether speech is of public or private concern requires us to examine

---

mentioned it in his petition for certiorari. . . . Snyder's claim arose out of Phelps' intentional acts at Snyder's son's funeral. . . . Nor did Snyder respond to the statement in the opposition to certiorari that "[t]hough the epic was asserted as a basis for the claims at trial, the petition . . . appears to be addressing only claims based on the picketing." . . . Snyder devoted only one paragraph in the argument section of his opening merits brief to the epic. Given the foregoing and the fact that exclusions from First an Internet posting may raise distinct issues in this context, we decline to consider the epic in deciding this case. . . .

[4] [3] The dissent attempts to draw parallels between this case and hypothetical cases involving defamation or fighting words. . . . But, as the court below noted, there is "no suggestion that the speech at issue falls within one of the categorical exclusions from First Amendment protection, such as those for obscenity or 'fighting words'." . . .

the content, form, and context of that speech, as revealed by the whole record. As in other First Amendment cases, the court is obligated to make an independent examination of the whole record in order to make sure that the judgment does not constitute a forbidden intrusion on the field of free expression. In considering content, form, and context, no factor is dispositive, and it is necessary to evaluate all the circumstances of the speech, including what was said, where it was said, and how it was said. [Citations and internal quotation marks omitted.]

The "content" of Westboro's signs plainly relates to broad issues of interest to society at large, rather than matters of "purely private concern." . . . The placards read "God Hates the USA/Thank God for 9/11," "America is Doomed," "Don't Pray for the USA," "Thank God for IEDs," "Fag Troops," "Semper Fi Fags," "God Hates Fags," "Maryland Taliban," "Fags Doom Nations," "Not Blessed Just Cursed," "Thank God for Dead Soldiers," "Pope in Hell," "Priests Rape Boys," "You're Going to Hell," and "God Hates You." . . . While these messages may fall short of refined social or political commentary, the issues they highlight — the political and moral conduct of the United States and its citizens, the fate of our Nation, homosexuality in the military, and scandals involving the Catholic clergy — are matters of public import. The signs certainly convey Westboro's position on those issues, in a manner designed . . . to reach as broad a public audience as possible. And even if a few of the signs — such as "You're Going to Hell" and "God Hates You" — were viewed as containing messages related to Matthew Snyder or the Snyders specifically, that would not change the fact that the overall thrust and dominant theme of Westboro's demonstration spoke to broader public issues.

Apart from the content of Westboro's signs, Snyder contends that the "context" of the speech — its connection with his son's funeral — makes the speech a matter of private rather than public concern. The fact that Westboro spoke in connection with a funeral, however, cannot by itself transform the nature of Westboro's speech. Westboro's signs, displayed on public land next to a public street, reflect the fact that the church finds much to condemn in modern society. Its speech is "fairly characterized as constituting speech on a matter of public concern," . . . and the funeral setting does not alter that conclusion.

Snyder argues that the church members in fact mounted a personal attack on Snyder and his family, and then attempted to "immunize their conduct by claiming that they were actually protesting the United States' tolerance of homosexuality or the supposed evils of the Catholic Church." . . . We are not concerned in this case that Westboro's speech on public matters was in any way contrived to insulate speech on a private matter from liability. Westboro had been actively engaged in speaking on the subjects addressed in its picketing long before it became aware of Matthew Snyder, and there can be no serious claim that Westboro's picketing did not represent its "honestly believed" views on public issues. . . .

Snyder goes on to argue that Westboro's speech should be afforded less than full First Amendment protection "not only because of the words" but also because the church members exploited the funeral "as a platform to bring their message to a broader audience." . . . There is no doubt that Westboro chose to stage its picketing at the Naval Academy, the Maryland State House, and Matthew Snyder's funeral to increase publicity for its views and because of the relation between those sites and its views — in the case of the military funeral, because Westboro believes that God is killing American soldiers as punishment for the Nation's sinful policies.

Westboro's choice to convey its views in conjunction with Matthew Snyder's funeral made the expression of those views particularly hurtful to many, especially to Matthew's father. The record makes clear that the applicable legal term — "emotional distress" — fails to capture fully the anguish Westboro's choice added to Mr. Snyder's already incalculable grief. But Westboro conducted its picketing peacefully on matters of public concern at a public place adjacent to a public street. Such space occupies a "special position in terms of First Amendment protection." . . . "[W]e have repeatedly referred to public streets as the archetype of a traditional public forum," noting that " '[t]ime out of mind' public streets and sidewalks have been used for public assembly and debate."[5] . . .

That said, even protected speech is not equally permissible in all places and at all times. Westboro's choice of where and when to conduct its picketing is not beyond the Government's regulatory reach — it is "subject to reasonable time, place, or manner restrictions" that are consistent with the standards announced in this Court's precedents. [Citations and internal quotation marks omitted.] . . .

. . . Simply put, the church members had the right to be where they were. Westboro alerted local authorities to its funeral protest and fully complied with police guidance on where the picketing could be staged. The picketing was conducted under police supervision some 1,000 feet from the church, out of the sight of those at the church. The protest was not unruly; there was no shouting, profanity, or violence.

The record confirms that any distress occasioned by Westboro's picketing turned on the content and viewpoint of the message conveyed, rather than any interference with the funeral itself. A group of parishioners standing at the very spot where Westboro stood, holding signs that said "God Bless America" and "God Loves You," would not have been subjected to liability. It was what Westboro said that exposed it to tort damages. Given that Westboro's speech was at a public place on a matter of public concern, that speech is entitled to "special protection" under the First Amendment. Such speech cannot be restricted simply because it is upsetting or arouses contempt. If there is a bedrock principle underlying the First Amendment, it is that the government may not prohibit the expression of an idea simply because society finds the idea itself offensive or disagreeable. . . . In a case such as this, a jury is unlikely to be neutral with respect to the content of [the]speech, posing a real danger of becoming an instrument for the suppression of vehement, caustic, and sometimes unpleasant expression. Such a risk is unacceptable; in public debate we must tolerate insulting, and even outrageous, speech in order to provideade quate breathing space' to the freedoms protected by the First Amendment. What Westboro said, in the whole context of how and where it chose to say it, is entitled

---

[5] [4] The dissent is wrong to suggest that the Court considers a public street "a free-fire zone in which otherwise actionable verbal attacks are shielded from liability." . . . The fact that Westboro conducted its picketing adjacent to a public street does not insulate the speech from liability, but instead heightens concerns that what is at issue is an effort to communicate to the public the church's views on matters of public concern. That is why our precedents so clearly recognize the special significance of this traditional public forum.

to "special protection" under the First Amendment, and that protection cannot be overcome by a jury finding that the picketing was outrageous. For all these reasons, the jury verdict imposing tort liability on Westboro for intentional infliction of emotional distress must be set aside. [Citations and internal quotation marks omitted.]

* * *

IV

Our holding today is narrow. We are required in First Amendment cases to carefully review the record, and the reach of our opinion here is limited by the particular facts before us. . . . Westboro believes that America is morally flawed; many Americans might feel the same about Westboro. Westboro's funeral picketing is certainly hurtful and its contribution to public discourse may be negligible. But Westboro addressed matters of public import on public property, in a peaceful manner, in full compliance with the guidance of local officials. The speech was indeed planned to coincide with Matthew Snyder's funeral, but did not itself disrupt that funeral, and Westboro's choice to conduct its picketing at that time and place did not alter the nature of its speech.

Speech is powerful. It can stir people to action, move them to tears of both joy and sorrow, and — as it did here — inflict great pain. On the facts before us, we cannot react to that pain by punishing the speaker. As a Nation we have chosen a different course — to protect even hurtful speech on public issues to ensure that we do not stifle public debate. That choice requires that we shield Westboro from tort liability for its picketing in this case.

The judgment of the United States Court of Appeals for the Fourth Circuit is affirmed.

* * *

JUSTICE BREYER, concurring [Omitted.]

JUSTICE ALITO, dissenting.

Our profound national commitment to free and open debate is not a license for the vicious verbal assault that occurred in this case. Petitioner Albert Snyder is not a public figure. He is simply a parent whose son, Marine Lance Corporal Matthew Snyder, was killed in Iraq. Mr. Snyder wanted what is surely the right of any parent who experiences such an incalculable loss: to bury his son in peace. But respondents, members of the Westboro Baptist Church, deprived him of that elementary right. They first issued a press release and thus turned Matthew's funeral into a tumultuous media event. They then appeared at the church, approached as closely as they could without trespassing, and launched a malevolent verbal attack on Matthew and his family at a time of acute emotional vulnerability. As a result, Albert Snyder suffered severe and lasting emotional injury. The Court now holds that the First Amendment protected respondents' right to brutalize Mr. Snyder. I cannot agree.

I

Respondents and other members of their church have strong opinions on certain moral, religious, and political issues, and the First Amendment ensures that they have almost limitless opportunities to express their views. . . . It does not follow, however, that they may intentionally inflict severe emotional injury on private persons at a time of intense emotional sensitivity by launching vicious verbal attacks that make no contribution to public debate. To protect against such injury, "most if not all jurisdictions"permit recovery in tort for the intentional infliction of emotional distress (or IIED). . . .

This is a very narrow tort with requirements that are rigorous, and difficult to satisfy. To recover, a plaintiff must show that the conduct at issue caused harm that was truly severe. A plaintiff must also establish that the defendant's conduct was so outrageous in character, and so extreme in degree, as to go beyond all possible bounds of decency, and to be regarded as atrocious, and utterly intolerable in a civilized community. Although the elements of the IIED tort are difficult to meet, respondents long ago abandoned any effort to show that those tough standards were not satisfied here. On appeal, they chose not to contest the sufficiency of the evidence. They did not dispute that Mr. Snyder suffered wounds that are truly severe and incapable of healing themselves. Nor did they dispute that their speech was so outrageous in character, and so extreme in degree, as to go beyond all possible bounds of decency, and to be regarded as atrocious, and utterly intolerable in a civilized community. Instead, they maintained that the First Amendment gave them a license to engage in such conduct. They are wrong. [Citations and internal quotation marks omitted.]

II

It is well established that a claim for the intentional infliction of emotional distress can be satisfied by speech. Indeed, what has been described as "[t]he leading case" recognizing this tort involved speech. [Citing *Wilkinson v. Downton*, (1897) Q.B. 57]. And although this Court has not decided the question, I think it is clear that the First Amendment does not entirely preclude liability for the intentional infliction of emotional distress by means of speech.

This Court has recognized that words may "by their very utterance inflict injury" and that the First Amendment does not shield utterances that form "no essential part of any exposition of ideas, and are of such slight social value as a step to truth that any benefit that may be derived from them is clearly outweighed by the social interest in order and morality." *Chaplinsky v. New Hampshire* (1942); see also *Cantwell v. Connecticut* (1940) ("[P]ersonal abuse is not in any proper sense communication of information or opinion safeguarded by the Constitution"). When grave injury is intentionally inflicted by means of an attack like the one at issue here, the First Amendment should not interfere with recovery.

III

In this case, respondents brutally attacked Matthew Snyder, and this attack, which was almost certain to inflict injury, was central to respondents' well-practiced strategy for attracting public attention. On the morning of Matthew Snyder's funeral, respondents could have chosen to stage their protest at countless locations. They could have picketed the United States Capitol, the White House, the Supreme Court, the Pentagon, or any of the more than 5,600 military recruiting stations in this country. They could have returned to the Maryland State House or the United States Naval Academy, where they had been the day before. They could have selected any public road where pedestrians are allowed. . . . They could have staged their protest in a public park. . . . They could have chosen any Catholic church where no funeral was taking place. . . . But of course, a small group picketing at any of these locations would have probably gone unnoticed. The Westboro Baptist Church, however, has devised a strategy that remedies this problem. As the Court notes, church members have protested at nearly 600 military funerals. . . . They have also picketed the funerals of police officers, firefighters, and the victims of natural disasters, accidents, and shocking crimes. And in advance of these protests, they issue press releases to ensure that their protests will attract public attention.

This strategy works because it is expected that respondents' verbal assaults will wound the family and friends of the deceased and because the media is irresistibly drawn to the sight of persons who are visibly in grief. The more outrageous the funeral protest, the more publicity the Westboro Baptist Church is able to obtain. Thus, when the church recently announced its intention to picket the funeral of a 9-year-old girl killed in the shooting spree in Tucson — proclaiming that she was "better off dead" — their announcement was national news, and the church was able to obtain free air time on the radio in exchange for canceling its protest. Similarly, in 2006, the church got air time on a talk radio show in exchange for canceling its threatened protest at the funeral of five Amish girls killed by a crazed gunman. In this case, respondents implemented the Westboro Baptist Church's publicity-seeking strategy. Their press release stated that they were going "to picket the funeral of Lance Cpl. Matthew A. Snyder" because "God Almighty killed Lance Cpl. Snyder. He died in shame, not honor — for a fag nation cursed by God . . . . Now in Hell — sine die." . . . This announcement guaranteed that Matthew's funeral would be transformed into a raucous media event and began the wounding process. It is well known that anticipation may heighten the effect of a painful event. On the day of the funeral, respondents, true to their word, displayed placards that conveyed the message promised in their press release. Signs stating "God Hates You" and "Thank God for Dead Soldiers" reiterated the message that God had caused Matthew's death in retribution for his sins. . . . Others, stating "You're Going to Hell" and "Not Blessed Just Cursed," conveyed the message that Matthew was "in Hell — sine die." . . .

Even if those who attended the funeral were not alerted in advance about respondents' intentions, the meaning of these signs would not have been missed. Since respondents chose to stage their protest at Matthew Snyder's funeral and not at any of the other countless available venues, a reasonable person would have assumed that there was a connection between the messages on the placards and the deceased. Moreover, since a church funeral is an event that naturally brings to mind thoughts about the afterlife, some of respondents' signs — *e.g.*, "God Hates You," "Not Blessed Just Cursed," and "You're Going to Hell" — would have likely been interpreted as referring to God's judgment of the deceased. Other signs would most naturally have been understood as suggesting — falsely — that Matthew was gay. Homosexuality was the theme of many of the signs. There were signs reading "God Hates Fags," "Semper Fi Fags," "Fags Doom Nations," and "Fag Troops." . . . Another placard depicted two men engaging in anal intercourse. A reasonable bystander seeing those signs would have likely concluded that they were meant to suggest that the deceased was a homosexual.

After the funeral, the Westboro picketers reaffirmed the meaning of their protest. They posted an online account entitled "The Burden of Marine Lance Cpl. Matthew A.Snyder. The Visit of Westboro Baptist Church to Help the Inhabitants of Maryland Connect the Dots!"[6] . . . The epic [the parties had referred to the Westboro Internet posting as the "epic"], however, is not a distinct claim but a piece of evidence that the jury considered in imposing liability for the claims now before this Court. The protest and the epic are parts of a single course of conduct that the jury found to constitute intentional infliction of emotional distress. . . . The Court's strange insistence that the epic "is not properly before us," . . . means that the Court has not actually made "an independent examination of the whole record." . . . And the Court's refusal to consider the epic contrasts sharply with its willingness to take notice of Westboro's protest activities at other times and locations. . . .

In light of this evidence, it is abundantly clear that respondents, going far beyond commentary on matters of public concern, specifically attacked Matthew Snyder because (1) he was a Catholic and (2) he was a member of the United States military. Both Matthew and petitioner were private figures, and this attack was not speech on a matter of public concern. While commentary on the Catholic Church or the United States military constitutes speech on matters of public concern, speech regarding Matthew Snyder's purely private conduct does not.

---

[6] [15] The Court refuses to consider the epic because it was not discussed. Belying any suggestion that they had simply made general comments about homosexuality, the Catholic Church, and the United States military, the "epic" addressed the Snyder family directly:

> "God blessed you, Mr. and Mrs. Snyder, with a resource and his name was Matthew. He was an arrow in your quiver! In thanks to God for the comfort the child could bring you, you had a DUTY to prepare that child to serve the LORD his GOD — PERIOD! You did JUST THE OPPOSITE — you raised him for the devil.
>
> . . . .
>
> "Albert and Julie RIPPED that body apart and taught Matthew to defy his Creator, to divorce, and to commit adultery. They taught him how to support the largest pedophile machine in the history of the entire world, the Roman Catholic monstrosity. Every dime they gave the Roman Catholic monster they condemned their own souls. They also, in supporting satanic Catholicism, taught Matthew to be an idolater.
>
> . . . .
>
> "Then after all that they sent him to fight for the United States of Sodom, a filthy country that is in lock step with his evil, wicked, and sinful manner of life, putting him in the cross hairs of a God that is so mad He has smoke coming from his nostrils and fire from his mouth! How dumb was that?" . . . .

* * *

IV

The Court concludes that respondents' speech was protected by the First Amendment for essentially three reasons, but none is sound.

First — and most important — the Court finds that "the overall thrust and dominant theme of [their] demonstration spoke to" broad public issues. . . . As I have attempted to show, this portrayal is quite inaccurate;respondents' attack on Matthew was of central importance. But in any event, I fail to see why actionable speech should be immunized simply because it is interspersed with speech that is protected. The First Amendment allows recovery for defamatory statements that are interspersed with nondefamatory statements on matters of public concern, and there is no good reason why respondents' attack on Matthew Snyder and his family should be treated differently.

Second, the Court suggests that respondents' personal attack on Matthew Snyder is entitled to First Amendment protection because it was not motivated by a private grudge, . . . but I see no basis for the strange distinction that the Court appears to draw. Respondents' motivation — "to increase publicity for its views," . . . — did not transform their statements attacking the character of a private figure into statements that made a contribution to debate on matters of public concern. Nor did their publicity-seeking motivation soften the sting of their attack. And as far as culpability is concerned, one might well think that wounding statements uttered in the heat of a private feud are less, not more, blameworthy than similar statements made as part of a cold and calculated strategy to slash a stranger as a means of attracting public attention.

Third, the Court finds it significant that respondents' protest occurred on a public street, but this fact alone should not be enough to preclude IIED liability. To be sure, statements made on a public street may be less likely to satisfy the elements of the IIED tort than statements made on private property, but there is no reason why a public street in close proximity to the scene of a funeral should be regarded as a free-fire zone in which otherwise actionable verbal attacks are shielded from liability. If the First Amendment permits the States to protect their residents from the harm inflicted by such attacks — and the Court does not hold otherwise — then the location of the tort should not be dispositive. A physical assault may occur without trespassing; it is no defense that the perpetrator had "the right to be where [he was]." . . . And the same should be true with respect to unprotected speech. Neither classic "fighting words" nor defamatory statements are immunized when they occur in a public place, and there is no good reason to treat a verbal assault based on the conduct or character of a private figure like Matthew Snyder any differently.

NOTES AND QUESTIONS

1. Notice that the Court refused to factor into its analysis the so-called "epic", *i.e.*, Westboro's post-demonstration Internet entry accusing the Snyders of raising their son "for the devil," teaching him to defy God, etc. The Court's refusal to factor those comments into its analysis, even though the so-called "epic" had been submitted to the jury, was because "Snyder never mentioned it in his petition for certiorari." Yet the Court also said that whether speech is of public or private concern is "determined by all the circumstances of the case." As Justice Alito pointed out in dissent, the Court in applying that all-the-circumstances test took "notice of Westboro's protest activities at other times and locations." Indeed the Court did factor into its analysis the fact that "Westboro had been actively engaged in speaking on the subjects addressed in its picketing long before it became aware of Matthew Snyder." If the Court rightly considered the "public" nature of Westboro's active engagement "in speaking on the subjects addressed in its picketing long before it became aware of Matthew Snyder," should it not also have considered the "private" nature of Westboro's Internet accusations against the Snyders?

2. Recall also that the Court dismissed Justice Alito's attempt at an analogy between speech constituting an intentional infliction of emotional distress and speech constituting defamation or "fighting words" by merely asserting that "there is no suggestion that the speech at issue falls within one of the categorical exclusions from First Amendment protection, such as those for obscenity or fighting words." Was Alito claiming that the speech at issue in the instant case *did* fall "within one of the categorical exclusions from First Amendment protection" or was he suggesting that the *rationales* for those categorical exclusions apply as well to speech constituting the intentional infliction of emotional distress? Since the Court acknowledged that "Westboro's funeral picketing is certainly hurtful and its contribution to public discourse may be negligible," should it have discussed Justice Alito's suggestion more thoroughly? If it had done so, and in light of its acknowledgement that "Westboro's funeral picketing is certainly hurtful and its contribution to public discourse may be negligible," what result?

3. At one point the Court acknowledged that "a few of the signs — such as "You're Going to Hell" and "God Hates You" — were viewed as containing messages related to Matthew Snyder or the Snyders specifically." Also, as the dissent pointed out, a reasonable bystander seeing the signs reading "God Hates Fags," "Semper Fi Fags," "Fags Doom Nations," and "Fag Troops" and the placard depicted two men engaging in anal intercourse would have likely concluded that they were meant to suggest that Matthew Snyder was a homosexual. Should the Court, instead of focusing as it did on "the overall thrust and dominant theme of Westboro's demonstration," at least have assessed whether those privately addressed epithets constituted the intentional infliction of emotional distress?

4. Can the federal government punish a man for intentionally and falsely claiming that he has received the Congressional Medal of Honor? One might think so. One might even hope so. In *United States v. Alvarez*, 132 S. Ct. 2537, 183 L. Ed. 2d 574 (2012), however, the Court held to the contrary. A plurality of four Justices (Kennedy, the Chief Justice, Ginsburg, and Sotomayor) saw the federal Stolen Valor Act as a content-based restriction on speech and as such, presumptively invalid under a strict-scrutiny standard. Although the plurality acknowledged that "content-based restrictions on speech have been permitted, as a general matter, only when confined to the few 'historic and traditional categories long familiar to the bar' [including] advocacy intended, and likely, to incite imminent lawless action, . . .

obscenity, . . . defamation, . . . speech integral to criminal conduct, . . . so-called 'fighting words,' . . . child pornography, . . . fraud, . . . true threats, . . . and speech presenting some grave and imminent threat the government has the power to prevent," the plurality reasoned that "[b]efore exempting a category of speech from the normal prohibition on content-based restrictions, . . . the Court must be presented with 'persuasive evidence that a novel restriction on content is part of a long (if heretofore unrecognized) tradition of proscription'." Justices Breyer and Kagan agreed that the federal restriction in question violated the First Amendment, but eschewed the categorical approach that the plurality had taken, and would have judged the restriction under an intermediate scrutiny rubric rather than the strict scrutiny used by the plurality. Justice Alito, Scalia, and Thomas dissented, pointing to a bevy of federal statutes that bear some similarity to the prohibition in the Stolen Valor Act, for example, the federal statutory crimes of falsely impersonating a federal officer, and of knowingly using, without authorization, the names of enumerated federal agencies in a manner reasonably calculated to convey the impression that a communication is approved or authorized by the agency — laws which the plurality also acknowledged. Impersonating and using the names of federal agencies would seem to involve speech of sorts. What is the operative First-Amendment difference between, on one hand, impersonating a federal official or falsely claiming federal-agency approval, and on the other hand, impersonating a Congressional-Medal-of-Honor recipient and falsely claiming congressional approbation of such an honor?

6.   Special Contexts

a.   Government Speech

AGENCY FOR INTERNATIONAL DEVELOPMENT v. ALLIANCE FOR OPEN SOCIETY INTERNATIONAL, INC.
133 S. Ct. 2321, 186 L. Ed. 2d 398 (2013)

ROBERTS, C.J., delivered the opinion of the Court, in which KENNEDY, GINSBURG, BREYER, ALITO, and SOTOMAYOR, JJ., joined. SCALIA, J., filed a dissenting opinion, in which THOMAS, J., joined. KAGAN, J., took no part in the consideration or decision of the case.

*   *   *

CHIEF JUSTICE ROBERTS delivered the opinion of the Court.

The United States Leadership Against HIV/AIDS, Tuberculosis, and Malaria Act of 2003 (Leadership Act), outlined a comprehensive strategy to combat the spread of HIV/AIDS around the world. As part of that strategy, Congress authorized the appropriation of billions of dollars to fund efforts by nongovernmental organizations to assist in the fight. The Act imposes two related conditions on that funding: First, no funds made available by the Act "may be used to promote or advocate the legalization or practice of prostitution or sex trafficking." And second, no funds may be used by an organization "that does not have a policy explicitly opposing prostitution and sex trafficking." This case concerns the second of these conditions, referred to as the Policy Requirement. The question is whether that funding condition violates a recipient's First Amendment rights.

I

*   *   *

In the Leadership Act, Congress directed the President to establish a "comprehensive, integrated" strategy to combat HIV/AIDS around the world.

*   *   *

The United States has enlisted the assistance of nongovernmental organizations to help achieve the many goals of the program.

*   *   *

Those funds, however, come with two conditions: First, no funds made available to carry out the Leadership Act "may be used to promote or advocate the legalization or practice of prostitution or sex trafficking." Second, no funds made available may "provide assistance to any group or organization that does not have a policy explicitly opposing prostitution and sex trafficking, except . . . to the Global Fund to Fight AIDS, Tuberculosis and Malaria, the World Health Organization, the International AIDS Vaccine Initiative or to any United Nations agency." It is this second condition — the Policy Requirement — that is at issue here.

The Department of Health and Human Services (HHS) and the United States Agency for International Development (USAID) are the federal agencies primarily responsible for overseeing implementation of the Leadership Act. To enforce the Policy Requirement, the agencies have directed that the recipient of any funding under the Act agree in the award document that it is opposed to "prostitution and sex trafficking because of the psychological and physical risks they pose for women, men, and children."

II

*   *   *

In 2005, respondents Alliance for Open Society International and Pathfinder International commenced this litigation, seeking a declaratory judgment that the Government's implementation of the Policy Requirement violated their First Amendment rights. Respondents sought a preliminary injunction barring the Government from cutting off their funding under the Act for the duration of the litigation, from unilaterally terminating their cooperative agreements with the United States, or from otherwise taking action solely on the basis of respondents' own privately funded speech. The District Court granted such a preliminary injunction, and the Government appealed.

While the appeal was pending, HHS and USAID issued guidelines on how recipients of Leadership Act funds could retain funding while working with affiliated organizations not bound by the Policy Requirement. The guidelines permit funding recipients to work with affiliated organizations that "engage [ ] in activities inconsistent with the recipient's opposition to the practices of prostitution and sex trafficking" as long as the recipients retain "objective integrity and independence from any affiliated organization." Whether sufficient separation exists is determined by the totality of the circumstances, including "but not . . . limited to" (1) whether the organizations are legally separate; (2) whether they have separate personnel; (3) whether they keep separate accounting records; (4) the degree of separation in the organizations' facilities; and (5) the extent to which signs and other forms of identification distinguish the organizations.

The Court of Appeals summarily remanded the case to the District Court to consider whether the preliminary injunction was still appropriate in light of the new guidelines. On remand, the District Court issued a new preliminary injunction along the same lines as the first, and the Government renewed its appeal.

The Court of Appeals affirmed, concluding that respondents had demonstrated a likelihood of success on the merits of their First Amendment challenge under this Court's "unconstitutional conditions" doctrine. Under this doctrine, the court reasoned, "the government may not place a condition on the receipt of a benefit or subsidy that infringes upon the recipient's constitutionally protected rights, even if the government has no obligation to offer the benefit in the first instance." And a condition that compels recipients "to espouse the government's position" on a subject of international debate could not be squared with the First Amendment. The court concluded that "the Policy Requirement, as implemented by the Agencies, falls well beyond what the Supreme Court . . . ha[s] upheld as permissible funding conditions."

* * *

We granted certiorari.

III

The Policy Requirement mandates that recipients of Leadership Act funds explicitly agree with the Government's policy to oppose prostitution and sex trafficking. It is, however, a basic First Amendment principle that "freedom of speech prohibits the government from telling people what they must say." *Rumsfeld v. Forum for Academic and Institutional Rights, Inc.*. "At the heart of the First Amendment lies the principle that each person should decide for himself or herself the ideas and beliefs deserving of expression, consideration, and adherence." Were it enacted as a direct regulation of speech, the Policy Requirement would plainly violate the First Amendment. The question is whether the Government may nonetheless impose that requirement as a condition on the receipt of federal funds.

A

The Spending Clause of the Federal Constitution grants Congress the power "[t]o lay and collect Taxes, Duties, Imposts and Excises, to pay the Debts and provide for the common Defence and general Welfare of the United States." The

Clause provides Congress broad discretion to tax and spend for the "general Welfare," including by funding particular state or private programs or activities. That power includes the authority to impose limits on the use of such funds to ensure they are used in the manner Congress intends. *Rust v. Sullivan* (1991) ("Congress' power to allocate funds for public purposes includes an ancillary power to ensure that those funds are properly applied to the prescribed use.").

As a general matter, if a party objects to a condition on the receipt of federal funding, its recourse is to decline the funds. This remains true when the objection is that a condition may affect the recipient's exercise of its First Amendment rights. See, *e.g.*, *United States v. American Liberty Assn., Inc.* (2003) (plurality opinion) (rejecting a claim by public libraries that conditioning funds for Internet access on the libraries' installing filtering software violated their First Amendment rights, explaining that "[t]o the extent that libraries wish to offer unfiltered access, they are free to do so without federal assistance").

At the same time, however, we have held that the Government " 'may not deny a benefit to a person on a basis that infringes his constitutionally protected . . . freedom of speech even if he has no entitlement to that benefit.' "

* * *

The dissent thinks that can only be true when the condition is not relevant to the objectives of the program (although it has its doubts about that), or when the condition is actually coercive, in the sense of an offer that cannot be refused. (opinion of SCALIA, J.). Our precedents, however, are not so limited. In the present context, the relevant distinction that has emerged from our cases is between conditions that define the limits of the government spending program — those that specify the activities Congress wants to subsidize — and conditions that seek to leverage funding to regulate speech outside the contours of the program itself. The line is hardly clear, in part because the definition of a particular program can always be manipulated to subsume the challenged condition. We have held, however, that "Congress cannot recast a condition on funding as a mere definition of its program in every case, lest the First Amendment be reduced to a simple semantic exercise."

A comparison of two cases helps illustrate the distinction: In *Regan v. Taxation With Representation of Washington*, the Court upheld a requirement that nonprofit organizations seeking tax-exempt status under 26 U.S.C. § 501(c)(3) not engage in substantial efforts to influence legislation. The tax-exempt status, we explained, "ha[d] much the same effect as a cash grant to the organization." And by limiting § 501(c)(3) status to organizations that did not attempt to influence legislation, Congress had merely "chose[n] not to subsidize lobbying." In rejecting the nonprofit's First Amendment claim, the Court highlighted — in the text of its opinion at the fact that the condition did not prohibit that organization from lobbying Congress altogether.

* * *

In *FCC v. League of Women Voters of California*, by contrast, the Court struck down a condition on federal financial assistance to noncommercial broadcast television and radio stations that prohibited all editorializing, including with private funds. (1984). Even a station receiving only one percent of its overall budget from the Federal Government, the Court explained, was "barred absolutely from all editorializing." Unlike the situation in *Regan*, the law provided no way for a station to limit its use of federal funds to noneditorializing activities, while using private funds "to make known its views on matters of public importance."

*   *   *

Our decision in *Rust v. Sullivan* elaborated on the approach reflected in *Regan and League of Women Voters*. In *Rust*, we considered Title X of the Public Health Service Act, a Spending Clause program that issued grants to nonprofit health-care organizations "to assist in the establishment and operation of voluntary family planning projects [to] offer a broad range of acceptable and effective family planning methods and services." The organizations received funds from a variety of sources other than the Federal Government for a variety of purposes. The Act, however, prohibited the Title X federal funds from being "used in programs where abortion is a method of family planning." To enforce this provision, HHS regulations barred Title X projects from advocating abortion as a method of family planning, and required grantees to ensure that their Title X projects were " 'physically and financially separate' " from their other projects that engaged in the prohibited activities.

*   *   *

The Court stressed that "Title X expressly distinguishes between a Title X *grantee* and a Title X *project*." The regulations governed only the scope of the grantee's Title X projects, leaving it "unfettered in its other activities." "The Title X *grantee* can continue to . . . engage in abortion advocacy; it simply is required to conduct those activities through programs that are separate and independent from the project that receives Title X funds." Because the regulations did not "prohibit[ ] the recipient from engaging in the protected conduct outside the scope of the federally funded program," they did not run afoul of the First Amendment.

B

As noted, the distinction drawn in these cases — between conditions that define the federal program and those that reach outside it — is not always self-evident. As Justice Cardozo put it in a related context, "Definition more precise must abide the wisdom of the future."

*   *   *

To begin, it is important to recall that the Leadership Act has two conditions relevant here. The first — unchallenged in this litigation — prohibits Leadership Act funds from being used "to promote or advocate the legalization or practice of prostitution or sex trafficking." The Government concedes that § 7631(e) by itself ensures that federal funds will not be used for the prohibited purposes.

The Policy Requirement therefore must be doing something more — and it is.

By demanding that funding recipients adopt — as their own — the Government's view on an issue of public concern, the condition by its very nature affects "protected conduct outside the scope of the federally funded program." A recipient cannot avow the belief dictated by the Policy Requirement when spending Leadership Act funds, and then turn around and assert a contrary belief, or claim neutrality, when participating in activities on its own time and dime. By requiring recipients to profess a specific belief, the Policy Requirement goes beyond defining the limits of the federally funded program to defining the recipient. ("our 'unconstitutional conditions' cases involve situations in which the Government has placed a condition on the *recipient* of the subsidy rather than on a particular program or service, thus effectively prohibiting the recipient from engaging in the protected conduct outside the scope of the federally funded program").

The Government contends that the affiliate guidelines, established while this litigation was pending, save the program. Under those guidelines, funding recipients are permitted to work with affiliated organizations that do not abide by the condition, as long as the recipients retain "objective integrity and independence" from the unfettered affiliates.

* * *

[This is not] sufficient. When we have noted the importance of affiliates in this context, it has been because they allow an organization bound by a funding condition to exercise its First Amendment rights outside the scope of the federal program. Affiliates cannot serve that purpose when the condition is that a funding recipient espouse a specific belief as its own. If the affiliate is distinct from the recipient, the arrangement does not afford a means for the *recipient* to express *its* beliefs. If the affiliate is more clearly identified with the recipient, the recipient can express those beliefs only at the price of evident hypocrisy.

* * *

The Government suggests that the Policy Requirement is necessary because, without it, the grant of federal funds could free a recipient's private funds "to be used to promote prostitution or sex trafficking." The Government offers no support for that assumption as a general matter, or any reason to believe it is true here. And if the Government's argument were correct, *League of Women Voters* would have come out differently, and much of the reasoning of *Regan* and *Rust* would have been beside the point.

The Government cites but one case to support that argument, *Holder v. Humanitarian Law Project*. That case concerned the quite different context of a ban on providing material support to terrorist organizations, where the record indicated that support for those organizations' nonviolent operations was funneled to support their violent activities.

Pressing its argument further, the Government contends that "if organizations awarded federal funds to implement Leadership Act programs could at the same time promote or affirmatively condone prostitution or sex trafficking, whether using public *or private funds*, it would undermine the government's program and confuse its message opposing prostitution and sex trafficking." But the Policy Requirement goes beyond preventing recipients from using private funds in a way that would undermine the federal program. It requires them to pledge allegiance to the

Government's policy of eradicating prostitution. As to that, we cannot improve upon what Justice Jackson wrote for the Court 70 years ago: "If there is any fixed star in our constitutional constellation, it is that no official, high or petty, can prescribe what shall be orthodox in politics, nationalism, religion, or other matters of opinion or force citizens to confess by word or act their faith therein."

* * *

The Policy Requirement compels as a condition of federal funding the affirmation of a belief that by its nature cannot be confined within the scope of the Government program. In so doing, it violates the First Amendment and cannot be sustained. The judgment of the Court of Appeals is affirmed.

It is so ordered.

KAGAN, J., took no part in the consideration or decision of this case.

JUSTICE SCALIA, with whom Justice THOMAS joins, dissenting.

* * *

The Constitution does not prohibit government spending that discriminates against, and injures, points of view to which the government is opposed; every government program which takes a position on a controversial issue does that. Anti-smoking programs injure cigar aficionados, programs encouraging sexual abstinence injure free-love advocates, etc. The constitutional prohibition at issue here is not a prohibition against discriminating against or injuring opposing points of view, but the First Amendment's prohibition against the coercing of speech. I am frankly dubious that a condition for eligibility to participate in a minor federal program such as this one runs afoul of that prohibition even when the condition is irrelevant to the goals of the program. Not every disadvantage is a coercion.

But that is not the issue before us here. Here the views that the Government demands an applicant forswear — or that the Government insists an applicant favor — are relevant to the program in question. The program is valid only if the Government is entitled to disfavor the opposing view (here, advocacy of or toleration of prostitution). And if the program can disfavor it, so can the selection of those who are to administer the program. There is no risk that this principle will enable the Government to discriminate arbitrarily against positions it disfavors. It would not, for example, permit the Government to exclude from bidding on defense contracts anyone who refuses to abjure prostitution. But here a central part of the Government's HIV/AIDS strategy is the suppression of prostitution, by which HIV is transmitted. It is entirely reasonable to admit to participation in the program only those who believe in that goal.

According to the Court, however, this transgresses a constitutional line between conditions that operate *inside* a spending program and those that control speech *outside* of it. I am at a loss to explain what this central pillar of the Court's opinion — this distinction that the Court itself admits is "hardly clear" and "not always self-evident" — has to do with the First Amendment. The distinction was alluded to, to be sure, in *Rust v. Sullivan* (1991), but not as (what the Court now makes it) an invariable requirement for First Amendment validity. That the pro-abortion speech prohibition was limited to "inside the program" speech was relevant in *Rust* because the program itself was not an anti-abortion program. The Government remained neutral on that controversial issue, but did not wish abortion to be promoted within its family-planning-services program. The statutory objective could not be impaired, in other words, by "outside the program" pro-abortion speech. The purpose of the limitation was to prevent Government funding from providing the *means* of pro-abortion propaganda, which the Government did not wish (and had no constitutional obligation) to provide. The situation here is vastly different. Elimination of prostitution is an objective of the HIV/AIDS program, and any promotion of prostitution — whether made inside or outside the program — *does* harm the program.

Of course the most obvious manner in which the admission to a program of an ideological opponent can frustrate the purpose of the program is by freeing up the opponent's funds for use in its ideological opposition. To use the Hamas example again: Subsidizing that organization's provision of social services enables the money that it would otherwise use for that purpose to be used, instead, for anti-American propaganda. Perhaps that problem does not exist in this case since the respondents do not affirmatively promote prostitution. But the Court's analysis categorically rejects that justification for ideological requirements in *all* cases, demanding "record indica[tion]" that "federal funding will simply supplant private funding, rather than pay for new programs." This seems to me quite naive. Money is fungible. The economic reality is that when NGOs can conduct their AIDS work on the Government's dime, they can expend greater resources on policies that undercut the Leadership Act. The Government need not establish by record evidence that this will happen. To make it a valid consideration in determining participation in federal programs, it suffices that this is a real and obvious risk.

*   *   *

The Court makes a head-fake at the unconstitutional conditions doctrine, but that doctrine is of no help. There is no case of ours in which a condition that is relevant to a statute's valid purpose and that is not in itself unconstitutional (*e.g.*, a religious-affiliation condition that violates the Establishment Clause) has been held to violate the doctrine. Moreover, as I suggested earlier, the contention that the condition here "coerces" respondents' speech is on its face implausible.

*   *   *

The majority cannot credibly say that this speech condition is coercive, so it does not. It pussyfoots around the lack of coercion by invalidating the Leadership Act for "*requiring* recipients to profess a specific belief" and "*demanding* that funding recipients adopt — as their own — the Government's view on an issue of public concern." (emphasis mine). But like King Cnut's commanding of the tides, here the Government's "requiring" and "demanding" have no coercive effect. In the end, and in the circumstances of this case, "compell[ing] *as a condition* of federal funding the affirmation of a belief," (emphasis mine), is no compulsion at all. It is the reasonable price of admission to a limited government-spending program that each organization remains free to accept or reject.

* * *

Ideological-commitment requirements such as the one here are quite rare; but making the choice between competing applicants on relevant ideological grounds is undoubtedly quite common. As far as the Constitution is concerned, it is quite impossible to distinguish between the two. If the government cannot demand a relevant ideological commitment as a condition of application, neither can it distinguish between applicants on a relevant ideological ground. And that is the real evil of today's opinion. One can expect, in the future, frequent challenges to the denial of government funding for relevant ideological reasons.

The Court's opinion contains stirring quotations. They serve only to distract attention from the elephant in the room: that the Government is not forcing *anyone* to say *anything*. What Congress has done here — requiring an ideological commitment relevant to the Government task at hand — is approved by the Constitution itself. Americans need not support the Constitution; they may be Communists or anarchists. But "[t]he Senators and Representatives . . . , and the Members of the several State Legislatures, and all executive and judicial Officers, both of the United States and of the several States, shall be bound by Oath or Affirmation, to support [the] Constitution." The Framers saw the wisdom of imposing affirmative ideological commitments prerequisite to assisting in the government's work. And so should we.

NOTES AND QUESTIONS

1. As discussed in the principal case, the Court, *Rust v. Sullivan* (1991) agreed in *dictum* that it would be unconstitutional for the government to condition a benefit or subsidy on a recipient's foregoing the exercise of a constitutional right — in *dictum*, because the Court in *Rust* found no such unconstitutional condition in the *Rust* case. With the possible exception of matters involving race, there is no more important social issue which divides Americans than does the question of abortion. How could the government silence anyone, even government employees, from expressing their point of view on this fundamentally important political question? Why is it that government grantees, under these circumstances, had, in effect, to surrender some of their First Amendment rights? The dissenters in *Rust* believed this was unconstitutional, but as the majority saw it that would have precluded the government from having a policy point of view entirely. Suppose you were a publisher hired to print the Federal Register (the official compendium of agency regulations). Could you claim that you had a First Amendment right to supply your own editorial commentary on some of the agency regulations? Is *Rust v. Sullivan* the same case?

2. Is it constitutionally permissible to require "family planning" clinics who accept federal funds to inform women who come to them seeking help obtaining an abortion that "We do not consider abortion an appropriate method of family planning"? This was one of the requirements which Congress, through the regulations issued from HHS, sought to impose on the acceptance of federal funds. Do you agree or disagree with the proposition that this raises First Amendment

problems? Is it the furtherance of government policy or a troubling interference with a protected constitutional right? Do you suppose that the federal officials who imposed the regulation referred to in the case were committed to the enforcement of a constitutionally-protected freedom to secure an abortion? Should this make a difference in the Court's treatment of the rule? One of the first acts of the Clinton administration was to lift the "gag rule" at issue in this case by directing that his Department of Health and Human Services simply not comply with the existing regulations. Was this lawful?

3.   The "unconstitutional condition" issue has re-surfaced in the implementation of a statutory provision requiring the National Endowment for the Arts (NEA) which instructs the NEA Chairperson to ensure that "artistic excellence and artistic merit are the criteria by which applications are judged, taking into consideration general standards of decency and respect for the diverse beliefs and values of the American public." 20 U.S.C. § 954(d). Is this constitutional? The issue came before the Court again in *NEA v. Finley*, decided in 1998. In defending this statute, the government argued that the Court's decisions precluding content and viewpoint discrimination are largely inapposite to a funding program that selectively subsidizes expressive conduct. For this proposition, President Clinton's Solicitor General relied heavily on the Court's decision in *Rust v. Sullivan*. The Solicitor General expansively quotes *Rust* for the proposition that "[t]he Government can, without violating the Constitution, selectively fund a program to encourage certain activities it believes to be in the public interest, without at the same time funding an alternative program. . . . In doing so, the Government has not discriminated on the basis of viewpoint; it has merely chosen to fund one activity to the exclusion of the other." 500 U.S. at 193. The Court held that the government has this funding latitude. There is a fundamental difference between government as patron and government as sovereign.

4.   In *Legal Services Corp. v. Velazquez*, 531 U.S. 533 (2001), the Court struck down a provision of the Legal Services Corporation Act that prevented LSC attorneys from using government funds for representations that involve efforts to amend or challenge the constitutionality of existing welfare law. The Court thought the program more like the limited public forum established by the University of Virginia, restrictions on which were struck down in *Rosenberger*: "Although the LSC program differs from the program at issue in *Rosenberger* in that its purpose is not to 'encourage a diversity of views,' the salient point is that, like the program in *Rosenberger*, the LSC program was designed to facilitate private speech, not to promote a governmental message."

> The LSC Act, like the scheme in *Rust*, does not create a public forum. Far from encouraging a diversity of views, it has always, as the Court accurately states, "placed restrictions on its use of funds." Nor does [the Act] discriminate on the basis of viewpoint, since it funds neither challenges to nor defenses of existing welfare law. The provision simply declines to subsidize a certain class of litigation, and under *Rust* that decision "does not infringe the right" to bring such litigation. . . . No litigant who, in the absence of LSC funding, would bring a suit challenging existing welfare law is deterred from doing so. *Rust* thus controls these cases and compels the conclusion that [it] is constitutional.

The Court contends that *Rust* is different because the program at issue subsidized government speech, while the LSC funds private speech. This is so unpersuasive it hardly needs response. If the private doctors' confidential advice to their patients at issue in *Rust* constituted "government speech," it is hard to imagine what subsidized speech would *not* be government speech. Moreover, the majority's contention that the subsidized speech in these cases is not government speech because the lawyers have a professional obligation to represent the interests of their clients founders on the reality that the doctors in *Rust* had a professional obligation to serve the interests of their patients. . . .

531 U.S. at 553–554. Who has the better argument here? Has the Court just created a special privilege for lawyers?

5. In *Pleasant Grove v. Summum*, 555 U.S. 460 (2009), Justice Alito wrote for a unanimous Court finding that Pleasant Grove could refuse acceptance of a religious monument for the City's park even as the park already included a Ten Commandments monument and close to a dozen others. The offerors of the monument of the "Seven Aphorisms" (teachings of the Gnostic Christian Church) argued that the park was a public forum in which the City had to accept all comers, subject only to content-neutral time, place and manner limits. Justice Alito did not deny that the Park was a public forum, but thought that forum analysis did not apply since "the placement of a permanent monument in a public park is best viewed as a form of government speech."

So did the City even have to explain its refusal? It's not clear, but it did, saying the other monuments — most of which were also privately donated — related to the City's history or organizations that had longstanding ties to the community. These justifications received virtually no attention because, said Justice Alito, when the government is "engaging in its own expressive conduct, then the Free Speech Clause has no application." The government spoke here by dictating the terms of acceptance of monuments.

But if that's the case, isn't there an Establishment Clause problem accepting one religious monument, but not another? No, said the Court, because the fact that a monument is seen as religious by a particular viewer does not suggest that this is the meaning the government wants to convey. Said the Justice, a city with an art museum doesn't necessarily agree with the artist. Well, all right, but isn't the museum then better understood as a public forum? If nebulous government expression frees the government from observing the many carefully constructed categories of protected speech, just about any claim of the government speaking would seem to prove way too much, would it not? In particular, what does the Court's explanation do to the endorsement test for religious displays?

Justices Stevens and Ginsburg concurred in the Court's opinion, calling it "persuasive," but they showed hesitation expanding the government speech doctrine, which they described as of "doubtful merit." Distinguishing *Rust*, these Justices wrote that this case did not implicate an expansion of the government speech doctrine, which they said was limited by the Establishment Clause and, somewhat cryptically, the Equal Protection Clause as well.

Justices Scalia and Thomas also concurred in the Alito opinion, but wrote separately to suggest the Establishment Clause hurdle could be surmounted, pointing out the *Van Orden* case allowing government speech in favor of the Ten Commandments, for reasons of history or secular message (prevention of delinquency).

Justice Breyer wrote separately to express the view that government speech doctrine is to be understood as a flexible rule of thumb that inquires into the purpose of free speech in the setting. He envisions a balancing test measuring the burden on speech against the government's interest. In this particular case, Justice Breyer's pragmatic balance favored the government, since too many monumental things in a park spoil its recreational purpose.

Justice Souter concurred only in the judgment, noting that the Court's analysis just papered over the Establishment Clause problems, which for him include improper endorsement or favoritism. Souter would call upon the reasonable objective observer to know where the limit may ultimately be to government speech immunity from the First Amendment.

6. In *United States Department of Agriculture v. United Foods, Inc.*, 533 U.S. 405 (2001), the Court may have fashioned another indirect limitation on government speech — or at least that aspect of government speech sought to be financed out of compelled assessments. In *United Foods*, the Court struck down a federal assessment for generic mushroom advertising. The Court divided over whether the issue should be analyzed under free speech doctrine, as a commercial speech question, or as garden-variety economic regulation. 6-3 the Court found the assessment to be contrary to First Amendment free speech protection that prevents government from compelling individuals to pay subsidies for speech to which they object. The respondents wanted to convey the message that branded mushrooms were superior to those grown by others and they objected to the generic advertising which contained the contrary message.

Just as the First Amendment may prevent the government from prohibiting speech, the Amendment may prevent the government from compelling individuals to express certain views, *see Wooley v. Maynard* (1977); *West Virginia Bd. of Ed. v. Barnette* (1943), or from compelling certain individuals to pay subsidies for speech to which they object. *See Abood v. Detroit Bd. of Ed.* (1977); *Keller v. State Bar of Cal.* (1990). A precedential problem for the Court, however, was that just a few years earlier, the Justices had sustained a compelled advertising initiative as part of a "marketing order" scheme in *Glickman v. Wileman Brothers & Elliott, Inc.* (1997) relating to California fruit trees. The Court attempted to differentiate *Glickman* by arguing that the mandated assessments there were ancillary to a more comprehensive regulatory program, which displaced competition to such an extent that marketing practices in the industry were exempt from the antitrust laws. By contrast, beyond the collection and disbursement of advertising funds in *United Foods*, there were no marketing orders that regulate how mushrooms may be produced and sold, no exemption from the antitrust laws, and nothing preventing individual producers from making their own marketing decisions. Justice Kennedy for the majority recognized that the law sometimes does permit compelled association (e.g., labor unions, bar associations), but such compelled association to advance legitimate purposes does not support compelled speech where there is a conflict of belief. Hence, we may have to be members of the state bar, but we do not have to contribute to the political activities of the bar that are not germane to its professional mission. *Keller v. State Bar of Cal.* (1990). So too, said the Court, a compelled subsidy for speech cannot be allowed where the context or bulk of the program is the speech, itself. The majority noted that the government did not fully argue whether its regulation could be sustained either under *Central Hudson*, as a commercial speech regulation substantially advancing a particular governmental interest, or as government speech, *see Rust*, so the Court did not address either.

Justices Breyer, Ginsburg and O'Connor dissented in *United Foods*, arguing that speech was not implicated in this matter of economic regulation because first, money isn't speech, and only money is required to be paid; second, the speech promoted advances the truthfulness of commercial transaction and hence is consistent with *Central Hudson*; and third, there is no special threat to freedom of belief or expression. Lamented the dissent: "The Court, in applying stricter First Amendment standards and finding them violated, sets an unfortunate precedent. That precedent suggests, perhaps requires, striking down any similar program that, for example, would require tobacco companies to contribute to an industry fund for advertising the harms of smoking or would use a portion of museum entry charges for a citywide campaign to promote the value of art." Are the dissenters correct? What's so bad about construing the First Amendment to prevent coerced assessments to finance government speech against the interests of those required to pay the assessments? Does the majority's rationale threaten to undermine the whole idea of government speech, itself, insofar as someone is always compelled to pay for it unwillingly?

The Court elaborated on the relationship between government speech and compelled assessments in *Johanns v. Livestock Marketing Association*, 544 U.S. 550 (2005). In *Livestock Marketing*, the issue was the constitutionality of the Beef Promotion and Research Act of 1985, which required beef producers to pay an assessment or check-off on all sales and importation of cattle. The check-off supported beef products generally and some of those subject to the assessment wanted to promote the superiority of grain-fed beef. The objecting producers sued claiming the beef act to be indistinguishable from that of *United Foods*, and that therefore they were being compelled to support messages contrary to the First Amendment. 6-3, the Supreme Court did not see it that way. Specifically, five Justices joined Justice Scalia's opinion which found the beef assessments to be protected government speech. The Court distinguished *United Foods*, and other cases, as the compelled subsidization of speech other than by the government itself. The government cannot compel speech or the subsidy of the speech of another, but no citizen can object to subsidizing the speech of the government, whether the subsidy is derived from general taxes or a special assessment as in *Livestock Marketing*. There were several concurring opinions accepting of this rationale. Justice Ginsburg also concurred, but on the grounds that the assessments are permissible economic regulation.

7. The Court first invalidated an outright compulsion of speech in *West Virginia Bd. of Ed. v. Barnette*, 319 U.S. 624 (1943). The state required every schoolchild to recite the Pledge of Allegiance while saluting the American flag, on pain of expulsion

from the public schools. The Court held that the First Amendment does not "le[ave] it open to public authorities to compel [a person] to utter" a message with which he does not agree. Likewise, in *Wooley v. Maynard*, 430 U.S. 705 (1977), the Court held that requiring a New Hampshire couple to bear the state's motto, "Live Free or Die," on their cars' license plates was an impermissible compulsion of expression. Obliging people to "use their private property as a 'mobile billboard' for the State's ideological message" amounted to impermissible compelled expression.

The principle of no compelled speech carried over to no compelled subsidization of private speech. Thus, while lawyers can be compelled to be members of the state bar and pay its annual dues and public-school teachers forced to join the labor union representing their "shop" or pay "service fees" equal to the union dues, the Court invalidated the use of the compulsory fees to fund speech on political matters. *See Keller v. State Bar of Cal.*, 496 U.S. 1 (1990); *Abood v. Detroit Bd. of Ed.*, 431 U.S. 209 (1977). These cases led directly to the invalidation of a compelled subsidy for advertising in *United Foods*, except where that advertising requirement was part of a larger program of economic regulation. *Glickman v. Wileman Brothers & Elliott, Inc.*, 521 U.S. 457 (1997) (which upheld the use of mandatory assessments to fund generic advertising promoting California tree fruit). The compelled support for generic advertising was held to be legitimately part of the Government's "collectivist" centralization of the market for tree fruit. In *Livestock Marketing*, there was no broader regulatory system in place, so absent the finding of government speech, the assessment under *United Foods* would have been invalid.

In reaching its holding, the Court found the speech attributable to the government, since the ads funded by the assessment originated with a board that was appointed in part by the Secretary of Agriculture, and in any event, the Secretary approved the final copy. The fact that the government received outside advice on marketing did not matter.

The principal dissent in *Livestock Marketing*, written by Justice Souter for Justices Stevens and Kennedy, argued that the government did not specifically identify the speech as its own, and therefore, it should not be entitled to be treated as government speech. While admitting that the "government has to say something," it has to say it clearly as its own in order for the democratic process to render the subsidization of government speech as tolerable. This is especially true, said the dissent, where a special assessment is employed. "If the judiciary is justified in keeping hands off special assessments on dissenters from government speech, it is because there is a practical opportunity for political response; esoteric knowledge on the part of a few will not do," said the dissent. Here, few taxpayers would realize it was the government, and not the objecting cattlemen themselves, who were behind the beef ads. The majority answered the dissent by pointing out that this was a facial challenge and nothing in the beef act required attribution to others than the government. The majority left open the door for an as-applied challenge that individual beef ads might be attributable to the objecting ranchers.

This much is plain, however: "Citizens may challenge compelled support of private speech, but have no First Amendment right not to fund government speech. And that is no less true when the funding is achieved through targeted assessments devoted exclusively to the program to which the assessed citizens object."

As noted above, a public-sector union can compel payment of a fee to further its union collective bargaining purpose, but not its political perspectives. With respect to the latter, *Abood* [and a later case *Chicago Teachers Union v. Hudson*, 475 U.S. 292 (1986)], establishes that those nonmembers required to pay agency shop fees for the collective bargaining efforts of a public union be given an opportunity to opt out of paying for the political speech portion of any union assessment. But what if a state enacts a law that requires a union to obtain the affirmative approval of its nonmembers — that is, to opt in? Does this pre-approval requirement unduly burden the speech or associational rights of the union?

In *Davenport v. Washington Education Association*, 551 U.S. 177(2007), Washington state voters approved an initiative which provided in part that union agency shop fees were not permitted to be used for political contributions unless the nonmember had given consent — that is, had affirmatively opted in — for such compelled fees to be used for that purpose. The Washington Education Association continued to use only the opt-out *Hudson* procedure, and faced litigation as a result. The Washington Supreme Court sided with the union, finding the "opt-in" requirement to be too burdensome on the associational rights of the union. While the case was pending, the Washington statute was amended to narrow the circumstances where the opt-in applied, but the amendment did not moot the case.

A unanimous Court, in an opinion by Justice Scalia, held that the statute did not violate the First Amendment as applied to public-sector unions. Noting that although previous precedent had not mandated an opt-in system, the Court still thought it "undeniably unusual for a government agency to give a private entity the power, in essence, to tax government employees." Justice Scalia considered it "counterintuitive" that a "modest limitation" such as an opt-in could violate the First Amendment, when the state had the power to repeal its agency shop provisions altogether, leaving the union no compensation for beneficial services rendered to non-members. The Washington Supreme Court had misinterpreted the *Hudson* case as setting forth mandatory procedures, when in fact they were only a constitutional floor to protect non-members, and states were free to go further to that end. In addition, the state high court had "read far too much" into the warning that "dissent is not to be presumed," because that precedent had only meant that a court should not enjoin use of all nonmember agency fees when a narrower remedy could be afforded.

Before the Supreme Court, the Washington Education Association had shifted the emphasis off the undue burden of the opt-in on its associational rights to argue that the statute violated its free speech rights because it regulated money that was lawfully in its hands. In particular, the union asserted that the state was drawing a content distinction, requiring affirmative consent only for election-related expenditures while permitting non-election expenditures without consent, subject only to the opt-out. In a portion of the opinion joined by six Justices (Justice Breyer, joined by Chief Justice Roberts and Justice Alito found these arguments not to have been sufficiently raised below and would not have reached them), Justice Scalia challenged the notion that this was a content limitation on union money. "What matters is that public-sector agency fees are in the union's possession only because Washington and its union-contracting government agencies have compelled their employees to pay those fees." Therefore, the statute "is [not] fairly described as a restriction on how the union can spend 'its' money; it is a condition placed upon the union's extraordinary *state* entitlement to acquire and spend *other people's* money."

Because the money was not fairly characterized as the union's money, the question became whether the statute was akin to an unconstitutional condition. The Court thought it was not. Assuming there was "no realistic possibility that official suppression of ideas is afoot," Justice Scalia said the apt analogy was not the government as regulatory, but the government as the provider of a subsidy or a forum. Just as the government may make content-based distinctions when it subsidizes speech and it can also exclude some subject matters from a nonpublic forum, provided that the restriction is viewpoint-neutral and reasonably advances the purpose of that forum, the government could control the use of compelled, non-member fees here. This statute was not an unconstitutional condition because it was "a reasonable, viewpoint-neutral limitation on the State's general authoriza- tion allowing public-sector unions to acquire and spend the money of government employees." The government's specific concern was with the integrity of the election process; in particular, the infusion into politics of non-member agency fees without the consent of the non-member.

8.   In *Chicago Teachers Union v. Hudson*, 475 U.S. 292 (1986), the Court identified procedural requirements that a public-sector union must meet in order to collect so-called "chargeable expenses" fees from nonmembers without violating their constitutional rights. *Chargeable expenses* are the union's monetary outlay for its collective-bargaining activity and they exclude outlay to be used for political, ideological, and other purposes not germane to collective bargaining. The Court in *Hudson* made it clear that procedures for collecting fees from nonmembers must be carefully tailored to minimize impingement on First Amendment rights. 475 U.S. 302–303. Indeed the Court's *Hudson* ruling has spawned a term of art known as "*Hudson* notice," a notification requirement whereby a public-sector union must give employees certain information about projected union expenditures, including its estimate of the percentage of its total expenditures in the coming year would be dedicated to chargeable collective-bargaining activities.

In *Knox v. SEIU*, 132 S. Ct. 2277, 183 L. Ed. 2d 281 (2012), the Court dealt with a California public-sector union's effort to comply with the *Hudson* notice require- ment. The Service Employees International Union, Local 1000 (SEIU), had sent out its regular annual *Hudson* notice informing employees what the agency fee would be for the year ahead. The notice. *Inter alia*, listed the monthly fee that employees would be expected to pay for the chargeable expenses, gave the employees 30 days in which to file any First Amendment objections to the listed union expenditures, and stated that the fee was subject to increase at any time without further notice. After the 30-day objection period had lapsed, the SEIU informed the employees that there would be a temporary 25% increase in monthly fees, justifying the increase as an "Emergency Temporary Assessment to Build a Political Fight-Back Fund" to be used "for a broad range of political expenses, including television and radio advertising, direct mail, voter registration, voter education, and get out the vote activities in our work sites and in our communities across California." Employees filed a class action on behalf of 28,000 nonunion employees who were forced to contribute money to the Political Fight-Back Fund. The Court struck down the increase, ruling that, under the First Amendment, "when a public-sector union imposes a special assessment or dues increase, the union must provide a fresh *Hudson* notice and may not exact any funds from nonmembers without their affirmative consent."

9.　Which brings us back to *Agency for International Development v. Alliance for Open Society International, Inc.*, 133 S. Ct. 2321; 186 L. Ed. 2d 398 (2013). Recall that the Act under review imposed two related conditions in its funding programs: First, no funds granted under the Leadership Act "may be used to promote or advocate the legalization or practice of prostitution or sex trafficking." And second, no funds may be utilized by an organization "that does not have a policy explicitly opposing prostitution and sex trafficking." The first condition, falling squarely within the *Rust* precedent, presented no problem. The second condition (referred to in the Court's opinion as the "Policy Requirement"), however, mandated that funding recipients "have a policy explicitly opposing prostitution and sex trafficking" — a policy that would obviously operate in all the operations of the recipient, not just those specifically within the program covered by the funding grant. The Court held that the second condition's Policy Requirement violated the First Amendment by compelling, as a condition of federal funding, the affirmation of "a belief that by its nature cannot be confined within the scope of the Government program." The Court summarized its rationale:

By demanding that funding recipients adopt — as their own — the Government's view on an issue of public concern, the condition by its very nature affects "protected conduct outside the scope of the federally funded program" [quoting from *Rust*]. A recipient cannot avow the belief dictated by the Policy Requirement when spending Leadership Act funds, and then turn around and assert a contrary belief, or claim neutrality, when participating in activities on its own time and dime. By requiring recipients to profess a specific belief, the Policy Requirement goes beyond defining the limits of the federally-funded program to defining the recipient. [Citing *Rust*:] ("our 'unconstitutional conditions' cases involve situations in which the Government has placed a condition on the *recipient* of the subsidy rather than on a particular program or service, thus effectively prohibiting the recipient from engaging in the protected conduct outside the scope of the federally funded program"). Why does the dissent think that this limitation is too constraining on the government? Individual Americans not using the government's dime can believe anything and say anything, writes the dissent, but when you take the government's money, receipt of that money can be hinged on the recipient holding the ideology favored by the government. Is this right? While the protections may be narrowing, hasn't the Supreme Court held that even government employees don't lose all free speech rights in the government workplace, itself? (See the *Garcetti* case, *infra*, in the next section. Why then is that acknowledgement of freedom not accorded to the grant recipients in *Agency for International Development*?

b. Public Employee Speech

GARCETTI v. CEBALLOS
547 U.S. 410 (2006)

JUSTICE KENNEDY delivered the opinion of the Court.

It is well settled that "a State cannot condition public employment on a basis that infringes the employee's constitutionally protected interest in freedom of expression." *Connick v. Myers* (1983). The question presented by the instant case is whether the First Amendment protects a government employee from discipline based on speech made pursuant to the employee's official duties.

I

Respondent Richard Ceballos has been employed since 1989 as a deputy district attorney for the Los Angeles County District Attorney's Office. During the period relevant to this case, Ceballos was a calendar deputy in the office's Pomona branch, and in this capacity he exercised certain supervisory responsibilities over other lawyers. In February 2000, a defense attorney contacted Ceballos about a pending criminal case. The defense attorney said there were inaccuracies in an affidavit used to obtain a critical search warrant. The attorney informed Ceballos that he had filed a motion to traverse, or challenge, the warrant, but he also wanted Ceballos to review the case. According to Ceballos, it was not unusual for defense attorneys to ask calendar deputies to investigate aspects of pending cases.

After examining the affidavit and visiting the location it described, Ceballos determined the affidavit contained serious misrepresentations. The affidavit called a long driveway what Ceballos thought should have been referred to as a separate roadway. Ceballos also questioned the affidavit's statement that tire tracks led from a stripped-down truck to the premises covered by the warrant. His doubts arose from his conclusion that the roadway's composition in some places made it difficult or impossible to leave visible tire tracks. . . .

Based on Ceballos' statements, a meeting was held to discuss the affidavit. Attendees included Ceballos, [and his supervisors] Sundstedt and Najera, as well as the warrant affiant and other employees from the sheriff's department. The meeting allegedly became heated, with one lieutenant sharply criticizing Ceballos for his handling of the case.

Despite Ceballos' concerns, Sundstedt decided to proceed with the prosecution, pending disposition of the defense motion to traverse. The trial court held a hearing on the motion. Ceballos was called by the defense and recounted his observations about the affidavit, but the trial court rejected the challenge to the warrant.

Ceballos claims that in the aftermath of these events he was subjected to a series of retaliatory employment actions. The actions included reassignment from his calendar deputy position to a trial deputy position, transfer to another courthouse, and denial of a promotion. Ceballos initiated an employment grievance, but the grievance was denied based on a finding that he had not suffered any retaliation.

Unsatisfied, Ceballos sued in the United States District Court for the Central District of California, asserting, as relevant here, a claim under 42 U.S.C. § 1983. He alleged petitioners violated the First and Fourteenth Amendments by retaliating against him based on his memo of March 2. . . . Noting that Ceballos wrote his memo pursuant to his employment duties, the [district] court concluded he was not entitled to First Amendment protection for the memo's contents. . . . The Court of Appeals for the Ninth Circuit reversed.

We granted *certiorari*, and we now reverse.

II

The First Amendment protects a public employee's right, in certain circumstances, to speak as a citizen addressing matters of public concern. See, *e.g.*, *Pickering; Connick; Rankin v. McPherson* (1987); *United States v. Treasury Employees* (1995).

Pickering provides a useful starting point in explaining the Court's doctrine. There the relevant speech was a teacher's letter to a local newspaper addressing issues including the funding policies of his school board. "The problem in any case," the Court stated, "is to arrive at a balance between the interests of the teacher, as a citizen, in commenting upon matters of public concern and the interest of the State, as an employer, in promoting the efficiency of the public services it performs through its employees." The Court found the teacher's speech "neither [was] shown nor can be presumed to have in any way either impeded the teacher's proper performance of his daily duties in the classroom or to have interfered with the regular operation of the schools generally." Thus, the Court concluded that "the interest of the school administration in limiting teachers' opportunities to contribute to public debate is not significantly greater than its interest in limiting a similar contribution by any member of the general public."

Pickering and the cases decided in its wake identify two inquiries to guide interpretation of the constitutional protections accorded to public employee speech. The first requires determining whether the employee spoke as a citizen on a matter of public concern. If the answer is no, the employee has no First Amendment cause of action based on his or her employer's reaction to the speech. If the answer is yes, then the possibility of a First Amendment claim arises. The question becomes whether the relevant government entity had an adequate justification for treating the employee differently from any other member of the general public. This consideration reflects the importance of the relationship between the speaker's expressions and employment. A government entity has broader discretion to restrict speech when it acts in its role as employer, but the restrictions it imposes must be directed at speech that has some potential to affect the entity's operations.

To be sure, conducting these inquiries sometimes has proved difficult. . . . When a citizen enters government service, the citizen by necessity must accept certain limitations on his or her freedom. See, *e.g.*, *Waters v. Churchill* (1994) (plurality opinion) ("[T]he government as employer indeed has far broader powers than does the government as sovereign"). Government employers, like private employers, need a significant degree of control over their employees' words and actions; without it, there would be little chance for the efficient provision of public services. Cf. *Connick* ("[G]overnment offices could not function if every employment decision became a constitutional matter"). Public employees, moreover, often occupy trusted positions in society. When they speak out, they can express views that contravene governmental policies or impair the proper performance of governmental functions.

At the same time, the Court has recognized that a citizen who works for the government is nonetheless a citizen. The First Amendment limits the ability of a public employer to leverage the employment relationship to restrict, incidentally or intentionally, the liberties employees enjoy in their capacities as private citizens. See *Perry v. Sindermann* (1972). So long as employees are speaking as citizens about matters of public concern, they must face only those speech restrictions that are necessary for their employers to operate efficiently and effectively.

The Court's employee-speech jurisprudence protects, of course, the constitutional rights of public employees. Yet the First Amendment interests at stake extend beyond the individual speaker. . . . "The interest at stake is as much the public's interest in receiving informed opinion as it is the employee's own right to disseminate it."

The Court's decisions, then, have sought both to promote the individual and societal interests that are served when employees speak as citizens on matters of public concern and to respect the needs of government employers attempting to perform their important public functions. Underlying our cases has been the premise that while the First Amendment invests public employees with certain rights, it does not empower them to "constitutionalize the employee grievance." *Connick.*

III

With these principles in mind we turn to the instant case. Respondent Ceballos believed the affidavit used to obtain a search warrant contained serious misrepresentations. He conveyed his opinion and recommendation in a memo to his supervisor. That Ceballos expressed his views inside his office, rather than publicly, is not dispositive. Employees in some cases may receive First Amendment protection for expressions made at work. See, *e.g.*, *Givhan v. Western Line Consol. School Dist.* (1979). Many citizens do much of their talking inside their respective workplaces, and it would not serve the goal of treating public employees like "any member of the general public," to hold that all speech within the office is automatically exposed to restriction.

The memo concerned the subject matter of Ceballos' employment, but this, too, is nondispositive. The First Amendment protects some expressions related to the speaker's job. As the Court noted in *Pickering*: "Teachers are, as a class, the members of a community most likely to have informed and definite opinions as to how funds allotted to the operation of the schools should be spent. Accordingly, it is essential that they be able to speak out freely on such questions without fear of retaliatory dismissal." The same is true of many other categories of public employees.

The controlling factor in Ceballos' case is that his expressions were made pursuant to his duties as a calendar deputy. ("Ceballos does not dispute that he prepared the memorandum 'pursuant to his duties as a prosecutor' "). That consideration — the fact that Ceballos spoke as a prosecutor fulfilling a responsibility to advise his supervisor about how best to proceed with a pending case — distinguishes Ceballos' case from those in which the First Amendment provides protection against discipline. We hold that when public employees make statements pursuant to their official duties, the employees are not speaking as citizens for First Amendment purposes, and the Constitution does not insulate their communications from employer discipline. . . . Restricting speech that owes its existence to a public employee's professional responsibilities does not infringe any liberties the employee might have enjoyed as a private citizen. It simply reflects the exercise of employer control over what the employer itself has commissioned or created. *Cf. Rosenberger v. Rector and Visitors of Univ. of Va.* (1995) ("[W]hen the government appropriates public funds to promote a particular policy of its own it is entitled to say what it wishes"). Contrast, for example, the expressions made by the speaker in *Pickering*, whose letter to the newspaper had no official significance and bore similarities to letters submitted by numerous citizens every day.

Ceballos did not act as a citizen when he went about conducting his daily professional activities, such as supervising attorneys, investigating charges, and preparing filings. In the same way he did not speak as a citizen by writing a memo that addressed the proper disposition of a pending criminal case. When he went to work and performed the tasks he was paid to perform, Ceballos acted as a government employee. The fact that his duties sometimes required him to speak or write does not mean his supervisors were prohibited from evaluating his performance.

This result is consistent with our precedents' attention to the potential societal value of employee speech. Refusing to recognize First Amendment claims based on government employees' work product does not prevent them from participating in public debate. The employees retain the prospect of constitutional protection for their contributions to the civic discourse. This prospect of protection, however, does not invest them with a right to perform their jobs however they see fit.

Our holding likewise is supported by the emphasis of our precedents on affording government employers sufficient discretion to manage their operations. Employers have heightened interests in controlling speech made by an employee in his or her professional capacity. Official communications have official consequences, creating a need for substantive consistency and clarity. Supervisors must ensure that their employees' official communications are accurate, demonstrate sound judgment, and promote the employer's mission. Ceballos' memo is illustrative. It demanded the attention of his supervisors and led to a heated meeting with employees from the sheriff's department. If Ceballos' superiors thought his memo was inflammatory or misguided, they had the authority to take proper corrective action.

Ceballos' proposed contrary rule, adopted by the Court of Appeals, would commit state and federal courts to a new, permanent, and intrusive role, mandating judicial oversight of communications between and among government employees and their superiors in the course of official business. This displacement of managerial discretion by judicial supervision finds no support in our precedents. . . . To hold otherwise would be to demand permanent judicial intervention in the conduct of governmental operations to a degree inconsistent with sound principles of federalism and the separation of powers.

The Court of Appeals based its holding in part on what it perceived as a doctrinal anomaly. The court suggested it would be inconsistent to compel public employers to tolerate certain employee speech made publicly but not speech made pursuant to an employee's assigned duties. This objection misconceives the theoretical underpinnings of our decisions. Employees who make public statements outside the course of performing their official duties retain some possibility of First Amendment protection because that is the kind of activity engaged in by citizens who do not work for the government. The same goes for writing a letter to a local newspaper, see *Pickering*, or discussing politics with a co-worker, see *Rankin*. When a public employee speaks pursuant to employment responsibilities, however, there is no relevant analogue to speech by citizens who are not government employees.

The Court of Appeals' concern also is unfounded as a practical matter. The perceived anomaly, it should be noted, is limited in scope: It relates only to the expressions an employee makes pursuant to his or her official responsibilities, not to statements or complaints (such as those at issue in cases like *Pickering* and *Connick*) that are made outside the duties of employment. If, moreover, a government employer is troubled by the perceived anomaly, it has the means at hand to avoid it. A public employer that wishes to encourage its employees to voice concerns privately retains the option of instituting internal policies and procedures that are receptive to employee criticism. Giving employees an internal forum for their speech will discourage them from concluding that the safest avenue of expression is to state their views in public.

Proper application of our precedents thus leads to the conclusion that the First Amendment does not prohibit managerial discipline based on an employee's expressions made pursuant to official responsibilities. Because Ceballos' memo falls into this category, his allegation of unconstitutional retaliation must fail.

IV

Exposing governmental inefficiency and misconduct is a matter of considerable significance. As the Court noted in *Connick*, public employers should, "as a matter of good judgment," be "receptive to constructive criticism offered by their employees." The dictates of sound judgment are reinforced by the powerful network of legislative enactments — such as whistle-blower protection laws and labor codes — available to those who seek to expose wrongdoing. Cases involving government attorneys implicate additional safeguards in the form of, for example, rules of conduct and constitutional obligations apart from the First Amendment. ("A member in government service shall not institute or cause to be instituted criminal charges when the member knows or should know that the charges are not supported by probable cause"); *Brady v. Maryland* (1963). These imperatives, as well as obligations arising from any other applicable constitutional provisions and mandates of the criminal and civil laws, protect employees and provide checks on supervisors who would order unlawful or otherwise inappropriate actions.

We reject, however, the notion that the First Amendment shields from discipline the expressions employees make pursuant to their professional duties. Our precedents do not support the existence of a constitutional cause of action behind every statement a public employee makes in the course of doing his or her job.

The judgment of the Court of Appeals is reversed, and the case is remanded for proceedings consistent with this opinion.

It is so ordered.

JUSTICE STEVENS, dissenting.

The proper answer to the question "whether the First Amendment protects a government employee from discipline based on speech made pursuant to the employee's official duties," is "Sometimes," not "Never." Of course a supervisor may take corrective action when such speech is "inflammatory or misguided." But what if it is just unwelcome speech because it reveals facts that the supervisor would rather not have anyone else discover?

Public employees are still citizens while they are in the office. The notion that there is a categorical difference between speaking as a citizen and speaking in the course of one's employment is quite wrong. Over a quarter of a century has passed since then-Justice Rehnquist, writing for a unanimous Court, rejected "the conclusion that a public employee forfeits his protection against governmental abridgment of freedom of speech if he decides to express his views privately rather than publicly." *Givhan v. Western Line Consol. School Dist.* (1979). We had no difficulty recognizing that the First Amendment applied when Bessie Givhan, an English teacher, raised concerns about the school's racist employment practices to the principal. Our silence as to whether or not her speech was made pursuant to her job duties demonstrates that the point was immaterial. That is equally true today, for it is senseless to let constitutional protection for exactly the same words hinge on whether they fall within a job description. Moreover, it seems perverse to fashion a new rule that provides employees with an incentive to voice their concerns publicly before talking frankly to their superiors. . . .

JUSTICE SOUTER, with whom JUSTICE STEVENS and JUSTICE GINSBURG join, dissenting.

The Court holds that "when public employees make statements pursuant to their official duties, the employees are not speaking as citizens for First Amendment purposes, and the Constitution does not insulate their communications from employer discipline." I respectfully dissent. I agree with the majority that a government employer has substantial interests in effectuating its chosen policy and objectives, and in demanding competence, honesty, and judgment from employees who speak for it in doing their work. But I would hold that private and public interests in addressing official wrongdoing and threats to health and safety can outweigh the government's stake in the efficient implementation of policy, and when they do public employees who speak on these matters in the course of their duties should be eligible to claim First Amendment protection.

I

*   *   *

The difference between a case like *Givhan* and this one is that the subject of Ceballos's speech fell within the scope of his job responsibilities, whereas choosing personnel was not what the teacher was hired to do. The effect of the majority's constitutional line between these two cases, then, is that a *Givhan* schoolteacher is protected when complaining to the principal about hiring policy, but a school personnel officer would not be if he protested that the principal disapproved of hiring minority job applicants. This is an odd place to draw a distinction, and while necessary judicial line-drawing sometimes looks arbitrary, any distinction obliges a court to justify its choice. Here, there is no adequate justification for the majority's line categorically denying *Pickering* protection to any speech uttered "pursuant to . . . official duties."

As all agree, the qualified speech protection embodied in *Pickering* balancing resolves the tension between individual and public interests in the speech, on the one hand, and the government's interest in operating efficiently without distraction or embarrassment by talkative or headline-grabbing employees. The need for a balance hardly disappears when an employee speaks on matters his job requires him to address; rather, it seems obvious that the individual and public value of such speech is no less, and may well be greater, when the employee speaks pursuant to his duties in addressing a subject he knows intimately for the very reason that it falls within his duties. . . .

Nothing accountable on the individual and public side of the *Pickering* balance changes when an employee speaks "pursuant" to public duties. On the side of the government employer, however, something is different, and to this extent, I agree with the majority of the Court. The majority is rightly concerned that the employee who speaks out on matters subject to comment in doing his own work has the greater leverage to create office uproars and fracture the government's authority to set policy to be carried out coherently through the ranks. "Official communications have official consequences, creating a need for substantive consistency and clarity. Supervisors must ensure that their employees' official communications are accurate, demonstrate sound judgment, and promote the employer's mission." Up to a point, then, the majority makes good points: government needs civility in the workplace, consistency in policy, and honesty and competence in public service.

But why do the majority's concerns, which we all share, require categorical exclusion of First Amendment protection against any official retaliation for things said on the job? Is it not possible to respect the unchallenged individual and public interests in the speech through a *Pickering* balance without drawing the strange line I mentioned before? . . .

The majority's position comes with no guarantee against fact-bound litigation over whether a public employee's statements were made "pursuant to . . . official duties." In fact, the majority invites such litigation by describing the enquiry as a "practical one," apparently based on the totality of employment circumstances. Are prosecutors' discretionary statements about cases addressed to the press on the courthouse steps made "pursuant to their official duties"? Are government nuclear scientists' complaints to their supervisors about a colleague's improper handling of radioactive materials made "pursuant" to duties?

II

The majority seeks support in two lines of argument extraneous to *Pickering* doctrine. The one turns on a fallacious reading of cases on government speech, the other on a mistaken assessment of protection available under whistle-blower statutes.

A

The majority accepts the fallacy propounded by the county petitioners and the Federal Government as *amicus* that any statement made within the scope of public employment is (or should be treated as) the government's own speech, and should thus be differentiated as a matter of law from the personal statements the First Amendment protects. The majority invokes the interpretation set out in *Rosenberger v. Rector and Visitors of Univ. of Va.* (1995), of *Rust v. Sullivan* (1991), which held there was no infringement of the speech rights of Title X funds recipients and their staffs when the Government forbade any on-the-job counseling in favor of abortion as a method of family planning. We have read *Rust* to mean that "when the government appropriates public funds to promote a particular policy of its own it is entitled to say what it wishes." *Rosenberger.*

The key to understanding the difference between this case and *Rust* lies in the terms of the respective employees' jobs and, in particular, the extent to which those terms require espousal of a substantive position prescribed by the government in advance. Some public employees are hired to "promote a particular policy" by broadcasting a particular message set by the government, but not everyone working for the government, after all, is hired to speak from a government manifesto. See *Legal Services Corporation v. Velazquez* (2001). There is no claim or indication that Ceballos was hired to perform such a speaking assignment. He was paid to enforce the law by constitutional action: to exercise the county government's prosecutorial power by acting honestly, competently, and constitutionally. The only sense in which his position apparently required him to hew to a substantive message was at the relatively abstract point of favoring respect for law and its evenhanded enforcement, subjects that are not at the level of controversy in this case and were not in *Rust.* Unlike the doctors in *Rust*, Ceballos was not paid to advance one specific policy among those legitimately available, defined by a specific message or limited by a particular message forbidden. The county government's interest in his speech cannot therefore be equated with the terms of a specific, prescribed, or forbidden substantive position comparable to the Federal Government's interest in *Rust*, and *Rust* is no authority for the notion that government may exercise plenary control over every comment made by a public employee in doing his job. . . .

B

The majority's second argument for its disputed limitation of *Pickering* doctrine is that the First Amendment has little or no work to do here owing to an assertedly comprehensive complement of state and national statutes protecting government whistle-blowers from vindictive bosses. But even if I close my eyes to the tenet that "[t]he applicability of a provision of the Constitution has never depended on the vagaries of state or federal law," *Board of Comm'rs, Wabaunsee Cty. v. Umbehr* (1996), the majority's counsel to rest easy fails on its own terms.

To begin with, speech addressing official wrongdoing may well fall outside protected whistle-blowing, defined in the classic sense of exposing an official's fault to a third party or to the public; the teacher in *Givhan*, for example, who raised the issue of unconstitutional hiring bias, would not have qualified as that sort of whistle-blower, for she was fired after a private conversation with the school principal. In any event, the combined variants of statutory whistle-blower definitions and protections add up to a patchwork, not a showing that worries may be remitted to legislatures for relief. Some state statutes protect all government workers, including the employees of municipalities and other subdivisions; others stop at state employees. Some limit protection to employees who tell their bosses before they speak out; others forbid bosses from imposing any requirement to warn. As for the federal Whistleblower Protection Act of 1989, current case law requires an employee complaining of retaliation to show "irrefragable proof" that the person criticized was not acting in good faith and in compliance with the law. . . . Most significantly, federal employees have been held to be unprotected for statements made in connection with normal employment duties, the very speech that the majority says will be covered by "the powerful network of legislative enactments . . . available to those who seek to expose wrongdoing." My point is not to disparage particular statutes or speak here to the merits of interpretations by other federal courts, but merely to show the current understanding of statutory protection: individuals doing the same sorts of governmental jobs and saying the same sorts of things addressed to civic concerns will get different protection depending on the local, state, or federal jurisdictions that happened to employ them.

*   *   *

JUSTICE BREYER, dissenting.

This case asks whether the First Amendment protects public employees when they engage in speech that both (1) involves matters of public concern and (2) takes place in the ordinary course of performing the duties of a government job. I write separately to explain why I cannot fully accept either the Court's or JUSTICE SOUTER's answer to the question presented.

I

I begin with what I believe is common ground:

Where a government employee speaks "as an employee upon matters only of personal interest," the First Amendment does not offer protection. *Connick v. Myers* (1983). Where the employee speaks "as a citizen . . . upon matters of public concern," the First Amendment offers protection but only where the speech survives a screening test. *Pickering v. Board of Ed. of Township High School Dist. 205, Will Cty.* (1968). That test, called, in legal shorthand, *"Pickering* balancing," requires a judge to "balance . . . the interests" of the employee "in commenting upon matters of public concern and the interest of the State, as an employer, in promoting the efficiency of the public services it performs through its employees."

Our prior cases do not decide what screening test a judge should apply in the circumstances before us, namely when the government employee both speaks upon a matter of public concern and does so in the course of his ordinary duties as a government employee.

II

The majority answers the question by holding that "when public employees make statements pursuant to their official duties, the employees are not speaking as citizens for First Amendment purposes, and the Constitution does not insulate their communications from employer discipline." In a word, the majority says, "never." That word, in my view, is too absolute . . . There may well be circumstances with special demand for constitutional protection of the speech at issue, where governmental justifications may be limited, and where administrable standards seem readily available — to the point where the majority's fears of department management by lawsuit are misplaced. In such an instance, I believe that courts should apply the *Pickering* standard, even though the government employee speaks upon matters of public concern in the course of his ordinary duties.

This is such a case.

First, the speech at issue is professional speech — the speech of a lawyer. Such speech is subject to independent regulation by canons of the profession. Those canons provide an obligation to speak in certain instances. And where that is so, the government's own interest in forbidding that speech is diminished. *Cf. Legal Services Corporation v. Velazquez* (2001) ("Restricting LSC [Legal Services Corporation] attorneys in advising their clients and in presenting arguments and analyses to the courts distorts the legal system by altering the traditional role of the attorneys"). See also *Polk County v. Dodson* (1981) ("[A] public defender is not amenable to administrative direction in the same sense as other employees of the State").

Second, the Constitution itself here imposes speech obligations upon the government's professional employee. A prosecutor has a constitutional obligation to learn of, to preserve, and to communicate with the defense about exculpatory and impeachment evidence in the government's possession. *Brady, supra.* . . .

Where professional and special constitutional obligations are both present, the need to protect the employee's speech is augmented, the need for broad government authority to control that speech is likely diminished, and administrable standards are quite likely available. Hence, I would find that the Constitution mandates special protection of employee speech in such circumstances. Thus I would apply the *Pickering* balancing test here.

III

While I agree with much of JUSTICE SOUTER's analysis, I believe that the constitutional standard he enunciates fails to give sufficient weight to the serious managerial and administrative concerns that the majority describes. The standard would instruct courts to apply *Pickering* balancing in all cases, but says that the government should prevail unless the employee (1) "speaks on a matter of unusual importance," and (2) "satisfies high standards of responsibility in the way he does it." JUSTICE SOUTER adds that "only comment on official dishonesty, deliberately unconstitutional action, other serious wrongdoing, or threats to health and safety can weigh out in an employee's favor."

There are, however, far too many issues of public concern, even if defined as "matters of unusual importance," for the screen to screen out very much. Government administration typically involves matters of public concern. Why else would government be involved? And "public issues," indeed, matters of "unusual importance," are often daily bread-and-butter concerns for the police, the intelligence agencies, the military, and many whose jobs involve protecting the public's health, safety, and the environment. . . .

The underlying problem with this breadth of coverage is that the standard (despite predictions that the government is likely to *prevail* in the balance unless the speech concerns "official dishonesty, deliberately unconstitutional action, other serious wrongdoing, or threats to health and safety,"), does not avoid the judicial need to *undertake the balance* in the first place. And this form of judicial activity — the ability of a dissatisfied employee to file a complaint, engage in discovery, and insist that the court undertake a balancing of interests — itself may interfere unreasonably with both the managerial function (the ability of the employer to control the way in which an employee performs his basic job) and with the use of other grievance-resolution mechanisms, such as arbitration, civil service review boards, and whistle-blower remedies, for which employees and employers may have bargained or which legislatures may have enacted.

At the same time, the list of categories substantially overlaps areas where the law already provides nonconstitutional protection through whistle-blower statutes and the like. That overlap diminishes the need for a constitutional forum and also means that adoption of the test would authorize federal Constitution-based legal actions that threaten to upset the legislatively struck (or administratively struck) balance that those statutes (or administrative procedures) embody.

IV

I conclude that the First Amendment sometimes does authorize judicial actions based upon a government employee's speech that both (1) involves a matter of public concern and also (2) takes place in the course of ordinary job-related duties. But it does so only in the presence of augmented need for constitutional protection and diminished risk of undue judicial interference with governmental management of the public's affairs. In my view, these conditions are met in this case and *Pickering* balancing is consequently appropriate.

With respect, I dissent.

NOTES AND QUESTIONS

1.   The basic constitutional doctrine which governs whether public employees may be terminated on the basis of the exercise of their First Amendment rights is as follows from *Waters v. Churchill*:

> To be protected, the speech must be on a matter of public concern, and the employee's interest in expressing herself on this matter must not be outweighed by any injury the speech could cause to the interest of the State, as an employer, in promoting the efficiency of the public services it performs through its employees.

511 U.S. at 668 (quoting *Connick v. Myers*, 461 U.S. 138, 142 (1983) (quoting *Pickering v. Bd. of Educ.*, 391 U.S. 563, 568 (1968))). Do you see that the standard has three elements, with the employee first proving an adverse employment action premised upon the employee's speech; second, that the speech was of public concern; and third, that the exercise of the speech right outweighs the government employer's interest in the efficient functioning of the office?

The Court followed *Garcetti* in *Borough of Duryea v. Guarnieri*, 131 S. Ct. 2488, 180 L. Ed. 2d 408 (2011). *Borough of Duryea* dealt with the borough's allegedly retaliatory firing of its police chief, Guarnieri. Guarnieri had filed a union grievance challenging his termination by the Borough Council. That grievance went to arbitration, which Guarnieri won. Thereupon the Borough Council reinstated Guarnieri, but it issued 11 particularized directives limiting and detailing the manner in which Guarnieri was to perform his employment duties. After another union grievance proceeding only partially resolved the situation, Guarnieri filed an action against the Council under 42 U.S.C. § 1983. Guarnieri based his challenge not on the Free Speech Clause, but rather on the Petition Clause, claiming an interference with his right to petition the government for a redress of his grievance. The Third Circuit upheld a jury verdict in Guarnieri's favor, holding that "a public employee who has petitioned the government through a formal mechanism such as the filing of a lawsuit or grievance is protected under the Petition Clause from retaliation for that activity, even if the petition concerns a matter of solely private concern." The Supreme Court, however, disagreed and indicated that the frame-work established in the *Garcetti* case is to be followed in Petition Clause cases:

> The framework used to govern Speech Clause claims by public employees, when applied to the Petition Clause, will protect both the interests of the government and the First Amendment right. If a public employee petitions as an employee on a matter of purely private concern, the employee's First Amendment interest must give way, as it does in speech cases.

An argument could perhaps be made that Guarnieri's situation involved matters that were not of "purely private concern", but because the *Garcetti* framework had not been followed in the court below, the Court remanded the case with instructions that that framework be applied to Guarnieri's situation.

2.   Do you think *Garcetti* will give rise to litigation over what is and is not within a public employee's job description? Can employers narrow their constitutional exposure by broadening this description? The Court opined that "[t]he proper inquiry is a practical one. Formal job descriptions often bear little resemblance to

the duties an employee actually is expected to perform, and the listing of a given task in an employee's written job description is neither necessary nor sufficient to demonstrate that conducting the task is within the scope of the employee's professional duties for First Amendment purposes." Does this statement make the likelihood of litigation even greater?

3. And what about law professors at public law schools? Their job description is presumably as wide as the principle of academic freedom, or after *Garcetti*, is it? The Court left the question open. "There is some argument that expression related to academic scholarship or classroom instruction," said the Justices, "implicates additional constitutional interests that are not fully accounted for by this Court's customary employee-speech jurisprudence. We need not, and for that reason do not, decide whether the analysis we conduct today would apply in the same manner to a case involving speech related to scholarship or teaching."

4. What if Ceballos were punished not for his internal memorandum, but because he spoke on the issue of unsupported search warrants before a local bar association? In all likelihood, the performance of his job did not require Ceballos to engage in such speech activity, but apparently, Ceballos did just that. Is this speech about the performance of his job which is not required by his job within the protection of the First Amendment? Justice Kennedy suggests the answer is "yes." Under the Court's opinion, when Ceballos gives a speech or writes a newspaper article complaining about the wrongdoing in question, rather than taking the matter to his supervisor, he is entitled to whatever constitutional protection *Pickering/ Connick* offers — that is, unless under the balancing test it undermines the work of the office. One thing for certain, *Garcetti* gives employees an incentive to go outside the established channels — to take their concerns to the newspapers, instead of up the established chain to their supervisors. In his dissent, Justice Souter noted that "[u]pon remand, it will be open to the Court of Appeals to consider the application of *Pickering* to any retaliation shown for other statements; not all of those statements would have been made pursuant to official duties in any obvious sense. . . ."

5. In *Waters v. Churchill* (1994), the Court imposed an obligation on employers seeking to sanction or dismiss a public employee on the basis of disruption to the workplace caused by speech on a matter of public concern to make reasonable investigation to determine the facts. In other words, a reviewing court may evaluate the reasonableness of the employers conclusions. While courts have recognized the special expertise and special needs of employers, the deference to their conclusions has never been complete. It is necessary that the decisionmaker reach its conclusion about what was said in good faith, rather than as a pretext; but it does not follow that good faith is sufficient, it must also be reasonable.

6. *Tennessee Secondary School Athletic Association v. Brentwood Academy*, 551 U.S. 291 (2007) held that an interscholastic athletic group, previously held by the Court to be a state actor in *Brentwood I* (2001), could enforce rules banning solicitation of high school athletic programs to middle school students. The restrictions allowed schools to make general announcements regarding their athletics, but coaches were not permitted to contact individual middle school students for the purpose of recruiting them for the high school team. A Brentwood

Academy coach who had sent out letters to individual eighth grade boys encouraging them to visit spring practices and "get[ ] involved as soon as possible" prompted the association to bring disciplinary proceedings against the school. The proceedings resulted in the school being banned from future tournaments for a number of years. In a largely unanimous opinion by Justice Stevens, the Court agreed that because the school voluntarily chose to join the association, it was subject to the association's rules.

Comparing the matter at hand to government employee speech cases, the majority held that "just as the government's interest in running an effective workplace can in some circumstances outweigh employee speech rights, so too can an athletic league's interest in enforcing its rules sometimes warrant curtailing the speech of its voluntary participants." Just as a government employee chooses to take on the employment, so the school chooses to take on the rules of the association, and therefore, its speech rights could be restricted. Unrefined, this is in tension with the unconstitutional condition doctrine explained in *Agency for International Development*. It is yet another reminder, however, that the First Amendment applies differently when the government is not acting solely as a regulator. However, the latitude to restrict speech is not unlimited. Justice Stevens alluded to the fact that speech restrictions on government employees must be necessary to operate an effective workplace, and so too, the athletic rules must be "necessary" to the accomplishment of the mission of the association. This places some limitation on speech conditions that can be voluntarily agreed to, but the Court did not elaborate, noting only that "[w]e need no empirical data to credit [the association's] common-sense conclusion that hard-sell tactics directed at middle school students could lead to exploitation, distort competition between high school teams, and foster an environment in which athletics are prized more highly than academics."

In a part of the opinion joined only by Justices Souter, Ginsburg, and Breyer, Justice Stevens relied on *Ohralik v. Ohio State Bar Association*, 436 U.S. 447 (1978), a case in which a rule prohibiting attorneys from "ambulance-chasing" was upheld. Acknowledging that the case had always been narrowly applied, Justice Stevens nevertheless likened *Ohralik* to the case at hand. Because the recruitment of middle school students to high school sports teams was, like legal solicitation, "inherently conducive to overreaching and other forms of misconduct," the cases were deemed analogous. Since the solicitation ban had been "more akin to a conduct regulation than a speech regulation" and "[struck] nowhere near the heart of the First Amendment," and because the schools were still free to advertise their programs to the community at large, no free speech violation had occurred.

Justice Kennedy, in a four-Justice concurrence, disagreed with the use of *Ohralik*. That case, he recognized, had always been limited to an attorney-client relationship, so much so that the Court had declined to apply it to an accountant-client relationship. More importantly, that holding left the opinion "open to the implication that the speech at issue is subject to state regulation whether or not the school has entered a voluntary contract with a state-sponsored association." This, Justice Kennedy wrote, "would be a dramatic expansion of *Ohralik* to a whole new field of endeavor." Because Justice Thomas, in his own concurrence, also disagreed with Justice Stevens' opinion, including the portion that relied on *Ohralik*, that portion is not binding precedent. Justice Thomas emphasized that, in his judgment, both the school and the association were private entities, and would reverse the previous opinion holding that the association was a state actor. Because he would hold that the association was not a state actor, in his opinion no First Amendment issues were involved at all. Therefore he concurred in the judgment that the policy did not violate the school's free speech rights.

7.   Beyond restricting an employee's speech, the First Amendment may be implicated if the government seeks to fire or refuse to promote an individual because of their political party affiliation. In *Elrod v. Burns*, 427 U.S. 347 (1976), a Court plurality under the late Justice Brennan found that party affiliation could not be used at least with respect to nonpolicymaking employees. In *Branti v. Finkel*, 445 U.S. 507 (1980), the Court extended the ruling when a Democratic administration sought to discharge two Republican public defenders. The Court disavowed the policymaking distinction and indicated that the essential inquiry was whether the government hiring authority could demonstrate that party affiliation is an appropriate requirement for the effective performance of the public office involved. The Court's decision in *Rutan v. Republican Party of Illinois*, 497 U.S. 62 (1990), extended the same principle to promotions, transfers and recalls after layoffs. Finally, in *O'Hare Truck Service Inc. v. Northlake, Ill.*, 518 U.S. 712 (1996), the Court applied the principle even to an independent contractor who lost his service contract for refusing to support the local political party. Justice Scalia has consistently dissented in this line of cases premised on the long history of political patronage, noting in particular, that even Supreme Court Justices owe their initial appointment to their political loyalties.

8.   An older line of cases allows government to prohibit its employees from engaging in partisan political activities, whether on the job or off. For example, the federal Hatch Act precludes government job holders from taking "an active part in political management or political campaigns." 5 U.S.C. § 7324 (1994). The Court accepted the limitation reasoning that public officials would be more even-handed if not involved politically. *United Public Workers v. Mitchell*, 330 U.S. 75 (1947). *Accord United States Civil Service Commission v. National Association of Letter Carriers, AFL-CIO*, 413 U.S. 548 (1973). While Justice Douglas strongly dissented arguing that "it was of no concern of Government what an employee does in his spare time, whether religion, recreation, social work, or politics is his hobby — unless what he does impairs efficiency or other facets of the merits of his job." *Id.* at 597 (Douglas, J., dissenting). What do you think? Would you be comfortable pursuing an important licensing matter for your business if the administrator was wearing the opposite political button from the one you were sporting?

9.   What about speech by judges or those seeking election as judges? May a state choose to have judges elected by the voters (rather than appointed, as is the case for federal judges) and then limit what judges can say during their election campaigns? In *Republican Party of Minnesota v. White*, 536 U.S. 765 (2002), the Court considered a Minnesota restriction barring candidates for judicial office from "announc[ing] his or her views on disputed legal or political issues." The Court held that the so-called "announce clause" violated the First Amendment:

There is an obvious tension between the article of Minnesota's popularly approved Constitution which provides that judges shall be elected, and the Minnesota Supreme Court's announce clause which places most subjects of interest to the voters off limits. The candidate-speech restrictions of all the other States that have them are also the product of judicial fiat. The disparity is perhaps unsurprising, since the ABA, which originated the announce clause, has long been an opponent of judicial elections. . . . That opposition may be well taken (it certainly had the support of the Founders of the Federal Government), but the First Amendment does not permit it to achieve its goal by leaving the principle of elections in place while preventing candidates from discussing what the elections are about. "[T]he greater power to dispense with elections altogether does not include the lesser power to conduct elections under conditions of state-imposed voter ignorance. If the State chooses to tap the energy and the legitimizing power of the democratic process, it must accord the participants in that process . . . the First Amendment rights that attach to their roles." . . .

Justice Ginsburg, joined by Justices Stevens, Souter, and Breyer, dissented. For them, Minnesota's announce clause was a legitimate method of insuring judicial independence and furthering due process:

Prohibiting a judicial candidate from pledging or promising certain results if elected directly promotes the State's interest in preserving public faith in the bench. When a candidate makes such a promise during a campaign, the public will no doubt perceive that she is doing so in the hope of garnering votes. And the public will in turn likely conclude that when the candidate decides an issue in accord with that promise, she does so at least in part to discharge her undertaking to the voters in the previous election and to prevent voter abandonment in the next. The perception of that unseemly *quid pro quo* — a judicial candidate's promises on issues in return for the electorate's votes at the polls — inevitably diminishes the public's faith in the ability of judges to administer the law without regard to personal or political self-interest.

Is the real problem judicial elections themselves? Justice Kennedy noted in concurrence that "By abridging speech based on its content, Minnesota impeaches its own system of free and open elections. . . . The State cannot opt for an elected judiciary and then assert that its democracy, in order to work as desired, compels the abridgement of speech." Kennedy cautioned the court to avoid criticizing the State's choice to use open elections as to do so would "implicitly condemn countless elected state judges without warrant." Interestingly, Justice O'Connor — the only Justice who has ever stood for election as a state court judge — argued strongly in a separate concurrence against the practice of electing judges. Apart from the announce clause, which she agreed could not withstand constitutional scrutiny, Justice O'Connor stated that she was "concerned that, even aside from what judicial candidates may say while campaigning, the very practice of electing judges undermines" the interest of fairness and impartiality. Elected judges, she argued, were aware that their decisions in cases affect election prospects, and even if judges resisted such pressure, the public would doubt the impartiality of elected judges. Beyond this, contested judicial elections often require substantial funds. *See*

Schotland, *Financing Judicial Elections, 2000: Change and Challenge*, 2001 L. Rev. Mich. State U. Detroit College of Law 849, 866 (reporting that in 2000, the 13 candidates in a partisan election for 5 seats on the Alabama Supreme Court spent an average of $1,092,076 on their campaigns); American Bar Association, Report and Recommendations of the Task Force on Lawyers' Political Contributions, pt. 2 (July 1998) (reporting that in 1995, one candidate for the Pennsylvania Supreme Court raised $1,848,142 in campaign funds, and that in 1986, $2,700,000 was spent on the race for Chief Justice of the Ohio Supreme Court). Wrote Justice O'Connor: "unless the pool of judicial candidates is limited to those wealthy enough to independently fund their campaigns, a limitation unrelated to judicial skill, the cost of campaigning requires judicial candidates to engage in fundraising. Yet relying on campaign donations may leave judges feeling indebted to certain parties or interest groups." Again, the public's confidence in judicial actors would lessen as they engaged in ever greater fundraising.

What is the counterpoint in support of judicial elections? Is it a sufficient justification for judicial elections at the state level that state court judges possess the power to make common law, and sometimes, shape state constitutions as well?

10.   And to round out our consideration of special contexts for speech, a word about student speech in public schools. This issue received attention in *Morse v. Frederick*, 551 U.S. 393 (2007) a case better remembered for its infantile student behavior than its legal development. At a school-sanctioned and school-supervised event, a high school principal saw some of her students unfurl a large banner reciting "Bong Hits 4 Jesus." The Court rather tendentiously asserted that the principal reasonably thought this conveyed a message promoting illegal drug use. Why was it important to the Court that the principal reasonably believed Frederick's speech was unprotected? Outside the schoolhouse, at least, what a public official thought was or was not reasonable would be largely irrelevant to the issue of whether a citizen's speech warranted constitutional protection. As Justice Stevens pointed out in his dissent, the reasonableness of the view that Frederick's message was unprotected speech is relevant to ascertaining whether qualified immunity should shield the principal from liability, not to whether her actions violated Frederick's constitutional rights. *Cf. Saucier v. Katz* (2001) ("The relevant, dispositive inquiry in determining whether a right is clearly established is whether it would be clear to a reasonable officer that his conduct was unlawful in the situation he confronted").

In any event, consistent with established school policy prohibiting such messages at school events, the principal directed the students to take down the banner. One student — among those who had brought the banner to the event — refused to do so. The principal confiscated the banner and later suspended the student. The Ninth Circuit held that the principal's actions violated the First Amendment, and that the student could sue the principal for damages. The Court reversed, finding illegal drug advocacy to be unprotected speech in the public school context and dismissed the damage action.

The case is useful for summarizing school speech cases. Those cases make clear that students do not "shed their constitutional rights to freedom of speech or expression at the schoolhouse gate." *Tinker v. Des Moines Independent Commu-*

nity School Dist. (1969) (students in classroom can wear a nondisruptive black armband protesting the Vietnam war). At the same time, "the constitutional rights of students in public school are not automatically coextensive with the rights of adults in other settings," *Bethel School Dist. No. 403 v. Fraser* (1986) (vulgarity in a school assembly need not be tolerated), and that the rights of students "must be 'applied in light of the special characteristics of the school environment.' " *Hazelwood School Dist. v. Kuhlmeier* (1988) (school newspaper done as part of school curriculum, subject to teacher's editorial decision-making). Consistent with these principles, the Court held that schools may take steps to safeguard those entrusted to their care from speech that can reasonably be regarded as encouraging illegal drug use. "We conclude that the school officials in this case did not violate the First Amendment by confiscating the pro-drug banner and suspending the student responsible for it."

Justice Thomas concurred, suggesting that if the Court was starting from scratch, students would not have First Amendment rights in school since teachers are the equivalent of parents during the school day. "In my view," wrote Justice Thomas, "the history of public education suggests that the First Amendment, as originally understood, does not protect student speech in public schools." Thomas thought it would be the better approach to dispense with *Tinker* altogether, and given the opportunity, he said, "I would do so." Justice Thomas argues that *stare decisis* is unwarranted since the *Tinker* Court claim that "[i]t can hardly be argued that either students or teachers shed their constitutional rights to freedom of speech or expression at the schoolhouse gate," was based on inapposite case law that was affirming the rights of private schools or parents, not student rights. For example, Thomas notes that "*Tinker* chiefly relies upon *Meyer v. Nebraska* (1923) (striking down a law prohibiting the teaching of German). However, *Meyer* involved a challenge by a *private* school, and the *Meyer* Court was quick to note that no " 'challenge [has] been made of the State's power to prescribe a curriculum for institutions which it supports.' " *Tinker* also relied on *Pierce v. Society of Sisters* (1925). But, as Justice Thomas points out, "*Pierce* has nothing to say on this issue either. *Pierce* simply upheld the right of parents to send their children to private school."

Would Thomas' view of *in loco parentis* trump other constitutional rights? After all, if public schools stand in for parents (who are not state actors and therefore free to censor student speech), is the "public school/parent" also free to instruct in matters of a favored religion (as a parent would) in disregard of the Establishment Clause? If your answer is to preclude such instruction, do you have a reasoned basis for distinguishing between one constitutional right and another?

Justice Alito and Kennedy were inclined oppositely from Justice Thomas. Justice Alito wrote: "I join the opinion of the Court on the understanding that (a) it goes no further than to hold that a public school may restrict speech that a reasonable observer would interpret as advocating illegal drug use and (b) it provides no support for any restriction of speech that can plausibly be interpreted as commenting on any political or social issue, including speech on issues such as 'the wisdom of the war on drugs or of legalizing marijuana for medicinal use' "

The dissenters (Stevens, Souter, and Ginsburg) agreed the principal should not be liable for guessing wrong about the protections of speech that obviously divide the Court, itself but also scoffed at the notion that there was any serious advocacy of illegal drug use. Said the dissent: "the First Amendment protects student speech if the message itself neither violates a permissible rule nor expressly advocates conduct that is illegal and harmful to students. This nonsense banner does neither, and the Court does serious violence to the First Amendment in upholding — indeed, lauding — a school's decision to punish Frederick for expressing a view with which it disagreed." Justice Breyer concurred only in the judgment without reaching the merits of the speech issue. How is this possible? Doesn't one have to determine the existence or nonexistence of a constitutional right before determining whether there was a violation of that right warranting money damages? In *Saucier v. Katz* (2001), the Court wrote that lower courts' "first inquiry must be whether a constitutional right would have been violated on the facts alleged." Only if there is a constitutional violation can lower courts proceed to consider whether the official is entitled to "qualified immunity."

Justice Breyer has advocated abandoning *Saucier*'s order-of-battle rule. *See Scott v. Harris* (2007) (Breyer, J., concurring); *Brosseau v. Haugen* (2004) (Breyer, J., concurring). Breyer's view is that courts should not reach constitutional questions prematurely ("[T]he rule violates the longstanding principle that courts should 'not . . . pass on questions of constitutionality . . . unless such adjudication is unavoidable.'" *Spector Motor Service, Inc. v. McLaughlin* (1944)). What is the justification for the *Saucier* rule? Presumably, it is to encourage the development of constitutional doctrine in the lower courts. Justice Breyer thinks this an overstated concern, since the rule only encourages an order of battle, it does not require it, and in any event, it does not bind the Supreme Court.

Chief Justice Roberts has also argued for not deciding issues prematurely and for narrow rulings that would promote unanimity, and presumably, greater clarity and stability in constitutional law. Here, the Chief Justice thought the merits had to be reached since Frederick wanted both monetary and injunctive relief. Qualified immunity might resolve the money issue, but the Court needed to assess the merits to evaluate whether an injunction was appropriate.

Putting aside the silly facts of this case, does the harm associated with illegal drug use merit a special speech category? Chief Justice Roberts notes that previous cases permitting greater latitude for school searches under the Fourth Amendment concluded that deterring drug use by schoolchildren is an "important — indeed, perhaps compelling" interest. In part, that is because studies indicate that:

> School years are the time when the physical, psychological, and addictive effects of drugs are most severe. Maturing nervous systems are more critically impaired by intoxicants than mature ones are; childhood losses in learning are lifelong and profound; children grow chemically dependent more quickly than adults, and their record of recovery is depressingly poor. And of course the effects of a drug-infested school are visited not just upon the users, but upon the entire student body and faculty, as the educational process is disrupted.

551 U.S. 393 at 407. Beyond the unique damage to the physiology of young people is a judicial concern with greater usage. *See generally* 1 NATIONAL INSTITUTE ON DRUG ABUSE, NATIONAL INSTITUTES OF HEALTH, MONITORING THE FUTURE: NATIONAL SURVEY RESULTS ON DRUG USE, 1975–2005, SECONDARY SCHOOL STUDENTS (2006). About half of American 12th graders have used an illicit drug, as have more than a third of 10th graders and about one-fifth of 8th graders. Nearly one in four 12th graders has used an illicit drug in the past month. Some 25% of high schoolers say that they have been offered, sold, or given an illegal drug on school property within the past year. Dept. of Health and Human Services, Centers for Disease Control and Prevention, Youth Risk Behavior Surveillance — United States, 2005, 55 Morbidity and Mortality Weekly Report, Surveillance Summaries, No. SS-5, p. 19 (June 9, 2006).

c. Speech Within Private Associations

ROBERTS v. UNITED STATES JAYCEES
468 U.S. 609 (1984)

JUSTICE BRENNAN delivered the opinion of the Court.

This case requires us to address a conflict between a State's efforts to eliminate gender-based discrimination against its citizens and the constitutional freedom of association asserted by members of a private organization. In the decision under review, the Court of Appeals for the Eighth Circuit concluded that, by requiring the United States Jaycees to admit women as full voting members, the Minnesota Human Rights Act violates the First and Fourteenth Amendment rights of the organization's members. We . . . now reverse.

A

The United States Jaycees (Jaycees), founded in 1920 as the Junior Chamber of Commerce, is a nonprofit membership corporation, incorporated in Missouri with national headquarters in Tulsa, Okla. The objective of the Jaycees, as set out in its bylaws, is to pursue

> "such educational and charitable purposes as will promote and foster the growth and development of young men's civic organizations in the United States, designed to inculcate in the individual membership of such organization a spirit of genuine Americanism and civic interest, and as a supplementary education institution to provide them with opportunity for personal development and achievement and an avenue for intelligent participation by young men in the affairs of their community, state and nation, and to develop true friendship and understanding among young men of all nations."

The organization's bylaws establish seven classes of membership, including individual or regular members, associate individual members, and local chapters. Regular membership is limited to young men between the ages of 18 and 35, while associate membership is available to individuals or groups ineligible for regular membership, principally women and older men. An associate member, whose dues are somewhat lower than those charged regular members, may not vote, hold local or national office, or participate in certain leadership training and awards programs. The bylaws define a local chapter as "[a]ny young men's organization of good repute existing in any community within the United States, organized for purposes similar to and consistent with those" of the national organization. The ultimate policymaking authority of the Jaycees rests with an annual national convention, consisting of delegates from each local chapter, with a national president and board of directors. At the time of trial in August 1981, the Jaycees had approximately 295,000 members in 7,400 local chapters affiliated with 51 state organizations. There were at that time about 11,915 associate members. The national organization's executive vice president estimated at trial that women associate members make up about two percent of the Jaycees' total membership.

New members are recruited to the Jaycees through the local chapters, although the state and national organizations are also actively involved in recruitment through a variety of promotional activities. A new regular member pays an initial fee followed by annual dues; in exchange, he is entitled to participate in all of the activities of the local, state, and national organizations. The national headquarters employs a staff to develop "program kits" for use by local chapters that are designed to enhance individual development, community development, and members' management skills. These materials include courses in public speaking and personal finances as well as community programs related to charity, sports, and public health. The national office also makes available to members a range of personal products, including travel accessories, casual wear, pins, awards, and other gifts. The programs, products, and other activities of the organization are all regularly featured in publications made available to the membership, including a magazine entitled "Future."

B

In 1974 and 1975, respectively, the Minneapolis and St. Paul chapters of the Jaycees began admitting women as regular members. Currently, the memberships and boards of directors of both chapters include a substantial proportion of women. As a result, the two chapters have been in violation of the national organization's bylaws for about 10 years. The national organization has imposed a number of sanctions on the Minneapolis and St. Paul chapters for violating the bylaws, including denying their members eligibility for state or national office or awards programs, and refusing to count their membership in computing votes at national conventions.

In December 1978, the president of the national organization advised both chapters that a motion to revoke their charters would be considered at a forthcoming meeting of the national board of directors in Tulsa. Shortly after receiving this notification, members of both chapters filed charges of discrimination with the Minnesota Department of Human Rights. The complaints alleged that the exclusion of women from full membership required by the national organization's bylaws violated the Minnesota Human Rights Act (Act), which provides in part:

"It is an unfair discriminatory practice:

"To deny any person the full and equal enjoyment of the goods, services, facilities, privileges, advantages, and accommodations of a place of public accommodation because of race, color, creed, religion, disability, national origin or sex."

The term "place of public accommodation" is defined in the Act as "a business, accommodation, refreshment, entertainment, recreation, or transportation facility of any kind, whether licensed or not, whose goods, services, facilities, privileges, advantages or accommodations are extended, offered, sold, or otherwise made available to the public."

After an investigation, the Commissioner of the Minnesota Department of Human Rights found probable cause to believe that the sanctions imposed on the local chapters by the national organization violated the statute and ordered that an evidentiary hearing be held before a state hearing examiner. Before that hearing took place, however, the national organization brought suit against various state officials, appellants here, in the United States District Court for the District of Minnesota, seeking declaratory and injunctive relief to prevent enforcement of the Act. The complaint alleged that, by requiring the organization to accept women as regular members, application of the Act would violate the male members' constitutional rights of free speech and association. With the agreement of the parties, the District Court dismissed the suit without prejudice, stating that it could be renewed in the event the state administrative proceeding resulted in a ruling adverse to the Jaycees.

The proceeding before the Minnesota Human Rights Department hearing examiner then went forward and, upon its completion, the examiner filed findings of fact and conclusions of law. The examiner concluded that the Jaycees organization is a "place of public accommodation" within the Act and that it had engaged in an unfair discriminatory practice by excluding women from regular membership. He ordered the national organization to cease and desist from discriminating against any member or applicant for membership on the basis of sex and from imposing sanctions on any Minnesota affiliate for admitting women. The Jaycees then filed a renewed complaint in the District Court, which in turn certified to the Minnesota Supreme Court the question whether the Jaycees organization is a "place of public accommodation" within the meaning of the State's Human Rights Act.

With the record of the administrative hearing before it, the Minnesota Supreme Court answered that question in the affirmative. Based on the Act's legislative history, the court determined that the statute is applicable to any "public business facility." It then concluded that the Jaycees organization (a) is a "business" in that it sells goods and extends privileges in exchange for annual membership dues; (b) is a "public" business in that it solicits and recruits dues-paying members based on unselective criteria; and (c) is a public business "facility" in that it conducts its activities at fixed and mobile sites within the State of Minnesota.

Subsequently, the Jaycees amended its complaint in the District Court to add a claim that the Minnesota Supreme Court's interpretation of the Act rendered it unconstitutionally vague and overbroad. The federal suit then proceeded to trial, after which the District Court entered judgment in favor of the state officials. On appeal, a divided Court of Appeals for the Eighth Circuit reversed. The Court of

Appeals determined that, because "the advocacy of political and public causes, selected by the membership, is a not insubstantial part of what [the Jaycees] does," the organization's right to select its members is protected by the freedom of association guaranteed by the First Amendment. It further decided that application of the Minnesota statute to the Jaycees' membership policies would produce a "direct and substantial" interference with that freedom, because it would necessarily result in "some change in the Jaycees' philosophical cast," and would attach penal sanctions to those responsible for maintaining the policy. The court concluded that the State's interest in eradicating discrimination is not sufficiently compelling to outweigh this interference with the Jaycees' constitutional rights, because the organization is not wholly "public," the state interest had been asserted selectively, and the antidiscrimination policy could be served in a number of ways less intrusive of First Amendment freedoms.

Finally, the court held, in the alternative, that the Minnesota statute is vague as construed and applied and therefore unconstitutional under the Due Process Clause of the Fourteenth Amendment. In support of this conclusion, the court relied on a statement in the opinion of the Minnesota Supreme Court suggesting that, unlike the Jaycees, the Kiwanis Club is "private" and therefore not subject to the Act. By failing to provide any criteria that distinguish such "private" organizations from the "public accommodations" covered by the statute, the Court of Appeals reasoned, the Minnesota Supreme Court's interpretation rendered the Act unconstitutionally vague.

II

Our decisions have referred to constitutionally protected "freedom of association" in two distinct senses. In one line of decisions, the Court has concluded that choices to enter into and maintain certain intimate human relationships must be secured against undue intrusion by the State because of the role of such relationships in safeguarding the individual freedom that is central to our constitutional scheme. In this respect, freedom of association receives protection as a fundamental element of personal liberty. In another set of decisions, the Court has recognized a right to associate for the purpose of engaging in those activities protected by the First Amendment — speech, assembly, petition for the redress of grievances, and the exercise of religion. The Constitution guarantees freedom of association of this kind as an indispensable means of preserving other individual liberties.

The intrinsic and instrumental features of constitutionally protected association may, of course, coincide. In particular, when the State interferes with individuals' selection of those with whom they wish to join in a common endeavor, freedom of association in both of its forms may be implicated. The Jaycees contend that this is such a case. Still, the nature and degree of constitutional protection afforded freedom of association may vary depending on the extent to which one or the other aspect of the constitutionally protected liberty is at stake in a given case. We therefore find it useful to consider separately the effect of applying the Minnesota statute to the Jaycees on what could be called its members' freedom of intimate association and their freedom of expressive association.

A

The Court has long recognized that, because the Bill of Rights is designed to secure individual liberty, it must afford the formation and preservation of certain kinds of highly personal relationships a substantial measure of sanctuary from unjustified interference by the State. Without precisely identifying every consideration that may underlie this type of constitutional protection, we have noted that certain kinds of personal bonds have played a critical role in the culture and traditions of the Nation by cultivating and transmitting shared ideals and beliefs; they thereby foster diversity and act as critical buffers between the individual and the power of the State. Moreover, the constitutional shelter afforded such relationships reflects the realization that individuals draw much of their emotional enrichment from close ties with others. Protecting these relationships from unwarranted state interference therefore safeguards the ability independently to define one's identity that is central to any concept of liberty.

The personal affiliations that exemplify these considerations, and that therefore suggest some relevant limitations on the relationships that might be entitled to this sort of constitutional protection, are those that attend the creation and sustenance of a family — marriage, childbirth, the raising and education of children, and cohabitation with one's relatives. Family relationships, by their nature, involve deep attachments and commitments to the necessarily few other individuals with whom one shares not only a special community of thoughts, experiences, and beliefs but also distinctively personal aspects of one's life. Among other things, therefore, they are distinguished by such attributes as relative smallness, a high degree of selectivity in decisions to begin and maintain the affiliation, and seclusion from others in critical aspects of the relationship. As a general matter, only relationships with these sorts of qualities are likely to reflect the considerations that have led to an understanding of freedom of association as an intrinsic element of personal liberty. Conversely, an association lacking these qualities — such as a large business enterprise — seems remote from the concerns giving rise to this constitutional protection. Accordingly, the Constitution undoubtedly imposes constraints on the State's power to control the selection of one's spouse that would not apply to regulations affecting the choice of one's fellow employees.

Between these poles, of course, lies a broad range of human relationships that may make greater or lesser claims to constitutional protection from particular incursions by the State. Determining the limits of state authority over an individual's freedom to enter into a particular association therefore unavoidably entails a careful assessment of where that relationship's objective characteristics locate it on a spectrum from the most intimate to the most attenuated of personal attachments. We need not mark the potentially significant points on this terrain with any precision. We note only that factors that may be relevant include size, purpose, policies, selectivity, congeniality, and other characteristics that in a particular case may be pertinent. In this case, however, several features of the Jaycees clearly place the organization outside of the category of relationships worthy of this kind of constitutional protection.

The undisputed facts reveal that the local chapters of the Jaycees are large and basically unselective groups. At the time of the state administrative hearing, the

Minneapolis chapter had approximately 430 members, while the St. Paul chapter had about 400. Apart from age and sex, neither the national organization nor the local chapters employ any criteria for judging applicants for membership, and new members are routinely recruited and admitted with no inquiry into their backgrounds. In fact, a local officer testified that he could recall no instance in which an applicant had been denied membership on any basis other than age or sex. Furthermore, despite their inability to vote, hold office, or receive certain awards, women affiliated with the Jaycees attend various meetings, participate in selected projects, and engage in many of the organization's social functions. Indeed, numerous nonmembers of both genders regularly participate in a substantial portion of activities central to the decision of many members to associate with one another, including many of the organization's various community programs, awards ceremonies, and recruitment meetings.

In short, the local chapters of the Jaycees are neither small nor selective. Moreover, much of the activity central to the formation and maintenance of the association involves the participation of strangers to that relationship. Accordingly, we conclude that the Jaycees chapters lack the distinctive characteristics that might afford constitutional protection to the decision of its members to exclude women. We turn therefore to consider the extent to which application of the Minnesota statute to compel the Jaycees to accept women infringes the group's freedom of expressive association.

B

An individual's freedom to speak, to worship, and to petition the government for the redress of grievances could not be vigorously protected from interference by the State unless a correlative freedom to engage in group effort toward those ends were not also guaranteed. According protection to collective effort on behalf of shared goals is especially important in preserving political and cultural diversity and in shielding dissident expression from suppression by the majority. Consequently, we have long understood as implicit in the right to engage in activities protected by the First Amendment a corresponding right to associate with others in pursuit of a wide variety of political, social, economic, educational, religious, and cultural ends. In view of the various protected activities in which the Jaycees engages, that right is plainly implicated in this case.

Government actions that may unconstitutionally infringe upon this freedom can take a number of forms. Among other things, government may seek to impose penalties or withhold benefits from individuals because of their membership in a disfavored group; it may attempt to require disclosure of the fact of membership in a group seeking anonymity; and it may try to interfere with the internal organization or affairs of the group. By requiring the Jaycees to admit women as full voting members, the Minnesota Act works an infringement of the last type. There can be no clearer example of an intrusion into the internal structure or affairs of an association than a regulation that forces the group to accept members it does not desire. Such a regulation may impair the ability of the original members to express only those views that brought them together. Freedom of association therefore plainly presupposes a freedom not to associate.

The right to associate for expressive purposes is not, however, absolute. Infringements on that right may be justified by regulations adopted to serve compelling state interests, unrelated to the suppression of ideas, that cannot be achieved through means significantly less restrictive of associational freedoms. We are persuaded that Minnesota's compelling interest in eradicating discrimination against its female citizens justifies the impact that application of the statute to the Jaycees may have on the male members' associational freedoms.

On its face, the Minnesota Act does not aim at the suppression of speech, does not distinguish between prohibited and permitted activity on the basis of viewpoint, and does not license enforcement authorities to administer the statute on the basis of such constitutionally impermissible criteria. Nor does the Jaycees contend that the Act has been applied in this case for the purpose of hampering the organization's ability to express its views. Instead, as the Minnesota Supreme Court explained, the Act reflects the State's strong historical commitment to eliminating discrimination and assuring its citizens equal access to publicly available goods and services. That goal, which is unrelated to the suppression of expression, plainly serves compelling state interests of the highest order.

* * *

. . . [T]he Jaycees has failed to demonstrate that the Act imposes any serious burdens on the male members' freedom of expressive association. See *Hishon v. King & Spalding* (1984) (law firm "has not shown how its ability to fulfill [protected] function[s] would be inhibited by a requirement that it consider [a woman lawyer] for partnership on her merits"). To be sure, as the Court of Appeals noted, a "not insubstantial part" of the Jaycees' activities constitutes protected expression on political, economic, cultural, and social affairs. Over the years, the national and local levels of the organization have taken public positions on a number of diverse issues, and members of the Jaycees regularly engage in a variety of civic, charitable, lobbying, fundraising, and other activities worthy of constitutional protection under the First Amendment. There is, however, no basis in the record for concluding that admission of women as full voting members will impede the organization's ability to engage in these protected activities or to disseminate its preferred views. The Act requires no change in the Jaycees' creed of promoting the interests of young men, and it imposes no restrictions on the organization's ability to exclude individuals with ideologies or philosophies different from those of its existing members. *Cf. Democratic Party of United States v. Wisconsin* [(1981)] (recognizing the right of political parties to "protect themselves 'from intrusion by those with adverse political principles' "). Moreover, the Jaycees already invites women to share the group's views and philosophy and to participate in much of its training and community activities. Accordingly, any claim that admission of women as full voting members will impair a symbolic message conveyed by the very fact that women are not permitted to vote is attenuated at best.

While acknowledging that "the specific content of most of the resolutions adopted over the years by the Jaycees has nothing to do with sex," the Court of Appeals nonetheless entertained the hypothesis that women members might have a different view or agenda with respect to these matters so that, if they are allowed to vote, "some change in the Jaycees' philosophical cast can reasonably be expected." It is similarly arguable that, insofar as the Jaycees is organized to promote the views of young men whatever those views happen to be, admission of women as voting members will change the message communicated by the group's speech because of the gender-based assumptions of the audience. Neither supposition, however, is supported by the record. In claiming that women might have a different attitude about such issues as the federal budget, school prayer, voting rights, and foreign relations, or that the organization's public positions would have a different effect if the group were not "a purely young men's association," the Jaycees relies solely on unsupported generalizations about the relative interests and perspectives of men and women. Although such generalizations may or may not have a statistical basis in fact with respect to particular positions adopted by the Jaycees, we have repeatedly condemned legal decisionmaking that relies uncritically on such assumptions. In the absence of a showing far more substantial than that attempted by the Jaycees, we decline to indulge in the sexual stereotyping that underlies appellee's contention that, by allowing women to vote, application of the Minnesota Act will change the content or impact of the organization's speech.

In any event, even if enforcement of the Act causes some incidental abridgment of the Jaycees' protected speech, that effect is no greater than is necessary to accomplish the State's legitimate purposes. . . .

III

We turn finally to appellee's contentions that the Minnesota Act, as interpreted by the State's highest court, is unconstitutionally vague and overbroad. The void-for-vagueness doctrine reflects the principle that "a statute which either forbids or requires the doing of an act in terms so vague that [persons] of common intelligence must necessarily guess at its meaning and differ as to its application, violates the first essential of due process of law." The requirement that government articulate its aims with a reasonable degree of clarity ensures that state power will be exercised only on behalf of policies reflecting an authoritative choice among competing social values, reduces the danger of caprice and discrimination in the administration of the laws, enables individuals to conform their conduct to the requirements of law, and permits meaningful judicial review.

We have little trouble concluding that these concerns are not seriously implicated by the Minnesota Act, either on its face or as construed in this case. In deciding that the Act reaches the Jaycees, the Minnesota Supreme Court used a number of specific and objective criteria — regarding the organization's size, selectivity, commercial nature, and use of public facilities — typically employed in determining the applicability of state and federal antidiscrimination statutes to the membership policies of assertedly private clubs. The Court of Appeals seemingly acknowledged that the Minnesota court's construction of the Act by use of these familiar standards ensures that the reach of the statute is readily ascertainable. It nevertheless concluded that the Minnesota court introduced a constitutionally fatal element of uncertainty into the statute by suggesting that the Kiwanis Club might be sufficiently "private" to be outside the scope of the Act. Like the dissenting judge in the Court of Appeals, however, we read the illustrative reference to the Kiwanis Club, which the record indicates has a formal procedure for choosing members on the basis of specific and selective criteria, as simply providing a further refinement of the standards used to determine whether an organization is "public" or "private." By offering this counter-example, the Minnesota Supreme Court's opinion provided the statute with more, rather than less, definite content.

The contrast between the Jaycees and the Kiwanis Club drawn by the Minnesota court also disposes of appellee's contention that the Act is unconstitutionally overbroad. The Jaycees argues that the statute is "susceptible of sweeping and improper application," because it could be used to restrict the membership decisions of wholly private groups organized for a wide variety of political, religious, cultural, or social purposes. Without considering the extent to which such groups may be entitled to constitutional protection from the operation of the Minnesota Act, we need only note that the Minnesota Supreme Court expressly rejected the contention that the Jaycees should "be viewed analogously to private organizations such as the Kiwanis International Organization." The state court's articulated willingness to adopt limiting constructions that would exclude private groups from the statute's reach, together with the commonly used and sufficiently precise standards it employed to determine that the Jaycees is not such a group, establish that the Act, as currently construed, does not create an unacceptable risk of application to a substantial amount of protected conduct.

*   *   *

JUSTICE O'CONNOR, concurring in part and concurring in the judgment.

*   *   *

I

The Court analyzes Minnesota's attempt to regulate the Jaycees' membership using a test that I find both overprotective of activities undeserving of constitutional shelter and underprotective of important First Amendment concerns. The Court declares that the Jaycees' right of association depends on the organization's making a "substantial" showing that the admission of unwelcome members "will change the message communicated by the group's speech." I am not sure what showing the Court thinks would satisfy its requirement of proof of a membership-message connection, but whatever it means, the focus on such a connection is objectionable.

. . . Whether an association is or is not constitutionally protected in the selection of its membership should not depend on what the association says or why its members say it.

*   *   *

. . . [T]his Court's case law recognizes radically different constitutional protections for expressive and nonexpressive associations. The First Amendment is offended by direct state control of the membership of a private organization engaged exclusively in protected expressive activity, but no First Amendment interest stands in the way of a State's rational regulation of economic transactions by or within a commercial association. The proper approach to analysis of First

Amendment claims of associational freedom is, therefore, to distinguish nonexpressive from expressive associations and to recognize that the former lack the full constitutional protections possessed by the latter.

II

Minnesota's attempt to regulate the membership of the Jaycees chapters operating in that State presents a relatively easy case for application of the expressive-commercial dichotomy. Both the Minnesota Supreme Court and the United States District Court, which expressly adopted the state court's findings, made findings of fact concerning the commercial nature of the Jaycees' activities. The Court of Appeals, which disagreed with the District Court over the legal conclusions to be drawn from the facts, did not dispute any of those findings. "The Jaycees is not a political party, or even primarily a political pressure group, but the advocacy of political and public causes, selected by the membership, is a not insubstantial part of what it does. . . . [A] good deal of what the [Jaycees] does indisputably comes within the right of association . . . in pursuance of the specific ends of speech, writing, belief, and assembly for redress of grievances."

There is no reason to question the accuracy of this characterization. Notwithstanding its protected expressive activities, the Jaycees — otherwise known as the Junior Chamber of Commerce — is, first and foremost, an organization that, at both the national and local levels, promotes and practices the art of solicitation and management. The organization claims that the training it offers its members gives them an advantage in business, and business firms do indeed sometimes pay the dues of individual memberships for their employees. Jaycees members hone their solicitation and management skills, under the direction and supervision of the organization, primarily through their active recruitment of new members. "One of the major activities of the Jaycees is the sale of memberships in the organization. It encourages continuous recruitment of members with the expressed goal of increasing membership. . . . The Jaycees itself refers to its members as customers and membership as a product it is selling. More than 80 percent of the national officers' time is dedicated to recruitment, and more than half of the available achievement awards are in part conditioned on achievement in recruitment." The organization encourages record-breaking performance in selling memberships: the current records are 348 for most memberships sold in a year by one person, 134 for most sold in a month, and 1,586 for most sold in a lifetime.

Recruitment and selling are commercial activities, even when conducted for training rather than for profit. The "not insubstantial" volume of protected Jaycees activity found by the Court of Appeals is simply not enough to preclude state regulation of the Jaycees' commercial activities. The State of Minnesota has a legitimate interest in ensuring nondiscriminatory access to the commercial opportunity presented by membership in the Jaycees. The members of the Jaycees may not claim constitutional immunity from Minnesota's antidiscrimination law by seeking to exercise their First Amendment rights through this commercial organization.

NOTES AND QUESTIONS

1.   Does the result in this case surprise you? Why can't the Jaycees discriminate on the basis of sex? Why doesn't the First Amendment, as incorporated through the Fourteenth, protect their right to associate with whom they choose? All seven of the Justices who participated in this case concurred in the outcome (Justices Burger and Blackmun did not participate — could the fact that they were both Minnesotans have anything to do with this?). Would you have predicted the unanimity?

2.   Justice Brennan appears to have ruled that some freedom of association, most notably that involving marriage, procreation, contraception, and family and children, is entitled to more protection than the associational freedom of the Jaycees. Why should this be the case? Justice Brennan did appear to be willing to concede that the Jaycees did have some freedom of association related to their expression of collective views and interests, but he claimed that the state's aim in reducing discrimination on the basis of gender trumped this associational freedom on the part of the Jaycees. Why should this be the case?

3.   Notice that Justice O'Connor (the court's only woman at the time) went so far as to suggest that the Jaycees were not really an expressive organization at all, but had as their purpose commercial rather than speech aims. Is there really a difference? Is O'Connor persuasive on this point? Imagine a Minnesota organization formed by lesbians to promote the success of lesbian-owned businesses in Minnesota. Suppose a heterosexual male or female (or alternatively, a gay male) seeks to become a member of the organization and is refused membership. Would this refusal be impermissible under Minnesota law? Would the Minnesota law, as applied to our hypothetical lesbian organization, violate the federal Constitution? Would you need more facts regarding the operation of our hypothetical organization before you could answer the question?

4.   The Court has suggested that an intimate association might be allowed greater latitude to discriminate. *See generally* Kenneth Karst, *The Freedom of Intimate Association*, 89 Yale L.J. 624 (1980). Relatedly, perhaps, in *Hurley v. Irish-American Gay, Lesbian, and Bisexual Group of Boston*, 515 U.S. 557 (1995), the Court allowed the private groups organizing the St. Patrick's Day Parade to exclude gays. A unanimous Court found the parade to be an expressive activity, with those organizing it having the right to exclude messages that were antagonistic to that expression.

BOY SCOUTS OF AMERICA v. DALE
530 U.S. 640 (2000)

Rehnquist, C.J., delivered the opinion of the Court.

*   *   *

Petitioners are the Boy Scouts of America and the Monmouth Council, a division of the Boy Scouts of America (collectively, Boy Scouts). The Boy Scouts is a private, not-for-profit organization engaged in instilling its system of values in young people. The Boy Scouts asserts that homosexual conduct is inconsistent with the values it seeks to instill. Respondent is James Dale, a former Eagle Scout whose adult membership in the Boy Scouts was revoked when the Boy Scouts learned that he is an avowed homosexual and gay rights activist. The New Jersey Supreme Court held that New Jersey's public accommodations law requires that the Boy Scouts admit Dale. This case presents the question whether applying New Jersey's public accommodations law in this way violates the Boy Scouts' First Amendment right of expressive association. We hold that it does.

* * *

II

In *Roberts v. United States Jaycees* (1984), we observed that "implicit in the right to engage in activities protected by the First Amendment" is "a corresponding right to associate with others in pursuit of a wide variety of political, social, economic, educational, religious, and cultural ends." This right is crucial in preventing the majority from imposing its views on groups that would rather express other, perhaps unpopular, ideas (stating that protection of the right to expressive association is "especially important in preserving political and cultural diversity and in shielding dissident expression from suppression by the majority"). Government actions that may unconstitutionally burden this freedom may take many forms, one of which is "intrusion into the internal structure or affairs of an association" like a "regulation that forces the group to accept members it does not desire." Forcing a group to accept certain members may impair the ability of the group to express those views, and only those views, that it intends to express. Thus, "[f]reedom of association . . . plainly presupposes a freedom not to associate."

The forced inclusion of an unwanted person in a group infringes the group's freedom of expressive association if the presence of that person affects in a significant way the group's ability to advocate public or private viewpoints. *New York State Club Assn., Inc. v. City of New York* (1988). But the freedom of expressive association, like many freedoms, is not absolute. We have held that the freedom could be overridden "by regulations adopted to serve compelling state interests, unrelated to the suppression of ideas, that cannot be achieved through means significantly less restrictive of associational freedoms."

To determine whether a group is protected by the First Amendment's expressive associational right, we must determine whether the group engages in "expressive association." The First Amendment's protection of expressive association is not reserved for advocacy groups. But to come within its ambit, a group must engage in some form of expression, whether it be public or private.

Because this is a First Amendment case where the ultimate conclusions of law are virtually inseparable from findings of fact, we are obligated to independently review the factual record to ensure that the state court's judgment does not unlawfully intrude on free expression. The record reveals the following. The Boy Scouts is a private, nonprofit organization. According to its mission statement:

> "It is the mission of the Boy Scouts of America to serve others by helping to instill values in young people and, in other ways, to prepare them to make ethical choices over their lifetime in achieving their full potential.

"The values we strive to instill are based on those found in the Scout Oath and Law:

"Scout Oath

"On my honor I will do my best

"To do my duty to God and my country

"and to obey the Scout Law;

"To help other people at all times;

"To keep myself physically strong,

"mentally awake, and morally straight.

"Scout Law

"A Scout is:

"Trustworthy Obedient

"Loyal Cheerful

"Helpful Thrifty

"Friendly Brave

"Courteous Clean

"Kind Reverent."

Thus, the general mission of the Boy Scouts is clear: "[T]o instill values in young people." The Boy Scouts seeks to instill these values by having its adult leaders spend time with the youth members, instructing and engaging them in activities like camping, archery, and fishing. During the time spent with the youth members, the scoutmasters and assistant scoutmasters inculcate them with the Boy Scouts' values — both expressly and by example. . . .

Given that the Boy Scouts engages in expressive activity, we must determine whether the forced inclusion of Dale as an assistant scoutmaster would significantly affect the Boy Scouts' ability to advocate public or private viewpoints. This inquiry necessarily requires us first to explore, to a limited extent, the nature of the Boy Scouts' view of homosexuality.

* * *

Obviously, the Scout Oath and Law do not expressly mention sexuality or sexual orientation. And the terms "morally straight" and "clean" are by no means self-defining. . . .

* * *

The Boy Scouts asserts that it "teach[es] that homosexual conduct is not morally straight," and that it does "not want to promote homosexual conduct as a legitimate form of behavior." We accept the Boy Scouts' assertion. We need not inquire further to determine the nature of the Boy Scouts' expression with respect to homosexuality. But because the record before us contains written evidence of the Boy Scouts' viewpoint, we look to it as instructive, if only on the question of the sincerity of the professed beliefs.

A 1978 position statement to the Boy Scouts' Executive Committee, signed by Downing B. Jenks, the President of the Boy Scouts, and Harvey L. Price, the Chief Scout Executive, expresses the Boy Scouts' "official position" with regard to "homosexuality and Scouting":

> "Q. May an individual who openly declares himself to be a homosexual be a volunteer Scout leader?
>
> "A. No. The Boy Scouts of America is a private, membership organization and leadership therein is a privilege and not a right. We do not believe that homosexuality and leadership in Scouting are appropriate. We will continue to select only those who in our judgment meet our standards and qualifications for leadership."

Thus, at least as of 1978 — the year James Dale entered Scouting — the official position of the Boy Scouts was that avowed homosexuals were not to be Scout leaders.

A position statement promulgated by the Boy Scouts in 1991 (after Dale's membership was revoked but before this litigation was filed) also supports its current view.

* * *

We must then determine whether Dale's presence as an assistant scoutmaster would significantly burden the Boy Scouts' desire to not "promote homosexual conduct as a legitimate form of behavior." As we give deference to an association's assertions regarding the nature of its expression, we must also give deference to an association's view of what would impair its expression. . . . That is not to say that an expressive association can erect a shield against antidiscrimination laws simply by asserting that mere acceptance of a member from a particular group would impair its message. But here Dale, by his own admission, is one of a group of gay Scouts who have "become leaders in their community and are open and honest about their sexual orientation." Dale was the copresident of a gay and lesbian organization at college and remains a gay rights activist. Dale's presence in the Boy Scouts would, at the very least, force the organization to send a message, both to the youth members and the world, that the Boy Scouts accepts homosexual conduct as a legitimate form of behavior.

Hurley [*v. Irish-American Gay, Lesbian, and Bisexual Group of Boston* (1995)] is illustrative on this point. There we considered whether the application of Massachusetts' public accommodations law to require the organizers of a private St. Patrick's Day parade to include among the marchers an Irish-American gay, lesbian, and bisexual group, GLIB, violated the parade organizers' First Amendment rights. We noted that the parade organizers did not wish to exclude the GLIB members because of their sexual orientations, but because they wanted to march behind a GLIB banner.

*   *   *

The New Jersey Supreme Court determined that the Boy Scouts' ability to disseminate its message was not significantly affected by the forced inclusion of Dale as an assistant scoutmaster.

We disagree. . . .

First, associations do not have to associate for the "purpose" of disseminating a certain message in order to be entitled to the protections of the First Amendment. An association must merely engage in expressive activity that could be impaired in order to be entitled to protection. For example, the purpose of the St. Patrick's Day parade in *Hurley* was not to espouse any views about sexual orientation, but we held that the parade organizers had a right to exclude certain participants nonetheless.

Second, even if the Boy Scouts discourages Scout leaders from disseminating views on sexual issues — a fact that the Boy Scouts disputes with contrary evidence — the First Amendment protects the Boy Scouts' method of expression. If the Boy Scouts wishes Scout leaders to avoid questions of sexuality and teach only by example, this fact does not negate the sincerity of its belief discussed above.

Third, the First Amendment simply does not require that every member of a group agree on every issue in order for the group's policy to be "expressive association." The Boy Scouts takes an official position with respect to homosexual conduct, and that is sufficient for First Amendment purposes. . . .

*   *   *

Having determined that the Boy Scouts is an expressive association and that the forced inclusion of Dale would significantly affect its expression, we inquire whether the application of New Jersey's public accommodations law to require that the Boy Scouts accept Dale as an assistant scoutmaster runs afoul of the Scouts' freedom of expressive association. We conclude that it does.

State public accommodations laws were originally enacted to prevent discrimination in traditional places of public accommodation — like inns and trains. Over time, the public accommodations laws have expanded to cover more places. New Jersey's statutory definition of " '[a] place of public accommodation' " is extremely broad. . . . As the definition of "public accommodation" has expanded from clearly commercial entities, such as restaurants, bars, and hotels, to membership organizations such as the Boy Scouts, the potential for conflict between state public accommodations laws and the First Amendment rights of organizations has increased.

*   *   *

We recognized in cases such as *Roberts* and [*Board of Directors of Rotary Int'l v. Rotary Club of*] *Duarte* [(1987)] that States have a compelling interest in eliminating discrimination against women in public accommodations. But in each of these cases we went on to conclude that the enforcement of these statutes would not materially interfere with the ideas that the organization sought to express.

*   *   *

In *Hurley*, we said that public accommodations laws "are well within the State's usual power to enact when a legislature has reason to believe that a given group is the target of discrimination, and they do not, as a general matter, violate the First or Fourteenth Amendments." But we went on to note that in that case "the Massachusetts [public accommodations] law has been applied in a peculiar way" because "any contingent of protected individuals with a message would have the right to participate in petitioners' speech, so that the communication produced by the private organizers would be shaped by all those protected by the law who wish to join in with some expressive demonstration of their own." And in the associational freedom cases such as *Roberts*, *Duarte*, and *New York State Club Assn.*, after finding a compelling state interest, the Court went on to examine whether or not the application of the state law would impose any "serious burden" on the organization's rights of expressive association. So in these cases, the associational interest in freedom of expression has been set on one side of the scale, and the State's interest on the other.

Dale contends that we should apply the intermediate standard of review enunciated in *United States v. O'Brien* (1968), to evaluate the competing interests. There the Court enunciated a four-part test for review of a governmental regulation that has only an incidental effect on protected speech — in that case the symbolic burning of a draft card. A law prohibiting the destruction of draft cards only incidentally affects the free speech rights of those who happen to use a violation of that law as a symbol of protest. But New Jersey's public accommodations law directly and immediately affects associational rights, in this case associational rights that enjoy First Amendment protection. Thus, *O'Brien* is inapplicable.

In *Hurley*, we applied traditional First Amendment analysis to hold that the application of the Massachusetts public accommodations law to a parade violated the First Amendment rights of the parade organizers. Although we did not explicitly deem the parade in *Hurley* an expressive association, the analysis we applied there is similar to the analysis we apply here. We have already concluded that a state requirement that the Boy Scouts retain Dale as an assistant scoutmaster would significantly burden the organization's right to oppose or disfavor homosexual conduct. The state interests embodied in New Jersey's public accommodations law do not justify such a severe intrusion on the Boy Scouts' rights to freedom of expressive association. That being the case, we hold that the First Amendment prohibits the State from imposing such a requirement through the application of its public accommodations law.

* * *

Justice Stevens' dissent makes much of its observation that the public perception of homosexuality in this country has changed. Indeed, it appears that homosexuality has gained greater societal acceptance. But this is scarcely an argument for denying First Amendment protection to those who refuse to accept these views. The First Amendment protects expression, be it of the popular variety or not. See, *e.g.*, *Texas v. Johnson* (1989). . . . And the fact that an idea may be embraced and advocated by increasing numbers of people is all the more reason to protect the First Amendment rights of those who wish to voice a different view.

* * *

We are not, as we must not be, guided by our views of whether the Boy Scouts' teachings with respect to homosexual conduct are right or wrong; public or judicial disapproval of a tenet of an organization's expression does not justify the State's effort to compel the organization to accept members where such acceptance would derogate from the organization's expressive message. "While the law is free to promote all sorts of conduct in place of harmful behavior, it is not free to interfere with speech for no better reason than promoting an approved message or discouraging a disfavored one, however enlightened either purpose may strike the government."

The judgment of the New Jersey Supreme Court is reversed, and the cause remanded for further proceedings not inconsistent with this opinion.

It is so ordered.

JUSTICE STEVENS, with whom JUSTICE SOUTER, JUSTICE GINSBURG and JUSTICE BREYER join, dissenting.

* * *

The majority holds that New Jersey's law violates BSA's right to associate and its right to free speech. But that law does not "impos[e] any serious burdens" on BSA's "collective effort on behalf of [its] shared goals," *Roberts v. United States Jaycees* (1984), nor does it force BSA to communicate any message that it does not wish to endorse. New Jersey's law, therefore, abridges no constitutional right of the Boy Scouts.

* * *

BSA's published guidance on that topic underscores this point. Scouts, for example, are directed to receive their sex education at home or in school, but not from the organization: "Your parents or guardian or a sex education teacher should give you the facts about sex that you must know." Boy Scout Handbook (1992). . . .

* * *

. . . Insofar as religious matters are concerned, BSA's bylaws state that it is "absolutely nonsectarian in its attitude toward . . . religious training." "The BSA does not define what constitutes duty to God or the practice of religion. This is the responsibility of parents and religious leaders." In fact, many diverse religious organizations sponsor local Boy Scout troops. Because a number of religious groups do not view homosexuality as immoral or wrong and reject discrimination against homosexuals,[7] it is exceedingly difficult to believe that BSA nonetheless adopts a

---

[7] [3] *See, e.g.*, Brief for Deans of Divinity Schools and Rabbinical Institutions as *Amicus Curiae* 8 ("The diverse religi[ous] traditions of this country present no coherent moral message that excludes gays and lesbians from participating as full and equal members of those institutions. Indeed, the movement among a number of the nation's major religious institutions for many decades has been toward public recognition of gays and lesbians as full members of moral communities, and acceptance of gays and lesbians as religious leaders, elders and clergy"); Brief for General Board of Church and Society of the United Methodist Church et al. as *Amicus Curiae* 3 (describing views of The United Methodist Church, the Episcopal Church, the Religious Action Center of Reform Judaism, the United Church Board of

single particular religious or moral philosophy when it comes to sexual orientation. . . . BSA surely is aware that some religions do not teach that homosexuality is wrong.

* * *

II

* * *

At most the 1991 and 1992 statements declare only that BSA believed "homosexual conduct is inconsistent with the requirement in the Scout Oath that a Scout be morally straight and in the Scout Law that a Scout be clean in word and deed." But New Jersey's law prohibits discrimination on the basis of sexual orientation. And when Dale was expelled from the Boy Scouts, BSA said it did so because of his sexual orientation, not because of his sexual conduct.[8]

* * *

Several principles are made perfectly clear by *Jaycees* and *Rotary Club*. First, to prevail on a claim of expressive association in the face of a State's antidiscrimination law, it is not enough simply to engage in some kind of expressive activity. Both the Jaycees and the Rotary Club engaged in expressive activity protected by the First Amendment, yet that fact was not dispositive. Second, it is not enough to adopt an openly avowed exclusionary membership policy. Both the Jaycees and the Rotary Club did that as well. Third, it is not sufficient merely to articulate some connection between the group's expressive activities and its exclusionary policy. The Rotary Club, for example, justified its male-only membership policy by pointing to the " 'aspect of fellowship . . . that is enjoyed by the [exclusively] male membership' " and by claiming that only with an exclusively male membership could it "operate effectively" in foreign countries.

Rather, in *Jaycees*, we asked whether Minnesota's Human Rights Law requiring the admission of women "impose[d] any serious burdens" on the group's "collective effort on behalf of [its] shared goals." . . .

The evidence before this Court makes it exceptionally clear that BSA has, at most, simply adopted an exclusionary membership policy and has no shared goal of disapproving of homosexuality. . . .

* * *

. . . A State's antidiscrimination law does not impose a "serious burden" or a "substantial restraint" upon the group's "shared goals" if the group itself is unable to identify its own stance with any clarity.

Homeland Ministries, and the Unitarian Universalist Association, all of whom reject discrimination on the basis of sexual orientation).

[8] [8] At oral argument, BSA's counsel was asked: "[W]hat if someone is homosexual in the sense of having a sexual orientation in that direction but does not engage in any homosexual conduct?" Counsel answered: "[I]f that person also were to take the view that the reason they didn't engage in that conduct [was because] it would be morally wrong . . . that person would not be excluded."

IV

The majority pretermits this entire analysis. It finds that BSA in fact " 'teach[es] that homosexual conduct is not morally straight.' " This conclusion, remarkably, rests entirely on statements in BSA's briefs. . . .

This is an astounding view of the law. I am unaware of any previous instance in which our analysis of the scope of a constitutional right was determined by looking at what a litigant asserts in his or her brief and inquiring no further. It is even more astonishing in the First Amendment area, because, as the majority itself acknowledges, "we are obligated to independently review the factual record." . . .

. . . More critically, that inquiry requires our independent analysis, rather than deference to a group's litigating posture. Reflection on the subject dictates that such an inquiry is required.

Surely there are instances in which an organization that truly aims to foster a belief at odds with the purposes of a State's antidiscrimination laws will have a First Amendment right to association that precludes forced compliance with those laws. But that right is not a freedom to discriminate at will, nor is it a right to maintain an exclusionary membership policy simply out of fear of what the public reaction would be if the group's membership were opened up. . . .

*   *   *

There is, of course, a valid concern that a court's independent review may run the risk of paying too little heed to an organization's sincerely held views. But unless one is prepared to turn the right to associate into a free pass out of antidiscrimination laws, an independent inquiry is a necessity. Though the group must show that its expressive activities will be substantially burdened by the State's law, if that law truly has a significant effect on a group's speech, even the subtle speaker will be able to identify that impact.

In this case, no such concern is warranted. It is entirely clear that BSA in fact expresses no clear, unequivocal message burdened by New Jersey's law.

V

Even if BSA's right to associate argument fails, it nonetheless might have a First Amendment right to refrain from including debate and dialogue about homosexuality as part of its mission to instill values in Scouts. It can, for example, advise Scouts who are entering adulthood and have questions about sex to talk "with your parents, religious leaders, teachers, or Scoutmaster," and, in turn, it can direct Scoutmasters who are asked such questions "not undertake to instruct Scouts, in any formalized manner, in the subject of sex and family life" because "it is not construed to be Scouting's proper area." Dale's right to advocate certain beliefs in a public forum or in a private debate does not include a right to advocate these ideas when he is working as a Scoutmaster. And BSA cannot be compelled to include a message about homosexuality among the values it actually chooses to teach its Scouts, if it would prefer to remain silent on that subject.

*   *   *

[A newspaper] article did say that Dale was co-president of the Lesbian/Gay Alliance at Rutgers University, and that group presumably engages in advocacy regarding homosexual issues. But surely many members of BSA engage in expressive activities outside of their troop, and surely BSA does not want all of that expression to be carried on inside the troop. For example, a Scoutmaster may be a member of a religious group that encourages its followers to convert others to its faith. Or a Scoutmaster may belong to a political party that encourages its members to advance its views among family and friends. Yet BSA does not think it is appropriate for Scoutmasters to proselytize a particular faith to unwilling Scouts or to attempt to convert them from one religion to another. Nor does BSA think it appropriate for Scouts or Scoutmasters to bring politics into the troop. From all accounts, then, BSA does not discourage or forbid outside expressive activity, but relies on compliance with its policies and trusts Scouts and Scoutmasters alike not to bring unwanted views into the organization. Of course, a disobedient member who flouts BSA's policy may be expelled. But there is no basis for BSA to presume that a homosexual will be unable to comply with BSA's policy not to discuss sexual matters any more than it would presume that politically or religiously active members could not resist the urge to proselytize or politicize during troop meetings. As BSA itself puts it, its rights are "not implicated unless a prospective leader presents himself as a role model inconsistent with Boy Scouting's understanding of the Scout Oath and Law."

* * *

The majority, though, does not rest its conclusion on the claim that Dale will use his position as a bully pulpit. Rather, it contends that Dale's mere presence among the Boy Scouts will itself force the group to convey a message about homosexuality — even if Dale has no intention of doing so. The majority holds that "[t]he presence of an avowed homosexual and gay rights activist in an assistant scoutmaster's uniform sends a distinc[t] . . . message," and, accordingly, BSA is entitled to exclude that message. . . .

The majority's argument relies exclusively on *Hurley v. Irish-American Gay, Lesbian and Bisexual Group of Boston, Inc.* (1995). In that case, petitioners John Hurley and the South Boston Allied War Veterans Council ran a privately operated St. Patrick's Day parade. Respondent, an organization known as "GLIB," represented a contingent of gays, lesbians, and bisexuals who sought to march in the petitioners' parade "as a way to express pride in their Irish heritage as openly gay, lesbian, and bisexual individuals." . . .

First, it was critical to our analysis that GLIB was actually conveying a message by participating in the parade — otherwise, the parade organizers could hardly claim that they were being forced to include any unwanted message at all. Our conclusion that GLIB was conveying a message was inextricably tied to the fact that GLIB wanted to march in a parade, as well as the manner in which it intended to march. We noted the "inherent expressiveness of marching [in a parade] to make a point," and in particular that GLIB was formed for the purpose of making a particular point about gay pride. . . .

Second, we found it relevant that GLIB's message "would likely be perceived" as the parade organizers' own speech. That was so because "[p]arades and demonstrations . . . are not understood to be so neutrally presented or selectively viewed" as, say, a broadcast by a cable operator, who is usually considered to be "merely 'a conduit' for the speech" produced by others. Rather, parade organizers are usually understood to make the "customary determination about a unit admitted to the parade."

Dale's inclusion in the Boy Scouts is nothing like the case in *Hurley*. His participation sends no cognizable message to the Scouts or to the world. Unlike GLIB, Dale did not carry a banner or a sign; he did not distribute any fact sheet; and he expressed no intent to send any message. If there is any kind of message being sent, then, it is by the mere act of joining the Boy Scouts. Such an act does not constitute an instance of symbolic speech under the First Amendment.

* * *

Furthermore, it is not likely that BSA would be understood to send any message, either to Scouts or to the world, simply by admitting someone as a member. Over the years, BSA has generously welcomed over 87 million young Americans into its ranks. In 1992 over one million adults were active BSA members. The notion that an organization of that size and enormous prestige implicitly endorses the views that each of those adults may express in a non-Scouting context is simply mind boggling. Indeed, in this case there is no evidence that the young Scouts in Dale's troop, or members of their families, were even aware of his sexual orientation, either before or after his public statements at Rutgers University. It is equally farfetched to assert that Dale's open declaration of his homosexuality, reported in a local newspaper, will effectively force BSA to send a message to anyone simply because it allows Dale to be an Assistant Scoutmaster. For an Olympic gold medal winner or a Wimbledon tennis champion, being "openly gay" perhaps communicates a message — for example, that openness about one's sexual orientation is more virtuous than concealment; that a homosexual person can be a capable and virtuous person who should be judged like anyone else; and that homosexuality is not immoral — but it certainly does not follow that they necessarily send a message on behalf of the organizations that sponsor the activities in which they excel. The fact that such persons participate in these organizations is not usually construed to convey a message on behalf of those organizations any more than does the inclusion of women, African-Americans, religious minorities, or any other discrete group. Surely the organizations are not forced by antidiscrimination laws to take any position on the legitimacy of any individual's private beliefs or private conduct.

* * *

I respectfully dissent.

JUSTICE SOUTER, with whom JUSTICE GINSBURG and JUSTICE BREYER join, dissenting.

* * *

. . . I conclude that BSA has not made out an expressive association claim, therefore, not because of what BSA may espouse, but because of its failure to make sexual orientation the subject of my unequivocal advocacy, using the channels it customarily employs to state its message.

* * *

If, on the other hand, an expressive association claim has met the conditions JUSTICE STEVENS describes as necessary, there may well be circumstances in which the antidiscrimination law must yield, as he says. It is certainly possible for an individual to become so identified with a position as to epitomize it publicly. When that position is at odds with a group's advocated position, applying an antidiscrimination statute to require the group's acceptance of the individual in a position of group leadership could so modify or muddle or frustrate the group's advocacy as to violate the expressive associational right. While it is not our business here to rule on any such hypothetical, it is at least clear that our estimate of the progressive character of the group's position will be irrelevant to the First Amendment analysis if such a case comes to us for decision.

NOTES AND QUESTIONS

1. Does the ruling in *Dale* extend to homosexual membership, as well as leadership?

2. Why was the Court so deferential to the Boy Scouts on the issue of whether they associate for the purpose of engaging in expressive activity and whether that expression would be unconstitutionally burdened by the forced inclusion of an unwanted leader? Is it because of the sensitivities of any First Amendment speech claim and that the Court (as an arm of government) should not sit in judgment of the worth of private expression? The Court's deference was criticized by the dissent, but would the dissent have been comfortable with forcing a national civil rights organization to accept a proclaimed Neo-Nazi as one of its leaders?

3. Lingering in the background of this case is whether status discrimination is ever appropriate. The military has attempted to avoid this dilemma with a "don't ask, don't tell" policy — basically, if a member of the service neither volunteers the fact of homosexual status or engages in homosexual practice, there is no basis to exclude such service member from the military. Would this have been a better course for the Boy Scouts? Or are there some sensitive positions (teachers, athletic coaches, etc.) where orientation raises its own moral dilemmas? The dissent notes that some churches caution, as a matter of morality, against any differentiation on the basis of homosexual orientation, but this is not true of all, as some mainline denominations view the orientation, itself, as inclined toward an immoral practice. *See generally,* Vatican Congregation for the Doctrine of Faith, *Responding to Legislative Proposals on Discrimination Against Homosexuals,* 22 ORIGINS 174, 176 (August 6, 1992) ("There are areas in which it is not unjust discrimination to take sexual orientation into account, for example, in the placement of children for adoption or foster care, in employment of teachers or athletic coaches, and in military recruitment.")

4. The dissent claims that the Boy Scouts were merely interested in the public's reaction. But what is wrong with that? Isn't public reaction merely the consequence of expression?

5. Associations may be protected from government regulation that requires disclosure of membership. Such disclosure may chill participation and thus it

requires a compelling state interest. *NAACP v. Alabama ex rel. Patterson*, 357 U.S. 449 (1958). However, in *Buckley v. Valeo*, 424 U.S. 1 (1976), the Court upheld a statute requiring every political candidate and committee to keep records of their contributors and to make these records available to the public. Because the Court felt that the disclosure requirements would curtail corruption in campaign finance, there was a significant governmental interest shown.

6. In 1996, nearly 60% of the voters of California by Proposition 198 changed California's closed partisan primary system, used to determine the nominees of political parties, to a blanket primary. Under this new system, all registered voters in a primary could vote for any candidate, regardless of the voter's prior political affiliation. Four political parties, including California's Republicans and Democrats, sought to enforce their respective rules prohibiting non-party members from voting in their primaries, alleging that California's blanket primary violated the First Amendment right of association. In a 7-2 decision, *California Democratic Party v. Jones*, 530 U.S. 567 (2000), the Court invalidated the blanket primary. Justice Scalia's opinion for the Court acknowledges the role states play in the regulation of elections. For example, states can require parties to use the primary format for selecting nominees, mandate a showing of some level of support before allowing candidates ballot space, or require party registration for a reasonable period of time before a primary election. States may not, however, "regulate freely" the processes by which political parties select their nominees. In making the point that the "corollary of the right to associate is the right to not associate," the majority reiterated the notion that political parties may limit control over their decisions to those who share their "interests and persuasions." And perhaps no decision is more important for a political party than nominee selection, which is, in the Court's view, "the crucial juncture at which the appeal to common principles may be translated into . . . political power." Thus, Proposition 198, in order to be held constitutional, needed to be narrowly tailored to serve a compelling state interest, and the Court rejected each of the seven interests proffered by the state as either not sufficiently compelling or as not narrowly tailored to the open-primary requirement.

In *Clingman v. Beaver*, 544 U.S. 581 (2005), the Court again gave substantial deference to the right of political parties to maintain their respective identities. While the issue in *Jones* was compelling parties to allow non-members to participate in their primaries, in *Clingman*, the issue was a state law that limited the right of parties to invite non-members to participate in their primaries. Specifically, under Oklahoma's semi-closed primary law, a political party was limited to inviting its own members and independents, but not the members of other parties.

In a previous decision, *Tashjian v. Republican Party of Conn.*, 479 U.S. 208 (1986), the Court struck down, as inconsistent with the First Amendment, a closed primary system that prevented a political party from inviting even independent voters to vote in the party's primary. 6-3, the Justices per Justice Thomas distinguished *Tashjian* and found the semi-closed primary in *Clingman* to be far less burdensome or severe. The Oklahoma law, noted the Court, does not regulate the internal processes of the Libertarian Party, its authority to exclude unwanted members, or its capacity to communicate with the public. Moreover, whatever burden on associational interests there was off-set by important regulatory interests, such as the preservation of political parties as viable and identifiable groups, the enabling of electioneering and party-building efforts, and relatedly, the guarding against party raiding or other types of gaming of the primary process, such as Democrats voting in the Libertarian primary to pick a third party candidate who would be most likely to split the Republican vote in the general election. Raiding the major parties seems to be exactly what the Libertarian Party had in mind in challenging the semi-closed primary, but the Court refused to let them, by applying less than strict scrutiny — which the Court said should be reserved for those cases, unlike this one, where there was more than "a minimal infringement on the rights to vote and of association" — that is, where the burden is severe. In a separate concurrence, Justices O'Connor and Breyer declined to join part of the Thomas majority (thereby making that part only a plurality) in order to make the point that the associational interests of the Libertarian and other minor parties are not insignificant, and, in an appropriate case, it might be possible for these parties to demonstrate how the entire constellation of state election laws — regulations limiting access to the ballot, for example — might combine to run afoul of protected associational interests. These concurring Justices also note that greater scrutiny is warranted where election restrictions have an air of self-dealing, suggesting they were put in place by those already in office to stifle electoral competition.

7. What about campaign finance restrictions? Are they an unconstitutional restriction on the freedom of speech and association? The Court has grappled with this complex area repeatedly over the past thirty years. In *Buckley v. Valeo*, 425 U.S. 1 (1976), the Court considered contributions and expenditures to both be forms of speech, with the former more susceptible to limitation. Spending limits go directly to speech, and the Court was unwilling to accept the notion that some speakers are less able than others to spend. In other words, as a matter of constitutional judgment, the Court does not share any public misgiving generally about the expensive nature of campaigns or how such expense may essentially limit public office to the wealthy or their friends. By contrast, campaign contribution limits are subject to lesser, albeit "closely drawn" scrutiny, the Court reasoned, because campaign contribution (unlike expenditure) limits "entail only a marginal restriction upon the contributor's ability to engage in free communication." Contribution limits are grounded in the important government interest in preventing "both the actual corruption threatened by large financial contributions and the eroding of public confidence in the electoral process through the appearance of corruption."

The Bipartisan Campaign Finance Act of 2003 ("BCRA") continued this theme, bringing into congressional purview so-called "soft money" and issue ads. Soft money was defined very generally as "money as yet unregulated under" the Federal Election Campaign Act of 1971 ("FECA"). FECA had previously only regulated "hard money," or money contributed to a candidate or his or her campaign committee for the purpose of influencing a federal election. Soft money was used to fund activities intended to influence state and local elections, mixed federal and state uses such as get out the vote drives, and to advertise the party in general, even if it mentioned a federal candidate. The BCRA also regulated so-called "issues ads," which had previously escaped regulation because they did not directly say, "Vote for Smith." Rather, an issue ad would highlight a politician's voting record on a specific topic, such as gun control, crime, or the protection of unborn life. And so, instead of saying "Vote for Jim Smith," an issue ad would say, "Here is Jim Smith's voting record on gun-control."

Groups across the political spectrum brought free speech challenges against BCRA. The named plaintiff was Senator Mitch McConnell, a top-ranking Republican Senator, but other plaintiffs included the ACLU, NOW, NRA, and National Right to Life. The challenge narrowly failed. As an initial matter, the Court reiterated the distinction that first emerged in the seminal decision of *Buckley v. Valeo* between campaign contributions and spending limits. Subject to the lesser level of review applicable to contributions, BCRA passed muster as it was closely tailored to address the compelling government interest of avoiding actual or apparent corruption in politics. Opponents argued that the law was overbroad because the record suggested that the "appearance of corruption" was no more than the usual give and take of politics or attention to constituents. Moreover, said the challengers, there were other narrower ways to address real corruption in politics, namely the federal bribery statutes. The Court rejected these arguments because anti-bribery laws reach only the most egregious uses of money to obtain influence. Thus, "[i]n speaking of 'improper influence' and 'opportunities for abuse' in addition to 'quid pro quo arrangements,' we [have] recognized a concern not confined to bribery of public officials, but extending to the broader threat from politicians too compliant with the wishes of large contributors."

Justice Scalia's dissent lamented that *McConnell v. Federal Election Comm'n* (2003), was

> a sad day for freedom of speech. Who could have imagined that the same Court which, within the past four years, has sternly disapproved of restrictions upon such inconsequential forms of expression as virtual child pornography, tobacco advertising, dissemination of illegally intercepted communications, and sexually explicit cable programming, would smile with favor upon a law that cuts to the heart of what the First Amendment is meant to protect: the right to criticize the government.

Given BCRA's complex regulatory scheme and attendant criminal penalties, a person running for a federal office is well in need of an attorney specializing in election and campaign finance law. Thus, yet another impediment has been erected to service by Americans of moderate wealth. Moreover, BCRA is widely perceived as benefiting incumbents over challengers generally. In his dissent, Justice Scalia mentioned that incumbents raise approximately three times more hard money than soft money and that donations from lobbyists to these same incumbents is substantially (approximately 92%) hard money. Is it a coincidence that incumbent members of Congress chose only to regulate soft money in BCRA?

Beyond access to public office, BCRA is said to favor some voices over others, even as the Court majority held that "contribution limits, like other measures aimed at protecting the integrity of the [political] process, tangibly benefit public participation in public debate." But the dissent and other critics of BCRA asked: is it fair that the New York Times (a multibillion dollar media corporation) can produce editorials advocating the election of a given candidate unrestrained by BRCA while the NRA or the ACLU can not? Keep in mind that the NRA and the ACLU are funded by contributions or modest annual membership fees (approximately $35 and $20 a year, respectively).

8.   In *Randall v. Sorrell* (2006), the Court considered the constitutionality of a Vermont campaign finance statute that limits both (1) the amounts that candidates for state office may spend on their campaigns (expenditure limitations) and (2) the amounts that individuals, organizations, and political parties may contribute to those campaigns (contribution limitations). The Court held both sets of limitations to be inconsistent with the First Amendment. Under the Court's precedent, the expenditure limits violated the First Amendment, *Buckley v. Valeo* (1976), and notwithstanding years and years of proof that an enormous amount of a public official's time is diverted to raising funds to stay in office, the Court stubbornly refused to reconsider whether money is actually the equivalent of speech or whether, even if money and speech are too close to disentangle, a cap on spending is not more equivalent to a time, place or manner restriction than substantive censorship. The contribution limits were unconstitutional because in their specific details (involving low maximum levels and other restrictions) they failed to satisfy the First Amendment's requirement of careful tailoring. That is to say, they imposed burdens upon First Amendment interests that (when viewed in light of the statute's legitimate objectives) are disproportionately severe. For various reasons, four Justices (Alito, Kennedy, Thomas and Scalia) concurred only in the judgment, reiterating skepticism about how well campaign finance reform resolved fundamental questions in the context of speech doctrine.

Justice Stevens' dissent candidly conceded the reality of modern day fundraising and its effect on fulfilling one's public responsibilities. He called for *Buckley* to be overruled in the following dissent:

JUSTICE STEVENS, dissenting.

> JUSTICE BREYER and JUSTICE SOUTER debate whether the *per curiam* decision in *Buckley v. Valeo* forecloses any constitutional limitations on candidate expenditures. This is plainly an issue on which reasonable minds can disagree. The *Buckley* Court never explicitly addressed whether the pernicious effects of endless fundraising can serve as a compelling state interest that justifies expenditure limits, yet its silence, in light of the record before it, suggests that it implicitly treated this proposed interest as insufficient. Assuming this to be true, however, I am convinced that *Buckley*'s holding on expenditure limits is wrong, and that the time has come to overrule it.

*   *   *

> As Justice White recognized, it is quite wrong to equate money and speech. To the contrary,

>> "[t]he burden on actual speech imposed by limitations on the spending of money is minimal and indirect. All rights of direct political expression and advocacy are retained. Even under the campaign laws as originally enacted, everyone was free to spend as much as they chose to amplify their views on general political issues, just not

specific candidates. The restrictions, to the extent they do affect speech, are viewpoint-neutral and indicate no hostility to the speech itself or its effects."

Accordingly, these limits on expenditures are far more akin to time, place, and manner restrictions than to restrictions on the content of speech. Like Justice White, I would uphold them "so long as the purposes they serve are legitimate and sufficiently substantial."

Buckley's conclusion to the contrary relied on the following oft-quoted metaphor:

"Being free to engage in unlimited political expression subject to a ceiling on expenditures is like being free to drive an automobile as far and as often as one desires on a single tank of gasoline."

But, of course, while a car cannot run without fuel, a candidate can speak without spending money. And while a car can only travel so many miles per gallon, there is no limit on the number of speeches or interviews a candidate may give on a limited budget. Moreover, provided that this budget is above a certain threshold, a candidate can exercise due care to ensure that her message reaches all voters. Just as a driver need not use a Hummer to reach her destination, so a candidate need not flood the airways with ceaseless sound-bites of trivial information in order to provide voters with reasons to support her.

. . . When the seasoned campaigners who were Members of the Congress that endorsed the expenditure limits in the Federal Election Campaign Act Amendments of 1974 concluded that a modest budget would not preclude them from effectively communicating with the electorate, they necessarily rejected the *Buckley* metaphor.

These campaigners also identified significant government interests favoring the imposition of expenditure limits. Not only do these limits serve as an important complement to corruption-reducing contribution limits, but they also "protect equal access to the political arena, [and] free candidates and their staffs from the interminable burden of fundraising." These last two interests are particularly acute. When campaign costs are so high that only the rich have the reach to throw their hats into the ring, we fail "to protect the political process from undue influence of large aggregations of capital and to promote individual responsibility for democratic government." States have recognized this problem, but *Buckley's* perceived ban on expenditure limits severely limits their options in dealing with it.

The interest in freeing candidates from the fundraising straitjacket is even more compelling. Without expenditure limits, fundraising devours the time and attention of political leaders, leaving them too busy to handle their public responsibilities effectively. . . .

Additionally, there is no convincing evidence that these important interests favoring expenditure limits are fronts for incumbency protection. . . .

One final point bears mention. Neither the opinions in *Buckley* nor those that form today's cacophony pay heed to how the Framers would have viewed candidate expenditure limits. This is not an unprincipled approach, as the historical context is "usually relevant but not necessarily dispositive." This is particularly true of contexts that are so different. At the time of the framing the accepted posture of the leading candidates was one of modesty, acknowledging a willingness to serve rather than a desire to compete. Speculation about how the Framers would have legislated if they had foreseen the era of televised sound-bites thus cannot provide us with definitive answers.

Nevertheless, I am firmly persuaded that the Framers would have been appalled by the impact of modern fundraising practices on the ability of elected officials to perform their public responsibilities. I think they would have viewed federal statutes limiting the amount of money that congressional candidates might spend in future elections as well within Congress' authority. And they surely would not have expected judges to interfere with the enforcement of expenditure limits that merely require candidates to budget their activities without imposing any restrictions whatsoever on what they may say in their speeches, debates, and interviews.

For the foregoing reasons, I agree with JUSTICE SOUTER that it would be entirely appropriate to allow further proceedings on expenditure limits to go forward in these cases. For the reasons given in Parts II and III of his dissent, I also agree that Vermont's contribution limits and presumption of coordinated expenditures by political parties are constitutional, and so join those portions of his opinion.

9.   In *FEC v. Wisconsin Right to Life, Inc. (WRTL)*, 551 U.S. 449 (2007), the Court, at the pen of the Chief Justice, invalidated the application of section 203 of BCRA. Section 203 of the Bipartisan Campaign Reform Act of 2002 (BCRA) makes it a federal crime for any corporation to broadcast, shortly before an election, any communication that names a federal candidate for elected office and is targeted to the electorate. In *McConnell v. Federal Election Comm'n* (2003), the Court considered whether § 203 was facially overbroad under the First Amendment because it captured within its reach not only campaign speech, or "express advocacy," but also speech about public issues more generally, or "issue advocacy," that mentions a candidate for federal office. The Court concluded that there was no overbreadth concern to the extent the speech in question was the "functional equivalent" of express campaign speech. . . . On the other hand, the Court "assumed" that the interests it had found to "justify the regulation of campaign speech might not apply to the regulation of genuine issue ads." . . . The Court nonetheless determined that § 203 was not facially overbroad. Even assuming § 203 "inhibited some constitutionally protected corporate and union speech," the Court concluded that those challenging the law on its face had failed to carry their "heavy burden" of establishing that *all* enforcement of the law should therefore be prohibited. . . .

In *WRTL*, the Court confronted an as-applied challenge. Resolving it required the Court to first determine whether the speech at issue was the "functional equivalent" of speech expressly advocating the election or defeat of a candidate for federal office, or instead a "genuine issue ad." . . . In drawing that line, said the Court,

> the First Amendment requires us to err on the side of protecting political speech rather than suppressing it. BCRA § 203 . . . makes it a crime for any labor union or incorporated entity . . . to use its general treasury funds to pay for any "electioneering communication." . . . BCRA's definition of "electioneering communication" is clear and expansive. It encompasses any broadcast, cable, or satellite communication that refers to a candidate for federal office and that is aired within 30 days of a federal primary election or 60 days of a federal general election in the jurisdiction in which that candidate is running for office. . . .

WRTL began broadcasting a radio advertisement entitled "Wedding." The transcript of "Wedding" reads as follows:

> "PASTOR: And who gives this woman to be married to this man?

> "BRIDE'S FATHER: Well, as father of the bride, I certainly could. But instead, I'd like to share a few tips on how to properly install drywall. Now you put the drywall up . . . .

> "VOICE-OVER: Sometimes it's just not fair to delay an important decision.

> "But in Washington it's happening. A group of Senators is using the filibuster delay tactic to block federal judicial nominees from a simple "yes" or "no" vote. So qualified candidates don't get a chance to serve.

> "It's politics at work, causing gridlock and backing up some of our courts to a state of emergency.

> "Contact Senators Feingold and Kohl and tell them to oppose the filibuster.

> "Visit: BeFair.org

> "Paid for by Wisconsin Right to Life (befair.org), which is responsible for the content of this advertising and not authorized by any candidate or candidate's committee." . . .

WRTL filed suit against the Federal Election Commission (FEC) on July 28, 2004, seeking declaratory and injunctive relief before a three-judge District Court. . . . WRTL alleged that BCRA's prohibition on the use of corporate treasury funds for "electioneering communications" as defined in the Act is unconstitutional as applied to "Wedding," and some similar ads.

WRTL rightly concedes that its ads are prohibited by BCRA § 203. Each ad clearly identifies Senator Feingold, who was running (unopposed) in the Wisconsin Democratic primary on September 14, 2004, and each ad would have been "targeted to the relevant electorate," . . . during the BCRA blackout period. WRTL further concedes that its ads do not fit under any of BCRA's exceptions to the term "electioneering communication." . . . The only question, then, is whether it is consistent with the First Amendment for BCRA § 203 to prohibit WRTL from running these three ads.

The Court held that, as applied, the *Government* must prove that applying BCRA to WRTL's ads furthers a compelling interest and is narrowly tailored to achieve that interest. The Court further reasoned that any test to distinguish constitutionally protected political speech from speech that BCRA may proscribe should provide a safe harbor for those who wish to exercise First Amendment rights. The Court rejected a test based on either intent to affect an election or the actual effect speech will have on an election or on a particular segment of the target audience. Such a test "puts the speaker . . . wholly at the mercy of the varied understanding of his hearers." Rather, a court should find that an ad is the functional equivalent of express advocacy only if the ad is susceptible of no reasonable interpretation other than as an appeal to vote for or against a specific candidate. Under this test, WRTL's ads were found to be plainly not the functional equivalent of express advocacy. First, their content is consistent with that of a genuine issue ad: The ads focus on a legislative issue, take a position on the issue, exhort the public to adopt that position, and urge the public to contact public officials with respect to the matter. Second, their content lacks indicia of express advocacy: The ads do not mention an election, candidacy, political party, or challenger; and they do not take a position on a candidate's character, qualifications, or fitness for office. Merely because an ad appeals to citizens to contact their elected representative is not enough. The Chief Justice concluded:

> Yet, as is often the case in this Court's First Amendment opinions, we have gotten this far in the analysis without quoting the Amendment itself: "Congress shall make no law . . . abridging the freedom of speech." The Framers' actual words put these cases in proper perspective. Our jurisprudence over the past 216 years has rejected an absolutist interpretation of those words, but when it comes to drawing difficult lines in the area of pure political speech — between what is protected and what the Government may ban — it is worth recalling the language we are applying. *McConnell* held that express advocacy of a candidate or his opponent by a corporation shortly before an election may be prohibited, along with the functional equivalent of such express advocacy. We have no occasion to revisit that determination today. But when it comes to defining what speech qualifies as the functional equivalent of express advocacy subject to such a ban — the issue we *do* have to decide — we give the benefit of the doubt to speech, not censorship. The First Amendment's command that "Congress shall make no law . . . abridging the freedom of speech" demands at least that.

10. The law regarding the permissibility of campaign expenditures in contests for federal (and, increasingly, state) office is one of the most impenetrable in all of constitutional law. If one were to be realistic (or perhaps cynical), one could view the struggle here as a battle between incumbents, who want to do all that they can to disadvantage challengers (can you understand how the legislation at issue in this case might lend itself to that interpretation?), and challengers who can at least point to the First Amendment's clear and absolute prohibition on the regulation of speech. As the Chief Justice reminds us towards the close of his opinion, the relevant text of the First Amendment is that "Congress shall make no law . . . abridging the freedom of speech. . . ." Why is it that those words don't mean that the BCRA (popularly referred to as "McCain-Feingold" because of its two prominent Senatorial sponsors) provision at issue is unconstitutional on its face? Would you have voted for "McCain-Feingold" had you been a member of Congress? Do you think it is more than a coincidence that the broadcast ads at issue in the case target Senator Feingold himself?

11. *F.E.C. v. WRTL* was one of the last cases to be decided in the October 2006 term, which was the first term of the Court in which Sandra Day O'Connor had been replaced by Samuel Alito. Liberals feared that Alito's replacing O'Connor would lead to a much more conservative approach on the Supreme Court, and this case (among a few others) was reported in the popular media to be a strong sign of that. Do you agree? What do you make of the Chief Justice's careful avoidance of overruling the not-yet-four-year old *McConnell* decision? Both Justice Scalia (in his concurring opinion) and Justice Souter (in his dissent) (not reprinted) claim that the relevant provision of McCain-Feingold has been declared unconstitutional, so that *McConnell* has, in effect, been reversed. Indeed, in a footnote Justice Scalia declared, "[T]he [Chief Justice's opinion's] attempt at distinguishing *McConnell* is unpersuasive enough, and the change in the law it works is substantial enough, that seven Justices of the Court, having widely divergent views concerning the constitutionality of the restrictions at issue, agree that the opinion effectively overrules *McConnell* without saying so. This faux judicial restraint is judicial obfuscation." Would you agree that the Chief Justice's opinion is "judicial obfuscation"? Is it significant that at his Senate Confirmation hearings the then Judge Roberts made clear that he saw the judicial role as a modest one?

12. What is the argument in support of the constitutionality of § 203 of the BCRA? Mostly it is the concern with the increasing amount of money being spent on political campaigns for federal office, and the possibility that corporate contributors expect some sort of *quid-pro-quo* for their contributions (or expenditures) on behalf of candidates for federal office. Justice Souter suggests that those making corporate contributions are undermining the likelihood that members of Congress will vote on the basis of what they honestly perceive to be in the public interest, and will, instead, reward "special interest" contributors to their campaigns. As Justice Souter puts it, this would serve to undermine "the elements summed up in the notion of political integrity," which political integrity Souter believes, is "a value second to none in a free society." Is he right about that? Is there any higher value "in a free society"? If there is, is there an expression of such a value or values in the First Amendment?

13. As the omitted dissent noted: it is surely correct that prior decisions of the Court have recognized a "Government interest in 'equalizing the relative ability of individuals and groups to influence the outcome of elections,'" but how, precisely ought we to reconcile that interest with the strictures of the First Amendment? Is it appropriate to draw distinctions between what can be done by corporations or unions on the one hand, and individuals on the other? Is it appropriate to draw distinctions between what can be done by PAC's, and what can be done using general corporate treasuries? Is it appropriate to distinguish between expenditures for broadcast and print ads? And, finally, is it appropriate to distinguish between expenditures regarding "issues," and those regarding express advocacy of a particular candidate? Justice Scalia argues that the lines drawn by the Court have resulted in the "irony" that its decisions upholding federal regulation of campaign expenditures have resulted in "wealthy individuals" dominating "political discourse," while "small, grass-roots organizations" like WRTL end up "muzzled." Is he right about that?

14. The Court invalidated the so-called "Millionaire's Amendment." *Davis v. FEC* (2008). The Amendment is triggered if, in a given congressional race, a wealthy candidate signals that he or she is going to spend more than $350,000 of personal funds to finance that candidacy. That gives rise to a right for the opponent to raise money beyond the usual contribution ceilings, and to coordinate financing with a political party, again exceeding limits. It also triggers heavy disclosure requirements on the wealthy candidates, some perhaps due on a daily basis. The Amendment did not survive review by Justice Samuel A. Alito, Jr., who wrote for a majority: "for Congress to use the election laws to influence the voters' choices . . . [t]he Constitution . . . confers upon voters, not Congress, the power to choose the Members of the House of Representatives." Thus, Congress may not legislate to "level electoral opportunities."

In invalidating the Amendment, Justice Alito was echoing sentiments that Justice Scalia once expressed in dissent in *Austin v. Michigan Chamber of Commerce* (1990), which upheld limits on the use of certain corporate funds for political purposes. It would seem that Justice Alito is signaling that Congress' power to stop corruption or to avoid its appearance does not extend to leveling the playing field among rich and poor candidates. Does this put the earlier precedent restricting corporate and union spending in doubt?

What's wrong with trying to even up sides? Justice Alito believes it interferes with a wealthy candidate's "natural advantage" of access to more money. Well, yeah, that was the point — the candidate with a big loudspeaker can be heard better, too, but that doesn't preclude the park from limiting all candidates to a more modest speaker system. Is a restriction on wealth any more of a content limit than turning the volume knob down? In both situations, the government doesn't care what is being said, does it?

Would it be better to avoid all this as some other countries do with the public funding of all campaigns and leave it at that — no private spending, or is that just substituting legislative choices for those of voters?

15. The date: January 27, 2010. The scene: a packed assemblage of members of the Legislative, Executive, and Judicial Branches of the Government of the United States of America. The event: The first State of the Union address of the current President of the United States. Frozen in time is the moment when Democrat members of Congress and the Obama administration stood wildly cheering around and over the backs of the seated members of the United States Supreme Court. President Obama had just declared that the Supreme Court had "reversed a century of law to open the floodgates for special interests — including foreign corporations — to spend without limit in our elections" when it issued its ruling in a case barely a week earlier. As the partisans whooped and cheered, Justice Samuel Alito was observed quietly mouthing the words, "Not true." Then, on March 9, 2010, two and a half months after the arguably unprecedented "frozen moment," Chief

Justice Roberts was addressing a group of University of Alabama law students, when one of the students asked a question of the Chief Justice. The student asked if it was appropriate for the President to criticize the Supreme Court during the State of the Union address. The Chief Justice replied that he had no problem with people criticizing the Supreme Court. He then, however, added an on-the-other-hand comment:

> "On the other hand," he continued, "there is the issue of the setting, the circumstances, and the decorum. The image of having the members of one branch of government, standing up, literally surrounding the Supreme Court, cheering and hollering while the court — according the requirements of protocol — has to sit there expressionless, I think is very troubling."

"Very troubling" in that, as the Chief Justice explained, the constitutionally mandated presidential State of the Union address had "degenerated to a political pep rally."

Citizens United v. Federal Election Commission, 558 U.S. 310 (2010), was the case that occasioned those memorable and newsworthy exchanges. *Citizens United* centered on 2 U.S.C. § 441b, an amendment to the federal Bipartisan Campaign Reform Act of 2002. The Citizens United organization wanted to make the movie *Hillary* available through video-on-demand within 30 days of the 2008 primary elections, a course of action that would constitute a violation of § 441b. In an opinion by Justice Kennedy, the Court struck down, as violative of Citizens United's free speech rights, § 441b's restrictions on corporate *independent* expenditures — the expenditures that expressly advocate the election or defeat of a candidate (the restrictions that applied to the *Citizens United* situation). The statute's prohibition on corporate *direct* expenditures to candidates, however, was untouched by the Court's ruling and still stands. In making its ruling the Court expressly overruled *Austin* v. *Michigan Chamber of Commerce* (1990) and the part of *McConnell* v. *Federal Election Commission* (2003) that had upheld § 441b's restrictions on corporate independent expenditures. The Court saw *Austin*'s "antidistortion" rationale as being inconsistent with prior case law that, according to the Court, had consistently and strongly upheld the application of First Amendment protections to corporations. The "antidistortion" rationale, heavily relied on in *Austin* and by the Federal Election Commission in *Citizens United*, had suggested that the government has a compelling interest in preventing "the corrosive and distorting effects of immense aggregations of wealth that are accumulated with the help of the corporate form and that have little or no correlation to the public's support for the corporation's political ideas." Not so, declared the Court.

16. First came *Davis v. FEC*, then came *Citizens United v. FEC*, and the well-publicized showdown at the State of the Union Address (*see supra*, Note 15). Now comes *Arizona Free Enterprise Club's Freedom Club v. Bennett*, 131 S. Ct. 2806, 180 L. Ed. 2d 664 (2011), and the voiding of the Arizona Citizens Clean Elections Act. All three cases resulted in the striking down of campaign finance laws, and all three resulted essentially (*i.e.*, when the concurrences-in-part and dissents-in-part are sorted out) in 5/4 decisions along the Court's familiar factional lines. With the *Arizona Free Enterprise Club's Freedom Club* case, however, the scene changes to the state level. Arizona's law was an effort, purely at the state level, to "even up the sides" in elections for state offices. Arizona's scheme was a state-run financing system whereby candidates for state office who accept the public financing could "receive additional money from the State in direct response to the campaign activities of privately financed candidates and independent expenditure groups." The way it worked was that once the privately financed candidate expended funds beyond the initially set public financing limit, the publicly financed candidate would be entitled to receive "one dollar for every dollar spent by an opposing privately financed candidate" and one dollar for every dollar spent by independent expenditure groups in support of the privately financed candidate or in opposition to the publicly financed candidate. Publicly funded candidates had to agree, among other things, to limit their expenditure of personal funds to $500, to participate in at least one public debate, to adhere to an overall expenditure cap, and to return all unspent public moneys to the State. There was, however, a ceiling amount. In the words of the Court, "Matching funds top out at two times the initial authorized grant of public funding to the publicly financed candidate." The Court ruled that the Arizona scheme was too much like the so-called "Millionaire's Amendment that had been invalidated in *Davis v. FEC*, and thus it substantially burdened political speech without a justifying compelling state interest. To the Court, the burden on free-speech rights was evident: "It is clear not only to us but to every other court to have considered the question after *Davis* that a candidate or independent group might not spend money if the direct result of that spending is additional funding to political adversaries."

17.   In *John Doe #1 v. Reed*, 130 S. Ct. 2811, 177 L. Ed. 2d 493 (2010), sustained the constitutionality of the State of Washington's Public Records Act's disclosure provisions. The provisions authorize private parties to obtain copies of "government documents," and it is understood that the term "government documents" covers documents containing the names and addresses of persons who sign petitions to place issues on the state's referendum ballots. A recent referendum in the state involved the question of whether there should be a state law giving benefits comparable to those enjoyed by married couples to same-sex couples. The Act was known locally and colloquially as the "Everything But Marriage Act." John Doe #1, as well as John Doe #2 and an organization called Project Marriage Washington, gathered 138,000 signatures of Washingtonians on a petition for the referendum, substantially in excess of the number required by law. Several organizations, including the Washington Coalition for Open Government and Washington Families Standing Together filed a request for copies of the signed petition containing the names and addresses of the 138,000 signers. Shortly thereafter, two other organizations, "WhoSigned.org" and "KnowThyNeighbor.org," had issued a press release indicating their intent to put the names of the petition signers on the Internet. The petitioners sought to enjoin the release of their names and addresses, claiming that the compelled disclosure of the signatory information would violate their rights under the First Amendment. The United States Supreme Court ruled against them.

The key point that determined the Court's ruling in the *John Doe* case was one of procedure. In their complaint, the petitioners had alleged two counts, Count 1, which alleged that the Public Records Act is unconstitutional as applied to referendum petitions, and Count 2, which alleged that "[t]he Public Records Act is unconstitutional as applied to the [referendum petition in question] because there is a reasonable probability that the signatories of the Referendum 71 petition will be subjected to threats, harassment, and reprisals." When both the federal district court and the court of appeals, made their final decisions in the case, however, their rulings were confined to Count I of the petitioners' complaint. The issue before the United States Supreme Court was, therefore, limited to the question of whether the State of Washington's Public records Act was unconstitutional as applied to referendum petitions *in general*. In essence that question was whether the Act was invalid *on its face*, *i.e.*, without reference to the referendum petition in question or to the "reasonable probability that the signatories of the referendum petition in question will be subjected to threats, harassment, and reprisals," as the petitioners' complaint phrased it in Count II. The Chief Justice, writing for the Court, acknowledged that "[t]he compelled disclosure of signatory information on referendum petitions is subject to review under the First Amendment," and announced that the test to justify a government-compelled disclosure on the kind in the *John Doe* case is "exacting scrutiny," requiring that the government show "a substantial relation between the disclosure requirement and a sufficiently important governmental interest." Having divorced his analysis from the issue of the petitioners being possibly subjected to threats, harassment, and reprisals, the Chief Justice had little trouble identifying the state's interest in rooting out fraud or mistake in the referendum process as being sufficiently important, and the disclosure requirement being substantially related to that interest. The Chief Justice did, however, caution that a genuine *"as applied"* challenge would certainly be available to litigants who present a proper case alleging a reasonable probability that they would be subjected to threats, harassment, and reprisals if the disclosure were ordered but, again, because of its procedural posture, this was not such a case.

18.   In *Christian Legal Society Chapter v. Martinez*, 130 S. Ct. 2971, 177 L. Ed. 2d 838 (2010), the Court, in an opinion by Justice Ginsburg, the upheld the University of California at Hastings' denial of Registered Student Organization status to a group of law students who had organized themselves as a chapter of the Christian Legal Society. The Christian Legal Society is a national group of lawyers and law students, and it oversees affiliated local chapters at various law schools. The trouble that gave rise to the *Christian Legal Society* case was the society's specifically Christian "Statement of Faith," including the beliefs of the society that sexual activity should not occur outside of marriage and that marriage exists only between a man and a woman. The Christian Legal Society thus interprets its bylaws to exclude from affiliation anyone who engages in "unrepentant homosexual conduct." Complicating matters somewhat was the fact that the University of California at Hastings has a "Policy on Nondiscrimination" which apparently applies university-wide and commits the university to avoid discriminating unlawfully on the basis of, among other things, religion, and suggests that, in the awarding of Registered Student Organization status, the Policy on Nondiscrimination prevents the university from discriminating against the Christian Legal Society students on the basis of their religious beliefs. In the early stages of the litigation, however, the University took the position that its Policy on Nondiscrimination has been understood as an "accept-all-applicants" policy. That accept-all-applicants understanding originated in a former dean's deposition testimony as her explanation of the meaning of the University's Policy on Nondiscrimination. Armed with the

newly minted understanding of the University's Policy on Nondiscrimination, the Court had no difficulty in reasoning the university's denial of Registered Student Organization status had not been on the basis of the Christian Legal Society students' religious beliefs, but rather on their unwillingness to allow active homosexual students and students who did not accept the Christian Legal Society's Statement of Faith to become full members — thus on the Christian Legal Society students' unwillingness to adhere to the University's Policy on Nondiscrimination.

19. We leave First Amendment free speech and related liberties now to turn to economic liberty. Part of this topic was covered in Chapter Six when we explored the express textual protections of vested contract and property rights. Most, if not all, standard texts on constitutional law fail to consider the relationship between personal and economic liberties in any depth, reflecting an odd modern dichotomy between the two. Should they be treated differently? In a classic article, Robert McCloskey argues that the primary reason personal liberties have been protected more than economic ones is that the former are of great importance to intellectuals, such as lawyers and law professors who populate the Court. Robert McCloskey, *Economic Due Process and the Supreme Court: An Exhumation and Reburial*, 1962 SUP. CT. REV. 34. It's McCloskey's view that economic liberty need not be effaced from constitutional protection, and that the "extreme of the past [*Lochner* era] ha[s] generated the extreme of the present." *Id.* at 43. Along the same lines, Justice Potter Stewart once observed that:

> [T]he dichotomy between personal liberties and property rights is a false one. Property does not have rights. People have rights. The right to enjoy property without unlawful deprivation, no less than the right to speak or the right to travel, is in truth, a "personal" right, whether the "property" in question be a welfare check, a home, or a savings account.

Lynch v. Household Fin. Corp., 405 U.S. 538, 552 (1972). Or might one add the right to pursue a lawful calling? For an excellent, scholarly appraisal of this topic, see BERNARD H. SIEGAN, ECONOMIC LIBERTIES AND THE CONSTITUTION (University of Chicago 1980). The late Professor Siegan, who devoted his entire academic professional life to the defense of economic liberty, inspired generations of lawyers to keep this cause alive. One of the most successful legal public interest organizations in America, the Institute for Justice, received its inspiration and early direction from Professor Siegan, a man of enormous generosity and unmistakeable kindness, The Institute has demonstrated repeatedly how one of the greatest defenses of civil right is to ensure that regulation is not used to block initiative and entrepreneurship. IJ's beneficiaries are often ethnically minority and of modest income, but all possess great initiative and a devotion to human liberty in every sense. Each year, top law students typically after their first year compete for a spot in IJ's highly competitive (in the best sense) summer internship and education programs. Professor Siegan — following a highly successful career in practice in Chicago — had a fulsome second scholarly life at the University of San Diego until his death in 2006. Before turning to the controversial subject of substantive economic due process, we examine the guarantees of privileges and immunities in Article IV and a related, similarly worded provision in the Fourteenth Amendment.

B. THE SECOND AMENDMENT

The reliance upon historical meaning or original understanding to determine the present meaning of constitutional terms is difficult to accomplish (few lawyers or judges are true historians or have access to historical materials) and highly controversial (some argue this makes the Constitution too wooden and incapable of meeting the needs of the present time. The benefit of relying upon original understanding is avoiding disputes over meaning by putatively relying upon an objective source of meaning for the words of the text outside of the individual will or predilection of the deciding judge. The instruction to follow the plain meaning of the text came early in our history. *See Sturges v. Crowninshield* (1819), a unanimous opinion of Chief Justice John Marshall instructing:

> [A]lthough the spirit of an instrument, especially of a constitution, is to be respected not less than its letter, yet the spirit is to be collected chiefly from its words. It would be dangerous in the extreme, to infer from extrinsic circumstances, that a case for which the words of an instrument expressly provide, shall be exempted from its operation. Where words conflict with each other, where the different clauses of an instrument bear upon each other, and would be inconsistent, unless the natural and common import of words be varied, construction becomes necessary, and a departure from the obvious meaning of words, is justifiable. But if, in any case, the plain meaning of a provision, not contradicted by any other provision in the same instrument, is to be disregarded, because we believe the framers of that instrument could not intend what they say, it must be one in which the absurdity and injustice of applying the provision to the case would be so monstrous, that all mankind would, without hesitation, unite in rejecting the application.

Sturges, 17 U.S. (4 Wheat) at 202–03. Chief Justice Marshall's view seems to comport most closely with that of Justice Antonin Scalia as described in his book, A MATTER OF INTERPRETATION: FEDERAL COURTS AND THE LAW (1997). The next case, however, indicates that historical claims of meaning are hardly uniform or without controversy. Judge Posner following this next decision declared that "it is evidence that the Supreme Court, in deciding constitutional cases, exercises a freewheeling discretion strongly flavored with ideology." Richard A. Posner, *In Defense of Looseness*, THE NEW REPUBLIC (August 27, 2008). Posner continues:

> The majority opinion, by Justice Antonin Scalia, concluded that the original, and therefore the authoritative, meaning of the Second Amendment is that Americans are entitled to possess pistols (and perhaps other weapons) for the defense of their homes. Scalia's entire analysis rests on this interpretive method, which denies the legitimacy of flexible interpretation designed to adapt the Constitution (so far as the text permits) to current conditions. The irony is that the "originalist" method would have yielded the opposite result.

DISTRICT OF COLUMBIA v. HELLER
554 U.S. 570 (2008)

JUSTICE SCALIA delivered the opinion of the Court.

We consider whether a District of Columbia prohibition on the possession of usable handguns in the home violates the Second Amendment to the Constitution.

I

The District of Columbia generally prohibits the possession of handguns. It is a crime to carry an unregistered firearm, and the registration of handguns is prohibited. Wholly apart from that prohibition, no person may carry a handgun without a license, but the chief of police may issue licenses for 1-year periods. District of Columbia law also requires residents to keep their lawfully owned firearms, such as registered long guns, "unloaded and dissembled or bound by a trigger lock or similar device" unless they are located in a place of business or are being used for lawful recreational activities.

Respondent Dick Heller is a D.C. special police officer authorized to carry a handgun while on duty at the Federal Judicial Center. He applied for a registration certificate for a handgun that he wished to keep at home, but the District refused. He thereafter filed a lawsuit in the Federal District Court for the District of Columbia seeking, on Second Amendment grounds, to enjoin the city from enforcing the bar on the registration of handguns, the licensing requirement insofar as it prohibits the carrying of a firearm in the home without a license, and the trigger-lock requirement insofar as it prohibits the use of "functional firearms within the home." The District Court dismissed respondent's complaint. The Court of Appeals for the District of Columbia Circuit, construing his complaint as seeking the right to render a firearm operable and carry it about his home in that condition only when necessary for self-defense, reversed. It held that the Second Amendment protects an individual right to possess firearms and that the city's total ban on handguns, as well as its requirement that firearms in the home be kept nonfunctional even when necessary for self-defense, violated that right. The Court of Appeals directed the District Court to enter summary judgment for respondent. We granted *certiorari*.

II

We turn first to the meaning of the Second Amendment.

A

The Second Amendment provides: "A well regulated Militia, being necessary to the security of a free State, the right of the people to keep and bear Arms, shall not be infringed." In interpreting this text, we are guided by the principle that "[t]he Constitution was written to be understood by the voters; its words and phrases were used in their normal and ordinary as distinguished from technical meaning."

Normal meaning may of course include an idiomatic meaning, but it excludes sec
or technical meanings that would not have been known to ordinary citizens in ___
founding generation.

The two sides in this case have set out very different interpretations of the
Amendment. Petitioners and today's dissenting Justices believe that it protects only
the right to possess and carry a firearm in connection with militia service.
Respondent argues that it protects an individual right to possess a firearm
unconnected with service in a militia, and to use that arm for traditionally lawful
purposes, such as self-defense within the home.

The Second Amendment is naturally divided into two parts: its prefatory clause
and its operative clause. The former does not limit the latter grammatically, but
rather announces a purpose. The Amendment could be rephrased, "Because a well
regulated Militia is necessary to the security of a free State, the right of the people
to keep and bear Arms shall not be infringed." Although this structure of the Second
Amendment is unique in our Constitution, other legal documents of the founding
era, particularly individual-rights provisions of state constitutions, commonly
included a prefatory statement of purpose.

Logic demands that there be a link between the stated purpose and the
command. The Second Amendment would be nonsensical if it read, "A well
regulated Militia, being necessary to the security of a free State, the right of the
people to petition for redress of grievances shall not be infringed." That requirement of logical connection may cause a prefatory clause to resolve an ambiguity in
the operative clause ("The separation of church and state being an important
objective, the teachings of canons shall have no place in our jurisprudence." The
preface makes clear that the operative clause refers not to canons of interpretation
but to clergymen.) But apart from that clarifying function, a prefatory clause does
not limit or expand the scope of the operative clause. " 'It is nothing unusual in acts
. . . for the enacting part to go beyond the preamble; the remedy often extends
beyond the particular act or mischief which first suggested the necessity of the
law.' " Therefore, while we will begin our textual analysis with the operative clause,
we will return to the prefatory clause to ensure that our reading of the operative
clause is consistent with the announced purpose.[9]

1. Operative Clause.

a. "Right of the People. The first salient feature of the operative clause is that
it codifies a "right of the people." The unamended Constitution and the Bill of
Rights use the phrase "right of the people" two other times, in the First
Amendment's Assembly-and-Petition Clause and in the Fourth Amendment's

---

[9] [4] JUSTICE STEVENS criticizes us for discussing the prologue last. But if a prologue can be used only
to clarify an ambiguous operative provision, surely the first step must be to determine whether the
operative provision is ambiguous. It might be argued, we suppose, that the prologue itself should be one
of the factors that go into the determination of whether the operative provision is ambiguous — but that
would cause the prologue to be used to produce ambiguity rather than just to resolve it. In any event,
even if we considered the prologue *along with* the operative provision we would reach the same result
we do today, since (as we explain) our interpretation of "the right of the people to keep and bear arms"
furthers the purpose of an effective militia no less than (indeed, more than) the dissent's interpretation.

Search-and-Seizure Clause. The Ninth Amendment uses very similar terminology ("The enumeration in the Constitution, of certain rights, shall not be construed to deny or disparage others retained by the people"). All three of these instances unambiguously refer to individual rights, not "collective" rights, or rights that may be exercised only through participation in some corporate body.

Three provisions of the Constitution refer to "the people" in a context other than "rights" — the famous preamble ("We the people"), § 2 of Article I (providing that "the people" will choose members of the House), and the Tenth Amendment (providing that those powers not given the Federal Government remain with "the States" or "the people"). Those provisions arguably refer to "the people'" acting collectively — but they deal with the exercise or reservation of powers, not rights. Nowhere else in the Constitution does a "right" attributed to "the people" refer to anything other than an individual right. . . .

This contrasts markedly with the phrase "the militia" in the prefatory clause. As we will describe below, the "militia" in colonial America consisted of a subset of "the people" — those who were male, able bodied, and within a certain age range. Reading the Second Amendment as protecting only the right to "keep and bear Arms" in an organized militia therefore fits poorly with the operative clause's description of the holder of that right as "the people."

We start therefore with a strong presumption that the Second Amendment right is exercised individually and belongs to all Americans.

b. "Keep and bear Arms." We move now from the holder of the right — "the people" — to the substance of the right: "to keep and bear Arms."

Before addressing the verbs "keep" and "bear," we interpret their object: "Arms." The 18th-century meaning is no different from the meaning today. The 1773 edition of Samuel Johnson's dictionary defined "arms" as "weapons of offence, or armour of defence." The term was applied, then as now, to weapons that were not specifically designed for military use and were not employed in a military capacity. For instance, Cunningham's legal dictionary gave as an example of usage: "Servants and labourers shall use bows and arrows on *Sundays*, &c. and not bear other arms." Although one founding-era thesaurus limited "arms" (as opposed to "weapons") to "instruments of offence *generally* made use of in war," even that source stated that all firearms constituted "arms."

Some have made the argument, bordering on the frivolous, that only those arms in existence in the 18th century are protected by the Second Amendment. We do not interpret constitutional rights that way. Just as the First Amendment protects modern forms of communications, *e.g., Reno v. American Civil Liberties Union* (1997), and the Fourth Amendment applies to modern forms of search, *e.g., Kyllo v. United States* (2001), the Second Amendment extends, prima facie, to all instruments that constitute bearable arms, even those that were not in existence at the time of the founding.

We turn to the phrases "keep arms" and "bear arms." Johnson defined "keep" as, most relevantly, "[t]o retain; not to lose," and "[t]o have in custody." . . . No party has apprised us of an idiomatic meaning of "keep Arms." Thus, the most natural reading of "keep Arms" in the Second Amendment is to "have weapons."

. . . Petitioners point to militia laws of the founding period that required militia members to "keep" arms in connection with militia service, and they conclude from this that the phrase "keep Arms" has a militia-related connotation. This is rather like saying that, since there are many statutes that authorize aggrieved employees to "file complaints" with federal agencies, the phrase "file complaints" has an employment-related connotation. "Keep arms" was simply a common way of referring to possessing arms, for militiamen *and everyone else.*

At the time of the founding, as now, to "bear' " meant to "carry." When used with "arms," however, the term has a meaning that refers to carrying for a particular purpose — confrontation. In *Muscarello v. United States* (1998), in the course of analyzing the meaning of "carries a firearm" in a federal criminal statute, JUSTICE GINSBURG wrote that "[s]urely a most familiar meaning is, as the Constitution's Second Amendment . . . indicate[s]: 'wear, bear, or carry . . . upon the person or in the clothing or in a pocket, for the purpose . . . of being armed and ready for offensive or defensive action in a case of conflict with another person.' " We think that JUSTICE GINSBURG accurately captured the natural meaning of "bear arms." Although the phrase implies that the carrying of the weapon is for the purpose of "offensive or defensive action," it in no way connotes participation in a structured military organization. From our review of founding-era sources, we conclude that this natural meaning was also the meaning that "bear arms" had in the 18th century. In numerous instances, "bear arms" was unambiguously used to refer to the carrying of weapons outside of an organized militia. The most prominent examples are those most relevant to the Second Amendment: Nine state constitutional provisions written in the 18th century or the first two decades of the 19th, which enshrined a right of citizens to "bear arms in defense of themselves and the state" or "bear arms in defense of himself and the state." It is clear from those formulations that "bear arms" did not refer only to carrying a weapon in an organized military unit. Justice James Wilson interpreted the Pennsylvania Constitution's armsbearing right, for example, as a recognition of the natural right of defense "of one's person or house" — what he called the law of "self preservation." . . .

The phrase "bear Arms" also had at the time of the founding an idiomatic meaning that was significantly different from its natural meaning: "to serve as a soldier, do military service, fight" or "to wage war." But it *unequivocally* bore that idiomatic meaning only when followed by the preposition "against,' " which was in turn followed by the target of the hostilities. See 2 OXFORD 21. (That is how, for example, our Declaration of Independence ¶ 28, used the phrase: "He has constrained our fellow Citizens taken Captive on the high Seas to bear Arms against their Country. . . .") Every example given by petitioners' *amici* for the idiomatic meaning of "bear arms" from the founding period either includes the preposition "against" or is not clearly idiomatic. Without the preposition, "bear arms" normally meant (as it continues to mean today) what JUSTICE GINSBURG's opinion in *Muscarello* said. In any event, the meaning of "bear arms" that petitioners and JUSTICE STEVENS propose is *not even* the (sometimes) idiomatic meaning. Rather, they manufacture a hybrid definition, whereby "bear arms" connotes the actual carrying of arms (and therefore is not really an idiom) but only in the service of an organized militia. No dictionary has ever adopted that definition, and we have been apprised of no source that indicates that it carried that meaning at the time of the founding. But it is easy to see why petitioners and the dissent are driven to the hybrid definition. Giving "bear Arms" its idiomatic meaning would cause the protected right to consist of the right to be a soldier or to wage war — an absurdity that no commentator has ever endorsed. See L. LEVY, ORIGINS OF THE BILL OF RIGHTS 135 (1999). Worse still, the phrase "keep and bear Arms" would be incoherent. The word "Arms" would have two different meanings at once: "weapons" (as the object of "keep") and (as the object of "bear") one-half of an idiom. It would be rather like saying "He filled and kicked the bucket" to mean "He filled the bucket and died." Grotesque.

Petitioners justify their limitation of "bear arms' " to the military context by pointing out the unremarkable fact that it was often used in that context — the same mistake they made with respect to "keep arms." It is especially unremarkable that the phrase was often used in a military context in the federal legal sources (such as records of congressional debate) that have been the focus of petitioners' inquiry. Those sources would have had little occasion to use it *except* in discussions about the standing army and the militia. . . .

JUSTICE STEVENS points to a study by *amici* supposedly showing that the phrase "bear arms" was most frequently used in the military context. Of course, as we have said, the fact that the phrase was commonly used in a particular context does not show that it is limited to that context, and, in any event, we have given many sources where the phrase was used in nonmilitary contexts. Moreover, the study's collection appears to include (who knows how many times) the idiomatic phrase "bear arms against," which is irrelevant. The *amici* also dismiss examples such as " 'bear arms . . . for the purpose of killing game' " because those uses are "expressly qualified." . . . That analysis is faulty. A purposive qualifying phrase that contradicts the word or phrase it modifies is unknown this side of the looking glass (except, apparently, in some courses on Linguistics). If "bear arms" means, as we think, simply the carrying of arms, a modifier can limit the purpose of the carriage ("for the purpose of self defense" or "to make war against the King"). But if "bear arms" means, as the petitioners and the dissent think, the carrying of arms only for military purposes, one simply cannot add "for the purpose of killing game." The right "to carry arms in the militia for the purpose of killing game" is worthy of the mad hatter. Thus, these purposive qualifying phrases positively establish that "to bear arms" is not limited to military use.

JUSTICE STEVENS places great weight on James Madison's inclusion of a conscientious-objector clause in his original draft of the Second Amendment: "but no person religiously scrupulous of bearing arms, shall be compelled to render military service in person." CREATING THE BILL OF RIGHTS 12 (H. Veit, K. Bowling, & C. Bickford eds. 1991) (hereinafter Veit). He argues that this clause establishes that the drafters of the Second Amendment intended "bear Arms" to refer only to military service.. It is always perilous to derive the meaning of an adopted provision from another provision deleted in the drafting process.[10] In any case, what JUSTICE

---

[10] [12] JUSTICE STEVENS finds support for his legislative history inference from the recorded views of one Antifederalist member of the House. "The claim that the best or most representative reading of the [language of the] amendments would conform to the understanding and concerns of [the Antifederalists]

STEVENS would conclude from the deleted provision does not follow. It was not meant to exempt from military service those who objected to going to war but had no scruples about personal gunfights. Quakers opposed the use of arms not just for militia service, but for any violent purpose whatsoever — so much so that Quaker frontiersmen were forbidden to use arms to defend their families, even though "[i]n such circumstances the temptation to seize a hunting rifle or knife in self-defense . . . must sometimes have been almost overwhelming." . . . Thus, the most natural interpretation of Madison's deleted text is that those opposed to carrying weapons for potential violent confrontation would not be "compelled to render military service," in which such carrying would be required.

* * *

c. Meaning of the Operative Clause. Putting all of these textual elements together, we find that they guarantee the individual right to possess and carry weapons in case of confrontation. This meaning is strongly confirmed by the historical background of the Second Amendment. We look to this because it has always been widely understood that the Second Amendment, like the First and Fourth Amendments, codified a *pre-existing* right. The very text of the Second Amendment implicitly recognizes the pre-existence of the right and declares only that it "shall not be infringed." As we said in *United States v. Cruikshank* (1876), "[t]his is not a right granted by the Constitution. Neither is it in any manner dependent upon that instrument for its existence. The second amendment declares that it shall not be infringed . . . ."

Between the Restoration and the Glorious Revolution, the Stuart Kings Charles II and James II succeeded in using select militias loyal to them to suppress political dissidents, in part by disarming their opponents. Under the auspices of the 1671 Game Act, for example, the Catholic James II had ordered general disarmaments of regions home to his Protestant enemies. These experiences caused Englishmen to be extremely wary of concentrated military forces run by the state and to be jealous of their arms. They accordingly obtained an assurance from William and Mary, in the Declaration of Right (which was codified as the English Bill of Rights), that Protestants would never be disarmed: "That the subjects which are Protestants may have arms for their defense suitable to their conditions and as allowed by law." 1 W. & M., c. 2, § 7, in 3 Eng. Stat. at Large 441 (1689). This right has long been understood to be the predecessor to our Second Amendment. It was clearly an individual right, having nothing whatever to do with service in a militia. To be sure, it was an individual right not available to the whole population, given that it was restricted to Protestants, and like all written English rights it was held only against the Crown, not Parliament. But it was secured to them as individuals, according to "libertarian political principles," not as members of a fighting force. By the time of the founding, the right to have arms had become fundamental for English subjects. Blackstone, whose works, we have said, "constituted the preeminent authority on English law for the founding generation," cited the arms provision of the Bill of Rights as one of the fundamental rights of Englishmen. His description of it cannot possibly be thought to tie it to militia or military service. It was, he said, "the

---

is . . . highly problematic." Rakove, *The Second Amendment: The Highest Stage of Originalism*, BOGUS 74, 81.

natural right of resistance and self-preservation," and "the right of having and using arms for self-preservation and defence." . . . Thus, the right secured in 1689 as a result of the Stuarts' abuses was by the time of the founding understood to be an individual right protecting against both public and private violence.

And, of course, what the Stuarts had tried to do to their political enemies, George III had tried to do to the colonists. In the tumultuous decades of the 1760's and 1770's, the Crown began to disarm the inhabitants of the most rebellious areas. That provoked polemical reactions by Americans invoking their rights as Englishmen to keep arms. They understood the right to enable individuals to defend themselves. As the most important early American edition of Blackstone's Commentaries (by the law professor and former Antifederalist St. George Tucker) made clear in the notes to the description of the arms right, Americans understood the "right of self-preservation" as permitting a citizen to "repe[l] force by force" when "the intervention of society in his behalf, may be too late to prevent an injury." 1 BLACKSTONE'S COMMENTARIES 145–146, n. 42 (1803) (hereinafter Tucker's Blackstone).

There seems to us no doubt, on the basis of both text and history, that the Second Amendment conferred an individual right to keep and bear arms. Of course the right was not unlimited, just as the First Amendment's right of free speech was not, see, *e.g., United States v. Williams* (2008). Thus, we do not read the Second Amendment to protect the right of citizens to carry arms for *any sort* of confrontation, just as we do not read the First Amendment to protect the right of citizens to speak for *any purpose*. Before turning to limitations upon the individual right, however, we must determine whether the prefatory clause of the Second Amendment comports with our interpretation of the operative clause.

2. Prefatory Clause.

The prefatory clause reads: "A well regulated Militia, being necessary to the security of a free State . . . ."

   a. "Well-Regulated Militia." In *United States v. Miller*, 307 U.S. 174, 179 (1939), we explained that "the Militia comprised all males physically capable of acting in concert for the common defense." That definition comports with founding-era sources.

Petitioners take a seemingly narrower view of the militia, stating that "[m]ilitias are the state- and congressionally- regulated military forces described in the Militia Clauses (art. I, § 8, cls.15–16)." Although we agree with petitioners' interpretive assumption that "militia" means the same thing in Article I and the Second Amendment, we believe that petitioners identify the wrong thing, namely, the organized militia. Unlike armies and navies, which Congress is given the power to create ("to raise . . . Armies"; "to provide . . . a Navy," Art. I, § 8, cls. 12–13), the militia is assumed by Article I already to be *in existence*. Congress is given the power to "provide for calling forth the militia," § 8, cl. 15; and the power not to create, but to "organiz[e]" it — and not to organize "a" militia, which is what one would expect if the militia were to be a federal creation, but to organize "the" militia, connoting a body already in existence, *ibid.,* cl. 16. This is fully consistent with the ordinary definition of the militia as all able-bodied men. From that pool, Congress has plenary power to organize the units that will make up an effective fighting force. That is what Congress did in the first militia Act, which specified that "each and every free able-bodied white male citizen of the respective states, resident therein, who is or shall be of the age of eighteen years, and under the age of forty-five years (except as is herein after excepted) shall severally and respectively be enrolled in the militia." Act of May 8, 1792, 1 Stat. 271. To be sure, Congress need not conscript every able-bodied man into the militia, because nothing in Article I suggests that in exercising its power to organize, discipline, and arm the militia, Congress must focus upon the entire body. Although the militia consists of all able bodied men, the federally organized militia may consist of a subset of them.

Finally, the adjective "well-regulated" implies nothing more than the imposition of proper discipline and training.

b. "Security of a Free State." The phrase "security of a free state" meant "security of a free polity," not security of each of the several States as the dissent below argued. Joseph Story wrote in his treatise on the Constitution that "the word 'state' is used in various senses [and in] its most enlarged sense, it means the people composing a particular nation or community." It is true that the term "State" elsewhere in the Constitution refers to individual States, but the phrase "security of a free state" and close variations seem to have been terms of art in 18th-century political discourse, meaning a " 'free country' " or free polity. . . .

There are many reasons why the militia was thought to be "necessary to the security of a free state." First, of course, it is useful in repelling invasions and suppressing insurrections. Second, it renders large standing armies unnecessary — an argument that Alexander Hamilton made in favor of federal control over the militia. Third, when the able-bodied men of a nation are trained in arms and organized, they are better able to resist tyranny.

3. Relationship between Prefatory Clause and Operative Clause

We reach the question, then: Does the preface fit with an operative clause that creates an individual right to keep and bear arms? It fits perfectly, once one knows the history that the founding generation knew and that we have described above. That history showed that the way tyrants had eliminated a militia consisting of all the able bodied men was not by banning the militia but simply by taking away the people's arms, enabling a select militia or standing army to suppress political opponents. This is what had occurred in England that prompted codification of the right to have arms in the English Bill of Rights. The debate with respect to the right to keep and bear arms, as with other guarantees in the Bill of Rights, was not over whether it was desirable (all agreed that it was) but over whether it needed to be codified in the Constitution. During the 1788 ratification debates, the fear that the federal government would disarm the people in order to impose rule through a standing army or select militia was pervasive in Antifederalist rhetoric. . . . Federalists responded that because Congress was given no power to abridge the ancient right of individuals to keep and bear arms, such a force could never oppress the people. It was understood across the political spectrum that the right helped to secure the ideal of a citizen militia, which might be necessary to oppose an oppressive military force if the constitutional order broke down. It is therefore entirely sensible that the Second Amendment's prefatory clause announces the purpose for which the right was codified: to prevent elimination of the militia. The prefatory clause does not suggest that preserving the militia was the only reason Americans valued the ancient right; most undoubtedly thought it even more important for self-defense and hunting. But the threat that the new Federal Government would destroy the citizens' militia by taking away their arms was the reason that right — unlike some other English rights — was codified in a written Constitution. JUSTICE BREYER's assertion that individual self-defense is merely a "subsidiary interest" of the right to keep and bear arms is profoundly mistaken. He bases that assertion solely upon the prologue — but that can only show that self-defense had little to do with the right's *codification*; it was the *central component* of the right itself.

Besides ignoring the historical reality that the Second Amendment was not intended to lay down a "novel principl[e]" but rather codified a right "inherited from our English ancestors," petitioners' interpretation does not even achieve the narrower purpose that prompted codification of the right. If, as they believe, the Second Amendment right is no more than the right to keep and use weapons as a member of an organized militia — if, that is, the *organized* militia is the sole institutional beneficiary of the Second Amendment's guarantee — it does not assure the existence of a "citizens' militia" as a safeguard against tyranny. For Congress retains plenary authority to organize the militia, which must include the authority to say who will belong to the organized force. That is why the first Militia Act's requirement that only whites enroll caused States to amend their militia laws to exclude free blacks. Thus, if petitioners are correct, the Second Amendment protects citizens' right to use a gun in an organization from which Congress has plenary authority to exclude them. It guarantees a select militia of the sort the Stuart kings found useful, but not the people's militia that was the concern of the founding generation.

B

Our interpretation is confirmed by analogous arms-bearing rights in state constitutions that preceded and immediately followed adoption of the Second Amendment. . . . Pennsylvania's Declaration of Rights of 1776 said: "That the people have a right to bear arms *for the defence of themselves*, and the state . . . ." . . . North Carolina also codified a right to bear arms in 1776: "That the people have a right to bear arms, for the defence of the State . . . ."Declaration of Rights § XVII. This could plausibly be read to support only a right to bear arms in a militia — but that is a peculiar way to make the point in a constitution that elsewhere repeatedly mentions the militia explicitly. . . .

. . . That of the nine state constitutional protections for the right to bear arms enacted immediately after 1789 at least seven unequivocally protected an individual citizen's right to self-defense is strong evidence that that is how the founding generation conceived of the right. . . .

The historical narrative that petitioners must endorse would thus treat the Federal Second Amendment as an odd outlier, protecting a right unknown in state constitutions or at English common law, based on little more than an overreading of the prefatory clause.

C

JUSTICE STEVENS relies on the drafting history of the Second Amendment — the various proposals in the state conventions and the debates in Congress. It is dubious to rely on such history to interpret a text that was widely understood to codify a pre-existing right, rather than to fashion a new one. But even assuming that this legislative history is relevant, JUSTICE STEVENS flatly misreads the historical record.

. . . New Hampshire's Proposal [for constitutional amendments], the Pennsylvania minority's proposal, and Samuel Adams' proposal in Massachusetts unequivocally referred to individual rights, as did two state constitutional provisions at the time. JUSTICE STEVENS' view thus relies on the proposition, unsupported by any evidence, that different people of the founding period had vastly different conceptions of the right to keep and bear arms. That simply does not comport with our longstanding view that the Bill of Rights codified venerable, widely understood liberties.

D

We now address how the Second Amendment was interpreted from immediately after its ratification through the end of the 19th century. Before proceeding, however, we take issue with JUSTICE STEVENS' equating of these sources with post enactment legislative history, a comparison that betrays a fundamental misunderstanding of a court's interpretive task. "Legislative history," of course, refers to the pre-enactment statements of those who drafted or voted for a law; it is considered persuasive by some, not because they reflect the general understanding of the disputed terms, but because the legislators who heard or read those statements presumably voted with that understanding. *Ibid.* "Postenactment legislative history," *ibid.*, a deprecatory contradiction in terms, refers to statements of those who drafted or voted for the law that are made after its enactment and hence could have had no effect on the congressional vote. It most certainly does not refer to the examination of a variety of legal and other sources to determine *the public understanding* of a legal text in the period after its enactment or ratification. That sort of inquiry is a critical tool of constitutional interpretation. As we will show, virtually all interpreters of the Second Amendment in the century after its enactment interpreted the amendment as we do.

1. Post-ratification Commentary

Three important founding-era legal scholars interpreted the Second Amendment in published writings. All three understood it to protect an individual right unconnected with militia service.

St. George Tucker's version of BLACKSTONE'S COMMENTARIES, as we explained above, conceived of the Blackstonian arms right as necessary for self-defense. He equated that right, absent the religious and class-based restrictions, with the

Second Amendment. See 2 TUCKER'S BLACKSTONE 143. In Note D, entitled, "View of the Constitution of the United States," Tucker elaborated on the Second Amendment: "This may be considered as the true palladium of liberty . . . . The right to self-defence is the first law of nature: in most governments it has been the study of rulers to confine the right within the narrowest limits possible. Wherever standing armies are kept up, and the right of the people to keep and bear arms is, under any colour or pretext whatsoever, prohibited, liberty, if not already annihilated, is on the brink of destruction." He believed that the English game laws had abridged the right by prohibiting "keeping a gun or other engine for the destruction of game." *Ibid.*, see also 2 *id.*, at 143, and nn. 40 and 41. He later grouped the right with some of the individual rights included in the First Amendment and said that if "a law be passed by congress, prohibiting" any of those rights, it would "be the province of the judiciary to pronounce whether any such act were constitutional, or not; and if not, to acquit the accused . . . ." It is unlikely that Tucker was referring to a person's being "accused" of violating a law making it a crime to bear arms in a state militia.

In 1825, William Rawle, a prominent lawyer who had been a member of the Pennsylvania Assembly that ratified the Bill of Rights, published an influential treatise, which analyzed the Second Amendment as follows:

> "The first [principle] is a declaration that a well regulated militia is necessary to the security of a free state; a proposition from which few will dissent. . . .

> "The corollary, from the first position is, that the right of the people to keep and bear arms shall not be infringed.

> "The prohibition is general. No clause in the constitution could by any rule of construction be conceived to give to congress a power to disarm the people. Such a flagitious attempt could only be made under some general pretence by a state legislature. But if in any blind pursuit of inordinate power, either should attempt it, this amendment may be appealed to as a restraint on both."

*   *   *

Joseph Story published his famous COMMENTARIES ON THE CONSTITUTION OF THE UNITED STATES in 1833. JUSTICE STEVENS suggests that "[t]here is not so much as a whisper" in Story's explanation of the Second Amendment that favors the individual-rights view. That is wrong. Story explained that the English Bill of Rights had also included a "right to bear arms," a right that, as we have discussed, had nothing to do with militia service. 3 STORY § 1858. He then equated the English right with the Second Amendment: "§ 1891. A similar provision [to the Second Amendment] in favour of protestants (for to them it is confined) is to be found in the bill of rights of 1688, it being declared, 'that the subjects, which are protestants, may have arms for their defence suitable to their condition, and as allowed by law.' But under various pretences the effect of this provision has been greatly narrowed; and it is at present in England more nominal than real, as a defensive privilege." (Footnotes omitted.) This comparison to the Declaration of Right would not make sense if the Second Amendment right was the right to use a gun in a militia, which was plainly not what the English right protected. As the Tennessee Supreme Court recognized 38 years after Story wrote his COMMENTARIES, "[t]he passage from Story, shows clearly that this right was intended . . . and was guaranteed to, and to be exercised and enjoyed by the citizen as such, and not by him as a soldier, or in defense solely of his political rights." Story's COMMENTARIES also cite as support Tucker and Rawle, both of whom clearly viewed the right as unconnected to militia service. In addition, in a shorter 1840 work Story wrote: "One of the ordinary modes, by which tyrants accomplish their purposes without resistance, is, by disarming the people, and making it an offence to keep arms, and by substituting a regular army in the stead of a resort to the militia."

Antislavery advocates routinely invoked the right to bear arms for self-defense. . . . In his famous Senate speech about the 1856 "Bleeding Kansas" conflict, Charles Sumner proclaimed: "The rifle has ever been the companion of the pioneer and, under God, his tutelary protector against the red man and the beast of the forest. Never was this efficient weapon more needed in just self-defence, than now in Kansas, and at least one article in our National Constitution must be blotted out, before the complete right to it can in any way be impeached. And yet such is the madness of the hour, that, in defiance of the solemn guarantee, embodied in the Amendments to the Constitution, that 'the right of the people to keep and bear arms shall not be infringed,' the people of Kansas have been arraigned for keeping and bearing them, and the Senator from South Carolina has had the face to say openly, on this floor, that they should be disarmed — of course, that the fanatics of Slavery, his allies and constituents, may meet no impediment."

We have found only one early 19th-century commentator who clearly conditioned the right to keep and bear arms upon service in the militia — and he recognized that the prevailing view was to the contrary. . . .

2. Pre-Civil War Case Law

The 19th-century cases that interpreted the Second Amendment universally support an individual right unconnected to militia service. . . . In *Nunn v. State*, 1 Ga. 243, 251 (1846), the Georgia Supreme Court construed the Second Amendment as protecting the "*natural* right of self-defence" and therefore struck down a ban on carrying pistols openly. Its opinion perfectly captured the way in which the operative clause of the Second Amendment furthers the purpose announced in the prefatory clause, in continuity with the English right: "The right of the whole people, old and young, men, women and boys, and not militia only, to keep and bear *arms* of every description, and not *such* merely as are used by the *militia*, shall not be *infringed*, curtailed, or broken in upon, in the smallest degree; and all this for the important end to be attained: the rearing up and qualifying a well-regulated militia, so vitally necessary to the security of a free State. Our opinion is, that any law, State or Federal, is repugnant to the Constitution, and void, which contravenes this *right*, originally belonging to our forefathers, trampled under foot by Charles I. and his two wicked sons and successors, re-established by the revolution of 1688, conveyed to this land of liberty by the colonists, and finally incorporated conspicuously in our own Magna Charta!"

* * *

Those who believe that the Second Amendment preserves only a militia-centered right place great reliance on the Tennessee Supreme Court's 1840 decision in *Aymette v. State*. The case does not stand for that broad proposition; in fact, the case does not mention the word "militia" at all, except in its quoting of the Second Amendment. *Aymette* held that the state constitutional guarantee of the right to "bear" arms did not prohibit the banning of concealed weapons. The opinion first recognized that both the state right and the federal right were descendents of the 1689 English right, but (erroneously, and contrary to virtually all other authorities) read that right to refer only to "protect[ion of] the public liberty" and "keep[ing] in awe those in power." The court then adopted a sort of middle position, whereby citizens were permitted to carry arms openly, unconnected with any service in a formal militia, but were given the right to use them only for the military purpose of banding together to oppose tyranny. This odd reading of the right is, to be sure, not the one we adopt — but it is not petitioners' reading either. More importantly, seven years earlier the Tennessee Supreme Court had treated the state constitutional provision as conferring a right "of all the free citizens of the State to keep and bear arms for their defence," *Simpson*; and 21 years later the court held that the "keep" portion of the state constitutional right included the right to personal self-defense: "[T]he right to keep arms involves, necessarily, the right to use such arms for all the ordinary purposes, and in all the ordinary modes usual in the country, and to which arms are adapted, limited by the duties of a good citizen in times of peace."

3. Post-Civil War Legislation.

In the aftermath of the Civil War, there was an outpouring of discussion of the Second Amendment in Congress and in public discourse, as people debated whether and how to secure constitutional rights for newly free slaves. . . . Blacks were routinely disarmed by Southern States after the Civil War. Those who opposed these injustices frequently stated that they infringed blacks' constitutional right to keep and bear arms. Needless to say, the claim was not that blacks were being prohibited from carrying arms in an organized state militia. A Report of the Commission of the Freedmen's Bureau in 1866 stated plainly: "[T]he civil law [of Kentucky] prohibits the colored man from bearing arms. . . . Their arms are taken from them by the civil authorities. . . . Thus, the right of the people to keep and bear arms as provided in the Constitution is *infringed*." . . .

*   *   *

The understanding that the Second Amendment gave freed blacks the right to keep and bear arms was reflected in congressional discussion of the bill, with even an opponent of it saying that the founding generation "were for every man bearing his arms about him and keeping them in his house, his castle, for his own defense." . . .

It was plainly the understanding in the post-Civil War Congress that the Second Amendment protected an individual right to use arms for self-defense.

4. Post-Civil War Commentators.

Every late-19th-century legal scholar that we have read interpreted the Second Amendment to secure an individual right unconnected with militia service. The most famous was the judge and professor Thomas Cooley, who wrote a massively popular 1868 TREATISE ON CONSTITUTIONAL LIMITATIONS. Concerning the Second Amendment it said: "Among the other defences to personal liberty should be mentioned the right of the people to keep and bear arms. . . . The alternative to a standing army is 'a well-regulated militia,' but this cannot exist unless the people are trained to bearing arms. How far it is in the power of the legislature to regulate this right, we shall not undertake to say, as happily there has been very little occasion to discuss that subject by the courts."

That Cooley understood the right not as connected to militia service, but as securing the militia by ensuring a populace familiar with arms, is made even clearer in his 1880 work, GENERAL PRINCIPLES OF CONSTITUTIONAL LAW. The Second Amendment, he said, "was adopted with some modification and enlargement from the English Bill of Rights of 1688, where it stood as a protest against arbitrary action of the overturned dynasty in disarming the people." In a section entitled "The Right in General," he continued:

> "It might be supposed from the phraseology of this provision that the right to keep and bear arms was only guaranteed to the militia; but this would be an interpretation not warranted by the intent. The militia, as has been elsewhere explained, consists of those persons who, under the law, are liable to the performance of military duty, and are officered and enrolled for service when called upon. But the law may make provision for the enrolment of all who are fit to perform military duty, or of a small number only, or it may wholly omit to make any provision at all; and if the right were limited to those enrolled, the purpose of this guaranty might be defeated altogether by the action or neglect to act of the government it was meant to hold in check. The meaning of the provision undoubtedly is, that the people, from whom the militia must be taken, shall have the right to keep and bear arms; and they need no permission or regulation of law for the purpose. . . ."

All other post-Civil War 19th-century sources we have found concurred with Cooley. . . .

E

We now ask whether any of our precedents forecloses the conclusions we have reached about the meaning of the Second Amendment.

United States v. Cruikshank (1876), in the course of vacating the convictions of members of a white mob for depriving blacks of their right to keep and bear arms, held that the Second Amendment does not by its own force apply to anyone other than the Federal Government. The opinion explained that the right "is not a right granted by the Constitution [or] in any manner dependent upon that instrument for its existence. The second amendment . . . means no more than that it shall not be infringed by Congress." States, we said, were free to restrict or protect the right under their police powers. The limited discussion of the Second Amendment in *Cruikshank* supports, if anything, the individual-rights interpretation. There was no claim in *Cruikshank* that the victims had been deprived of their right to carry arms in a militia; indeed, the Governor had disbanded the local militia unit the year before the mob's attack. We described the right protected by the Second Amendment as " 'bearing arms for a lawful purpose' " and said that "the people [must] look for their protection against any violation by their fellow citizens of the rights it recognizes" to the States' police power. That discussion makes little sense if it is only a right to bear arms in a state militia.

*   *   *

JUSTICE STEVENS places overwhelming reliance upon this Court's decision in *United States v. Miller* (1939). "[H]undreds of judges," we are told, "have relied on the view of the amendment we endorsed there," and "[e]ven if the textual and historical arguments on both side of the issue were evenly balanced, respect for the well-settled views of all of our predecessors on this Court, and for the rule of law itself . . . would prevent most jurists from endorsing such a dramatic upheaval in the law." And what is, according to JUSTICE STEVENS, the holding of *Miller* that demands such obeisance? That the Second Amendment "protects the right to keep and bear arms for certain military purposes, but that it does not curtail the legislature's power to regulate the nonmilitary use and ownership of weapons."

Nothing so clearly demonstrates the weakness of JUSTICE STEVENS' case. *Miller* did not hold that and cannot possibly be read to have held that. The judgment in the case upheld against a Second Amendment challenge two men's federal convictions for transporting an unregistered short-barreled shotgun in interstate commerce, in violation of the National Firearms Act. It is entirely clear that the Court's basis for saying that the Second Amendment did not apply was *not* that the defendants were "bear[ing] arms" not "for . . . military purposes" but for "nonmilitary use." Rather, it was that the *type of weapon at issue* was not eligible for Second Amendment protection: "In the absence of any evidence tending to show that the possession or use of a [shortbarreled shotgun] at this time has some reasonable relationship to the preservation or efficiency of a well regulated militia, we cannot say that the Second Amendment guarantees the right to keep and bear *such an instrument*." "Certainly," the Court continued, "it is not within judicial notice that this weapon is any part of the ordinary military equipment or that its use could contribute to the common defense." *Ibid.* Beyond that, the opinion provided no explanation of the content of the right. This holding is not only consistent with, but positively suggests, that the Second Amendment confers an individual right to keep and bear arms (though only arms that "have some reasonable relationship to the preservation or efficiency of a well regulated militia"). Had the Court believed that the Second Amendment protects only those serving in the militia, it would have been odd to examine the character of the weapon rather than simply note that the two crooks were not militiamen. . . . *Miller* stands only for the proposition that the Second Amendment right, whatever its nature, extends only to certain types of weapons.

It is particularly wrongheaded to read *Miller* for more than what it said, because the case did not even purport to be a thorough examination of the Second Amendment. . . .

* * *

We conclude that nothing in our precedents forecloses our adoption of the original understanding of the Second Amendment. It should be unsurprising that such a significant matter has been for so long judicially unresolved. For most of our history, the Bill of Rights was not thought applicable to the States, and the Federal Government did not significantly regulate the possession of firearms by law-abiding citizens. Other provisions of the Bill of Rights have similarly remained unilluminated for lengthy periods. This Court first held a law to violate the First Amendment's guarantee of freedom of speech in 1931, almost 150 years after the Amendment was ratified, see *Near v. Minnesota* (1931), and it was not until after World War II that we held a law invalid under the Establishment Clause, see *Illinois ex rel. McCollum v. Board of Ed.* (1948). Even a question as basic as the scope of proscribable libel was not addressed by this Court until 1964, nearly two centuries after the founding. *New York Times Co. v. Sullivan* (1964).

It is demonstrably not true that, as JUSTICE STEVENS claims, "for most of our history, the invalidity of Second-Amendment-based objections to firearms regulations has been well settled and uncontroversial." For most of our history the question did not present itself.

III

Like most rights, the right secured by the Second Amendment is not unlimited. . . . For example, the majority of the 19th-century courts to consider the question held that prohibitions on carrying concealed weapons were lawful under the Second Amendment or state analogues. Although we do not undertake an exhaustive historical analysis today of the full scope of the Second Amendment, nothing in our opinion should be taken to cast doubt on longstanding prohibitions on the possession of firearms by felons and the mentally ill, or laws forbidding the carrying of firearms in sensitive places such as schools and government buildings, or laws imposing conditions and qualifications on the commercial sale of arms.

We also recognize another important limitation on the right to keep and carry arms. *Miller* said, as we have explained, that the sorts of weapons protected were those "in common use at the time." We think that limitation is fairly supported by the historical tradition of prohibiting the carrying of "dangerous and unusual weapons." . . .

It may be objected that if weapons that are most useful in military service — M-16 rifles and the like — may be banned, then the Second Amendment right is completely detached from the prefatory clause. But as we have said, the conception of the militia at the time of the Second Amendment's ratification was the body of all citizens capable of military service, who would bring the sorts of lawful weapons that they possessed at home to militia duty. It may well be true today that a militia, to be as effective as militias in the 18th century, would require sophisticated arms that are highly unusual in society at large. Indeed, it may be true that no amount of small arms could be useful against modern-day bombers and tanks. But the fact that modern developments have limited the degree of fit between the prefatory clause and the protected right cannot change our interpretation of the right.

IV

We turn finally to the law at issue here. As we have said, the law totally bans handgun possession in the home. It also requires that any lawful firearm in the home be disassembled or bound by a trigger lock at all times, rendering it inoperable.

As the quotations earlier in this opinion demonstrate, the inherent right of self-defense has been central to the Second Amendment right. The handgun ban amounts to a prohibition of an entire class of "arms" that is overwhelmingly chosen by American society for that lawful purpose. The prohibition extends, moreover, to the home, where the need for defense of self, family, and property is most acute. Under any of the standards of scrutiny that we have applied to enumerated constitutional rights,[11] banning from the home "the most preferred firearm in the nation to 'keep' and use for protection of one's home and family," 478 F.3d at 400, would fail constitutional muster.

Few laws in the history of our Nation have come close to the severe restriction of the District's handgun ban. And some of those few have been struck down. . . . It is no answer to say, as petitioners do, that it is permissible to ban the possession of handguns so long as the possession of other firearms (*i.e.*, long guns) is allowed. It is enough to note, as we have observed, that the American people have considered the handgun to be the quintessential self-defense weapon. There are many reasons that a citizen may prefer a handgun for home defense: It is easier to store in a location that is readily accessible in an emergency; it cannot easily be redirected or wrestled away by an attacker; it is easier to use for those without the upper body strength to lift and aim a long gun; it can be pointed at a burglar with one hand while the other hand dials the police. Whatever the reason, handguns are the most popular weapon chosen by Americans for self-defense in the home, and a complete prohibition of their use is invalid.

We must also address the District's requirement (as applied to respondent's handgun) that firearms in the home be rendered and kept inoperable at all times. This makes it impossible for citizens to use them for the core lawful purpose of self-defense and is hence unconstitutional. The District argues that we should interpret this element of the statute to contain an exception for self defense. But we think that is precluded by the unequivocal text, and by the presence of certain other enumerated exceptions. . . .

---

[11] [27] JUSTICE STEVENS correctly notes that this law, like almost all laws, would pass rational-basis scrutiny. But rational-basis scrutiny is a mode of analysis we have used when evaluating laws under constitutional commands that are themselves prohibitions on irrational laws. *Engquist v. Oregon Dept. of Agriculture* (2008) In those cases, "rational basis" is not just the standard of scrutiny, but the very substance of the constitutional guarantee. Obviously, the same test could not be used to evaluate the extent to which a legislature may regulate a specific, enumerated right, be it the freedom of speech, the guarantee against double jeopardy, the right to counsel, or the right to keep and bear arms. *United States v. Carolene Products Co.*, 304 U.S. 144, 152, n. 4 (1938) ("There may be narrower scope for operation of the presumption of constitutionality [*i.e.*, narrower than that provided by rational-basis review] when legislation appears on its face to be within a specific prohibition of the Constitution, such as those of the first ten amendments. . . ."). If all that was required to overcome the right to keep and bear arms was a rational basis, the Second Amendment would be redundant with the separate constitutional prohibitions on irrational laws, and would have no effect.

Apart from his challenge to the handgun ban and the trigger-lock requirement respondent asked the District Court to enjoin petitioners from enforcing the separate licensing requirement "in such a manner as to forbid the carrying of a firearm within one's home or possessed land without a license." . . . Before this Court petitioners have stated that "if the handgun ban is struck down and respondent registers a handgun, he could obtain a license, assuming he is not otherwise disqualified," by which they apparently mean if he is not a felon and is not insane. Respondent conceded at oral argument that he does not "have a problem with . . . licensing" and that the District's law is permissible so long as it is "not enforced in an arbitrary and capricious manner." We therefore assume that petitioners' issuance of a license will satisfy respondent's prayer for relief and do not address the licensing requirement.

JUSTICE BREYER has devoted most of his separate dissent to the handgun ban. He says that, even assuming the Second Amendment is a personal guarantee of the right to bear arms, the District's prohibition is valid. He first tries to establish this by founding-era historical precedent, pointing to various restrictive laws in the colonial period. . . . Of the laws he cites, only one offers even marginal support for his assertion. A 1783 Massachusetts law forbade the residents of Boston to "take into" or "receive into" "any Dwelling House, Stable, Barn, Out-house, Ware-house, Store, Shop or other Building" loaded firearms, and permitted the seizure of any loaded firearms that "shall be found' " there. That statute's text and its prologue, which makes clear that the purpose of the prohibition was to eliminate the danger to firefighters posed by the "depositing of loaded Arms' " in buildings, give reason to doubt that colonial Boston authorities would have enforced that general prohibition against someone who temporarily loaded a firearm to confront an intruder (despite the law's application in that case). In any case, we would not stake our interpretation of the Second Amendment upon a single law, in effect in a single city, that contradicts the overwhelming weight of other evidence regarding the right to keep and bear arms for defense of the home. The other laws JUSTICE BREYER cites are gunpowder-storage laws that he concedes did not clearly prohibit loaded weapons, but required only that excess gunpowder be kept in a special container or on the top floor of the home. Nothing about those fire-safety laws undermines our analysis; they do not remotely burden the right of self defense as much as an absolute ban on handguns. Nor, correspondingly, does our analysis suggest the invalidity of laws regulating the storage of firearms to prevent accidents.

JUSTICE BREYER points to other founding-era laws that he says "restricted the firing of guns within the city limits to at least some degree" in Boston, Philadelphia and New York. Those laws provide no support for the severe restriction in the present case. The New York law levied a fine of 20 shillings on anyone who fired a gun in certain places (including houses) on New Year's Eve and the first two days of January, and was aimed at preventing the "great Damages . . . frequently done on [those days] by persons going House to House, with Guns and other Firearms and being often intoxicated with Liquor." It is inconceivable that this law would have been enforced against a person exercising his right to self-defense on New Year's Day against such drunken hooligans. . . .

A broader point about the laws that JUSTICE BREYER cites: All of them punished the discharge (or loading) of guns with a small fine and forfeiture of the weapon (or in a few cases a very brief stay in the local jail), not with significant criminal penalties. They are akin to modern penalties for minor public-safety infractions like speeding or jaywalking. And although such public-safety laws may not contain exceptions for self-defense, it is inconceivable that the threat of a jaywalking ticket would deter someone from disregarding a "Do Not Walk" sign in order to flee an attacker, or that the Government would enforce those laws under such circumstances. Likewise, we do not think that a law imposing a 5-shilling fine and forfeiture of the gun would have prevented a person in the founding era from using a gun to protect himself or his family from violence, or that if he did so the law would be enforced against him. The District law, by contrast, far from imposing a minor fine, threatens citizens with a year in prison (five years for a second violation) for even obtaining a gun in the first place. JUSTICE BREYER moves on to make a broad jurisprudential point: He criticizes us for declining to establish a level of scrutiny for evaluating Second Amendment restrictions. He proposes, explicitly at least, none of the traditionally expressed levels (strict scrutiny, intermediate scrutiny, rational basis), but rather a judge-empowering "'nterest balancing inquiry" that "asks whether the statute burdens a protected interest in a way or to an extent that is out of proportion to the statute's salutary effects upon other important governmental interests." After an exhaustive discussion of the arguments for and against gun control, JUSTICE BREYER arrives at his interest-balanced answer: because handgun violence is a problem, because the law is limited to an urban area, and because there were somewhat similar restrictions in the founding period (a false proposition that we have already discussed), the interest-balancing inquiry results in the constitutionality of the handgun ban. QED.

We know of no other enumerated constitutional right whose core protection has been subjected to a freestanding "interest-balancing" approach. The very enumeration of the right takes out of the hands of government — even the Third Branch of Government — the power to decide on a case-by-case basis whether the right is *really worth* insisting upon. A constitutional guarantee subject to future judges' assessments of its usefulness is no constitutional guarantee at all. Constitutional rights are enshrined with the scope they were understood to have when the people adopted them, whether or not future legislatures or (yes) even future judges think that scope too broad. We would not apply an "interest-balancing" approach to the prohibition of a peaceful neo-Nazi march through Skokie. *National Socialist Party of America v. Skokie* (1977) *(per curiam)*. The First Amendment contains the freedom-of-speech guarantee that the people ratified, which included exceptions for obscenity, libel, and disclosure of state secrets, but not for the expression of extremely unpopular and wrong-headed views. The Second Amendment is no different. Like the First, it is the very *product* of an interest-balancing by the people — which JUSTICE BREYER would now conduct for them anew. And whatever else it leaves to future evaluation, it surely elevates above all other interests the right of law-abiding, responsible citizens to use arms in defense of hearth and home.

JUSTICE BREYER chides us for leaving so many applications of the right to keep and bear arms in doubt, and for not providing extensive historical justification for those regulations of the right that we describe as permissible. But since this case represents this Court's first in-depth examination of the Second Amendment, one should not expect it to clarify the entire field, any more than *Reynolds v. United*

States (1879), our first in-depth Free Exercise Clause case, left that area in a state of utter certainty. And there will be time enough to expound upon the historical justifications for the exceptions we have mentioned if and when those exceptions come before us.

In sum, we hold that the District's ban on handgun possession in the home violates the Second Amendment, as does its prohibition against rendering any lawful firearm in the home operable for the purpose of immediate self-defense. Assuming that Heller is not disqualified from the exercise of Second Amendment rights, the District must permit him to register his handgun and must issue him a license to carry it in the home.

*   *   *

We are aware of the problem of handgun violence in this country, and we take seriously the concerns raised by the many *amici* who believe that prohibition of handgun ownership is a solution. The Constitution leaves the District of Columbia a variety of tools for combating that problem, including some measures regulating handguns, But the enshrinement of constitutional rights necessarily takes certain policy choices off the table. These include the absolute prohibition of handguns held and used for self-defense in the home. Undoubtedly some think that the Second Amendment is outmoded in a society where our standing army is the pride of our Nation, where well-trained police forces provide personal security, and where gun violence is a serious problem. That is perhaps debatable, but what is not debatable is that it is not the role of this Court to pronounce the Second Amendment extinct.

We affirm the judgment of the Court of Appeals. It is so ordered.

JUSTICE STEVENS, with whom JUSTICE SOUTER, JUSTICE GINSBURG, and JUSTICE BREYER join, dissenting.

The question presented by this case is not whether the Second Amendment protects a "collective right" or an "individual right." Surely it protects a right that can be enforced by individuals. But a conclusion that the Second Amendment protects an individual right does not tell us anything about the scope of that right.

Guns are used to hunt, for self-defense, to commit crimes, for sporting activities, and to perform military duties. The Second Amendment plainly does not protect the right to use a gun to rob a bank; it is equally clear that it *does* encompass the right to use weapons for certain military purposes. Whether it also protects the right to possess and use guns for nonmilitary purposes like hunting and personal self-defense is the question presented by this case. The text of the Amendment, its history, and our decision in *United States v. Miller* (1939), provide a clear answer to that question.

The Second Amendment was adopted to protect the right of the people of each of the several States to maintain a well-regulated militia. It was a response to concerns raised during the ratification of the Constitution that the power of Congress to disarm the state militias and create a national standing army posed an intolerable threat to the sovereignty of the several States. Neither the text of the Amendment nor the arguments advanced by its proponents evidenced the slightest interest in limiting any legislature's authority to regulate private civilian uses of firearms. Specifically, there is no indication that the Framers of the Amendment intended to enshrine the common-law right of self-defense in the Constitution.

In 1934, Congress enacted the National Firearms Act, the first major federal firearms law. Upholding a conviction under that Act, this Court held that, "[i]n the absence of any evidence tending to show that possession or use of a 'shotgun having a barrel of less than eighteen inches in length' at this time has some reasonable relationship to the preservation or efficiency of a well regulated militia, we cannot say that the Second Amendment guarantees the right to keep and bear such an instrument." *Miller*. The view of the Amendment we took in *Miller* — that it protects the right to keep and bear arms for certain military purposes, but that it does not curtail the Legislature's power to regulate the nonmilitary use and ownership of weapons — is both the most natural reading of the Amendment's text and the interpretation most faithful to the history of its adoption.

* * *

The opinion the Court announces today fails to identify any new evidence supporting the view that the Amendment was intended to limit the power of Congress to regulate civilian uses of weapons. . . .

Even if the textual and historical arguments on both sides of the issue were evenly balanced, respect for the well-settled views of all of our predecessors on this Court, and for the rule of law itself, would prevent most jurists from endorsing such a dramatic upheaval in the law. As Justice Cardozo observed years ago, the "labor of judges would be increased almost to the breaking point if every past decision could be reopened in every case, and one could not lay one's own course of bricks on the secure foundation of the courses laid by others who had gone before him."

* * *

I

The text of the Second Amendment is brief. It provides: "A well regulated Militia, being necessary to the security of a free State, the right of the people to keep and bear Arms, shall not be infringed." Three portions of that text merit special focus: the introductory language defining the Amendment's purpose, the class of persons encompassed within its reach, and the unitary nature of the right that it protects. *"A well regulated Militia, being necessary to the security of a free State."* The preamble to the Second Amendment makes three important points. It identifies the preservation of the militia as the Amendment's purpose; it explains that the militia is necessary to the security of a free State; and it recognizes that the militia must be "well regulated." In all three respects it is comparable to provisions in several State Declarations of Rights that were adopted roughly contemporaneously with the Declaration of Independence. Those state provisions highlight the importance members of the founding generation attached to the maintenance of state militias; they also underscore the profound fear shared by many in that era of the dangers posed by standing armies. While the need for state militias has not been a matter of significant public interest for almost two centuries, that fact should not obscure the contemporary concerns that animated the Framers.

The parallels between the Second Amendment and these state declarations, and the Second Amendment's omission of any statement of purpose related to the right to use firearms for hunting or personal self-defense, is especially striking in light of the fact that the Declarations of Rights of Pennsylvania and Vermont *did* expressly protect such civilian uses at the time. . . . The contrast between those two declarations and the Second Amendment reinforces the clear statement of purpose announced in the Amendment's preamble. It confirms that the Framers' single-minded focus in crafting the constitutional guarantee "to keep and bear arms" was on military uses of firearms, which they viewed in the context of service in state militias.

The preamble thus both sets forth the object of the Amendment and informs the meaning of the remainder of its text. Such text should not be treated as mere surplusage, for "[i]t cannot be presumed that any clause in the constitution is intended to be without effect."

The Court today tries to denigrate the importance of this clause of the Amendment by beginning its analysis with the Amendment's operative provision and returning to the preamble merely "to ensure that our reading of the operative clause is consistent with the announced purpose." That is not how this Court ordinarily reads such texts, and it is not how the preamble would have been viewed at the time the Amendment was adopted. . . . Without identifying any language in the text that even mentions civilian uses of firearms, the Court proceeds to "find" its preferred reading in what is at best an ambiguous text, and then concludes that its reading is not foreclosed by the preamble. Perhaps the Court's approach to the text is acceptable advocacy, but it is surely an unusual approach for judges to follow.

"The right of the people"

The centerpiece of the Court's textual argument is its insistence that the words "the people" as used in the Second Amendment must have the same meaning, and protect the same class of individuals, as when they are used in the First and Fourth Amendments. According to the Court, in all three provisions — as well as the Constitution's preamble, section 2 of Article I, and the Tenth Amendment — "the term unambiguously refers to all members of the political community, not an unspecified subset." But the Court *itself* reads the Second Amendment to protect a "subset" significantly narrower than the class of persons protected by the First and Fourth Amendments; when it finally drills down on the substantive meaning of the Second Amendment, the Court limits the protected class to "law-abiding, respon-sible citizens." But the class of persons protected by the First and Fourth Amendments is *not* so limited; for even felons (and presumably irresponsible citizens as well) may invoke the protections of those constitutional provisions.

The Court offers no way to harmonize its conflicting pronouncements.

The Court also overlooks the significance of the way the Framers used the phrase "the people" in these constitutional provisions. In the First Amendment, no words define the class of individuals entitled to speak, to publish, or to worship; in that Amendment it is only the right peaceably to assemble, and to petition the

Government for a redress of grievances, that is described as a right of "the people." These rights contemplate collective action. . . .

Similarly, the words "the people" in the Second Amendment refer back to the object announced in the Amendment's preamble. They remind us that it is the collective action of individuals having a duty to serve in the militia that the text directly protects and, perhaps more importantly, that the ultimate purpose of the Amendment was to protect the States' share of the divided sovereignty created by the Constitution.

* * *

"To keep and bear Arms"

Although the Court's discussion of these words treats them as two "phrases" — as if they read "to keep" and "to bear" — they describe a unitary right: to possess arms if needed for military purposes and to use them in conjunction with military activities.

. . . Had the Framers wished to expand the meaning of the phrase "bear arms" to encompass civilian possession and use, they could have done so by the addition of phrases such as "for the defense of themselves," as was done in the Pennsylvania and Vermont Declarations of Rights. The *unmodified* use of "bear arms," by contrast, refers most naturally to a military purpose, as evidenced by its use in literally dozens of contemporary texts. The absence of any reference to civilian uses of weapons tailors the text of the Amendment to the purpose identified in its preamble. But when discussing these words, the Court simply ignores the preamble.

* * *

The Amendment's use of the term "keep" in no way contradicts the military meaning conveyed by the phrase "bear arms" and the Amendment's preamble. To the contrary, a number of state militia laws in effect at the time of the Second Amendment's drafting used the term "keep" to describe the requirement that militia members store their arms at their homes, ready to be used for service when necessary. . . .

This reading is confirmed by the fact that the clause protects only one right, rather than two. It does not describe a right "to keep arms" and a separate right "to bear arms." Rather, the single right that it does describe is both a duty and a right to have arms available and ready for military service, and to use them for military purposes when necessary. Different language surely would have been used to protect nonmilitary use and possession of weapons from regulation if such an intent had played any role in the drafting of the Amendment.

* * *

When each word in the text is given full effect, the Amendment is most naturally read to secure to the people a right to use and possess arms in conjunction with service in a well-regulated militia. So far as appears, no more than that was contemplated by its drafters or is encompassed within its terms. Even if the meaning of the text were genuinely susceptible to more than one interpretation, the burden would remain on those advocating a departure from the purpose identified in the preamble and from settled law to come forward with persuasive new arguments or evidence. The textual analysis offered by respondent and embraced by the Court falls far short of sustaining that heavy burden. . . .

II

The proper allocation of military power in the new Nation was an issue of central concern for the Framers. The compromises they ultimately reached, reflected in Article I's Militia Clauses and the Second Amendment, represent quintessential examples of the Framers' "splitting the atom of sovereignty."

Two themes relevant to our current interpretive task ran through the debates on the original Constitution. "On the one hand, there was a widespread fear that a national standing Army posed an intolerable threat to individual liberty and to the sovereignty of the separate States." . . . On the other hand, the Framers recognized the dangers inherent in relying on inadequately trained militia members "as the primary means of providing for the common defense"; during the Revolutionary War, "[t]his force, though armed, was largely untrained, and its deficiencies were the subject of bitter complaint." In order to respond to those twin concerns, a compromise was reached: Congress would be authorized to raise and support a national Army[12] and Navy, and also to organize, arm, discipline, and provide for the calling forth of "the Militia.' " U.S. Const., Art. I, § 8, cls.12–16. The President, at the same time, was empowered as the "Commander in Chief of the Army and Navy of the United States, and of the Militia of the several States, when called into the actual Service of the United States." Art. II, § 2. But, with respect to the militia, a significant reservation was made to the States: Although Congress would have the power to call forth, organize, arm, and discipline the militia, as well as to govern "such Part of them as may be employed in the Service of the United States," the States respectively would retain the right to appoint the officers and to train the militia in accordance with the discipline prescribed by Congress. Art. I, § 8, cl. 16.[13]

But the original Constitution's retention of the militia and its creation of divided authority over that body did not prove sufficient to allay fears about the dangers posed by a standing army. For it was perceived by some that Article I contained a significant gap: While it empowered Congress to organize, arm, and discipline the militia, it did not prevent Congress from providing for the militia's *dis* armament. . . . The Anti-Federalists were ultimately unsuccessful in persuading state ratifi-

---

[12] [18] "[B]ut no Appropriation of Money to that Use [raising and supporting Armies] shall be for a longer Term than two Years."U.S. Const., Art I, § 8, cl. 12.

[13] [20] The Court assumes — incorrectly, in my view — that even when a state militia was not called into service, Congress would have had the power to exclude individuals from enlistment in that state militia. That assumption is not supported by the text of the Militia Clauses of the original Constitution, which confer upon Congress the power to "organiz[e], ar[m], and disciplin[e], the Militia," Art. I, § 8, cl. 16, but not the power to say who will be members of a state militia. It is also flatly inconsistent with the Second Amendment. The States' power to create their own militias provides an easy answer to the Court's complaint that the right as I have described it is empty because it merely guarantees "citizens' right to use a gun in an organization from which Congress has plenary authority to exclude them."

cation conventions to condition their approval of the Constitution upon the eventual inclusion of any particular amendment. But a number of States did propose to the first Federal Congress amendments reflecting a desire to ensure that the institution of the militia would remain protected under the new Government. The proposed amendments sent by the States of Virginia, North Carolina, and New York focused on the importance of preserving the state militias and reiterated the dangers posed by standing armies. New Hampshire sent a proposal that differed significantly from the others; while also invoking the dangers of a standing army, it suggested that the Constitution should more broadly protect the use and possession of weapons, without tying such a guarantee expressly to the maintenance of the militia. . . .

* * *

With all of these sources upon which to draw, it is strikingly significant that Madison's first draft omitted any mention of nonmilitary use or possession of weapons. . . . Madison's decision to model the Second Amendment on the distinctly military Virginia proposal is therefore revealing, since it is clear that he considered and rejected formulations that would have unambiguously protected civilian uses of firearms. When Madison prepared his first draft, and when that draft was debated and modified, it is reasonable to assume that all participants in the drafting process were fully aware of the other formulations that would have protected civilian use and possession of weapons and that their choice to craft the Amendment as they did represented a rejection of those alternative formulations. Madison's initial inclusion of an exemption for conscientious objectors sheds revelatory light on the purpose of the Amendment. It confirms an intent to describe a duty as well as a right, and it unequivocally identifies the military character of both. The objections voiced to the conscientious-objector clause only confirm the central meaning of the text. Although records of the debate in the Senate, which is where the conscientious-objector clause was removed, do not survive, the arguments raised in the House illuminate the perceived problems with the clause: Specifically, there was concern that Congress "can declare who are those religiously scrupulous, and prevent them from bearing arms." The ultimate removal of the clause, therefore, only serves to confirm the purpose of the Amendment — to protect against congressional disarmament, by whatever means, of the States' militias.

* * *

The history of the adoption of the Amendment thus describes an overriding concern about the potential threat to state sovereignty that a federal standing army would pose, and a desire to protect the States' militias as the means by which to guard against that danger. But state militias could not effectively check the prospect of a federal standing army so long as Congress retained the power to disarm them, and so a guarantee against such disarmament was needed. . . .

III

Although it gives short shrift to the drafting history of the Second Amendment, the Court dwells at length on four other sources: the 17th-century English Bill of Rights; BLACKSTONE'S COMMENTARIES ON THE LAWS OF ENGLAND; postenactment commentary on the Second Amendment; and post-Civil War legislative history. All of these sources shed only indirect light on the question before us, and in any event offer little support for the Court's conclusion.

*   *   *

The English Bill of Rights

The Court's reliance on Article VII of the 1689 English Bill of Rights — which, like most of the evidence offered by the Court today, was considered in *Miller* — is misguided both because Article VII was enacted in response to different concerns from those that motivated the Framers of the Second Amendment, and because the guarantees of the two provisions were by no means coextensive. . . .

Blackstone's Commentaries

The Court's reliance on BLACKSTONE'S COMMENTARIES ON THE LAWS OF ENGLAND is unpersuasive for the same reason as its reliance on the English Bill of Rights. Blackstone's invocation of 'the natural right of resistance and self-preservation,' " and " 'the right of having and using arms for self-preservation and defence,' " referred specifically to Article VII in the English Bill of Rights. The excerpt from Blackstone offered by the Court, therefore, is, like Article VII itself, of limited use in interpreting the very differently worded, and differently historically situated, Second Amendment.

What *is* important about Blackstone is the instruction he provided on reading the sort of text before us today. Blackstone described an interpretive approach that gave far more weight to preambles than the Court allows. Counseling that "[t]he fairest and most rational method to interpret the will of the legislator, is by exploring his intentions at the time when the law was made, by *signs* the most natural and probable," Blackstone explained that "[i]f words happen to be still dubious, we may establish their meaning from the context; with which it may be of singular use to compare a word, or a sentence, whenever they are ambiguous, equivocal, or intricate. Thus, the proeme, or preamble, is often called in to help the construction of an act of parliament." . . .

Postenactment Commentary

The Court also excerpts, without any real analysis, commentary by a number of additional scholars, some near in time to the framing and others post-dating it by close to a century. Those scholars are for the most part of limited relevance in construing the guarantee of the Second Amendment: Their views are not altogether clear, they tended to collapse the Second Amendment with Article VII of the English Bill of Rights, and they appear to have been unfamiliar with the drafting history of the Second Amendment.

The most significant of these commentators was Joseph Story. Contrary to the Court's assertions, however, Story actually supports the view that the Amendment was designed to protect the right of each of the States to maintain a well-regulated militia. When Story used the term "palladium" in discussions of the Second

Amendment, he merely echoed the concerns that animated the Framers of the Amendment and led to its adoption. An excerpt from his 1833 COMMENTARIES ON THE CONSTITUTION OF THE UNITED STATES — the same passage cited by the Court in *Miller* — merits reproducing at some length: "The importance of [the Second Amendment] will scarcely be doubted by any persons who have duly reflected upon the subject. The militia is the natural defence of a free country against sudden foreign invasions, domestic insurrections, and domestic usurpations of power by rulers. It is against sound policy for a free people to keep up large military establishments and standing armies in time of peace, both from the enormous expenses with which they are attended and the facile means which they afford to ambitious and unprincipled rulers to subvert the government, or trample upon the rights of the people. The right of the citizens to keep and bear arms has justly been considered as the palladium of the liberties of a republic, since it offers a strong moral check against the usurpation and arbitrary power of rulers, and will generally, even if these are successful in the first instance, enable the people to resist and triumph over them. And yet, though this truth would seem so clear, and the importance of a well-regulated militia would seem so undeniable, it cannot be disguised that, among the American people, there is a growing indifference to any system of militia discipline, and a strong disposition, from a sense of its burdens, to be rid of all regulations. How it is practicable to keep the people duly armed without some organization, it is difficult to see. There is certainly no small danger that indifference may lead to disgust, and disgust to contempt; and thus gradually undermine all the protection intended by the clause of our national bill of rights." 2 J. STORY, COMMENTARIES ON THE CONSTITUTION OF THE UNITED STATES § 1897, pp. 620–621 (4th ed. 1873) (footnote omitted).

Story thus began by tying the significance of the Amendment directly to the paramount importance of the militia. He then invoked the fear that drove the Framers of the Second Amendment — specifically, the threat to liberty posed by a standing army. An important check on that danger, he suggested, was a "well-regulated militia," for which he assumed that arms would have to be kept and, when necessary, borne. There is not so much as a whisper in the passage above that Story believed that the right secured by the Amendment bore any relation to private use or possession of weapons for activities like hunting or personal self-defense.

*   *   *

IV

The brilliance of the debates that resulted in the Second Amendment faded into oblivion during the ensuing years, for the concerns about Article I's Militia Clauses that generated such pitched debate during the ratification process and led to the adoption of the Second Amendment were short lived.

*   *   *

Thus, for most of our history, the invalidity of Second-Amendment-based objections to firearms regulations has been well settled and uncontroversial. Indeed, the Second Amendment was not even mentioned in either full House of Congress during the legislative proceedings that led to the passage of the 1934 Act.

Yet enforcement of that law produced the judicial decision that confirmed the status of the Amendment as limited in reach to military usage. After reviewing many of the same sources that are discussed at greater length by the Court today, the *Miller* Court unanimously concluded that the Second Amendment did not apply to the possession of a firearm that did not have "some reasonable relationship to the preservation or efficiency of a well regulated militia." The key to that decision did not, as the Court belatedly suggests, turn on the difference between muskets and sawed-off shotguns; it turned, rather, on the basic difference between the military and nonmilitary use and possession of guns. Indeed, if the Second Amendment were not limited in its coverage to military uses of weapons, why should the Court in *Miller* have suggested that some weapons but not others were eligible for Second Amendment protection? If use for self-defense were the relevant standard, why did the Court not inquire into the suitability of a particular weapon for self-defense purposes?

Perhaps in recognition of the weakness of its attempt to distinguish *Miller*, the Court argues in the alternative that *Miller* should be discounted because of its decisional history. It is true that the appellee in *Miller* did not file a brief or make an appearance, although the court below had held that the relevant provision of the National Firearms Act violated the Second Amendment (albeit without any reasoned opinion). But, as our decision in *Marbury v. Madison*, in which only one side appeared and presented arguments, demonstrates, the absence of adversarial presentation alone is not a basis for refusing to accord *stare decisis* effect to a decision of this Court. Of course, if it can be demonstrated that new evidence or arguments were genuinely not available to an earlier Court, that fact should be given special weight as we consider whether to overrule a prior case. But the Court does not make that claim, because it cannot. . . .

*   *   *

V

The Court concludes its opinion by declaring that it is not the proper role of this Court to change the meaning of rights "enshrine[d]" in the Constitution. But the right the Court announces was not "enshrined" in the Second Amendment by the Framers; it is the product of today's law-changing decision. The majority's exegesis has utterly failed to establish that as a matter of text or history, "the right of law-abiding, responsible citizens to use arms in defense of hearth and home" is "elevate[d] above all other interests" by the Second Amendment.

Until today, it has been understood that legislatures may regulate the civilian use and misuse of firearms so long as they do not interfere with the preservation of a well-regulated militia. The Court's announcement of a new constitutional right to own and use firearms for private purposes upsets that settled understanding, but leaves for future cases the formidable task of defining the scope of permissible regulations. Today judicial craftsmen have confidently asserted that a policy choice that denies a "law-abiding, responsible citize[n]" the right to keep and use weapon s in the home for self-defense is "off the table." Given the presumption that most citizens are law abiding, and the reality that the need to defend oneself may suddenly arise in a host of locations outside the home, I fear that the District's policy choice may well be just the first of an unknown number of dominoes to be knocked off the table.

I do not know whether today's decision will increase the labor of federal judges to the "breaking point" envisioned by Justice Cardozo, but it will surely give rise to a far more active judicial role in making vitally important national policy decisions than was envisioned at any time in the 18th, 19th, or 20th centuries.

The Court properly disclaims any interest in evaluating the wisdom of the specific policy choice challenged in this case, but it fails to pay heed to a far more important policy choice — the choice made by the Framers themselves. The Court would have us believe that over 200 years ago, the Framers made a choice to limit the tools available to elected officials wishing to regulate civilian uses of weapons, and to authorize this Court to use the common-law process of case-by-case judicial lawmaking to define the contours of acceptable gun control policy. Absent compelling evidence that is nowhere to be found in the Court's opinion, I could not possibly conclude that the Framers made such a choice.

For these reasons, I respectfully dissent.

JUSTICE BREYER, with whom JUSTICE STEVENS, JUSTICE SOUTER, and JUSTICE GINSBURG join, dissenting.

We must decide whether a District of Columbia law that prohibits the possession of handguns in the home violates the Second Amendment. The majority, relying upon its view that the Second Amendment seeks to protect a right of personal self-defense, holds that this law violates that Amendment. In my view, it does not.

I

The majority's conclusion is wrong for two independent reasons. The first reason is that set forth by JUSTICE STEVENS — namely, that the Second Amendment protects militia-related, not self-defense-related, interests. These two interests are sometimes intertwined. To assure 18th-century citizens that they could keep arms for militia purposes would necessarily have allowed them to keep arms that they could have used for self-defense as well. But self-defense alone, detached from any militia-related objective, is not the Amendment's concern.

The second independent reason is that the protection the Amendment provides is not absolute. The Amendment permits government to regulate the interests that it serves. Thus, irrespective of what those interests are — whether they do or do not include an independent interest in self-defense — the majority's view cannot be correct unless it can show that the District's regulation is unreasonable or inappropriate in Second Amendment terms.

This the majority cannot do.

In respect to the first independent reason, I agree with JUSTICE STEVENS, and I join his opinion. In this opinion I shall focus upon the second reason. I shall show that the District's law is consistent with the Second Amendment even if that Amendment is interpreted as protecting a wholly separate interest in individual self-defense. That is so because the District's regulation, which focuses upon the presence of handguns in high-crime urban areas, represents a permissible legislative response to a serious, indeed life-threatening, problem.

Thus I here assume that one objective (but, as the majority concedes, *ante*, at 26, not the *primary* objective) of those who wrote the Second Amendment was to help assure citizens that they would have arms available for purposes of self-defense. Even so, a legislature could reasonably conclude that the law will advance goals of great public importance, namely, saving lives, preventing injury, and reducing crime. The law is tailored to the urban crime problem in that it is local in scope and thus affects only a geographic area both limited in size and entirely urban; the law concerns handguns, which are specially linked to urban gun deaths and injuries, and which are the overwhelmingly favorite weapon of armed criminals; and at the same time, the law imposes a burden upon gun owners that seems proportionately no greater than restrictions in existence at the time the Second Amendment was adopted. In these circumstances, the District's law falls within the zone that the Second Amendment leaves open to regulation by legislatures.

II

*   *   *

This historical evidence demonstrates that a self-defense assumption is the *beginning*, rather than the *end*, of any constitutional inquiry. That the District law impacts self-defense merely raises *questions* about the law's constitutionality. But to answer the questions that are raised (that is, to see whether the statute is unconstitutional) requires us to focus on practicalities, the statute's rationale, the problems that called it into being, its relation to those objectives — in a word, the details. There are no purely logical or conceptual answers to such questions. All of which to say that to raise a self-defense question is not to answer it.

III

I therefore begin by asking a process-based question: How is a court to determine whether a particular firearm regulation (here, the District's restriction on handguns) is consistent with the Second Amendment? What kind of constitutional standard should the court use? How high a protective hurdle does the Amendment erect? The question matters. The majority is wrong when it says that the District's law is unconstitutional "[u]nder any of the standards of scrutiny that we have applied to enumerated constitutional rights." How could that be? It certainly would not be unconstitutional under, for example, a "rational basis" standard, which requires a court to uphold regulation so long as it bears a "rational relationship" to a "legitimate governmental purpose." *Heller v. Doe* (1993). The law at issue here, which in part seeks to prevent gun-related accidents, at least bears a "rational relationship" to that "legitimate" life-saving objective. . . .

Respondent proposes that the Court adopt a "strict scrutiny" test, which would require reviewing with care each gun law to determine whether it is "narrowly tailored to achieve a compelling governmental interest." But the majority implicitly, and appropriately, rejects that suggestion by broadly approving a set of laws —

prohibitions on concealed weapons, forfeiture by criminals of the Second Amendment right, prohibitions on firearms in certain locales, and governmental regulation of commercial firearm sales — whose constitutionality under a strict scrutiny standard would be far from clear.

Indeed, adoption of a true strict-scrutiny standard for evaluating gun regulations would be impossible. That is because almost every gun-control regulation will seek to advance (as the one here does) a "primary concern of every government — a concern for the safety and indeed the lives of its citizens." The Court has deemed that interest, as well as "the Government's general interest in preventing crime," to be "compelling," and the Court has in a wide variety of constitutional contexts found such public-safety concerns sufficiently forceful to justify restrictions on individual liberties, *e.g., Brandenburg v. Ohio* (1969) (*per curiam*) (First Amendment free speech rights); *Sherbert v. Verner* (1963) (First Amendment religious rights). . . . Thus, any attempt *in theory* to apply strict scrutiny to gun regulations will *in practice* turn into an interest-balancing inquiry, with the interests protected by the Second Amendment on one side and the governmental public-safety concerns on the other, the only question being whether the regulation at issue impermissibly burdens the former in the course of advancing the latter.

I would simply adopt such an interest-balancing inquiry explicitly. The fact that important interests lie on both sides of the constitutional equation suggests that review of gun-control regulation is not a context in which a court should effectively presume either constitutionality (as in rational-basis review) or unconstitutionality (as in strict scrutiny). Rather, "where a law significantly implicates competing constitutionally protected interests in complex ways," the Court generally asks whether the statute burdens a protected interest in a way or to an extent that is out of proportion to the statute's salutary effects upon other important governmental interests. See *Nixon v. Shrink Missouri Government PAC* (2000) (BREYER, J., concurring). Any answer would take account both of the statute's effects upon the competing interests and the existence of any clearly superior less restrictive alternative. Contrary to the majority's unsupported suggestion that this sort of "proportionality" approach is unprecedented, the Court has applied it in various constitutional contexts, including election-law cases, speech cases, and due process cases. 528 U.S., at 403 (citing examples where the Court has taken such an approach); *e.g., Thompson v. Western States Medical Center* (2002) (BREYER, J., dissenting) (commercial speech); *Burdick v. Takushi* (1992) (election regulation); *Mathews v. Eldridge* (1976) (procedural due process); *Pickering v. Board of Ed. of Township High School Dist. 205* (1968) (government employee speech). In applying this kind of standard the Court normally defers to a legislature's empirical judgment in matters where a legislature is likely to have greater expertise and greater institutional factfinding capacity. *Turner Broadcasting System, Inc. v. FCC* (1997). Nonetheless, a court, not a legislature, must make the ultimate constitutional conclusion, exercising its "independent judicial judgment" in light of the whole record to determine whether a law exceeds constitutional boundaries.

The above-described approach seems preferable to a more rigid approach here for a further reason. Experience as much as logic has led the Court to decide that in one area of constitutional law or another the interests are likely to prove stronger on one side of a typical constitutional case than on the other. Here, we have little prior experience. Courts that *do* have experience in these matters have uniformly taken an approach that treats empirically-based legislative judgment with a degree of deference. . . .

IV

*   *   *

A

No one doubts the constitutional importance of the statute's basic objective, saving lives. But there is considerable debate about whether the District's statute helps to achieve that objective.

*   *   *

The upshot is a set of studies and counterstudies that, at most, could leave a judge uncertain about the proper policy conclusion. But from respondent's perspective any such uncertainty is not good enough. That is because legislators, not judges, have primary responsibility for drawing policy conclusions from empirical fact. And, given that constitutional allocation of decisionmaking responsibility, the empirical evidence presented here is sufficient to allow a judge to reach a firm *legal* conclusion. In particular this Court, in First Amendment cases applying intermediate scrutiny, has said that our" "sole obligation" in reviewing a legislature's "predictive judgments" is "to assure that, in formulating its judgments," the legislature "has drawn reasonable inferences based on substantial evidence." And judges, looking at the evidence before us, should agree that the District legislature's predictive judgments satisfy that legal standard.

That is to say, the District's judgment, while open to question, is nevertheless supported by "substantial evidence." There is no cause here to depart from the standard set forth in *Turner*, for the District's decision represents the kind of empirically based judgment that legislatures, not courts, are best suited to make. In fact, deference to legislative judgment seems particularly appropriate here, where the judgment has been made by a local legislature, with particular knowledge of local problems and insight into appropriate local solutions. *Los Angeles v. Alameda Books, Inc.* (2002) (plurality opinion) ("[W]e must acknowledge that the Los Angeles City Council is in a better position than the Judiciary to gather and evaluate data on local problems"). Different localities may seek to solve similar problems in different ways, and a "city must be allowed a reasonable opportunity to experiment with solutions to admittedly serious problems." *Renton v. Playtime Theatres, Inc.* (1986). "The Framers recognized that the most effective democracy occurs at local levels of government, where people with firsthand knowledge of local problems have more ready access to public officials responsible for dealing with them." *Garcia v. San Antonio Metropolitan Transit Authority* (1985) (Powell, J., dissenting) (citing THE FEDERALIST No. 17 (A. Hamilton)). We owe that democratic process some substantial weight in the constitutional calculus. For these reasons, I conclude that the District's statute properly seeks to further the sort of life-preserving and public-safety interests that the Court has called "compelling."

B

I next assess the extent to which the District's law burdens the interests that the Second Amendment seeks to protect. Respondent and his *amici,* as well as the majority, suggest that those interests include: (1) the preservation of a "well regulated Militia"; (2) safeguarding the use of firearms for sporting purposes, *e.g.,* hunting and marksmanship; and (3) assuring the use of firearms for self-defense. For argument's sake, I shall consider all three of those interests here.

*   *   *

3

The District's law does prevent a resident from keeping a loaded handgun in his home. And it consequently makes it more difficult for the householder to use the handgun for self-defense in the home against intruders, such as burglars. . . . To that extent the law burdens to some degree an interest in self-defense that for present purposes I have assumed the Amendment seeks to further.

C

In weighing needs and burdens, we must take account of the possibility that there are reasonable, but less restrictive alternatives. Are there *other* potential measures that might similarly promote the same goals while imposing lesser restrictions? Here I see none.

The reason there is no clearly superior, less restrictive alternative to the District's handgun ban is that the ban's very objective is to reduce significantly the number of handguns in the District, say, for example, by allowing a law enforcement officer immediately to assume that *any* handgun he sees is an *illegal* handgun. And there is no plausible way to achieve that objective other than to ban the guns.

*   *   *

D

The upshot is that the District's objectives are compelling; its predictive judgments as to its law's tendency to achieve those objectives are adequately supported; the law does impose a burden upon any self-defense interest that the Amendment seeks to secure; and there is no clear less restrictive alternative. I turn now to the final portion of the "permissible regulation" question: Does the District's law *disproportionately* burden Amendment-protected interests? Several considerations, taken together, convince me that it does not.

*   *   *

V

The majority derides my approach as "judge-empowering." I take this criticism seriously, but I do not think it accurate. As I have previously explained, this is an approach that the Court has taken in other areas of constitutional law. Application of such an approach, of course, requires judgment, but the very nature of the approach — requiring careful identification of the relevant interests and evaluating the law's effect upon them — limits the judge's choices; and the method's necessary transparency lays bare the judge's reasoning for all to see and to criticize. The majority's methodology is, in my view, substantially less transparent than mine. At a minimum, I find it difficult to understand the reasoning that seems to underlie certain conclusions that it reaches.

* * *

At the same time the majority ignores a more important question: Given the purposes for which the Framers enacted the Second Amendment, how should it be applied to modern-day circumstances that they could not have anticipated? Assume, for argument's sake, that the Framers did intend the Amendment to offer a degree of self-defense protection. Does that mean that the Framers also intended to guarantee a right to possess a loaded gun near swimming pools, parks, and playgrounds? That they would not have cared about the children who might pick up a loaded gun on their parents' bedside table? That they (who certainly showed concern for the risk of fire) would have lacked concern for the risk of accidental deaths or suicides that readily accessible loaded handguns in urban areas might bring? Unless we believe that they intended future generations to ignore such matters, answering questions such as the questions in this case requires judgment — judicial judgment exercised within a framework for constitutional analysis that guides that judgment and which makes its exercise transparent. One cannot answer those questions by combining inconclusive historical research with judicial *ipse dixit*.

The argument about method, however, is by far the less important argument surrounding today's decision. Far more important are the unfortunate consequences that today's decision is likely to spawn. Not least of these, as I have said, is the fact that the decision threatens to throw into doubt the constitutionality of gun laws throughout the United States. I can find no sound legal basis for launching the courts on so formidable and potentially dangerous a mission. In my view, there simply is no untouchable constitutional right guaranteed by the Second Amendment to keep loaded handguns in the house in crime-ridden urban areas.

VI

For these reasons, I conclude that the District's measure is a proportionate, not a disproportionate, response to the compelling concerns that led the District to adopt it. And, for these reasons as well as the independently sufficient reasons set forth by JUSTICE STEVENS, I would find the District's measure consistent with the Second Amendment's demands. With respect, I dissent.

NOTES AND QUESTIONS

1. In *District of Columbia v. Heller* (2008), the Court per Justice Scalia 5-4 found that the Second Amendment protects an individual right to own a handgun in one's home against a handgun limitation traceable to federal authority. DC's handgun ban was total, except for peace officers; one needed a license to have a gun in one's home, but none could be obtained as the local law was applied. One could have a long gun (a rifle), but it had to be disassembled or have a trigger lock.

2.   As an under-interpreted provision in the Constitution, the Second Amendment provided an opportunity to test the integrity and utility of the original understanding method of interpretation. As suggested by the material introducing the case, original understanding posits that constitutional provisions should not be interpreted in light of their modern consequence, but in light of their ratified meaning, with words being interpreted in reference to their understanding at the time of ratification, not the specific intent of any particular drafter. Justice Scalia, who wrote majority in *Heller*, is the strongest proponent of this methodology. It is meant to check judicial abuse and to allow cases to be decided as much as possible in accordance with the law as written and independent of the predilections of particular Justices. Did the theory resolve *Heller*, since both Justice Scalia for the majority and Justice Stevens for the dissent employed a careful historical examination of the amendment and reached exactly opposite conclusions?

3.   The language to be construed: "a well regulated militia being necessary to the security of a Free State, the right of the people to keep and bear arms shall not be infringed." Prior to *Heller*, many thought that the second half of the text was to be construed only in reference to its preamble. Justice Scalia concludes instead that the first 13 words of the amendment are "a purpose," but not *the* purpose. Your co-authors are in disagreement about the originalist legitimacy of this move by Justice Scalia. Professor Kmiec thinks the Scalia view to be questionable given that the concern with having a militia as a counterpoint to government tyranny fits both the history and the text. It also fit structure as an answer to the threat of abuse of Congress' own Article I militia organizing authority. Dean Eastman, as noted below, believes Justice Scalia is informing the text with an appreciation of a natural law right of self-defense. As for "the right of the people" language, both majority and dissent agree that this suggests an individually enforceable right, but that tells us nothing about its scope — specifically whether that scope must have a militia-nexus. What do you think?

4.   Of course, sometimes text, history, context, and structure have been contradicted by longstanding precedent which, by reason of reliance, merits adherence. *United States v. Miller* in 1939 arguably saw the Second Amendment as militia-related, and it was a precedent followed by virtually every lower federal court since it had been decided. Justice Scalia argues that *Miller* holds only that a short-barreled shotgun was not "ordinary military equipment" because it was not the type, men bearing arms would be expected to bring when called to militia service.

5.   The dissent saw the opinion as legislating from the bench. Wrote Justice Stevens for the four dissenters quoting *Miller*, "the signification attributed to the term Militia appears from the debates in the convention, the history and legislation of colonies and states, and the writings of approved commentators." In light of that, Justice Stevens concluded: "Until today, it has been understood that legislatures may regulate the civilian use and misuse of firearms so long as they do not interfere with the preservation of a well regulated militia. The court's announcement of a new

constitutional right to own and use firearms for private purposes upsets that settled understanding, but leaves for future cases the formidable task of defining the scope of permissible regulations."

6.   But there is another view of originalism possibly in play as well, one which heretofore has been championed largely by Justice Thomas but to which Justice Scalia's opinion appears to give credence. That view holds, with substantial evidentiary basis in the founding-era debates, that the Bill of Rights merely recognizes (rather than creates) pre-existing natural rights. All of your co-authors think this view has credibility. It is possible that Justice Scalia is also accepting of this view — at least in this case — since he makes reference to 19th century case law approving of the perspective. In this regard, the Court makes several references to this "natural law" view of the Second Amendment right, concluding that the Second Amendment necessarily codifies a deeper right to self-defense, against both private thugs and government tyrants.

7.   But assuming Justice Scalia is in fact now willing to judicially enforce the text of the Constitution only as informed by the natural law (a proposition we will see Justice Scalia denies outside of the gun context), how exactly does he know that the natural law includes a right to possess a handgun for self-defense. A link to "the militia," allows the right to be defined in relation to a historical purpose. Isn't it possible to see handguns as contrary to any natural law right insofar as gun usage has its own inherent dangers or just simply in light of the number of handgun deaths each year in urban areas including DC?

8.   In *McDonald v. City of Chicago*, 130 S. Ct. 3020, 177 L. Ed. 2d 894 (2010), the Court held that the rights under the Second Amendment are "fully applicable to the States." A clear majority of five, led by Justice Alito held that § 1 of the 14th Amendment incorporates the 2nd Amendment and makes it applicable to the states, but only a plurality held that the Due Process Clause is the incorporating agent. Justice Thomas's concurrence contained a characteristically bold attack on the much-criticized *Slaughter-House* interpretation of the 14th Amendment's Privileges or Immunities Clause and on the on the illogic of using a "*process*" clause as the grounding for the recognition of fundamental *substantive* rights when the Privileges or Immunities Clause would seem more logically to protect substantive rights. Justice Alito, for the plurality on that issue, declined to reconsider the *Slaughter-House Cases*, 83 U.S. (16 Wall.) 36 (1873), simply because doing so would disturb several decades of past Due Process decisions:

> We see no need to reconsider that interpretation here. For many decades, the question of the rights protected by the Fourteenth Amendment against state infringement has been analyzed under the Due Process Clause of that Amendment and not under the Privileges or Immunities Clause. We therefore decline to disturb the *Slaughter-House* holding.

The City of Chicago had argued "a right set out in the Bill of Rights applies to the States only if that right is an indispensable attribute of *any* 'civilized' legal system" — the point being that the right to keep and bear arms can hardly be considered "an indispensable attribute of *any* 'civilized' legal system." Some early formulations of the test seemed to suggest such a criterion (*e.g.*, *Palko v. Connecticut*, 302 U.S. 319 (1937)). The case law requirements as understood by Justice Alito for the majority, however, focused on two later formulations:

> [W]e must decide [wrote Justice Alito] whether the right to keep and bear arms is fundamental to *our* scheme of ordered liberty [citing *Duncan v. Louisiana*, 391 U.S. 145 (1968)], or as we have said in a related context, whether this right is "deeply rooted in this Nation's history and tradition" [citing *Washington v. Glucksberg*, 521 U.S. 702 (1997)].

Justice Alito, for the majority, found that the right to keep and bear arms clearly fit in with the *Duncan/Glucksberg* formulation's emphasis on *American* history and tradition. Justice Breyer in dissent did not attack Justice Alito's use of the *Duncan/Glucksberg* formulation. Instead he attacked Alito's use of *history* as the *sole* determinant in the application of the *Duncan/Glucksberg* formulation, and suggested an additional set of factors for selective-incorporation determinations:

> I . . . think it proper, above all where history provides no clear answer, to look to other factors in considering whether a right is sufficiently "fundamental" to remove it from the political process in every State. I would include among those factors the nature of the right; any contemporary disagreement about whether the right is fundamental; the extent to which incorporation will further other, perhaps more basic, constitutional aims; and the extent to which incorporation will advance or hinder the Constitution's structural aims, including its division of powers among different governmental institutions (and the people as well). Is incorporation needed, for example, to further the Constitution's effort to ensure that the government treats each individual with equal respect? Will it help maintain the democratic form of government that the Constitution foresees? In a word, will incorporation prove consistent, or inconsistent, with the Constitution's efforts to create governmental institutions well suited to the carrying out of its constitutional promises?

9. Leaving the disputes over the meaning of Second Amendment and supposed gun rights, it is worth recalling that English Bill of Rights facilitated the ascendency of William and Mary to the throne. While the Bill of Rights, and their passage by Parliament and acceptance by William and Mary, went fairly far to justify and legitimate the Glorious Revolution, there was still a need for a clearer philosophical and political underpinning for the deposing of James. In other words, there was a need for someone to justify the Glorious Revolution in the manner that Milton tried to justify the beheading of Charles I. This philosophical justification came with the work of John Locke, our final, and most important, reading in this section.

C. ECONOMIC LIBERTY

1. Privileges *and* Immunities

The Privileges and Immunities Clause in Article IV, Section 2, reads "The Citizens of each State shall be entitled to all Privileges and Immunities of Citizens in the several states." Under this Clause, there can be no discrimination against out-of-state residents with regard either to express constitutional rights or those economic liberties that relate to livelihood. Thus, the primary focus of Article IV, as it has been interpreted, is the avoidance of interstate discrimination, not the promotion or safeguarding of economic liberty, per se. At various points in history, however, the clause has been argued to have a larger purpose. The Republican abolitionists, for example, in the 19th century posited that it was the intent of Article IV, Section 2 to establish an unbreakable connection between United States citizenship and certain fundamental rights. When this proposition was doubted, the post-Civil War Congress approved the Fourteenth Amendment's Privileges or Immunities Clause to protect certain fundamental rights, including life and liberty, acquiring and possessing property, pursuing one's trade or calling, and in general, happiness. We first take up the non-discrimination interpretation of Article IV, and then turn our attention to the Fourteenth Amendment and, in particular, efforts to secure economic liberty under the Privileges or Immunities Clause and the Due Process Clause of Section 1 of that Amendment.

a.   Historical Origins

Article IV, Section 2 is traced by one writer to the concept of "alien friends" in the Magna Carta. R. HOWELL, THE PRIVILEGES AND IMMUNITIES OF STATE CITIZENSHIP 9–13 (1918). More proximately, Article IV repeats a provision of the Articles of Confederation:

> ARTICLE IV. The better to secure and perpetuate mutual friendship and intercourse among the people of the different States in this Union, the free inhabitants of each of these States, paupers, vagabonds and fugitives from justice excepted, shall be entitled to all privileges and immunities of free citizens in the several states; and the people of each State shall have free ingress and regress to and from any other State, and shall enjoy therein all the privileges of trade and commerce, subject to the same duties, impositions and restrictions as the inhabitants thereof respectively, provided that such restriction shall not extend so far as to prevent the removal of property imported into any State, to any other State of which the owner is an inhabitant; provided also that no imposition, duties or restriction shall be laid by any State, on the property of the United States, or either of them.

ARTICLES OF CONFEDERATION art. IV (1781), *reprinted in* 1 U.S.C. at xlv (1994).

Joseph Story explains that this provision in the Articles of Confederation gave rise to confusion:

> It was remarked by the Federalist, that there is a strange confusion in this language. Why the terms, *free inhabitants*, are used in one part of the article, *free citizens* in another, and *people* in another; or what is meant by superadding to "all privileges and immunities of free citizens," "all the privileges of trade and commerce," cannot easily be determined.

3 JOSEPH STORY, COMMENTARIES ON THE CONSTITUTION OF THE UNITED STATES § 1799, at 673 (photo. reprint 1991) (Boston, Hilliard, Gray & Co. 1833). Story then writes:

> The provision in the constitution [Article IV, Section 2] avoids all this ambiguity. It is plain and simple in its language; and its object is not easily to be mistaken. Connected with the exclusive power of naturalization in the

national government, it puts at rest many of the difficulties, which affected the construction of the article of the confederation. It is obvious, that, if the citizens of each state were to be deemed aliens to each other, they could not take, or hold real estate, or other privileges, except as other aliens. The intention of this clause was to confer on them, if one may so say, a general citizenship; and to communicate all the privileges and immunities, which the citizens of the same state would be entitled to under the like circumstances.

Id. § 1800, at 674–75 (footnotes omitted).

If the purpose of Article IV is the conferral of "general citizenship," it might be thought that this idea would have been more easily and directly achieved with a national, rather than a federalist, government. As discussed in Chapter Four, however, this was not the American objective. The several states were to remain sovereign political communities, possessing large amounts of reserved lawmaking authority. Such lawmaking authority allows for experimentation and different public policy decisions respecting what goods and services are to be provided publicly, and what privately. Thus, the American attachment to federalism mandated that state governments retain some authority to draw distinctions between residents and nonresidents. Politically, nonresidents are denied the vote. Socially, group benefits logically are limited to contributing members of the group. While it is true that there is not a perfect correlation between residency and those who contribute state tax resources (states do tax nonresidents engaged in business within the state and impose sales taxes on nonresidents, for example), residents are perceived as contributing more to state revenue. This perception thus allows states to restrict some state-provided goods to residents, or to favor residents in some way, such as with reduced tuition costs at the state university. *Vlandis v. Kline*, 412 U.S. 441 (1973).

Nevertheless, Article IV does create a general citizenship, and that citizenship entails certain fundamental rights because states cannot draw resident/nonresident distinctions with respect to at least some fundamental or basic rights. The importance of this general citizenship was explained by James Wilson:

James Wilson, *Of Man, as a Member of a Confederation —*
A History of Confederacies
in 1 THE WORKS OF JAMES WILSON 313–14
(James DeWitt Andrews ed., Chicago, Callaghan & Co. 1896) (1791)

When we say, that the government of those states, which unite in the same confederacy, ought to be of the same nature; it is not to be understood, that there should be a precise and exact uniformity in all their particular establishments and laws. It is sufficient that the fundamental principles of their laws and constitutions be consistent and congenial; and that some general rights and privileges should be diffused indiscriminately among them. Among these, the rights and privileges of naturalization hold an important place. Of such consequence was the intercommunication of these rights and privileges in the opinion of my Lord Bacon, that he considered them as the strongest of all bonds to cement and to preserve the union of states. "Let us take a view," says he, "and we shall find, that wheresoever kingdoms and states have been united, and that union incorporated by a bond of mutual naturalization, you shall never observe them afterwards, upon any occasion of trouble or otherwise, to break and sever again." Machiavel, when he inquires concerning the causes, to which Rome was indebted for her splendour and greatness, assigns none of stronger or more extensive operation than this — she easily compounded and incorporated with strangers. This important subject has received a proportioned degree of attention in forming the constitution of the United States. "The citizens of each state shall be entitled to all privileges and immunities of citizens in the several states." In addition to this, the congress have power to "establish a uniform rule of naturalization throughout the United States."

Though a union of laws is, by no means, necessary to a union of states; yet a similarity in their code of *publick* laws is a most desirable object. The publick law is the great sinew of government. The sinews of the different governments, composing the union, should, as far as it can be effected, be equally strong. "In this point," says my Lord Bacon, "the rule holdeth, which was pronounced by an ancient father, touching the diversity of rites in the church; for finding the vesture of the queen in the psalm (who prefigured the church) was of divers colours; and finding again that Christ's coat was without a seam, concludeth well, in veste varietas sit, scissura non sit."

b. Giving Definition

Corfield v. Coryell was the first attempt to give greater definition to what constitutes these basic privileges and immunities of citizenship. We previously saw *Corfield* in Chapter Two, when we discussed the importance of natural law for the interpretation of the Constitution. *Corfield* was a trespass action for seizing a certain boat, called the Hiram, that had been captured after it was found oyster raking in a cove contrary to local ordinance. The local ordinance provided that those raking oysters in the seabed belonging to the state had either to be state inhabitants or on-board a vessel "owned by some person, inhabitant of, and actually residing in this state." The ordinance was argued to violate the Privileges and Immunities Clause in Article IV. The court disagreed, finding oyster raking not to be one of those fundamental privileges, in part because the court understands the oyster beds to be under the unique and preservative influence of the particular state. As interesting as the ownership of oysters may be, our interest is in the court's description of the fundamental privileges and immunities of citizens. Turn back to Chapter Two to see Justice Washington's listing.

The Court touched upon the overlap between the Privileges and Immunities Clause and the dormant Commerce Power in *McBurney v. Young*, 133 S. Ct. 1709, 185 L. Ed. 2d 758 (2013). The Commonwealth of Virginia's Freedom of Information Act (FOIA), provides that "all public records shall be open to inspection and copying by any citizens of the Commonwealth," but it grants no such right to non-Virginians. Two out-of-staters sued, asserting that the Virginia FOIA violated their rights under the Privileges and Immunities Clause of Art. IV of the United States Constitution, and also violated the dormant Commerce Power. The out-of-staters argued, *inter alia*, that the Virginia FOIA violated the opportunity to pursue a common calling (one of the out-of-staters had a business of obtaining real estate tax records on clients' behalf from state and local governments across the United

States). The Court acknowledged that "the Privileges and Immunities Clause protects the right of citizens to 'ply their trade, practice their occupation, or pursue a common calling' [quoting from *Hicklin*]," but it only does so, the Court asserted "when those laws were enacted for the protectionist purpose of burdening out-of-state citizens" [citing *Hicklin* and *Supreme Court of New Hampshire v. Piper*, discussed below]. The Court ruled that the Act, although treating Virginia citizens and out-of-staters differently, did not have a protectionist aim, in that there was no intent on the part of the Virginia legislature "to provide a competitive economic advantage for Virginia citizens." The out-of-staters had also made the "sweeping claim that the challenged provision of the Virginia FOIA violates the Privileges and Immunities Clause because it denies them the right to access public information on equal terms with citizens of the Commonwealth [of Virginia]." The Court took the occasion to announce that "there is no constitutional right to obtain all the information provided by FOIA laws." Having found that the Virginia legislature had no protectionist motivation in enacting its FOIA, the Court had no trouble disposing of the out-of-staters' dormant Commerce Power argument. The Virginia FOIA was neither discriminatory nor excessively burdensome. The Court even opined that Virginia's FOIA could be defended under the market-participant doctrine:

> Insofar as there is a "market" for public documents in Virginia, it is a market for a product that the Commonwealth has created and of which the Commonwealth is the sole manufacturer. We have held that a State does not violate the dormant Commerce Clause when, having created a market through a state program, it "limits benefits generated by [that] state program to those who fund the state treasury and whom the State was created to serve." [Quoting from *Reeves, Inc. v. Stake* (1980).]

Citizenship for Article IV purposes does not include corporations. *Paul v. Virginia*, 75 U.S. (8 Wall.) 168 (1868) (out of state insurance firm was not a citizen within the scope of Article IV, even as it may be a citizen of the place of incorporation for purposes of diversity jurisdiction). As for human persons, citizenship is treated as the equivalent of residence. *Hicklin v. Orbeck*, 437 U.S. 518, 524 n.8 (1978) (citizenship and residence are "essentially interchangeable"). *United Bldg. and Constr. Trades Council v. Mayor of Camden*, 465 U.S. 208, 216 (1984). As indicated in *Corfield*, the court found the Privileges and Immunities Clause not to be implicated where the question was distribution of public resources "owned" by the state in question. Professor Jonathan Varat writes: "[s]ome, but not all, public benefits can be reserved for the exclusive or preferential use of the state's inhabitants. The task of separating which can and cannot be reserved poses impressive obstacles." Jonathan D. Varat, *State "Citizenship" and Interstate Equality*, 48 U. CHI. L. REV. 487, 492 (1981). While dispositive in *Corfield*, and some later cases, *e.g.*, *McCready v. Virginia*, 94 U.S. 391 (1877) (state power to forbid planting of oysters in state tideland upheld), in *Hicklin v. Orbeck*, 437 U.S. 518 (1978), the Court refused to let Alaska condition contracts for the extraction of oil and gas on an employment preference for state residents. In *Hicklin*, state ownership of the resource was described as "a factor — although often the crucial factor — to be considered in evaluating whether the statute's discrimination against noncitizens violates the Clause." 437 U.S. at 529. In *Hicklin*, the Court reasoned that Alaska's ownership interest in oil and gas was too "attenuated" to allow discrimination against nonresidents. *Id.*

Overlap with the dormant Commerce Clause. The Privileges and Immunities Clause and the dormant Commerce Clause are mutually reinforcing, but not entirely coincident. *Hicklin*, 437 U.S. at 531–32. As earlier discussed in Chapter Four, the focus of the dormant Commerce Clause is the avoidance of burdens on interstate commerce; whereas, the Privileges and Immunities Clause is intended to preclude states from discriminating against citizens of other states in favor of its own. *Hague v. CIO*, 307 U.S. 496, 511 (1939). How do the clauses differ otherwise? For starters, corporations may sue under the dormant Commerce Clause. In addition, there are several exceptions to the dormant Commerce Clause which don't carry over to privileges and immunities analysis. First, Congress may expressly remove a dormant Commerce Clause limitation by legislative approval. Second, when a state or local government is acting as a market participant, there is no application of the dormant Commerce Clause. Thus, in *White v. Massachusetts Council of Construction Employers, Inc.*, 460 U.S. 204 (1983), a city requirement that 50 percent of those hired for city construction be city residents did not violate the dormant Commerce Clause, but a similar restriction was held to transgress privileges and immunities. *United Bldg. and Constr. Trades Council v. Mayor of Camden*, 465 U.S. 208 (1984).

Defining Privileges and Immunities. *Corfield* is the basic exposition. Many of these rights are expressly protected by the Bill of Rights, and hence, when they are violated, there is little need to state a separate cause of action under the Privileges and Immunities Clause. *Duncan v. Louisiana*, 391 U.S. 145, 166 (1968) (Black, J. concurring) ("What more precious 'privilege' of American citizenship could there be than that privilege to claim the protections of our great Bill of Rights?"). But occasionally a case arises separately, *e.g.*, *Blake v. McClung*, 172 U.S. 239 (1898) (in-state creditor could not be favored over out-of-state creditor with regard to disposition of insolvent's property; to provide such favoritism is to disregard the privilege of owning and disposing of property).

In *Supreme Court of New Hampshire v. Piper*, 470 U.S. 274 (1985), the differentiation between in-state and out-of-state residents related to membership in the New Hampshire bar. Admission was limited to state residents, and this frustrated Katherine Piper's plan to keep her home with a favorable mortgage rate across the state line in Vermont. Piper challenged the Supreme Court of New Hampshire's bar admission rule arguing that it violated Article IV privileges and immunities. The Court agreed, rejecting the various arguments put forward by the state that the state court would be unable to supervise the behavior of an out-of-state attorney, the out-of-state counsel would be less able to perform pro bono and other occasionally required services and might be less familiar with the local bar rules. In the end, however, none of these arguments carried the day, and the Court reiterated that the scope of privileges and immunities under Art. IV is limited to those privileges and immunities that bear on the vitality of the nation as a single entity, and based upon precedent, found no reason not to include the occupation of lawyering to be within that category of occupations important to the nation's economy. By contrast, the Supreme Court of New Hampshire argued that lawyers were officers of the court and thus entangled with state sovereignty, such that the profession should be outside the Privileges and Immunities Clause. The U.S. Supreme Court rejected the notion, reasoning that a lawyer is not really an officer of the state in any political policy sense, and therefore, there is no reason to exclude nonresidents from the bar.

There was only one dissent in *Piper*, and it was the opinion of Justice Rehnquist. Rehnquist was a noted Federalist and, therefore, it is not surprising that he would have sympathy for the interest of the state, but the opinion is more subtle than that, and the dissent is worth reading because it captures a nobility for legal practice that for a variety of reasons seems less present than it should be. Rehnquist argues, for example, that law practice is by its very nature non-national and that the nature of our union is such that each state can endorse different philosophies and respond to different interests in different ways. Wrote the Justice: "I believe that the practice of law differs from other trades and businesses for Art. IV, sec. 2 purposes. . . . The reason that the practice of law should be treated differently is that law is one occupation that does not readily translate across state lines. Certain aspects of legal practice are distinctly and intentionally non-national. In this regard one might see this country's legal system as the antithesis of the norms embodied in the Article IV privileges and immunities clause." Rehnquist also objected to the Court applying the least restrictive means analysis as being too intrusive upon state interests. Rehnquist's sensitivities and sentimentality notwithstanding, the legal standard that applies in this area prescribes that the state not discriminate against nonresidents absent a substantial reason for doing so, and then only if that discrimination bears a substantial relationship to the advancement of that reason and is the least restrictive means to accomplish the objective.

NOTES AND QUESTIONS

1. What if the form of the discrimination was not exclusion, but merely differential licensing? In *Ward v. Maryland*, 79 U.S. (12 Wall.) 418 (1870), the Court invalidated a higher licensing fee for non-residential traders of goods, and in *Toomer v. Witsell*, 334 U.S. 385 (1948), the Court struck down a $2,500 license fee for nonresident commercial shrimp fisherman, when residents paid only $25. The Court stated: "one of the privileges which the clause guarantees to citizens of State A is that of doing business in State B on terms of substantial equality with citizens of that State." 334 U.S. at 396.

2. However, discrimination is allowed when the activity is not economic livelihood or a fundamental constitutional right. Thus, in *Baldwin v. Fish and Game Commission*, 436 U.S. 371 (1978), the Court allowed substantially higher elk-hunting license fees for out of state residents, writing, "[the sport] is not a means to the nonresident's livelihood. . . . Equality in access to Montana elk is not basic to the maintenance or well-being of the union." *Id.* at 388. The Court explained in *Baldwin* that the underlying purpose of the Privileges and Immunities Clause in Article IV was to promote a level of interstate harmony, or at least not to allow practices that "frustrate the purposes of the formation of the Union." *Id.* at 387. State discrimination with respect to nonessential activities does not pose the risk of such frustration.

3. Theoretically, as suggested in *Piper*, a state or locality may continue discrimination if it has a substantial reason for doing so and the discrimination itself bears a substantial relationship to the advancement of that reason. In evaluating the substantiality of the relationship between the discrimination and the state's objective, the Court asks if the state could employ less restrictive means. *Piper*, 470 U.S. at 284. The Court has not yet supplied a case that adequately meets this justification. In *Toomer v. Witsell*, 334 U.S. 385 (1948), for example, the Court noted that the state could eliminate the danger of excessive trawling through less restrictive means than discrimination against nonresidents: restricting the type of equipment used in its fisheries, graduating license fees according to the size of the boats, or charging nonresidents a differential to compensate for the added enforcement burden they imposed. *Id.* at 398–99. Chief Justice Rehnquist thought the least restrictive means inquiry too judicially intrusive. *Piper*, 470 U.S. at 294–95 (Rehnquist, J., dissenting).

4. Note that the Court decides in favor of Ms. Piper because of the discrimination with respect to a fundamental interest, and not merely because of interference with a fundamental interest — namely, the pursuit of a calling or trade. In the *Slaughter-House Cases* considered in the next section, the pursuit of one's lawful occupation is argued to be a protected privilege of all citizens in the fashion of Justice Washington in *Corfield*. In *Piper*, the Court lamely characterizes *Corfield* as representing a theory of "natural rights . . . discarded long ago," 470 U.S. at 281 n.10. The Court cites for this cavalier disregard of natural law originalism, a 1939 opinion dealing with labor picketing and the First Amendment. Examining that opinion, one does not see any reasoned basis for the disregard of natural law. Indeed, all the Court observes in the earlier cited case is that:

> At one time it was thought that [the privileges and immunities of Article IV] recognized a group of rights which, according to the jurisprudence of the day, were classed as "natural rights"; and that the purpose of the section was to create rights of citizens of the United States by guaranteeing the citizens of every State the recognition of this group of rights by every other State. Such was the view of Justice Washington.

Hague v. CIO, 307 U.S. 496, 511 (1939) (citing *Corfield*).

5. Even though the Court has limited Article IV privileges and immunities to ferreting out improper discrimination between resident and nonresident, it recognizes that licensing laws and grants of exclusive franchises may result from less than pure motive. For example, the Court in a footnote in *Piper* mentions that "[a] former president of the American Bar Association has suggested another possible reason for the rule [excluding nonresident lawyers]: 'Many of the states that have erected fences against out-of-state lawyers have done so primarily to protect their own lawyers from professional competition.' This reason is not 'substantial.' " 470 U.S. at 285 n.18 (quoting Chesterfield Smith, *Time for a National Practice of Law Act*, 64 A.B.A. J. 557, 557 (1978)). The Court went on to observe that "[t]he Privileges and Immunities Clause was designed primarily to prevent such economic protectionism." *Id.* True enough, but the fact that Article IV privilege and immunity analysis is confined to discrimination and separated from its natural rights origin makes it more difficult for the Court to protect all citizens from such illicit, protectionist use of public power. Many thought the Fourteenth Amendment Privileges or Immunities Clause would rectify this difficulty.

2. Privileges *or* Immunities

The Fourteenth Amendment adopted after the Civil War provides, in part: "No State shall make or enforce any law which shall abridge the privileges or immunities of the citizens of the United States." In Chapters Two and Four, we briefly raised the issue of whether this provision was intended to apply (or "incorporate") the Bill of Rights to the states. Justice Hugo Black thought so, writing that these words "seem to me an eminently reasonable way of expressing the idea that henceforth the Bill of Rights shall apply to the States." *Duncan v. Louisiana*, 391 U.S. 145, 166 (Black, J., concurring). There is much historical dispute here, however. In an extensive article, Professor Charles Fairman argues that "Congress would not have attempted [incorporation by this means], the country would not have stood for it, the legislatures would not have ratified." Charles Fairman, *Does the Fourteenth Amendment Incorporate the Bill of Rights? The Original Understanding*, 2 Stan. L. Rev. 5, 137 (1949). The most prominent framers of the Fourteenth Amendment spoke differently. Senator Howard, for example, referenced Justice Washington's earlier articulation of privileges and immunities in *Corfield*, indicating that "[s]uch is the character of the privileges and immunities spoken of in the second section of the fourth article of the Constitution. [And t]o these privileges and immunities . . . should be added the personal rights guarantied and secured by the first eight amendments of the Constitution." Cong. Globe, 39th Cong., 1st Sess. 2765 (1866).

Whatever the intent of the 39th Congress that drafted the Fourteenth Amendment Privileges or Immunities Clause, the claim that this provision places limits upon the states either with natural law rights like those articulated in *Corfield* or the express Bill of Rights was narrowly defeated in the *Slaughter-House Cases*, 83 U.S. (16 Wall.) 36 (1873). *Slaughter-House* involved a state-granted monopoly to the Crescent City Live-Stock and Slaughter-House Company, which greatly diminished the economic liberties of competing houses and the suppliers of meat products. Writing for the Court, Justice Miller nevertheless sustained the government-imposed monopoly on the dubious ground that the Fourteenth Amendment merely had the purpose of establishing or affirming the freedom of slaves, and little else. Justice Miller explicitly refused to apply the Bill of Rights to the states pursuant to the Privileges or Immunities Clause, as Senator Howard had described, because he said:

> [S]uch a construction . . . would constitute this court a perpetual censor upon all legislation of the States, on the civil rights of their own citizens, with authority to nullify such as it did not approve as consistent with those rights, as they existed at the time of the adoption of the amendment.

Id. at 78. Instead, Justice Miller's conception of the protected privileges or immunities of federal citizenship were so abstract and inconsequential that it prompted the dissenters to write that if such is all the amendment means, "it was a vain and idle enactment, which accomplished nothing, and most unnecessarily excited Congress and the people on its passage." *Id.* at 96 (Field, J., dissenting).

The *Slaughter-House* opinion remained highly controverted. More than a decade later, the case was before the Court in another form in *Butchers' Union Slaughter-House and Live-Stock Landing Co. v. Crescent City Live-Stock Landing and Slaughter-House Co.*, 111 U.S. 746 (1884). In 1879, the Louisiana state constitution was amended to outlaw the previously granted monopoly. Crescent City, the holder of the monopoly, went to Court arguing that the amendment was an unconstitutional impairment of contract. The members of the Court were entirely agreed that Louisiana could repeal the previous monopoly, but for very different reasons. Justice Miller, who wrote the first *Slaughter-House* opinion, justified the repeal with the proposition that no sovereign can bargain away the police power, a proposition discussed in Chapter Six. The concurring justices, however, were still smarting from Justice Miller's earlier *Slaughter-House* opinion. Justice Bradley categorically argued that the original grant of monopoly was wrongful, as "all mere monopolies are odious and against common right." *Id.* at 761 (Bradley, J., concurring). To not recognize this would be to abridge the basic privileges or immunities of all citizens, he argued.

NOTES AND QUESTIONS

1. *Slaughter-House* was decided 5-4, but even that does not fully reflect the division on the Court. The case yielded the majority opinion authored by Justice Miller, and three separate dissenting opinions: one written by Justice Stephen Field (joined by Chief Justice Salmon Chase, and Justices Swayne and Bradley), another by Justice Bradley with Justice Swayne, and finally, Justice Swayne writing individually. Legal historian Michael Kent Curtis believes the outcome in *Slaughter-House* reflects a "strange reading of the language of the Fourteenth Amendment" and that "[t]he history of abuses that led to the amendment received superficial and cursory attention at best," while legislative history "received no attention at all." Michael Kent Curtis, No State Shall Abridge 175, 173 (1986).

2. The Fourteenth Amendment was intended to re-order the state-federal balance. That this was so can be seen in the fact that the Butcher's Association in *Slaughter-House* was represented by John A. Campbell, a former justice of the Supreme Court who had resigned when his home state of Alabama seceded from the Union prior to the Civil War. Former Justice Campbell's prior actions tend to give even greater credence to his losing argument in favor of a position that would allow the national (if you will, Union) Supreme Court to set aside state action contrary to a nationally defined set of privileges or immunities. Indeed, Campbell, himself, recognized the profound shift from pre-Civil War position, writing:

> The doctrine of the "States-Rights party," led in modern times by Mr. Calhoun, was, that there was no citizenship in the whole United States, except *sub modo* and by the permission of the States. . . . The fourteenth amendment struck at, and forever destroyed, all such doctrines. . . . By it the national principle has received an indefinite enlargement. The tie between the United States and every citizen in every part of its own jurisdiction has been made intimate and familiar.

The Slaughter House Cases, 83 U.S. (16 Wall.) 36, 52–53 (1873) (argument of John A. Campbell on behalf of The Butchers' Benevolent Association of New Orleans).

The full argument of former Justice Campbell can be found in the official report of the case, 83 U.S. (16 Wall.) at 44–57.

3. Civil Rights Is More Than Equality. The decimation of the Privileges or Immunities Clause in *Slaughter-House* transformed the modern concept of civil right from a guarantee of inalienable or natural right to a concept almost totally focused on equality. As we discuss in Chapter Eight, equal treatment under law is no small matter, yet, this exclusive focus was not in keeping with the original understanding of the Fourteenth Amendment. As Alfred Avins, a scholar of the post-Civil War era writes, the framers of the Fourteenth Amendment intended "to confer certain civil or natural rights on all persons, white as well as black, and not merely to abolish racial discrimination." THE RECONSTRUCTION AMENDMENTS' DEBATES at vii (Alfred Avins ed., 1967). The original conception of civil right or liberty which the drafters of the Fourteenth Amendment had carried forward, was that of Sir William Blackstone, who defined civil liberty as "no other than natural liberty so far restrained by human laws (and no farther) as is necessary and expedient for the general advantage of the publick." 1 WILLIAM BLACKSTONE, COMMENTARIES *125 (citing JUSTINIAN, INSTITUTES 1.3.1). Similarly, Senator John Sherman a few years after the drafting of the Privileges or Immunities Clause reflected:

> What are those privileges and immunities? Are they only those defined in the Constitution, the rights secured by the [Bill of Rights]? Not at all. The great fountainhead, the great reservoir of the rights of an American citizen is in the common law. . . .
>
> *   *   *
>
> . . . [And such] right must be determined from time to time by the judicial tribunals, and in determining it they will look first at the Constitution of the United States as the primary fountain of authority. If that does not define the right they will look for the unenumerated powers to the Declaration of American Independence, . . . [and] to the common law of England. . . .

CONG. GLOBE, 42d Cong., 2d Sess. 843–44 (1872). Without question, those who crafted the Privileges or Immunities Clause expected that economic liberty would be protected. Representative John A. Bingham, the principal author of the first section of the 14th Amendment, included within its scope "the liberty . . . to work in an honest calling and contribute by your own toil in some sort to the support of yourself, to the support of your fellowmen, and to be secure in the enjoyment of the fruits of your toil." CONG. GLOBE, 42d Cong., 1st Sess. app. 86 (1871). But, of course, even if there is a general right of economic liberty, does that mean that the Court is to second-guess every legislative restriction of that right? Assuming for the sake of argument, *Slaughter-House* to be in error on the content of privilege or immunity does not answer this further question. And the difficulty of giving answer became clear to the Court as it tried to correct the damage done in *Slaughter-House* by bootstrapping freedom of contract into the Due Process Clause. We will thus return to this question after we examine the *Lochner, Nebbia,* and *Carolene Products* cases, below.

4. Civil Liberty and Equality Have Common Cause. As an historical matter, it should be recognized that protecting equality and economic liberty were interrelated. Following the Civil War, various southern states and localities effectively tried to negate emancipation by precluding the economic liberty of the freedmen with the so-called "Black Codes." As one report to Congress put it:

> The opposition to the negro's controlling his own labor, carrying on business independently on his own account — in one word, working for his own benefit — showed itself in a variety of ways. Here and there municipal regulations were gotten up heavily taxing or otherwise impeding those trades and employments in which colored people are most likely to engage.

S. Exec. Doc. No. 39-2, at 24 (1865), *reprinted in* The Reconstruction Amendments' Debates, *supra*, at 90. To counteract these Black Codes, Congress passed the Civil Rights Act of 1866, providing that all citizens shall "have the same right . . . to make and enforce contracts, to sue, be parties, and give evidence, to inherit, purchase, lease, sell, hold, and convey real and personal property, and to full and equal benefit of all laws." Civil Rights Act of 1866, ch. 31, § 1, 14 Stat. 27, 27 (codified as amended at 42 U.S.C. §§ 1981–1982 (1994)). President Andrew Johnson vetoed this legislation. Concerned that Congress lacked authority, Section 2 had been construed only to secure such privileges and immunities as each state chose to give its own citizens and states were merely prohibited from discriminating in favor of its own citizens. Some in Congress argued that Article IV was a broader security of natural right generally, and on this and other grounds, Congress overrode the veto. Nevertheless, the Fourteenth Amendment resulted to erase any doubt about congressional authority. Thus, Senator Jacob Howard would explain that under the original Privileges and Immunities Clause of Article IV, Section 2 and the Bill of Rights, "the States are not restrained from violating the principles embraced in them except by their own local constitutions. [By contrast, the] great object of the [Fourteenth] amendment is . . . to restrain the power of the States and compel them at all times to respect these great fundamental guarantees." Cong. Globe, 39th Cong., 1st Sess. 2766 (1866).

5. The Evil of Monopoly. No one wants a slaughter-house in their backyard, so the legislation in the *Slaughter-House Cases* did have some obvious public health merit. However, the record also established that "legislative bribery had greased passage of the law, with its most immediate beneficiaries — the seventeen participants in the corporation it established — adroitly distributing shares of stock and cash." Charles A. Lofgren, The Plessy Case 67 (1987). It was not the inspection and health aspects of the law that deserved scrutiny, but the arguably unnecessary grant of monopoly. The common law of England condemned all monopolies, not merely because of the increase in price and deterioration in quality of goods (although this is often economically undeniable), but as Justice Field recognized, because of the interference with the liberty of citizens to pursue the maintenance of family through any lawful trade or occupation. At common law, regulated monopolies or those that arose from grants of special privilege from the government were especially suspect. Economic monopolies are constrained by market competition; government monopolies are more durable and thus pernicious because of their legal protection. This was a well-established point of common law inherited by the American colonies. Justice Field observed in dissent that:

The common law of England is the basis of the jurisprudence of the United States. It was brought to this country by the colonists, together with the English statutes, and was established here so far as it was applicable to their condition. That law and the benefit of such of the English statutes as existed at the time of their colonization, and which they had by experience found to be applicable to their circumstances, were claimed by the Congress of the United Colonies in 1774 as a part of their "indubitable rights and liberties." Of the statutes, the benefits of which was thus claimed, the statute of James I against monopolies was one of the most important. And when the Colonies separated from the mother country no privilege was more fully recognized or more completely incorporated into the fundamental law of the country than that every free subject in the British empire was entitled to pursue his happiness by following any of the known established trades and occupations of the country, subject only to such restraints as equally affected all others. The immortal document which proclaimed the independence of the country declared as self-evident truths that the Creator had endowed all men "with certain unalienable rights, and that among these are life, liberty, and the pursuit of happiness; and that to secure these rights governments are instituted among men."

The Slaughter-House Cases, 83 U.S. (16 Wall.) at 104–05 (Field, J., dissenting) (footnote omitted).

6. Is Louisiana Special? It might be argued that as the only civil law jurisdiction in the United States, common law dislike of monopoly was irrelevant to the outcome in *Slaughter-House*. However, Justice Field pointed out in part of his dissent not reprinted that Louis XVI abolished all trade monopolies in 1776, and that this law prevailed in the French colony at the time of its cession to the United States. *Id.* at 105 (Field, J., dissenting).

7. Slaughtered by *Slaughter-House*. From the time of its decision to the present, *Slaughter-House* has done considerable damage to the cause of economic liberty. Almost immediately, for example, the Court used *Slaughter-House* to uphold an Illinois law that forbade qualified women from practicing law. *Bradwell v. Illinois*, 83 U.S. (16 Wall.) 130 (1872). So too, the majority's reasoning that the Privileges or Immunities Clause referred only to minor features of national citizenship was used to argue that Congress lacked remedial authority to address racial segregation in public accommodations. THE RECONSTRUCTION AMENDMENTS' DEBATES, *supra*, at xxiv. *Slaughter-House* thus prompted the impulse for the Court to distort other provisions of the Constitution in order to reach that which would have been better addressed under the privileges or immunities rubric, with its direct philosophical linkage to the Declaration of Independence and natural law. To address racial discrimination in public accommodations, the Court nourished an ever-expanding view of the commerce power, and with far less judicial warrant, elaborated substantive due process to temporarily ensure economic liberty.

8. Can *Slaughter-House* Be Overruled? For a while there was academic speculation to that effect. The late Professor Philip Kurland has observed that the Privileges or Immunities Clause "is in repose, it is not yet dead." Philip B. Kurland, *The Privileges or Immunities Clause, "Its Hour Come Round at Last"?*, 1972

WASH. U. L.Q. 405, 413. It turns out that was optimistic on the part of Professor Kurland who expired first. The Court did contemplate relying upon privileges or immunities for its contemporary interpretation of the Second Amendment, but Justice Alito decided that too much time had passed and too many alternative constructions of the Constitution could be undertaken to resolve whether or not the right to own a handgun for purposes of private self-defense independent of any Militia obligation could be decided on other constitutional grounds without disinterring 14th Amendment privileges or immunities.

9. Before his appointment to the Supreme Court, Justice Clarence Thomas speculated that:

> While it may be idle to think in terms of overruling the *Slaughter-House Cases*, there is an even more important point to be emphasized here. It goes to the fundamental rights of the American regime — those of life, liberty, and property. These rights are inalienable ones, given to man by his Creator, and did not simply come from a piece of paper.

Clarence Thomas, *The Higher Law Background of the Privileges or Immunities Clause of the Fourteenth Amendment*, 12 HARV. J.L. & PUB. POL'Y 63, 68 (1989) (footnotes omitted). In fact, much of *Slaughter-House* has been overruled — at least that which narrowed the scope of the Equal Protection and Due Process Clauses. Justice Miller's prediction that the Equal Protection Clause would likely never have application outside the area of racial discrimination has proven entirely false, as gender, alienage and legitimacy, for example, have come within its reach. *See* Chapter Eight. Similarly, as discussed in the section immediately below, during the first third of the 20th century, the Due Process Clause was employed by the Court to protect economic liberty. *Compare Lochner v. New York*, 198 U.S. 45 (1905), *with Nebbia v. New York*, 291 U.S. 502 (1933). The modern Court has backed away from this, however, finding the due process-based protection of economic liberty to be judicial activism, and insufficiently attentive to majority or legislative outcome. Oddly, the Court continues the very same substantive due process theory to create contraceptive and abortion rights. *See* Chapter Nine and Joseph D. Grano, *Teaching* Roe *and* Lochner, 42 WAYNE L. REV. 1973 (1996) (demonstrating that *Roe* and *Lochner* are the same cases from a methodological perspective because both single out certain unenumerated liberties for special protection without textual guidance).

The dichotomy between the protection of abortion-related and other personal liberties, and the post-*Lochner* disregard of economic liberty is orchestrated by footnote 4 in *United States v. Carolene Products*, 304 U.S. 144 (1938). Conservative legal theorists resist any efforts to revive or strengthen the judicial protection of economic liberty under either privileges or immunities or due process analysis, thinking, perhaps mistakenly, this to be the only principled position against judicial activism. *But see* Douglas W. Kmiec, *Natural Law Originalism or Why Justice Scalia (Almost) Gets It Right*, 21 HARV. J.L. & PUB. POL'Y 627 (1997). Justice Thomas likewise writes.

> The best defense of . . . the judicial restraint [and] limited government[] is the higher law political philosophy of the Founding Fathers. Contrary to the worst fears of my conservative allies, such a view is far from being a

license for . . . a roving judiciary. Rather, natural rights and higher law arguments are the best defense of liberty and of limited government. . . . Rather than being a justification of the worst type of judicial activism, higher law is the only alternative to the willfulness of both run-amok majorities and run-amok judges.

Thomas, *supra*, at 64–65. The 14th Amendment Privileges or Immunities Clause has been given a new life of sorts by Justice Stevens in the following case. As you will see, this provision of the 14th Amendment becomes a part of the justification for the constitutional right to travel.

SAENZ v. ROE
526 U.S. 489 (1999)

JUSTICE STEVENS delivered the opinion of the Court.

In 1992, California enacted a statute limiting the maximum welfare benefits available to newly arrived residents. The scheme limits the amount payable to a family that has resided in the State for less than 12 months to the amount payable by the State of the family's prior residence. The questions presented by this case are whether the 1992 statute was constitutional when it was enacted and, if not, whether an amendment to the Social Security Act enacted by Congress in 1996 affects that determination.

* * *

III

The word "travel" is not found in the text of the Constitution. Yet the "constitutional right to travel from one State to another" is firmly embedded in our jurisprudence. . . . The right is so important that it is "assertable against private interference as well as governmental action . . . a virtually unconditional personal right, guaranteed by the Constitution to us all."

In *Shapiro v. Thompson* (1969), we reviewed the constitutionality of three statutory provisions that denied welfare assistance to residents of Connecticut, the District of Columbia, and Pennsylvania, who had resided within those respective jurisdictions less than one year immediately preceding their applications for assistance. Without pausing to identify the specific source of the right, we began by noting that the Court had long "recognized that the nature of our Federal Union and our constitutional concepts of personal liberty unite to require that all citizens be free to travel throughout the length and breadth of our land uninhibited by statutes, rules, or regulations which unreasonably burden or restrict this move-ment." We squarely held that it was "constitutionally impermissible" for a State to enact durational residency requirements for the purpose of inhibiting the migration by needy persons into the State. We further held that a classification that had the effect of imposing a penalty on the exercise of the right to travel violated the Equal Protection Clause "unless shown to be necessary to promote a compelling govern-mental interest," and that no such showing had been made.

In this case California argues that [the state statute] was not enacted for the impermissible purpose of inhibiting migration by needy persons and that, unlike the legislation reviewed in *Shapiro*, it does not penalize the right to travel because new arrivals are not ineligible for benefits during their first year of residence. California submits that, instead of being subjected to the strictest scrutiny, the statute should be upheld if it is supported by a rational basis and that the State's legitimate interest in saving over $10 million a year satisfies that test. Although the United States did not elect to participate in the proceedings in the District Court or the Court of Appeals, it has participated as *amicus curiae* in this Court. It has advanced the novel argument that the enactment of [a federal statute] allows the States to adopt a "specialized choice-of-law-type provision" that "should be subject to an intermediate level of constitutional review," merely requiring that durational residency requirements be "substantially related to an important governmental objective." The debate about the appropriate standard of review, together with the potential relevance of the federal statute, persuades us that it will be useful to focus on the source of the constitutional right on which respondents rely.

IV

The "right to travel" discussed in our cases embraces at least three different components. It protects the right of a citizen of one State to enter and to leave another State, the right to be treated as a welcome visitor rather than an unfriendly alien when temporarily present in the second State, and, for those travelers who elect to become permanent residents, the right to be treated like other citizens of that State.

It was the right to go from one place to another, including the right to cross state borders while en route, that was vindicated in *Edwards v. California* (1941), which invalidated a state law that impeded the free interstate passage of the indigent. . . . Given that [the state law here] imposed no obstacle to respondents' entry into California, we think the State is correct when it argues that the statute does not directly impair the exercise of the right to free interstate movement. For the purposes of this case, therefore, we need not identify the source of that particular right in the text of the Constitution. The right of "free ingress and regress to and from" neighboring States, which was expressly mentioned in the text of the Articles of Confederation, may simply have been "conceived from the beginning to be a necessary concomitant of the stronger Union the Constitution created."

The second component of the right to travel is, however, expressly protected by the text of the Constitution. The first sentence of Article IV, § 2, provides:

> "The Citizens of each State shall be entitled to all Privileges and Immunities of Citizens in the several States."

Thus, by virtue of a person's state citizenship, a citizen of one State who travels in other States, intending to return home at the end of his journey, is entitled to enjoy the "Privileges and Immunities of Citizens in the several States" that he visits.[15] This provision removes "from the citizens of each State the disabilities of

---

[15] [14] *Corfield v. Coryell* (1823) (Washington, J-., on circuit) ("fundamental" rights protected by the

alienage in the other States." . . . Those protections are not "absolute," but the Clause "does bar discrimination against citizens of other States where there is no substantial reason for the discrimination beyond the mere fact that they are citizens of other States." There may be a substantial reason for requiring the nonresident to pay more than the resident for a hunting license, but our cases have not identified any acceptable reason for qualifying the protection afforded by the Clause for "the 'citizen of State A who ventures into State B' to settle there and establish a home." Permissible justifications for discrimination between residents and nonresidents are simply inapplicable to a nonresident's exercise of the right to move into another State and become a resident of that State.

What is at issue in this case, then, is this third aspect of the right to travel — the right of the newly arrived citizen to the same privileges and immunities enjoyed by other citizens of the same State. That right is protected not only by the new arrival's status as a state citizen, but also by her status as a citizen of the United States.[16] That additional source of protection is plainly identified in the opening words of the Fourteenth Amendment:

> "All persons born or naturalized in the United States, and subject to the jurisdiction thereof, are citizens of the United States and of the State wherein they reside. No State shall make or enforce any law which shall abridge the privileges or immunities of citizens of the United States; . . . ."

Despite fundamentally differing views concerning the coverage of the Privileges or Immunities Clause of the Fourteenth Amendment, most notably expressed in the majority and dissenting opinions in the *Slaughter-House Cases* (1872), it has always been common ground that this Clause protects the third component of the right to travel. Writing for the majority in the *Slaughter-House Cases*, Justice Miller explained that one of the privileges conferred by this Clause "is that a citizen of the United States can, of his own volition, become a citizen of any State of the Union by a bona fide residence therein, with the same rights as other citizens of that State." Justice Bradley, in dissent, used even stronger language to make the same point:

> "The states have not now, if they ever had, any power to restrict their citizenship to any classes or persons. A citizen of the United States has a perfect constitutional right to go to and reside in any State he chooses, and to claim citizenship therein, and an equality of rights with every other citizen; and the whole power of the nation is pledged to sustain him in that right. He is not bound to cringe to any superior, or to pray for any act of grace, as a means of enjoying all the rights and privileges enjoyed by other citizens."

---

privileges and immunities clause include "the right of a citizen of one state to pass through, or to reside in any other state").

   16 [15] The Framers of the Fourteenth Amendment modeled this Clause upon the "Privileges and Immunities" Clause found in Article IV. Cong. Globe, 39th Cong., 1st Sess., 1033–1034 (1866) (statement of Rep. Bingham). In *Dred Scott v. Sandford*, 15 L.Ed. 691, 19 How. 393 (1856), this Court had limited the protection of Article IV to rights under state law and concluded that free blacks could not claim citizenship. The Fourteenth Amendment overruled this decision. The Amendment's Privileges and Immunities Clause and Citizenship Clause guaranteed the rights of newly freed black citizens by ensuring that they could claim the state citizenship of any State in which they resided and by precluding that State from abridging their rights of national citizenship.

That newly arrived citizens "have two political capacities, one state and one federal," adds special force to their claim that they have the same rights as others who share their citizenship. Neither mere rationality nor some intermediate standard of review should be used to judge the constitutionality of a state rule that discriminates against some of its citizens because they have been domiciled in the State for less than a year. The appropriate standard may be more categorical than that articulated in *Shapiro*, but it is surely no less strict.

V

* * *

It is undisputed that respondents and the members of the class that they represent are citizens of California and that their need for welfare benefits is unrelated to the length of time that they have resided in California. We thus have no occasion to consider what weight might be given to a citizen's length of residence if the bona fides of her claim to state citizenship were questioned. Moreover, because whatever benefits they receive will be consumed while they remain in California, there is no danger that recognition of their claim will encourage citizens of other States to establish residency for just long enough to acquire some readily portable benefit, such as a divorce or a college education, that will be enjoyed after they return to their original domicile.

* * *

California must therefore explain not only why it is sound fiscal policy to discriminate against those who have been citizens for less than a year, but also why it is permissible to apply such a variety of rules within that class.

These classifications may not be justified by a purpose to deter welfare applicants from migrating to California for three reasons. First, although it is reasonable to assume that some persons may be motivated to move for the purpose of obtaining higher benefits, the empirical evidence reviewed by the District Judge, which takes into account the high cost of living in California, indicates that the number of such persons is quite small — surely not large enough to justify a burden on those who had no such motive. Second, California has represented to the Court that the legislation was not enacted for any such reason. Third, even if it were, as we squarely held in *Shapiro v. Thompson* (1969), such a purpose would be unequivocally impermissible.

* * *

VI

The question that remains is whether congressional approval of durational residency requirements in the 1996 amendment to the Social Security Act somehow resuscitates the constitutionality of [the state law]. That question is readily answered, for we have consistently held that Congress may not authorize the States to violate the Fourteenth Amendment. Moreover, the protection afforded to the citizen by the Citizenship Clause of that Amendment is a limitation on the powers of the National Government as well as the States.

Article I of the Constitution grants Congress broad power to legislate in certain areas. Those legislative powers are, however, limited not only by the scope of the Framers' affirmative delegation, but also by the principle "that they may not be exercised in a way that violates other specific provisions of the Constitution."

Citizens of the United States, whether rich or poor, have the right to choose to be citizens "of the State wherein they reside." The States, however, do not have any right to select their citizens.

*   *   *

The judgment of the Court of Appeals is affirmed.

CHIEF JUSTICE REHNQUIST, with whom JUSTICE THOMAS joins, dissenting.

The Court today breathes new life into the previously dormant Privileges or Immunities Clause of the Fourteenth Amendment. . . . Because I do not think any provision of the Constitution — and surely not a provision relied upon for only the second time since its enactment 130 years ago — requires this result, I dissent.

I

Much of the Court's opinion is unremarkable and sound. The right to travel clearly embraces the right to go from one place to another, and prohibits States from impeding the free interstate passage of citizens.

*   *   *

I also have no difficulty with aligning the right to travel with the protections afforded by the Privileges and Immunities Clause of Article IV, § 2, to nonresidents who enter other States "intending to return home at the end of [their] journey.'' Nonresident visitors of other States should not be subject to discrimination solely because they live out of State.

Finally, I agree with the proposition that a "citizen of the United States can, of his own volition, become a citizen of any State of the Union by a bona fide residence therein, with the same rights as other citizens of that State." *Slaughter-House Cases* (1872).

But I cannot see how the right to become a citizen of another State is a necessary "component" of the right to travel, or why the Court tries to marry these separate and distinct rights. A person is no longer "traveling" in any sense of the word when he finishes his journey to a State which he plans to make his home. Indeed, under the Court's logic, the protections of the Privileges or Immunities Clause recognized in this case come into play only when an individual stops traveling with the intent to remain and become a citizen of a new State. The right to travel and the right to become a citizen are distinct, their relationship is not reciprocal, and one is not a "component" of the other. Indeed, the same dicta from the *Slaughter-House Cases* quoted by the Court actually treats the right to become a citizen and the right to travel as separate and distinct rights under the Privileges or Immunities Clause of the Fourteenth Amendment. At most, restrictions on an individual's right to become a citizen indirectly affect his calculus in deciding whether to exercise his right to travel in the first place, but such an attenuated and uncertain relationship is no ground for folding one right into the other.

No doubt the Court has, in the past 30 years, essentially conflated the right to travel with the right to equal state citizenship in striking down durational residence requirements similar to the one challenged here. *See, e.g., Shapiro v. Thompson* (1969) (striking down 1-year residence before receiving any welfare benefit); *Dunn v. Blumstein*, 405 U.S. 330 (1972) (striking down 1-year residence before receiving the right to vote in state elections); [*Memorial Hospital v.*] *Maricopa County*, 415 U.S. at 280–283 (striking down 1-year county residence before receiving entitlement to nonemergency hospitalization or emergency care). These cases marked a sharp departure from the Court's prior right-to-travel cases because in none of them was travel itself prohibited.

Instead, the Court in these cases held that restricting the provision of welfare benefits, votes, or certain medical benefits to new citizens for a limited time impermissibly "penalized" them under the Equal Protection Clause of the Fourteenth Amendment for having exercised their right to travel. . . . In other cases, the Court recognized that laws dividing new and old residents had little to do with the right to travel and merely triggered an inquiry into whether the resulting classification rationally furthered a legitimate government purpose. *See Zobel v. Williams* 457 U.S. 55 (1982); *Hooper v. Bernalillo County Assessor*, 472 U.S. 612 (1985).

*   *   *

The Court today tries to clear much of the underbrush created by these prior right-to-travel cases, abandoning its effort to define what residence requirements deprive individuals of "important rights and benefits" or "penalize" the right to travel. Under its new analytical framework, a State, outside certain ill-defined circumstances, cannot classify its citizens by the length of their residence in the State without offending the Privileges or Immunities Clause of the Fourteenth Amendment. The Court thus departs from *Shapiro* and its progeny, and, while paying lipservice to the right to travel, the Court does little to explain how the right to travel is involved at all.

*   *   *

II

In unearthing from its tomb the right to become a state citizen and to be treated equally in the new State of residence, however, the Court ignores a State's need to assure that only persons who establish a bona fide residence receive the benefits provided to current residents of the State.

*   *   *

. . . [T]he Court has consistently recognized that while new citizens must have the same opportunity to enjoy the privileges of being a citizen of a State, the States retain the ability to use bona fide residence requirements to ferret out those who intend to take the privileges and run. . . . "[R]esidence" requires "both physical presence and an intention to remain". . . .

While the physical presence element of a bona fide residence is easy to police, the subjective intent element is not. It is simply unworkable and futile to require States to inquire into each new resident's subjective intent to remain. Hence, States employ objective criteria such as durational residence requirements to test a new resident's resolve to remain before these new citizens can enjoy certain in-state benefits. Recognizing the practical appeal of such criteria, this Court has repeatedly sanctioned the State's use of durational residence requirements before new residents receive in-state tuition rates at state universities. *Starns v. Malkerson*, 401 U.S. 985 (1971) (upholding 1-year residence requirement for in-state tuition). . . . The Court has done the same in upholding a 1-year residence requirement for eligibility to obtain a divorce in state courts, see *Sosna v. Iowa*, 419 U.S. 393 (1975), and in upholding political party registration restrictions that amounted to a durational residency requirement for voting in primary elections, see *Rosario v. Rockefeller*, 410 U.S. 752 (1973).

If States can require individuals to reside in-state for a year before exercising the right to educational benefits, the right to terminate a marriage, or the right to vote in primary elections that all other state citizens enjoy, then States may surely do the same for welfare benefits. Indeed, there is no material difference between a 1-year residence requirement applied to the level of welfare benefits given out by a State, and the same requirement applied to the level of tuition subsidies at a state university. The welfare payment here and in-state tuition rates are cash subsidies provided to a limited class of people, and California's standard of living and higher education system make both subsidies quite attractive. Durational residence requirements were upheld when used to regulate the provision of higher education subsidies, and the same deference should be given in the case of welfare payments. . . .

The Court today recognizes that States retain the ability to determine the bona fides of an individual's claim to residence, but then tries to avoid the issue. It asserts that because respondents' need for welfare benefits is unrelated to the length of time they have resided in California, it has "no occasion to consider what weight might be given to a citizen's length of residence if the bona fides of her claim to state citizenship were questioned." But I do not understand how the absence of a link between need and length of residency bears on the State's ability to objectively test respondents' resolve to stay in California. There is no link between the need for an education or for a divorce and the length of residence, and yet States may use length of residence as an objective yardstick to channel their benefits to those whose intent to stay is legitimate.

In one respect, the State has a greater need to require a durational residence for welfare benefits than for college eligibility. The impact of a large number of new residents who immediately seek welfare payments will have a far greater impact on a State's operating budget than the impact of new residents seeking to attend a state university. In the case of the welfare recipients, a modest durational residence requirement to allow for the completion of an annual legislative budget cycle gives the State time to decide how to finance the increased obligations.

The Court tries to distinguish education and divorce benefits by contending that the welfare payment here will be consumed in California, while a college education or a divorce produces benefits that are "portable" and can be enjoyed after individuals return to their original domicile. But this "you can't take it with you" distinction is more apparent than real, and offers little guidance to lower courts who must apply this rationale in the future.

* * *

I therefore believe that the durational residence requirement challenged here is a permissible exercise of the State's power to "assur[e] that services provided for its residents are enjoyed only by residents." The 1-year period established in [the state law here] is the same period this Court approved in *Starns* and *Sosna*. The requirement does not deprive welfare recipients of all benefits; indeed, the limitation has no effect whatsoever on a recipient's ability to enjoy the full 5-year period of welfare eligibility; to enjoy the full range of employment, training, and accompanying supportive services; or to take full advantage of health care benefits under Medicaid. This waiting period does not preclude new residents from all cash payments, but merely limits them to what they received in their prior State of residence. Moreover, as the Court recognizes, any pinch resulting from this limitation during the 1-year period is mitigated by other programs such as homeless assistance and an increase in food stamp allowance. The 1-year period thus permissibly balances the new resident's needs for subsistence with the State's need to ensure the bona fides of their claim to residence.

Finally, Congress' express approval of durational residence requirements for welfare recipients like the one established by California only goes to show the reasonableness of a law like [the state law here]. The National Legislature, where people from Mississippi as well as California are represented, has recognized the need to protect state resources in a time of experimentation and welfare reform. . . .

JUSTICE THOMAS, with whom THE CHIEF JUSTICE joins, dissenting.

I join THE CHIEF JUSTICE's dissent. . . . In my view, the majority attributes a meaning to the Privileges or Immunities Clause that likely was unintended when the Fourteenth Amendment was enacted and ratified.

The Privileges or Immunities Clause of the Fourteenth Amendment provides that "[n]o State shall make or enforce any law which shall abridge the privileges or immunities of citizens of the United States." U.S. Const., Amdt. 14, § 1. Unlike the Equal Protection and Due Process Clauses, which have assumed near-talismanic status in modern constitutional law, the Court all but read the Privileges or Immunities Clause out of the Constitution in the *Slaughter-House Cases* (1872).

* * *

Unlike the majority, I would look to history to ascertain the original meaning of the Clause. At least in American law, the phrase (or its close approximation) appears to stem from the 1606 Charter of Virginia, which provided that "all and every the Persons being our Subjects, which shall dwell and inhabit within every or any of the said several Colonies . . . shall HAVE and enjoy all Liberties, Franchises, and Immunities . . . as if they had been abiding and born, within this our Realme of England." Years later, as tensions between England and the American Colonies increased, the colonists adopted resolutions reasserting their entitlement to the privileges or immunities of English citizenship.[17]

The Constitution, which superceded the Articles of Confederation, similarly guarantees that "[t]he Citizens of each State shall be entitled to all Privileges and Immunities of Citizens in the several States." Art. IV, § 2, cl. 1.

Justice Bushrod Washington's landmark opinion in *Corfield v. Coryell* (1825), reflects this historical understanding.

Washington rejected the proposition that the Privileges and Immunities Clause guaranteed equal access to all public benefits (such as the right to harvest oysters in public waters) that a State chooses to make available. Instead, he endorsed the colonial-era conception of the terms "privileges" and "immunities," concluding that Article IV encompassed only fundamental rights that belong to all citizens of the United States.

Justice Washington's opinion in *Corfield* indisputably influenced the Members of Congress who enacted the Fourteenth Amendment. When Congress gathered to debate the Fourteenth Amendment, members frequently, if not as a matter of course, appealed to *Corfield*, arguing that the Amendment was necessary to guarantee the fundamental rights that Justice Washington identified in his opinion. . . .

That Members of the 39th Congress appear to have endorsed the wisdom of Justice Washington's opinion does not, standing alone, provide dispositive insight into their understanding of the Fourteenth Amendment's Privileges or Immunities Clause. Nevertheless, their repeated references to the *Corfield* decision, combined with what appears to be the historical understanding of the Clause's operative terms, supports the inference that, at the time the Fourteenth Amendment was adopted, people understood that "privileges or immunities of citizens" were fundamental rights, rather than every public benefit established by positive law. Accordingly, the majority's conclusion — that a State violates the Privileges or Immunities Clause when it "discriminates" against citizens who have been domiciled in the State for less than a year in the distribution of welfare benefit — appears contrary to the original understanding and is dubious at best.

. . . The *Slaughter-House Cases* sapped the Clause of any meaning. Although the majority appears to breathe new life into the Clause today, it fails to address its

---

[17] [3] *See, e.g., The Massachusetts Resolves, in* PROLOGUE TO REVOLUTION: SOURCES AND DOCUMENTS ON THE STAMP ACT CRISIS 56 (E. Morgan ed. 1959) ("Resolved, That there are certain essential Rights of the British Constitution of Government, which are founded in the Law of God and Nature, and are the common Rights of Mankind — Therefore, . . . Resolved that no Man can justly take the Property of another without his Consent . . . this inherent Right, together with all other essential Rights, Liberties, Privileges and Immunities of the People of Great Britain have been fully confirmed to them by Magna Charta"). . . .

historical underpinnings or its place in our constitutional jurisprudence. Because I believe that the demise of the Privileges or Immunities Clause has contributed in no small part to the current disarray of our Fourteenth Amendment jurisprudence, I would be open to reevaluating its meaning in an appropriate case. Before invoking the Clause, however, we should endeavor to understand what the framers of the Fourteenth Amendment thought that it meant. We should also consider whether the Clause should displace, rather than augment, portions of our equal protection and substantive due process jurisprudence. The majority's failure to consider these important questions raises the specter that the Privileges or Immunities Clause will become yet another convenient tool for inventing new rights, limited solely by the "predilections of those who happen at the time to be Members of this Court."

I respectfully dissent.

NOTES AND QUESTIONS

1.   California's welfare benefits are some of the highest in the nation, and state leaders thought it fiscally prudent to limit the welfare benefits of new residents in order to save over ten million dollars, coordinate other assistance programs, and, frankly, to keep from becoming a "welfare magnet." With these rational legislative thoughts, California may have reasoned it could allocate its own funds, but it was wrong. Why does the Court, including two of the Court's strongest federalism advocates — Justices Scalia and O'Connor — deny California this latitude?

2.   Justice Stevens' majority opinion in *Saenz* argues that Justice Miller's meager holding in *Slaughter-House* is enough to secure the Golden State's largesse for the new residents, but was that your impression of *Slaughter-House*? Said Stevens: "[d]espite fundamentally differing views concerning the coverage of the Privileges or Immunities Clause, . . . it has always been common ground that this Clause protects [the right of the newly arrived citizen to the same privileges and immunities enjoyed by other citizens of the same State]." Maybe, except that notwithstanding the claim of "common ground" over the dicta in *Slaughter-House*, the Fourteenth Amendment Privileges or Immunities Clause had never been applied in that categorical way. Indeed, in over 130 years, the Clause had never been used at all, save in a minor tax dispute the Court rather promptly overruled.

3.   Remember that the words privileges *and* immunities also appear in Article IV distinct from the Privileges *or* Immunities Clause in the Fourteenth Amendment. Article IV is basically a limited nondiscrimination principle between residents and visitors, and thus, Article IV has no application in *Saenz* dealing with two classes of residents. Moreover, according to the Court, Article IV was intended to "fuse into one Nation, a collection of independent, sovereign States." As interpreted by the modern Supreme Court, such distinctions need only be avoided with regard to a somewhat uncertain category of fundamental liberties, like lawyering in a neighboring state, but not, say, differentially calculated elk hunting fees.

4.   So where does the right to travel fit into the Fourteenth Amendment? In *Saenz*, Justice Stevens more or less re-made the Privileges or Immunities Clause of the Fourteenth Amendment into both the right to travel from state to state and the right of new residents to be treated as well as old ones. Chief Justice Rehnquist

thought this a ruse. "I cannot see how the right to become a citizen of another State," Rehnquist wrote in dissent, "is a necessary 'component' of the right to travel." The only reason the Court "unearth[ed] from its tomb" the Privileges or Immunities Clause, argued Rehnquist, was to clean up its decidedly messy right to travel cases that "in the past 30 years, essentially conflated the right to travel with the right to equal citizenship." Most of these cases dealt with durational residency requirements, with the Court inquiring whether restricting the provision of welfare benefits, voting, or medical assistance to new residents for a limited time impermissibly penalized them under the Equal Protection Clause. To some degree, the Court's earlier cases turned on a judicial assessment of the importance of a right like voting, but as the Chief Justice observes, in light of *Saenz*, outside a few ill-defined circumstances, states generally can no longer classify their citizens by the length of their residence. And the noted qualification of "a few ill-defined circumstances" is only the majority's assertion in *Saenz* that differences between in-state and out-of-state college tuition levels and state waiting periods for divorce are somehow still okay.

5. The most interesting opinion in *Saenz* may be the dissent of Justice Thomas. Justice Thomas agrees with the Chief Justice that the Fourteenth Amendment Privileges or Immunities Clause has nothing to do with a durational residency requirement for a welfare benefit, but Justice Thomas is far more congenial to exhuming privileges or immunities generally. Writes Justice Thomas: "[b]ecause I believe that the demise of the Privileges or Immunities Clause has contributed in no small part to the current disarray of our Fourteenth Amendment jurisprudence, I would be open to reevaluating its meaning in an appropriate case. Before invoking the Clause, however, we should endeavor to understand what the framers of the Fourteenth Amendment thought that it meant."

Justice Thomas traces the language to 17th century colonial charters, noting that scholars have attributed the specific use of the language in the Fourteenth Amendment to support for the 1866 Civil Rights Act and its protection of contract and property rights that were being denied the freed slaves. In addition, it appears that some drafters of the Fourteenth Amendment thought the Privileges or Immunities Clause would secure from state infringement all of the rights expressed in the first Eight Amendments, as well as those unenumerated fundamental rights anchored in common law tradition, or as it is sometimes formulated, "those rights, common to all men which no man or state may rightfully take away." Natural law formulations like these can be abused by partisans of many stripes, but as the criticism of the *Slaughter-House* majority across the scholarly spectrum discloses, the price for judicially ignoring natural rights is often abdication of them. On the social side of liberty, the protection of the rights to marry, procreate, live in extended families, and direct the upbringing of children have all been discovered in modern times by recurring "to the most specific level at which a relevant tradition protecting, or denying protection to, the asserted right can be identified." *Michael H. v. Gerald D.* (1989). Is there any principled reason not to employ the same type of careful judicial inquiry in the economic realm? What would an historically accurate definition of privileges or immunities be? Justice Field, in dissent in *Slaughter-House*, gave this description: "the right to pursue a lawful employment in a lawful manner, without other restraint than such as equally affects all persons."

Justice Thomas cautioned that without its proper historical grounding, the Clause "will become yet another convenient tool for inventing new rights, limited solely by the 'predilections of those who happen at the time to be Members of this Court.'" Substantive economic due process, which we take up next, is often pointed to as the archetypical example of where personal judicial "predilections" first became part of the Court's opinions.

3. Substantive Economic Due Process

Slaughter-House both undermined the privileges or immunities envisioned by the Fourteenth Amendment, and cursorily dismissed the Butchers' Association's alternative ground for recovery, due process. The Court wrote:

> [U]nder no construction of that provision that we have ever seen, or any that we deem admissible, can the restraint imposed by the State of Louisiana upon the exercise of their trade by the butchers of New Orleans be held to be a deprivation of property within the meaning of that provision.

83 U.S. (16 Wall.) 36, 81 (1873). In essence, the Court was saying due process relates to procedure, and no more. More recently, Justice Scalia has written that he agrees, since the Clause "[b]y its inescapable terms . . . guarantees only process. . . . To say otherwise is to abandon textualism, and to render democratically adopted texts mere springboards for judicial lawmaking." ANTONIN SCALIA, A MATTER OF INTERPRETATION 24–25 (1997). The counter to this argument is that textualism requires context, and specifically, the natural law context of the framers to protect certain fundamental rights. This is what we saw the early Supreme Court do in *Calder v. Bull*, 3 U.S. (3 Dall.) 386 (1798), *Fletcher v. Peck*, 10 U.S. (6 Cranch) 87 (1810), and *Terrett v. Taylor*, 13 U.S. (9 Cranch) 43 (1815), discussed in Chapter Two. When Justice Scalia argues that the first substantive use of due process was to uphold slavery in *Dred Scott v. Sanford*, 60 U.S. (19 How.) 393 (1856) (*see* Chapter Five), he thus omits this crucial bit of originalism. No one can justify *Dred Scott*, then or now; however, its lack of justification, too, depends upon the recognition that, despite the political compromise of the Fugitive Slave Clause in the original Constitution (Article IV, Section 2, Paragraph 3), providing for the return of escaping slaves, the founders understood slavery to be a disregard of the basic human dignity of all persons recognized by the natural law. *See* THE FEDERALIST No. 54 (James Madison) (describing slavery as a legal artifice, not part of the natural order).

But does due process guarantee economic liberty? Dissenting Justices Field and Bradley thought so in *Slaughter-House*. Bradley wrote:

> [T]he individual citizen, as a necessity, must be left free to adopt such calling, profession, or trade as may seem to him most conducive to that end. Without this right he cannot be a freeman. This right to choose one's calling is an essential part of that liberty which is the object of government to protect; and a calling, when chosen, is a man's property and right. Liberty and property are not protected where these rights are arbitrarily assailed.

83 U.S. (16 Wall.) at 116 (Bradley, J., dissenting). In other words, the Due Process Clause guaranteed not just procedure, but limited the ability of states to adopt arbitrary laws at all.

The year after *Slaughter-House*, the Court seemed effectively to adopt the Field and Bradley dissenting view and began to articulate economic liberty as a judicially-protectible fundamental interest. In *Loan Association v. Topeka*, 87 U.S. (20 Wall.) 655 (1874), the Court invalidated a city ordinance that authorized the issuance of bonds "to encourage the establishment of manufactories and such other enterprises." *Id.* at 42 (statement of the case). These bonds would be paid for by public monies raised through taxation, even as the proceeds of the bonds were primarily of benefit to private manufacturing concerns. Justice Miller, who had refused to find economic freedom to be a privilege or immunity of citizenship and who quickly dismissed due process as a basis for such liberty, wrote the majority opinion, in which he found the bonding authority to be beyond the legislative power and an invasion of private right.

Students who read the full opinion in *Loan Association* often inquire whether the Court was following earlier natural law principles. It would seem to insofar as it protects the economic resources of one private party from being expropriated for the benefit of another. From 1874 to 1897, the Court continued this thinking and to hint that the Due Process Clause placed a substantive limit on the activities of government. In *Munn v. Illinois*, 94 U.S. 113 (1877), the Court sustained the regulation of grain warehouses because the business was "affected with the public interest"; however, the Court indicated that absent that interrelationship, the regulation of business would violate due process. *Id.* at 125–26. In a subsequent case, the Court upheld state regulation of railroad rates, but did so with the caveat that "[t]he question of the reasonableness of a rate of charge for transportation by a railroad company . . . is eminently a question for judicial investigation, requiring due process of law for its determination." *Chicago, Milwaukee & St. Paul Ry. Co. v. Minnesota*, 134 U.S. 418, 458 (1890). Similarly, in *Mugler v. Kansas*, 123 U.S. 623 (1887), the Court found no reason to set aside the prohibition of the sale of alcoholic beverages, but noted that if "a statute purporting to have been enacted to protect the public health, the public morals, or the public safety, has no real or substantial relation to those objects, or is a palpable invasion of rights secured by the fundamental law, it is the duty of the courts to so adjudge, and thereby give effect to the Constitution." *Id.* at 661. A year earlier, the Court made it clear that corporations could bring suit under the Fourteenth Amendment because they would be treated as "persons." *Santa Clara County v. Southern Pacific R.R. Co.*, 118 U.S. 394, 396 (1886) (statement of facts) (Chief Justice Waite stated before oral argument that the Court would not hear argument on whether a corporation constitutes a "person" under the Equal Protection Clause, as the Court was "all of the opinion that it does."). Remember that corporations are not "persons" under the Privileges or Immunities Clause, so this difference invited corporate litigation.

In 1897, a Louisiana law prohibiting payments on insurance policies issued by non-Louisiana companies that were not licensed to do business in the state was struck down. *Allgeyer v. Louisiana*, 165 U.S. 578 (1897). In *Allgeyer*, the Court made it plain that substantive due process protected economic liberty, writing:

> The "liberty" mentioned in [the Fourteenth Amendment is] deemed to embrace the right of . . . citizen[s] to be free in the enjoyment of all [their] faculties; to be free to use them in all lawful ways; to live and work where [they] will; to earn [their] livelihood by any lawful calling; to pursue any

livelihood or avocation; and for that purpose to enter into all contacts which may be proper, necessary, and essential to [their] carrying out to a successful completion the purposes above mentioned.

Id. at 589. This was the formal beginning to an era of judicial intervention in favor of freedom of contract that would not end until the Depression of the 1930s led to political demands for extensive government regulation of the free market, at least during economic emergency. The constitutional doctrine came to be known as "Lochnerism," after the next case.

LOCHNER v. NEW YORK
198 U.S. 45 (1905)

MR. JUSTICE PECKHAM . . . delivered the opinion of the court:

[New York Law provided that "No employee shall be required or permitted to work in a biscuit, bread, or cake bakery or confectionery establishment more than sixty hours in any one week, or more than ten hours in any one day, unless for the purpose of making a shorter work day on the last day of the week; nor more hours in any one week than will make an average of ten hours per day for the number of days during such week in which such employee shall work."]

The indictment, it will be seen, charges that [Lochner] violated . . . the labor law of the State of New York, in that he wrongfully and unlawfully required and permitted an employee working for him to work more than sixty hours in one week. . . . The mandate of the statute, that "no employee shall be required or permitted to work," is the substantial equivalent of an enactment that "no employee shall contract or agree to work," more than ten hours per day, and as there is no provision for special emergencies the statute is mandatory in all cases. It is not an act merely fixing the number of hours which shall constitute a legal day's work, but an absolute prohibition upon the employer, permitting, under any circumstances, more than ten hours work to be done in his establishment. The employee may desire to earn the extra money, which would arise from his working more than the prescribed time, but this statute forbids the employer from permitting the employee to earn it.

The statute necessarily interferes with the right of contract between the employer and employees, concerning the number of hours in which the latter may labor in the bakery of the employer. The general right to make a contract in relation to his business is part of the liberty of the individual protected by the Fourteenth Amendment of the Federal Constitution. *Allgeyer v. Louisiana* (1897). Under that provision no state can deprive any person of life, liberty or property without due process of law. The right to purchase or to sell labor is part of the liberty protected by this amendment, unless there are circumstances which exclude the right. There are, however, certain powers, existing in the sovereignty of each State in the Union, somewhat vaguely termed police powers, the exact description and limitation of which have not been attempted by the courts. Those powers, broadly stated and without, at present, any attempt at a more specific limitation, relate to the safety, health, morals and general welfare of the public. Both property and liberty are held on such reasonable conditions as may be imposed by the governing power of the

State in the exercise of those powers, and with such conditions the Fourteenth Amendment was not designed to interfere.

*   *   *

It must, of course, be conceded that there is a limit to the valid exercise of the police power by the State. There is no dispute concerning this general proposition. Otherwise the Fourteenth Amendment would have no efficacy and the legislatures of the States would have unbounded power, and it would be enough to say that any piece of legislation was enacted to conserve the morals, the health or the safety of the people; such legislation would be valid, no matter how absolutely without foundation the claim might be. . . .

This is not a question of substituting the judgment of the court for that of the legislature. If the act be within the power of the State it is valid, although the judgment of the court might be totally opposed to the enactment of such a law. But the question would still remain: Is it within the police power of the State? and that question must be answered by the court.

The question whether this act is valid as a labor law, pure and simple, may be dismissed in a few words. There is no reasonable ground for interfering with the liberty of person or the right of free contract, by determining the hours of labor, in the occupation of a baker. There is no contention that bakers as a class are not equal in intelligence and capacity to men in other trades or manual occupations, or that they are not able to assert their rights and care for themselves without the protecting arm of the State, interfering with their independence of judgment and of action. They are in no sense wards of the State. Viewed in the light of a purely labor law, with no reference whatever to the question of health, we think that a law like the one before us involves neither the safety, the morals nor the welfare of the public, and that the interest of the public is not in the slightest degree affected by such an act. The law must be upheld, if at all, as a law pertaining to the health of the individual engaged in the occupation of a baker. It does not affect any other portion of the public than those who are engaged in that occupation. Clean and wholesome bread does not depend upon whether the baker works but ten hours per day or only sixty hours a week. The limitation of the hours of labor does not come within the police power on that ground.

It is a question of which of two powers or rights shall prevail — the power of the State to legislate or the right of the individual to liberty of person and freedom of contract. The mere assertion that the subject relates though but in a remote degree to the public health does not necessarily render the enactment valid. The act must have a more direct relation, as a means to an end, and the end itself must be appropriate and legitimate, before an act can be held to be valid which interferes with the general right of an individual to be free in his person and in his power to contract in relation to his own labor.

. . . Although found in what is called a labor law of the state, the court of appeals has upheld the act as one relating to the public health, — in other words, as a health law. One of the judges of the court of appeals, in upholding the law, stated that, in his opinion, the regulation in question could not be sustained unless they were able to say, from common knowledge, that working in a bakery and candy factory was an unhealthy employment. The judge held that, while the evidence was not uniform, it still led him to the conclusion that the occupation of a baker or confectioner was unhealthy and tended to result in diseases of the respiratory organs. Three of the judges dissented from that view, and they thought the occupation of a baker was not to such an extent unhealthy as to warrant the interference of the legislature with the liberty of the individual.

We think the limit of the police power has been reached and passed in this case. There is, in our judgment, no reasonable foundation for holding this to be necessary or appropriate as a health law to safeguard the public health or the health of the individuals who are following the trade of a baker. If this statute be valid, and if, therefore, a proper case is made out in which to deny the right of an individual, *sui juris*, as employer or employee, to make contracts for the labor of the latter under the protection of the provisions of the Federal Constitution, there would seem to be no length to which legislation of this nature might not go. . . .

We think that, [unlike in *Holden v. Hardy* (1898), where we upheld maximum hour restrictions on coal miners,] there can be no fair doubt that the trade of a baker, in and of itself, is not an unhealthy one to that degree which would authorize the legislature to interfere with the right to labor, and with the right of free contract on the part of the individual, either as employer or employee. In looking through statistics regarding all trades and occupations, it may be true that the trade of a baker does not appear to be as healthy as some other trades, and is also vastly more healthy than still others. To the common understanding the trade of a baker has never been regarded as an unhealthy one. . . . There must be more than the mere fact of the possible existence of some small amount of unhealthiness to warrant legislative interference with liberty. It is unfortunately true that labor, even in any department, may possibly carry with it the seeds of unhealthiness. But are we all, on that account, at the mercy of legislative majorities? A printer, a tinsmith, a locksmith, a carpenter, a cabinetmaker, a dry goods clerk, a bank's, a lawyer's or a physician's clerk, or a clerk in almost any kind of business, would all come under the power of the legislature, on this assumption. No trade, no occupation, no mode of earning one's living, could escape this all-pervading power, and the acts of the legislature in limiting the hours of labor in all employments would be valid, although such limitation might seriously cripple the ability of the laborer to support himself and his family. In our large cities there are many buildings into which the sun penetrates for but a short time in each day, and these buildings are occupied by people carrying on the business of bankers, brokers, lawyers, real estate, and many other kinds of business, aided by many clerks, messengers, and other employees. Upon the assumption of the validity of this act under review, it is not possible to say that an act, prohibiting lawyers' or bank clerks, or others, from contracting to labor for their employers more than eight hours a day would be invalid. . . .

. . . The act is not, within any fair meaning of the term, a health law, but is an illegal interference with the rights of individuals, both employers and employees, to make contracts regarding labor upon such terms as they may think best, or which they may agree upon with the other parties to such contracts. Statutes of the nature of that under review, limiting the hours in which grown and intelligent men may labor to earn their living, are mere meddlesome interferences with the rights of the individual, and they are not saved from condemnation by the claim that they are passed in the exercise of the police power and upon the subject of the health of the individual whose rights are interfered with, unless there be some fair ground, reasonable in and of itself, to say that there is material danger to the public health or to the health of the employees, if the hours of labor are not curtailed. If this be not clearly the case the individuals, whose rights are thus made the subject of legislative interference, are under the protection of the Federal Constitution regarding their liberty of contract as well as of person; and the legislature of the State has no power to limit their right as proposed in this statute. All that it could properly do has been done by it with regard to the conduct of bakeries, as provided for in the other sections of the act. These several sections provide for the inspection of the premises where the bakery is carried on, with regard to furnishing proper wash rooms and waterclosets, apart from the bake room, also with regard to providing proper drainage, plumbing and painting; the sections, in addition, provide for the height of the ceiling, the cementing or tiling of floors, where necessary in the opinion of the factory inspector, and for other things of that nature; alterations are also provided for and are to be made where necessary in the opinion of the inspector, in order to comply with the provisions of the statute. These various sections may be wise and valid regulations, and they certainly go to the full extent of providing for the cleanliness and the healthiness, so far as possible, of the quarters in which bakeries are to be conducted. Adding to all these requirements, a prohibition to enter into any contract of labor in a bakery for more than a certain number of hours a week, is, in our judgment, so wholly beside the matter of a proper, reasonable and fair provision, as to run counter to that liberty of person and of free contract provided for in the Federal Constitution.

. . . In our judgment it is not possible in fact to discover the connection between the number of hours a baker may work in the bakery and the healthful quality of the bread made by the workman. The connection, if any exist, is too shadowy and thin to build any argument for the interference of the legislature. If the man works ten hours a day it is all right, but if ten and a half or eleven his health is in danger and his bread may be unhealthy, and, therefore, he shall not be permitted to do it. This, we think, is unreasonable and entirely arbitrary. . . .

*   *   *

It is impossible for us to shut our eyes to the fact that many of the laws of this character, while passed under what is claimed to be the police power for the purpose of protecting the public health or welfare, are, in reality, passed from other motives. . . .

. . . It seems to us that the real object and purpose were simply to regulate the hours of labor between the master and his employees (all being men, *sui juris*), in a private business, not dangerous in any degree to morals or in any real and substantial degree, to the health of the employees. Under such circumstances the freedom of master and employee to contract with each other in relation to their employment, and in defining the same, cannot be prohibited or interfered with, without violating the Federal Constitution.

*   *   *

MR. JUSTICE HARLAN, with whom MR. JUSTICE WHITE and MR. JUSTICE DAY concurred, dissenting.

*   *   *

Granting then that there is a liberty of contract which cannot be violated even under the sanction of direct legislative enactment, but assuming, as according to settled law we may assume, that such liberty of contract is subject to such regulations as the State may reasonably prescribe for the common good and the well-being of society, what are the conditions under which the judiciary may declare such regulations to be in excess of legislative authority and void? Upon this point there is no room for dispute; for, the rule is universal that a legislative enactment, Federal or state, is never to be disregarded or held invalid unless it be, beyond question, plainly and palpably in excess of legislative power. . . . If there be doubt as to the validity of the statute, that doubt must therefore be resolved in favor of its validity, and the courts must keep their hands off, leaving the legislature to meet the responsibility for unwise legislation. If the end which the legislature seeks to accomplish be one to which its power extends, and if the means employed to that end, although not the wisest or best, are yet not plainly and palpably unauthorized by law, then the court cannot interfere. In other words, when the validity of a statute is questioned, the burden of proof, so to speak, is upon those who assert it to be unconstitutional. *McCulloch v. Maryland*, 4 Wheat. 316, 421.

*   *   *

. . . Whether or not this be wise legislation it is not the province of the court to inquire. Under our systems of government the courts are not concerned with the wisdom or policy of legislation. So that in determining the question of power to interfere with liberty of contract, the court may inquire whether the means devised by the State are germane to an end which may be lawfully accomplished and have a real or substantial relation to the protection of health, as involved in the daily work of the persons, male and female, engaged in bakery and confectionery establishments. But when this inquiry is entered upon I find it impossible, in view of common experience, to say that there is here no real or substantial relation between the means employed by the State and the end sought to be accomplished by its legislation. . . .

*   *   *

I take leave to say that the New York statute, in the particulars here involved, cannot be held to be in conflict with the Fourteenth Amendment, without enlarging the scope of the Amendment far beyond its original purpose and without bringing under the supervision of this court matters which have been supposed to belong exclusively to the legislative departments of the several States when exerting their conceded power to guard the health and safety of their citizens by such regulations as they in their wisdom deem best. Health laws of every description constitute, said Chief Justice Marshall, a part of that mass of legislation which "embraces everything within the territory of a state, not surrendered to the General Government; all which can be most advantageously exercised by the States themselves." A decision that the New York statute is void under the Fourteenth Amendment will, in my opinion, involve consequences of a far-reaching and mischievous character; for such a decision would seriously cripple the inherent power of the States to care for the lives, health and well-being of their citizens. Those are matters which can be best controlled by the states. The preservation of the just powers of the States is quite as vital as the preservation of the powers of the General Government.

* * *

MR. JUSTICE HOLMES dissenting.

I regret sincerely that I am unable to agree with the judgment in this case, and that I think it my duty to express my dissent.

This case is decided upon an economic theory which a large part of the country does not entertain. If it were a question whether I agreed with that theory, I should desire to study it further and long before making up my mind. But I do not conceive that to be my duty, because I strongly believe that my agreement or disagreement has nothing to do with the right of a majority to embody their opinions in law. It is settled by various decisions of this court that state constitutions and state laws may regulate life in many ways which we as legislators might think as injudicious or if you like as tyrannical as this, and which equally with this interfere with the liberty to contract. Sunday laws and usury laws are ancient examples. A more modern one is the prohibition of lotteries. The liberty of the citizen to do as he likes so long as he does not interfere with the liberty of others to do the same, which has been a shibboleth for some well-known writers, is interfered with by school laws, by the Post office, by every state or municipal institution which takes his money for purposes thought desirable, whether he likes it or not. The 14th Amendment does not enact Mr. Herbert Spencer's Social Statics. . . .

. . . I think that the word liberty, in the Fourteenth Amendment is perverted when it is held to prevent the natural outcome of a dominant opinion, unless it can be said that a rational and fair man necessarily would admit that the statute proposed would infringe fundamental principles as they have been understood by the traditions of our people and our law. It does not need research to show that no such sweeping condemnation can be passed upon the statute before us. A reasonable man might think it a proper measure on the score of health. Men whom I certainly could not pronounce unreasonable would uphold it as a first instalment of a general regulation of the hours of work. Whether in the latter aspect it would be open to the charge of inequality I think it unnecessary to discuss.

NOTES AND QUESTIONS

1. Because of his famous line that the "14th Amendment does not enact Mr. Herbert Spencer's Social Statics," Holmes is often argued to be "expressly reject[ing] the majority's premise that the Constitution should be used to limit government regulation and protect a laissez-faire economy." ERWIN CHEMERINSKY, CONSTITUTIONAL LAW PRINCIPLES AND POLICIES 482 (1997). But is that entirely true? What does Holmes mean in his dissent when he states that:

> [T]he word liberty, in the Fourteenth Amendment is perverted when it is
> held to prevent the natural outcome of a dominant opinion, unless it can be

said that a rational and fair man necessarily would admit that the statute proposed would infringe fundamental principles as they have been understood by the traditions of our people and our law.

198 U.S. at 76 (Holmes, J., dissenting). Doesn't that statement admit of a natural law limitation on government power, informed by tradition and the common law, even as Holmes in this particular case disagrees with the majority that a regulation of a baker's hours violates that tradition?

2. *Lochner* established or confirmed a number of judicial statements that had been made in dicta prior to it: freedom of contract related to the carrying out of a trade or profession was within the protected liberty of the Fifth and Fourteenth Amendment Due Process Clauses, 198 U.S. at 53; liberty may be limited by government power if the limitation truly relates to health and safety (the "police power"), *id.*; and the Court must carefully inquire as to whether the regulation is within its proper police power scope, *id.* at 56. On the last point, the Court was particularly concerned that government regulation was being too frequently used to redistribute wealth to the politically favored, rather than addressing genuine public purposes. The use of substantive due process to prevent wealth redistribution began in the shadow of slavery as Chief Justice Taney said that a person's property right in his slave could not be extinguished simply by the slave's act of moving to a free state. This was contrary to the common law of England, which found slavery to be so repulsive and so antagonistic to natural law principles that English law proclaimed its existence to be only in those places where the narrow positive law allowed it. Had the Court learned the lesson of the evils of monopoly that it disregarded in *Slaughter-House*? Or was the Court now overcorrecting and intruding too deeply into matters that, while related remotely to the principle of economic liberty, require the specific policy determination of the legislature? Justice Harlan's dissent in *Lochner* thought the latter, arguing that bakers suffered from serious health problems, including prolonged exposure to flour dust and intense heat.

3. With respect to concerns about the *public* health (as opposed to the *private* health of individual workers), is a minor who works more than 10 hours a day any more likely to cause harm *to others* than a baker? Does the fact that mining is more inherently dangerous than baking to those engaged in it effect the *public health* calculus in the least? The Court subsequently allowed maximum hour laws for women, but not minimum wage laws. *Compare Muller v. Oregon*, 208 U.S. 412 (1908) (this case gave rise to the expression "Brandeis brief" [not a compliment] in which not yet Supreme Court Justice Louis Brandeis filed a brief of 113 pages supporting the limitation of women's efforts outside domestic work), *with Adkins v. Children's Hospital*, 261 U.S. 525 (1923) (finding women perfectly capable of fending for themselves in the negotiation of wages). Brandeis argued in his brief, and the Court accepted, that maximum hour restrictions on women protected the *public's* interest in insuring that women would be available for child-rearing. Is that more, or less, of a legitimate governmental interest than was claimed by New York in *Lochner*? Would you support using the Due Process Clause to invalidate such a law today?

4. For a while following *Lochner*, the Court upheld the natural right of economic liberty under the auspices of the Due Process Clause. For example, the

Court invalidated irrational barriers to entry into trade or business. *New State Ice Co. v. Liebmann*, 285 U.S. 262 (1932) (striking down permitting requirements that tended to create monopoly in the ice business). Tartly, the Court observed that government power cannot be used "to prevent a shoemaker from making or selling shoes because shoemakers already in that occupation can make and sell all the shoes that are needed." *Id.* at 279.

5.   Much academic criticism of *Lochner* is not principled, but merely advocacy for an activist government that sets prices and otherwise favors the public or quasi-public delivery of goods, rather than the private market. For scholarly criticism of this position, see RICHARD EPSTEIN, TAKINGS: PRIVATE PROPERTY AND THE POWER OF EMINENT DOMAIN (1985); and BERNARD SIEGAN, ECONOMIC LIBERTIES AND THE CONSTITUTION (1980). The Institute for Justice in Washington DC makes a principled defense of substantive economic due process as a means of addressing economic protectionism, which is often deeply embedded in regulatory initiatives and disguised under the flag of public health.

6.   Today, of course, maximum hour restrictions and a host of other work-place regulations are commonplace; the *Lochner* Court's protection of economic liberty eventually gave way to deference by the Court to the regulatory state. Why did the *Lochner* era end? Professor Laurence Tribe writes:

> In large measure . . . it was the economic realities of the Depression. . . .
> The legal "freedom" of contract and property came increasingly to be seen
> as an illusion, subject as it was to impersonal economic forces. Positive
> government intervention came to be more widely accepted as essential to
> economic survival, and legal doctrines would henceforth have to operate
> from that premise.

LAURENCE TRIBE, AMERICAN CONSTITUTIONAL LAW § 8-6, at 578 (2d ed. 1988). In the face of the tens of millions unemployed during the 1930s, Professor Tribe is surely right. However, given the thankfully transient nature of the Depression, should the fundamental right of economic liberty have been abandoned or merely deferred until the passing of a temporary or unusual economic circumstance? In *Nebbia v. New York*, 291 U.S. 502 (1933), the first Justice Roberts would be said to have switched his skepticism of government intervention in the face of the great economic distress of the 1930s and saved the court from the prospects of Court Packing.

7.   *Nebbia* indulges a level of economic regulation greater than that acknowledged by the Court previously. Why? As noted earlier, in the late 19th and early 20th centuries, the Court relied upon the fact that certain industries were "affected with the public interest" in order to justify regulation. *See Munn v. Illinois*, 94 U.S. 113, 126 (1876). In *Nebbia*, the Court denies the significance of this earlier explanation, writing:

> It is true that the court cited a statement from Lord Hale's *De Portibus
> Maris*, to the effect that when private property is "affected with a public
> interest, it ceases to be *juris privati* only"; but the court proceeded at once
> to define what it understood by the expression, saying: "Property does
> become clothed with a public interest when used in a manner to make it of

public consequence, and affect the community at large." Thus understood, "affected with a public interest" is the equivalent of "subject to the exercise of the police power"; and it is plain that nothing more was intended by the expression.

291 U.S. at 532–33 (quoting *Munn*, 94 U.S. at 126). Notwithstanding the disclaimer, was the abandonment of the "public interest" limitation on the police power a break with the common law, and the natural law protection of economic liberty? As Justice McReynolds illustrates in his dissent:

> [N]othing [in *Munn*] sustains the notion that the ordinary business of dealing in commodities is charged with a public interest and subject to legislative control. The contrary has been distinctly announced. To undertake now to attribute a repudiated implication to that opinion is to affirm that it means what this Court has declared again and again was not intended. The painstaking effort there to point out that certain businesses like ferries, mills, etc., were subject to legislative control at common law and then to show that warehousing at Chicago occupied like relation to the public would have been pointless if "affected with a public interest" only means that the public has serious concern about the perpetuity and success of the undertaking. That is true of almost all ordinary business affairs. Nothing in the opinion lends support, directly or otherwise, to the notion that in times of peace a legislature may fix the price of ordinary commodities — grain, meat, milk, cotton, etc.

Id. at 555–56 (McReynolds, J., dissenting).

8.   *Nebbia* thus signaled the beginning of the end of meaningful review of questions pertaining to economic liberty under the Due Process Clause. A few years later, for example, the Court upheld a minimum wage law for women. *West Coast Hotel Co v. Parrish*, 300 U.S. 379 (1937). Dissenting, Justice Sutherland bemoaned the loss of the presumption in favor of economic freedom. "[F]reedom of contract was the general rule and restraint the exception; and . . . the power to abridge that freedom could only be justified by the existence of exceptional circumstances." *Id.* at 406 (Sutherland, J., dissenting). The modern highly deferential standard of review applied by the Court presumes not economic freedom, but the constitutionality of regulation.

9.   The rethinking in *Nebbia* occurred in conjunction with a similar qualification of the application of the constitutional provision forbidding the impairment of contract. *See Home Bldg. & Loan Ass'n v. Blaisdell*, 290 U.S. 398 (1934) (upholding a state mortgage foreclosure moratorium law). Recall, however, from our discussion in Chapter Six that the impairment accepted in *Blaisdell* was viewed as minor and not vitiating the underlying contract. What's more, that impairment was again viewed as necessary to meet an emergency. After the emergency passed, the Court — initially, at least — returned to an undiminished enforcement of the Contract Clause.

10.   Lochnerism may have ended less from an abandonment of fundamental principle, than a threatened change in personnel yielding a noticeable change of perspective. We aspire to be a nation under law, but it is undeniable that our

imperfect human nature must apply that law. The imperfections of human nature were well on display in Franklin Roosevelt's attempt to pack the Supreme Court with his political partisans. Following his landslide re-election in 1936, Roosevelt proposed that Congress adopt legislation increasing the size of the Court by one new Justice for each over the age of 70 who had served for 10 or more years on any federal court up to a maximum of 15 Justices. Practically, this would have allowed Roosevelt to add six new justices and rid himself of a judiciary that believed federal power ought to be limited to enumerated subjects. Roosevelt claimed in a radio address that his proposal was simply inspired by a desire for "new blood" to carry out the heavy burdens of the judiciary. Chief Justice Charles Evans Hughes responded in a letter to the Senate that no new blood was needed, thank you. The Chief Justice said the Court was fully abreast of its work and more Justices would add, not subtract, from the complexity of the work. The Congress was appalled by the President's action and the Senate Judiciary Committee recommended that Roosevelt's proposal was "a needless, futile, and utterly dangerous abandonment of constitutional principle. . . . It is a measure which should be so emphatically rejected that its parallel will never again be presented to the free representatives of the free people of America." SENATE COMM. ON THE JUDICIARY, REORGANIZATION OF THE FEDERAL JUDICIARY, S. REP. No. 75-711, at 23 (1937). It was. Nevertheless, the message did not go unheard at the Supreme Court. While Justice Owen Roberts in particular denied being affected by the threatened reorganization plan (*see* Felix Frankfurter, *Mr. Justice Roberts*, 104 U. PA. L. REV. 311 (1955) (arguing that Roberts' later pro-FDR votes began before the Court packing plan was announced)), Justice Roberts became more cordial to governmental efforts to regulate economic matters. His opinion above in *Nebbia* was already primed in that direction. Roosevelt's ill-conceived plan is discussed at length in ROBERT JACKSON, THE STRUGGLE FOR JUDICIAL SUPREMACY (1941). Death and retirement allowed Roosevelt to have his way with the Court in any event. Between the years 1937 and 1941, Roosevelt made eight appointments.

11.   The next case illustrates the Court's present disposition to uphold virtually any economic regulation so long as it has some conceivable rational basis, even if it is the Court, and not the legislature, that conceives of it. As Justice Stone writes:

> [T]he existence of facts supporting the legislative judgment is to be presumed, for regulatory legislation affecting ordinary commercial trans-actions is not to be pronounced unconstitutional unless in the light of the facts made known or generally assumed it is of such a character as to preclude the assumption that it rests upon some rational basis.

United States v. Carolene Products Co., 304 U.S. 144, 152 (1938). The following case also contains a famous footnote (note 4) that is held responsible for creating the present-day anomaly of heightened due process review for personal liberties, like speech, but almost nonexistent review for economic freedom.

UNITED STATES v. CAROLENE PRODUCTS CO.
304 U.S. 144 (1938)

MR. JUSTICE STONE delivered the opinion of the Court.

The question for decision is whether the "Filled Milk Act" of Congress of March 4, 1923, which prohibits the shipment in interstate commerce of skimmed milk compounded with any fat or oil other than milk fat, so as to resemble milk or cream, transcends the power of Congress to regulate interstate commerce or infringes the Fifth Amendment.

*   *   *

Second. [We find t]he prohibition of shipment of [Carolene's] product in interstate commerce does not infringe the Fifth Amendment. . . .

. . . [W]e might rest decision wholly on the presumption of constitutionality. But affirmative evidence also sustains the statute. In twenty years evidence has steadily accumulated of the danger to the public health from the general consumption of foods which have been stripped of elements essential to the maintenance of health. The Filled Milk Act was adopted by Congress after committee hearings, in the course of which eminent scientists and health experts testified. An extensive investigation was made of the commerce in milk compounds in which vegetable oils have been substituted for natural milk fat, and of the effect upon the public health of the use of such compounds as a food substitute for milk. The conclusions drawn from evidence presented at the hearings were embodied in reports of the House Committee on Agriculture, and the Senate Committee on Agriculture and Forestry. Both committees concluded, as the statute itself declares, that the use of filled milk as a substitute for pure milk is generally injurious to health and facilitates fraud on the public.

*   *   *

There is nothing in the Constitution which compels a legislature, either national or state, to ignore such evidence, nor need it disregard the other evidence which amply supports the conclusions of the Congressional committees that the danger is greatly enhanced where an inferior product, like [Carolene Products'], is indistinguishable from a valuable food of almost universal use, thus making fraudulent distribution easy and protection of the consumer difficult.

Here the prohibition of the statute is inoperative unless the product is "in imitation or semblance of milk, cream, or skimmed milk, whether or not condensed." Whether in such circumstance the public would be adequately protected by the prohibition of false labels and false branding imposed by the Pure Food and Drugs Act, or whether it was necessary to go farther and prohibit a substitute food product thought to be injurious to health if used as a substitute when the two are not distinguishable, was a matter for the legislative judgment and not that of courts. . . .

*   *   *

Third. We may assume for present purposes that no pronouncement of a legislature can forestall attack upon the constitutionality of the prohibition which it enacts by applying opprobrious epithets to the prohibited act, and that a statute would deny due process which precluded the disproof in judicial proceedings of all facts which would show or tend to show that a statute depriving the suitor of life, liberty, or property had a rational basis.

But such we think is not the purpose or construction of the statutory characterization of filled milk as injurious to health and as a fraud upon the public. There is no need to consider it here as more than a declaration of the legislative findings deemed to support and justify the action taken as a constitutional exertion of the legislative power, aiding informed judicial review, as do the reports of legislative committees, by revealing the rationale of the legislation. Even in the absence of such aids the existence of facts supporting the legislative judgment is to be presumed, for regulatory legislation affecting ordinary commercial transactions is not to be pronounced unconstitutional unless in the light of the facts made known or generally assumed it is of such a character as to preclude the assumption that it rests upon some rational basis within the knowledge and experience of the legislators.[19] The present statutory findings affect [Carolene Products] no more than the reports of the Congressional committees and since in the absence of the statutory findings they would be presumed, their incorporation in the statute is no more prejudicial than surplusage.

Where the existence of a rational basis for legislation whose constitutionality is attacked depends upon facts beyond the sphere of judicial notice, such facts may properly be made the subject of judicial inquiry, and the constitutionality of a statute predicated upon the existence of a particular state of facts may be challenged by showing to the court that those facts have ceased to exist. Similarly we recognize that the constitutionality of a statute, valid on its face, may be assailed by proof of facts tending to show that the statute as applied to a particular article is without support in reason because the article, although within the prohibited class, is so different from others of the class as to be without the reason for the prohibition, though the effect of such proof depends on the relevant circumstances of each case, as for example the administrative difficulty of excluding the article from the regulated class. But by their very nature such inquiries, where the legislative judgment is drawn in question, must be restricted to the issue whether any state of facts either known or which could reasonably be assumed affords

---

[19] [4] There may be narrower scope for operation of the presumption of constitutionality when legislation appears on its face to be within a specific prohibition of the Constitution, such as those of the first ten Amendments, which are deemed equally specific when held to be embraced within the Fourteenth.

It is unnecessary to consider now whether legislation which restricts those political processes which can ordinarily be expected to bring about repeal of undesirable legislation, is to be subjected to more exacting judicial scrutiny under the general prohibitions of the Fourteenth Amendment than are most other types of legislation.

Nor need we enquire whether similar considerations enter into the review of statutes directed at particular religious, or national, or racial minorities: whether prejudice against discrete and insular minorities may be a special condition, which tends seriously to curtail the operation of those political processes ordinarily to be relied upon to protect minorities, and which may call for a correspondingly more searching judicial inquiry.

support for it. Here [Carolene Products] challenges the validity of the statute on its face and it is evident from all the considerations presented to Congress, and those of which we may take judicial notice, that the question is at least debatable whether commerce in filled milk should be left unregulated, or in some measure restricted, or wholly prohibited. As that decision was for Congress, neither the finding of a court arrived at by weighing the evidence, nor the verdict of a jury can be substituted for it.

*   *   *

Mr. Justice Black concurs in the result and in all of the opinion except the part marked "Third."

Mr. Justice McReynolds thinks that the judgment should be affirmed.

Mr. Justice Cardozo and Mr. Justice Reed took no part in the consideration or decision of this case.

Mr. Justice Butler, [concurring].

I concur in the result. Prima facie the facts alleged in the indictment are sufficient to constitute a violation of the statute. But they are not sufficient conclusively to establish guilt of the accused. At the trial it may introduce evidence to show that the declaration of the Act that the described product is injurious to public health and that the sale of it is a fraud upon the public are without any substantial foundation. The provisions on which the indictment rests should if possible be construed to avoid the serious question of constitutionality. If construed to exclude from interstate commerce wholesome food products that demonstrably are neither injurious to health nor calculated to deceive, they are repugnant to the Fifth Amendment. The allegation of the indictment that Milnut "is an adulterated article of food, injurious to the public health," tenders an issue of fact to be determined upon evidence.

NOTES AND QUESTIONS

1. Does the dichotomy between personal and economic liberties created in *Carolene Products* and maintained thereafter by the Court make sense? Since 1937, not a single law dealing with an economic question has been found invalid by the Court under substantive due process analysis. In *Williamson v. Lee Optical of Oklahoma*, 348 U.S. 483 (1955), for example, the Court upheld Oklahoma's requirement that only licensed optometrists and ophthalmologists could fit eyeglasses or replicate existing lenses, thus prohibiting opticians from replacing eyeglasses without a prescription and protecting optometrists and ophthalmologosists from competition. Noted the Court: "The day is gone when this Court uses the Due Process Clause of the Fourteenth Amendment to strike down state laws, regulatory of business and industrial conditions, because they may be unwise, improvident, or out of harmony with a particular school of thought." *But cf. BMW* *of North America, Inc. v. Gore*, 517 U.S. 559 (1996) (using due process to find a punitive damage award by a jury of $2 million for a scratched automobile to be "grossly excessive" discussed in Chapter Six). Didn't the natural law thinking of the founders understand government's primary purpose to be the preservation of property and the economic liberty or initiative that gives rise to it?

For an assessment of *Carolene Products* calling for its re-examination, see Geoffrey P. Miller, *The True Story of* Carolene Products, 1987 Sup. Ct. Rev. 397 (1987).

The Court further solidified its use of deferential rational-basis analysis for economic liberties cases in *Armour v. City of Indianapolis*, 132 S. Ct. 2073, 182 L. Ed. 2d 998 (2012), but not without a dissent by the Chief Justice and Justices Scalia and Alito. The City of Indianapolis had been operating its sewer-construction assessments under a plan whereby the property owners in a new-sewer area would each be assessed an equal amount. The property owners could pay the assessed amount in a lump sum up front or, if they so choose, by installment (with interest) for up to 30 years. Approximately one year into one particular sewer-construction project, the City changed its assessment scheme so that the vast majority of the sewer construction costs were borne by revenue from municipal bonds. With the changeover, the City notified the installment payers that they were under no obligation to make any further payments. The City, however, declined to return any of the monies of those property owners who had paid in a lump sum up front. The result was that 38 of the property owners (those who had chosen to pay up front) had to pay some $9,278 for their new sewers, whereas the other 142 property owners got their sewers for less than $1,000. The 38 property owners sued the City under an Equal Protection theory. Justice Breyer, writing for the 6-member majority, held that the City had a rational basis (*i.e.*, reducing its administrative costs) for treating the two groups of property owners differently.

Citing *Carolene Products* and its progeny, the Court meandered through several of its own past formulations of deferential rational-basis analysis:

> . . . [T]his case falls directly within the scope of our precedents holding such a law constitutionally valid if there is a plausible policy reason for the classification, the legislative facts on which the classification is apparently based rationally may have been considered to be true by the governmental decisionmaker, and the relationship of the classification to its goal is not so attenuated as to render the distinction arbitrary or irrational. . . . And it falls within the scope of our precedents holding that there is such a plausible reason if there is any reasonably conceivable state of facts that could provide a rational basis for the classification. . . .

> Moreover, analogous precedent warns us that we are not to pronounce this classification unconstitutional unless in the light of the facts made known or generally assumed it is of such a character as to preclude the assumption that it rests upon some rational basis within the knowledge and experience of the legislators. . . . Further, because the classification is presumed constitutional, the burden is on the one attacking the legislative arrangement to negative every conceivable basis which might support it. [Citations and quotation marks omitted.]

The Chief Justice, writing for the dissenters, relied on *Allegheny Pittsburgh Coal Co. v. Commission of Webster Cty.*, 488 U.S. 336 (1989). In *Allegheny Pittsburgh*, the Court had held that a county failed to comport with equal protection requirements when it assessed property taxes primarily on the basis of purchase price, with no appropriate adjustments over time, resulting in disparate assessments approximating the 9 to 1 ratio that is operative in the *Armour* case. *Allegheny Pittsburgh* had called that a "gross disparity" in tax levels. The majority, however, took note of the fact that *Allegheny Pittsburgh* was a "lone" case-law decision, influenced somewhat by a state constitutional provision demanding that taxation be equal and uniform.

2. *Slaughter-House* was earlier said to disregard natural rights, including the right to economic liberty, arguably intended to be protected by the Privileges or Immunities Clause. Does natural law originalism answer whether legislation like that in *Lochner, Nebbia*, and *Carolene Products* is valid or invalid? Perhaps one can argue that the natural law of the American founding operates on two levels: first, establishing economic liberty, and against unnecessary restraint in matters of trade or calling, as a privilege of citizenship, but second, that save for the exceptional case, such natural law precept is to be applied by the legislature, not the Court. In this way, might natural law be distinguished from noninterpretivism and the less consistent and uncharted course of the *Lochner* majority? If so, specific claims like the right to be free of particular educational requirements for a given occupational license cannot be said to arise inexorably from immutable aspects of human nature and justice. Burdensome or debateable occupational licensing requirements may be economically unwise, but such arguments are better aimed at the legislature. By contrast, the judiciary might be expected to safeguard the fundamental right of economic liberty, itself, where state imposed monopolies stand as insurmountable. As one writer put it well:

> [Natural law] principles and precepts[, like the injunction to seek the good or the proscription against killing or theft,] are incapable by themselves of governing action, — for different reasons, . . . : in the case of principles, because they specify only the end, and action depends on specification of means; in the case of precepts, because they specify the means only generally and without reference to the contingent circumstances which are always involved in action.

Harold R. McKinnon, *Natural Law and Positive Law*, 23 NOTRE DAME L. REV. 125, 134–35 (1948). It is the contingent circumstances that make rules the usual subject of positive law, and far different from principles and precepts. In this may also lie the difference between a fundamental privilege or immunity and a spuriously substantive due process violation. As Professor Philip Kurland observes: "only the privileges or immunities clause speaks to matters of substance; certainly the language of due process and equal protection does not." Philip B. Kurland, *The Privileges or Immunities Clause, "Its Hour Come Round at Last"?*, 1972 WASH. U. L.Q. 405, 406.

3. The manageability of judicial application of the Privileges or Immunities Clause, and the protection of economic liberty, may also increase over time as articulated by Justice Bradley in his dissent in *Slaughter-House*:

Like the prohibition against passing a law impairing the obligation of a contract, it would execute itself. The point would be regularly raised, in a suit at law, and settled by final reference to the Federal court. As the privileges and immunities protected are only those fundamental ones which belong to every citizen, they would soon become so far defined as to cause but a slight accumulation of business in the Federal courts. Besides, the recognized existence of the law would prevent its frequent violation.

83 U.S. at 123–24.

4.   Can the Court effectively balance a proper posture of judicial restraint with the needed protection of individual right? For one thoughtful suggestion, see Rosalie Berger Levinson, *Protection Against Government Abuse of Power: Has the Court Taken the Substance Out of Substantive Due Process?*, 16 U. Dayton L. Rev. 313 (1991) (discussing concerns that justify a narrow interpretation of substantive due process and proposing a balanced approach that maintains the guarantees of substantive due process while minimizing the impact on democratic policy).

Chapter 5

A GOVERNMENT COMMITMENT TO EQUALITY

The premise of equality is explicit in the Declaration of Independence ("all men are created equal"), and upon this premise the founders debunked the earlier notion that some were Divinely entitled to rule over others. Equality of human creation under God meant plainly that if law was to have binding authority it was to be premised upon the consent of the governed. If no one had an entitlement to rule, then assent to live under that rule would be needed. Of course, the noble premise of equality was besmirched in our national record by the institution of slavery. How the framers who knew slavery to be against natural and common law, as recorded in English cases, could tolerate this vast disregard of the human nature is a story of perhaps necessary political expediency in the forming of a union, but expediency nonetheless.

The original constitutional document is also anomalous by containing no explicit provision providing for equal treatment under law. This would not be added until after the Civil War and the Fourteenth Amendment ("No state shall . . . deny to any person within its jurisdiction the equal protection of the laws.") Even when added, the provision went largely ignored until the mid-20th century. To this day, the Constitution does not explicitly exact a promise of equality from the federal government, though such has been judicially required. *Bolling v. Sharpe*, 347 U.S. 497 (1954) (reading the Equal Protection Clause into the Fifth Amendment due process limitation on the federal government).

What the equal protection inquiry is about is the appropriateness of government classification. Most laws draw distinctions. For example, to obtain a work permit one frequently needs to be 16 or older. Thus, those under the age of 16 are being treated differently than the rest of the population. Similarly, those under the age of majority (18 or 21 in most jurisdictions) may be excused from contracts they enter into. These distinctions or classifications are almost always upheld so long as the government has some rational basis for them — *e.g.*, protecting children from work or economic commitment inconsistent with their age or maturity.

You will see that the equal protection analysis of the modern Court will often proceed in three steps: an identification of the classification, the application of the appropriate level of judicial scrutiny (deferential, intermediate, or strict), and an assessment of whether the government's explanation for the classification meets the applicable level of scrutiny. In this Chapter, we primarily concentrate on classifications that warrant either strict or intermediate scrutiny. For example, classifications based on race need a compelling governmental interest to survive this most careful review. Intermediate scrutiny is applicable to gender distinctions in law. This standard requires a lesser justification, but still an "important" one, and the government bears the burden of proving that its classification substantially advances that important justification. We will also take a look at classifications that affect an exercise of a fundamental right, namely, voting, and discover that the Court has crafted a special concept of numerical equality out of the Equal Protection Clause — namely, the guarantee of one person/one vote.

Most classifications under law not implicating a suspect classification like race or a fundamental right are reviewed under the rational basis standard. This is a highly deferential standard. The Court will uphold a statute or regulation if the Court can conceive of any legitimate governmental purpose served by the statute or regulation. The burden of proof is on those challenging such classification, and only rarely, as in the case of *Romer v. Evans* dealing with a sexual orientation classification, has the Court found it to be wanting. Thus, in *Hodel v. Irving*, 452 U.S. 314 (1981), the Court stated: "[s]ocial and economic legislation . . . that does not employ suspect classifications or impinge in fundamental rights must be upheld against equal protection attack when the legislative means are rationally related to a legitimate government purpose. Moreover, such legislation carries with it a presumption of rationality that can only be overcome by a clear showing of arbitrariness and irrationality." *Id.* at 331–332. In *Federal Communications Commission v. Beach Communications, Inc.*, 508 U.S. 307 (1993), the Court further illustrated its deference at this level by observing that "those attacking the rationality of the legislative classification have the burden to negate every conceivable basis which might support it." *Id.* at 315. Again, this is seldom accomplished, but not impossible, as we will see when we turn to *Bush v. Gore* in section B, and *Romer v. Evans* in Section D below and *Lawrence v. Texas* in Chapter 6. While it is rare for traditional equal protection review — that is, a case not involving either a suspect classification or implicating a fundamental right — to result in invalidation, a much different story exists with regard to the use of race as a class. Sadly, this was not always true. Prior to the Civil War, several provisions of the original Constitution protected the institution of slavery. Article I, section 9 prevented Congress from banning the importation of slaves before 1808. Article IV, section 2 — the so-called fugitive slave clause — required the return of escaping slaves. In *Prigg v. Pennsylvania*, 41 U.S. (16 Pet.) 539 (1842), discussed in the case below, the Court invalidated a state law that prohibited the use of force or violence to return an escaped slave.

A. RACE

1. Slavery

It is a difficult but necessary question: why did the United States, a nation founded on principles of natural law, tolerate such a terrible institution as chattel slavery? There is no easy answer to this question, but the readings that follow provide at least some basis on which to consider it.

RECORDS OF THE FEDERAL CONVENTION
(August 22, 1787)
[*2:369; Madison, 22 Aug.*]

[The convention continued the discussion of the text that would later become

Article 1, Section 9, Clause 1, which reads "The Migration or Importation of such Persons as any of the States now existing shall think proper to admit, shall not be prohibited by the Congress prior to the Year one thousand eight hundred and eight, but a Tax or duty may be imposed on such Importation, not exceeding ten dollars for each Person."]

Mr. Sherman was for leaving the clause as it stands. He disapproved of the slave trade: yet as the States were now possessed of the right to import slaves, as the public good did not require it to be taken from them, & as it was expedient to have as few objections as possible to the proposed scheme of Government, he thought it best to leave the matter as we find it. He observed that the abolition of slavery seemed to be going on in the U. S. & that the good sense of the several States would probably by degrees compleat it. He urged on the Convention the necessity of despatching its business.

Col. Mason. This infernal trafic originated in the avarice of British Merchants. The British Govt. constantly checked the attempts of Virginia to put a stop to it. The present question concerns not the importing States alone but the whole Union. The evil of having slaves was experienced during the late war. Had slaves been treated as they might have been by the Enemy, they would have proved dangerous instruments in their hands. But their folly dealt by the slaves, as it did by the Tories. He mentioned the dangerous insurrections of the slaves in Greece and Sicily; and the instructions given by Cromwell to the Commissioners sent to Virginia, to arm the servants & slaves, in case other means of obtaining its submission should fail. Maryland & Virginia he said had already prohibited the importation of slaves expressly. N. Carolina had done the same in substance. All this would be in vain if S. Carolina & Georgia be at liberty to import. The Western people are already calling out for slaves for their new lands; and will fill that Country with slaves if they can be got thro' S. Carolina & Georgia. Slavery discourages arts & manufactures. The poor despise labor when performed by slaves. They prevent the immigration of Whites, who really enrich & strengthen a Country. They produce the most pernicious effect on manners. Every master of slaves is born a petty tyrant. They bring the judgment of heaven on a Country. As nations can not be rewarded or punished in the next world they must be in this. By an inevitable chain of causes & effects providence punishes national sins, by national calamities. He lamented that some of our Eastern brethren had from a lust of gain embarked in this nefarious traffic. As to the States being in possession of the Right to import, this was the case with many other rights, now to be properly given up. He held it essential in every point of view, that the Genl. Govt. should have power to prevent the increase of slavery.

*   *   *

Mr. Pinkney — If slavery be wrong, it is justified by the example of all the world. He cited the case of Greece Rome & other antient States; the sanction given by France England, Holland & other modern States. In all ages one half of mankind have been slaves. If the S. States were let alone they will probably of themselves stop importations. He wd. himself as a Citizen of S. Carolina vote for it. An attempt to take away the right as proposed will produce serious objections to the Constitution which he wished to see adopted.

General Pinkney declared it to be his firm opinion that if himself& all his colleagues were to sign the Constitution & use their personal influence, it would be of no avail towards obtaining the assent of their Constituents. S. Carolina & Georgia cannot do without slaves. As to Virginia she will gain by stopping the importations. Her slaves will rise in value, & she has more than she wants. It would be unequal to require S. C. & Georgia to confederate on such unequal terms. He said the Royal assent before the Revolution had never been refused to S. Carolina as to Virginia. He contended that the importation of slaves would be for the interest of the whole Union. The more slaves, the more produce to employ the carrying trade; The more consumption also, and the more of this, the more of revenue for the common treasury. He admitted it to be reasonable that slaves should be dutied like other imports, but should consider a rejection of the clause as an exclusion of S. Carola from the Union.

* * *

Mr. Dickenson considered it as inadmissible on every principle of honor & safety that the importation of slaves should be authorized to the States by the Constitution. The true question was whether the national happiness would be promoted or impeded by the importation, and this question ought to be left to the National Govt. not to the States particularly interested. If Engd. & France permit slavery, slaves are at the same time excluded from both those Kingdoms. Greece and Rome were made unhappy by their slaves. He could not believe that the Southn. States would refuse to confederate on the account apprehended; especially as the power was not likely to be immediately exercised by the Genl. Government.

* * *

Mr. Rutlidge. If the Convention thinks that N. C; S. C. & Georgia will ever agree to the plan, unless their right to import slaves be untouched, the expectation is vain. The people of those States will never be such fools as to give up so important an interest. He was strenuous agst. striking out the Section, and seconded the motion of Genl. Pinkney for a commitment.

* * *

Mr. Randolph was for committing in order that some middle ground might, if possible, be found. He could never agree to the clause as it stands. He wd. sooner risk the constitution — He dwelt on the dilemma to which the Convention was exposed. By agreeing to the clause, it would revolt the Quakers, the Methodists, and many others in the States having no slaves. On the other hand, two States might be lost to the Union.

PENNSYLVANIA RATIFYING CONVENTION
December 3–4, 1787
Remarks of James Wilson, Elliot 2:451–53, 484–86

With respect to the clause restricting Congress from prohibiting the *migration or importation of such persons* as any of the states now existing shall think proper to admit, prior to the year 1808, the honorable gentleman says that this clause is not only dark, but intended to grant to Congress, for that time, the power to admit the importation of *slaves*. No such thing was intended. But I will tell you what was done, and it gives me high pleasure that so much was done. Under the present Confederation, the states may admit the importation of slaves as long as they please; but by this article, after the year 1808, the Congress will have power to prohibit such importation, notwithstanding the disposition of any state to the contrary. I consider this as laying the foundation for banishing slavery out of this country; and though the period is more distant than I could wish, yet it will produce the same kind, gradual change, which was pursued in Pennsylvania. It is with much satisfaction I view this power in the general government, whereby they may lay an interdiction on this reproachful trade: but an immediate advantage is also obtained; for a tax or duty may be imposed on such importation, not exceeding ten dollars for each person; and this, sir, operates as a partial prohibition; it was all that could be obtained. I am sorry it was no more; but from this I think there is reason to hope, that yet a few years, and it will be prohibited altogether; and in the mean time, the *new* states which are to be formed will be under *the control* of Congress in this particular, and slaves will never be introduced amongst them. The gentleman says that it is unfortunate in another point of view: it means to prohibit the introduction of white people from Europe, as this tax may deter them from coming amongst us. A little impartiality and attention will discover the care that the Convention took in selecting their language. The words are, "the migration or importation of such persons, &c., shall not be prohibited by Congress prior to the year 1808, but a tax or duty may be imposed on such importation." It is observable here that the term *migration* is dropped, when a tax or duty is mentioned, so that Congress have power to impose the tax only on those imported.

FEDERALIST No. 42 (Madison)

It were doubtless to be wished that the power of prohibiting the importation of slaves, had not been postponed until the year 1808, or rather that it had been suffered to have immediate operation. But it is not difficult to account either for this restriction on the general government, or for the manner in which the whole clause is expressed. It ought to be considered as a great point gained in favor of humanity, that a period of twenty years may terminate for ever within these States, a traffic which has so long and so loudly upbraided the barbarism of modern policy; that within that period it will receive a considerable discouragement from the foederal Government, and may be totally abolished by a concurrence of the few States which continue the unnatural traffic, in the prohibitory example which has been given by so great a majority of the Union. Happy would it be for the unfortunate Africans, if an equal prospect lay before them, of being redeemed from the oppressions of their European brethren! Attempts have been made to pervert this clause into an objection against the Constitution, by representing it on one side as a criminal toleration of an illicit practice, and on another, as calculated to prevent voluntary and beneficial emigrations from Europe to America. I mention these misconstructions, not with a view to give them an answer, for they deserve none; but as specimens of the manner and spirit in which some have thought fit to conduct their opposition to the proposed government.

In the years following the ratification of the Constitution, debates developed about the admission of new slave states and new free states — because either admission would alter the balance of power in the Senate and the House. Eventually, the pro-slavery and anti-slavery factions came to an understanding: those new states north of the southern border of Missouri would be free states, and those new states south of it would be slave states. Under this "Missouri Compromise," Congress attempted to admit Missouri as a state on condition that slavery be kept out of the new territories north of latitude 36 degrees, 30 minutes. Dred Scott was born a slave in Virginia around 1799. In 1830, Dred Scott and his master moved to Missouri, which was a slave state. Four years later, a surgeon in the U.S. army named Dr. John Emerson bought Scott and moved him to the free state of Illinois. In 1836, Scott and Emerson moved to Fort Snelling, Wisconsin Territory. The Missouri Compromise prohibited slavery in this territory. That same year, Scott married a slave named Harriet. In 1838, the Emersons and the Scotts moved back to Missouri where the Scotts had two daughters. Emerson died in 1843 and left his possessions, including the Scotts, to his widow Irene. In 1846, Scott asked Mrs. Emerson if he could work for his freedom. Mrs. Emerson refused.

Scott sued Mrs. Emerson in a Missouri court for "false imprisonment" and battery. Scott argued that he was being held illegally because he had become a free man as soon as he had lived in a free state. He claimed he was taken to a slave state against his will. Many slaves had sued their owners in this way and won their freedom in the past. In 1847, Emerson won in the Missouri Circuit court based on a legal error. Scott's lawyers failed to prove that she was holding Scott as a slave. Scott's lawyers moved successfully for a new trial.

By the time the new case went to trial in 1850, Mrs. Emerson had moved to Massachusetts leaving her brother, John Sanford, in charge of Scott's case. The jury agreed that Scott and his family should be freed in accordance with the doctrine "once free, always free." The case was appealed to the Missouri Supreme Court in 1852, where breaking with its own precedent, two of the three judges found for Emerson and Sanford. William Scott wrote the decision of the court, stating that states have the power to refuse to enforce the laws of other states.

Sanford was legally recognized as Scott's owner in 1853. Sanford moved to New York, leaving the Scotts in Missouri. Scott filed a new lawsuit in federal court based on their diversity of citizenship. The clerk of the federal court mistakenly added a letter to Sanford's name, so the case permanently became *Dred Scott v. John F.A. Sandford*.

In 1854, the U.S. Court for the District of Missouri heard the case. John Sanford argued that the federal court lacked jurisdiction since Dred Scott was not a citizen. Judge Wells disagreed, but then on the merits instructed the jury to apply only the laws of Missouri in its decision. The jury found in favor of Sanford, and Dred Scott appealed to the Supreme Court of the United States.

Some historians believe that Chief Justice Taney hoped that his decision in the Dred Scott case would help prevent, not create, future disputes over slavery. Scott lost, and so did a Nation unable to come to terms with its natural law principles.

SCOTT v. SANDFORD
60 U.S. (19 How.) 393 (1856)

(excerpted for clarity)

MR. CHIEF JUSTICE TANEY delivered the opinion of the court.

* * *

[Was Scott a citizen?]

. . . Can a negro, whose ancestors were imported into this country, and sold as slaves, become a member of the political community formed and brought into existence by the Constitution of the United States, and as such become entitled to all the rights, and privileges, and immunities, guarantied by that instrument to the citizen? One of which rights is the privilege of suing in a court of the United States in the cases specified in the Constitution.

We think they [people of African ancestry] are not [citizens], and that they are not included, and were not intended to be included, under the word "citizens" in the Constitution, and can therefore claim none of the rights and privileges which that instrument provides for and secures to citizens of the United States.

[Were slaves people within the terms of the Declaration?]

. . . [T]he legislation and histories of the times, and the language used in the Declaration of Independence, show, that neither the class of persons who had been imported as slaves, nor their descendants, whether they had become free or not, were then acknowledged as a part of the people, nor intended to be included in the general words used in that memorable instrument.

For if they were so received, and entitled to the privileges and immunities of citizens, it would exempt them from the operation of the special laws and from the police regulations which they considered to be necessary for their own safety. It would give to persons of the negro race, who were recognized as citizens in any one State of the Union, the right to enter every other State whenever they pleased . . . to go where they pleased at every hour of the day or night without molestation, unless they committed some violation of law for which a white man would be punished; and it would give them the full liberty of speech in public and in private upon all subjects upon which its own citizens might speak; to hold public meetings upon political affairs, and to keep and carry arms wherever they went. And all of this would be done in the face of the subject race of the same color, both free and slaves, and inevitably producing discontent and insubordination among them, and endangering the peace and safety of the State.

[Did Congress have authority to pass the Missouri Compromise?]

The act of Congress, upon which the plaintiff relies, declares that slavery and involuntary servitude, except as a punishment for crime, shall be forever prohibited in all that part of the territory ceded by France, under the name of Louisiana, which lies north of thirty-six degrees thirty minutes north latitude, and not included within the limits of Missouri. And the difficulty which meets us at the threshold of this part of the inquiry is, whether Congress was authorized to pass this law under any of the powers granted to it by the Constitution; for if the authority is not given by that instrument, it is the duty of this court to declare it void and inoperative, and incapable of conferring freedom upon any one who is held as a slave under the laws of any one of the States.

There is certainly no power given by the Constitution to the Federal Government to establish or maintain colonies bordering on the United States or at a distance, to be ruled and governed at its own pleasure; nor to enlarge its territorial limits in any way, except by the admission of new States. That power is plainly given; and if a new State is admitted, it needs no further legislation by Congress, because the Constitution itself defines the relative rights and powers, and duties of the State, and the citizens of the State, and the Federal Government. But no power is given to acquire a Territory to be held and governed permanently in that character.

. . . [I]t may be safely assumed that citizens of the United States who migrate to a Territory belonging to the people of the United States, cannot be ruled as mere colonists, dependent upon the will of the General Government, and to be governed by any laws it may think proper to impose. The principle upon which our Governments rests is the union of States, sovereign and independent within their own limits in . . . their internal and domestic concerns, and bound together as one people by a General Government, possessing certain enumerated and restricted powers, delegated to it by the people of the several States. . . .

[If Scott is no longer a slave, has private property been taken?]

. . . [T]he rights of private property have been guarded with . . . care. Thus the rights of property are united with the rights of person, and placed on the same ground by the Fifth Amendment to the Constitution, which provides that no person shall be deprived of life, liberty, and property, without due process of law. And an act of Congress which deprives a citizen of the United States of his liberty or property, merely because he came himself or brought his property into a particular Territory of the United States, and who had committed no offence against the laws, could hardly be dignified with the name of due process of law.

*   *   *

Mr. Justice McLean, dissenting.

*   *   *

There is no averment in this plea which shows or conduces to show an inability in the plaintiff to sue. . . . He [Scott] is averred to have had a negro ancestry, but this does not show that he is not a citizen of Missouri, within the meaning of the act of Congress authorizing him to sue in the Circuit Court. It has never been held necessary, to constitute a citizen within the act, that he should have the qualifications of an elector. Females and minors may sue in the Federal courts, and so may any individual who has a permanent domicile in the State under whose laws his rights are protected, and to which he owes allegiance.

Being born under our Constitution and laws, no naturalization is required, as one of foreign birth, to make him a citizen. The most general and appropriate definition of the term citizen is "a freeman." Being a freeman, and having his domicile in a State different from that of the defendant, he is a citizen within the act of Congress, and the courts of the Union are open to him.

In the great and leading case of *Prigg v. The State of Pennsylvania* [(1842)], this court say that, by the general law of nations, no nation is bound to recognize the state of slavery, as found within its territorial dominions, where it is in opposition to its own policy and institutions, in favor of the subjects of other nations where slavery is organized. If it does it, it is as a matter of comity, and not as a matter of international right. The state of slavery is deemed to be a mere municipal regulation, founded upon and limited to the range of the territorial laws. This was fully recognized in *Somersett's case* [(1772)], which was decided before the American Revolution.

*   *   *

I will now consider the relation which the Federal Government bears to slavery in the States:

Slavery is emphatically a State institution. In the ninth section of the first article of the Constitution, it is provided "that the migration or importation of such persons as any of the States now existing shall think proper to admit, shall not be prohibited by the Congress prior to the year 1808, but a tax or duty may be imposed on such importation, not exceeding ten dollars for each person."

In the Convention, it was proposed by a committee of eleven to limit the importation of slaves to the year 1800, when Mr. Pinckney moved to extend the time to the year 1808. This motion was carried. . . . In opposition to the motion, Mr. Madison said: "Twenty years will produce all the mischief that can be apprehended from the liberty to import slaves; so long a term will be more dishonorable to the American character than to say nothing about it in the Constitution."

The provision in regard to the slave trade shows clearly that Congress considered slavery a State institution, to be continued and regulated by its individual sovereignty; and to conciliate that interest, the slave trade was continued twenty years, not as a general measure, but for the "benefit of such States as shall think proper to encourage it."

*   *   *

In the formation of the Federal Constitution, care was taken to confer no power on the Federal Government to interfere with this institution in the States. In the provision respecting the slave trade, in fixing the ratio of representation, and providing for the reclamation of fugitives from labor, slaves were referred to as persons, and in no other respect are they considered in the Constitution.

We need not refer to the mercenary spirit which introduced the infamous traffic in slaves, to show the degradation of negro slavery in our country. This system was imposed upon our colonial settlements by the mother country, and it is due to truth to say that the commercial colonies and States were chiefly engaged in the traffic. But we know as a historical fact, that James Madison, that great and good man, a leading member in the Federal Convention, was solicitous to guard the language of that instrument so as not to convey the idea that there could be property in man.

I prefer the lights of Madison, Hamilton, and Jay, as a means of construing the Constitution in all its bearings, rather than to look behind that period, into a traffic which is now declared to be piracy, and punished with death by Christian nations. I do not like to draw the sources of our domestic relations from so dark a ground. Our independence was a great epoch in the history of freedom; and while I admit the Government was not made especially for the colored race, yet many of them were citizens of the New England States, and exercised the rights of suffrage when the Constitution was adopted, and it was not doubted by any intelligent person that its tendencies would greatly ameliorate their condition.

Many of the States, on the adoption of the Constitution, or shortly afterward, took measures to abolish slavery within their respective jurisdictions; and it is a well-known fact that a belief was cherished by the leading men, South as well as North, that the institution of slavery would gradually decline, until it would become extinct. The increased value of slave labor, in the culture of cotton and sugar, prevented the realization of this expectation. Like all other communities and States, the South were influenced by what they considered to be their own interests.

* * *

On the 13th of July, the Ordinance of 1787 was passed, "for the government of the United States territory northwest of the river Ohio," with but one dissenting vote. This instrument provided there should be organized in the territory not less than three nor more than five States, designating their boundaries. It was passed while the Federal Convention was in session, about two months before the Constitution was adopted by the Convention. The members of the Convention must therefore have been well acquainted with the provisions of the Ordinance. It provided for a temporary Government, as initiatory to the formation of State Governments. Slavery was prohibited in the territory.

* * *

If Congress may establish a Territorial Government in the exercise of its discretion, it is a clear principle that a court cannot control that discretion. This being the case, I do not see on what ground the act [Missouri Compromise] is held [by the Supreme Court majority's opinion in the *Scott* case] to be void. It did not purport to forfeit property, or take it for public purposes. It only prohibited slavery; in doing which, it followed the ordinance of 1787.

* * *

When Dred Scott, his wife and children, were removed from Fort Snelling to Missouri, in 1838, they were free, as the law was then settled, and continued for fourteen years afterwards, up to 1852, when the above decision was made. Prior to this, for nearly thirty years, as Chief Justice Gamble declares, the residence of a master with his slave in the State of Illinois, or in the Territory north of Missouri, where slavery was prohibited by the act called the Missouri compromise, would manumit the slave as effectually as if he had executed a deed of emancipation. . . . Such was the settled law of Missouri until the decision of [*Dred*] *Scott* [*v.*] *Emerson.*

NOTES AND QUESTIONS

1. You have just read excerpts from one of the most important constitutional law decisions ever rendered, and the one believed by nearly every constitutional law professor to have been decided egregiously wrongly. Note that Chief Justice Taney's majority opinion has two important foci — (1) the question whether Dred Scott, even if he were not a slave, was a citizen of the United States qualified to bring a lawsuit in a federal court, and (2) the question whether Congress possessed the power to forbid slavery in the territories. Chief Justice Taney addresses a third question, whether Scott's temporary residence in Illinois, a free state, could give him his freedom, but that question turns on the interpretation of Missouri law, and is not as important as the other two questions, which can only be answered by reference to the first principles involved in our constitutional order.

2. Consider the first question — was Dred Scott a "citizen" as that word was employed in the constitutional and statutory provisions which permitted "citizens" of different states to bring suit in federal courts? Taney says, "No," because he finds that even free blacks were not regarded as members of the body which originally made up "the people of the United States." Who has the better of this argument, Taney or the dissent? Note the dissent's evidence on the point — principally that there were several states at the time of the Constitution which permitted blacks to vote, and who accorded them full state citizenship. Does this successfully meet Taney's argument? How does he come to grips with this problem? Why did seven out of the nine Justices apparently agree with Taney? Would you be surprised to learn that in late 1997, no member of *H-Law*, the legal history Internet discussion list, was able to produce a single pre-Civil War decision in which a free black or a woman was permitted to bring suit as a plaintiff? Did this mean that Taney got the "citizenship" question right — at least as a matter of law?

3. Generally speaking, those who have condemned the *Dred Scott* opinion have done so because of what they have found to be the racist attitudes manifested by Chief Justice Taney and his brethren. Was Taney a racist? Do his views on the merits or demerits of members of the African American race influence his opinion? Does he claim that they do? Moreover, does he believe that current attitudes toward blacks should determine the constitutional law questions involved? What then should? Why was it so important that the questions at issue in *Dred Scott* be settled? Perhaps you have learned enough American history to know that during the years 1830 to 1860 the United States was roiled in sectional controversy over many issues relating to slavery, and, in particular, whether slavery ought to be allowed in the Territories, those lands, principally acquired through purchase from foreign governments, that would eventually become states. Indeed, perhaps it is not too much to say that *Scott v. Sanford* is not just about the claims to freedom of a particular former slave, but is about the continued validity of the institution of slavery itself.

4. Is slavery constitutional? At one level this is a fatuous question, since the Constitution very clearly provides both for the counting of unfree persons in determining representation in Congress and also for the return of fugitive slaves ("persons held to service"). Indeed, were it not for these nods in the direction of the legitimacy of Southern slavery, the Constitution would never have been ratified in the Southern states. At another level, however, even the Constitution itself implicitly condemns slavery, as it carries the potential for the eventual restriction of the slave trade. During debate over the Missouri compromise, some members of Congress argued that the Article IV Guarantee Clause codified the Declaration's mandate of government by consent and therefore barred the spread of slavery beyond the original states where it was protected by the Constitution's compromises. *See* John C. Eastman, *The Declaration of Independence as Viewed from the States, in* SCOTT GERBER, ED., THE DECLARATION OF INDEPENDENCE: ORIGINS AND IMPACT (Congressional Quarterly Press 2002). There were also plenty of Northern abolitionists who argued that slavery violated a higher natural law than the Constitution, and that even the Constitution itself could not justify it. Many of these abolitionists were willing to and did risk injury and death for their views. Their argument, essentially, was that slavery was against natural law and the law of God. Is this a somewhat problematic argument, since the Bible itself references slavery, without denunciation? Of course, perhaps the Bible's references to slavery are simply that whatever one's status, slave or free, it is irrelevant to one's religious duty. The common law, as an embodiment of natural law applied to human circumstance, is far more explicitly condemning of slavery. You will have already noticed the statement quoted from Lord Mansfield's famous opinion in *Somerset v. Stewart*, 98 Eng. Rep. 499, 510 (K.B. 1772):

> The state of slavery is of such a nature, that it is incapable of being introduced on any reasons, moral or political; but only positive law, which preserves its force long after the reasons, occasion, and time itself from whence it was created, is erased from memory: it's so odious, that nothing can be suffered to support it, but positive law.

Lord Mansfield, after uttering these words, freed a black man who had been held as a slave in Virginia and brought to England temporarily by his Virginia master. The gist of Mansfield's holding was that since slavery was not permitted in England, Somerset had to be set free. Mansfield's words and his holding were influential in several American decisions, and his views gave comfort to the enemies of slavery right up to the Civil War. Mansfield's views were declared to be the law of America, as well, in Justice Story's influential treatise, COMMENTARIES ON THE CONFLICT OF LAWS § 96 (Boston, Little, Brown & Co. 4th ed. 1852), and Story clearly believed that slavery was contrary to the law of nations, which he believed to be founded on natural law. *See also* Story's opinion in *United States v. The La Jeune Eugenie*, 26 F. Cas. 832, 846 (C.C.D. Mass. 1822) (No. 15,551).

5. Why, then, if slavery was contrary to the law of nations and the law of nature, does Taney determine that Congress is barred from ensuring that the basic postulate of the law of nature, the equality of all men, whatever their race, is enforced in the territories? What does Taney mean when he says that there is no "law of nations" standing between a slaveholder and his property? Doesn't the law of nations, as part of the common law, have force in America, even as an implicit part of the Constitution? And doesn't this mean that property in slaves might be dealt with on a different footing than other property? In other words, even if the Due Process Clause of the Fifth Amendment might bar Congress from depriving persons of all of their property merely because they chose to live in a territory, might property in slaves still be singled out for different treatment, since such property was condemned by the law of nations and the law of nature? You will have noticed that this is a point made by both of the dissenters in the case. Why isn't it persuasive to Taney? Remember that Taney's philosophy of constitutional interpretation is "original understanding." Is his opinion with regard to the Due Process Clause consistent with this constitutional philosophy? At the end of the 18th century virtually all federal jurists would have said that the common law (with its attendant law of nations and law of nature) was a part of the Constitution. When Taney ignores or seems unaware of this, isn't he betraying his own jurisprudence? Do members of the modern Court who subscribe to original understanding without reference to natural law commit the same error?

6. Whatever the correctness of Taney's views, his opinion served as a bloody shirt for anti-slavery advocates, who saw in it the potential for the establishment of slavery — by the Court — in all the states. Was this a fair reading of the opinion? You may remember Abraham Lincoln's famous statement about how a "house divided" could not stand, and consequently the country could not endure forever half slave and half free — it had to become entirely one or the other. Can you understand why some people believe that *Scott v. Sanford* caused the Civil War? Lincoln not only condemned the *Dred Scott* opinion in his famous debates with Judge Douglas in 1858, but boldly took the position that the Declaration of Independence's words had to be read to apply to blacks as well as whites — a position which you will remember Taney rejected. For these debates, which established Lincoln's reputation and eventually made him a nominee for President, *see, e.g.*, CREATED EQUAL? THE COMPLETE LINCOLN-DOUGLAS DEBATES OF 1858 (Paul M. Angle ed., 1958).

7. Both those who fought for the South in defense of their "peculiar institution" and those who fought for the North against slavery and for Union believed that they had God on their side. The North emerged victorious, and in the debates over the Post-Civil War Amendments, which eventually abolished slavery (the Thirteenth Amendment), and made blacks citizens (the Fourteenth Amendment), their advocates referred often to the natural law of human equality. The Thirteenth Amendment at first foundered in the House of Representatives in 1864, and its opponents, such as Representative C.A. White, argued that an Amendment overruling slavery would be "unconstitutional" because of the Constitution's foundation in the positive law of property (an argument not unlike that of Justice Taney). The Thirteenth Amendment was finally passed by Congress in 1865, and ratified by the requisite three quarters majority of the states, but only after such

ratification was, in effect, demanded by President Johnson in the exercise of his powers as commander-in-chief over the still subjugated Southern states. Eventually the Fourteenth Amendment was similarly passed under threats, this time as a condition of readmission to the Union for the Southern states. From that time to this, some Southern partisans and others have argued that the Reconstruction Amendments ought to be of suspect validity, since they were, in effect, "passed at gunpoint." Perhaps their grounding in American common law, and natural law theories of equality have never allowed this "gunpoint" argument to gain much headway. Did the Thirteenth Amendment, the Civil Rights Act of 1866 (which gave the newly freed blacks the property and contract rights of their white fellow Americans), and the Fourteenth Amendment (designed, at least in part, to give a firmer constitutional basis to the 1866 Civil Rights Act) finally win equality for African Americans? The following cases explore this problem.

8. Those wishing to examine further Taney's and the dissenters' constitutional theories should begin with the recent brilliant article by Mark A. Graber, *Desperately Ducking Slavery*: Dred Scott *and Contemporary Constitutional Theory*, 14 CONST. COMMENTARY 271 (1997), which builds a dispassionate case for the correctness of Taney's views, but which also suggests the validity of some of the views of the dissenters, and gives a full summary of current constitutional theorists' inability to analyze the case on its own terms.

2. Civil Rights and Non-Discrimination

PLESSY v. FERGUSON
163 U.S. 537 (1896)

MR. JUSTICE BROWN . . . delivered the opinion of the court.

This case turns upon the constitutionality of an act of the General Assembly of the State of Louisiana, passed in 1890, providing for separate railway carriages for the white and colored races.

The first section of the statute enacts "that all railway companies carrying passengers in their coaches in this State, shall provide equal but separate accommodations for the white, and colored races, by providing two or more passenger coaches for each passenger train, or by dividing the passenger coaches by a partition so as to secure separate accommodations: . . . No person or persons, shall be admitted to occupy seats in coaches, other than the ones assigned to them, on account of the race they belong to."

By the second section it was enacted "that the officers of such passenger trains shall have power and are hereby required to assign each passenger to the coach or compartment used for the race to which such passenger belongs; any passenger insisting on going into a coach or compartment to which by race he does not belong, shall be liable to a fine of twenty-five dollars, or in lieu thereof to imprisonment for a period of not more than twenty days in the parish prison, and any officer of any railroad insisting on assigning a passenger to a coach or compartment other than the one set aside for the race to which said passenger belongs, shall be liable to a fine of twenty-five dollars, or in lieu thereof to imprisonment for a period of not more than twenty days in the parish prison; and should any passenger refuse to occupy the coach or compartment to which he or she is assigned by the officer of such railway, said officer shall have power to refuse to carry such passenger on his train, and for such refusal neither he nor the railway company which he represents shall be liable for damages in any of the courts of this State."

The third section . . . [includes] a proviso that "nothing in this act shall be construed as applying to nurses attending children of the other race." . . .

The information filed in the criminal District Court charged in substance that Plessy, being a passenger between two stations within the State of Louisiana, was assigned by officers of the company to the coach used for the race to which he belonged, but he insisted upon going into a coach used by the race to which he did not belong. Neither in the information nor plea was his particular race or color averred.

*   *   *

The constitutionality of this act is attacked upon the ground that it conflicts both with the Thirteenth Amendment of the Constitution, abolishing slavery, and the Fourteenth Amendment, which prohibits certain restrictive legislation on the part of the States.

1. That it does not conflict with the Thirteenth Amendment, which abolished slavery and involuntary servitude, except as a punishment for crime, is too clear for argument. Slavery implies involuntary servitude — a state of bondage; the ownership of mankind as a chattel, or at least the control of the labor and services of one man for the benefit of another, and the absence of a legal right to the disposal of his own person, property and services. This amendment was said in the *Slaughter-House Cases* [(1872)], to have been intended primarily to abolish slavery, as it had been previously known in this country, and that it equally forbade Mexican peonage or the Chinese coolie trade, when they amounted to slavery or involuntary servitude, and that the use of the word "servitude" was intended to prohibit the use of all forms of involuntary slavery, of whatever class or name. It was intimated, however, in that case that this amendment was regarded by the statesmen of that day as insufficient to protect the colored race from certain laws which had been enacted in the Southern States, imposing upon the colored race onerous disabilities and burdens, and curtailing their rights in the pursuit of life, liberty and property to such an extent that their freedom was of little value; and that the Fourteenth Amendment was devised to meet this exigency.

So, too, in the *Civil Rights Cases* [(1883)], it was said that the act of a mere individual, the owner of an inn, a public conveyance or place of amusement, refusing accommodations to colored people, cannot be justly regarded as imposing any badge of slavery or servitude upon the applicant, but only as involving an ordinary civil injury, properly cognizable by the laws of the State, and presumably subject to redress by those laws until the contrary appears. . . .

A statute which implies merely a legal distinction between the white and colored races — a distinction which is founded in the color of the two races, and which must always exist so long as white men are distinguished from the other race by color —

has no tendency to destroy the legal equality of the two races, or re-establish a state of involuntary servitude. . . .

2. By the Fourteenth Amendment, all persons born or naturalized in the United States, and subject to the jurisdiction thereof, are made citizens of the United States and of the State wherein they reside; and the States are forbidden from making or enforcing any law which shall abridge the privileges or immunities of citizens of the United States, or shall deprive any person of life, liberty or property without due process of law, or deny to any person within their jurisdiction the equal protection of the laws.

The proper construction of this amendment was first called to the attention of this court in the *Slaughter-House Cases*, which involved, however, not a question of race, but one of exclusive privileges. The case did not call for any expression of opinion as to the exact rights it was intended to secure to the colored race, but it was said generally that its main purpose was to establish the citizenship of the negro; to give definitions of citizenship of the United States and of the States, and to protect from the hostile legislation of the States the privileges and immunities of citizens of the United States, as distinguished from those of citizens of the States.

The object of the amendment was undoubtedly to enforce the absolute equality of the two races before the law, but in the nature of things it could not have been intended to abolish distinctions based upon color, or to enforce social, as distinguished from political equality, or a commingling of the two races upon terms unsatisfactory to either. Laws permitting, and even requiring, their separation in places where they are liable to be brought into contact do not necessarily imply the inferiority of either race to the other, and have been generally, if not universally, recognized as within the competency of the state legislatures in the exercise of their police power. The most common instance of this is connected with the establishment of separate schools for white and colored children, which has been held to be a valid exercise of the legislative power even by courts of States where the political rights of the colored race have been longest and most earnestly enforced.

One of the earliest of these cases is that of *Roberts v. City of Boston* [(Mass. 1849)], in which the Supreme Judicial Court of Massachusetts held that the general school committee of Boston had power to make provision for the instruction of colored children in separate schools established exclusively for them, and to prohibit their attendance upon the other schools. "The great principle," said Chief Justice Shaw, "advanced by the learned and eloquent advocate for the plaintiff," [Mr. Charles Sumner,] "is, that by the constitution and laws of Massachusetts, all persons without distinction of age or sex, birth or color, origin or condition, are equal before the law. . . . But, when this great principle comes to be applied to the actual and various conditions of persons in society, it will not warrant the assertion, that men and women are legally clothed with the same civil and political powers, and that children and adults are legally to have the same functions and be subject to the same treatment; but only that the rights of all, as they are settled and regulated by law, are equally entitled to the paternal consideration and protection of the law for their maintenance and security." It was held that the powers of the committee extended to the establishment of separate schools for children of different ages, sexes and colors. . . . Similar laws have been enacted by Congress under its general power of legislation over the District of Columbia, as well as by the legislatures of many of the States, and have been generally, if not uniformly, sustained by the courts.

Laws forbidding the intermarriage of the two races may be said in a technical sense to interfere with the freedom of contract, and yet have been universally recognized as within the police power of the State.

The distinction between laws interfering with the political equality of the negro and those requiring the separation of the two races in schools, theatres and railway carriages has been frequently drawn by this court. Thus in *Strauder v. West Virginia* [(1879)], it was held that a law of West Virginia limiting to white male persons, 21 years of age and citizens of the State, the right to sit upon juries, was a discrimination which implied a legal inferiority in civil society, which lessened the security of the right of the colored race, and was a step toward reducing them to a condition of servility. Indeed, the right of a colored man that, in the selection of jurors to pass upon his life, liberty and property, there shall be no exclusion of his race, and no discrimination against them because of color, has been asserted in a number of cases. So, where the laws of a particular locality or the charter of a particular railway corporation has provided that no person shall be excluded from the cars on account of color, we have held that this meant that persons of color should travel in the same car as white ones, and that the enactment was not satisfied by the company's providing cars assigned exclusively to people of color, though they were as good as those which they assigned exclusively to white persons.

Upon the other hand, where a statute of Louisiana required those engaged in the transportation of passengers among the States to give to all persons travelling within that State, upon vessels employed in that business, equal rights and privileges in all parts of the vessel, without distinction on account of race or color, and subjected to an action for damages the owner of such a vessel, who excluded colored passengers on account of their color from the cabin set aside by him for the use of whites, it was held to be so far as it applied to interstate commerce, unconstitutional and void. The court in this case, however, expressly disclaimed that it had anything whatever to do with the statute as a regulation of internal commerce, or affecting anything else than commerce among the States.

In the *Civil Rights Cases*, it was held that an act of Congress, entitling all persons within the jurisdiction of the United States to the full and equal enjoyment of the accommodations, advantages, facilities and privileges of inns, public convey-ances, on land or water, theatres and other places of public amusement, and made applicable to citizens of every race and color, regardless of any previous condition of servitude, was unconstitutional and void, upon the ground that the Fourteenth Amendment was prohibitory upon the States only, and the legislation authorized to be adopted by Congress for enforcing it was not direct legislation on matters respecting which the States were prohibited from making or enforcing certain laws, or doing certain acts, but was corrective legislation, such as might be necessary or proper for counteracting and redressing the effect of such laws or acts. In delivering the opinion of the court Mr. Justice Bradley observed that the Fourteenth Amendment "does not invest Congress with power to legislate upon subjects that are within the domain of state legislation; but to provide modes of relief against state legislation, or state action, of the kind referred to. It does not authorize Congress to create a code of municipal law for the regulation of private rights; but to provide modes of redress against the operation of state laws, and the action of state officers, executive or judicial, when these are subversive of the fundamental rights specified in the amendment. Positive rights and privileges are undoubtedly secured by the Fourteenth Amendment; but they are secured by way of prohibition against state laws and state proceedings affecting those rights and privileges, and by power given to Congress to legislate for the purpose of carrying such prohibition into effect; and such legislation must necessarily be predicated upon such supposed state laws or state proceedings, and be directed to the correction of their operation and effect."

Much nearer, and, indeed, almost directly in point, is the case of the *Louisville, New Orleans &c. Railway v. Mississippi* [(1890)], wherein the railway company was indicted for a violation of a statute of Mississippi, enacting that all railroads carrying passengers should provide equal, but separate, accommodations for the white and colored races, by providing two or more passenger cars for each passenger train, or by dividing the passenger cars by a partition, so as to secure separate accommodations. The case was presented in a different aspect from the one under consideration, inasmuch as it was an indictment against the railway company for failing to provide the separate accommodations, but the question considered was the constitutionality of the law. In that case, the Supreme Court of Mississippi had held that the statute applied solely to commerce within the State, and, that being the construction of the state statute by its highest court, was accepted as conclusive. "If it be a matter," said the court, "respecting commerce wholly within a State, and not interfering with commerce between the States, then, obviously, there is no violation of the commerce clause of the Federal Constitution. . . . No question arises under this section, as to the power of the State to separate in different compartments interstate passengers, or affect, in any manner, the privileges and rights of such passengers. All that we can consider is, whether the State has the power to require that railroad trains within her limits shall have separate accommodations for the two races; that affecting only commerce within the State is no invasion of the power given to Congress by the commerce clause."

A like course of reasoning applies to the case under consideration, since the Supreme Court of Louisiana . . . held that the statute in question did not apply to interstate passengers, but was confined in its application to passengers travelling exclusively within the borders of the State. . . . Similar statutes for the separation of the two races upon public conveyances were held to be constitutional [in cases from the state courts of Pennsylvania, Michigan, Illinois, Tennessee, and several other cases from the lower federal courts and from the Interstate Commerce Commission].

*   *   *

In this connection, it is also suggested by the learned counsel for the plaintiff in error that the same argument that will justify the state legislature in requiring railways to provide separate accommodations for the two races will also authorize them to require separate cars to be provided for people whose hair is of a certain color, or who are aliens, or who belong to certain nationalities, or to enact laws requiring colored people to walk upon one side of the street, and white people upon the other, or requiring white men's houses to be painted white, and colored men's black, or their vehicles or business signs to be of different colors, upon the theory that one side of the street is as good as the other, or that a house or vehicle of one color is as good as one of another color. The reply to all this is that every exercise of the police power must be reasonable, and extend only to such laws as are enacted in good faith for the promotion for the public good, and not for the annoyance or oppression of a particular class. Thus in *Yick Wo v. Hopkins* [(1886)], it was held by this court that a municipal ordinance of the city of San Francisco, to regulate the carrying on the public laundries within the limits of the municipality, violated the provisions of the Constitution of the United States, if it conferred upon the municipal authorities arbitrary power, at their own will, and without regard to discretion, in the legal sense, of the term, to give or withhold consent as to persons or places, without regard to the competency of the persons applying, or the propriety of the places selected for the carrying on the business. It was held to be a covert attempt on the part of the municipality to make an arbitrary and unjust discrimination against the Chinese race. While this was the case of a municipal ordinance, a like principle has been held to apply to acts of a state legislature passed in the exercise of the police power.

So far, then, as a conflict with the Fourteenth Amendment is concerned, the case reduces itself to the question whether the statute of Louisiana is a reasonable regulation, and with respect to this there must necessarily be a large discretion on the part of the legislature. In determining the question of reasonableness it is at liberty to act with reference to the established usages, customs and traditions of the people, and with a view to the promotion of their comfort, and the preservation of the public peace and good order. Gauged by this standard, we cannot say that a law which authorizes or even requires the separation of the two races in public conveyances is unreasonable, or more obnoxious to the Fourteenth Amendment than the acts of Congress requiring separate schools for colored children in the District of Columbia, the constitutionality of which does not seem to have been questioned, or the corresponding acts of state legislatures.

We consider the underlying fallacy of the plaintiff's argument to consist in the assumption that the enforced separation of the two races stamps the colored race with a badge of inferiority. If this be so, it is not by reason of anything found in the act, but solely because the colored race chooses to put that construction upon it. The argument necessarily assumes that if, as has been more than once the case, and is not unlikely to be so again, the colored race should become the dominant power in the state legislature, and should enact a law in precisely similar terms, it would thereby relegate the white race to an inferior position. We imagine that the white race, at least, would not acquiesce in this assumption. The argument also assumes that social prejudices may be overcome by legislation, and that equal rights cannot be secured to the negro except by an enforced commingling of the two races. We cannot accept this proposition. If the two races are to meet upon terms of social equality, it must be the result of natural affinities, a mutual appreciation of each other's merits and a voluntary consent of individuals. As was said by the Court of Appeals of New York in *People v. Gallagher* [(1883)], "this end can neither be accomplished nor promoted by laws which conflict with the general sentiment of the community upon whom they are designed to operate. When the government, therefore, has secured to each of its citizens equal rights before the law and equal opportunities for improvement and progress, it has accomplished the end for which it was organized and performed all of the functions respecting social advantages with which it is endowed." Legislation is powerless to eradicate racial instincts or to abolish distinctions based upon physical differences, and the attempt to do so can only result in accentuating the difficulties of the present situation. If the civil and political rights of both races be equal one cannot be inferior to the other civilly or politically. If one race be inferior to the other socially, the Constitution of the United States cannot put them upon the same plane.

The judgment of the court below is, therefore,

Affirmed.

Mr. Justice Harlan dissenting.

*   *   *

In respect of civil rights, common to all citizens, the Constitution of the United States does not, I think, permit any public authority to know the race of those entitled to be protected in the enjoyment of such rights. Every true man has pride of race, and under appropriate circumstances when the rights of others, his equals before the law, are not to be affected, it is his privilege to express such pride and to take such action based upon it as to him seems proper. But I deny that any legislative body or judicial tribunal may have regard to the race of citizens when the civil rights of those citizens are involved. Indeed, such legislation, as that here in question, is inconsistent not only with that equality of rights which pertains to citizenship, National and State, but with the personal liberty enjoyed by every one within the United States.

*   *   *

It is one thing for railroad carriers to furnish, or to be required by law to furnish, equal accommodations for all whom they are under a legal duty to carry. It is quite another thing for government to forbid citizens of the white and black races from traveling in the same public conveyance, and to punish officers of railroad companies for permitting persons of the two races to occupy the same passenger coach. If a State can prescribe, as a rule of civil conduct, that whites and blacks shall not travel as passengers in the same railroad coach, why may it not so regulate the use of the streets of its cities and towns as to compel white citizens to keep on one side of a street and black citizens to keep on the other? Why may it not, upon like grounds, punish whites and blacks who ride together in street cars or in open vehicles on a public road or street? Why may it not require sheriffs to assign whites to one side of a court-room and blacks to the other? And why may it not also prohibit the commingling of the two races in the galleries of legislative halls or in public assemblages convened for the considerations of the political questions of the day? Further, if this statute of Louisiana is consistent with the personal liberty of citizens, why may not the State require the separation in railroad coaches of native and naturalized citizens of the United States, or of Protestants and Roman

Catholics?

The answer given at the argument to these questions was that regulations of the kind they suggest would be unreasonable, and could not, therefore, stand before the law. Is it meant that the determination of questions of legislative power depends upon the inquiry whether the statute whose validity is questioned is, in the judgment of the courts, a reasonable one, taking all the circumstances into consideration? A statute may be unreasonable merely because a sound public policy forbade its enactment. But I do not understand that the courts have anything to do with the policy or expediency of legislation. A statute may be valid, and yet, upon grounds of public policy, may well be characterized as unreasonable. . . . [T]he legislative intention being clearly ascertained, "the courts have no other duty to perform than to execute the legislative will, without any regard to their views as to the wisdom or justice of the particular enactment." There is a dangerous tendency in these latter days to enlarge the functions of the courts, by means of judicial interference with the will of the people as expressed by the legislature. Our institutions have the distinguishing characteristic that the three departments of government are coordinate and separate. Each must keep within the limits defined by the Constitution. And the courts best discharge their duty by executing the will of the law-making power, constitutionally expressed, leaving the results of legisla- tion to be dealt with by the people through their representatives. Statutes must always have a reasonable construction. Sometimes they are to be construed strictly; sometimes, liberally, in order to carry out the legislative will. But however construed, the intent of the legislature is to be respected, if the particular statute in question is valid, although the courts, looking at the public interests, may conceive the statute to be both unreasonable and impolitic. . . .

The white race deems itself to be the dominant race in this country. And so it is, in prestige, in achievements, in education, in wealth and in power. So, I doubt not, it will continue to be for all time, if it remains true to its great heritage and holds fast to the principles of constitutional liberty. But in view of the Constitution, in the eye of the law, there is in this country no superior, dominant, ruling class of citizens. There is no caste here. Our Constitution is color-blind, and neither knows nor tolerates classes among citizens. In respect of civil rights, all citizens are equal before the law. The humblest is the peer of the most powerful. The law regards man as man, and takes no account of his surroundings or of his color when his civil rights as guaranteed by the supreme law of the land are involved. It is, therefore, to be regretted that this high tribunal, the final expositor of the fundamental law of the land, has reached the conclusion that it is competent for a State to regulate the enjoyment by citizens of their civil rights solely upon the basis of race.

In my opinion, the judgment this day rendered will, in time, prove to be quite as pernicious as the decision made by this tribunal in the *Dred Scott* case. . . .

* * *

BROWN v. BOARD OF EDUCATION
347 U.S. 483 (1954)

MR. CHIEF JUSTICE WARREN delivered the opinion of the Court.

These cases come to us from the States of Kansas, South Carolina, Virginia, and Delaware. They are premised on different facts and different local conditions, but a common legal question justifies their consideration together in this consolidated opinion.

In each of the cases, minors of the Negro race, through their legal representatives, seek the aid of the courts in obtaining admission to the public schools of their community on a nonsegregated basis. In each instance, they had been denied admission to schools attended by white children under laws requiring or permitting segregation according to race. This segregation was alleged to deprive the plaintiffs of the equal protection of the laws under the Fourteenth Amendment. In each of the cases other than the Delaware case, a three-judge federal district court denied relief to the plaintiffs on the so-called "separate but equal" doctrine announced by this Court in *Plessy v. Ferguson* [(1896)]. Under that doctrine, equality of treatment is accorded when the races are provided substantially equal facilities, even though these facilities be separate. In the Delaware case, the Supreme Court of Delaware adhered to that doctrine, but ordered that the plaintiffs be admitted to the white schools because of their superiority to the Negro schools.

The plaintiffs contend that segregated public schools are not "equal" and cannot be made "equal," and that hence they are deprived of the equal protection of the laws. . . .

[Pursuant to our request, there was r]eargument [which] was largely devoted to the circumstances surrounding the adoption of the Fourteenth Amendment in 1868. It covered exhaustively consideration of the Amendment in Congress, ratification by the states, then existing practices in racial segregation, and the views of proponents and opponents of the Amendment. This discussion and our own investigation convince us that, although these sources cast some light, it is not enough to resolve the problem with which we are faced. At best, they are inconclusive. The most avid proponents of the post-[Civil] War Amendments undoubtedly intended them to remove all legal distinctions among "all persons born or naturalized in the United States." Their opponents, just as certainly, were antagonistic to both the letter and the spirit of the Amendments and wished them to have the most limited effect. What others in Congress and the state legislatures had in mind cannot be determined with any degree of certainty.

An additional reason for the inconclusive nature of the Amendment's history, with respect to segregated schools, is the status of public education at that time. In the South, the movement toward free common schools, supported by general taxation, had not yet taken hold. Education of white children was largely in the hands of private groups. Education of Negroes was almost nonexistent, and practically all of the race were illiterate. In fact, any education of Negroes was forbidden by law in some states. Today, in contrast, many Negroes have achieved outstanding success in the arts and sciences as well as in the business and professional world. It is true that public school education at the time of the Amendment had advanced further in the North, but the effect of the Amendment on Northern States was generally ignored in the congressional debates. Even in the North, the conditions of public education did not approximate those existing today. The curriculum was usually rudimentary; ungraded schools were common in rural areas; the school term was but three months a year in many states; and compulsory school attendance was virtually unknown. As a consequence, it is not surprising that there should be so little in the history of the Fourteenth Amendment relating to its intended effect on public education.

In the first cases in this Court construing the Fourteenth Amendment, decided shortly after its adoption, the Court interpreted it as proscribing all state-imposed discriminations against the Negro race.[1]

The doctrine of "separate but equal" did not make its appearance in this Court until 1896 in the case of *Plessy v. Ferguson*, involving not education but transportation. American courts have since labored with the doctrine for over half a century. In this Court, there have been six cases involving the "separate but equal" doctrine in the field of public education. In [two of these cases], the validity of the doctrine itself was not challenged. In more recent cases, all on the graduate school level, inequality was found in that specific benefits enjoyed by white students were denied to Negro students of the same educational qualifications. In none of these cases was it necessary to re-examine the doctrine to grant relief to the Negro plaintiff. And in [one of these cases,] *Sweatt v. Painter* [(1950)], the Court expressly reserved decision on the question whether *Plessy v. Ferguson* should be held inapplicable to public education.

In the instant cases, that question is directly presented. Here, unlike *Sweatt v. Painter*, there are findings below that the Negro and white schools involved have been equalized, or are being equalized, with respect to buildings, curricula, qualifications and salaries of teachers, and other "tangible" factors. Our decision, therefore, cannot turn on merely a comparison of these tangible factors in the Negro and white schools involved in each of the cases. We must look instead to the effect of segregation itself on public education.

In approaching this problem, we cannot turn the clock back to 1868 when the Amendment was adopted, or even to 1896 when *Plessy v. Ferguson* was written. We must consider public education in the light of its full development and its present

---

[1] [5] *Slaughter-House Cases* (1873); *Strauder v. West Virginia* (1880):

"It ordains that no State shall deprive any person of life, liberty, or property, without due process of law, or deny to any person within its jurisdiction the equal protection of the laws. What is this but declaring that the law in the States shall be the same for the black as for the white; that all persons, whether colored or white, shall stand equal before the laws of the States, and, in regard to the colored race, for whose protection the amendment was primarily designed, that no discrimination shall be made against them by law because of their color? The words of the amendment, it is true, are prohibitory, but they contain a necessary implication of a positive immunity, or right, most valuable to the colored race, — the right to exemption from unfriendly legislation against them distinctively as colored, — exemption from legal discriminations, implying inferiority in civil society, lessening the security of their enjoyment of the rights which others enjoy, and discriminations which are steps towards reducing them to the condition of a subject race."

place in American life throughout the Nation. Only in this way can it be determined if segregation in public schools deprives these plaintiffs of the equal protection of the laws.

Today, education is perhaps the most important function of state and local governments. Compulsory school attendance laws and the great expenditures for education both demonstrate our recognition of the importance of education to our democratic society. It is required in the performance of our most basic public responsibilities, even service in the armed forces. It is the very foundation of good citizenship. Today it is a principal instrument in awakening the child to cultural values, in preparing him for later professional training, and in helping him to adjust normally to his environment. In these days, it is doubtful that any child may reasonably be expected to succeed in life if he is denied the opportunity of an education. Such an opportunity, where the state has undertaken to provide it, is a right which must be made available to all on equal terms.

We come then to the question presented: Does segregation of children in public schools solely on the basis of race, even though the physical facilities and other "tangible" factors may be equal, deprive the children of the minority group of equal educational opportunities? We believe that it does.

In *Sweatt v. Painter, supra,* in finding that a segregated law school for Negroes could not provide them equal educational opportunities, this Court relied in large part on "those qualities which are incapable of objective measurement but which make for greatness in a law school." In *McLaurin v. Oklahoma State Regents* [(1950)], [another 14th Amendment education case involving a graduate school], the Court, in requiring that a Negro admitted to a white graduate school be treated like all other students, again resorted to intangible considerations: ". . . his ability to study, to engage in discussions and exchange views with other students, and, in general, to learn his profession." Such considerations apply with added force to children in grade and high schools. To separate them from others of similar age and qualifications solely because of their race generates a feeling of inferiority as to their status in the community that may affect their hearts and minds in a way unlikely ever to be undone. The effect of this separation on their educational opportunities was well stated by a finding in the Kansas case by a court which nevertheless felt compelled to rule against the Negro plaintiffs:

> "Segregation of white and colored children in public schools has a detrimental effect upon the colored children. The impact is greater when it has the sanction of the law; for the policy of separating the races is usually interpreted as denoting the inferiority of the negro group. A sense of inferiority affects the motivation of a child to learn. Segregation with the sanction of law, therefore, has a tendency to [retard] the educational and mental development of negro children and to deprive them of some of the benefits they would receive in a racial[ly] integrated school system."

Whatever may have been the extent of psychological knowledge at the time of *Plessy v. Ferguson,* this finding is amply supported by modern authority.[2]

---

[2] [11] K.B. Clark, Effect of Prejudice and Discrimination on Personality Development (Midcentury

Any language in *Plessy v. Ferguson* contrary to this finding is rejected.

We conclude that in the field of public education the doctrine of "separate but equal" has no place. Separate educational facilities are inherently unequal. Therefore, we hold that the plaintiffs and others similarly situated for whom the actions have been brought are, by reason of the segregation complained of, deprived of the equal protection of the laws guaranteed by the Fourteenth Amendment.

NOTES AND QUESTIONS

1. There is universal agreement in the American legal academy to the proposition that *Plessy* was wrongly decided and *Brown* was correct. How could a majority have reached the conclusion that it did in *Plessy*? Is it simply that the times were different, as the *Brown* Court all but implicitly concedes? Should different times make for different constitutional law? What do you make of Earl Warren's famous suggestion in *Brown* that one can't "turn the clock back"? 347 U.S. at 492. Can clocks be turned back? Some philosophers, most notably the famous Christian apologist C.S. Lewis, have gone so far as to suggest that turning back the clock may be the only rational strategy when the times have gone badly wrong. Should one ever turn back the clock in constitutional law?

2. What's wrong with the "separate but equal" doctrine enunciated in *Plessy*? Would it surprise you to learn that the owners of the public transportation providers in *Plessy* were hoping for a ruling that would remove the necessity to operate parallel accommodations in transportation? What are the economic aspects of state-supported racial discrimination? Is it efficient or inefficient, and should this be a concern?

3. Note Justice Harlan's eloquent dissent in *Plessy*, and, in particular his assertion that the Constitution is "color-blind." 163 U.S. at 559 (Harlan, J., dissenting). Where does this idea come from, and do you agree? Were the framers of the Constitution "color-blind"? Was the document they produced? Is natural law "color blind"? Do you find any help in deciding whether *Brown* was correctly reasoned in the dissenting opinions in *Dred Scott*? Generally those people who believe that *Dred Scott* was the worst decision ever rendered by the Supreme Court believe that *Brown* was the best. Would you have guessed this? Are the constitutional theories implemented in the majority opinions in the two cases fundamentally at odds, as well as their substantive conclusions?

Are there any explicit references to race in the body of the Constitution? Should the Thirteenth or Fourteenth Amendments be construed as implementing a "color-blind" society, even if the Constitution did not? Clearly the Thirteenth and Fourteenth Amendments were designed to overrule *Dred Scott*. Is *Plessy* consistent with this historical understanding? Why, by the way, did the plaintiffs in *Plessy*

White House Conference on Children and Youth, 1950); Witmer and Kotinsky, Personality in the Making, ch. 6 (1952); Deutscher & Chein, *The Psychological Effects of Enforced Segregation: A Survey of Social Science Opinion*, 26 J. Psychol. 259 (1948); Chein, *What are the Psychological Effects of Segregation Under Conditions of Equal Facilities?*, 3 Int. J. Opinion & Attitude Res. 229 (1949); Brameld, Educational Costs, in Discrimination and National Welfare 44–48 (MacIver ed., 1949); Frazier, The Negro in the United States 674–81 (1949). And see generally Myrdal, An American Dilemma (1944).

believe that they had a case to make under the Thirteenth Amendment, and why did the court reject their claim?

4. Does *Brown* completely overrule *Plessy*? If not, to what extent is *Plessy* still good law after *Brown*? Do you suppose the doctrines in *Plessy* have any remaining force today? Is this because of what *Brown* decided, or for other reasons?

5. *Brown* was a unanimous decision. Can you understand why *Brown* is universally regarded as the most important Supreme Court case of the 20th century? What do you think of the principles of constitutional interpretation that triumph in *Brown*? Are they the same as those that you have observed in other Supreme Court decisions? How, by the way, would Chief Justice John Roberts and Justices Scalia, Thomas, and Alito to pick the Court's currently most conservative members, have decided *Brown*? Would *Plessy* have been overruled by the trio of Justices — O'Connor, Kennedy, and Souter — who refused to overrule *Roe v. Wade* in *Planned Parenthood v. Casey*? See Chapter 6 discussing these abortion decisions. Would their principles of *stare decisis* have required an affirmance of *Plessy* in *Brown*? Ask yourself this question when you read *Casey* in the following Chapter.

6. Consider *Brown*'s famous "footnote 11," one of the most famous in all constitutional law. What is its significance? Can *Brown* be explained without reference to the social psychological data collected in footnote 11? Footnote 11 exists to buttress the conclusion that forced separation of the races harms the black race, at least with regard to elementary school education. Why wasn't such an argument persuasive in *Plessy*?

7. Does *Brown* end state-sponsored racial separation? What is the extent of its reach? In a series of short *per curiam* opinions rendered shortly after *Brown*, the Court struck down segregation at public beaches and bathhouses, *Mayor and City Council of Baltimore v. Dawson* (1955); at municipal golf courses, *Holmes v. City of Atlanta* (1955); and on city buses, *Gayle v. Browder* (1956), merely citing to *Brown* in each instance without further discussion. Do these decisions necessarily follow from the rationale adopted in *Brown*? With them, must *Brown* be viewed as establishing a principled objection to segregation *per se* that was not expressly articulated in the *Brown* opinion itself?

3. Vestiges of Discrimination — The Difficulty of Past Racial Effect

FREEMAN v. PITTS
503 U.S. 467 (1992)

JUSTICE KENNEDY delivered the opinion of the Court.

DeKalb County, Georgia, is a major suburban area of Atlanta. This case involves a court-ordered desegregation decree for the DeKalb County School System (DCSS). DCSS now serves some 73,000 students in kindergarten through high school and is the 32nd largest elementary and secondary school system in the Nation.

DCSS has been subject to the supervision and jurisdiction of the United States District Court for the Northern District of Georgia since 1969, when it was ordered to dismantle its dual school system. In 1986, petitioners filed a motion for final dismissal. The District Court ruled that DCSS had not achieved unitary status in all respects but had done so in student attendance and three other categories. In its order the District Court relinquished remedial control as to those aspects of the system in which unitary status had been achieved, and retained supervisory authority only for those aspects of the school system in which the district was not in full compliance. The Court of Appeals for the Eleventh Circuit reversed, holding that a district court should retain full remedial authority over a school system until it achieves unitary status in six categories at the same time for several years. We now reverse the judgment of the Court of Appeals. . . .

I

A

For decades before our decision in *Brown v. Board of Education* (1954) (*Brown I*) . . . DCSS was segregated by law. DCSS' initial response to the mandate of [a later decision by the Supreme Court in *Brown v. Board of Education*, known as *"Brown II,"* which mandated desegregation of the nation's public schools "with all deliberate speed,"] was an all too familiar one. Interpreting "all deliberate speed" as giving latitude to delay steps to desegregate, DCSS took no positive action toward desegregation until the 1966–1967 school year, when it did nothing more than adopt a freedom of choice transfer plan. Some black students chose to attend former *de jure* white schools, but the plan had no significant effect on the former *de jure* black schools.

In 1968, we decided *Green v. School Bd. of New Kent County.* We held that adoption of a freedom of choice plan does not, by itself, satisfy a school district's mandatory responsibility to eliminate all vestiges of a dual system. . . . Concerned by more than a decade of inaction, we stated that " '[t]he time for mere "deliberate speed" has run out.' " We said that the obligation of school districts once segregated by law was to come forward with a plan that "promises realistically to work, and promises realistically to work *now*." . . .

Within two months of our ruling in *Green*, respondents, who are black school-children and their parents, instituted this class action in the United States District Court for the Northern District of Georgia. After the suit was filed, DCSS voluntarily began working with the Department of Health, Education, and Welfare to devise a comprehensive and final plan of desegregation. The District Court, in June 1969, entered a consent order approving the proposed plan, which was to be implemented in the 1969–1970 school year. The order abolished the freedom of choice plan and adopted a neighborhood school attendance plan that had been proposed by DCSS and accepted by the Department of Health, Education, and Welfare subject to a minor modification. Under the plan all of the former *de jure* black schools were closed, and their students were reassigned among the remaining neighborhood schools. The District Court retained jurisdiction.

Between 1969 and 1986, respondents sought only infrequent and limited judicial intervention into the affairs of DCSS. They did not request significant changes in student attendance zones or student assignment policies. In 1976, DCSS was ordered to expand its Majority-to-Minority (M-to-M) student transfer program, allowing students in a school where they are in the majority race to transfer to a school where they are in the minority; to establish a biracial committee to oversee the transfer program and future boundary line changes; and to reassign teachers so that the ratio of black to white teachers in each school would be, in substance, similar to the racial balance in the school population systemwide. From 1977 to 1979, the District Court approved a boundary line change for one elementary school attendance zone and rejected DCSS proposals to restrict the M-to-M transfer program. In 1983, DCSS was ordered to make further adjustments to the M-to-M transfer program.

In 1986, petitioners filed a motion for final dismissal of the litigation. They sought a declaration that DCSS had satisfied its duty to eliminate the dual education system. . . . The District Court approached the question whether DCSS had achieved unitary status by asking whether DCSS was unitary with respect to each of the factors identified in *Green*. The court considered an additional factor that is not named in *Green*: the quality of education being offered to the white and black student populations.

The District Court found DCSS to be "an innovative school system that has travelled the often long road to unitary status almost to its end," noting that "the court has continually been impressed by the successes of the DCSS and its dedication to providing a quality education for all students within that system." It found that DCSS is a unitary system with regard to student assignments, transportation, physical facilities, and extracurricular activities, and ruled that it would order no further relief in those areas. The District Court stopped short of dismissing the case, however, because it found that DCSS was not unitary in every respect. The court said that vestiges of the dual system remain in the areas of teacher and principal assignments, resource allocation, and quality of education. DCSS was ordered to take measures to address the remaining problems.

B

Proper resolution of any desegregation case turns on a careful assessment of its facts. Here, as in most cases where the issue is the degree of compliance with a school desegregation decree, a critical beginning point is the degree of racial imbalance in the school district. . . . This inquiry is fundamental, for under the former *de jure* regimes racial exclusion was both the means and the end of a policy motivated by disparagement of, or hostility towards, the disfavored race. In accord with this principle, the District Court began its analysis with an assessment of the current racial mix in the schools throughout DCSS and the explanation for the racial imbalance it found. Respondents did not contend on appeal that the findings of fact were clearly erroneous, and the Court of Appeals did not find them to be erroneous. The Court of Appeals did disagree with the conclusion reached by the District Court respecting the need for further supervision of racial balance in student assignments.

In the extensive record that comprises this case, one fact predominates: Remarkable changes in the racial composition of the county presented DCSS and the District Court with a student population in 1986 far different from the one they set out to integrate in 1969. Between 1950 and 1985, DeKalb County grew from 70,000 to 450,000 in total population, but most of the gross increase in student enrollment had occurred by 1969, the relevant starting date for our purposes. Although the public school population experienced only modest changes between 1969 and 1986 (remaining in the low 70,000s), a striking change occurred in the racial proportions of the student population. The school system that the District Court ordered desegregated in 1969 had 5.6% black students; by 1986 the percentage of black students was 47%.

To compound the difficulty of working with these radical demographic changes, the northern and southern parts of the county experienced much different growth patterns. The District Court found that "[a]s the result of these demographic shifts, the population of the northern half of DeKalb County is now predominantly white and the southern half of DeKalb County is predominantly black." . . . Most of the growth in the nonwhite population in the southern portion of the county was due to the migration of black persons from the city of Atlanta. . . .

The District Court made findings with respect to the number of nonwhite citizens in the northern and southern parts of the county for the years 1970 and 1980 without making parallel findings with respect to white citizens. Yet a clear picture does emerge. During the relevant period, the black population in the southern portion of the county experienced tremendous growth while the white population did not, and the white population in the northern part of the county experienced tremendous growth while the black population did not.

The demographic changes that occurred during the course of the desegregation order are an essential foundation for the District Court's analysis of the current racial mix of DCSS. As the District Court observed, the demographic shifts have had "an immense effect on the racial compositions of the DeKalb County schools." From 1976 to 1986, enrollment in elementary schools declined overall by 15%, while black enrollment in elementary schools increased by 86%. During the same period, overall high school enrollment declined by 16%, while black enrollment in high schools increased by 119%. These effects were even more pronounced in the southern portion of DeKalb County.

Concerned with racial imbalance in the various schools of the district, respondents presented evidence that during the 1986–1987 school year DCSS had the following features: (1) 47% of the students attending DCSS were black; (2) 50% of the black students attended schools that were over 90% black; (3) 62% of all black students attended schools that had more than 20% more blacks than the system-wide average; (4) 27% of white students attended schools that were more than 90% white; (5) 59% of the white students attended schools that had more than 20% more whites than the system-wide average; (6) of the 22 DCSS high schools, five had student populations that were more than 90% black, while five other schools had student populations that were more than 80% white; and (7) of the 74 elementary schools in DCSS, 18 are over 90% black, while 10 are over 90% white.

Respondents argued in the District Court that this racial imbalance in student assignment was a vestige of the dual system, rather than a product of independent demographic forces. In addition to the statistical evidence that the ratio of black students to white students in individual schools varied to a significant degree from the system-wide average, respondents contended that DCSS had not used all available desegregative tools in order to achieve racial balancing. Respondents pointed to the following alleged shortcomings in DCSS' desegregative efforts: (1) DCSS did not break the county into subdistricts and racially balance each subdistrict; (2) DCSS failed to expend sufficient funds for minority learning opportunities; (3) DCSS did not establish community advisory organizations; (4) DCSS did not make full use of the freedom of choice plan; (5) DCSS did not cluster schools, that is, it did not create schools for separate grade levels which could be used to establish a feeder pattern; (6) DCSS did not institute its magnet school program as early as it might have; and (7) DCSS did not use busing to facilitate urban to suburban exchanges.

According to the District Court, respondents conceded that the 1969 order assigning all students to their neighborhood schools "effectively desegregated the DCSS for a period of time" with respect to student assignment. The District Court noted, however, that despite this concession respondents contended there was an improper imbalance in two schools even in 1969. Respondents made much of the fact that despite the small percentage of blacks in the county in 1969, there were then two schools that contained a majority of black students. . . .

The District Court found the racial imbalance in these schools was not a vestige of the prior *de jure* system. It observed that both the . . . schools were *de jure* white schools before the freedom of choice plan was put in place. It cited expert witness testimony that [one of the schools,] Terry Mill[,] had become a majority black school as a result of demographic shifts unrelated to the actions of petitioners or their predecessors. In 1966, the overwhelming majority of students at Terry Mill were white. By 1967, due to migration of black citizens from Atlanta into DeKalb County — and into the neighborhood surrounding the Terry Mill school in particular — 23% of the students at Terry Mill were black. By 1968, black students constituted 50% of the school population at Terry Mill. By 1969, when the plan was put into effect, the percentage of black students had grown to 76. In accordance with the evidence of demographic shifts, and in the absence of any evidence to suggest that the former dual system contributed in any way to the rapid racial transformation of the Terry Mill student population, the District Court found that the pre-1969 unconstitutional acts of petitioners were not responsible for the high percentage of black students at the Terry Mill school in 1969. Its findings in this respect are illustrative of the problems DCSS and the District Court faced in integrating the whole district.

Although the District Court found that DCSS was desegregated for at least a short period under the court-ordered plan of 1969, it did not base its finding that DCSS had achieved unitary status with respect to student assignment on that circumstance alone. Recognizing that "the achievement of unitary status in the area of student assignment cannot be hedged on the attainment of such status for a brief moment," the District Court examined the interaction between DCSS policy and demographic shifts in DeKalb County.

The District Court noted that DCSS had taken specific steps to combat the effects of demographics on the racial mix of the schools. Under the 1969 order, a biracial committee had reviewed all proposed changes in the boundary lines of school attendance zones. Since the original desegregation order, there had been about 170 such changes. It was found that only three had a partial segregative effect. An expert testified, and the District Court found, that even those changes had no significant effect on the racial mix of the school population, given the tremendous demographic shifts that were taking place at the same time.

The District Court also noted that DCSS, on its own initiative, started an M-to-M program in the 1972 school year. The program was a marked success. Participation increased with each passing year, so that in the 1986–1987 school year, 4,500 of the 72,000 students enrolled in DCSS participated. An expert testified that the impact of an M-to-M program goes beyond the number of students transferred because students at the receiving school also obtain integrated learning experiences. The District Court found that about 19% of the students attending DCSS had an integrated learning experience as a result of the M-to-M program.

In addition, in the 1980's, DCSS instituted a magnet school program in schools located in the middle of the county. The magnet school programs included a performing arts program, two science programs, and a foreign language program. There was testimony in the District Court that DCSS also had plans to operate additional magnet programs in occupational education and gifted and talented education, as well as a preschool program and an open campus. By locating these programs in the middle of the county, DCSS sought to attract black students from the southern part of the county and white students from the northern part.

Further, the District Court found that DCSS operates a number of experience programs integrated by race, including a writing center for fifth and seventh graders, a driving range, summer school programs, and a dialectical speech program. DCSS employs measures to control the racial mix in each of these special areas.

In determining whether DCSS has achieved unitary status with respect to student assignment, the District Court saw its task as one of deciding if petitioners "have accomplished maximum practical desegregation of the DCSS or if the DCSS must still do more to fulfill their affirmative constitutional duty." Petitioners and respondents presented conflicting expert testimony about the potential effects that desegregative techniques not deployed might have had upon the racial mix of the schools. The District Court found that petitioners' experts were more reliable, citing their greater familiarity with DCSS, their experience, and their standing within the expert community. The District Court made these findings:

> "[The actions of DCSS] achieved maximum practical desegregation from 1969 to 1986. The rapid population shifts in DeKalb County were not caused by any action on the part of the DCSS. These demographic shifts were inevitable as the result of suburbanization, that is, work opportunities arising in DeKalb County as well as the City of Atlanta, which attracted blacks to DeKalb; the decline in the number of children born to white families during this period while the number of children born to black families did not decrease; blockbusting of formerly white neighborhoods leading to selling and buying of real estate in the DeKalb area on a highly

dynamic basis; and the completion of Interstate 20, which made access from DeKalb County into the City of Atlanta much easier. . . . There is no evidence that the school system's previous unconstitutional conduct may have contributed to this segregation. This court is convinced that any further actions taken by defendants, while the actions might have made marginal adjustments in the population trends, would not have offset the factors that were described above and the same racial segregation would have occurred at approximately the same speed."

The District Court added:

"[A]bsent massive bussing, which is not considered as a viable option by either the parties or this court, the magnet school program and the M-to-M program, which the defendants voluntarily implemented and to which the defendants obviously are dedicated, are the most effective ways to deal with the effects on student attendance of the residential segregation existing in DeKalb County at this time."

Having found no constitutional violation with respect to student assignment, the District Court next considered the other *Green* factors, beginning with faculty and staff assignments. The District Court first found that DCSS had fulfilled its constitutional obligation with respect to hiring and retaining minority teachers and administrators. DCSS has taken active steps to recruit qualified black applicants and has hired them in significant numbers, employing a greater percentage of black teachers than the statewide average. The District Court also noted that DCSS has an "equally exemplary record" in retention of black teachers and administrators. Nevertheless, the District Court found that DCSS had not achieved or maintained a ratio of black to white teachers and administrators in each school to approximate the ratio of black to white teachers and administrators throughout the system. In other words, a racial imbalance existed in the assignment of minority teachers and administrators. The District Court found that in the 1984–1985 school year, seven schools deviated by more than 10% from the system-wide average of 26.4% minority teachers in elementary schools and 24.9% minority teachers in high schools. The District Court also found that black principals and administrators were over-represented in schools with high percentages of black students and underrepresented in schools with low percentages of black students.

The District Court found the crux of the problem to be that DCSS has relied on the replacement process to attain a racial balance in teachers and other staff and has avoided using mandatory reassignment. DCSS gave as its reason for not using mandatory reassignment that the competition among local school districts is stiff, and that it is difficult to attract and keep qualified teachers if they are required to work far from their homes. In fact, because teachers prefer to work close to their homes, DCSS has a voluntary transfer program in which teachers who have taught at the same school for a period of three years may ask for a transfer. Because most teachers request to be transferred to schools near their homes, this program makes compliance with the objective of racial balance in faculty and staff more difficult.

The District Court stated that it was not "unsympathetic to the difficulties that DCSS faces in this regard," but . . . ordered DCSS to devise a plan to achieve compliance with [prior Supreme Court precedent requiring racial balance in teachers and staff] noting that "[i]t would appear that such compliance will necessitate reassignment of both teachers and principals." With respect to faculty, the District Court noted that [this] would not be difficult, citing petitioners' own estimate that most schools' faculty could conform by moving, at most, two or three teachers.

Addressing the more ineffable category of quality of education, the District Court rejected most of respondents' contentions that there was racial disparity in the provision of certain educational resources (*e.g.*, teachers with advanced degrees, teachers with more experience, library books), contentions made to show that black students were not being given equal educational opportunity. The District Court went further, however, and examined the evidence concerning achievement of black students in DCSS. It cited expert testimony praising the overall educational program in the district, as well as objective evidence of black achievement: Black students at DCSS made greater gains on the Iowa Tests of Basic Skills than white students, and black students at DCSS are more successful than black students nationwide on the Scholastic Aptitude Test. . . .

* * *

Despite its finding that there was no intentional violation, the District Court found that DCSS had not achieved unitary status with respect to quality of education because teachers in schools with disproportionately high percentages of white students tended to be better educated and have more experience than their counterparts in schools with disproportionately high percentages of black students, and because per-pupil expenditures in majority white schools exceeded per-pupil expenditures in majority black schools. From these findings, the District Court ordered DCSS to equalize spending and remedy the other problems.

The final *Green* factors considered by the District Court were: (1) physical facilities, (2) transportation, and (3) extracurricular activities. The District Court noted that although respondents expressed some concerns about the use of portable classrooms in schools in the southern portion of the county, they in effect conceded that DCSS has achieved unitary status with respect to physical facilities.

In accordance with its factfinding, the District Court held that it would order no further relief in the areas of student assignment, transportation, physical facilities, and extracurricular activities. The District Court, however, did order DCSS to establish a system to balance teacher and principal assignments and to equalize per-pupil expenditures throughout DCSS. Having found that blacks were represented on the school board and throughout DCSS administration, the District Court abolished the biracial committee as no longer necessary.

Both parties appealed to the United States Court of Appeals for the Eleventh Circuit. The Court of Appeals affirmed the District Court's ultimate conclusion that DCSS has not yet achieved unitary status, but reversed the District Court's ruling that DCSS has no further duties in the area of student assignment. The Court of Appeals held that the District Court erred by considering the six *Green* factors as separate categories. The Court of Appeals rejected the District Court's incremental approach, . . . and held that a school system achieves unitary status only after it has satisfied all six factors at the same time for several years. Because, under this test,

DCSS had not achieved unitary status at any time, the Court of Appeals held that DCSS could "not shirk its constitutional duties by pointing to demographic shifts occurring prior to unitary status." The Court of Appeals held that petitioners bore the responsibility for the racial imbalance, and in order to correct that imbalance would have to take actions that "may be administratively awkward, inconvenient, and even bizarre in some situations," such as pairing and clustering of schools, drastic gerrymandering of school zones, grade reorganization, and busing. . . .

II

Two principal questions are presented. The first is whether a district court may relinquish its supervision and control over those aspects of a school system in which there has been compliance with a desegregation decree if other aspects of the system remain in noncompliance. As we answer this question in the affirmative, the second question is whether the Court of Appeals erred in reversing the District Court's order providing for incremental withdrawal of supervision in all the circumstances of this case.

A

The duty and responsibility of a school district once segregated by law is to take all steps necessary to eliminate the vestiges of the unconstitutional *de jure* system. . . .

The objective of *Brown I* was made more specific by our holding in *Green* that the duty of a former *de jure* district is to "take whatever steps might be necessary to convert to a unitary system in which racial discrimination would be eliminated root and branch." We also identified various parts of the school system which, in addition to student attendance patterns, must be free from racial discrimination before the mandate of *Brown* is met: faculty, staff, transportation, extracurricular activities, and facilities. The *Green* factors are a measure of the racial identifiability of schools in a system that is not in compliance with *Brown*, and we instructed the District Courts to fashion remedies that address all these components of elementary and secondary school systems.

The concept of unitariness has been a helpful one in defining the scope of the district courts' authority, for it conveys the central idea that a school district that was once a dual system must be examined in all of its facets, both when a remedy is ordered and in the later phases of desegregation when the question is whether the district courts' remedial control ought to be modified, lessened, or withdrawn. But, as we explained last Term . . . , the term "unitary" is not a precise concept:

> "[I]t is a mistake to treat words such as 'dual' and 'unitary' as if they were actually found in the Constitution. . . . Courts have used the terms 'dual' to denote a school system which has engaged in intentional segregation of students by race, and 'unitary' to describe a school system which has been brought into compliance with the command of the Constitution. We are not sure how useful it is to define these terms more precisely, or to create subclasses within them."

It follows that we must be cautious not to attribute to the term a utility it does not have. . . .

That the term "unitary" does not have fixed meaning or content is not inconsistent with the principles that control the exercise of equitable power. The essence of a court's equity power lies in its inherent capacity to adjust remedies in a feasible and practical way to eliminate the conditions or redress the injuries caused by unlawful action. Equitable remedies must be flexible if these underlying principles are to be enforced with fairness and precision. . . .

Our application of these guiding principles in *Pasadena Bd. of Education v. Spangler* (1976), is instructive. There we held that a District Court exceeded its remedial authority in requiring annual readjustment of school attendance zones in the Pasadena school district when changes in the racial makeup of the schools were caused by demographic shifts "not attributed to any segregative acts on the part of the [school district]." In so holding we said:

> "It may well be that petitioners have not yet totally achieved the unitary system contemplated by . . . [the earlier desegregation case,] *Swann* [*v. Charlotte-Mecklenburg Bd. of Education* (1970) (which approved of busing as a remedy to achieve racial balance)]. There has been, for example, dispute as to the petitioners' compliance with those portions of the plan specifying procedures for hiring and promoting teachers and administrators. ["] . . .

[Nevertheless, t]oday, [we hold that] . . . [a] federal court in a school desegregation case has the discretion to order an incremental or partial withdrawal of its supervision and control. This discretion derives both from the constitutional authority which justified its intervention in the first instance and its ultimate objectives in formulating the decree. The authority of the court is invoked at the outset to remedy particular constitutional violations. In construing the remedial authority of the district courts, we have been guided by the principles that "judicial powers may be exercised only on the basis of a constitutional violation," and that "the nature of the violation determines the scope of the remedy." A remedy is justifiable only insofar as it advances the ultimate objective of alleviating the initial constitutional violation.

We have said that the court's end purpose must be to remedy the violation and, in addition, to restore state and local authorities to the control of a school system that is operating in compliance with the Constitution. Partial relinquishment of judicial control, where justified by the facts of the case, can be an important and significant step in fulfilling the district court's duty to return the operations and control of schools to local authorities. . . . [F]ederal judicial supervision of local school systems was intended as a "temporary measure." Although this temporary measure has lasted decades, the ultimate objective has not changed — to return school districts to the control of local authorities. A transition phase in which control is relinquished in a gradual way is an appropriate means to this end.

As we have long observed, "local autonomy of school districts is a vital national tradition." Returning schools to the control of local authorities at the earliest practicable date is essential to restore their true accountability in our governmental system. When the school district and all state entities participating with it in operating the schools make decisions in the absence of judicial supervision, they can be held accountable to the citizenry, to the political process, and to the courts in the ordinary course. As we discuss below, one of the prerequisites to relinquishment of control in whole or in part is that a school district has demonstrated its commitment to a course of action that gives full respect to the equal protection guarantees of the Constitution. Yet it must be acknowledged that the potential for discrimination and racial hostility is still present in our country, and its manifestations may emerge in new and subtle forms after the effects of *de jure* segregation have been eliminated. It is the duty of the State and its subdivisions to ensure that such forces do not shape or control the policies of its school systems. . . .

We hold that, in the course of supervising desegregation plans, federal courts have the authority to relinquish supervision and control of school districts in incremental stages, before full compliance has been achieved in every area of school operations. . . . In particular, the district court may determine that it will not order further remedies in the area of student assignments where racial imbalance is not traceable, in a proximate way, to constitutional violations.

A court's discretion to order the incremental withdrawal of its supervision in a school desegregation case must be exercised in a manner consistent with the purposes and objectives of its equitable power. Among the factors which must inform the sound discretion of the court in ordering partial withdrawal are the following: whether there has been full and satisfactory compliance with the decree in those aspects of the system where supervision is to be withdrawn; whether retention of judicial control is necessary or practicable to achieve compliance with the decree in other facets of the school system; and whether the school district has demonstrated, to the public and to the parents and students of the once disfavored race, its good-faith commitment to the whole of the court's decree and to those provisions of the law and the Constitution that were the predicate for judicial intervention in the first instance.

In considering these factors, a court should give particular attention to the school system's record of compliance. . . .

* * *

B

We reach now the question whether the Court of Appeals erred in prohibiting the District Court from returning to DCSS partial control over some of its affairs. . . .

It was an appropriate exercise of its discretion for the District Court to address the elements of a unitary system discussed in *Green*, to inquire whether other elements ought to be identified, and to determine whether minority students were being disadvantaged in ways that required the formulation of new and further remedies to ensure full compliance with the court's decree. Both parties agreed that quality of education was a legitimate inquiry in determining DCSS' compliance with the desegregation decree, and the trial court found it workable to consider the point in connection with its findings on resource allocation. . . . The District Court's approach illustrates that the *Green* factors need not be a rigid framework. It illustrates also the uses of equitable discretion. By withdrawing control over areas where judicial supervision is no longer needed, a district court can concentrate both its own resources and those of the school district on the areas where the effects of *de jure* discrimination have not been eliminated and further action is necessary in order to provide real and tangible relief to minority students.

The Court of Appeals' rejection of the District Court's order rests on related premises: first, that given noncompliance in some discrete categories, there can be no partial withdrawal of judicial control; and second, until there is full compliance, heroic measures must be taken to ensure racial balance in student assignments system wide. Under our analysis and our precedents, neither premise is correct.

The Court of Appeals was mistaken in ruling that our opinion in *Swann* requires "awkward," "inconvenient," and "even bizarre" measures to achieve racial balance in student assignments in the late phases of carrying out a decree, when the imbalance is attributable neither to the prior *de jure* system nor to a later violation by the school district but rather to independent demographic forces. In *Swann* we undertook to discuss the objectives of a comprehensive desegregation plan and the powers and techniques available to a district court in designing it at the outset. We confirmed that racial balance in school assignments was a necessary part of the remedy in the circumstances there presented. In the case before us the District Court designed a comprehensive plan for desegregation of DCSS in 1969, one that included racial balance in student assignments. The desegregation decree was designed to achieve maximum practicable desegregation. Its central remedy was the closing of black schools and the reassignment of pupils to neighborhood schools, with attendance zones that achieved racial balance. The plan accomplished its objective in the first year of operation, before dramatic demographic changes altered residential patterns. For the entire 17-year period respondents raised no substantial objection to the basic student assignment system, as the parties and the District Court concentrated on other mechanisms to eliminate the *de jure* taint.

That there was racial imbalance in student attendance zones was not tantamount to a showing that the school district was in noncompliance with the decree or with its duties under the law. Racial balance is not to be achieved for its own sake. It is to be pursued when racial imbalance has been caused by a constitutional violation. Once the racial imbalance due to the *de jure* violation has been remedied, the school district is under no duty to remedy imbalance that is caused by demographic factors. . . .

The findings of the District Court that the population changes which occurred in DeKalb County were not caused by the policies of the school district, but rather by independent factors, are consistent with the mobility that is a distinct characteristic of our society. In one year (from 1987 to 1988) over 40 million Americans, or 17.6% of the total population, moved households. Over a third of those people moved to a different county, and over six million migrated between States. In such a society it is inevitable that the demographic makeup of school districts, based as they are on political subdivisions such as counties and municipalities, may undergo rapid change.

The effect of changing residential patterns on the racial composition of schools, though not always fortunate, is somewhat predictable. Studies show a high correlation between residential segregation and school segregation. The District Court in this case heard evidence tending to show that racially stable neighborhoods are not likely to emerge because whites prefer a racial mix of 80% white and 20% black, while blacks prefer a 50-50 mix.

Where resegregation is a product not of state action but of private choices, it does not have constitutional implications. It is beyond the authority and beyond the practical ability of the federal courts to try to counteract these kinds of continuous and massive demographic shifts. . . .

In one sense of the term, vestiges of past segregation by state decree do remain in our society and in our schools. Past wrongs to the black race, wrongs committed by the State and in its name, are a stubborn fact of history. And stubborn facts of history linger and persist. But though we cannot escape our history, neither must we overstate its consequences in fixing legal responsibilities. The vestiges of segregation that are the concern of the law in a school case may be subtle and intangible but nonetheless they must be so real that they have a causal link to the *de jure* violation being remedied. It is simply not always the case that demographic forces causing population change bear any real and substantial relation to a *de jure* violation. . . .

As the *de jure* violation becomes more remote in time and these demographic changes intervene, it becomes less likely that a current racial imbalance in a school district is a vestige of the prior *de jure* system. The causal link between current conditions and the prior violation is even more attenuated if the school district has demonstrated its good faith. In light of its finding that the demographic changes in DeKalb County are unrelated to the prior violation, the District Court was correct to entertain the suggestion that DCSS had no duty to achieve system-wide racial balance in the student population. It was appropriate for the District Court to examine the reasons for the racial imbalance before ordering an impractical, and no doubt massive, expenditure of funds to achieve racial balance after 17 years of efforts to implement the comprehensive plan in a district where there were fundamental changes in demographics, changes not attributable to the former *de jure* regime or any later actions by school officials. The District Court's determination to order instead the expenditure of scarce resources in areas such as the quality of education, where full compliance had not yet been achieved, underscores the uses of discretion in framing equitable remedies.

To say, as did the Court of Appeals, that a school district must meet all six *Green* factors before the trial court can declare the system unitary and relinquish its control over school attendance zones, and to hold further that racial balancing by all necessary means is required in the interim, is simply to vindicate a legal phrase. The law is not so formalistic. . . .

We next consider whether retention of judicial control over student attendance is necessary or practicable to achieve compliance in other facets of the school system. Racial balancing in elementary and secondary school student assignments may be a legitimate remedial device to correct other fundamental inequities that were themselves caused by the constitutional violation. We have long recognized that the *Green* factors may be related or interdependent. Two or more *Green* factors may be intertwined or synergistic in their relation, so that a constitutional violation in one area cannot be eliminated unless the judicial remedy addresses other matters as well. We have observed, for example, that student segregation and faculty segregation are often related problems. . . .

There was no showing that racial balancing was an appropriate mechanism to cure other deficiencies in this case. . . .

. . . [T]he good-faith compliance of the district with the court order over a reasonable period of time is a factor to be considered in deciding whether or not jurisdiction could be relinquished. A history of good-faith compliance is evidence that any current racial imbalance is not the product of a new *de jure* violation, and enables the district court to accept the school board's representation that it has accepted the principle of racial equality and will not suffer intentional discrimination in the future.

When a school district has not demonstrated good faith under a comprehensive plan to remedy ongoing violations, we have without hesitation approved comprehensive and continued district court supervision.

*   *   *

The judgment is reversed, and the case is remanded to the Court of Appeals. . . .

*   *   *

Justice Thomas took no part in the consideration or decision of this case.

Justice Scalia, concurring.

*   *   *

Almost a quarter century ago, in *Green v. School Bd. of New Kent County* (1968), this Court held that school systems which had been enforcing *de jure* segregation at the time of *Brown* had not merely an obligation to assign students and resources on a race-neutral basis but also an "affirmative duty" to "desegregate," that is, to achieve insofar as practicable racial balance in their schools. This holding has become such a part of our legal fabric that there is a tendency, reflected in the Court of Appeals opinion in this case, to speak as though the Constitution requires such racial balancing. Of course it does not: The Equal Protection Clause reaches only those racial imbalances shown to be intentionally caused by the State. . . .

*   *   *

Racially imbalanced schools are hence the product of a blend of public and private actions, and any assessment that they would not be segregated, or would not be *as* segregated, in the absence of a particular one of those factors is guesswork. It is similarly guesswork, of course, to say that they *would* be segregated, or would be *as* segregated, in the absence of one of those factors. Only in rare cases such as this one . . . , where the racial imbalance had been temporarily corrected after the abandonment of *de jure* segregation, can it be asserted with any degree of confidence that the past discrimination is no longer playing a proximate role. Thus, allocation of the burden of proof foreordains the result in almost all of the "vestige of past discrimination" cases. If, as is normally the case under our equal protection jurisprudence (and in the law generally), we require the plaintiffs to establish the asserted facts entitling them to relief — that the racial imbalance they wish corrected is at least in part the vestige of an old *de jure* system — the plaintiffs will almost always lose. Conversely, if we alter our normal approach and require the school authorities to establish the negative — that the imbalance is *not* attributable to their past discrimination — the plaintiffs will almost always win.

Since neither of these alternatives is entirely palatable, an observer unfamiliar with the history surrounding this issue might suggest that we avoid the problem by requiring only that the school authorities establish a regime in which parents are free to disregard neighborhood-school assignment, and to send their children (with transportation paid) to whichever school they choose. So long as there is free choice, he would say, there is no reason to require that the schools be made identical. The constitutional right is equal racial access to schools, not access to racially equal schools; whatever racial imbalances such a free-choice system might produce would be the product of private forces. We apparently envisioned no more than this in our initial post-*Brown* cases. It is also the approach we actually adopted in *Bazemore v. Friday* (1986), which concerned remedies for prior *de jure* segregation of state university-operated clubs and services.

But we ultimately charted a different course with respect to public elementary and secondary schools. We concluded in *Green* that a "freedom of choice" plan was not necessarily sufficient, and later applied this conclusion to all jurisdictions with a history of intentional segregation. . . . Thus began judicial recognition of an "affirmative duty" to desegregate, achieved by allocating the burden of negating causality to the defendant. Our post-*Green* cases provide that, once state-enforced school segregation is shown to have existed in a jurisdiction in 1954, there arises a presumption, effectively irrebuttable (because the school district cannot prove the negative), that any current racial imbalance is the product of that violation, at least if the imbalance has continuously existed.

In the context of elementary and secondary education, the presumption was extraordinary in law but not unreasonable in fact. . . . The extent and recency of the prior discrimination, and the improbability that young children (or their parents) would use "freedom of choice" plans to disrupt existing patterns "warrant[ed] a presumption [that] schools that are substantially disproportionate in their racial composition" were remnants of the *de jure* system.

But granting the merits of this approach at the time of *Green*, it is now 25 years later. "From the very first, federal supervision of local school systems was intended as a *temporary* measure to remedy past discrimination." We envisioned it as temporary partly because "[n]o single tradition in public education is more deeply rooted than local control over the operation of schools," and because no one's interest is furthered by subjecting the Nation's educational system to "judicial tutelage for the indefinite future." But we also envisioned it as temporary, I think, because the rational basis for the extraordinary presumption of causation simply must dissipate as the *de jure* system and the school boards who produced it recede further into the past. Since a multitude of private factors has shaped school systems in the years after abandonment of *de jure* segregation — normal migration, population growth (as in this case), "white flight" from the inner cities, increases in the costs of new facilities — the percentage of the current makeup of school systems attributable to the prior, government-enforced discrimination has diminished with each passing year, to the point where it cannot realistically be assumed to be a significant factor.

At some time, we must acknowledge that it has become absurd to assume, without any further proof, that violations of the Constitution dating from the days when Lyndon Johnson was President, or earlier, continue to have an appreciable effect upon current operation of schools. We are close to that time. While we must continue to prohibit, without qualification, all racial discrimination in the operation of public schools, and to afford remedies that eliminate not only the discrimination but its identified consequences, we should consider laying aside the extraordinary, and increasingly counterfactual, presumption of *Green*. We must soon revert to the ordinary principles of our law, of our democratic heritage, and of our educational tradition: that plaintiffs alleging equal protection violations must prove intent and causation and not merely the existence of racial disparity; that public schooling, even in the South, should be controlled by locally elected authorities acting in conjunction with parents; and that it is "desirable" to permit pupils to attend "schools nearest their homes."

JUSTICE SOUTER, concurring. [Omitted.]

JUSTICE BLACKMUN, with whom JUSTICE STEVENS and JUSTICE O'CONNOR join, concurring in the judgment. [Omitted.]

NOTES AND QUESTIONS

1. Reading between the lines of this case you can get some notion of what happened in the almost forty years which elapsed between *Brown* and *Freeman*. There was massive resistance, especially in the South, to the *Brown* case, and in particular to the Supreme Court's effectively making the federal courts the supervisors of the local school systems instead of state and local governments. As the years dragged on, and as many school systems, particularly in the South, remained virtually segregated, the federal courts devised a variety of new strategies for dealing with the problem. You have read, for example in *Freeman*, about the watershed decision in *Green v. County School Board of New Kent County*, 391 U.S. 430 (1968), an opinion by the great liberal Justice William Brennan, in which he held that on the facts before him a so-called "freedom of choice" plan, which allowed school children the option of choosing whether to attend a predominantly-white or a predominately-black school, did not meet the constitutional mandate expressed in *Brown*, because it failed to eradicate the "dual school system" condemned in *Brown*. But *Green*, in many ways, represented a radically different approach to school desegregation than that taken in *Brown*. *Brown* had only required that the state not dictate by law the schools students were to attend based on their race. Paradoxically, when *Green* required positive steps by the states to end the dual school systems, the states and localities found themselves actually required, once again, to assign pupils to schools based on their races, and the era of school busing, based on the race of students, began. The constitutional imprimatur approving of busing to

achieve racial balance was secured in the 1971 decision of *Swann v. Charlotte-Meckenbourg Board of Education*, 402 U.S. 1 (1971), when the Supreme Court approved of a district court's order that school children be taken by buses away from their neighborhood schools, in order to achieve racial balance in a public school system.

2. You can probably discern from the opinions in *Freeman*, and particularly that of Justice Scalia, the results of decisions such as *Green* and *Swann*. For many school districts, they ended the concept of "neighborhood schools," in the interests of racial integration. Was this what *Brown* intended? Does *Freeman* represent a departure from, or a return to the aims of *Brown*? *See* Michael Heise, *Assessing the Efficacy of School Desegregation*, 46 SYRACUSE L. REV. 1093 (1996) ("Too many students particularly those from low-income families attending inner-city public schools, may bear a disproportionate share of desegregation's [economic, educational, and other] costs"); *but see* Bernard James & Julie M. Hoffman, Brown *in State Hands: State Policymaking and Educational Equality after* Freeman v. Pitts, 20 HASTINGS CONST. L.Q. 521 (1993) (arguing that the legacy of *Brown*'s equality principle has been turned over to the states after *Freeman* and that state constitutional notions of equality thus take on greater importance).

3. One of the effects of *Brown* was "white flight," the movement of whites who feared the consequences of racial integration in the pubic schools to the suburbs, which, for a while at least, were not as racially mixed as the inner cities. Is the decline in the quality of urban education, which followed "white flight," a consequence of *Brown*? Should the Court have followed a strategy of insisting that school administrations be expanded so that both suburban and urban areas be administered together, in order to achieve racial balance and defeat the plans of those who fled from the urban schools? Cf., *Milliken v. Bradley*, 418 U.S. 717 (1974) (precluding an inter-district or multi-district remedy where there was no evidence that district boundaries were drawn purposefully on racial lines). Would a better strategy have been to insist on state-wide equality of per pupil expenditures? Such a strategy appears to be gaining in some states, though the proposition has yet to win universal acceptance. Who should be making decisions about how much is spent in local school systems — the federal courts, the federal legislature, the state legislatures, or local governments? What light does *Freeman* cast on the problem? Is race an intractable problem in American law? Consider the next group of cases.

4. Proving Discriminatory Intent

WASHINGTON v. DAVIS
426 U.S. 229 (1976)

MR. JUSTICE WHITE delivered the opinion of the Court.

This case involves the validity of a qualifying test administered to applicants for positions as police officers in the District of Columbia Metropolitan Police Department. . . .

I

This action began on April 10, 1970, when two Negro police officers filed suit against the then Commissioner of the District of Columbia, the Chief of the District's Metropolitan Police Department, and the Commissioners of the United States Civil Service Commission. An amended complaint, filed December 10, alleged that the promotion policies of the Department were racially discriminatory and sought a declaratory judgment and an injunction. The respondents Harley and Sellers were permitted to intervene, their amended complaint asserting that their applications to become officers in the Department had been rejected, and that the Department's recruiting procedures discriminated on the basis of race against black applicants by . . . a written personnel test which excluded a disproportionately high number of Negro applicants. . . . Respondents then filed a motion for partial summary judgment with respect to the recruiting phase of the case, seeking a declaration that the test administered to those applying to become police officers is "unlawfully discriminatory and thereby in violation of the due process clause of the Fifth Amendment." . . . The District of Columbia defendants, petitioners here, and the federal parties also filed motions for summary judgment. . . . The District Court granted petitioners' and denied respondents' motions.

According to the findings and conclusions of the District Court, to be accepted by the Department and to enter an intensive 17-week training program, the police recruit was required to satisfy certain physical and character standards, to be a high school graduate or its equivalent, and to receive a grade of at least 40 out of 80 on "Test 21," which is "an examination that is used generally throughout the federal service," which "was developed by the Civil Service Commission, not the Police Department," and which was "designed to test verbal ability, vocabulary, reading and comprehension."

The validity of Test 21 was the sole issue before the court on the motions for summary judgment. The District Court noted that there was no claim of "an intentional discrimination or purposeful discriminatory acts" but only a claim that Test 21 bore no relationship to job performance and "has a highly discriminatory impact in screening out black candidates." Respondents' evidence, the District Court said, warranted three conclusions: "(a) The number of black police officers, while substantial, is not proportionate to the population mix of the city. (b) A higher percentage of blacks fail the Test than whites. (c) The Test has not been validated to establish its reliability for measuring subsequent job performance." This showing was deemed sufficient to shift the burden of proof to the defendants in the action, petitioners here; but the court nevertheless concluded that on the undisputed facts respondents were not entitled to relief. The District Court relied on several factors. Since August 1969, 44% of new police force recruits had been black; that figure also represented the proportion of blacks on the total force and was roughly equivalent to 20- to 29-year-old blacks in the 50-mile radius in which the recruiting efforts of the Police Department had been concentrated. It was undisputed that the Department had systematically and affirmatively sought to enroll black officers many of whom passed the test but failed to report for duty. The District Court rejected the assertion that Test 21 was culturally slanted to favor whites and was "satisfied that the undisputable facts prove the test to be reasonably and directly related to the requirements of the police recruit training program and that it is neither so designed nor operates [*sic*] to discriminate against otherwise qualified blacks." It was thus not necessary to show that Test 21 was not only a useful indicator of training school performance but had also been validated in terms of job performance — "The lack of job performance validation does not defeat the Test, given its direct relationship to recruiting and the valid part it plays in this process." The District Court ultimately concluded that "[t]he proof is wholly lacking that a police officer qualifies on the color of his skin rather than ability" and that the Department "should not be required on this showing to lower standards or to abandon efforts to achieve excellence."

. . . [R]espondents brought the case to the Court of Appeals claiming that their summary judgment motion, which rested on purely constitutional grounds, should have been granted. The tendered constitutional issue was whether the use of Test 21 invidiously discriminated against Negroes and hence denied them due process of law contrary to the commands of the Fifth Amendment. The Court of Appeals, addressing that issue, announced that it would be guided by *Griggs v. Duke Power Co.* (1971), a case involving the interpretation and application of Title VII of the Civil Rights Act of 1964, and held that the statutory standards elucidated in that case were to govern the due process question tendered in this one. The court went on to declare that lack of discriminatory intent in designing and administering Test 21 was irrelevant; the critical fact was rather that a far greater proportion of blacks — four times as many — failed the test than did whites. This disproportionate impact, standing alone and without regard to whether it indicated a discriminatory purpose, was held sufficient to establish a constitutional violation, absent proof by petitioners that the test was an adequate measure of job performance in addition to being an indicator of probable success in the training program, a burden which the court ruled petitioners had failed to discharge. That the Department had made substantial efforts to recruit blacks was held beside the point and the fact that the racial distribution of recent hirings and of the Department itself might be roughly equivalent to the racial makeup of the surrounding community, broadly conceived, was put aside as a "comparison [not] material to this appeal." . . .

II

Because the Court of Appeals erroneously applied the legal standards applicable to Title VII cases in resolving the constitutional issue before it, we reverse its judgment in respondents' favor. . . .

As the Court of Appeals understood Title VII, employees or applicants proceeding under it need not concern themselves with the employer's possibly discriminatory purpose but instead may focus solely on the racially differential impact of the challenged hiring or promotion practices. This is not the constitutional rule. We have never held that the constitutional standard for adjudicating claims of invidious racial discrimination is identical to the standards applicable under Title VII, and we decline to do so today.

The central purpose of the Equal Protection Clause of the Fourteenth Amendment is the prevention of official conduct discriminating on the basis of race. It is also true that the Due Process Clause of the Fifth Amendment contains an equal protection component prohibiting the United States from invidiously discriminating between individuals or groups. *Bolling v. Sharpe* (1954). But our cases have not embraced the proposition that a law or other official act, without regard to whether it reflects a racially discriminatory purpose, is unconstitutional *solely* because it has a racially disproportionate impact.

Almost 100 years ago, *Strauder v. West Virginia* (1880) established that the exclusion of Negroes from grand and petit juries in criminal proceedings violated the Equal Protection Clause, but the fact that a particular jury or a series of juries does not statistically reflect the racial composition of the community does not in itself make out an invidious discrimination forbidden by the Clause. "A purpose to discriminate must be present which may be proven by systematic exclusion of eligible jurymen of the proscribed race or by unequal application of the law to such an extent as to show intentional discrimination." . . .

The rule is the same in other contexts. *Wright v. Rockefeller* (1964) upheld a New York congressional apportionment statute against claims that district lines had been racially gerrymandered. The challengers did not prevail because they failed to prove that the New York Legislature "was either motivated by racial considerations or in fact drew the districts on racial lines". . . .

The school desegregation cases have also adhered to the basic equal protection principle that the invidious quality of a law claimed to be racially discriminatory must ultimately be traced to a racially discriminatory purpose. That there are both predominantly black and predominantly white schools in a community is not alone violative of the Equal Protection Clause. The essential element of *de jure* segregation is "a current condition of segregation resulting from intentional state action." . . . The Court has also recently rejected allegations of racial discrimination based solely on the statistically disproportionate racial impact of various provisions of the Social Security Act because "[t]he acceptance of appellants' constitutional theory would render suspect each difference in treatment among the grant classes, however lacking in racial motivation and however otherwise rational the treatment might be."

This is not to say that the necessary discriminatory racial purpose must be express or appear on the face of the statute, or that a law's disproportionate impact is irrelevant in cases involving Constitution-based claims of racial discrimination. . . . It is also clear from the cases dealing with racial discrimination in the selection of juries that the systematic exclusion of Negroes is itself such an "unequal application of the law . . . as to show intentional discrimination." A prima facie case of discriminatory purpose may be proved as well by the absence of Negroes on a particular jury combined with the failure of the jury commissioners to be informed of eligible Negro jurors in a community, or with racially non-neutral selection procedures. With a prima facie case made out, "the burden of proof shifts to the State to rebut the presumption of unconstitutional action by showing that permissible racially neutral selection criteria and procedures have produced the monochromatic result."

Necessarily, an invidious discriminatory purpose may often be inferred from the totality of the relevant facts. . . . It is also not infrequently true that the discriminatory impact — in the jury cases for example, the total or seriously disproportionate exclusion of Negroes from jury venires — may for all practical purposes demonstrate unconstitutionality because in various circumstances the discrimination is very difficult to explain on nonracial grounds. Nevertheless, we have not held that a law, neutral on its face and serving ends otherwise within the power of government to pursue, is invalid under the Equal Protection Clause simply because it may affect a greater proportion of one race than of another. . . .

As an initial matter, we have difficulty understanding how a law establishing a racially neutral qualification for employment is nevertheless racially discriminatory and denies "any person . . . equal protection of the laws" simply because a greater proportion of Negroes fail to qualify than members of other racial or ethnic groups. Had respondents, along with all others who had failed Test 21, whether white or black, brought an action claiming that the test denied each of them equal protection of the laws as compared with those who had passed with high enough scores to qualify them as police recruits, it is most unlikely that their challenge would have been sustained. Test 21, which is administered generally to prospective Government employees, concededly seeks to ascertain whether those who take it have acquired a particular level of verbal skill; and it is untenable that the Constitution prevents the Government from seeking modestly to upgrade the communicative abilities of its employees rather than to be satisfied with some lower level of competence, particularly where the job requires special ability to communicate orally and in writing. Respondents, as Negroes, could no more successfully claim that the test denied them equal protection than could white applicants who also failed. The conclusion would not be different in the face of proof that more Negroes than whites had been disqualified by Test 21. That other Negroes also failed to score well would, alone, not demonstrate that respondents individually were being denied equal protection of the laws by the application of an otherwise valid qualifying test being administered to prospective police recruits.

Nor on the facts of the case before us would the disproportionate impact of Test 21 warrant the conclusion that it is a purposeful device to discriminate against Negroes and hence an infringement of the constitutional rights of respondents as well as other black applicants. As we have said, the test is neutral on its face and rationally may be said to serve a purpose the Government is constitutionally empowered to pursue. Even agreeing with the District Court that the differential racial effect of Test 21 called for further inquiry, we think the District Court correctly held that the affirmative efforts of the Metropolitan Police Department to recruit black officers, the changing racial composition of the recruit classes and of the force in general, and the relationship of the test to the training program negated any inference that the Department discriminated on the basis of race or that "a police officer qualifies on the color of his skin rather than ability."

Under Title VII, Congress provided that when hiring and promotion practices disqualifying substantially disproportionate numbers of blacks are challenged, discriminatory purpose need not be proved, and that it is an insufficient response to demonstrate some rational basis for the challenged practices. It is necessary, in addition, that they be "validated" in terms of job performance in any one of several ways, perhaps by ascertaining the minimum skill, ability, or potential necessary for the position at issue and determining whether the qualifying tests are appropriate for the selection of qualified applicants for the job in question. However this process proceeds, it involves a more probing judicial review of, and less deference to, the seemingly reasonable acts of administrators and executives than is appropriate under the Constitution where special racial impact, without discriminatory purpose, is claimed. We are not disposed to adopt this more rigorous standard for the purposes of applying the Fifth and the Fourteenth Amendments in cases such as this.

A rule that a statute designed to serve neutral ends is nevertheless invalid, absent compelling justification, if in practice it benefits or burdens one race more than another would be far reaching and would raise serious questions about, and perhaps invalidate, a whole range of tax, welfare, public service, regulatory, and licensing statutes that may be more burdensome to the poor and to the average black than to the more affluent white.

Given that rule, such consequences would perhaps be likely to follow. However, in our view, extension of the rule beyond those areas where it is already applicable by reason of statute, such as in the field of public employment, should await legislative prescription.

III

The judgment of the Court of Appeals accordingly is reversed.

Mr. Justice Stevens, concurring. [Omitted.]

Mr. Justice Brennan, with whom Mr. Justice Marshall joins, dissenting. [Omitted.]

NOTES AND QUESTIONS

1.   Under this case, what is the standard required to show unconstitutional racial discrimination? There seems to be a clear finding that a disproportionately high number of African-American applicants failed the written personnel test at issue. The plaintiffs believed that this disproportionate impact was enough to show a violation of the Equal Protection Clause, and the court of appeals apparently agreed. Why did the Supreme Court reject this argument?

2.   Note than in its decision of the case the majority departs from the standard under anti-discrimination statutory law (Title VII of the Civil Rights Act of 1964, 42 U.S.C. §§ 2000e to 2000e-17 (1994)), under which the showing of disproportionate impact would be enough to make out a presumption of a violation. The constitutional standard, according to the majority, is stricter, and requires an actual intent to discriminate. While the Court indicates that one must look to the totality of the circumstances, and disproportionate impact is one factor to be examined, given the circumstances of the case at bar, where the test seemed neutral on its face, and where there were efforts made to recruit black officers, the Court determined that there was no intent to discriminate.

3.   Why, then, do you suppose a dissenting opinion was filed by Justices Brennan and Marshall? Should intent be the test for a constitutional violation, or should disparate impact be enough? How, by the way, can Congress adopt an impact

standard in Title VII if the constitutional standard is based on intent?

4. In *Alexander v. Sandoval*, 532 U.S. 275 (2001), the Court used another statutory interpretation case to speculate further about the constitutionality of disparate impact statutes. *Alexander v. Sandoval* involved a class action claim that Alabama's policy of administering driver's license exams only in English violated U.S. Department of Transportation regulations forbidding recipients of federal funds from engaging in practices that have a disproportionate effect on the basis of national origin.

The Court, by a 5-4 majority, per Justice Scalia, concluded that, under Title VI of the Civil Rights Act of 1964, there is no private right of action to claim a disparate impact violation of federal regulations. In reaching this result, the Court largely relied upon established precedent against implying a private cause of action where none is intended by Congress. Justice Scalia noted that Title VI itself has been interpreted by the Court to forbid only intentional discrimination — disparate treatment — but the Department of Transportation regulations at issue went beyond that to ban actions that have only a disproportionate effect.

The Court seemed to do a partial about-face in *Jackson v. Birmingham Bd. of Education*, 544 U.S. 167 (2005), which involved a girl's basketball coach who was allegedly fired for complaining about disparities between boys and girls programs and who then asserted that the cause of action under Title IX that the Court had previously implied under Title IX extended to his claim of retaliation. The lower court, relying on *Alexander v. Sandoval*, rejected the claim, noting that courts may not allow a private right of action without explicit congressional intent. Moreover, said the lower courts, Title IX was nearly identical to Title VI except that it bars discrimination on the basis of sex, not race.

By a margin of 5 to 4, in an opinion by Justice O'Connor, the Court disagreed. It didn't matter, said Justice O'Connor, that Jackson was an "indirect" victim of discrimination, since Title IX is intended not only to prevent the use of federal dollars to support discriminatory practices, but also to provide citizens effective protection against those practices. Jackson would not be protected against retaliation for objecting to the discriminatory practice. Thus, the majority claimed to distinguish *Sandoval*. It is not a question of implying a discriminatory prohibition because retaliation against a person who speaks out against sex discrimination is the victim of intentional discrimination on the basis of sex.

The dissent, written by Justice Thomas, argued that the majority's opinion is contrary to the plain terms of Title IX. It is evident said the dissent that "retaliatory conduct" is qualitatively not the same as discrimination "on the basis of sex." In any event, Congress certainly had not spoken "unambiguously in imposing conditions on funding recipients through its spending power." Protecting whistleblowers may be wise policy, but Congress had not provided for it, and it is not up to the Court to expand liability. Wrote the dissent, "[b]y crafting its own additional enforcement mechanism, the majority returns this Court to the days in which it created remedies out of whole cloth to effectuate its vision of congressional purpose. In doing so, the majority substitutes its policy judgments for the bargains struck by Congress, as reflected in the statute's text." The majority reiterated in response that retaliation, itself, was a form of sex discrimination, and it was not imposing an unexpected condition on federal funds, since the Court had construed the previously implied Title IX private cause of action broadly and implementing regulations clearly covered retaliation.

5.   Returning to the distinction between disparate treatment and impact, in *Alexander v. Sandoval*, Alabama chose not to raise the constitutionality of reaching disparate impact. For reasons of its own, Alabama chose not to raise the constitutionality of reaching disparate impact. Nevertheless, in a footnote, Justice Scalia noted that "[w]e cannot help observing . . . how strange it is to say that disparate-impact regulations" implement Title VI when the statute "permits the very behavior that the regulations forbid."

As *Washington v. Davis* (1976) makes apparent, the Court has treated the difference between disparate treatment (intentional conduct) and disparate impact (unintended consequence) as one of kind, not degree. And the Court has been especially jealous of the Congress expanding or redefining the meaning of constitutional terms. *See, e.g.*, *City of Boerne v. Flores* (1997), where Congress was not allowed to expand the free exercise guarantee. If Congress can't do it, then executive agencies cannot either. This is especially true when executive agencies seek to impose their expansive regulations on the states, who were not forewarned in the acceptance of the federal money, as the Court has required since *Atascadero State Hospital v. Scanlon* (1985).

As these notes explore, the difference between intent and impact can be blurred in practice by the assessment of circumstantial evidence, including impact of indirect changes in procedures and the like. Pragmatically, many businesses simply hire by the numbers or settle cases where practices are alleged to have disproportionate impact. Defendants do have the opportunity to rebut disparate impact claims by proving that the challenged practices are justified by some "necessity," but this is often difficult and costly. These defendants are clearly advantaged by the indirect reminder in *Alexander* that intent remains the constitutional standard.

6.   An older example of where the intent/impact line was observed is *Village of Arlington Heights v. Metropolitan Housing Development Corp.* (1977). Metropolitan Housing Development Corporation (MHDC) applied to petitioner, the Village of Arlington Heights, Ill., for the rezoning of a 15-acre parcel from single-family to multiple-family classification. Using federal financial assistance, MHDC planned to build 190 clustered townhouse units for low- and moderate-income tenants. The Village denied the rezoning request. MHDC, joined by other plaintiffs brought suit alleging the denial was racially discriminatory and that it violated, *inter alia*, the Fourteenth Amendment and the Fair Housing Act of 1968. Following a bench trial, the District Court entered judgment for the Village, and respondents appealed. The Court of Appeals for the Seventh Circuit reversed, finding that the "ultimate effect" of the denial was racially discriminatory, and that the refusal to rezone therefore violated the Fourteenth Amendment. Finding a lack of intent, the Supreme Court reversed, but it suggested how intent might be infered from unusual process.

In particular, when the Plan Commission considered the MHDC proposal at a series of three public meetings, which drew large crowds. Some of the comments, both from opponents and supporters, addressed what was referred to as the "social issue" — the desirability or undesirability of introducing at this location in

Arlington Heights low- and moderate-income housing, housing that would probably be racially integrated.

Many of the opponents, however, focused on the zoning aspects of the petition, stressing two arguments. First, the area always had been zoned single-family, and the neighboring citizens had built or purchased there in reliance on that classification. Rezoning threatened to cause a measurable drop in property value for neighboring sites. Second, the Village's apartment policy, adopted by the Village Board in 1962 and amended in 1970, called for R-5 zoning primarily to serve as a buffer between single-family development and land uses thought incompatible, such as commercial or manufacturing districts. Lincoln Green did not meet this requirement, as it adjoined no commercial or manufacturing district.

Relying upon *Washington v. Davis* (1976), the Court stated that official action will not be held unconstitutional solely because it results in a racially disproportionate impact.

> . . . "Disproportionate impact is not irrelevant, but it is not the sole touchstone of an invidious racial discrimination." Proof of racially discriminatory intent or purpose is required to show a violation of the Equal Protection Clause. . . .

> *Davis* does not require a plaintiff to prove that the challenged action rested solely on racially discriminatory purposes. Rarely can it be said that a legislature or administrative body operating under a broad mandate made a decision motivated solely by a single concern, or even that a particular purpose was the "dominant" or "primary" one. In fact, it is because legislators and administrators are properly concerned with balancing numerous competing considerations that courts refrain from reviewing the merits of their decisions, absent a showing of arbitrariness or irrationality. But racial discrimination is not just another competing consideration. When there is a proof that a discriminatory purpose has been a motivating factor in the decision, this judicial deference is no longer justified.

But the Court admitted that finding the intent-based "smoking gun" evidence was rare. As a consequence, it was appropriate wrote Justice Powell for the Court to inquire into the impact of the official action — whether it "bears more heavily on one race than another," since this may provide an important starting point. "Sometimes a clear pattern," said the Court, "unexplainable on grounds other than race, emerges from the effect of the state action even when the governing legislation appears neutral on its face."

> The historical background of the decision is one evidentiary source, particularly if it reveals a series of official actions taken for invidious purposes. The specific sequence of events leading up to the challenged decision also may shed some light on the decisionmaker's purposes. For example, if the property involved here always had been zoned R-5 but suddenly was changed to R-3 when the town learned of MHDC's plans to erect integrated housing, we would have a far different case. Departures from the normal procedural sequence also might afford evidence that

improper purposes are playing a role. Substantive departures too may be relevant, particularly if the factors usually considered important by the decisionmaker strongly favor a decision contrary to the one reached.

The legislative or administrative history may be highly relevant, especially where there are contemporary statements by members of the decisionmaking body, minutes of its meetings, or reports. In some extraordinary instances the members might be called to the stand at trial to testify concerning the purpose of the official action, although even then such testimony frequently will be barred by privilege.

This circumstantial evidence was missing, and as a consequence, that the Village's decision carried a discriminatory "ultimate effect" was without independent constitutional significance. That, of course, did not preclude the statutory Fair Housing claim, since the FHA is an effects-based statute. 42 U.S.C. § 3601 *et seq.*

7. The Court has maintained the requirement of discriminatory intent or purpose in other cases. In *Mobile v. Bolden*, 446 U.S. 55 (1980), the Court refused to invalidate at-large voting in a predominately white town, writing "only if there is purposeful discrimination can there be a violation of the Equal Protection Clause. . . . [T]his principle applies to claims of racial discrimination affecting voting just as it does to other claims of racial discrimination." *Id.* at 67. Similarly, in *McClesky v. Kemp*, 481 U.S. 279 (1987), the Court refused to rely on statistical disparity in the administration of the death penalty to find an equal protection violation.

5. Civil Right or Preference?

We move now to a discussion of the use of racial preference in public decision making. In *City of Richmond v. Croson*, 488 U.S. 469 (1969), the Court, per Justice O'Connor, held that "generalized assertions" of past racial discrimination could not justify a racial set-aside in the award of public contracts. The City Council of Richmond, Virginia, had required that companies doing business with the city subcontract 30 percent of their business to minority business enterprises. While over 50% of the population in Richmond was black, only. 67% of the city's prime contracts had been awarded to minority contractors. The City's legal counsel opined that the set-aside would be constitutional since the Supreme Court had previously approved a 10% set-aside in *Fullilove v. Klutznick*, 448 U.S. 448 (1980), in federal contracting. The Supreme Court ruled otherwise when the J.A. Croson Company challenged the program as a "rigid" racial quota. Justice O'Connor's opinion noted that the 30 percent set-aside figure had not been linked with "any injury suffered by anyone." Distinguishing *Fullilove*, the Court noted that Congress had documented widespread discrimination in the construction industry. Moreover, the fact that "Congress may identify and redress the effects of society-wide discrimination does not mean that, *a fortiori*, the States and their political subdivisions are free to decide that such remedies are appropriate." Congress, she noted, has a specific mandate to enforce the Fourteenth Amendment, while the states are constrained by it. At a minimum, the use of a racial preference by a state must be tied to a showing of prior discrimination by the state or its political subdivision and the preference must be narrowly tailored to remedy that prior discrimination, which would necessarily mean employing race-neutral means of greater inclusiveness first. Justice O'Connor left open the possibility that the Constitution would also permit a city to be racially sensitive in its contracting practice to avoid becoming a passive participant in the demonstrable discrimination of others, but here, there simply was no particularized showing of discrimination of any kind. Allowing unrefined claims of past discrimination to serve as the basis for racial quotas would subvert constitutional values. Wrote Justice O'Connor: "The dream of a Nation of equal citizens in a society where race is irrelevant to personal opportunity and achievement would be lost in a mosaic of shifting preferences based on inherently unmeasurable claims of past wrongs."

Justice Marshall, joined by Justices Brennan and Blackmun, dissented, in the following terms:

A

Today, for the first time, a majority of this Court has adopted strict scrutiny as its standard of Equal Protection Clause review of race-conscious remedial measures. . . .

Racial classifications "drawn on the presumption that one race is inferior to another or because they put the weight of government behind racial hatred and separatism" warrant the strictest judicial scrutiny because of the very irrelevance of these rationales. By contrast, racial classifications drawn for the purpose of remedying the effects of discrimination that itself was race based have a highly pertinent basis: the tragic and indelible fact that discrimination against blacks and other racial minorities in this Nation has pervaded our Nation's history and continues to scar our society. As I stated in *Fullilove*: "Because the consideration of race is relevant to remedying the continuing effects of past racial discrimination, and because governmental programs employing racial classifications for remedial purposes can be crafted to avoid stigmatization, . . . such programs should not be subjected to conventional 'strict scrutiny' — scrutiny that is strict in theory, but fatal in fact."

* * *

B

I am also troubled by the majority's assertion that, even if it did not believe generally in strict scrutiny of race-based remedial measures, "the circumstances of this case" require this Court to look upon the Richmond City Council's measure with the strictest scrutiny. The sole such circumstance which the majority cites, however, is the fact that blacks in Richmond are a "dominant racial grou[p]" in the city. In support of this characterization of dominance, the majority observes that "blacks constitute approximately 50% of the population of the city of Richmond" and that "[f]ive of the nine seats on the City Council are held by blacks."

While I agree that the numerical and political supremacy of a given racial group is a factor bearing upon the level of scrutiny to be applied, this Court has never held that numerical inferiority, standing alone, makes a racial group "suspect" and thus entitled to strict scrutiny review. Rather, we have identified *other* "traditional indicia of suspectness": whether a group has been "saddled with such disabilities, or subjected to such a history of purposeful unequal treatment, or relegated to such a position of political powerlessness as to command extraordinary protection from the majoritarian political process."

It cannot seriously be suggested that nonminorities in Richmond have any "history of purposeful unequal treatment." . . .

In my view, the "circumstances of this case," underscore the importance of *not* subjecting to a strict scrutiny straitjacket the increasing number of cities which have recently come under minority leadership and are eager to rectify, or at least prevent the perpetuation of, past racial discrimination. In many cases, these cities will be the ones with the most in the way of prior discrimination to rectify. Richmond's leaders had just witnessed decades of publicly sanctioned racial discrimination in virtually all walks of life — discrimination amply documented in the decisions of the federal judiciary. This history of "purposefully unequal treatment" forced upon minorities, not imposed by them, should raise an inference that minorities in Richmond had much to remedy — and that the 1983 set-aside was undertaken with sincere remedial goals in mind, not "simple racial politics."

*   *   *

C

Today's decision, finally, is particularly noteworthy for the daunting standard it imposes upon States and localities contemplating the use of race-conscious measures to eradicate the present effects of prior discrimination and prevent its perpetuation. The majority restricts the use of such measures to situations in which a State or locality can put forth "a prima facie case of a constitutional or statutory violation." In so doing, the majority calls into question the validity of the business set-asides which dozens of municipalities across this Nation have adopted on the authority of *Fullilove*.

Notice that Justice O'Connor's majority opinion leaves open the possibility that the Federal government has more freedom than the states to engage in allegedly benign racial discrimination pursuant to Section 5 of the Fourteenth Amendment. This issue was first addressed in *Metro Broadcasting, Inc. v. Federal Communications Commission*, 497 U.S. 547 (1990), in which a badly divided 5-4 Court upheld congressional preferences for minority-owned businesses in broadcast licensing. Writing for the Court, the late Justice Brennan asserted that the federal government somehow was held to a lesser standard of equality than the states in *Richmond v. Croson*. This was an unstable outcome, as the next case reflects.

ADARAND CONSTRUCTORS, INC. v. PENA
515 U.S. 200 (1995)

JUSTICE O'CONNOR announced the judgment of the Court and delivered an opinion with respect to Parts I, II, III-A, III-B, III-D, and IV, which is for the Court except insofar as it might be inconsistent with the views expressed in JUSTICE SCALIA'S concurrence, and an opinion with respect to Part III-C in which JUSTICE KENNEDY joins.

Petitioner Adarand Constructors, Inc., claims that the Federal Government's practice of giving general contractors on government projects a financial incentive to hire subcontractors controlled by "socially and economically disadvantaged individuals," and in particular, the Government's use of race-based presumptions in identifying such individuals, violates the equal protection component of the Fifth Amendment's Due Process Clause. . . .

I

In 1989, the Central Federal Lands Highway Division (CFLHD), which is part of the United States Department of Transportation (DOT), awarded the prime contract for a highway construction project in Colorado to Mountain Gravel & Construction Company. Mountain Gravel then solicited bids from subcontractors for the guardrail portion of the contract. Adarand, a Colorado-based highway construction company specializing in guardrail work, submitted the low bid. Gonzales Construction Company also submitted a bid.

The prime contract's terms provide that Mountain Gravel would receive additional compensation if it hired subcontractors certified as small businesses controlled by "socially and economically disadvantaged individuals." Gonzales is certified as such a business; Adarand is not. Mountain Gravel awarded the subcontract to Gonzales, despite Adarand's low bid, and Mountain Gravel's Chief Estimator has submitted an affidavit stating that Mountain Gravel would have accepted Adarand's bid, had it not been for the additional payment it received by hiring Gonzales instead. Federal law requires that a subcontracting clause similar to the one used here must appear in most federal agency contracts, and it also requires the clause to state that "the contractor shall presume that socially and economically disadvantaged individuals include Black Americans, Hispanic Americans, Native Americans, Asian Pacific Americans, and other minorities, or any other individual found to be disadvantaged by the [Small Business] Administration pursuant to section 8(a) of the Small Business Act." Adarand claims that the presumption set forth in that statute discriminates on the basis of race in violation of the Federal Government's Fifth Amendment obligation not to deny anyone equal protection of the laws.

These fairly straightforward facts implicate a complex scheme of federal statutes and regulations, to which we now turn. The Small Business Act declares it to be "the policy of the United States that small business concerns, [and] small business concerns owned and controlled by socially and economically disadvantaged individuals, . . . shall have the maximum practicable opportunity to participate in the performance of contracts let by any Federal agency." The Act defines "socially disadvantaged individuals" as "those who have been subjected to racial or ethnic prejudice or cultural bias because of their identity as a member of a group without regard to their individual qualities," and it defines "economically disadvantaged individuals" as "those socially disadvantaged individuals whose ability to compete in the free enterprise system has been impaired due to diminished capital and credit opportunities as compared to others in the same business area who are not socially disadvantaged."

In furtherance of [its] policy . . . the Act establishes "[t]he Government-wide goal for participation by small business concerns owned and controlled by socially and economically disadvantaged individuals" at "not less than 5 percent of the total value of all prime contract and subcontract awards for each fiscal year." It also requires the head of each Federal agency to set agency-specific goals for participation by businesses controlled by socially and economically disadvantaged individuals.

The Small Business Administration (SBA) has implemented these statutory directives in a variety of ways, two of which are relevant here. One is the "8(a) program," which is available to small businesses controlled by socially and economically disadvantaged individuals as the SBA has defined those terms. The 8(a) program confers a wide range of benefits on participating businesses, one of which is automatic eligibility for subcontractor compensation provisions of the kind at issue in this case. To participate in the 8(a) program, a business must be "small," . . . and it must be 51% owned by individuals who qualify as "socially and economically disadvantaged." The SBA presumes that Black, Hispanic, Asian Pacific, Subcontinent Asian, and Native Americans, as well as "members of other groups designated from time to time by SBA," are "socially disadvantaged." It also allows any individual not a member of a listed group to prove social disadvantage "on the basis of clear and convincing evidence". . . . Social disadvantage is not enough to establish eligibility, however; SBA also requires each 8(a) program participant to prove "economic disadvantage". . . .

The other SBA program relevant to this case is the "8(d) subcontracting program," which unlike the 8(a) program is limited to eligibility for subcontracting provisions like the one at issue here. In determining eligibility, the SBA presumes social disadvantage based on membership in certain minority groups, just as in the 8(a) program, and again appears to require an individualized, although "less restrictive," showing of economic disadvantage. A different set of regulations, however, says that members of minority groups wishing to participate in the 8(d) subcontracting program are entitled to a race-based presumption of social *and* economic disadvantage. We are left with some uncertainty as to whether participation in the 8(d) subcontracting program requires an individualized showing of economic disadvantage. In any event, in both the 8(a) and the 8(d) programs, the presumptions of disadvantage are rebuttable if a third party comes forward with evidence suggesting that the participant is not, in fact, either economically or socially disadvantaged.

The contract giving rise to the dispute in this case came about as a result of the Surface Transportation and Uniform Relocation Assistance Act of 1987 ("STURAA"), a DOT appropriations measure. [It] provides that "not less than 10 percent" of the appropriated funds "shall be expended with small business concerns owned and controlled by socially and economically disadvantaged individuals." STURAA adopts the Small Business Act's definition of "socially and economically disadvantaged individual," including the applicable race-based presumptions, and adds that "women shall be presumed to be socially and economically disadvantaged individuals for purposes of this subsection." STURAA also requires the Secretary of Transportation to establish "minimum uniform criteria for State governments to use in certifying whether a concern qualifies for purposes of this subsection." The Secretary has [issued] . . . regulations [which] say that the certifying authority should presume both social and economic disadvantage (*i.e.*, eligibility to participate) if the applicant belongs to certain racial groups, or is a woman. As with the SBA programs, third parties may come forward with evidence in an effort to rebut the presumption of disadvantage for a particular business.

The operative clause in the contract in this case reads as follows:

> "*Subcontracting*. This subsection is supplemented to include a Disadvantaged Business Enterprise (DBE) Development and Subcontracting Provision as follows:
>
>> "Monetary compensation is offered for awarding subcontracts to small business concerns owned and controlled by socially and economically disadvantaged individuals. . . .
>>
>> "A small business concern will be considered a DBE after it has been certified as such by the U.S. Small Business Administration or any State Highway Agency. . . . If the Contractor requests payment under this provision, the Contractor shall furnish the engineer with acceptable evidence of the subcontractor(s') DBE certification and shall furnish one certified copy of the executed subcontract(s).
>>
>> "The Contractor will be paid an amount computed as follows:
>>
>> "1. If a subcontract is awarded to one DBE, 10 percent of the final amount of the approved DBE subcontract, not to exceed 1.5 percent of the original contract amount.
>>
>> "2. If subcontracts are awarded to two or more DBEs, 10 percent of the final amount of the approved DBE subcontracts, not to exceed 2 percent of the original contract amount."

To benefit from this clause, Mountain Gravel had to hire a subcontractor who had been certified as a small disadvantaged business by the SBA, a state highway agency, or some other certifying authority acceptable to the Contracting Officer. . . .

After losing the guardrail subcontract to Gonzales, Adarand filed suit against various federal officials in the United States District Court for the District of Colorado, claiming that the race-based presumptions involved in the use of subcontracting compensation clauses violate Adarand's right to equal protection. The District Court granted the Government's motion for summary judgment. The Court of Appeals for the Tenth Circuit affirmed. It understood our decision in *Fullilove v. Klutznick* (1980), to have adopted "a lenient standard, resembling intermediate scrutiny, in assessing" the constitutionality of federal race-based action. Applying that "lenient standard," as further developed in *Metro Broadcasting, Inc. v. FCC* (1990), the Court of Appeals upheld the use of subcontractor compensation clauses. . . .

* * *

III

[The Government] urge[s] that "[t]he Subcontracting Compensation Clause program is . . . a program based on *disadvantage,* not on race," and thus that it is subject only to "the most relaxed judicial scrutiny." To the extent that the statutes and regulations involved in this case are race neutral, we agree. [The Government] concede[s], however, that "the race-based rebuttable presumption used in some certification determinations under the Subcontracting Compensation Clause" is subject to some heightened level of scrutiny. The parties disagree as to what that level should be. . . .

Adarand's claim arises under the Fifth Amendment to the Constitution, which provides that "No person shall . . . be deprived of life, liberty, or property, without due process of law." Although this Court has always understood that Clause to provide some measure of protection against *arbitrary* treatment by the Federal Government, it is not as explicit a guarantee of *equal* treatment as the Fourteenth Amendment, which provides that "No *State* shall . . . deny to any person within its jurisdiction the equal protection of the laws" (emphasis added). Our cases have accorded varying degrees of significance to the difference in the language of those two Clauses. We think it necessary to revisit the issue here.

A

Through the 1940s, this Court had routinely taken the view in non-race-related cases that, "[u]nlike the Fourteenth Amendment, the Fifth contains no equal protection clause and it provides no guaranty against discriminatory legislation by Congress." When the Court first faced a Fifth Amendment equal protection challenge to a federal racial classification, it adopted a similar approach, with most unfortunate results. In *Hirabayashi v. United States* (1943), the Court considered a curfew applicable only to persons of Japanese ancestry. The Court observed — correctly — that "[d]istinctions between citizens solely because of their ancestry are by their very nature odious to a free people whose institutions are founded upon the doctrine of equality," and that "racial discriminations are in most circumstances irrelevant and therefore prohibited." But it also [held] that the Fifth Amendment "restrains only such discriminatory legislation by Congress as amounts to a denial of due process," and upheld the curfew because "circumstances within the knowledge of those charged with the responsibility for maintaining the national defense afforded a rational basis for the decision which they made."

Eighteen months later, the Court again approved wartime measures directed at persons of Japanese ancestry. *Korematsu v. United States* (1944), concerned an order that completely excluded such persons from particular areas. The Court did not address the view, expressed in cases like *Hirabayashi* . . . that the Federal Government's obligation to provide equal protection differs significantly from that of the States. Instead, it began by noting that "all legal restrictions which curtail the civil rights of a single racial group are immediately suspect . . . [and] courts must subject them to the most rigid scrutiny." . . . But in spite of the "most rigid scrutiny" standard it had just set forth, the Court then inexplicably relied on "the principles we announced in the *Hirabayashi* case," to conclude that, although "exclusion from the area in which one's home is located is a far greater deprivation than constant confinement to the home from 8 p.m. to 6 a.m.," the racially discriminatory order was nonetheless within the Federal Government's power.

In *Bolling v. Sharpe* (1954) [a companion case to *Brown*, forbidding legally-mandated segregation in the District of Columbia's schools], the Court for the first time explicitly questioned the existence of any difference between the obligations of the Federal Government and the States to avoid racial classifications. *Bolling* did note that "[t]he 'equal protection of the laws' is a more explicit safeguard of prohibited unfairness than 'due process of law.' " But *Bolling* then concluded that, "[i]n view of [the] decision that the Constitution prohibits the states from maintaining racially segregated public schools, it would be unthinkable that the same Constitution would impose a lesser duty on the Federal Government."

Bolling's facts concerned school desegregation, but its reasoning was not so limited. . . .

Later cases in contexts other than school desegregation did not distinguish between the duties of the States and the Federal Government to avoid racial classifications. . . .

. . . Thus, in 1975, the Court stated explicitly that "this Court's approach to Fifth Amendment equal protection claims has always been precisely the same as to equal protection claims under the Fourteenth Amendment." We do not understand a few contrary suggestions appearing in cases in which we found special deference to the political branches of the Federal Government to be appropriate to detract from this general rule.

B

. . . In 1978, the Court confronted the question whether race-based governmental action designed to *benefit* such groups [which had previously suffered discrimination] should also be subject to "the most rigid scrutiny." *Regents of Univ. of California v. Bakke* (1978) involved an equal protection challenge to a state-run medical school's practice of reserving a number of spaces in its entering class for minority students. The petitioners argued that "strict scrutiny" should apply only to "classifications that disadvantage 'discrete and insular minorities.' " *Bakke* did not produce an opinion for the Court, but Justice Powell's opinion announcing the Court's judgment rejected the argument. In a passage joined by Justice White, Justice Powell wrote that "[t]he guarantee of equal protection cannot mean one thing when applied to one individual and something else when applied to a person of another color." . . . On the other hand, four Justices in *Bakke* would have applied a less stringent standard of review to racial classifications "designed to further remedial purposes." And four Justices thought the case should be decided on statutory grounds.

Two years after *Bakke*, . . . [i]n *Fullilove v. Klutznick* (1980), the Court upheld Congress' inclusion of a 10% set-aside for minority-owned businesses in the Public Works Employment Act of 1977. As in *Bakke*, there was no opinion for the Court.

Chief Justice Burger, in an opinion joined by Justices White and Powell, observed that "[a]ny preference based on racial or ethnic criteria must necessarily receive a most searching examination to make sure that it does not conflict with constitutional guarantees." That opinion, however, "d[id] not adopt, either expressly or implicitly, the formulas of analysis articulated in such cases as [*Bakke*]." It employed instead a two-part test which asked, first, "whether the *objectives* of th[e] legislation are within the power of Congress," and second, "whether the limited use of racial and ethnic criteria, in the context presented, is a constitutionally permissible *means* for achieving the congressional objectives." It then upheld the program under that test, adding at the end of the opinion that the program also "would survive judicial review under either 'test' articulated in the several *Bakke* opinions." Justice Powell wrote separately to express his view that the plurality opinion had essentially applied "strict scrutiny" as described in his *Bakke* opinion. . . . Justice Stewart (joined by then-JUSTICE REHNQUIST) dissented, arguing that the Constitution required the Federal Government to meet the same strict standard as the States when enacting racial classifications, and that the program before the Court failed that standard. JUSTICE STEVENS also dissented, arguing that "[r]acial classifications are simply too pernicious to permit any but the most exact connection between justification and classification," and that the program before the Court could not be characterized "as a 'narrowly tailored' remedial measure." Justice Marshall (joined by Justices Brennan and Blackmun) concurred in the judgment, reiterating the view of four Justices in *Bakke* that any race-based governmental action designed to "remed[y] the present effects of past racial discrimination" should be upheld if it was "substantially related" to the achievement of an "important governmental objective" — *i.e.*, such action should be subjected only to what we now call "intermediate scrutiny."

In *Wygant v. Jackson Board of Ed.* (1986), the Court considered a Fourteenth Amendment challenge to another form of remedial racial classification. The issue in *Wygant* was whether a school board could adopt race-based preferences in determining which teachers to lay off. Justice Powell's plurality opinion observed that "the level of scrutiny does not change merely because the challenged classification operates against a group that historically has not been subject to governmental discrimination," and stated the two-part inquiry as "whether the layoff provision is supported by a compelling state purpose and whether the means chosen to accomplish that purpose are narrowly tailored." In other words, "racial classifications of any sort must be subjected to 'strict scrutiny.'" The plurality then concluded that the school board's interest in "providing minority role models for its minority students, as an attempt to alleviate the effects of societal discrimination," was not a compelling interest that could justify the use of a racial classification. It added that "[s]ocietal discrimination, without more, is too amorphous a basis for imposing a racially classified remedy," and insisted instead that "a public employer . . . must ensure that, before it embarks on an affirmative-action program, it has convincing evidence that remedial action is warranted. That is, it must have sufficient evidence to justify the conclusion that there has been prior discrimination." Justice White concurred only in the judgment, although he agreed that the school board's asserted interests could not, "singly or together, justify this racially discriminatory layoff policy." Four Justices dissented, three of whom again argued for intermediate scrutiny of remedial race-based government action.

The Court's failure to produce a majority opinion in *Bakke, Fullilove*, and *Wygant* left unresolved the proper analysis for remedial race-based governmental action. Lower courts found this lack of guidance unsettling.

The Court resolved the issue, at least in part, in . . . *Richmond v. J.A. Croson Co.* (1989). . . .

With *Croson*, the Court finally agreed that the Fourteenth Amendment requires strict scrutiny of all race-based action by state and local governments. But *Croson* of course had no occasion to declare what standard of review the Fifth Amendment requires for such action taken by the Federal Government. . . .

. . . [T]he Court's cases through *Croson* had established three general propositions with respect to governmental racial classifications. First, skepticism: " 'any preference based on racial or ethnic criteria must necessarily receive a most searching examination.' " Second, consistency: "[T]he standard of review under the Equal Protection Clause is not dependent on the race of those burdened or benefitted by a particular classification". . . . And third, congruence: "Equal protection analysis in the Fifth Amendment area is the same as that under the Fourteenth Amendment." Taken together, these three propositions lead to the conclusion that any person, of whatever race, has the right to demand that any governmental actor subject to the Constitution justify any racial classification subjecting that person to unequal treatment under the strictest judicial scrutiny. . . .

A year later, however, the Court took a surprising turn. *Metro Broadcasting, Inc. v. FCC* [(1990)], involved a Fifth Amendment challenge to two race-based policies of the Federal Communications Commission. In *Metro Broadcasting*, the Court repudiated the long-held notion that "it would be unthinkable that the same Constitution would impose a lesser duty on the Federal Government" than it does on a State to afford equal protection of the laws. It did so by holding that "benign" federal racial classifications need only satisfy intermediate scrutiny, even though *Croson* had recently concluded that such classifications enacted by a State must satisfy strict scrutiny. "[B]enign" federal racial classifications, the Court said, " — even if those measures are not 'remedial' in the sense of being designed to compensate victims of past governmental or societal discrimination — are constitutionally permissible to the extent that they serve *important* governmental objectives within the power of Congress and are *substantially related* to achievement of those objectives." (emphasis added). The Court did not explain how to tell whether a racial classification should be deemed "benign," other than to express "confidence that an 'examination of the legislative scheme and its history' will separate benign measures from other types of racial classifications."

Applying this test, the Court first noted that the FCC policies at issue did not serve as a remedy for past discrimination. Proceeding on the assumption that the policies were nonetheless "benign," it concluded that they served the "important governmental objective" of "enhancing broadcast diversity," and that they were "substantially related" to that objective. It therefore upheld the policies.

By adopting intermediate scrutiny as the standard of review for congressionally mandated "benign" racial classifications, *Metro Broadcasting* departed from prior cases in two significant respects. First, it turned its back on *Croson*'s explanation of why strict scrutiny of all governmental racial classifications is essential:

> "Absent searching judicial inquiry into the justification for such race-based measures, there is simply no way of determining what classifications are 'benign' or 'remedial' and what classifications are in fact motivated by illegitimate notions of racial inferiority or simple racial politics. Indeed, the purpose of strict scrutiny is to 'smoke out' illegitimate uses of race by assuring that the legislative body is pursuing a goal important enough to warrant use of a highly suspect tool. The test also ensures that the means chosen 'fit' this compelling goal so closely that there is little or no possibility that the motive for the classification was illegitimate racial prejudice or stereotype." (plurality opinion of O'CONNOR, J.).

We adhere to that view today, despite the surface appeal of holding "benign" racial classifications to a lower standard, because "it may not always be clear that a so-called preference is in fact benign," *Bakke* (opinion of Powell, J.). "[M]ore than good motives should be required when government seeks to allocate its resources by way of an explicit racial classification system."

Second, *Metro Broadcasting* squarely rejected one of the three propositions established by the Court's earlier equal protection cases, namely, congruence between the standards applicable to federal and state racial classifications, and in so doing also undermined the other two — skepticism of all racial classifications and consistency of treatment irrespective of the race of the burdened or benefited group. . . .

The three propositions undermined by *Metro Broadcasting* all derive from the basic principle that the Fifth and Fourteenth Amendments to the Constitution protect *persons*, not *groups*. It follows from that principle that all governmental action based on race — a *group* classification long recognized as "in most circumstances irrelevant and therefore prohibited" — should be subjected to detailed judicial inquiry to ensure that the *personal* right to equal protection of the laws has not been infringed. . . . Accordingly, we hold today that all racial classifications, imposed by whatever federal, state, or local governmental actor, must be analyzed by a reviewing court under strict scrutiny. In other words, such classifications are constitutional only if they are narrowly tailored measures that further compelling governmental interests. To the extent that *Metro Broadcasting* is inconsistent with that holding, it is overruled.

*   *   *

C

"Although adherence to precedent is not rigidly required in constitutional cases, any departure from the doctrine of *stare decisis* demands special justification." In deciding whether this case presents such justification, we recall Justice Frankfurter's admonition that "*stare decisis* is a principle of policy and not a mechanical formula of adherence to the latest decision, however recent and questionable, when such adherence involves collision with a prior doctrine more embracing in its scope, intrinsically sounder, and verified by experience." Remaining true to an "intrinsically sounder" doctrine established in prior cases better serves the values of *stare decisis* than would following a more recently decided case inconsistent with the decisions that came before it; the latter course would simply compound the recent error and would likely make the unjustified break from previously established doctrine complete. In such a situation, "special justification" exists to depart from the recently decided case.

As we have explained, *Metro Broadcasting* undermined important principles of this Court's equal protection jurisprudence, established in a line of cases stretching back over fifty years. Those principles together stood for an "embracing" and "intrinsically soun[d]" understanding of equal protection "verified by experience," namely, that the Constitution imposes upon federal, state, and local governmental actors the same obligation to respect the personal right to equal protection of the laws. . . .

* * *

It is worth pointing out the difference between the applications of *stare decisis* in this case and in *Planned Parenthood of Southeastern Pa. v. Casey* (1992). *Casey* explained how considerations of *stare decisis* inform the decision whether to overrule a long-established precedent that has become integrated into the fabric of the law. Overruling precedent of that kind naturally may have consequences for "the ideal of the rule of law." In addition, such precedent is likely to have engendered substantial reliance, as was true in *Casey* itself. But in this case, as we have explained, we do not face a precedent of that kind, because *Metro Broadcasting* itself *departed* from our prior cases — and did so quite recently. By refusing to follow *Metro Broadcasting*, then, we do not depart from the fabric of the law; we restore it. . . .

* * *

D

Our action today makes explicit what Justice Powell thought implicit in the *Fullilove* lead opinion: Federal racial classifications, like those of a State, must serve a compelling governmental interest, and must be narrowly tailored to further that interest. Of course, it follows that to the extent (if any) that *Fullilove* held federal racial classifications to be subject to a less rigorous standard, it is no longer controlling. But we need not decide today whether the program upheld in *Fullilove* would survive strict scrutiny as our more recent cases have defined it.

Some have questioned the importance of debating the proper standard of review of race-based legislation. But we agree with JUSTICE STEVENS that, "[b]ecause racial characteristics so seldom provide a relevant basis for disparate treatment, and because classifications based on race are potentially so harmful to the entire body politic, it is especially important that the reasons for any such classification be clearly identified and unquestionably legitimate" and that "[r]acial classifications are simply too pernicious to permit any but the most exact connection between justification and classification." We think that requiring strict scrutiny is the best way to ensure that courts will consistently give racial classifications that kind of detailed examination, both as to ends and as to means. . . .

Finally, we wish to dispel the notion that strict scrutiny is "strict in theory, but fatal in fact." *Fullilove, supra* (Marshall, J., concurring in judgment). The unhappy persistence of both the practice and the lingering effects of racial discrimination against minority groups in this country is an unfortunate reality, and government is not disqualified from acting in response to it. As recently as 1987, for example, every Justice of this Court agreed that the Alabama Department of Public Safety's "pervasive, systematic, and obstinate discriminatory conduct" justified a narrowly tailored race-based remedy. See *United States v. Paradise* (1987). When race-based action is necessary to further a compelling interest, such action is within constitutional constraints if it satisfies the "narrow tailoring" test this Court has set out in previous cases.

IV

Because our decision today alters the playing field in some important respects, we think it best to remand the case to the lower courts for further consideration in light of the principles we have announced. The Court of Appeals, following *Metro Broadcasting* and *Fullilove*, analyzed the case in terms of intermediate scrutiny. It upheld the challenged statutes and regulations because it found them to be "narrowly tailored to achieve [their] *significant governmental purpose* of providing subcontracting opportunities for small disadvantaged business enterprises." (emphasis added). The Court of Appeals did not decide the question whether the interests served by the use of subcontractor compensation clauses are properly described as "compelling." It also did not address the question of narrow tailoring in terms of our strict scrutiny cases, by asking, for example, whether there was "any consideration of the use of race-neutral means to increase minority business participation" in government contracting, *Croson*, or whether the program was appropriately limited such that it "will not last longer than the discriminatory effects it is designed to eliminate," *Fullilove* (Powell, J., concurring).

*   *   *

Accordingly, the judgment of the Court of Appeals is vacated, and the case is remanded for further proceedings consistent with this opinion.

JUSTICE SCALIA, concurring in part and concurring in the judgment.

I join the opinion of the Court, except Part III-C, and except insofar as it may be inconsistent with the following: In my view, government can never have a "compelling interest" in discriminating on the basis of race in order to "make up" for past racial discrimination in the opposite direction. Individuals who have been wronged by unlawful racial discrimination should be made whole; but under our Constitution there can be no such thing as either a creditor or a debtor race. That concept is alien to the Constitution's focus upon the individual, and its rejection of dispositions based on race, or based on blood, see III, § 3 ("[N]o Attainder of Treason shall work Corruption of Blood"); Art. I, § 9, cl. 8 ("No Title of Nobility shall be granted by the United States"). To pursue the concept of racial entitlement — even for the most admirable and benign of purposes — is to reinforce and preserve for future mischief the way of thinking that produced race slavery, race privilege and race hatred. In the eyes of government, we are just one race here. It is American.

*   *   *

JUSTICE THOMAS, concurring in part and concurring in the judgment.

I agree with the majority's conclusion that strict scrutiny applies to *all* government classifications based on race. I write separately, however, to express my disagreement with the premise underlying JUSTICE STEVENS' and JUSTICE GINSBURG's dissents: that there is a racial paternalism exception to the principle of equal protection. I believe that there is a "moral [and] constitutional equivalence," between laws designed to subjugate a race and those that distribute benefits on the basis of race in order to foster some current notion of equality. Government cannot make us equal; it can only recognize, respect, and protect us as equal before the law.

That these programs may have been motivated, in part, by good intentions cannot provide refuge from the principle that under our Constitution, the government may not make distinctions on the basis of race. As far as the Constitution is concerned, it is irrelevant whether a government's racial classifications are drawn by those who wish to oppress a race or by those who have a sincere desire to help those thought to be disadvantaged. There can be no doubt that the paternalism that appears to lie at the heart of this program is at war with the principle of inherent equality that underlies and infuses our Constitution. see Declaration of Independence ("We hold these truths to be self-evident, that all men are created equal, that they are endowed by their Creator with certain unalienable Rights, that among these are Life, Liberty, and the pursuit of Happiness").

These programs not only raise grave constitutional questions, they also undermine the moral basis of the equal protection principle. Purchased at the price of immeasurable human suffering, the equal protection principle reflects our Nation's understanding that such classifications ultimately have a destructive impact on the individual and our society. Unquestionably, "[i]nvidious [racial] discrimination is an engine of oppression." It is also true that "[r]emedial" racial preferences may reflect "a desire to foster equality in society." But there can be no doubt that racial paternalism and its unintended consequences can be as poisonous and pernicious as any other form of discrimination. So-called "benign" discrimination teaches many that because of chronic and apparently immutable handicaps, minorities cannot compete with them without their patronizing indulgence. Inevitably, such programs engender attitudes of superiority or, alternatively, provoke resentment among those who believe that they have been wronged by the government's use of race. These programs stamp minorities with a badge of inferiority and may cause them to develop dependencies or to adopt an attitude that they are "entitled" to preferences. . . .

In my mind, government-sponsored racial discrimination based on benign prejudice is just as noxious as discrimination inspired by malicious prejudice. In each instance, it is racial discrimination, plain and simple.

JUSTICE STEVENS, with whom JUSTICE GINSBURG joins, dissenting.

Instead of deciding this case in accordance with controlling precedent, the Court today delivers a disconcerting lecture about the evils of governmental racial classifications. . . .

The Court's concept of "consistency" assumes that there is no significant difference between a decision by the majority to impose a special burden on the members of a minority race and a decision by the majority to provide a benefit to certain members of that minority notwithstanding its incidental burden on some members of the majority. In my opinion that assumption is untenable. There is no moral or constitutional equivalence between a policy that is designed to perpetuate a caste system and one that seeks to eradicate racial subordination. Invidious discrimination is an engine of oppression, subjugating a disfavored group to enhance or maintain the power of the majority. Remedial race-based preferences reflect the opposite impulse: a desire to foster equality in society. . . .

The consistency that the Court espouses would disregard the difference between a "No Trespassing" sign and a welcome mat. It would treat a Dixiecrat Senator's decision to vote against Thurgood Marshall's confirmation in order to keep African Americans off the Supreme Court as on a par with President Johnson's evaluation of his nominee's race as a positive factor. It would equate a law that made black citizens ineligible for military service with a program aimed at recruiting black soldiers. An attempt by the majority to exclude members of a minority race from a regulated market is fundamentally different from a subsidy that enables a relatively small group of newcomers to enter that market. An interest in "consistency" does not justify treating differences as though they were similarities.

The Court's explanation for treating dissimilar race-based decisions as though they were equally objectionable is a supposed inability to differentiate between "invidious" and "benign" discrimination. But the term "affirmative action " is common and well understood. Its presence in everyday parlance shows that people understand the difference between good intentions and bad. . . .

Indeed, our jurisprudence has made the standard to be applied in cases of invidious discrimination turn on whether the discrimination is "intentional," or whether, by contrast, it merely has a discriminatory "effect." *Washington v. Davis* (1976). Surely this distinction is at least as subtle, and at least as difficult to apply, as the usually obvious distinction between a measure intended to benefit members of a particular minority race and a measure intended to burden a minority race. . . .

Second, *Metro Broadcasting*'s holding rested on more than its application of "intermediate scrutiny." Indeed, I have always believed that, labels notwithstanding, the FCC program we upheld in that case would have satisfied any of our various standards in affirmative-action cases — including the one the majority fashions today. What truly distinguishes *Metro Broadcasting* from our other affirmative-action precedents is the distinctive goal of the federal program in that case. Instead of merely seeking to remedy past discrimination, the FCC program was intended to achieve future benefits in the form of broadcast diversity. Reliance on race as a legitimate means of achieving diversity was first endorsed by Justice Powell in *Regents of Univ. of California v. Bakke* (1978). Later, in *Wygant v. Jackson Board of Ed.* (1986), I also argued that race is not always irrelevant to governmental decisionmaking; in response, JUSTICE O'CONNOR correctly noted that, although the School Board had relied on an interest in providing black teachers to serve as role models for black students, that interest "should not be confused with the very different goal of promoting racial diversity among the faculty." She then added that, because the school board had not relied on an interest in diversity, it was not "necessary to discuss the magnitude of that interest or its applicability in this case."

Thus, prior to *Metro Broadcasting*, the interest in diversity had been mentioned in a few opinions, but it is perfectly clear that the Court had not yet decided whether that interest had sufficient magnitude to justify a racial classification. *Metro Broadcasting*, of course, answered that question in the affirmative. The majority today overrules *Metro Broadcasting* only insofar as it is "inconsistent with [the] holding" that strict scrutiny applies to "benign" racial classifications promulgated by the Federal Government. The proposition that fostering diversity may provide a sufficient interest to justify such a program is *not* inconsistent with the Court's holding today — indeed, the question is not remotely presented in this case — and I do not take the Court's opinion to diminish that aspect of our decision in *Metro Broadcasting*.

JUSTICE SOUTER, with whom JUSTICE GINSBURG and JUSTICE BREYER join, dissenting.

As the Court's opinion explains in detail, the scheme in question provides financial incentives to general contractors to hire subcontractors who have been certified as disadvantaged business enterprises on the basis of certain race-based presumptions. These statutes (or the originals, of which the current ones are reenactments) have previously been justified as providing remedies for the continuing effects of past discrimination, see, *e.g., Fullilove*, and the Government has so defended them in this case. Since petitioner has not claimed the obsolescence of any particular fact on which the *Fullilove* Court upheld the statute, no issue has come up to us that might be resolved in a way that would render *Fullilove* inapposite.

In these circumstances, I agree with JUSTICE STEVENS's conclusion that *stare decisis* compels the application of *Fullilove*. Although *Fullilove* did not reflect doctrinal consistency, its several opinions produced a result on shared grounds that petitioner does not attack: that discrimination in the construction industry had been subject to government acquiescence, with effects that remain and that may be addressed by some preferential treatment falling within the congressional power under § 5 of the Fourteenth Amendment. Once *Fullilove* is applied, as JUSTICE STEVENS points out, it follows that the statutes in question here (which are substantially better tailored to the harm being remedied than the statute endorsed in *Fullilove*) pass muster under Fifth Amendment due process and Fourteenth Amendment equal protection.

JUSTICE GINSBURG, with whom JUSTICE BREYER joins, dissenting [omitted].

NOTES AND QUESTIONS

1. *Adarand,* if possible, created even more of a stir than did *Richmond v. Croson.* You will remember that *Richmond* suggested, and *Metro Broadcasting* held, that the federal government had more freedom to engage in "benign" racial

classifications than did the state governments. Suddenly, in 1995, that was no longer the case, and even very recent federal court precedents were no longer good law. Why? What, if anything, had changed? Was it that the Court in 1995 came to see the validity of Justice O'Connor's reasoning in dissent in *Metro Broadcasting* that "[m]odern equal protection doctrine has recognized only one [sufficient] interest [for employing a racial classification]: remedying the effects of racial discrimination. The interest in increasing diversity of broadcast viewpoints is clearly not a compelling interest." 497 U.S. at 612 (O'Connor, J., dissenting).

Does Justice O'Connor's view now prevail? Has diversity as a rationale, say for racial preference in an educational setting, been ruled off-limits? A decade prior to *Adarand*, a plurality of the Court articulated in *Wygant v. Jackson Bd. of Ed.*, 476 U.S. 267 (1986) (holding that a school board could not use race-based preferences to determine teacher layoffs), that a compelling governmental interest only exists when it seeks to remedy prior discrimination. As Justice Powell wrote for the Court's plurality: "[A] public employer . . . must ensure that, before it embarks on an affirmative-action program, it has convincing evidence that remedial action is warranted. That is, it must have sufficient evidence to justify the conclusion that there has been prior discrimination." *Id.* at 277. Again, does this mean that racial preference is now off-limits for non-remedial purposes?

In *Adarand*, the Court properly reminds us that because our Nation is still beset by "both the practice and the lingering effects of racial discrimination against minority groups," strict scrutiny is not " 'strict in theory, but fatal in fact.' " 515 U.S. at 237 (quoting *Fullilove v. Klutznick*, 448 U.S. 448, 519 (1980) (Marshall, J., concurring in the judgment) (*Fullilove* upheld a federal government set-aside for minority businesses, but its plurality opinion failed to supply a coherent rationale.)). However, does the general recognition of these "lingering effects" allow the transforming of the very constitutional standard of remedying prior discrimination clarified in *Wygant, Croson*, and *Adarand*, into a broad undifferentiated claim of advancing diversity?

Answering the question is somewhat complicated, in part, because there remains disagreement among members of the Court on the manner in which prior discrimination is to be proven. Justice Scalia, for example, argues that "government can never have a 'compelling interest' in discriminating on the basis of race in order to 'make up' for past racial discrimination in the opposite direction." 515 U.S. at 239 (Scalia, J., concurring in part and concurring in the judgment). Similarly, Justice Thomas characterizes racial preferences by the government as a type of "paternalism" that is "at war with the principle of inherent equality that underlies and infuses our Constitution." *Id.* at 240 (Thomas, J., concurring in part and concurring in the judgment) (referencing The Declaration of Independence para. 1 (U.S. 1776)). By comparison, Justice O'Connor speculated in *Croson* that a state may act to prevent itself from being used as a "passive participant" in private discrimination. 488 U.S. at 491–92 (plurality opinion of O'Connor, J.).

2. Note Justice Scalia's consistent position that no racial classifications are supportable under the Fourteenth Amendment. Note also the strong opinion by Justice Thomas, the Court's only African-American Justice. What disturbs him about the racial classification at issue, given that the classification was made in

order to help African Americans? Justice Thomas was the subject of powerful criticism for his affirmative action constitutional opinions, given that he was supposedly himself the beneficiary of affirmative action. Or was he? Before Thomas assumed the bench, he was one of the most vocal proponents of the notion that natural law ought to be a part of constitutional jurisprudence. Do you see any signs of that in his opinion in this case?

3. What about societal discrimination? Whatever differences remain on the Court concerning the demonstration of prior discrimination (see Note 1 above), a clear majority of the Court subscribes to the belief articulated by the plurality in *Wygant* that "[i]n the absence of particularized findings [of prior discrimination], a court could uphold remedies that are ageless in their reach into the past, and timeless in their ability to affect the future." 476 U.S. at 276 (plurality opinion). Likewise, Justice O'Connor writes: "I agree with the plurality that a governmental agency's interest in remedying 'societal' discrimination, that is, discrimination not traceable to its own actions, cannot be deemed sufficiently compelling to pass constitutional muster under strict scrutiny." *Id.* at 288 (O'Connor, J., concurring in part and concurring in the judgment).

4. So what about racial diversity, then, in say, an educational setting? In *Regents of the University of California v. Bakke*, 438 U.S. 265 (1978), the Court could reach no majority opinion in a case dealing with the reservation of 16 slots in the UC Davis medical school for minority students. Four Justices assumed that racial affirmative action might be reviewed under intermediate scrutiny, a proposition since rejected by the Court, and Justice Powell opined that while the reservation of places was unconstitutional, race could be used by admissions committees as a "factor" to enhance diversity. There is considerable question whether Justice Powell's suggestion remains good law. Justice O'Connor made glancing reference to the Powell's view in *Wygant*, but as one appellate court determined in rejecting the race-based admission policy of the University of Texas law school: "The . . . argument is not persuasive. Justice O'Connor's statement is purely descriptive and [does] not purport to express her approval or disapproval of diversity as a compelling interest." *Hopwood v. Texas*, 78 F.3d 932, 845 n.27, *cert. denied*, 116 S. Ct. 2581 (1996). Duke law professor Walter Dellinger, while serving President Clinton in the Department of Justice, records that the Court has *never* accepted diversity as a constitutionally sufficient justification for racial preference. Office of Legal Counsel Memorandum to General Counsels, Re: *Adarand* at 12 (available on Westlaw at 1995 DLR 125 d33 (June 29, 1995).

5. But can't racial diversity be justified on the same basis as school desegregation? This, too, seems difficult. The discretion federal courts have to integrate student bodies is necessarily linked in *Swann v. Charlotte-Mecklenburg Bd. of Educ.*, 402 U.S. 1 (1971), and other similar cases to a finding of past discrimination or publicly imposed segregation (*i.e.*, a "dual school system"). *See, e.g., Keyes v. School District No. 1, Denver, Colorado*, 413 U.S. 189 (1973) (specifically adhering to the distinction between de jure and de facto discrimination, which mirrors the distinction later drawn by the Court between discrimination by the governmental entity, itself, and societal discrimination). It was only if school authorities failed in their affirmative obligation to eliminate the official and egregious segregation condemned in *Brown v. Board of Education*, 347 U.S. 483 (1954), and following

cases, that the equitable authority of district courts could be invoked. 402 U.S. at 15. Even in the face of clearly demonstrated past discrimination, the Court was careful to note in *Swann* that "the constitutional command to desegregate schools does not mean that every school in every community must always reflect the racial composition of the school system as a whole." *Id.* at 24. Undifferentiated claims for the non-remedial use of race in public decisions have unfortunately marred the otherwise admirable effort of federal judges to address the real harms of past discrimination in the school context. *See, e.g., Missouri v. Jenkins,* 515 U.S. 70 (1995) (finding the order of teacher salary increases and similar measures to enhance the "desegregative attractiveness" of the schools to far exceed the scope of the constitutional violation and thus the district court's equitable discretion) ("[W]ithout an interdistrict violation and interdistrict effect, there is no constitutional wrong calling for an interdistrict remedy." 515 U.S. at 87). One writer puts the problem of justifying a diversity claim this way:

> [T]he diversity rationale neatly disposes of pesky questions about when affirmative action will end. Compensatory affirmative action was always advertised as temporary, and the passage of time has created . . . legal . . . problems. The legal problem is that those affirmative action programs that the Court approved as having an adequate factual predicate must also, in order to gain approval, have a self-destruct mechanism. And as the most egregious forms of discrimination are reined in, the likelihood of new court-ordered affirmative action remedies drops precipitously. . . . Since diversity is unrelated to historical wrongs, its rationale . . . applies in *perpetuity.* . . .

RICHARD D. KAHLENBERG, THE REMEDY: CLASS, RACE, AND AFFIRMATIVE ACTION 39–40 (1996) (emphasis added). Justice O'Connor recognized the inherent problem with diversity claims when she wrote in *Croson* for the plurality that "[t]he dissent's watered down version of equal protection review effectively assures that race will always be relevant in American life, and that the 'ultimate goal' of 'eliminat[ing] entirely from government decisionmaking such irrelevant factors as a human being's race' . . . will never be achieved." 488 U.S. at 495 (plurality opinion of O'Connor, J.) (quoting *Wygant,* 476 U.S. at 320 (Stevens, J., dissenting)).

6. Isn't diversity a good way to secure necessary services to underserved areas or populations? This certainly has surface plausibility. However, as Justice Powell found in *Bakke,* there was "virtually no evidence" the preference for minority applicants was "either needed or geared to promote that goal." 438 U.S. at 310. The simple fact is: race as proxy is racial stereotype. "[T]he use of a racial characteristic to establish a presumption that the individual also possesses other, and socially relevant, characteristics, exemplifies, encourages and legitimizes the mode of thought and behavior that underlies most prejudice and bigotry in modern America." Richard A. Posner, *The* DeFunis *Case and the Constitutionality of Preferential Treatment of Racial Minorities,* 1974 SUP. CT. REV. 12 (1974). Are race-neutral and more narrowly tailored programs more effective means of facilitating such objectives? *See* Eugene Volokh, *Race as Proxy, and Religion as Proxy,* 43 UCLA L. REV. 2059, 2064–70 (1996) (arguing that there are better ways). "Social scientists may debate how peoples' thoughts and behavior reflect their background, but the Constitution provides that the government may not allocate

benefits or burdens among individuals based on the assumption that race or ethnicity determines how they act or think." *Metro Broadcasting v. Federal Communications Commission*, 497 U.S. at 602 (O'Connor, J., dissenting).

7. Could it be that diversity claims are simply not well addressed by clumsy or anonymous set-aside mechanisms that large public bureaucracies employ, and that diversity would be better pursued voluntarily by private actors in contexts where the effect of race on individual life can be meaningfully considered without subverting the principle of equal justice under law? *See* Douglas W. Kmiec, *The Abolition of Public Racial Preference — An Invitation to Private Racial Sensitivity*, 11 Notre Dame J.L. Ethics & Pub. Pol'y 1 (1997). Diversity can enrich debate and discussion, but it can also aggravate racial division. Professor Robert Alt writes:

> The inevitable conclusion to which this system leads is that if you are not my color, you are not qualified to police me, to represent me, or to judge me; you do not know my experiences, and therefore you lack legitimacy. . . . [I]t is [just] this sort of racial classification and segregation that the Equal Protection Clause and Civil Rights Act [were] intended to prevent, not to foster.

Robert D. Alt, *Toward Equal Protection*, 36 Washburn L.J. 179, 189 (1997). Diversity as an abstract concept remains high-sounding, but it may have more troubling implications than first thought. Perhaps the most troubling is that some see diversity as "discarding the aspiration of color blindness in the long run. . . . [T]he . . . advocates of diversity argue that the color-blind ideal was wrong all along. Race does matter, and it always will. . . ." Kahlenberg, *supra*, at 28. Would the elder Justice Harlan see diversity thus conceived as antithetical to the Constitution? The Court took up the question in the following twin cases involving the University of Michigan's undergraduate and law school admissions programs.

GRUTTER v. BOLLINGER
539 U.S. 306 (2003)

Justice O'Connor delivered the opinion of the Court.

This case requires us to decide whether the use of race as a factor in student admissions by the University of Michigan Law School (Law School) is unlawful.

I

A

The Law School ranks among the Nation's top law schools. . . . The Law School sought to ensure that its efforts to achieve student body diversity complied with this Court's most recent ruling on the use of race in university admissions. See *Regents of Univ. of Cal. v. Bakke* (1978). . . .

The hallmark of that policy is its focus on academic ability coupled with a flexible assessment of applicants' talents, experiences, and potential "to contribute to the learning of those around them." The policy requires admissions officials to evaluate each applicant based on all the information available in the file, including a personal statement, letters of recommendation, and an essay describing the ways in which the applicant will contribute to the life and diversity of the Law School. In reviewing an applicant's file, admissions officials must consider the applicant's undergraduate grade point average (GPA) and Law School Admissions Test (LSAT) score because they are important (if imperfect) predictors of academic success in law school. The policy stresses that "no applicant should be admitted unless we expect that applicant to do well enough to graduate with no serious academic problems."

. . . The policy requires admissions officials to look beyond grades and test scores to other criteria that are important to the Law School's educational objectives. So-called " 'soft' variables" such as "the enthusiasm of recommenders, the quality of the undergraduate institution, the quality of the applicant's essay, and the areas and difficulty of undergraduate course selection" are all brought to bear in assessing an "applicant's likely contributions to the intellectual and social life of the institution."

. . . The policy does not restrict the types of diversity contributions eligible for "substantial weight" in the admissions process, but instead recognizes "many possible bases for diversity admissions." The policy does, however, reaffirm the Law School's longstanding commitment to "one particular type of diversity," that is, "racial and ethnic diversity with special reference to the inclusion of students from groups which have been historically discriminated against, like African-Americans, Hispanics and Native Americans, who without this commitment might not be represented in our student body in meaningful numbers." By enrolling a " 'critical mass' of [underrepresented] minority students," the Law School seeks to "ensur[e] their ability to make unique contributions to the character of the Law School."

The policy does not define diversity "solely in terms of racial and ethnic status." Nor is the policy "insensitive to the competition among all students for admission to the [L]aw [S]chool." Rather, the policy seeks to guide admissions officers in "producing classes both diverse and academically outstanding, classes made up of students who promise to continue the tradition of outstanding contribution by Michigan Graduates to the legal profession."

B

Petitioner Barbara Grutter is a white Michigan resident who applied to the Law School in 1996 with a 3.8 grade point average and 161 LSAT score. The Law School initially placed petitioner on a waiting list, but subsequently rejected her application. . . . .

Petitioner further alleged that her application was rejected because the Law School uses race as a "predominant" factor, giving applicants who belong to certain minority groups "a significantly greater chance of admission than students with similar credentials from disfavored racial groups." Petitioner also alleged that respondents "had no compelling interest to justify their use of race in the admissions process." Petitioner requested compensatory and punitive damages, an order requiring the Law School to offer her admission, and an injunction prohibiting the Law School from continuing to discriminate on the basis of race.

* * *

During the 15-day bench trial, the parties introduced extensive evidence concerning the Law School's use of race in the admissions process. Dennis Shields, Director of Admissions when petitioner applied to the Law School, testified that he did not direct his staff to admit a particular percentage or number of minority students, but rather to consider an applicant's race along with all other factors.

* * *

[Petitioner's expert, Dr. Kinley Larntz] concluded that membership in certain minority groups " 'is an extremely strong factor in the decision for acceptance,' " and that applicants from these minority groups " 'are given an extremely large allowance for admission' " as compared to applicants who are members of nonfavored groups. Dr. Larntz conceded, however, that race is not the predominant factor in the Law School's admissions calculus.

* * *

In the end, the District Court concluded that the Law School's use of race as a factor in admissions decisions was unlawful. Applying strict scrutiny, the District Court determined that the Law School's asserted interest in assembling a diverse student body was not compelling because "the attainment of a racially diverse class . . . was not recognized as such by *Bakke* and is not a remedy for past discrimination." . . .

Sitting en banc, the Court of Appeals reversed. . . . Four dissenting judges would have held the Law School's use of race unconstitutional. . . .

* * *

II

A

Since this Court's splintered decision in *Bakke*, Justice Powell's opinion announcing the judgment of the Court has served as the touchstone for constitutional analysis of race-conscious admissions policies. . . .

Justice Powell began by stating that "[t]he guarantee of equal protection cannot mean one thing when applied to one individual and something else when applied to a person of another color. . . ." First, Justice Powell rejected an interest in " 'reducing the historic deficit of traditionally disfavored minorities in medical schools and in the medical profession' " as an unlawful interest in racial balancing. Second, Justice Powell rejected an interest in remedying societal discrimination because such measures would risk placing unnecessary burdens on innocent third parties "who bear no responsibility for whatever harm the beneficiaries of the special admissions program are thought to have suffered." Third, Justice Powell rejected an interest in "increasing the number of physicians who will practice in communities currently underserved," concluding that even if such an interest could be compelling in some circumstances the program under review was not "geared to promote that goal."

Justice Powell approved the university's use of race to further only one interest: "the attainment of a diverse student body." With the important proviso that "constitutional limitations protecting individual rights may not be disregarded," Justice Powell grounded his analysis in the academic freedom that "long has been viewed as a special concern of the First Amendment." . . .

Justice Powell was, however, careful to emphasize that in his view race "is only one element in a range of factors a university properly may consider in attaining the goal of a heterogeneous student body." For Justice Powell, "[i]t is not an interest in simple ethnic diversity, in which a specified percentage of the student body is in effect guaranteed to be members of selected ethnic groups," that can justify the use of race. Rather, "[t]he diversity that furthers a compelling state interest encompasses a far broader array of qualifications and characteristics of which racial or ethnic origin is but a single though important element."

*   *   *

For the reasons set out below, today we endorse Justice Powell's view that student body diversity is a compelling state interest that can justify the use of race in university admissions.

B

The Equal Protection Clause provides that no State shall "deny to any person within its jurisdiction the equal protection of the laws." U.S. Const., Amdt. 14, § 2. Because the Fourteenth Amendment "protect[s] *persons*, not *groups*," all "governmental action based on race — a *group* classification long recognized as in most circumstances irrelevant and therefore prohibited — should be subjected to detailed judicial inquiry to ensure that the *personal* right to equal protection of the laws has not been infringed." . . .

We have held that all racial classifications imposed by government "must be analyzed by a reviewing court under strict scrutiny." This means that such classifications are constitutional only if they are narrowly tailored to further compelling governmental interests. "Absent searching judicial inquiry into the justification for such race-based measures," we have no way to determine what "classifications are 'benign' or 'remedial' and what classifications are in fact motivated by illegitimate notions of racial inferiority or simple racial politics." . . .

Strict scrutiny is not "strict in theory, but fatal in fact." Although all governmental uses of race are subject to strict scrutiny, not all are invalidated by it. . . .

Context matters when reviewing race-based governmental action under the Equal Protection Clause. . . .

III

A

With these principles in mind, we turn to the question whether the Law School's use of race is justified by a compelling state interest. Before this Court, as they have throughout this litigation, respondents assert only one justification for their use of race in the admissions process: obtaining "the educational benefits that flow from a diverse student body." . . .

*   *   *

The Law School's educational judgment that such diversity is essential to its educational mission is one to which we defer. . . .

We have long recognized that, given the important purpose of public education and the expansive freedoms of speech and thought associated with the university environment, universities occupy a special niche in our constitutional tradition. . . .

As part of its goal of "assembling a class that is both exceptionally academically qualified and broadly diverse," the Law School seeks to "enroll a 'critical mass' of minority students." The Law School's interest is not simply "to assure within its student body some specified percentage of a particular group merely because of its race or ethnic origin." That would amount to outright racial balancing, which is patently unconstitutional. *Freeman v. Pitts* (1992) ("Racial balance is not to be achieved for its own sake"). Rather, the Law School's concept of critical mass is defined by reference to the educational benefits that diversity is designed to produce.

These benefits are substantial. As the District Court emphasized, the Law School's admissions policy promotes "cross-racial understanding," helps to break down racial stereotypes, and "enables [students] to better understand persons of different races." These benefits are "important and laudable," because "classroom discussion is livelier, more spirited, and simply more enlightening and interesting" when the students have "the greatest possible variety of backgrounds."

The Law School's claim of a compelling interest is further bolstered by its *amici*, who point to the educational benefits that flow from student body diversity. In addition to the expert studies and reports entered into evidence at trial, numerous studies show that student body diversity promotes learning outcomes, and "better prepares students for an increasingly diverse workforce and society, and better prepares them as professionals." . . .

These benefits are not theoretical but real, as major American businesses have made clear that the skills needed in today's increasingly global marketplace can only be developed through exposure to widely diverse people, cultures, ideas, and viewpoints. . . . To fulfill its mission, the military "must be selective in admissions for training and education for the officer corps, *and* it must train and educate a highly qualified, racially diverse officer corps in a racially diverse setting." We agree that "[i]t requires only a small step from this analysis to conclude that our country's other most selective institutions must remain both diverse and selective."

* * *

Moreover, universities, and in particular, law schools, represent the training ground for a large number of our Nation's leaders. . . . A handful of these schools accounts for 25 of the 100 United States Senators, 74 United States Courts of Appeals judges, and nearly 200 of the more than 600 United States District Court judges.

* * *

The Law School does not premise its need for critical mass on "any belief that minority students always (or even consistently) express some characteristic minority viewpoint on any issue." To the contrary, diminishing the force of such stereotypes is both a crucial part of the Law School's mission, and one that it cannot accomplish with only token numbers of minority students. Just as growing up in a particular region or having particular professional experiences is likely to affect an individual's views, so too is one's own, unique experience of being a racial minority in a society, like our own, in which race unfortunately still matters. The Law School has determined, based on its experience and expertise, that a "critical mass" of underrepresented minorities is necessary to further its compelling interest in securing the educational benefits of a diverse student body.

B

Even in the limited circumstance when drawing racial distinctions is permissible to further a compelling state interest, government is still "constrained in how it may pursue that end: [T]he means chosen to accomplish the [government's] asserted purpose must be specifically and narrowly framed to accomplish that purpose."

* * *

To be narrowly tailored, a race-conscious admissions program cannot use a quota system — it cannot "insulat[e] each category of applicants with certain desired qualifications from competition with all other applicants." Instead, a university may consider race or ethnicity only as a " 'plus' in a particular applicant's file," without "insulat[ing] the individual from comparison with all other candidates for the available seats." In other words, an admissions program must be "flexible enough to consider all pertinent elements of diversity in light of the particular qualifications of each applicant, and to place them on the same footing for consideration, although not necessarily according them the same weight."

. . . It follows from this mandate that universities cannot establish quotas for members of certain racial groups or put members of those groups on separate admissions tracks. Nor can universities insulate applicants who belong to certain racial or ethnic groups from the competition for admission. Universities can, however, consider race or ethnicity more flexibly as a "plus" factor in the context of individualized consideration of each and every applicant.

* * *

THE CHIEF JUSTICE believes that the Law School's policy conceals an attempt to achieve racial balancing, and cites admissions data to contend that the Law School discriminates among different groups within the critical mass. (dissenting opinion).

*   *   *

Here, the Law School engages in a highly individualized, holistic review of each applicant's file, giving serious consideration to all the ways an applicant might contribute to a diverse educational environment. The Law School affords this individualized consideration to applicants of all races. There is no policy, either *de jure* or *de facto*, of automatic acceptance or rejection based on any single "soft" variable. Unlike the program at issue in *Gratz v. Bollinger*, the Law School awards no mechanical, predetermined diversity "bonuses" based on race or ethnicity. . . .

We also find that, like the Harvard plan Justice Powell referenced in *Bakke*, the Law School's race-conscious admissions program adequately ensures that all factors that may contribute to student body diversity are meaningfully considered alongside race in admissions decisions. With respect to the use of race itself, all underrepresented minority students admitted by the Law School have been deemed qualified. . . .

The Law School does not, however, limit in any way the broad range of qualities and experiences that may be considered valuable contributions to student body diversity. To the contrary, the 1992 policy makes clear "[t]here are many possible bases for diversity admissions," and provides examples of admittees who have lived or traveled widely abroad, are fluent in several languages, have overcome personal adversity and family hardship, have exceptional records of extensive community service, and have had successful careers in other fields. The Law School seriously considers each "applicant's promise of making a notable contribution to the class by way of a particular strength, attainment, or characteristic — *e.g.*, an unusual intellectual achievement, employment experience, nonacademic performance, or personal background." All applicants have the opportunity to highlight their own potential diversity contributions through the submission of a personal statement, letters of recommendation, and an essay describing the ways in which the applicant will contribute to the life and diversity of the Law School.

What is more, the Law School actually gives substantial weight to diversity factors besides race. The Law School frequently accepts nonminority applicants with grades and test scores lower than underrepresented minority applicants (and other nonminority applicants) who are rejected. This shows that the Law School seriously weighs many other diversity factors besides race that can make a real and dispositive difference for nonminority applicants as well. By this flexible approach, the Law School sufficiently takes into account, in practice as well as in theory, a wide variety of characteristics besides race and ethnicity that contribute to a diverse student body. JUSTICE KENNEDY speculates that "race is likely outcome determinative for many members of minority groups" who do not fall within the upper range of LSAT scores and grades. (dissenting opinion). But the same could be said of the Harvard plan discussed approvingly by Justice Powell in *Bakke*, and indeed of any plan that uses race as one of many factors.

Petitioner and the United States argue that the Law School's plan is not narrowly tailored because race-neutral means exist to obtain the educational benefits of student body diversity that the Law School seeks. We disagree. Narrow tailoring does not require exhaustion of every conceivable race-neutral alternative. Nor does it require a university to choose between maintaining a reputation for excellence or fulfilling a commitment to provide educational opportunities to members of all racial groups. . . . Narrow tailoring does, however, require serious, good faith consideration of workable race-neutral alternatives that will achieve the diversity the university seeks.

We agree with the Court of Appeals that the Law School sufficiently considered workable race-neutral alternatives. The District Court took the Law School to task for failing to consider race-neutral alternatives such as "using a lottery system" or "decreasing the emphasis for all applicants on undergraduate GPA and LSAT scores." But these alternatives would require a dramatic sacrifice of diversity, the academic quality of all admitted students, or both.

The Law School's current admissions program considers race as one factor among many, in an effort to assemble a student body that is diverse in ways broader than race. Because a lottery would make that kind of nuanced judgment impossible, it would effectively sacrifice all other educational values, not to mention every other kind of diversity. So too with the suggestion that the Law School simply lower admissions standards for all students, a drastic remedy that would require the Law School to become a much different institution and sacrifice a vital component of its educational mission. The United States advocates "percentage plans," recently adopted by public undergraduate institutions in Texas, Florida, and California to guarantee admission to all students above a certain class rank threshold in every high school in the State. The United States does not, however, explain how such plans could work for graduate and professional schools. Moreover, even assuming such plans are race-neutral, they may preclude the university from conducting the individualized assessments necessary to assemble a student body that is not just racially diverse, but diverse along all the qualities valued by the university. We are satisfied that the Law School adequately considered race-neutral alternatives currently capable of producing a critical mass without forcing the Law School to abandon the academic selectivity that is the cornerstone of its educational mission.

We acknowledge that "there are serious problems of justice connected with the idea of preference itself." Narrow tailoring, therefore, requires that a race-conscious admissions program not unduly harm members of any racial group. Even remedial race-based governmental action generally "remains subject to continuing oversight to assure that it will work the least harm possible to other innocent persons competing for the benefit." To be narrowly tailored, a race-conscious admissions program must not "unduly burden individuals who are not members of the favored racial and ethnic groups."

We are satisfied that the Law School's admissions program does not. Because the Law School considers "all pertinent elements of diversity," it can (and does) select nonminority applicants who have greater potential to enhance student body diversity over underrepresented minority applicants.

*   *   *

We are mindful, however, that "[a] core purpose of the Fourteenth Amendment was to do away with all governmentally imposed discrimination based on race."

Accordingly, race-conscious admissions policies must be limited in time. This requirement reflects that racial classifications, however compelling their goals, are potentially so dangerous that they may be employed no more broadly than the interest demands. Enshrining a permanent justification for racial preferences would offend this fundamental equal protection principle. We see no reason to exempt race-conscious admissions programs from the requirement that all governmental use of race must have a logical end point. The Law School, too, concedes that all "race-conscious programs must have reasonable durational limits."

In the context of higher education, the durational requirement can be met by sunset provisions in race-conscious admissions policies and periodic reviews to determine whether racial preferences are still necessary to achieve student body diversity. Universities in California, Florida, and Washington State, where racial preferences in admissions are prohibited by state law, are currently engaged in experimenting with a wide variety of alternative approaches. . . .

* * *

It has been 25 years since Justice Powell first approved the use of race to further an interest in student body diversity in the context of public higher education. Since that time, the number of minority applicants with high grades and test scores has indeed increased. We expect that 25 years from now, the use of racial preferences will no longer be necessary to further the interest approved today.

IV

In summary, the Equal Protection Clause does not prohibit the Law School's narrowly tailored use of race in admissions decisions to further a compelling interest in obtaining the educational benefits that flow from a diverse student body. . . .

It is so ordered.

JUSTICE GINSBURG, with whom JUSTICE BREYER joins, concurring.

* * *

However strong the public's desire for improved education systems may be, it remains the current reality that many minority students encounter markedly inadequate and unequal educational opportunities. Despite these inequalities, some minority students are able to meet the high threshold requirements set for admission to the country's finest undergraduate and graduate educational institutions. As lower school education in minority communities improves, an increase in the number of such students may be anticipated. From today's vantage point, one may hope, but not firmly forecast, that over the next generation's span, progress toward nondiscrimination and genuinely equal opportunity will make it safe to sunset affirmative action.

* * *

CHIEF JUSTICE REHNQUIST, with whom JUSTICE SCALIA, JUSTICE KENNEDY, and JUSTICE THOMAS join, dissenting.

. . . I do not believe that the University of Michigan Law School's (Law School) means are narrowly tailored to the interest it asserts. The Law School claims it must take the steps it does to achieve a " 'critical mass' " of underrepresented minority students. But its actual program bears no relation to this asserted goal. Stripped of its "critical mass" veil, the Law School's program is revealed as a naked effort to achieve racial balancing.

*   *   *

Before the Court's decision today, we consistently applied the same strict scrutiny analysis regardless of the government's purported reason for using race and regardless of the setting in which race was being used. We rejected calls to use more lenient review in the face of claims that race was being used in "good faith" because " '[m]ore than good motives should be required when government seeks to allocate its resources by way of an explicit racial classification system.' " . . .

Although the Court recites the language of our strict scrutiny analysis, its application of that review is unprecedented in its deference.

*   *   *

In practice, the Law School's program bears little or no relation to its asserted goal of achieving "critical mass." Respondents explain that the Law School seeks to accumulate a "critical mass" of *each* underrepresented minority group. But the record demonstrates that the Law School's admissions practices with respect to these groups differ dramatically and cannot be defended under any consistent use of the term "critical mass."

From 1995 through 2000, the Law School admitted between 1,130 and 1,310 students. Of those, between 13 and 19 were Native American, between 91 and 108 were African Americans, and between 47 and 56 were Hispanic. If the Law School is admitting between 91 and 108 African Americans in order to achieve "critical mass," thereby preventing African American students from feeling "isolated or like spokespersons for their race," one would think that a number of the same order of magnitude would be necessary to accomplish the same purpose for Hispanics and Native Americans. Similarly, even if all of the Native American applicants admitted in a given year matriculate, which the record demonstrates is not at all the case, how can this possibly constitute a "critical mass" of Native Americans in a class of over 350 students? In order for this pattern of admission to be consistent with the Law School's explanation of "critical mass," one would have to believe that the objectives of "critical mass" offered by respondents are achieved with only half the number of Hispanics and one sixth the number of Native Americans as compared to African Americans. But respondents offer no race specific reasons for such disparities. Instead, they simply emphasize the importance of achieving "critical mass," without any explanation of why that concept is applied differently among the three underrepresented minority groups.

These different numbers, moreover, come only as a result of substantially different treatment among the three underrepresented minority groups, as is apparent in an example offered by the Law School and highlighted by the Court: The school asserts that it "frequently accepts nonminority applicants with grades and test scores lower than underrepresented minority applicants (and other nonminority applicants) who are rejected." Specifically, the Law School states that "[s]ixty-nine minority applicants were rejected between 1995 and 2000 with at least a 3.5 [Grade Point Average (GPA)] and a [score of] 159 or higher on the [Law School Admissions Test (LSAT)]" while a number of Caucasian and Asian American applicants with similar or lower scores were admitted.

Review of the record reveals only 67 such individuals. Of these 67 individuals, *56* were Hispanic, while only 6 were African American, and only 5 were Native American. This discrepancy reflects a consistent practice. For example, in 2000, 12 Hispanics who scored between a 159–160 on the LSAT and earned a GPA of 3.00 or higher applied for admission and only 2 were admitted. Meanwhile, 12 African Americans in the same range of qualifications applied for admission and all 12 were admitted. Likewise, that same year, 16 Hispanics who scored between a 151–153 on the LSAT and earned a 3.00 or higher applied for admission and only 1 of those applicants was admitted. Twenty-three similarly qualified African Americans applied for admission and 14 were admitted.

These statistics have a significant bearing on petitioner's case. Respondents have *never* offered any race specific arguments explaining why significantly more individuals from one underrepresented minority group are needed in order to achieve "critical mass" or further student body diversity. They certainly have not explained why Hispanics, who they have said are among "the groups most isolated by racial barriers in our country," should have their admission capped out in this manner. The Law School's disparate admissions practices with respect to these minority groups demonstrate that its alleged goal of "critical mass" is simply a sham. . . . Surely strict scrutiny cannot permit these sort of disparities without at least some explanation.

Only when the "critical mass" label is discarded does a likely explanation for these numbers emerge. The Court states that the Law School's goal of attaining a "critical mass" of underrepresented minority students is not an interest in merely " 'assur[ing] within its student body some specified percentage of a particular group merely because of its race or ethnic origin.' " The Court recognizes that such an interest "would amount to outright racial balancing, which is patently unconstitutional." . . .

But the correlation between the percentage of the Law School's pool of applicants who are members of the three minority groups and the percentage of the admitted applicants who are members of these same groups is far too precise to be dismissed as merely the result of the school paying "some attention to [the] numbers."

*   *   *

For example, in 1995, when 9.7% of the applicant pool was African American, 9.4% of the admitted class was African American. By 2000, only 7.5% of the applicant pool was African American, and 7.3% of the admitted class was African American. This correlation is striking. . . . The tight correlation between the percentage of applicants and admittees of a given race, therefore, must result from careful race based planning by the Law School. It suggests a formula for admission based on the aspirational assumption that all applicants are equally qualified academically, and therefore that the proportion of each group admitted should be the same as the proportion of that group in the applicant pool.

Not only do respondents fail to explain this phenomenon, they attempt to obscure it. ("The Law School's minority enrollment percentages . . . diverged from the percentages in the applicant pool by as much as 17.7% from 1995–2000"). But the divergence between the percentages of underrepresented minorities in the applicant pool and in the *enrolled* classes is not the only relevant comparison. In fact, it may not be the most relevant comparison. The Law School cannot precisely control which of its admitted applicants decide to attend the university. But it can and, as the numbers demonstrate, clearly does employ racial preferences in extending offers of admission. Indeed, the ostensibly flexible nature of the Law School's admissions program that the Court finds appealing, appears to be, in practice, a carefully managed program designed to ensure proportionate representation of applicants from selected minority groups.

I do not believe that the Constitution gives the Law School such free rein in the use of race. The Law School has offered no explanation for its actual admissions practices and, unexplained, we are bound to conclude that the Law School has managed its admissions program, not to achieve a "critical mass," but to extend offers of admission to members of selected minority groups in proportion to their statistical representation in the applicant pool. But this is precisely the type of racial balancing that the Court itself calls "patently unconstitutional."

Finally, I believe that the Law School's program fails strict scrutiny because it is devoid of any reasonably precise time limit on the Law School's use of race in admissions. . . . The Court suggests a possible 25-year limitation on the Law School's current program. . . . The Court, in an unprecedented display of deference under our strict scrutiny analysis, upholds the Law School's program despite its obvious flaws. We have said that when it comes to the use of race, the connection between the ends and the means used to attain them must be precise. But here the flaw is deeper than that; it is not merely a question of "fit" between ends and means. Here the means actually used are forbidden by the Equal Protection Clause of the Constitution.

JUSTICE KENNEDY, dissenting [omitted].

JUSTICE SCALIA, with whom JUSTICE THOMAS joins, concurring in part and dissenting in part.

I join the opinion of THE CHIEF JUSTICE. As he demonstrates, the University of Michigan Law School's mystical "critical mass" justification for its discrimination by race challenges even the most gullible mind. The admissions statistics show it to be a sham to cover a scheme of racially proportionate admissions.

I also join Parts I through VII of JUSTICE THOMAS's opinion. I find particularly unanswerable his central point: that the allegedly "compelling state interest" at issue here is not the incremental "educational benefit" that emanates from the fabled "critical mass" of minority students, but rather Michigan's interest in maintaining a "prestige" law school whose normal admissions standards disproportionately exclude blacks and other minorities. If that is a compelling state interest, everything is.

I add the following: The "educational benefit" that the University of Michigan seeks to achieve by racial discrimination consists, according to the Court, of " 'cross-racial understanding,' " and " 'better prepar[ation of] students for an increasingly diverse workforce and society,' " all of which is necessary not only for work, but also for good "citizenship." This is not, of course, an "educational benefit" on which students will be graded on their Law School transcript (Works and Plays Well with Others: B+) or tested by the bar examiners (Q: Describe in 500 words or less your cross-racial understanding). For it is a lesson of life rather than law — essentially the same lesson taught to (or rather learned by, for it cannot be "taught" in the usual sense) people three feet shorter and twenty years younger than the full-grown adults at the University of Michigan Law School, in institutions ranging from Boy Scout troops to public-school kindergartens. If properly considered an "educational benefit" at all, it is surely not one that is either uniquely relevant to law school or uniquely "teachable" in a formal educational setting. *And therefore:* If it is appropriate for the University of Michigan Law School to use racial discrimination for the purpose of putting together a "critical mass" that will convey generic lessons in socialization and good citizenship, surely it is no less appropriate — indeed, *particularly* appropriate — for the civil service system of the State of Michigan to do so. There, also, those exposed to "critical masses" of certain races will presumably become better Americans, better Michiganders, better civil servants. And surely private employers cannot be criticized — indeed, should be praised — if they also "teach" good citizenship to their adult employees through a patriotic, all-American system of racial discrimination in hiring. The nonminority individuals who are deprived of a legal education, a civil service job, or any job at all by reason of their skin color will surely understand.

Unlike a clear constitutional holding that racial preferences in state educational institutions are impermissible, or even a clear anticonstitutional holding that racial preferences in state educational institutions are OK, today's *Grutter-Gratz* split double header seems perversely designed to prolong the controversy and the litigation. [*Gratz v. Bollinger*, 539 U.S. 244 (2003), decided the same day as *Grutter*, was a parallel case involving the University of Michigan's undergraduate affirmative action program, under which applications were rated on a point scale, with 150 points being the maximum. Minority students were given a 20-point bonus. The Court ruled the program unconstitutional. *Gratz* is explored in the Notes following this case. — Eds.] Some future lawsuits will presumably focus on whether the discriminatory scheme in question contains enough evaluation of the applicant "as an individual," and sufficiently avoids "separate admissions tracks" to fall under *Grutter* rather than *Gratz*. Some will focus on whether a university has gone beyond the bounds of a " 'good faith effort' " and has so zealously pursued its "critical mass" as to make it an unconstitutional *de facto* quota system, rather than merely " 'a permissible goal.' " Other lawsuits may focus on whether, in the particular setting at issue, any educational benefits flow from racial diversity. (That issue was not contested in *Grutter*; and while the opinion accords "a degree of deference to a university's academic decisions," "deference does not imply abandonment or abdication of judicial review.") Still other suits may challenge the bona fides of the institution's expressed commitment to the educational benefits of diversity that immunize the discriminatory scheme in *Grutter*. (Tempting targets, one would suppose, will be those universities that talk the talk of multiculturalism and racial diversity in the courts but walk the walk of tribalism and racial segregation on their campuses — through minority only student organizations, separate minority housing opportunities, separate minority student centers, even separate minority only graduation ceremonies.) And still other suits may claim that the institution's racial preferences have gone below or above the mystical *Grutter*-approved "critical mass." Finally, litigation can be expected on behalf of minority groups intentionally short changed in the institution's composition of its generic minority "critical mass." I do not look forward to any of these cases. The Constitution proscribes government discrimination on the basis of race, and state-provided education is no exception.

JUSTICE THOMAS, with whom JUSTICE SCALIA joins as to Parts I–VII, concurring in part and dissenting in part.

Frederick Douglass, speaking to a group of abolitionists almost 140 years ago, delivered a message lost on today's majority:

> "[I]n regard to the colored people, there is always more that is benevolent, I perceive, than just, manifested towards us. What I ask for the negro is not benevolence, not pity, not sympathy, but simply *justice*. The American people have always been anxious to know what they shall do with us. . . . I have had but one answer from the beginning. Do nothing with us! Your doing with us has already played the mischief with us. Do nothing with us! If the apples will not remain on the tree of their own strength, if they are worm-eaten at the core, if they are early ripe and disposed to fall, let them fall! . . . And if the negro cannot stand on his own legs, let him fall also. All I ask is, give him a chance to stand on his own legs! Let him alone! . . . [Y]our interference is doing him positive injury." What the Black Man Wants: An Address Delivered in Boston, Massachusetts, on 26 January 1865.

Like Douglass, I believe blacks can achieve in every avenue of American life without the meddling of university administrators. Because I wish to see all students succeed whatever their color, I share, in some respect, the sympathies of those who sponsor the type of discrimination advanced by the University of Michigan Law School (Law School). The Constitution does not, however, tolerate institutional devotion to the status quo in admissions policies when such devotion ripens into racial discrimination. Nor does the Constitution countenance the unprecedented deference the Court gives to the Law School, an approach inconsistent with the very concept of "strict scrutiny."

No one would argue that a university could set up a lower general admission standard and then impose heightened requirements only on black applicants. Similarly, a university may not maintain a high admission standard and grant exemptions to favored races. The Law School, of its own choosing, and for its own purposes, maintains an exclusionary admissions system that it knows produces racially disproportionate results. Racial discrimination is not a permissible solution to the self-inflicted wounds of this elitist admissions policy.

The majority upholds the Law School's racial discrimination not by interpreting the people's Constitution, but by responding to a faddish slogan of the cognoscenti. Nevertheless, I concur in part in the Court's opinion. First, I agree with the Court insofar as its decision, which approves of only one racial classification, confirms that further use of race in admissions remains unlawful. Second, I agree with the Court's holding that racial discrimination in higher education admissions will be illegal in 25 years. (stating that racial discrimination will no longer be narrowly tailored, or "necessary to further" a compelling state interest, in 25 years). I respectfully dissent from the remainder of the Court's opinion and the judgment, however, because I believe that the Law School's current use of race violates the Equal Protection Clause and that the Constitution means the same thing today as it will in 300 months.

* * *

IV

The interest in remaining elite and exclusive that the majority thinks so obviously critical requires the use of admissions "standards" that, in turn, create the Law School's "need" to discriminate on the basis of race. The Court validates these admissions standards by concluding that alternatives that would require "a dramatic sacrifice of . . . the academic quality of all admitted students," need not be considered before racial discrimination can be employed. In the majority's view, such methods are not required by the "narrow tailoring" prong of strict scrutiny because that inquiry demands, in this context, that any race-neutral alternative work " 'about as well.' " The majority errs, however, because race-neutral alternatives must only be "workable," and do "about as well" *in vindicating the compelling state interest*. The Court never explicitly holds that the Law School's desire to retain the status quo in "academic selectivity" is itself a compelling state interest, and, as I have demonstrated, it is not. Therefore, the Law School should be forced to choose between its classroom aesthetic and its exclusionary admissions system — it cannot have it both ways.

With the adoption of different admissions methods, such as accepting all students who meet minimum qualifications, the Law School could achieve its vision of the racially aesthetic student body without the use of racial discrimination. The Law School concedes this, but the Court holds, implicitly and under the guise of narrow tailoring, that the Law School has a compelling state interest in doing what it wants to do. I cannot agree. First, under strict scrutiny, the Law School's assessment of the benefits of racial discrimination and devotion to the admissions status quo are not entitled to any sort of deference, grounded in the First Amendment or anywhere else. Second, even if its "academic selectivity" must be maintained at all costs along with racial discrimination, the Court ignores the fact that other top law schools have succeeded in meeting their aesthetic demands without racial discrimination.

A

The Court bases its unprecedented deference to the Law School — deference antithetical to strict scrutiny — on an idea of "educational autonomy" grounded in the First Amendment. In my view, there is no basis for a right of public universities to do what would otherwise violate the Equal Protection Clause.

* * *

B

1

The Court's deference to the Law School's conclusion that its racial experimentation leads to educational benefits will, if adhered to, have serious collateral consequences. The Court relies heavily on social science evidence to justify its deference. The Court never acknowledges, however, the growing evidence that racial (and other sorts) of heterogeneity actually impairs learning among black students. *See, e.g.*, Flowers & Pascarella, *Cognitive Effects of College Racial Composition on African American Students After 3 Years of College*, 40 J. OF COLLEGE STUDENT DEVELOPMENT 669, 674 (1999) (concluding that black students experience superior cognitive development at Historically Black Colleges (HBCs) and that, even among blacks, "a substantial diversity moderates the cognitive effects of attending an HBC"); Allen, *The Color of Success: African American College Student Outcomes at Predominantly White and Historically Black Public Colleges and Universities*, 62 HARV. EDUC. REV. 26, 35 (1992) (finding that black students attending HBCs report higher academic achievement than those attending predominantly white colleges).

* * *

The sky has not fallen at Boalt Hall at the University of California, Berkeley, for example. Prior to Proposition 209's adoption of Cal. Const., Art. 1, § 31(a), which bars the State from "grant[ing] preferential treatment . . . on the basis of race . . . in the operation of . . . public education," Boalt Hall enrolled 20 blacks and 28 Hispanics in its first year class for 1996. In 2002, without deploying express racial discrimination in admissions, Boalt's entering class enrolled 14 blacks and 36 Hispanics. Total underrepresented minority student enrollment at Boalt Hall now exceeds 1996 levels. Apparently the Law School cannot be counted on to be as resourceful. The Court is willfully blind to the very real experience in California and elsewhere, which raises the inference that institutions with "reputation[s] for excellence," rivaling the Law School's have satisfied their sense of mission without resorting to prohibited racial discrimination.

V

Putting aside the absence of any legal support for the majority's reflexive deference, there is much to be said for the view that the use of tests and other measures to "predict" academic performance is a poor substitute for a system that gives every applicant a chance to prove he can succeed in the study of law. The rallying cry that in the absence of racial discrimination in admissions there would be a true meritocracy ignores the fact that the entire process is poisoned by numerous exceptions to "merit." For example, in the national debate on racial discrimination in higher education admissions, much has been made of the fact that elite institutions utilize a so-called "legacy" preference to give the children of alumni an advantage in admissions. This, and other, exceptions to a "true" meritocracy give the lie to protestations that merit admissions are in fact the order of the day at the Nation's universities. The Equal Protection Clause does not, however, prohibit the use of unseemly legacy preferences or many other kinds of arbitrary admissions procedures. What the Equal Protection Clause does prohibit are classifications made on the basis of race. So while legacy preferences can stand under the Constitution, racial discrimination cannot. I will not twist the Constitution to invalidate legacy preferences or otherwise impose my vision of higher education admissions on the Nation. The majority should similarly stay its impulse to validate faddish racial discrimination the Constitution clearly forbids.

*   *   *

VI

Putting aside what I take to be the Court's implicit rejection of *Adarand*'s holding that beneficial and burdensome racial classifications are equally invalid, I must contest the notion that the Law School's discrimination benefits those admitted as a result of it. The Court spends considerable time discussing the impressive display of *amicus* support for the Law School in this case from all corners of society. But nowhere in any of the filings in this Court is any evidence that the purported "beneficiaries" of this racial discrimination prove themselves by performing at (or even near) the same level as those students who receive no preferences. *Cf.* Thernstrom & Thernstrom, *Reflections on the Shape of the River*, 46 UCLA L. Rev. 1583, 1605–1608 (1999) (discussing the failure of defenders of racial discrimination in admissions to consider the fact that its "beneficiaries" are underperforming in the classroom).

The silence in this case is deafening to those of us who view higher education's purpose as imparting knowledge and skills to students, rather than a communal, rubber-stamp, credentialing process. The Law School is not looking for those students who, despite a lower LSAT score or undergraduate grade point average, will succeed in the study of law. The Law School seeks only a façade — it is sufficient that the class looks right, even if it does not perform right.

The Law School tantalizes unprepared students with the promise of a University of Michigan degree and all of the opportunities that it offers. These overmatched students take the bait, only to find that they cannot succeed in the cauldron of competition. And this mismatch crisis is not restricted to elite institutions. See T. Sowell, Race and Culture 176–177 (1994) ("Even if most minority students are able to meet the normal standards at the 'average' range of colleges and universities, the systematic mismatching of minority students begun at the top can mean that such students are generally overmatched throughout all levels of higher education"). Indeed, to cover the tracks of the aestheticists, this cruel farce of racial discrimination must continue — in selection for the Michigan Law Review, see University of Michigan Law School Student Handbook 2002–2003, (noting the presence of a "diversity plan" for admission to the review), and in hiring at law firms and for judicial clerkships until the "beneficiaries" are no longer tolerated. While these students may graduate with law degrees, there is no evidence that they have received a qualitatively better legal education (or become better lawyers) than if they had gone to a less "elite" law school for which they were better prepared. And the aestheticists will never address the real problems facing "underrepresented minorities," instead continuing their social experiments on other people's children.

Beyond the harm the Law School's racial discrimination visits upon its test subjects, no social science has disproved the notion that this discrimination "engender[s] attitudes of superiority or, alternatively, provoke[s] resentment among those who believe that they have been wronged by the government's use of race." "These programs stamp minorities with a badge of inferiority and may cause them to develop dependencies or to adopt an attitude that they are 'entitled' to preferences."

It is uncontested that each year, the Law School admits a handful of blacks who would be admitted in the absence of racial discrimination. Who can differentiate between those who belong and those who do not? The majority of blacks are admitted to the Law School because of discrimination, and because of this policy all are tarred as undeserving. This problem of stigma does not depend on determinacy as to whether those stigmatized are actually the "beneficiaries" of racial discrimination. When blacks take positions in the highest places of government, industry, or academia, it is an open question today whether their skin color played a part in their advancement. The question itself is the stigma — because either racial discrimination did play a role, in which case the person may be deemed "otherwise unqualified," or it did not, in which case asking the question itself unfairly marks those blacks who would succeed without discrimination. Is this what the Court means by "visibly open"?

* * *

VII

As the foregoing makes clear, I believe the Court's opinion to be, in most respects, erroneous. I do, however, find two points on which I agree.

A

First, I note that the issue of unconstitutional racial discrimination among the groups the Law School prefers is not presented in this case, because petitioner has never argued that the Law School engages in such a practice, and the Law School maintains that it does not. I join the Court's opinion insofar as it confirms that this type of racial discrimination remains unlawful. Under today's decision, it is still the case that racial discrimination that does not help a university to enroll an unspecified number, or "critical mass," of underrepresented minority students is unconstitutional. Thus, the Law School may not discriminate in admissions between similarly situated blacks and Hispanics, or between whites and Asians. This is so because preferring black to Hispanic applicants, for instance, does nothing to further the interest recognized by the majority today. Indeed, the majority describes such racial balancing as "patently unconstitutional." Like the Court, I express no opinion as to whether the Law School's current admissions program runs afoul of this prohibition.

B

The Court also holds that racial discrimination in admissions should be given another 25 years before it is deemed no longer narrowly tailored to the Law School's fabricated compelling state interest. While I agree that in 25 years the practices of the Law School will be illegal, they are, for the reasons I have given, illegal now. The majority does not and cannot rest its time limitation on any evidence that the gap in credentials between black and white students is shrinking or will be gone in that timeframe. In recent years there has been virtually no change, for example, in the proportion of law school applicants with LSAT scores of 165 and higher who are black. In 1993 blacks constituted 1.1% of law school applicants in that score range, though they represented 11.1% of all applicants. In 2000 the comparable numbers were 1.0% and 11.3%. No one can seriously contend, and the Court does not, that the racial gap in academic credentials will disappear in 25 years. Nor is the Court's holding that racial discrimination will be unconstitutional in 25 years made contingent on the gap closing in that time.

Indeed, the very existence of racial discrimination of the type practiced by the Law School may impede the narrowing of the LSAT testing gap. An applicant's LSAT score can improve dramatically with preparation, but such preparation is a cost, and there must be sufficient benefits attached to an improved score to justify additional study. Whites scoring between 163 and 167 on the LSAT are routinely rejected by the Law School, and thus whites aspiring to admission at the Law School have every incentive to improve their score to levels above that range. (showing that in 2000, 209 out of 422 white applicants were rejected in this scoring range). Blacks, on the other hand, are nearly guaranteed admission if they score above 155. (showing that 63 out of 77 black applicants are accepted with LSAT scores above 155). As admission prospects approach certainty, there is no incentive for the black applicant to continue to prepare for the LSAT once he is reasonably assured of achieving the requisite score. It is far from certain that the LSAT test-taker's behavior is responsive to the Law School's admissions policies. Nevertheless, the possibility remains that this racial discrimination will help fulfill the bigot's prophecy about black underperformance — just as it confirms the conspiracy theorist's belief that "institutional racism" is at fault for every racial disparity in our society.

* * *

For the immediate future, however, the majority has placed its *imprimatur* on a practice that can only weaken the principle of equality embodied in the Declaration of Independence and the Equal Protection Clause. "Our Constitution is color-blind, and neither knows nor tolerates classes among citizens." *Plessy v. Ferguson* (1896) (Harlan, J., dissenting). It has been nearly 140 years since Frederick Douglass asked the intellectual ancestors of the Law School to "[d]o nothing with us!" and the Nation adopted the Fourteenth Amendment. Now we must wait another 25 years to see this principle of equality vindicated. I therefore respectfully dissent from the remainder of the Court's opinion and the judgment.

NOTES AND QUESTIONS

1.   How deferential was the Court to the University in *Grutter*? And was this deference consistent with prior equal protection precedent and strict scrutiny? Is there some other constitutional basis to giving deference to universities especially? Arguably, academic freedom has a constitutional root. Justice Thomas in his dissent in *Grutter* noted that "the constitutionalization of 'academic freedom' began with the concurring opinion of Justice Frankfurter in *Sweezy v. New Hampshire*, 354 U.S. 234 (1957). Sweezy, a Marxist economist, was investigated by the Attorney General of New Hampshire on suspicion of being a subversive. The prosecution sought, *inter alia*, the contents of a lecture Sweezy had given at the University of New Hampshire. The Court held that the investigation violated due process." But what does this have to do with race conscious admissions? Justice Thomas thought not much. Do you agree?

2.   In a parallel case involving the University of Michigan's undergraduate admission's affirmative action program, *Gratz v. Bollinger*, 539 U.S. 244 (2003), Justice O'Connor, who authored the principal opinion in *Grutter*, joined an opinion by Chief Justice Rehnquist and the other *Grutter* dissenters holding that the undergraduate program was unconstitutional. The University employed a "selection index," on which an applicant could score a maximum of 150 points. Applicants with a score of 100 or more were automatically admitted; applicants with scores of 90–99 were usually admitted after an individualized review; applicants with scores between 75 and 89 were usually denied, but could be admitted after an individualized review; and applicants with scores of 74 and below were almost always denied admission, although individualized review was also possible for some in this range as well. Points were awarded for high school GPA, standardized test scores, strength of high school, in-state residency, alumni relationship, personal essay, and personal achievement. "Underrepresented minorities" were awarded up to 20 points based solely on membership in the racial or ethnic minority group. The Court, by a 5-4 vote, found that this point system had "the effect of making 'the factor of race . . . decisive' for virtually every minimally qualified underrepresented minority applicant," and therefore unconstitutional even under the Court's holding in *Grutter*.

3.   In *Gratz*, Justice Ginsburg dissented, arguing that "[o]ne can reasonably anticipate . . . that colleges and universities will seek to maintain their minority enrollment . . . whether or not they can do so in full candor through adoption of affirmative action plans of the kind here at issue." Does this suggest that Justice Ginsburg believes the University of Michigan and other public institutions would have pursued race conscious admissions policies, whether or not the Court accepted them? That would seem to be the case, since Justice Ginsburg goes on to say that "[i]f honesty is the best policy, surely Michigan's accurately described, fully disclosed College affirmative action program is preferable to achieving similar numbers through winks, nods, and disguises." Chief Justice Rehnquist thought

these comments "remarkable" since they hardly support giving deference to the University "whose academic judgment we are told in *Grutter v. Bollinger*," was worthy of deference." Since when, the Chief Justice wondered, do we change the Constitution so that "it conforms to the conduct of the universities"?

4.   Can private universities now also use race to achieve diversity in admissions? In previous cases, the Court has explained that actions that would violate the Equal Protection Clause of the Fourteenth Amendment if committed by a private institution accepting federal funds would also violate Title VI. *See Alexander v. Sandoval* (2001). But is the converse true? That is, just because a public university has been given latitude to use race if it chooses under the Equal Protection Clause, does that necessarily tell us that a statutory prohibition against race-based decisions now permits this as well? Isn't it the intent of the Congress at the time the particular statute was enacted that governs? After all, with respect to 42 U.S.C. § 1981 as well, which applies to private and public parties, the Court has explained that the provision was "meant, by its broad terms, to proscribe discrimination in the making or enforcement of contracts against, or in favor of, any race." *McDonald v. Santa Fe Trail Transp. Co.* (1976). The court has even held that a contract for educational services is a "contract" for purposes of § 1981. *See Runyon v. McCrary* (1976). And it is well-settled that purposeful discrimination that violates the Equal Protection Clause of the Fourteenth Amendment will also violate § 1981 *See General Building Contractors Assn., Inc. v. Pennsylvania* (1982). At the end of her opinion in *Grutter*, Justice O'Connor declares (without elaboration) that a public university law school, Michigan, has no statutory liability since Title VI and 1981 have been construed "co-extensively" with the Equal Protection Clause. Assuming that to be so, does *Grutter* preclude the Congress from amending these laws to expressly prohibit that which the Court has permitted? To prohibit private and public institutions, or just private? It is clear that states retain the authority to deny what the federal Constitution has been construed to permit, as California has expressly prohibited preferential treatment on the basis of race, sex, color, ethnicity or national origin in its State Constitution? Cal. Const. Art I, § 31(a).

5.   Given that race-based decision making is so odious in our history, why do you think the Court did not tell Michigan Law just to employ an admissions test other than the LSAT upon which minority students, on average, do not perform well? In this regard, Justice Thomas noted in a portion of the dissent not reprinted that "there is nothing ancient, honorable, or constitutionally protected about 'selective' admissions. The University of Michigan should be well aware that alternative methods have historically been used for the admission of students, for it brought to this country the German certificate system in the late 19th century. *See* H. WECHSLER, THE QUALIFIED STUDENT 16–39 (1977) (hereinafter QUALIFIED STUDENT). Under this system, a secondary school was certified by a university so that any graduate who completed the course offered by the school was offered admission to the university. The certification regime supplemented, and later virtually replaced (at least in the Midwest), the prior regime of rigorous subject matter entrance examinations. The facially race-neutral 'percent plans' now used in Texas, California, and Florida are in many ways the descendents of the certificate system."

So what prompts universities to use highly selective examinations? Justice Thomas continues: Certification was replaced by selective admissions in the beginning of the 20th century, as universities sought to exercise more control over the composition of their student bodies. Since its inception, selective admissions has been the vehicle for racial, ethnic, and religious tinkering and experimentation by university administrators. The initial driving force for the relocation of the selective function from the high school to the universities was the same desire to select racial winners and losers that the Law School exhibits today. Columbia, Harvard, and others infamously determined that they had 'too many' Jews, just as today the Law School argues it would have 'too many' whites or Asian-Americans if it could not discriminate in its admissions process. *See* QUALIFIED STUDENT 155–168 (Columbia); H. BROUN & G. BRITT, CHRISTIANS ONLY: A STUDY IN PREJUDICE 53–54 (1931) (Harvard)."

"Columbia employed intelligence tests precisely because Jewish applicants, who were predominantly immigrants, scored worse on such tests. Thus, Columbia could claim (falsely)that " '[w]e have not eliminated boys because they were Jews and do not propose to do so. We have honestly attempted to eliminate the lowest grade of applicant [through the use of intelligence testing] and it turns out that a good many of the low grade men are New York City Jews.' " Letter from Herbert E. Hawkes, dean of Columbia College, to E.B. Wilson, June 16, 1922 (reprinted in QUALIFIED STUDENT 160–161). In other words, the tests were adopted with full knowledge of their disparate impact. *Cf., DeFunis v. Odegaard*, 416 U.S. 312, 335 (1974) (*per curiam*) (Douglas, J., dissenting)." If all this is true, why isn't use of a testing regimen with full knowledge of its disparate impact, an equal protection violation?

6. If you think the LSAT a reasonable measure of likely success in law school (and later the bar exam — and there is some positive correlation), is Michigan or another public university authorized to employ race if it means sacrificing these "learning outcomes," as Justice O'Connor described them? Could it be that the legal permission to take the extraordinary step of employing race is necessarily hinged on the institution being fully capable of carrying out its educational mission *and* achieving diversity?

There is much in Justice O'Connor's opinion to suggest that only the most elite educational institutions will be able to accomplish both goals and that therefore, public (and vicariously) private institutions that cannot do so are *not* permitted by the Constitution to shape their decisions by race. Justice O'Connor specifically links approval of the Michigan law school pursuit of a "critical mass" of minority students to the fact that the law school "ranks among the Nation's top law schools" and that admission to such a selective institution is a prelude to power and essential to creating leaders for private and public contexts, whether politics, the military, or business.

Arguably, that highly selective institutions satisfy these educational outcomes is what allows them to satisfy strict scrutiny and demonstrate a compelling governmental interest. It is also what allows Justice O'Connor to remain faithful to the Court's precedents, many of which she authored, that demand nothing less. To be sure, this is obscured somewhat by the presumption of good faith that the majority gives the Michigan law school. As the dissenters point out, the presumption seems incongruous given how the factual record illustrates that minority students were admitted to Michigan with significantly lower credentials than their white and Asian counterparts. These facts lead Justice Kennedy — who states explicitly that he shares the view articulated by the late Justice Powell that race can be used in admissions as a nonpredominant factor — to believe that the majority had "abandoned or manipulated [or] distort[ed] [the] real and accepted meaning" of strict scrutiny.

While that is possible, of course, it should not be assumed that Justice O'Connor intended to overturn decades of precedent establishing that there is only one Equal Protection Clause, and that it applies to black and white alike, regardless of whether the government's desired classification is said to help or hurt the particular group. There is nothing in the majority opinion to suggest that Justice O'Connor formally abandons "searching judicial inquiry for race-based measures" or the proposition that there is no way to determine whether classifications are "benign" or "remedial." She cites both with approval. Instead, Justice O'Connor writes: "context matters," and the context that matters most are the words with which she begins her opinion: in the case under review the sought-after diversity occurs within one of the Nation's top schools.

When Justice Thomas in dissent argues that Michigan ought to be made to choose between its elite status and the diversity that it seeks, Justice O'Connor rejects that notion. She calls the prospect of lowering admissions standards, "a drastic remedy that would require the Law School to become a much different institution and sacrifice a vital component of its educational mission." It is for this same reason that Justice O'Connor finds that the Michigan law school has acted in a "narrowly tailored" manner without having exhausted all race-neutral means to achieve diversity, as the Bush administration had urged the Court. Percentage plans and lotteries do have greater racial fairness, but the law school does not need to consider them since that would force the school "to abandon the academic selectivity that is the cornerstone of its educational mission."

But which schools would qualify as elite? Certainly, it is open to debate at any given time how many universities or law schools see themselves as elite or selective, and therefore, as qualifying for this rare constitutional dispensation. Each school has unique features that make it attractive, but the reality is that applicants with high grades and test scores rationally seek out places, on average, that have large endowments and the traditions and faculties which give rise to them. All sides in the affirmative action debate also concede that for reasons that remain perplexing and intractable (and that cry out to be addressed in noncosmetic ways), far too few minority students fall within the upper ranges of the entrance exam. Of the 4,461 applicants to law school who had scores in roughly the 93rd percentile in 2002, 29 were black. About 25–30 law schools consistently and exclusively take their nonminority students from this range. Is that the contextual universe Justice O'Connor was writing about? If so, the opinion is far less of a blockbuster, but then, it would also keep the use of race to the extraordinary.

7. Didn't the Court previously reject the diversity model in *Wygant* when it refused to accept a minority role model argument? Is *Wygant* still good law? If the Court defers to the law school's judgment that a racially mixed student body confers educational benefits to all, then why would the *Wygant* Court not defer to the school board's judgment with respect to the benefits a racially mixed faculty confers?

8. In your own law school environment, do you see the benefits of diversity of viewpoint and experience regularly in classroom discussion? Justice Thomas thought that unlikely. He writes: " '[D]iversity,' for all of its devotees, is more a fashionable catchphrase than it is a useful term, especially when something as serious as racial discrimination is at issue." Because the Equal Protection Clause renders the color of one's skin constitutionally irrelevant to the law school's mission, he referred to the Michigan law school's interest as an "aesthetic." That is, the Law School wants to have a certain appearance, from the shape of the desks and tables in its classrooms to the color of the students sitting at them.

The aesthetic label was also intended to suggest that affirmative action does little for the least advantaged poor. Justice Thomas again writes: "It must be remembered that the Law School's racial discrimination does nothing for those too poor or uneducated to participate in elite higher education and therefore presents only an illusory solution to the challenges facing our Nation." Do you agree? Or does the inclusion of diversity "trickle down" somehow to encourage all?

9. Does affirmative action skirt the real issue? As an *amicus* for the Center for New Black Leadership authored by the Institute for Justice observes: "the real cause of racial disparities in post-secondary education [is] a severe racial gap in academic achievement in the K-12 years, owing significantly to the concentration of economically disadvantaged black and Hispanic students in defective inner-city public schools." The 2000 National Assessment of Educational Progress (NAEP) found that 63 %of black and 56 %of Hispanic fourth-graders are below the most basic levels of proficiency in reading. The average black 17-year-old is three to five years behind in reading and science and math. All of this shows up of course on college and law school entrance exams. And racial preferences do nothing to close this gap. THERNSTROM AND THERNSTROM, AMERICA IN BLACK AND WHITE (1997). Arguably, preferences make the situation worse by creating the illusion of improvement when the underlying reality is left unaddressed. The absence of racial preference, of course, would shatter the illusion. But as the *New York Times* concluded: "ending affirmative action [in California and elsewhere] has had one unpublicized and profoundly desirable consequence: it has forced the universit[ies] to try to expand the pool of eligible minority students." James Traub, *The Class of Prop. 209*, NEW YORK TIMES at 44 (May 2, 1999).

10. Is there a better way? Some public and private universities have begun to realize that action is needed years before students apply. On the private side, the University of Southern California was recently named Time Magazine's "University of the Year" for an elaborate and well-conceived effort enlisting college students and professors to help educationally disadvantaged students build their skills for college admission. Most recently, it has added a web-site directed at middle and high school students (and their parents and counselors) to help them prepare for college with detailed planning tools extending into 8th grade. Similar efforts are now underway in public education at Berkeley, the University of Washington, and Wisconsin. Of course, increased opportunities for parents to choose among available primary and secondary school options to escape failing schools or school systems are thought helpful as well see *Zelman v. Simmons-Harris*, 536 U.S. 639 (2002) (upholding the Cleveland school voucher program for low and moderate income students).

11. Obviously, affirmative action gives us much to think about. Even if *Grutter* applies outside elite institutions, it is important to remember that it did come with some explicit limits. In endorsing Justice Powell's views in *Bakke*, the Court accepted many qualifications for the use of race in university admissions: applicant review must be on an individual basis; the process must not be a disguised attempt to achieve racial balance; and one minority racial group cannot be preferred or played off against another. A faculty cannot spuriously conclude that it wants more African Americans, say, than Hispanics. That's not an overall critical mass of minority students but racial balancing, said the majority, which would be "patently unconstitutional." On the last point, Justices Scalia and Thomas joined the majority in partial concurrence.

12. In *Fisher v. University of Texas at Austin*, 133 S. Ct. 2411 (2013), the Court shed further light on the curious strict-scrutiny-with-deference approach that it had taken in the *Grutter* case. *Fisher* involved a University of Texas program that considers race as one of various factors in its undergraduate admissions process — a program not completely dissimilar to the University of Michigan School of Law program sustained as constitutional in the *Grutter* case. The District Court and the Court of Appeals in the *Fisher* case, noting the similarity, applied what they understood to be the *Grutter* strict-scrutiny-with-deference approach and granted summary judgment to the University. The Supreme Court vacated the lower court judgment and remanded the case to the Court of Appeals. The Court of Appeals had read *Grutter* in too deferential a manner and had held, on the compelling-government-interest part of the test, that Ms. Fisher could *only* challenge whether the University's decision to use race as a factor in admissions was a good-faith effort to achieve "diversity". Moreover the Court of Appeals had presumed that the University acted in good faith and placed on Ms. Fisher the burden of rebutting that presumption. And finally, the Court of Appeals had also concluded that the narrow-tailoring inquiry — like the compelling-interest inquiry — is undertaken with a degree of deference to the Universit[y]."

The Supreme Court essentially held: Wrong, Wrong, and Wrong. True, the Court does defer to "a university's educational judgment that "diversity" is essential to its educational mission but, the Court explained, a court "should ensure that there is a reasoned, principled explanation for the academic decision." And "[t]he University must prove that the means chosen by the University to attain diversity are narrowly tailored to that goal. On this point, the University receives no deference." And a "reviewing court must ultimately be satisfied that no workable race-neutral alternatives would produce the educational benefits of diversity. If a nonracial approach . . . could promote the substantial interest about as well and at tolerable administrative expense . . . , then the university may not consider race."

At one point the Court seemed to entertain fleetingly the thought of revisiting the strict-scrutiny-with-deference approach used in *Grutter*:

> There is disagreement about whether *Grutter* was consistent with the principles of equal protection in approving this compelling interest in diversity. [Citing Justice Scalia's and Justice Thomas's concurrences and Justice Ginsburg's dissent.] But the parties here do not ask the Court to revisit that aspect of *Grutter*'s holding.

Indeed, Justice Thomas, in a lengthy dissent, called for the overruling of *Grutter*.

13. In *Parents Involved in Community Schools v. Seattle School District No.1* (2007), the Chief Justice, writing mostly for a plurality, but with the partial concurrence of Justice Kennedy also in part for the Court, invalidated voluntarily adopted student assignment plans that rely upon race to determine which public schools certain children may attend. The Seattle school district classifies children as white or nonwhite; the Jefferson County school district as black or "other." In Seattle, this racial classification is used to allocate slots in oversubscribed high schools. In Jefferson County, it is used to make certain elementary school assignments and to rule on transfer requests. In each case, the school district relies upon an individual student's race in assigning that student to a particular school, so that the racial balance at the school falls within a predetermined range based on the racial composition of the school district as a whole. Parents of students denied assignment to particular schools under these plans solely because of their race brought suit, contending that allocating children to different public schools on the basis of race violated the Fourteenth Amendment guarantee of equal protection. The Court of Appeals below upheld the plans. The Supreme Court granted *certiorari*, and reversed.

A key factor in the reversal for the Chief Justice was that neither school district was engaged in illegal segregation. The Washington school district in Seattle had never been found to be discriminatory and the Jefferson County, Kentucky school district had operated under a desegregation decree until 2000, when the District Court dissolved the decree after finding that the district had achieved unitary status by eliminating "[t]o the greatest extent practicable" the vestiges of its prior policy of segregation. In 2001, after the decree had been dissolved, Jefferson County adopted the voluntary student assignment plan at issue in this case.

14. Assume a child is told that she cannot attend a given school because of her race. Those were the facts of *Brown*. Are the facts in *Parents Involved* equivalent? Walter Dellinger who served President Clinton as head of the Office of Legal Counsel argues with considerable conviction that the two cases are entirely different. *Brown* excluded on the basis of hatred, he contends, while *Parents Involved* excluded for the noble purpose of ensuring the integration of the races. To think the two situations the same, or even similar, argues Professor Dellinger, who for many years was a distinguished full-time member of the Duke Law faculty, is to be "profoundly misguided." Do you agree? Would the excluded child agree? Consider the underlying logic of Professor Dellinger's argument:

> Why is it so critical that we "get beyond race" in every possible way? Get beyond despising or disliking [or] oppressing people because of their race, yes. But avoiding any consideration of race as though it were toxic? I don't understand that. The court's decision is everything conservatives should abhor. It is a form of social engineering dictated from Washington. It ignores the principle of local control of schools [and] sets aside the judgment of elected officials. . . . It equates the well-intentioned and inclusive programs supported by both white and black people in Louisville and Seattle with the whole grotesquerie of racially oppressive practices which came down . . . from slavery and the Black Codes. The plurality

opinion is elegantly reasoned . . . [b]ut it fails the very first lesson taught to preschoolers who watch *Sesame Street*: "Which of These Things Is Not Like the Others?"

Walter E. Dellinger, *Everything Conservatives Should Abhor*, SLATE http://www.slate.com/articles/life/the_breakfast_table/features/2007/a_supreme_court_conversation/everything_conservatives_should_abhor.html (June 29, 2007).

15. What, if anything, does *Parents Involved* mean for diversity outside the educational setting — specifically, in the work-place? Title VII makes it unlawful to "discriminate" against any individual in employment *"because of"* race, sex, and other protected characteristics. Elsewhere in the text, we note the anomaly of Title VII of the Civil Rights Act of 1964 making unlawful employment practices with discriminatory impact or effect when the Equal Protection Clause requires intent for a constitutional violation. In theory, Congress' authority for the broader sweep of Title VII, which applies to public and private employers, is the prophylactic nature of section 5 of the Fourteenth Amendment with respect to public actors and the commerce power with respect to both. That said, Congress cannot presumably use either power to discriminate on the basis of race. Yet consider the Court's decision in *United Steelworkers of America v. Weber*, 443 U.S. 193 (1979), which held that Title VII permitted a voluntary race-conscious affirmative action plan that sought to "eliminate manifest racial imbalances in traditionally segregated job categories." Title VII permitted the plan, the Court explained, because it sought to "break[] down old patterns of racial segregation and hierarchy"; did not "unnecessarily trammel" the interests of non-minority employees; and was temporary.

The *Weber* reasoning also decided *Johnson v. Transportation Agency*, 480 U.S. 616 (1987), where the Court again rejected a Title VII challenge to an affirmative action plan. Paul Johnson claimed, unsuccessfully, that his employer violated Title VII when it promoted Diane Joyce over him. The Court found the employer's explicit consideration of Joyce's sex was permissible because it "was made pursuant to an Agency plan that directed that sex or race be taken into account for the purpose of remedying under-representation." Again the Court noted that the plan was remedying "a conspicuous . . . imbalance in traditionally segregated job categories." The *Johnson* Court did issue this caution: "blind hiring by the numbers" could "fairly be called into question," and the Court cautioned against decisions "made by reflexive adherence to a numerical standard." The caution can fairly be said to be incorporated into *Grutter*'s equal protection analysis, especially in light of *Gratz* (combined, these cases stand for the proposition that race can be a plus factor so long as it involves individualized consideration and that consideration is not overly mechanical or quota-like).

After *Grutter* and *Gratz*, a number of appellate courts decided against racially conscious diversity programs in both the public and private sector see *Alexander v. City of Milwaukee*, 474 F.3d 437 (7th Cir. 2007); *Lomack v. City of Newark*, 463 F.3d 303 (3d Cir. 2006); *Kohlbek v. City of Omaha*, 447 F.3d 552 (8th Cir. 2006); *Dean v. City of Shreveport*, 438 F.3d 448 (5th Cir. 2006); *Biondo v. City of Chicago*, 382 F.3d 680 (7th Cir. 2004); *Frank v. Xerox Corp.*, 347 F.3d 130, 133, 137 (5th Cir. 2003). Now that *Parents Involved* has reaffirmed *Grutter*'s conclusion that racial balancing is "patently unconstitutional," does that mean that *Weber*'s allowance of race consciousness in employment for "manifest imbalance" is open to question? Or is responding to a "manifest imbalance" a remedy for past intentional discrimination? Does the diversity rationale in *Grutter* make sense when applied to employment, or is it limited to higher education?

And how does Justice Kennedy's concurrence fit into this? While his opinion allows for some race consciousness on a macro level — thus, perhaps permitting employer outreach — does it insulate from challenge an employer who turns away an individual because of his race, the facts of *Weber*?

16.   Should the Court give deference to state government in other areas of core state functions in which states have employed racial classifications, such as when assessing California's practice of initially segregating prison inmates by race until individual determinations as to race-based gang membership can be made? Justice O'Connor, writing for the Court in *Johnson v. California*, 543 U.S. 499 (2005), held that strict scrutiny, rather than the more deferential level of scrutiny customarily utilized when assessing a state's legitimate penological interests, must be applied for "*all* racial classifications" "in order to 'smoke out' illegitimate uses of race by assuring that [government] is pursuing a goal important enough to warrant [such] a highly suspect tool." Is this holding consistent with the deference the Court gave to the Michigan law school in *Grutter*? If not, what explains the difference? Has the Court effectively resurrected its holding in *Metro Broadcasting, Inc. v. FCC* (1990), overruled in *Adarand Constructors, Inv. v. Pena*, that lesser scrutiny applies when assessing so-called "benign" racial classifications such as affirmative action than when assessing "invidious" classifications? What will California need to show on remand to the trial court, in order to keep its inmate housing program in place?

17.   Is the use of race acceptable in the drawing of voting districts? Some argue that it is since such districts have a long history of being gerrymandered in numerous ways reflecting such things as politics, ethnicity and urban vs. suburban proclivities. Why, it is claimed, should race be any different? The Court tries to answer in the next case.

MILLER v. JOHNSON
515 U.S. 900 (1995)

JUSTICE KENNEDY delivered the opinion of the Court.

The constitutionality of Georgia's congressional redistricting plan is at issue here. In *Shaw v. Reno* (1993), we held that a plaintiff states a claim under the Equal Protection Clause by alleging that a state redistricting plan, on its face, has no rational explanation save as an effort to separate voters on the basis of race. The question we now decide is whether Georgia's new Eleventh District gives rise to a valid equal protection claim under the principles announced in *Shaw*, and, if so, whether it can be sustained nonetheless as narrowly tailored to serve a compelling governmental interest.

I

A

The Equal Protection Clause of the Fourteenth Amendment provides that no State shall "deny to any person within its jurisdiction the equal protection of the laws." Its central mandate is racial neutrality in governmental decisionmaking. Though application of this imperative raises difficult questions, the basic principle is straightforward: "Racial and ethnic distinctions of any sort are inherently suspect and thus call for the most exacting judicial examination. . . . This perception of racial and ethnic distinctions is rooted in our Nation's constitutional and demographic history." *Regents of Univ. of California v. Bakke* (1978) (opinion of Powell, J.). This rule obtains with equal force regardless of "the race of those burdened or benefited by a particular classification." *Richmond v. J.A. Croson Co.* (1989) (SCALIA, J., concurring in judgment); *Adarand Constructors, Inc. v. Pena* [(1995)]. Laws classifying citizens on the basis of race cannot be upheld unless they are narrowly tailored to achieving a compelling state interest.

. . . Applying this basic Equal Protection analysis in the voting rights context, we held that "redistricting legislation that is so bizarre on its face that it is 'unexplainable on grounds other than race,' . . . demands the same close scrutiny that we give other state laws that classify citizens by race."

This case requires us to apply the principles articulated in *Shaw* to the most recent congressional redistricting plan enacted by the State of Georgia.

B

In 1965, the Attorney General designated Georgia a covered jurisdiction under § 4(b) of the Voting Rights Act (Act). In consequence, § 5 of the Act requires Georgia to obtain either administrative preclearance by the Attorney General or approval by the United States District Court for the District of Columbia of any change in a "standard, practice, or procedure with respect to voting" made after November 1, 1964. The preclearance mechanism applies to congressional redistricting plans, and requires that the proposed change "not have the purpose and will not have the effect of denying or abridging the right to vote on account of race or color." . . .

Between 1980 and 1990, one of Georgia's 10 congressional districts was a majority-black district, that is, a majority of the district's voters were black. The 1990 Decennial Census indicated that Georgia's population of 6,478,216 persons, 27% of whom are black, entitled it to an additional eleventh congressional seat, prompting Georgia's General Assembly to redraw the State's congressional districts. Both the House and the Senate adopted redistricting guidelines which, among other things, required single-member districts of equal population, contiguous geography, nondilution of minority voting strength, fidelity to precinct lines where possible, and compliance with §§ 2 and 5 of the Act. Only after these requirements were met did the guidelines permit drafters to consider other ends, such as maintaining the integrity of political subdivisions, preserving the core of existing districts, and avoiding contests between incumbents.

A special session opened in August 1991, and the General Assembly submitted a congressional redistricting plan to the Attorney General for preclearance on October 1, 1991. The legislature's plan contained two majority-minority districts, the Fifth and Eleventh, and an additional district, the Second, in which blacks comprised just over 35% of the voting age population. Despite the plan's increase in the number of majority-black districts from one to two and the absence of any evidence of an intent to discriminate against minority voters, the Department of Justice refused preclearance on January 21, 1992. The Department's objection letter noted a concern that Georgia had created only two majority-minority districts, and that the proposed plan did not "recognize" certain minority populations by placing them in a majority-black district.

. . . A new plan was enacted and submitted for preclearance. This second attempt assigned the black population in Central Georgia's Baldwin County to the Eleventh District and increased the black populations in the Eleventh, Fifth and Second Districts. The Justice Department refused preclearance again, relying on alternative plans proposing three majority-minority districts. One of the alternative schemes relied on by the Department was the so-called "max-black" plan, drafted by the American Civil Liberties Union (ACLU) for the General Assembly's black caucus. The key to the ACLU's plan was the "Macon/Savannah trade." The dense black population in the Macon region would be transferred from the Eleventh District to the Second, converting the Second into a majority-black district, and the Eleventh District's loss in black population would be offset by extending the Eleventh to include the black populations in Savannah. Pointing to the General Assembly's refusal to enact the Macon/Savannah swap into law, the Justice Department concluded that Georgia had "failed to explain adequately" its failure to create a third majority-minority district. . . .

Twice spurned, the General Assembly set out to create three majority-minority districts to gain preclearance. Using the ACLU's "max-black" plan as its benchmark, the General Assembly enacted a plan that

> "bore all the signs of [the Justice Department's] involvement: The black population of Meriwether County was gouged out of the Third District and attached to the Second District by the narrowest of land bridges; Effingham and Chatham Counties were split to make way for the Savannah extension, which itself split the City of Savannah; and the plan as a whole split 26 counties, 23 more than the existing congressional districts."

The new plan also enacted the Macon/Savannah swap necessary to create a third majority-black district. The Eleventh District lost the black population of Macon, but picked up Savannah, thereby connecting the black neighborhoods of metropolitan Atlanta and the poor black populace of coastal Chatham County, though 260 miles apart in distance and worlds apart in culture. In short, the social, political and economic makeup of the Eleventh District tells a tale of disparity, not community. . . . The Almanac of American Politics has this to say about the Eleventh District: "Geographically, it is a monstrosity, stretching from Atlanta to Savannah. Its core is the plantation country in the center of the state, lightly populated, but heavily black. It links by narrow corridors the black neighborhoods in Augusta, Savannah and southern DeKalb County." Georgia's plan included three majority-black districts, though, and received Justice Department preclearance on April 2, 1992.

Elections were held under the new congressional redistricting plan on November 4, 1992, and black candidates were elected to Congress from all three majority-black districts. On January 13, 1994, appellees, five white voters from the Eleventh District, filed this action. . . . As residents of the challenged Eleventh District, . . . [t]heir suit alleged that Georgia's Eleventh District was a racial gerrymander and so a violation of the Equal Protection Clause as interpreted in *Shaw v. Reno.* A three-judge court was convened . *,* . , and the United States and a number of Georgia residents intervened in support of the defendant-state officials.

A majority of the District Court panel agreed that the Eleventh District was invalid under *Shaw*, with one judge dissenting. After sharp criticism of the Justice Department for its use of partisan advocates in its dealings with state officials and for its close cooperation with the ACLU's vigorous advocacy of minority district maximization, the majority turned to a careful interpretation of our opinion in *Shaw*. It read *Shaw* to require strict scrutiny whenever race is the "overriding, predominant force" in the redistricting process. Citing much evidence of the legislature's purpose and intent in creating the final plan, as well as the irregular shape of the district . . . , the court found that race was the overriding and predominant force in the districting determination. The court proceeded to apply strict scrutiny. Though rejecting proportional representation as a compelling interest, it was willing to assume that compliance with the Voting Rights Act would be a compelling interest. As to the latter, however, the court found that the Act did not require three majority-black districts, and that Georgia's plan for that reason was not narrowly tailored to the goal of complying with the Act.

* * *

II

A

Finding that the "evidence of the General Assembly's intent to racially gerry-mander the Eleventh District is overwhelming, and practically stipulated by the parties involved," the District Court held that race was the predominant, overriding factor in drawing the Eleventh District. Appellants do not take issue with the court's factual finding of this racial motivation. Rather, they contend that evidence of a legislature's deliberate classification of voters on the basis of race cannot alone suffice to state a claim under *Shaw*. They argue that, regardless of the legislature's purposes, a plaintiff must demonstrate that a district's shape is so bizarre that it is unexplainable other than on the basis of race, and that appellees failed to make that showing here. Appellants' conception of the constitutional violation misapprehends our holding in *Shaw* and the Equal Protection precedent upon which *Shaw* relied.

Shaw recognized a claim "analytically distinct" from a vote dilution claim. Whereas a vote dilution claim alleges that the State has enacted a particular voting scheme as a purposeful device "to minimize or cancel out the voting potential of racial or ethnic minorities," an action disadvantaging voters of a particular race, the essence of the equal protection claim recognized in *Shaw* is that the State has used race as a basis for separating voters into districts. Just as the State may not, absent extraordinary justification, segregate citizens on the basis of race in its public parks, buses, golf courses, beaches, and schools, so did we recognize in *Shaw* that it may not separate its citizens into different voting districts on the basis of race. The idea is a simple one: "At the heart of the Constitution's guarantee of equal protection lies the simple command that the Government must treat citizens 'as individuals, not "as simply components of a racial, religious, sexual or national class." ' " *Metro Broadcasting, Inc. v. FCC* (1990). When the State assigns voters on the basis of race, it engages in the offensive and demeaning assumption that voters of a particular race, because of their race, "think alike, share the same political interests, and will prefer the same candidates at the polls." Race-based assignments "embody stereotypes that treat individuals as the product of their race, evaluating their thoughts and efforts — their very worth as citizens — according to a criterion barred to the Government by history and the Constitution." . . . As we concluded in *Shaw*:

> "Racial classifications with respect to voting carry particular dangers. Racial gerrymandering, even for remedial purposes, may balkanize us into competing racial factions; it threatens to carry us further from the goal of a political system in which race no longer matters — a goal that the Fourteenth and Fifteenth Amendments embody, and to which the Nation continues to aspire. . . ."

Our observation in *Shaw* of the consequences of racial stereotyping was not meant to suggest that a district must be bizarre on its face before there is a constitutional violation. . . . Our circumspect approach and narrow holding in *Shaw* did not erect an artificial rule barring accepted equal protection analysis in other redistricting cases. Shape is relevant not because bizarreness is a necessary element of the constitutional wrong or a threshold requirement of proof, but because it may be persuasive circumstantial evidence that race for its own sake, and not other districting principles, was the legislature's dominant and controlling rationale in drawing its district lines. The logical implication, as courts applying *Shaw* have recognized, is that parties may rely on evidence other than bizarreness to establish race-based districting.

. . . We recognized in *Shaw* that, outside the districting context, statutes are subject to strict scrutiny under the Equal Protection Clause not just when they contain express racial classifications, but also when, though race neutral on their face, they are motivated by a racial purpose or object. In the rare case, where the effect of government action is a pattern " 'unexplainable on grounds other than race,' " "[t]he evidentiary inquiry is . . . relatively easy." As early as *Yick Wo v. Hopkins* (1886), the Court recognized that a laundry permit ordinance was administered in a deliberate way to exclude all Chinese from the laundry business; and in *Gomillion v. Lightfoot* (1960), the Court concluded that the redrawing of Tuskegee, Alabama's municipal boundaries left no doubt that the plan was designed to exclude blacks. In those cases, however, it was the presumed racial purpose of state action, not its stark manifestation, that was the constitutional violation. . . . In the absence of a pattern as stark as those in *Yick Wo* or *Gomillion*, "impact alone is not determinative, and the Court must look to other evidence" of race-based decisionmaking.

* * *

B

Federal-court review of districting legislation represents a serious intrusion on the most vital of local functions. It is well settled that "reapportionment is primarily the duty and responsibility of the State." Electoral districting is a most difficult subject for legislatures, and so the States must have discretion to exercise the political judgment necessary to balance competing interests. Although race-based decisionmaking is inherently suspect, until a claimant makes a showing sufficient to support that allegation the good faith of a state legislature must be presumed. The courts, in assessing the sufficiency of a challenge to a districting plan, must be sensitive to the complex interplay of forces that enter a legislature's redistricting calculus. Redistricting legislatures will, for example, almost always be aware of racial demographics; but it does not follow that race predominates in the redistricting process. The distinction between being aware of racial considerations and being motivated by them may be difficult to make. This evidentiary difficulty, together with the sensitive nature of redistricting and the presumption of good faith that must be accorded legislative enactments, requires courts to exercise extraordinary caution in adjudicating claims that a state has drawn district lines on the basis of race. The plaintiff's burden is to show, either through circumstantial evidence of a district's shape and demographics or more direct evidence going to legislative purpose, that race was the predominant factor motivating the legislature's decision to place a significant number of voters within or without a particular district. To make this showing, a plaintiff must prove that the legislature subordinated traditional race-neutral districting principles, including but not limited to compactness, contiguity, respect for political subdivisions or communities defined by actual shared interests, to racial considerations. Where these or other race-neutral considerations are the basis for redistricting legislation, and are not subordinated to race, a state can "defeat a claim that a district has been gerrymandered on racial lines." . . .

In our view, the District Court applied the correct analysis, and its finding that race was the predominant factor motivating the drawing of the Eleventh District was not clearly erroneous. The court found it was "exceedingly obvious" from the shape of the Eleventh District, together with the relevant racial demographics, that the drawing of narrow land bridges to incorporate within the District outlying appendages containing nearly 80% of the district's total black population was a deliberate attempt to bring black populations into the district. Although by comparison with other districts the geometric shape of the Eleventh District may not seem bizarre on its face, when its shape is considered in conjunction with its racial and population densities, the story of racial gerrymandering seen by the District Court becomes much clearer. . . . The District Court had before it considerable additional evidence showing that the General Assembly was motivated by a predominant, overriding desire to assign black populations to the Eleventh District and thereby permit the creation of a third majority-black district in the Second.

The court found that "it became obvious," both from the Justice Department's objection letters and the three preclearance rounds in general, "that [the Justice Department] would accept nothing less than abject surrender to its maximization agenda." . . . The State admitted that it " 'would not have added those portions of Effingham and Chatham Counties that are now in the [far southeastern extension of the] present Eleventh Congressional District but for the need to include additional black population in that district to offset the loss of black population caused by the shift of predominantly black portions of Bibb County in the Second Congressional District which occurred in response to the Department of Justice's March 20th, 1992, objection letter.' " It conceded further that "[t]o the extent that precincts in the Eleventh Congressional District are split, a substantial reason for their being split was the objective of increasing the black population of that district." And in its brief to this Court, the State concedes that "[i]t is undisputed that Georgia's eleventh is the product of a desire by the General Assembly to create a majority black district." . . . On this record, we fail to see how the District Court could have reached any conclusion other than that race was the predominant factor in drawing Georgia's Eleventh District. . . .

* * *

. . . As a result, Georgia's congressional redistricting plan cannot be upheld unless it satisfies strict scrutiny, our most rigorous and exacting standard of constitutional review.

III

To satisfy strict scrutiny, the State must demonstrate that its districting legislation is narrowly tailored to achieve a compelling interest. There is a "significant state interest in eradicating the effects of past racial discrimination." The State does not argue, however, that it created the Eleventh District to remedy past discrimination, and with good reason: There is little doubt that the State's true interest in designing the Eleventh District was creating a third majority-black district to satisfy the Justice Department's preclearance demands. Whether or not in some cases compliance with the Voting Rights Act, standing alone, can provide a compelling interest independent of any interest in remedying past discrimination, it cannot do so here. As we suggested in *Shaw*, compliance with federal antidiscrimination laws cannot justify race-based districting where the challenged district was not reasonably necessary under a constitutional reading and application of those laws. The congressional plan challenged here was not required by the Voting Rights Act under a correct reading of the statute. . . .

We do not accept the contention that the State has a compelling interest in complying with whatever preclearance mandates the Justice Department issues. When a state governmental entity seeks to justify race-based remedies to cure the effects of past discrimination, we do not accept the government's mere assertion that the remedial action is required. Rather, we insist on a strong basis in evidence of the harm being remedied. "The history of racial classifications in this country suggests that blind judicial deference to legislative or executive pronouncements of necessity has no place in equal protection analysis." Our presumptive skepticism of all racial classifications prohibits us as well from accepting on its face the Justice Department's conclusion that racial districting is necessary under the Voting Rights

Act. Where a State relies on the Department's determination that race-based districting is necessary to comply with the Voting Rights Act, the judiciary retains an independent obligation in adjudicating consequent equal protection challenges to ensure that the State's actions are narrowly tailored to achieve a compelling interest. Were we to accept the Justice Department's objection itself as a compelling interest adequate to insulate racial districting from constitutional review, we would be surrendering to the Executive Branch our role in enforcing the constitutional limits on race-based official action. We may not do so.

For the same reasons, we think it inappropriate for a court engaged in constitutional scrutiny to accord deference to the Justice Department's interpretation of the Act. Although we have deferred to the Department's interpretation in certain statutory cases, we have rejected agency interpretations to which we would otherwise defer where they raise serious constitutional questions. When the Justice Department's interpretation of the Act compels race-based districting, it by definition raises a serious constitutional question, and should not receive deference.

Georgia's drawing of the Eleventh District was not required under the Act because there was no reasonable basis to believe that Georgia's earlier enacted plans violated § 5. Wherever a plan is "ameliorative," a term we have used to describe plans increasing the number of majority-minority districts, it "cannot violate § 5 unless the new apportionment itself so discriminates on the basis of race or color as to violate the Constitution." Georgia's first and second proposed plans increased the number of majority-black districts from 1 out of 10 (10%) to 2 out of 11 (18.18%). These plans were "ameliorative" and could not have violated § 5's non-retrogression principle. Acknowledging as much, the United States now relies on the fact that the Justice Department may object to a state proposal either on the ground that it has a prohibited purpose or a prohibited effect. The Government justifies its preclearance objections on the ground that the submitted plans violated § 5's purpose element. The key to the Government's position . . . is and always has been that Georgia failed to proffer a nondiscriminatory purpose for its refusal in the first two submissions to take the steps necessary to create a third majority-minority district.

The Government's position is insupportable. "[A]meliorative changes, even if they fall short of what might be accomplished in terms of increasing minority representation, cannot be found to violate section 5 unless they so discriminate on the basis of race or color as to violate the Constitution." Although it is true we have held that the State has the burden to prove a nondiscriminatory purpose under § 5, Georgia's Attorney General provided a detailed explanation for the State's initial decision not to enact the max-black plan. The District Court accepted this explanation, and found an absence of any discriminatory intent. The State's policy of adhering to other districting principles instead of creating as many majority-minority districts as possible does not support an inference that the plan "so discriminates on the basis of race or color as to violate the Constitution," and thus cannot provide any basis under § 5 for the Justice Department's objection.

Instead of grounding its objections on evidence of a discriminatory purpose, it would appear the Government was driven by its policy of maximizing majority-black districts. In utilizing § 5 to require States to create majority-minority districts wherever possible, the Department of Justice expanded its authority under the statute beyond what Congress intended and we have upheld.

* * *

IV

The Voting Rights Act, and its grant of authority to the federal courts to uncover official efforts to abridge minorities' right to vote, has been of vital importance in eradicating invidious discrimination from the electoral process and enhancing the legitimacy of our political institutions. Only if our political system and our society cleanse themselves of that discrimination will all members of the polity share an equal opportunity to gain public office regardless of race. As a Nation we share both the obligation and the aspiration of working toward this end. The end is neither assured nor well served, however, by carving electorates into racial blocs. "If our society is to continue to progress as a multiracial democracy, it must recognize that the automatic invocation of race stereotypes retards that progress and causes continued hurt and injury." It takes a shortsighted and unauthorized view of the Voting Rights Act to invoke that statute, which has played a decisive role in redressing some of our worst forms of discrimination, to demand the very racial stereotyping the Fourteenth Amendment forbids.

* * *

JUSTICE O'CONNOR, concurring. [Omitted.]

JUSTICE STEVENS, dissenting.

* * *

In *Shaw v. Reno* (1993), the Court crafted a new cause of action with two novel, troubling features. First, the Court misapplied the term "gerrymander," previously used to describe grotesque line-drawing by a dominant group to maintain or enhance its political power at a minority's expense, to condemn the efforts of a majority (whites) to share its power with a minority (African Americans). Second, the Court dispensed with its previous insistence in vote dilution cases on a showing of injury to an identifiable group of voters, but it failed to explain adequately what showing a plaintiff must make to establish standing to litigate the newly minted *Shaw* claim. Neither in *Shaw* itself nor in the cases decided today has the Court coherently articulated what injury this cause of action is designed to redress. Because respondents have alleged no legally cognizable injury, they lack standing, and these cases should be dismissed.

Even assuming the validity of *Shaw*, I cannot see how respondents in these cases could assert the injury the Court attributes to them. Respondents, plaintiffs below, are white voters in Georgia's Eleventh Congressional District. The Court's conclusion that they have standing to maintain a *Shaw* claim appears to rest on a theory that their placement in the Eleventh District caused them " 'representational harms.' " The *Shaw* Court explained the concept of "representational harms" as follows: "When a district obviously is created solely to effectuate the perceived common interests of one racial group, elected officials are more likely to believe that their primary obligation is to represent only the members of that group, rather than their constituency as a whole." Although the *Shaw* Court attributed representational harms solely to a message sent by the legislature's action, those harms can only come about if the message is received — that is, first, if all or most black voters support the same candidate, and, second, if the successful candidate ignores the interests of her white constituents. Respondents' standing, in other words, ultimately depends on the very premise the Court purports to abhor: that voters of a particular race " 'think alike, share the same political interests, and will prefer the same candidates at the polls.' " This generalization, as the Court recognizes, is "offensive and demeaning."

* * *

The Court attempts an explanation in these cases by equating the injury it imagines respondents have suffered with the injuries African Americans suffered under segregation. The heart of respondents' claim, by the Court's account, is that "a State's assignment of voters on the basis of race," violates the Equal Protection Clause for the same reason a State may not "segregate citizens on the basis of race in its public parks, buses, golf courses, beaches, and schools." This equation, however, fails to elucidate the elusive *Shaw* injury. Our desegregation cases redressed the *exclusion* of black citizens from public facilities reserved for whites. In this case, in contrast, any voter, black or white, may live in the Eleventh District. What respondents contest is the *inclusion* of too many black voters in the District as drawn. In my view, if respondents allege no vote dilution, that inclusion can cause them no conceivable injury.

The Court's equation of *Shaw* claims with our desegregation decisions is inappropriate for another reason. In each of those cases, legal segregation frustrated the public interest in diversity and tolerance by barring African Americans from joining whites in the activities at issue. The districting plan here, in contrast, serves the interest in diversity and tolerance by increasing the likelihood that a meaningful number of black representatives will add their voices to legislative debates. "There is no moral or constitutional equivalence between a policy that is designed to perpetuate a caste system and one that seeks to eradicate racial subordination." . . .

Equally distressing is the Court's equation of traditional gerrymanders, designed to maintain or enhance a dominant group's power, with a dominant group's decision to share its power with a previously underrepresented group. In my view, districting plans violate the Equal Protection Clause when they "serve no purpose other than to favor one segment — whether racial, ethnic, religious, economic, or political — that may occupy a position of strength at a particular point in time, or to disadvantage a politically weak segment of the community." In contrast, I do not see how a districting plan that favors a politically weak group can violate equal protection. The Constitution does not mandate any form of proportional representation, but it certainly permits a State to adopt a policy that promotes fair representation of different groups. . . .

The Court's refusal to distinguish an enactment that helps a minority group from enactments that cause it harm is especially unfortunate at the intersection of race and voting, given that African Americans and other disadvantaged groups have struggled so long and so hard for inclusion in that most central exercise of our democracy. I have long believed that treating racial groups differently from other identifiable groups of voters, as the Court does today, is itself an invidious racial classification. Racial minorities should receive neither more nor less protection than other groups against gerrymanders. *A fortiori*, racial minorities should not be less eligible than other groups to benefit from districting plans the majority designs to aid them.

* * *

JUSTICE GINSBURG, with whom JUSTICE STEVENS and JUSTICE BREYER join, and with whom JUSTICE SOUTER joins except as to Part III-B, dissenting.

Two Terms ago, in *Shaw v. Reno* (1993), this Court took up a claim "analytically distinct" from a vote dilution claim. *Shaw* authorized judicial intervention in "extremely irregular" apportionments, in which the legislature cast aside traditional districting practices to consider race alone. . . .

Today the Court expands the judicial role, announcing that federal courts are to undertake searching review of any district with contours "predominant[ly] motivat[ed]" by race: "[S]trict scrutiny" will be triggered not only when traditional districting practices are abandoned, but also when those practices are "subordinated to" — given less weight than — race. Applying this new "race-as-predominant-factor" standard, the Court invalidates Georgia's districting plan even though Georgia's Eleventh District, the focus of today's dispute, bears the imprint of familiar districting practices. . . .

I

At the outset, it may be useful to note points on which the Court does not divide. First, we agree that federalism and the slim judicial competence to draw district lines weigh heavily against judicial intervention in apportionment decisions; as a rule, the task should remain within the domain of state legislatures. Second, for most of our Nation's history, the franchise has not been enjoyed equally by black citizens and white voters. To redress past wrongs and to avert any recurrence of exclusion of blacks from political processes, federal courts now respond to Equal Protection Clause and Voting Rights Act complaints of state action that dilutes minority voting strength. Third, to meet statutory requirements, state legislatures must sometimes consider race as a factor highly relevant to the drawing of district lines. Finally, state legislatures may recognize communities that have a particular racial or ethnic makeup, even in the absence of any compulsion to do so, in order to account for interests common to or shared by the persons grouped together. See *Shaw* ("[W]hen members of a racial group live together in one community, a reapportionment plan that concentrates members of the group in one district and excludes them from others may reflect wholly legitimate purposes.").

Therefore, the fact that the Georgia General Assembly took account of race in drawing district lines — a fact not in dispute — does not render the State's plan invalid. . . .

* * *

II

A

Before *Shaw v. Reno* (1993), this Court invoked the Equal Protection Clause to justify intervention in the quintessentially political task of legislative districting in two circumstances: to enforce the one-person-one-vote requirement, see *Reynolds v. Sims* (1964); and to prevent dilution of a minority group's voting strength.

In *Shaw*, the Court recognized a third basis for an equal protection challenge to a State's apportionment plan. The Court wrote cautiously, emphasizing that judicial intervention is exceptional: Strict judicial scrutiny is in order, the Court declared, if a district is "so extremely irregular on its face that it rationally can be viewed only as an effort to segregate the races for purposes of voting."

. . . The problem in *Shaw* was not the plan architects' consideration of race as relevant in redistricting. Rather, in the Court's estimation, it was the virtual exclusion of other factors from the calculus. Traditional districting practices were cast aside, the Court concluded, with race alone steering placement of district lines.

B

The record before us does not show that race similarly overwhelmed traditional districting practices in Georgia. Although the Georgia General Assembly prominently considered race in shaping the Eleventh District, race did not crowd out all other factors, as the Court found it did in North Carolina's delineation of the *Shaw* district.

In contrast to the snake-like North Carolina district inspected in *Shaw*, Georgia's Eleventh District is hardly "bizarre," "extremely irregular," or "irrational on its face." Instead, the Eleventh District's design reflects significant consideration of "traditional districting factors (such as keeping political subdivisions intact) and the usual political process of compromise and trades for a variety of nonracial reasons." The District covers a core area in central and eastern Georgia, and its total land area of 6,780 square miles is about average for the State. The border of the Eleventh District runs 1,184 miles, in line with Georgia's Second District, which has a 1,243-mile border, and the State's Eighth District, with a border running 1,155 miles.

Nor does the Eleventh District disrespect the boundaries of political subdivisions. Of the 22 counties in the District, 14 are intact and 8 are divided. That puts the Eleventh District at about the state average in divided counties. By contrast, of the Sixth District's 5 counties, none are intact, and of the Fourth District's four counties, just one is intact. Seventy-one percent of the Eleventh District's boundaries track the borders of political subdivisions. Of the State's 11 districts, 5 score worse than the Eleventh District on this criterion, and 5 score better. Eighty-three percent of the Eleventh District's geographic area is composed of intact counties, above average for the State's congressional districts. And notably, the Eleventh

District's boundaries largely follow precinct lines.

Evidence at trial similarly shows that considerations other than race went into determining the Eleventh District's boundaries. For a "political reason" — to accommodate the request of an incumbent State Senator regarding the placement of the precinct in which his son lived — the DeKalb County portion of the Eleventh District was drawn to include a particular (largely white) precinct. The corridor through Effingham County was substantially narrowed at the request of a (white) State Representative. In Chatham County, the District was trimmed to exclude a heavily black community in Garden City because a State Representative wanted to keep the city intact inside the neighboring First District. The Savannah extension was configured by "the narrowest means possible" to avoid splitting the city of Port Wentworth.

Georgia's Eleventh District, in sum, is not an outlier district shaped without reference to familiar districting techniques. Tellingly, the District that the Court's decision today unsettles is not among those on a statistically calculated list of the 28 most bizarre districts in the United States, a study prepared in the wake of our decision in *Shaw*.

C

The Court suggests that it was not Georgia's legislature, but the U.S. Department of Justice, that effectively drew the lines, and that Department officers did so with nothing but race in mind. Yet the "Max-Black" plan advanced by the Attorney General was not the plan passed by the Georgia General Assembly. [As the dissenting District Judge below stated,] "The Max-Black plan did influence to some degree the shape of the ultimate Eleventh District. . . . [But] the actual Eleventh is *not* identical to the Max-Black plan. The Eleventh, to my eye, is significantly different in shape in many ways. These differences show . . . consideration of other matters beyond race. . . ."

And although the Attorney General refused preclearance to the first two plans approved by Georgia's legislature, the State was not thereby disarmed; Georgia could have demanded relief from the Department's objections by instituting a civil action in the United States District Court for the District of Columbia, with ultimate review in this Court. Instead of pursuing that avenue, the State chose to adopt the plan here in controversy — a plan the State forcefully defends before us. We should respect Georgia's choice by taking its position on brief as genuine.

D

Along with attention to size, shape, and political subdivisions, the Court recognizes as an appropriate districting principle, "respect for . . . communities defined by actual shared interests." The Court finds no community here, however, because a report in the record showed "fractured political, social, and economic interests within the Eleventh District's black population."

But ethnicity itself can tie people together, as volumes of social science literature have documented — even people with divergent economic interests. For this reason, ethnicity is a significant force in political life. . . .

To accommodate the reality of ethnic bonds, legislatures have long drawn voting districts along ethnic lines. Our Nation's cities are full of districts identified by their ethnic character — Chinese, Irish, Italian, Jewish, Polish, Russian, for example. The creation of ethnic districts reflecting felt identity is not ordinarily viewed as offensive or demeaning to those included in the delineation.

III

To separate permissible and impermissible use of race in legislative apportionment, the Court orders strict scrutiny for districting plans "predominantly motivated" by race. No longer can a State avoid judicial oversight by giving — as in this case — genuine and measurable consideration to traditional districting practices. Instead, a federal case can be mounted whenever plaintiffs plausibly allege that other factors carried less weight than race. This invitation to litigate against the State seems to me neither necessary nor proper.

A

The Court derives its test from diverse opinions on the relevance of race in contexts distinctly unlike apportionment. The controlling idea, the Court says, is " 'the simple command [at the heart of the Constitution's guarantee of equal protection] that the Government must treat citizens as individuals, not as simply components of a racial, religious, sexual or national class.' "

In adopting districting plans, however, States do not treat people as individuals. Apportionment schemes, by their very nature, assemble people in groups. States do not assign voters to districts based on merit or achievement, standards States might use in hiring employees or engaging contractors. Rather, legislators classify voters in groups — by economic, geographical, political, or social characteristics — and then "reconcile the competing claims of [these] groups."

That ethnicity defines some of these groups is a political reality. Until now, no constitutional infirmity has been seen in districting Irish or Italian voters together, for example, so long as the delineation does not abandon familiar apportionment practices. If Chinese-Americans and Russian-Americans may seek and secure group recognition in the delineation of voting districts, then African-Americans should not be dissimilarly treated. Otherwise, in the name of equal protection, we would shut out "the very minority group whose history in the United States gave birth to the Equal Protection Clause."

B

Under the Court's approach, judicial review of the same intensity, *i.e.*, strict scrutiny, is in order once it is determined that an apportionment is predominantly motivated by race. It matters not at all, in this new regime, whether the apportionment dilutes or enhances minority voting strength. As very recently observed, however, "[t]here is no moral or constitutional equivalence between a policy that is designed to perpetuate a caste system and one that seeks to eradicate racial subordination." *Adarand Constructors, Inc. v. Pena* (STEVENS, J., dissenting).

Special circumstances justify vigilant judicial inspection to protect minority voters — circumstances that do not apply to majority voters. A history of exclusion from state politics left racial minorities without clout to extract provisions for fair representation in the lawmaking forum. The equal protection rights of minority voters thus could have remained unrealized absent the Judiciary's close surveillance. The majority, by definition, encounters no such blockage. White voters in Georgia do not lack means to exert strong pressure on their state legislators. The force of their numbers is itself a powerful determiner of what the legislature will do that does not coincide with perceived majority interests.

State legislatures like Georgia's today operate under federal constraints imposed by the Voting Rights Act — constraints justified by history and designed by Congress to make once-subordinated people free and equal citizens. But these federal constraints do not leave majority voters in need of extraordinary judicial solicitude. The Attorney General, who administers the Voting Rights Act's preclearance requirements, is herself a political actor. She has a duty to enforce the law Congress passed, and she is no doubt aware of the political cost of venturing too far to the detriment of majority voters. Majority voters, furthermore, can press the State to seek judicial review if the Attorney General refuses to preclear a plan that the voters favor. Finally, the Act is itself a political measure, subject to modification in the political process.

C

The Court's disposition renders redistricting perilous work for state legislatures. Statutory mandates and political realities may require States to consider race when drawing district lines. But today's decision is a counterforce; it opens the way for federal litigation if "traditional . . . districting principles" arguably were accorded less weight than race. Genuine attention to traditional districting practices and avoidance of bizarre configurations seemed, under *Shaw,* to provide a safe harbor. In view of today's decision, that is no longer the case.

NOTES AND QUESTIONS

1. You will have been able to discern that this case, like *Shaw v. Reno,* came about because of vigorous Justice Department efforts to secure more African-American and other minority representatives in Congress. Is that a worthy goal? Or is there something unsavory in the notion that representatives should be selected on the basis that they are of a particular race or ethnic group? The majority in the case seems to believe that racial re-districting is, in a sense, a betrayal of American notions of equality, notions presumably based not only in the Equal Protection Clause of the Fourteenth Amendment, but also in the Declaration of Independence and in natural law. Do you agree?

2. The dissenters argue that the Supreme Court has gone even further in this case than it did in *Shaw v. Reno* to interfere with the "political process," and that such interference with a state's attempt to draw its own representational boundaries (albeit with a thumb on the scale provided by the Justice Department) is

unwarranted. Do you agree? Do you discern a trend in the Supreme Court's decisions that seems to be moving in a different direction from the cases that followed the landmark decisions in *Brown, Green,* and *Swann*? Race, as indicated already, continues to be one of the most intractable problems in American society. What should be the role of the courts in ameliorating that problem, or do they have much of a role to play?

3.   *Miller* establishes that race cannot be a predominant factor in the drawing of district lines. After *Miller,* a plurality of the Court led by Justice O'Connor indicated that predominance meant more than race consciousness, it meant that legitimate districting principles were subordinated to race. *Bush v. Vera,* 517 U.S. 952, 962 (1996). And in *Hunt v. Cromartie,* 526 U.S. 541 (1999), the Court held that it was inappropriate to determine whether race predominates as a matter of summary judgment where the state contends that it was not attempting to employ race, but party affiliation, in the redrawing of the same district (District 12, North Carolina) that was at issue in *Shaw v. Reno* (1993). Applying the normal presumptions, the Court said summary judgment was only appropriate where there is no genuine issue of material fact and the moving party is entitled to judgment as a matter of law. Those challenging District 12 had, however, offered only circumstantial evidence of racial predominance (bizarre shape; lack of compactness; disregard for political subdivision [the only district in the State containing no undivided county]), and the state did contest the alleged racial motivation, arguing that it was attempting to "protect incumbents, to adhere to traditional districting criteria, and to preserve the existing partisan balance in the State's congressional delegation. . . ." In addition, factual evidence tended to show that there was a high correlation between race and party in North Carolina. Given that the District court was obliged to assume the state's explanations as true for purposes of evaluating the summary judgment claim (the nonmoving party's evidence is to be believed and all justifiable inferences are to be drawn in that party's favor), the challengers were not entitled to judgment as a matter of law. "Our prior decisions have made clear that a jurisdiction may engage in constitutional political gerrymandering, even if it so happens that the most loyal Democrats happen to be black Democrats and even if the State were conscious of that fact."

In response to the Court's remand, the District Court conducted a 3 day trial and once again found that the congressional district was premised upon race. 5-4, the Supreme Court overturned the District Court as "clearly erroneous." *Easley v. Cromartie,* 532 U.S. 234 (2001). Writing for the Court, Justice Breyer articulated the view that those challenging a district as motivated predominantly by race have a heavy burden. Race must not just be a factor, but the predominant one; that is, one unexplainable on grounds other than race. This considerable burden reflects that districting is a legislative decision. Said Justice Breyer: "Caution is especially appropriate in this case, where the State has articulated a legitimate political explanation for its districting decision, and the voting population is one in which race and political affiliation are highly correlated." Justice Thomas wrote for the dissent, arguing that the Court had engaged in its own factfinding and improperly set aside the trial court. The dissent noted that the District Court used objective measures to find the legislative district "could not have been explained by political [that is, nonracial] motives."

4. Elaborating on its recognition in *Cromartie* that redistricting is fundamentally a legislative decision, the Supreme Court in *Georgia v. Ashcroft*, 539 U.S. 461 (2003), held that it was permissible for a legislature to choose to create "black influence districts" rather than a few districts in which blacks were a large enough majority of the voting age population to ensure the election of a candidate of their choice, and therefore remanded the case to the district court to consider whether pre-clearance was required once the entire effect of the redistricting plan was considered. "Section 5 gives States the flexibility to implement the type of plan that Georgia has submitted for preclearance — a plan that increases the number of districts with a majority-black voting age population, even if it means that in some of those districts, minority voters will face a somewhat reduced opportunity to elect a candidate of their choice." Thus, Justice O'Connor (writing for the five-member majority) held, because "the Voting Rights Act, as properly interpreted, should encourage the transition to a society where race no longer matters: a society where integration and color-blindness are not just qualities to be proud of, but are simple facts of life." *But see Grutter v. Bollinger, supra.*

5. What justifications remain for using race at all in districting? Here, the Court is divided. Justices Thomas and Scalia believe that strict scrutiny is appropriate whenever race is intentionally used in districting, whether or not it predominates. The dissenters in these cases (Justices Stevens, Souter, Ginsburg, and Breyer) would rather freely allow the use of race to create so-called majority-minority districts. In *Shaw v. Hunt*, 517 U.S. 899 (1996), the Court expressly held that compliance with the views of the Justice Department, especially as it applied section 5 of the Voting Rights Act, could not be used to justify the use of race. Section 5 requires pre-clearance by the Department of changes by states with a history of racial discrimination in voting matters. An unanswered question is whether compliance with section 2 of that Act, which prohibits changes in election systems with discriminatory effect (as opposed to intent), could justify a policy of maximizing minority districts. The Court implies a negative answer since the refusal to use race, itself, to maximize minority districts has not been viewed by the Court as an action with a prohibited discriminatory impact.

6. The Voting Rights Act, like Title VII of the Civil Rights Act, has provisions precluding not just racial intent, but racial impact. Given that the standard for an equal protection violation is purposeful or intentional discrimination, by what authority has Congress passed such legislation? If your thought is section 5 of the Fourteenth Amendment, the answer may not be sufficient. While the Voting Rights Act or Title VII may employ more lenient evidentiary means to identify constitutional violations, such means do not permit a public decision maker to make use of race in ways not permitted by the Constitution. According to the Court, race cannot be used for non-remedial purposes in employment and it must not be a predominant factor in the drawing of district lines. When Congress penalizes the racial impact of a neutral practice either in employment or voting, is Congress seeking to contradict the Court's fundamental requirement of racial intent for an equal protection violation? In *City of Boerne v. Flores*, 521 U.S. 507 (1997) (considered in Chapter Five), the Court invalidated the Religious Freedom Restoration Act (RFRA) by which Congress sought to explicitly displace the Court's interpretation of the Free Exercise Clause with a standard of its own choosing. Is Congress displacing the

Court's view of equal protection in the Voting Rights Act or Title VII? As important as Congress' Fourteenth Amendment enforcement power is, does it include substantively rewriting constitutional text? In this regard, the Court held in *Boerne* that "Congress does not enforce a constitutional right by changing what the right is. It has been given the power 'to enforce,' not the power to determine what constitutes a constitutional violation. Were it not so, what Congress would be enforcing would no longer be, in any meaningful sense, the 'provisions of [the Constitution].' " 521 U.S. 519 (1997). "If Congress could define its own powers by altering the Fourteenth Amendment's meaning, no longer would the Constitution be 'superior paramount law, unchangeable by ordinary means.' It would be 'on a level with ordinary legislative acts, and, like other acts, . . . alterable when the legislature shall please to alter it.' " *Id.* at 529 (citing *Marbury v. Madison*, 5 U.S. (1 Cranch) 137, 177 (1803)).

7. In *Perry v. Perez*, 132 S. Ct. 934 (2012), the Court faced a complexity, if not a dilemma, caused by the 2010 census. The 2010 census showed an enormous increase in Texas' population, necessitating that the State redraw its electoral districts for the United States Congress and for its state legislative branches. Texas, being a "covered jurisdiction" under § 5 of the federal Voting Rights Act of 1965, the Texas legislature enacted redistricting plans. The State then submitted its legislature's redistricting plans to the United States District Court for the District of Columbia for the "preclearance" required under the Voting Rights Act. "Preclearance" requires the covered jurisdiction to demonstrate that its proposed changes have neither the purpose nor effect "of denying or abridging the right to vote on account of race or color." While that preclearance suit was pending in the District of Columbia, various plaintiffs sued in the United States District Court for the Western District of Texas, claiming that Texas's newly enacted redistricting plans violate § 2 of the Voting Rights Act and discriminate against Latinos and African-Americans by diluting their voting strength.

With the 2012 primaries and elections approaching, it became clear to the federal district court in Texas that the State's newly enacted plans would not receive preclearance from the United States District Court for the District of Columbia in time for the 2012 elections. Normally, in such a scenario, the older, original districting scheme would be used in the primaries and elections. But in this case, Texas's old districting lines had been rendered so anachronistic by the demographics of the enormous increase in population that using them would clearly run afoul of the one-person, one-vote requirement of the Constitution. Hence the dilemma.

Feeling the weight of that dilemma, the United States District Court for the Western District of Texas sought to solve it by going forward with its case and drafting its own redistricting plans for the Texas state and national legislative districts. The United States Supreme Court held that the district court had erred in doing so, and remanded the case for further proceedings.

The United States Supreme Court at first seemed to deepen the dilemma when it announced the basic principle involving preclearances:

Where a State has sought preclearance in the District Court for the District of Columbia, § 5 [of the Voting Rights Act] allows only that court to determine whether the state plan complies with § 5. . . . [O]ther district courts may not address the merits of § 5 challenges.

The case in the district court in Texas, however, involved alleged violations of the Equal Protection Clause and § 2, not § 5, of the Voting Rights Act. With that circumstance in mind, the United States Supreme Court said:

> Where a State's plan faces challenges under the Constitution or § 2 of the Voting Rights Act, a district court should still be guided by [the challenged state redistricting] plan, except to the extent those legal challenges are shown to have a likelihood of success on the merits.

The Court further acknowledged that "serious constitutional questions" involving "intrusion on state sovereignty" are raised when the United States District Court for the District of Columbia handles § 5 cases, and cautioned that those questions "would only be exacerbated if § 5 required a district court to wholly ignore the State's policies in drawing maps that will govern a State's elections, without any reason to believe those state policies are unlawful." The Court then applied that sensitivity to the § 2 case that was before it, noting that while the district court had purported to "give effect to as much of the policy judgments in the [Texas] Legislature's enacted map as possible," it had also indicated that it was drawing an "independent map," following "neutral principles that advance the interest of the collective public good," and had ultimately asserted that it "was not required to give any deference to the [Texas] Legislature's enacted plan." In a *per curiam* opinion, the Court concluded:

> To the extent the [United States] District Court [for the Western District of Texas] exceeded its mission to draw interim maps that do not violate the Constitution or the Voting Rights Act, and substituted its own concept of "the collective public good" for the Texas Legislature's determination of which policies serve "the interests of the citizens of Texas," the court erred.

8. Before moving on to consider gender and other bases of classification, mention of the topic of voting allows us to see another implication of the concept of equal protection.

B.　NUMERICAL EQUALITY — ONE PERSON/ONE VOTE

Equal protection has also been applied in the context of malapportionment — that is, the failure to keep voting districts of reasonably equal population. Applying equal protection to this issue was controversial since it was initially thought that voting was a political right to be determined by the political branches, most notably the state legislatures, of the several states. In *Baker v. Carr*, 369 U.S. 186 (1962), the Court concluded that a constitutional equal protection challenge was not solely a political question, and the issue was brought — over vigorous dissent — before the Supreme Court. The first case to articulate the one person/one vote standard was *Gray v. Sanders*, 372 U.S. 368 (1963), involving a challenge to the method of electing members to the Georgia House of Representatives. The Court asserted that "[t]he conception of political equality from the Declaration of Independence, to Lincoln's Gettysburg Address, to the Fifteenth, Seventeenth, and Nineteenth Amendments can mean only one thing — one person, one vote." *Id.* at 381. The Court subsequently applied this principle to districts for the U.S. House of Representatives in *Wesberry v. Sanders*, 376 U.S. 1 (1964). Perhaps all this seems obvious to us today. However, a moment's reflection reveals that the national legislature — the Congress — does not fully follow this principle. The Senate of the United States is made up of two representatives from each state regardless of population. This was part of the so-called great compromise at the 1787 constitutional convention, whereby regional, and to some extent slavery-determined, differences were assuaged by having a bicameral legislature made up of both population- and non-population-based interests in its composition. Why shouldn't the same political latitude be allowed within the states? Might not an individual state that is mostly rural and concerned with agricultural matters not want to counterbalance the urban interests of a singularly large city within the boundaries of the state? Of course, then the urban interests might be offended. As the mayor of Nashville complained about the situation in Tennessee litigated in *Baker*, the state was governed "by the hog lot and the cow pasture." ED CRAY, CHIEF JUSTICE: A BIOGRAPHY OF EARL WARREN 379 (1997).

One real problem confronted by the Court in *Baker* was the Supreme Court's prior opinion in *Colegrove v. Green*, 328 U.S. 549 (1946), written by Justice Frankfurter, which refused to interfere with the apportionment of Illinois congressional districts, even though population disparities in them ran as high as nine to one. Justice Frankfurter passionately dissented in *Baker*. He accused the majority, among other things, of imperiling the Court's high standing in American society and of producing an "umbrageous disposition." 369 U.S. at 267 (Frankfurter, J., dissenting). Why was there such obvious ire behind his opinion? Felix Frankfurter was undoubtedly one of the most talented men ever to sit on the Supreme Court. He was a professor at Harvard when he was nominated by President Franklin D. Roosevelt, and he was very much sympathetic to the New Deal. He was, then, very much a liberal in politics. Once on the Court, however, he became a champion for "judicial restraint" — that is, for articulating the view that the Court weakened its legitimacy when it took on social issues that, in Frankfurter's opinion, more properly belonged to other branches of government, or perhaps to the states rather than the federal government. When Frankfurter realized that a majority of the Court in *Baker* was going to repudiate his conclusion in *Colegrove* that apportionment was a "political question" that the Supreme Court should not touch, Frankfurter declared to his clerks that "[t]his is the darkest day in the history of the Court." CRAY, *supra*, at 382. Was he right? Whether or not it was the darkest day in the history of the Court, it was certainly a dark day for Frankfurter. Ten days after Brennan's opinion for the Court was announced in *Baker*, Frankfurter suffered a "massive stroke that left his left side paralyzed." *Id.* at 385. It is quite likely that the redistricting decision contributed to the tension and exertion that resulted in this crippling affliction. It was, Earl Warren's biographer notes, "the last and greatest blow" to Frankfurter, whose philosophy had been abandoned by his brethren. *Id.* The term in which *Baker* was decided was Frankfurter's last. Six months after the decision, realizing that he no longer had the physical capacity to participate fully in the work of the Court, Frankfurter submitted his resignation to the President. This marked "the end of an era." *Id.* When Frankfurter left the Court it was left to Justice Harlan to carry on Frankfurter's role as a champion of judicial restraint. You will be able to evaluate how well Harlan performed his task by considering his dissent in the case that follows — one made inevitable by *Baker*. The essence of Harlan's problem with what the majority decided *sub silentio* in *Baker* was that he could find no Fourteenth Amendment declaration that each person's vote ought to be counted equally. What was implicit in *Baker* became explicit in *Reynolds v. Sims*.

REYNOLDS v. SIMS
377 U.S. 533 (1964)

Mr. Chief Justice Warren delivered the opinion of the Court.

* * *

I.

On August 26, 1961, the original plaintiffs . . . , residents, taxpayers and voters of Jefferson County, Alabama, filed a complaint in the United States District Court for the Middle District of Alabama, in their own behalf and on behalf of all similarly situated Alabama voters, challenging the apportionment of the Alabama Legislature. . . . The complaint alleged a deprivation of rights under the Alabama Constitution and under the Equal Protection Clause of the Fourteenth Amendment. . . .

* * *

Plaintiffs below alleged that the last apportionment of the Alabama Legislature was based on the 1900 federal census, despite the requirement of the State Constitution that the legislature be reapportioned decennially. They asserted that, since the population growth in the State from 1900 to 1960 had been uneven, Jefferson and other counties were now victims of serious discrimination with respect to the allocation of legislative representation. As a result of the failure of the legislature to reapportion itself, plaintiffs asserted, they were denied "equal suffrage in free and equal elections . . . and the equal protection of the laws" in violation of the Alabama Constitution and the Fourteenth Amendment to the Federal Constitution . . . and that, while the Alabama Supreme Court had found that the legislature had not complied with the State Constitution in failing to reapportion according to population decennially, that court had nevertheless indicated that it would not interfere with matters of legislative reapportionment.

* * *

On April 14, 1962, the District Court . . . [r]elying on our decision in *Baker v. Carr* . . . found jurisdiction, justiciability and standing. . . . [T]he Court stated that if the legislature complied with the Alabama constitutional provision requiring legislative representation to be based on population there could be no objection on federal constitutional grounds to such an apportionment. The Court further indicated that, if the legislature failed to act, or if its actions did not meet constitutional standards, it would be under a "clear duty" to take some action on the matter prior to the November 1962 general election. . . . Subsequently, plaintiffs were permitted to amend their complaint by adding a further prayer for relief, which asked the District Court to reapportion the Alabama Legislature provisionally so that the rural strangle hold would be relaxed enough to permit it to reapportion itself.

On July 12, 1962, an extraordinary session of the Alabama Legislature adopted two reapportionment plans to take effect for the 1966 elections. One was a proposed constitutional amendment, referred to as the "67-Senator Amendment." It provided for a House of Representatives consisting of 106 members, apportioned by giving one seat to each of Alabama's 67 counties and distributing the others according to population by the "equal proportions" method. Using this formula, the constitutional amendment specified the number of representatives allotted to each county until a new apportionment could be made on the basis of the 1970 census. The Senate was to be composed of 67 members, one from each county. The legislation provided that the proposed amendment should be submitted to the voters for ratification at the November 1962 general election.

The other reapportionment plan was embodied in a statutory measure adopted by the legislature and signed into law by the Alabama Governor, and was referred to as the "Crawford-Webb Act." It was enacted as standby legislation to take effect in 1966 if the proposed constitutional amendment should fail of passage by a majority of the State's voters, or should the federal courts refuse to accept the proposed amendment. . . . The act provided for a Senate consisting of 35 members, representing 35 senatorial districts established along county lines, and altered only a few of the former districts. In apportioning the 106 seats in the Alabama House of Representatives, the statutory measure gave each county one seat, and apportioned the remaining 39 on a rough population basis, under a formula requiring increasingly more population for a county to be accorded additional seats. . . .

*   *   *

On July 21, 1962, the District Court held that the inequality of the existing representation in the Alabama Legislature violated the Equal Protection Clause of the Fourteenth Amendment, a finding which the Court noted had been "generally conceded" by the parties to the litigation, since population growth and shifts had converted the 1901 scheme, as perpetuated some 60 years later, into an invidiously discriminatory plan completely lacking in rationality. . . . Population-variance ratios of up to about 41-to-1 existed in the Senate, and up to about 16-to-1 in the House. . . .

*   *   *

II.

Undeniably the Constitution of the United States protects the right of all qualified citizens to vote, in state as well as in federal elections. A consistent line of decisions by this Court in cases involving attempts to deny or restrict the right of suffrage has made this indelibly clear. . . . The right to vote freely for the candidate of one's choice is of the essence of a democratic society, and any restrictions on that right strike at the heart of representative government. And the right of suffrage can be denied by a debasement or dilution of the weight of a citizen's vote just as effectively as by wholly prohibiting the free exercise of the franchise.

In *Baker v. Carr* (1962) we held that a claim asserted under the Equal Protection Clause challenging the constitutionality of a State's apportionment of seats in its legislature, on the ground that the right to vote of certain citizens was effectively impaired since debased and diluted, in effect presented a justiciable controversy subject to adjudication by federal courts. The spate of similar cases filed and decided by lower courts since our decision in *Baker* amply shows that the problem of state legislative malapportionment is one that is perceived to exist in a large number of the States. In *Baker*, a suit involving an attack on the apportionment of seats in the Tennessee Legislature, we remanded to the District Court, which had dismissed the action, for consideration on the merits. We intimated no view as to the proper constitutional standards for evaluating the validity of a state legislative apportionment scheme. Nor did we give any consideration to the question of appropriate remedies. . . .

In *Gray v. Sanders* (1963) we held that the Georgia county unit system, applicable in statewide primary elections, was unconstitutional since it resulted in a dilution of the weight of the votes of certain Georgia voters merely because of where they resided. After indicating that the Fifteenth and Nineteenth Amendments prohibit a State from overweighting or diluting votes on the basis of race or sex, we stated . . . that "there is no indication in the Constitution that homesite or occupation affords a permissible basis for distinguishing between qualified voters within the State." And, finally, we concluded: "The conception of political equality from the Declaration of Independence, to Lincoln's Gettysburg Address, to the Fifteenth, Seventeenth, and Nineteenth Amendments can mean only one thing — one person, one vote."

We stated in *Gray*, however, that that case,

> "unlike *Baker v. Carr*, . . . does not involve a question of the degree to which the Equal Protection Clause of the Fourteenth Amendment limits the authority of a State Legislature in designing the geographical districts from which representatives are chosen either for the State Legislature or for the Federal House of Representatives. . . . Nor does it present the question, inherent in the bicameral form of our Federal Government, whether a State may have one house chosen without regard to population."

Of course, in these cases we are faced with the problem not presented in *Gray* — that of determining the basic standards and stating the applicable guidelines for implementing our decision in *Baker v. Carr*.

In *Wesberry v. Sanders* (1964), decided earlier this Term, we held that attacks on the constitutionality of congressional districting plans enacted by state legislatures do not present nonjusticiable questions and should not be dismissed generally for "want of equity." We determined that the constitutional test for the validity of congressional districting schemes was one of substantial equality of population among the various districts established by a state legislature for the election of members of the Federal House of Representatives.

In that case we decided that an apportionment of congressional seats which "contracts the value of some votes and expands that of others" is unconstitutional, since "the Federal Constitution intends that when qualified voters elect members of Congress each vote be given as much weight as any other vote. . . ." We concluded that the constitutional prescription for election of members of the House of Representatives "by the People," construed in its historical context, "means that as nearly as is practicable one man's vote in a congressional election is to be worth as much as another's." . . . We found further, in *Wesberry*, that "our Constitution's plain objective" was that "of making equal representation for equal numbers of people the fundamental goal." . . .

* * *

III.

A predominant consideration in determining whether a State's legislative apportionment scheme constitutes an invidious discrimination violative of rights asserted under the Equal Protection Clause is that the rights allegedly impaired are individual and personal in nature. . . .

Legislators represent people, not trees or acres. Legislators are elected by voters, not farms or cities or economic interests. As long as ours is a representative form of government, and our legislatures are those instruments of government elected directly by and directly representative of the people, the right to elect legislators in a free and unimpaired fashion is a bedrock of our political system. It could hardly be gainsaid that a constitutional claim had been asserted by an allegation that certain otherwise qualified voters had been entirely prohibited from voting for members of their state legislature. And, if a State should provide that the votes of citizens in one part of the State should be given two times, or five times, or 10 times the weight of votes of citizens in another part of the State, it could hardly be contended that the right to vote of those residing in the disfavored areas had not been effectively diluted. . . . Of course, the effect of state legislative districting schemes which give the same number of representatives to unequal numbers of constituents is identical. Overweighting and overvaluation of the votes of those living here has the certain effect of dilution and undervaluation of the votes of those living there. The resulting discrimination against those individual voters living in disfavored areas is easily demonstrable mathematically. Their right to vote is simply not the same right to vote as that of those living in a favored part of the State. . . . Weighting the votes of citizens differently, by any method or means, merely because of where they happen to reside, hardly seems justifiable. . . .

* * *

We are told that the matter of apportioning representation in a state legislature is a complex and many-faceted one. We are advised that States can rationally consider factors other than population in apportioning legislative representation. We are admonished not to restrict the power of the States to impose differing views as to political philosophy on their citizens. We are cautioned about the dangers of entering into political thickets and mathematical quagmires. Our answer is this: a denial of constitutionally protected rights demands judicial protection; our oath and our office require no less of us. . . . To the extent that a citizen's right to vote is debased, he is that much less a citizen. The fact that an individual lives here or there is not a legitimate reason for overweighting or diluting the efficacy of his vote. . . . [T]he basic principle of representative government remains, and must remain, unchanged — the weight of a citizen's vote cannot be made to depend on where he lives. . . . This is the clear and strong command of our Constitution's Equal Protection Clause. This is an essential part of the concept of a government of laws and not men. This is at the heart of Lincoln's vision of "government of the people, by the people, [and] for the people." The Equal Protection Clause demands no less than substantially equal state legislative representation for all citizens, of all places as well as of all races.

IV.

We hold that, as a basic constitutional standard, the Equal Protection Clause requires that the seats in both houses of a bicameral state legislature must be apportioned on a population basis. Simply stated, an individual's right to vote for state legislators is unconstitutionally impaired when its weight is in a substantial fashion diluted when compared with votes of citizens living in other parts of the State. Since, under neither the existing apportionment provisions nor either of the proposed plans was either of the houses of the Alabama Legislature apportioned on a population basis, the District Court correctly held that all three of these schemes were constitutionally invalid. Furthermore, the existing apportionment, and also to a lesser extent the apportionment under the Crawford-Webb Act, presented little more than crazy quilts, completely lacking in rationality, and could be found invalid on that basis alone. Although the District Court presumably found the apportionment of the Alabama House of Representatives under the 67-Senator Amendment to be acceptable, we conclude that the deviations from a strict population basis are too egregious to permit us to find that that body, under this proposed plan, was apportioned sufficiently on a population basis so as to permit the arrangement to be constitutionally sustained. . . .

Legislative apportionment in Alabama is signally illustrative and symptomatic of the seriousness of this problem in a number of the States. At the time this litigation was commenced, there had been no reapportionment of seats in the Alabama Legislature for over 60 years. Legislative inaction, coupled with the unavailability of any political or judicial remedy, had resulted, with the passage of years, in the perpetuated scheme becoming little more than an irrational anachronism. . . .

V.

Since neither of the houses of the Alabama Legislature, under any of the three plans considered by the District Court, was apportioned on a population basis, we would be justified in proceeding no further. However, one of the proposed plans, that contained in the so-called 67-Senator Amendment, at least superficially resembles the scheme of legislative representation followed in the Federal Congress. Under this plan, each of Alabama's 67 counties is allotted one senator, and no counties are given more than one Senate seat. Arguably, this is analogous to the allocation of two Senate seats, in the Federal Congress, to each of the 50 States, regardless of population. Seats in the Alabama House, under the proposed constitutional amendment, are distributed by giving each of the 67 counties at least one, with the remaining 39 seats being allotted among the more populous counties on a population basis. This scheme, at least at first glance, appears to resemble that prescribed for the Federal House of Representatives, where the 435 seats are distributed among the States on a population basis, although each State, regardless of its population, is given at least one Congressman. . . .

Much has been written since our decision in *Baker v. Carr* about the applicability of the so-called federal analogy to state legislative apportionment arrangements. After considering the matter, the court below concluded that no conceivable analogy could be drawn between the federal scheme and the apportionment of seats in the Alabama Legislature under the proposed constitutional amendment. We agree with the District Court, and find the federal analogy inapposite and irrelevant to state legislative districting schemes. . . . [T]he Founding Fathers clearly had no intention of establishing a pattern or model for the apportionment of seats in state legislatures when the system of representation in the Federal Congress was adopted. Demonstrative of this is the fact that the Northwest Ordinance, adopted in the same year, 1787, as the Federal Constitution, provided for the apportionment of seats in territorial legislatures solely on the basis of population.

The system of representation in the two Houses of the Federal Congress is one ingrained in our Constitution, as part of the law of the land. It is one conceived out of compromise and concession indispensable to the establishment of our federal republic. Arising from unique historical circumstances, it is based on the consideration that in establishing our type of federalism a group of formerly independent States bound themselves together under one national government. . . .

Political subdivisions of States — counties, cities, or whatever — never were and never have been considered as sovereign entities. Rather, they have been traditionally regarded as subordinate governmental instrumentalities created by the State to assist in the carrying out of state governmental functions. . . .

Thus, we conclude that the plan contained in the 67-Senator Amendment for apportioning seats in the Alabama Legislature cannot be sustained by recourse to the so-called federal analogy. Nor can any other inequitable state legislative apportionment scheme be justified on such an asserted basis. This does not necessarily mean that such a plan is irrational or involves something other than a "republican form of government." We conclude simply that such a plan is impermissible for the States under the Equal Protection Clause, since perforce resulting, in virtually every case, in submergence of the equal population principle in at least one house of a state legislature.

Since we find the so-called federal analogy inapposite to a consideration of the constitutional validity of state legislative apportionment schemes, we necessarily hold that the Equal Protection Clause requires both houses of a state legislature to be apportioned on a population basis. . . .

*   *   *

VI.

By holding that as a federal constitutional requisite both houses of a state legislature must be apportioned on a population basis, we mean that the Equal Protection Clause requires that a State make an honest and good faith effort to construct districts, in both houses of its legislature, as nearly of equal population as is practicable. We realize that it is a practical impossibility to arrange legislative districts so that each one has an identical number of residents, or citizens, or voters. Mathematical exactness or precision is hardly a workable constitutional requirement.

* * *

A State may legitimately desire to maintain the integrity of various political subdivisions, insofar as possible, and provide for compact districts of contiguous territory in designing a legislative apportionment scheme. Valid considerations may underlie such aims. Indiscriminate districting, without any regard for political subdivision or natural or historical boundary lines, may be little more than an open invitation to partisan gerrymandering. Single-member districts may be the rule in one State, while another State might desire to achieve some flexibility by creating multimember or floterial districts. Whatever the means of accomplishment, the overriding objective must be substantial equality of population among the various districts, so that the vote of any citizen is approximately equal in weight to that of any other citizen in the State.

History indicates, however, that many States have deviated, to a greater or lesser degree, from the equal-population principle in the apportionment of seats in at least one house of their legislatures. So long as the divergences from a strict population standard are based on legitimate considerations incident to the effectuation of a rational state policy, some deviations from the equal-population principle are constitutionally permissible with respect to the apportionment of seats in either or both of the two houses of a bicameral state legislature. But neither history alone, nor economic or other sorts of group interests, are permissible factors in attempting to justify disparities from population-based representation. Citizens, not history or economic interests, cast votes. Considerations of area alone provide an insufficient justification for deviations from the equal-population principle. Again, people, not land or trees or pastures, vote. Modern developments and improvements in transportation and communications make rather hollow, in the mid-1960's, most claims that deviations from population-based representation can validly be based solely on geographical considerations. Arguments for allowing such deviations in order to insure effective representation for sparsely settled areas and to prevent legislative districts from becoming so large that the availability of access of citizens to their representatives is impaired are today, for the most part, unconvincing.

A consideration that appears to be of more substance in justifying some deviations from population-based representation in state legislatures is that of insuring some voice to political subdivisions, as political subdivisions. Several factors make more than insubstantial claims that a State can rationally consider according political subdivisions some independent representation in at least one body of the state legislature, as long as the basic standard of equality of population among districts is maintained. Local governmental entities are frequently charged with various responsibilities incident to the operation of state government. In many States much of the legislature's activity involves the enactment of so-called local legislation, directed only to the concerns of particular political subdivisions. And a State may legitimately desire to construct districts along political subdivision lines to deter the possibilities of gerrymandering. However, permitting deviations from population-based representation does not mean that each local governmental unit or political subdivision can be given separate representation, regardless of population. Carried too far, a scheme of giving at least one seat in one house to each political subdivision (for example, to each county) could easily result, in many States, in a total subversion of the equal-population principle in that legislative body. . . .

VII.

One of the arguments frequently offered as a basis for upholding a State's legislative apportionment arrangement, despite substantial disparities from a population basis in either or both houses, is grounded on congressional approval, incident to admitting States into the Union, of state apportionment plans containing deviations from the equal-population principle. Proponents of this argument contend that congressional approval of such schemes, despite their disparities from population-based representation, indicates that such arrangements are plainly sufficient as establishing a "republican form of government." As we stated in *Baker v. Carr*, some questions raised under the Guaranty Clause are nonjusticiable, where "political" in nature and where there is a clear absence of judicially manageable standards. Nevertheless, it is not inconsistent with this view to hold that, despite congressional approval of state legislative apportionment plans at the time of admission into the Union, even though deviating from the equal-population principle here enunciated, the Equal Protection Clause can and does require more. And an apportionment scheme in which both houses are based on population can hardly be considered as failing to satisfy the Guaranty Clause requirement. Congress presumably does not assume, in admitting States into the Union, to pass on all constitutional questions relating to the character of state governmental organization. In any event, congressional approval, however well-considered, could hardly validate an unconstitutional state legislative apportionment. . . .

VIII.

That the Equal Protection Clause requires that both houses of a state legislature be apportioned on a population basis does not mean that States cannot adopt some reasonable plan for periodic revision of their apportionment schemes. Decennial reapportionment appears to be a rational approach to readjustment of legislative representation in order to take into account population shifts and growth. . . . While we do not intend to indicate that decennial reapportionment is a constitutional requisite, compliance with such an approach would clearly meet the minimal requirements for maintaining a reasonably current scheme of legislative representation. And we do not mean to intimate that more frequent reapportionment would not be constitutionally permissible or practically desirable. But if reapportionment were accomplished with less frequency, it would assuredly be constitutionally suspect.

* * *

X.

We do not consider here the difficult question of the proper remedial devices which federal courts should utilize in state legislative apportionment cases. Remedial techniques in this new and developing area of the law will probably often differ with the circumstances of the challenged apportionment and a variety of local conditions. It is enough to say now that, once a State's legislative apportionment scheme has been found to be unconstitutional, it would be the unusual case in which a court would be justified in not taking appropriate action to insure that no further elections are conducted under the invalid plan. . . .

We feel that the District Court in this case acted in a most proper and commendable manner. It initially acted wisely in declining to stay the impending primary election in Alabama, and properly refrained from acting further until the Alabama Legislature had been given an opportunity to remedy the admitted discrepancies in the State's legislative apportionment scheme, while initially stating some of its views to provide guidelines for legislative action. And it correctly recognized that legislative reapportionment is primarily a matter for legislative consideration and determination, and that judicial relief becomes appropriate only when a legislature fails to reapportion according to federal constitutional requisites in a timely fashion after having had an adequate opportunity to do so. Additionally, the court below acted with proper judicial restraint, after the Alabama Legislature had failed to act effectively in remedying the constitutional deficiencies in the State's legislative apportionment scheme, in ordering its own temporary reapportionment plan into effect, at a time sufficiently early to permit the holding of elections pursuant to that plan without great difficulty, and in prescribing a plan admittedly provisional in purpose so as not to usurp the primary responsibility for reapportionment which rests with the legislature.

We find, therefore, that the action taken by the District Court in this case, in ordering into effect a reapportionment of both houses of the Alabama Legislature for purposes of the 1962 primary and general elections, by using the best parts of the two proposed plans which it had found, as a whole, to be invalid, was an appropriate and well-considered exercise of judicial power. . . . In retaining jurisdiction while deferring a hearing on the issuance of a final injunction in order to give the provisionally reapportioned legislature an opportunity to act effectively, the court below proceeded in a proper fashion. Since the District Court evinced its realization that its ordered reapportionment could not be sustained as the basis for conducting the 1966 election of Alabama legislators, and avowedly intends to take some further action should the reapportioned Alabama Legislature fail to enact a constitutionally valid, permanent apportionment scheme in the interim, we affirm the judgment below and remand the cases for further proceedings consistent with the views stated in this opinion.

It is so ordered.

MR. JUSTICE CLARK, concurring in the affirmance.

The Court goes much beyond the necessities of this case in laying down a new "equal population" principle for state legislative apportionment. . . .

It seems to me that all that the Court need say in this case is that each plan considered by the trial court is "a crazy quilt," clearly revealing invidious discrimination in each house of the Legislature and therefore violative of the Equal Protection Clause. . . .

I, therefore, do not reach the question of the so-called "federal analogy." But in my view, if one house of the State Legislature meets the population standard, representation in the other house might include some departure from it so as to take into account, on a rational basis, other factors in order to afford some representation to the various elements of the State. . . .

MR. JUSTICE STEWART. [Omitted.]

MR. JUSTICE HARLAN, dissenting.

In these cases the Court holds that seats in the legislatures . . . are apportioned in ways that violate the Federal Constitution. Under the Court's ruling it is bound to follow that the legislatures in all but a few of the other . . . States will meet the same fate. These decisions, with *Wesberry v. Sanders* (1964) involving congressional districting by the States, and *Gray v. Sanders* (1963) relating to elections for statewide office, have the effect of placing basic aspects of state political systems under the pervasive overlordship of the federal judiciary. Once again, I must register my protest.

PRELIMINARY STATEMENT.

Today's holding is that the Equal Protection Clause of the Fourteenth Amendment requires every State to structure its legislature so that all the members of each house represent substantially the same number of people; other factors may be given play only to the extent that they do not significantly encroach on this basic "population" principle. Whatever may be thought of this holding as a piece of political ideology — and even on that score the political history and practices of this country from its earliest beginnings leave wide room for debate — I think it demonstrable that the Fourteenth Amendment does not impose this political tenet on the States or authorize this Court to do so.

The Court's constitutional discussion . . . is remarkable . . . for its failure to address itself at all to the Fourteenth Amendment as a whole or to the legislative history of the Amendment pertinent to the matter at hand. Stripped of aphorisms, the Court's argument boils down to the assertion that appellees' right to vote has been invidiously "debased" or "diluted" by systems of apportionment which entitle them to vote for fewer legislators than other voters, an assertion which is tied to the Equal Protection Clause only by the constitutionally frail tautology that "equal" means "equal."

Had the Court paused to probe more deeply into the matter, it would have found that the Equal Protection Clause was never intended to inhibit the States in choosing any democratic method they pleased for the apportionment of their legislatures. This is shown by the language of the Fourteenth Amendment taken as a whole, by the understanding of those who proposed and ratified it, and by the political practices of the States at the time the Amendment was adopted. It is confirmed by numerous state and congressional actions since the adoption of the Fourteenth Amendment, and by the common understanding of the Amendment as evidenced by subsequent constitutional amendments and decisions of this Court before *Baker v. Carr* made an abrupt break with the past in 1962.

The failure of the Court to consider any of these matters cannot be excused or explained by any concept of "developing" constitutionalism. It is meaningless to speak of constitutional "development" when both the language and history of the controlling provisions of the Constitution are wholly ignored. Since it can, I think, be shown beyond doubt that state legislative apportionments, as such, are wholly free of constitutional limitations, save such as may be imposed by the Republican Form of Government Clause (Const., Art. IV, § 4), the Court's action now bringing them within the purview of the Fourteenth Amendment amounts to nothing less than an exercise of the amending power by this Court.

So far as the Federal Constitution is concerned, the complaints in these cases should all have been dismissed below for failure to state a cause of action, because what has been alleged or proved shows no violation of any constitutional right.

* * *

I.

* * *

. . . In my judgment, today's decisions are refuted by the language of the Amendment which they construe and by the inference fairly to be drawn from subsequently enacted Amendments. They are unequivocally refuted by history and by consistent theory and practice from the time of the adoption of the Fourteenth Amendment until today.

II.

The Court's elaboration of its new "constitutional" doctrine indicates how far — and how unwisely — it has strayed from the appropriate bounds of its authority. The consequence of today's decision is that in all but the handful of States which may already satisfy the new requirements, the local District Court or, it may be, the state courts, are given blanket authority and the constitutional duty to supervise apportionment of the State Legislatures. It is difficult to imagine a more intolerable and inappropriate interference by the judiciary with the independent legislatures of the States.

* * *

. . . [T]hese cases do not mark the end of reapportionment problems in the courts. Predictions once made that the courts would never have to face the problem of actually working out an apportionment have proved false. This Court, however, continues to avoid the consequences of its decisions, simply assuring us that the lower courts "can and . . . will work out more concrete and specific standards." Deeming it "expedient" not to spell out "precise constitutional tests," the Court contents itself with stating "only a few rather general considerations."

Generalities cannot obscure the cold truth that cases of this type are not amenable to the development of judicial standards. No set of standards can guide a court which has to decide how many legislative districts a State shall have, or what the shape of the districts shall be, or where to draw a particular district line. No judicially manageable standard can determine whether a State should have single-member districts or multimember districts or some combination of both. No such standard can control the balance between keeping up with population shifts and having stable districts. In all these respects, the courts will be called upon to make particular decisions with respect to which a principle of equally populated districts will be of no assistance whatsoever. Quite obviously, there are limitless possibilities for districting consistent with such a principle. Nor can these problems be avoided by judicial reliance on legislative judgments so far as possible. Reshaping or combining one or two districts, or modifying just a few district lines, is no less a matter of choosing among many possible solutions, with varying political consequences, than reapportionment broadside.[3]

The Court ignores all this, saying only that "what is marginally permissible in one State may be unsatisfactory in another, depending on the particular circumstances of the case." It is well to remember that the product of today's decisions will not be readjustment of a few districts in a few States which most glaringly depart from the principle of equally populated districts. It will be a redetermination, extensive in many cases, of legislative districts in all but a few States.

Although the Court — necessarily, as I believe — provides only generalities in elaboration of its main thesis, its opinion nevertheless fully demonstrates how far removed these problems are from fields of judicial competence. Recognizing that "indiscriminate districting" is an invitation to "partisan gerrymandering," the Court nevertheless excludes virtually every basis for the formation of electoral districts other than "indiscriminate districting." In one or another of today's opinions, the Court declares it unconstitutional for a State to give effective consideration to any of the following in establishing legislative districts:

(1) history;

(2) "economic or other sorts of group interests";

(3) area;

(4) geographical considerations;

(5) a desire "to insure effective representation for sparsely settled areas";

(6) "availability of access of citizens to their representatives";

---

[3] [62] It is not mere fancy to suppose that in order to avoid problems of this sort, the Court may one day be tempted to hold that all state legislators must be elected in statewide elections.

(7) theories of bicameralism (except those approved by the Court);

(8) occupation;

(9) "an attempt to balance urban and rural power";

(10) the preference of a majority of voters in the State.

So far as presently appears, the *only* factor which a State may consider, apart from numbers, is political subdivisions. But even "a clearly rational state policy" recognizing this factor is unconstitutional if "population is submerged as the controlling consideration. . . ."

I know of no principle of logic or practical or theoretical politics, still less any constitutional principle, which establishes all or any of these exclusions. Certain it is that the Court's opinion does not establish them. So far as the Court says anything at all on this score, it says only that "legislators represent people, not trees or acres"; that "citizens, not history or economic interests, cast votes"; that "people, not land or trees or pastures, vote." All this may be conceded. But it is surely equally obvious, and, in the context of elections, more meaningful to note that people are not ciphers and that legislators can represent their electors only by speaking for their interests — economic, social, political — many of which do reflect the place where the electors live. The Court does not establish, or indeed even attempt to make a case for the proposition that conflicting interests within a State can only be adjusted by disregarding them when voters are grouped for purposes of representation.

CONCLUSION.

. . . What is done today deepens my conviction that judicial entry into this realm is profoundly ill-advised and constitutionally impermissible. As I have said before, I believe that the vitality of our political system, on which in the last analysis all else depends, is weakened by reliance on the judiciary for political reform; in time a complacent body politic may result.

These decisions also cut deeply into the fabric of our federalism. What must follow from them may eventually appear to be the product of state legislatures. Nevertheless, no thinking person can fail to recognize that the aftermath of these cases, however desirable it may be thought in itself, will have been achieved at the cost of a radical alteration in the relationship between the States and the Federal Government, more particularly the Federal Judiciary. Only one who has an overbearing impatience with the federal system and its political processes will believe that that cost was not too high or was inevitable.

Finally, these decisions give support to a current mistaken view of the Constitution and the constitutional function of this Court. This view, in a nutshell, is that every major social ill in this country can find its cure in some constitutional "principle," and that this Court should "take the lead" in promoting reform when other branches of government fail to act. The Constitution is not a panacea for every blot upon the public welfare, nor should this Court, ordained as a judicial body, be thought of as a general haven for reform movements. The Constitution is an instrument of government, fundamental to which is the premise that in a diffusion of governmental authority lies the greatest promise that this Nation will realize liberty for all its citizens. This Court, limited in function in accordance with that premise, does not serve its high purpose when it exceeds its authority, even to satisfy justified impatience with the slow workings of the political process. For when, in the name of constitutional interpretation, the Court *adds* something to the Constitution that was deliberately excluded from it, the Court in reality substitutes its view of what should be so for the amending process.

*   *   *

NOTES AND QUESTIONS

1. Warren's biographer calls the case you have just read "the most influential of the 170 majority opinions he would write, more important than *Brown*, more important than the communist cases that so angered his critics, more important than the criminal law decisions that purportedly had loosed a crime wave upon the nation." ED CRAY, CHIEF JUSTICE: A BIOGRAPHY OF EARL WARREN 432 (1997). Why do you suppose *Reynolds* is regarded as so important? Earl Warren appears to have been passionate about the case because he thought his Court was correcting an evil which had resulted in the exclusion of Southern African Americans from state legislatures, and, indeed, a generation after *Reynolds*, 3,000 black men and women held elective office in the United States, whereas before *Reynolds*, almost none did. *Id.* at 437. Another effect of *Reynolds*, perhaps unintended by Warren, was that after decades of domination of Southern legislatures by the Democratic party, "the two-party system had returned." *Id.* These ends seem worthy, but did they justify the means used?

2. There can be no doubt that the Alabama constitutional mandate for reapportionment was ignored by the Alabama legislature. It does not seem too difficult to conclude that the rights of Alabamans were violated (and this, and this alone may be why Justice Stewart concurred in the result in the case), but should there be a federal judicial remedy for such a violation of a state constitution? Does *Baker v. Carr* answer that question?

3. What of the particular selection scheme for the bicameral legislature which the Alabama Constitution mandates? If the Court bases its grant of relief in part on the Alabama Constitution's requirement of decennial updates, why does it depart from the Alabama Constitution, and declare that one House of the Alabama Legislature may not represent counties, while the other represents the population? What's wrong with the so-called "federal analogy" (on which the "67-Senator Amendment" was based)? The analogy is based on the federal scheme whereby the Senate represents the states and the House of Representatives represents the people. Why is it a violation of the Fourteenth Amendment when a state seeks to emulate the governmental model of the Federal Government? If it is unconstitutional for a state to do that, why is it still constitutional at the federal level? The Fourteenth Amendment forbids only state action, of course, but aren't there principles of due process, equity, or perhaps natural law that would also impose equal protection obligations on the federal government? Justice Warren calls the Alabama plans clearly "discriminatory, arbitrary and irrational," 377 U.S. at 547, but if they are simply an attempt to replicate the federal system is this characterization valid?

4.   But moving back to the problem of what the state legislatures can and cannot do with regard to apportionment, is it necessarily correct that just as the Fifteenth and Nineteenth Amendments prohibit a state from overweighting or diluting votes on the basis of race or sex, votes may not be "diluted" on the basis of where a person resides? The Chief Justice's pronouncement that "[t]he Equal Protection Clause demands no less than substantially equal state legislative representation for all citizens, of all places as well as of all races," 377 U.S. at 568, has a fine ring to it, and even rhymes, but is it a *non sequitur*? Might it well be a non-arbitrary and quite rational, albeit discriminatory, decision to make sure that urban voters do not always have their way against rural voters? Is it made less arbitrary and less irrational by the fact that throughout most of our history America has been an agricultural and pastoral place, even though the majority of our population is not now so situated? Is it true, as the Court declared in *Gray v. Sanders*, that "[t]he conception of political equality from the Declaration of Independence, to Lincoln's Gettysburg Address, to the Fifteenth, Seventeenth, and Nineteenth Amendments can mean only one thing — one person, one vote"? *Gray v. Sanders*, 372 U.S. 368, 381 (1963). How do each of these Amendments (to say nothing of the Gettysburg Address and the Declaration) lead to that conclusion? Would the framers have agreed with this interpretation of the political tradition they were founding?

5.   "One person, one vote," which comes from *Gray v. Sanders* (why, by the way, is that case, which invalidated malapportionment in the Georgia House, not dispositive of *Reynolds*? Is it that *Reynolds* requires *both* houses of a state legislature to be apportioned by population?), is some of the most famous language used in *Reynolds*, and *Reynolds* is often taken to stand for that proposition. More pungent, perhaps, is the language of Chief Justice Warren making a correlate point: "Legislators represent people, not trees or acres. Legislators are elected by voters, not farms or cities or economic interests." *Reynolds*, 377 U.S. at 562. Is he right? Do legislators represent only the people, or is something more at stake? The one person/one vote standard was applied to districts for the U.S. House of Representatives in *Wesberry v. Sanders*, 376 U.S. 1 (1964). Local governments were covered in *Avery v. Midland County*, 390 U.S. 474 (1968). Even limited governing bodies, like school districts, are now within the rule. *Hadley v. Junior College District*, 397 U.S. 50 (1970). The rule of one person/one vote does not require mathematical exactness, but it is more demanding for the U.S. House than for state and local offices.

6.   The only dissent is that of Justice Harlan, who relies on "detailed analysis of the history, drafting, language and ratification of the Fourteenth Amendment." Gordon E. Baker, Reynolds v. Sims, *in* THE OXFORD COMPANION TO THE SUPREME COURT OF THE UNITED STATES 732, 733 (Kermit L. Hall et al. eds., 1992). Which part of his analysis is most convincing? Chief Justice Warren also purports to rely on history. Who does the better job? Why do you suppose that Harlan was unable to gather any other votes in support of his position? At issue in *Reynolds* and its accompanying cases were redistricting decisions for six state legislatures, and one week later the Court handed down similar rulings, without accompanying opinions, invalidating apportionment in ten other states. Indeed, it appears that *Reynolds* declared the invalidity of "at least one house in nearly all state legislatures . . . and

both houses in most." Baker, *supra*, at 732. Which is more likely, that fifty state legislatures got it wrong, or that eight men on the Supreme Court did? Can you understand why shortly after *Reynolds* (and several other Warren Court decisions involving criminal law and racial integration) billboards even began to appear in some rural areas with the legend "Impeach Earl Warren"? He was never impeached, of course, but he was subjected to more vilification than any other Chief Justice before or since, with the possible exception of Chief Justice Taney. Did he deserve the calumny?

7. Justice Harlan is concerned that the majority is dangerously undercutting federalism, and he is similarly disturbed by the Court's "judicial activism to cure perceived social ills." Baker, *supra*, at 733. Do you agree with Harlan's basic point, that "[t]he Constitution is not a panacea for every blot upon the public welfare, nor should th[e] Court, ordained as a judicial body, be thought of as a general haven for reform movements"? *Reynolds*, 377 U.S. at 624–25 (Harlan, J., dissenting). Why would he believe in such a limited role for the Supreme Court? Would Frankfurter have agreed? Who, if anyone, today maintains this Harlan/Frankfurter legacy? Would you?

8. An issue related to the proportionality of voting districts is the enumeration of the general population for the purpose of apportioning congressional representation among the states. Article I, section 2, clause 3 of the Constitution provides: "The actual Enumeration shall be made within . . . every subsequent Term of ten Years, in such Manner as they [the Congress] shall by Law direct." Section 2 of the Fourteenth Amendment provides that "Representatives shall be apportioned among the several States according to their respective numbers. . . ." Dictionaries contemporaneous with the founding define "enumeration" as actual counting, not estimation. The Congressional Census Acts have similarly so required; indeed, the Acts of 1810 through 1950 required census enumerators to visit each home in person. Thus, it came as a significant departure from tradition when the Clinton administration proposed to use statistical sampling methods (methods of estimation) to arrive at part of the Census for the Year 2000. The plan was challenged by private citizens who would suffer a loss of representation under the estimated methods or who would be adversely affected by intrastate redistricting. To meet the *Reynolds* standard, many states use population numbers generated by the Census. Members of Congress also filed suit alleging a congressional interest in the composition of the House. In *Department of Commerce v. United States House of Representatives*, 525 U.S. 316 (1999), the Court held that the private parties had standing and that the Census Act requires actual enumeration (counting) not estimation or sampling for apportionment purposes.

9. The next case is well-known, and while not everyone was satisfied with either the effective political outcome or its remedial considerations, it was apparent to seven Justices that the case presented a basic equal protection problem that could not survive even the most lenient standard of judicial examination. The majority of the Court and Justices Souter and Breyer in dissent were in common agreement that disparate standards could not be applied in different electoral jurisdictions to otherwise identical facts. As Justices Souter and Breyer explained: "It is true that the Equal Protection Clause does not forbid the use of a variety of voting mechanisms within a jurisdiction, even though different mechanisms will have

different levels of effectiveness in recording voters' intentions; local variety can be justified by concerns about cost, the potential value of innovation, and so on. But evidence in the record here suggests that a different order of disparity obtains under rules for determining a voter's intent that have been applied (and could continue to be applied) to identical types of ballots used in identical brands of machines and exhibiting identical physical characteristics (such as 'hanging' or 'dimpled' chads). . . . [We] can conceive of no legitimate state interest served by these differing treatments of the expressions of voters' fundamental rights. The differences appear wholly arbitrary." (Souter and Breyer, JJ., dissenting). To be wholly arbitrary in classification in reference to voting was not constitutionally permissible.

BUSH v. GORE
531 U.S. 98 (2000)

PER CURIAM

On December 8, 2000, the Supreme Court of Florida ordered that the Circuit Court of Leon County tabulate by hand 9,000 ballots in Miami-Dade County. It also ordered the inclusion in the certified vote totals of 215 votes identified in Palm Beach County and 168 votes identified in Miami-Dade County for Vice President Albert Gore, Jr., and Senator Joseph Lieberman, Democratic Candidates for President and Vice President. The court further held that relief would require manual recounts in all Florida counties where so-called "undervotes" had not been subject to manual tabulation. The court ordered all manual recounts to begin at once. Governor Bush and Richard Cheney, Republican Candidates for the Presidency and Vice Presidency, filed an emergency application for a stay of this mandate. On December 9, we granted the application, treated the application as a petition for a writ of certiorari, and granted certiorari.

On November 8, 2000, the day following the Presidential election, the Florida Division of Elections reported that petitioner, Governor Bush, had received 2,909,135 votes, and respondent, Vice President Gore, had received 2,907,351 votes, a margin of 1,784 for Governor Bush. Because Governor Bush's margin of victory was less than "one-half of a percent of the votes cast," an automatic machine recount was conducted under . . . the election code, the results of which showed Governor Bush still winning the race but by a diminished margin. Vice President Gore then sought manual recounts in Volusia, Palm Beach, Broward, and Miami-Dade Counties, pursuant to Florida's election protest provisions. . . . A dispute arose concerning the deadline for local county canvassing boards to submit their returns to the Secretary of State (Secretary). The Secretary declined to waive the November 14 deadline imposed by statute. The Florida Supreme Court, however, set the deadline at November 26. We granted certiorari and vacated the Florida Supreme Court's decision, finding considerable uncertainty as to the grounds on which it was based. On December 11, the Florida Supreme Court issued a decision on remand reinstating that date.

On November 26, the Florida Elections Canvassing Commission certified the results of the election and declared Governor Bush the winner of Florida's 25 electoral votes. On November 27, Vice President Gore, pursuant to Florida's contest provisions, filed a complaint in Leon County Circuit Court contesting the certification. He sought relief pursuant to [Florida law] which provides that "[r]eceipt of a number of illegal votes or rejection of a number of legal votes sufficient to change or place in doubt the result of the election" shall be grounds for a contest. The Circuit Court denied relief, stating that Vice President Gore failed to meet his burden of proof. He appealed to the First District Court of Appeal, which certified the matter to the Florida Supreme Court.

* * *

The [Florida] Supreme Court held that Vice President Gore had satisfied his burden of proof with respect to his challenge to Miami-Dade County's failure to tabulate, by manual count, 9,000 ballots on which the machines had failed to detect a vote for President ("undervotes"). Noting the closeness of the election, the Court explained that "[o]n this record, there can be no question that there are legal votes within the 9,000 uncounted votes sufficient to place the results of this election in doubt." A "legal vote," as determined by the Supreme Court, is "one in which there is a 'clear indication of the intent of the voter.' " The court therefore ordered a hand recount of the 9,000 ballots in Miami-Dade County. Observing that the contest provisions vest broad discretion in the circuit judge to "provide any relief appropriate under such circumstances," the Supreme Court further held that the Circuit Court could order "the Supervisor of Elections and the Canvassing Boards, as well as the necessary public officials, in all counties that have not conducted a manual recount or tabulation of the undervotes to do so forthwith, said tabulation to take place in the individual counties where the ballots are located."

The Supreme Court also determined that both Palm Beach County and Miami-Dade County, in their earlier manual recounts had identified a net gain of 215 and 168 legal votes for Vice President Gore. Rejecting the Circuit Court's conclusion that Palm Beach County lacked the authority to include the 215 net votes submitted past the November 26 deadline, the Supreme Court explained that the deadline was not intended to exclude votes identified after that date through ongoing manual recounts. As to Miami-Dade County, the Court concluded that although the 168 votes identified were the result of a partial recount, they were "legal votes [that] could change the outcome of the election." The Supreme Court therefore directed the Circuit Court to include those totals in the certified results, subject to resolution of the actual vote total from the Miami-Dade partial recount.

The petition presents the following questions: whether the Florida Supreme Court established new standards for resolving Presidential election contests, thereby violating Art. II, § 1, cl. 2, of the United States Constitution and failing to comply with 3 U.S.C. § 5, and whether the use of standardless manual recounts violates the Equal Protection and Due Process Clauses. With respect to the equal protection question, we find a violation of the Equal Protection Clause.

II

A

The closeness of this election, and the multitude of legal challenges which have followed in its wake, have brought into sharp focus a common, if heretofore unnoticed, phenomenon. Nationwide statistics reveal that an estimated 2% of ballots cast do not register a vote for President for whatever reason, including deliberately choosing no candidate at all or some voter error, such as voting for two candidates or insufficiently marking a ballot. . . . In certifying election results, the votes eligible for inclusion in the certification are the votes meeting the properly established legal requirements.

This case has shown that punch card balloting machines can produce an unfortunate number of ballots which are not punched in a clean, complete way by the voter. After the current counting, it is likely legislative bodies nationwide will examine ways to improve the mechanisms and machinery for voting.

B

The individual citizen has no federal constitutional right to vote for electors for the President of the United States unless and until the state legislature chooses a statewide election as the means to implement its power to appoint members of the Electoral College. U.S. Const., Art. II, § 1. This is the source for the statement in *McPherson v. Blacker*, 146 U.S. 1, 35 (1892), that the State legislature's power to select the manner for appointing electors is plenary; it may, if it so chooses, select the electors itself, which indeed was the manner used by State legislatures in several States for many years after the Framing of our Constitution. History has now favored the voter, and in each of the several States the citizens themselves vote for Presidential electors. When the state legislature vests the right to vote for President in its people, the right to vote as the legislature has prescribed is fundamental; and one source of its fundamental nature lies in the equal weight accorded to each vote and the equal dignity owed to each voter. The State, of course, after granting the franchise in the special context of Article II, can take back the power to appoint electors. ("[T]here is no doubt of the right of the legislature to resume the power at any time, for it can neither be taken away nor abdicated").

The right to vote is protected in more than the initial allocation of the franchise. Equal protection applies as well to the manner of its exercise. Having once granted the right to vote on equal terms, the State may not, by later arbitrary and disparate treatment, value one person's vote over that of another. It must be remembered that "the right of suffrage can be denied by a debasement or dilution of the weight of a citizen's vote just as effectively as by wholly prohibiting the free exercise of the franchise." *Reynolds v. Sims*, 377 U.S. 533, 555 (1964).

There is no difference between the two sides of the present controversy on these basic propositions. Respondents say that the very purpose of vindicating the right to vote justifies the recount procedures now at issue. The question before us, however, is whether the recount procedures the Florida Supreme Court has adopted are consistent with its obligation to avoid arbitrary and disparate treatment of the members of its electorate.

Much of the controversy seems to revolve around ballot cards designed to be perforated by a stylus but which, either through error or deliberate omission, have not been perforated with sufficient precision for a machine to count them. In some cases a piece of the card — a chad — is hanging, say by two corners. In other cases there is no separation at all, just an indentation.

The Florida Supreme Court has ordered that the intent of the voter be discerned from such ballots. For purposes of resolving the equal protection challenge, it is not necessary to decide whether the Florida Supreme Court had the authority under the legislative scheme for resolving election disputes to define what a legal vote is and to mandate a manual recount implementing that definition. The recount mechanisms implemented in response to the decisions of the Florida Supreme Court do not satisfy the minimum requirement for non-arbitrary treatment of voters necessary to secure the fundamental right. Florida's basic command for the count of legally cast votes is to consider the "intent of the voter". . . . This is unobjectionable as an abstract proposition and a starting principle. The problem inheres in the absence of specific standards to ensure its equal application. The formulation of uniform rules to determine intent based on these recurring circumstances is practicable and, we conclude, necessary.

The law does not refrain from searching for the intent of the actor in a multitude of circumstances; and in some cases the general command to ascertain intent is not susceptible to much further refinement. In this instance, however, the question is not whether to believe a witness but how to interpret the marks or holes or scratches on an inanimate object, a piece of cardboard or paper which, it is said, might not have registered as a vote during the machine count. The factfinder confronts a thing, not a person. The search for intent can be confined by specific rules designed to ensure uniform treatment.

The want of those rules here has led to unequal evaluation of ballots in various respects. . . . As seems to have been acknowledged at oral argument, the standards for accepting or rejecting contested ballots might vary not only from county to county but indeed within a single county from one recount team to another.

The record provides some examples. A monitor in Miami-Dade County testified at trial that he observed that three members of the county canvassing board applied different standards in defining a legal vote. And testimony at trial also revealed that at least one county changed its evaluative standards during the counting process. Palm Beach County, for example, began the process with a 1990 guideline which precluded counting completely attached chads, switched to a rule that considered a vote to be legal if any light could be seen through a chad, changed back to the 1990 rule, and then abandoned any pretense of a *per se* rule, only to have a court order that the county consider dimpled chads legal. This is not a process with sufficient guarantees of equal treatment.

An early case in our one person, one vote jurisprudence arose when a State accorded arbitrary and disparate treatment to voters in its different counties. *Gray v. Sanders* (1963). The Court found a constitutional violation. We relied on these principles in the context of the Presidential selection process in *Moore v. Ogilvie*, 394 U.S. 814 (1969), where we invalidated a county-based procedure that diluted the influence of citizens in larger counties in the nominating process. There we observed that "[t]he idea that one group can be granted greater voting strength than another is hostile to the one man, one vote basis of our representative government."

The State Supreme Court ratified this uneven treatment. It mandated that the recount totals from two counties, Miami-Dade and Palm Beach, be included in the certified total. The court also appeared to hold *sub silentio* that the recount totals from Broward County, which were not completed until after the original November 14 certification by the Secretary of State, were to be considered part of the new certified vote totals even though the county certification was not contested by Vice President Gore. Yet each of the counties used varying standards to determine what was a legal vote. Broward County used a more forgiving standard than Palm Beach County, and uncovered almost three times as many new votes, a result markedly disproportionate to the difference in population between the counties.

In addition, the recounts in these three counties were not limited to so-called undervotes but extended to all of the ballots. The distinction has real consequences. A manual recount of all ballots identifies not only those ballots which show no vote but also those which contain more than one, the so-called overvotes. Neither category will be counted by the machine. This is not a trivial concern. At oral argument, respondents estimated there are as many as 110,000 overvotes statewide. As a result, the citizen whose ballot was not read by a machine because he failed to vote for a candidate in a way readable by a machine may still have his vote counted in a manual recount; on the other hand, the citizen who marks two candidates in a way discernable by the machine will not have the same opportunity to have his vote count, even if a manual examination of the ballot would reveal the requisite indicia of intent. Furthermore, the citizen who marks two candidates, only one of which is discernable by the machine, will have his vote counted even though it should have been read as an invalid ballot. The State Supreme Court's inclusion of vote counts based on these variant standards exemplifies concerns with the remedial processes that were under way.

That brings the analysis to yet a further equal protection problem. The votes certified by the court included a partial total from one county, Miami-Dade. The Florida Supreme Court's decision thus gives no assurance that the recounts included in a final certification must be complete. Indeed, it is respondent's submission that it would be consistent with the rules of the recount procedures to include whatever partial counts are done by the time of final certification, and we interpret the Florida Supreme Court's decision to permit this. This accommodation no doubt results from the truncated contest period established by the Florida Supreme Court in *Bush I* [*Bush v. Palm Beach County Canvassing Board*], at respondents' own urging. The press of time does not diminish the constitutional concern. A desire for speed is not a general excuse for ignoring equal protection guarantees.

In addition to these difficulties the actual process by which the votes were to be counted under the Florida Supreme Court's decision raises further concerns. That order did not specify who would recount the ballots. The county canvassing boards were forced to pull together ad hoc teams comprised of judges from various Circuits who had no previous training in handling and interpreting ballots. Furthermore, while others were permitted to observe, they were prohibited from objecting during the recount.

The recount process, in its features here described, is inconsistent with the minimum procedures necessary to protect the fundamental right of each voter in the special instance of a statewide recount under the authority of a single state judicial officer. Our consideration is limited to the present circumstances, for the problem of equal protection in election processes generally presents many complexities.

. . . The question before the Court is not whether local entities, in the exercise of their expertise, may develop different systems for implementing elections. Instead, we are presented with a situation where a state court with the power to assure uniformity has ordered a statewide recount with minimal procedural safeguards. When a court orders a statewide remedy, there must be at least some assurance that the rudimentary requirements of equal treatment and fundamental fairness are satisfied.

Given the Court's assessment that the recount process underway was probably being conducted in an unconstitutional manner, the Court stayed the order directing the recount so it could hear this case and render an expedited decision. The contest provision, as it was mandated by the State Supreme Court, is not well calculated to sustain the confidence that all citizens must have in the outcome of elections. The State has not shown that its procedures include the necessary safeguards. The problem, for instance, of the estimated 110,000 overvotes has not been addressed, although Chief Justice Wells called attention to the concern in his dissenting opinion.

Upon due consideration of the difficulties identified to this point, it is obvious that the recount cannot be conducted in compliance with the requirements of equal protection and due process without substantial additional work. It would require not only the adoption (after opportunity for argument) of adequate statewide standards for determining what is a legal vote, and practicable procedures to implement them, but also orderly judicial review of any disputed matters that might arise. In addition, the Secretary of State has advised that the recount of only a portion of the ballots requires that the vote tabulation equipment be used to screen out undervotes, a function for which the machines were not designed. If a recount of overvotes were also required, perhaps even a second screening would be necessary. Use of the equipment for this purpose, and any new software developed for it, would have to be evaluated for accuracy by the Secretary of State, as required by [Florida law].

The Supreme Court of Florida has said that the legislature intended the State's electors to "participat[e] fully in the federal electoral process," as provided in 3 U.S.C. § 5. That statute, in turn, requires that any controversy or contest that is designed to lead to a conclusive selection of electors be completed by December 12. That date is upon us, and there is no recount procedure in place under the State Supreme Court's order that comports with minimal constitutional standards. Because it is evident that any recount seeking to meet the December 12 date will be unconstitutional for the reasons we have discussed, we reverse the judgment of the Supreme Court of Florida ordering a recount to proceed.

Seven Justices of the Court agree that there are constitutional problems with the recount ordered by the Florida Supreme Court that demand a remedy. (SOUTER, J., dissenting); (BREYER, J., dissenting). The only disagreement is as to the remedy. Because the Florida Supreme Court has said that the Florida Legislature intended to obtain the safe-harbor benefits of 3 U.S.C. § 5, JUSTICE BREYER's proposed remedy — remanding to the Florida Supreme Court for its ordering of a constitutionally proper contest until December 18 — contemplates action in violation of the Florida election code, and hence could not be part of an "appropriate" order authorized by [Florida Statute].

* * *

None are more conscious of the vital limits on judicial authority than are the members of this Court, and none stand more in admiration of the Constitution's design to leave the selection of the President to the people, through their legislatures, and to the political sphere. When contending parties invoke the process of the courts, however, it becomes our unsought responsibility to resolve the federal and constitutional issues the judicial system has been forced to confront.

The judgment of the Supreme Court of Florida is reversed, and the case is remanded for further proceedings not inconsistent with this opinion.

It is so ordered.

CHIEF JUSTICE REHNQUIST, with whom JUSTICE SCALIA and JUSTICE THOMAS join, concurring. [Omitted.]

JUSTICE STEVENS, with whom JUSTICE GINSBURG and JUSTICE BREYER join, dissenting. [Omitted.]

JUSTICE SOUTER, with whom JUSTICE BREYER joins and with whom JUSTICE STEVENS and JUSTICE GINSBURG join with regard to all but Part C, dissenting.

The Court should not have reviewed either *Bush v. Palm Beach County Canvassing Bd.* [*Bush I*] or this case, and should not have stopped Florida's attempt to recount all undervote ballots, by issuing a stay of the Florida Supreme Court's orders during the period of this review. If this Court had allowed the State to follow the course indicated by the opinions of its own Supreme Court, it is entirely possible that there would ultimately have been no issue requiring our review, and political tension could have worked itself out in the Congress following the procedure provided in 3 U.S.C. § 15. The case being before us, however, its resolution by the majority is another erroneous decision.

* * *

B

The issue is whether the judgment of the state supreme court has displaced the state legislature's provisions for election contests: is the law as declared by the court different from the provisions made by the legislature, to which the national

Constitution commits responsibility for determining how each State's Presidential electors are chosen? See U.S. Const., Art. II, § 1, cl. 2. Bush does not, of course, claim that any judicial act interpreting a statute of uncertain meaning is enough to displace the legislative provision and violate Article II; statutes require interpretation, which does not without more affect the legislative character of a statute within the meaning of the Constitution. What Bush does argue, as I understand the contention, is that the interpretation was so unreasonable as to transcend the accepted bounds of statutory interpretation, to the point of being a nonjudicial act and producing new law untethered to the legislative act in question.

The majority view is in each instance within the bounds of reasonable interpretation, and the law as declared is consistent with Article II.

The statute does not define a "legal vote," the rejection of which may affect the election. The State Supreme Court was therefore required to define it, and in doing that the court looked to another election statute, dealing with damaged or defective ballots, which contains a provision that no vote shall be disregarded "if there is a clear indication of the intent of the voter as determined by a canvassing board." The court read that objective of looking to the voter's intent as indicating that the legislature probably meant "legal vote" to mean a vote recorded on a ballot indicating what the voter intended. It is perfectly true that the majority might have chosen a different reading. *E.g.*, (defining "legal votes" as "votes properly executed in accordance with the instructions provided to all registered voters in advance of the election and in the polling places"). But even so, there is no constitutional violation in following the majority view; Article II is unconcerned with mere disagreements about interpretive merits.

*   *   *

C

*   *   *

Petitioners have raised an equal protection claim (or, alternatively, a due process claim, see generally *Logan v. Zimmerman Brush Co.* (1982)), in the charge that unjustifiably disparate standards are applied in different electoral jurisdictions to otherwise identical facts. It is true that the Equal Protection Clause does not forbid the use of a variety of voting mechanisms within a jurisdiction, even though different mechanisms will have different levels of effectiveness in recording voters' intentions; local variety can be justified by concerns about cost, the potential value of innovation, and so on. But evidence in the record here suggests that a different order of disparity obtains under rules for determining a voter's intent that have been applied (and could continue to be applied) to identical types of ballots used in identical brands of machines and exhibiting identical physical characteristics (such as "hanging" or "dimpled" chads). I can conceive of no legitimate state interest served by these differing treatments of the expressions of voters' fundamental rights. The differences appear wholly arbitrary.

In deciding what to do about this, we should take account of the fact that electoral votes are due to be cast in six days. I would therefore remand the case to the courts of Florida with instructions to establish uniform standards for evaluating the several types of ballots that have prompted differing treatments, to be applied within and among counties when passing on such identical ballots in any further recounting (or successive recounting) that the courts might order.

* * *

I respectfully dissent.

JUSTICE GINSBURG with whom JUSTICE STEVENS joins, and with whom JUSTICE SOUTER and JUSTICE BREYER join as to Part I, dissenting. [Omitted.]

JUSTICE BREYER, with whom JUSTICE STEVENS and JUSTICE GINSBURG join except as to Part I-A-1, and with whom JUSTICE SOUTER joins as to Part I, dissenting. [Omitted.]

NOTES AND QUESTIONS

1.   Did the U.S. Supreme Court have to get involved? Wasn't this just an issue of state law or a nonjusticiable political dispute? Seven Justices apparently thought not since, according to the per curiam opinion, basic principles of equal protection require that once a state has granted the people the right to vote for presidential electors, "the State may not, by later arbitrary and disparate treatment, value one person's vote over that of another." True, at an earlier point in our history, the Court might have been inclined to treat this matter as a nonjusticiable political question, but modernly, such judicial reticence in the voting context cannot be reconciled with decisions like *Baker v. Carr* and *Reynolds v. Sims* (1964). Remember that in *Baker* and *Reynolds*, the Court applied equal protection principles to establish the one person/one vote maxim in the context of voting districts that were malapportioned in terms of population. A vote is diluted when 10,000 voters in one district have the same number of political representatives in the legislative assembly as 100,000 voters in another. By parity of reasoning, inequality results in a statewide race for presidential electors when an incomplete or ambiguously completed ballot in one county is counted and in another is discarded. The inequality is magnified when the same types of ballots are differently treated even within the same county, which counsel for Vice President Gore conceded was occurring at oral argument. In other words, it was a bit of a free for all. Count first; figure out the standards later. How would you feel if your professor graded each final exam in this class by a different standard, and if asked what standard she applied, proclaimed that it varied from bluebook to bluebook?

2.   But what about the differences in voting machine technology? As the Court discovered, punch card machines are less reliable than optical scanners. Does the failure to supply the best or most fool-proof equipment to all counties violate equal protection? The Court doesn't say, and it is highly unlikely. First, the Court emphasizes that its ruling pertains to the unique risks and circumstances before it — namely, a *judicially* mandated *recount* of real, *inanimate objects* (the ballots). In the Court's words, "[o]ur consideration is limited to the present circumstances, for the problem of equal protection in election processes generally presents many complexities." For example, the case does not answer whether it is unconstitutional to allow local decision-makers to employ different types of machines in the future;

in other words, to have the discretion to update voting equipment in a non-discriminatory, rational way as scarce equipment budgets permit. This would seem minimally rational, even if not ideal. Second, the recount process is especially susceptible to abuse because it occurs after the fact, in essence allowing the contesting candidate an opportunity to manipulate the recount in light of his initial losing margin. Third, when the judiciary inserts itself into election recounts, it must at least anticipate basic due process questions like who will count the votes and how objections can be made and disposed.

3.   Was the decision in *Bush* politically motivated? There was a good deal of unfortunate public commentary, even from members of the legal academy, that more than suggested this possibility in intemperate language. The Court civilly and concisely anticipated this criticism in its opinion, characterizing the matter before it as an "unsought responsibility to resolve . . . federal and constitutional issues." Indeed, in fairness to the Court, it went out of its way to avoid ruling on federal grounds. The first time the dispute was presented to the Court in *Bush v. Palm Beach County Canvassing Board*, 531 U.S. 70 (2000), *vacating* and *remanding* 772 So. 2d 1220 (Fla. 2000) (*Bush I*), the Court unanimously returned the matter to the state for clarification. In *Bush I*, the central issue was not equal protection — because the absence of a recount standard had yet to fully manifest itself — but whether the Florida Supreme Court had faithfully followed the state election code. Normally, the Court defers to a state court's interpretation of a state statute, but Article II, section 1, clause 2 posed the unique circumstance in which the state legislature was acting pursuant not to its own reserved power, but power delegated by the federal Constitution. In that circumstance, it was unresolved whether a state court, even a state supreme court acting under the state constitution, could substantially vary the legislative will. In *Bush I*, a unanimous Court reasoned that: "It is fundamental that state courts be left free and unfettered by us in interpreting their state constitutions. But it is equally important that ambiguous or obscure adjudications by state courts do not stand as barriers to a determination by this Court of the validity under the federal constitution of state action." Nevertheless, the Court did not immediately decide the issue, but remanded asking the Florida Supreme Court whether it saw the Florida Constitution as circumscribing the legislature's authority under Article II, section 1, clause 2.

4.   Why didn't the fracas end there? That is, why didn't the Florida Supreme Court rule that it was merely interpreting the state election code, and not judicially altering it pursuant to equitable or state constitutional power? Well, here the compressed sequence of events took over. The state court would ultimately get around to saying just that, but not until December 11, 2000. *Palm Beach County Canvassing Bd. v. Harris*, 772 So. 2d 1273 (Fla. 2000). The U.S. Supreme Court had asked for clarification on December 4, and while a week is normally quite expeditious, it was an eternity in the context of this closely fought presidential election. Following the state high court's first opinion, Governor Bush had been certified the winner by state election officials. This triggered a contest by Vice President Gore, which he lost at trial and appealed to the Florida Supreme Court on December 7. At this point, the Florida Supreme Court could have insulated its ultimate determination from further U.S. Supreme Court review by doing two things: affirming the state trial court ruling denying the Gore contest or reversing

it (with a full statewide recount of all ballots pursuant to a uniform standard) and briefly answering the Court's query from *Bush I* that it had not used the state constitution to undermine the legislative will. In allocating its work load, however, the state high court chose to answer the appeal first on December 8 and wait until December 11 to answer the U.S. Supreme Court. As it turned out, this only highlighted the equal protection concerns, since by a vote of 4-3 in *Gore v. Harris*, 772 So. 2d 1243 (Fla. 2000), the state high court authorized a qualified statewide recount that had already been comprised with ballots that had only been counted pursuant to its previous opinion which had been unanimously vacated in *Bush I* and had yet to be satisfactorily justified and re-issued.

5.　　Was the Vice President entitled to further recounts? As noted above, this closely divided the state supreme court, and had it not raised basic equal protection concerns, might have been resolved entirely without further U.S. Supreme Court review. The essential issue under the Florida code was whether Mr. Gore had demonstrated sufficient evidence to "change or place in doubt the result of the election." The four justice majority thought the Vice President had done so merely by showing the existence of a number of so-called "undervotes" in selective — that is, heavily Democratic — counties. The dissent thought the Vice President's county-based evidence wholly wanting since he needed to show not just that the result would be different in a single county or set of favored counties, but statewide. As dissenting Justice Major Harding reasoned: "the selective recounting requested by [Vice President Gore] is not available under the election contest provisions of [the Florida code]. Such an application does not provide for a more accurate reflection of the will of the voters but, rather, allows for an unfair distortion of the statewide vote. It is patently unlawful to permit the recount of [undervotes] in a single county to determine the outcome of the November 7, 2000 election for the next President of the United States. We are a nation of laws, and we have survived and prospered as a free nation because we have adhered to the rule of law. Fairness is achieved by following the rules." The dissent's point went unanswered by the state high court majority triggering the principal case.

6.　　But wait a minute, isn't it unprecedented for the U.S. Supreme Court to rule that a state court interpretation of state law violates the federal Constitution? Unprecedented, no; rare, yes. In *Fairfax's Devisee v. Hunter's Lessee*, 11 U.S. (7 Cranch) 603 (1813), the Supreme Court early in our history disagreed with the Supreme Court of Appeals of Virginia that a 1782 state law had extinguished the property interests of one Denny Fairfax, so that a 1789 ejectment order against Fairfax supported by a 1785 state law did not constitute a future confiscation under the 1783 peace treaty with Great Britain. Other more contemporary, but not numerous, examples can be found from the protection of civil rights. In *NAACP v. Alabama ex rel. Patterson*, 357 U.S. 449 (1958), it was argued that the Court was without jurisdiction because the petitioner had not pursued the correct appellate remedy in Alabama's state courts. Petitioners had sought a state-law writ of certiorari in the Alabama Supreme Court when a writ of mandamus, according to that court, was proper. The Court found this state-law ground inadequate to defeat its jurisdiction because it was "unable to reconcile the procedural holding of the Alabama Supreme Court" with prior Alabama precedent. *Id.* at 456. The purported state-law ground was so novel, in the Court's independent estimation, that "petitioner could not fairly be deemed to have been apprised of its existence." *Id.* at 457. Similarly, six years later in *Bouie v. City of Columbia*, 378 U.S. 347 (1964), the state court had held, contrary to precedent, that the state trespass law applied to black sit-in demonstrators who had consent to enter private property but were then asked to leave. Relying upon *NAACP*, the Court concluded that the South Carolina Supreme Court's interpretation of a state penal statute had impermissibly broadened the scope of that statute beyond what a fair reading provided, in violation of due process.

7.   Wouldn't it have been more prudent to simply reverse and remand and allow Florida to figure out whether it could get the counting done in time in accordance with federal constitutional principle? While this is much obscured in public commentary and even confused a bit by the Court's own dicta, that is technically what the Court did. The Supreme Court reversed and remanded, it did not dismiss. But, of course, it was by then December 12, and this date was clearly thought by at least five of the seven Justices who raised the equal protection concern to be pivotal. The date was not significant because of federal statute alone — the so-called, "safe harbor" provision in 3 U.S.C. § 5 — but because the Florida Supreme Court had held that the Florida legislature had wanted to take advantage of that date. Said the Court in its Per Curiam, "[t]he Supreme Court of Florida has said that the legislature intended the State's electors to 'participat[e] fully in the federal electoral process,' as provided in 3 U.S.C. § 5. . . . That statute, in turn, requires that any controversy or contest that is designed to lead to a conclusive selection of electors be completed by December 12. That date is upon us, and there is no recount procedure in place under the State Supreme Court's order that comports with minimal constitutional standards."

The absence of time to do a constitutionally sufficient recount had also been noted in dissent by Chief Justice Wells of the Florida Supreme Court, who observed that: in the four days remaining, "all questionable ballots must be reviewed by the judicial officer appointed to discern the intent of the voter in a process open to the public. Fairness dictates that a provision be made for either party to object to how a particular ballot is counted. Additionally, this short time period must allow for judicial review. I respectfully submit this cannot be completed without taking Florida's presidential electors outside the safe harbor provision, creating the very real possibility of disenfranchising those nearly 6 million voters who are able to correctly cast their ballots on election day." (Wells, C.J., dissenting.)

8.   It is not entirely true that Florida would have been disenfranchised if it missed the December 12th date. The actual casting of the vote by presidential electors was not required to take place until December 18th and the votes would not be opened and counted until January 6, 2001. This prompted Justice Stevens to write in dissent in the principal case that the majority acted "on the basis of the deadlines set forth in Title 3 of the United States Code. But . . . those provisions merely provide rules of decision for Congress to follow when selecting among conflicting slates of electors. They do not prohibit a State from counting what the majority concedes to be legal votes until a bona fide winner is determined. Indeed, in 1960, Hawaii appointed two slates of electors and Congress chose to count the one appointed on January 4, 1961, well after the Title 3 deadlines. Josephson & Ross, *Repairing the Electoral College*, 22 J. LEGIS. 145, 166, n. 154 (1996)." Would this have

been a better course? Before you answer, remember that the Florida legislature was in session and preparing — if the U.S. Supreme Court decided against Governor Bush, who had been certified the winner, to substitute its hand-chosen set of Bush electors.

The possibility of competing slates did not trouble Justice Breyer, who thought this had been well provided for by the political process in the Electoral Count Act in Title 3. As he observed, that Act sets out rules for the congressional determination of disputes. Justice Breyer reasoned: "If, for example, a state submits a single slate of electors, Congress must count those votes unless both Houses agree that the votes 'have not been . . . regularly given.' 3 U.S.C. § 15. If, as occurred in 1876, one or more states submits two sets of electors, then Congress must determine whether a slate has entered the safe harbor of § 5, in which case its votes will have 'conclusive' effect. If, as also occurred in 1876, there is controversy about 'which of two or more of such State authorities is the lawful tribunal' authorized to appoint electors, then each House shall determine separately which votes are 'supported by the decision of such State so authorized by its law.' If the two Houses of Congress agree, the votes they have approved will be counted. If they disagree, then 'the votes of the electors whose appointment shall have been certified by the executive of the State, under the seal thereof, shall be counted.'" *Ibid.*

It was this "detailed, comprehensive scheme for counting electoral votes," that suggested to Justice Breyer that there was "no reason to believe that federal law either foresees or requires resolution of such a political issue by this Court."

9. **Historical perspective.** Just after the 1876 Presidential election, Florida, South Carolina, and Louisiana each sent two slates of electors to Washington. Without these states, Tilden, the Democrat, had 184 electoral votes, one short of the number required to win the Presidency. With those States, Hayes, his Republican opponent, would have had 185. In order to choose between the two slates of electors, Congress decided to appoint an electoral commission composed of five Senators, five Representatives, and five Supreme Court Justices. Initially the Commission was to be evenly divided between Republicans and Democrats, with Justice David Davis, an Independent, to possess the decisive vote. However, when at the last minute the Illinois Legislature elected Justice Davis to the United States Senate, the final position on the Commission was filled by Supreme Court Justice Joseph P. Bradley. When the Commission divided along partisan lines, the deciding vote fell to Justice Bradley. He decided to accept the votes by the Republican electors, and thereby awarded the Presidency to Hayes.

Justice Breyer remarks that Justice Bradley immediately became the subject of vociferous attacks. "Bradley was accused of accepting bribes, of being captured by railroad interests, and of an eleventh-hour change in position after a night in which his house 'was surrounded by the carriages' of Republican partisans and railroad officials. C. Woodward, *Reunion and Reaction* 159–160 (1966)." For Justice Breyer the history lesson is that Bradley's participation did not lend legitimacy to the Court and the "Congress that later enacted the Electoral Count Act knew it."

10. Was the Court's legitimacy enhanced or prejudiced by its ruling in the principal case? The opinions continue to run strongly in both directions. Harvard's Professor Dershowitz has penned a book summarizing and advocating the com-

plaints against the Court's resolution. ALAN DERSHOWITZ, SUPREME INJUSTICE (2001). Ambassador Kmiec is more accepting of the Court's ruling, writing in popular commentary immediately following the decision that "[t]he ruling of the U.S. Supreme Court was not along partisan or ideological lines. As the justices pointedly observed in the opinion, 'seven justices of the court agree that there are constitutional problems with the recount ordered by the Florida Supreme Court that demand a remedy.' " Kmiec, *The Court's Decision is Law, Not Politics*, L.A. TIMES B11 (December 14, 2000).

Justice Breyer's historical reference is interesting, but not entirely parallel to *Bush v. Gore* where the Justices participated because an aggrieved litigant brought the case to them, not in an extra-judicial capacity like the isolated Justice Bradley in the 1876 election. In this regard, Yale's Professor Paul Kahn commented that: "The rule of law is our national myth . . . and the institutional locus of that [myth] is the U.S. Supreme Court. . . . Its legitimacy comes not from its knowledge of legal science nor from the justices' political appointments, but from the capacity to persuade us that the rule of law is the rule of the people. At that moment, we overcome the divide between law and politics." Paul W. Kahn, *The Call to Law Is a Call to a Faith in Higher Politics*, L.A. TIMES, B7 (November 24, 2000).

11.   Does the right to vote include the right *not* to have to show identification when doing so? No, or not yet. In *Crawford v. Marion County Election Board* (2008), Indiana had enacted an election law requiring citizens voting in person to present government issued photo identification. This was alleged to impose an unconstitutional burden, especially on the elderly and the less affluent, and to the extent that there is a correlation between those groups and the Democratic Party, a disadvantage drawn along party lines.

All very interesting, said Justice Stevens for the majority, but the state interests for requiring government issued photo identification to vote were sufficiently weighty to justify any limitation imposed on voters. Indiana had a valid interest in deterring and detecting voter fraud. That interest existed even though there wasn't a lot of fraud in Indiana, and Indiana was largely worried about voter impersonation and like practices that happened in other states. Noting that Indiana's identification cards are free, they nevertheless involve some inconvenience like going down to the Bureau of Motor Vehicles, which most people rank with visiting the dentist. Moreover, the Court accepted the speculation that the burden of this requirement would fall mostly on elderly persons born out of state who may have difficulty obtaining the necessary birth certificates and other proof of identification that one needs to get identification. While it would be easy to imagine someone within the category of the poor or the elderly being overly burdened, the Court took the position that the statute is presumptively valid with those challenging having the heavy burden of persuasion that it is invalid in all of its applications. That's the nature of a facial challenge. As the Court points out, "given the fact that petitioners have advanced a broad attack on the constitutionality of [the statute], seeking relief that would invalidate the statute in all its applications, they bear a heavy burden of persuasion." The challengers couldn't meet that standard in *Crawford*. The court reasoned that on the basis of the evidence in the record it, wasn't possible to quantify either the magnitude of the burden on the narrow class of voters for whom the ID requirement would be difficult — the elderly and the indigent — and that even if quantified, there would be difficulty measuring it against the law's anti-fraud justification. The record said virtually nothing about the difficulties faced by either indigent voters or, say, voters with religious objections to being photographed. And, said the Court, even if a particular burden was shown, the remedy still in all likelihood would not be to invalidate the entire statute. As for the suspicion that Republicans had imposed the ID requirement in an effort to dampen Democratic turnout, the Court said "if a nondiscriminatory law is supported by valid neutral justifications, those justification should not be disregarded simply because partisan interest may have provided one motivation for the votes of individual legislators."

12.   We now move from racial discrimination and the "numerical" concept of equal protection as it applies to voting, to tackle another problematic area for the courts, that of gender discrimination. As you read these cases, ask yourself whether the Court's opinions in this area have been more consistent or clear than those regarding racial classifications.

C.   GENDER

MINOR v. HAPPERSETT
88 U.S. (21 Wall.) 162 (1874)

The CHIEF JUSTICE [WAITE] delivered the opinion of the court.

*   *   *

If the right of suffrage is one of the necessary privileges of a citizen of the United States, then the constitution and laws of Missouri confining it to men are in violation of the Constitution of the United States, as amended, and consequently void. The direct question is, therefore, presented whether all citizens are necessarily voters.

*   *   *

The [Fourteenth] amendment did not add to the privileges and immunities of a citizen. It simply furnished an additional guaranty for the protection of such as he already had. No new voters were necessarily made by it. Indirectly it may have had that effect, because it may have increased the number of citizens entitled to suffrage under the constitution and laws of the States, but it operates for this purpose, if at all, through the States and the State laws, and not directly upon the citizen.

It is clear, therefore, we think, that the Constitution has not added the right of suffrage to the privileges and immunities of citizenship as they existed at the time it was adopted. This makes it proper to inquire whether suffrage was coextensive with the citizenship of the States at the time of its adoption. If it was, then it may with force be argued that suffrage was one of the rights which belonged to citizenship, and in the enjoyment of which every citizen must be protected. But if it was not, the contrary may with propriety be assumed.

When the Federal Constitution was adopted, all the States, with the exception of Rhode Island and Connecticut, had constitutions of their own. These two continued to act under their charters from the Crown. Upon an examination of those constitutions we find that in no State were all citizens permitted to vote. Each State determined for itself who should have that power. Thus, in New Hampshire, "every male inhabitant of each town and parish with town privileges, and places unincorporated in the State, of twenty-one years of age and upwards, excepting paupers and persons excused from paying taxes at their own request," were its voters; in Massachusetts "every male inhabitant of twenty-one years of age and upwards, having a freehold estate within the commonwealth of the annual income of three pounds, or any estate of the value of sixty pounds;" in Rhode Island "such as are admitted free of the company and society" of the colony; in Connecticut such persons as had "maturity in years, quiet and peaceable behavior, a civil conversation, and forty shillings freehold or forty pounds personal estate," if so certified by the selectmen; in New York "every male inhabitant of full age who shall have personally resided within one of the counties of the State for six months immediately preceding the day of election . . . if during the time aforesaid he shall have been a freeholder, possessing a freehold of the value of twenty pounds within the county, or have rented a tenement therein of the yearly value of forty shillings, and been rated and actually paid taxes to the State;" in New Jersey "all inhabitants . . . of full age who are worth fifty pounds, proclamation-money, clear estate in the same, and have resided in the county in which they claim a vote for twelve months immediately preceding the election;" in Pennsylvania "every freeman of the age of twenty-one years, having resided in the State two years next before the election, and within that time paid a State or county tax which shall have been assessed at least six months before the election;". . . .

In this condition of the law in respect to suffrage in the several States it cannot for a moment be doubted that if it had been intended to make all citizens of the United States voters, the framers of the Constitution would not have left it to implication. . . .

But if further proof is necessary to show that no such change was intended, it can easily be found both in and out of the Constitution. By Article 4, section 2, it is provided that "the citizens of each State shall be entitled to all the privileges and immunities of citizens in the several States." If suffrage is necessarily a part of citizenship, then the citizens of each State must be entitled to vote in the several States precisely as their citizens are. . . .

And still again, after the adoption of the fourteenth amendment, it was deemed necessary to adopt a fifteenth, as follows: "The right of citizens of the United States to vote shall not be denied or abridged by the United States, or by any State, on account of race, color, or previous condition of servitude." The fourteenth amendment had already provided that no State should make or enforce any law which should abridge the privileges or immunities of citizens of the United States. If suffrage was one of these privileges or immunities, why amend the Constitution to prevent its being denied on account of race, &c.? . . .

It is true that the United States guarantees to every State a republican form of government. It is also true that no State can pass a bill of attainder, and that no person can be deprived of life, liberty, or property without due process of law. All these several provisions of the Constitution must be construed in connection with the other parts of the instrument, and in the light of the surrounding circumstances.

The guaranty is of a republican form of government. No particular government is designated as republican, neither is the exact form to be guaranteed, in any manner especially designated. Here, as in other parts of the instrument, we are compelled to resort elsewhere to ascertain what was intended.

The guaranty necessarily implies a duty on the part of the States themselves to provide such a government. All the States had governments when the Constitution was adopted. In all the people participated to some extent, through their representatives elected in the manner specially provided. These governments the Constitution did not change. They were accepted precisely as they were, and it is, therefore, to be presumed that they were such as it was the duty of the States to provide. Thus we have unmistakable evidence of what was republican in form, within the meaning of that term as employed in the Constitution.

As has been seen, all the citizens of the States were not invested with the right of suffrage. In all, save perhaps New Jersey, this right was only bestowed upon men and not upon all of them. Under these circumstances it is certainly now too late to contend that a government is not republican, within the meaning of this guaranty in the Constitution, because women are not made voters.

The same may be said of the other provisions just quoted. Women were excluded from suffrage in nearly all the States by the express provision of their constitutions and laws. If that had been equivalent to a bill of attainder, certainly its abrogation would not have been left to implication. Nothing less than express language would have been employed to effect so radical a change. So also of the amendment which declares that no person shall be deprived of life, liberty, or property without due process of law, adopted as it was as early as 1791. If suffrage was intended to be included within its obligations, language better adapted to express that intent would most certainly have been employed. The right of suffrage, when granted, will be protected. He who has it can only be deprived of it by due process of law, but in order to claim protection he must first show that he has the right.

But we have already sufficiently considered the proof found upon the inside of the Constitution. That upon the outside is equally effective.

The Constitution was submitted to the States for adoption in 1787, and was ratified by nine States in 1788, and finally by the thirteen original States in 1790. Vermont was the first new State admitted to the Union, and it came in under a constitution which conferred the right of suffrage only upon men of the full age of twenty-one years, having resided in the State for the space of one whole year next before the election, and who were of quiet and peaceable behavior. This was in 1791. . . . No new State has ever been admitted to the Union which has conferred the right of suffrage upon women, and this has never been considered a valid objection to her admission. On the contrary, as is claimed in the argument, the right of suffrage was withdrawn from women as early as 1807 in the State of New Jersey, without any attempt to obtain the interference of the United States to prevent it. Since then the governments of the insurgent States have been reorganized under a requirement that before their representatives could be admitted to seats in Congress they must have adopted new constitutions, republican in form. In no one of these constitutions was suffrage conferred upon women, and yet the States have all been restored to their original position as States in the Union.

Besides this, citizenship has not in all cases been made a condition precedent to the enjoyment of the right of suffrage. Thus, in Missouri, persons of foreign birth, who have declared their intention to become citizens of the United States, may under certain circumstances vote. The same provision is to be found in the constitutions of Alabama, Arkansas, Florida, Georgia, Indiana, Kansas, Minnesota, and Texas.

Certainly, if the courts can consider any question settled, this is one. . . . Our province is to decide what the law is, not to declare what it should be.

We have given this case the careful consideration its importance demands. If the law is wrong, it ought to be changed; but the power for that is not with us. . . .

NOTES AND QUESTIONS

1. Why don't the reconstruction amendments, particularly the Fourteenth Amendment's guarantee of equal protection, guarantee a woman's right to vote? By the way, was the argument supporting the right of women to vote grounded in the Equal Protection Clause? If not, why not? Does it surprise you that the Court was unanimous in its decision in the case? It would not be until 1920 that this case would be overruled by amendment. More on that after the next case.

2. Note that the Court holds that the reconstruction amendments' guarantees of citizenship do not necessarily guarantee the franchise. Did this understanding of these amendments last throughout the twentieth century? This case, as well as *United States v. Anthony*, 24 F. Cas. 829 (N.D.N.Y. 1873) (No. 14,459), which follows, were closely contemporary with the Fourteenth and Fifteenth Amendments. Do they help us discern the original understanding of their text? Have the courts been faithful to that original understanding?

UNITED STATES v. ANTHONY
24 F. Cas. 829 (N.D.N.Y. 1873) (No. 14,459)

HUNT, CIRCUIT JUSTICE . . . ruled as follows:

The defendant is indicted under the act of congress of May 31st, 1870, for having voted for a representative in congress, in November, 1872. Among other things, that act makes it an offence for any person knowingly to vote for such representative without having a lawful right to vote. It is charged that the defendant thus voted, she not having a right to vote, because she is a woman. The defendant insists that she has a right to vote; and that the provision of the constitution of this state, limiting the right to vote to persons of the male sex, is in violation of the fourteenth amendment of the constitution of the United States, and is void.

The thirteenth, fourteenth and fifteenth amendments were designed mainly for the protection of the newly emancipated negroes, but full effect must, nevertheless, be given to the language employed. . . .

The fourteenth amendment creates and defines citizenship of the United States. It had long been contended, and had been held by many learned authorities, and had never been judicially decided to the contrary, that there was no such thing as a citizen of the United States, except as that condition arose from citizenship of some state. No mode existed, it was said, of obtaining a citizenship of the United States, except by first becoming a citizen of some state. This question is now at rest. The fourteenth amendment defines and declares who shall be citizens of the United States, to wit, "all persons born or naturalized in the United States, and subject to the jurisdiction thereof." The latter qualification was intended to exclude the children of foreign representatives and the like. With this qualification, every person born in the United States or naturalized is declared to be a citizen of the United States and of the state wherein he resides.

After creating and defining citizenship of the United States, the fourteenth amendment provides, that "no state shall make or enforce any law which shall abridge the privileges or immunities of citizens of the United States." This clause is intended to be a protection, not to all our rights, but to our rights as citizens of the United States only; that is, to rights existing or belonging to that condition or capacity. The expression, citizen of a state, used in the previous paragraph, is carefully omitted here. In article 4, § 2, subd. 1, of the constitution of the United States, it had been already provided, that "the citizens of each state shall be entitled to all privileges and immunities of citizens in the several states." The rights of citizens of the states and of citizens of the United States are each guarded by these different provisions. That these rights are separate and distinct, was held in the *Slaughter-House Cases*, recently decided by the supreme court. . . .

* * *

HUNT, CIRCUIT JUSTICE, in denying the motion, said, in substance:

The whole law of the case has been reargued, and I have given the best consideration in my power to the arguments presented. But for the evident earnestness of the learned counsel for the defendant, for whose ability and integrity I have the highest respect, I should have no hesitation. . . .

The learned counsel insists, however, that an error was committed in directing the jury to render a verdict of guilty. This direction, he argues, makes the verdict that of the court and not of the jury, and it is contended that the provisions of the constitution looking to and securing a trial by jury in criminal cases have been violated.

The right of trial by jury in civil as well as in criminal cases is a constitutional right. The second section of the first article of the constitution of the state of New York provides, that "the trial by jury, in all cases in which it has been heretofore used, shall remain inviolate forever." Articles six and seven of the amendments to the constitution of the United States contain a similar provision. Yet, in cases where the facts are all conceded, or where they are proved and uncontradicted by evidence, it has always been the practice of the courts to take the case from the jury and decide it as a question of law. No counsel has ever disputed the right of the court to do so. No respectable counsel will venture to doubt the correctness of such practice. . . . The right of a trial by jury in a criminal case is not more distinctly secured than it is in a civil case. In each class of cases this right exists only in respect of a disputed fact. To questions of fact the jury respond. Upon questions of law, the decision of the court is conclusive, and the jury are bound to receive the law as declared by the court. Such is the established practice in criminal as well as in civil cases, and this practice is recognized by the highest authorities. It has been so held by the former supreme court of this state, and by the present court of appeals of this state.

At a circuit court of the United States, held by Judges Woodruff and Blatchford, upon deliberation and consultation, it was decided, that, in a criminal case, the court was not bound to submit the case to the jury, there being no sufficient evidence to justify a conviction, and the court accordingly instructed the jury to find a verdict of not guilty. The district attorney now states, that, on several occasions, since he has been in office, Judge Hall, being of opinion that the evidence did not warrant a conviction, has directed the jury to find a verdict of not guilty.

In the case of *People v. Bennett* (N.Y. 1872), the court of appeals of the state of New York, through its chief justice, uses the following language:

> "Contrary to an opinion formerly prevailing, it has been settled that the juries are not judges of the law, as well as the facts, in criminal cases, but that they must take the law from the court. All questions of law during the trial are to be determined by the court, and it is the duty of the jury to regard and abide by such determination. . . . I can see no reason, therefore, why the court may not, in a case presenting a question of law only, instruct the jury to acquit the prisoner, or to direct an acquittal, and enforce the direction, nor why it is not the duty of the court to do so. This results from the rule, that the jury must take the law as adjudged by the court, and I think it is a necessary result."

In these cases the question, in each instance, was, whether the court had power to direct a verdict of not guilty to be rendered. But the counsel for defendant expressly admits that the authority which justifies a direction to acquit will, in a proper case, justify a direction to convict; that it is a question of power; and that, if the power may be exercised in favor of the defendant, it may be exercised against him. . . . The duty of the jury to take the law from the court is the same, whether it is favorable to the defendant, or unfavorable to him. . . .

In the present case, the court had decided, as matter of law, that Miss Anthony was not a legal voter. It had also decided, as matter of law, that, knowing every fact in the case, and intending to do just what she did, she had knowingly voted, not having a right to vote, and that her belief did not affect the question. Every fact in the case was undisputed. There was no inference to be drawn or point made on the facts, that could, by possibility, alter the result. It was, therefore, not only the right, but it seems to me, upon the authorities, the plain duty of the judge to direct a verdict of guilty. The motion for a new trial is denied.

The defendant was thereupon sentenced to pay a fine of $100 and the costs of the prosecution.

NOTES AND QUESTIONS

1. Susan Anthony was one of the great champions of female suffrage, and was willing to suffer the consequences of the criminal justice system to make her views

known. Does she get a fair trial in this case? What do you make of the directed verdict of guilty? Have you ever encountered that before? Is Judge Hunt convincing in his argument for such a procedural move?

2.   Ms. Anthony and her fellow suffragettes had been arguing since even before the time of the Civil War that to deprive women of the vote, and, indeed to relegate them to the second-class citizenship to which they were subject under the common law, was a violation of the law of nature and nature's God. Such was the point of the famous "Seneca Falls Resolutions" in 1848, a set of propositions that resulted from the first women's rights convention, held in Seneca Falls, New York.

3.   Not until the Constitution was amended to provide, in Amendment Nineteen (ratified in 1920), that "the right of citizens of the United States to vote shall not be denied or abridged by the United States or by any state on account of sex," U.S. Const., amend. XIX, did Susan Anthony's views become part of the Constitution. For many years the text that was to become the Nineteenth Amendment was known as the "Anthony Amendment," in fitting tribute. A woman's suffrage amendment was first introduced into Congress in 1868. Why did it take more than fifty years to secure its passage?

4.   In the 19th century, women were legally precluded from entering various professions. For example, in *Bradwell v. Illinois*, 16 U.S. (Wall.) 130 (1872), the Court upheld an Illinois law that denied women a license to practice law. One member of the Court reasoned: "The paramount destiny and mission of women are to fulfill the noble and benign offices of wife and mother. This is the law of the [C]reator. And the rules of civil society must be adapted in the general constitution of things, and cannot be based on exceptional cases." *Id.* at 141 (Bradley, J. concurring). Is this a misstatement, or at least misapplication of natural law? Is it one thing to recognize the undeniable importance of women in the nurturing and stability of family life and another to require under law that *all* women see this as their "paramount destiny and mission"? In modern gender analysis, is it possible to rid the law of this inflexibility without denigrating the significance of the choice many modern women still make, either with or without a market career, to dedicate extraordinary time to the well-being of families?

In *Goesart v. Cleary*, 335 U.S. 464 (1948), the Court upheld a Michigan law preventing the licensing of women as bartenders unless the bar was owned by her husband or father. Justice Frankfurter, a well-known liberal appointed to the bench by FDR from the Harvard Law School, stated: "Michigan could, beyond question, forbid all women from working behind a bar." *Id.* at 465. Again, even assuming such moral judgments are defensible as a matter of philosophy, isn't this an example of a disregard of the natural law precept articulated by Thomas Aquinas that every vice ought not be prohibited under law? In the 1970s, the Court began to eliminate these distinctions and the legal issue turned to the level of judicial scrutiny to be applied to gender classifications. Ultimately, the Court settled on intermediate scrutiny in *Craig v. Boren*, 429 U.S. 190 (1976) (invalidating a state law that allowed women to drink some alcohol at 18; while men were precluded until 21). Similarly, in *Mississippi University for Women v. Hogan*, 458 U.S. 718 (1982), the Court used intermediate scrutiny to declare unconstitutional the practice of limiting a state nursing school to women. We saw in our review of the cases regarding racial discrimination movement since, at least in recent years, toward a "color blind Constitution." Is the current attitude toward gender discrimination in support of a "gender blind Constitution"? Consider the important case which follows.

UNITED STATES v. VIRGINIA
518 U.S. 515 (1996)

JUSTICE GINSBURG delivered the opinion of the Court.

Virginia's public institutions of higher learning include an incomparable military college, Virginia Military Institute (VMI). The United States maintains that the Constitution's equal protection guarantee precludes Virginia from reserving exclusively to men the unique educational opportunities VMI affords. We agree.

I

Founded in 1839, VMI is today the sole single-sex school among Virginia's 15 public institutions of higher learning. VMI's distinctive mission is to produce "citizen-soldiers," men prepared for leadership in civilian life and in military service. VMI pursues this mission through pervasive training of a kind not available anywhere else in Virginia. Assigning prime place to character development, VMI uses an "adversative method" modeled on English public schools and once characteristic of military instruction. VMI constantly endeavors to instill physical and mental discipline in its cadets and impart to them a strong moral code. The school's graduates leave VMI with heightened comprehension of their capacity to deal with duress and stress, and a large sense of accomplishment for completing the hazardous course.

VMI has notably succeeded in its mission to produce leaders; among its alumni are military generals, Members of Congress, and business executives. The school's alumni overwhelmingly perceive that their VMI training helped them to realize their personal goals. VMI's endowment reflects the loyalty of its graduates; VMI has the largest per-student endowment of all public undergraduate institutions in the Nation.

* * *

II

A

* * *

VMI cadets live in spartan barracks where surveillance is constant and privacy nonexistent; they wear uniforms, eat together in the mess hall, and regularly participate in drills. Entering students are incessantly exposed to the rat line, "an extreme form of the adversative model," comparable in intensity to Marine Corps boot camp. Tormenting and punishing, the rat line bonds new cadets to their fellow sufferers and, when they have completed the 7-month experience, to their former tormentors.

VMI's "adversative model" is further characterized by a hierarchical "class system" of privileges and responsibilities, a "dyke system" for assigning a senior class mentor to each entering class "rat," and a stringently enforced "honor code," which prescribes that a cadet " 'does not lie, cheat, steal nor tolerate those who do.' "

VMI attracts some applicants because of its reputation as an extraordinarily challenging military school, and "because its alumni are exceptionally close to the school." "[W]omen have no opportunity anywhere to gain the benefits of [the system of education at VMI]."

B

In 1990, prompted by a complaint filed with the Attorney General by a female high-school student seeking admission to VMI, the United States sued the Commonwealth of Virginia and VMI, alleging that VMI's exclusively male admission policy violated the Equal Protection Clause of the Fourteenth Amendment. . . .

* * *

The District Court ruled in favor of VMI, however, and rejected the equal protection challenge pressed by the United States. That court correctly recognized that *Mississippi Univ. for Women v. Hogan* (1982), was the closest guide. There, this Court underscored that a party seeking to uphold government action based on sex must establish an "exceedingly persuasive justification" for the classification. To succeed, the defender of the challenged action must show "at least that the classification serves important governmental objectives and that the discriminatory means employed are substantially related to the achievement of those objectives."

The District Court reasoned that education in "a single-gender environment, be it male or female," yields substantial benefits. VMI's school for men brought diversity to an otherwise coeducational Virginia system, and that diversity was "enhanced by VMI's unique method of instruction." If single-gender education for males ranks as an important governmental objective, it becomes obvious, the District Court concluded, that the *only* means of achieving the objective "is to exclude women from the all-male institution — VMI."

"Women are [indeed] denied a unique educational opportunity that is available only at VMI," the District Court acknowledged. But "[VMI's] single-sex status would be lost, and some aspects of the [school's] distinctive method would be altered" if women were admitted: "Allowance for personal privacy would have to be made," "[p]hysical education requirements would have to be altered, at least for the women," the adversative environment could not survive unmodified. Thus, "sufficient constitutional justification" had been shown, the District Court held, "for continuing [VMI's] single-sex policy."

The Court of Appeals for the Fourth Circuit disagreed and vacated the District Court's judgment. The appellate court held: "The Commonwealth of Virginia has not . . . advanced any state policy by which it can justify its determination, under an announced policy of diversity, to afford VMI's unique type of program to men and not to women."

*   *   *

The parties agreed that "some women can meet the physical standards now imposed on men," and the court was satisfied that "neither the goal of producing citizen soldiers nor VMI's implementing methodology is inherently unsuitable to women." The Court of Appeals, however, accepted the District Court's finding that "at least these three aspects of VMI's program — physical training, the absence of privacy, and the adversative approach — would be materially affected by coeducation." Remanding the case, the appeals court assigned to Virginia, in the first instance, responsibility for selecting a remedial course. The court suggested these options for the State: Admit women to VMI; establish parallel institutions or programs; or abandon state support, leaving VMI free to pursue its policies as a private institution. In May 1993, this Court denied certiorari.

C

In response to the Fourth Circuit's ruling, Virginia proposed a parallel program for women: Virginia Women's Institute for Leadership (VWIL). The 4-year, state-sponsored undergraduate program would be located at Mary Baldwin College, a private liberal arts school for women, and would be open, initially, to about 25 to 30 students. Although VWIL would share VMI's mission — to produce "citizen-soldiers" — the VWIL program would differ, as does Mary Baldwin College, from VMI in academic offerings, methods of education, and financial resources.

The average combined SAT score of entrants at Mary Baldwin is about 100 points lower than the score for VMI freshmen. Mary Baldwin's faculty holds "significantly fewer Ph.D.'s than the faculty at VMI," and receives significantly lower salaries. While VMI offers degrees in liberal arts, the sciences, and engineering, Mary Baldwin, at the time of trial, offered only bachelor of arts degrees. A VWIL student seeking to earn an engineering degree could gain one, without public support, by attending Washington University in St. Louis, Missouri, for two years, paying the required private tuition.

Experts in educating women at the college level composed the Task Force charged with designing the VWIL program; Task Force members were drawn from Mary Baldwin's own faculty and staff. Training its attention on methods of instruction appropriate for "most women," the Task Force determined that a military model would be "wholly inappropriate" for VWIL.

VWIL students would participate in ROTC programs and a newly established, "largely ceremonial" Virginia Corps of Cadets, but the VWIL House would not have a military format, and VWIL would not require its students to eat meals together or to wear uniforms during the school day. In lieu of VMI's adversative method, the VWIL Task Force favored "a cooperative method which reinforces self-esteem." In addition to the standard bachelor of arts program offered at Mary Baldwin, VWIL students would take courses in leadership, complete an off-campus leadership externship, participate in community service projects, and assist in arranging a speaker series.

Virginia represented that it will provide equal financial support for in-state VWIL students and VMI cadets and the VMI Foundation agreed to supply a $5.4625 million endowment for the VWIL program. Mary Baldwin's own endowment is about $19 million; VMI's is $131 million. Mary Baldwin will add $35 million to its endowment based on future commitments; VMI will add $220 million. The VMI Alumni Association has developed a network of employers interested in hiring VMI graduates. The Association has agreed to open its network to VWIL graduates, but those graduates will not have the advantage afforded by a VMI degree.

D

Virginia returned to the District Court seeking approval of its proposed remedial plan, and the court decided the plan met the requirements of the Equal Protection Clause. The District Court again acknowledged evidentiary support for these determinations. "[T]he VMI methodology could be used to educate women and, in fact, some women . . . may prefer the VMI methodology to the VWIL methodology." But the "controlling legal principles," the District Court decided, "do not require the Commonwealth to provide a mirror image VMI for women." The court anticipated that the two schools would "achieve substantially similar outcomes." It concluded: "If VMI marches to the beat of a drum, then Mary Baldwin marches to the melody of a fife and when the march is over, both will have arrived at the same destination."

A divided Court of Appeals affirmed the District Court's judgment. . . .

"[P]roviding the option of a single-gender college education may be considered a legitimate and important aspect of a public system of higher education," the appeals court observed; that objective, the court added, is "not pernicious." Moreover, the court continued, the adversative method vital to a VMI education "has never been tolerated in a sexually heterogeneous environment." The method itself "was not designed to exclude women," the court noted, but women could not be accommodated in the VMI program, the court believed, for female participation in VMI's adversative training "would destroy . . . any sense of decency that still permeates the relationship between the sexes."

* * *

The Fourth Circuit denied rehearing en banc. . . .

III

The cross-petitions in this case present two ultimate issues. First, does Virginia's exclusion of women from the educational opportunities provided by VMI — extraordinary opportunities for military training and civilian leadership development — deny to women "capable of all of the individual activities required of VMI cadets," the equal protection of the laws guaranteed by the Fourteenth Amendment? Second, if VMI's "unique" situation — as Virginia's sole single-sex public institution of higher education — offends the Constitution's equal protection principle, what is the remedial requirement?

IV

We note, once again, the core instruction of this Court's pathmarking decisions in *J.E.B. v. Alabama ex rel. T.B.* (1994), and *Mississippi Univ. for Women*: Parties who seek to defend gender-based government action must demonstrate an "exceedingly persuasive justification" for that action.

Today's skeptical scrutiny of official action denying rights or opportunities based on sex responds to volumes of history. As a plurality of this Court acknowledged a generation ago, "our Nation has had a long and unfortunate history of sex discrimination." *Frontiero v. Richardson* (1973). Through a century plus three decades and more of that history, women did not count among voters composing "We the People"; not until 1920 did women gain a constitutional right to the franchise. And for a half century thereafter, it remained the prevailing doctrine that government, both federal and state, could withhold from women opportunities accorded men so long as any "basis in reason" could be conceived for the discrimination.

In 1971, for the first time in our Nation's history, this Court ruled in favor of a woman who complained that her State had denied her the equal protection of its laws. *Reed v. Reed* (1971) (holding unconstitutional Idaho Code prescription that, among " 'several persons claiming and equally entitled to administer [a decedent's estate], males must be preferred to females' "). Since *Reed*, the Court has repeatedly recognized that neither federal nor state government acts compatibly with the equal protection principle when a law or official policy denies to women, simply because they are women, full citizenship stature — equal opportunity to aspire, achieve, participate in and contribute to society based on their individual talents and capacities.

. . . To summarize the Court's current directions for cases of official classification based on gender: Focusing on the differential treatment or denial of opportunity for which relief is sought, the reviewing court must determine whether the proffered justification is "exceedingly persuasive." The burden of justification is demanding and it rests entirely on the State. The State must show "at least that the [challenged] classification serves 'important governmental objectives and that the discriminatory means employed' are 'substantially related to the achievement of those objectives.' " . . .

The heightened review standard our precedent establishes does not make sex a proscribed classification. Supposed "inherent differences" are no longer accepted as a ground for race or national origin classifications. See *Loving v. Virginia* (1967). Physical differences between men and women, however, are enduring: "[T]he two sexes are not fungible; a community made up exclusively of one [sex] is different from a community composed of both."

"Inherent differences" between men and women, we have come to appreciate, remain cause for celebration, but not for denigration of the members of either sex or for artificial constraints on an individual's opportunity. Sex classifications may be used to compensate women "for particular economic disabilities [they have] suffered," to "promote equal employment opportunity," to advance full development of the talent and capacities of our Nation's people. But such classifications may not be used, as they once were to create or perpetuate the legal, social, and economic inferiority of women.

Measuring the record in this case against the review standard just described, we conclude that Virginia has shown no "exceedingly persuasive justification" for excluding all women from the citizen-soldier training afforded by VMI. . . . Because the remedy proffered by Virginia — the Mary Baldwin VWIL program — does not cure the constitutional violation, *i.e.*, it does not provide equal opportunity, we reverse the Fourth Circuit's final judgment in this case.

V

. . . Virginia . . . asserts two justifications in defense of VMI's exclusion of women. First, the Commonwealth contends, "single-sex education provides important educational benefits" and the option of single-sex education contributes to "diversity in educational approaches." Second, the Commonwealth argues, "the unique VMI method of character development and leadership training," the school's adversative approach, would have to be modified were VMI to admit women. . . .

A

. . . Virginia has not shown that VMI was established, or has been maintained, with a view to diversifying, by its categorical exclusion of women, educational opportunities within the State. In cases of this genre, our precedent instructs that "benign" justifications proffered in defense of categorical exclusions will not be accepted automatically; a tenable justification must describe actual state purposes, not rationalizations for actions in fact differently grounded.

Mississippi Univ. for Women is immediately in point. There the State asserted, in justification of its exclusion of men from a nursing school, that it was engaging in "educational affirmative action" by "compensat[ing] for discrimination against women." Undertaking a "searching analysis," the Court found no close resemblance between "the alleged objective" and "the actual purpose underlying the discriminatory classification[.]" Pursuing a similar inquiry here, we reach the same conclusion.

Neither recent nor distant history bears out Virginia's alleged pursuit of diversity through single-sex educational options. In 1839, when the State established VMI, a range of educational opportunities for men and women was scarcely contemplated. Higher education at the time was considered dangerous for women;[9] reflecting

---

[9] [9] Dr. Edward H. Clarke of Harvard Medical School, whose influential book, Sex in Education, went through 17 editions, was perhaps the most well-known speaker from the medical community opposing higher education for women. He maintained that the physiological effects of hard study and academic competition with boys would interfere with the development of girls' reproductive organs. See E. CLARKE, SEX IN EDUCATION 38–39, 62–63 (1873); *id.*, at 127 ("identical education of the two sexes is a crime before God and humanity, that physiology protests against, and that experience weeps over"); see also H.

widely held views about women's proper place, the Nation's first universities and colleges — for example, Harvard in Massachusetts, William and Mary in Virginia — admitted only men. VMI was not at all novel in this respect: In admitting no women, VMI followed the lead of the State's flagship school, the University of Virginia, founded in 1819.

"[N]o struggle for the admission of women to a state university," a historian has recounted, "was longer drawn out, or developed more bitterness, than that at the University of Virginia." In 1879, the State Senate resolved to look into the possibility of higher education for women, recognizing that Virginia " 'has never, at any period of her history,' " provided for the higher education of her daughters, though she " 'has liberally provided for the higher education of her sons.' " Despite this recognition, no new opportunities were instantly open to women.

Virginia eventually provided for several women's seminaries and colleges. Farmville Female Seminary became a public institution in 1884. Two women's schools, Mary Washington College and James Madison University, were founded in 1908; another, Radford University, was founded in 1910. By the mid-1970's, all four schools had become coeducational.

* * *

. . . [W]e find no persuasive evidence in this record that VMI's male-only admission policy "is in furtherance of a state policy of 'diversity.' " . . . A purpose genuinely to advance an array of educational options, as the Court of Appeals recognized, is not served by VMI's historic and constant plan — a plan to "affor[d] a unique educational benefit only to males." However "liberally" this plan serves the State's sons, it makes no provision whatever for her daughters. That is not *equal* protection.

B

Virginia next argues that VMI's adversative method of training provides educational benefits that cannot be made available, unmodified, to women. Alterations to accommodate women would necessarily be "radical," so "drastic," Virginia asserts, as to transform, indeed "destroy," VMI's program. Neither sex would be favored by the transformation, Virginia maintains: Men would be deprived of the unique opportunity currently available to them; women would not gain that opportunity because their participation would "eliminat[e] the very aspects of [the] program that distinguish [VMI] from . . . other institutions of higher education in Virginia."

* * *

In support of its initial judgment for Virginia, a judgment rejecting all equal

---

MAUDSLEY, SEX IN MIND AND IN EDUCATION 17 (1874) ("It is not that girls have not ambition, nor that they fail generally to run the intellectual race [in coeducational settings], but it is asserted that they do it at a cost to their strength and health which entails life-long suffering, and even incapacitates them for the adequate performance of the natural functions of their sex."); C. MEIGS, FEMALES AND THEIR DISEASES 350 (1848) (after five or six weeks of "mental and educational discipline," a healthy woman would "lose . . . the habit of menstruation" and suffer numerous ills as a result of depriving her body for the sake of her mind).

protection objections presented by the United States, the District Court made "findings" on "gender-based developmental differences." These "findings" restate the opinions of Virginia's expert witnesses, opinions about typically male or typically female "tendencies." For example, "[m]ales tend to need an atmosphere of adversativeness," while "[f]emales tend to thrive in a cooperative atmosphere." "I'm not saying that some women don't do well under [the] adversative model," VMI's expert on educational institutions testified, "undoubtedly there are some [women] who do"; but educational experiences must be designed "around the rule," this expert maintained, and not "around the exception."

The United States does not challenge any expert witness estimation on average capacities or preferences of men and women. Instead, the United States emphasizes that time and again since this Court's turning point decision in *Reed v. Reed* (1971), we have cautioned reviewing courts to take a "hard look" at generalizations or "tendencies" of the kind pressed by Virginia, and relied upon by the District Court. State actors controlling gates to opportunity, we have instructed, may not exclude qualified individuals based on "fixed notions concerning the roles and abilities of males and females."

It may be assumed, for purposes of this decision, that most women would not choose VMI's adversative method. As Fourth Circuit Judge Motz observed, however, in her dissent from the Court of Appeals' denial of rehearing en banc, it is also probable that "many men would not want to be educated in such an environment." Education, to be sure, is not a "one size fits all" business. The issue, however, is not whether "women — or men — should be forced to attend VMI"; rather, the question is whether the State can constitutionally deny to women who have the will and capacity, the training and attendant opportunities that VMI uniquely affords.

* * *

VI

In the second phase of the litigation, Virginia presented its remedial plan — maintain VMI as a male-only college and create VWIL as a separate program for women. The plan met District Court approval. The Fourth Circuit, in turn, deferentially reviewed the State's proposal and decided that the two single-sex programs directly served Virginia's reasserted purposes: single-gender education, and "achieving the results of an adversative method in a military environment." Inspecting the VMI and VWIL educational programs to determine whether they "afford[ed] to both genders benefits comparable in substance, [if] not in form and detail," the Court of Appeals concluded that Virginia had arranged for men and women opportunities "sufficiently comparable" to survive equal protection evaluation. The United States challenges this "remedial" ruling as pervasively misguided.

A

A remedial decree, this Court has said, must closely fit the constitutional violation; it must be shaped to place persons unconstitutionally denied an opportunity or advantage in "the position they would have occupied in the absence of [discrimination]." The constitutional violation in this case is the categorical exclusion of women from an extraordinary educational opportunity afforded men. A proper remedy for an unconstitutional exclusion, we have explained, aims to "eliminate [so far as possible] the discriminatory effects of the past" and to "bar like discrimination in the future."

Virginia chose not to eliminate, but to leave untouched, VMI's exclusionary policy. For women only, however, Virginia proposed a separate program, different in kind from VMI and unequal in tangible and intangible facilities. Having violated the Constitution's equal protection requirement, Virginia was obliged to show that its remedial proposal "directly address[ed] and relate[d] to" the violation, the equal protection denied to women ready, willing, and able to benefit from educational opportunities of the kind VMI offers. Virginia described VWIL as a "parallel program," and asserted that VWIL shares VMI's mission of producing "citizen-soldiers" and VMI's goals of providing "education, military training, mental and physical discipline, character . . . and leadership development." If the VWIL program could not "eliminate the discriminatory effects of the past," could it at least "bar like discrimination in the future"? A comparison of the programs said to be "parallel" informs our answer. . . .

VWIL affords women no opportunity to experience the rigorous military training for which VMI is famed. Instead, the VWIL program "deemphasize[s]" military education, and uses a "cooperative method" of education "which reinforces self-esteem[.]"

VWIL students participate in ROTC and a "largely ceremonial" Virginia Corps of Cadets, but Virginia deliberately did not make VWIL a military institute. The VWIL House is not a military-style residence and VWIL students need not live together throughout the 4-year program, eat meals together, or wear uniforms during the school day. VWIL students thus do not experience the "barracks" life "crucial to the VMI experience," the spartan living arrangements designed to foster an "egalitarian ethic." . . .

VWIL students receive their "leadership training" in seminars, externships, and speaker series, episodes and encounters lacking the "[p]hysical rigor, mental stress, . . . minute regulation of behavior, and indoctrination in desirable values" made hallmarks of VMI's citizen-soldier training. . . .

Virginia maintains that these methodological differences are "justified pedagogically," based on "important differences between men and women in learning and developmental needs," "psychological and sociological differences" Virginia describes as "real" and "not stereotypes." The Task Force charged with developing the leadership program for women, drawn from the staff and faculty at Mary Baldwin College, "determined that a military model and, especially VMI's adversative method, would be wholly inappropriate for educating and training *most women*." . . .

As earlier stated, generalizations about "the way women are," estimates of what is appropriate for *most women*, no longer justify denying opportunity to women whose talent and capacity place them outside the average description. Notably, Virginia never asserted that VMI's method of education suits *most men*. It is also revealing that Virginia accounted for its failure to make the VWIL experience "the entirely militaristic experience of VMI" on the ground that VWIL "is planned for women who do not necessarily expect to pursue military careers." By that reasoning, VMI's "entirely militaristic" program would be inappropriate for men in general or as a group, for "[o]nly about 15% of VMI cadets enter career military service."

In contrast to the generalizations about women on which Virginia rests, we note again these dispositive realties: VMI's "implementing methodology" is not "inherently unsuitable to women," "some women . . . do well under [the] adversative model," "some women, at least, would want to attend [VMI] if they had the opportunity," "some women are capable of all of the individual activities required of VMI cadets," and "can meet the physical standards [VMI] now impose[s] on men[.]" It is on behalf of these women that the United States has instituted this suit, and it is for them that a remedy must be crafted,[10] a remedy that will end their exclusion from a state-supplied educational opportunity for which they are fit, a decree that will "bar like discrimination in the future."

B

In myriad respects other than military training, VWIL does not qualify as VMI's equal. VWIL's student body, faculty, course offerings, and facilities hardly match VMI's. Nor can the VWIL graduate anticipate the benefits associated with VMI's 157-year history, the school's prestige, and its influential alumni network.

*   *   *

Virginia, in sum, while maintaining VMI for men only, has failed to provide any "comparable single-gender women's institution." Instead, the Commonwealth has created a VWIL program fairly appraised as a "pale shadow" of VMI in terms of the range of curricular choices and faculty stature, funding, prestige, alumni support and influence.

Virginia's VWIL solution is reminiscent of the remedy Texas proposed 50 years ago, in response to a state trial court's 1946 ruling that, given the equal protection guarantee, African Americans could not be denied a legal education at a state facility. *Sweatt v. Painter* (1950). Reluctant to admit African Americans to its flagship University of Texas Law School, the State set up a separate school for Heman Sweatt and other black law students. As originally opened, the new school had no independent faculty or library, and it lacked accreditation. Nevertheless, the

---

[10] [19] Admitting women to VMI would undoubtedly require alterations necessary to afford members of each sex privacy from the other sex in living arrangements, and to adjust aspects of the physical training programs. Brief for Petitioner 27–29; *cf.* note following 10 U.S.C. § 4342 (academic and other standards for women admitted to the Military, Naval, and Air Force Academies "shall be the same as those required for male individuals, except for those minimum essential adjustments in such standards required because of physiological differences between male and female individuals"). Experience shows such adjustments are manageable. U.S. MILITARY ACADEMY, A. VITTERS, N. KINZER, & J. ADAMS, REPORT OF ADMISSION OF WOMEN (Project Athena I–IV) (1977–1980) (4-year longitudinal study of the admission of women to West Point); DEFENSE ADVISORY COMMITTEE ON WOMEN IN THE SERVICES, REPORT ON THE INTEGRATION AND PERFORMANCE OF WOMEN AT WEST POINT 17–18 (1992).

state trial and appellate courts were satisfied that the new school offered Sweatt opportunities for the study of law "substantially equivalent to those offered by the State to white students at the University of Texas."

Before this Court considered the case, the new school had gained "a faculty of five full-time professors; a student body of 23; a library of some 16,500 volumes serviced by a full-time staff; a practice court and legal aid association; and one alumnus who had become a member of the Texas Bar." This Court contrasted resources at the new school with those at the school from which Sweatt had been excluded. The University of Texas Law School had a full-time faculty of 16, a student body of 850, a library containing over 65,000 volumes, scholarship funds, a law review, and moot court facilities.

More important than the tangible features, the Court emphasized, are "those qualities which are incapable of objective measurement but which make for greatness" in a school, including "reputation of the faculty, experience of the administration, position and influence of the alumni, standing in the community, traditions and prestige." Facing the marked differences reported in the *Sweatt* opinion, the Court unanimously ruled that Texas had not shown "substantial equality in the [separate] educational opportunities" the State offered. Accordingly, the Court held, the Equal Protection Clause required Texas to admit African Americans to the University of Texas Law School. In line with *Sweatt*, we rule here that Virginia has not shown substantial equality in the separate educational opportunities the State supports at VWIL and VMI.

C

When Virginia tendered its VWIL plan, the Fourth Circuit did not inquire whether the proposed remedy, approved by the District Court, placed women denied the VMI advantage in "the position they would have occupied in the absence of [discrimination]." Instead, the Court of Appeals considered whether the State could provide, with fidelity to the equal protection principle, separate and unequal educational programs for men and women.

. . . [T]he appeals court declared the substantially different and significantly unequal VWIL program satisfactory. The court reached that result by revising the applicable standard of review. The Fourth Circuit displaced the standard developed in our precedent and substituted a standard of its own invention.

We have earlier described the deferential review in which the Court of Appeals engaged, a brand of review inconsistent with the more exacting standard our precedent requires. . . . [T]he Court of Appeals candidly described its own analysis as one capable of checking a legislative purpose ranked as "pernicious," but generally according "deference to [the] legislative will." Recognizing that it had extracted from our decisions a test yielding "little or no scrutiny of the effect of a classification directed at [single-gender education]," the Court of Appeals devised another test, a "substantive comparability" inquiry and proceeded to find that new test satisfied.

The Fourth Circuit plainly erred in exposing Virginia's VWIL plan to a deferential analysis, for "all gender-based classifications today" warrant "heightened scrutiny." Valuable as VWIL may prove for students who seek the program offered, Virginia's remedy affords no cure at all for the opportunities and advantages withheld from women who want a VMI education and can make the grade. In sum, Virginia's remedy does not match the constitutional violation; the State has shown no "exceedingly persuasive justification" for withholding from women qualified for the experience premier training of the kind VMI affords.

VII

A generation ago, "the authorities controlling Virginia higher education" despite long established tradition, agreed "to innovate and favorably entertain[ed] the [then] relatively new idea that there must be no discrimination by sex in offering educational opportunity." Commencing in 1970, Virginia opened to women "educational opportunities at the Charlottesville campus that [were] not afforded in other [State-operated] institutions." . . .

VMI, too, offers an educational opportunity no other Virginia institution provides, and the school's "prestige" — associated with its success in developing "citizen-soldiers" — is unequaled. Virginia has closed this facility to its daughters and, instead, has devised for them a "parallel program," with a faculty less impressively credentialed and less well paid, more limited course offerings, fewer opportunities for military training and for scientific specialization. VMI, beyond question, "possesses to a far greater degree" than the VWIL program "those qualities which are incapable of objective measurement but which make for greatness in a . . . school," including "position and influence of the alumni, standing in the community, traditions and prestige." Women seeking and fit for a VMI-quality education cannot be offered anything less, under the State's obligation to afford them genuinely equal protection.

A prime part of the history of our Constitution, historian Richard Morris recounted, is the story of the extension of constitutional rights and protections to people once ignored or excluded. VMI's story continued as our comprehension of "We the People" expanded. There is no reason to believe that the admission of women capable of all the activities required of VMI cadets would destroy the Institute rather than enhance its capacity to serve the "more perfect Union."

. . . [T]he case is remanded for further proceedings consistent with this opinion.

It is so ordered.

JUSTICE THOMAS took no part in the consideration or decision of this case.

CHIEF JUSTICE REHNQUIST, concurring in judgment. [omitted]

JUSTICE SCALIA, dissenting.

Today the Court shuts down an institution that has served the people of the Commonwealth of Virginia with pride and distinction for over a century and a half. To achieve that desired result, it rejects (contrary to our established practice) the factual findings of two courts below, sweeps aside the precedents of this Court, and ignores the history of our people. As to facts: it explicitly rejects the finding that there exist "gender-based developmental differences" supporting Virginia's restriction of the "adversative" method to only a men's institution, and the finding that the all-male composition of the Virginia Military Institute (VMI) is essential to that institution's character. As to precedent: it drastically revises our established standards for reviewing sex-based classifications. And as to history: it counts for nothing the long tradition, enduring down to the present, of men's military colleges supported by both States and the Federal Government.

Much of the Court's opinion is devoted to deprecating the closed-mindedness of our forebears with regard to women's education, and even with regard to the treatment of women in areas that have nothing to do with education. Closed-minded they were — as every age is, including our own, with regard to matters it cannot guess, because it simply does not consider them debatable. The virtue of a democratic system with a First Amendment is that it readily enables the people, over time, to be persuaded that what they took for granted is not so, and to change their laws accordingly. That system is destroyed if the smug assurances of each age are removed from the democratic process and written into the Constitution. So to counterbalance the Court's criticism of our ancestors, let me say a word in their praise: they left us free to change. The same cannot be said of this most illiberal Court, which has embarked on a course of inscribing one after another of the current preferences of the society (and in some cases only the counter-majoritarian preferences of the society's law-trained elite) into our Basic Law. Today it enshrines the notion that no substantial educational value is to be served by an all-men's military academy — so that the decision by the people of Virginia to maintain such an institution denies equal protection to women who cannot attend that institution but can attend others. Since it is entirely clear that the Constitution of the United States — the old one — takes no sides in this educational debate, I dissent.

* * *

IV

* * *

A

Under the constitutional principles announced and applied today, single-sex public education is unconstitutional. By going through the motions of applying a balancing test — asking whether the State has adduced an "exceedingly persuasive justification" for its sex-based classification — the Court creates the illusion that government officials in some future case will have a clear shot at justifying some sort of single-sex public education. Indeed, the Court seeks to create even a greater illusion than that: It purports to have said nothing of relevance to *other* public schools at all. "We address specifically and only an educational opportunity recognized . . . as 'unique'. . . ."

The Supreme Court of the United States does not sit to announce "unique" dispositions. Its principal function is to establish *precedent* — that is, to set forth principles of law that every court in America must follow. . . .

And the rationale of today's decision is sweeping: for sex-based classifications, a redefinition of intermediate scrutiny that makes it indistinguishable from strict scrutiny. Indeed, the Court indicates that if any program restricted to one sex is "uniqu[e]," it must be opened to members of the opposite sex "who have the will and capacity" to participate in it. I suggest that the single-sex program that will not be capable of being characterized as "unique" is not only unique but nonexistent.

In any event, regardless of whether the Court's rationale leaves some small amount of room for lawyers to argue, it ensures that single-sex public education is functionally dead. The costs of litigating the constitutionality of a single-sex education program, and the risks of ultimately losing that litigation, are simply too high to be embraced by public officials. Any person with standing to challenge any sex-based classification can haul the State into federal court and compel it to establish by evidence (presumably in the form of expert testimony) that there is an "exceedingly persuasive justification" for the classification. Should the courts happen to interpret that vacuous phrase as establishing a standard that is not utterly impossible of achievement, there is considerable risk that whether the standard has been met will not be determined on the basis of the record evidence — indeed, that will necessarily be the approach of any court that seeks to walk the path the Court has trod today. No state official in his right mind will buy such a high-cost, high-risk lawsuit by commencing a single-sex program. The enemies of single-sex education have won. . . .

This is especially regrettable because, as the District Court here determined, educational experts in recent years have increasingly come to "suppor[t] [the] view that substantial educational benefits flow from a single-gender environment, be it male or female, *that cannot be replicated in a coeducational setting*." . . . Until quite recently, some public officials have attempted to institute new single-sex programs, at least as experiments. In 1991, for example, the Detroit Board of Education announced a program to establish three boys-only schools for inner-city youth; it was met with a lawsuit, a preliminary injunction was swiftly entered by a District Court that purported to rely on *Hogan*, and the Detroit Board of Education voted to abandon the litigation and thus abandon the plan[.] Today's opinion assures that no such experiment will be tried again.

B

There are few extant single-sex public educational programs. The potential of today's decision for widespread disruption of existing institutions lies in its application to *private* single-sex education. Government support is immensely important to private educational institutions. Mary Baldwin College — which designed and runs VWIL — notes that private institutions of higher education in the 1990–1991 school year derived approximately 19 percent of their budgets from federal, state, and local government funds, *not including financial aid to students*. Charitable status under the tax laws is also highly significant for private educational institutions, and it is certainly not beyond the Court that rendered today's decision to hold that a donation to a single-sex college should be deemed contrary to public policy and therefore not deductible if the college discriminates on the basis of sex.

* * *

The only hope for state-assisted single-sex private schools is that the Court will not apply in the future the principles of law it has applied today. That is a substantial hope, I am happy and ashamed to say. After all, did not the Court today abandon the principles of law it has applied in our earlier sex-classification cases? And does not the Court positively invite private colleges to rely upon our ad-hocery by assuring them this case is "unique"? I would not advise the foundation of any new single-sex college (especially an all-male one) with the expectation of being allowed to receive any government support; but it is too soon to abandon in despair those single-sex colleges already in existence. It will certainly be possible for this Court to write a future opinion that ignores the broad principles of law set forth today, and that characterizes as utterly dispositive the opinion's perceptions that VMI was a uniquely prestigious all-male institution, conceived in chauvinism, etc., etc. I will not join that opinion.

* * *

Justice Brandeis said it is "one of the happy incidents of the federal system that a single courageous State may, if its citizens choose, serve as a laboratory; and try novel social and economic experiments without risk to the rest of the country." *New State Ice Co. v. Liebmann* (1932) (dissenting opinion). But it is one of the unhappy incidents of the federal system that a self-righteous Supreme Court, acting on its Members' personal view of what would make a "more perfect Union," (a criterion only slightly more restrictive than a "more perfect world"), can impose its own favored social and economic dispositions nationwide. As today's disposition, and others this single Term, show, this places it beyond the power of a "single courageous State," not only to introduce novel dispositions that the Court frowns upon, but to reintroduce, or indeed even adhere to, disfavored dispositions that are centuries old. The sphere of self-government reserved to the people of the Republic is progressively narrowed.

* * *

In an odd sort of way, it is precisely VMI's attachment to such old-fashioned concepts as manly "honor" that has made it, and the system it represents, the target of those who today succeed in abolishing public single-sex education. The record contains a booklet that all first-year VMI students (the so-called "rats") were required to keep in their possession at all times. Near the end there appears the following period-piece, entitled "The Code of a Gentleman":

> "Without a strict observance of the fundamental Code of Honor, no man, no matter how 'polished,' can be considered a gentleman. The honor of a gentleman demands the inviolability of his word, and the incorruptibility of his principles. He is the descendant of the knight, the crusader; he is the defender of the defenseless and the champion of justice . . . or he is not a Gentleman.

> "A Gentleman . . .

"Does not discuss his family affairs in public or with acquaintances.

"Does not speak more than casually about his girl friend.

"Does not go to a lady's house if he is affected by alcohol. He is temperate in the use of alcohol.

"Does not lose his temper; nor exhibit anger, fear, hate, embarrassment, ardor or hilarity in public.

"Does not hail a lady from a club window.

"A gentleman never discusses the merits or demerits of a lady.

"Does not mention names exactly as he avoids the mention of what things cost.

"Does not borrow money from a friend, except in dire need. Money borrowed is a debt of honor, and must be repaid as promptly as possible. Debts incurred by a deceased parent, brother, sister or grown child are assumed by honorable men as a debt of honor.

"Does not display his wealth, money or possessions.

"Does not put his manners on and off, whether in the club or in a ballroom. He treats people with courtesy, no matter what their social position may be.

"Does not slap strangers on the back nor so much as lay a finger on a lady.

"Does not 'lick the boots of those above' nor 'kick the face of those below him on the social ladder.'

"Does not take advantage of another's helplessness or ignorance and assumes that no gentleman will take advantage of him."

I do not know whether the men of VMI lived by this Code; perhaps not. But it is powerfully impressive that a public institution of higher education still in existence sought to have them do so. I do not think any of us, women included, will be better off for its destruction.

NOTES AND QUESTIONS

1. What is the argument for invoking the Fourteenth Amendment as a prohibition on gender discrimination? For example, if Susan B. Anthony was unsuccessful in arguing that the Fourteenth Amendment gave her the right to vote, why should it give young Virginia women the right to enter VMI? Why doesn't "separate but equal" work in this case, or does it? Was the VMI program really premised upon gender stereotypes or is it simply that single-gender education can, for some people, be particularly effective? Does it matter that empirical studies tend to suggest that teenage girls in secondary school do particularly well in a single-sex environment? *See* Rodney K. Smith, *When Ignorance Is Not Bliss: In Search of Racial and Gender Equality in Intercollegiate Athletics*, 61 Mo. L. Rev. 329 (1996) (discussing gender and racial inequities that permeate college athletics and arguing

that an academically prejudicial reluctance on the part of scholars to study the subject is perpetuating the problem).

2.   Why is "intermediate scrutiny" the appropriate test for gender discrimination? Why not "rational basis" or "strict scrutiny"? Is gender, unlike race, a sometimes acceptable criteria for public decision making? What are those times? Is Justice Scalia correct that the majority actually uses a "strict scrutiny" test? Why the need for a middle or a middle and a half tier? Is he correct that publically-funded single-sex education is now unconstitutional? Justice Scalia's opinion boils down to the simple contention that the Court is legislating its value preferences into constitutional law. Why does he believe this, and do you agree?

3.   Not all gender classifications have been struck down. In *Michael M. v. Superior Court*, 450 U.S. 464 (1981), the Court upheld a statutory rape law that punishes men for having sexual intercourse with a women under 18, but not vice versa, and in *Rostker v. Goldberg*, 453 U.S. 57 (1981), the Court sustained the federal law that requires only men to register for the military draft. Are these gender distinctions in doubt in light of *VMI*? Are gender distinctions ever acceptable on the theory of anatomical or biological difference? In *Dothard v. Rawlinson*, 433 U.S. 321 (1977), the Court upheld the exclusion of women from so-called "contact positions" in an all-male prison. *Michael M.* was premised on the belief that the consequences of teenage pregnancy are naturally harder for a female who must bear the pregnancy, and hence, the law could rationally distinguish between male and female penalties under the rape statute. Do you agree? If so, do these biological differences also justify the exemption from the draft?

4.   Are classifications that benefit women contrary to equal protection? Sometimes. For example, in *Orr v. Orr*, 440 U.S. 268 (1979), the Court struck an Alabama law that allowed alimony to women, but not men. Similarly, in *Califano v. Goldfarb*, 430 U.S. 199 (1977), a provision of the federal law providing benefits to a surviving spouse was invalidated because it gave preference to a surviving wife, but required a surviving husband to prove that he received half of his support from his wife. Given that, statistically, there are still more dependent women than men, why is it wrong for legislatures to take cognizance of this fact? Should the law be used as a form of social engineering to undo, or create incentives to undo, choices made by spouses in their individual lives? Not all legal preferences for women have been invalidated, either. For example, in *Califano v. Webster*, 430 U.S. 313 (1977), the Court upheld more favorable benefits calculation for women under the Social Security Act than men. Similarly, in *Schlesinger v. Ballard*, 419 U.S. 498 (1975), a Navy regulation that allowed women four additional years to obtain promotion in rank than men before involuntary discharge was accepted. Are some benefits under law for women based on stereotype and others designed to redress past discrimination? Does Justice Ginsburg in *VMI* rule out a state-run single-sex institution for women?

5.   While thus far our study of equal protection has been of race and gender classifications, others sometimes exist under law. Do any others require heightened scrutiny? Yes, with regard to aliens and illegitimate children, but it's a bit complicated. Because the text of the equal protection clause extends to "persons," and not merely citizens, aliens may not be discriminated against, except in

particular cases mentioned below. *See Graham v. Richardson*, 403 U.S. 365 (1971) (invalidating a Pennsylvania law that excluded aliens from state public assistance). The Court in *Graham* applied strict scrutiny, reasoning that aliens were a particularly disabled class since they are unable to vote and may often be the target of economic protectionism or bias. However, strict scrutiny does not apply to the exclusion of aliens from the right to vote, itself, or public office or service on a jury. These matters of basic citizenship or self-government can be reserved to citizens, and the government needs only a rational basis to do so. *See, e.g., Foley v. Connelie*, 435 U.S. 291 (1978) (upholding a state law requiring citizenship to be a police officer). *Accord Ambach v. Norwich*, 441 U.S. 68 (1979) (citizenship required for public school teacher). Aliens may also be excluded because of Congress' plenary authority over immigration. Thus, in *Matthews v. Diaz*, 426 U.S. 67 (1976), the Court upheld the federal exclusion of those aliens who had not been admitted for permanent residence and resided in America for at least five years from Medicaid benefits. Thus, unlike state and local governments who are bound by the Court's decision in *Graham, supra*, Congress and the President in the implementation of foreign policy, of which immigration is a part, may discriminate against aliens for rational reasons. *Cf., Hampton v. Wong*, 426 U.S. 88 (1976) (the deference does not extend to federal decisions made by subordinate agencies unless they are directly implementing immigration or foreign policy). In a decision of some controversy, the Supreme Court held in *Plyler v. Doe*, 457 U.S. 202 (1982), that it was irrational for a state to exclude the children of illegal aliens from public schools unless they reimbursed the school system. The Court, as a matter of social compassion, saw the children as "blameless," and that in any event, creating an illiterate sub-class would simply aggravate crime and other social problems. Chief Justice Burger in dissent thought the matter better handled by the legislature since neither a fundamental right nor suspect class was implicated. California responded to *Plyler* by passing Proposition 187 denying undocumented aliens a public education. A lower court has invalidated the measure as preempted by Congress' immigration authority. *League of United American Citizens v. Wilson*, 908 F. Supp. 755 (C.D. Cal. 1995).

Illegitimate children are accorded intermediate scrutiny in the Court's cases. For example, in *Trimble v. Gordon*, 430 U.S. 762 (1977), the Court struck an Illinois law that prevented illegitimate children from inheriting from a father who died without a will. *Cf. Labine v. Vincent*, 401 U.S. 532 (1971), a state law denying inheritance from the father of an illegitimate child unless the child has been formally acknowledged during the father's lifetime is constitutional. The Court thus appears unwilling to deny all benefits or privileges to illegitimate children, but willing to accept reasonable distinctions within the class of illegitimate children.

6. Other classifications — those premised upon age, wealth, and disability, for example — are subject to rational basis review. In *Massachusetts Board of Retirement v. Murgia*, 427 U.S. 307 (1976), the Court sustained a Massachusetts law requiring police officers to retire at age 50. Unlike race or gender, age is a stage that all reach, it is not an immutable characteristic and states must have reasonable discretion to make policy judgments about its effect on given responsibilities. Nor has the Court applied heightened scrutiny to wealth. For example, in *Dandridge v. Williams*, 397 U.S. 471 (1970), the Court sustained a welfare cap on families regardless of the size of the family. Different laws affect income groups differently, and again, the Court was unwilling to second-guess the legislature in matters of policy. In any event, one's relative wealth is also not immutable and therefore less likely to be the basis of invidious distinction. Finally, with respect to disability, the Court, too, has applied a rational basis standard, though occasionally one with a "bite." In *City of Cleburne v. Cleburne Living Center, Inc.*, 473 U.S. 432 (1985), the Court invalidated a special permit requirement for a group home for the mentally disabled, even though its general deference in economic and land use matters would have led to the opposite result. Since the local ordinance allowed for other congregate uses in the same place, like boarding houses and fraternities, the Court could discern no rational basis — other than bias — for the permit requirement's application to the mentally disabled.

7.   In recent years, the issue of gay rights has presented the Court with some opportunity to evaluate whether sexual orientation is a legitimate basis for legal characterization. The issue is complicated because much religious and moral teaching finds homosexual practice to be spiritually or culturally disordered. *See, e.g.*, John M. Finnis, *Law, Morality and "Sexual Orientation"*, 69 Notre Dame L. Rev. 1049, 1070–76 (1994) (arguing that homosexual activity may be banned because it is against the common good and different than heterosexual activity that is an authentic union and open to the possibility, though not the certainty, of childbirth); Robert P. George & Gerard V. Bradley, *Marriage and the Liberal Imagination*, 84 Geo. L.J. 301, 318–20 (1995) (arguing that homosexual activity is intrinsically immoral and that "the state ought not to institutionalize . . . same sex [marriage]"); *but see also* Michael J. Perry, *The Morality of Homosexual Conduct: A Response to John Finnis*, 9 Notre Dame J.L. Ethics & Pub. Pol'y 41, 47 49 (1995) (questioning Finnis' premise that only the sexual union of a married couple can be a "single reality"). The issue is further complicated by the fact that sexual orientation classifications arguably implicate both status and conduct. Because of the former, there are political calls to treat sexual orientation classifications as the equivalent of race or gender classifications, and thus entitled to heightened scrutiny. Thus far, the Court has not reached that result — at least, not explicitly. The classification side of the sexual orientation debate is taken up in *Romer v. Evans*, below.

The conduct aspect of the sexual orientation debate, on the other hand, invokes notions of liberty and hence of the potential for heightened scrutiny under the "fundamental rights" aspect of equal protection analysis. That aspect of the debate, and the Court's contribution to it, is taken up in Chapter 9.

D.   SEXUAL ORIENTATION

ROMER v. EVANS
517 U.S. 620 (1996)

Justice Kennedy delivered the opinion of the Court.

One century ago, the first Justice Harlan admonished this Court that the Constitution "neither knows nor tolerates classes among citizens." *Plessy v.*

Ferguson (1896) (dissenting opinion). Unheeded then, those words now are understood to state a commitment to the law's neutrality where the rights of persons are at stake. The Equal Protection Clause enforces this principle and today requires us to hold invalid a provision of Colorado's Constitution.

I

The enactment challenged in this case is an amendment to the Constitution of the State of Colorado, adopted in a 1992 statewide referendum. The parties and the state courts refer to it as "Amendment 2," its designation when submitted to the voters. The impetus for the amendment and the contentious campaign that preceded its adoption came in large part from ordinances that had been passed in various Colorado municipalities. For example, the cities of Aspen and Boulder and the City and County of Denver each had enacted ordinances which banned discrimination in many transactions and activities, including housing, employment, education, public accommodations, and health and welfare services. What gave rise to the statewide controversy was the protection the ordinances afforded to persons discriminated against by reason of their sexual orientation. Amendment 2 repeals these ordinances to the extent they prohibit discrimination on the basis of "homosexual, lesbian or bisexual orientation, conduct, practices or relationships."

Yet Amendment 2, in explicit terms, does more than repeal or rescind these provisions. It prohibits all legislative, executive or judicial action at any level of state or local government designed to protect the named class, a class we shall refer to as homosexual persons or gays and lesbians. . . .

Soon after Amendment 2 was adopted, this litigation to declare its invalidity and enjoin its enforcement was commenced in the District Court for the City and County of Denver. Among the plaintiffs (respondents here) were homosexual persons, some of them government employees. They alleged that enforcement of Amendment 2 would subject them to immediate and substantial risk of discrimination on the basis of their sexual orientation. . . .

The trial court granted a preliminary injunction to stay enforcement of Amendment 2, and an appeal was taken to the Supreme Court of Colorado. Sustaining the interim injunction and remanding the case for further proceedings, the State Supreme Court held that Amendment 2 was subject to strict scrutiny under the Fourteenth Amendment because it infringed the fundamental right of gays and lesbians to participate in the political process. To reach this conclusion, the state court relied on our voting rights cases, and on our precedents involving discriminatory restructuring of governmental decisionmaking. On remand, the State advanced various arguments in an effort to show that Amendment 2 was narrowly tailored to serve compelling interests, but the trial court found none sufficient. It enjoined enforcement of Amendment 2, and the Supreme Court of Colorado, in a second opinion, affirmed the ruling. We granted certiorari and now affirm the judgment, but on a rationale different from that adopted by the State Supreme Court.

II

The State's principal argument in defense of Amendment 2 is that it puts gays and lesbians in the same position as all other persons. So, the State says, the measure does no more than deny homosexuals special rights. This reading of the amendment's language is implausible. We rely not upon our own interpretation of the amendment but upon the authoritative construction of Colorado's Supreme Court. The state court, deeming it unnecessary to determine the full extent of the amendment's reach, found it invalid even on a modest reading of its implications. The critical discussion of the amendment . . . is as follows:

> "The immediate objective of Amendment 2 is, at a minimum, to repeal existing statutes, regulations, ordinances, and policies of state and local entities that barred discrimination based on sexual orientation.

> "The 'ultimate effect' of Amendment 2 is to prohibit any governmental entity from adopting similar, or more protective statutes, regulations, ordinances, or policies in the future unless the state constitution is first amended to permit such measures."

Sweeping and comprehensive is the change in legal status effected by this law. So much is evident from the ordinances that the Colorado Supreme Court declared would be void by operation of Amendment 2. Homosexuals, by state decree, are put in a solitary class with respect to transactions and relations in both the private and governmental spheres. The amendment withdraws from homosexuals, but no others, specific legal protection from the injuries caused by discrimination, and it forbids reinstatement of these laws and policies.

The change that Amendment 2 works in the legal status of gays and lesbians in the private sphere is far-reaching, both on its own terms and when considered in light of the structure and operation of modern anti-discrimination laws. That structure is well illustrated by contemporary statutes and ordinances prohibiting discrimination by providers of public accommodations. "At common law, innkeepers, smiths, and others who 'made profession of a public employment,' were prohibited from refusing, without good reason, to serve a customer." The duty was a general one and did not specify protection for particular groups. The common law rules, however, proved insufficient in many instances, and it was settled early that the Fourteenth Amendment did not give Congress a general power to prohibit discrimination in public accommodations, *Civil Rights Cases* (1883). In consequence, most States have chosen to counter discrimination by enacting detailed statutory schemes.

Colorado's state and municipal laws typify this emerging tradition of statutory protection and follow a consistent pattern. . . .

These statutes and ordinances also depart from the common law by enumerating the groups or persons within their ambit of protection. Enumeration is the essential device used to make the duty not to discriminate concrete and to provide guidance for those who must comply. In following this approach, Colorado's state and local governments have not limited anti-discrimination laws to groups that have so far been given the protection of heightened equal protection scrutiny under our cases. [sex, illegitimacy, race, ancestry] Rather, they set forth an extensive catalogue of traits which cannot be the basis for discrimination, including age, military status, marital status, pregnancy, parenthood, custody of a minor child, political affiliation, physical or mental disability of an individual or of his or her associates — and, in recent times, sexual orientation.

Amendment 2 bars homosexuals from securing protection against the injuries that these public-accommodations laws address. That in itself is a severe consequence, but there is more. Amendment 2, in addition, nullifies specific legal protections for this targeted class in all transactions in housing, sale of real estate, insurance, health and welfare services, private education, and employment.

Not confined to the private sphere, Amendment 2 also operates to repeal and forbid all laws or policies providing specific protection for gays or lesbians from discrimination by every level of Colorado government. The State Supreme Court cited two examples of protections in the governmental sphere that are now rescinded and may not be reintroduced. The first is Colorado Executive Order D0035 (1990), which forbids employment discrimination against " 'all state employees, classified and exempt' on the basis of sexual orientation." Also repealed, and now forbidden, are "various provisions prohibiting discrimination based on sexual orientation at state colleges." The repeal of these measures and the prohibition against their future reenactment demonstrates that Amendment 2 has the same force and effect in Colorado's governmental sector as it does elsewhere and that it applies to policies as well as ordinary legislation.

Amendment 2's reach may not be limited to specific laws passed for the benefit of gays and lesbians. It is a fair, if not necessary, inference from the broad language of the amendment that it deprives gays and lesbians even of the protection of general laws and policies that prohibit arbitrary discrimination in governmental and private settings. At some point in the systematic administration of these laws, an official must determine whether homosexuality is an arbitrary and thus forbidden basis for decision. Yet a decision to that effect would itself amount to a policy prohibiting discrimination on the basis of homosexuality, and so would appear to be no more valid under Amendment 2 than the specific prohibitions against discrimination the state court held invalid.

If this consequence follows from Amendment 2, as its broad language suggests, it would compound the constitutional difficulties the law creates. The state court did not decide whether the amendment has this effect, however, and neither need we. In the course of rejecting the argument that Amendment 2 is intended to conserve resources to fight discrimination against suspect classes, the Colorado Supreme Court made the limited observation that the amendment is not intended to affect many anti-discrimination laws protecting non-suspect classes. . . .

III

The Fourteenth Amendment's promise that no person shall be denied the equal protection of the laws must co-exist with the practical necessity that most legislation classifies for one purpose or another, with resulting disadvantage to various groups or persons. We have attempted to reconcile the principle with the reality by stating that, if a law neither burdens a fundamental right nor targets a suspect class, we will uphold the legislative classification so long as it bears a rational relation to some legitimate end.

Amendment 2 fails, indeed defies, even this conventional inquiry. First, the amendment has the peculiar property of imposing a broad and undifferentiated disability on a single named group, an exceptional and, as we shall explain, invalid form of legislation. Second, its sheer breadth is so discontinuous with the reasons offered for it that the amendment seems inexplicable by anything but animus toward the class that it affects; it lacks a rational relationship to legitimate state interests.

Taking the first point, even in the ordinary equal protection case calling for the most deferential of standards, we insist on knowing the relation between the classification adopted and the object to be attained. . . . In the ordinary case, a law will be sustained if it can be said to advance a legitimate government interest, even if the law seems unwise or works to the disadvantage of a particular group, or if the rationale for it seems tenuous. . . . By requiring that the classification bear a rational relationship to an independent and legitimate legislative end, we ensure that classifications are not drawn for the purpose of disadvantaging the group burdened by the law.

Amendment 2 confounds this normal process of judicial review. It is at once too narrow and too broad. It identifies persons by a single trait and then denies them protection across the board. The resulting disqualification of a class of persons from the right to seek specific protection from the law is unprecedented in our jurisprudence. The absence of precedent for Amendment 2 is itself instructive; "[d]iscriminations of an unusual character especially suggest careful consideration to determine whether they are obnoxious to the constitutional provision."

It is not within our constitutional tradition to enact laws of this sort. Central both to the idea of the rule of law and to our own Constitution's guarantee of equal protection is the principle that government and each of its parts remain open on impartial terms to all who seek its assistance. " 'Equal protection of the laws is not achieved through indiscriminate imposition of inequalities.' " Respect for this principle explains why laws singling out a certain class of citizens for disfavored legal status or general hardships are rare. A law declaring that in general it shall be more difficult for one group of citizens than for all others to seek aid from the government is itself a denial of equal protection of the laws in the most literal sense. "The guaranty of 'equal protection of the laws is a pledge of the protection of equal laws.' "

Davis v. Beason (1890), not cited by the parties but relied upon by the dissent, is not evidence that Amendment 2 is within our constitutional tradition, and any reliance upon it as authority for sustaining the amendment is misplaced. In *Davis*, the Court approved an Idaho territorial statute denying Mormons, polygamists, and advocates of polygamy the right to vote and to hold office because, as the Court construed the statute, it "simply excludes from the privilege of voting, or of holding any office of honor, trust or profit, those who have been convicted of certain offences, and those who advocate a practical resistance to the laws of the Territory and justify and approve the commission of crimes forbidden by it." To the extent *Davis* held that persons advocating a certain practice may be denied the right to vote, it is no longer good law. *Brandenburg v. Ohio* (1969) (per curiam). To the extent it held that the groups designated in the statute may be deprived of the right to vote because of their status, its ruling could not stand without surviving strict scrutiny, a most doubtful outcome. To the extent *Davis* held that a convicted felon may be denied the right to vote, its holding is not implicated by our decision and is unexceptionable.

A second and related point is that laws of the kind now before us raise the inevitable inference that the disadvantage imposed is born of animosity toward the class of persons affected. "[I]f the constitutional conception of 'equal protection of the laws' means anything, it must at the very least mean that a bare . . . desire to harm a politically unpopular group cannot constitute a legitimate governmental interest." Even laws enacted for broad and ambitious purposes often can be explained by reference to legitimate public policies which justify the incidental disadvantages they impose on certain persons. Amendment 2, however, in making a general announcement that gays and lesbians shall not have any particular protections from the law, inflicts on them immediate, continuing, and real injuries that outrun and belie any legitimate justifications that may be claimed for it. We conclude that, in addition to the far-reaching deficiencies of Amendment 2 that we have noted, the principles it offends, in another sense, are conventional and venerable; a law must bear a rational relationship to a legitimate governmental purpose, and Amendment 2 does not.

The primary rationale the State offers for Amendment 2 is respect for other citizens' freedom of association, and in particular the liberties of landlords or employers who have personal or religious objections to homosexuality. Colorado also cites its interest in conserving resources to fight discrimination against other groups. The breadth of the Amendment is so far removed from these particular justifications that we find it impossible to credit them. We cannot say that Amendment 2 is directed to any identifiable legitimate purpose or discrete objective. It is a status-based enactment divorced from any factual context from which we could discern a relationship to legitimate state interests; it is a classification of persons undertaken for its own sake, something the Equal Protection Clause does not permit. "[C]lass legislation . . . [is] obnoxious to the prohibitions of the Fourteenth Amendment. . . ."

We must conclude that Amendment 2 classifies homosexuals not to further a proper legislative end but to make them unequal to everyone else. This Colorado cannot do. A State cannot so deem a class of persons a stranger to its laws. . . .

JUSTICE SCALIA, with whom THE CHIEF JUSTICE and JUSTICE THOMAS join, dissenting.

The Court has mistaken a Kulturkampf for a fit of spite. The constitutional amendment before us here is not the manifestation of a " 'bare . . . desire to harm' " homosexuals, but is rather a modest attempt by seemingly tolerant Coloradans to preserve traditional sexual mores against the efforts of a politically powerful minority to revise those mores through use of the laws. That objective, and the means chosen to achieve it, are not only unimpeachable under any constitutional doctrine hitherto pronounced (hence the opinion's heavy reliance upon principles of righteousness rather than judicial holdings); they have been specifically approved by the Congress of the United States and by this Court.

In holding that homosexuality cannot be singled out for disfavorable treatment, the Court contradicts a decision, unchallenged here, pronounced only 10 years ago, see *Bowers v. Hardwick* (1986), and places the prestige of this institution behind the proposition that opposition to homosexuality is as reprehensible as racial or religious bias. Whether it is or not is *precisely* the cultural debate that gave rise to the Colorado constitutional amendment (and to the preferential laws against which the amendment was directed). Since the Constitution of the United States says nothing about this subject, it is left to be resolved by normal democratic means, including the democratic adoption of provisions in state constitutions. This Court has no business imposing upon all Americans the resolution favored by the elite class from which the Members of this institution are selected, pronouncing that "animosity" toward homosexuality is evil. I vigorously dissent.

* * *

Today's opinion has no foundation in American constitutional law, and barely pretends to. The people of Colorado have adopted an entirely reasonable provision which does not even disfavor homosexuals in any substantive sense, but merely denies them preferential treatment. Amendment 2 is designed to prevent piecemeal deterioration of the sexual morality favored by a majority of Coloradans, and is not only an appropriate means to that legitimate end, but a means that Americans have employed before. Striking it down is an act, not of judicial judgment, but of political will. I dissent.

NOTES AND QUESTIONS

1. What does Justice Scalia mean when he says, dissenting, that "[t]he Court has mistaken a Kulturkampf for a fit of spite." *Romer*, 517 U.S. at 636 (Scalia, J., dissenting). What does that have to do with constitutional law? It was often said in the late twentieth century that the United States was engaged in a cultural civil war, but as this edition goes to press in 2014, the war over same-sex marriage at least seems to be winding down rather unexpectedly without serious skirmish. What happened? Increasingly same sex marriage is accepted by the people through a legislative means. Yet, there is genuine uncertainty over how to accommodate religious beliefs that preclude formal cooperation with such unions or relationships. It is conceded by all that no religion ought to be forced to change its doctrine or to extend marital blessing to that which is unrecognized by the particular faith tradition. What is in dispute beyond that, however, is the extent to which church property that is otherwise available as a public accommodation, (*e.g.*, the church hall) can be withheld from a same-sex related use or the extent to which a member of the religious congregation can refuse to, say, provide flowers or catering services. Obviously, the farther one moves from the essential or core religious practice toward auxiliary services the more a denial of that service seems appropriately condemned as discrimination, rather than religious liberty. But, as is obvious as well, it is an extremely sensitive subject on both sides.

2. *Romer* is to some degree an example of the occasional inconsistent application of the deferential rational basis standard. There have been a few other examples. As mentioned earlier in this Chapter, in *City of Cleburne v. Cleburne*

Living Center, 473 U.S. 432 (1985), the Court ostensibly used rational basis review to invalidate a zoning ordinance that irrationally (but no more so than many land use requirements) excluded a home for the mentally disabled from a residential district. Today, such practices would violate the federal Fair Housing Act, as amended, but *Cleburne* pre-dated that amendment. Also, *Metropolitan Life Insurance Company v. Ward*, 470 U.S. 869 (1985), invalidated an Alabama law that taxed in-state insurers much less than out-of-state companies.

3. In *Equality Foundation of Greater Cincinnati, Inc. v. City of Cincinnati*, 54 F.3d 261 (6th Cir. 1995), the appellate court held that sexual orientation was not a suspect classification. The court thus approved a city charter amendment providing that the "City of Cincinnati and its various Boards and Commissions may not enact, adopt, enforce or administer any ordinance, regulation, rule or policy which provides that homosexual, lesbian, or bisexual orientation, status, conduct, or relationship constitutes, entitles, or otherwise provides a person with the basis to have any claim of minority or protected status, quota preference or other preferential treatment." The appellate court found sexual orientation not to be a suspect class with the following reasoning:

> Assuming *arguendo* the truth of the scientific theory that sexual orientation is a "characteristic beyond the control of the individual" as found by the trial court, the reality remains that no law can successfully be drafted that is calculated to burden or penalize, or to benefit or protect, an unidentifiable group or class of individuals whose identity is defined by subjective and unapparent characteristics such as innate desires, drives, and thoughts. Those persons having a homosexual "orientation" simply do not, as such, comprise an identifiable class. Many homosexuals successfully conceal their orientation. Because homosexuals generally are not identifiable "on sight" unless they elect to be so identifiable by conduct (such as public displays of homosexual affection or self-proclamation of homosexual tendencies), they cannot constitute a suspect class or a quasi-suspect class because "they do not [necessarily] exhibit obvious, immutable, or distinguishing characteristics that define them as a discrete group[.]"

> Therefore, *Bowers v. Hardwick* and its progeny command that, as a matter of law, gays, lesbians, and bisexuals cannot constitute either a "suspect class" or a "quasi-suspect class," and, accordingly, the district court's application of the intermediate heightened scrutiny standard to the constitutional analysis of the Amendment was erroneous.

Bowers v. Hardwick (1986) held that homosexual sodomy was not a protected liberty under the Due Process Clause of the Fourteenth Amendment, and as discussed in the next Chapter, has since been overruled in *Lawrence v. Texas* (2003), which found a privacy protection for intimate sexual activity in one's home under a due process analysis. Does the overruling of *Bowers* affect the determination of whether or not sexual orientation is a suspect class? The Sixth Circuit's decision in *Equality Foundation*, itself, was vacated and remanded for further consideration in light of the Court's decision in *Romer*. Justices Scalia and Thomas and the Chief Justice dissented from that remand.

The view that sexual orientation is *not* a suspect classification was nominally adhered to by the Supreme Judicial Court of Massachusetts in *Goodridge v. Department of Public Health*, 440 Mass. 309 (2003), which nevertheless found that Massachusetts' statutory definition of marriage as between one man and one woman was unconstitutional even under rational basis review. The California Supreme Court, on the other hand, held in *In re Marriage Cases*, 43 Cal. 4th 757 (2008), that sexual orientation *is* a suspect classification, and further that the fundamental right to marry could not be denied same-sex couples under the Equal Protection Clause of the California constitution. The extension of marriage to same sex couples was subsequently overturned by voter initiative in November 2008 (Proposition 8), although both the validity of Proposition 8, and whether it has retroactive effect, remain to be determined by a subsequent legal challenge still pending at the time of publication.

4. The issues surrounding sexual orientation are not easy questions and the moral and cultural issues at stake go to the heart of the Republic. What would the natural law thinkers that influenced the Nation's founding have to say on this subject?. *See* Raymond B. Marcin, *Natural Law, Homosexual Conduct, and the Public Policy Exception*, 32 CREIGHTON L. REV. 67 (1998). In the next Chapter — devoted to issues of family and even life, itself — we conclude these materials exploring constitutional theory and application in light of the Nation's natural law premises and related history.

UNITED STATES v. WINDSOR
133 S. Ct. 2675 (2013)

JUSTICE KENNEDY delivered the opinion of the Court.

Two women then resident in New York were married in a lawful ceremony in Ontario, Canada, in 2007. Edith Windsor and Thea Spyer returned to their home in New York City. When Spyer died in 2009, she left her entire estate to Windsor. Windsor sought to claim the [federal] estate tax exemption for surviving spouses. She was barred from doing so, however, by a federal law, the Defense of Marriage Act, which excludes a same-sex partner from the definition of "spouse" as that term is used in federal statutes. Windsor paid the taxes but filed suit to challenge the constitutionality of this provision. The United States District Court and the Court of Appeals ruled that this portion of the statute is unconstitutional and ordered the United States to pay Windsor a refund. This Court granted certiorari and now affirms the judgment in Windsor's favor.

I

In 1996, as some States were beginning to consider the concept of same-sex marriage . . . and before any State had acted to permit it, Congress enacted the Defense of Marriage Act (DOMA) . . . . DOMA contains two operative sections: Section 2, which has not been challenged here, allows States to refuse to recognize same-sex marriages performed under the laws of other States. . . .

Section 3 is at issue here. It . . . provide[s] a federal definition of "marriage" and "spouse" . . . as follows:

> "In determining the meaning of any Act of Congress, or of any ruling, regulation, or interpretation of the various administrative bureaus and agencies of the United States, the word 'marriage' means only a legal union between one man and one woman as husband and wife, and the word 'spouse' refers only to a person of the opposite sex who is a husband or a wife." . . .

The definitional provision does not by its terms forbid States from enacting laws permitting same-sex marriages or civil unions or providing state benefits to residents in that status. The enactment's comprehensive definition of marriage for purposes of all federal statutes and other regulations or directives covered by its terms, however, does control over 1,000 federal laws in which marital or spousal status is addressed as a matter of federal law. . . .

* * *

While [Windsor's] tax refund suit was pending, the Attorney General of the United States notified the Speaker of the House of Representatives . . . that the Department of Justice would no longer defend the constitutionality of DOMA's § 3. Noting that "the Department has previously defended DOMA against . . . challenges involving legally married same-sex couples," . . . the Attorney General informed Congress that "the President has concluded that given a number of factors, including a documented history of discrimination, classifications based on sexual orientation should be subject to a heightened standard of scrutiny." . . . The Department of Justice has submitted many . . . letters over the years refusing to defend laws it deems unconstitutional . . . . This case is unusual, however, because the . . . letter . . . reflected the Executive's own conclusion, relying on a definition still being debated and considered in the courts, that heightened equal protection scrutiny should apply to laws that classify on the basis of sexual orientation.

Although "the President . . . instructed the Department not to defend the statute in *Windsor*," he also decided "that Section 3 will continue to be enforced by the Executive Branch" and that the United States had an "interest in providing Congress a full and fair opportunity to participate in the litigation of those cases." . . . The stated rationale for this dual-track procedure (determination of unconstitutionality coupled with ongoing enforcement) was to "recogniz[e] the judiciary as the final arbiter of the constitutional claims raised." . . .

In response to the notice from the Attorney General, the Bipartisan Legal Advisory Group (BLAG) of the House of Representatives voted to intervene in the litigation to defend the constitutionality of § 3 of DOMA. The Department of Justice did not oppose limited intervention by BLAG. The District Court denied BLAG's motion to enter the suit as of right, [but] did grant intervention by BLAG as an interested party. . . .

On the merits of the tax refund suit, the District Court . . . held that § 3 of DOMA is unconstitutional and ordered the Treasury to refund the tax with interest. . . . [T]he Court of Appeals for the Second Circuit affirmed the District Court's judgment. It applied heightened scrutiny to classifications based on sexual orientation, as both the Department and Windsor had urged. The United States has not complied with the judgment. Windsor has not received her refund, and the Executive Branch continues to enforce § 3 of DOMA.

In granting certiorari on the question of the constitutionality of § 3 of DOMA, the Court requested argument on two additional questions: whether the United States' agreement with Windsor's legal position precludes further review and whether BLAG has standing to appeal the case. All parties agree that the Court has jurisdiction to decide this case; and, with the case in that framework, the Court appointed Professor Vicki Jackson as *amicus curiae* to argue the position that the Court lacks jurisdiction to hear the dispute. . . .

* * *

II

[The Court first dealt with the issue of justiciability in the context of President Obama's order to the Attorney General, made during the District Court proceedings, not to defend the constitutionality of § 3 of DOMA, ostensibly removing adverseness from the main issue in the case. The Court ruled that since the Executive branch of the federal government, although conceding the unconstitutionality of § 3, was nonetheless refusing to pay the refund that the plaintiff had sought and that the District Court eventually ordered, an economic injury was still at stake and the case was, at the District Court level at least, an Article III controversy. When the District Court ruled in favor of the plaintiff (Windsor) in the curious circumstance in which the defendant (United States) was in agreement with the main tenet of the court's ruling (that § 3 was unconstitutional), an appellate anomaly resulted — both sides had won. Nonetheless, the Court decided that the Executive branch, in refusing to pay the tax refund ordered by the District Court, retained a stake sufficient to support Article III jurisdiction on appeal, and the participation of BLAG supplied the needed adverseness required by prudential limits on the exercise of jurisdiction.]

III

. . . It seems fair to conclude that, until recent years, many citizens had not even considered the possibility that two persons of the same sex might aspire to occupy the same status and dignity as that of a man and woman in lawful marriage. For marriage between a man and a woman no doubt had been thought of by most people as essential to the very definition of that term and to its role and function throughout the history of civilization. That belief, for many who long have held it, became even more urgent, more cherished when challenged. For others, however, came the beginnings of a new perspective, a new insight. Accordingly some States concluded that same-sex marriage ought to be given recognition and validity in the law for those same-sex couples who wish to define themselves by their commitment to each other. The limitation of lawful marriage to heterosexual couples, which for centuries had been deemed both necessary and fundamental, came to be seen in New York and certain other States as an unjust exclusion.

Slowly at first and then in rapid course, the laws of New York came to acknowledge the urgency of this issue for same-sex couples who wanted to affirm their commitment to one another before their children, their family, their friends, and their community. And so New York recognized same-sex marriages performed elsewhere; and then it later amended its own marriage laws to permit same-sex marriage. New York, in common with, as of this writing, 11 other States and the District of Columbia, decided that same-sex couples should have the right to marry and so live with pride in themselves and their union and in a status of equality with all other married persons. After a statewide deliberative process that enabled its citizens to discuss and weigh arguments for and against same-sex marriage, New York acted to enlarge the definition of marriage to correct what its citizens and elected representatives perceived to be an injustice that they had not earlier known or understood. . . .

Against this background of lawful same-sex marriage in some States, the design, purpose, and effect of DOMA should be considered as the beginning point in deciding whether it is valid under the Constitution. By history and tradition the definition and regulation of marriage, as will be discussed in more detail, has been treated as being within the authority and realm of the separate States. Yet it is further established that Congress, in enacting discrete statutes, can make determinations that bear on marital rights and privileges. . . . [T]he general principle [is] that when the Federal Government acts in the exercise of its own proper authority, it has a wide choice of the mechanisms and means to adopt. [Citing *McCulloch v. Maryland* (1819).] Congress has the power both to ensure efficiency in the administration of its programs and to choose what larger goals and policies to pursue.

*   *   *

Though [several examples cited by the Court] establish the constitutionality of limited federal laws that regulate the meaning of marriage in order to further federal policy, DOMA has a far greater reach; for it enacts a directive applicable to over 1,000 federal statutes and the whole realm of federal regulations. And its operation is directed to a class of persons that the laws of New York, and of 11 other States, have sought to protect. . . .

In order to assess the validity of that intervention it is necessary to discuss the extent of the state power and authority over marriage as a matter of history and tradition. State laws defining and regulating marriage, of course, must respect the constitutional rights of persons, see, *e.g., Loving v. Virginia* (1967); but, subject to those guarantees, "regulation of domestic relations" is "an area that has long been regarded as a virtually exclusive province of the States." *Sosna v. Iowa* (1975).

The recognition of civil marriages is central to state domestic relations law applicable to its residents and citizens. . . . The definition of marriage is the foundation of the State's broader authority to regulate the subject of domestic relations with respect to the "[p]rotection of offspring, property interests, and the enforcement of marital responsibilities." [Quoting *Williams v. North Carolina* (1942).] "[T]he states, at the time of the adoption of the Constitution, possessed full power over the subject of marriage and divorce . . . [and] the Constitution delegated no authority to the Government of the United States on the subject of marriage and divorce." [Quoting *Haddock v. Haddock* (1906).]

Consistent with this allocation of authority, the Federal Government, through our history, has deferred to state-law policy decisions with respect to domestic relations. . . . In order to respect this principle, the federal courts, as a general rule, do not adjudicate issues of marital status even when there might otherwise be a basis for federal jurisdiction. See *Ankenbrandt v. Richards* (1992). Federal courts will not hear divorce and custody cases even if they arise in diversity because of "the virtually exclusive primacy . . . of the States in the regulation of domestic relations." [Quoting *Ankenbrandt* (Blackmun, J., concurring in judgment).]

The significance of state responsibilities for the definition and regulation of marriage dates to the Nation's beginning; for "when the Constitution was adopted the common understanding was that the domestic relations of husband and wife and parent and child were matters reserved to the States." . . . Marriage laws vary in some respects from State to State. For example, the required minimum age is 16 in Vermont, but only 13 in New Hampshire. . . . Likewise the permissible degree of consanguinity can vary(most States permit first cousins to marry, but a handful — such as Iowa and Washington . . . — prohibit the practice). But these rules are in every event consistent within each State.

Against this background DOMA rejects the long-established precept that the incidents, benefits, and obligations of marriage are uniform for all married couples within each State, though they may vary, subject to constitutional guarantees, from one State to the next. Despite these considerations, it is unnecessary to decide whether this federal intrusion on state power is a violation of the Constitution because it disrupts the federal balance.

The State's power in defining the marital relation is of central relevance in this case quite apart from principles of federalism. Here the State's decision to give this class of persons the right to marry conferred upon them a dignity and status of immense import. When the State used its historic and essential authority to define the marital relation in this way, its role and its power in making the decision enhanced the recognition, dignity, and protection of the class in their own community. DOMA, because of its reach and extent, departs from this history and tradition of reliance on state law to define marriage. " '[D]iscriminations of an unusual character especially suggest careful consideration to determine whether they are obnoxious to the constitutional provision.' " [Quoting *Romer*; in turn, quoting *Louisville Gas & Elec. Co. v. Coleman* (1928)).]

The Federal Government uses this state-defined class for the opposite purpose — to impose restrictions and disabilities. That result requires this Court now to address whether the resulting injury and indignity is a deprivation of an essential part of the liberty protected by the Fifth Amendment. What the State of New York treats as alike the federal law deems unlike by a law designed to injure the same class the State seeks to protect.

In acting first to recognize and then to allow same-sex marriages, New York was responding "to the initiative of those who [sought] a voice in shaping the destiny of their own times." [Quoting *Bond v. United States* (2011).] These actions were without doubt a proper exercise of its sovereign authority within our federal system, all in the way that the Framers of the Constitution intended. The dynamics of state government in the federal system are to allow the formation of consensus respecting the way the members of a discrete community treat each other in their daily contact and constant interaction with each other.

The States' interest in defining and regulating the marital relation, subject to constitutional guarantees, stems from the understanding that marriage is more than a routine classification for purposes of certain statutory benefits. Private, consensual sexual intimacy between two adult persons of the same sex may not be punished by the State, and it can form "but one element in a personal bond that is more enduring." [Quoting *Lawrence v. Texas* (2003).] By its recognition of the validity of same-sex marriages performed in other jurisdictions and then by authorizing same-sex unions and same-sex marriages, New York sought to give further protection and dignity to that bond. For same-sex couples who wished to be married, the State acted to give their lawful conduct a lawful status. This status is a far-reaching legal acknowledgment of the intimate relationship between two people, a relationship deemed by the State worthy of dignity in the community equal with all other marriages. It reflects both the community's considered perspective on the historical roots of the institution of marriage and its evolving understanding of the meaning of equality.

IV

DOMA seeks to injure the very class New York seeks to protect. By doing so it violates basic due process and equal protection principles applicable to the Federal Government. See U. S. CONST., AMDT. 5; *Bolling v. Sharpe* (1954). The Constitution's guarantee of equality "must at the very least mean that a bare congressional desire to harm a politically unpopular group cannot" justify disparate treatment of that group. [Quoting *Department of Agriculture v. Moreno* (1973).] In determining whether a law is motived by an improper animus or purpose, "'[d]iscriminations of an unusual character'" especially require careful consideration. [Quoting *Moreno*; in turn, quoting *Romer*.] DOMA cannot survive under these principles. The responsibility of the States for the regulation of domestic relations is an important indicator of the substantial societal impact the State's classifications have in the daily lives and customs of its people. DOMA's unusual deviation from the usual tradition of recognizing and accepting state definitions of marriage here operates to deprive same-sex couples of the benefits and responsibilities that come with the federal recognition of their marriages. This is strong evidence of a law having the purpose and effect of disapproval of that class. The avowed purpose and practical effect of the law here in question are to impose a disadvantage, a separate status, and so a stigma upon all who enter into same-sex marriages made lawful by the unquestioned authority of the States.

The history of DOMA's enactment and its own text demonstrate that interference with the equal dignity of same-sex marriages, a dignity conferred by the States in the exercise of their sovereign power, was more than an incidental effect of the federal statute. It was its essence. The House Report announced its conclusion that "it is both appropriate and necessary for Congress to do what it can to defend the institution of traditional heterosexual marriage. . . . H. R. 3396 is appropriately entitled the 'Defense of Marriage Act.' The effort to redefine 'marriage' to extend to homosexual couples is a truly radical proposal that would fundamentally alter the institution of marriage." . . . The House concluded that DOMA expresses "both moral disapproval of homosexuality, and a moral conviction that heterosexuality better comports with traditional (especially Judeo-Christian) morality." . . . The stated purpose of the law was to promote an "interest in protecting the traditional moral teachings reflected in heterosexual-only marriage laws." . . . Were there any doubt of this far-reaching purpose, the title of the Act confirms it: The Defense of Marriage.

The arguments put forward by BLAG are just as candid about the congressional purpose to influence or interfere with state sovereign choices about who may be married. As the title and dynamics of the bill indicate, its purpose is to discourage enactment of state same-sex marriage laws and to restrict the freedom and choice of couples married under those laws if they are enacted. The congressional goal was "to put a thumb on the scales and influence a state's decision as to how to shape its own marriage laws." [Quoting *Massachusetts v. United States Dept. of Health and Human Servs.* (1st Cir. 2012).] The Act's demonstrated purpose is to ensure that if any State decides to recognize same-sex marriages, those unions will be treated as second-class marriages for purposes of federal law. This raises a most serious question under the Constitution's Fifth Amendment.

DOMA's operation in practice confirms this purpose. When New York adopted a law to permit same-sex marriage, it sought to eliminate inequality; but DOMA frustrates that objective through a system-wide enactment with no identified connection to any particular area of federal law. DOMA writes inequality into the entire United States Code. The particular case at hand concerns the estate tax, but DOMA is more than a simple determination of what should or should not be allowed as an estate tax refund. Among the over 1,000 statutes and numerous federal regulations that DOMA controls are laws pertaining to Social Security, housing, taxes, criminal sanctions, copyright, and veterans' benefits.

DOMA's principal effect is to identify a subset of state-sanctioned marriages and make them unequal. The principal purpose is to impose inequality, not for other reasons like governmental efficiency. Responsibilities, as well as rights, enhance the dignity and integrity of the person. And DOMA contrives to deprive some couples married under the laws of their State, but not other couples, of both rights and responsibilities. By creating two contradictory marriage regimes within the same State, DOMA forces same-sex couples to live as married for the purpose of state law but unmarried for the purpose of federal law, thus diminishing the stability and predictability of basic personal relations the State has found it proper to acknowledge and protect. By this dynamic DOMA undermines both the public and private significance of state-sanctioned same-sex marriages; for it tells those couples, and all the world, that their otherwise valid marriages are unworthy of federal recognition. This places same-sex couples in an unstable position of being in a second-tier marriage. The differentiation demeans the couple, whose moral and sexual choices the Constitution protects, see *Lawrence* . . . , and whose relationship the State has sought to dignify. And it humiliates tens of thousands of children now being raised by same-sex couples. The law in question makes it even more difficult for the children to understand the integrity and closeness of their own family and its concord with other families in their community and in their daily lives.

Under DOMA, same-sex married couples have their lives burdened, by reason of government decree, in visible and public ways. By its great reach, DOMA touches many aspects of married and family life, from the mundane to the profound. It prevents same-sex married couples from obtaining government healthcare benefits they would otherwise receive. . . . It deprives them of the Bankruptcy Code's special protections for domestic-support obligations. . . . It forces them to follow a complicated procedure to file their state and federal taxes jointly. . . . It prohibits them from being buried together in veterans' cemeteries. . . . For certain married couples, DOMA's unequal effects are even more serious. The federal penal code makes it a crime to "assaul[t], kidna[p], or murde[r] . . . a member of the immediate family" of "a United States official, a United States judge, [or] a Federal law enforcement officer," . . . with the intent to influence or retaliate against that official . . . . Although a "spouse" qualifies as a member of the officer's "immediate family," . . . DOMA makes this protection inapplicable to same-sex spouses.

DOMA also brings financial harm to children of same-sex couples. It raises the cost of health care for families by taxing health benefits provided by employers to their workers' same-sex spouses. . . . And it denies or reduces benefits allowed to families upon the loss of a spouse and parent, benefits that are an integral part of family security. . . .

DOMA divests married same-sex couples of the duties and responsibilities that are an essential part of married life and that they in most cases would be honored to accept were DOMA not in force. For instance, because it is expected that spouses will support each other as they pursue educational opportunities, federal law takes into consideration a spouse's income in calculating a student's federal financial aid eligibility. . . . Same-sex married couples are exempt from this requirement. The same is true with respect to federal ethics rules. Federal executive and agency officials are prohibited from "participat[ing] personally and substantially" in matters as to which they or their spouses have a financial interest. . . . A similar statute prohibits Senators, Senate employees, and their spouses from accepting high-value gifts from certain sources, . . . and another mandates detailed financial disclosures by numerous high-ranking officials and their spouses. . . . Under DOMA, however, these Government-integrity rules do not apply to same-sex spouses.

*   *   *

The power the Constitution grants it also restrains. And though Congress has great authority to design laws to fit its own conception of sound national policy, it cannot deny the liberty protected by the Due Process Clause of the Fifth Amendment.

What has been explained to this point should more than suffice to establish that the principal purpose and the necessary effect of this law are to demean those persons who are in a lawful same-sex marriage. This requires the Court to hold, as it now does, that DOMA is unconstitutional as a deprivation of the liberty of the person protected by the Fifth Amendment of the Constitution.

The liberty protected by the Fifth Amendment's Due Process Clause contains within it the prohibition against denying to any person the equal protection of the laws. . . . While the Fifth Amendment itself withdraws from Government the power to degrade or demean in the way this law does, the equal protection guarantee of the Fourteenth Amendment makes that Fifth Amendment right all the more specific and all the better understood and preserved.

The class to which DOMA directs its restrictions and restraints are those persons who are joined in same-sex marriages made lawful by the State. DOMA singles out a class of persons deemed by a State entitled to recognition and protection to enhance their own liberty. It imposes a disability on the class by refusing to acknowledge a status the State finds to be dignified and proper. DOMA instructs all federal officials, and indeed all persons with whom same-sex couples interact, including their own children, that their marriage is less worthy than the marriages of others. The federal statute is invalid, for no legitimate purpose overcomes the purpose and effect to disparage and to injure those whom the State, by its marriage laws, sought to protect in personhood and dignity. By seeking to displace this protection and treating those persons as living in marriages less respected than others, the federal statute is in violation of the Fifth Amendment. This opinion and its holding are confined to those lawful marriages.

The judgment of the Court of Appeals for the Second Circuit is affirmed.

Chief Justice Roberts, dissenting. [Omitted.]

Justice Scalia, with whom Justice Thomas joins, and with whom The Chief Justice joins as to Part I, dissenting. [Some footnotes have been omitted.]

This case is about power in several respects. It is about the power of our people to govern themselves, and the power of this Court to pronounce the law. Today's opinion aggrandizes the latter, with the predictable consequence of diminishing the former. We have no power to decide this case. And even if we did, we have no power under the Constitution to invalidate this democratically adopted legislation. The Court's errors on both points spring forth from the same diseased root: an exalted conception of the role of this institution in America.

I

A

[Justice Scalia critiqued the majority opinion's treatment of the justiciability issue. This part of Justice Scalia's dissent appears earlier in these materials.]

B

[Justice Scalia critiqued the treatment of the justiciability issue in Justice Alito's dissenting opinion. Omitted]

II

* * *

A

There are many remarkable things about the majority's merits holding. The first is how rootless and shifting its justifications are. For example, the opinion starts with seven full pages about the traditional power of States to define domestic relations — initially fooling many readers, I am sure, into thinking that this is a federalism opinion. But we are eventually told that "it is unnecessary to decide whether this federal intrusion on state power is a violation of the Constitution," and that "[t]he State's power in defining the marital relation is of central relevance in this case quite apart from principles of federalism" because "the State's decision to give this class of persons the right to marry conferred upon them a dignity and status of immense import." . . . But no one questions the power of the States to define marriage (with the concomitant conferral of dignity and status), so what is the point of devoting seven pages to describing how long and well established that power is? Even after the opinion has formally disclaimed reliance upon principles of federalism, mentions of "the usual tradition of recognizing and accepting state definitions of marriage" continue. . . . What to make of this? The opinion never explains. My guess is that the majority, while reluctant to suggest that defining the meaning of "marriage" in federal statutes is unsupported by any of the Federal Government's enumerated powers,[11] nonetheless needs some rhetorical basis to support its pretense that today's prohibition of laws excluding same-sex marriage is confined to the Federal Government (leaving the second, state-law shoe to be dropped later, maybe next Term). But I am only guessing.

Equally perplexing are the opinion's references to "the Constitution's guarantee of equality." . . . Near the end of the opinion, we are told that although the "equal protection guarantee of the Fourteenth Amendment makes [the] Fifth Amendment [due process] right all the more specific and all the better understood and preserved" — what can that mean? — "the Fifth Amendment itself withdraws from Government the power to degrade or demean in the way this law does." . . . The only possible interpretation of this statement is that the Equal Protection Clause, even the Equal Protection Clause as incorporated in the Due Process Clause, is not the basis for today's holding.

But the portion of the majority opinion that explains why DOMA is unconstitutional (Part IV) begins by citing *Bolling v. Sharpe* (1954), *Department of Agriculture v. Moreno* (1973), and *Romer v. Evans* (1996) — *all* of which are equal-protection cases.[12] And those three cases are the only authorities that the Court

---

[11] [4] Such a suggestion would be impossible, given the Federal Government's long history of making pronouncements regarding marriage — for example, conditioning Utah's entry into the Union upon its prohibition of polygamy. See Act of July 16, 1894, ch. 138, § 3, 28 Stat. 108 ("The constitution [of Utah]" must provide "perfect toleration of religious sentiment," "*Provided*, That polygamous or plural marriages are forever prohibited").

[12] [5] Since the Equal Protection Clause technically applies only against the States, see U. S. CONST., AMDT. 14, *Bolling* and *Moreno*, dealing with federal action, relied upon "the equal protection component

cites in Part IV about the Constitution's meaning, except for its citation of *Lawrence v. Texas* . . . (2003) (not an equal-protection case) to support its passing assertion that the Constitution protects the "moral and sexual choices" of same-sex couples . . . .

Moreover, if this is meant to be an equal-protection opinion, it is a confusing one. The opinion does not resolve and indeed does not even mention what had been the central question in this litigation: whether, under the Equal Protection Clause, laws restricting marriage to a man and a woman are reviewed for more than mere rationality. That is the issue that divided the parties and the court below . . . . In accord with my previously expressed skepticism about the Court's "tiers of scrutiny"approach, I would review this classification only for its rationality. . . . As nearly as I can tell, the Court agrees with that; its opinion does not apply strict scrutiny, and its central propositions are taken from rational-basis cases like *Moreno*. But the Court certainly does not *apply* anything that resembles that deferential framework. See *Heller v. Doe* (1993) (a classification "'must be upheld . . . if there is any reasonably conceivable state of facts'" that could justify it).

The majority opinion need not get into the strict-vs.-rational-basis scrutiny question, and need not justify its holding under either, because it says that DOMA is unconstitutional as "a deprivation of the liberty of the person protected by the Fifth Amendment of the Constitution" . . . ; that it violates "basic due process" principles . . . ; and that it inflicts an "injury and indignity" of a kind that denies "an essential part of the liberty protected by the Fifth Amendment" . . . . The majority never utters the dread words "substantive due process," perhaps sensing the disrepute into which that doctrine has fallen, but that is what those statements mean. Yet the opinion does not argue that same-sex marriage is"deeply rooted in this Nation's history and tradition" [quoting *Washington v. Glucksberg* (1997)], a claim that would of course be quite absurd. So would the further suggestion (also necessary, under our substantive-due-process precedents) that a world in which DOMA exists is one bereft of "ordered liberty." . . . (quoting *Palko v. Connecticut* (1937)). Some might conclude that this loaf could have used a while longer in the oven. But that would be wrong; it is already overcooked. The most expert care in preparation cannot redeem a bad recipe. The sum of all the Court's nonspecific hand-waving is that this law is invalid (maybe on equal-protection grounds, maybe on substantive-due-process grounds, and perhaps with some amorphous federalism component playing a role) because it is motivated by a "'bare . . . desire to harm'" couples in same-sex marriages. . . . It is this proposition with which I will therefore engage.

B

As I have observed before, the Constitution does not forbid the government to enforce traditional moral and sexual norms. See *Lawrence v. Texas* (2003) (SCALIA, J., dissenting). I will not swell the U. S. Reports with restatements of that point. It is enough to say that the Constitution neither requires nor forbids our society to approve of same-sex marriage, much as it neither requires nor forbids us to approve

---

of the Due Process Clause of the Fifth Amendment," [quoting *Moreno*.]

of no-fault divorce, polygamy, or the consumption of alcohol.

However, even setting aside traditional moral disapproval of same-sex marriage (or indeed same-sex sex), there are many perfectly valid — indeed, downright boring — justifying rationales for this legislation. Their existence ought to be the end of this case. For they give the lie to the Court's conclusion that only those with hateful hearts could have voted "aye" on this Act. And more importantly, they serve to make the contents of the legislators' hearts quite irrelevant: "It is a familiar principle of constitutional law that this Court will not strike down an otherwise constitutional statute on the basis of an alleged illicit legislative motive." *United States v. O'Brien* (1968). Or at least it was a familiar principle. By holding to the contrary, the majority has declared open season on any law that (in the opinion of the law's opponents and any panel of like-minded federal judges) can be characterized as mean-spirited.

The majority concludes that the only motive for this Act was the "bare . . . desire to harm a politically unpopular group." . . . Bear in mind that the object of this condemnation is not the legislature of some once-Confederate Southern state (familiar objects of the Court's scorn), . . . but our respected coordinate branches, the Congress and Presidency of the United States. Laying such a charge against them should require the most extraordinary evidence, and I would have thought that every attempt would be made to indulge a more anodyne explanation for the statute. The majority does the opposite — affirmatively concealing from the reader the arguments that exist in justification. It makes only a passing mention of the "arguments put forward" by the Act's defenders, and does not even trouble to paraphrase or describe them. . . . I imagine that this is because it is harder to maintain the illusion of the Act's supporters as unhinged members of a wild-eyed lynch mob when one first describes their views as *they* see them.

To choose just one of these defenders' arguments, DOMA avoids difficult choice-of-law issues that will now arise absent a uniform federal definition of marriage. . . . Imagine a pair of women who marry in Albany and then move to Alabama, which does not "recognize as valid any marriage of parties of the same sex." . . . When the couple files their next federal tax return, may it be a joint one? Which State's law controls, for federal-law purposes: their State of celebration (which recognizes the marriage) or their State of domicile (which does not)? (Does the answer depend on whether they were just visiting in Albany?) Are these questions to be answered as a matter of federal common law, or perhaps by borrowing a State's choice-of-law rules? If so, *which* State's? And what about States where the status of an out-of-state same-sex marriage is an unsettled question under local law? . . . DOMA avoided all of this uncertainty by specifying which marriages would be recognized for federal purposes. That is a classic purpose for a definitional provision.

Further, DOMA preserves the intended effects of prior legislation against then-unforeseen changes in circumstance. When Congress provided (for example) that a special estate-tax exemption would exist for spouses, this exemption reached only *opposite-sex* spouses — those being the only sort that were recognized in any State at the time of DOMA's passage. When it became clear that changes in state law might one day alter that balance, DOMA's definitional section was enacted to ensure that state-level experimentation did not automatically alter the basic operation of federal law, unless and until Congress made the further judgment to do so on its own. That is not animus — just stabilizing prudence. Congress has hardly demonstrated itself unwilling to make such further, revising judgments upon due deliberation. *See, e.g.,* Don't Ask, Don't Tell Repeal Act of 2010 . . . .

The Court mentions none of this. Instead, it accuses the Congress that enacted this law and the President who signed it of something much worse than, for example, having acted in excess of enumerated federal powers — or even having drawn distinctions that prove to be irrational.

Those legal errors may be made in good faith, errors though they are. But the majority says that the supporters of this Act acted with malice — with the "*purpose*" . . . "to disparage and to injure" same-sex couples. It says that the motivation for DOMA was to "demean" . . . ; to "impose inequality" . . . ; to "impose . . . a stigma" . . . ; to deny people "equal dignity" . . . ; to brand gay people as "unworthy" . . . ; and to "*humiliat*[*e*]" their children . . . (emphasis added).

I am sure these accusations are quite untrue. To be sure (as the majority points out), the legislation is called the Defense of Marriage Act. But to defend traditional marriage is not to condemn, demean, or humiliate those who would prefer other arrangements, any more than to defend the Constitution of the United States is to condemn, demean, or humiliate other constitutions. To hurl such accusations so casually demeans this institution. In the majority's judgment, any resistance to its holding is beyond the pale of reasoned disagreement. To question its high-handed invalidation of a presumptively valid statute is to act (the majority is sure) with the purpose to "disparage," "injure," "degrade," "demean," and "humiliate" our fellow human beings, our fellow citizens, who are homosexual. All that, simply for supporting an Act that did no more than codify an aspect of marriage that had been unquestioned in our society for most of its existence — indeed, had been unquestioned in virtually all societies for virtually all of human history. It is one thing for a society to elect change; it is another for a court of law to impose change by adjudging those who oppose it *hostes humani generis*, enemies of the human race.

* * *

The penultimate sentence of the majority's opinion is a naked declaration that "[t]his opinion and its holding are confined" to those couples "joined in same-sex marriages made lawful by the State." . . . I have heard such "bald, unreasoned disclaimer[s]" before. [Citing *Lawrence.*] When the Court declared a constitutional right to homosexual sodomy, we were assured that the case had nothing, nothing at all to do with "whether the government must give formal recognition to any relationship that homosexual persons seek to enter." . . . Now we are told that DOMA is invalid because it "demeans the couple, whose moral and sexual choices the Constitution protects," . . . — with an accompanying citation of *Lawrence*. It takes real cheek for today's majority to assure us, as it is going out the door, that a constitutional requirement to give formal recognition to same-sex marriage is not at issue here — when what has preceded that assurance is a lecture on how superior the majority's moral judgment in favor of same-sex marriage is to the Congress's hateful moral judgment against it. I promise you this: The only thing that will "confine" the Court's holding is its sense of what it can get away with.

* * *

In my opinion . . . , the view that this Court will take of state prohibition of same-sex marriage is indicated beyond mistaking by today's opinion. As I have said, the real rationale of today's opinion, whatever disappearing trail of its legalistic argle-bargle one chooses to follow, is that DOMA is motivated by " 'bare . . . desire to harm' " couples in same-sex marriages. . . . How easy it is, indeed how inevitable, to reach the same conclusion with regard to state laws denying same-sex couples marital status. Consider how easy (inevitable) it is to make the following substitutions in a passage from today's opinion . . . :

> "*This state law's* principal effect is to identify a subset of *constitutionally protected sexual relationships*, see *Lawrence*, and make them unequal. The principal purpose is to impose inequality, not for other reasons like governmental efficiency. Responsibilities, as well as rights, enhance the dignity and integrity of the person. And *this state law* contrives to deprive some couples *enjoying constitutionally protected sexual relationships*, but not other couples, of both rights and responsibilities."

Or try this passage . . . :

> "*This state law* tells those couples, and all the world, that their otherwise valid *relationships* are unworthy of *state* recognition. This places same-sex couples in an unstable position of being in a second-tier *relationship*. The differentiation demeans the couple, whose moral and sexual choices the Constitution protects, see *Lawrence* . . . ."

Or this . . . — which does not even require alteration, except as to the invented number:

> "And it humiliates thousands of children now being raised by same-sex couples. The law in question makes it even more difficult for the children to understand the integrity and closeness of their own family and its concord with other families in their community and in their daily lives."

Similarly transposable passages — deliberately transposable, I think — abound. In sum, that Court which finds it so horrific that Congress irrationally and hatefully robbed same-sex couples of the "personhood and dignity" which state legislatures conferred upon them, will of a certitude be similarly appalled by state legislatures' irrational and hateful failure to acknowledge that "personhood and dignity" in the first place. . . . As far as this Court is concerned, no one should be fooled; it is just a matter of listening and waiting for the other shoe.

By formally declaring anyone opposed to same-sex marriage an enemy of human decency, the majority arms well every challenger to a state law restricting marriage to its traditional definition. Henceforth those challengers will lead with this Court's declaration that there is "no legitimate purpose" served by such a law, and will claim that the traditional definition has "the purpose and effect to disparage and to injure" the "personhood and dignity" of same-sex couples . . . . The majority's limiting assurance will be meaningless in the face of language like that, as the majority well knows. That is why the language is there. The result will be a judicial distortion of our society's debate over marriage — a debate that can seem in need of our clumsy "help" only to a member of this institution.

As to that debate: Few public controversies touch an institution so central to the lives of so many, and few inspire such attendant passion by good people on all sides. Few public controversies will ever demonstrate so vividly the beauty of what our Framers gave us, a gift the Court pawns today to buy its stolen moment in the spotlight: a system of government that permits us to rule *ourselves*. Since DOMA's passage, citizens on all sides of the question have seen victories and they have seen defeats. There have been plebiscites, legislation, persuasion, and loud voices — in other words, democracy. Victories in one place for some . . . are offset by victories in other places for others . . . . Even in a *single State*, the question has come out differently on different occasions. . . .

In the majority's telling, this story is black-and-white: Hate your neighbor or come along with us. The truth is more complicated. It is hard to admit that one's political opponents are not monsters, especially in a struggle like this one, and the challenge in the end proves more than today's Court can handle. Too bad. A reminder that disagreement over something so fundamental as marriage can still be politically legitimate would have been a fit task for what in earlier times was called the judicial temperament. We might have covered ourselves with honor today, by promising all sides of this debate that it was theirs to settle and that we would respect their resolution. We might have let the People decide. But that the majority will not do. Some will rejoice in today's decision, and some will despair at it; that is the nature of a controversy that matters so much to so many. But the Court has cheated both sides, robbing the winners of an honest victory, and the losers of the peace that comes from a fair defeat. We owed both of them better.

I dissent.

JUSTICE ALITO, with whom JUSTICE THOMAS joins as to Parts II and III, dissenting. [Omitted.]

NOTES AND QUESTIONS

1. The Court of Appeals in *Windsor* applied heightened scrutiny to the sexual-orientation classification inherent in § 3 of DOMA, as both the Department and Windsor had urged. Did Justice Kennedy for the majority apply heightened scrutiny as well? What test, if any, did he apply in ruling § 3 of DOMA to be unconstitutional?

2. In footnote 4 in his dissent, Justice Scalia mentioned "polygamous or plural marriages," albeit in a slightly different context. If one or more states were to define "marriage" so as to be inclusive of polygamous or plural marriage," would the rationale in Justice Kennedy's majority opinion fit that scenario? If not, why not?

3. What are the implications of Justice Kennedy's majority opinion for a case challenging a state's definition of "marriage: as an exclusively heterosexual union? Justice Scalia in dissent wrote, "[T]he view that this Court will take of state

prohibition of same-sex marriage is indicated beyond mistaking by today's opinion." If, as Justice Kennedy for the majority asserts, with respect to DOMA, that "[t]he Constitution's guarantee of equality must at the very least mean that a bare congressional desire to harm a politically unpopular group cannot justify disparate treatment of that group," wouldn't that rhetoric apply to any state that prohibits same-sex marriage?

4. In his majority opinion, Justice Kennedy wrote, "[N]o legitimate purpose overcomes the purpose and effect [of DOMA] to disparage and to injure those whom the State, by its marriage laws, sought to protect in personhood and dignity." Was it the "purpose" of the 342 members of the House of Representatives, the 85 Senators, and President Clinton to disparage and to injure those whom the states might choose, in the post-1996 future, to "protect in personhood and dignity"? Or was the original "purpose" of those who enacted DOMA in 1996 overridden, at least in the mind of Justice Kennedy and the other four signers of the majority opinion, by changes in the political and social climate? If the latter, shouldn't the changes in the political and social climate reflect themselves in the representative branches of government, rather than in the judiciary? Justice Scalia, in dissent, further summarized the various statements in Justice Kennedy's majority opinion: "[T]he majority says that the supporters of this Act acted with malice — with the '*purpose*' . . . 'to disparage and to injure' same-sex couples. It says that the motivation for DOMA was to 'demean' . . . ; to 'impose inequality' . . . ; to 'impose . . . a stigma' . . . ; to deny people 'equal dignity' . . . ; to brand gay people as 'unworthy' . . . ; and to '*humiliat[e]*' their children . . . (emphasis added)." Again, was it the purpose of the members of Congress and the President of the United States to do all those heinous things to gay people *and their children*?

5. Does the Constitution secure the religious liberty of those faiths that are disapproving of active homosexual practice and/or marriage? Could a broad exemption be given without running afoul of the equality due same-sex couples as *Windsor* suggests? Does the majority reasoning reject or evaluate at all the underlying religious claims? Is there room for religious liberty under the majority's accusatory rhetoric aimed at those who accept the condemnations of homosexual conduct and sexually active homosexual relationships that are explicit in the Jewish Bible, the Christian New Testament, and the Quran of Islam? For example:

> Thou shalt not lie with mankind, as with womankind: it *is* abomination. Leviticus 18:22

> If a man also lie with mankind, as he lieth with a woman, both of them have committed an abomination: they shall surely be put to death; their blood *shall be* upon them. Leviticus 20:13

The Holy Scriptures: A Jewish Bible According to the Masoretic Text (Tel Aviv, Israel: Sinai Publishing House, 1984)

> Wherefore God also gave them up to uncleanness through the lusts of their own hearts, to dishonour their own bodies between themselves: Who changed the truth of God into a lie, and worshipped and served the creature more than the Creator, who is blessed for ever. Amen. For this cause God gave them up unto vile affections: for even their women did change the

natural use into that which is against nature: And likewise also the men, leaving the natural use of the woman, burned in their lust one toward another; men with men working that which is unseemly, and receiving in themselves that recompence of their error which was meet. Romans 1:26–28

Know ye not that the unrighteous shall not inherit the kingdom of God? Be not deceived: neither fornicators, nor idolaters, nor adulterers, nor effeminate, nor abusers of themselves with mankind, Nor thieves, nor covetous, nor drunkards, nor revilers, nor extortioners, shall inherit the kingdom of God. I Corinthians 6:9-10

HOLY BIBLE: KING JAMES VERSION

If two men among you are guilty of lewdness, punish them both. If they repent and amend, leave them alone; for God [Allah] is Oft-returning, Most Merciful. Sura iv:16

We also (sent) Lut: He said to his people: "Do ye commit lewdness such as no people in creation (ever) committed before you? For ye practice your lusts on men in preference to women: ye are indeed a people transgressing beyond bounds." Sura vii:80-81

Of all creatures in the world, will ye approach males, and leave those whom God has created for you to be your mates? Nay, ye are a people transgressing (all limits)! Sura xxvi:165-66

THE HOLY QUR'AN: TEXT, TRANSLATION AND COMMENTARY, trans. Abdullah Yusuf Ali (Elmhurst, N.Y.: Tahrike Tarsile Qur'an, Inc., 2001)

6.   Some religious denominations do approve of same-sex marriage. The United Church in Christ voted in 2005 to allow same-sex marriages. The Unitarian Universalist Association of Congregations also officially sanctioned same-sex marriage in 1996. The Episcopal and Presbyterian Churches permit the blessing of same-sex unions, and while "blessings" are not marriages, individual Episcopal priests decide whether or not to perform a same-sex ceremony. The Presbyterian Church has however voted down changing the definition of marriage to between "two people" instead of "two genders."

Views on same-sex marriage among non-Christian religions also vary. Reform and Conservative Jewish congregations allow same-sex marriages. The Reconstructionist movement also allows gay marriages. But each group lets rabbis opt-out of officiating same-sex ceremonies. The Orthodox Union — which is the principal Orthodox Jewish entity in the U.S. — disapproves of same-sex marriage, as does Islamic teaching.

Neither Hinduism nor Buddhism have official stances on same sex marriage, but instruction on matters of sexuality discourages homosexual behavior as without virtue. Should the government (judges, legislators or the executive) be taking sides on something that divides faith traditions in this manner? Given the differences in view, should marriage be considered the province of religion to decide freely as their understanding of doctrine instructs, such that the state should get out of the marriage business. This position was explored by Ambassador Kmiec on "The

Colbert Report," http://www.colbertnation.com/the-colbert-report-videos/224791/ april-16-2009/douglas-kmiec (April 17, 2009), and in the national media, *see, e.g.*, Michael A. Lindenberger, *A Gay Marriage Solution: End Marriage?*, TIME MAGAZINE, March 16, 2009.

Chapter 6

A GOVERNMENT OF IMPERFECT KNOWLEDGE — OF INKBLOTS, LIBERTY AND LIFE ITSELF

We asked at the beginning of our exploration into the history and nature of the Constitution whether this founding document was an end in itself or a means to some larger end, such as the pursuit of happiness, or more simply, a good life. As the original meaning we have recovered reveals, the structural provisions of the Constitution divide and limit government power, so that individual liberty might be preserved. This liberty or personal freedom is further secured by express subject matter restraints on the power of government primarily in the Bill of Rights and the Fourteenth Amendment. In this way, the Constitution is not the source of our liberty, but its guarantor. The Constitution constrains governments, federal and state, from interfering *unnecessarily* with particularly vital freedoms, such as speech, religion, and the ownership of property.

Does the Constitution then facilitate the larger end of a good life? Yes, but it is primarily up to each citizen to pursue that end through the prudent exercise of liberty. It was Madison who opined that only a virtuous citizen could be free. That is because any freedom can be abused. Free speech permits the search for truth and wisdom, but it also allows libel and perjury and forms of entertainment that degrade. The free exercise of religion for a great many will be an indispensable opening to an understanding of God, but for a few it invites or shields counter-cultural practices or rituals that threaten the civic order. Property can provide a level of economic security for individual and family and human flourishing through work within a larger civilized community, or it can be abused to magnify environmental harms or to deny a just wage to an employee.

As a general matter, most people would agree that it is not the job of the government to instruct in matters of virtue. Especially to the extent that virtue is derived from religion, the Constitution makes it abundantly clear that the federal government is not to prescribe (establish) or proscribe (as in prohibiting free exercise) the particular ways individuals come to know God. Yet, in the past fifty years especially, the federal government has undertaken to be our moral instructor. The expansion of the commerce power has allowed Congress to speak its mind on everything from lottery tickets to civil rights. So too, in giving meaning to words like "liberty" and "equal protection," the Court necessarily supplies at least a minimalist conception of what is, and is not, an accepted exercise of liberty. For example, in *Board of Regents v. Roth*, 408 U.S. 564 (1972), the Court said:

> "While this Court has not attempted to define with exactness the liberty . . . guaranteed [by the Fifth and Fourteenth Amendments], the term . . . denotes not merely freedom from bodily restraint but also the right of the individual to contract, to engage in any of the common occupations of life,

to acquire useful knowledge, to marry, establish a home and bring up children, to worship God according to the dictates of his own conscience, and generally to enjoy those privileges long recognized . . . as essential to the orderly pursuit of happiness by free men." In a Constitution for a free people, there can be no doubt that the meaning of "liberty" must be broad indeed.

Id. at 572 (quoting *Meyer v. Nebraska*, 262 U.S. 390, 399 (1923) (discussed below)). Notice that the Court's definition includes both enumerated or textual rights, like the free exercise of religion, but also other non-textual rights, such as the right to marry and to bring up children. Part of the task of this Chapter is to explore why the Court has found some non-textual rights, but denied others.

The federal government, pursuant to its enumerated powers, or the states by their reserved powers, may restrain liberty. To give an obvious example, Congress has the enumerated power to "coin Money [and] regulate the Value thereof," and therefore, federal laws limiting counterfeiting are a fully justifiable limitation upon the liberty one might otherwise have to print currency. U.S. Const., art. I, § 8, cl. 5. So too, under the Tenth Amendment, the "police powers," that by tradition are described as the maintenance of the health, safety, morals, and general welfare of the community, are reserved to the states so that life and property can be protected with laws punishing murder and theft. U.S. Const., amend. X. There is general agreement that neither the fraud of the counterfeiter, the violence of the murderer, nor the intrusion of the thief are exercises of liberty that need be tolerated. But what of other practices? In this Chapter, we will explore claims that constitutionally-protected liberty includes the right to marry, to engage in homo-sexual sodomy, and to have access to contraceptives, abortion, and assisted suicide. None of these matters are dealt with expressly in the text of the Constitution, and yet, we modernly turn to the Supreme Court to evaluate whether such claimed liberties exist or are legitimate. Where these libertarian claims have succeeded, ask yourself as you read the cases if the Court is drawing upon any discernible moral principle, such as the natural law, in reaching its decisions. As a formal matter, the legal theory involved in most of them is the rather stark proposition that the Due Process Clause substantively limits government infringements of these liberties. In a few cases, mention will be made of the Ninth Amendment, providing that the "enumeration in the Constitution, of certain rights, shall not be construed to deny or disparage others retained by the people."

To what rights (liberties) is the Ninth Amendment referring? In the context of hearings on his nomination to the Supreme Court, the late federal Judge Robert Bork remarked that he did not know, analogizing the provision to an indecipherable inkblot. Judge Bork stated:

I do not think you can use the Ninth Amendment unless you know something of what it means. For example, if you had an amendment that says "Congress shall make no" and then there is an inkblot, and you cannot read the rest of it, and that is the only copy you have, I do not think the court can make up what might be under the inkblot.

The Bork Disinformers, WALL ST. J., Oct. 5, 1987, at 22. For a scholarly elaboration of the Bork view, *see* Thomas B. McAffee, *A Critical Guide to the Ninth*

Amendment, 69 TEMP. L. REV. 61 (1996) (explaining the *Griswold v. Connecticut* debate and concluding that a "rights-foundationalist theory of the Constitution . . . carries the potential to privilege judicial views of the 'natural law,' or political morality, over the views of the people who are the source of their office"). Since no part of the Constitution ought to be assumed meaningless or superfluous, the Amendment must have more significance than an inkblot, but what?

At a minimum, the Amendment on its face appears to be a rule of construction. It states, after all, that the enumeration of the Bill of Rights "shall not be *construed* to deny or disparage others retained by the people." U.S. Const., amend. IX (emphasis added). Ninth Amendment scholar Professor Randy E. Barnett thus observes: "the Ninth Amendment stands ready to respond to a crabbed construction that limits the scope of this protection to the enumerated rights." Randy E. Barnett, *Reconceiving the Ninth Amendment*, 74 CORNELL L. REV. 1, 42 (1988). However, broader claims are made for the Ninth Amendment. Professor Laurence Tribe understands the Ninth Amendment as "a uniquely central text in any attempt to take seriously the process of *construing* the Constitution." Laurence H. Tribe, *Contrasting Constitutional Visions: Of Real and Unreal Differences*, 22 HARV. C.R.-C.L. L. REV. 95, 100 (1987). For him, both textual and nontextual rights and liberties rely upon the Ninth Amendment as their supporting ground. Others suggest that the Ninth Amendment is a denial of government power. Harvard historian Raoul Berger sees the Ninth Amendment as an " 'affirmation that rights exist independently of government, that they constitute an area of no-power.' " Raoul Berger, *The Ninth Amendment*, 66 CORNELL L. REV. 1, 9 (1980) (quoting Leslie W. Dunbar, *James Madison and the Ninth Amendment*, 42 VA. L. REV. 627, 641 (1956)).

All well and good, but don't we still need to know just what rights are retained by the people? This raises the problem of imperfect knowledge alluded to in the title to this Chapter. Upon further reflection after his confirmation failed, Judge Bork posited that the retained rights refer to those that are guaranteed outside the federal constitution in "state constitutions, statutes and common law." ROBERT BORK, THE TEMPTING OF AMERICA 184 (1990) (citing Russell Caplan, *The History and Meaning of the Ninth Amendment*, 69 VA. L. REV. 223 (1983)). The reference to the common law is an especially apt one because it reminds us that the founders' conception of retained rights was much shaped by the common or natural law idea that rights are derived from reasoned reflection upon human nature over time, and not located, as Alexander Hamilton observed, in musty parchments. But what can we know from a reasoned reflection upon human nature?

Philosophy of any type asks what we can know about ourselves and our world, and this in turn, raises the age-old problem of whether anything can be known by reason at all. Skeptics, like Montaigne for example, denied the accessibility of such knowledge by unaided reason. Montaigne writes:

> [T]here cannot be first principles for men, unless the Divinity has revealed them; all the rest — beginning, middle, and end — is nothing but dreams and smoke. . . . [E]very human presupposition and every enunciation has as much authority as another. . . . The impression of certainty is a certain token of folly and extreme uncertainty.

Michel de Montaigne, *Apology for Raymond Sebond, in* THE ESSAYS (1588), *reprinted in* 23 GREAT BOOKS OF THE WESTERN WORLD 248, 301 (Mortimer J. Adler ed. & Donald M. Frame trans., 2d ed., Encyclopaedia Britannica 1990). Modernly, this may be the credo of much of the legal academy, but none of the framers assumed this extreme position, and thus what we might call "natural law originalism" does not either. Jefferson, after all, premised the independence of the American republic upon "truths," not only known, but held to be "self-evident."

But is such knowledge merely assertion on Jefferson's part? Long before Jefferson, in the *Metaphysics*, Aristotle confronted the extreme skepticism of those who would assert that all propositions are either true, or the converse, that all are false. Again, this is to claim that nothing can be truly known, a proposition that violates Jefferson's practical assertion of self-evidence, and more subtly, the philosophical principle of noncontradiction that something cannot both be and not be at the same time. (Thus, Thomas Aquinas writes: "the first indemonstrable principle is that *the same thing cannot be affirmed and denied at the same time,* which is based on the notion of *being* and *not-being*; and on this principle all others are based, as is stated in [the] *Metaphysics.*" 1 THOMAS AQUINAS, SUMMA THEOLOGICA I–II, Q. 94, art. 2, at 1009 (Fathers of the English Dominican Province trans., Benziger Brothers 1947) (citing ARISTOTLE, METAPHYSICS bk. 4, ch. 3). Any skeptic who maintains otherwise would necessarily contradict himself. As the modern expositor of the great book tradition, Mortimer Adler writes, "if all propositions are true, then the proposition 'Some propositions are false' is also true; if all propositions are false, the proposition 'All propositions are false' is also false." 1 THE SYNTOPICON: AN INDEX TO THE GREAT IDEAS 686 (Mortimer J. Adler ed., 2d ed. 1990).

Now the principle of noncontradiction may seem far removed from constitutional interpretation, but it is not. While Montaigne declared there were no "first principles" knowable to reason alone to guide us, the cases in this Chapter illustrate the Court's search for these first principles. You will need to make up your own mind if the Court has been faithful to Jefferson's idea that human natural right flows from the self-evident premise that we exist, from the fact of being, itself (in Jefferson's terminology, that "[we] are endowed by [our] Creator with certain unalienable Rights." THE DECLARATION OF INDEPENDENCE para. 2 (U.S. 1776)). The most controversial and sensitive topics of constitutional discourse interrelate with the Court's performance here. As Professor Michael Zuckert has written in his superb book explicating the natural rights foundation of the American republic, "[t]he truths about the institution of government . . . follow from the truths about prepolitical society as the truths about the postpolitical situation follow from the truths about the institution of government." MICHAEL P. ZUCKERT, THE NATURAL RIGHTS REPUBLIC 48 (1996). As Zuckert explains, the pre-political recognition of the self-evident truth that all human beings are "created equal" and endowed with unalienable rights leads directly to the subsidiary truth that no human being has a natural right to govern another. Thus, just power comes from the consent of the governed and governments are instituted to secure the pre-political, unalienable rights. Governments that fail this purpose may be, post-politically, "alter[ed] or abolish[ed]." *Id.* at 47 (quoting THE DECLARATION OF INDEPENDENCE para. 2 (U.S. 1776)).

Assuming natural rights are knowable in the manner suggested, and that these rights give meaning to the constitutional concept of liberty, there is the further question of whether such rights are instructive to legislative bodies only or whether they are to be judicially enforced. Madison arguably thought the judiciary had a role, and that it was not a role wholly limited to constitutional text. First, in introducing the Bill of Rights in Congress, Madison reflected on the purpose of what would become the Ninth Amendment, stating:

> It has been objected . . . against a bill of rights, that, by enumerating particular exceptions to the grant of power, it would disparage those rights which were not placed in that enumeration; and it might follow by implication, that those rights which were not singled out, were intended to be assigned into the hands of the General Government, and were consequently insecure. This is one of the most plausible arguments I have ever heard urged against the admission of a bill of rights into this system; but, I conceive, that may be guarded against. I have attempted it, as gentlemen may see by turning to [what would become the Ninth Amendment].

1 ANNALS OF CONG. 439 (Joseph Gales ed., 1789) (a more complete version of this speech is reproduced in Chapter Two). But Madison's method for guarding against the encroachment of unenumerated rights was thought too indeterminate. Governor Randolph of Virginia argued that "there was no criterion by which it could be determined whether any other particular right was retained or not." Letter from Hardin Burnley to James Madison (Nov. 28, 1789), *in* 12 THE PAPERS OF JAMES MADISON 455, 456 (Charles F. Hobson et al. eds., 1979) (stating Randolph's objections). Madison denied the problem, but he also tried to answer it, positing that "if [the amendments] are incorporated into the constitution, independent tribunals of justice will consider themselves in a peculiar manner the guardians of those rights; they will be an impenetrable bulwark against every assumption of power in the legislative or executive." 1 ANNALS OF CONG. 439 (Joseph Gales ed., 1789).

Before exploring more attenuated claims of liberty, it should be noted that the Court has always assumed that liberty in the Fifth and Fourteenth Amendments means "freedom from bodily restraint." *Board of Regents v. Roth*, 408 U.S. 564, 572 (1972). Much of your course work in criminal law and procedure concerns this aspect of liberty, and it will not be repeated here. Numerous provisions of the Bill of Rights concern procedures that the government must follow before restraining the physical liberty of a person. For example, the Eighth Amendment prohibits excessive bail and the Sixth Amendment includes the right to a "speedy and public trial, by an impartial jury" and the right "to be informed of the nature and cause of the accusation [of a crime]" and "to be confronted [by] witnesses." U.S. Const., amend. VI. Similarly, some of the colloquial aspects of American criminal justice are judicial glosses on these provisions, such as the presumption of innocence, *Taylor v. Kentucky*, 436 U.S. 478 (1978), and the requirement of proof beyond a reasonable doubt, *In re Winship*, 397 U.S. 358 (1970).

Due process must also be afforded a person whose liberty is sought to be deprived in a civil proceeding. *Addington v. Texas*, 441 U.S. 418, 425 (1979). In *Kansas v. Hendricks*, 521 U.S. 346 (1997), the Court upheld a state statute that provides for the involuntary and indeterminate commitment in a mental hospital of a person charged with a sexually violent act, like rape or sexual exploitation of a child, and who has been proven beyond a reasonable doubt to have a mental abnormality that leaves him unable to control his sexual conduct. Sexually Violent Predators Act, Kan. Stat. Ann. §§ 59-29a01 to -29a15 (1994). Due process was satisfied, said the Court, because Hendricks' continued confinement was premised upon a showing of his dangerousness and mental incapacity. 521 U.S. at 360. The Court also found that such commitment does not count as criminal incarceration for purposes of the Double Jeopardy Clause, amend. V, cl. 2, or the Ex Post Facto Clause, Article I, § 9, cl. 3. 521 U.S. at 361–68.

Moving beyond mere freedom from physical restraint, let's examine what else the Court has found essential to "ordered liberty."

A. NATURAL LAW ECHOES — PARENTAL AND FAMILY RIGHTS

1. Directing the Upbringing of Children

The next two cases are viewed as the foundation of the substantive due process right to direct the upbringing of children. In *Meyer v. Nebraska*, 262 U.S. 390 (1923), the Court invalidates a state law prohibiting the teaching in languages other than English in public schools. *Pierce v. Society of Sisters of the Holy Names of Jesus and Mary*, 268 U.S. 510 (1925), strikes down an Oregon law requiring all children to attend public schools. The third case, *Troxel v. Granville*, 530 U.S. 57 (2000), is a recent application of the same principle.

MEYER v. NEBRASKA
262 U.S. 390 (1923)

MR. JUSTICE MCREYNOLDS delivered the opinion of the Court.

Plaintiff in error was tried and convicted in the District Court for Hamilton County, Nebraska, under an information which charged that on May 25, 1920, while an instructor in Zion Parochial School, he unlawfully taught the subject of reading in the German language. . . .

The Supreme Court of the State affirmed the judgment of conviction [writing:]

> The salutary purpose of the statute is clear. The Legislature had seen the baneful effects of permitting foreigners, who had taken residence in this country, to rear and educate their children in the language of their native land. The result of that condition was found to be inimical to our own safety. . . . The obvious purpose of this statute was that the English language should be and become the mother tongue of all children reared in this state. The enactment of such a statute comes reasonably within the police power of the state.

* * *

The problem for our determination is whether the statute as construed and applied unreasonably infringes the liberty guaranteed to the plaintiff in error by the Fourteenth Amendment:

"No state shall . . . deprive any person of life, liberty, or property, without due process of law."

While this court has not attempted to define with exactness the liberty thus guaranteed, the term has received much consideration and some of the included things have been definitely stated. Without doubt, it denotes not merely freedom from bodily restraint but also the right of the individual to contract, to engage in any of the common occupations of life, to acquire useful knowledge, to marry, establish a home and bring up children, to worship God according to the dictates of his own conscience, and generally to enjoy those privileges long recognized at common law as essential to the orderly pursuit of happiness by free men. *Slaughter-House Cases.* The established doctrine is that this liberty may not be interfered with, under the guise of protecting the public interest, by legislative action which is arbitrary or without reasonable relation to some purpose within the competency of the State to effect. Determination by the Legislature of what constitutes proper exercise of police power is not final or conclusive but is subject to supervision by the courts.

*   *   *

. . . Corresponding to the right of control [meaning parental control over the upbringing of a child], it is the natural duty of the parent to give his children education suitable to their station in life. . . .

*   *   *

Practically, education of the young is only possible in schools conducted by especially qualified persons who devote themselves thereto. The calling always has been regarded as useful and honorable, essential, indeed, to the public welfare. Mere knowledge of the German language cannot reasonably be regarded as harmful. Heretofore it has been commonly looked upon as helpful and desirable. Plaintiff in error taught this language in school as part of his occupation. His right thus to teach and the right of parents to engage him so to instruct their children, we think, are within the liberty of the Amendment.

The challenged statute forbids the teaching in school of any subject except in English; also the teaching of any other language until the pupil has attained and successfully passed the eighth grade, which is not usually accomplished before the age of twelve. The Supreme Court of the State has held that "the so-called ancient or dead languages" are not "within the spirit or the purpose of the act." *Neb. Dist. of Evangelical Lutheran Synod v. McKelvie,* (Neb. 1922). Latin, Greek, Hebrew are not proscribed; but German, French, Spanish, Italian, and every other alien speech are within the ban. Evidently the Legislature has attempted materially to interfere with the calling of modern language teachers, with the opportunities of pupils to acquire knowledge, and with the power of parents to control the education of their own.

*   *   *

That the State may do much, go very far, indeed, in order to improve the quality of its citizens, physically, mentally and morally, is clear; but the individual has certain fundamental rights which must be respected. The protection of the

Constitution extends to all, to those who speak other languages as well as to those born with English on the tongue. Perhaps it would be highly advantageous if all had ready understanding of our ordinary speech, but this cannot be coerced by methods which conflict with the Constitution — a desirable end cannot be promoted by prohibited means.

For the welfare of his Ideal Commonwealth, Plato suggested a law which should provide: "That the wives of our guardians are to be common, and their children are to be common, and no parent is to know his own child, nor any child his parent. . . . The proper officers will take the offspring of the good parents to the pen or fold, and there they will deposit them with certain nurses who dwell in a separate quarter; but the offspring of the inferior, or of the better when they chance to be deformed, will be put away in some mysterious, unknown place, as they should be." In order to submerge the individual and develop ideal citizens, Sparta assembled the males at seven into barracks and intrusted their subsequent education and training to official guardians. Although such measures have been deliberately approved by men of great genius, their ideas touching the relation between individual and State were wholly different from those upon which our institutions rest; and it hardly will be affirmed that any Legislature could impose such restrictions upon the people of a State without doing violence to both letter and spirit of the Constitution.

The desire of the legislature to foster a homogeneous people with American ideals prepared readily to understand current discussions of civic matters is easy to appreciate. Unfortunate experiences during the late war and aversion toward every character of truculent adversaries were certainly enough to quicken that aspiration. But the means adopted, we think, exceed the limitations upon the power of the State and conflict with rights assured to plaintiff in error. The interference is plain enough and no adequate reason therefore in time of peace and domestic tranquility has been shown.

The power of the State to compel attendance at some school and to make reasonable regulations for all schools, including a requirement that they shall give instructions in English, is not questioned. Nor has challenge been made of the State's power to prescribe a curriculum for institutions which it supports. Those matters are not within the present controversy. Our concern is with the prohibition approved by the [Nebraska] Supreme Court. . . . We are constrained to conclude that the statute as applied is arbitrary and without reasonable relation to any end within the competency of the State.

*   *   *

Reversed.

Mr. Justice Holmes and Mr. Justice Sutherland, dissent. [Omitted.]

PIERCE v. SOCIETY OF THE SISTERS OF THE HOLY NAMES OF JESUS AND MARY
268 U.S. 510 (1925)

MR. JUSTICE McREYNOLDS delivered the opinion of the Court.

* * *

The challenged act, effective September 1, 1926, requires every parent, guardian, or other person having control or charge or custody of a child between eight and sixteen years to send him "to a public school for the period of time a public school shall be held during the current year" in the district where the child resides; and failure so to do is declared a misdemeanor. . . . The manifest purpose is to compel general attendance at public schools by normal children, between eight and sixteen, who have not completed the eighth grade. And without doubt enforcement of the statute would seriously impair, perhaps destroy, the profitable features of appellees' business and greatly diminish the value of their property.

Appellee, the Society of Sisters, is an Oregon corporation, organized in 1880, with power to care for orphans, educate and instruct the youth, establish and maintain academies or schools, and acquire necessary real and personal property. It has long devoted its property and effort to the secular and religious education and care of children, and has acquired the valuable good will of many parents and guardians. It conducts interdependent primary and high schools and junior colleges, and maintains orphanages for the custody and control of children between eight and sixteen. In its primary schools many children between those ages are taught the subjects usually pursued in Oregon public schools during the first eight years. Systematic religious instruction and moral training according to the tenets of the Roman Catholic Church are also regularly provided. . . . The Compulsory Education Act of 1922 has already caused the withdrawal from its schools of children who would otherwise continue, and their income has steadily declined. The appellants, public officers, have proclaimed their purpose strictly to enforce the statute.

After setting out the above facts, the Society's bill alleges that the enactment conflicts with the right of parents to choose schools where their children will receive appropriate mental and religious training, the right of the child to influence the parents' choice of a school, the right of schools and teachers therein to engage in a useful business or profession, and is accordingly repugnant to the Constitution and void. And, further, that unless enforcement of the measure is enjoined the corporation's business and property will suffer irreparable injury.

* * *

No question is raised concerning the power of the State reasonably to regulate all schools, to inspect, supervise and examine them, their teachers and pupils; to require that all children of proper age attend some school, that teachers shall be of good moral character and patriotic disposition, that certain studies plainly essential to good citizenship must be taught, and that nothing be taught which is manifestly inimical to the public welfare.

The inevitable practical result of enforcing the Act under consideration would be destruction of appellees' primary schools, and perhaps all other private primary schools for normal children within the State of Oregon. These parties are engaged in a kind of undertaking not inherently harmful, but long regarded as useful and meritorious. Certainly there is nothing in the present records to indicate that they have failed to discharge their obligations to patrons, students or the State. And there are no peculiar circumstances or present emergencies which demand extraordinary measures relative to primary education.

Under the doctrine of *Meyer v. Nebraska*, we think it entirely plain that the Act of 1922 unreasonably interferes with the liberty of parents and guardians to direct the upbringing and education of children under their control. As often heretofore pointed out, rights guaranteed by the Constitution may not be abridged by legislation which has no reasonable relation to some purpose within the competency of the State. The fundamental theory of liberty upon which all governments in this Union repose excludes any general power of the State to standardize its children by forcing them to accept instruction from public teachers only. The child is not the mere creature of the State; those who nurture him and direct his destiny have the right, coupled with the high duty, to recognize and prepare him for additional obligations.

Appellees are corporations, and therefore, it is said, they cannot claim for themselves the liberty which the Fourteenth Amendment guarantees. Accepted in the proper sense, this is true. But they have business and property for which they claim protection. These are threatened with destruction through the unwarranted compulsion which appellants are exercising over present and prospective patrons of their schools. And this court has gone very far to protect against loss threatened by such action. *Truax v. Raich* [(1915)]; *Truax v. Corrigan* [(1921)]; *Terrace v. Thompson* [(1923)].

Generally it is entirely true, as urged by counsel, that no person in any business has such an interest in possible customers as to enable him to restrain exercise of proper power of the State upon the ground that he will be deprived of patronage. But the injunctions here sought are not against the exercise of any *proper* power. Appellees asked protection against arbitrary, unreasonable and unlawful interference with their patrons and the consequent destruction of their business and property. Their interest is clear and immediate, within the rule approved in *Truax v. Raich, Truax v. Corrigan,* and *Terrace v. Thompson, supra,* and many other cases where injunctions have issued to protect business enterprises against interference with the freedom of patrons or customers.

*   *   *

The decrees below [grant of injunctive relief] are affirmed.

TROXEL v. GRANVILLE
530 U.S. 57 (2000)

JUSTICE O'CONNOR announced the judgment of the Court and delivered an opinion, in which THE CHIEF JUSTICE, JUSTICE GINSBURG, and JUSTICE BREYER join.

Section 26.10.160(3) of the Revised Code of Washington permits "[a]ny person" to petition a superior court for visitation rights "at any time," and authorizes that court to grant such visitation rights whenever "visitation may serve the best interest of the child." Petitioners Jenifer and Gary Troxel petitioned a Washington Superior Court for the right to visit their grandchildren, Isabelle and Natalie Troxel. Respondent Tommie Granville, the mother of Isabelle and Natalie, opposed the petition. The case ultimately reached the Washington Supreme Court, which held that § 26.10.160(3) unconstitutionally interferes with the fundamental right of parents to rear their children.

I

Tommie Granville and Brad Troxel shared a relationship that ended in June 1991. The two never married, but they had two daughters, Isabelle and Natalie. Jenifer and Gary Troxel are Brad's parents, and thus the paternal grandparents of Isabelle and Natalie. After Tommie and Brad separated in 1991, Brad lived with his parents and regularly brought his daughters to his parents' home for weekend visitation. Brad committed suicide in May 1993. Although the Troxels at first continued to see Isabelle and Natalie on a regular basis after their son's death, Tommie Granville informed the Troxels in October 1993 that she wished to limit their visitation with her daughters to one short visit per month.

. . . At trial, the Troxels requested two weekends of overnight visitation per month and two weeks of visitation each summer. Granville did not oppose visitation altogether, but instead asked the court to order one day of visitation per month with no overnight stay. . . .

* * *

The Washington Court of Appeals reversed the lower court's visitation order and dismissed the Troxels' petition for visitation, holding that nonparents lack standing to seek visitation under §§ 26.10.160(3) unless a custody action is pending. In the Court of Appeals' view, that limitation on nonparental visitation actions was "consistent with the constitutional restrictions on state interference with parents' fundamental liberty interest in the care, custody, and management of their children." . . .

The Washington Supreme Court granted the Troxels' petition for review and, after consolidating their case with two other visitation cases, affirmed. The court disagreed with the Court of Appeals' decision on the statutory issue and found that the plain language of § 26.10.160(3) gave the Troxels standing to seek visitation, irrespective of whether a custody action was pending. The Washington Supreme Court nevertheless agreed with the Court of Appeals' ultimate conclusion that the Troxels could not obtain visitation of Isabelle and Natalie pursuant to § 26.10.160(3).

The court rested its decision on the Federal Constitution, holding that § 26.10.160(3) unconstitutionally infringes on the fundamental right of parents to rear their children. In the court's view, there were at least two problems with the nonparental visitation statute. First, according to the Washington Supreme Court, the Constitution permits a State to interfere with the right of parents to rear their children only to prevent harm or potential harm to a child. Section 26.10.160(3) fails that standard because it requires no threshold showing of harm. Second, by allowing " 'any person' to petition for forced visitation of a child at 'any time' with the only requirement being that the visitation serve the best interest of the child," the Washington visitation statute sweeps too broadly. "It is not within the province of the state to make significant decisions concerning the custody of children merely because it could make a 'better' decision." The Washington Supreme Court held that "[p]arents have a right to limit visitation of their children with third persons," and that between parents and judges, "the parents should be the ones to choose whether to expose their children to certain people or ideas."

II

The demographic changes of the past century make it difficult to speak of an average American family. The composition of families varies greatly from household to household. While many children may have two married parents and grandparents who visit regularly, many other children are raised in single-parent households. In 1996, children living with only one parent accounted for 28 percent of all children under age 18 in the United States. Understandably, in these single-parent households, persons outside the nuclear family are called upon with increasing frequency to assist in the everyday tasks of child rearing. In many cases, grandparents play an important role. For example, in 1998, approximately 4 million children — or 5.6 percent of all children under age 18 — lived in the household of their grandparents.

The Fourteenth Amendment provides that no State shall "deprive any person of life, liberty, or property, without due process of law." We have long recognized that the Amendment's Due Process Clause, like its Fifth Amendment counterpart, "guarantees more than fair process." The Clause also includes a substantive component that "provides heightened protection against government interference with certain fundamental rights and liberty interests."

The liberty interest at issue in this case — the interest of parents in the care, custody, and control of their children — is perhaps the oldest of the fundamental liberty interests recognized by this Court. More than 75 years ago, in *Meyer v. Nebraska* (1923), we held that the "liberty" protected by the Due Process Clause includes the right of parents to "establish a home and bring up children" and "to control the education of their own." Two years later, in *Pierce v. Society of Sisters* (1925), we again held that the "liberty of parents and guardians" includes the right "to direct the upbringing and education of children under their control." We explained in *Pierce* that "[t]he child is not the mere creature of the State; those who nurture him and direct his destiny have the right, coupled with the high duty, to recognize and prepare him for additional obligations." We returned to the subject in *Prince v. Massachusetts* (1944), and again confirmed that there is a constitutional dimension to the right of parents to direct the upbringing of their children. "It is cardinal with us that the custody, care and nurture of the child reside first in the parents, whose primary function and freedom include preparation for obligations the state can neither supply nor hinder."

In subsequent cases also, we have recognized the fundamental right of parents to make decisions concerning the care, custody, and control of their children. (citing cases) In light of this extensive precedent, it cannot now be doubted that the Due Process Clause of the Fourteenth Amendment protects the fundamental right of parents to make decisions concerning the care, custody, and control of their children.

Section 26.10.160(3), as applied to Granville and her family in this case, unconstitutionally infringes on that fundamental parental right. The Washington nonparental visitation statute is breathtakingly broad. According to the statute's text, "*any person* may petition the court for visitation rights *at any time*," and the court may grant such visitation rights whenever "visitation may serve *the best interest of the child*." § 26.10.160(3) (emphases added). That language effectively permits any third party seeking visitation to subject any decision by a parent concerning visitation of the parent's children to state-court review.

. . . The Troxels did not allege, and no court has found, that Granville was an unfit parent. That aspect of the case is important, for there is a presumption that fit parents act in the best interests of their children.

The problem here is not that the Washington Superior Court intervened, but that when it did so, it gave no special weight at all to Granville's determination of her daughters' best interests. More importantly, it appears that the Superior Court applied exactly the opposite presumption.

The judge's comments suggest that he presumed the grandparents' request should be granted unless the children would be "impact[ed] adversely." In effect, the judge placed on Granville, the fit custodial parent, the burden of disproving that visitation would be in the best interest of her daughters.

The decisional framework employed by the Superior Court directly contravened the traditional presumption that a fit parent will act in the best interest of his or her child. In an ideal world, parents might always seek to cultivate the bonds between grandparents and their grandchildren. Needless to say, however, our world is far from perfect, and in it the decision whether such an intergenerational relationship would be beneficial in any specific case is for the parent to make in the first instance. And, if a fit parent's decision of the kind at issue here becomes subject to judicial review, the court must accord at least some special weight to the parent's own determination.

Finally, we note that there is no allegation that Granville ever sought to cut off visitation entirely. Rather, the present dispute originated when Granville informed the Troxels that she would prefer to restrict their visitation with Isabelle and Natalie to one short visit per month and special holidays.

Considered together with the Superior Court's reasons for awarding visitation to the Troxels, the combination of these factors demonstrates that the visitation order in this case was an unconstitutional infringement on Granville's fundamental right to make decisions concerning the care, custody, and control of her two daughters.

Because we rest our decision on the sweeping breadth of § 26.10.160(3) and the application of that broad, unlimited power in this case, we do not consider the primary constitutional question passed on by the Washington Supreme Court — whether the Due Process Clause requires all nonparental visitation statutes to include a showing of harm or potential harm to the child as a condition precedent to granting visitation. We do not, and need not, define today the visitation context. In this respect, we agree with JUSTICE KENNEDY that the constitutionality of any standard for awarding visitation turns on the specific manner in which that standard is applied and that the constitutional protections in this area are best "elaborated with care." (dissenting opinion). Because much state-court adjudication in this context occurs on a case-by-case basis, we would be hesitant to hold that specific nonparental visitation statutes violate the Due Process Clause as a per se matter.

Accordingly, the judgment of the Washington Supreme Court is affirmed.

JUSTICE SOUTER, concurring in the judgment. (omitted)

JUSTICE THOMAS, concurring in the judgment.

I write separately to note that neither party has argued that our substantive due process cases were wrongly decided and that the original understanding of the Due Process Clause precludes judicial enforcement of unenumerated rights under that constitutional provision. As a result, I express no view on the merits of this matter, and I understand the plurality as well to leave the resolution of that issue for another day.[1]

Consequently, I agree with the plurality that this Court's recognition of a fundamental right of parents to direct the upbringing of their children resolves this case. Our decision in *Pierce v. Society of Sisters* (1925), holds that parents have a fundamental constitutional right to rear their children, including the right to determine who shall educate and socialize them. The opinions of the plurality, JUSTICE KENNEDY, and JUSTICE SOUTER recognize such a right, but curiously none of them articulates the appropriate standard of review. I would apply strict scrutiny to infringements of fundamental rights. Here, the State of Washington lacks even a legitimate governmental interest — to say nothing of a compelling one — in second-guessing a fit parent's decision regarding visitation with third parties. On this basis, I would affirm the judgment below.

---

[1] [*] This case also does not involve a challenge based upon the Privileges and Immunities Clause and thus does not present an opportunity to reevaluate the meaning of that Clause. See *Saenz v. Roe* (1999) (THOMAS, J., dissenting).

JUSTICE STEVENS, dissenting [omitted].

JUSTICE SCALIA, dissenting.

In my view, a right of parents to direct the upbringing of their children is among the "unalienable Rights" with which the Declaration of Independence proclaims "all Men . . . are endowed by their Creator." And in my view that right is also among the "othe[r] [rights] retained by the people" which the Ninth Amendment says the Constitution's enumeration of rights "shall not be construed to deny or disparage." The Declaration of Independence, however, is not a legal prescription conferring powers upon the courts; and the Constitution's refusal to "deny or disparage" other rights is far removed from affirming any one of them, and even farther removed from authorizing judges to identify what they might be, and to enforce the judges' list against laws duly enacted by the people. Consequently, while I would think it entirely compatible with the commitment to representative democracy set forth in the founding documents to argue, in legislative chambers or in electoral campaigns, that the state has no power to interfere with parents' authority over the rearing of their children, I do not believe that the power which the Constitution confers upon me as a judge entitles me to deny legal effect to laws that (in my view) infringe upon what is (in my view) that unenumerated right.

Only three holdings of this Court rest in whole or in part upon a substantive constitutional right of parents to direct the upbringing of their children — two of them from an era rich in substantive due process holdings that have since been repudiated. See *Meyer v. Nebraska* (1923); *Pierce v. Society of Sisters* (1925); *Wisconsin v. Yoder* (1972). The sheer diversity of today's opinions persuades me that the theory of unenumerated parental rights underlying these three cases has small claim to stare decisis protection. A legal principle that can be thought to produce such diverse outcomes in the relatively simple case before us here is not a legal principle that has induced substantial reliance. While I would not now overrule those earlier cases (that has not been urged), neither would I extend the theory upon which they rested to this new context.

Judicial vindication of "parental rights" under a Constitution that does not even mention them requires (as JUSTICE KENNEDY's opinion rightly points out) not only a judicially crafted definition of parents, but also — unless, as no one believes, the parental rights are to be absolute — judicially approved assessments of "harm to the child" and judicially defined gradations of other persons (grandparents, extended family, adoptive family in an adoption later found to be invalid, long-term guardians, etc.) who may have some claim against the wishes of the parents. If we embrace this unenumerated right, I think it obvious — whether we affirm or reverse the judgment here, or remand as JUSTICE STEVENS or JUSTICE KENNEDY would do — that we will be ushering in a new regime of judicially prescribed, and federally prescribed, family law. I have no reason to believe that federal judges will be better at this than state legislatures; and state legislatures have the great advantages of doing harm in a more circumscribed area, of being able to correct their mistakes in a flash, and of being removable by the people.[2]

---

[2] [2] I note that respondent is asserting only, on her own behalf, a substantive due process right to

For these reasons, I would reverse the judgment below.

JUSTICE KENNEDY, dissenting.

                              *   *   *

Turning to the question whether harm to the child must be the controlling standard in every visitation proceeding, there is a beginning point that commands general, perhaps unanimous, agreement in our separate opinions: As our case law has developed, the custodial parent has a constitutional right to determine, without undue interference by the state, how best to raise, nurture, and educate the child. The parental right stems from the liberty protected by the Due Process Clause of the Fourteenth Amendment. *Pierce* and *Meyer*, had they been decided in recent times, may well have been grounded upon First Amendment principles protecting freedom of speech, belief, and religion. Their formulation and subsequent interpretation have been quite different, of course; and they long have been interpreted to have found in Fourteenth Amendment concepts of liberty an independent right of the parent in the "custody, care and nurture of the child," free from state intervention. The principle exists, then, in broad formulation; yet courts must use considerable restraint, including careful adherence to the incremental instruction given by the precise facts of particular cases, as they seek to give further and more precise definition to the right.

On the question whether one standard must always take precedence over the other in order to protect the right of the parent or parents, "[o]ur Nation's history, legal traditions, and practices" do not give us clear or definitive answers. The consensus among courts and commentators is that at least through the 19th century there was no legal right of visitation; court-ordered visitation appears to be a 20th-century phenomenon. . . .

To say that third parties have had no historical right to petition for visitation does not necessarily imply, as the Supreme Court of Washington concluded, that a parent has a constitutional right to prevent visitation in all cases not involving harm. . . .

                              *   *   *

Indeed, contemporary practice should give us some pause before rejecting the best interests of the child standard in all third-party visitation cases, as the Washington court has done. The standard has been recognized for many years as a basic tool of domestic relations law in visitation proceedings. Since 1965 all 50 States have enacted a third-party visitation statute of some sort. . . . In light of the inconclusive historical record and case law, as well as the almost universal adoption of the best interests standard for visitation disputes, I would be hard pressed to conclude the right to be free of such review in all cases is itself " 'implicit in the concept of ordered liberty.' " In my view, it would be more appropriate to conclude that the constitutionality of the application of the best interests standard depends on more specific factors. In short, a fit parent's right vis-a-vis a complete stranger

---

direct the upbringing of her own children, and is not asserting, on behalf of her children, their First Amendment rights of association or free exercise. I therefore do not have occasion to consider whether, and under what circumstances, the parent could assert the latter enumerated rights.

is one thing; her right vis-a-vis another parent or a de facto parent may be another. The protection the Constitution requires, then, must be elaborated with care, using the discipline and instruction of the case law system. We must keep in mind that family courts in the 50 States confront these factual variations each day, and are best situated to consider the unpredictable, yet inevitable, issues that arise. . . .

* * *

NOTES AND QUESTIONS

1. Is the liberty recognized in *Meyer*, *Pierce*, and *Troxel* a fundamental right demanding strict scrutiny or some lesser standard of review? Prior to *Troxel*, modern Supreme Court dicta supported the proposition that the right to educate one's children is deserving of strict scrutiny, and both the plurality and Justice Thomas seem inclined in this direction in *Troxel*, itself. *See, e.g., Employment Div. v. Smith*, 494 U.S. 872, 881 (1990) (equating the "right of parents . . . to direct the education of their children" with "freedom of speech and of the press"); *Griswold v. Connecticut*, 381 U.S. 479, 482 (1965) (referring to the right to direct the education of one's children as if it were fundamental); *id.* at 498 (Goldberg, J., concurring) (noting that the rights recognized in *Pierce* and *Meyer* are fundamental). Not surprisingly, some state authorities, like the Washington Supreme Court in *Troxel*, also have concluded that the right of parents to direct the education of their children is fundamental. *See, e.g., Michigan Dep't of Soc. Services v. Emmanuel Baptist Preschool*, 455 N.W.2d 1, 16 (Mich. 1990) (Cavanagh, J., concurring); *Sheridan Rd. Baptist Church v. Department of Educ.*, 396 N.W.2d 373, 407–09 (Mich. 1986) (Riley, J., dissenting) (finding the right to direct the education of one's children to be a fundamental right); *Ohio v. Whisner*, 351 N.E.2d 750, 769 (Ohio 1976) ("it has long been recognized that the right of a parent to guide the education, including the religious education, of his or her children is indeed a 'fundamental right' guaranteed by the due process clause of the Fourteenth Amendment.").

So does *Troxel* clarify the status of this right or not? The answer is unfortunately not. The plurality is content to rest its opinion on the sweep of the Washington visitation statute. Justice Thomas refrains from answering the question as well, and Justice Scalia admits that the natural rights of parents exist, but refuses to defend them judicially. Indeed, Justice Scalia's opinion may be the most perplexing insofar as he proclaims "the theory of unenumerated parental rights underlying these three cases has small claim to stare decisis protection." Do you agree? What support does Justice Scalia give for disregarding what even he concedes was one of the natural rights for which the Constitution was framed? Because Justice Scalia is an opponent of the unenumerated right claim to terminate a pregnancy (abortion), is he driven to this conclusion by symmetry — *i.e.*, a belief that he must neither be pro- nor anti-parent? Is this a correct understanding of natural law? Judicial restraint? Justice Scalia's view seems to be grounded in his textualism: parental rights are not mentioned in the Constitution, so he has no authority to vindicate them against state legislation. But is it so clear that parental rights are not protected by the text of the Constitution? Are they not a "privilege or immunity" of citizenship protected both by Article IV and the Fourteenth Amendment? *See*

Corfield v. Coryell, supra, Chapter 1. Why do you think Justice Scalia is unwilling to give effect to this constitutional text?

The casual willingness of the Court to leave the issue ambiguous belies the general importance of the parental right to the average citizen. In this regard, the right has taken on increased relevance because of the interest and success of home schooling. *See, e.g., Michigan v. DeJonge,* 501 N.W.2d 127 (Mich. 1993) (Michigan's teacher certification requirement violated the Free Exercise Clause and parents' right to direct the upbringing of their children, as the state failed to demonstrate that the requirement achieved its interest by the least restrictive means); *but see Michigan v. Bennett,* 501 N.W.2d 106 (Mich. 1993) (upholding the certification requirement as applied to home school parents who raised the parental right apart from a claim of religious freedom. The *Bennett* court also characterized the parental right as not fundamental, seemingly putting the Michigan court at odds with the contrary dicta in *DeJonge*).

As a matter of policy, many states have rejected the archaic notion that certified instruction is necessary for home schools. Within the last decade, over twenty states have repealed teacher certification requirements for home schools. Neal Devins, *Fundamentalist Christian Educators v. State: An Inevitable Compromise,* 60 GEO. WASH. L. REV. 818, 819 (1992). Besides Michigan, only two states, California and Alabama, appear to mandate teacher certification in home schools. Cal. Educ. Code § 48224 (1993); Ala. Code § 16-28-5 (1995). Alabama, however, exempts "church schools" from the teacher certification requirement, Ala. Code § 16-28-1(2) (1995). Although Kansas bars the usual home school, *In re Sawyer,* 672 P.2d 1093 (Kan. 1983), it permits private, denominational, and parochial instruction by "competent" instructors. Kan. Stat. Ann. § 72-1111 (1992), § 121, 1996 Kan. Sess. Laws 1274, 1404.

2.   Apart from the issue of home schooling, the Supreme Court has held that the right to direct the upbringing of one's children is not absolute. This is not dispositive of the fundamental/non-fundamental debate, however, because no fundamental right is absolute, that is, free of limitation. Thus, in *Prince v. Massachusetts,* 321 U.S. 158 (1944), the Court sustained the application of child labor laws to prevent parents from engaging a nine-year-old girl in the solicitation practices of Jehovah's Witnesses parents.

Prince is somewhat unusual because where parental rights are motivated by religious belief, it is normally a formidable constitutional combination. Judicial deference to parents here coincides with the teaching of many, if not all, faiths that parents have the primary responsibility for the education of their children. This education, it is supposed, will include not just the tenets of the family's faith tradition, but also the common virtues necessary to lead a responsible life, such as prudence (making informed decisions), temperance (avoiding excess — a virtue spoken of extensively by Aristotle), courage (the ability to see a task to its completion), and justice (being honorable in our dealings with others; fulfilling the obligation of what we owe). For a practical, readable account of the role of family in the pursuit of virtue for children, see DOUGLAS W. KMIEC, CEASE-FIRE ON THE FAMILY (1995). Contrasted with Ambassador Kmiec's view should be that of Professor Barbara Woodhouse who argues that the state should assume a larger role in the governance of children in order to break down the "attachment to the patriarchal family." Barbara Bennett Woodhouse, *Who Owns the Child? Meyer and Pierce and the Child as Property*, 33 Wm. & Mary L. Rev. 995, 997 (1992). Professor Woodhouse's vision of the child is "as public resource and public ward, entitled both to make claims upon the community and to be claimed by the community." *Id.* at 1091. But is this "vision" sufficient to accomplish the role played throughout recorded western civilization? As Dean Bruce Hafen of the Brigham Young Law School notes:

> [T]he cultural patterns of American family life have contributed enormously to the ultimate purposes of a democratic society by providing the stability and the structure that are essential to sustaining individual liberty over the long term.

* * *

> . . . Only in the master-apprentice relationship of parent and child, committed to one another by the bonds of kinship, can the skills, normative standards, and virtues that maintain our cultural bedrock be transmitted.

Bruce C. Hafen, *The Constitutional Status of Marriage, Kinship, and Sexual Privacy — Balancing the Individual and Social Interests*, 81 Mich. L. Rev. 463, 473, 478 (1983) (footnote omitted).

3.   The decision in *Prince* should be contrasted with that of *Wisconsin v. Yoder*, 406 U.S. 205 (1972), discussed in Chapter Two. In *Yoder* it will be recalled, the Court allowed Amish parents to educate their children at home after the eighth grade, notwithstanding compulsory school requirements. The Court observed that:

> [A] State's interest in universal education, however highly we rank it, is not totally free from a balancing process when it impinges on fundamental rights and interests, such as those specifically protected by the Free Exercise Clause of the First Amendment, and the traditional interest of parents with respect to the religious upbringing of their children.

Id. at 214.

Alfonso v. Fernandez, 606 N.Y.S.2d 259 (N.Y. App. Div. 1993), reveals a frequent source of conflict between parental and school direction. In this case, parents brought suit against New York city public high schools, claiming that the schools' condom distribution program violated their due process and free exercise rights because the program did not contain a parental consent or opt-out provision. The New York Supreme Court, Appellate Division, held that such a program violated the parents' due process rights to "direct the upbringing of their children." *Id.* at 261. The parents, said the New York court, "enjoy a well-recognized liberty interest in rearing and educating their children in accord with their own views." *Id.* at 265. Thus, the court said that a parental consent or opt-out provision is required under the Due Process Clause. Contrast *Alfonso* with *Curtis v. School Committee*, 652 N.E.2d 580 (Mass. 1995). In *Curtis*, the Massachusetts Supreme Judicial Court upheld the constitutionality of a school condom distribution program against a due process and free exercise challenge by some of the students' parents. The Massachusetts court, critical of the *Alfonso* court, found that because the parents' children were not forced to participate in the program, their parental liberties were not violated, and an opt-out provision or parental consent was unnecessary to preserve the program's constitutionality. *Id.* at 586–87.

2. Family-Related Rights Beyond Parenting

a. Marriage

LOVING v. VIRGINIA
388 U.S. 1 (1967)

MR. CHIEF JUSTICE WARREN delivered the opinion of the Court.

This case presents a constitutional question never addressed by this Court: whether a statutory scheme adopted by the State of Virginia to prevent marriages between persons solely on the basis of racial classifications violates the Equal Protection and Due Process Clauses of the Fourteenth Amendment. For reasons which seem to us to reflect the central meaning of those constitutional commands, we conclude that these statutes cannot stand consistently with the Fourteenth Amendment.

In June 1958, two residents of Virginia, Mildred Jeter, a Negro woman, and Richard Loving, a white man, were married in the District of Columbia pursuant to its laws. Shortly after their marriage, the Lovings returned to Virginia and established their marital abode in Caroline County. At the October Term, 1958, of the Circuit Court of Caroline County, a grand jury issued an indictment charging the Lovings with violating Virginia's ban on interracial marriages. On January 6, 1959, the Lovings pleaded guilty to the charge and were sentenced to one year in jail; however, the trial judge suspended the sentence for a period of 25 years on the condition that the Lovings leave the State and not return to Virginia together for 25 years. . . .

*   *   *

The Supreme Court of Appeals upheld the constitutionality of the antimiscege-nation statutes and, after modifying the sentence, affirmed the convictions. The Lovings appealed this decision, and we noted probable jurisdiction. . . .

The two statutes under which appellants were convicted and sentenced are part of a comprehensive statutory scheme aimed at prohibiting and punishing interracial marriages. The Lovings were convicted of violating § 20-58 of the Virginia Code:

> "*Leaving State to evade law* — If any white person and colored person shall go out of this State, for the purpose of being married, and with the intention of returning, and be married out of it, and afterwards return to and reside in it, cohabiting as man and wife, they shall be punished as provided in § 20-59, and the marriage shall be governed by the same law as if it had been solemnized in this State. The fact of their cohabitation here as man and wife shall be evidence of their marriage."

Section 20-59, which defines the penalty for miscegenation, provides:

> *"Punishment for marriage.* — If any white person intermarry with a colored person, or any colored person intermarry with a white person, he shall be guilty of a felony and shall be punished by confinement in the penitentiary for not less than one nor more than five years." . . .

*   *   *

Virginia is now one of 16 States which prohibit and punish marriages on the basis of racial classifications.[3]

Penalties for miscegenation arose as an incident to slavery and have been common in Virginia since the colonial period. The present statutory scheme dates from the adoption of the Racial Integrity Act of 1924, passed during the period of extreme nativism which followed the end of the First World War. The central features of this Act, and current Virginia law, are the absolute prohibition of a "white person" marrying other than another "white person," a prohibition against issuing marriage licenses until the issuing official is satisfied that the applicants' statements as to their race are correct, certificates of "racial composition" to be kept by both local and state registrars, and the carrying forward of earlier prohibitions against racial intermarriage.

I.

*   *   *

While the state court is no doubt correct in asserting that marriage is a social relation subject to the State's police power, the State does not contend in its argument before this Court that its powers to regulate marriage are unlimited notwithstanding the commands of the Fourteenth Amendment. Nor could it do so in light of *Meyer v. Nebraska* (1923), and *Skinner v. Oklahoma* (1942). Instead, the State argues that the meaning of the Equal Protection Clause, as illuminated by the statements of the Framers, is only that state penal laws containing an interracial element as part of the definition of the offense must apply equally to whites and Negroes in the sense that members of each race are punished to the same degree. Thus, the State contends that, because its miscegenation statutes punish equally

---

[3] [5] After the initiation of this litigation, Maryland repealed its prohibitions against interracial marriage, Md. Laws 1967, c. 6, leaving Virginia and 15 other States with statutes outlawing interracial marriage: Alabama, Ala. Const., Art. 4, § 102, Ala. Code, Tit. 14, § 360 (1958); Arkansas, Ark. Stat. Ann. § 55-104 (1947); Delaware, Del. Code Ann., Tit. 13, § 101 (1953); Florida, Fla. Const., Art. 16, § 24, Fla. Stat. § 741.11 (1965); Georgia, Ga. Code Ann. § 53-106 (1961); Kentucky, Ky. Rev. Stat. Ann. § 402.020 (Supp. 1966); Louisiana, La. Rev. Stat. § 14:79 (1950); Mississippi, Miss. Const., Art. 1 § 26 Miss. Code Ann. § 459 (1956); Missouri, Mo. Rev. Stat. § 451.020 (Supp. 1966); North Carolina, N. C. Const., Art. XIV, § 8, N. C. Gen. Stat. § 14-181 (1953); Oklahoma, Okla. Stat., Tit 43, § 12 (Supp. 1965); South Carolina, S. C. Const., Art. 3, § 33, S. C. Code Ann. § 20-7 (1962); Tennessee, Tenn. Const., Art. 11,§ 14, Tenn. Code Ann. § 36-402 (1955); Texas, Tex. Pen. Code, Art. 492 (1952); West Virginia, W. Va. Code Ann. § 4697 (1961). Over the past 15 years, 14 States have repealed laws outlawing interracial marriages: Arizona, California, Colorado, Idaho, Indiana, Maryland, Montana, Nebraska, Nevada, North Dakota, Oregon, South Dakota, Utah, and Wyoming. The first state court to recognize that miscegenation statutes violate the Equal Protection Clause was the Supreme Court of California. *Perez v. Sharp*, 198 P.2d 17 (Cal. 1948).

both the white and the Negro participants in an interracial marriage, these statutes, despite their reliance on racial classifications, do not constitute an invidious discrimination based upon race. . . .

*   *   *

. . . We have rejected the proposition that the debates in the Thirty-ninth Congress or in the state legislatures which ratified the Fourteenth Amendment supported the theory advanced by the State, that the requirement of equal protection of the laws is satisfied by penal laws defining offenses based on racial classifications so long as white and Negro participants in the offense were similarly punished.

. . . As we [have previously] demonstrated, the Equal Protection Clause requires the consideration of whether the classifications drawn by any statute constitute an arbitrary and invidious discrimination. The clear and central purpose of the Fourteenth Amendment was to eliminate all official state sources of invidious racial discrimination in the States. *Slaughter-House Cases.*

There can be no question but that Virginia's miscegenation statutes rest solely upon distinctions drawn according to race. The statutes proscribe generally accepted conduct if engaged in by members of different races. Over the years, this Court has consistently repudiated "[d]istinctions between citizens solely because of their ancestry" as being "odious to a free people whose institutions are founded upon the doctrine of equality." At the very least, the Equal Protection Clause demands that racial classifications, especially suspect in criminal statutes, be subjected to the "most rigid scrutiny," and, if they are ever to be upheld, they must be shown to be necessary to the accomplishment of some permissible state objective, independent of the racial discrimination which it was the object of the Fourteenth Amendment to eliminate. Indeed, two members of this Court have already stated that they "cannot conceive of a valid legislative purpose . . . which makes the color of a person's skin the test of whether his conduct is a criminal offense." *McLaughlin v. Florida* (1964) (STEWART, J., joined by DOUGLAS, J., concurring).

There is patently no legitimate overriding purpose independent of invidious racial discrimination which justifies this classification. . . .

II.

These statutes also deprive the Lovings of liberty without due process of law in violation of the Due Process Clause of the Fourteenth Amendment. The freedom to marry has long been recognized as one of the vital personal rights essential to the orderly pursuit of happiness by free men.

Marriage is one of the "basic civil rights of man," fundamental to our very existence and survival. *Skinner v. Oklahoma* (1942). To deny this fundamental freedom on so unsupportable a basis as the racial classifications embodied in these statutes, classifications so directly subversive of the principle of equality at the heart of the Fourteenth Amendment, is surely to deprive all the State's citizens of liberty without due process of law. The Fourteenth Amendment requires that the freedom of choice to marry not be restricted by invidious racial discriminations. Under our Constitution, the freedom to marry, or not marry, a person of another race resides with the individual and cannot be infringed by the State.

These convictions must be reversed. It is so ordered.

Mr. Justice Stewart, concurring. [Omitted.]

NOTES AND QUESTIONS

1.   Marriage is said to have deep roots in history and tradition, and therefore, it must be recognized as a nontextual constitutional right. Why is marriage so important? Does the stability of marriage and family have much to do with the level of civility and achievement in the larger culture? Tocqueville wrote: "Certainly of all Countries in the world America is the one in which the marriage tie is most respected and where the highest and truest conception of conjugal happiness has been conceived." Alexis de Tocqueville, Democracy in America 291 (J.P. Mayer ed. & George Lawrence trans., Doubleday 1969) (1850). The marriage root is far deeper than the American experience, of course. Biblically, marriage is represented in the following way:

> Have ye not read, that he who made man from the beginning, Made them male and female? And he [Christ] said: For this cause shall a man leave father and mother, and shall cleave to his wife, and they two shall be in one flesh. Therefore now they are not two, but one flesh. What, therefore, God hath joined together, let no man put asunder.

Matthew 19:4-6.

2.   Unlike some religious conceptions of marriage, the constitutional right to marry includes the right to divorce. *Boddie v. Connecticut*, 401 U.S. 371 (1971). In *Boddie*, the Court invalidated a state law as it applied to an indigent that required the payment of filing fees and costs in a divorce proceeding. The theory: preventing someone from divorcing also prevents them from marrying someone else. Given the often negative consequences of divorce on the individuals involved, their children, and the larger community, *see* Barbara Dafoe Whitehead, The Divorce Culture (1997), is the Court really protecting the natural right of marriage by facilitating its termination? Or is the Court's conception of marriage merely that of individual, personal autonomy, as opposed to a lifetime promise and assumption of duty to others — most notably, spouse and children? At one time, a Wisconsin law prevented an individual from marrying if he or she had a minor child not in his or her custody and the individual was in arrears on child support. The Court invalidated the law in *Zablocki v. Redhail*, 434 U.S. 374 (1978), under the Equal Protection Clause. Again, the Court waxed eloquent about the decision to marry being "on the same level of importance as decisions relating to procreation, childbirth, child rearing, and family relationships." *Id.* at 386. Admitting that the state had a substantial interest in seeing to the prompt payment of child support, the Court thought the state had better alternatives to further its interest, such as wage garnishment or civil or criminal penalties for default. *Id.* at 388–91.

3. Insofar as the Court recognizes marriage to be a fundamental right and it does so based not upon the text of the Constitution (marriage is not mentioned) or even the more mundane authority of statute, but rather based on its own discernment of the truth of human nature, is this further evidence that natural law is inescapable? Will this reliance upon human nature result in common ground being found between advocates of same-sex marriage and, say, those who support the understanding of life beginning at conception — based upon natural law?

b. Procreation

SKINNER v. OKLAHOMA
316 U.S. 535 (1942)

MR. JUSTICE DOUGLAS delivered the opinion of the Court.

This case touches a sensitive and important area of human rights. Oklahoma deprives certain individuals of a right which is basic to the perpetuation of a race — the right to have offspring. Oklahoma has decreed the enforcement of its law against petitioner, overruling his claim that it violated the Fourteenth Amendment. Because that decision raised grave and substantial constitutional questions, we granted the petition for certiorari.

The statute involved is Oklahoma's Habitual Criminal Sterilization Act. That Act defines an "habitual criminal" as a person who, having been convicted two or more times for crimes "amounting to felonies involving moral turpitude," either in an Oklahoma court or in a court of any other State, is thereafter convicted of such a felony in Oklahoma and is sentenced to a term of imprisonment in an Oklahoma penal institution. Machinery is provided for the institution by the Attorney General of a proceeding against such a person in the Oklahoma courts for a judgment that such person shall be rendered sexually sterile. Notice, an opportunity to be heard, and the right to a jury trial are provided. The issues triable in such a proceeding are narrow and confined. If the court or jury finds that the defendant is an "habitual criminal" and that he "may be rendered sexually sterile without detriment to his or her general health," then the court "shall render judgment to the effect that said defendant be rendered sexually sterile" by the operation of vasectomy in case of a male, and of salpingectomy in case of a female. Only one other provision of the Act is material here, . . . which provides that "offenses arising out of the violation of the prohibitory laws, revenue acts, embezzlement, or political offenses, shall not come or be considered within the terms of this Act."

Petitioner was convicted in 1926 of the crime of stealing chickens, and was sentenced to the Oklahoma State Reformatory. In 1929 he was convicted of the crime of robbery with firearms, and was sentenced to the reformatory. In 1934 he was convicted again of robbery with firearms, and was sentenced to the penitentiary. He was confined there in 1935 when the Act was passed. In 1936 the Attorney General instituted proceedings against him. Petitioner in his answer challenged the Act as unconstitutional by reason of the Fourteenth Amendment. A jury trial was had. The court instructed the jury that the crimes of which petitioner had been convicted were felonies involving moral turpitude, and that the only question for the jury was whether the operation of vasectomy could be performed on petitioner without detriment to his general health. The jury found that it could be. A judgment directing that the operation of vasectomy be performed on petitioner was affirmed by the Supreme Court of Oklahoma by a five to four decision.

Several objections to the constitutionality of the Act have been pressed upon us. . . . We pass those points without intimating an opinion on them, for there is a feature of the Act which clearly condemns it. That is, its failure to meet the requirements of the equal protection clause of the Fourteenth Amendment.

We do not stop to point out all of the inequalities in this Act. A few examples will suffice. In Oklahoma, grand larceny is a felony. Larceny is grand larceny when the property taken exceeds $20 in value. Embezzlement is punishable "in the manner prescribed for feloniously stealing property of the value of that embezzled." Hence, he who embezzles property worth more than $20 is guilty of a felony. A clerk who appropriates over $20 from his employer's till and a stranger who steals the same amount are thus both guilty of felonies. If the latter repeats his act and is convicted three times, he may be sterilized. But the clerk is not subject to the pains and penalties of the Act no matter how large his embezzlements nor how frequent his convictions. A person who enters a chicken coop and steals chickens commits a felony; and he may be sterilized if he is thrice convicted. If, however, he is a bailee of the property and fraudulently appropriates it, he is an embezzler. Hence, no matter how habitual his proclivities for embezzlement are and no matter how often his conviction, he may not be sterilized. . . .

It was stated in *Buck v. Bell* [(1927)] that the claim that state legislation violates the equal protection clause of the Fourteenth Amendment is "the usual last resort of constitutional arguments." Under our constitutional system the States in determining the reach and scope of particular legislation need not provide "abstract symmetry" They may mark and set apart the classes and types of problems according to the needs and as dictated or suggested by experience. . . .

But the instant legislation runs afoul of the equal protection clause, though we give Oklahoma that large deference which the rule of the foregoing cases requires. We are dealing here with legislation which involves one of the basic civil rights of man. Marriage and procreation are fundamental to the very existence and survival of the race. The power to sterilize, if exercised, may have subtle, far reaching and devastating effects. In evil or reckless hands it can cause races or types which are inimical to the dominant group to wither and disappear. There is no redemption for the individual whom the law touches. Any experiment which the State conducts is to his irreparable injury. He is forever deprived of a basic liberty. We mention these matters not to reexamine the scope of the police power of the States. We advert to them merely in emphasis of our view that strict scrutiny of the classification which a State makes in a sterilization law is essential, lest unwittingly, or otherwise, invidious discriminations are made against groups or types of individuals in violation of the constitutional guaranty of just and equal laws. The guaranty of "equal protection of the laws is a pledge of the protection of equal laws." When the law lays an unequal hand on those who have committed intrinsically the same quality of offense and sterilizes one and not the other, it has made as invidious a discrimination as if it had selected a particular race or nationality for oppressive treatment. Sterilization of those who have thrice committed grand larceny, with immunity for those who are embezzlers, is a clear, pointed, unmistakable discrimination. Oklahoma makes no attempt to say that he who commits larceny by trespass or trick or fraud has biologically inheritable traits which he who commits embezzlement lacks. . . . In terms of fines and imprisonment the crimes of larceny and embezzlement rate the same under the Oklahoma code. Only when it comes to sterilization are the pains and penalties of the law different. The equal protection clause would indeed be a formula of empty words if such conspicuously artificial lines could be drawn. . . .

*   *   *

Reversed.

Mr. Chief Justice Stone, concurring.

I concur in the result, but I am not persuaded that we are aided in reaching it by recourse to the equal protection clause.

If Oklahoma may resort generally to the sterilization of criminals on the assumption that their propensities are transmissible to future generations by inheritance, I seriously doubt that the equal protection clause requires it to apply the measure to all criminals in the first instance, or to none.

Moreover, if we must presume that the legislature knows — what science has been unable to ascertain — that the criminal tendencies of any class of habitual offenders are transmissible regardless of the varying mental characteristics of its individuals, I should suppose that we must likewise presume that the legislature, in its wisdom, knows that the criminal tendencies of some classes of offenders are more likely to be transmitted than those of others. And so I think the real question we have to consider is not one of equal protection, but whether the wholesale condemnation of a class to such an invasion of personal liberty, without opportunity to any individual to show that his is not the type of case which would justify resort to it, satisfies the demands of due process.

There are limits to the extent to which the presumption of constitutionality can be pressed, especially where the liberty of the person is concerned (see *United States v. Carolene Products Co.*, 304 U.S. 144, 152, n. 4) and where the presumption is resorted to only to dispense with a procedure which the ordinary dictates of prudence would seem to demand for the protection of the individual from arbitrary action. Although petitioner here was given a hearing to ascertain whether sterilization would be detrimental to his health, he was given none to discover whether his criminal tendencies are of an inheritable type. Undoubtedly a state may, after appropriate inquiry, constitutionally interfere with the personal liberty of the individual to prevent the transmission by inheritance of his socially injurious tendencies. *Buck v. Bell.* But until now we have not been called upon to say that it may do so without giving him a hearing and opportunity to challenge the existence as to him of the only facts which could justify so drastic a measure.

Science has found and the law has recognized that there are certain types of mental deficiency associated with delinquency which are inheritable. But the State does not contend — nor can there be any pretense — that either common knowledge or experience, or scientific investigation, has given assurance that the criminal tendencies of any class of habitual offenders are universally or even generally inheritable. In such circumstances, inquiry whether such is the fact in the case of any particular individual cannot rightly be dispensed with. Whether the procedure by which a statute carries its mandate into execution satisfies due process is a matter of judicial cognizance. A law which condemns, without hearing, all the individuals of a class to so harsh a measure as the present because some or even many merit condemnation, is lacking in the first principles of due process. And so, while the state may protect itself from the demonstrably inheritable tendencies of the individual which are injurious to society, the most elementary notions of due process would seem to require it to take appropriate steps to safeguard the liberty of the individual by affording him, before he is condemned to an irreparable injury in his person, some opportunity to show that he is without such inheritable tendencies. The state is called on to sacrifice no permissible end when it is required to reach its objective by a reasonable and just procedure adequate to safeguard rights of the individual which concededly the Constitution protects.

Mr. Justice Jackson concurring.

I join the Chief Justice in holding that the hearings provided are too limited in the context of the present Act to afford due process of law. I also agree with the opinion of Mr. Justice Douglas that the scheme of classification set forth in the Act denies equal protection of the law. I disagree with the opinion of each in so far as it rejects or minimizes the grounds taken by the other.

*   *   *

I also think the present plan to sterilize the individual in pursuit of a eugenic plan to eliminate from the race characteristics that are only vaguely identified and which in our present state of knowledge are uncertain as to transmissibility presents other constitutional questions of gravity. This Court has sustained such an experiment with respect to an imbecile, a person with definite and observable characteristics, where the condition had persisted through three generations and afforded grounds for the belief that it was transmissible and would continue to manifest itself in generations to come. *Buck v. Bell.*

There are limits to the extent to which a legislatively represented majority may conduct biological experiments at the expense of the dignity and personality and natural powers of a minority — even those who have been guilty of what the majority define as crimes. But this Act falls down before reaching this problem, which I mention only to avoid the implication that such a question may not exist because not discussed. On it I would also reserve judgment.

NOTES AND QUESTIONS

1. Is it extraordinary to think of government-imposed sterilization? Prior to *Skinner*, the Court upheld the power of the government to impose involuntary sterilization. In *Buck v. Bell*, 274 U.S. 200 (1927), the Court ruled that it was

constitutional for Virginia to involuntarily sterilize the mentally retarded. The Court's opinion in *Buck* was written by Oliver Wendell Holmes, an antagonist of the American natural law tradition. Holmes explained his opposition by writing: "[t]he jurists who believe in natural law seem to me to be in that naive state of mind that accepts what has been familiar and accepted by them and their neighbors as something that must be accepted by all men everywhere." Oliver Wendell Holmes, *Natural Law*, 32 HARV. L. REV. 40, 41 (1918). What Carrie Bell, the 18-year-old woman in *Buck* asked to have accepted were the fundamental elements of her human personhood. However, Justice Holmes responded cooly: "It is better for all the world, if instead of waiting to execute degenerate offspring for crime, or to let them starve for their imbecility, society can prevent those who are manifestly unfit from continuing their kind. . . . Three generations of imbeciles are enough." 274 U.S. at 207. The reasoning in *Skinner* disavows this stark proposition, even as it does not formally overrule *Buck*.

Justice Holmes' coarse language drew rebuke from many, but especially from law faculties of religious schools. For example, the late Professor Edward Barrett of Notre Dame reminded his students of the decision in *Buck* to urge them never to remain complacent when the integrity of the human person was at stake. How many law school graduates, Professor Barrett wondered, were prepared to

> cut through at once to the fallacious "inarticulate premise" of Justice Holmes' defense of compulsory sterilization (less than ten years before Hitler): "the principle that sustains compulsory vaccination is broad enough to cover the cutting of the Fallopian tubes?" How many [students educated in the tradition of natural law originalism] were content, like Justice Butler, to "dissent without opinion?" How many more, charmed by the word-witchery of Holmes, silently acquiesced? All teaching is an act of faith.

Edward Barrett, *The "Catholic" Law School and the Natural Law — The Notre Dame Experiment*, 56 HOMILETIC & PASTORAL REV. 904, 905–06 (1956) (quoting *Buck*, 274 U.S. at 207). What is the "fallacious logic" Barrett assails? On what principle can anyone distinguish state-required immunization from state-required sterilization? From what source does that principle derive?

2.   As a precise matter of constitutional adjudication, *Skinner* is mostly an equal protection case. As explained by Justice Douglas, the law discriminates among similarly situated people, the larcenist and the embezzler for example, in respect to the exercise of what the Court describes as "one of the basic civil rights of man." 316 U.S. at 541. We discussed equal protection at length in Chapter 5; there, we saw that it was generally inappropriate for government to draw distinctions among individuals on the basis of suspect (race, national origin, and sometimes alienage) or quasi-suspect (gender, illegitimacy) classifications. If these classifications are employed, the government needs a compelling or important governmental purpose, respectively. *Skinner* illustrates another aspect of equal protection review. Where a fundamental right is at issue, government distinctions among individuals with respect to that right are all suspect. Other fundamental rights triggering this analysis include voting, *see, e.g., Harper v. Virginia Bd. of Elections*, 383 U.S. 663 (1966) (holding that the Equal Protection Clause forbids states from conditioning the right to vote on the affluence of the voter or on the payment of a fee); *Reynolds*

v. Sims, 377 U.S. 533 (1964) (finding that the Constitution requires a standard of one person/one vote), access to the court system, *see, e.g., Douglas v. California*, 372 U.S. 353 (1963) (right to counsel for indigents); *Griffin v. Illinois*, 351 U.S. 12 (1956) (free transcripts for indigents in a criminal proceeding); *M.L.B. v. S.L.J.*, 519 U.S. 102 (1996) (right to free transcript in civil custody proceeding because of the fundamental parent-child relationship), and interstate travel, *Shapiro v. Thompson*, 394 U.S. 618 (1969) (one-year residency requirement to receive welfare was an unconstitutional infringement of the travel right. Right to travel cases may also be handled as a privilege or immunity of citizenship, *see* Chapter 4). It is possible for equal protection analysis to apply as well with respect to any of the textual Bill of Rights, although violations of free speech and religion, for example, are frequently dealt with directly within the terms of their separate history and case authority.

c. Family Living Arrangements

The importance of the family to the well-being of the nation cannot be understated. Professor Sylvia Law writes that to the founders: "The family was the central economic unit of society, both producing and consuming almost all goods and services. . . . Custom and law strongly encouraged family formation and virtually everyone lived in a family." Sylvia A. Law, *The Founders on Families*, 39 U. Fla. L. Rev. 583, 591–92 (1987). The family, of course, pre-dates the State and has long been recognized as its own sovereignty. As one 17th century writer observed:

> A family is a little church, and a little commonwealth, at least a lively representation thereof, whereby trial may be made of such as are fit for any place of authority, or of subjection, in church or commonwealth. Or rather, it is as a school wherein the first principles and grounds of government are learned; whereby men are fitted to greater matters in church and commonwealth.

William Gouge, Of Domesticall Duties (1622), *quoted in* John Demos, *Images of the American Family, Then and Now, in* Changing Images of the Family 43, 46 (Virginia Tufte & Barbara Myerhoff eds., 1979).

In *Moore v. City of East Cleveland*, 431 U.S. 494 (1977), the Court manifested respect for the extended family as well — that is, family based on kinship (blood, marriage or adoption) relationships. In *Moore*, the Court invalidated a municipal ordinance that so narrowly defined family that it precluded a grandmother from living with her two grandsons, who were cousins, rather than brothers. (The city was by this awkward means attempting to keep public school enrollments in balance.) *Moore*'s respect for the extended family is consistent with original understanding. In the words of one commentator:

> From our colonial beginnings, and throughout most of the republican experience, American legal and cultural systems gave broad and deep support to large families and to family-based economic enterprise. To get intact families started in the new world, colonial charters offered free inheritable land and protection against taxes. To encourage the creation of large families, special incentives were offered such as additional land or longer tax exemptions for each newborn child.

Robert Kimball Shinkoskey, *Without Law*, FAM. AMERICA (Rockford Inst. Ctr. on the Family in Am., Rockford, Il.), Jan. 1993, at 1, 3.

Moore's solicitude for the family does not extend to unrelated individuals. In *Village of Belle Terre v. Boraas*, 416 U.S. 1 (1974), the Court upheld a zoning ordinance limiting the number of individuals not related by "blood, marriage, or adoption" who could live together. A group of college students were thereby precluded from sharing a rented house. The Court held that the ordinance infringed no fundamental right and thus the applicable standard was whether the statute bore a rational relationship to a permissible state objective. *Id.* at 8–9. The Court concluded that Belle Terre met this standard because the state's objective, "[a] quiet place where yards are wide, people few, and motor vehicles restricted [provided] legitimate guidelines in a land-use project addressed to family needs." *Id.* at 9. A similar distinction between related and unrelated individuals was drawn in *Smith v. Organization of Foster Families for Equality and Reform*, 431 U.S. 816 (1977) (upholding a pre-removal hearing for foster parents only where the foster child had been in the home for 18 months or more). Unlike biological parents, the state, said the Court, "has been a partner from the outset" in the foster child context. *Id.* at 845.

Indirect economic pressures arising from the structure of government benefit programs that may cause related family members to live apart do not fall within the *Moore* holding. For example, in *Lyng v. Castillo*, 477 U.S. 635 (1986), the Court sustained the federal provision of food stamps to household units, consisting of parents, children, and siblings who live together. Effectively, this meant that families or households received less food assistance if they lived together than if they lived apart. Because the law did not "order" relatives to live separately, but only created an economic incentive to do so, it did not transgress the fundamental right articulated in *Moore*. *Id.* at 638–39. The Court is more deferential generally when a government benefit, rather than a prohibition, is said to have a negative impact on the family. Thus, in *Bowen v. Gilliard*, 483 U.S. 587 (1987), the Court allowed Aid to Families with Dependent Children to be calculated in relation to the income of parents and siblings living together, even if again, that meant they received less than if they lived apart. This may be unwise social policy, but the Court held that Congress' power is plenary when it defines " 'the scope and the duration of the entitlement to . . . benefits, and to increase, to decrease, or to terminate those benefits.' " *Id.* at 598 (quoting *Atkins v. Parker*, 472 U.S. 115, 129 (1985)).

MICHAEL H. v. GERALD D.
491 U.S. 110 (1989)

JUSTICE SCALIA announced the judgment of the Court and delivered an opinion, in which THE CHIEF JUSTICE joins, and in all but footnote 6 of which JUSTICE O'CONNOR and JUSTICE KENNEDY join.

Under California law, a child born to a married woman living with her husband is presumed to be a child of the marriage. Cal. Evid. Code Ann. § 621 (Supp. 1989). The presumption of legitimacy may be rebutted only by the husband or wife, and then only in limited circumstances. The instant appeal presents the claim that this presumption infringes upon the due process rights of a man who wishes to establish his paternity of a child born to the wife of another man, and the claim that it infringes upon the constitutional right of the child to maintain a relationship with her natural father.

I

The facts of this case are, we must hope, extraordinary. On May 9, 1976, in Las Vegas, Nevada, Carole D., an international model, and Gerald D., a top executive in a French oil company, were married. The couple established a home in Playa del Rey, California, in which they resided as husband and wife when one or the other was not out of the country on business. In the summer of 1978, Carole became involved in an adulterous affair with a neighbor, Michael H. In September 1980, she conceived a child, Victoria D., who was born on May 11, 1981. Gerald was listed as father on the birth certificate and has always held Victoria out to the world as his daughter. Soon after delivery of the child, however, Carole informed Michael that she believed he might be the father.

In the first three years of her life, Victoria remained always with Carole, but found herself within a variety of quasi-family units. In October 1981, Gerald moved to New York City to pursue his business interests, but Carole chose to remain in California. At the end of that month, Carole and Michael had blood tests of themselves and Victoria, which showed a 98.07% probability that Michael was Victoria's father. In January 1982, Carole visited Michael in St. Thomas, where his primary business interests were based. There Michael held Victoria out as his child. In March, however, Carole left Michael and returned to California, where she took up residence with yet another man, Scott K. Later that spring, and again in the summer, Carole and Victoria spent time with Gerald in New York City, as well as on vacation in Europe. In the fall, they returned to Scott in California.

In November 1982, rebuffed in his attempts to visit Victoria, Michael filed a filiation action in California Superior Court to establish his paternity and right to visitation. In March 1983, the court appointed an attorney and guardian ad litem to represent Victoria's interests. Victoria then filed a cross-complaint asserting that if she had more than one psychological or *de facto* father, she was entitled to maintain her filial relationship, with all of the attendant rights, duties, and obligations, with both. In May 1983, Carole filed a motion for summary judgment. During this period, from March through July 1983, Carole was again living with Gerald in New York. In August, however, she returned to California, became involved once again with Michael, and instructed her attorneys to remove the summary judgment motion from the calendar.

For the ensuing eight months, when Michael was not in St. Thomas he lived with Carole and Victoria in Carole's apartment in Los Angeles and held Victoria out as his daughter. In April 1984, Carole and Michael signed a stipulation that Michael was Victoria's natural father. Carole left Michael the next month, however, and instructed her attorneys not to file the stipulation. In June 1984, Carole reconciled with Gerald and joined him in New York, where they now live with Victoria and two other children since born into the marriage.

In May 1984, Michael and Victoria, through her guardian ad litem, sought visitation rights for Michael *pendente lite*. To assist in determining whether visitation would be in Victoria's best interests, the Superior Court appointed a psychologist to evaluate Victoria, Gerald, Michael, and Carole. The psychologist recommended that Carole retain sole custody, but that Michael be allowed continued contact with Victoria pursuant to a restricted visitation schedule. The court concurred and ordered that Michael be provided with limited visitation privileges *pendente lite*.

On October 19, 1984, Gerald, who had intervened in the action, moved for summary judgment on the ground that under Cal. Evid. Code § 621 there were no triable issues of fact as to Victoria's paternity. This law provides that "the issue of a wife cohabiting with her husband, who is not impotent or sterile, is conclusively presumed to be a child of the marriage." Cal. Evid. Code Ann. § 621(a) (Supp. 1989). The presumption may be rebutted by blood tests, but only if a motion for such tests is made, within two years from the date of the child's birth, either by the husband or, if the natural father has filed an affidavit acknowledging paternity, by the wife. §§ 621(c) and (d).

On January 28, 1985, having found that affidavits submitted by Carole and Gerald sufficed to demonstrate that the two were cohabiting at conception and birth and that Gerald was neither sterile nor impotent, the Superior Court granted Gerald's motion for summary judgment, rejecting Michael's and Victoria's challenges to the constitutionality of § 621. The court also denied their motions for continued visitation pending the appeal under Cal. Civ. Code § 4601, which provides that a court may, in its discretion, grant "reasonable visitation rights . . . to any . . . person having an interest in the welfare of the child." Cal. Civ. Code Ann. § 4601 (Supp. 1989). It found that allowing such visitation would "violat[e] the intention of the Legislature by impugning the integrity of the family unit."

*   *   *

III

*   *   *

. . . Michael contends as a matter of substantive due process that, because he has established a parental relationship with Victoria, protection of Gerald's and Carole's marital union is an insufficient state interest to support termination of that relationship. This argument is, of course, predicated on the assertion that Michael has a constitutionally protected liberty interest in his relationship with Victoria.

It is an established part of our constitutional jurisprudence that the term "liberty" in the Due Process Clause extends beyond freedom from physical restraint. *See, e.g., Pierce v. Society of Sisters* (1925); *Meyer v. Nebraska* (1923). Without that core textual meaning as a limitation, defining the scope of the Due Process Clause "has at times been a treacherous field for this Court," giving "reason for concern lest the only limits to . . . judicial intervention become the predilections of those who happen at the time to be Members of this Court." *Moore v. East Cleveland* (1977). . . . In an attempt to limit and guide interpretation of the Clause, we have insisted not merely that the interest denominated as a "liberty" be "fundamental" (a concept that, in isolation, is hard to objectify), but also that it be an interest traditionally protected by our society.[4] As we have put it, the Due Process Clause affords only those protections "so rooted in the traditions and conscience of our people as to be ranked as fundamental." *Snyder v. Massachusetts* (1934) (Cardozo, J.). Our cases reflect "continual insistence upon respect for the teachings of history [and] solid recognition of the basic values that underlie our society. . . ." *Griswold v. Connecticut* (1965) (Harlan, J., concurring in judgment).

This insistence that the asserted liberty interest be rooted in history and tradition is evident, as elsewhere, in our cases according constitutional protection to certain parental rights. . . . [These cases] rest not upon such isolated factors but upon the historic respect — indeed, sanctity would not be too strong a term — traditionally accorded to the relationships that develop within the unitary family.[5] . . .

Thus, the legal issue in the present case reduces to whether the relationship between persons in the situation of Michael and Victoria has been treated as a protected family unit under the historic practices of our society, or whether on any other basis it has been accorded special protection. We think it impossible to find that it has. In fact, quite to the contrary, our traditions have protected the marital family (Gerald, Carole, and the child they acknowledge to be theirs) against the sort of claim Michael asserts.

The presumption of legitimacy was a fundamental principle of the common law. Traditionally, that presumption could be rebutted only by proof that a husband was incapable of procreation or had had no access to his wife during the relevant period. H. NICHOLAS, ADULTURINE BASTARDY 9–10 (1836) (citing BRACTON, DE LEGIBUS ET CONSUETUDINIBUS ANGLIAE, bk. i, ch. 9, at 6; bk. ii, ch. 29, at 63, ch. 32, at 70 (1569)). As explained by Blackstone, nonaccess could only be proved "if the husband be out of the kingdom of England (or, as the law somewhat loosely phrases it, *extra quatuor maria* [beyond the four seas]) for above nine months. . . ." 1 BLACKSTONE'S COMMENTARIES 456 (J. Chitty ed., 1826). And, under the common law both in England and here, "neither husband nor wife [could] be a witness to prove access or nonaccess." J. SCHOULER, LAW OF THE DOMESTIC RELATIONS § 225, at 306 (3d ed. 1882). The primary policy rationale underlying the common law's severe restrictions on

---

[4] [2] We do not understand what JUSTICE BRENNAN has in mind by an interest "that society traditionally has thought important . . . without protecting it." The protection need not take the form of an explicit constitutional provision or statutory guarantee, but it must at least exclude (all that is necessary to decide the present case) a societal tradition of enacting laws *denying* the interest. Nor do we understand why our practice of limiting the Due Process Clause to traditionally protected interests turns the Clause "into a redundancy." Its purpose is to prevent future generations from lightly casting aside important traditional values — not to enable this Court to invent new ones.

[5] [3] JUSTICE BRENNAN asserts that only a "pinched conception of 'the family' " would exclude Michael, Carole, and Victoria from protection. We disagree. The family unit accorded traditional respect in our society, which we have referred to as the "unitary family," is typified, of course, by the marital family, but also includes the household of unmarried parents and their children. Perhaps the concept can be expanded even beyond this, but it will bear no resemblance to traditionally respected relationships — and will thus cease to have any constitutional significance — if it is stretched so far as to include the relationship established between a married woman, her lover, and their child, during a 3-month sojourn in St. Thomas, or during a subsequent 8-month period when, if he happened to be in Los Angeles, he stayed with her and the child.

rebuttal of the presumption appears to have been an aversion to declaring children illegitimate, thereby depriving them of rights of inheritance and succession, and likely making them wards of the state. A secondary policy concern was the interest in promoting the "peace and tranquillity of States and families," a goal that is obviously impaired by facilitating suits against husband and wife asserting that their children are illegitimate. . . .

We have found nothing in the older sources, nor in the older cases, addressing specifically the power of the natural father to assert parental rights over a child born into a woman's existing marriage with another man. Since it is Michael's burden to establish that such a power (at least where the natural father has established a relationship with the child) is so deeply embedded within our traditions as to be a fundamental right, the lack of evidence alone might defeat his case. But the evidence shows that even in modern times — when, as we have noted, the rigid protection of the marital family has in other respects been relaxed — the ability of a person in Michael's position to claim paternity has not been generally acknowledged. . . .

Moreover, even if it were clear that one in Michael's position generally possesses, and has generally always possessed, standing to challenge the marital child's legitimacy, that would still not establish Michael's case. . . . What counts is whether the States in fact award substantive parental rights to the natural father of a child conceived within, and born into, an extant marital union that wishes to embrace the child. We are not aware of a single case, old or new, that has done so. This is not the stuff of which fundamental rights qualifying as liberty interests are made.[6]

---

6 [6] JUSTICE BRENNAN criticizes our methodology in using historical traditions specifically relating to the rights of an adulterous natural father, rather than inquiring more generally "whether parenthood is an interest that historically has received our attention and protection." There seems to us no basis for the contention that this methodology is "nove[l]." For example, in *Bowers v. Hardwick*, 478 U.S. 186 (1986) [overruled in *Lawrence v. Texas*, 539 U.S. 558 (2003) — Eds.], we noted that at the time the Fourteenth Amendment was ratified all but 5 of the 37 States had criminal sodomy laws, that all 50 of the States had such laws prior to 1961, and that 24 States and the District of Columbia continued to have them; and we concluded from that record, regarding that very specific aspect of sexual conduct, that "to claim that a right to engage in such conduct is 'deeply rooted in this Nation's history and tradition' or 'implicit in the concept of ordered liberty' is, at best, facetious." In *Roe v. Wade*, 410 U.S. 113 (1973), we spent about a fifth of our opinion negating the proposition that there was a longstanding tradition of laws proscribing abortion.

We do not understand why, having rejected our focus upon the societal tradition regarding the natural father's rights vis-à-vis a child whose mother is married to another man, JUSTICE BRENNAN would choose to focus instead upon "parenthood." Why should the relevant category not be even more general — perhaps "family relationships"; or "personal relationships"; or even "emotional attachments in general"? Though the dissent has no basis for the level of generality it would select, we do: We refer to the most specific level at which a relevant tradition protecting or denying protection to, the asserted right can be identified. If, for example, there were no societal tradition, either way, regarding the rights of the natural father of a child adulterously conceived, we would have to consult, and (if possible) reason from, the traditions regarding natural fathers in general. But there is such a more specific tradition, and it unqualifiedly denies protection to such a parent.

One would think that JUSTICE BRENNAN would appreciate the value of consulting the most specific tradition available, since he acknowledges that "[e]ven if we can agree . . . that 'family' and 'parenthood' are part of the good life, it is absurd to assume that we can agree on the content of those terms and destructive to pretend that we do." Because such general traditions provide such imprecise guidance, they permit judges to dictate rather than discern the society's views. The need, if arbitrary decision-

. . . It is a question of legislative policy and not constitutional law whether California will allow the presumed parenthood of a couple desiring to retain a child conceived within and born into their marriage to be rebutted.

We do not accept JUSTICE BRENNAN's criticism that this result "squashes" the liberty that consists of "the freedom not to conform." It seems to us that reflects the erroneous view that there is only one side to this controversy — that one disposition can expand a "liberty" of sorts without contracting an equivalent "liberty" on the other side. Such a happy choice is rarely available. Here, to *provide* protection to an adulterous natural father is to *deny* protection to a marital father, and vice versa. If Michael has a "freedom not to conform" (whatever that means), Gerald must equivalently have a "freedom to conform." One of them will pay a price for asserting that "freedom" — Michael by being unable to act as father of the child he has adulterously begotten, or Gerald by being unable to preserve the integrity of the traditional family unit he and Victoria have established. Our disposition does not choose between these two "freedoms," but leaves that to the people of California. JUSTICE BRENNAN's approach chooses one of them as the constitutional imperative, on no apparent basis except that the unconventional is to be preferred.

IV

* * *

The judgment of the California Court of Appeal is

Affirmed.

JUSTICE O'CONNOR, with whom JUSTICE KENNEDY joins, concurring in part.

I concur in all but footnote 6 of JUSTICE SCALIA's opinion. This footnote sketches a mode of historical analysis to be used when identifying liberty interests protected by the Due Process Clause of the Fourteenth Amendment that may be somewhat inconsistent with our past decisions in this area. *Griswold v. Connecticut*; *Eisenstadt v. Baird*. On occasion the Court has characterized relevant traditions protecting asserted rights at levels of generality that might not be "the most specific level" available. *Loving v. Virginia*, 388 U.S. 1 (1967). I would not foreclose the

---

making is to be avoided, to adopt the most specific tradition as the point of reference — or at least to announce, as JUSTICE BRENNAN declines to do, some other criterion for selecting among the innumerable relevant traditions that could be consulted — is well enough exemplified by the fact that in the present case JUSTICE BRENNAN's opinion and JUSTICE O'CONNOR's opinion, which disapproves this footnote, *both* appeal to tradition, but on the basis of the tradition they select reach opposite results. Although assuredly having the virtue (if it be that) of leaving judges free to decide as they think best when the unanticipated occurs, a rule of law that binds neither by text nor by any particular, identifiable tradition is no rule of law at all.

Finally, we may note that this analysis is not inconsistent with the result in cases such as *Griswold v. Connecticut*, or *Eisenstadt v. Baird*, 405 U.S. 438 (1972). None of those cases acknowledged a longstanding and still extant societal tradition withholding the very right pronounced to be the subject of a liberty interest and then rejected it. JUSTICE BRENNAN must do so here. In this case, the existence of such a tradition, continuing to the present day, refutes any possible contention that the alleged right is "so rooted in the traditions and conscience of our people as to be ranked as fundamental," or "implicit in the concept of ordered liberty."

unanticipated by the prior imposition of a single mode of historical analysis.

JUSTICE STEVENS, concurring in the judgment. [Omitted.]

JUSTICE BRENNAN, with whom JUSTICE MARSHALL and JUSTICE BLACKMUN join, dissenting.

*   *   *

I

Once we recognized that the "liberty" protected by the Due Process Clause of the Fourteenth Amendment encompasses more than freedom from bodily restraint, today's plurality opinion emphasizes, the concept was cut loose from one natural limitation on its meaning. This innovation paved the way, so the plurality hints, for judges to substitute their own preferences for those of elected officials. Dissatisfied with this supposedly unbridled and uncertain state of affairs, the plurality casts about for another limitation on the concept of liberty.

It finds this limitation in "tradition." Apparently oblivious to the fact that this concept can be as malleable and as elusive as "liberty" itself, the plurality pretends that tradition places a discernible border around the Constitution. The pretense is seductive; it would be comforting to believe that a search for "tradition" involves nothing more idiosyncratic or complicated than poring through dusty volumes on American history. Yet, . . . the plurality has not found the objective boundary that it seeks.

*   *   *

Today's plurality, however, does not ask whether parenthood is an interest that historically has received our attention and protection; the answer to that question is too clear for dispute. Instead, the plurality asks whether the specific variety of parenthood under consideration — a natural father's relationship with a child whose mother is married to another man — has enjoyed such protection.

*   *   *

In construing the Fourteenth Amendment to offer shelter only to those interests specifically protected by historical practice, moreover, the plurality ignores the kind of society in which our Constitution exists. We are not an assimilative, homogeneous society, but a facilitative, pluralistic one, in which we must be willing to abide someone else's unfamiliar or even repellent practice because the same tolerant impulse protects our own idiosyncracies (sic) Even if we can agree, therefore, that "family" and "parenthood" are part of the good life, it is absurd to assume that we can agree on the content of those terms and destructive to pretend that we do. In a community such as ours, "liberty" must include the freedom not to conform. The plurality today squashes this freedom by requiring specific approval from history before protecting anything in the name of liberty.

The document that the plurality construes today is unfamiliar to me. It is not the living charter that I have taken to be our Constitution; it is instead a stagnant, archaic, hidebound document steeped in the prejudices and superstitions of a time long past. *This* Constitution does not recognize that times change, does not see that sometimes a practice or rule outlives its foundations. I cannot accept an interpretive method that does such violence to the charter that I am bound by oath to uphold.

II

* * *

Thus, to describe the issue in this case as whether the relationship existing between Michael and Victoria "has been treated as a protected family unit under the historic practices of our society, or whether on any other basis it has been accorded special protection," is to reinvent the wheel. The better approach — indeed, the one commanded by our prior cases and by common sense — is to ask whether the specific parent-child relationship under consideration is close enough to the interests that we already have protected to be deemed an aspect of "liberty" as well. On the facts before us, therefore, the question is not what "level of generality" should be used to describe the relationship between Michael and Victoria, but whether the relationship under consideration is sufficiently substantial to qualify as a liberty interest under our prior cases.

* * *

JUSTICE WHITE, with whom JUSTICE BRENNAN joins, dissenting [omitted].

NOTES AND QUESTIONS

1. *Michael H.* raises the issue of the interest of unmarried fathers. As you might guess, and as *Michael H.* illustrates, they are treated with far less judicial deference than those of married fathers, or for that matter, married parents. For example, in *Santosky v. Kramer*, 455 U.S. 745 (1982), the Court held that a parent's custodial right can be terminated only upon a showing of clear and convincing evidence. "The fundamental liberty interest of natural parents in the care, custody, and management of their child" is protected by the Fourteenth Amendment. *Id.* at 753. By contrast, in *Lehr v. Robertson*, 463 U.S. 248 (1983), the Court allowed an unmarried father's interest in his progeny to be terminated without notice or hearing. The Court made special note of the fact that the father had shown no interest in the child in terms of either support or paternity. *Id.* at 251–52.

Nevertheless, unmarried parents do have a constitutionally-protected interest where they have demonstrated "a full commitment to the responsibilities of parenthood by 'coming forward to participate in the rearing of [their] child[ren].'" *Lehr*, 463 U.S. at 261 (quoting *Caban v. Mohammed*, 441 U.S. 380, 392 (1979)). Thus, in the earlier case of *Stanley v. Illinois*, 405 U.S. 645 (1972), it was a due process and equal protection violation for Illinois to terminate an unmarried father's interest in custody when the father had lived for eighteen years with the children and their mother until her death.

2. *Michael H.* is most often cited because of Justice Scalia's instruction of how the Court should articulate non-textual fundamental rights. How convincing do you find his argument? Here, Justice Scalia wrote only for himself and Chief Justice Rehnquist, yet, the methodology is of considerable importance and the subject of much debate. In directing the Court to protect nontextual rights under the Due Process Clause at their most specific level of abstraction, Justice Scalia was providing a mechanism for constitutional flexibility over time as well as judicial restraint. The Court's most activist member in modern time, the late William Brennan, strongly objected to the Court's, and in particular, Scalia's defense of the liberty of the traditional family, but not others. Justice Brennan argued for accepting "someone else's unfamiliar or even repellent practice[s]," *id.* at 141 (Brennan, J., dissenting), including those of an individual engaging in adultery who wished to insert himself unwelcomely into the rearing of a child being raised by the married spouse who bore the pain of his spouse's infidelity. Notwithstanding Justice Brennan's severe dissent, the Court has relied upon Justice Scalia's approach several times since. For example, in *Reno v. Flores*, 507 U.S. 292 (1993), the Justices described as "mere novelty" the claim that the government as custodial guardian of immigrant children was constitutionally required to provide the best schooling and health care at the highest possible funding level. *Id.* at 303. The claim was "novel," said the Court, because it could not in any way be considered "rooted in the traditions and conscience of our people." *Id.* (quoting *Snyder v. Massachusetts*, 291 U.S. 97, 105 (1934)). Similarly, as we will see below, the Court employed the *Michael H.* approach to reject the claimed assisted suicide right.

3. When Justice Scalia's approach is not followed the Court tends to go off in far less precise directions in the discovery of implied fundamental rights. For a scholarly appraisal of the methods employed, see David Crump, *How Do the Courts Really Discover Unenumerated Fundamental Rights? Cataloguing the Methods of Judicial Alchemy*, 19 HARV. J.L. & PUB. POL'Y 795 (1996) (demonstrating how current judicial practice uses multiple and complex legal formulae to create fundamental rights perhaps often derived from personal inclination or experience).

B. THE NINTH AMENDMENT — A RIGHT OF PRIVACY?

1. Contraception

GRISWOLD v. CONNECTICUT
381 U.S. 479 (1965)

MR. JUSTICE DOUGLAS delivered the opinion of the Court.

Appellant Griswold is Executive Director of the Planned Parenthood League of Connecticut. Appellant Buxton is a licensed physician and a professor at the Yale Medical School who served as Medical Director for the League at its Center in New Haven — a center open and operating from November 1 to November 10, 1961, when appellants were arrested.

They gave information, instruction, and medical advice to *married persons* as to the means of preventing conception. . . .

The statutes whose constitutionality is involved in this appeal are §§ 53-32 and 54-196 of the General Statutes of Connecticut (1958 rev.). The former provides:

"Any person who uses any drug, medicinal article or instrument for the purpose of preventing conception shall be fined not less than fifty dollars or imprisoned not less than sixty days nor more than one year or be both fined and imprisoned."

Section 54-196 provides:

"Any person who assists, abets, counsels, causes, hires or commands another to commit any offense may be prosecuted and punished as if he were the principal offender."

The appellants were found guilty as accessories and fined $100 each, against the claim that the accessory statute as so applied violated the Fourteenth Amendment. . . .

We think that appellants have standing to raise the constitutional rights of the married people with whom they had a professional relationship. . . .

* * *

Coming to the merits, we are met with a wide range of questions that implicate the Due Process Clause of the Fourteenth Amendment. Overtones of some arguments suggest that *Lochner v. New York* [(1905)] should be our guide. But we decline that invitation. . . . We do not sit as a super-legislature to determine the wisdom, need, and propriety of laws that touch economic problems, business affairs, or social conditions. This law, however, operates directly on an intimate relation of husband and wife and their physician's role in one aspect of that relation.

The association of people is not mentioned in the Constitution nor in the Bill of Rights. The right to educate a child in a school of the parents' choice — whether public or private or parochial — is also not mentioned. Nor is the right to study any particular subject or any foreign language. Yet the First Amendment has been construed to include certain of those rights.

By *Pierce v. Society of Sisters*, the right to educate one's children as one chooses is made applicable to the States by the force of the First and Fourteenth Amendments. By *Meyer v. Nebraska*, the same dignity is given the right to study the German language in a private school. In other words, the State may not, consistently with the spirit of the First Amendment, contract the spectrum of available knowledge. The right of freedom of speech and press includes not only the right to utter or to print, but the right to distribute, the right to receive, the right to read and freedom of inquiry, freedom of thought, and freedom to teach — indeed the freedom of the entire university community. Without those peripheral rights the specific rights would be less secure. And so we reaffirm the principle of the *Pierce* and the *Meyer* cases.

In *NAACP v. Alabama* [(1958)] we protected the "freedom to associate and privacy in one's associations," noting that freedom of association was a peripheral First Amendment right. Disclosure of membership lists of a constitutionally valid association, we held, was invalid "as entailing the likelihood of a substantial restraint upon the exercise by petitioner's members of their right to freedom of association." In other words, the First Amendment has a penumbra where privacy is protected from governmental intrusion. . . .

Those cases involved more than the "right of assembly" — a right that extends to all irrespective of their race or ideology. The right of "association," like the right of belief, is more than the right to attend a meeting; it includes the right to express one's attitudes or philosophies by membership in a group or by affiliation with it or by other lawful means. Association in that context is a form of expression of opinion; and while it is not expressly included in the First Amendment its existence is necessary in making the express guarantees fully meaningful.

The foregoing cases suggest that specific guarantees in the Bill of Rights have penumbras, formed by emanations from those guarantees that help give them life and substance. Various guarantees create zones of privacy. The right of association contained in the penumbra of the First Amendment is one, as we have seen. The Third Amendment in its prohibition against the quartering of soldiers "in any house" in time of peace without the consent of the owner is another facet of that privacy. The Fourth Amendment explicitly affirms the "right of the people to be secure in their persons, houses, papers, and effects, against unreasonable searches and seizures." The Fifth Amendment in its Self-Incrimination Clause enables the citizen to create a zone of privacy which government may not force him to surrender to his detriment. The Ninth Amendment provides: "The enumeration in the Constitution, of certain rights, shall not be construed to deny or disparage others retained by the people."

*   *   *

We have had many controversies over these penumbral rights of "privacy and repose." These cases bear witness that the right of privacy which presses for recognition here is a legitimate one.

The present case, then, concerns a relationship lying within the zone of privacy created by several fundamental constitutional guarantees. And it concerns a law which, in forbidding the *use* of contraceptives rather than regulating their manufacture or sale, seeks to achieve its goals by means having a maximum destructive impact upon that relationship. Such a law cannot stand in light of the familiar principle, so often applied by this Court, that a "governmental purpose to control or prevent activities constitutionally subject to state regulation may not be achieved by means which sweep unnecessarily broadly and thereby invade the area of protected freedoms." Would we allow the police to search the sacred precincts of marital bedrooms for telltale signs of the use of contraceptives? The very idea is repulsive to the notions of privacy surrounding the marriage relationship.

We deal with a right of privacy older than the Bill of Rights — older than our political parties, older than our school system. Marriage is a coming together for better or for worse, hopefully enduring, and intimate to the degree of being sacred. It is an association that promotes a way of life, not causes; a harmony in living, not political faiths; a bilateral loyalty, not commercial or social projects. Yet it is an association for as noble a purpose as any involved in our prior decisions.

Reversed.

MR. JUSTICE GOLDBERG, whom THE CHIEF JUSTICE and MR. JUSTICE BRENNAN join, concurring.

I agree with the Court that Connecticut's birth-control law unconstitutionally intrudes upon the right of marital privacy, and I join in its opinion and judgment. Although I have not accepted the view that "due process" as used in the Fourteenth Amendment includes all of the first eight Amendments, I do agree that the concept of liberty protects those personal rights that are fundamental, and is not confined to the specific terms of the Bill of Rights. My conclusion that the concept of liberty is not so restricted and that it embraces the right of marital privacy though that right is not mentioned explicitly in the Constitution is supported both by numerous decisions of this Court, referred to in the Court's opinion, and by the language and history of the Ninth Amendment. In reaching the conclusion that the right of marital privacy is protected, as being within the protected penumbra of specific guarantees of the Bill of Rights, the Court refers to the Ninth Amendment. I add these words to emphasize the relevance of that Amendment to the Court's holding.

* * *

This Court, in a series of decisions, has held that the Fourteenth Amendment absorbs and applies to the States those specifics of the first eight amendments which express fundamental personal rights. The language and history of the Ninth Amendment reveal that the Framers of the Constitution believed that there are additional fundamental rights, protected from governmental infringement, which exist alongside those fundamental rights specifically mentioned in the first eight constitutional amendments.

The Ninth Amendment reads, "The enumeration in the Constitution, of certain rights, shall not be construed to deny or disparage others retained by the people." The Amendment is almost entirely the work of James Madison. It was introduced in Congress by him and passed the House and Senate with little or no debate and virtually no change in language. It was proffered to quiet expressed fears that a bill of specifically enumerated rights[7] could not be sufficiently broad to cover all essential rights and that the specific mention of certain rights would be interpreted as a denial that others were protected.[8]

---

[7] [3] Madison himself had previously pointed out the dangers of inaccuracy resulting from the fact that "no language is so copious as to supply words and phrases for every complex idea." THE FEDERALIST No. 37, at 236 (James Madison) (Cooke ed., 1961).

[8] [4] Alexander Hamilton was opposed to a bill of rights on the ground that it was unnecessary because the Federal Government was a government of delegated powers and it was not granted the power to intrude upon fundamental personal rights. THE FEDERALIST No. 84, at 578–79 (Alexander Hamilton) (Cooke ed., 1961). He also argued,

"I go further, and affirm that bills of rights, in the sense and in the extent in which they are contended for, are not only unnecessary in the proposed constitution, but would even be dangerous. They would contain various exceptions to powers which are not granted; and on this very account, would afford a colourable pretext to claim more than were granted. For why declare that things shall not be done which there is no power to do? Why for instance, should it be said, that the liberty of the press shall not be restrained, when no power is given by which

In presenting the proposed Amendment, Madison said:

> "It has been objected also against a bill of rights, that, by enumerating particular exceptions to the grant of power, it would disparage those rights which were not placed in that enumeration; and it might follow by implication, that those rights which were not singled out, were intended to be assigned into the hands of the General Government, and were consequently insecure. This is one of the most plausible arguments I have ever heard urged against the admission of a bill of rights into this system; but, I conceive, that it may be guarded against. I have attempted it, as gentlemen may see by turning to the last clause of the fourth resolution [the Ninth Amendment]." 1 ANNALS OF CONG. 439 (Gales and Seaton eds., 1834).

Mr. Justice Story wrote of this argument against a bill of rights and the meaning of the Ninth Amendment:

> "In regard to . . . [a] suggestion, that the affirmance of certain rights might disparage others, or might lead to argumentative implications in favor of other powers, it might be sufficient to say that such a course of reasoning could never be sustained upon any solid basis. . . . But a conclusive answer is, that such an attempt may be interdicted (as it has been) by a positive declaration in such a bill of rights that the enumeration of certain rights shall not be construed to deny or disparage others retained by the people." 2 JOSEPH STORY, COMMENTARIES ON THE CONSTITUTION OF THE UNITED STATES 626–27 (5th ed. 1891).

He further stated, referring to the Ninth Amendment:

> "This clause was manifestly introduced to prevent any perverse or ingenious misapplication of the well known maxim, that an affirmation in particular cases implies a negation in all others; and, *e converso*, that a negation in particular cases implies an affirmation in all others." *Id.* at 651.

These statements of Madison and Story make clear that the Framers did not intend that the first eight amendments be construed to exhaust the basic and fundamental rights which the Constitution guaranteed to the people.[9]

While this Court has had little occasion to interpret the Ninth Amendment, "[i]t cannot be presumed that any clause in the constitution is intended to be without effect." *Marbury v. Madison* [(1803)]. In interpreting the Constitution, "real effect should be given to all the words it uses." *Myers v. United States* [(1926)]. The Ninth Amendment to the Constitution may be regarded by some as a recent discovery and

---

restrictions may be imposed? I will not contend that such a provision would confer a regulating power; but it is evident that it would furnish, to men disposed to usurp, a plausible pretence for claiming that power." *Id.* at 579.

The Ninth Amendment and the Tenth Amendment, which provides, "The powers not delegated to the United States by the Constitution, nor prohibited by it to the States, are reserved to the States respectively, or to the people," were apparently also designed in part to meet the above-quoted argument of Hamilton.

[9] [5] The Tenth Amendment similarly made clear that the States and the people retained all those powers not expressly delegated to the Federal Government.

may be forgotten by others, but since 1791 it has been a basic part of the Constitution which we are sworn to uphold. To hold that a right so basic and fundamental and so deep-rooted in our society as the right of privacy in marriage may be infringed because that right is not guaranteed in so many words by the first eight amendments to the Constitution is to ignore the Ninth Amendment and to give it no effect whatsoever. Moreover, a judicial construction that this fundamental right is not protected by the Constitution because it is not mentioned in explicit terms by one of the first eight amendments or elsewhere in the Constitution would violate the Ninth Amendment, which specifically states that "[t]he enumeration in the Constitution, of certain rights, shall not be *construed* to deny or disparage others retained by the people." (Emphasis added.)

A dissenting opinion suggests that my interpretation of the Ninth Amendment somehow "broaden[s] the powers of this Court." With all due respect, I believe that it misses the import of what I am saying. I do not take the position of my Brother BLACK in his dissent in *Adamson v. California*, 332 U.S. 46, 68, that the entire Bill of Rights is incorporated in the Fourteenth Amendment, and I do not mean to imply that the Ninth Amendment is applied against the States by the Fourteenth. Nor do I mean to state that the Ninth Amendment constitutes an independent source of rights protected from infringement by either the States or the Federal Government. Rather, the Ninth Amendment shows a belief of the Constitution's authors that fundamental rights exist that are not expressly enumerated in the first eight amendments and an intent that the list of rights included there not be deemed exhaustive. As any student of this Court's opinions knows, this Court has held, often unanimously, that the Fifth and Fourteenth Amendments protect certain fundamental personal liberties from abridgment by the Federal Government or the States. The Ninth Amendment simply shows the intent of the Constitution's authors that other fundamental personal rights should not be denied such protection or disparaged in any other way simply because they are not specifically listed in the first eight constitutional amendments. I do not see how this broadens the authority of the Court; rather it serves to support what this Court has been doing in protecting fundamental rights.

Nor am I turning somersaults with history in arguing that the Ninth Amendment is relevant in a case dealing with a *State's* infringement of a fundamental right. While the Ninth Amendment — and indeed the entire Bill of Rights — originally concerned restrictions upon *federal* power, the subsequently enacted Fourteenth Amendment prohibits the States as well from abridging fundamental personal liberties. And, the Ninth Amendment, in indicating that not all such liberties are specifically mentioned in the first eight amendments, is surely relevant in showing the existence of other fundamental personal rights, now protected from state, as well as federal, infringement. In sum, the Ninth Amendment simply lends strong support to the view that the "liberty" protected by the Fifth and Fourteenth Amendments from infringement by the Federal Government or the States is not restricted to rights specifically mentioned in the first eight amendments.

In determining which rights are fundamental, judges are not left at large to decide cases in light of their personal and private notions. Rather, they must look to the "traditions and [collective] conscience of our people" to determine whether a principle is "so rooted [there] . . . as to be ranked as fundamental." The inquiry is whether a right involved "is of such a character that it cannot be denied without violating those 'fundamental principles of liberty and justice which lie at the base of all our civil and political institutions'. . . ." "Liberty" also "gains content from the emanations of . . . specific [constitutional] guarantees" and "from experience with the requirements of a free society."

I agree fully with the Court that, applying these tests, the right of privacy is a fundamental personal right, emanating "from the totality of the constitutional scheme under which we live." Mr. Justice Brandeis, dissenting in *Olmstead v. United States* [(1928)], comprehensively summarized the principles underlying the Constitution's guarantees of privacy:

> "The protection guaranteed by the [Fourth and Fifth] amendments is much broader in scope. The makers of our Constitution undertook to secure conditions favorable to the pursuit of happiness. They recognized the significance of man's spiritual nature, of his feelings and of his intellect. They knew that only a part of the pain, pleasure and satisfactions of life are to be found in material things. They sought to protect Americans in their beliefs, their thoughts, their emotions and their sensations. They conferred, as against the Government, the right to be let alone — the most comprehensive of rights and the right most valued by civilized men."

The Connecticut statutes here involved deal with a particularly important and sensitive area of privacy — that of the marital relation and the marital home. This Court recognized in *Meyer v. Nebraska*, that the right "to marry, establish a home and bring up children" was an essential part of the liberty guaranteed by the Fourteenth Amendment. In *Pierce v. Society of Sisters*, the Court held unconstitutional an Oregon Act which forbade parents from sending their children to private schools because such an act "unreasonably interferes with the liberty of parents and guardians to direct the upbringing and education of children under their control." As this Court said in *Prince v. Massachusetts* [(1944)], the *Meyer* and *Pierce* decisions "have respected the private realm of family life which the state cannot enter."

I agree with MR. JUSTICE HARLAN's statement in his dissenting opinion in *Poe v. Ullman* [(1961)]: "Certainly the safeguarding of the home does not follow merely from the sanctity of property rights. The home derives its pre-eminence as the seat of family life. And the integrity of that life is something so fundamental that it has been found to draw to its protection the principles of more than one explicitly granted Constitutional right. . . . Of this whole 'private realm of family life' it is difficult to imagine what is more private or more intimate than a husband and wife's marital relations."

The entire fabric of the Constitution and the purposes that clearly underlie its specific guarantees demonstrate that the rights to marital privacy and to marry and raise a family are of similar order and magnitude as the fundamental rights specifically protected.

Although the Constitution does not speak in so many words of the right of privacy in marriage, I cannot believe that it offers these fundamental rights no protection. The fact that no particular provision of the Constitution explicitly forbids the State from disrupting the traditional relation of the family — a relation as old and as fundamental as our entire civilization — surely does not show that the Government was meant to have the power to do so. Rather, as the Ninth Amendment expressly recognizes, there are fundamental personal rights such as this one, which are protected from abridgment by the Government though not specifically mentioned in the Constitution.

My Brother STEWART, while characterizing the Connecticut birth control law as "an uncommonly silly law," would nevertheless let it stand on the ground that it is not for the courts to " 'substitute their social and economic beliefs for the judgment of legislative bodies, who are elected to pass laws.' " Elsewhere, I have stated that "[w]hile I quite agree with Mr. Justice Brandeis that . . . 'a . . . State may . . . serve as a laboratory; and try novel social and economic experiments,' I do not believe that this includes the power to experiment with the fundamental liberties of citizens. . . ." The vice of the dissenters' views is that it would permit such experimentation by the States in the area of the fundamental personal rights of its citizens. I cannot agree that the Constitution grants such power either to the States or to the Federal Government.

The logic of the dissents would sanction federal or state legislation that seems to me even more plainly unconstitutional than the statute before us. Surely the Government, absent a showing of a compelling subordinating state interest, could not decree that all husbands and wives must be sterilized after two children have been born to them. Yet by their reasoning such an invasion of marital privacy would not be subject to constitutional challenge because, while it might be "silly," no provision of the Constitution specifically prevents the Government from curtailing the marital right to bear children and raise a family. While it may shock some of my Brethren that the Court today holds that the Constitution protects the right of marital privacy, in my view it is far more shocking to believe that the personal liberty guaranteed by the Constitution does not include protection against such totalitarian limitation of family size, which is at complete variance with our constitutional concepts. Yet, if upon a showing of a slender basis of rationality, a law outlawing voluntary birth control by married persons is valid, then, by the same reasoning, a law requiring compulsory birth control also would seem to be valid. In my view, however, both types of law would unjustifiably intrude upon rights of marital privacy which are constitutionally protected.

In a long series of cases this Court has held that where fundamental personal liberties are involved, they may not be abridged by the States simply on a showing that a regulatory statute has some rational relationship to the effectuation of a proper state purpose. "Where there is a significant encroachment upon personal liberty, the State may prevail only upon showing a subordinating interest which is compelling." . . .

Although the Connecticut birth-control law obviously encroaches upon a fundamental personal liberty, the State does not show that the law serves any "subordinating [state] interest which is compelling" or that it is "necessary . . . to the accomplishment of a permissible state policy." The State, at most, argues that there is some rational relation between this statute and what is admittedly a legitimate subject of state concern — the discouraging of extra-marital relations. It says that preventing the use of birth-control devices by married persons helps prevent the indulgence by some in such extra-marital relations. The rationality of this justification is dubious, particularly in light of the admitted widespread availability to all persons in the State of Connecticut, unmarried as well as married, of birth-control devices for the prevention of disease, as distinguished from the prevention of conception. But, in any event, it is clear that the state interest in safeguarding marital fidelity can be served by a more discriminately tailored statute, which does not, like the present one, sweep unnecessarily broadly, reaching far beyond the evil sought to be dealt with and intruding upon the privacy of all married couples. Here, as elsewhere, "[p]recision of regulation must be the touchstone in an area so closely touching our most precious freedoms." The State of Connecticut does have statutes, the constitutionality of which is beyond doubt, which prohibit adultery and fornication. These statutes demonstrate that means for achieving the same basic purpose of protecting marital fidelity are available to Connecticut without the need to "invade the area of protected freedoms."

Finally, it should be said of the Court's holding today that it in no way interferes with a State's proper regulation of sexual promiscuity or misconduct. As my Brother HARLAN so well stated in his dissenting opinion in *Poe v. Ullman* [(1961)]:

> "Adultery, homosexuality and the like are sexual intimacies which the State forbids . . . but the intimacy of husband and wife is necessarily an essential and accepted feature of the institution of marriage, an institution which the State not only must allow, but which always and in every age it has fostered and protected. It is one thing when the State exerts its power either to forbid extra-marital sexuality . . . or to say who may marry, but it is quite another when, having acknowledged a marriage and the intimacies inherent in it, it undertakes to regulate by means of the criminal law the details of that intimacy."

In sum, I believe that the right of privacy in the marital relation is fundamental and basic — a personal right "retained by the people" within the meaning of the Ninth Amendment. Connecticut cannot constitutionally abridge this fundamental right, which is protected by the Fourteenth Amendment from infringement by the States. I agree with the Court that petitioners' convictions must therefore be reversed.

MR. JUSTICE HARLAN, concurring in the judgment.

I fully agree with the judgment of reversal, but find myself unable to join the Court's opinion. The reason is that it seems to me to evince an approach to this case very much like that taken by my Brothers BLACK and STEWART in dissent, namely: the Due Process Clause of the Fourteenth Amendment does not touch this Connecticut statute unless the enactment is found to violate some right assured by the letter or penumbra of the Bill of Rights.

In other words, what I find implicit in the Court's opinion is that the "incorporation" doctrine may be used to *restrict* the reach of Fourteenth Amendment Due Process. For me this is just as unacceptable constitutional doctrine as is the use of the "incorporation" approach to *impose* upon the States all the requirements of the

Bill of Rights as found in the provisions of the first eight amendments and in the decisions of this Court interpreting them.

In my view, the proper constitutional inquiry in this case is whether this Connecticut statute infringes the Due Process Clause of the Fourteenth Amendment because the enactment violates basic values "implicit in the concept of ordered liberty," *Palko v. Connecticut* [(1937)]. For reasons stated at length in my dissenting opinion in *Poe v. Ullman*, I believe that it does. While the relevant inquiry may be aided by resort to one or more of the provisions of the Bill of Rights, it is not dependent on them or any of their radiations. The Due Process Clause of the Fourteenth Amendment stands, in my opinion, on its own bottom.

A further observation seems in order respecting the justification of my Brothers BLACK and STEWART for their "incorporation" approach to this case. Their approach does not rest on historical reasons, . . . but on the thesis that by limiting the content of the Due Process Clause of the Fourteenth Amendment to the protection of rights which can be found elsewhere in the Constitution, in this instance in the Bill of Rights, judges will thus be confined to "interpretation" of specific constitutional provisions, and will thereby be restrained from introducing their own notions of constitutional right and wrong into the "vague contours of the Due Process Clause."

While I could not more heartily agree that judicial "self restraint" is an indispensable ingredient of sound constitutional adjudication, I do submit that the formula suggested for achieving it is more hollow than real. "Specific" provisions of the Constitution, no less than "due process," lend themselves as readily to "personal" interpretations by judges whose constitutional outlook is simply to keep the Constitution in supposed "tune with the times." . . .

Judicial self-restraint will not, I suggest, be brought about in the "due process" area by the historically unfounded incorporation formula long advanced by my Brother BLACK, and now in part espoused by my Brother STEWART. It will be achieved in this area, as in other constitutional areas, only by continual insistence upon respect for the teachings of history, solid recognition of the basic values that underlie our society, and wise appreciation of the great roles that the doctrines of federalism and separation of powers have played in establishing and preserving American freedoms. . . .

MR. JUSTICE WHITE, concurring in the judgment.

In my view this Connecticut law as applied to married couples deprives them of "liberty" without due process of law, as that concept is used in the Fourteenth Amendment. I therefore concur in the judgment of the Court reversing these convictions under Connecticut's aiding and abetting statute.

* * *

. . . There is no serious contention that Connecticut thinks the use of artificial or external methods of contraception immoral or unwise in itself, or that the anti-use statute is founded upon any policy of promoting population expansion. Rather, the statute is said to serve the State's policy against all forms of promiscuous or illicit sexual relationships, be they premarital or extramarital, concededly a permissible and legitimate legislative goal.

Without taking issue with the premise that the fear of conception operates as a deterrent to such relationships in addition to the criminal proscriptions Connecticut has against such conduct, I wholly fail to see how the ban on the use of contraceptives by married couples in any way reinforces the State's ban on illicit sexual relationships. Connecticut does not bar the importation or possession of contraceptive devices; they are not considered contraband material under state law, and their availability in that State is not seriously disputed. The only way Connecticut seeks to limit or control the availability of such devices is through its general aiding and abetting statute whose operation in this context has been quite obviously ineffective and whose most serious use has been against birth-control clinics rendering advice to married, rather than unmarried, persons. . . .

In these circumstances one is rather hard pressed to explain how the ban on use by married persons in any way prevents use of such devices by persons engaging in illicit sexual relations and thereby contributes to the State's policy against such relationships. Neither the state courts nor the State before the bar of this Court has tendered such an explanation. It is purely fanciful to believe that the broad proscription on use facilitates discovery of use by persons engaging in a prohibited relationship or for some other reason makes such use more unlikely and thus can be supported by any sort of administrative consideration. Perhaps the theory is that the flat ban on use prevents married people from possessing contraceptives and without the ready availability of such devices for use in the marital relationship, there will be no or less temptation to use them in extramarital ones. This reasoning rests on the premise that married people will comply with the ban in regard to their marital relationship, notwithstanding total nonenforcement in this context and apparent nonenforcibility, but will not comply with criminal statutes prohibiting extramarital affairs and the anti-use statute in respect to illicit sexual relationships, a premise whose validity has not been demonstrated and whose intrinsic validity is not very evident. At most the broad ban is of marginal utility to the declared objective. A statute limiting its prohibition on use to persons engaging in the prohibited relationship would serve the end posited by Connecticut in the same way, and with the same effectiveness, or ineffectiveness, as the broad anti-use statute under attack in this case. I find nothing in this record justifying the sweeping scope of this statute, with its telling effect on the freedoms of married persons, and therefore conclude that it deprives such persons of liberty without due process of law.

Mr. Justice Black, with whom Mr. Justice Stewart joins, dissenting.

* * *

The Court talks about a constitutional "right of privacy" as though there is some constitutional provision or provisions forbidding any law ever to be passed which might abridge the "privacy" of individuals. But there is not. There are, of course, guarantees in certain specific constitutional provisions which are designed in part to protect privacy at certain times and places with respect to certain activities. . . .

One of the most effective ways of diluting or expanding a constitutionally guaranteed right is to substitute for the crucial word or words of a constitutional guarantee another word or words, more or less flexible and more or less restricted in meaning. This fact is well illustrated by the use of the term "right of privacy" as a comprehensive substitute for the Fourth Amendment's guarantee against "unreasonable searches and seizures." "Privacy" is a broad, abstract and ambiguous concept which can easily be shrunken in meaning but which can also, on the other hand, easily be interpreted as a constitutional ban against many things other than searches and seizures. . . . I like my privacy as well as the next one, but I am nevertheless compelled to admit that government has a right to invade it unless prohibited by some specific constitutional provision. For these reasons I cannot agree with the Court's judgment and the reasons it gives for holding this Connecticut law unconstitutional.

. . . I think that if properly construed neither the Due Process Clause nor the Ninth Amendment, nor both together, could under any circumstances be a proper basis for invalidating the Connecticut law. I discuss the due process and Ninth Amendment arguments together because on analysis they turn out to be the same thing — merely using different words to claim for this Court and the federal judiciary power to invalidate any legislative act which the judges find irrational, unreasonable or offensive.

The due process argument which my Brothers HARLAN and WHITE adopt here is based, as their opinions indicate, on the premise that this Court is vested with power to invalidate all state laws that it considers to be arbitrary, capricious, unreasonable, or oppressive, or this Court's belief that a particular state law under scrutiny has no "rational or justifying" purpose, or is offensive to a "sense of fairness and justice." If these formulas based on "natural justice," or others which mean the same thing, are to prevail, they require judges to determine what is or is not constitutional on the basis of their own appraisal of what laws are unwise or unnecessary. The power to make such decisions is of course that of a legislative body. Surely it has to be admitted that no provision of the Constitution specifically gives such blanket power to courts to exercise such a supervisory veto over the wisdom and value of legislative policies and to hold unconstitutional those laws which they believe unwise or dangerous. I readily admit that no legislative body, state or national, should pass laws that can justly be given any of the invidious labels invoked as constitutional excuses to strike down state laws. But perhaps it is not too much to say that no legislative body ever does pass laws without believing that they will accomplish a sane, rational, wise and justifiable purpose. While I completely subscribe to the holding of *Marbury v. Madison*, and subsequent cases, that our Court has constitutional power to strike down statutes, state or federal, that violate commands of the Federal Constitution, I do not believe that we are granted power by the Due Process Clause or any other constitutional provision or provisions to measure constitutionality by our belief that legislation is arbitrary, capricious or unreasonable, or accomplishes no justifiable purpose, or is offensive to our own notions of "civilized standards of conduct." Such an appraisal of the wisdom of legislation is an attribute of the power to make laws, not of the power to interpret them. . . .

. . . I merely point out that the reasoning stated in *Meyer* and *Pierce* was the same natural law due process philosophy which many later opinions repudiated, and which I cannot accept. . . .

My Brother GOLDBERG has adopted the recent discovery[10] that the Ninth Amendment as well as the Due Process Clause can be used by this Court as authority to strike down all state legislation which this Court thinks violates "fundamental principles of liberty and justice," or is contrary to the "traditions and [collective] conscience of our people." . . . That Amendment was passed, not to broaden the powers of this Court or any other department of "the General Government," but, as every student of history knows, to assure the people that the Constitution in all its provisions was intended to limit the Federal Government to the powers granted expressly or by necessary implication. If any broad, unlimited power to hold laws unconstitutional because they offend what this Court conceives to be the "[collective] conscience of our people" is vested in this Court by the Ninth Amendment, the Fourteenth Amendment, or any other provision of the Constitution, it was not given by the Framers, but rather has been bestowed on the Court by the Court. . . .

I repeat so as not to be misunderstood that this Court does have power, which it should exercise, to hold laws unconstitutional where they are forbidden by the Federal Constitution. My point is that there is no provision of the Constitution which either expressly or impliedly vests power in this Court to sit as a supervisory agency over acts of duly constituted legislative bodies and set aside their laws because of the Court's belief that the legislative policies adopted are unreasonable, unwise, arbitrary, capricious or irrational. . . .

* * *

MR. JUSTICE STEWART, whom MR. JUSTICE BLACK joins, dissenting. [Omitted.]

NOTES AND QUESTIONS

1. Note that Justice Douglas expressly declines to locate the contraceptive right in the Due Process Clause of the Fourteenth Amendment, writing "[o]vertones of some arguments suggest that *Lochner v. New York* should be our guide. But we decline that invitation" 381 U.S. at 481–82. Did the Court really avoid *Lochner*, or was Justice Douglas' recital of reliance upon the penumbras of the First, Third, Fourth, and Fifth Amendments merely a smokescreen? Could *Lochner* and *Griswold* have been distinguished simply by noting that in the former the Court's action was prompted largely by disagreement with the adopted economic policy even though the maximum hour law could have been easily enforced, while in *Griswold* the Connecticut law was largely unenforceable, except in the rarest of circumstances or with a severe invasion of marital privacy? In this regard, unlike the abortion cases that would build on *Griswold*, this case did not establish any

---

[10] [12] See PATTERSON, THE FORGOTTEN NINTH AMENDMENT (1955). Mr. Patterson urges that the Ninth Amendment be used to protect unspecified "natural and inalienable rights." *Id.* at 4. The Introduction by Roscoe Pound states that "there is a marked revival of natural law ideas throughout the world. Interest in the Ninth Amendment is a symptom of that revival." *Id.* at iii.

undifferentiated right of reproductive autonomy, but concentrated on avoiding intrusion into the marital bedroom.

2.   Do you think that Justice White is correct in his concurring opinion that the Connecticut law fails even the rational basis standard? White failed to see "how the ban on the use of contraceptives by married couples in any way reinforce[d] the State's ban on illicit sexual relationships." *Id.* at 505 (White, J., concurring in the judgment). But is that really so far-fetched? Later, the Supreme Court will argue that abortion is necessary to facilitate the participation of women in the "economic and social life of the nation." *Casey v. Planned Parenthood*, 505 U.S. 833, 835 (1992). If some women are willing to undergo a more costly and physically intrusive abortion procedure to not have their lives fettered with obligations to children, might they not also more willingly engage in sexual relationships, licit or illicit, if contraception also avoids the consequences of pregnancy and childbirth?

3.   Contraception as a moral matter remains highly controversial, especially in the Christian (most notably Catholic) tradition. One writer states, for example:

> By its very nature, contraceptive behavior seeks to take apart what God in His wisdom has put together — the procreative and the affective aspects of sexual relations. Natural Family Planning, on the other hand, respects God's order of creation; it respects the alternating periods of fertility and infertility that God has established and the integrity of the sexual act as God intends it.

JOHN F. KIPPLEY, BIRTH CONTROL AND CHRISTIAN DISCIPLESHIP 16 (1985). Artificial contraception has also been described as a grave evil that can lead to the degradation of women and a distortion of the meaning and purpose of human sexuality, as both an unconditional gift of self and, should the union produce children, a responsible willingness to assume the duties of parenting. The Catholic position is summarized:

> Within [the cultural climate in which the sense of God and of man is eclipsed], the *body* is no longer perceived as a properly personal reality, a sign and place of relations with others, with God and with the world. It is reduced to pure materiality: it is simply a complex of organs, functions and energies to be used according to the sole criteria of pleasure and efficiency. Consequently, *sexuality* too is depersonalized and exploited: from being the sign, place and language of love, that is, of the gift of self and acceptance of another, in all the other's richness as a person, it increasingly becomes the occasion and instrument for self-assertion and the selfish satisfaction of personal desires and instincts. Thus the original import of human sexuality is distorted and falsified, and the two meanings, unitive and procreative, inherent in the very nature of the conjugal act, are artificially separated: in this way the marriage union is betrayed and its fruitfulness is subjected to the caprice of the couple. *Procreation* then becomes the "enemy" to be avoided in sexual activity: if it is welcomed, this is only because it expresses a desire, or indeed the intention, to have a child "at all costs", and not because it signifies the complete acceptance of the other and therefore an openness to the richness of life which the child represents.

POPE JOHN PAUL II, THE GOSPEL OF LIFE [EVANGELIUM VITAE] No. 23, at 42–43 (1995).

Despite the moral difficulty with contraception, eminent Catholic theologians have argued against incorporating any distinctively religious view into law. For example, in a memorandum to Cardinal Richard Cushing in the mid-1960s, Father John Courtney Murray, S.J., a renowned scholar of Catholic theology noted that "[i]t is not the function of civil law to prescribe everything that is morally right and to forbid everything that is morally wrong." JOHN COURTNEY MURRAY, S.J., *Memo. to Cardinal Cushing on Contraception Legislation, in* BRIDGING THE SACRED AND THE SECULAR 81, 82 (J. Leon Hooper, S.J. ed., 1994). A matter of public morality only arises, wrote Murray, when "a practice seriously undermines the foundations of society or gravely damages the moral life of the community as such." *Id.* Father Murray was especially mindful of the fact that there "must be a reasonable correspondence between the moral standards generally recognized by the conscience of the community and the legal statutes concerning public morality. Otherwise laws will be unenforceable and ineffective and they will be resented as undue restrictions on civil or personal freedom." *Id.* at 83. In this regard, Murray noted that the practice of contraception had become widespread, and as a matter of "responsible parenthood," had received some religious sanction among other denominations. *Id.* Thus, he thought individuals also had the right to make up their own mind about the practice as a matter of religious freedom. Father Murray urged the Cardinal to instruct Catholics to be open about stating their moral objection to contraception, but not to use law "to enforce upon the whole community moral standards that the community itself does not accept." *Id.* at 85–86. Religious believers, he said, must "lift the standards of public morality in all its dimensions, not by appealing to law and police action, but by the integrity of their Christian lives." *Id.* at 86. Do you see why the church could not apply the same argument to abortion and assisted suicide?

For an extended treatment of this argument, see DOUGLAS W. KMIEC, CAN A CATHOLIC SUPPORT HIM? ASKING THE BIG QUESTION ABOUT BARACK OBAMA (Overlook Press, 2008).

EISENSTADT v. BAIRD
405 U.S. 438 (1972)

MR. JUSTICE BRENNAN delivered the opinion of the Court.

Appellee William Baird was convicted at a bench trial in the Massachusetts Superior Court under Massachusetts General Laws Ann., c. 272, § 21, first, for exhibiting contraceptive articles in the course of delivering a lecture on contraception to a group of students at Boston University and, second, for giving a young woman a package of Emko vaginal foam at the close of his address.[11] The Massachusetts Supreme Judicial Court unanimously set aside the conviction for exhibiting contraceptives on the ground that it violated Baird's First Amendment rights, but by a four-to-three vote sustained the conviction for giving away the foam.

---

[11] [1] . . . The Court of Appeals below described the recipient of the foam as "an unmarried adult woman." 429 F.2d 1398, 1399 (1970). . . .

Massachusetts v. Baird (Mass. 1969). Baird subsequently filed a petition for a federal writ of habeas corpus, which the District Court dismissed. On appeal, however, the Court of Appeals for the First Circuit vacated the dismissal and remanded the action with directions to grant the writ discharging Baird. This appeal by the Sheriff of Suffolk County, Massachusetts, followed. . . . We affirm.

Massachusetts General Laws Ann., c. 272, § 21, under which Baird was convicted, provides a maximum five-year term of imprisonment for "whoever . . . gives away . . . any drug, medicine, instrument or article whatever for the prevention of conception," except as authorized in § 21A. Under § 21A, "[a] registered physician may administer to or prescribe for any married person drugs or articles intended for the prevention of pregnancy or conception. . . ." As interpreted by the State Supreme Judicial Court, these provisions make it a felony for anyone, other than a registered physician or pharmacist acting in accordance with the terms of § 21A, to dispense any article with the intention that it be used for the prevention of conception. The statutory scheme distinguishes among three distinct classes of distributees — *first*, married persons may obtain contraceptives to prevent pregnancy, but only from doctors or druggists on prescription; *second*, single persons may not obtain contraceptives from anyone to prevent pregnancy; and, *third*, married or single persons may obtain contraceptives from anyone to prevent, not pregnancy, but the spread of disease. . . .

The legislative purposes that the statute is meant to serve are not altogether clear. . . .[12]

* * *

II

The basic principles governing application of the Equal Protection Clause of the Fourteenth Amendment are familiar. As THE CHIEF JUSTICE only recently explained in *Reed v. Reed* (1971):

> "In applying that clause, this Court has consistently recognized that the Fourteenth Amendment does not deny to States the power to treat different classes of persons in different ways. The Equal Protection Clause of that amendment does, however, deny to States the power to legislate that different treatment be accorded to persons placed by a statute into different classes on the basis of criteria wholly unrelated to the objective of that statute. A classification 'must be reasonable, not arbitrary, and must rest upon some ground of difference having a fair and substantial relation to the object of the legislation, so that all persons similarly circumstanced shall be treated alike.' "

The question for our determination in this case is whether there is some ground of

---

[12] [3] Appellant suggests that the purpose of the Massachusetts statute is to promote marital fidelity as well as to discourage premarital sex. Under § 21A, however, contraceptives may be made available to married persons without regard to whether they are living with their spouses or the uses to which the contraceptives are to be put. Plainly the legislation has no deterrent effect on extramarital sexual relations.

difference that rationally explains the different treatment accorded married and unmarried persons under Massachusetts General Laws Ann., c. 272, §§ 21 and 21A.[13] For the reasons that follow, we conclude that no such ground exists.

First. Section 21 stems from Mass. Stat. 1879, c. 159, § 1, which prohibited, without exception, distribution of articles intended to be used as contraceptives. In *Massachusetts v. Allison* (Mass. 1917), the Massachusetts Supreme Judicial Court explained that the law's "plain purpose is to protect purity, to preserve chastity, to encourage continence and self restraint, to defend the sanctity of the home, and thus to engender in the State and nation a virile and virtuous race of men and women." Although the State clearly abandoned that purpose with the enactment of § 21A, at least insofar as the illicit sexual activities of married persons are concerned, see n. 3, *supra*, the court reiterated in *Sturgis v. Attorney General* [(Mass. 1970)] that the object of the legislation is to discourage premarital sexual intercourse. Conceding that the State could, consistently with the Equal Protection Clause, regard the problems of extramarital and premarital sexual relations as "[e]vils . . . of different dimensions and proportions, requiring different remedies," we cannot agree that the deterrence of premarital sex may reasonably be regarded as the purpose of the Massachusetts law.

It would be plainly unreasonable to assume that Massachusetts has prescribed pregnancy and the birth of an unwanted child as punishment for fornication, which is a misdemeanor under Massachusetts General Laws Ann., c. 272, § 18. Aside from the scheme of values that assumption would attribute to the State, it is abundantly clear that the effect of the ban on distribution of contraceptives to unmarried persons has at best a marginal relation to the proffered objective. . . . Nor, in making contraceptives available to married persons without regard to their intended use, does Massachusetts attempt to deter married persons from engaging in illicit sexual relations with unmarried persons. Even on the assumption that the fear of pregnancy operates as a deterrent to fornication, the Massachusetts statute is thus so riddled with exceptions that deterrence of premarital sex cannot reasonably be regarded as its aim.

Moreover, §§ 21 and 21A on their face have a dubious relation to the State's criminal prohibition on fornication. As the Court of Appeals explained, "Fornication is a misdemeanor [in Massachusetts], entailing a thirty dollar fine, or three months in jail. Violation of the present statute is a felony, punishable by five years in prison. We find it hard to believe that the legislature adopted a statute carrying a five-year penalty for its possible, obviously by no means fully effective, deterrence of the commission of a ninety-day misdemeanor." Even conceding the legislature a full measure of discretion in fashioning means to prevent fornication, and recognizing that the State may seek to deter prohibited conduct by punishing more severely those who facilitate than those who actually engage in its commission, we, like the Court of Appeals, cannot believe that in this instance Massachusetts has chosen to

---

[13] [7] Of course, if we were to conclude that the Massachusetts statute impinges upon fundamental freedoms under *Griswold*, the statutory classification would have to be not merely *rationally related* to a valid public purpose but *necessary* to the achievement of a *compelling* state interest. . . . [W]e do not have to address the statute's validity under that test because the law fails to satisfy even the more lenient equal protection standard.

expose the aider and abetter who simply *gives away* a contraceptive to *20* times the *90-day* sentence of the offender himself. The very terms of the State's criminal statutes, coupled with the *de minimis* effect of §§ 21 and 21A in deterring fornication, thus compel the conclusion that such deterrence cannot reasonably be taken as the purpose of the ban on distribution of contraceptives to unmarried persons.

Second. . . .

. . . "If there is need to have a physician prescribe (and a pharmacist dispense) contraceptives, that need is as great for unmarried persons as for married persons." . . .[14] Furthermore, we must join the Court of Appeals in noting that not all contraceptives are potentially dangerous. As a result, if the Massachusetts statute were a health measure, it would not only invidiously discriminate against the unmarried, but also be overbroad with respect to the married. . . . "In this posture," as the Court of Appeals concluded, "it is impossible to think of the statute as intended as a health measure for the unmarried, and it is almost as difficult to think of it as so intended even as to the married."

* * *

Third. If the Massachusetts statute cannot be upheld as a deterrent to fornication or as a health measure, may it, nevertheless, be sustained simply as a prohibition on contraception? The Court of Appeals analysis "led inevitably to the conclusion that, so far as morals are concerned, it is contraceptives per se that are considered immoral — to the extent that *Griswold* will permit such a declaration." The Court of Appeals went on to hold:

> "To say that contraceptives are immoral as such, and are to be forbidden to unmarried persons who will nevertheless persist in having intercourse, means that such persons must risk for themselves an unwanted pregnancy, for the child, illegitimacy, and for society, a possible obligation of support. Such a view of morality is not only the very mirror image of sensible legislation; we consider that it conflicts with fundamental human rights. In the absence of demonstrated harm, we hold it is beyond the competency of the state."

We need not and do not, however, decide that important question in this case because, whatever the rights of the individual to access to contraceptives may be, the rights must be the same for the unmarried and the married alike.

If under *Griswold* the distribution of contraceptives to married persons cannot be prohibited, a ban on distribution to unmarried persons would be equally impermissible. It is true that in *Griswold* the right of privacy in question inhered in the marital relationship. Yet the marital couple is not an independent entity with a

---

[14] [8] Appellant insists that the unmarried have no right to engage in sexual intercourse and hence no health interest in contraception that needs to be served. The short answer to this contention is that the same devices the distribution of which the State purports to regulate when their asserted purpose is to forestall pregnancy are available without any controls whatsoever so long as their asserted purpose is to prevent the spread of disease. It is inconceivable that the need for health controls varies with the purpose for which the contraceptive is to be used when the physical act in all cases is one and the same.

mind and heart of its own, but an association of two individuals each with a separate intellectual and emotional makeup. If the right of privacy means anything, it is the right of the *individual*, married or single, to be free from unwarranted governmental intrusion into matters so fundamentally affecting a person as the decision whether to bear or beget a child.

On the other hand, if *Griswold* is no bar to a prohibition on the distribution of contraceptives, the State could not, consistently with the Equal Protection Clause, outlaw distribution to unmarried but not to married persons. In each case the evil, as perceived by the State, would be identical, and the underinclusion would be invidious. . . . We hold that by providing dissimilar treatment for married and unmarried persons who are similarly situated, Massachusetts General Laws Ann., c. 272, §§ 21 and 21A, violate the Equal Protection Clause. The judgment of the Court of Appeals is

Affirmed.

MR. JUSTICE POWELL and MR. JUSTICE REHNQUIST took no part in the consideration or decision of this case.

MR. JUSTICE DOUGLAS, concurring. [Omitted.]

MR. JUSTICE WHITE, with whom MR. JUSTICE BLACKMUN joins, concurring in the result [omitted].

MR. CHIEF JUSTICE BURGER, dissenting.

* * *

It is revealing, I think, that those portions of the majority and concurring opinions rejecting the statutory limitation on distributors rely on no particular provision of the Constitution. I see nothing in the Fourteenth Amendment or any other part of the Constitution that even vaguely suggests that these medicinal forms of contraceptives must be available in the open market. I do not challenge *Griswold v. Connecticut, supra*, despite its tenuous moorings to the text of the Constitution, but I cannot view it as controlling authority for this case. The Court was there confronted with a statute flatly prohibiting the use of contraceptives, not one regulating their distribution. I simply cannot believe that the limitation on the class of lawful distributors has significantly impaired the right to use contraceptives in Massachusetts. By relying in *Griswold* in the present context, the Court has passed beyond the penumbras of the specific guarantees into the uncircumscribed area of personal predilections.

NOTES AND QUESTIONS

1. In *Eisenstadt*, the Court concludes: "[W]hatever the rights of the individual to access to contraceptives may be, the rights must be the same for the unmarried and the married alike." 405 U.S. at 453. However, wasn't the right to use

contraceptives premised on marital privacy in *Griswold*? If so, why did the Court in *Eisenstadt* feel compelled to expand the right to unmarried individuals? The answer may lie in the fact that the *Eisenstadt* Court lost sight of the fact that the fundamental right offended in *Griswold* was marriage, and *its* associated right of privacy, and not an undifferentiated right of privacy. Note, too, that the *Eisenstadt* Court interchanges a prohibition on contraceptive use and a prohibition on distribution, even as the latter has far fewer, if any, privacy implications. Nevertheless, the Court in *Eisenstadt* writes:

> If under *Griswold* the distribution of contraceptives to married persons cannot be prohibited, a ban on distribution to unmarried persons would be equally impermissible. It is true that in *Griswold* the right of privacy in question inhered in the marital relationship. Yet the marital couple is not an independent entity with a mind and heart of its own, but an association of two individuals each with a separate intellectual and emotional makeup. If the right of privacy means anything, it is the right of the *individual*, married or single, to be free from unwarranted governmental intrusion into matters so fundamentally affecting a person as the decision whether to bear or beget a child.

> On the other hand, if *Griswold* is no bar to a prohibition on the distribution of contraceptives, the State could not, consistently with the Equal Protection Clause, outlaw distribution to unmarried but not to married persons. In each case the evil, as perceived by the State, would be identical, and the underinclusion would be invidious.

Id. at 453–54.

2.   Justice Brennan argues that "[i]t would be plainly unreasonable to assume that Massachusetts has prescribed pregnancy and the birth of an unwanted child as punishment for fornication." 405 U.S. at 448. Yet later in *Michael M. v. Superior Court*, 450 U.S. 464 (1981), California's statutory rape law would be upheld against an equal protection challenge, even though men alone could be held criminally liable for the act of sexual intercourse with a female under the age of 18 not one's wife. In *Michael M.*, Justice Rehnquist writing for a plurality of the Court reasoned:

> Because virtually all of the significant harmful and inescapably identifiable consequences of teenage pregnancy fall on the young female, a legislature acts well within its authority when it elects to punish only the participant who, by nature, suffers few of the consequences of his conduct. . . . Moreover, the risk of pregnancy itself constitutes a substantial deterrence to young females.

Id. at 473. True, Justice Brennan dissented in *Michael M.*, but whose argument is more in line with human nature? Aren't the consequences and difficulties of giving birth outside the stability and structure of marriage some disincentive to sexual intercourse by unmarried individuals?

3.   Given that some contraceptives do have sometimes profound health effects, why wasn't Chief Justice Burger correct that the state could rightly limit the distribution of contraceptives to those under the supervision of a licensed pharmacist? *See, e.g.*, E. Daly et al., *Risk of Venous Thromboembolism in Users of*

Hormone Replacement Therapy, 348 LANCET 977 (1996) (finding an increased risk of deep vein thrombosis in users of oral contraceptives); D.B. Thomas & R.M. Ray, *Oral Contraceptives and Invasive Adenocarcinomas and Adenosquamous Carcinomas of the Uterine Cervix, The World Health Organization Collaborative Study of Neoplasia and Steroid Contraceptives*, 144 AM. J. EPIDEMIOLOGY 281 (1996) (finding an increased risk of cervical cancer in users of oral contraceptives); F. Levi et al., *Oral Contraceptives, Menopausal Hormone Replacement Treatment and Breast Cancer Risk*, 5 EUR. J. CANCER PREVENTION 259 (1996) (confirming that breast cancer is related to oral contraceptive use and concluding that such findings ought to be considered in any risk/health assessment and public health evaluation).

4.   After *Eisenstadt*, the Court leaped from clearing legal hurdles in the way of unmarried access to contraceptives to doing the same with respect to minors. In the meantime, the Court had decided *Roe v. Wade*, 410 U.S. 113 (1973), finding a right of reproductive autonomy protected under Fourteenth Amendment "liberty," and thus, it was relatively easy for the Court to invalidate a New York law that made it a crime to sell or distribute contraceptives to minors under the age of 16. *Carey v. Population Services Int'l*, 431 U.S. 678 (1977). Again, Justice Brennan wrote for the Court, stating: "[s]ince the State may not impose a blanket prohibition, or even a blanket requirement of parental consent, on the choice of a minor to terminate her pregnancy, the constitutionality of a blanket prohibition of the distribution of contraceptives to minors is *a fortiori* foreclosed." *Id.* at 694.

5.   The imprecision in the identification of the fundamental right has been identified by the Justices, themselves, as a serious or at least problematic source of judicial error. Interestingly, while their methodologies differ, both Justice Scalia in *Michael H.*, and as we will shortly see, Justice Souter in the context of assisted suicide, bemoan the failure of the Court to speak at the proper level of "generality" (Scalia), 491 U.S. at 127 n.6, or "exactitude" (Souter), *Washington v. Glucksberg*, 521 U.S. 702, 772 (1997) (Souter, J., concurring).

2. Abortion

There is no more controversial subject in American constitutional law than that of abortion. In 1973 when *Roe* was decided, 31 states had laws prohibiting abortion except to save the life of the mother. Clark D. Forsythe, *The Effective Enforcement of Abortion Law Before* Roe v. Wade, *in* THE SILENT SUBJECT 179, 194 (Brad Stetson ed., 1996). Just before *Roe v. Wade*, 410 U.S. 113 (1973), Michigan and North Dakota voters overwhelmingly rejected liberalization of their state abortion restrictions. *Id.* If nontextual fundamental rights originate in the history and tradition of the nation, abortion presents the stark anomaly of the crime made into fundamental right.

ROE v. WADE
410 U.S. 113 (1973)

Mr. Justice Blackmun delivered the opinion of the Court.

This Texas federal appeal and its Georgia companion, *Doe v. Bolton*, present constitutional challenges to state criminal abortion legislation. The Texas statutes under attack here are typical of those that have been in effect in many States for approximately a century. The Georgia statutes, in contrast, have a modern cast and are a legislative product that, to an extent at least, obviously reflects the influences of recent attitudinal change, of advancing medical knowledge and techniques, and of new thinking about an old issue.

We forthwith acknowledge our awareness of the sensitive and emotional nature of the abortion controversy, of the vigorous opposing views, even among physicians, and of the deep and seemingly absolute convictions that the subject inspires. One's philosophy, one's experiences, one's exposure to the raw edges of human existence, one's religious training, one's attitudes toward life and family and their values, and the moral standards one establishes and seeks to observe, are all likely to influence and to color one's thinking and conclusions about abortion.

* * *

Our task, of course, is to resolve the issue by constitutional measurement, free of emotion and of predilection. We seek earnestly to do this, and, because we do, we . . . place some emphasis upon, medical and medical-legal history and what that history reveals about man's attitudes toward the abortion procedure over the centuries. We bear in mind, too, Mr. Justice Holmes' admonition in his now-vindicated dissent in *Lochner v. New York* (1905):

> "[The Constitution] is made for people of fundamentally differing views, and the accident of our finding certain opinions natural and familiar, or novel, and even shocking, ought not to conclude our judgment upon the question whether statutes embodying them conflict with the Constitution of the United States."

I

The Texas statutes that concern us here . . . make it a crime to "procure an abortion," . . . except with respect to "an abortion procured or attempted by medical advice for the purpose of saving the life of the mother." . . .

Texas first enacted a criminal abortion statute in 1854. . . .

II

Jane Roe, a single woman who was residing in Dallas County, Texas, instituted this federal action in March 1970 against the District Attorney of the county. She sought a declaratory judgment that the Texas criminal abortion statutes were unconstitutional on their face, and an injunction restraining the defendant from enforcing the statutes.

Roe alleged that she was unmarried and pregnant; that she wished to terminate her pregnancy by an abortion "performed by a competent, licensed physician, under safe, clinical conditions"; that she was unable to get a "legal" abortion in Texas because her life did not appear to be threatened by the continuation of her pregnancy; and that she could not afford to travel to another jurisdiction in order to secure a legal abortion under safe conditions. She claimed that the Texas statutes were unconstitutionally vague and that they abridged her right of personal privacy, protected by the First, Fourth, Fifth, Ninth, and Fourteenth Amendments. By an amendment to her complaint Roe purported to sue "on behalf of herself and all other women" similarly situated.

*   *   *

IV

We are next confronted with issues of justiciability, standing, and abstention. . . .

*   *   *

Viewing Roe's case as of the time of its filing and thereafter until as late as May, there can be little dispute that it then presented a case or controversy and that, wholly apart from the class aspects, she, as a pregnant single woman thwarted by the Texas criminal abortion laws, had standing to challenge those statutes. . . .

The appellee notes, however, that the record does not disclose that Roe was pregnant at the time of the District Court hearing on May 22, 1970, or on the following June 17 when the court's opinion and judgment were filed. And he suggests that Roe's case must now be moot because she and all other members of her class are no longer subject to any 1970 pregnancy.

The usual rule in federal cases is that an actual controversy must exist at stages of appellate or certiorari review, and not simply at the date the action is initiated. But when, as here, pregnancy is a significant fact in the litigation, the normal 266-day human gestation period is so short that the pregnancy will come to term before the usual appellate process is complete. If that termination makes a case moot, pregnancy litigation seldom will survive much beyond the trial stage, and appellate review will be effectively denied. Our law should not be that rigid. Pregnancy often comes more than once to the same woman, and in the general population, if man is to survive, it will always be with us. Pregnancy provides a classic justification for a conclusion of nonmootness. It truly could be "capable of repetition, yet evading review."

We, therefore, agree with the District Court that Jane Roe had standing to undertake this litigation, that she presented a justiciable controversy, and that the termination of her 1970 pregnancy has not rendered her case moot.

*   *   *

V

The principal thrust of appellant's attack on the Texas statutes is that they improperly invade a right, said to be possessed by the pregnant woman, to choose to terminate her pregnancy. Appellant would discover this right in the concept of personal "liberty" embodied in the Fourteenth Amendment's Due Process Clause; or in personal marital, familial, and sexual privacy said to be protected by the Bill of Rights or its penumbras, see *Griswold v. Connecticut* (1965); *Eisenstadt v. Baird* (1972), or among those rights reserved to the people by the Ninth Amendment, *Griswold* (Goldberg, J., concurring). Before addressing this claim, we feel it desirable briefly to survey, in several aspects, the history of abortion, for such insight as that history may afford us, and then to examine the state purposes and interests behind the criminal abortion laws.

VI

It perhaps is not generally appreciated that the restrictive criminal abortion laws in effect in a majority of States today are of relatively recent vintage. Those laws, generally proscribing abortion or its attempt at any time during pregnancy except when necessary to preserve the pregnant woman's life, are not of ancient or even of common-law origin. Instead, they derive from statutory changes effected, for the most part, in the latter half of the 19th century.

1. Ancient attitudes. . . . Greek and Roman law afforded little protection to the unborn. If abortion was prosecuted in some places, it seems to have been based on a concept of a violation of the father's right to his offspring. Ancient religion did not bar abortion.

2. The Hippocratic Oath. What then of the famous Oath that has stood so long as the ethical guide of the medical profession . . . ? The Oath varies somewhat according to the particular translation, but in any translation the content is clear: "I will give no deadly medicine to anyone if asked. . . . Similarly, I will not give to a woman an abortive remedy."

. . . The Oath was not uncontested even in Hippocrates' day; only the Pythagorean school of philosophers frowned upon the related act of suicide. Most Greek thinkers, on the other hand, commended abortion, at least prior to viability. See PLATO, REPUBLIC, V, 461; ARISTOTLE, POLITICS, VII, 1335b 25. For the Pythagoreans, however, it was a matter of dogma. For them the embryo was animate from the moment of conception, and abortion meant destruction of a living being. The abortion clause of the Oath, therefore, "echoes Pythagorean doctrines," and "[i]n no other stratum of Greek opinion were such views held or proposed in the same spirit of uncompromising austerity."

. . . But with the end of antiquity a decided change took place. Resistance against suicide and against abortion became common. The Oath came to be popular. The emerging teachings of Christianity were in agreement with the Pythagorean ethic. The Oath "became the nucleus of all medical ethics" and "was applauded as the embodiment of truth." . . .

3. The common law. It is undisputed that at common law, abortion performed

before "quickening" — the first recognizable movement of the fetus in utero, appearing usually from the 16th to the 18th week of pregnancy — was not an indictable offense. The absence of a common-law crime for pre-quickening abortion appears to have developed from a confluence of earlier philosophical, theological, and civil and canon law concepts of when life begins. These disciplines variously approached the question in terms of the point at which the embryo or fetus became "formed" or recognizably human, or in terms of when a "person" came into being, that is, infused with a "soul" or "animated." A loose consensus evolved in early English law that these events occurred at some point between conception and live birth. This was "mediate animation." Although Christian theology and the canon law came to fix the point of animation at 40 days for a male and 80 days for a female, a view that persisted until the 19th century, there was otherwise little agreement about the precise time of formation or animation. There was agreement, however, that prior to this point the fetus was to be regarded as part of the mother, and its destruction, therefore, was not homicide. Due to continued uncertainty about the precise time when animation occurred, to the lack of any empirical basis for the 40-80-day view, and perhaps to Aquinas' definition of movement as one of the two first principles of life, Bracton focused upon quickening as the critical point. The significance of quickening was echoed by later common-law scholars and found its way into the received common law in this country.

Whether abortion of a quick fetus was a felony at common law, or even a lesser crime, is still disputed. Bracton, writing early in the 13th century, thought it homicide. But the later and predominant view, following the great common-law scholars, has been that it was, at most, a lesser offense. In a frequently cited passage, Coke took the position that abortion of a woman "quick with childe" is "a great misprision, and no murder." Blackstone followed, saying that while abortion after quickening had once been considered manslaughter (though not murder), "modern law" took a less severe view. A recent review of the common-law precedents argues, however, that those precedents contradict Coke and that even post-quickening abortion was never established as a common-law crime. This is of some importance because while most American courts ruled, in holding or dictum, that abortion of an unquickened fetus was not criminal under their received common law, others followed Coke in stating that abortion of a quick fetus was a "misprision," a term they translated to mean "misdemeanor." That their reliance on Coke on this aspect of the law was uncritical and, apparently in all the reported cases, dictum (due probably to the paucity of common-law prosecutions for post-quickening abortion), makes it now appear doubtful that abortion was ever firmly established as a common-law crime even with respect to the destruction of a quick fetus.

4. The English statutory law. England's first criminal abortion statute . . . came in 1803. It made abortion of a quick fetus a capital crime, but it provided lesser penalties for the felony of abortion before quickening, and thus preserved the "quickening" distinction. . . .

5. The American law. In this country, the law in effect in all but a few States until mid-19th century was the pre-existing English common law. Connecticut, the first State to enact abortion legislation, adopted in 1821 that part of Lord Ellenborough's Act that related to a woman "quick with child." The death penalty was not imposed.

Abortion before quickening was made a crime in that State only in 1860. In 1828, New York enacted legislation that, in two respects, was to serve as a model for early anti-abortion statutes. First, while barring destruction of an unquickend fetus as well as a quick fetus, it made the former only a misdemeanor, but the latter second-degree manslaughter. Second, it incorporated a concept of therapeutic abortion by providing that an abortion was excused if it "shall have been necessary to preserve the life of such mother, or shall have been advised by two physicians to be necessary for such purpose." By 1840, when Texas had received the common law, only eight American States had statutes dealing with abortion. It was not until after the War Between the States that legislation began generally to replace the common law. Most of these initial statutes dealt severely with abortion after quickening but were lenient with it before quickening. . . .

Gradually, in the middle and late 19th century the quickening distinction disappeared from the statutory law of most States and the degree of the offense and the penalties were increased. By the end of the 1950's a large majority of the jurisdictions banned abortion, however and whenever performed, unless done to save or preserve the life of the mother. . . . In the past several years, however, a trend toward liberalization of abortion statutes has resulted in adoption, by about one-third of the States, of less stringent laws. . . .

It is thus apparent that at common law, at the time of the adoption of our Constitution, and throughout the major portion of the 19th century, abortion was viewed with less disfavor than under most American statutes currently in effect. Phrasing it another way, a woman enjoyed a substantially broader right to terminate a pregnancy than she does in most States today. At least with respect to the early stage of pregnancy, and very possibly without such a limitation, the opportunity to make this choice was present in this country well into the 19th century. Even later, the law continued for some time to treat less punitively an abortion procured in early pregnancy.

6. The position of the American Medical Association. The anti-abortion mood prevalent in this country in the late 19th century was shared by the medical profession. Indeed, the attitude of the profession may have played a significant role in the enactment of stringent criminal abortion legislation during that period.

An AMA Committee on Criminal Abortion was appointed in May 1857. It presented its report to the Twelfth Annual Meeting. That report observed that the Committee had been appointed to investigate criminal abortion "with a view to its general suppression." It deplored abortion and its frequency and it listed three causes of "this general demoralization":

> "The first of these causes is a wide-spread popular ignorance of the true character of the crime — a belief, even among mothers themselves, that the foetus is not alive till after the period of quickening.

> "The second of the agents alluded to is the fact that the profession themselves are frequently supposed careless of foetal life. . . .

> "The third reason of the frightful extent of this crime is found in the grave defects of our laws, both common and statute, as regards the independent and actual existence of the child before birth, as a living being.

These errors, which are sufficient in most instances to prevent conviction, are based, and only based, upon mistaken and exploded medical dogmas. With strange inconsistency, the law fully acknowledges the foetus in utero and its inherent rights, for civil purposes; while personally and as criminally affected, it fails to recognize it, and to its life as yet denies all protection."

The Committee then offered, and the Association adopted, resolutions protesting "against such unwarrantable destruction of human life," calling upon state legislatures to revise their abortion laws, and requesting the cooperation of state medical societies "in pressing the subject."

Except for periodic condemnation of the criminal abortionist, no further formal AMA action took place until 1967. In that year, the Committee on Human Reproduction urged the adoption of a stated policy of opposition to induced abortion, except when there is "documented medical evidence" of a threat to the health or life of the mother, or that the child "may be born with incapacitating physical deformity or mental deficiency," or that a pregnancy "resulting from legally established statutory or forcible rape or incest may constitute a threat to the mental or physical health of the patient". . . .

In 1970, . . . the House of Delegates adopted . . . resolutions[, which] emphasized "the best interests of the patient," "sound clinical judgment," and "informed patient consent," in contrast to "mere acquiescence to the patient's demand." The resolutions asserted that abortion is a medical procedure that should be performed by a licensed physician in an accredited hospital only after consultation with two other physicians and in conformity with state law, and that no party to the procedure should be required to violate personally held moral principles. . . .

*   *   *

VII

Three reasons have been advanced to explain historically the enactment of criminal abortion laws in the 19th century and to justify their continued existence.

It has been argued occasionally that these laws were the product of a Victorian social concern to discourage illicit sexual conduct. Texas, however, does not advance this justification in the present case, and it appears that no court or commentator has taken the argument seriously. The appellants and *amici* contend, moreover, that this is not a proper state purpose at all and suggest that, if it were, the Texas statutes are overbroad in protecting it since the law fails to distinguish between married and unwed mothers.

A second reason is concerned with abortion as a medical procedure. When most criminal abortion laws were first enacted, the procedure was a hazardous one for the woman. . . . Abortion mortality was high. Even after 1900, and perhaps until as late as the development of antibiotics in the 1940's, standard modern techniques such as dilation and curettage were not nearly so safe as they are today. Thus, it has been argued that a State's real concern in enacting a criminal abortion law was to protect the pregnant woman, that is, to restrain her from submitting to a procedure that placed her life in serious jeopardy.

Modern medical techniques have altered this situation. Appellants and various *amici* refer to medical data indicating that abortion in early pregnancy, that is, prior to the end of the first trimester, although not without its risk, is now relatively safe. Mortality rates for women undergoing early abortions, where the procedure is legal, appear to be as low as or lower than the rates for normal childbirth. Consequently, any interest of the State in protecting the woman from an inherently hazardous procedure, except when it would be equally dangerous for her to forgo it, has largely disappeared. Of course, important state interests in the areas of health and medical standards do remain. The State has a legitimate interest in seeing to it that abortion, like any other medical procedure, is performed under circumstances that insure maximum safety for the patient. . . . Moreover, the risk to the woman increases as her pregnancy continues. Thus, the State retains a definite interest in protecting the woman's own health and safety when an abortion is proposed at a late stage of pregnancy.

The third reason is the State's interest — some phrase it in terms of duty — in protecting prenatal life. Some of the argument for this justification rests on the theory that a new human life is present from the moment of conception. The State's interest and general obligation to protect life then extends, it is argued, to prenatal life. Only when the life of the pregnant mother herself is at stake, balanced against the life she carries within her, should the interest of the embryo or fetus not prevail. Logically, of course, a legitimate state interest in this area need not stand or fall on acceptance of the belief that life begins at conception or at some other point prior to live birth. In assessing the State's interest, recognition may be given to the less rigid claim that as long as at least potential life is involved, the State may assert interests beyond the protection of the pregnant woman alone.

It is with these interests, and the weight to be attached to them, that this case is concerned.

VIII

The Constitution does not explicitly mention any right of privacy. In a line of decisions, however, . . . the Court has recognized that a right of personal privacy, or a guarantee of certain areas or zones of privacy, does exist under the Constitution. In varying contexts, the Court or individual Justices have, indeed, found at least the roots of that right in the First Amendment, *Stanley v. Georgia* (1969); in the Fourth and Fifth Amendments, *Terry v. Ohio* (1968); in the penumbras of the Bill of Rights, *Griswold v. Connecticut* (1969); in the Ninth Amendment, *id.* (Goldberg, J., concurring); or in the concept of liberty guaranteed by the first section of the Fourteenth Amendment, see *Meyer v. Nebraska* (1923). These decisions make it clear that only personal rights that can be deemed "fundamental" or "implicit in the concept of ordered liberty," *Palko v. Connecticut* (1937), are included in this guarantee of personal privacy. They also make it clear that the right has some extension to activities relating to marriage, *Loving v. Virginia* (1967); procreation, *Skinner v. Oklahoma* (1942); contraception, *Eisenstadt v. Baird*; family relationships, *Prince v. Massachusetts* (1944); and child rearing and education,

Pierce v. Society of Sisters (1925), *Meyer v. Nebraska, supra.*

This right of privacy, whether it be founded in the Fourteenth Amendment's concept of personal liberty and restrictions upon state action, as we feel it is, or, as the District Court determined, in the Ninth Amendment's reservation of rights to the people, is broad enough to encompass a woman's decision whether or not to terminate her pregnancy. The detriment that the State would impose upon the pregnant woman by denying this choice altogether is apparent. Specific and direct harm medically diagnosable even in early pregnancy may be involved. Maternity, or additional offspring, may force upon the woman a distressful life and future. Psychological harm may be imminent. Mental and physical health may be taxed by child care. There is also the distress, for all concerned, associated with the unwanted child, and there is the problem of bringing a child into a family already unable, psychologically and otherwise, to care for it. In other cases, as in this one, the additional difficulties and continuing stigma of unwed motherhood may be involved. All these are factors the woman and her responsible physician necessarily will consider in consultation.

On the basis of elements such as these, appellant and some *amici* argue that the woman's right is absolute and that she is entitled to terminate her pregnancy at whatever time, in whatever way, and for whatever reason she alone chooses. With this we do not agree. Appellant's arguments that Texas either has no valid interest at all in regulating the abortion decision, or no interest strong enough to support any limitation upon the woman's sole determination, are unpersuasive. The Court's decisions recognizing a right of privacy also acknowledge that some state regulation in areas protected by that right is appropriate. As noted above, a State may properly assert important interests in safeguarding health, in maintaining medical standards, and in protecting potential life. At some point in pregnancy, these respective interests become sufficiently compelling to sustain regulation of the factors that govern the abortion decision. The privacy right involved, therefore, cannot be said to be absolute. In fact, it is not clear to us that the claim asserted by some *amici* that one has an unlimited right to do with one's body as one pleases bears a close relationship to the right of privacy previously articulated in the Court's decisions. The Court has refused to recognize an unlimited right of this kind in the past. *Jacobson v. Massachusetts* (1905) (vaccination); *Buck v. Bell* (1927) (sterilization).

We, therefore, conclude that the right of personal privacy includes the abortion decision, but that this right is not unqualified and must be considered against important state interests in regulation.

*   *   *

Where certain "fundamental rights" are involved, the Court has held that regulation limiting these rights may be justified only by a "compelling state interest," and that legislative enactments must be narrowly drawn to express only the legitimate state interests at stake.

*   *   *

IX

*   *   *

A. The appellee and certain *amici* argue that the fetus is a "person" within the language and meaning of the Fourteenth Amendment. In support of this, they outline at length and in detail the well-known facts of fetal development. If this suggestion of personhood is established, the appellant's case, of course, collapses, for the fetus' right to life would then be guaranteed specifically by the Amendment. The appellant conceded as much on reargument. On the other hand, the appellee conceded on reargument that no case could be cited that holds that a fetus is a person within the meaning of the Fourteenth Amendment.

The Constitution does not define "person" in so many words. Section 1 of the Fourteenth Amendment contains three references to "person." The first, in defining "citizens," speaks of "persons born or naturalized in the United States." The word also appears both in the Due Process Clause and in the Equal Protection Clause. "Person" is used in other places in the Constitution. . . . But in nearly all these instances, the use of the word is such that it has application only postnatally. None indicates, with any assurance, that it has any possible prenatal application.

All this, together with our observation, *supra*, that throughout the major portion of the 19th century prevailing legal abortion practices were far freer than they are today, persuades us that the word "person," as used in the Fourteenth Amendment, does not include the unborn. . . .

This conclusion, however, does not of itself fully answer the contentions raised by Texas, and we pass on to other considerations.

B. The pregnant woman cannot be isolated in her privacy. She carries an embryo and, later, a fetus, if one accepts the medical definitions of the developing young in the human uterus. The situation therefore is inherently different from marital intimacy, or bedroom possession of obscene material, or marriage, or procreation, or education, with which *Eisenstadt* and *Griswold, Stanley, Loving, Skinner* and *Pierce* and *Meyer* were respectively concerned. As we have intimated above, it is reasonable and appropriate for a State to decide that at some point in time another interest, that of health of the mother or that of potential human life, becomes significantly involved. The woman's privacy is no longer sole and any right of privacy she possesses must be measured accordingly.

Texas urges that, apart from the Fourteenth Amendment, life begins at conception and is present throughout pregnancy, and that, therefore, the State has a compelling interest in protecting that life from and after conception. We need not resolve the difficult question of when life begins. When those trained in the respective disciplines of medicine, philosophy, and theology are unable to arrive at any consensus, the judiciary, at this point in the development of man's knowledge, is not in a position to speculate as to the answer.

It should be sufficient to note briefly the wide divergence of thinking on this most sensitive and difficult question. There has always been strong support for the view that life does not begin until live birth. This was the belief of the Stoics. It appears to be the predominant, though not the unanimous, attitude of the Jewish faith. It may be taken to represent also the position of a large segment of the Protestant community, insofar as that can be ascertained; organized groups that have taken a formal position on the abortion issue have generally regarded abortion as a matter for the conscience of the individual and her family. As we have noted, the common law found greater significance in quickening. Physicians and their scientific colleagues have regarded that event with less interest and have tended to focus either upon conception, upon live birth, or upon the interim point at which the fetus becomes "viable," that is, potentially able to live outside the mother's womb, albeit with artificial aid. Viability is usually placed at about seven months (28 weeks) but may occur earlier, even at 24 weeks. The Aristotelian theory of "mediate animation," that held sway throughout the Middle Ages and the Renaissance in Europe, continued to be official Roman Catholic dogma until the 19th century, despite opposition to this "ensoulment" theory from those in the Church who would recognize the existence of life from the moment of conception. The latter is now, of course, the official belief of the Catholic Church. As one *amicus* brief discloses, this is a view strongly held by many non-Catholics as well, and by many physicians. Substantial problems for precise definition of this view are posed, however, by new embryological data that purport to indicate that conception is a "process" over time, rather than an event, and by new medical techniques such as menstrual extraction, the "morning-after" pill, implantation of embryos, artificial insemination, and even artificial wombs.

In areas other than criminal abortion, the law has been reluctant to endorse any theory that life, as we recognize it, begins before life birth or to accord legal rights to the unborn except in narrowly defined situations and except when the rights are contingent upon live birth. For example, the traditional rule of tort law denied recovery for prenatal injuries even though the child was born alive. That rule has been changed in almost every jurisdiction. In most States, recovery is said to be permitted only if the fetus was viable, or at least quick, when the injuries were sustained, though few courts have squarely so held. In a recent development, generally opposed by the commentators, some States permit the parents of a stillborn child to maintain an action for wrongful death because of prenatal injuries. Such an action, however, would appear to be one to vindicate the parents' interest and is thus consistent with the view that the fetus, at most, represents only the potentiality of life. Similarly, unborn children have been recognized as acquiring rights or interests by way of inheritance or other devolution of property, and have been represented by guardians ad litem. Perfection of the interests involved, again, has generally been contingent upon live birth. In short, the unborn have never been recognized in the law as persons in the whole sense.

X

In view of all this, we do not agree that, by adopting one theory of life, Texas may override the rights of the pregnant woman that are at stake. We repeat, however, that the State does have an important and legitimate interest in preserving and protecting the health of the pregnant woman, whether she be a resident of the State or a non-resident who seeks medical consultation and treatment there, and that it has still another important and legitimate interest in protecting the potentiality of human life. These interests are separate and distinct. Each grows in substantiality as the woman approaches term and, at a point during pregnancy, each becomes "compelling."

With respect to the State's important and legitimate interest in the health of the mother, the "compelling" point, in the light of present medical knowledge, is at approximately the end of the first trimester. This is so because of the now-established medical fact, referred to above, that until the end of the first trimester mortality in abortion may be less than mortality in normal childbirth. It follows that, from and after this point, a State may regulate the abortion procedure to the extent that the regulation reasonably relates to the preservation and protection of maternal health. Examples of permissible state regulation in this area are requirements as to the qualifications of the person who is to perform the abortion; as to the licensure of that person; as to the facility in which the procedure is to be performed, that is, whether it must be a hospital or may be a clinic or some other place of less-than-hospital status; as to the licensing of the facility; and the like.

This means, on the other hand, that, for the period of pregnancy prior to this "compelling" point, the attending physician, in consultation with his patient, is free to determine, without regulation by the State, that, in his medical judgment, the patient's pregnancy should be terminated. If that decision is reached, the judgment may be effectuated by an abortion free of interference by the State.

With respect to the State's important and legitimate interest in potential life, the "compelling" point is at viability. This is so because the fetus then presumably has the capability of meaningful life outside the mother's womb. State regulation protective of fetal life after viability thus has both logical and biological justifications. If the State is interested in protecting fetal life after viability, it may go so far as to proscribe abortion during that period, except when it is necessary to preserve the life or health of the mother.

Measured against these standards, Art. 1196 of the Texas Penal Code, in restricting legal abortions to those "procured or attempted by medical advice for the purpose of saving the life of the mother," sweeps too broadly. The statute makes no distinction between abortions performed early in pregnancy and those performed later, and it limits to a single reason, "saving" the mother's life, the legal justification for the procedure. The statute, therefore, cannot survive the constitutional attack made upon it here.

*   *   *

XI

To summarize and to repeat:

1. A state criminal abortion statute of the current Texas type, that excepts from criminality only a life-saving procedure on behalf of the mother, without regard to pregnancy stage and without recognition of the other interests involved, is violative of the Due Process Clause of the Fourteenth Amendment.

(a) For the stage prior to approximately the end of the first trimester, the abortion decision and its effectuation must be left to the medical judgment of the pregnant woman's attending physician.

(b) For the stage subsequent to approximately the end of the first trimester, the State, in promoting its interest in the health of the mother, may, if it chooses, regulate the abortion procedure in ways that are reasonably related to maternal health.

(c) For the stage subsequent to viability, the State in promoting its interest in the potentiality of human life may, if it chooses, regulate, and even proscribe, abortion except where it is necessary, in appropriate medical judgment, for the preservation of the life or health of the mother.

2. The State may define the term "physician," as it has been employed in the preceding paragraphs of this Part XI of this opinion, to mean only a physician currently licensed by the State, and may proscribe any abortion by a person who is not a physician as so defined.

*   *   *

This holding, we feel, is consistent with the relative weights of the respective interests involved, with the lessons and examples of medical and legal history, with the lenity of the common law, and with the demands of the profound problems of the present day. The decision leaves the State free to place increasing restrictions on abortion as the period of pregnancy lengthens, so long as those restrictions are tailored to the recognized state interests. The decision vindicates the right of the physician to administer medical treatment according to his professional judgment up to the points where important state interests provide compelling justifications for intervention. Up to those points, the abortion decision in all its aspects is inherently, and primarily, a medical decision, and basic responsibility for it must rest with the physician. If an individual practitioner abuses the privilege of exercising proper medical judgment, the usual remedies, judicial and intra-professional, are available.

XII

*   *   *

We find it unnecessary to decide whether the District Court erred in withholding injunctive relief, for we assume the Texas prosecutorial authorities will give full credence to this decision that the present criminal abortion statutes of that State are unconstitutional.

Affirmed in part and reversed in part.

MR. JUSTICE STEWART, concurring.

In 1963, this Court purported to sound the death knell for the doctrine of substantive due process, a doctrine under which many state laws had in the past been held to violate the Fourteenth Amendment. As Mr. Justice Black's opinion for the Court in [*Ferguson v.*] *Skrupa* put it: "We have returned to the original constitutional proposition that courts do not substitute their social and economic beliefs for the judgment of legislative bodies, who are elected to pass laws."

Barely two years later, in *Griswold*, the Court held a Connecticut birth control law unconstitutional. In view of what had been so recently said in *Skrupa*, the Court's opinion in *Griswold* understandably did its best to avoid reliance on the Due Process Clause of the Fourteenth Amendment as the ground for decision. Yet, the Connecticut law did not violate any provision of the Bill of Rights, nor any other specific provision of the Constitution. So it was clear to me then, and it is equally clear to me now, that the *Griswold* decision can be rationally understood only as a holding that the Connecticut statute substantively invaded the "liberty" that is protected by the Due Process Clause of the Fourteenth Amendment. As so understood, *Griswold* stands as one in a long line of pre-*Skrupa* cases decided under the doctrine of substantive due process, and I now accept it as such.

* * *

As Mr. Justice Harlan once wrote: "[T]he full scope of the liberty guaranteed by the Due Process Clause cannot be found in or limited by the precise terms of the specific guarantees elsewhere provided in the Constitution. This 'liberty' is not a series of isolated points priced out in terms of the taking of property; the freedom of speech, press, and religion; the right to keep and bear arms; the freedom from unreasonable searches and seizures; and so on. It is a rational continuum which, broadly speaking, includes a freedom from all substantial arbitrary impositions and purposeless restraints . . . and which also recognizes, what a reasonable and sensitive judgment must, that certain interests require particularly careful scrutiny of the state needs asserted to justify their abridgment." In the words of Mr. Justice Frankfurter, "Great concepts like . . . 'liberty' . . . were purposely left to gather meaning from experience. For they relate to the whole domain of social and economic fact, and the statesmen who founded this Nation knew too well that only a stagnant society remains unchanged."

Several decisions of this Court make clear that freedom of personal choice in matters of marriage and family life is one of the liberties protected by the Due Process Clause of the Fourteenth Amendment. *Loving v. Virginia, Griswold v. Connecticut, Pierce v. Society of Sisters, Meyer v. Nebraska.* As recently as last Term, in *Eisenstadt*, we recognized "the right of the individual, married or single, to be free from unwarranted governmental intrusion into matters so fundamentally affecting a person as the decision whether to bear or beget a child." That right necessarily includes the right of a woman to decide whether or not to terminate her pregnancy. Certainly the interests of a woman in giving of her physical and emotional self during pregnancy and the interests that will be affected throughout her life by the birth and raising of a child are of a far greater degree of significance and personal intimacy than the right to send a child to private school protected in *Pierce*, or the right to teach a foreign language protected in *Meyer*." Clearly, therefore, the Court today is correct in holding that the right asserted by Jane Roe is embraced within the personal liberty protected by the Due Process Clause of the Fourteenth Amendment.

It is evident that the Texas abortion statute infringes that right directly. Indeed, it is difficult to imagine a more complete abridgment of a constitutional freedom than that worked by the inflexible criminal statute now in force in Texas. The question then becomes whether the state interests advanced to justify this abridgment can survive the "particularly careful scrutiny" that the Fourteenth Amendment here requires.

The asserted state interests are protection of the health and safety of the pregnant woman, and protection of the potential future human life within her. These are legitimate objectives, amply sufficient to permit a State to regulate abortions as it does other surgical procedures, and perhaps sufficient to permit a State to regulate abortions more stringently or even to prohibit them in the late stages of pregnancy. But such legislation is not before us, and I think the Court today has thoroughly demonstrated that these state interests cannot constitutionally support the broad abridgment of personal liberty worked by the existing Texas law. Accordingly, I join the Court's opinion holding that that law is invalid under the Due Process Clause of the Fourteenth Amendment.

MR. JUSTICE REHNQUIST, dissenting.

*   *   *

While the Court's opinion quotes from the dissent of Mr. Justice Holmes in *Lochner v. New York* (1905), the result it reaches is more closely attuned to the majority opinion of Mr. Justice Peckham in that case. As in *Lochner* and similar cases applying substantive due process standards to economic and social welfare legislation, the adoption of the compelling state interest standard will inevitably require this Court to examine the legislative policies and pass on the wisdom of these policies in the very process of deciding whether a particular state interest put forward may or may not be "compelling." The decision here to break pregnancy into three distinct terms and to outline the permissible restrictions the State may impose in each one, for example, partakes more of judicial legislation than it does of a determination of the intent of the drafters of the Fourteenth Amendment.

The fact that a majority of the States reflecting, after all, the majority sentiment in those States, have had restrictions on abortions for at least a century is a strong indication, it seems to me, that the asserted right to an abortion is not "so rooted in the traditions and conscience of our people as to be ranked as fundamental." Even today, when society's views on abortion are changing, the very existence of the debate is evidence that the "right" to an abortion is not so universally accepted as the appellant would have us believe.

To reach its result, the Court necessarily has had to find within the scope of the Fourteenth Amendment a right that was apparently completely unknown to the drafters of the Amendment. As early as 1821, the first state law dealing directly with abortion was enacted by the Connecticut Legislature. By the time of the adoption of the Fourteenth Amendment in 1868, there were at least 36 laws enacted by state or territorial legislatures limiting abortion. While many States have amended or updated their laws, 21 of the laws on the books in 1868 remain in effect today. Indeed, the Texas statute struck down today was, as the majority notes, first enacted in 1857 and "has remained substantially unchanged to the present time."

There apparently was no question concerning the validity of this provision or of any of the other state statutes when the Fourteenth Amendment was adopted. The only conclusion possible from this history is that the drafters did not intend to have the Fourteenth Amendment withdraw from the States the power to legislate with respect to this matter.

III

Even if one were to agree that the case that the Court decides were here, and that the enunciation of the substantive constitutional law in the Court's opinion were proper, the actual disposition of the case by the Court is still difficult to justify. The Texas statute is struck down in toto, even though the Court apparently concedes that at later periods of pregnancy Texas might impose these selfsame statutory limitations on abortion. My understanding of past practice is that a statute found to be invalid as applied to a particular plaintiff, but not unconstitutional as a whole, is not simply "struck down" but is, instead, declared unconstitutional as applied to the fact situation before the Court.

For all of the foregoing reasons, I respectfully dissent.

NOTES AND QUESTIONS

1.   Recent scholarship questions Justice Blackmun's history. As Clark D. Forsythe, president of Americans United for Life, writes:

> [T]he Court relied almost entirely on the work of one law professor, Cyril Means, who happened to be chief counsel for [the National Abortion Rights Action League]. . . . [T]here can be no question, if the historical facts are considered, that abortion was considered a crime of some degree by the common law at *every* stage of gestation and was *never* protected as a right.

Clark D. Forsythe, *The Effective Enforcement of Abortion Law Before* Roe v. Wade, *in* THE SILENT SUBJECT 183 (Brad Stetson ed., 1996). Regardless of one's view of the issue, there is indeed evidence that abortion prohibitions date back at least to the 13th century, and an excellent catalogue of the common law cases prohibiting the practice can be found in Brief for the American Academy of Medical Ethics at 13 n.18, *Hope v. Perales*, 634 N.E.2d 183 (N.Y. 1994) (No. 23); *see also,* Joseph W. Dellapenna, *The Historical Case Against Abortion,* 13 CONTINUITY 59 (1989). Feminist historians have documented several 17th century cases in colonial America of the crime of abortion. *See* JULIA CHERRY SPRUILL, WOMEN'S LIFE AND WORK IN THE SOUTHERN COLONIES 325–26 (1972).

The most obvious explanation for some of these historical differences of opinion was the difficulty of determining the existence of an early pregnancy until well into the 20th century. Pregnancy tests as late as the 1960s were unreliable. CLINICAL OBSTETRICS 110–14 (Carl J. Pauerstein ed., 1987). The common law therefore focused on quickening, the first physical movement of the child felt by the mother, but this often does not occur until 16–18 weeks in the pregnancy. It was impossible to treat abortion and homicide as one, not by reason of moral approval, but because of evidentiary difficulty. As a mid-19th century treatise explained: "[t]he signs of abortion, as obtained by an *examination of the female,* are not very certain in their character. . . . When abortion occurs in the early months, it leaves but slight and evanescent traces behind it." 3 FRANCIS WHARTON & MORETON STILLE, A TREATISE ON

MEDICAL JURISPRUDENCE § 107, at 77 (Philadelphia, Kay & Brother, 4th ed. 1884).

2. Does *Roe* forsake the principle of the sanctity of human life? Is this departure from natural law principle required or contemplated by constitutional text? Without any firm grounding in history, and even less in text, Justice Blackmun argues:

> This right of privacy, whether it be founded in the Fourteenth Amendment's conception of personal liberty and restrictions upon state action, as we feel it is, or, . . . in the Ninth Amendment's reservation of rights to the people, is broad enough to encompass a woman's decision whether or not to terminate her pregnancy.

410 U.S. at 153. Categorizing abortion as a fundamental, but not absolute, right, the Court held that any state restriction must be in pursuit of a compelling interest and "narrowly drawn to express only the legitimate state interests at stake." *Id.* at 155.

Because the word "persons" is employed in the text of the Constitution and these persons are guaranteed due process as well as equal protection, the *Roe* Court needed to exclude unborn children from legal "personhood" and thus, the protection of the law. *Cf.*, Raymond B. Marcin, *"Posterity" in the Preamble and a Positivist Pro-Life Position*, 38 AM. J. JURIS. 273 (1993) ("the Constitution can and perhaps should be interpreted [from a positivist perspective] as [protecting] the right to life of fetuses or unborn children"). Yet, the Court states:

> The Constitution does not define "person" in so many words. Section 1 of the Fourteenth Amendment contains three references to "person." The first, in defining "citizens," speaks of "persons born or naturalized in the United States." The word also appears both in the Due Process Clause and the Equal Protection Clause. . . . But in nearly all these instances, the use of the word is such that it has application only postnatally. None indicates, with any assurance that it has any possible prenatal application. [Emphasis added.]

Id. at 157 (footnote omitted). Do you find the Court's reasoning persuasive? Why did Justice Blackmun use the hedging expressions "*nearly* all" and "with any *assurance*"? Professor Marcin has argued in a more recent article that Justice Blackmun, in his listing of all the usages of the word "person" in the Constitution, omitted the usage of one variant of the plural form of the word "person," *i.e.*, the word "People" in the Constitution's Preamble — a usage that is declarative of the Constitution's intent to secure the Blessings of Liberty to ourselves *and our Posterity* [emphasis added]. See Raymond B. Marcin, *God's Littlest Children and the Right to Live: The Case for a Positivist Overturning of* Roe, 25 JOURNAL OF CONTEMPORARY HEALTH LAW AND POLICY 38 (2008).

The careful reader may have noticed that Justice Blackmun, throughout his opinion, frequently used the term "mother" in referring to the pregnant woman. Of whom is she the mother?

3. The decision in *Roe* incorporated what became known as a trimester analysis. During the first three months of pregnancy, states were allowed only to protect maternal health and regulate abortion as they would medical procedures generally — effectively, this meant no specialized abortion regulation; in the second trimester, the government "may, if it chooses, regulate the abortion procedure in ways that are reasonably related to maternal health," *id.* at 164, and in the last trimester — after viability — the government may prohibit abortions except if necessary to preserve the life or health of the mother. Presumably, the state's interest in prenatal life was recognized in these last months, but the health exception was open-ended. In particular, the "health" of the mother exception was given an expansive definition in the companion case of *Doe v. Bolton*, 410 U.S. 179 (1973). Justice Blackmun wrote that an abortion may be directed by the exercise of professional judgment "in the light of all factors — physical, emotional, psychological, familial, and the woman's age — relevant to the well-being of the patient." *Id.* at 192.

Justices White and Rehnquist dissented in *Roe*. White called the opinion "an exercise of raw judicial power" that in his view was "improvident." 410 U.S. at 222 (White, J., dissenting). Both of the dissenting justices would have left the matter to state legislatures.

4. *Roe* triggered great controversy. John Hart Ely wrote that:

> The problem with *Roe* is not so much that it bungles the question it sets itself, but rather that it sets itself a question the Constitution has not made the Court's business.

* * *

> . . . [*Roe* is] a very bad decision. . . . It is bad because it is bad constitutional law, or rather because it is *not* constitutional law and gives almost no sense of an obligation to try to be.

John Hart Ely, *The Wages of Crying Wolf: A Comment on* Roe v. Wade, 82 YALE L.J. 920, 943, 947 (1973). But can *Roe* really be singled out in this way, given the Court's earlier decision in say, *Eisenstadt*? What distinguishes *Roe* from the nontextual recognition of the right to marry or to direct the upbringing of children? If your answer is that marriage and parenting are consistent with human life and its development, while abortion is the opposite, is this a natural law argument, and is it the kind of argument that can be made to the Supreme Court? Of course, if the criticism of *Roe* is that it devalues human life, isn't the very premise of that assessment a natural law one in the sense that it depends upon a belief that what counts as life is a natural fact to be discovered. However, Frances Olsen argues, "[t]he value of life is not a simple attribute of any particular life form, something that can be discovered. Culturally created, the value of life rests on social meanings, and, importantly, on sexual politics." Frances Olsen, *Unraveling Compromise*, 103 HARV. L. REV. 105, 127–28 (1989). If you think Ms. Olsen is on to something, was it also true that the value of slave life was the product of "social meanings" and racial politics?

By 1989, the Court, with some new members appointed by President Reagan, seemed ready to overrule *Roe*. Five times, President Reagan had his Solicitor General ask the Supreme Court to re-consider *Roe*, but each time the Court refused. *Roe* is reaffirmed below with some greater limitations, but reaffirmed nonetheless. We have excerpted the opinion below because of its near 100-page length, but we begin first with the case caption for your reference and a brief summary of our own, the excerpts from the prevailing joint opinion and from the dissents follow.

PLANNED PARENTHOOD OF SOUTHEASTERN PENNSYLVANIA v. CASEY
505 U.S. 833 (1992)

[In an opinion authored by JUSTICE O'CONNOR, JUSTICE KENNEDY, and JUSTICE SOUTER, the Court affirms the abortion right found in *Roe*, but qualifies it, such that it is now subject to reasonable regulation especially after the first trimester, but reaching farther back to the beginning of the pregnancy at least in theory. The Court here formally reiterated and held that a woman's interest predominates in the first six months of pregnancy, and is partially counterbalanced by the interests of the state in potential life in the first and second trimesters. In the last or final three months of pregnancy, subject to a health exception the government may proscribe the practice of abortion altogether. Since the word "health" has been broadly interpreted to mean or include mental health, and even at that, to encompass matters of depression, it is not difficult for a woman to find a doctor willing to indicate that an abortion affects health right up to the moment of birth. As a consequence, *Casey*'s reaffirmation of the abortion right, while less one-sided than the opinion in *Roe* and better reasoned to be sure nevertheless amounts to an elaborate *ipse dixit* in its favor.

The result also amounts to a bit of doctrinal incoherence insofar as what had previously been thought of as fundamental right is now subjected to a battery of limitations that the Court would not permit a true fundamental right to be subjected to without an extraordinary or compelling governmental interest. Pennsylvania asserts a number of interests and virtually all of them are sustained including waiting periods, information keeping requirements and adequate counseling, among other things. Only notice given to the spouse, concluded the governing joint opinion, is invalid on its face, with these justices believing that there was a risk of spousal abuse or other related forms of intimidation that the statute did not adequately address and for that reason the spousal notice was construed to be an undue burden (the new test for constitutionality in the abortion context) on the abortion right.

Casey is a long opinion; and we urge students to the extent that their time permits to read the opinion in its entirety. In terms of effect however, this opinion moderates the categorical treatment of the implicit liberty to terminate a pregnancy found by Justice Blackmun in *Roe*, but it is no more satisfying to the opponents of the practice, often as a result of sincere religious objection to the frightful dismemberment of an unborn.

An important subtext of the *Casey* opinion are strong dissents written by Justice Scalia and Chief Justice Rehnquist both of whom seriously question the credibility of the Court in undertaking to give answer where the text of the Constitution is wholly silent and where one would think the best silence beckons legislatures of the states or the people respectively. The argument that federalism should insulate states from interference by the federal government when states are occupying its own traditional policy areas receives very little attention here, though the reader should be alert to it, because following the election of President Obama and his first two nominees for the Supreme Court — Sonia Sotomayor and Elena Kagan — federalism objection will lead to invalidation of a significant section of the federal Defense of Marriage Act (DOMA). It is a different time, a different court.

In the core of the *Casey* opinion, there is a statement that the abortion right needed reaffirmation because it is only through the judicial precedents warranting the continued existence of the practice as lawful that a woman's place in the social and economic marketplace can be enjoyed. The opponents of abortion are quick to say the Court is in essence giving its approval to the sacrifice of a child so that a parent can find employment. This enrages opponents of the practice including advocates for a strong conception of an international human right to life — a right based solely upon the intrinsic dignity of being part of the human race. The notion that this dignity can be sacrificed so that a mother can complete the memo writing of a lawyer or the negotiations of a CEO is said to be repugnant. Nevertheless, it is undoubtedly true that employers in the culture at large have done very little to make it easy for a woman or a man to devote more balanced time to the raising of a family together with market employment.

Casey signaled that the Court was withdrawing from the micromanagement of state regulation of the abortion practice. The opinion is long and it collapses the first and second trimesters and nominally concedes that the state does have an interest in unborn life from the very moment of conception, but it is not likely that this formulation will make any difference in the near-term, though someone seeking to address this matter will find the powerful rhetoric of the opinions a useful source for argument. It is a less useful source for understanding. Herewith a few of those excerpts: — Eds.]

I

Liberty finds no refuge in a jurisprudence of doubt. Yet 19 years after our holding that the Constitution protects a woman's right to terminate her pregnancy in its early stages, *Roe v. Wade* (1973), that definition of liberty is still questioned. Joining the respondents as *amicus curiae*, the United States, as it has done in five other cases in the last decade, again asks us to overrule *Roe*.

At issue in these cases are five provisions of the Pennsylvania Abortion Control Act of 1982, as amended in 1988 and 1989. 18 Pa. Cons. Stat. §§ 3203–3220 (1990). The Act requires that a woman seeking an abortion give her informed consent prior to the abortion procedure, and specifies that she be provided with certain information at least 24 hours before the abortion is performed. § 3205. For a minor to obtain an abortion, the Act requires the informed consent of one of her parents, but provides for a judicial bypass option if the minor does not wish to or cannot obtain a parent's consent. § 3206. Another provision of the Act requires that, unless certain exceptions apply, a married woman seeking an abortion must sign a statement indicating that she has notified her husband of her intended abortion. § 3209. The Act exempts compliance with these three requirements in the event of a "medical emergency," which is defined in § 3203 of the Act. In addition to the above provisions regulating the performance of abortions, the Act imposes certain reporting requirements on facilities that provide abortion services. §§ 3207(b), 3214(a), 3214(f).

*   *   *

After considering the fundamental constitutional questions resolved by *Roe*, principles of institutional integrity, and the rule of *stare decisis*, we are led to conclude this: the essential holding of *Roe v. Wade* should be retained and once again reaffirmed.

It must be stated at the outset and with clarity that *Roe*'s essential holding, the holding we reaffirm, has three parts. First is recognition of the right of the woman to choose to have an abortion before viability and to obtain it without undue interference from the State. Before viability, the State's interests are not strong enough to support a prohibition of abortion or the imposition of a substantial obstacle to the woman's effective right to elect the procedure. Second is a confirmation of the State's power to restrict abortions after fetal viability, if the law contains exceptions for pregnancies which endanger the woman's life or health. And third is the principle that the State has legitimate interests from the outset of the pregnancy in protecting the health of the woman and the life of the fetus that may become a child. These principles do not contradict one another; and we adhere to each.

II

Constitutional protection of the woman's decision to terminate her pregnancy derives from the Due Process Clause of the Fourteenth Amendment. It declares that no State shall "deprive any person of life, liberty, or property, without due process of law." . . .

The most familiar of the substantive liberties protected by the Fourteenth Amendment are those recognized by the Bill of Rights. We have held that the Due Process Clause of the Fourteenth Amendment incorporates most of the Bill of Rights against the States. *See, e.g., Duncan v. Louisiana* (1968). It is tempting, as a means of curbing the discretion of federal judges, to suppose that liberty encompasses no more than those rights already guaranteed to the individual against federal interference by the express provisions of the first eight Amendments to the Constitution. But of course this Court has never accepted that view.

*   *   *

Neither the Bill of Rights nor the specific practices of States at the time of the adoption of the Fourteenth Amendment marks the outer limits of the substantive sphere of liberty which the Fourteenth Amendment protects. *See* U.S. Const., Amdt. 9. . . .

The inescapable fact is that adjudication of substantive due process claims may call upon the Court in interpreting the Constitution to exercise that same capacity which by tradition courts always have exercised: reasoned judgment. Its boundaries are not susceptible of expression as a simple rule. That does not mean we are free to invalidate state policy choices with which we disagree; yet neither does it permit us to shrink from the duties of our office. . . .

* * *

Our law affords constitutional protection to personal decisions relating to marriage, procreation, contraception, family relationships, child rearing, and education. . . . These matters, involving the most intimate and personal choices a person may make in a lifetime, choices central to personal dignity and autonomy, are central to the liberty protected by the Fourteenth Amendment. At the heart of liberty is the right to define one's own concept of existence, of meaning, of the universe, and of the mystery of human life. . . .

* * *

III

A

The obligation to follow precedent begins with necessity, and a contrary necessity marks its outer limit. . . .

* * *

It will be recognized, of course, that *Roe* stands at an intersection of two lines of decisions, but in whichever doctrinal category one reads the case, the result for present purposes will be the same. The *Roe* Court itself placed its holding in the succession of cases most prominently exemplified by *Griswold v. Connecticut.* When it is so seen, *Roe* is clearly in no jeopardy, since subsequent constitutional developments have neither disturbed, nor do they threaten to diminish, the scope of recognized protection accorded to the liberty relating to intimate relationships, the family, and decisions about whether or not to beget or bear a child.

* * *

Nor will courts building upon *Roe* be likely to hand down erroneous decisions as a consequence. Even on the assumption that the central holding of *Roe* was in error, that error would go only to the strength of the state interest in fetal protection, not to the recognition afforded by the Constitution to the woman's liberty. . . .

* * *

The underlying substance of this legitimacy is of course the warrant for the Court's decisions in the Constitution and the lesser sources of legal principle on which the Court draws. . . . Thus, the Court's legitimacy depends on making legally principled decisions under circumstances in which their principled character is sufficiently plausible to be accepted by the Nation.

The need for principled action to be perceived as such is implicated to some degree whenever this, or any other appellate court, overrules a prior case. This is not to say, of course, that this Court cannot give a perfectly satisfactory explanation in most cases. . . .

In two circumstances, however, the Court would almost certainly fail to receive the benefit of the doubt in overruling prior cases. There is, first, a point beyond which frequent overruling would overtax the country's belief in the Court's good faith. Despite the variety of reasons that may inform and justify a decision to overrule, we cannot forget that such a decision is usually perceived (and perceived correctly) as, at the least, a statement that a prior decision was wrong. . . .

. . . Where, in the performance of its judicial duties, the Court decides a case in such a way as to resolve the sort of intensely divisive controversy reflected in *Roe* and those rare, comparable cases, its decision has a dimension that the resolution of the normal case does not carry. It is the dimension present whenever the Court's interpretation of the Constitution calls the contending sides of a national controversy to end their national division by accepting a common mandate rooted in the Constitution.

*   *   *

A decision to overrule *Roe*'s essential holding under the existing circumstances would address error, if error there was, at the cost of both profound and unnecessary damage to the Court's legitimacy, and to the Nation's commitment to the rule of law. It is therefore imperative to adhere to the essence of *Roe*'s original decision, and we do so today.

IV

*   *   *

Before viability, *Roe* and subsequent cases treat all governmental attempts to influence a woman's decision on behalf of the potential life within her as unwarranted. This treatment is, in our judgment, incompatible with the recognition that there is a substantial state interest in potential life throughout pregnancy.

The very notion that the State has a substantial interest in potential life leads to the conclusion that not all regulations must be deemed unwarranted. Not all burdens on the right to decide whether to terminate a pregnancy will be undue. In our view, the undue burden standard is the appropriate means of reconciling the State's interest with the woman's constitutionally protected liberty.

The concept of an undue burden has been utilized by the Court as well as individual Members of the Court, including two of us, in ways that could be considered inconsistent. Because we set forth a standard of general application to which we intend to adhere, it is important to clarify what is meant by an undue burden.

A finding of an undue burden is shorthand for the conclusion that a state regulation has the purpose or effect of placing a substantial obstacle in the path of a woman seeking an abortion of a nonviable fetus. A statute with this purpose is invalid because the means chosen by the State to further the interest in potential life must be calculated to inform the woman's free choice, not hinder it. And a statute which, while furthering the interest in potential life or some other valid state interest, has the effect of placing a substantial obstacle in the path of a woman's choice cannot be considered a permissible means of serving its legitimate ends. To the extent that the opinions of the Court or of individual Justices use the undue burden standard in a manner that is inconsistent with this analysis, we set out what in our view should be the controlling standard. . . .

Some guiding principles should emerge. What is at stake is the woman's right to make the ultimate decision, not a right to be insulated from all others in doing so. Regulations which do no more than create a structural mechanism by which the State, or the parent or guardian of a minor, may express profound respect for the life of the unborn are permitted, if they are not a substantial obstacle to the woman's exercise of the right to choose. Unless it has that effect on her right of choice, a state measure designed to persuade her to choose childbirth over abortion will be upheld if reasonably related to that goal. Regulations designed to foster the health of a woman seeking an abortion are valid if they do not constitute an undue burden.

. . . We give this summary:

(a) To protect the central right recognized by *Roe v. Wade* while at the same time accommodating the State's profound interest in potential life, we will employ the undue burden analysis as explained in this opinion. An undue burden exists, and therefore a provision of law is invalid, if its purpose or effect is to place a substantial obstacle in the path of a woman seeking an abortion before the fetus attains viability.

(b) We reject the rigid trimester framework of *Roe v. Wade*. To promote the State's profound interest in potential life, throughout pregnancy the State may take measures to ensure that the woman's choice is informed, and measures designed to advance this interest will not be invalidated as long as their purpose is to persuade the woman to choose childbirth over abortion. These measures must not be an undue burden on the right.

(c) As with any medical procedure, the State may enact regulations to further the health or safety of a woman seeking an abortion. Unnecessary health regulations that have the purpose or effect of presenting a substantial obstacle to a woman seeking an abortion impose an undue burden on the right.

(d) Our adoption of the undue burden analysis does not disturb the central holding of *Roe v. Wade*, and we reaffirm that holding. Regardless of whether exceptions are made for particular circumstances, a State may not prohibit any woman from making the ultimate decision to terminate her pregnancy before viability.

(e) We also reaffirm *Roe*'s holding that "subsequent to viability, the State in promoting its interest in the potentiality of human life may, if it chooses, regulate, and even proscribe, abortion except where it is necessary, in appropriate medical judgment, for the preservation of the life or health of the mother."

These principles control our assessment of the Pennsylvania statute, and we now turn to the issue of the validity of its challenged provisions [and we uphold all but the spousal notice provision as explained below].

* * *

C

Section 3209 of Pennsylvania's abortion law provides, except in cases of medical emergency, that no physician shall perform an abortion on a married woman without receiving a signed statement from the woman that she has notified her spouse that she is about to undergo an abortion. The woman has the option of providing an alternative signed statement certifying that her husband is not the man who impregnated her; that her husband could not be located; that the pregnancy is the result of spousal sexual assault which she has reported; or that the woman believes that notifying her husband will cause him or someone else to inflict bodily injury upon her. A physician who performs an abortion on a married woman without receiving the appropriate signed statement will have his or her license revoked, and is liable to the husband for damages.

The District Court heard the testimony of numerous expert witnesses, and made detailed findings of fact regarding the effect of this statute. These included:

"273. The vast majority of women consult their husbands prior to deciding to terminate their pregnancy. . . .

* * *

"279. The 'bodily injury' exception could not be invoked by a married woman whose husband, if notified, would, in her reasonable belief, threaten to (a) publicize her intent to have an abortion to family, friends or acquaintances; (b) retaliate against her in future child custody or divorce proceedings; (c) inflict psychological intimidation or emotional harm upon her, her children or other persons; (d) inflict bodily harm on other persons such as children, family members or other loved ones; or (e) use his control over finances to deprive of necessary monies for herself or her children. . . ."

. . . The American Medical Association (AMA) has published a summary of the recent research in this field, which indicates that in an average 12-month period in this country, approximately two million women are the victims of severe assaults by their male partners. . . .

Other studies fill in the rest of this troubling picture. Physical violence is only the most visible form of abuse. Psychological abuse, particularly forced social and economic isolation of women, is also common. . . .

The limited research that has been conducted with respect to notifying one's husband about an abortion, although involving samples too small to be representative, also supports the District Court's findings of fact. The vast majority of women notify their male partners of their decision to obtain an abortion. In many cases in which married women do not notify their husbands, the pregnancy is the result of an extramarital affair. Where the husband is the father, the primary reason women do not notify their husbands is that the husband and wife are experiencing marital difficulties, often accompanied by incidents of violence.

* * *

. . . Respondents argue that since some of these women will be able to notify their husbands without adverse consequences or will qualify for one of the exceptions, the statute affects fewer than one percent of women seeking abortions. For this reason, it is asserted, the statute cannot be invalid on its face. We disagree with respondents' basic method of analysis.

The analysis does not end with the one percent of women upon whom the statute operates; it begins there. Legislation is measured for consistency with the Constitution by its impact on those whose conduct it affects. . . .

* * *

This conclusion is in no way inconsistent with our decisions upholding parental notification or consent requirements. Those enactments, and our judgment that they are constitutional, are based on the quite reasonable assumption that minors will benefit from consultation with their parents and that children will often not realize that their parents have their best interests at heart. We cannot adopt a parallel assumption about adult women.

We recognize that a husband has a "deep and proper concern and interest . . . in his wife's pregnancy and in the growth and development of the fetus she is carrying." With regard to the children he has fathered and raised, the Court has recognized his "cognizable and substantial" interest in their custody. If these cases concerned a State's ability to require the mother to notify the father before taking some action with respect to a living child raised by both, therefore, it would be reasonable to conclude as a general matter that the father's interest in the welfare of the child and the mother's interest are equal.

Before birth, however, the issue takes on a very different cast. It is an inescapable biological fact that state regulation with respect to the child a woman is carrying will have a far greater impact on the mother's liberty than on the father's. . . . ["]Inasmuch as it is the woman who physically bears the child and who is the more directly and immediately affected by the pregnancy, as between the two, the balance weighs in her favor." This conclusion rests upon the basic nature of marriage and the nature of our Constitution: "[T]he marital couple is not an independent entity with a mind and heart of its own, but an association of two individuals each with a separate intellectual and emotional makeup. If the right of privacy means anything, it is the right of the *individual*, married or single, to be free from unwarranted governmental intrusion into matters so fundamentally affecting a person as the decision whether to bear or beget a child." *Eisenstadt v. Baird.* . . .

The judgment . . . is affirmed in part and reversed in part. . . .

It is so ordered.

JUSTICE STEVENS, concurring in part and dissenting in part [omitted].

JUSTICE BLACKMUN, concurring in part, concurring in the judgment in part, and dissenting in part.

* * *

IV

In one sense, the Court's approach is worlds apart from that of THE CHIEF JUSTICE[,] JUSTICE SCALIA[and JUSTICES WHITE and THOMAS]. And yet, in another sense, the distance between the two approaches is short — the distance is but a single vote.

I am 83 years old. I cannot remain on this Court forever, and when I do step down, the confirmation process for my successor well may focus on the issue before us today. That, I regret, may be exactly where the choice between the two worlds will be made.

CHIEF JUSTICE REHNQUIST, with whom JUSTICE WHITE, JUSTICE SCALIA, and JUSTICE THOMAS join, concurring in the judgment in part and dissenting in part.

The joint opinion, following its newly minted variation on *stare decisis*, retains the outer shell of *Roe v. Wade* (1973), but beats a wholesale retreat from the substance of that case. We believe that *Roe* was wrongly decided, and that it can and should be overruled consistently with our traditional approach to *stare decisis* in constitutional cases. We would . . . uphold the challenged provisions of the Pennsylvania statute in their entirety.

I

* * *

. . . Although they reject the trimester framework that formed the underpinning of *Roe*, JUSTICES O'CONNOR, KENNEDY, and SOUTER adopt a revised undue burden standard to analyze the challenged regulations. We conclude, however, that such an outcome is an unjustified constitutional compromise, one which leaves the Court in a position to closely scrutinize all types of abortion regulations despite the fact that it lacks the power to do so under the Constitution.

* * *

We have held that a liberty interest protected under the Due Process Clause of the Fourteenth Amendment will be deemed fundamental if it is "implicit in the concept of ordered liberty." . . .

In construing the phrase "liberty" incorporated in the Due Process Clause of the Fourteenth Amendment, we have recognized that its meaning extends beyond freedom from physical restraint. In *Pierce v. Society of Sisters* (1925), we held that it included a parent's right to send a child to private school; in *Meyer v. Nebraska* (1923), we held that it included a right to teach a foreign language in a parochial school. Building on these cases, we have held that the term "liberty" includes a right to marry, *Loving v. Virginia* (1967); a right to procreate, *Skinner v. Oklahoma ex rel. Williamson* (1942); and a right to use contraceptives, *Griswold v. Connecticut* (1965); *Eisenstadt v. Baird* (1972). But a reading of these opinions makes clear that they do not endorse any all-encompassing "right of privacy."

. . . We are now of the view that, in terming this right fundamental, the Court in *Roe* read the earlier opinions upon which it based its decision much too broadly. Unlike marriage, procreation, and contraception, abortion "involves the purposeful termination of a potential life." *Harris v. McRae*, 448 U.S. 297, 325 (1980). The abortion decision must therefore "be recognized as *sui generis*, different in kind from the others that the Court has protected under the rubric of personal or family privacy and autonomy." One cannot ignore the fact that a woman is not isolated in her pregnancy, and that the decision to abort necessarily involves the destruction of a fetus.

* * *

JUSTICE SCALIA, with whom THE CHIEF JUSTICE, JUSTICE WHITE, and JUSTICE THOMAS join, concurring in the judgment in part and dissenting in part.

. . . The States may, if they wish, permit abortion on demand, but the Constitution does not *require* them to do so. The permissibility of abortion, and the limitations upon it, are to be resolved like most important questions in our democracy: by citizens trying to persuade one another and then voting. As the Court acknowledges, "where reasonable people disagree the government can adopt one position or the other." . . . A State's choice between two positions on which reasonable people can disagree is constitutional even when (as is often the case) it intrudes upon a "liberty" in the absolute sense. Laws against bigamy, for example — with which entire societies of reasonable people disagree — intrude upon men and women's liberty to marry and live with one another. But bigamy happens not to be a liberty specially "protected" by the Constitution.

That is, quite simply, the issue in these cases: not whether the power of a woman to abort her unborn child is a "liberty" in the absolute sense; or even whether it is a liberty of great importance to many women. Of course it is both. The issue is whether it is a liberty protected by the Constitution of the United States. I am sure it is not. I reach that conclusion not because of anything so exalted as my views concerning the "concept of existence, of meaning, of the universe, and of the mystery of human life." Rather, I reach it for the same reason I reach the conclusion that bigamy is not constitutionally protected — because of two simple facts: (1) the Constitution says absolutely nothing about it, and (2) the longstanding traditions of American society have permitted it to be legally proscribed.[15]

---

[15] [1] The Court's suggestion that adherence to tradition would require us to uphold laws against interracial marriage is entirely wrong. Any tradition in that case was contradicted *by a text* — an Equal Protection Clause that explicitly establishes racial equality as a constitutional value. *Loving v. Virginia* (1967). The enterprise launched in *Roe v. Wade* (1973), by contrast, sought to *establish* "in the teeth of a clear, contrary tradition" a value found nowhere in the constitutional text. There is, of course, no comparable tradition barring recognition of a "liberty interest" in carrying one's child to term free from state efforts to kill it. For that reason, it does not follow that the Constitution does not protect childbirth

* * *

The Imperial Judiciary lives. It is instructive to compare this Nietzschean vision of us unelected, life-tenured judges — leading a Volk who will be "tested by following," and whose very "belief in themselves" is mystically bound up in their "understanding" of a Court that "speak[s] before all others for their constitutional ideals" — with the somewhat more modest role envisioned for these lawyers by the Founders.

> "The judiciary . . . has . . . no direction either of the strength or of the wealth of the society, and can take no active resolution whatever. It may truly be said to have neither Force nor Will, but merely judgment. . . ." THE FEDERALIST No. 78.

Or, again, to compare this ecstasy of a Supreme Court in which there is, especially on controversial matters, no shadow of change or hint of alteration ("There is a limit to the amount of error that can plausibly be imputed to prior Courts"), with the more democratic views of a more humble man:

> "[T]he candid citizen must confess that if the policy of the Government upon vital questions affecting the whole people is to be irrevocably fixed by decisions of the Supreme Court, . . . the people will have ceased to be their own rulers, having to that extent practically resigned their Government into the hands of that eminent tribunal." A. Lincoln, First Inaugural Address (Mar. 4, 1861).

It is particularly difficult, in the circumstances of the present decision, to sit still for the Court's lengthy lecture upon the virtues of "constancy," of "remain[ing] steadfast," and adhering to "principle." Among the five Justices who purportedly adhere to *Roe*, at most three agree upon the *principle* that constitutes adherence (the joint opinion's "undue burden" standard) — and that principle is inconsistent with *Roe*. To make matters worse, two of the three, in order thus to remain steadfast, had to abandon previously stated positions. It is beyond me how the Court expects these accommodations to be accepted "as grounded truly in principle, not as compromises with social and political pressures having, as such, no bearing on the principled choices that the Court is obliged to make." The only principle the Court "adheres" to, it seems to me, is the principle that the Court must be seen as standing by *Roe*. That is not a principle of law (which is what I thought the Court was talking about), but a principle of *Realpolitik* — and a wrong one at that.

I cannot agree with, indeed I am appalled by, the Court's suggestion that the decision whether to stand by an erroneous constitutional decision must be strongly influenced — *against* overruling, no less — by the substantial and continuing public opposition the decision has generated. The Court's judgment that any other course would "subvert the Court's legitimacy" must be another consequence of reading the error-filled history book that described the deeply divided country brought together by *Roe*. In my history-book, the Court was covered with dishonor and deprived of

---

simply because it does not protect abortion. The Court's contention that the only way to protect childbirth is to protect abortion shows the utter bankruptcy of constitutional analysis deprived of tradition as a validating factor. It drives one to say that the only way to protect the right to eat is to acknowledge the constitutional right to starve oneself to death.

legitimacy by *Dred Scott v. Sandford* (1857), an erroneous (and widely opposed) opinion that it did not abandon, rather than by *West Coast Hotel Co. v. Parrish* (1937), which produced the famous "switch in time" from the Court's erroneous (and widely opposed) constitutional opposition to the social measures of the New Deal. . . .

But whether it would "subvert the Court's legitimacy" or not, the notion that we would decide a case differently from the way we otherwise would have in order to show that we can stand firm against public disapproval is frightening. It is a bad enough idea, even in the head of someone like me, who believes that the text of the Constitution, and our traditions, say what they say and there is no fiddling with them. But when it is in the mind of a Court that believes the Constitution has an evolving meaning; that the Ninth Amendment's reference to "othe[r]" rights is not a disclaimer, but a charter for action; and that the function of this Court is to "speak before all others for [the people's] constitutional ideals" unrestrained by meaningful text or tradition — then the notion that the Court must adhere to a decision for as long as the decision faces "great opposition" and the Court is "under fire" acquires a character of almost czarist arrogance. We are offended by these marchers who descend upon us, every year on the anniversary of *Roe*, to protest our saying that the Constitution requires what our society has never thought the Constitution requires. These people who refuse to be "tested by following" must be taught a lesson. We have no Cossacks, but at least we can stubbornly refuse to abandon an erroneous opinion that we might otherwise change — to show how little they intimidate us.

*   *   *

We should get out of this area, where we have no right to be, and where we do neither ourselves nor the country any good by remaining.

NOTES AND QUESTIONS

1.   *Roe* was criticized for its reliance upon the Due Process Clause, rather than the Equal Protection Clause. *See, e.g.*, Ruth Bader Ginsburg, *Some Thoughts on Autonomy and Equality in Relation to* Roe v. Wade, 63 N.C. L. REV. 375, 383 (1985). Does the Court in *Casey* address that criticism by its allusion to the importance of abortion to a woman's participation in the "economic and social life of the nation"? 505 U.S. at 835. If women must have the option of terminating pregnancies to be equal participants in our national economic life, is there something amiss in our economic system? In any event, since gender is a quasi-suspect class that can be employed to further an important governmental interest, wouldn't the interest in potential life — which the *Casey* Court says exists throughout the pregnancy — justify most abortion regulations?

2.   Justice Blackmun wrote in *Roe v. Wade* that "[w]e need not resolve the difficult question of when life begins. When those trained in . . . medicine . . . are unable to arrive at any consensus, the judiciary, at this point in the development of man's knowledge, is not in a position to speculate as to the answer." 410 U.S. at 159. Does the Court's focus on viability in *Roe*, and again in *Casey*, effectively decide this question? Justice Scalia has commented: Chief Justice Taney and the *Dred Scott*

decision. *Dred Scott* is the only other decision in the history of our nation (aside from *Roe*) in which a class of human beings (Blacks, slave *or free*, in *Dred Scott*) were defined as not being "People" within the meaning of the Constitution and hence outside its protections.

3.   In rendering its reaffirmation of abortion in *Casey v. Planned Parenthood*, the Court concluded that the "factual underpinnings of *Roe's* central holding" have not changed. 505 U.S. at 864. Yet, in its very lengthy opinion, the Court nowhere discusses modern science. The late Dr. Jerome LeJeune, M.D., Ph.D., the world-famous geneticist from the University of Paris who is credited with discovering the first chromosomal abnormality in man, Down's Syndrome, however, stated well before *Casey* that there is a specific and unique human being present from the moment of conception. According to LeJeune this is not inference, but a deduction. It is just plain observation. Moreover, in Dr. LeJeune's view this is the consensus of scientists everywhere. In LeJeune's words, "[t]o accept the fact that after fertilization has taken place a new human has come into being is no longer a matter of taste or opinion. The human nature of the human being from conception to old age is not a metaphysical contention, it is plain experimental evidence." *The Human Life Bill: Hearings on S. 158 Before the Subcomm. on Separation of Powers of the Senate Comm. on the Judiciary*, 97th Cong. 10 (1982) (statement of Dr. Jerome LeJeune).

Scientists today can make direct observation of the chromosomal and molecular structure of the first cell of life because of a method developed by Dr. Alec Jeffreys of Leicester University (U.K.) for extracting molecules of DNA (deoxyribonucleic acid), the so-called building block of life. With Dr. Jeffreys' methodology, scientists are able to demonstrate that each person — from the moment of the first fertilized cell — is unique. In essence, there is a "bar code" for a person, much like the codes on products in the supermarket, with one very important difference: no two persons in the world have exactly the same code. If John and Mary Doe decide to have a child, Baby Doe is a unique individual like none other to recur in the universe. Should the scientifically-provable uniqueness of the unborn child determine personhood? Does it matter that only a small amount of genetic information is fully expressed in a fertilized egg? Or is genetic expression less important than the fact that *all* of the genetic information that a person will ever have is contained in the first cell, whether it is expressed or not? After all, genetic expression does not end at birth, but continues throughout life. Surely, no one would seriously argue that a six month old infant could be denied nutrition because of insufficient genetic expression, would they?

4.   Maybe the distinction between born and unborn can be found in the fact that there is an absence of differentiated neurons or a functioning brain stem in the fertilized cell. Since those without such functions are said to be "brain dead" at the other end of life, perhaps that is why the unborn child is claimed to be not yet "alive." This, however, ignores that withdrawing life support from a person in a vegetative state does nothing to revive the brain stem; whereas, it is the violent intervention of abortion that stops the development of the brain stem and nervous system in the unborn child. In *Vacco v. Quill*, 521 U.S. 793 (1997), dealing with assisted suicide, we will see the Court reject an analogy between withdrawing life support and affirmatively assisting in the killing of patient.

5.   When Texas defended its criminal prohibition of abortion in *Roe*, the nature of fetal development was premised upon inference. Anyone who has ever listened to the audio tape of the oral argument knows that the Court and the advocates had only a rudimentary understanding of science at the time *Roe* was decided. Yet, the science of the unborn was far fuller at the time of *Casey*. In *Roe*, Justice Blackmun wrote: "[i]f this suggestion of personhood is established, the [pro-abortion] case, of course, collapses," 410 U.S. at 156; did he forget? Or can the law declare personhood to be one thing, when scientific fact affirms another? What would the founders say in the tradition of natural law originalism? Justice James Wilson, who both signed the Declaration of Independence and the Constitution, sagely counseled that "law can never attain either the extent or the elevation of a science, unless it be raised upon the science of man." 1 JAMES WILSON, THE WORKS OF JAMES WILSON 197 (Robert Green McCloskey ed., Belknap Press 1967) (1804).

6.   After *Casey*, the constitutionality of regulation of abortion practice depends upon whether the regulation, at least prior to viability, constitutes an undue burden. But what exactly is an undue burden? The joint opinion of Justices Kennedy, O'Connor and Souter define it as a law with the "purpose or effect [of placing] a substantial obstacle in the path of a woman seeking an abortion" 505 U.S. at 878. By the same token, the *Casey* opinion articulates that the state has a profound interest in unborn life throughout the pregnancy and "may take measures to ensure that the woman's choice is informed, and measures designed to advance this interest will not be invalidated as long as their purpose is to persuade the woman to choose childbirth over abortion." *Id.* But aren't measures designed to favor childbirth, obstacles? If the answer is yes, then why are they tolerated? Presumably, it is because they are not undue burdens or undue obstacles. Caught in this circular thought pattern, the most one can say is — states are permitted to encourage life (and thereby discourage abortion), but not too much.

Post-*Casey*, the following types of abortion restrictions, all considered in *Casey*, are likely constitutional: a 24 hour waiting period, 505 U.S. at 885–886; an informed consent requirement calling for the provision of truthful, nonmisleading information about the nature of the abortion procedure, associated health risks, as well as information about the development of the unborn child, *id.* at 838; and medical recordkeeping and reporting requirements specifying the name of the abortionist, marital status of the woman, prior pregnancies, and fetal condition, *id.* at 900. Recordkeeping laws that do not preserve the confidentiality of the woman choosing to take the life of her unborn child may, under pre-*Casey* decision, be open to constitutional doubt *e.g., Thornburgh v. American College of Obstetricians and Gynecologists*, 476 U.S. at 766 (characterizing the record requirements there as "extreme" with identification of the patient being their only "obvious" purpose). In addition, in an earlier decision, *Webster v. Reproductive Health Services*, a plurality of the Court and a separate concurring opinion by Justice O'Connor accepted responsible testing of the unborn child to determine viability. As Justice O'Connor wrote, "[i]t is clear to me that requiring the performance of examinations and tests useful to determining whether a fetus is viable, when viability is possible, and when it would not be medically imprudent to do so, does not impose an undue burden on a woman's abortion decision." 492 U.S. at 530.

While pre-*Casey* decisions invalidated most abortion method restrictions, *Casey* more forthrightly acknowledges the state's interest in unborn life throughout the pregnancy, so it is possible that requirements that abortions be performed in a hospital setting (today, most are not, rather they are performed in "clinics" very loosely defined) might be sustained. In the earlier decision of *Planned Parenthood of Kansas City, Mo. v. Ashcroft*, a state law requiring a second physician where an abortion is performed after viability was sustained. 462 U.S. at 486.

Parental notice or consent requirements applicable to unmarried minors are constitutional, subject to the availability of an alternative judicial procedure that would allow authorization of the abortion where a court finds that the minor is sufficiently mature to make her own decision or where the court independently finds the abortion to be in her best interests. *Bellotti v. Baird*, 443 U.S. 622 (1979) (invalidating a two parent consent requirement because it did not provide for a sufficiently porous judicial by-pass). See also *Hodgson v. Minnesota*, 497 U.S. 417 (1990), upholding a two parent notification requirement applicable to minors, so long as a judicial by-pass mechanism was available. Given that parents have the right — perhaps a fundamental right — to direct the upbringing of their children, why is it that the state can preempt parental direction in this morally sensitive context? Generally, parental consent is required whenever a medical procedure is performed on a minor child. Given that *Casey* more completely recognizes the interest of the state in discouraging abortion based upon its generalized interest in the preservation of human life, why isn't the specific, familial interest of a grandparent in the life of an unborn grandchild equally weighty?

Another anomaly is the Court's refusal to acknowledge a spouse's interest in being informed of an abortion decision. *Casey*, of course, invalidates even a highly qualified spousal notification. 505 U.S. at 887–98. In so doing, the joint opinion without record evidence tends to assume widespread spousal abuse and thereby makes dysfunctional marriages the norm. Apart from the dubious sociology, the invalidation of the notice requirement is seemingly a misapplication of the undue burden standard. As the Chief Justice points out in dissent, "[i]n most instances the notification requirement operates without difficulty." *See* footnote 2 of the Chief Justice's dissenting opinion (not included above). Admitting that some marriages are troubled by abuse, the Pennsylvania statute did not require spousal notice where the woman could reasonably believe that it would result in her bodily harm. A husband's interest in procreation within marriage is substantial — and again, more personal than the state's generalized interest in the preservation of life — and yet, the Court fails to explain persuasively why this substantial interest cannot be credited.

Apart from restrictions on abortion, the government is under no constitutional obligation to subsidize the practice. In other words, the existence of a constitutional right, perhaps especially a highly controverted one like abortion, implies no obligation on the part of the government to facilitate its exercise. In *Maher v. Roe*, the Court wrote that the judicial discovery of an abortion right "implies no limitation on the authority of a State to make a value judgment favoring childbirth over abortion, and to implement that judgment by the allocation of public funds." 432 U.S. at 474. Thus, the state prohibition of the use of Medicaid funds for abortions in *Maher* "place[d] no obstacles — absolute or otherwise — in the pregnant woman's path to an abortion. An indigent woman who desires an abortion suffers no disadvantage as a consequence of Connecticut's decision to fund childbirth." *Id.* The Court has also sustained express federal restrictions on the use of public funds for abortion. *Harris v. McRae*, 448 U.S. 297, 302 (1980) (sustaining the Hyde amendment prohibiting federal funding of abortion, except in limited cases). In *Rust v. Sullivan*, 500 U.S. 173 (1991), the Court upheld the ability of government to fund only speech that promotes its interest in childbirth. "[The] Government can, without violating the Constitution, selectively fund a program to encourage certain activities it believes to be in the public interest, without at the same time funding an alternate program which seeks to deal with the problem another way. In so doing, the Government has not discriminated on the basis of viewpoint; it has merely chosen to fund one activity to the exclusion of another." *Id.* at 193.

7.   Previously we mentioned the troubling imprecision in the Court's identification of nontextual fundamental rights. From a natural law respect for family, marriage, and procreation, the Court moved — without explicit justification — to an unrefined concept of privacy, and then, liberty, that included largely unfettered access to contraception and abortion by married and unmarried alike. As suggested in *Casey*, the Court had already allowed the sweep of these privacy rights to remove reasonable distinctions between an adult and a minor child. *See, e.g.*, *Carey v. Population Services Int'l*, 431 U.S. 678 (1977), where a plurality of the Court extended the abortion right of privacy to minors, asserting "the right to privacy in connection with decisions affecting procreation extends to minors as well as to adults." *Id.* at 693. Some might argue that discovering implied rights in "natural law" is no more precise than loose formulations of "implicit in ordered liberty" and other similar terminology that the Court has employed from time to time; however, as you surely recognize by now, the natural law tradition is a longstanding jurisprudential effort (much of which was introduced in Chapters One and Two) to discern human good from human nature, itself. In addition, the Framers expressly adopted this natural law system in premising the claim of constitutional liberty and inalienable right upon the "laws of nature and nature's God." Do you believe, like the Framers did, that human nature is knowable? Does the very make-up of yourself instruct you in the basics of how to live? If it is fair to say that by reasoned reflection, you can determine what foods are compatible with your body, what clothing is appropriate for the external climate, and what knowledge brings happiness and fulfillment, might it not also be true that by the same course of deductive reasoning some exercises of liberty will be more readily seen to promote human good? Are the vaguer formulations of "ordered liberty" or "fundamental notions of fair play" less helpful because they do not specifically avert to the philosophical system identified by the framers and declared to be the basis of our independence? Do overly broad and untethered ideas of autonomy tend to dissolve into constitutional right claims that not only do not further human nature, but also disregard (slavery) or destroy (abortion) it? *Cf.*, David Crump, *How Do the Courts Really Discover Unenumerated Fundamental Rights? Cataloguing the Methods of Judicial Alchemy*, 19 HARV. J.L. & PUB. POL'Y 795 (1996) (demonstrating how current judicial practice uses convulted legal formulae to create fundamental rights from personal inclinations).

8.   The Supreme Court proclaims in *Casey* that every person has "the right to define [their] own concept of existence, of meaning, of the universe, and of the mystery of human life," 505 U.S. at 852, but natural law originalism, as restated by John Locke, gave God the benefit of the doubt in such matters. As Locke's thinking is summarized:

> [H]uman beings are the creation or "workmanship" of God; they therefore belong to God, are his property. From this fact derives a set of prescriptions under the natural law; these mainly have the form of limitations on what human beings may do: they may not use force, *i.e.*, directly harm each other, for they belong to God, not to each other; they may not harm themselves, *e.g.*, they may not commit suicide, for the same reason; and they may not indirectly harm each other through taking more than their fair share of the goods of the external world.

Michael P. Zuckert, *Do Natural Rights Derive from Natural Law?*, 21 HARV. J.L. & PUB. POL'Y 695 (1997) (referencing JOHN LOCKE, QUESTIONS CONCERNING THE LAW OF NATURE (Robert Horwitz et al. trans., 1990)). And it is our equality vis-a-vis a transcendent God that supplies the necessary insight for democratic rule. When all are created equal, no one has a superior right to govern. *See* HARRY V. JAFFA, ORIGINAL INTENT AND THE FRAMERS OF THE CONSTITUTION 62–63 (1994) (indicating that the legitimacy of the consent of the governed is a reciprocal of natural human equality). The passage from *Casey* mentioned above is sometimes denigratingly referred to as the Court's "mystery passage." It was this mystery passage that led lower courts to find an assisted suicide right. *See Compassion in Dying v. Washington*, 79 F.3d 790, 813 (9th Cir. 1996), *rev'd sub nom. Washington v. Glucksberg*, 521 U.S. 702 (1997); *Quill v. Vacco*, 80 F.2d 716, 730 (2d Cir. 1996), *rev'd*, 521 U.S. 793 (1997). When you read the Supreme Court's ruling in the assisted suicide cases below consider whether the Court has retrenched from the mystery passage. In particular, does the Court indicate that its decision about what aspects of personal autonomy are to receive constitutional protection must be more than a "philosophical exercise"? "That many of the rights and liberties protected by the Due Process Clause sound in personal autonomy," said the Court, "does not warrant the sweeping conclusion that any and all important, intimate, and personal decisions are so protected." 521 U.S. at 727. For a claim of personal autonomy to be protected, the claim must be "deeply rooted in our history and traditions, or so fundamental to our concept of constitutionally ordered liberty, that they are protected by the Fourteenth Amendment." *Id.*

9.   Are contraception and abortion related? Consider the following:

> But despite their differences of nature and moral gravity, contraception and abortion are often closely connected, as fruits of the same tree. It is true that in many cases contraception and even abortion are practised under the pressure of real life difficulties, which nonetheless can never exonerate from striving to observe God's law fully. Still, in very many other instances such practices are rooted in a hedonistic mentality unwilling to accept responsibility in matters of sexuality, and they imply a self-centered concept of freedom, which regards procreation as an obstacle to personal fulfillment. The life which could result from a sexual encounter thus

becomes an enemy to be avoided at all costs, and abortion becomes the only possible decisive response to failed contraception.

The close connection which exists, in mentality, between the practice of contraception and that of abortion is becoming increasingly obvious. It is being demonstrating in an alarming way by the development of chemical products, intrauterine devices and vaccines which, distributed with the same ease as contraceptives, really act as abortifacients in the very early stages of the development of the life of the new human being.

POPE JOHN PAUL II, THE GOSPEL OF LIFE [EVANGELIUM VITAE] No. 13, at 28–29 (1995).

10.   There is another aspect to the abortion debate that warrants mention. Several studies have indicated that there may be a correlation between abortion and increased risk of breast cancer. Another recent study has shown a strong correlation between legalized abortion and sexually transmitted diseases:

Our regression results show that abortion legalization led to an increase of sexually transmitted diseases; this result is robust to a wide range of time periods and covariates and is constant across the sexes. The point estimates indicate that legalization caused an increase in the gonorrhea and syphilis rates potentially as large as 25 percent. . . . If a similar abortion effect exists for other STDs, which we could not examine because of data limitations, additional treatment expenditures might amount to more than $4 billion annually.

Klick and Stratmann, 32 J. LEGAL STUDIES 407 (June 2003). What effect, if any, should this kind of evidence have on the states' ability to regulate or restrict abortion as a means of protecting maternal health?

11.   In *Stenberg v. Carhart* (2000), the Court, 5-4, invalidated a Nebraska prohibition on the so-called "partial-birth" abortion procedure which takes the life of the unborn child by means of stabbing in the back of the skull when all but the head of the child has been delivered, as opposed to the more common procedure after the initial weeks of dissection and reassembly for missing parts. The Court found the absence of a broadly worded health exception for the mother and the possibility that a doctor might inadvertently start with the dissection procedure and end up with the other created an impermissible undue burden on a woman's decision before fetal viability.

12.   In *Ayotte v. Planned Parenthood of Northern New England* (2000), the Court unanimously held that if enforcing a statute that regulates access to abortion would be unconstitutional in medical emergencies, the proper judicial response is not to invalidate the statute entirely if lower courts may be able to render narrower declaratory and injunctive relief. The problem in *Ayotte* was the absence of a medical emergency exception to either parental consent or a judicial by-pass of parental consent (which still might be too slow if an emergency occurred). In writing for the Court, Justice O'Connor stated:

Three interrelated principles inform our approach to remedies. First, we try not to nullify more of a legislature's work than is necessary, for we know that "[a] ruling of unconstitutionality frustrates the intent of the elected representatives of the people." . . . Accordingly, the "normal rule" is that "partial, rather than facial, invalidation is the required course," such that a "statute may . . . be declared invalid to the extent that it reaches too far, but otherwise left intact."

Second, mindful that our constitutional mandate and institutional competence are limited, we restrain ourselves from "rewrit[ing] state law to conform it to constitutional requirements" even as we strive to salvage it. Our ability to devise a judicial remedy that does not entail quintessentially legislative work often depends on how clearly we have already articulated the background constitutional rules at issue and how easily we can articulate the remedy. . . .

Third, the touchstone for any decision about remedy is legislative intent, for a court cannot use its remedial powers to circumvent the intent of the legislature." . . . All the while, we are wary of legislatures who would rely on our intervention, for "[i]t would certainly be dangerous if the legislature could set a net large enough to catch all possible offenders, and leave it to the courts to step inside" to announce to whom the statute may be applied. "This would, to some extent, substitute the judicial for the legislative department of the government."

Finding that the court below had used the most "blunt" remedy — permanently enjoining the enforcement of New Hampshire's parental notification law and thereby invalidating it entirely — the Court agreed with New Hampshire that the lower courts need not have invalidated the law wholesale . . .

13.   It was not immediately clear how significant *Ayotte* was. On the one hand, it did not signify that the Court intends to regularize abortion jurisprudence, such that it will now follow the more customary, and demanding, standard for proving facial invalidity — namely, that a law has no conceivable constitutional application. Since at least *Casey*, the Court has seemingly applied a standard in only the abortion context that is inclined toward invalidity — whether a significant fraction of the subset of women affected by a regulation are unduly burdened. In *Casey* itself, this invalidated the spousal notice requirement even though an overwhelming percentage of women either experienced no burden in informing their spouse or fell within one of several exceptions for an abusive spouse and the like.

14.   The Court stressed, as it had before, that states do have the right to require parental involvement. Under the Court's precedent, such laws must include a parental "bypass," allowing a pregnant minor to seek approval from a judge for an abortion when consulting parents would not be in the girl's best interests. Such a bypass procedure must be timely and confidential. New Hampshire's law had such a bypass, but the Court was not convinced the judges could act swiftly enough by this means to address an emergency health issue.

GONZALES v. CARHART
550 U.S. 124 (2007)

JUSTICE KENNEDY delivered the opinion of the Court.

These cases require us to consider the validity of the Partial-Birth Abortion Ban Act of 2003 (Act), a federal statute regulating abortion procedures. In recitations preceding its operative provisions the Act refers to the Court's opinion in *Stenberg v. Carhart* (2000), which also addressed the subject of abortion procedures used in the later stages of pregnancy. Compared to the state statute at issue in *Stenberg*, the Act is more specific concerning the instances to which it applies and in this respect more precise in its coverage. We conclude the Act should be sustained against the objections lodged by the broad, facial attack brought against it.

* * *

[Two lower courts] enjoined the Attorney General from enforcing the Act.

I

A

The Act proscribes a particular manner of ending fetal life,[16] so it is necessary here, as it was in *Stenberg*, to discuss abortion procedures in some detail. . . .

---

[16] [24] The operative provisions of the Act provide in relevant part:

"(a) Any physician who, in or affecting interstate or foreign commerce, knowingly performs a partial-birth abortion and thereby kills a human fetus shall be fined under this title or imprisoned not more than 2 years, or both. This subsection does not apply to a partial-birth abortion that is necessary to save the life of a mother whose life is endangered by a physical disorder, physical illness, or physical injury, including a life-endangering physical condition caused by or arising from the pregnancy itself. This subsection takes effect 1 day after the enactment.

"(b) As used in this section —

"(1) the term 'partial-birth abortion' means an abortion in which the person performing the abortion —

"(A) deliberately and intentionally vaginally delivers a living fetus until, in the case of a head-first presentation, the entire fetal head is outside the body of the mother, or, in the case of breech presentation, any part of the fetal trunk past the navel is outside the body of the mother, for the purpose of performing an overt act that the person knows will kill the partially delivered living fetus; and

"(B) performs the overt act, other than completion of delivery, that kills the partially delivered living fetus; and

"(2) the term 'physician' means a doctor of medicine or osteopathy legally authorized to practice medicine and surgery by the State in which the doctor performs such activity, or any other individual legally authorized by the State to perform abortions: *Provided, however*, That any individual who is not a physician or not otherwise legally authorized by the State to perform abortions, but who nevertheless directly performs a partial-birth abortion, shall be subject to the provisions of this section.

. . . .

(d)(1) A defendant accused of an offense under this section may seek a hearing before the

Abortion methods vary depending to some extent on the preferences of the physician and, of course, on the term of the pregnancy and the resulting stage of the unborn child's development. Between 85 and 90 percent of the approximately 1.3 million abortions performed each year in the United States take place in the first three months of pregnancy, which is to say in the first trimester. The most common first-trimester abortion method is vacuum aspiration (otherwise known as suction curettage) in which the physician vacuums out the embryonic tissue. Early in this trimester an alternative is to use medication, such as mifepristone (commonly known as RU-486), to terminate the pregnancy. The Act does not regulate these procedures.

Of the remaining abortions that take place each year, most occur in the second trimester. The surgical procedure referred to as "dilation and evacuation" or "D & E" is the usual abortion method in this trimester. . . .

A doctor must first dilate the cervix at least to the extent needed to insert surgical instruments into the uterus and to maneuver them to evacuate the fetus. . . .

After sufficient dilation the surgical operation can commence. The woman is placed under general anesthesia or conscious sedation. The doctor, often guided by ultrasound, inserts grasping forceps through the woman's cervix and into the uterus to grab the fetus. The doctor grips a fetal part with the forceps and pulls it back through the cervix and vagina, continuing to pull even after meeting resistance from the cervix. The friction causes the fetus to tear apart. For example, a leg might be ripped off the fetus as it is pulled through the cervix and out of the woman. The process of evacuating the fetus piece by piece continues until it has been completely removed. A doctor may make 10 to 15 passes with the forceps to evacuate the fetus in its entirety, though sometimes removal is completed with fewer passes. Once the fetus has been evacuated, the placenta and any remaining fetal material are suctioned or scraped out of the uterus. The doctor examines the different parts to ensure the entire fetal body has been removed.

Some doctors, especially later in the second trimester, may kill the fetus a day or two before performing the surgical evacuation. They inject digoxin or potassium chloride into the fetus, the umbilical cord, or the amniotic fluid. Fetal demise may cause contractions and make greater dilation possible. Once dead, moreover, the fetus' body will soften, and its removal will be easier. Other doctors refrain from injecting chemical agents, believing it adds risk with little or no medical benefit.

The abortion procedure that was the impetus for the numerous bans on "partial-birth abortion," including the Act, is a variation of this standard D & E. The

---

State Medical Board on whether the physician's conduct was necessary to save the life of the mother whose life was endangered by a physical disorder, physical illness, or physical injury, including a life-endangering physical condition caused by or arising from the pregnancy itself.

"(2) The findings on that issue are admissible on that issue at the trial of the defendant. Upon a motion of the defendant, the court shall delay the beginning of the trial for not more than 30 days to permit such a hearing to take place.

"(e) A woman upon whom a partial-birth abortion is performed may not be prosecuted under this section, for a conspiracy to violate this section, or for an offense under section 2, 3, or 4 of this title based on a violation of this section."

medical community has not reached unanimity on the appropriate name for this D & E variation. It has been referred to as "intact D & E," "dilation and extraction" (D & X), and "intact D & X." For discussion purposes this D & E variation will be referred to as intact D & E.

* * *

Intact D & E gained public notoriety when, in 1992, Dr. Martin Haskell gave a presentation describing his method of performing the operation. Dilation and Extraction. In the usual intact D & E the fetus' head lodges in the cervix, and dilation is insufficient to allow it to pass. Haskell explained the next step as follows:

> "At this point, the right-handed surgeon slides the fingers of the left [hand] along the back of the fetus and 'hooks' the shoulders of the fetus with the index and ring fingers (palm down).

> "While maintaining this tension, lifting the cervix and applying traction to the shoulders with the fingers of the left hand, the surgeon takes a pair of blunt curved Metzenbaum scissors in the right hand. He carefully advances the tip, curved down, along the spine and under his middle finger until he feels it contact the base of the skull under the tip of his middle finger.

> "[T]he surgeon then forces the scissors into the base of the skull or into the foramen magnum. Having safely entered the skull, he spreads the scissors to enlarge the opening.

> "The surgeon removes the scissors and introduces a suction catheter into this hole and evacuates the skull contents. With the catheter still in place, he applies traction to the fetus, removing it completely from the patient."

This is an abortion doctor's clinical description. Here is another description from a nurse who witnessed the same method performed on a 26 1/2-week fetus and who testified before the Senate Judiciary Committee:

> "Dr. Haskell went in with forceps and grabbed the baby's legs and pulled them down into the birth canal. Then he delivered the baby's body and the arms — everything but the head. The doctor kept the head right inside the uterus. . . .

> "The baby's little fingers were clasping and unclasping, and his little feet were kicking. Then the doctor stuck the scissors in the back of his head, and the baby's arms jerked out, like a startle reaction, like a flinch, like a baby does when he thinks he is going to fall.

> "The doctor opened up the scissors, stuck a high-powered suction tube into the opening, and sucked the baby's brains out. Now the baby went completely limp. . . .

> "He cut the umbilical cord and delivered the placenta. He threw the baby in a pan, along with the placenta and the instruments he had just used."

Dr. Haskell's approach is not the only method of killing the fetus once its head lodges in the cervix. . . . Others continue to pull the fetus out of the woman until it disarticulates at the neck, in effect decapitating it. These doctors then grasp the head with forceps, crush it, and remove it.

. . . Another doctor testified he crushes a fetus' skull not only to reduce its size but also to ensure the fetus is dead before it is removed. For the staff to have to deal with a fetus that has "some viability to it, some movement of limbs," according to this doctor, "[is] always a difficult situation."

D & E and intact D & E are not the only second-trimester abortion methods. Doctors also may abort a fetus through medical induction. The doctor medicates the woman to induce labor, and contractions occur to deliver the fetus. Induction, which unlike D & E should occur in a hospital, can last as little as 6 hours but can take longer than 48. It accounts for about five percent of second-trimester abortions before 20 weeks of gestation and 15 percent of those after 20 weeks. Doctors turn to two other methods of second-trimester abortion, hysterotomy and hysterectomy, only in emergency situations because they carry increased risk of complications. In a hysterotomy, as in a cesarean section, the doctor removes the fetus by making an incision through the abdomen and uterine wall to gain access to the uterine cavity. A hysterectomy requires the removal of the entire uterus. These two procedures represent about .07% of second-trimester abortions.

B

After Dr. Haskell's procedure received public attention, with ensuing and increasing public concern, bans on "partial birth abortion" proliferated. By the time of the *Stenberg* decision, about 30 States had enacted bans designed to prohibit the procedure. In 1996, Congress also acted to ban partial-birth abortion. President Clinton vetoed the congressional legislation, and the Senate failed to override the veto. Congress approved another bill banning the procedure in 1997, but President Clinton again vetoed it. In 2003, after this Court's decision in *Stenberg*, Congress passed the Act at issue here. On November 5, 2003, President Bush signed the Act into law. It was to take effect the following day.

The Act responded to *Stenberg* in two ways. First, Congress made factual findings. . . . Congress found, among other things, that "[a] moral, medical, and ethical consensus exists that the practice of performing a partial-birth abortion . . . is a gruesome and inhumane procedure that is never medically necessary and should be prohibited."

Second, and more relevant here, the Act's language differs from that of the Nebraska statute struck down in *Stenberg*.

* * *

C

[The lower courts] concluded the Act was unconstitutional for two reasons. First, it determined the Act was unconstitutional because it lacked an exception allowing the procedure where necessary for the health of the mother. Second, the District

Court found the Act deficient because it covered not merely intact D & E but also certain other D & Es. . . .

* * *

II

The principles set forth in the joint opinion in *Planned Parenthood of South-eastern Pa. v. Casey*, (1992), did not find support from all those who join the instant opinion (SCALIA, J., joined by THOMAS, J., *inter alios*, concurring in judgment in part and dissenting in part). Whatever one's views concerning the *Casey* joint opinion, it is evident a premise central to its conclusion — that the government has a legitimate and substantial interest in preserving and promoting fetal life — would be repudiated were the Court now to affirm the judgments of the Courts of Appeals.

Casey involved a challenge to *Roe v. Wade* (1973). The opinion contains this summary:

> "It must be stated at the outset and with clarity that *Roe*'s essential holding, the holding we reaffirm, has three parts. First is a recognition of the right of the woman to choose to have an abortion before viability and to obtain it without undue interference from the State. Before viability, the State's interests are not strong enough to support a prohibition of abortion or the imposition of a substantial obstacle to the woman's effective right to elect the procedure. Second is a confirmation of the State's power to restrict abortions after fetal viability, if the law contains exceptions for pregnancies which endanger the woman's life or health. And third is the principle that the State has legitimate interests from the outset of the pregnancy in protecting the health of the woman and the life of the fetus that may become a child. These principles do not contradict one another; and we adhere to each."

Though all three holdings are implicated in the instant cases, it is the third that requires the most extended discussion; for we must determine whether the Act furthers the legitimate interest of the Government in protecting the life of the fetus that may become a child.

To implement its holding, *Casey* rejected both *Roe*'s rigid trimester framework and the interpretation of *Roe* that considered all previability regulations of abortion unwarranted. . . .

We assume the following principles for the purposes of this opinion. Before viability, a State may not prohibit any woman from making the ultimate decision to terminate her pregnancy. "It also may not impose upon this right an undue burden, which exists if a regulation's 'purpose or effect is to place a substantial obstacle in the path of a woman seeking an abortion before the fetus attains viability.' " On the other hand, "[r]egulations which do no more than create a structural mechanism by which the State, or the parent or guardian of a minor, may express profound respect for the life of the unborn are permitted, if they are not a substantial obstacle to the woman's exercise of the right to choose." [*Casey*, in short, struck a balance. The balance was central to its holding. We now apply its standard to the cases at bar.]

III

*   *   *

We conclude that the Act is not void for vagueness, does not impose an undue burden from any overbreadth, and is not invalid on its face.

A

The Act punishes "knowingly perform[ing]" a "partial-birth abortion." It defines the unlawful abortion in explicit terms.

First, the person performing the abortion must "vaginally delive[r] a living fetus." The Act does not restrict an abortion procedure involving the delivery of an expired fetus. The Act, furthermore, is inapplicable to abortions that do not involve vaginal delivery (for instance, hysterotomy or hysterectomy). The Act does apply both previability and postviability because, by common understanding and scientific terminology, a fetus is a living organism while within the womb, whether or not it is viable outside the womb. We do not understand this point to be contested by the parties.

Second, the Act's definition of partial-birth abortion requires the fetus to be delivered "until, in the case of a head-first presentation, the entire fetal head is outside the body of the mother, or, in the case of breech presentation, any part of the fetal trunk past the navel is outside the body of the mother." The Attorney General concedes, and we agree, that if an abortion procedure does not involve the delivery of a living fetus to one of these "anatomical 'landmarks' " — where, depending on the presentation, either the fetal head or the fetal trunk past the navel is outside the body of the mother — the prohibitions of the Act do not apply.

Third, to fall within the Act, a doctor must perform an "overt act, other than completion of delivery, that kills the partially delivered living fetus." For purposes of criminal liability, the overt act causing the fetus' death must be separate from delivery. And the overt act must occur after the delivery to an anatomical landmark. This is because the Act proscribes killing "the partially delivered" fetus, which, when read in context, refers to a fetus that has been delivered to an anatomical landmark.

Fourth, the Act contains scienter requirements concerning all the actions involved in the prohibited abortion. To begin with, the physician must have "deliberately and intentionally" delivered the fetus to one of the Act's anatomical landmarks. If a living fetus is delivered past the critical point by accident or inadvertence, the Act is inapplicable. In addition, the fetus must have been delivered "for the purpose of performing an overt act that the [doctor] knows will kill [it]." If either intent is absent, no crime has occurred. This follows from the general principle that where scienter is required no crime is committed absent the requisite state of mind.

B

Respondents contend the language described above is indeterminate, and they thus argue the Act is unconstitutionally vague on its face. "As generally stated, the void-for-vagueness doctrine requires that a penal statute define the criminal offense with sufficient definiteness that ordinary people can understand what conduct is prohibited and in a manner that does not encourage arbitrary and discriminatory enforcement." The Act satisfies both requirements.

The Act provides doctors "of ordinary intelligence a reasonable opportunity to know what is prohibited." . . . Unlike the statutory language in *Stenberg* that prohibited the delivery of a "substantial portion" of the fetus — where a doctor might question how much of the fetus is a substantial portion — the Act defines the line between potentially criminal conduct on the one hand and lawful abortion on the other. Doctors performing D & E will know that if they do not deliver a living fetus to an anatomical landmark they will not face criminal liability.

This conclusion is buttressed by the intent that must be proved to impose liability. . . . The Act requires the doctor deliberately to have delivered the fetus to an anatomical landmark. Because a doctor performing a D & E will not face criminal liability if he or she delivers a fetus beyond the prohibited point by mistake, the Act cannot be described as "a trap for those who act in good faith."

Respondents likewise have failed to show that the Act should be invalidated on its face because it encourages arbitrary or discriminatory enforcement. Just as the Act's anatomical landmarks provide doctors with objective standards, they also "establish minimal guidelines to govern law enforcement." Respondents' arguments concerning arbitrary enforcement, furthermore, are somewhat speculative. This is a preenforcement challenge, where "no evidence has been, or could be, introduced to indicate whether the [Act] has been enforced in a discriminatory manner or with the aim of inhibiting [constitutionally protected conduct]." The Act is not vague.

C

We next determine whether the Act imposes an undue burden, as a facial matter, because its restrictions on second-trimester abortions are too broad. A review of the statutory text discloses the limits of its reach. The Act prohibits intact D & E; and, notwithstanding respondents' arguments, it does not prohibit the D & E procedure in which the fetus is removed in parts.

1

The Act prohibits a doctor from intentionally performing an intact D & E. The dual prohibitions of the Act, both of which are necessary for criminal liability, correspond with the steps generally undertaken during this type of procedure. . . .

The Act excludes most D & Es in which the fetus is removed in pieces, not intact. If the doctor intends to remove the fetus in parts from the outset, the doctor will not have the requisite intent to incur criminal liability. . . .

A comparison of the Act with the Nebraska statute struck down in *Stenberg* confirms this point. The statute in *Stenberg* prohibited "deliberately and intentionally delivering into the vagina a living unborn child, or a substantial portion thereof, for the purpose of performing a procedure that the person performing such procedure knows will kill the unborn child and does kill the unborn child." The Court concluded that this statute encompassed D & E because "D & E will often involve a physician pulling a 'substantial portion' of a still living fetus, say, an arm or leg, into the vagina prior to the death of the fetus." The Court also rejected the limiting interpretation urged by Nebraska's Attorney General that the statute's reference to a "procedure" that "kill[s] the unborn child" was to a distinct procedure, not to the abortion procedure as a whole.

Congress, it is apparent, responded to these concerns because the Act departs in material ways from the statute in *Stenberg*. . . .

The identification of specific anatomical landmarks to which the fetus must be partially delivered also differentiates the Act from the statute at issue in *Stenberg*. . . .

By adding an overt-act requirement Congress sought further to meet the Court's objections to the state statute considered in *Stenberg*. . . .

The canon of constitutional avoidance, finally, extinguishes any lingering doubt as to whether the Act covers the prototypical D & E procedure. "[T]he elementary rule is that every reasonable construction must be resorted to, in order to save a statute from unconstitutionality." It is true this longstanding maxim of statutory interpretation has, in the past, fallen by the wayside when the Court confronted a statute regulating abortion. The Court at times employed an antagonistic "canon of construction under which in cases involving abortion, a permissible reading of a statute [was] to be avoided at all costs." *Casey* put this novel statutory approach to rest. *Stenberg* need not be interpreted to have revived it. We read that decision instead to stand for the uncontroversial proposition that the canon of constitutional avoidance does not apply if a statute is not "genuinely susceptible to two constructions." In *Stenberg* the Court found the statute covered D & E. Here, by contrast, interpreting the Act so that it does not prohibit standard D & E is the most reasonable reading and understanding of its terms.

2

*   *   *

IV

Under the principles accepted as controlling here, the Act, as we have interpreted it, would be unconstitutional "if its purpose or effect is to place a substantial obstacle in the path of a woman seeking an abortion before the fetus attains viability" (plurality opinion). The abortions affected by the Act's regulations take place both previability and postviability; so the quoted language and the undue burden analysis it relies upon are applicable. The question is whether the Act, measured by its text in this facial attack, imposes a substantial obstacle to late-term, but previability, abortions. The Act does not on its face impose a substantial obstacle, and we reject this further facial challenge to its validity.

A

The Act's purposes are set forth in recitals preceding its operative provisions. A description of the prohibited abortion procedure demonstrates the rationale for the congressional enactment. The Act proscribes a method of abortion in which a fetus is killed just inches before completion of the birth process. Congress stated as follows: "Implicitly approving such a brutal and inhumane procedure by choosing not to prohibit it will further coarsen society to the humanity of not only newborns, but all vulnerable and innocent human life, making it increasingly difficult to protect such life." The Act expresses respect for the dignity of human life.

Congress was concerned, furthermore, with the effects on the medical community and on its reputation caused by the practice of partial-birth abortion. The findings in the Act explain:

> "Partial-birth abortion . . . confuses the medical, legal, and ethical duties of physicians to preserve and promote life, as the physician acts directly against the physical life of a child, whom he or she had just delivered, all but the head, out of the womb, in order to end that life."

There can be no doubt the government "has an interest in protecting the integrity and ethics of the medical profession." *Washington v. Glucksberg*. Under our precedents it is clear the State has a significant role to play in regulating the medical profession.

Casey reaffirmed these governmental objectives. The government may use its voice and its regulatory authority to show its profound respect for the life within the woman. A central premise of the opinion was that the Court's precedents after *Roe* had "undervalue[d] the State's interest in potential life." The plurality opinion indicated "[t]he fact that a law which serves a valid purpose, one not designed to strike at the right itself, has the incidental effect of making it more difficult or more expensive to procure an abortion cannot be enough to invalidate it." This was not an idle assertion. The three premises of *Casey* must coexist. The third premise, that the State, from the inception of the pregnancy, maintains its own regulatory interest in protecting the life of the fetus that may become a child, cannot be set at naught by interpreting *Casey's* requirement of a health exception so it becomes tantamount to allowing a doctor to choose the abortion method he or she might prefer. Where it has a rational basis to act, and it does not impose an undue burden, the State may use its regulatory power to bar certain procedures and substitute others, all in furtherance of its legitimate interests in regulating the medical profession in order to promote respect for life, including life of the unborn.

The Act's ban on abortions that involve partial delivery of a living fetus furthers the Government's objectives. No one would dispute that, for many, D & E is a procedure itself laden with the power to devalue human life. Congress could nonetheless conclude that the type of abortion proscribed by the Act requires specific regulation because it implicates additional ethical and moral concerns that justify a special prohibition. Congress determined that the abortion methods it proscribed had a "disturbing similarity to the killing of a newborn infant," and thus it was concerned with "draw[ing] a bright line that clearly distinguishes abortion and infanticide." The Court has in the past confirmed the validity of drawing boundaries to prevent certain practices that extinguish life and are close to actions that are condemned. *Glucksberg* found reasonable the State's "fear that permitting assisted suicide will start it down the path to voluntary and perhaps even involuntary euthanasia."

Respect for human life finds an ultimate expression in the bond of love the mother has for her child. The Act recognizes this reality as well. Whether to have an abortion requires a difficult and painful moral decision. While we find no reliable data to measure the phenomenon, it seems unexceptionable to conclude some women come to regret their choice to abort the infant life they once created and sustained. Severe depression and loss of esteem can follow.

In a decision so fraught with emotional consequence some doctors may prefer not to disclose precise details of the means that will be used, confining themselves to the required statement of risks the procedure entails. From one standpoint this ought not to be surprising. Any number of patients facing imminent surgical procedures would prefer not to hear all details, lest the usual anxiety preceding invasive medical procedures become the more intense. This is likely the case with the abortion procedures here in issue.

It is, however, precisely this lack of information concerning the way in which the fetus will be killed that is of legitimate concern to the State. The State has an interest in ensuring so grave a choice is well informed. It is self-evident that a mother who comes to regret her choice to abort must struggle with grief more anguished and sorrow more profound when she learns, only after the event, what she once did not know: that she allowed a doctor to pierce the skull and vacuum the fast-developing brain of her unborn child, a child assuming the human form.

It is a reasonable inference that a necessary effect of the regulation and the knowledge it conveys will be to encourage some women to carry the infant to full term, thus reducing the absolute number of late-term abortions. The medical profession, furthermore, may find different and less shocking methods to abort the fetus in the second trimester, thereby accommodating legislative demand. The State's interest in respect for life is advanced by the dialogue that better informs the political and legal systems, the medical profession, expectant mothers, and society as a whole of the consequences that follow from a decision to elect a late-term abortion.

It is objected that the standard D & E is in some respects as brutal, if not more, than the intact D & E, so that the legislation accomplishes little. What we have already said, however, shows ample justification for the regulation. Partial-birth abortion, as defined by the Act, differs from a standard D & E because the former occurs when the fetus is partially outside the mother to the point of one of the Act's anatomical landmarks. It was reasonable for Congress to think that partial-birth abortion, more than standard D & E, "undermines the public's perception of the appropriate role of a physician during the delivery process, and perverts a process during which life is brought into the world." There would be a flaw in this Court's logic, and an irony in its jurisprudence, were we first to conclude a ban on both D & E and intact D & E was overbroad and then to say it is irrational to ban only intact D & E because that does not proscribe both procedures. In sum, we reject the contention that the congressional purpose of the Act was "to place a substantial obstacle in the path of a woman seeking an abortion."

B

The Act's furtherance of legitimate government interests bears upon, but does not resolve, the next question: whether the Act has the effect of imposing an unconstitutional burden on the abortion right because it does not allow use of the barred procedure where "necessary, in appropriate medical judgment, for [the] preservation of the . . . health of the mother." *Ayotte.* The prohibition in the Act would be unconstitutional, under precedents we here assume to be controlling, if it "subject[ed] [women] to significant health risks." In *Ayotte* the parties agreed a health exception to the challenged parental-involvement statute was necessary "to avert serious and often irreversible damage to [a pregnant minor's] health." Here, by contrast, whether the Act creates significant health risks for women has been a contested factual question. The evidence presented in the trial courts and before Congress demonstrates both sides have medical support for their position.

. . . Abortion doctors testified, for example, that intact D & E decreases the risk of cervical laceration or uterine perforation because it requires fewer passes into the uterus with surgical instruments and does not require the removal of bony fragments of the dismembered fetus, fragments that may be sharp. Respondents also presented evidence that intact D & E was safer both because it reduces the risks that fetal parts will remain in the uterus and because it takes less time to complete. Respondents, in addition, proffered evidence that intact D & E was safer for women with certain medical conditions or women with fetuses that had certain anomalies.

These contentions were contradicted by other doctors who testified in the District Courts and before Congress. They concluded that the alleged health advantages were based on speculation without scientific studies to support them. They considered D & E always to be a safe alternative.

There is documented medical disagreement whether the Act's prohibition would ever impose significant health risks on women. . . .

The question becomes whether the Act can stand when this medical uncertainty persists. The Court's precedents instruct that the Act can survive this facial attack. The Court has given state and federal legislatures wide discretion to pass legislation in areas where there is medical and scientific uncertainty.

This traditional rule is consistent with *Casey*, which confirms the State's interest in promoting respect for human life at all stages in the pregnancy. Physicians are not entitled to ignore regulations that direct them to use reasonable alternative procedures. The law need not give abortion doctors unfettered choice in the course of their medical practice, nor should it elevate their status above other physicians in the medical community. In *Casey* the controlling opinion held an informed-consent requirement in the abortion context was "no different from a requirement that a doctor give certain specific information about any medical procedure." . . .

Medical uncertainty does not foreclose the exercise of legislative power in the abortion context any more than it does in other contexts. The medical uncertainty over whether the Act's prohibition creates significant health risks provides a sufficient basis to conclude in this facial attack that the Act does not impose an undue burden.

The conclusion that the Act does not impose an undue burden is supported by other considerations. Alternatives are available to the prohibited procedure. As we have noted, the Act does not proscribe D & E. One District Court found D & E to have extremely low rates of medical complications. *Planned Parenthood, supra,* at 1000, 112 S.Ct. 2791. Another indicated D & E was "generally the safest method of abortion during the second trimester."

*   *   *

In reaching the conclusion the Act does not require a health exception we reject certain arguments made by the parties on both sides of these cases. On the one hand, the Attorney General urges us to uphold the Act on the basis of the congressional findings alone. Although we review congressional fact finding under a deferential standard, we do not in the circumstances here place dispositive weight on Congress' findings. The Court retains an independent constitutional duty to review factual findings where constitutional rights are at stake. See *Crowell v. Benson* (1932) ("In cases brought to enforce constitutional rights, the judicial power of the United States necessarily extends to the independent determination of all questions, both of fact and law, necessary to the performance of that supreme function").

V

The considerations we have discussed support our further determination that these facial attacks should not have been entertained in the first instance. In these circumstances the proper means to consider exceptions is by as-applied challenge. The Government has acknowledged that preenforcement, as-applied challenges to the Act can be maintained. This is the proper manner to protect the health of the woman if it can be shown that in discrete and well-defined instances a particular condition has or is likely to occur in which the procedure prohibited by the Act must be used. In an as-applied challenge the nature of the medical risk can be better quantified and balanced than in a facial attack.

The latitude given facial challenges in the First Amendment context is inapplicable here. Broad challenges of this type impose "a heavy burden" upon the parties maintaining the suit. *Rust v. Sullivan* (1991). What that burden consists of in the specific context of abortion statutes has been a subject of some question. *Compare Ohio v. Akron Center for Reproductive Health* (1990) ("[B]ecause appellees are making a facial challenge to a statute, they must show that no set of circumstances exists under which the Act would be valid" (internal quotation marks omitted)), *with Casey* (opinion of the Court) (indicating a spousal-notification statute would impose an undue burden "in a large fraction of the cases in which [it] is relevant" and holding the statutory provision facially invalid). We need not resolve that debate.

As the previous sections of this opinion explain, respondents have not demonstrated that the Act would be unconstitutional in a large fraction of relevant cases. *Casey* (opinion of the Court). We note that the statute here applies to all instances in which the doctor proposes to use the prohibited procedure, not merely those in which the woman suffers from medical complications. It is neither our obligation nor within our traditional institutional role to resolve questions of constitutionality with respect to each potential situation that might develop. "[I]t would indeed be undesirable for this Court to consider every conceivable situation which might possibly arise in the application of complex and comprehensive legislation." For this reason, "[a]s-applied challenges are the basic building blocks of constitutional adjudication."

The Act is open to a proper as-applied challenge in a discrete case. No as-applied challenge need be brought if the prohibition in the Act threatens a woman's life because the Act already contains a life exception.

* * *

Respondents have not demonstrated that the Act, as a facial matter, is void for vagueness, or that it imposes an undue burden on a woman's right to abortion based on its overbreadth or lack of a health exception. For these reasons the judgments of the Courts of Appeals for the Eighth and Ninth Circuits are reversed.

It is so ordered.

JUSTICE THOMAS, with whom JUSTICE SCALIA joins, concurring.

I join the Court's opinion because it accurately applies current jurisprudence, including *Planned Parenthood of Southeastern Pa. v. Casey* (1992). I write separately to reiterate my view that the Court's abortion jurisprudence, including *Casey* and *Roe v. Wade* (1973), has no basis in the Constitution. I also note that whether the Act constitutes a permissible exercise of Congress' power under the Commerce Clause is not before the Court. The parties did not raise or brief that issue; it is outside the question presented; and the lower courts did not address it.

JUSTICE GINSBURG, with whom JUSTICE STEVENS, JUSTICE SOUTER, and JUSTICE BREYER join, dissenting. . . .

Taking care to speak plainly, the *Casey* Court restated and reaffirmed *Roe*'s essential holding.

* * *

Seven years ago, in *Stenberg v. Carhart* (2000), the Court invalidated a Nebraska statute criminalizing the performance of a medical procedure that, in the political arena, has been dubbed "partial-birth abortion." With fidelity to the *Roe-Casey* line of precedent, the Court held the Nebraska statute unconstitutional in part because it lacked the requisite protection for the preservation of a woman's health.

Today's decision is alarming. It refuses to take *Casey* and *Stenberg* seriously. It tolerates, indeed applauds, federal intervention to ban nationwide a procedure found necessary and proper in certain cases by the American College of Obstetricians and Gynecologists (ACOG). It blurs the line, firmly drawn in *Casey*, between previability and postviability abortions. And, for the first time since *Roe*, the Court blesses a prohibition with no exception safeguarding a woman's health.

I dissent from the Court's disposition. Retreating from prior rulings that abortion restrictions cannot be imposed absent an exception safeguarding a woman's health, the Court upholds an Act that surely would not survive under the close scrutiny that previously attended state-decreed limitations on a woman's reproductive choices.

I

A

As *Casey* comprehended, at stake in cases challenging abortion restrictions is a woman's "control over her [own] destiny." "There was a time, not so long ago," when women were "regarded as the center of home and family life, with attendant special responsibilities that precluded full and independent legal status under the Constitution." Those views, this Court made clear in *Casey*, "are no longer consistent with our understanding of the family, the individual, or the Constitution." Women, it is now acknowledged, have the talent, capacity, and right "to participate equally in the economic and social life of the Nation." Their ability to realize their full potential, the Court recognized, is intimately connected to "their ability to control their reproductive lives." Thus, legal challenges to undue restrictions on abortion procedures do not seek to vindicate some generalized notion of privacy; rather, they center on a woman's autonomy to determine her life's course, and thus to enjoy equal citizenship stature.

In keeping with this comprehension of the right to reproductive choice, the Court has consistently required that laws regulating abortion, at any stage of pregnancy and in all cases, safeguard a woman's health.

* * *

In *Stenberg*, we expressly held that a statute banning intact D & E was unconstitutional in part because it lacked a health exception.

* * *

II

A

The Court offers flimsy and transparent justifications for upholding a nationwide ban on intact D & E *sans* any exception to safeguard a women's health. Today's ruling, the Court declares, advances "a premise central to [*Casey*'s] conclusion" — *i.e.*, the Government's "legitimate and substantial interest in preserving and promoting fetal life." But the Act scarcely furthers that interest: The law saves not a single fetus from destruction, for it targets only a *method* of performing abortion.

. . .

As another reason for upholding the ban, the Court emphasizes that the Act does not proscribe the nonintact D & E procedure. But why not, one might ask. Nonintact D & E could equally be characterized as "brutal," involving as it does "tear[ing] [a fetus] apart" and "ripp[ing] off" its limbs. "[T]he notion that either of these two equally gruesome procedures . . . is more akin to infanticide than the other, or that the State furthers any legitimate interest by banning one but not the other, is simply irrational." *Stenberg* (STEVENS, J., concurring). . . .

Ultimately, the Court admits that "moral concerns" are at work, concerns that could yield prohibitions on any abortion. ("Congress could . . . conclude that the type of abortion proscribed by the Act requires specific regulation because it implicates additional ethical and moral concerns that justify a special prohibition."). Notably, the concerns expressed are untethered to any ground genuinely serving the Government's interest in preserving life. By allowing such concerns to carry the day and case, overriding fundamental rights, the Court dishonors our precedent. *See, e.g., Casey* ("Some of us as individuals find abortion offensive to our most basic principles of morality, but that cannot control our decision. Our obligation is to define the liberty of all, not to mandate our own moral code."); *Lawrence v. Texas* (Though "[f]or many persons [objections to homosexual conduct] are not trivial concerns but profound and deep convictions accepted as ethical and moral principles," the power of the State may not be used "to enforce these views on the whole society through operation of the criminal law" (citing *Casey*).

* * *

B

In cases on a "woman's liberty to determine whether to [continue] her pregnancy," this Court has identified viability as a critical consideration. . . .

Today, the Court blurs that line, maintaining that "[t]he Act [legitimately] appl[ies] both previability and postviability because . . . a fetus is a living organism while within the womb, whether or not it is viable outside the womb." Instead of drawing the line at viability, the Court refers to Congress' purpose to differentiate "abortion and infanticide" based not on whether a fetus can survive outside the womb, but on where a fetus is anatomically located when a particular medical procedure is performed. . . .

III

A

The Court further confuses our jurisprudence when it declares that "facial attacks" are not permissible in "these circumstances," *i.e.*, where medical uncertainty exists.

* * *

B

If there is anything at all redemptive to be said of today's opinion, it is that the Court is not willing to foreclose entirely a constitutional challenge to the Act. "The Act is open," the Court states, "to a proper as-applied challenge in a discrete case."

* * *

The Court envisions that in an as-applied challenge, "the nature of the medical risk can be better quantified and balanced." But it should not escape notice that the record already includes hundreds and hundreds of pages of testimony identifying "discrete and well-defined instances" in which recourse to an intact D & E would better protect the health of women with particular conditions. . . .

The Court's allowance only of an "as-applied challenge in a discrete case" jeopardizes women's health and places doctors in an untenable position. Even if courts were able to carve-out exceptions through piecemeal litigation for "discrete and well-defined instances," women whose circumstances have not been anticipated by prior litigation could well be left unprotected. In treating those women, physicians would risk criminal prosecution, conviction, and imprisonment if they exercise their best judgment as to the safest medical procedure for their patients. The Court is thus gravely mistaken to conclude that narrow as-applied challenges are "the proper manner to protect the health of the woman."

IV

* * *

For the reasons stated, I dissent from the Court's disposition and would affirm the judgments before us for review.

NOTES AND QUESTIONS

1.   How deferential should the Court be to congressional findings enforcing the provisions of the Fourteenth Amendment? Justice Ginsburg in dissent thought little deference was warranted, especially in light of the fact the District Courts found some of Congress' recitals to be in error or superseded. For example, Congress determined no medical schools provide instruction on the prohibited procedure, whereas, the District Judge found some evidence of teaching of the procedure in a few medical school programs. Likewise, the District Court doubted the existence of a medical consensus that the prohibited procedure is never medically necessary. Isn't there something curious here? Would it be appropriate for Congress ever to modify free speech protections on the supposition that a consensus of speech experts viewed a given form of speech to be of no value? But then, is the abortion right qualitatively different than free speech insofar as it, unlike abortion, is textual? Why shouldn't Congress have a greater power of definitional refinement when the right in question is an unenumerated product of judicial reasoning, rather than the product of the people by ratification?

Maybe the level of deference ought to depend on the magnitude of the risk. Speech is important to human flourishing, but isn't health at the very core of well being? Justice Ginsburg reasoned that in the face of medical uncertainty, the doubt ought to be resolved to leave no margin for error. Would that have stacked the deck against the state's interest in pre-natal life that is part of the *Casey* balance? Justice Kennedy posited that a "zero tolerance policy" would strike down legitimate abortion regulations, like the partial birth ban, if some part of the medical community were disinclined to follow the proscription. "This is too exacting a standard to impose on the legislative power," wrote Kennedy. "Considerations of marginal safety, including the balance of risks, are within the legislative competence when the regulation is rational and in pursuit of legitimate ends. When standard medical options are available, mere convenience does not suffice to displace them; and if some procedures have different risks than others, it does not follow that the State is altogether barred from imposing reasonable regulations. The Act is not invalid on its face where there is uncertainty over whether the barred procedure is ever necessary to preserve a woman's health, given the availability of other abortion procedures that are considered to be safe alternatives."

2.   Justice Kennedy angers the dissent by speaking of a "bond of love between mother and child." Indeed, the majority posits that a woman suffers adverse health effects by giving consent to a practice bordering on infanticide. "Women who have abortions come to regret their choices, and consequently suffer from '[s]evere depression and loss of esteem.'" Kennedy speculates that the gruesome nature of the partial birth procedure would tempt doctors to leave women inadequately informed of "the different procedures and their attendant risks." Hence, by the majority's reasoning, it is not just the state's interest in prenatal life that is honored by the ban, but also the state's interest in maternal health. Justice Ginsburg refuses to concede these adverse health effects of having an abortion, emphasizing instead the greater depression of "delivering and parenting a child that [the mother] did not intend to have" (quoting a policy study favoring abortion). Is the abortion right in *Casey* about choice or about the promotion of the pro-abortion side of the choice?

3.   Out of date? The reference to the relationship of mother and child is also denigrated as outdated thinking by the dissent. "This way of thinking reflects ancient notions about women's place in the family and under the Constitution — ideas that have long since been discredited," writes Justice Ginsburg. What is intended by this observation? Presumably, Justice Ginsburg is affirming the incontestable point that women have as much right as men to pursue marketplace opportunities outside the home, and not that it is "outdated" to favor motherhood over abortion.

4.   A new equality rationale for abortion? In a thoughtful essay for the *Los Angeles Times* (April 20, 2007), Professor Cass Sunstein of the University of Chicago noted correctly that Justice Ginsburg in her dissent in *Carhart* sought to re-anchor the abortion right on equality rather than liberty or privacy which has been the originally claimed basis for the right in *Roe* and *Casey*. Professor Sunstein observes that, "for Ginsburg, this alternative understanding of the right to choose has concrete implications." Elaborating Ginsburg's point, Sunstein argues that "for supporters of the right to choose, the sex equality argument has considerable advantages over the privacy argument. Much more than the right to privacy, the ban on sex discrimination is firmly entrenched in constitutional doctrines." But are men and women similarly situated with respect to pregnancy?

Basic principles of equal protection require that those who are alike or similarly situated be treated in like manner; they do not require collapsing or disregarding actual gender differences. Professor Sunstein addresses this matter of gender difference in this fashion: "True, men cannot become pregnant, and it is tempting to think that, for that reason, abortion restrictions cannot possibly create a problem of discrimination. But perhaps this argument has things backward. In our society, isn't there an equality problem if laws target only women's bodies and leave men's bodies alone?" It's not clear what Professor Sunstein means by this singular "targeting of women's bodies." In one sense, given the differences between men and women's bodies, it arguably is little more than a restatement of the question are men and women different? If they are, it is not gender discrimination to treat them differently.

Yet, both Professor Sunstein and Justice Ginsburg are onto something important. It can only be grasped, however, if the claimed link between abortion and equality is broken. Perhaps Justice Ginsburg is mistaken to indulge the legal premise that equates the equal citizenship of women as hinged primarily upon abortion. In this respect, perhaps the source of inequality is not the unavailability of a given abortion procedure, but the failure of social or work environments to simultaneously accommodate the birth of a child and a women's professional or other market skills. Ginsburg puts the whole burden of accommodation on the woman. Her attempted re-framing in the dissent of the abortion precedents from being anchored upon liberty and privacy to equal protection does not solve this.

Given the profound religious, scientific, and cultural controversy that abortion represents, should a woman's equal citizenship (or market opportunities) be made to depend upon a woman's willingness to undergo the normatively-contested practice? Perhaps the real truth of Justice Ginsburg's (and derivatively Professor Sunstein's) equality insight is this: women, but not men, are disadvantaged by society and in the economic marketplace by pregnancy. The solution, however, may not lie in putting a legal thumb on the scale in favor of terminating pregnancies, but in reforming the culture and the marketplace to accommodate women as they are — not as the market (or the men still dominating it) would like them.

Justice Ginsburg is highly intelligent. Despite brilliance and erudition, she was turned away early in her legal career by Felix Frankfurter for a Supreme Court clerkship and a dozen New York law firms. Matters have improved for women law graduates, but by how much? How many corporations or law firms meaningfully structure work environments to make it possible for a woman to fully participate in the economic and social life of the nation without having to beg for special treatment, or, as is implied or even explicit, in Justice Ginsburg's equal citizenship remark, to face a choice between work and family that men do not have to face?

5. *Carhart* upholds the federal ban on its face, leaving open the possibility of an "as applied" challenge. Is it clear how an as applied challenge would be brought by a woman facing an immediate medical decision? What would have to be shown to prevail as applied that was not shown facially? And on the subject of facial challenges, note that the Court does not realign the abortion jurisprudence with the general and more demanding facial challenge standard that applies outside the abortion context (*i.e.*, a challenger must demonstrate that there is no conceivable

application of the contested statute that would be constitutional as to any Justice Ginsburg insists that a provision restricting access to abortion "mu̲s̲ ̲ ̲ ̲ ̲ judged by reference to those [women] for whom it is an actual rather than an irrelevant restriction." In other words, as she sees it, it does not matter that a statute is constitutional in many, if not most, cases. For the dissent, a facial challenge can be brought not just when a large fraction of women are affected, but when any individual woman might be. Justice Ginsburg thus argues "[t]here is, in short, no fraction because the numerator and denominator are the same: The health exception reaches only those cases where a woman's health is at risk. Perhaps for this reason, in mandating safeguards for women's health, we have never before invoked the 'large fraction' test." In other words, the health exception for Justice Ginsburg may be exercised by any woman who has a doctor willing to assert it on her behalf. Is this formulation then abortion on demand? If it is, is it consistent with the carefully calibrated competing interests recognized in *Casey*?

3. Assisted Suicide

WASHINGTON v. GLUCKSBERG
521 U.S. 702 (1997)

CHIEF JUSTICE REHNQUIST delivered the opinion of the Court.

The question presented in this case is whether Washington's prohibition against "caus[ing]" or "aid[ing]" a suicide offends the Fourteenth Amendment to the United States Constitution. We hold that it does not.

. . . Today, Washington law provides: "a person is guilty of promoting a suicide attempt when he knowingly causes or aids another person to attempt suicide." "Promoting a suicide attempt" is a felony, punishable by up to five years' imprisonment and up to a $10,000 fine. At the same time, Washington's Natural Death Act, enacted in 1979, states that the "withholding or withdrawal of life-sustaining treatment" at a patient's direction "shall not, for any purpose, constitute a suicide."

. . . In January 1994, [four physicians who practice in Washington], along with three gravely ill, pseudonymous plaintiffs who have since died and Compassion in Dying, a nonprofit organization that counsels people considering physician-assisted suicide, sued in the United States District Court, seeking a declaration that [the prohibition against assisted suicide] is, on its face, unconstitutional.

The plaintiffs asserted "the existence of a liberty interest protected by the Fourteenth Amendment which extends to a personal choice by a mentally competent, terminally ill adult to commit physician-assisted suicide." Relying primarily on *Planned Parenthood v. Casey* and *Cruzan v. Director, Missouri Dept. of Health*, the District Court agreed, and concluded that Washington's assisted-suicide ban is unconstitutional because it "places an undue burden on the exercise of [that] constitutionally protected liberty interest." The District Court also decided that the Washington statute violated the Equal Protection Clause's requirement that " 'all persons similarly situated . . . be treated alike.' "

A panel of the Court of Appeals for the Ninth Circuit reversed, emphasizing that "[i]n the two hundred and five years of our existence no constitutional right to aid in killing oneself has ever been asserted and upheld by a court of final jurisdiction." The Ninth Circuit reheard the case en banc, reversed the panel's decision, and affirmed the District Court. . . .

I

We begin, as we do in all due-process cases, by examining our Nation's history, legal traditions, and practices. In almost every State — indeed, in almost every western democracy — it is a crime to assist a suicide. The States' assisted-suicide bans are not innovations. Rather, they are longstanding expressions of the States' commitment to the protection and preservation of all human life. . . .

More specifically, for over 700 years, the Anglo-American common-law tradition has punished or otherwise disapproved of both suicide and assisting suicide. In the 13th century, Henry de Bracton, one of the first legal-treatise writers, observed that "[j]ust as a man may commit felony by slaying another so may he do so by slaying himself." 2 BRACTON ON LAWS AND CUSTOMS OF ENGLAND 423 (§ 150) (G. Woodbine ed., S. Thorne trans., 1968). The real and personal property of one who killed himself to avoid conviction and punishment for a crime were forfeit to the king. . . . Centuries later, Sir William Blackstone, whose Commentaries on the Laws of England not only provided a definitive summary of the common law but was also a primary legal authority for 18th and 19th century American lawyers, referred to suicide as "self-murder" and "the pretended heroism, but real cowardice, of the Stoic philosophers, who destroyed themselves to avoid those ills which they had not the fortitude to endure. . . ." 4 W. BLACKSTONE, COMMENTARIES *189. . . .

For the most part, the early American colonies adopted the common-law approach. . . .

Over time, however, the American colonies abolished the[] harsh common-law penalties [associated with suicide]. . . . [T]he movement away from the common law's harsh sanctions did not represent an acceptance of suicide; rather, . . . this change reflected the growing consensus that it was unfair to punish the suicide's family for his wrongdoing. . . .

That suicide remained a grievous, though nonfelonious, wrong is confirmed by the fact that colonial and early state legislatures and courts did not retreat from prohibiting assisting suicide. Swift, in his early 19th century treatise on the laws of Connecticut, stated that "[i]f one counsels another to commit suicide, and the other by reason of the advice kills himself, the advisor is guilty of murder as principal." 2 Z. SWIFT, A DIGEST OF THE LAWS OF THE STATE OF CONNECTICUT 270 (1823). This was the well established common-law view. . . . And the prohibitions against assisting suicide never contained exceptions for those who were near death. Rather, "[t]he life of those to whom life ha[d] become a burden — of those who [were] hopelessly diseased or fatally wounded — nay, even the lives of criminals condemned to death, [were] under the protection of law, equally as the lives of those who [were] in the full tide of life's enjoyment, and anxious to continue to live." *Blackburn v. State* (1872).

The earliest American statute explicitly to outlaw assisting suicide was enacted in New York in 1828. . . . By the time the Fourteenth Amendment was ratified, it was a crime in most States to assist a suicide. . . .

Though deeply rooted, the States' assisted-suicide bans have in recent years been reexamined and, generally, reaffirmed. Because of advances in medicine and technology, Americans today are increasingly likely to die in institutions, from chronic illnesses. Public concern and democratic action are therefore sharply focused on how best to protect dignity and independence at the end of life, with the result that there have been many significant changes in state laws and in the attitudes these laws reflect. Many States, for example, now permit "living wills," surrogate health-care decisionmaking, and the withdrawal or refusal of life-sustaining medical treatment. At the same time, however, voters and legislators continue for the most part to reaffirm their States' prohibitions on assisting suicide.

The Washington statute at issue in this case was enacted in 1975 as part of a revision of that State's criminal code. . . . In 1991, Washington voters rejected a ballot initiative which, had it passed, would have permitted a form of physician-assisted suicide. Washington then added a provision to the Natural Death Act expressly excluding physician-assisted suicide.

California voters rejected an assisted-suicide initiative similar to Washington's in 1993. On the other hand, in 1994, voters in Oregon enacted, also through ballot initiative, that State's "Death With Dignity Act," which legalized physician-assisted suicide for competent, terminally ill adults.[17] Since the Oregon vote, many proposals to legalize assisted-suicide have been and continue to be introduced in the States' legislatures, but none has been enacted. And just last year, Iowa and Rhode Island joined the overwhelming majority of States explicitly prohibiting assisted suicide. Also, on April 30, 1997, President Clinton signed the Federal Assisted Suicide Funding Restriction Act of 1997, which prohibits the use of federal funds in support of physician-assisted suicide.

* * *

Attitudes toward suicide itself have changed since Bracton, but our laws have consistently condemned, and continue to prohibit, assisting suicide. Despite changes in medical technology and notwithstanding an increased emphasis on the importance of end-of-life decisionmaking, we have not retreated from this prohibition. Against this backdrop of history, tradition, and practice, we now turn to respondents' constitutional claim.

II

The Due Process Clause guarantees more than fair process, and the "liberty" it protects includes more than the absence of physical restraint. The Clause also provides heightened protection against government interference with certain fundamental rights and liberty interests. In a long line of cases, we have held that,

---

[17] [14] Ore. Rev. Stat. §§ 127.800 et seq. (1996); Lee v. Oregon, 891 F. Supp. 1429 (Ore. 1995) (Oregon Act does not provide sufficient safeguards for terminally ill persons and therefore violates the Equal Protection Clause), vacated, 107 F.3d 1382 (9th Cir. 1997), cert. denied sub nom. Lee v. Harcleroad, 522 U.S. 927 (1997)].

in addition to the specific freedoms protected by the Bill of Rights, the "liberty" specially protected by the Due Process Clause includes the rights to marry, *Loving v. Virginia* (1967); to have children, *Skinner v. Oklahoma ex rel. Williamson* (1942); to direct the education and upbringing of one's children, *Meyer v. Nebraska* (1923); *Pierce v. Society of Sisters* (1925); to marital privacy, *Griswold v. Connecticut* (1965); to use contraception, *ibid*; *Eisenstadt v. Baird* (1972); to bodily integrity, *Rochin v. California* (1952), and to abortion, *Casey, supra*. We have also assumed, and strongly suggested, that the Due Process Clause protects the traditional right to refuse unwanted lifesaving medical treatment. *Cruzan*.

But we "ha[ve] always been reluctant to expand the concept of substantive due process because guideposts for responsible decisionmaking in this unchartered area are scarce and open-ended." By extending constitutional protection to an asserted right or liberty interest, we, to a great extent, place the matter outside the arena of public debate and legislative action. We must therefore "exercise the utmost care whenever we are asked to break new ground in this field," lest the liberty protected by the Due Process Clause be subtly transformed into the policy preferences of the members of this Court.

Our established method of substantive-due-process analysis has two primary features: First, we have regularly observed that the Due Process Clause specially protects those fundamental rights and liberties which are, objectively, "deeply rooted in this Nation's history and tradition," and "implicit in the concept of ordered liberty," such that "neither liberty nor justice would exist if they were sacrificed." Second, we have required in substantive-due-process cases a "careful description" of the asserted fundamental liberty interest. Our Nation's history, legal traditions, and practices thus provide the crucial "guideposts for responsible decisionmaking," that direct and restrain our exposition of the Due Process Clause. . . .

JUSTICE SOUTER, relying on Justice Harlan's dissenting opinion in *Poe v. Ullman*, would largely abandon this restrained methodology, and instead ask "whether [Washington's] statute sets up one of those 'arbitrary impositions' or 'purposeless restraints' at odds with the Due Process Clause of the Fourteenth Amendment" (quoting *Poe* (1961) (Harlan, J., dissenting)).[18] In our view, however, the development of this Court's substantive-due-process jurisprudence, described briefly above, has been a process whereby the outlines of the "liberty" specially protected by the Fourteenth Amendment — never fully clarified, to be sure, and perhaps not capable of being fully clarified — have at least been carefully refined by concrete examples involving fundamental rights found to be deeply rooted in our legal

---

[18] [17] In JUSTICE SOUTER's opinion, Justice Harlan's *Poe* dissent supplies the "modern justification" for substantive-due-process review. (SOUTER, J., concurring in judgment). But although Justice Harlan's opinion has often been cited in due-process cases, we have never abandoned our fundamental-rights-based analytical method. Just four Terms ago, six of the Justices now sitting joined the Court's opinion in *Reno v. Flores*, 507 U.S. 292, 301–305 (1993); *Poe* was not even cited. And in *Cruzan*, neither the Court's nor the concurring opinions relied on *Poe*; rather, we concluded that the right to refuse unwanted medical treatment was so rooted in our history, tradition, and practice as to require special protection under the Fourteenth Amendment. True, the Court relied on Justice Harlan's dissent in *Casey*, but, as *Flores* demonstrates, we did not in so doing jettison our established approach. Indeed, to read such a radical move into the Court's opinion in *Casey* would seem to fly in the face of that opinion's emphasis on *stare decisis*.

tradition. This approach tends to rein in the subjective elements that are necessarily present in due-process judicial review. In addition, by establishing a threshold requirement — that a challenged state action implicate a fundamental right — before requiring more than a reasonable relation to a legitimate state interest to justify the action, it avoids the need for complex balancing of competing interests in every case.

Turning to the claim at issue here, . . . the question before us is whether the "liberty" specially protected by the Due Process Clause includes a right to commit suicide which itself includes a right to assistance in doing so.

We now inquire whether this asserted right has any place in our Nation's traditions. Here, as discussed above, we are confronted with a consistent and almost universal tradition that has long rejected the asserted right, and continues explicitly to reject it today, even for terminally ill, mentally competent adults. To hold for respondents, we would have to reverse centuries of legal doctrine and practice, and strike down the considered policy choice of almost every State.

Respondents contend, however, that the liberty interest they assert *is* consistent with this Court's substantive-due-process line of cases, if not with this Nation's history and practice. Pointing to *Casey* and *Cruzan*, respondents read our jurisprudence in this area as reflecting a general tradition of "self-sovereignty," and as teaching that the "liberty" protected by the Due Process Clause includes "basic and intimate exercises of personal autonomy" . . . .

In *Cruzan*, we considered whether Nancy Beth Cruzan, who had been severely injured in an automobile accident and was in a persistent vegetative state, "ha[d] a right under the United States Constitution which would require the hospital to withdraw life-sustaining treatment" at her parents' request. . . . "[F]or purposes of [that] case, we assume[d] that the United States Constitution would grant a competent person a constitutionally protected right to refuse lifesaving hydration and nutrition." We concluded that, notwithstanding this right, the Constitution permitted Missouri to require clear and convincing evidence of an incompetent patient's wishes concerning the withdrawal of life-sustaining treatment.

*   *   *

The right assumed in *Cruzan*, however, was not simply deduced from abstract concepts of personal autonomy. Given the common-law rule that forced medication was a battery, and the long legal tradition protecting the decision to refuse unwanted medical treatment, our assumption was entirely consistent with this Nation's history and constitutional traditions. The decision to commit suicide with the assistance of another may be just as personal and profound as the decision to refuse unwanted medical treatment, but it has never enjoyed similar legal protection. Indeed, the two acts are widely and reasonably regarded as quite distinct. See *Vacco v. Quill* [the companion case below]. . . .

[R]espondents also rely on *Casey*. . . .

. . . Respondents emphasize the statement in *Casey* that:

> "At the heart of liberty is the right to define one's own concept of existence, of meaning, of the universe, and of the mystery of human life. Beliefs about

these matters could not define the attributes of personhood were they formed under compulsion of the State."

By choosing this language, the Court's opinion in *Casey* described, in a general way and in light of our prior cases, those personal activities and decisions that this Court has identified as so deeply rooted in our history and traditions, or so fundamental to our concept of constitutionally ordered liberty, that they are protected by the Fourteenth Amendment. The opinion moved from the recognition that liberty necessarily includes freedom of conscience and belief about ultimate considerations to the observation that "though the abortion decision may originate within the zone of conscience and belief, it is *more than a philosophic exercise.*" That many of the rights and liberties protected by the Due Process Clause sound in personal autonomy does not warrant the sweeping conclusion that any and all important, intimate, and personal decisions are so protected, *San Antonio Independent School Dist. v. Rodriguez* (1973), and *Casey* did not suggest otherwise.

The history of the law's treatment of assisted suicide in this country has been and continues to be one of the rejection of nearly all efforts to permit it. That being the case, our decisions lead us to conclude that the asserted "right" to assistance in committing suicide is not a fundamental liberty interest protected by the Due Process Clause. The Constitution also requires, however, that Washington's assisted-suicide ban be rationally related to legitimate government interests. . . . Washington's assisted-suicide ban implicates a number of state interests.

First, Washington has an "unqualified interest in the preservation of human life." The State's prohibition on assisted suicide, like all homicide laws, both reflects and advances its commitment to this interest. . . .

Respondents admit that "[t]he State has a real interest in preserving the lives of those who can still contribute to society and enjoy life." . . . Washington, however, has rejected this sliding-scale approach and, through its assisted-suicide ban, insists that all persons' lives, from beginning to end, regardless of physical or mental condition, are under the full protection of the law. As we have previously affirmed, the States "may properly decline to make judgments about the 'quality' of life that a particular individual may enjoy," *Cruzan*. This remains true, as *Cruzan* makes clear, even for those who are near death.

Relatedly, all admit that suicide is a serious public-health problem, especially among persons in otherwise vulnerable groups. . . .

Those who attempt suicide — terminally ill or not — often suffer from depression or other mental disorders. [The] New York [State] Task Force [on Life and the Law found that] more than 95% of those who commit suicide had a major psychiatric illness at the time of death; among the terminally ill, uncontrolled pain is a "risk factor" because it contributes to depression. . . . The New York Task Force, however, expressed its concern that, because depression is difficult to diagnose, physicians and medical professionals often fail to respond adequately to seriously ill patients' needs. Thus, legal physician-assisted suicide could make it more difficult for the State to protect depressed or mentally ill persons, or those who are suffering from untreated pain, from suicidal impulses.

The State also has an interest in protecting the integrity and ethics of the medical profession. In contrast to the Court of Appeals' conclusion that "the integrity of the medical profession would [not] be threatened in any way by [physician-assisted suicide]," the American Medical Association, like many other medical and physicians' groups, has concluded that "[p]hysician-assisted suicide is fundamentally incompatible with the physician's role as healer." American Medical Association, Code of Ethics § 2.211 (1994). . . . And physician-assisted suicide could, it is argued, undermine the trust that is essential to the doctor-patient relationship by blurring the time-honored line between healing and harming.

Next, the State has an interest in protecting vulnerable groups — including the poor, the elderly, and disabled persons — from abuse, neglect, and mistakes. . . . If physician-assisted suicide were permitted, many might resort to it to spare their families the substantial financial burden of end-of-life health-care costs.

The State's interest here goes beyond protecting the vulnerable from coercion; it extends to protecting disabled and terminally ill people from prejudice, negative and inaccurate stereotypes, and "societal indifference." . . .

Finally, the State may fear that permitting assisted suicide will start it down the path to voluntary and perhaps even involuntary euthanasia. The Court of Appeals struck down Washington's assisted-suicide ban only "as applied to competent, terminally ill adults who wish to hasten their deaths by obtaining medication prescribed by their doctors." Washington insists, however, that the impact of the court's decision will not and cannot be so limited. If suicide is protected as a matter of constitutional right, it is argued, "every man and woman in the United States must enjoy it." The Court of Appeals' decision, and its expansive reasoning, provide ample support for the State's concerns. . . .

This concern is further supported by evidence about the practice of euthanasia in the Netherlands. The Dutch government's own study revealed that in 1990, there were 2,300 cases of voluntary euthanasia (defined as "the deliberate termination of another's life at his request"), 400 cases of assisted suicide, and more than 1,000 cases of euthanasia without an explicit request. In addition to these latter 1,000 cases, the study found an additional 4,941 cases where physicians administered lethal morphine overdoses without the patients' explicit consent. Physician-Assisted Suicide and Euthanasia in the Netherlands: A Report of Chairman Charles T. Canady, at 12–13 (citing Dutch study). This study suggests that, despite the existence of various reporting procedures, euthanasia in the Netherlands has not been limited to competent, terminally ill adults who are enduring physical suffering, and that regulation of the practice may not have prevented abuses in cases involving vulnerable persons, including severely disabled neonates and elderly persons suffering from dementia. . . .

We need not weigh exactly the relative strengths of these various interests. They are unquestionably important and legitimate, and Washington's ban on assisted suicide is at least reasonably related to their promotion and protection. We therefore hold that [the Washington assisted suicide ban] does not violate the Fourteenth Amendment, either on its face or "as applied to competent, terminally ill adults who wish to hasten their deaths by obtaining medication prescribed by their doctors."

*   *   *

Throughout the Nation, Americans are engaged in an earnest and profound debate about the morality, legality, and practicality of physician-assisted suicide. Our holding permits this debate to continue, as it should in a democratic society. The decision of the en banc Court of Appeals is reversed, and the case is remanded for further proceedings consistent with this opinion.

JUSTICE O'CONNOR, concurring [in both *Glucksberg*, and in *Vacco v. Quill*, a companion case to *Glucksberg*, which follows].

*   *   *

. . . I join the Court's opinions because <u>I agree that there is no generalized right to "commit suicide."</u> But respondents urge us to address the narrower question whether a mentally competent person who is experiencing great suffering has a constitutionally cognizable interest in controlling the circumstances of his or her imminent death. I see no need to reach that question in the context of the facial challenges to the New York and Washington laws at issue here. The parties and *amici* agree that in these States a patient who is suffering from a terminal illness and who is experiencing great pain has no legal barriers to obtaining medication, from qualified physicians, to alleviate that suffering, even to the point of causing unconsciousness and hastening death. . . .

*   *   *

In sum, there is no need to address the question whether suffering patients have a constitutionally cognizable interest in obtaining relief from the suffering that they may experience in the last days of their lives. There is no dispute that dying patients in Washington and New York can obtain palliative care, even when doing so would hasten their deaths. The difficulty in defining terminal illness and the risk that a dying patient's request for assistance in ending his or her life might not be truly voluntary justifies the prohibitions on assisted suicide we uphold here.

JUSTICE STEVENS, concurring in the judgments [of both *Glucksberg* and *Vacco*].

*   *   *

I

*   *   *

Today, the Court decides that Washington's statute prohibiting assisted suicide is not invalid "on its face," that is to say, in all or most cases in which it might be applied. That holding, however, does not foreclose the possibility that some applications of the statute might well be invalid.

*   *   *

III

The state interests supporting a general rule banning the practice of physician-assisted suicide do not have the same force in all cases. . . .

Many terminally ill people find their lives meaningful even if filled with pain or dependence on others. Some find value in living through suffering; some have an abiding desire to witness particular events in their families' lives; many believe it a sin to hasten death. Individuals of different religious faiths make different judgments and choices about whether to live on under such circumstances. There are those who will want to continue aggressive treatment; those who would prefer terminal sedation; and those who will seek withdrawal from life-support systems and death by gradual starvation and dehydration. Although as a general matter the State's interest in the contributions each person may make to society outweighs the person's interest in ending her life, this interest does not have the same force for a terminally ill patient faced not with the choice of whether to live, only of how to die. Allowing the individual, rather than the State, to make judgments " 'about the "quality" of life that a particular individual may enjoy,' " does not mean that the lives of terminally-ill, disabled people have less value than the lives of those who are healthy. Rather, it gives proper recognition to the individual's interest in choosing a final chapter that accords with her life story, rather than one that demeans her values and poisons memories of her. . . .

. . . I agree that the State has a compelling interest in preventing persons from committing suicide because of depression, or coercion by third parties. But the State's legitimate interest in preventing abuse does not apply to an individual who is not victimized by abuse, who is not suffering from depression, and who makes a rational and voluntary decision to seek assistance in dying. . . .

Relatedly, the State and *amici* express the concern that patients whose physical pain is inadequately treated will be more likely to request assisted suicide. Encouraging the development and ensuring the availability of adequate pain treatment is of utmost importance; palliative care, however, cannot alleviate all pain and suffering. . . .

The final major interest asserted by the State is its interest in preserving the traditional integrity of the medical profession. The fear is that a rule permitting physicians to assist in suicide is inconsistent with the perception that they serve their patients solely as healers. But for some patients, it would be a physician's refusal to dispense medication to ease their suffering and make their death tolerable and dignified that would be inconsistent with the healing role. . . .

As the New York State Task Force on Life and the Law recognized, a State's prohibition of assisted suicide is justified by the fact that the " 'ideal' " case in which "patients would be screened for depression and offered treatment, effective pain medication would be available, and all patients would have a supportive committed family and doctor" is not the usual case. Although, as the Court concludes today, these *potential* harms are sufficient to support the State's general public policy against assisted suicide, they will not always outweigh the individual liberty interest of a particular patient. Unlike the Court of Appeals, I would not say as a categorical matter that these state interests are invalid as to the entire class of terminally ill, mentally competent patients. <u>I do not, however, foreclose the possibility that an</u> <u>individual plaintiff seeking to hasten her death, or a doctor whose assistance was</u> <u>sought, could prevail in a more particularized challenge. Future cases will deter-</u> <u>mine whether such a challenge may succeed.</u>

*   *   *

JUSTICE SOUTER, concurring in the judgment.

*   *   *

II

*   *   *

Before the ratification of the Fourteenth Amendment, substantive constitutional review resting on a theory of unenumerated rights occurred largely in the state courts applying state constitutions that commonly contained either due process clauses like that of the Fifth Amendment (and later the Fourteenth) or the textual antecedents of such clauses, repeating Magna Carta's guarantee of "the law of the land." On the basis of such clauses, or of general principles untethered to specific constitutional language, state courts evaluated the constitutionality of a wide range of statutes.

*   *   *

Even in this early period, however, this Court anticipated the developments that would presage both the Civil War and the ratification of the Fourteenth Amendment, by making it clear on several occasions that it too had no doubt of the judiciary's power to strike down legislation that conflicted with important but unenumerated principles of American government. In most such instances, after declaring its power to invalidate what it might find inconsistent with rights of liberty and property, the Court nevertheless went on to uphold the legislative acts under review. *See, e.g., Wilkinson v. Leland* (1829); *Calder v. Bull* (1798) (opinion of Chase, J.); see also *Corfield v. Coryell*, 6 F. Cas. (1823). But in *Fletcher v. Peck* (1810), the Court went further. It struck down an act of the Georgia legislature that purported to rescind a sale of public land *ab initio* and reclaim title for the State, and so deprive subsequent, good-faith purchasers of property conveyed by the original grantees. The Court rested the invalidation on alternative sources of authority: the specific prohibitions against bills of attainder, *ex post facto* laws, laws impairing contracts in Article I, § 10 of the Constitution; and "general principles which are common to our free institutions," by which Chief Justice Marshall meant that a simple deprivation of property by the State could not be an authentically "legislative" act.

Fletcher was not, though, the most telling early example of such review. For its most salient instance in this Court before the adoption of the Fourteenth Amendment was, of course, the case that the Amendment would in due course overturn, *Dred Scott v. Sandford* (1857). Unlike *Fletcher, Dred Scott* was textually based on a due process clause (in the Fifth Amendment, applicable to the national government), and it was in reliance on that clause's protection of property that the Court invalidated the Missouri Compromise. This substantive protection of an owner's property in a slave taken to the territories was traced to the absence of any enumerated power to affect that property granted to the Congress by Article I of the Constitution, *id.*, the implication being that the government had no legitimate interest that could support the earlier congressional compromise. The ensuing judgment of history needs no recounting here.

After the ratification of the Fourteenth Amendment, with its guarantee of due process protection against the States, interpretation of the words "liberty" and "property" as used in due process clauses became a sustained enterprise, with the Court generally describing the due process criterion in converse terms of reasonableness or arbitrariness. That standard is fairly traceable to Justice Bradley's dissent in the *Slaughter-House Cases*, in which he said that a person's right to choose a calling was an element of liberty (as the calling, once chosen, was an aspect of property) and declared that the liberty and property protected by due process are not truly recognized if such rights may be "arbitrarily assailed."[19] After that, opinions comparable to those that preceded *Dred Scott* expressed willingness to review legislative action for consistency with the Due Process Clause even as they upheld the laws in question.

The theory became serious, however, beginning with *Allgeyer v. Louisiana* (1897), where the Court invalidated a Louisiana statute for excessive interference with Fourteenth Amendment liberty to contract, and offered a substantive interpretation of "liberty," that in the aftermath of the so-called Lochner Era has been scaled back in some respects, but expanded in others, and never repudiated in principle. The Court said that Fourteenth Amendment liberty includes "the right of the citizen to be free in the enjoyment of all his faculties; to be free to use them in all lawful ways; to live and work where he will; to earn his livelihood by any lawful calling; to pursue any livelihood or avocation; and for that purpose to enter into all contracts which may be proper, necessary and essential to his carrying out to a successful conclusion the purposes above mentioned." *Id.* "[W]e do not intend to hold that in no such case can the State exercise its police power," the Court added, but "[w]hen and how far such power may be legitimately exercised with regard to these subjects must be left for determination to each case as it arises."

Although this principle was unobjectionable, what followed for a season was, in the realm of economic legislation, the echo of *Dred Scott. Allgeyer* was succeeded within a decade by *Lochner v. New York* (1905), and the era to which that case gave

---

[19] [6] The *Slaughter-House Cases* are important, of course, for their holding that the Privileges or Immunities Clause was no source of any but a specific handful of substantive rights. *Slaughter-House Cases*, 16 Wall., at 74–80. To a degree, then, that decision may have led the Court to look to the Due Process Clause as a source of substantive rights. In *Twining v. New Jersey*, 211 U.S. 78, 95–97 (1908), for example, the Court of the Lochner Era acknowledged the strength of the case against *Slaughter-House*'s interpretation of the Privileges or Immunities Clause but reaffirmed that interpretation without questioning its own frequent reliance on the Due Process Clause as authorization for substantive judicial review. J. ELY, DEMOCRACY AND DISTRUST 14–30 (1980) (arguing that the Privileges or Immunities Clause and not the Due Process Clause is the proper warrant for courts' substantive oversight of state legislation). But the courts' use of due process clauses for that purpose antedated the 1873 decision, as we have seen, and would in time be supported in the *Poe* dissent, as we shall see.

its name, famous now for striking down as arbitrary various sorts of economic regulations that post-New Deal courts have uniformly thought constitutionally sound. Compare, *e.g.*, *id.* (finding New York's maximum-hours law for bakers "unreasonable and entirely arbitrary"), *and Adkins v. Children's Hospital of D.C.* (1923) (holding a minimum wage law "so clearly the product of a naked, arbitrary exercise of power that it cannot be allowed to stand under the Constitution of the United States"), with *West Coast Hotel Co. v. Parrish* (1937) (overruling *Adkins* and approving a minimum-wage law on the principle that "regulation which is reasonable in relation to its subject and is adopted in the interests of the community is due process"). As the parentheticals here suggest, while the cases in the *Lochner* line routinely invoked a correct standard of constitutional arbitrariness review, they harbored the spirit of *Dred Scott* in their absolutist implementation of the standard they espoused.

Even before the deviant economic due process cases had been repudiated, however, the more durable precursors of modern substantive due process were reaffirming this Court's obligation to conduct arbitrariness review, beginning with *Meyer v. Nebraska* (1923). Without referring to any specific guarantee of the Bill of Rights, the Court invoked precedents from the *Slaughter-House Cases* through *Adkins* to declare that the Fourteenth Amendment protected "the right of the individual to contract, to engage in any of the common occupations of life, to acquire useful knowledge, to marry, establish a home and bring up children, to worship God according to the dictates of his own conscience, and generally to enjoy those privileges long recognized at common law as essential to the orderly pursuit of happiness by free men." The Court then held that the same Fourteenth Amendment liberty included a teacher's right to teach and the rights of parents to direct their children's education without unreasonable interference by the States, with the result that Nebraska's prohibition on the teaching of foreign languages in the lower grades was, "arbitrary and without reasonable relation to any end within the competency of the State." See also *Pierce v. Society of Sisters* (1925) (finding that a statute that all but outlawed private schools lacked any "reasonable relation to some purpose within the competency of the State"); *Palko v. Connecticut* (1937) ("even in the field of substantive rights and duties the legislative judgment, if oppressive and arbitrary, may be overridden by the courts"; "Is that [injury] to which the statute has subjected [the appellant] a hardship so acute and shocking that our polity will not endure it? Does it violate those fundamental principles of liberty and justice which lie at the base of all our civil and political institutions?") (citation and internal quotation marks omitted).

After *Meyer* and *Pierce*, two further opinions took the major steps that lead to the modern law. The first was not even in a due process case but one about equal protection, *Skinner v. Oklahoma ex rel. Williamson* (1942), where the Court emphasized the "fundamental" nature of individual choice about procreation and so foreshadowed not only the later prominence of procreation as a subject of liberty protection, but the corresponding standard of "strict scrutiny," in this Court's Fourteenth Amendment law. *Skinner*, that is, added decisions regarding procreation to the list of liberties recognized in *Meyer* and *Pierce* and loosely suggested, as a gloss on their standard of arbitrariness, a judicial obligation to scrutinize any impingement on such an important interest with heightened care. In so doing, it suggested a point that Justice Harlan would develop, that the kind and degree of justification that a sensitive judge would demand of a State would depend on the importance of the interest being asserted by the individual.

The second major opinion leading to the modern doctrine was Justice Harlan's *Poe* dissent just cited, the conclusion of which was adopted in *Griswold v. Connecticut* (1965), and the authority of which was acknowledged in *Planned Parenthood of Southeastern Pa. v. Casey* (1992). The dissent is important for three things that point to our responsibilities today. The first is Justice Harlan's respect for the tradition of substantive due process review itself, and his acknowledgement of the Judiciary's obligation to carry it on. For two centuries American courts, and for much of that time this Court, have thought it necessary to provide some degree of review over the substantive content of legislation under constitutional standards of textual breadth. The obligation was understood before *Dred Scott* and has continued after the repudiation of *Lochner*'s progeny, most notably on the subjects of segregation in public education, *Bolling v. Sharpe* (1954), interracial marriage, *Loving v. Virginia* (1967), marital privacy and contraception, *Carey v. Population Services Int'l* (1977), *Griswold v. Connecticut, supra*, abortion, *Planned Parenthood of Southeastern Pa. v. Casey* (1992) (joint opinion of O'CONNOR, KENNEDY, and SOUTER, JJ.), *Roe v. Wade* (1973), personal control of medical treatment, *Cruzan v. Director, Mo. Dept. of Health* (1990) (O'CONNOR, J., concurring); *id.* (BRENNAN, J., dissenting); *id.* (STEVENS, J., dissenting); see also *id.* (majority opinion), and physical confinement, *Foucha v. Louisiana* (1992). This enduring tradition of American constitutional practice is, in Justice Harlan's view, nothing more than what is required by the judicial authority and obligation to construe constitutional text and review legislation for conformity to that text. See *Marbury v. Madison* (1803). Like many judges who preceded him and many who followed, he found it impossible to construe the text of due process without recognizing substantive, and not merely procedural, limitations. "Were due process merely a procedural safeguard it would fail to reach those situations where the deprivation of life, liberty or property was accomplished by legislation which by operating in the future could, given even the fairest possible procedure in application to individuals, nevertheless destroy the enjoyment of all three." The text of the Due Process Clause thus imposes nothing less than an obligation to give substantive content to the words "liberty" and "due process of law."

* * *

JUSTICE GINSBURG, concurring in the judgments [of both *Glucksberg* and *Vacco*].

I concur in the Court's judgments in these cases substantially for the reasons stated by JUSTICE O'CONNOR in her concurring opinion.

JUSTICE BREYER, concurring in the judgments [of both *Glucksberg* and *Vacco*].

I believe that JUSTICE O'CONNOR's views, which I share, have greater legal significance than the Court's opinion suggests. I join her separate opinion, except insofar as it joins the majority. And I concur in the judgments. I shall briefly explain how I differ from the Court.

. . . I do not agree . . . with the Court's formulation of that claimed "liberty" interest. The Court describes it as a "right to commit suicide with another's assistance." But I would not reject the respondents' claim without considering a different formulation, for which our legal tradition may provide greater support. That formulation would use words roughly like a "right to die with dignity." But irrespective of the exact words used, at its core would lie personal control over the manner of death, professional medical assistance, and the avoidance of unnecessary and severe physical suffering — combined.

* * *

I do not believe, however, that this Court need or now should decide whether or a not such a right is "fundamental." That is because, in my view, the avoidance of severe physical pain (connected with death) would have to comprise an essential part of any successful claim and because, as JUSTICE O'CONNOR points out, the laws before us do not *force* a dying person to undergo that kind of pain. . . .

Medical technology, we are repeatedly told, makes the administration of pain-relieving drugs sufficient, except for a very few individuals for whom the ineffectiveness of pain control medicines can mean, not pain, but the need for sedation which can end in a coma. . . .

This legal circumstance means that the state laws before us do not infringe directly upon the (assumed) central interest (what I have called the core of the interest in dying with dignity) as, by way of contrast, the state anticontraceptive laws at issue in *Poe* did interfere with the central interest there at stake — by bringing the State's police powers to bear upon the marital bedroom.

Were the legal circumstances different — for example, were state law to prevent the provision of palliative care, including the administration of drugs as needed to avoid pain at the end of life — then the law's impact upon serious and otherwise unavoidable physical pain (accompanying death) would be more directly at issue. And as JUSTICE O'CONNOR suggests, the Court might have to revisit its conclusions in these cases.

VACCO v. QUILL
521 U.S. 793 (1997)

CHIEF JUSTICE REHNQUIST delivered the opinion of the Court.

In New York, as in most States, it is a crime to aid another to commit or attempt suicide, but patients may refuse even lifesaving medical treatment. The question presented by this case is whether New York's prohibition on assisting suicide therefore violates the Equal Protection Clause of the Fourteenth Amendment. We hold that it does not.

The Equal Protection Clause commands that no State shall "deny to any person within its jurisdiction the equal protection of the laws." This provision creates no substantive rights. . . .

New York's statutes outlawing assisting suicide affect and address matters of profound significance to all New Yorkers alike. They neither infringe fundamental rights nor involve suspect classifications. *Washington v. Glucksberg.* . . .

On their faces, neither New York's ban on assisting suicide nor its statutes permitting patients to refuse medical treatment treat anyone differently than anyone else or draw any distinctions between persons. *Everyone*, regardless of physical condition, is entitled, if competent, to refuse unwanted lifesaving medical treatment; *no one* is permitted to assist a suicide. Generally speaking, laws that apply evenhandedly to all "unquestionably comply" with the Equal Protection Clause. . . .

. . . Unlike the Court of Appeals, we think the distinction between assisting suicide and withdrawing life-sustaining treatment, a distinction widely recognized and endorsed in the medical profession[20] and in our legal traditions, is both important and logical; it is certainly rational.

The distinction comports with fundamental legal principles of causation and intent. First, when a patient refuses life-sustaining medical treatment, he dies from an underlying fatal disease or pathology; but if a patient ingests lethal medication prescribed by a physician, he is killed by that medication.

Furthermore, a physician who withdraws, or honors a patient's refusal to begin, life-sustaining medical treatment purposefully intends, or may so intend, only to respect his patient's wishes and "to cease doing useless and futile or degrading things to the patient when [the patient] no longer stands to benefit from them." The same is true when a doctor provides aggressive palliative care; in some cases, painkilling drugs may hasten a patient's death, but the physician's purpose and intent is, or may be, only to ease his patient's pain. A doctor who assists a suicide, however, "must, necessarily and indubitably, intend primarily that the patient be made dead." . . .

*   *   *

This Court has also recognized, at least implicitly, the distinction between letting a patient die and making that patient die. In *Cruzan v. Director, Mo. Dept. of Health* (1990), we concluded that "[t]he principle that a competent person has a constitutionally protected liberty interest in refusing unwanted medical treatment may be inferred from our prior decisions," and we assumed the existence of such a right for purposes of that case. But our assumption of a right to refuse treatment was grounded not, as the Court of Appeals supposed, on the proposition that patients have a general and abstract "right to hasten death," but on well established,

---

[20] [6] The American Medical Association emphasizes the "fundamental difference between refusing life-sustaining treatment and demanding a life-ending treatment." American Medical Association, Council on Ethical and Judicial Affairs, *Physician-Assisted Suicide*, 10 Issues in Law & Medicine 91, 93 (1994); see also American Medical Association, Council on Ethical and Judicial Affairs, *Decisions Near the End of Life*, 267 JAMA 2229, 2230–2231, 2233 (1992) ("The withdrawing or withholding of life-sustaining treatment is not inherently contrary to the principles of beneficence and nonmaleficence," but assisted suicide "is contrary to the prohibition against using the tools of medicine to cause a patient's death"); New York State Task Force on Life and the Law, When Death is Sought: Assisted Suicide and Euthanasia in the Medical Context 108 (1994) ("[Professional organizations] consistently distinguish assisted suicide and euthanasia from the withdrawing or withholding of treatment, and from the provision of palliative treatments or other medical care that risk fatal side effects"). . . .

traditional rights to bodily integrity and freedom from unwanted touching. . . .

For all these reasons, we disagree with respondents' claim that the distinction between refusing lifesaving medical treatment and assisted suicide is "arbitrary" and "irrational." . . .

The judgment of the Court of Appeals is reversed.

JUSTICE O'CONNOR, concurring [in both *Vacco* and *Glucksberg*. *See* JUSTICE O'CONNOR's concurring opinion in *Glucksberg*].

JUSTICE STEVENS, concurring in the judgments [of both *Vacco* and *Glucksberg*].

* * *

IV

In New York, a doctor must respect a competent person's decision to refuse or to discontinue medical treatment even though death will thereby ensue, but the same doctor would be guilty of a felony if she provided her patient assistance in committing suicide. Today we hold that the Equal Protection Clause is not violated by the resulting disparate treatment of two classes of terminally ill people who may have the same interest in hastening death. I agree that the distinction between permitting death to ensue from an underlying fatal disease and causing it to occur by the administration of medication or other means provides a constitutionally sufficient basis for the State's classification. Unlike the Court, however, I am not persuaded that in all cases there will in fact be a significant difference between the intent of the physicians, the patients or the families in the two situations.

There may be little distinction between the intent of a terminally-ill patient who decides to remove her life-support and one who seeks the assistance of a doctor in ending her life; in both situations, the patient is seeking to hasten a certain, impending death. The doctor's intent might also be the same in prescribing lethal medication as it is in terminating life support. A doctor who fails to administer medical treatment to one who is dying from a disease could be doing so with an intent to harm or kill that patient. Conversely, a doctor who prescribes lethal medication does not necessarily intend the patient's death — rather that doctor may seek simply to ease the patient's suffering and to comply with her wishes. The illusory character of any differences in intent or causation is confirmed by the fact that the American Medical Association unequivocally endorses the practice of terminal sedation — the administration of sufficient dosages of pain-killing medication to terminally ill patients to protect them from excruciating pain even when it is clear that the time of death will be advanced. The purpose of terminal sedation is to ease the suffering of the patient and comply with her wishes, and the actual cause of death is the administration of heavy doses of lethal sedatives. This same intent and causation may exist when a doctor complies with a patient's request for lethal medication to hasten her death.

Thus, although the differences the majority notes in causation and intent between terminating life-support and assisting in suicide support the Court's rejection of the respondents' facial challenge, these distinctions may be inapplicable to particular terminally ill patients and their doctors. Our holding today in *Vacco v. Quill* that the Equal Protection Clause is not violated by New York's classification, just like our holding in *Washington v. Glucksberg* that the Washington statute is not invalid on its face, does not foreclose the possibility that some applications of the New York statute may impose an intolerable intrusion on the patient's freedom.

*   *   *

JUSTICE SOUTER, concurring in the judgment.

Even though I do not conclude that assisted suicide is a fundamental right entitled to recognition at this time, I accord the claims raised by the patients and physicians in this case and *Washington v. Glucksberg* a high degree of importance, requiring a commensurate justification. The reasons that lead me to conclude in *Glucksberg* that the prohibition on assisted suicide is not arbitrary under the due process standard also support the distinction between assistance to suicide, which is banned, and practices such as termination of artificial life support and death-hastening pain medication, which are permitted. I accordingly concur in the judgment of the Court.

JUSTICE GINSBURG, concurring in the judgments [of both *Vacco* and *Glucksberg*].

I concur in the Court's judgments in these cases substantially for the reasons stated by JUSTICE O'CONNOR in her concurring opinion.

JUSTICE BREYER, concurring in the judgments [of both *Vacco* and *Glucksberg*]. [Omitted.]

NOTES AND QUESTIONS

1.   How does the Court disavow a right to assisted suicide, after it has declared an abortion right? Aren't they both exercises of personal autonomy? Chief Justice Rehnquist writes that even as "many of the rights and liberties protected by the Due Process Clause sound in personal autonomy does not warrant the sweeping conclusion that any and all important, intimate, and personal decisions are so protected. . . ." But, why not? Presumably, the Chief Justice's answer is that the constitutional protection of personal liberty has a boundary, but where can it be found? His answer: in the "deeply rooted" traditions of our nation, as reflected in our history. Alternatively stated, only those personal activities that are "so fundamental to our concept of constitutionally ordered liberty" are protected. Assisted suicide does not fall within this category because of its common law condemnation going back 700 years before the nation itself. *See* Robert A. Destro, *The Scope of the Fourteenth Amendment Liberty Interest: Does the Constitution Encompass a Right to Define Oneself Out of Existence? An Exchange of Views with John A. Powell, Legal Director, American Civil Liberties Union,* 10 ISSUES L. & MED. 183 (1994) (asserting that arguments in favor of a "right to suicide fail because they assume . . . that the right to be a homicide victim — by one's own hand or that of another — is (or should be) one of the liberties protected by the Bill of Rights").

2. How significantly does Justice Souter's due process methodology based upon Justice Harlan's earlier dissenting opinion in *Poe v. Ullman* differ from that of the Court? Chief Justice Rehnquist suggests that the Souter/Harlan view is prone to subjectivity, and therefore, judicial misuse. Do you agree? Justice Souter proclaims that substantive due process is important and is a proper function of the Court, but that it cannot depend then on "extratextual absolutes." By this is Justice Souter disavowing his allegiance to the natural law principles — the self-evident truths — that underlie the Constitution? If Justice Souter does not wish to depend on first principle, isn't he inevitably led merely to impose his own view of what *he* thinks is reasonable? Justice Souter tries to soften this conclusion by writing that he sees his function as merely a benign supervisor of clashing principles, substituting his view "only when [the government has reached an outcome that] falls outside the realm of the reasonable." Reasonable to whom, and by what standard? Similarly, Justice Souter talks about judicial protection of only fundamental rights or those "truly deserving constitutional stature." He then identifies these, however, in relation to either "in constitutional text, or those exemplified by 'traditions from which [the Nation] developed,' or revealed by contrast with 'the traditions from which it broke.'"

3. Justice Souter pointedly attempts to distinguish his approach from that which invalidated the Missouri Compromise and kept Dred Scott a slave, but is the attempt comprehensible once he separates himself from the natural law? It is surely understandable to interpret the word "person" in the Constitution as including all human beings in light of their "created" natures and accompanying unalienable rights, but once these "absolutist failings," as Justice Souter disparages them, are disavowed, why wasn't Chief Justice Taney correct that the Court was duty-bound to protect whatever the positive law declares to be property? The significance of recognizing the created or transcendent origin of personhood, as our founding Declaration does, cannot be understated in this regard. Indeed, religious leaders frequently make this point. For example, John Cardinal O'Connor writes:

> I am not sure that even a sense of humanity, even a recognition that the unborn, the cancer-ridden, the vulnerable are persons will change anything. What will change it? I am not sure that anything will change it except a recognition of the sacredness of the human person, not simply the humanity, but that human beings belong to God. As St. Paul says, "You are not your own. You have been purchased, and at what a price! So glorify God in your body." No, human beings will not be safe unless we recognize they are sacred persons.

John Cardinal O'Connor, *"You Are Not Your Own" A Teaching From St. Paul Has Everything To Do With* Roe v. Wade, 37 Cath. Law. 261, 266 (1997) (quoting 1 *Corinthians* 6:19–20).

4. In description, the Souter method seems tame or restrained. "Only," he says, "when the legislation's justifying principle, critically valued, is so far from being commensurate with the individual interest as to be arbitrarily or pointlessly applied that the statute must give way." Unfortunately, since Justice Souter is one of the principle architects of the reformed reaffirmation of the abortion right, the description does not seem to match application. After all, can it really be said that the state's desire to preserve unborn life is arbitrary and pointless? Similarly, Justice Souter goes to great length to insist that his weighing of "clashing principles" notion only properly works if the principles are described at the right level of detail or generality. In making his argument, Justice Souter highlights how the prohibition against the use of contraceptives foundered because the regulation invaded the *marital* bedroom. A broader claim for constitutional protection for sexual relations outside marriage, he states, would "be shot-through by exception." Since the Justice implies that the state might legitimately enforce such limits outside the marital relationship, one wonders why his voice was not heard in *Romer v. Evans*, discussed in Chapter 5.

5. Outside of Justice Souter's attempt to re-center constitutional due process analysis upon "nuanced" judicial balancing, the common theme among the concurrences is to reserve the right to revisit the issue if state laws against assisting suicide as applied prevent the provision of palliative care. Only Justice Stevens explains the origin of this reserved authority. Curiously, he describes the interest in "hastening death," as he calls it, as a pre-societal liberty traceable to the fact that "it [is] self-evident that all men were endowed by their Creator with liberty as one of the cardinal unalienable rights." Unfortunately, Justice Stevens fails to then explain how an *un*alienable right (that is, one incapable of sale or forfeiture even by the person holding the right) produces a liberty interest that includes unnatural or premature alienation.

6. The Court's opinion in *Vacco* rejecting the equal protection challenge is in some ways a better reflection of natural law than *Glucksberg*'s refusal to find a due process violation. In *Glucksberg*, the Court supplies less an affirmation of the unalienability of human life, except by reference to the common law sources that contain that affirmation, than a refusal to impose a judicial outcome that would have preempted the debate about the "morality, legality, and practicality of physician-assited suicide." The Court in *Glucksberg* proclaims that its "holding permits this debate to continue, as it should in a democratic society." By contrast, the *Vacco* opinion suggests that even democratic debate cannot lead to immoral end, at least not given "fundamental legal principles of causation and intent" that the Court claims aptly distinguish a refusal of continued care, including a withdrawal of treatment, from the affirmative aiding of the taking of life.

7. In 1994, Oregon voters approved a so-called "Death With Dignity Act," by a narrow margin permitting doctors to prescribe lethal medications at a dying patient's request. Initially, the Act was enjoined in the view that the law treated terminal patients unequally under the law. *Lee v. Oregon*, 891 F. Supp. 1429 (D. Or. 1995). Applying deferential rational basis, the district judge found that the terminally ill were being singled out irrationally and denied protections that otherwise applied to medical patients. Specifically, the court found that the duty of reasonable care to which all other patients were entitled was suspended with regard to the terminally ill and replaced with a subjective good faith standard. *Id.* at 1437. The Ninth Circuit reversed and vacated the lower court judgment finding that even if the unequal standard existed there was no adversely affected plaintiff with standing before the court. 107 F.3d 1382 (9th Cir.), *cert. denied sub nom. Lee v. Harcleroad*, 522 U.S. 927 (1997).

For a while it looked as if Oregon might repeal the Act. However, in November 1997, Oregon voters defeated a repeal measure, and thus, Oregon law presently provides that a doctor may prescribe on request a lethal dosage of oral mediation to a terminally ill person who is deemed to have less than six months to live. The person receiving the drugs must wait 15 days before self-administering them.

While many religions have spoken out strongly against assisted suicide, as the Court's decisions make plain there are non-religious reasons for concern as well. For a superb appraisal of these considerations by an eminent scholar well before the controversy made its way to the Court, see Yale Kamisar, *Some Non-Religious Views Against Proposed "Mercy-Killing" Legislation*, 42 Minn. L. Rev. 969 (1958), and later views in Yale Kamisar, *The "Right to Die": On Drawing (and Erasing) Lines*, 35 Duq. L. Rev. 481 (1996) (arguing that *Quill* and *Compassion in Dying* imprudently erased the line between foregoing life-sustaining medical treatment and actively intervening to bring about death). For articles advising the Court to be hesitant about resolving the issue prematurely, see Thomas W. Mayo, *Constitutionalizing the "Right to Die"*, 49 Md. L. Rev. 103 (1990); *see also*, Victor G. Rosenblum & Clarke D. Forsythe, *The Right to Assisted Suicide: Protection of Autonomy or an Open Door to Social Killing?*, 6 Issues L. & Med. 3 (1990) (discussing the legalization of assisted suicide in light of a clear historical understanding of the nation's legal and medical foundations, and calling on the medical profession to resist the transformation from "healers" to "killers"); and see Richard S. Meyers, *An Analysis of the Constitutionality of Laws Banning Assisted Suicide from the Perspective of Catholic Moral Teaching*, 72 U. Det. Mercy L. Rev. 771 (1996) (examining two approaches to the constitutionality of laws banning assisted suicide: the "liberal" position hinged on personal "choice" and autonomy and the "conservative" position based on objective moral standards from history and tradition).

4. Homosexual Conduct

In *Bowers v. Hardwick*, 478 U.S. 186 (1986), the Court, 5-4, held that homosexual sodomy was not a protected liberty interest, and therefore, Georgia could make it unlawful. Justice White wrote for the majority:

> [W]e think it evident that none of the rights announced in those cases bears any resemblance to the claimed constitutional right of homosexuals to engage in acts of sodomy that is asserted in this case. No connection between family, marriage, or procreation on the one hand and homosexual activity on the other has been demonstrated, either by the Court of Appeals or by respondent. Moreover, any claim that these cases nevertheless stand for the proposition that any kind of private sexual conduct between consenting adults is constitutionally insulated from state proscription is unsupportable. Indeed, the Court's opinion in *Carey* [*v. Population Services International* (1977)] twice asserted that the privacy right, which the *Griswold* [*v. Connecticut* (1965)] line of cases found to be one of the protections provided by the Due Process Clause, did not reach so far.

> Precedent aside, however, respondent would have us announce, as the Court of Appeals did, a fundamental right to engage in homosexual sodomy.

This we are quite unwilling to do. It is true that despite the language of the Due Process Clauses of the Fifth and Fourteenth Amendments, which appears to focus only on the processes by which life, liberty, or property is taken, the cases are legion in which those Clauses have been interpreted to have substantive content, subsuming rights that to a great extent are immune from federal or state regulation or proscription. Among such cases are those recognizing rights that have little or no textual support in the constitutional language. . . .

Striving to assure itself and the public that announcing rights not readily identifiable in the Constitution's text involves much more than the imposition of the Justices' own choice of values on the States and the Federal Government, the Court has sought to identify the nature of the rights qualifying for heightened judicial protection. In *Palko v. Connecticut* (1937), it was said that this category includes those fundamental liberties that are "implicit in the concept of ordered liberty," such that "neither liberty nor justice would exist if [they] were sacrificed." A different description of fundamental liberties appeared in *Moore v. East Cleveland* (1977) (opinion of POWELL, J.), where they are characterized as those liberties that are "deeply rooted in this Nation's history and tradition."

It is obvious to us that neither of these formulations would extend a fundamental right to homosexuals to engage in acts of consensual sodomy. Proscriptions against that conduct have ancient roots. Sodomy was a criminal offense at common law and was forbidden by the laws of the original 13 States when they ratified the Bill of Rights. In 1868, when the Fourteenth Amendment was ratified, all but 5 of the 37 States in the Union had criminal sodomy laws. In fact, until 1961, all 50 States outlawed sodomy, and today, 24 States and the District of Columbia continue to provide criminal penalties for sodomy performed in private and between consenting adults. Against this background, to claim that a right to engage in such conduct is "deeply rooted in this Nation's history and tradition" or "implicit in the concept of ordered liberty" is, at best, facetious.

*   *   *

Even if the conduct at issue here is not a fundamental right, respondent asserts that there must be a rational basis for the law and that there is none in this case other than the presumed belief of a majority of the electorate in Georgia that homosexual sodomy is immoral and unacceptable. This is said to be an inadequate rationale to support the law. The law, however, is constantly based on notions of morality, and if all laws representing essentially moral choices are to be invalidated under the Due Process Clause, the courts will be very busy indeed. Even respondent makes no such claim, but insists that majority sentiments about the morality of homosexuality should be declared inadequate. We do not agree, and are unpersuaded that the sodomy laws of some 25 States should be invalidated on this basis.

Justice Blackmun, the author of *Roe v. Wade*, filed a vigorous dissent in *Bowers*. Blackmun claimed that the case was not about a "fundamental right to engage in homosexual sodomy," but rather was about "the most comprehensive of rights and the right most valued by civilized men . . . the right to be let alone." Was he right about that? Where does this right come from? The Constitution is about forming a "more perfect union" — a community — not about being left alone, right? Is that why the majority rejected Blackmun's claim, or was the majority merely reflecting the historical disapproval of homosexual practice? Can a state, then, decide to express that disapproval in law? Consider the next case.

LAWRENCE v. TEXAS
539 U.S. 558 (2003)

JUSTICE KENNEDY delivered the opinion of the Court.

[Liberty protects the person from unwarranted government intrusions into a dwelling or other private places.] In our tradition the State is not omnipresent in the home. And there are other spheres of our lives and existence, outside the home, where the State should not be a dominant presence. Freedom extends beyond spatial bounds. Liberty presumes an autonomy of self that includes freedom of thought, belief, expression, and certain intimate conduct. The instant case involves liberty of the person both in its spatial and more transcendent dimensions.

I

The question before the Court is the validity of a Texas statute making it a crime for two persons of the same sex to engage in certain intimate sexual conduct.

In Houston, Texas, officers of the Harris County Police Department were dispatched to a private residence in response to a reported weapons disturbance. They entered an apartment where one of the petitioners, John Geddes Lawrence, resided. The right of the police to enter does not seem to have been questioned. The officers observed Lawrence and another man, Tyron Garner, engaging in a sexual act. The two petitioners were arrested, held in custody over night, and charged and convicted before a Justice of the Peace.

The complaints described their crime as "deviate sexual intercourse, namely anal sex, with a member of the same sex (man)." . . . The statute defines "[d]eviate sexual intercourse" as follows:

> "(A) any contact between any part of the genitals of one person and the mouth or anus of another person; or

> "(B) the penetration of the genitals or the anus of another person with an object."

* * *

The Court of Appeals for the Texas Fourteenth District considered the petitioners' federal constitutional arguments under both the Equal Protection and Due Process Clauses of the Fourteenth Amendment. After hearing the case en banc the court, in a divided opinion, rejected the constitutional arguments and affirmed the convictions. The majority opinion indicates that the Court of Appeals considered our decision in *Bowers v. Hardwick*, (1986), to be controlling on the federal due process aspect of the case. *Bowers* then being authoritative, this was proper.

* * *

The petitioners were adults at the time of the alleged offense. Their conduct was in private and consensual.

II

We conclude the case should be resolved by determining whether the petitioners were free as adults to engage in the private conduct in the exercise of their liberty under the Due Process Clause of the Fourteenth Amendment to the Constitution. For this inquiry we deem it necessary to reconsider the Court's holding in *Bowers*.

* * *

The Court began its substantive discussion in *Bowers* as follows: "The issue presented is whether the Federal Constitution confers a fundamental right upon homosexuals to engage in sodomy and hence invalidates the laws of the many States that still make such conduct illegal and have done so for a very long time." That statement, we now conclude, discloses the Court's own failure to appreciate the extent of the liberty at stake. To say that the issue in *Bowers* was simply the right to engage in certain sexual conduct demeans the claim the individual put forward, just as it would demean a married couple were it to be said marriage is simply about the right to have sexual intercourse. . . . When sexuality finds overt expression in intimate conduct with another person, the conduct can be but one element in a personal bond that is more enduring. The liberty protected by the Constitution allows homosexual persons the right to make this choice.

Having misapprehended the claim of liberty there presented to it, and thus stating the claim to be whether there is a fundamental right to engage in consensual sodomy, the *Bowers* Court said: "Proscriptions against that conduct have ancient roots." In academic writings, and in many of the scholarly *amicus* briefs filed to assist the Court in this case, there are fundamental criticisms of the historical premises relied upon by the majority and concurring opinions in *Bowers*. We need not enter this debate in the attempt to reach a definitive historical judgment, but the following considerations counsel against adopting the definitive conclusions upon which *Bowers* placed such reliance.

At the outset it should be noted that there is no longstanding history in this country of laws directed at homosexual conduct as a distinct matter. Beginning in colonial times there were prohibitions of sodomy derived from the English criminal laws passed in the first instance by the Reformation Parliament of 1533.

. . . The early American sodomy laws were not directed at homosexuals as such but instead sought to prohibit nonprocreative sexual activity more generally. This does not suggest approval of homosexual conduct. It does tend to show that this particular form of conduct was not thought of as a separate category from like conduct between heterosexual persons.

* * *

To the extent that there were any prosecutions for the acts in question, 19th-century evidence rules imposed a burden that would make a conviction more difficult to obtain even taking into account the problems always inherent in prosecuting consensual acts committed in private. Under then-prevailing standards, a man could not be convicted of sodomy based upon testimony of a consenting partner, because the partner was considered an accomplice. A partner's testimony, however, was admissible if he or she had not consented to the act or was a minor, and therefore incapable of consent. . . . In all events that infrequency makes it difficult to say that society approved of a rigorous and systematic punishment of the consensual acts committed in private and by adults. The longstanding criminal prohibition of homosexual sodomy upon which the *Bowers* decision placed such reliance is as consistent with a general condemnation of nonprocreative sex as it is with an established tradition of prosecuting acts because of their homosexual character.

* * *

American laws targeting same-sex couples did not develop until the last third of the 20th century. The reported decisions concerning the prosecution of consensual, homosexual sodomy between adults for the years 1880–1995 are not always clear in the details, but a significant number involved conduct in a public place.

* * *

In summary, the historical grounds relied upon in *Bowers* are more complex than the majority opinion and the concurring opinion by Chief Justice Burger indicate. Their historical premises are not without doubt and, at the very least, are overstated.

It must be acknowledged, of course, that the Court in *Bowers* was making the broader point that for centuries there have been powerful voices to condemn homosexual conduct as immoral. The condemnation has been shaped by religious beliefs, conceptions of right and acceptable behavior, and respect for the traditional family. For many persons these are not trivial concerns but profound and deep convictions accepted as ethical and moral principles to which they aspire and which thus determine the course of their lives. These considerations do not answer the question before us, however. The issue is whether the majority may use the power of the State to enforce these views on the whole society through operation of the criminal law. "Our obligation is to define the liberty of all, not to mandate our own moral code." *Planned Parenthood of Southeastern Pa. v. Casey.*

Chief Justice Burger joined the opinion for the Court in *Bowers* and further explained his views as follows: "Decisions of individuals relating to homosexual conduct have been subject to state intervention throughout the history of Western civilization. Condemnation of those practices is firmly rooted in Judeao-Christian moral and ethical standards." . . . [W]e think that our laws and traditions in the past half century are of most relevance here. These references show an emerging awareness that liberty gives substantial protection to adult persons in deciding how to conduct their private lives in matters pertaining to sex.

This emerging recognition should have been apparent when *Bowers* was decided.

In 1955 the American Law Institute promulgated the Model Penal Code and made clear that it did not recommend or provide for "criminal penalties for consensual sexual relations conducted in private." ALI, Model Penal Code § 213.2, Comment 2, p. 372 (1980). It justified its decision on three grounds: (1) The prohibitions undermined respect for the law by penalizing conduct many people engaged in; (2) the statutes regulated private conduct not harmful to others; and (3) the laws were arbitrarily enforced and thus invited the danger of blackmail. . . .

In *Bowers* the Court referred to the fact that before 1961 all 50 States had outlawed sodomy, and that at the time of the Court's decision 24 States and the District of Columbia had sodomy laws. . . .

The sweeping references by Chief Justice Burger to the history of Western civilization and to Judeo-Christian moral and ethical standards did not take account of other authorities pointing in an opposite direction. A committee advising the British Parliament recommended in 1957 repeal of laws punishing homosexual conduct. . . .

Of even more importance, almost five years before *Bowers* was decided the European Court of Human Rights considered a case with parallels to *Bowers* and to today's case. An adult male resident in Northern Ireland alleged he was a practicing homosexual who desired to engage in consensual homosexual conduct. The laws of Northern Ireland forbade him that right. He alleged that he had been questioned, his home had been searched, and he feared criminal prosecution. The court held that the laws proscribing the conduct were invalid under the European Convention on Human Rights. *Dudgeon v. United Kingdom*, 45 Eur. Ct. H.R. (1981) & ¶ 52. Authoritative in all countries that are members of the Council of Europe (21 nations then, 45 nations now), the decision is at odds with the premise in *Bowers* that the claim put forward was insubstantial in our Western civilization.

In our own constitutional system the deficiencies in *Bowers* became even more apparent in the years following its announcement. The 25 States with laws prohibiting the relevant conduct referenced in the *Bowers* decision are reduced now to 13, of which 4 enforce their laws only against homosexual conduct. In those States where sodomy is still proscribed, whether for same-sex or heterosexual conduct, there is a pattern of nonenforcement with respect to consenting adults acting in private. The State of Texas admitted in 1994 that as of that date it had not prosecuted anyone under those circumstances.

Two principal cases decided after *Bowers* cast its holding into even more doubt. In *Planned Parenthood of Southeastern Pa. v. Casey* (1992), the Court reaffirmed the substantive force of the liberty protected by the Due Process Clause. The *Casey* decision again confirmed that our laws and tradition afford constitutional protection to personal decisions relating to marriage, procreation, contraception, family relationships, child rearing, and education. In explaining the respect the Constitution demands for the autonomy of the person in making these choices, we stated as follows:

"These matters, involving the most intimate and personal choices a person may make in a lifetime, choices central to personal dignity and autonomy, are central to the liberty protected by the Fourteenth Amendment. At the heart of liberty is the right to define one's own concept of existence, of meaning, of the universe, and of the mystery of human life. Beliefs about these matters could not define the attributes of personhood were they formed under compulsion of the State."

Persons in a homosexual relationship may seek autonomy for these purposes, just as heterosexual persons do. The decision in *Bowers* would deny them this right.

The second post-*Bowers* case of principal relevance is *Romer v. Evans* (1996). . . .

As an alternative argument in this case, counsel for the petitioners and some *amici* contend that *Romer* provides the basis for declaring the Texas statute invalid under the Equal Protection Clause. That is a tenable argument, but we conclude the instant case requires us to address whether *Bowers* itself has continuing validity. Were we to hold the statute invalid under the Equal Protection Clause some might question whether a prohibition would be valid if drawn differently, say, to prohibit the conduct both between same-sex and different-sex participants.

Equality of treatment and the due process right to demand respect for conduct protected by the substantive guarantee of liberty are linked in important respects, and a decision on the latter point advances both interests. . . . The central holding of *Bowers* has been brought in question by this case, and it should be addressed. Its continuance as precedent demeans the lives of homosexual persons.

* * *

The doctrine of *stare decisis* is essential to the respect accorded to the judgments of the Court and to the stability of the law. It is not, however, an inexorable command.

* * *

Bowers was not correct when it was decided, and it is not correct today. It ought not to remain binding precedent. *Bowers v. Hardwick* should be and now is overruled.

The present case does not involve minors. It does not involve persons who might be injured or coerced or who are situated in relationships where consent might not easily be refused. It does not involve public conduct or prostitution. It does not involve whether the government must give formal recognition to any relationship that homosexual persons seek to enter. The case does involve two adults who, with full and mutual consent from each other, engaged in sexual practices common to a homosexual lifestyle. The petitioners are entitled to respect for their private lives. The State cannot demean their existence or control their destiny by making their private sexual conduct a crime. Their right to liberty under the Due Process Clause gives them the full right to engage in their conduct without intervention of the government. "It is a promise of the Constitution that there is a realm of personal liberty which the government may not enter." The Texas statute furthers no legitimate state interest which can justify its intrusion into the personal and private life of the individual.

Had those who drew and ratified the Due Process Clauses of the Fifth

Amendment or the Fourteenth Amendment known the components of liberty in its manifold possibilities, they might have been more specific. They did not presume to have this insight. They knew times can blind us to certain truths and later generations can see that laws once thought necessary and proper in fact serve only to oppress. As the Constitution endures, persons in every generation can invoke its principles in their own search for greater freedom.

The judgment of the Court of Appeals for the Texas Fourteenth District is reversed, and the case is remanded for further proceedings not inconsistent with this opinion.

It is so ordered.

JUSTICE O'CONNOR, concurring in the judgment.

The Court today overrules *Bowers v. Hardwick* (1986). I joined *Bowers*, and do not join the Court in overruling it. Nevertheless, I agree with the Court that Texas' statute banning same-sex sodomy is unconstitutional. Rather than relying on the substantive component of the Fourteenth Amendment's Due Process Clause, as the Court does, I base my conclusion on the Fourteenth Amendment's Equal Protection Clause.

The Equal Protection Clause of the Fourteenth Amendment "is essentially a direction that all persons similarly situated should be treated alike." *Cleburne v. Cleburne Living Center, Inc.* (1982). Under our rational basis standard of review, "legislation is presumed to be valid and will be sustained if the classification drawn by the statute is rationally related to a legitimate state interest."

Laws such as economic or tax legislation that are scrutinized under rational basis review normally pass constitutional muster, since "the Constitution presumes that even improvident decisions will eventually be rectified by the democratic processes." We have consistently held, however, that some objectives, such as "a bare . . . desire to harm a politically unpopular group," are not legitimate state interests. When a law exhibits such a desire to harm a politically unpopular group, we have applied a more searching form of rational basis review to strike down such laws under the Equal Protection Clause.

We have been most likely to apply rational basis review to hold a law unconstitutional under the Equal Protection Clause where, as here, the challenged legislation inhibits personal relationships. In *Department of Agriculture v. Moreno*, for example, we held that a law preventing those households containing an individual unrelated to any other member of the household from receiving food stamps violated equal protection because the purpose of the law was to " 'discriminate against hippies.' " The asserted governmental interest in preventing food stamp fraud was not deemed sufficient to satisfy rational basis review. In *Eisenstadt v. Baird* (1972), we refused to sanction a law that discriminated between married and unmarried persons by prohibiting the distribution of contraceptives to single persons. Likewise, in *Cleburne v. Cleburne Living Center, supra*, we held that it was irrational for a State to require a home for the mentally disabled to obtain a special use permit when other residences — like fraternity houses and apartment buildings — did not have to obtain such a permit. And in *Romer v. Evans*, we disallowed a state statute that "impos[ed] a broad and undifferentiated disability on a single named group" — specifically, homosexuals. The dissent apparently agrees that if these cases have *stare decisis* effect, Texas' sodomy law would not pass scrutiny under the Equal Protection Clause, regardless of the type of rational basis review that we apply.

The statute at issue here makes sodomy a crime only if a person "engages in deviate sexual intercourse with another individual of the same sex." Sodomy between opposite-sex partners, however, is not a crime in Texas. . . .

* * *

Texas attempts to justify its law, and the effects of the law, by arguing that the statute satisfies rational basis review because it furthers the legitimate governmental interest of the promotion of morality. In *Bowers*, we held that a state law criminalizing sodomy as applied to homosexual couples did not violate substantive due process. We rejected the argument that no rational basis existed to justify the law, pointing to the government's interest in promoting morality. The only question in front of the Court in *Bowers* was whether the substantive component of the Due Process Clause protected a right to engage in homosexual sodomy. *Bowers* did not hold that moral disapproval of a group is a rational basis under the Equal Protection Clause to criminalize homosexual sodomy when heterosexual sodomy is not punished.

This case raises a different issue than *Bowers*: whether, under the Equal Protection Clause, moral disapproval is a legitimate state interest to justify by itself a statute that bans homosexual sodomy, but not heterosexual sodomy. It is not. Moral disapproval of this group, like a bare desire to harm the group, is an interest that is insufficient to satisfy rational basis review under the Equal Protection Clause. . . .

* * *

Texas argues, however, that the sodomy law does not discriminate against homosexual persons. Instead, the State maintains that the law discriminates only against homosexual conduct. While it is true that the law applies only to conduct, the conduct targeted by this law is conduct that is closely correlated with being homosexual. . . .

* * *

Whether a sodomy law that is neutral both in effect and application, would violate the substantive component of the Due Process Clause is an issue that need not be decided today. I am confident, however, that so long as the Equal Protection Clause requires a sodomy law to apply equally to the private consensual conduct of homosexuals and heterosexuals alike, such a law would not long stand in our democratic society. In the words of Justice Jackson:

> "The framers of the Constitution knew, and we should not forget today, that there is no more effective practical guaranty against arbitrary and unreasonable government than to require that the principles of law which officials would impose upon a minority be imposed generally. Conversely, nothing

opens the door to arbitrary action so effectively as to allow those officials to pick and choose only a few to whom they will apply legislation and thus to escape the political retribution that might be visited upon them if larger numbers were affected."

That this law as applied to private, consensual conduct is unconstitutional under the Equal Protection Clause does not mean that other laws distinguishing between heterosexuals and homosexuals would similarly fail under rational basis review. Texas cannot assert any legitimate state interest here, such as national security or preserving the traditional institution of marriage. Unlike the moral disapproval of same-sex relations — the asserted state interest in this case — other reasons exist to promote the institution of marriage beyond mere moral disapproval of an excluded group.

A law branding one class of persons as criminal solely based on the State's moral disapproval of that class and the conduct associated with that class runs contrary to the values of the Constitution and the Equal Protection Clause, under any standard of review. I therefore concur in the Court's judgment that Texas' sodomy law banning "deviate sexual intercourse" between consenting adults of the same sex, but not between consenting adults of different sexes, is unconstitutional.

JUSTICE SCALIA, with whom THE CHIEF JUSTICE and JUSTICE THOMAS join, dissenting.

*   *   *

Most of today's opinion has no relevance to its actual holding — that the Texas statute "furthers no legitimate state interest which can justify" its application to petitioners under rational-basis review. (overruling *Bowers* to the extent it sustained Georgia's anti-sodomy statute under the rational-basis test). Though there is discussion of "fundamental proposition[s]," and "fundamental decisions," nowhere does the Court's opinion declare that homosexual sodomy is a "fundamental right" under the Due Process Clause; nor does it subject the Texas law to the standard of review that would be appropriate (strict scrutiny) if homosexual sodomy *were* a "fundamental right." Thus, while overruling the *outcome* of *Bowers*, the Court leaves strangely untouched its central legal conclusion: "[R]espondent would have us announce . . . a fundamental right to engage in homosexual sodomy. This we are quite unwilling to do." Instead the Court simply describes petitioners' conduct as "an exercise of their liberty" — which it undoubtedly is — and proceeds to apply an unheard-of form of rational-basis review that will have far-reaching implications beyond this case.

I

I begin with the Court's surprising readiness to reconsider a decision rendered a mere 17 years ago in *Bowers v. Hardwick*. I do not myself believe in rigid adherence to *stare decisis* in constitutional cases; but I do believe that we should be consistent rather than manipulative in invoking the doctrine. Today's opinions in support of reversal do not bother to distinguish — or indeed, even bother to mention — the paean to *stare decisis* coauthored by three Members of today's majority in *Planned Parenthood v. Casey*. There, when *stare decisis* meant preservation of judicially invented abortion rights, the widespread criticism of *Roe* was strong reason to *reaffirm* it:

> "Where, in the performance of its judicial duties, the Court decides a case in such a way as to resolve the sort of intensely divisive controversy reflected in *Roe*[,] . . . its decision has a dimension that the resolution of the normal case does not carry. . . . [T]o overrule under fire in the absence of the most compelling reason . . . would subvert the Court's legitimacy beyond any serious question."

Today, however, the widespread opposition to *Bowers*, a decision resolving an issue as "intensely divisive" as the issue in *Roe*, is offered as a reason in favor of *overruling* it. Gone, too, is any "enquiry" (of the sort conducted in *Casey*) into whether the decision sought to be overruled has "proven 'unworkable.' "

Today's approach to *stare decisis* invites us to overrule an erroneously decided precedent (including an "intensely divisive" decision) *if*: (1) its foundations have been "eroded" by subsequent decisions, (2) it has been subject to "substantial and continuing" criticism; and (3) it has not induced "individual or societal reliance" that counsels against overturning. The problem is that *Roe* itself — which today's majority surely has no disposition to overrule — satisfies these conditions to at least the same degree as *Bowers*.

* * *

 . . . "[T]here has been," the Court says, "no individual or societal reliance on *Bowers* of the sort that could counsel against overturning its holding . . . ." It seems to me that the "societal reliance" on the principles confirmed in *Bowers* and discarded today has been overwhelming. Countless judicial decisions and legislative enactments have relied on the ancient proposition that a governing majority's belief that certain sexual behavior is "immoral and unacceptable" constitutes a rational basis for regulation. *See, e.g., Williams v. Pryor* (C.A.11 2001) (citing *Bowers* in upholding Alabama's prohibition on the sale of sex toys on the ground that "[t]he crafting and safeguarding of public morality . . . indisputably is a legitimate government interest under rational basis scrutiny"); *Milner v. Apfel* (C.A.7 1998) (citing *Bowers* for the proposition that "[l]egislatures are permitted to legislate with regard to morality . . . rather than confined to preventing demonstrable harms"); *Holmes v. California Army National Guard* (C.A.9 1997) (relying on *Bowers* in upholding the federal statute and regulations banning from military service those who engage in homosexual conduct); *Owens v. State* (1999) (relying on *Bowers* in holding that "a person has no constitutional right to engage in sexual intercourse, at least outside of marriage"); *Sherman v. Henry* (Tex.1996) (relying on *Bowers* in rejecting a claimed constitutional right to commit adultery). We ourselves relied extensively on *Bowers* when we concluded, in *Barnes v. Glen Theatre, Inc.* (1991), that Indiana's public indecency statute furthered "a substantial government interest in protecting order and morality," (plurality opinion). State laws against bigamy, same-sex marriage, adult incest, prostitution, masturbation, adultery, fornication, bestiality, and obscenity are likewise sustainable only in light of *Bowers'* validation of laws based on moral choices. Every single one of these laws is called into question by today's decision; the Court makes no effort to cabin the scope of its decision to exclude them from its holding (noting "an emerging awareness that liberty gives substantial protection to adult persons in deciding how to conduct their private lives *in matters pertaining to sex*" (emphasis added)). The impossibility of distinguishing homosexuality from other traditional "morals" offenses is precisely why *Bowers* rejected the rational-basis challenge. "The law," it said, "is constantly based on notions of morality, and if all laws representing essentially moral choices are to be invalidated under the Due Process Clause, the courts will be very busy indeed."

* * *

What a massive disruption of the current social order, therefore, the overruling of *Bowers* entails. Not so the overruling of *Roe*, which would simply have restored the regime that existed for centuries before 1973, in which the permissibility of and restrictions upon abortion were determined legislatively State-by-State. *Casey*, however, chose to base its *stare decisis* determination on a different "sort" of reliance. "[P]eople," it said, "have organized intimate relationships and made choices that define their views of themselves and their places in society, in reliance on the availability of abortion in the event that contraception should fail." This falsely assumes that the consequence of overruling *Roe* would have been to make abortion unlawful. It would not; it would merely have *permitted* the States to do so. Many States would unquestionably have declined to prohibit abortion, and others would not have prohibited it within six months (after which the most significant reliance interests would have expired). Even for persons in States other than these, the choice would not have been between abortion and childbirth, but between abortion nearby and abortion in a neighboring State.

To tell the truth, it does not surprise me, and should surprise no one, that the Court has chosen today to revise the standards of *stare decisis* set forth in *Casey*. It has thereby exposed *Casey*'s extraordinary deference to precedent for the result-oriented expedient that it is.

II

* * *

The Texas law undoubtedly imposes constraints on liberty. So do laws prohibiting prostitution, recreational use of heroin, and, for that matter, working more than 60 hours per week in a bakery. But there is no right to "liberty" under the Due Process Clause, though today's opinion repeatedly makes that claim. . . . The Fourteenth Amendment *expressly allows* States to deprive their citizens of "liberty," *so long as* "*due process of law*" *is provided*:

> "No state shall . . . deprive any person of life, liberty, or property, *without due process of law*." Amdt. 14 (emphasis added).

Our opinions applying the doctrine known as "substantive due process" hold that the Due Process Clause prohibits States from infringing *fundamental* liberty interests, unless the infringement is narrowly tailored to serve a compelling state interest. *Washington v. Glucksberg*.

* * *

Bowers held, first, that criminal prohibitions of homosexual sodomy are not subject to heightened scrutiny because they do not implicate a "fundamental right" under the Due Process Clause. Noting that "[p]roscriptions against that conduct have ancient roots," that "[s]odomy was a criminal offense at common law and was forbidden by the laws of the original 13 States when they ratified the Bill of Rights," *ibid.*, and that many States had retained their bans on sodomy, *Bowers* concluded that a right to engage in homosexual sodomy was not " 'deeply rooted in this Nation's history and tradition.' "

The Court today does not overrule this holding. Not once does it describe homosexual sodomy as a "fundamental right" or a "fundamental liberty interest" nor does it subject the Texas statute to strict scrutiny. Instead, having failed to establish that the right to homosexual sodomy is " 'deeply rooted in this Nation's history and tradition,' " the Court concludes that the application of Texas's statute to petitioners' conduct fails the rational-basis test, and overrules *Bowers*' holding to the contrary. "The Texas statute furthers no legitimate state interest which can justify its intrusion into the personal and private life of the individual."

III

*   *   *

The Court's description of "the state of the law" at the time of *Bowers* only confirms that *Bowers* was right. The Court points to *Griswold v. Connecticut* (1965). But that case *expressly disclaimed* any reliance on the doctrine of "substantive due process," and grounded the so-called "right to privacy" in penumbras of constitutional provisions *other than* the Due Process Clause. *Eisenstadt v. Baird* (1972), likewise had nothing to do with "substantive due process"; it invalidated a Massachusetts law prohibiting the distribution of contraceptives to unmarried persons solely on the basis of the Equal Protection Clause. Of course *Eisenstadt* contains well known dictum relating to the "right to privacy," but this referred to the right recognized in *Griswold* — a right penumbral to the *specific* guarantees in the Bill of Rights, and not a "substantive due process" right.

Roe v. Wade recognized that the right to abort an unborn child was a "fundamental right" protected by the Due Process Clause. The *Roe* Court, however, made no attempt to establish that this right was " 'deeply rooted in this Nation's history and tradition' "; instead, it based its conclusion that "the Fourteenth Amendment's concept of personal liberty . . . is broad enough to encompass a woman's decision whether or not to terminate her pregnancy" on its own normative judgment that anti-abortion laws were undesirable. We have since rejected *Roe*'s holding that regulations of abortion must be narrowly tailored to serve a compelling state interest, see *Planned Parenthood v. Casey* (joint opinion of O'CONNOR, KENNEDY, and SOUTER, JJ.); (REHNQUIST, C.J., concurring in judgment in part and dissenting in part) — and thus, by logical implication, *Roe*'s holding that the right to abort an unborn child is a "fundamental right." . . .

*   *   *

It is (as *Bowers* recognized) entirely irrelevant whether the laws in our long national tradition criminalizing homosexual sodomy were "directed at homosexual conduct as a distinct matter." Whether homosexual sodomy was prohibited by a law targeted at same-sex sexual relations or by a more general law prohibiting both homosexual and heterosexual sodomy, the only relevant point is that it *was* criminalized — which suffices to establish that homosexual sodomy is not a right "deeply rooted in our Nation's history and tradition." The Court today agrees that homosexual sodomy was criminalized and thus does not dispute the facts on which *Bowers actually* relied.

* * *

Realizing that fact, the Court instead says: "[W]e think that our laws and traditions in the past half century are of most relevance here. These references show *an emerging awareness* that liberty gives substantial protection to adult persons in deciding how to conduct their private lives *in matters pertaining to sex.*" Apart from the fact that such an "emerging awareness" does not establish a "fundamental right," the statement is factually false. States continue to prosecute all sorts of crimes by adults "in matters pertaining to sex": prostitution, adult incest, adultery, obscenity, and child pornography. Sodomy laws, too, have been enforced "in the past half century," in which there have been 134 reported cases involving prosecutions for consensual, adult, homosexual sodomy. . . .

In any event, an "emerging awareness" is by definition not "deeply rooted in this Nation's history and tradition[s]," as we have said "fundamental right" status requires. Constitutional entitlements do not spring into existence because some States choose to lessen or eliminate criminal sanctions on certain behavior. Much less do they spring into existence, as the Court seems to believe, because *foreign nations* decriminalize conduct. . . .

IV

I turn now to the ground on which the Court squarely rests its holding: the contention that there is no rational basis for the law here under attack. This proposition is so out of accord with our jurisprudence — indeed, with the jurisprudence of *any* society we know — that it requires little discussion.

The Texas statute undeniably seeks to further the belief of its citizens that certain forms of sexual behavior are "immoral and unacceptable," — the same interest furthered by criminal laws against fornication, bigamy, adultery, adult incest, bestiality, and obscenity. *Bowers* held that this *was* a legitimate state interest. The Court today reaches the opposite conclusion. The Texas statute, it says, "furthers *no legitimate state interest* which can justify its intrusion into the personal and private life of the individual." The Court embraces instead Justice Stevens' declaration in his *Bowers* dissent, that "the fact that the governing majority in a State has traditionally viewed a particular practice as immoral is not a sufficient reason for upholding a law prohibiting the practice." This effectively decrees the end of all morals legislation. If, as the Court asserts, the promotion of majoritarian sexual morality is not even a *legitimate* state interest, none of the above-mentioned laws can survive rational-basis review.

V

Finally, I turn to petitioners' equal-protection challenge, which no Member of the Court save JUSTICE O'CONNOR embraces: On its face the law applies equally to all persons. Men and women, heterosexuals and homosexuals, are all subject to its prohibition of deviate sexual intercourse with someone of the same sex. To be sure, the law does distinguish between the sexes insofar as concerns the partner with whom the sexual acts are performed: men can violate the law only with other men, and women only with other women. But this cannot itself be a denial of equal protection, since it is precisely the same distinction regarding partner that is drawn in state laws prohibiting marriage with someone of the same sex while permitting marriage with someone of the opposite sex.

The objection is made, however, that the antimiscegenation laws invalidated in *Loving v. Virginia* (1967), similarly were applicable to whites and blacks alike, and only distinguished between the races insofar as the *partner* was concerned. In *Loving*, however, we correctly applied heightened scrutiny, rather than the usual rational-basis review, because the Virginia statute was "designed to maintain White Supremacy." A racially discriminatory purpose is always sufficient to subject a law to strict scrutiny, even a facially neutral law that makes no mention of race.

JUSTICE O'CONNOR argues that the discrimination in this law which must be justified is not its discrimination with regard to the sex of the partner but its discrimination with regard to the sexual proclivity of the principal actor.

* * *

Of course the same could be said of any law. A law against public nudity targets "the conduct that is closely correlated with being a nudist," and hence "is targeted at more than conduct"; it is "directed toward nudists as a class." But be that as it may. Even if the Texas law *does* deny equal protection to "homosexuals as a class," that denial *still* does not need to be justified by anything more than a rational basis, which our cases show is satisfied by the enforcement of traditional notions of sexual morality.

JUSTICE O'CONNOR simply decrees application of "a more searching form of rational basis review" to the Texas statute. The cases she cites do not recognize such a standard, and reach their conclusions only after finding, as required by conventional rational-basis analysis, that no conceivable legitimate state interest supports the classification at issue. See *Romer v. Evans* (1973). Nor does JUSTICE O'CONNOR explain precisely what her "more searching form" of rational-basis review consists of. It must at least mean, however, that laws exhibiting "'a . . . desire to harm a politically unpopular group,'" are invalid *even though* there may be a conceivable rational basis to support them.

This reasoning leaves on pretty shaky grounds state laws limiting marriage to opposite-sex couples. JUSTICE O'CONNOR seeks to preserve them by the conclusory statement that "preserving the traditional institution of marriage" is a legitimate state interest. But "preserving the traditional institution of marriage" is just a kinder way of describing the State's *moral disapproval* of same-sex couples. Texas's interest could be recast in similarly euphemistic terms: "preserving the traditional sexual mores of our society." In the jurisprudence JUSTICE O'CONNOR has seemingly created, judges can validate laws by characterizing them as "preserving the traditions of society" (good); or invalidate them by characterizing them as "expressing moral disapproval" (bad).

* * *

Today's opinion is the product of a Court, which is the product of a law-profession culture, that has largely signed on to the so-called homosexual agenda, by which I mean the agenda promoted by some homosexual activists directed at eliminating the moral opprobrium that has traditionally attached to homosexual conduct. I noted in an earlier opinion the fact that the American Association of Law Schools (to which any reputable law school *must* seek to belong) excludes from membership any school that refuses to ban from its job-interview facilities a law firm (no matter how small) that does not wish to hire as a prospective partner a person who openly engages in homosexual conduct.

* * *

Let me be clear that I have nothing against homosexuals, or any other group, promoting their agenda through normal democratic means. Social perceptions of sexual and other morality change over time, and every group has the right to persuade its fellow citizens that its view of such matters is the best. That homosexuals have achieved some success in that enterprise is attested to by the fact that Texas is one of the few remaining States that criminalize private, consensual homosexual acts. But persuading one's fellow citizens is one thing, and imposing one's views in absence of democratic majority will is something else. I would no more *require* a State to criminalize homosexual acts — or, for that matter, display *any* moral disapprobation of them — than I would *forbid* it to do so. What Texas has chosen to do is well within the range of traditional democratic action, and its hand should not be stayed through the invention of a brand-new "constitutional right" by a Court that is impatient of democratic change. It is indeed true that "later generations can see that laws once thought necessary and proper in fact serve only to oppress," and when that happens, later generations can repeal those laws. But it is the premise of our system that those judgments are to be made by the people, and not imposed by a governing caste that knows best.

One of the benefits of leaving regulation of this matter to the people rather than to the courts is that the people, unlike judges, need not carry things to their logical conclusion. The people may feel that their disapprobation of homosexual conduct is strong enough to disallow homosexual marriage, but not strong enough to criminalize private homosexual acts — and may legislate accordingly. The Court today pretends that it possesses a similar freedom of action, so that that we need not fear judicial imposition of homosexual marriage, as has recently occurred in Canada (in a decision that the Canadian Government has chosen not to appeal). At the end of its opinion — after having laid waste the foundations of our rational-basis jurisprudence — the Court says that the present case "does not involve whether the government must give formal recognition to any relationship that homosexual persons seek to enter." Do not believe it. More illuminating than this bald, unreasoned disclaimer is the progression of thought displayed by an earlier passage in the Court's opinion, which notes the constitutional protections afforded to "personal decisions relating to *marriage*, procreation, contraception, family relationships, child rearing, and education," and then declares that "[p]ersons in a homosexual relationship may seek autonomy for these purposes, just as heterosexual persons do." Today's opinion dismantles the structure of constitutional law that has permitted a distinction to be made between heterosexual and homosexual unions, insofar as formal recognition in marriage is concerned. If moral disapprobation of homosexual conduct is "no legitimate state interest" for purposes of proscribing that conduct, and if, as the Court coos (casting aside all pretense of neutrality), "[w]hen sexuality finds overt expression in intimate conduct with another person, the conduct can be but one element in a personal bond that is more enduring;" what justification could there possibly be for denying the benefits of marriage to homosexual couples exercising "[t]he liberty protected by the Constitution"? Surely not the encouragement of procreation, since the sterile and the elderly are allowed to marry. This case "does not involve" the issue of homosexual marriage only if one entertains the belief that principle and logic have nothing to do with the decisions of this Court. Many will hope that, as the Court comfortingly assures us, this is so.

The matters appropriate for this Court's resolution are only three: Texas's prohibition of sodomy neither infringes a "fundamental right" (which the Court does not dispute), nor is unsupported by a rational relation to what the Constitution considers a legitimate state interest, nor denies the equal protection of the laws. I dissent.

JUSTICE THOMAS, dissenting.

I join JUSTICE SCALIA's dissenting opinion. I write separately to note that the law before the Court today "is . . . uncommonly silly." If I were a member of the Texas Legislature, I would vote to repeal it. Punishing someone for expressing his sexual preference through noncommercial consensual conduct with another adult does not appear to be a worthy way to expend valuable law enforcement resources.

Notwithstanding this, I recognize that as a member of this Court I am not empowered to help petitioners and others similarly situated. My duty, rather, is to "decide cases 'agreeably to the Constitution and laws of the United States.' " And, just like Justice Stewart in *Griswold*, I "can find [neither in the Bill of Rights nor any other part of the Constitution a] general right of privacy," or as the Court terms it today, the "liberty of the person both in its spatial and more transcendent dimensions."

NOTES AND QUESTIONS

1. Is this case faithful to any of the methods the Court has historically used to discover unenumerated fundamental rights? The Court is quite right that "history and tradition are the starting point but not in all cases the ending point of the substantive due process inquiry." An asserted "fundamental liberty interest" must not only be "deeply rooted in this Nation's history and tradition," *Washington v. Glucksberg*, 521 U.S. 702, 721 (1997), but it must *also* be "implicit in the concept of

ordered liberty," so that "neither liberty nor justice would exist if [it] were sacrificed." Do you think the right of intimate privacy is so "deeply rooted"? After all, no one in this case disputes that sodomy generally was a *criminal* act throughout our history, not a matter of right, do they? Is it enough to say that a claim unsupported by history and tradition, and thus not deserving of "heightened scrutiny," should still be protected? Was the problem here simply that laws that cannot be meaningfully enforced are inherently irrational and arbitrary? Wouldn't that have been a far narrower, perhaps better holding, reflecting what philosophers for millennia, including Thomas Aquinas, knew well: that one cannot enact every virtue or prohibit every vice in law? Everyone conceded that sodomy statutes, down through the ages, had never been applied, and that it was applied here largely by the accident of the false report of gun activity. If that is the case, why did the Court reach out to decide this dispute or decide it on the sweeping grounds that it did?

Justice Scalia thinks the Court took the case in order to take "sides in the culture war, departing from its role of assuring, as neutral observer, that the democratic rules of engagement are observed." First, is there such a war or is this merely the natural tendency to ask questions even about what appears to be even well-settled matters like marriage and family? Justice Scalia may be right that "many Americans do not want persons who openly engage in homosexual conduct as partners in their business, as scoutmasters for their children, as teachers in their children's schools, or as boarders in their home," but if that is the case shouldn't we as a people, in order to insure that we are not acting out of hate or stereotype, be asked to give a clear answer as to why sexual relations within marriage are culturally important and why they are reserved to a man and woman? Did Texas make adequate defense? But, absent the presence of either suspect class or fundamental right, is it the place of the Court to even ask or opine? The dissent writes: "in most States what the Court calls 'discrimination' against those who engage in homosexual acts is perfectly legal; that proposals to ban such 'discrimination' under Title VII have repeatedly been rejected by Congress, *see* Employment Non-Discrimination Act of 1994, S. 2238, 103d Cong., 2d Sess. (1994); Civil Rights Amendments, H.R. 5452, 94th Cong., 1st Sess. (1975); that in some cases such 'discrimination' is *mandated* by federal statute, *see* 10 U.S.C. § 654(b)(1) (mandating discharge from the armed forces of any service member who engages in or intends to engage in homosexual acts); and that in some cases such 'discrimination' is a constitutional right, *see Boy Scouts of America v. Dale* (2000)."

2.   A political firestorm, of sorts, erupted after an Associated Press interview with Pennsylvania's Republican Senator Rick Santorum, on April 7, 2003, where he was commenting on the fact that the Texas sodomy legislation was before the Court, and he stated that:

> We have laws in states, like the one at the Supreme Court right now, that has sodomy laws and they were there for a purpose. Because, again, I would argue, they undermine the basic tenets of our society and the family. And if the Supreme Court says that you have the right to consensual sex within your home, then you have the right to bigamy, you have the right to polygamy, you have the right to incest, you have the right to adultery. You have the right to anything. Does that undermine the fabric of our society?

I would argue yes, it does. It all comes from, I would argue, this right to privacy that doesn't exist in my opinion in the United States Constitution . . . .

Now that six Justices of the United States Supreme Court have declared that Texas may not punish homosexual acts between willing adults, does this mean that Senator Santorum was correct? Is there a way in which the Supreme Court's reading of the "right to privacy" can be limited so that polygamy, incest, adultery, or any other sexual acts between willing adults do not necessarily receive constitutional protection?

3. Carried to its logical extreme, Justice Antonin Scalia in his dissent opined that the ruling seriously hobbles state morals legislation. Indeed, promoting morality through law is all but declared irrational. Yet, perhaps the case should not be over-read. Justice Anthony Kennedy disclaimed any purpose other than securing basic privacy. His ruling, he said, does not involve the government giving formal recognition to any relationship (which presumably means he is not endorsing gay marriage) and does not involve minors, coercion, or public activity such as disqualification from the military for overt conduct.

The analytical problem is why these matters should remain undisturbed — other than that the Court controls its own docket.

TABLE OF CASES

[References are to pages]

[References are to pages]

[References are to pages]

[References are to pages]

[References are to pages]

[References are to pages]

M

N

[References are to pages]

[References are to pages]

[References are to pages]

[References are to pages]

Table of Articles

Table of Articles

INDEX

[References are to pages.]

I-1

[References are to pages.]

[References are to pages.]